MCSA/MCSE

Self-Paced Training Kit

Microsoft

WINDOWS 2000 SERVER

Microsoft

2

Second Edition

Exam 70-215

PUBLISHED BY
Microsoft Press
A Division of Microsoft Corporation
One Microsoft Way
Redmond, Washington 98052-6399

Library of Congress Cataloging-in-Publication Data
MCSE Training Kit--Microsoft Windows 2000 Server / Microsoft Corporation.
        p. cm.
    Includes index.
    ISBN 1-57231-903-8
    ISBN 0-7356-1767-8 (Second Edition)
    1. Electronic data processing personnel--Certification.   2. Microsoft
software--Examinations--Study guides.   3. Microsoft Windows 2000 server.   I. Microsoft
Corporation.

    QA76.3 .M33455   2000
    005.7'13769--dc21   99-059501

Printed and bound in the United States of America.

1 2 3 4 5 6 7 8 9   QWT   7 6 5 4 3 2

Distributed in Canada by H.B. Fenn and Company Ltd.

A CIP catalogue record for this book is available from the British Library.

Microsoft Press books are available through booksellers and distributors worldwide. For further informa-tion about international editions, contact your local Microsoft Corporation office or contact Microsoft Press International directly at fax (425) 936-7329. Visit our Web site at www.microsoft.com/mspress. Send comments to *tkinput@microsoft.com*.

Acquisitions Editor: Jeff Madden
Project Editor: Lynn Finnel

Authors: Bob Sheldon and Ethan Wilansky
Body Part No. X08-73011

Contents

Part 1   Self-Paced Training for Microsoft Windows 2000 Server

Chapter 1   Introduction to Microsoft Windows 2000   1

Chapter 11   Microsoft Windows 2000 Security   619

Part 2   Preparation for MCP Exam 70-215

About This Book

Welcome to the *MCSE Training Kit—Microsoft Windows 2000 Server.* This book is organized in two parts. Part 1 is a self-paced training course designed to teach you how to set up and support the Microsoft Windows 2000 Server operating system, and prepare you for the related Microsoft Certified Professional exam 70-215: Installing, Configuring, and Administering Microsoft Windows 2000 Server. Part 2 is designed to give you a focused, timesaving way to identify the information you need to know to pass the exam, and is accompanied by a realistic electronic assessment tool to help you become familiar with the types of questions that you will encounter on MCP exam 70-215. By reviewing the objectives and sample questions in Part 2, you can focus on the specific skills you need to improve before taking the exam.

Before You Begin Part 1

Part 1 teaches you how to install and configure Microsoft Windows 2000 Server. After a brief introduction to the features in all editions of Windows 2000, you will learn how to install Windows 2000 Server through manual and automated installation routines. After installation, you will learn about the various file systems and disk management functions available in Windows 2000 Server. Administering the operating system and Active Directory services is explored because these are integral to your understanding of Windows 2000. In addition, you will learn about network protocols, routing and remote access, and other application server functions such as Terminal Services. Additionally, you will be introduced to monitoring and optimizing Windows 2000 Server.

Note For more information on becoming a Microsoft Certified Systems Engineer, see the section titled "The Microsoft Certified Professional Program" later in this chapter.

Each chapter in Part 1 is divided into lessons. Many lessons include hands-on procedures that allow you to practice or demonstrate a particular concept or skill. Each chapter ends with a short summary of all chapter lessons and a set of review questions to test your knowledge of the chapter material.

The "Getting Started" section of this chapter provides important setup instructions that describe the hardware and software requirements to complete the procedures in this course. It also provides information about the networking configuration necessary to complete some of the hands-on procedures. Read this section thoroughly before you start the lessons.

Intended Audience

This book was developed for information technology (IT) professionals who need to design, plan, implement, and support Windows 2000 Server or who plan to take the related Microsoft Certified Professional exam Exam 70-215: Installing, Configuring, and Administering Microsoft Windows 2000 Server.

Prerequisites

This course requires that students meet the following prerequisites:

- Knowledge of the fundamentals of current networking technology

- Ability to navigate the Windows operating system interface (preferably, the Windows 95, Windows 98, Windows NT, or Windows 2000 interface)

- At least six months of experience supporting a network, or successful completion of the Networking Essentials, Hands-On Self-Paced Training for Supporting Local and Wide Area Networks course is recommended

- Experience with basic internal and external operating system commands like CD, Dir, Fdisk, and Format

- A practical knowledge of accessing and changing PC computer BIOS settings

- Previous training or knowledge of Microsoft Windows 2000 Professional

- Previous training or knowledge of Windows NT Server is not required but will facilitate the learning process

Reference Materials

You might find the following reference materials useful:

- *MCP Magazine Online.* Available online at *http://www.mcpmag.com.*
- Microsoft Web site (*http://www.microsoft.com*) and *Microsoft TechNet Technical Plus* available monthly on CD-ROM and the Microsoft Web site.
- *Microsoft Windows 2000 Server Resource Kit.* Microsoft Press, 1999.
- *MCSE Training Kit–Microsoft Windows 2000 Professional.* Microsoft Press, 2000.
- *MCSE Training Kit–Networking Essentials Plus*, 3rd ed. Microsoft Press, 1999.
- Silberschatz A and P. Galvin. *Operating System Concepts,* 5th ed. Addison-Wesley Publishing Company, 1998. This is just one of many good text books that explores operating systems fundamentals.
- *Windows NT Magazine* (soon to be renamed *Windows 2000 Magazine*). This online magazine can be found at *http://www.winntmag.com* and is published by Duke Communications.
- Sysinternals Freeware Web site: *http://www.sysinternals.com.*

About the CD-ROM

The Supplemental Course Materials CD-ROM contains a variety of informational aids that may be used throughout this book. This includes supplemental articles and files used in hands-on exercises. These files can be used directly from the CD-ROM or copied onto your hard drive. The CD-ROM also includes an online version of the book, Internet Explorer 6.0, and an electronic assessment program for exam 70-215. For more information regarding the contents and use of the Supplemental Course Materials CD-ROM, see the README.TXT file located in the root directory of the CD-ROM.

Features of This Book

Each chapter opens with a "Before You Begin" section, which prepares you for completing the chapter.

▶ The chapters are then broken down into lessons. Many of the lessons contain exercises that give you an opportunity to use the skills presented or explore the part of the application described. All exercises offer step-by-step procedures that are identified with a symbol like the one to the left of this paragraph.

The "Review" section at the end of each chapter allows you to test what you have learned in the chapter's lessons.

Appendix A, "Questions and Answers" contains all of Part 1's questions and corresponding answers.

Notes

Several types of Notes appear throughout the lessons.

- Notes marked **Tip** contain explanations of possible results or alternative methods.

- Notes marked **Important** contain information that is essential to completing a task.

- Notes marked **Note** contain supplemental information.

- Notes marked **Caution** contain warnings about possible loss of data.

Conventions

The following conventions are used throughout Part 1.

Notational Conventions

- Characters or commands that you type appear in **bold** type.

- *Italic* in syntax statements indicates placeholders for variable information. *Italic* is also used for book titles and URLs.

- Names of files and folders appear in Title Caps, except when you are to type them directly. Unless otherwise indicated, you can use all lowercase letters when you type a file name in a dialog box or at a command prompt.

- File name extensions appear in all lowercase.

- Acronyms appear in all uppercase.

- Monospace type represents code samples, examples of screen text, or entries that you might type at a command prompt or in initialization files.

- Angle brackets < > are used in syntax statements to enclose optional items. For example, *<filename>* in command syntax indicates that you can choose to type a file name with the command. Type only the information within the brackets, not the brackets themselves.

- Icons represent specific sections in the book as described in the following table.

Icon	Represents
	A file contained on the CD-ROM. Some files are needed to complete a hands-on practice; others contain supplemental information about the topic being discussed. The purpose of the file and its location are described in the accompanying text.
	A hands-on exercise. You should perform the exercise to give yourself an opportunity to use the skills presented in the lesson.
	Chapter review questions. These questions at the end of each chapter allow you to test what you have learned in the lessons. You will find the answers to the review questions in the Questions and Answers appendix at the end of the book.

Keyboard Conventions

- A plus sign (+) between two key names means that you must press those keys at the same time. For example, "Press Alt+Tab" means that you hold down Alt while you press Tab.

- A comma (,) between two or more key names means that you must press each of the keys consecutively, not together. For example, "Press Alt, F, X" means that you press and release each key in sequence. "Press Alt+W, L" means that you first press Alt and W together, and then release them and press L.

- You can choose menu commands with the keyboard. Press the Alt key to activate the menu bar, and then sequentially press the keys that correspond to the highlighted or underlined letter of the menu name and the command name. For some commands, you can also press a key combination listed in the menu.

- You can select or clear check boxes or option buttons in dialog boxes with the keyboard. Press the Alt key, and then press the key that corresponds to the underlined letter of the option name. Alternately, you can press Tab until the option is highlighted, and then press the spacebar to select or clear the check box or option button.

- You can cancel the display of a dialog box by pressing the Esc key.

Chapter and Appendix Overview

This self-paced training course combines descriptive text, notes, hands-on procedures, and review questions to teach you to install and configure Windows 2000 Server. It is designed to be completed from beginning to end, but you can choose a customized track and complete only the sections that interest you. (See the next section, "Finding the Best Starting Point for You" for more information.) If you choose the customized track option, see the "Before You Begin" section in each chapter. Any hands-on procedures that require preliminary work from preceding chapters refer to the appropriate chapters.

Part 1 is divided into the following chapters:

- The "About This Book" section contains a self-paced training overview and introduces the components of this training. Read this section thoroughly to get the greatest educational value from this self-paced training and to plan which lessons you will complete. Following the setup information outlined in "About This Book" is critical to the successful completion of the exercises in this training kit.

- Chapter 1, "Introduction to Microsoft Windows 2000," summarizes Windows 2000 features, operating system architecture, and Windows 2000 directory services.

- Chapter 2, "Installing and Configuring Microsoft Windows 2000 Server," covers how to prepare, install, upgrade, and troubleshoot a Windows 2000 Server installation.

- Chapter 3, "Unattended Installations of Microsoft Windows 2000 Server," covers how to prepare for and automate the installation of Windows 2000 Server and server applications.

- Chapter 4, "Microsoft Windows 2000 File Systems," explores disk management basics, Windows 2000 file systems, and file system security.

- Chapter 5, "Advanced File Systems," explores the Distributed File System and the File Replication Service.

- Chapter 6, "Active Directory Services," describes how to plan, implement, and administer Active Directory services.

- Chapter 7, "Administering Microsoft Windows 2000 Server," covers how to use the MMC, administer user and group accounts, and implement group policies.

- Chapter 8, "Administering Print Services," provides an overview of Windows 2000 printing, including how to install, administer, and connect a network printer. The chapter also explores the relationship between Active Directory services and printing.

- Chapter 9, "Network Protocols and Services," introduces network protocols, and provides details about TCP/IP, DHCP, WINS, and DNS.

- Chapter 10, "Routing and Remote Access Service," covers routing and remote access features, including how to install RAS and VPN and use RRAS tools.

- Chapter 11, "Microsoft Windows 2000 Security," explores PKI, public key technologies, and Kerberos in Windows 2000. The chapter also covers security configuration tools and implementing auditing in Windows 2000.

- Chapter 12, "Reliability and Availability," discusses how to manage hardware devices and drivers, implement Windows 2000 backup, build a disaster protection strategy, and recover from a disaster.

- Chapter 13, "Monitoring and Optimization," describes monitoring and optimizing Windows 2000 performance, provides an overview of SNMP, and discusses how to use Performance Console, Network Monitor, and Task Manager.

- Chapter 14, "Microsoft Windows 2000 Application Servers," discusses how to install and configure Internet Information Services 5.0, Telnet services, and Terminal Services.

Following Part 2 you will find:

- Appendix A, "Questions and Answers," lists all the review questions from Part 1 showing the page number where the question appears and the suggested answer.

- Appendix B, "Sample Answer Files for Unattended Setup," provides information about creating an unattended setup file.

- Appendix C, "Installing Service Packs," provides information about installing and administering service packs in Windows 2000.

Finding the Best Starting Point For You

Because Part 1 is self-paced, you can skip some lessons and visit them later. Note, however, that in many cases you must complete exercises in each chapter before completing exercises in later chapters. Use the following table to find the best starting point for you.

If you	Follow this learning path
Are preparing to take the Microsoft Certified Professional exam Exam 70-215: Installing, Configuring, and Administering Microsoft Windows 2000 Server	Read the "Getting Started" section. Then work through Chapters 1 and 2. Work through the remaining chapters in any order. Carefully read the "Before You Begin" of each chapter to determine exercise dependencies from previous chapters.
Are reviewing information about specific topics from the exam	Use the "Where to Find Specific Skills in This Book" section that follows this table.

Where to Find Specific Skills in This Book

The following tables provide a list of the skills measured on certification exam Exam 70-215: Installing, Configuring, and Administering Microsoft Windows 2000 Server. The table lists the skill, and where in this book you will find the lesson relating to that skill. For sample questions to help gauge your readiness for exam 70-215, see Part 2, "Preparation for MCP Exam 70-215."

Note Skills required for exams are subject to change without prior notice and at the sole discretion of Microsoft.

Installing Windows 2000 Server

Skills Being Measured	Location in Book Chapter	Lesson
Perform an attended installation of Windows 2000 Server.	2	1–2
Perform an unattended installation of Windows 2000 Server.	3	1–3
• Create unattended answer files by using Setup Manager to automate the installation of Windows 2000 Server.	3	1–3
• Create and configure automated methods for installation of Windows 2000.	3	1–3

Skills Being Measured	Location in Book Chapter	Lesson
Upgrade a server from Microsoft Windows NT 4.0.	2	3
Deploy service packs.	12	1
Troubleshoot failed installations.	2	4

Installing, Configuring, and Troubleshooting Access to Resources

Skills Being Measured	Location in Book Chapter	Lesson
Install and configure network services for interoperability.	14	1–4
	9	3–5
Monitor, configure, troubleshoot, and control access to printers.	8	2–5
Monitor, configure, troubleshoot, and control access to files, folders, and shared folders.	4	1–4
	5	1–2
	14	1–2
▪ Configure, manage, and troubleshoot a stand-alone Distributed file system (Dfs).	5	1
▪ Configure, manage, and troubleshoot a domain-based Distributed file system (Dfs).	5	1
	6	3
▪ Monitor, configure, troubleshoot, and control local security on files and folders.	4	4
▪ Monitor, configure, troubleshoot, and control access to files and folders in a shared folder.	4	4
▪ Monitor, configure, troubleshoot, and control access to files and folders via Web services.	14	1–2
Monitor, configure, troubleshoot, and control access to Web sites.	14	1–2

Configuring and Troubleshooting Hardware Devices and Drivers

Skills Being Measured	Location in Book	
	Chapter	Lesson
Configure hardware devices.	12	1
Configure driver signing options.	12	1
Update device drivers.	12	1
Troubleshoot problems with hardware.	12	1

Managing, Monitoring, and Optimizing System Performance, Reliability, and Availability

Skills Being Measured	Location in Book	
	Chapter	Lesson
Monitor and optimize usage of system resources.	13	2–5
Manage processes.	13	5
▪ Set priorities, and start and stop processes.	13	5
Optimize disk performance.	13	1
Manage and optimize availability of system state data and user data.	12	1–4
Recover systems and user data.	12	2, 4
▪ Recover systems and user data by using Windows Backup.	12	2, 4
▪ Troubleshoot system restoration by using Safe Mode.	12	4
▪ Recover systems and user data by using the Recovery Console.	12	4

Managing, Configuring, and Troubleshooting Storage Use

Skills Being Measured	Location in Book	
	Chapter	Lesson
Monitor, configure, and troubleshoot disks and volumes.	12	3
	13	1
Configure data compression.	13	1

Skills Being Measured	Location in Book	
	Chapter	**Lesson**
Monitor and configure disk quotas.	13	1
Recover from disk failures.	12	4

Configuring and Troubleshooting Windows 2000 Network Connections

Skills Being Measured	Location in Book	
	Chapter	**Lesson**
Install, configure, and troubleshoot shared access.	4	4
Install, configure, and troubleshoot a virtual private network (VPN).	10	4
Install, configure, and troubleshoot network protocols.	9	1, 2
Install and configure network services.	9	3–5
	13	4
Configure, monitor, and troubleshoot remote access.	10	1–3, 5
• Configure inbound connections.	10	1–3
• Create a remote access policy.	10	3
• Configure a remote access profile.	10	1–3
Install, configure, monitor, and troubleshoot Terminal Services.	14	4
• Remotely administer servers by using Terminal Services.	14	4
• Configure Terminal Services for application sharing.	14	4
• Configure applications for use with Terminal Services.	14	4
Install, configure, and troubleshoot network adapters and drivers.	2	1, 2
	9	2
	12	1

Implementing, Monitoring, and Troubleshooting Security

Skills Being Measured	Location in Book	
	Chapter	Lesson
Encrypt data on a hard disk by using Encrypting File System (EFS).	11	2
Implement, configure, manage, and troubleshoot policies in a Windows 2000 environment.	7	4
• Implement, configure, manage, and troubleshoot Local Policy in a Windows 2000 environment.	7	4
• Implement, configure, manage, and troubleshoot System Policy in a Windows 2000 environment.	7	4
Implement, configure, manage, and troubleshoot auditing.	11	5
Implement, configure, manage, and troubleshoot local accounts.	7	2
Implement, configure, manage, and troubleshoot Account Policy.	7	2, 4
Implement, configure, manage, and troubleshoot security by using the Security Configuration Tool Set.	11	4

Getting Started

This self-paced training course contains hands-on procedures to help you learn about Windows 2000 Server.

To complete some of these procedures, you must have two networked computers or be connected to a larger network. Ideally, the network used for the exercises in this kit should not be an isolated network. Both computers must be capable of running Windows 2000 Server.

Caution Several exercises may require you to make changes to your servers. This may have undesirable results if you are connected to a larger network. Check with your network administrator before attempting these exercises.

The first computer will be designated as Computer 1 with a computer name of Server01. The second computer will be designated as Computer 2 with a computer name of Server02. Both computers must be capable of running Windows 2000 Server. If you have only one computer, read the steps and familiarize yourself with the procedures as best you can. Computer 1 and Computer 2 are described in more detail in the "Setup Instructions" section of this document.

Exercises and explanations of procedures in the text use drop-down menus to demonstrate how to navigate through Windows interface elements, like the Microsoft Management Console (MMC). Many objects appearing in the Windows interface can also be accessed through Context menus. If you use right-handed mouse settings, the Context menus are accessed by pointing at an object and right-clicking the mouse. If you use left handed mouse settings, the Context menus are accessed by pointing at an object and left-clicking the mouse.

Hardware Requirements

Each computer must have the following minimum configuration. All hardware should be on the Microsoft Windows 2000 Server Hardware Compatibility List (HCL).

- 133 MHz or higher Pentium-compatible CPU
- 128 MB of RAM
- 2 GB free space for the boot partition (the partition containing the operating system files) and other files created through exercises in this course.
- 500 MB of unallocated space on the computer that will become Server01 through exercises in this kit (the unallocated space will be partitioned in Chapter 4 exercises)
- 12X CD-ROM drive
- VGA monitor (800 x 600 resolution or better recommended)
- Microsoft Mouse or compatible pointing device
- A modem in Computer 1 and a modem in Computer 2
- Optional: Internet access

There are a number of methods for determining whether your hardware is on the HCL. The following list shows some of these methods:

- Check \Support\Hcl.txt on the Windows 2000 Server installation CD-ROM.

- Review the most up-to-date list of supported hardware at the Microsoft Windows Hardware Quality Labs Web site at *http://www.microsoft.com/hcl/default.asp*.

- If this URL fails, go to the Microsoft homepage at *http://www.microsoft.com* and perform a search using the keyword "HCL."

Software Requirements

The following software is required to complete the procedures in this course:

- Windows 2000 Server CD-ROM or Windows 2000 Server 120-Day evaluation version CD-ROM. Installation for either version of the software is covered in Chapters 2 and 3.

- A Windows 32-bit operating system (Windows 9*x*, Windows NT 3.51, or Windows NT 4.0) running on Computer 2 to perform an unattended installation of Windows 2000 as covered in Chapter 3.

A 120-day evaluation copy of Microsoft Windows 2000 Server is included in this training kit.

About the eBook

The Supplemental Course Materials CD-ROM includes an online version of the book that you can view on screen using Microsoft Internet Explorer 5.01 or later. For installation information, see the README.TXT file included in the root directory of the Supplemental Course Materials CD-ROM.

Note You must have the CD inserted in your CD-ROM drive for the online version of the book to run properly.

Setup Instructions

Set up your computer according to the manufacturer's instructions.

For the exercises that require networked computers, you need to make sure the computers can communicate with each other. The first computer (Computer 1) will be designated as a domain controller, and will be assigned the computer account name Server01 and the domain name microsoft.com. This computer will act as a domain controller in microsoft.com.

The second computer (Computer 2) will be assigned the computer account name of Server02 and the domain name of microsoft.com. It will act as a member server for most of the optional exercises in this course.

Preparing for Windows 2000 Server Training

The installation of Windows 2000 Server is part of this kit and is covered in Chapters 2 and 3. To reduce the possibility of difficulty in completing these exercises, your computers should contain only HCL-approved equipment, exceed the minimum hardware requirements, and be networked together in an isolated network. Ideally, each computer should have 3 GB of disk capacity and 128 MB of RAM available for the operating system and contain only software that is part of this training.

Throughout this kit you will see references to the following environment variables:

- %systemroot% points to the directory containing the Windows 2000 operating system files. Typically, %systemroot% will resolve to C:\winnt.

- %windir% points to the same location as %systemroot% and is also used in Windows 95 and Windows 98.

- %systemdrive% points to the root of the boot partition. If you installed Windows 2000 in C:\winnt then this environment variable points to C:.

Before You Begin Part 2

Part 2 will help you evaluate your readiness for the MCP Exam 70-215: Installing, Configuring, and Administering Microsoft Windows 2000 Server. When you pass this exam, you earn core credit toward Microsoft Certified Systems Engineer (MCSE) certification. In addition, when you pass this exam you achieve Microsoft Certified Professional status.

Note You can find a complete list of MCP exams and their related objectives on the Microsoft Certified Professional Web site at *http://www.microsoft.com/mcp/*.

The Components of Part 2

An electronic assessment program for Exam 70-215 is provided on the Supplemental Course Materials CD. This program is a practice certification test that helps you evaluate your skills. It provides instant scoring feedback so that you can determine areas in which additional study may be helpful before you take the certification exam. Although your score on the electronic assessment does not necessarily indicate what your score will be on the certification exam, it does give you the opportunity to answer questions that are similar to those on the actual certification exam.

Part 2 is organized by the exam's objectives. Each chapter of the book pertains to one of the seven primary groups of objectives on the actual exam, called the *Objective Domains*. Each Objective Domain lists the tested skills you need to master to adequately answer the exam questions. Because the certification exams focus on real-world skills, the Tested Skills and Suggested Practices lists provide practices that emphasize the practical application of the exam objectives. Each Objective Domain also provides suggestions for further reading or additional resources to help you understand the objectives and increase your ability to perform the task or skills specified by the objectives.

Within each Objective Domain, you will find the related objectives that are covered on the exam. Each objective provides you with the following:

- **Key terms** you must know to understand the objective. Knowing these terms can help you answer the objective's questions correctly.

- Several sample exam questions with the correct answers. The answers are accompanied by explanations of each correct and incorrect answer. (These questions match the questions on the electronic assessment.)

Use the electronic assessment to determine the exam objectives that you need to study, and then use the book to learn more about those particular objectives and discover additional study materials to supplement your knowledge. You can also use the book to research the answers to specific sample test questions. Keep in mind that to pass the exam, you should understand not only the answer to the question, but also the concepts on which the correct answer is based.

MCP Exam Prerequisites

No exams or classes are required before you take the Installing, Configuring, and Administering Microsoft Windows 2000 Server exam. However, in addition to the skills tested by the exam, you should have a working knowledge of the operation and support of hardware and software on Windows 2000 Server computers. This knowledge should include:

- Using the Windows 2000 operating system interface.
- Using Windows 2000 Server utilities, including TCP/IP utilities and internal and external operating system commands.
- Knowledge of the fundamentals of current networking technology.
- Practical knowledge of accessing and changing PC computer BIOS settings.
- Installing application software.
- Installing hardware devices, such as memory, communication peripherals, and disk drives.
- Successful completion of Part 1, "Self-Paced Training for Microsoft Windows 2000 Server" is recommended.

Note After you have determined that you are ready for the exam, use the Get More MCP Information link provided in the home page of the electronic assessment tool for information on scheduling for the exam. You can schedule exams up to six weeks in advance, or as late as one working day before the exam date.

Know the Products

Microsoft's certification program relies on exams that measure your ability to perform a specific job function or set of tasks. Microsoft develops the exams by analyzing the tasks performed by people who are currently working in the field. Therefore, the specific knowledge, skills, and abilities relating to the job are reflected in the certification exam.

Because the certification exams are based on real-world tasks, you need to gain hands-on experience with the applicable technology in order to master the exam. In a sense, you might consider hands-on experience in an organizational environment to be a prerequisite for passing an MCP exam. Many of the questions relate directly to Microsoft products or technology, so use opportunities at your organization or home to practice using the relevant tools.

Using the Electronic Assessment and Part 2

Although you can use the electronic assessment and Part 2 in a number of ways, you might start your studies by taking the electronic assessment as a pretest. After completing the exam, review your results for each Objective Domain and focus your studies first on the Objective Domains for which you received the lowest scores. The electronic assessment allows you to print your results, and a printed report of how you fared can be useful when reviewing the exam material in this book.

After you have taken the electronic assessment, use Part 2 to learn more about the Objective Domains that you find difficult and to find listings of appropriate study materials that may supplement your knowledge. By reviewing why the answers are correct or incorrect, you can determine if you need to study the objective topics more.

You can also use Part 2 to focus on the exact objectives that you need to master. Each objective in the book contains several questions that help you determine if you understand the information related to that particular skill. Part 2 is also designed for you to answer each question before turning the page to review the correct answer.

The best method to prepare for the MCP exam is to use Part 2 in conjunction with the electronic assessment and other study material. Thoroughly studying and practicing the material combined with substantial real-world experience can help you fully prepare for the MCP exam.

Understanding the Conventions for Part 2

Before you begin Part 2, it is important that you understand the terms and conventions used in the electronic assessment and book.

Question Numbering System

The electronic assessment and Part 2 of the book contain reference numbers for each question. Understanding the numbering format will help you use this part of the training kit more effectively. When Microsoft creates the exams, the questions are grouped by job skills called *Objectives*. These Objectives are then organized by sections known as *Objective Domains*. Each question can be identified by the Objective Domain and the Objective it covers. The question numbers follow this format:

Test Number.Objective Domain.Objective.Question Number

For example, question number 70-215.02.01.003 means this is question three (003) for the first Objective (01) in the second Objective Domain (02) of the Installing, Configuring, and Administering Microsoft Windows 2000 Server exam (70-215). Each question is numbered based on its presentation in the printed book. You can use this numbering system to reference questions on the electronic assessment or in Part 2 of the book. Even though the questions in the book are organized by objective, questions in the electronic assessment and actual certification exam are presented in random order.

Notational Conventions

- Characters or commands that you type appear in **bold lowercase** type.
- Variable information and URLs are *italicized*. *Italic* is also used for book titles.
- Acronyms, Filenames, and Utilities appear in FULL CAPITALS.

Notes

Notes appear throughout the book.

- Notes marked *Caution* contain information you will want to know before continuing with the book's material.
- Notes marked *Note* contain supplemental information.
- Notes marked *Tip* contain helpful process hints.

Using the Electronic Assessment

The electronic assessment simulates the actual MCP exam. Each iteration of the electronic assessment consists of 50 questions covering all the objectives for the Installing, Configuring, and Administering Microsoft Windows 2000 Server exam. (MCP certification exams consist of approximately 50 questions.) Just like a real certification exam, you see questions from the objectives in random order during the practice test. Similar to the certification exam, the electronic assessment allows you to mark questions and review them after you finish the test.

To increase its value as a study aid, you can take the electronic assessment multiple times. Each time you are presented with a different set of questions in a revised order; however, some questions may be repeated.

If you have used one of the certification exam preparation tests available from Microsoft, the electronic assessment should look familiar. The difference is that this electronic assessment gives you the opportunity to learn as you take the exam.

Installing and Running
the Electronic Assessment Software

Before you begin using the electronic assessment, you need to install the software. You need a computer with the following minimum configuration:

- Multimedia PC with a 75 MHz Pentium or higher processor
- Microsoft Internet Explorer 5.01 or later
- If you do not have Internet Explorer 5.01, you can download it for free from *http://www.microsoft.com/ie/*
- 16 MB RAM for Windows 95 or Windows 98, or
- 32 MB RAM for Windows NT, or
- 64 MB RAM for Windows 2000
- 17 MB of available hard disk space
- A double-speed CD-ROM drive or better
- Super VGA display with at least 256 colors

▶ **To install the electronic assessment**

1. Insert the Supplemental Course Materials compact disc into your CD-ROM drive.

   A starting menu will display automatically, with links to the resources included on the CD-ROM. Click the link to the exam you want to install.

2. Click Next.

   The License Agreement dialog box appears.

3. To continue with the installation of the electronic assessment engine, you must accept the License Agreement by clicking Yes.

4. The Choose Destination Location dialog box appears showing a default installation directory. Either accept the default or change the installation directory if needed. Click Next to copy the files to your hard drive.

5. A Question dialog box appears asking whether you would like Setup to create a desktop shortcut for this program. If you click Yes, an icon will be placed on your desktop.

6. The Setup Complete dialog box appears. Select whether you want to view the README.TXT file after closing the Setup program, and then click Finish.

The electronic assessment software is completely installed. If you chose to view the README.TXT file, it will launch in a new window. For optimal viewing enable word wrap.

▶ To start the electronic assessment

1. From the Start menu, point to Programs, point to MCSE Readiness Review, and then click MCSE RR Exam 70-215.

   The electronic assessment program starts.

2. Click Start Test.

   Information about the electronic assessment program appears.

3. Click OK.

Note The electronic assessment programs are designed to run independently of other electronic assessment programs and will not run simultaneously.

Taking the Electronic Assessment

The electronic assessment consists of 50 multiple-choice questions, and as in the certification exam, you can skip questions or mark them for later review. Each exam question contains a question number that you can use to refer back to Part 2 of the book.

Before you end the electronic assessment, you should make sure to answer all the questions. When the exam is graded, unanswered questions are counted as incorrect and will lower your score. Similarly, on the actual certification exam you should complete all questions or they will be counted as incorrect. No trick questions appear on the exam. The correct answer will always be among the list of choices. Some questions may have more than one correct answer, and this will be indicated in the question. A good strategy is to eliminate the most obvious incorrect answers first to make it easier for you to select the correct answer.

You have 75 minutes to complete the electronic assessment. During the exam you will see a timer indicating the amount of time you have remaining. This will help you to gauge the amount of time you should use to answer each question and to complete the exam. The amount of time you are given on the actual certification exam varies with each exam. Generally, certification exams take approximately 100 minutes to complete.

Ending and Grading the Electronic Assessment

When you click the Score Test button, you have the opportunity to review the questions you marked or left incomplete. (This format is not similar to the one used on the actual certification exam, in which you can verify whether you are satisfied with your answers and then click the Grade Test button.) The electronic assessment is graded when you click the Score Test button, and the software presents your section scores and your total score.

You can always end a test without grading your electronic assessment by clicking the Home button.

After your electronic assessment is graded, you can view the correct and incorrect answers by clicking the Review Questions button.

Interpreting the Electronic Assessment Results

The Score screen shows you the number of questions in each Objective Domain section, the number of questions you answered correctly, and a percentage grade for each section. You can use the Score screen to determine where to spend additional time studying. On the actual certification exam, the number of questions and passing score will depend on the exam you are taking. The electronic assessment records your score each time you grade an exam so that you can track your progress over time.

▸ **To view your progress and exam records**

1. From the electronic assessment Main menu, click View History. Your scores will appear.

2. Click on a test attempt date/time to view your score for each objective domain.

    Review these scores to determine which Objective Domains you should study further. You can also use the scores to determine your progress.

Ordering More Questions

Self Test Software offers practice tests to help you prepare for a variety of MCP certification exams. These practice tests contain hundreds of additional questions and are similar to the electronic assessment. For a fee, you can order exam practice tests for this exam and other Microsoft certification exams. Click on the Order More Questions link on the electronic assessment home page for more information.

Using Part 2 of This Book

You can use Part 2 of the book as a supplement to the electronic assessment, or as a standalone study aid. If you decide to use the book as a standalone study aid, review the Table of Contents to find topics of interest or an appropriate starting point for you. To get the greatest benefit from the book, use the electronic assessment as a pretest to determine the Objective Domains for which you should spend the most study time. Or, if you would like to research specific questions while taking the electronic assessment, you can use the question number located on the question screen to reference the question number in the book.

One way to determine areas in which additional study may be helpful is to carefully review your individual section scores from the electronic assessment and note objective areas in which your score could be improved. The section scores correlate to the Objective Domains listed in the book.

Review the Objectives

Each Objective Domain in the book contains an introduction and a list of practice skills. Each list of practice skills describes suggested tasks you can perform to help you understand the objectives. Some of the tasks suggest reading additional material, while others are hands-on practices with software or hardware. You should pay particular attention to the hands-on practices, as the certification exam reflects real-world knowledge you can gain only by working with the software or technology. Increasing your real-world experience with the relevant products and technologies will improve your performance on the exam.

Once you have chosen the objectives you would like to study, turn to the Table of Contents to locate the objectives in Part 2 of the book. You can study each objective separately, but you may need to understand the concepts explained in other objectives.

Make sure you understand the key terms for each objective. You will need a thorough understanding of these terms to answer the objective's questions correctly. Key term definitions are located in the glossary of the electronic assessment program, which is located on the Supplemental Course Materials compact disc.

Review the Questions

Each odd-numbered page contains one or two questions followed by the possible answers. After you review the question and select a probable answer, you can turn to the Answer section to determine whether you answered the question correctly. (For information about the question numbering format, see "Question Numbering System," earlier in this introduction.)

Part 2 briefly discusses each possible answer and explains why each answer is correct or incorrect. After reviewing each explanation, if you feel you need more information about a topic, question, or answer, refer to the Further Readings section for that domain for more information.

The answers to the questions in Part 2 and the electronic assessment are based on current industry specifications and standards. However, the information provided by the answers is subject to change as technology improves and changes.

The Microsoft Certified Professional Program

The Microsoft Certified Professional (MCP) program is the best method to prove your command of current Microsoft products and technologies. Microsoft, an industry leader in certification, is on the forefront of testing methodology. Our exams and corresponding certifications are developed to validate your mastery of critical competencies as you design and develop, or implement and support, solutions with Microsoft products and technologies. Computer professionals who become Microsoft certified are recognized as experts industry-wide.

The Microsoft Certified Professional program offers eight certifications, based on specific areas of technical expertise:

- *Microsoft Certified Professional (MCP).* Demonstrated in-depth knowledge of at least one Microsoft operating system. Candidates may pass additional Microsoft certification exams to further qualify their skills with Microsoft BackOffice products, development tools, or desktop programs.

- *Microsoft Certified Professional + Internet.* MCPs with a specialty in the Internet are qualified to plan security, install and configure server products, manage server resources, extend servers to run scripts, monitor and analyze performance, and troubleshoot problems.

- *Microsoft Certified Professional + Site Building.* Demonstrated what it takes to plan, build, maintain, and manage Web sites using Microsoft technologies and products.

- *Microsoft Certified Systems Administrator (MCSA)* on Microsoft Windows 2000. Individuals who implement, manage, and troubleshoot existing network and system environments based on the Microsoft Windows 2000 and Windows .NET Server operating systems.

- *Microsoft Certified Systems Engineer (MCSE).* Qualified to effectively plan, implement, maintain, and support information systems in a wide range of computing environments with Microsoft Windows NT Server and the Microsoft BackOffice integrated family of server software.

- *Microsoft Certified Systems Engineer + Internet.* MCSEs with an advanced qualification to enhance, deploy, and manage sophisticated intranet and Internet solutions that include a browser, proxy server, host servers, database, and messaging and commerce components. In addition, an MCSE+Internet-certified professional is able to manage and analyze Web sites.

- *Microsoft Certified Database Administrator (MCDBA).* Individuals who derive physical database designs, develop logical data models, create physical databases, create data services by using Transact-SQL, manage and maintain databases, configure and manage security, monitor and optimize databases, and install and configure Microsoft SQL Server.

- *Microsoft Certified Solution Developer (MCSD).* Qualified to design and develop custom business solutions with Microsoft development tools, technologies, and platforms, including Microsoft Office and Microsoft BackOffice.

- *Microsoft Certified Trainer (MCT).* Instructionally and technically qualified to deliver Microsoft Official Curriculum through a Microsoft Certified Technical Education Center (CTEC).

Microsoft Certification Benefits

Microsoft certification, one of the most comprehensive certification programs available for assessing and maintaining software-related skills, is a valuable measure of an individual's knowledge and expertise. Microsoft certification is awarded to individuals who have successfully demonstrated their ability to perform specific tasks and implement solutions with Microsoft products. Not only does this provide an objective measure for employers to consider, it provides guidance for what an individual should know to be proficient. And as with any skills-assessment and benchmarking measure, certification brings a variety of benefits: to the individual, to employers, and to organizations.

Microsoft Certification Benefits for Individuals

As a Microsoft Certified Professional, you receive many benefits:

- Industry recognition of your knowledge and proficiency with Microsoft products and technologies.

- Access to technical and product information directly from Microsoft through a secured area of the MCP Web Site.

- MSDN Online Certified Membership that helps you tap into the best technical resources, connect to the MCP community, and gain access to valuable resources and services. (Some MSDN Online benefits may be available in English only or may not be available in all countries.) See the MSDN Web site for a growing list of certified member benefits.

- Logos to enable you to identify your Microsoft Certified Professional status to colleagues or clients.

- Invitations to Microsoft conferences, technical training sessions, and special events.

- A Microsoft Certified Professional certificate.

- Subscription to *Microsoft Certified Professional Magazine* (North America only), a career and professional development magazine.

Additional benefits, depending on your certification and location, include:

- A complimentary one-year subscription to the Microsoft TechNet Technical Plus, providing valuable information on monthly CD-ROMs.

- A one-year subscription to the Microsoft Beta Evaluation program. This benefit provides you with up to 12 free monthly CD-ROMs containing beta software (English only) for many of Microsoft's newest software products.

Microsoft Certification Benefits for Employers and Organizations

Through certification, computer professionals can maximize the return on investment in Microsoft technology. Research shows that Microsoft certification provides organizations with:

- Excellent return on training and certification investments by providing a standard method of determining training needs and measuring results.

- Increased customer satisfaction and decreased support costs through improved service, increased productivity and greater technical self-sufficiency.

- Reliable benchmark for hiring, promoting and career planning.

- Recognition and rewards for productive employees by validating their expertise.

- Retraining options for existing employees so they can work effectively with new technologies.

- Assurance of quality when outsourcing computer services.

Requirements for Becoming a Microsoft Certified Professional

The certification requirements differ for each certification and are specific to the products and job functions addressed by the certification.

To become a Microsoft Certified Professional, you must pass rigorous certification exams that provide a valid and reliable measure of technical proficiency and expertise. These exams are designed to test your expertise and ability to perform a role or task with a product, and are developed with the input of professionals in the industry. Questions in the exams reflect how Microsoft products are used in actual organizations, giving them "real-world" relevance.

Microsoft Certified Product Specialists are required to pass one operating system exam. Candidate may pass additional Microsoft certification exams to further qualify their skills with Microsoft BackOffice products, development tools, or desktop applications.

Microsoft Certified Professional + Internet specialists are required to pass the prescribed Microsoft Windows NT Server 4.0, TCP/IP, and Microsoft Internet Information System exam series.

Microsoft Certified Professionals with a specialty in site building are required to pass two exams covering Microsoft FrontPage, Microsoft Site Server, and Microsoft Visual InterDev technologies to provide a valid and reliable measure of technical proficiency and expertise.

Microsoft Certified Systems Engineers are required to pass a series of core Microsoft Windows operating system and networking exams, and BackOffice technology elective exams.

Microsoft Certified Systems Engineers + Internet specialists are required to pass seven operating system exams and two elective exams that provide a valid and reliable measure of technical proficiency and expertise.

Microsoft Certified Database Administrators are required to pass three core exams and one elective exam that provide a valid and reliable measure of technical proficiency and expertise.

Microsoft Certified Solution Developers are required to pass two core Microsoft Windows operating system technology exams and two BackOffice technology elective exams.

Microsoft Certified Trainers are required to meet instructional and technical requirements specific to each Microsoft Official Curriculum course they are certified to deliver. In the United States and Canada, call Microsoft at (800) 636-7544 for more information on becoming a Microsoft Certified Trainer or visit *http://www.microsoft.com/traincert/mcp/*. Outside the United States and Canada, contact your local Microsoft subsidiary.

Technical Training for Computer Professionals

Technical training is available in a variety of ways, with instructor-led classes, online instruction, or self-paced training available at thousands of locations worldwide.

Self-paced Training

For motivated learners who are ready for the challenge, self-paced instruction is the most flexible, cost-effective way to increase your knowledge and skills.

A full line of self-paced print and computer-based training materials is available direct from the source—Microsoft Press. Microsoft Official Curriculum courseware kits designed for advanced computer system professionals are available from Microsoft Press and the Microsoft Developer Division. Self-paced training kits from Microsoft Press feature print-based instructional materials, along with CD-ROM–based product software, multimedia presentations, lab exercises, and practice files. The Mastering Series provides in-depth, interactive training on CD-ROM for experienced developers. These are all great ways to prepare for Microsoft Certified Professional (MCP) exams.

Online Training

For a more flexible alternative to instructor-led classes, turn to online instruction. It's as near as the Internet and it's ready whenever you are. Learn at your own pace and on your own schedule in a virtual classroom, often with easy access to an online instructor. Without ever leaving your desk, you can gain the expertise you need. Online instruction covers a variety of Microsoft products and technologies. It includes options ranging from Microsoft Official Curriculum to choices available nowhere else. It's training on demand, with access to learning resources 24 hours a day. Online training is available through Microsoft Certified Technical Education Centers.

Microsoft Certified Technical Education Centers

Microsoft Certified Technical Education Centers (CTECs) are the best source for instructor-led training that can help you prepare to become a Microsoft Certified Professional. The Microsoft CTEC program is a worldwide network of qualified technical training organizations that provide authorized delivery of Microsoft Official Curriculum courses by Microsoft Certified Trainers to computer professionals.

For a listing of CTEC locations in the United States and Canada, visit *http://www.microsoft.com/traincert/CTEC/*.

Technical Support

Every effort has been made to ensure the accuracy of this book and the contents of the companion disc. If you have comments, questions, or ideas regarding this book or the companion disc, please send them to Microsoft Press using either of the following methods:

E-mail:
TKINPUT@MICROSOFT.COM

Postal Mail:
Microsoft Press
Attn: *MCSE Training Kit–Microsoft Windows 2000 Server* Editor
One Microsoft Way
Redmond, WA 98052-6399

Microsoft Press provides corrections for books through the World Wide Web at the following address:

http://www.microsoft.com/mspress/support/

Please note that product support is not offered through the above mail addresses. For further information regarding Microsoft software support options, please connect to *http://www.microsoft.com/support/* or call Microsoft Support Network Sales at (800) 936-3500.

P A R T   1

Self-Paced Training for
Microsoft Windows 2000 Server

C H A P T E R   1

Introduction to Microsoft Windows 2000

About This Chapter

This chapter introduces you to the Microsoft Windows 2000 operating system. It describes the various editions of Windows 2000 and provides an overview of the operating system architecture. This chapter also discusses the concept of directory services and introduces you to Active Directory services, the centralized directory service included in Windows 2000 Server, Advanced Server, and Windows 2000 Datacenter Server.

Before You Begin

There are no special requirements to complete the lessons in this chapter, although a working knowledge of Microsoft Windows NT is helpful.

Lesson 1: Overview of Windows 2000

This lesson introduces you to the family of Windows 2000 products, which includes Windows 2000 Professional, Windows 2000 Server, Windows 2000 Advanced Server, and Windows 2000 Datacenter Server. The lesson goes on to describe the features and benefits of Windows 2000, with a focus on features specific to Windows 2000 Professional and Windows 2000 Server.

After this lesson, you will be able to

- Describe the key features of the four editions of Windows 2000 and identify how these editions differ from one another

Estimated lesson time: 15 minutes

Editions of Windows 2000

Windows 2000 is a multipurpose operating system with integrated support for client/server and peer-to-peer networks. The Windows 2000 family of products has been designed to increase reliability, deliver higher levels of system availability, and provide for scalability from a small network to a large enterprise network. Windows 2000 incorporates technologies that reduce the total cost of ownership by allowing organizations to increase the value of their existing investments while lowering overall computing costs. In addition, Windows 2000 incorporates comprehensive Internet and applications support, building on the success of Windows NT Server 4.0 as an Internet-aware, application-enabled server operating system.

Microsoft has released four editions of Windows 2000: Windows 2000 Professional, Windows 2000 Server, Windows 2000 Advanced Server, and Windows 2000 Datacenter Server. These products support an advanced PC-based, client/server infrastructure that lowers costs and allows an organization to adapt quickly to change. The Windows 2000 platform provides administrators with more control over their networks and client/server infrastructure, maximizing flexibility while supporting the kind of centralized control typically associated with a mainframe/terminal model.

Windows 2000 Professional

Windows 2000 Professional is the main Microsoft desktop operating system for businesses of all sizes. It is a high-performance, secure-network client computer and corporate desktop operating system that incorporates the best business features of Windows 98 and builds in the traditional strengths of Windows NT Workstation. Windows 2000 Professional includes a simplified user interface, plug and play capabilities, enhanced power management, and support for a broad range of hardware devices. In addition, Windows 2000 Professional significantly extends the manageability, reliability, and security of Windows NT because of its new file encryption system and application management tools.

Windows 2000 Server

Windows 2000 Server is a file, print, and application server, as well as a Web-server platform, and contains all the features of Windows 2000 Professional plus many new server-specific functions. At the core of Windows 2000 is a complete set of infrastructure services based on Active Directory services. Active Directory services centralizes the management of users, groups, security services, and network resources. Windows 2000 Server supports uniprocessor systems to four-way symmetric multiprocessing (SMP) systems with up to 4 gigabytes (GB) of physical memory. It includes the multipurpose capabilities required for workgroups and branch offices as well as for departmental deployments of file and print servers, application servers, Web servers, and communication servers. Windows 2000 Server is ideal for small-to-medium sized enterprise application deployments.

Windows 2000 Advanced Server

Windows 2000 Advanced Server is a more powerful departmental and application server operating system that includes the full feature set of Windows 2000 Server and adds the advanced high availability and improved scalability required for enterprise and larger departmental solutions. Windows 2000 Advanced Server supports eight-way SMP and integrates high-availability two-way clustering, and it is ideal for database-intensive work. Hardware that is designed around the Intel Physical Address Extensions (PAEs) allows Windows 2000 Advanced Server to take advantage of more physical memory.

Windows 2000 Datacenter Server

Windows 2000 Datacenter Server is a specialized high-end version of Windows 2000 Server designed for large-scale enterprise solutions. Windows 2000 Datacenter Server is optimized for large data warehouses, econometric analysis, large-scale simulations in science and engineering, online transaction processing (OLTP), and server consolidation projects. It is also ideal for large-scale Internet Service Providers (ISPs) and Web site hosting. Windows 2000 Datacenter Server includes the full feature set of Windows 2000 Advanced Server, providing load balancing services and enhancing clustering services by supporting four-way clustering. It is a specialized high-end version of Windows 2000 Server that supports up to 16-way SMP and up to 32-way SMP through original equipment manufacturer (OEM) operating system enhancements.

Features of Windows 2000

The following table describes the features and benefits of Windows 2000. The table includes information specific to Windows 2000 Professional and Windows 2000 Server.

Feature	Benefit
Lower total cost of ownership	Reduces the cost of running and administering a network by providing automatic installation and upgrading of applications, and by simplifying the setup and configuration of client computers.
	Reduces the number of calls to support by providing the familiar Microsoft Windows interface for users and administrators, including wizards and interactive help.
	Reduces the need for administrators to travel to desktop computers to upgrade the operating system.
Security	Authenticates users before they gain access to resources or data on a computer or the network.
	Provides local and network security and auditing for files, folders, printers, and other resources.
	Supports the Kerberos protocol and public key infrastructure (PKI) security.
Directory services	Stores information about network resources, such as user accounts, applications, print resources, and security information.
	Provides the services that permit users to gain access to resources throughout the entire Windows 2000 network and to locate users, computers, and other resources. Also enables administrators to manage and secure these resources.
	Windows 2000 Server Stores and manages Active Directory services information in the directory, which is the database that stores information about network resources, such as computers and printers. Active Directory services makes this information available to users and applications. It also enables administrators to control access to resources.
Performance and scalability	Supports SMP on computers that are configured with multiple micro processors. Also supports multitasking for system processes and programs.
	Windows 2000 Server Supports up to four microprocessors. Windows 2000 Server computers are typically configured as a file and print server or application server, such as Terminal Services.
	Windows 2000 Professional Supports up to two microprocessors.

Feature	Benefit
Networking and communication services	Provides built-in support for the most popular network protocols, including TCP/IP and IPX/SPX.
	Provides connectivity with Novell NetWare, UNIX, and AppleTalk.
	Provides dial-up networking, which lets mobile users connect to a computer running Windows 2000.
	Windows 2000 Server Supports 256 simultaneous inbound dial-up sessions.
	Windows 2000 Professional Supports one inbound dial-up networking session.
Internet integration	Integrates users' desktops with the Internet, thereby removing the distinction between the local computer and the Internet. Users can securely browse the network, intranet, and Internet for resources, as well as send and receive e-mail messages.
	Windows 2000 Server Includes Microsoft Internet Information Server (IIS), which is a secure Web-server platform used to host Internet and intranet Web sites on network servers.
	Windows 2000 Professional Provides a personal Web server, which enables users to host personal Web sites.
Integrated administration tools	Provides the means to create customized tools to manage local and remote computers with a single standard interface.
	Provides the means to incorporate third-party administrative tools into the standard interface.
Hardware support	Supports universal serial bus (USB), an external bus standard that eliminates many constraints of earlier computer peripherals.
	Supports Plug and Play hardware, which Windows 2000 automatically detects, installs, and configures.

Lesson Summary

Windows 2000 consists of a family of four products: Windows 2000 Professional, Windows 2000 Server, Windows 2000 Advanced Server, and Windows 2000 Datacenter Server. Windows 2000 Professional is a desktop operating system with integrated support for client/server and peer-to-peer networks. Windows 2000 Server contains all the features of Windows 2000 Professional plus many new server-specific functions. Windows 2000 Server is well suited as a file and print server or application server, such as a Web-server platform. Windows 2000 Advanced Server is a more powerful departmental and application server operating system that builds on Windows 2000 Server by providing two-way clustering and load balancing. Windows 2000 Datacenter Server includes all the features of Windows 2000 Advanced Server, but supports four-way clustering, more processors, and more than 10,000 simultaneous users. It is the most powerful server operating system ever offered by Microsoft for large-scale enterprise solutions.

Lesson 2: Operating System Architecture

Windows 2000 is an object-based system. In other words, it is a modular operating system made up of small, self-contained software components that work together to perform operating system tasks. Each component provides a set of functions that act as an interface to the rest of the system.

After this lesson, you will be able to

- Identify the main components of the Windows 2000 operating system architecture

- Distinguish those components in the user mode layer from those in the kernel mode layer

- Identify the characteristics of kernel mode drivers, including Windows Driver Model (WDM) drivers

Estimated lesson time: 45 minutes

Windows 2000 Architectural Overview

Windows 2000 is a portable operating system designed to run on Complex Instruction Set Computing (CISC)-based computers. Because of this, devices and their drivers are both hardware-configurable and software-configurable. Windows 2000 is always preemptible and always interruptible, and it is designed to run uniformly on uniprocessor and SMP platforms, ensuring that code being executed on one processor does not simultaneously access and modify data being accessed and modified from another processor. Windows 2000 supports packet-driven input/output (I/O) with reusable I/O request packets (IRPs) and asynchronous I/O so that the originator of an I/O request can continue to be executed, rather than waiting for its I/O request to be completed. To support the various functionality, Windows 2000 is designed to be a modular system made up of a set of objects that can be broken into two major layers: user mode and kernel mode.

Figure 1.1 provides an overview of the Windows 2000 operating system architecture. Like all operating systems, Windows 2000 contains many lines of code designed to make computer hardware available to applications. Figure 1.1 merely provides a conceptual framework for understanding how the code fits together. Therefore, diagrams from different sources may vary from this one.

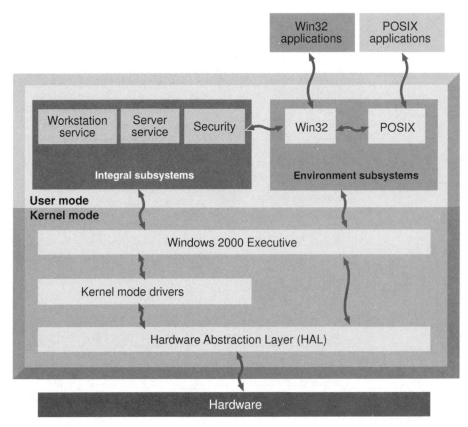

Figure 1.1 Overview of the Microsoft Windows 2000 operating system architecture

User Mode

The user mode layer of Windows 2000 is made up of a set of components referred to as *subsystems*. A subsystem passes I/O requests to the appropriate kernel mode driver through the I/O systems services. The subsystem insulates its end users and applications from having to know anything about kernel mode components. The user mode layer is made up of two kinds of subsystems: environment subsystems and integral subsystems.

Environment Subsystems

Environment subsystems allow Windows 2000 to run applications written for different operating systems. These subsystems emulate different operating systems by presenting the application programming interfaces (APIs) that the applications need to be available. The environment subsystems accept the API calls made by the application, convert the API calls into a format understood by Windows 2000, and then pass the converted API to Executive components running in kernel mode.

The following table describes the environment subsystems in Windows 2000.

Environment subsystem	Function
Win32	Controls Win32-based applications and provides an environment for Win16 and Microsoft MS-DOS–based applications.
POSIX	Provides APIs for POSIX-based applications. *POSIX* refers to the portable operating system interface standard developed by the Institute of Electrical and Electronics Engineers (IEEE) to ensure portability of applications across different platforms.

The environment subsystems and the applications that run within them have no direct access to hardware or device drivers. They are limited to an assigned address space. Environment subsystems are forced to use hard disk space as virtual memory whenever the system needs memory. In addition, these subsystems run at a lower priority than kernel mode processes. Consequently, they have less access to CPU cycles than processes that run in kernel mode.

Note Microsoft Enterprise Memory Architecture (EMA), part of Windows 2000 Advanced Server and Windows 2000 Datacenter Server, can make larger amounts of physical RAM available to applications, thereby improving their performance.

Integral Subsystems

Integral subsystems perform essential operating system functions. The following table describes some of the important integral subsystems.

Integral subsystem	Function
Security	Creates security tokens and tracks rights and permissions associated with user accounts. The subsystem accepts user logon requests and initiates logon authentication. The Security subsystem also tracks which system resources are audited.
Workstation service	A networking integral subsystem that provides an API to access the network redirector. The Workstation service allows a Windows 2000 computer to access the network.
Server service	A networking integral subsystem that provides an API to access the network server. The Server service allows a Windows 2000 computer to provide network resources.

Kernel Mode

The kernel mode layer of the Windows 2000 architecture has access to system data and hardware. Kernel mode provides direct access to memory and is executed in a protected memory area. It determines when a particular sequence of code is run by following prioritizing criteria. Every thread has an associated priority attribute. The kernel mode also prioritizes hardware and software interrupts so that some kernel mode code runs at higher interrupt request levels (IRQLs). The kernel mode consists of several components with well-defined functionality isolated in each component: the Executive, the Hardware Abstraction Level (HAL), and the set of kernel mode drivers.

Windows 2000 Executive

The Executive performs most of the I/O and object management, including security. Various components within the Executive, such as the Virtual Memory Manager (VMM) and the I/O Manager, define one or more object types. These components provide system services and internal routines. System services are available to both the user mode subsystems and to other Executive components. Internal routines are available only to other components within the Executive. No component is allowed to access any instance of another component's object types directly. The component must call the exported support routines in order to use another component's objects. Each component exports kernel-only support routines that manipulate instances of its object types when these routines are called. If the underlying implementation of a support routine changes over time, its caller remains portable because the interface to the defining component does not change.

The following table includes the kernel mode components contained in the Executive.

Component	Function
I/O Manager	Provides core services for device drivers and translates user-mode read and write commands into read or write IRPs. It manages all the other main operating system IRPs. The I/O Manager manages input from and the delivery of output to different devices. The I/O Manager includes the following components:
	File systems Accept the oriented I/O requests and translate them into device-specific calls. The network redirector and the network server are both implemented as file system drivers.
	Device drivers Low-level drivers that directly manipulate hardware to accept input or to write output.
	Cache Manager Improves disk I/O by storing disk reads in system memory. Cache Manager also improves write performance by caching writes to disk in the background.
Security reference monitor	Enforces security policies on the local computer.
Interprocess Communication (IPC) Manager	Manages communication between clients and servers. The IPC Manager manages communication between environmental subsystems and the Executive. The subsystem acts like a client requesting information, and the Executive acts like a server to satisfy the request for information. The IPC Manager includes the following two components:
	Local Procedure Call (LPC) facility Manages communication when clients and servers exist on the same computer.
	Remote Procedure Call (RPC) facility Manages communication when clients and servers exist on separate computers.
Virtual Memory Manager (VMM)	Implements and controls virtual memory, a memory management that provides a private address space for each process and protects that address space. The VMM allows the operating system to use peripheral hard disk storage as if it is actually part of the physical memory. Virtual memory uses both physical memory and disk storage. The VMM also controls demand for paging, allowing the use of disk space as a storage area to move code and data in and out of physical RAM.

Component	Function
Process Manager	Creates and terminates processes and threads. A process is a program or part of a program, and a thread is a specific set of commands within a program. The Process Manager also suspends and resumes threads, and stores and retrieves information about processes and threads.
Plug and Play (PnP) Manager	Maintains central control of the Plug and Play process. The PnP Manager supports boot-time Plug and Play activity and interfaces with HAL, the Executive, and device drivers. It maintains central control, directing bus drivers to perform enumeration and configuration and directing device drivers to add and start devices. The PnP Manager coordinates with the user mode PnP counterpart to pause or remove devices as appropriate.
Power Manager	Controls power management APIs, coordinates power events, and generates power management IRPs. For example, when several devices request to be turned off, the Power Manager collects those requests, determines which requests must be serialized, and then generates appropriate power management IRPs.
Window Manager and graphical device interface (GDI)	Manages the display system. These two components, implemented as a single device driver named Win32k.sys, perform the following functions: **Window Manager** Controls window displays and manages screen output. Window Manager is also responsible for receiving input from devices such as the keyboard and the mouse and then passing messages to applications that are receiving input. **GDI** Contains the functions that are required for drawing and manipulating graphics.
Object Manager	Creates, manages, and deletes objects that represent operating system resources, such as processes, threads, and data structures.

Hardware Abstraction Layer (HAL)

The HAL virtualizes, or hides, the hardware interface details, making Windows 2000 more portable across different hardware architectures. The HAL contains the hardware-specific code that handles I/O interfaces, interrupt controllers, and multiprocessor communication mechanisms. This layer was originally designed to allow Windows 2000 to run on both Intel-based and other platforms, such as Alpha-based systems, without having to maintain two separate versions of the Windows 2000 Executive.

Note Support for Alpha-based hardware was discontinued after Windows 2000 Release Candidate One. See the Supplemental Course Materials CD-ROM (\chapt01\articles\compaq.html) that accompanies this book.

The HAL is implemented as a dynamic-link library and is responsible for all hardware-level, platform-specific support needed by every component in the system. The HAL exports support routines that hide platform-specific hardware details about caches, I/O buses, and interrupt controllers; and provides an interface between the platform's hardware and the system's software components.

Kernel Mode Drivers

Like the Windows 2000 operating system, kernel mode drivers are implemented as discrete, modular components with a well-defined set of required functionality. All kernel mode drivers, including Windows Driver Model (WDM) drivers, include a set of system-defined standard driver routines and some internal routines, depending on individual device requirements. To all other components in the system, including user mode code, a connection to a device is represented as an open operation of a file object in I/O Manager. However, within the I/O system, the logical, virtual, and physical devices for each driver are represented as device objects. Each driver's load image is represented as a driver object within I/O Manager. I/O Manager defines the object types for file objects, device objects, and driver objects. Drivers use objects by calling kernel mode support routines exported by I/O Manager and other system components.

Kernel mode drivers share many of the design goals of Windows 2000, including all of the following:

- Portability from one platform to another
- Configurability of hardware and software
- Always preemptible and always interruptible
- Multiprocessor-safe on multiprocessor platforms
- Object-based
- Packet-driven I/O with reusable IRPs
- Support for asynchronous I/O

There are three basic types of kernel mode drivers: highest-level drivers, intermediate drivers, and lowest-level drivers, as shown in Figure 1.2.

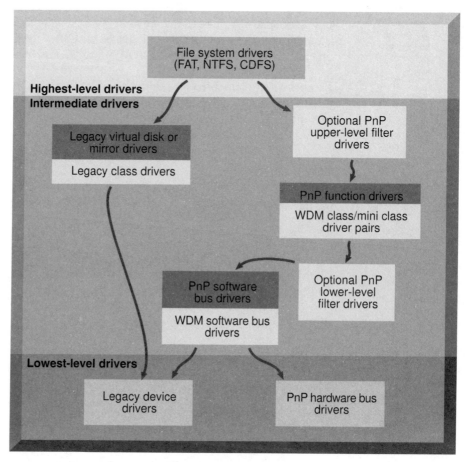

Figure 1.2 The three types of kernel mode drivers

Each type of kernel mode driver has a slightly different structure and quite different functionality. The following table provides an overview of each type of driver. Note that Windows Driver Model (WDM) drivers are included in the intermediate level.

Driver type	Description
Highest-level drivers	Includes such files system drivers (FSDs) as the system-supplied file allocation table (FAT), NT file system (NTFS), and Compact Disk File System (CDFS) drivers. Highest-level drivers always depend on support from underlying lower-level drivers. Although an FSD may or may not get support from one or more intermediate drivers, every FSD depends on support from one or more underlying peripheral device drivers.
Intermediate drivers	Includes such drivers as a virtual disk, mirror, or device-type–specific class driver. Intermediate drivers depend on support from underlying lower-level drivers. Intermediate drivers also include the following drivers:
	PnP function drivers that control specific peripheral devices on an I/O controlled by a PnP hardware bus driver;
	PnP filter drivers that insert themselves above or below PnP function drivers in the driver stack for a peripheral device;
	Any system-supplied class driver that exports a system-defined WDM class/miniport interface;
	PnP software bus drivers that present a set of child devices to which higher-level class, function, or filter drivers can attach themselves;
	WDM software bus drivers.
Lowest-level drivers	Includes such drivers as PnP hardware bus drivers that control an I/O bus on which some number of peripheral devices are connected. Lowest-level drivers do not depend on lower-level drivers but control physical peripheral devices such as buses. Lowest-level drivers also include legacy Windows NT device drivers that control a physical peripheral device directly, such as the small computer system interface (SCSI) host bus adapter driver.

Windows Driver Model (WDM)

Some Windows 2000 kernel model drivers are also WDM drivers. WDM drivers are a subset of the intermediate level of kernel mode drivers. The WDM specification defines the architecture for hardware drivers and interfaces to the operating system. Devices that conform to WDM device driver architecture benefit from a common set of WDM I/O services and a planned binary compatibility between Windows 2000 and Windows 98 operating systems.

To help decrease the effort necessary for hardware vendors to support all Windows platforms, WDM enables devices designed for either Windows 2000 or Windows 98 to be installed and used with computers running under either operating system.

This driver model is based on a class/miniport structure that provides modular, extensible architectures for device support. WDM is a core technology for the Simply Interactive PC (SIPC) and Zero Administration initiatives and for new PnP device support for USB, IEEE 1394, and the OnNow power management initiative.

Each WDM class abstracts many of the common details involved in controlling similar devices. For example, consider five separate devices attached to a USB. If each driver for each device separately contained all the code needed to talk to its device over the USB, there would be five very large drivers, consisting mainly of the same code, to deal with USB communications issues. With WDM, driver developers write the generally smaller code pieces (miniports) that talk to their hardware directly and call the appropriate class driver to do the bulk of the common tasks. Another significant advantage of writing miniports is that it decreases the likelihood of introducing bugs into device driver code.

WDM Layered Architecture

WDM is a multiple-layer driver architecture that uses special class drivers to provide cross-platform support. Driver classes are layers of abstraction that allow WDM drivers to be used in both Windows 2000 and Windows 98. There are four different classes of drivers:

- Miniport drivers
- Class drivers
- OS services
- Virtualization drivers

For each bus class and hardware device class supported by WDM, Windows 2000 provides a class driver. Because Microsoft provides all platform-specific integration support for WDM, only miniports are required to be written for all hardware devices whose classes are supported by Microsoft.

Miniport Drivers   Miniport drivers are already implemented in Windows NT in the classes of SCSI and network adapters. With Windows 2000, the concept of miniport drivers has been widened to include the USB support. Miniport drivers have the following attributes:

- Indirect control of hardware through a specific bus class driver
- Source and binary compatibility across Windows platforms
- Dynamic loading and unloading
- Hardware-specific functionality only
- Capacity to expose multiple class interfaces

Class Drivers   A class driver is best conceptualized as a driver for drivers. Class drivers provide interfaces between different layers of the WDM architecture. The lower layer of a class driver communicates with the class-specific interface exposed by a miniport driver. The upper edge of top-level class drivers is operating system-specific. Class drivers also have the following capabilities:

- Class-specific functions, not hardware-specific or bus-specific, except for bus-type class drivers
- Dynamic loading and unloading
- Class-specific functions only (such as enumeration)
- Capacity to expose a single class-specific interface to multiple client layers

OS Services   The OS services layer is always specific to the operating system. This layer abstracts all the operating system specific functionality from the miniport layers beneath it. This functionality includes:

- Thread management
- Heap management
- Event services

Virtualization Drivers   Virtualization drivers have been a part of Microsoft Windows since the release of version 3.0. They are the familiar .vxd files in Windows 95 and the .386 files in earlier versions of Windows. Virtualization drivers under WDM have some very specific functions. The functions virtualize the interfaces of legacy hardware and send class-specific commands to the appropriate device. For instance, an MS-DOS game running under Windows would use the virtualization driver to work with a USB-based joystick.

These drivers do not access hardware directly but act as go-betweens so that legacy software or hardware can work correctly under the new architecture.

The WDM driver support for Windows 2000 includes:

- Stream class driver to support kernel-mode streaming of data for video capture, MPEG decoders, audio, DVD-ROM, and broadcast architectures
- Human Interface Devices (HID) class driver to support input devices
- USB class driver
- IEEE 1394 bus class driver

Lesson Summary

Windows 2000 is a modular operating system made up of small, self-contained software components that work together to perform operating system tasks. Windows 2000 consists of a set of objects that can be broken into two major layers: user mode and kernel mode. The main components of the user mode layer are a set of subsystems that insulate end users and applications from having to know anything about kernel mode components. There are two kinds of subsystems: environment and integral. The main components of the kernel mode layer are the Executive, the HAL, and the kernel mode drivers. The Executive performs most of the I/O and object management, including security. The HAL hides the hardware interface details and handles I/O interfaces, interrupt controllers, and multiprocessor communication mechanisms. Kernel mode drivers are implemented as discrete, modular components with a well-defined set of required functionality. There are three types of kernel mode drivers: highest-level drivers, intermediate drivers, and lowest-level drivers. Windows Driver Model (WDM) drivers are a subset of intermediate kernel mode drivers.

Lesson 3: Windows 2000 Directory Services

A *directory* is a stored collection of information about objects that are all related to one another in some way. You can compare a network directory to a telephone directory, which stores the names, addresses and phone numbers of individuals and businesses. The telephone directory is a collection of attributes (names and addresses) that can be used as search properties to locate information about objects (phone numbers) that are stored in the directory. In much the same way, a *directory service* uniquely identifies users and resources on a network and provides a way to organize and access those users and resources.

After this lesson, you will be able to

- Describe the functions of a directory service
- Identify the differences between workgroups and domains
- Describe Active Directory services and its functions and identify the components of the Active Directory structure

Estimated lesson time: 45 minutes

Introduction to Directory Services

In a distributed computing system or a public computer network such as the Internet, many objects are necessary to support that system, such as users, file servers, printers, fax servers, applications, and databases. Users want to easily and efficiently locate and use these objects. Administrators want to manage how these objects are used. If all the information needed to use and manage these objects is stored in a centralized location, the process of locating and managing these resources can be vastly simplified. This is when a directory service becomes useful.

The terms directory and directory service refer to the directories found in public and private networks. A directory is a database of network objects that can be referenced in many different ways. It stores information related to the network resources to facilitate locating and managing these resources. A directory service differs from a directory in that it is both the *source* of the directory information and the *services* making the information available to the users.

A directory service provides the means to organize and simplify access to resources of a networked computer system. It makes it possible to find an object based on one or more of its attributes. For example, administrators may not know the exact name of an object, but chances are they know one or more of the attributes of that object. With a directory service, they can query the directory to get a list of objects that match the known attributes. For instance, they could query the directory for all color printer objects that are associated with the third floor attribute (or maybe a location attribute that has been set to "third floor").

You can use a directory service to perform a number of functions:

- Enforce security to protect the objects in its database from outside intruders or from internal users who do not have permission to access those objects

- Replicate a directory to other computers in the network to make it available to more users and make it resistant to failure

- Partition a directory into multiple stores that are located on different computers across the network. This makes more space available to the directory as a whole and allows the storage of a large numbers of objects

A directory service is both an administration tool and an end-user tool. The larger a network becomes, the more resources there are to manage. As the number of resource objects in a network grows, the more necessary the directory service becomes.

Workgroups and Domains

As stated earlier, a directory service provides a way to organize and simplify access to network resources. However, to facilitate that access, Windows 2000 supports two types of networks: workgroups and domains.

Windows 2000 Workgroups

A *workgroup* is a logical grouping of networked computers that share resources, such as files and printers. A domain is a logical grouping of network computers that share a central directory database that contains user accounts and security information for the domain. A workgroup is sometimes referred to as a peer-to-peer network because all computers in the workgroup can share resources as equals, without a dedicated server, as shown in Figure 1.3. Each Windows 2000 Server computer and Windows 2000 Professional computer in the workgroup maintains a local security database, which contains a list of user accounts and resource security information for that computer.

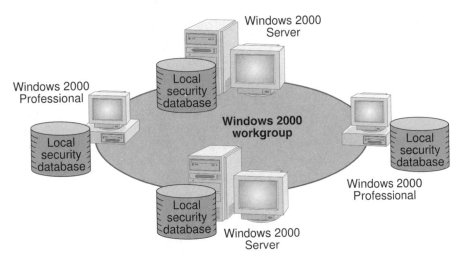

Figure 1.3 A Windows 2000 workgroup

Because each computer in the workgroup maintains a local security database, the administration of user accounts and resource security is decentralized. A user must have a user account on each computer that the user needs to access. Any changes to user accounts, such as changing a password or adding a new account, must be made on each computer. If you forget to add a new user account to one of the computers, the new user will not be able to log on to that computer and will not be able to access resources on it.

Windows 2000 workgroups provide the following advantages:

- A workgroup does not require a computer running Windows 2000 Server to hold centralized security information.

- A workgroup is simple to design and implement; it does not require the extensive planning and administration that a domain requires.

- A workgroup is convenient for a limited number of computers in close proximity, although a workgroup becomes impractical in environments with more than 10 computers.

- A workgroup is well suited to small groups of technical users who do not require central administration.

Note In a workgroup, a computer running Windows 2000 Server is called a stand-alone server.

Windows 2000 Domains

A *Windows 2000 domain* is a logical grouping of network computers that share a central directory database. A directory database contains user accounts and security information for the domain. In Windows 2000, the directory database is known as the directory and is the database portion of Active Directory services, which is the Windows 2000 directory service. In a domain, the directory resides on computers that are configured as domain controllers (Figure 1.4). A *domain controller* is a server that manages all security-related user/domain interactions and centralizes administration.

Note In Windows NT domains, domain controllers are either backup domain controllers (BDCs) or primary domain controllers (PDCs). In Windows 2000 domains, there is only one type of domain controller. All domain controllers are peers.

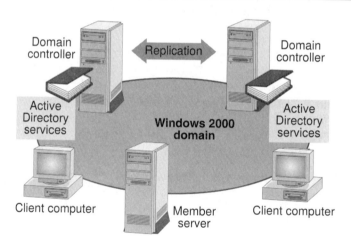

Figure 1.4 A Windows 2000 domain

A domain does not refer to a single location or a specific type of network configuration. The computers in a domain can share physical proximity on a small local area network (LAN) or can be located in different corners of the world, communicating over various kinds of connections, including analog connections, Integrated Services Digital Networks (ISDNs), or Digital Subscriber Lines (DSLs). Domains are discussed in more detail in the following section, "Windows 2000 Active Directory Services."

Windows 2000 domains provide the following advantages:

- A domain provides centralized administration because all user information is stored centrally.

- A domain provides a single logon process for users to gain access to network resources, such as file, print, and application resources for which they have permissions. A user can log on to one computer and access resources on another computer in the network as long as that user has appropriate permissions to the resource.

- A domain provides scalability so that you can create very large networks.

Windows 2000 Active Directory Services

Active Directory services is the directory service included in Windows 2000. Active Directory services provides a single point of network management, allowing you to add, remove, and relocate users and resources easily.

Active Directory services includes the directory, which stores information about network resources, as well as all the services that make the information available and useful. The resources stored in the directory, such as user data, printers, servers, databases, groups, computers, and security policies, are known as objects.

Active Directory Features

Active Directory services organizes resources hierarchically in domains. A *domain* is a logical grouping of servers and other network resources under a single domain name. The domain is the basic unit of replication and security in a Windows 2000 network.

Each domain includes one or more domain controllers. A *domain controller* is a Windows 2000 Server computer that stores a complete replica of the domain directory. To simplify administration, all domain controllers in Active Directory services are peers, so you can make changes to any domain controller and the updates are replicated to all other domain controllers in the domain.

Scalability

In Active Directory services, the directory stores information by using *partitions*, which are logical dividers that organize the directory into sections and permit storage of a large number of objects. Therefore, the directory can expand as an organization grows, allowing you to scale from a small installation with a few hundred objects to a large installation with millions of objects.

Open Standards Support

Active Directory services integrates the Internet concept of a namespace with Windows NT directory services. This integration allows you to unify and manage the multiple namespaces that now exist in the heterogeneous software and hardware environments of corporate networks. Active Directory services uses the Domain Name System (DNS) for its name system and can exchange information with any application or directory that uses Lightweight Directory Access Protocol (LDAP). Active Directory services also shares information with other directory services that support LDAP versions 2 and 3, such as Novell Directory Services (NDS).

The Domain Name System (DNS)

Because Active Directory services uses DNS as its domain naming and location service, Windows 2000 domain names are also DNS names. Windows 2000 Server uses dynamic DNS, which enables client computers with dynamically assigned addresses to register directly with the DNS server and update the DNS table dynamically. Dynamic DNS can eliminate the need for other Internet naming services, such as Windows Internet Naming Service (WINS).

Note For Active Directory services and associated client software to function correctly, you must have installed and configured the DNS service.

Lightweight Directory Access Protocol (LDAP)

Active Directory services further embraces Internet standards by directly supporting LDAP. LDAP is an Internet standard (RFC 1777) for accessing directory services. It was developed as a simpler alternative to the X.500 Directory Access Protocol (DAP). X.500 is a set of standards defining a distributed directory service, developed by the International Standards Organization (ISO). Active Directory services supports both LDAP versions 2 and 3. Active Directory uses LDAP to exchange information between directories and applications.

Note RFC 1777 is located on the Supplemental Course Materials CD-ROM (\chapt01\articles\RFC 1777.txt) that accompanies this book.

Support for Standard Name Formats

Active Directory services supports several common name formats. As a result, users and applications can access Active Directory services by using the format they are most familiar with. The following table describes some standard name formats supported by Active Directory services.

Format	Description
RFC 822	RFC 822 names are in the form *username@domainname* and are familiar to most users as Internet e-mail addresses.
LDAP URLs and X.500	LDAP names use X.500's attributed naming. An LDAP URL specifies the server holding Active Directory services and the attributed name of the object. For example:
	LDAP://servername.myco.com/CN=jimsmith,OU=sys, OU=product,OU=division,O=myco,C=US.
Universal Naming Convention (UNC)	Active Directory services supports the UNC used in Windows 2000-based networks to refer to shared volumes, printers, and files. For example:
	\\servername.myco.com\xl\budget.xls.

At any time, the interface determines the name standard that may be used. Sometimes any of the naming standards may be used (for example, during logon), while at other times a particular standard will be required. (For instance, the LDP utility, an Active Directory support tool, requires the LDAP naming convention.)

The Active Directory Structure

Windows 2000 Active Directory services provides a method for designing a directory structure tailored to the needs of your organization. Therefore, you should examine your organization's business structure and operations before installing Active Directory services.

Active Directory services separates the network into two structures: logical and physical.

Logical Structure

In Active Directory services, you organize resources in a logical structure. Grouping resources logically enables you to find a resource by its name rather than its physical location.

Objects

An *object* is a distinct named set of attributes that represents a network resource. Object *attributes* are characteristics of objects in the directory. For example, the attributes of a user might include the user's first and last names, department, and e-mail address.

In Active Directory services, you can organize objects in *classes*, which are logical groupings of objects. For example, a class of objects might be users, groups, computers, domains, or organizational units.

Note Container objects are objects that can contain other objects. For example, a domain is a container object.

Organizational Units

An *organizational unit* (OU) is a container object that you use to organize objects within a domain into logical administrative groups. An OU can contain objects such as user accounts, groups, computers, printers, applications, file shares, and other OUs. The OU hierarchy within a domain is independent of the structure of other domains—each domain can implement its own OU hierarchy.

Domains

The core unit of the logical structure in Active Directory services is the domain. Grouping objects into one or more domains allows you to reflect your company's organization within your network.

All network objects exist within a domain, and each domain stores information only about the objects it contains. Theoretically, a domain directory can contain up to 10 million objects, but one million objects per domain is the supported (tested) limit.

A domain is a security boundary. Access to domain objects is controlled by Access Control Lists (ACLs), which are populated with Access Control Entries (ACEs). All security polices and settings, such as administrative rights, security policies, and ACLs, do not cross from one domain to another. The domain administrator has absolute rights to set policies only within that domain.

Note A domain is called a *partition* of Active Directory services. All domains within a forest make up Active Directory services. (Forests are described later in this section.)

A typical domain will have the following types of computers:

- **Domain controllers running Windows 2000 Server** Each domain controller stores and maintains a copy of the directory. Domain controllers are discussed in more detail later in this section.

- **Member servers running Windows 2000 Server** A member server is one that is not configured as a domain controller. A member server does not store directory information and cannot authenticate users. Member servers provide shared resources such as shared folders or printers.

- **Client computers running Windows 2000 Professional** Client computers run a user's desktop environment and allow the user to gain access to resources in the domain.

Trees

A *tree* is a grouping or hierarchical arrangement of one or more Windows 2000 domains that allows global resource sharing. A tree can consist of a single Windows 2000 domain. However, you can create a larger contiguous namespace by joining multiple domains in a hierarchical structure.

The following illustration (Figure 1.5) provides an example of a parent domain (microsoft.com) and two child domains (dev.microsoft.com and product.microsoft.com).

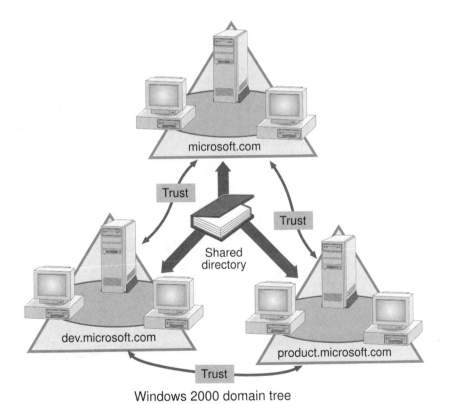

Windows 2000 domain tree

Figure 1.5 A domain tree

All domains in a tree share information and resources to function as a single unit. There is only one directory in a domain tree, but each domain maintains a portion of the directory that contains the user account information for the users in that domain. Within a tree, a user who logs on in one domain can use resources in another domain, as long as the user has the appropriate permissions.

Windows 2000 combines the directory information from all domains into a single directory, which makes the information of each domain globally accessible. In addition, each domain automatically provides a subset of its domain information in Active Directory services to an index, which resides on domain controllers. Users search this index to locate other users, computers, resources, and applications throughout the domain tree. All domains within a single tree share a common *schema*, which is a formal definition of all object types you can store in an Active Directory deployment. In addition, all domains within a single tree share a common *global catalog*, which is the central repository of information about objects in a tree or forest.

All domains within a single tree also share a common namespace and a hierarchical naming structure. A *namespace* is a set of naming rules that provides the hierarchical structure, or path, of the tree. Following DNS standards, the domain name of a child domain is the relative name of that child domain appended with the name of the parent domain. A domain tree name should map to a company's registered Internet name.

In Active Directory services, a tree is defined by:

- A hierarchy of domains
- A contiguous namespace
- Kerberos transitive trust relationships between the domains
- A common schema
- A global catalog capable of listing any object in the tree

Forests

A *forest* is a grouping of one or more trees. Forests allow organizations to group divisions (or two organizations to combine their networks) that do not use the same naming scheme, operate independently, yet need to communicate with the entire organization.

The trees in the forest share the same schema and rules on how objects work together. All domains in a forest have the same global catalog and configuration container.

A forest is defined by:

- One or more sets of trees

- Disjointed namespaces between these trees

- Kerberos transitive trust relationships between the trees

- A common schema

- A global catalog capable of listing any object in the forest

The objects of the domain trees that make up a forest are available to all user objects in the forest. However, when accessing objects in the forest but in different trees, the user must know the fully qualified domain name or must at least become comfortable with viewing multiple fully qualified domain names when browsing the internal network for resources.

Trust Relationships

The domains in a tree are joined together transparently through two-way, Kerberos transitive trust relationships. A *Kerberos transitive trust* simply means that if Domain A trusts Domain B, and Domain B trusts Domain C, then Domain A trusts Domain C. Therefore, a domain joining a tree immediately has trust relationships established with every domain in the tree. These trust relationships make all the objects in all the domains of the tree available to all other domains in the tree.

A trust relationship is a link between at least two domains in which the trusting domain honors the logon authentication of the trusted domain. User accounts and groups defined in a trusted domain can be given rights and resource permissions in a trusting domain, even though those accounts do not exist in the trusting domain's directory database. Figure 1.6 shows the difference between Windows NT two-way trusts and the simplified model of transitive trusts in Windows 2000.

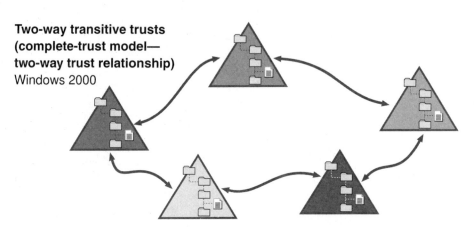

One-way explicit trusts
Windows NT 4.0

**Two-way transitive trusts
(complete-trust model—
two-way trust relationship)**
Windows 2000

Figure 1.6 Trust relationships among Windows NT domains and Windows 2000 domains

In Windows NT 4.0 and earlier versions, inter-domain trust relationships are defined by one-way trusted domain accounts between domain controllers. Each trust must be established and managed individually. Management of explicit one-way trust relationships between domains on a large network is a complex task.

Transitive Trust Relationships   The network administrator can define explicit one-way trust accounts for specific domains when a two-way trust is not appropriate. This capability is provided to support connections to existing Windows NT 4.0 and earlier domains, and to allow the configuration of trust relationships with domains in other forests.

Windows 2000 Trust Relationships   When a domain is joined to a Windows 2000 domain tree, a trust relationship is automatically established between the new domain and the root or parent domain of the tree. Transitive trust is a feature of the Kerberos system, which provides the distributed authentication and authorization in Windows 2000 computers.

Note   You can define explicit one-way trust relationships as necessary through the domain properties in the Active Directory Sites And Services snap-in. A *snap-in* is a type of tool that you can add to a console supported by Microsoft Management Console (MMC). MMC and snap-ins are discussed in detail in Chapter 6, "Administering Microsoft Windows 2000 Server."

Physical Structure

The physical structure of Active Directory services affects the efficiency of replication among the domain controllers.

Domain Controllers

A domain controller is a Windows 2000 Server computer that stores a replica of the directory partition (local domain database). All domain controllers in a domain have a complete replica of the domain's portion of the directory. When you perform an action that results in an update to the directory, Windows 2000 automatically replicates the update to all other domain controllers in the domain. Certain important updates, such as a password change or a user account being locked out, are replicated immediately throughout the domain.

In a domain, you create a user account once, which Windows 2000 records in the directory. When a user logs on to a computer in the domain, a domain controller checks the directory for the user name, password, and logon restrictions to authenticate the user. When there are multiple domain controllers, they periodically replicate their directory information. Only computers running Windows 2000 Server, Advanced Server, or Datacenter Server can be designated as domain controllers.

Sites

The concept of a site has become familiar in the implementation of Microsoft BackOffice family of products. This concept is included in the implementation of Active Directory services; however, it is different than the site concept in some BackOffice products, such as Microsoft Exchange. In Windows 2000 Active Directory services, the site concept uses existing Internet Protocol (IP) subnets to determine site boundaries for replication traffic considerations. The basic difference between sites in Active Directory services and other BackOffice products is that in Active Directory sites are defined as a range of IP subnets. In BackOffice products such as Microsoft Exchange Server, a site is a logical grouping of servers that can be specified without regard to physical location of the servers themselves.

Basically, an Active Directory site is a collection of IP subnet ranges. For example, a site can be defined as the subnet ranges 192.168.10.0/24 to 192.168.20.0/24. Another site on the other side of a WAN link can be 172.20.10.0/24 to 172.20.20.0/24. However, both sites can be part of the same Windows 2000 domain.

Note The /24 nomenclature used in the previous example represents 24 bits enabled from left to right, or 255.255.255.0. A /22 nomenclature would represent 255.255.252.0, or 22 bits enabled from left to right.

One of the benefits of Active Directory services is that domains can span geography with different topologies connected by WAN links and still remain transparent to the user. However, available WAN bandwidth is always a consideration. By defining groups of local subnets as sites, administrators can control the replication traffic between subnets, and therefore between sites. The result is reduced replication traffic over WAN links.

The idea of a site is also used for a client locating a domain controller to validate logon credentials. A user from one site could be sitting at a workstation in another site. For the user to get validated, a domain controller in the user's site might need to be located. Comparing the site of the user and the site of the workstation (i.e., comparing the subnets) will help locate an appropriate domain controller.

Lesson Summary

A directory service provides the means to organize and simplify access to resources of a networked computer system. Windows 2000 supports secure network environments in which users are able to share common resources, regardless of network size. Windows 2000 supports two types of networks: workgroups and domains. Windows 2000 includes Active Directory services, a directory service that provides a single point of network management. Active Directory services allows you to add, remove, and relocate users and resources easily. It completely separates the logical structure of the domain hierarchy from the physical structure. The logical structure is made up of objects, OUs, domains, trees, and forests. When a domain is joined to a Windows 2000 domain tree, a Kerberos transitive trust relationship is automatically established between the new domain and the root or parent domain of the tree. The physical structure of the domain hierarchy is made up of domain controllers and sites.

Review

The following questions are intended to reinforce key information presented in this chapter. If you are unable to answer a question, review the appropriate lesson and then try the question again. Answers to the questions can be found in Appendix A, "Questions and Answers."

1. A client has asked you to recommend the appropriate server edition(s) of Windows 2000 for his environment. Your recommendation is based on the following characteristics:

   - All remote offices are connected to the corporate headquarters and data center by high-speed (greater than 10 Mbps) connections.

   - All 10,000 users run Windows 2000 Professional or Windows 98.

   And the following functional requirements:

   - All sites will access a high-availability server cluster running a Microsoft SQL Server 7.0 database. A two-server cluster with six processors per computer is adequate, and there are no plans to upgrade the cluster.

   - All other servers will run an edition of Windows 2000 to provide Active Directory services, basic file and print services, and dial-in access to the network.

   - These servers will run anywhere from one to four processors. Processor sizing will be based on the number of users supported at each site. For example, a small remote site will contain a single processor server while all servers in the corporate site will contain four processors. For simplicity, one server edition of Windows 2000 will be selected for all computers serving this role.

   - Each domain in Active Directory services will support 2500 users.

2. Why is a WDM driver preferred over legacy Windows NT drivers?

3. How does Windows 2000 protect Executive services from user mode applications?

4. What component of the Executive makes Windows 2000 preemptible?

5. What is the primary difference between a workgroup and a domain?

6. What is the structure and purpose of a directory service?

C H A P T E R   2

Installing and Configuring Microsoft Windows 2000 Server

About This Chapter

This chapter prepares you for running a Windows 2000 Server installation. It outlines the type of information you should gather to prepare for your installation and describes the steps you should take before you begin. The chapter then takes you through the phases of a normal installation and continues with a discussion of upgrading to Windows 2000 Server. The chapter finishes with a lesson on troubleshooting the Windows 2000 Server installation.

Before You Begin

To complete the lessons in this chapter, you must have

- A computer that meets the minimum hardware requirements as outlined in "About This Book."
- A copy of the Windows 2000 Server installation CD-ROM.

Lesson 1: Preparing to Install Windows 2000 Server

Before you can begin to install Windows 2000 Server, you must prepare for the installation by gathering information and making decisions about how you want to install the software. This lesson gives you the foundation you need to install Windows 2000 Server. It describes the tasks that you should complete before moving on to the installation.

After this lesson, you will be able to

- Prepare to install Windows 2000 Server by completing preinstallation tasks such as identifying hardware requirements and gathering the necessary installation information

Estimated lesson time: 90 minutes

Preparing for Installation

During installation, the Windows 2000 Setup program asks you to provide information about how to install and configure Windows 2000. You should gather all the necessary information. Good preparation helps you avoid problems during and after the installation.

Before you begin the Windows 2000 installation process, review the list of tasks outlined in the table below. Each task is discussed in greater detail in the sections that follow. Initially, you should complete only the first two tasks in this table—verifying that your computer meets the minimum hardware requirements and checking hardware compatibility. The remaining tasks are completed during the actual installation of Windows 2000 Server, which you will perform in the exercises later in this chapter. This table is meant only to prepare you for the installation so that you can install Windows 2000 Server without any unnecessary delays.

Task

| Verify that your computer meets the minimum hardware requirements. For example, your hard disk should meet the minimum space requirements and preferably have a minimum of 2 gigabytes (GB) of free disk space. | ■ |

| Check all hardware (network adapters, video drivers, sound cards, CD-ROM drives, PC cards, and so on) for compatibility by checking the Windows 2000 Hardware Compatibility List (HCL). | ■ |

Task

Identify how you want to partition the hard disk drive on which you are going to install Windows 2000 Server.	■
Choose a file system that meets your requirements and provides the services you need. Choose NTFS unless you need to run more than one operating system on your computer.	■
Select a licensing mode. You can switch to per-seat from per-server mode after installation, but not to per-server from per-seat.	■
Choose the type of network group (workgroup or domain) your computer will join. If you are joining a domain, you need additional information such as the domain name and the computer account name created for you. With an administrator account and password in the domain, you can create a computer account in the domain.	■
Determine whether to perform a new installation or upgrade an existing version of Windows NT Server. Windows NT Workstation and Windows 9x cannot be upgraded to Windows 2000 Server.	■
Select an installation method: Setup boot disks, CD-ROM, or over-the-network.	■
Choose which components you need to install, such as Networking Services or Microsoft Indexing Service.	■

In addition to the tasks in the checklist, you should perform the following tasks to prepare for installation and to eliminate potential problems.

Working with Domain Name System (DNS)

When you create a Windows 2000 domain, the DNS service must be running and configured. If you are joining a domain, you must know the DNS name of the domain that your computer is joining. If DNS is not running, it is installed automatically when you create a domain controller or when you promote a server to a domain controller.

Recording Information

You should write down the following information: previous operating system (if any), name of the computer (if on a network), name of the workgroup or domain (if on a network), and the IP address (if there is no Dynamic Host Configuration Protocol [DHCP] server or an existing DHCP server will not be used for dynamic IP addressing).

Backing Up Files

Before you install Windows 2000 Server, you should back up the files that you want to preserve. You can back up files to a disk, a tape drive, or another computer on the network.

Uncompressing the Drive

Uncompress any DriveSpace or DoubleSpace volumes before installing Windows 2000. You should not install Windows 2000 on a compressed drive unless the drive was compressed with the NTFS compression utility. DriveSpace or DoubleSpace volumes are created in Windows 9x. Windows 9x cannot be upgraded to Windows 2000 Server but can coexist on the same computer running Windows 2000 Server.

Disabling Disk Mirroring

If you are installing a clean copy of Windows 2000 and you have Windows NT disk mirroring installed on your target computer, disable it before running Setup. You can re-enable disk mirroring after completing the installation. If you are upgrading to Windows 2000, you can leave Windows NT mirroring enabled during Setup.

Note Disabling hardware level disk mirroring to complete a new installation of Windows 2000 is not necessary since the operating system is unaware of redundant array of inexpensive disks (RAID) implemented in hardware.

Disconnecting UPS Devices

If you have UPS equipment connected to your target computer, disconnect the connecting serial cable before running Setup. Windows 2000 Setup attempts to automatically detect devices connected to serial ports, and UPS equipment can cause problems with the detection process.

Reviewing Applications

Before starting the Windows 2000 Server Setup program, be sure to read Readme.doc (in the root directory of the Windows 2000 Server installation CD-ROM) for information regarding applications that need to be disabled or removed before running Setup. You may need to remove virus-scanning software, third-party network services, or client software before running the Windows 2000 Server installation.

Checking the Boot Sector for Viruses

A boot sector virus will cause the installation of Windows 2000 to fail. To verify that the boot sector is not infected with a virus, run the Makedisk.bat file in the \Valueadd\3rdparty\CA_antiv directory on the Windows 2000 Server installation CD-ROM. The Makedisk.bat utility creates a diskette that is used to check the boot sector. After creating this diskette, boot the computer with the diskette inserted. This will run a boot sector virus check. After the utility has run, remove the diskette and proceed to the next preinstallation step.

Gathering Materials

Gather the following materials to prepare for the Windows 2000 installation:

- Read any documentation pertaining to installing Windows 2000 for updated installation information. Review the pertinent .txt and .doc files located on the Windows 2000 Server installation CD-ROM.

- Make sure you have all device driver disks and configuration settings for third-party hardware, including any third-party device driver disks and documentation.

- Have the Windows 2000 Server installation CD-ROM or a network share with the Windows 2000 Server files available.

- Format four 3.5-inch 1.44 MB floppy disks (if creating optional Setup Startup disks).

Important Windows NT 4.0 Setup disks are not compatible with Windows 2000.

Minimum Hardware Requirements

You should be familiar with the minimum hardware requirements necessary to install and operate Windows 2000 Server so that you can determine whether your system meets these requirements. The minimum installation requirements for Windows 2000 are listed in the following table.

Component	Minimum requirement
Processor	32-bit Pentium 133 MHz.
Free hard disk space	One or more hard disks where %systemroot% (C:\WINNT by default) is located on a partition with at least 1.0 GB of hard disk free space (2 GB is recommended).

Component	Minimum requirement
Memory	128 MB of RAM.
Display	VGA monitor capable of 800 x 600 (1024 x 768 recommended).
CD-ROM drive	12x or faster recommended; not required for network installations.
Additional drives	High-density 3.5-inch disk drive, unless your CD-ROM is bootable and supports starting the Setup program from a CD-ROM.
Optional components	Mouse or other pointing device.
	For network installation: a network adapter and an MS-DOS–based network operating system that permits connection to a server containing the Windows 2000 Setup files.

Hardware Compatibility

Windows 2000 Setup automatically checks your hardware and software and reports any potential conflicts. However, to ensure a successful installation, you should make sure that your computer hardware is compatible with Windows 2000 Server before starting the setup process. To do this, verify that your hardware is on the HCL. The HCL is included on your Windows 2000 Server installation CD-ROM in the Support folder in Hcl.txt. The HCL lists each hardware model that has passed the Hardware Compatibility Tests (HCTs). The list also indicates which devices Windows 2000 Server supports. Testing is conducted by Windows Hardware Quality Labs (WHQL) and by some hardware vendors. Installing Windows 2000 Server on a computer that does not have hardware listed in the HCL might not be successful.

Note Microsoft releases an updated HCL on a regular basis. Review the most up-to-date list of supported hardware at the Microsoft WHQL Web site, *http://www.microsoft.com/hwtest/hcl*. If this URL fails, try *http://www.microsoft.com/isapi/redir.dll?prd=Win2000HCL&pver=1*. This URL should direct you to the WHQL Web site. If it doesn't display the WHQL Web site, search *http://www.microsoft.com* by using the keyword "HCL."

A hardware model is "supported" if it is listed on the HCL and you are using a Microsoft-supplied driver to control that hardware. The term "unsupported" does not imply anything about the relative quality of hardware or of third-party drivers. Many unsupported computers and devices work correctly with Windows 2000. However, the Windows 2000 support staff at Microsoft does not offer a full range of support services for problems specific to unsupported hardware or drivers.

Microsoft supports only those devices on the HCL. If one of the computer's devices is not on the HCL, contact the device manufacturer to request a Windows 2000 driver, if it exists.

Disk Partitions

The Windows 2000 Server Setup program allows you to install Windows 2000 Server onto an existing partition or to create a partition and then install Windows 2000 onto the new one. During installation, the Setup program examines the hard disk. Depending on the state of the disk, you will be provided with some or all of the following partitioning options during the installation:

- If the entire hard disk is unpartitioned, you must create and size the installation partition.

- If the disk has partitions, but there is enough unpartitioned disk space, you can create and size the installation partition by using that unpartitioned space.

- If there is an existing partition that is large enough, you can install Windows 2000 Server onto that partition.

- If the hard disk has an existing partition, you can delete it to create more unpartitioned disk space and then use that unpartitioned space to create the Windows 2000 partition.

- If you specify any action that will cause information to be erased, you will be prompted to confirm your choice. If you delete an existing partition, you will cause any data on that partition to be erased. Performing a new installation of Windows 2000 on a partition that contains another operating system will cause that operating system to be overwritten.

Although you can use the Windows 2000 Setup program to create other partitions, you should create and size only the installation partition. After Windows 2000 is installed, use the Disk Management tool to partition any remaining unpartitioned space on the hard disk.

Sizing the Installation Partition

The Windows 2000 Server Setup program requires a boot partition of at least 1 GB of free space to install all Windows 2000 operating system files. However, it is recommended that you create a boot partition of at least 2 GB to allow for future installations of files and programs, such as the Windows 2000 paging file, operating system tools, and operating system updates. The boot partition holds the core operating system files.

The system partition is the partition that holds the files needed to begin the initial load of Windows 2000. On an *x*86-based computer, the operating system starts from the system partition. This means that Windows 2000 looks for certain files, such as Ntldr, Ntdetect.com, and Boot.ini in the root directory, usually the C: drive (Disk 0) when the computer is started. The operating system cannot start unless the system partition is marked active.

The boot partition is where Windows 2000 Server is installed. It contains the operating system parent directory (Winnt, by default), the \System32 subdirectory, the Windows 2000 kernel, and all other files required to run the operating system. If Windows 2000 Server is installed on the active partition, it is both the boot and system partition.

The disk partition where you store Windows 2000 files must be on a permanent hard disk and must have enough unused disk space to hold all the files. This partition must be formatted either with the NTFS (NTFS 4.0 or NTFS 5.0) or with the FAT16 or FAT32 file systems. However, you cannot install Windows 2000 to a FAT16 or FAT32 partition that has implemented disk compression, such as Microsoft DriveSpace.

Note In Windows 2000, if you choose to format NTFS during the installation, it will format the partition directly to NTFS. In previous versions, the partition was formatted FAT and then converted to NTFS. This new process allows you to create partitions larger than 4 GB.

Winnt.exe and Winnt32.exe, the Setup executable files, report an error if they are unable to find a drive with enough free disk space available (greater than 1 GB), or if the drive specified with the /t: or /tempdrive: switch has insufficient free disk space. If such an error occurs, you must free some disk space and then run Winnt or Winnt32 again.

Windows 2000 looks for certain files in the root directory of the active partition when you start your computer; however, the Windows 2000 operating system may be installed on another drive, such as drive D, as long as the drive is configured with a supported file system. If you want to dual-boot your computer to operating systems that do not support NTFS, such as Windows 98, drive C must be FAT16 or FAT32.

If a system's hard disk contains basic input/output system (BIOS) controlled partitions, other file systems such as network file system (NFS), stripe sets, volume sets, or mirrors, those elements appear on the Setup screen as partitions of an unknown type. To avoid deleting elements inadvertently, do not use Setup to delete partitions that are displayed as unknown.

If you are installing a new copy of Windows 2000 on a partition mirrored in software, you must disable mirroring before running Setup and then reestablish mirroring after installation is complete. However, if you are upgrading Windows NT Server versions 3.51 or 4.0 or Windows 2000 Server, you can leave mirroring enabled during Setup.

Do not install Windows 2000 or upgrade to Windows 2000 on a compressed drive unless the drive was compressed with the NTFS file system compression utility. Uncompress a Windows 9x DriveSpace or DoubleSpace volume before running Windows 2000 Setup on it.

If you are setting up a dual-boot configuration of Windows 2000 with another operating system such as MS-DOS, Windows 3.0, Windows 95, Windows 98, or Windows NT, install Windows 2000 onto its own partition. Although it is possible to install Windows 2000 onto the same partition as an existing operating system, it is highly recommended that you install Windows 2000 onto a separate partition, because the Windows 2000 Setup program can overwrite files in the Program Files folder installed by other operating systems.

File Systems

When you are installing Windows 2000 Setup onto unpartitioned disk space, you are prompted to select the file system that should be used to format the partition. You should decide which file system to use before installing Windows 2000 Server. Windows 2000 supports NTFS and the FAT file system. There are two FAT file systems: FAT16 and FAT32.

NTFS

Windows 2000 supports NTFS, a file system with all the basic capabilities of FAT, plus advanced storage features such as security, compression, and better scalability to large volumes. Windows 2000 and Windows NT are the only operating systems designed to access data on a local hard disk that is formatted with NTFS.

Note There are third-party utilities designed to provide access to NTFS partitions from MS-DOS and other operating systems; however, these utilities are not supported by Microsoft.

Windows 2000 includes a new version of NTFS: NTFS version 5.0. NTFS version 5.0 offers many performance enhancements and a host of new features including per-user disk quotas, file encryption, and reparse points. Reparse points are used to extend file system features. Applications can trap open operations against file system objects and execute their own code before returning file data. (Reparse points are discussed in more detail in Chapter 4, "Microsoft Windows 2000 File Systems.") You can also add disk space to NTFS version 5.0 volumes without rebooting.

NTFS requires Windows 2000 or Windows NT. If the computer is booted under a different operating system, that operating system is not able to access the NTFS partitions.

You should use NTFS when the Windows 2000 partition requires any of the following features:

- **File-level and directory-level local security** NTFS allows you to control access to files and directories regardless of whether access is local or over the network.

- **Disk compression** NTFS compresses files to store more data on the partition.

- **Disk quotas** NTFS allows you to control disk usage on a per-user basis.

- **Encryption** NTFS allows you to encrypt file data on the physical hard disk.

NTFS is generally the recommended file system. It is the only one that supports Active Directory services, which includes many important features such as domains and domain-based security. However, in certain cases it might be necessary to use a FAT16 or FAT32 partition in certain dual-boot situations. If you plan to promote a server to a domain controller, format the installation partition with NTFS.

FAT16 and FAT32

The FAT16 and FAT32 file systems allow access by, and compatibility with, more than one operating system. To boot between Windows 2000 and another operating system, the Windows 2000 system partition must be formatted either with the FAT16 or the FAT32 file system. If you select FAT and the partition is smaller than 2048 MB, Setup formats the hard drive as FAT16. On partitions larger than 2 GB, Setup automatically formats the hard drive as FAT32.

Note Windows 2000 supports FAT32 volumes of any size created by Windows 95 OSR2 or Windows 98. However, Windows 2000 formats FAT32 volumes only up to 32 GB in size. This limitation stems from memory constraints in recovery utilities such as Autochk.

FAT16 and FAT32 do not offer many of the features supported by NTFS, such as file-level security. Therefore, in most situations, you should format the hard disk with NTFS. The only reason to use FAT16 or FAT32 is for dual booting. If you are setting up a computer for dual booting, you would have to format only the system partition as FAT16 or FAT32. For example, if drive C is the system partition, you could format drive C as FAT16 or FAT32 and format drive D as NTFS. However, Microsoft does not recommend dual booting a server.

File System Considerations

If the system and boot partitions are different partitions, Windows 2000 Setup will format only the boot partition by default. You must take additional steps during setup to format the system partition. Use the following guidelines and the table below to help you decide which file system format to use for your system partition.

- You may use an existing partition that is already formatted. The default option keeps the existing file system intact, preserving all files on that partition.

- You can convert an existing partition to NTFS to make use of Windows 2000 security and other file system enhancements. This option preserves existing files, but only Windows 2000 has access to that partition.

- You can reformat an existing partition either to NTFS or to the FAT file system, which erases all existing files on that partition. If you choose to reformat the partition as NTFS, remember that only Windows 2000 and Windows NT has access to that partition.

- You should choose the FAT option if your system partition is smaller than 2 GB and you want to gain access to that partition when running MS-DOS, Windows 3.x, Windows 95, Windows 98, or OS/2 on this computer. Setup formats the disk with FAT.

- You should choose the FAT32 option if you are dual-booting with the OSR2 release of Windows 95 or Windows 98 and you have a system partition larger than 2 GB. Setup formats the disk with FAT32.

- You should choose the NTFS option if you are running Windows 2000 and you want to take advantage of the features in NTFS. (See the following table.) Setup formats the boot partition with NTFS version 5.0.

Note You cannot convert FAT16 volumes to FAT32 in Windows 2000.

The following table compares the different features of the three file systems supported by Windows 2000:

Operating system	FAT16	FAT32	NTFS
Overall compatibility	Recognized by MS-DOS, Windows 3.x, Windows 95, Windows 98, Windows NT, Windows 2000, and OS/2.	Recognized only by Windows 95 OSR2, Windows 98, and Windows 2000.	Recognized only by Windows NT and Windows 2000. When the computer is running another operating system (such as MS-DOS, Windows 95, Windows 98, or OS/2), that operating system cannot gain access to files on an NTFS volume on the same computer.
Supported by MS-DOS and Windows 3.x	Yes	No	No
Supported by Windows 95 pre-OSR2 releases	Yes	No	No
Supported by Windows 95 OSR2 and Windows 98	Yes	Yes	No
Supported by Windows NT 3.51	Yes	No	Yes, but Windows NT 3.51 does not support NTFS version 5.0.
Supported by Windows NT 4.0	Yes	No	Yes. Windows NT 4.0 supports NTFS version 5.0 with Service Pack 4 or later installed.
Supported by Windows 2000	Yes	Yes	Yes

Licensing

Windows 2000 Server supports two licensing modes: Per Server and Per Seat. In Per Server mode, Client Access Licenses (CALs) are assigned to a server. In Per Seat mode, each computer that accesses the Windows 2000 Server computer requires a separate CAL.

Per-Server Licensing

With Per Server licensing, CALs are assigned to a particular server. Each CAL allows one connection per client computer to the server for basic network services. You must have at least as many CALs that are dedicated to the server as the maximum number of client computers that could be used to connect concurrently to that server.

Per Server licensing is preferred by small companies with only one computer running Windows 2000 Server. It is also useful for Internet or remote-access servers where client computers might not be licensed as Windows 2000 network client computers. In this situation, Per Server licensing allows you to specify a maximum number of concurrent server connections and reject any additional logon attempts.

Note If you are unsure which licensing mode to use, choose Per Server because you can change, only once, from Per Server to Per Seat licensing at no additional cost (by double-clicking the Licensing icon in the Control Panel). It is not necessary to notify Microsoft to make this change. This is a one-way conversion; you cannot convert from Per Seat to Per Server.

Per-Seat Licensing

The Per Seat licensing mode requires a separate CAL for each client computer used to access Windows 2000 Server for basic network services. After a client computer has a CAL, it can be used to access any computer running Windows 2000 Server on the enterprise network. Per Seat licensing is often more economical for large networks in which client computers will be used to connect to more than one server.

With Terminal Services, the licensing mode is usually Per Seat, except with the Terminal Services Internet Connector license, where the mode would always be Per Server. If you plan to use Terminal Services, you need to install two components: Terminal Services and Terminal Services Licensing.

Client Access License (CAL)

A CAL gives client computers the right to connect to computers running Windows 2000 Server so that the client computers can connect to network services, shared folders, and print resources. When you install Windows 2000 Server, you must choose a CAL mode: Per Seat or Per Server.

The following services do not require CALs:

- Anonymous or authenticated access to Windows 2000 Server with Microsoft Internet Information Services (IIS) version 4.0 or a Web-server application that provides Hypertext Transfer Protocol (HTTP) sharing of Hypertext Markup Language (HTML) files

- Telnet and File Transfer Protocol (FTP) connections

Note If your company uses Microsoft BackOffice products, you must also have licenses for the BackOffice products. A Windows 2000 license does not cover BackOffice products.

Workgroups and Domains

During installation, you must choose the type of network you want the computer to join. A computer running Windows 2000 can join one of two types of networks: workgroup or domain.

Joining a Workgroup

When joining a workgroup, assign a workgroup name to the computer. The workgroup name assigned can be the name of an existing workgroup or the name of a workgroup created during installation. Whether assigning a new workgroup name or using an existing one, the computer appears as a member of that workgroup when other computer users in the network browse for network resources.

A domain and a workgroup can share the same name. However, consider the following:

- The workgroup computers are not members of the domain and are not included in domain administration.

- The workgroup computers appear with the domain computers in Windows 2000 Explorer.

Joining a Domain

During installation, the Windows 2000 Setup wizard provides access to join an existing domain. The wizard stops for the DNS name of the domain.

Before a computer running Windows NT or Windows 2000 can join a domain, a computer account must be created in or added to the domain database. Only users who have the Join A Computer To The Domain permission can create a computer account. Members of the Administrators, Domain Administrators, or Account Operators groups have this user right by default.

When joining a domain, create a computer account for that computer in advance, or create it during the installation process by selecting the check box Create A Computer Account In The Domain. Next, supply a user account and password that have the authority to add computer accounts in the domain. By default, this must be an Administrator account.

Note When joining a domain, even if the computer account has been previously created, domain credentials must be supplied.

At least one domain controller and one DNS server must be online when installing a computer in the domain. If you install Windows 2000 Server as a stand-alone server without joining a domain, you can join a domain later by using the Network Identification tab in the System Properties dialog box, as shown in Figure 2.1.

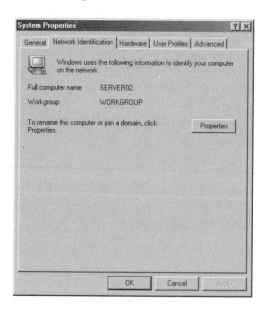

Figure 2.1 The Network Identification tab in the System Properties dialog box

Upgrade or New Installation

Before running Windows 2000 Server Setup, you need to determine whether to upgrade your existing installation of Windows NT or to perform a new installation.

Upgrading is the process of installing Windows 2000 Server in a directory that currently contains certain versions of Windows NT. An upgrade automatically installs Windows 2000 Server into the same directory as the currently installed operating system. The versions of Windows NT from which you can upgrade are:

- Windows NT Server 3.51
- Windows NT Server 4.0 Server or Windows NT 4.0 Terminal Server

If you have Windows NT 4.0 Server Enterprise Edition, you can upgrade to Windows 2000 Advanced Server, but not to Windows 2000 Server. If you have a version of Windows NT Server earlier than 3.51, you cannot upgrade directly to Windows 2000 Server; you must first upgrade to Windows NT Server 3.51 or 4.0. Additionally, Windows NT Workstation and Windows 2000 Professional cannot be upgraded to Windows 2000 Server.

Installing, in contrast with upgrading, is the process of placing the operating system in a new directory, wiping out the previous operating system at setup, or installing Windows 2000 Server on a disk or disk partition with no previous operating system. If you want to perform a new installation on a disk partition that contains applications you want to keep, you will need to back them up and reinstall them after installing Windows 2000 Server.

If you want to perform a new installation of Windows 2000 Server on a partition that previously contained Windows 2000 Server, and you have documents under My Documents that you want to save, back up the documents in the Documents and Settings directory and copy the documents back into the folder after completing the installation. My Documents points to subdirectories below the Documents and Settings directory.

Installation Methods

There are three methods available to install Windows 2000 Server on the Intel platform:

- Setup boot disk
- CD-ROM
- Over-the-network

Setup Boot Disks

Windows 2000 Server is distributed on a CD-ROM and includes four setup floppy disks. These Setup boot disks are required if you are installing Windows 2000 Server on an *x*86-based computer that is not running MS-DOS or a Windows operating system and does not support the bootable CD-ROM format. These disks also let you start Windows 2000 later, when it might not be able to start on its own because of a computer error, and to initiate an emergency repair.

You can create a set of Setup Boot disks by running Makeboot.exe or Makebt32.exe from the \Bootdisk directory on the Windows 2000 Server installation CD-ROM. Makeboot.exe is a 16-bit DOS application that runs on MS-DOS, 16-bit operating systems like Windows 3.11, and Windows 9*x*. Makebt32.exe is a 32-bit application that runs on Windows NT and Windows 2000.

After the initial setup load process, Windows 2000 starts and the remainder of setup runs under Windows 2000, which is helpful for troubleshooting. For example, the install process displays a standard Windows 2000 error check code if an error occurs during setup.

To start an installation of Windows 2000 Server by using the Setup Boot disks, you should first turn off the computer, insert the disk labeled Windows 2000 Setup Boot Disk into drive A, and then turn on your computer. Setup starts automatically.

Note If you are installing Windows 2000 Server on a computer with no previous operating system, and you are using an MS-DOS boot floppy disk (performing an over-the-network setup), you have to format the drive first. However, if you are using the Windows 2000 Setup disks to start Setup, you can format the drive during Setup.

During loading from the Setup boot floppies, the bar at the bottom of the screen displays the Windows 2000 components being loaded. These components are described in the following sections.

Setup Disk One

The Setupldr.bin file starts the Setup. The computer is inspected and machine identification data is collected. If a driver is not found for the fixed disk that contains the boot partition, you might need to load a third-party driver. Follow the instructions in Setup to load a third-party SCSI or RAID controller driver. The text mode portion of Windows 2000 Setup is loaded. The Ntkrnlmp.exe file loads the Windows 2000 Executive.

Setup Disk Two

This disk loads the HAL, configuration tools, fonts, locale-specific data, drivers, and controllers. Windows 2000 Setup continues to run in text mode.

Setup Disk Three

This disk loads the Compaq drive array and disk controller drivers. During this process, Setup detects the appropriate drivers for the system and loads the dynamic volume support (dmboot1). Windows 2000 Setup continues to run in Text mode.

Setup Disk Four

This disk loads the floppy disk drivers; SCSI CD-ROM, floppy, and fixed drive drivers; and file system drivers (FAT, NTFS, and CDFS). Windows 2000 is loaded and takes over the setup process. The Welcome screen appears, and you can choose whether to set up Windows 2000, repair an existing version of Windows 2000, or quit Setup. At this point, the CD-ROM drive is accessed. Setup searches for previous versions of Windows and any existing partitions. You can delete existing partitions and create new ones. After configuring the partitions, you must choose a file system (NTFS or FAT). The partition is then formatted. When formatting is complete, file copy begins. After the files are copied, the system reboots. Remove any floppy disks before the reboot.

Beyond Disk Four

After the system reboots, Windows 2000 Setup starts in GUI mode. CD-ROM files continue to be copied to the hard disk. Setup detects and installs devices and then prompts for user information. You must then choose which components to install. From there, choose the type of network installation (typical or custom) and the type of network (workgroup or domain) to join. Setup builds the file list and installs and configures the components.

Bootable CD-ROM

If your Windows 2000 Server installation files are on compact disc and your computer's BIOS supports the Bootable CD-ROM (no-emulation mode) format, insert the Windows 2000 Server compact disc into the CD-ROM drive and then turn off your computer. When you turn your computer back on, Setup starts automatically.

When Setup requests that you remove the CD-ROM from the CD-ROM drive, do so on bootable CD-ROM systems. Otherwise, Setup starts again on the following boot.

Important Although your system might support bootable CD-ROMs, you might have to modify your system BIOS to boot to the CD-ROM.

If your computer is running an operating system such as Windows 95, Windows 98, or Windows NT and you insert the Windows 2000 installation CD-ROM while the computer is running, the Windows 2000 Setup Wizard dialog box appears (provided you haven't turned off AutoPlay).

Over-the-Network (Server-Based)

The Windows 2000 Server system files must be available over the network. Copy the Windows 2000 installation CD-ROM, or at a minimum, the source directory (\I386), to a directory on the hard disk of a network server and share the directory. Creating a distribution folder is discussed in more detail in Chapter 3, "Performing an Unattended Installation of Microsoft Windows 2000 Server."

Upgrading Windows 95, Windows 98, or Windows NT

If your computer is currently running Windows 95, Windows 98, or Windows NT, connect to the system files over the network and run (double-click) Winnt32.exe, located in the I386 directory. Only Windows NT Server can be upgraded to Windows 2000 Server. None of the other Windows operating systems can be upgraded to Windows 2000 Server. If you are installing Windows 2000 Server on a Windows NT Server computer, you are prompted to select Upgrade to Windows 2000 Server or Install Windows 2000 Server. In all other cases, you are prompted to Install Windows 2000 Server.

Upgrading Windows NT Server retains most system settings, preferences, and application installations. If you prefer a dual-boot configuration, choose the Install Windows 2000 Server option. Press Enter or click Next to continue.

Installing New or Upgrading Current Version

If you do not have Windows 95, Windows 98, or Windows NT installed, you need to run MS-DOS and an MS-DOS network client to establish your connection to the shared network folder containing the Setup files.

Running the MS-DOS network client, connect to the system files over the network and run Winnt.exe, which is located on the network share.

The MS-DOS computer needs 500 KB of free conventional memory to run the setup routine successfully. Make sure you have loaded Emm386.exe and are loading all device drivers high.

Tip To free some memory, run LoadHigh Winnt.exe to load portions of Winnt.exe high.

You should be running Smartdrv.exe or your installation will be slow, lasting from 4 to 12 hours.

Choosing Which Components to Install

Windows 2000 Server includes a wide variety of core components, including a number of administrative tools, which are automatically installed by Setup. In addition, you can choose from a number of components that extend the functionality of Windows 2000 Server. These components can be installed at Setup time or added afterward (through the Add/Remove Windows Components option within Control Panel's Add/Remove Programs application).

Choosing more of these components means providing more capabilities on the server. However, you should choose only the components you need, since each component requires additional disk space. The following table will help you choose the components you need in your installation.

Possible Server Function	Optional Components to Consider Installing
DHCP, DNS, or WINS server (in a TCP/IP network)	Dynamic Host Configuration Protocol (DHCP), DNS, or Windows Internet Name Service (WINS)—all part of Networking Services
Centralized administration of networks	Management and Monitoring Tools
	Remote Installation Services
Authentication and secure communication	Internet Authentication Services (part of Networking Services)
	Certificate Services
File access	Microsoft Indexing Service
	Remote Storage
	Other Network File and Print Services (support for NetWare, Macintosh, and UNIX). NetWare client computers are supported through Gateway Services for NetWare (GSNW). The Directory Service Migration Tool installs GSNW if NetWare Directory Service (NDS) is not installed.
Print access	Other Network File and Print Services (support for NetWare, Macintosh, and UNIX)

Possible Server Function	Optional Components to Consider Installing
Terminal services	Terminal Services
	Terminal Services Licensing
Application support	Message Queuing Services
	Quality of Service (QoS) Admission Control Service (part of Networking Services)
Internet (Web) infrastructure	Internet Information Services (IIS)
	Site Server and Lightweight Directory Access Protocol (part of Networking Services)
Phone and fax support	Connection Manager Administration Kit and Connection Point Services (part of Management and Monitoring Tools)
Multimedia communications	Windows Media Services
Support for a variety of client operating systems	Other Network File and Print Services (support for NetWare, Macintosh, and UNIX)

The following table describes each of the optional components and is designed to work with the previous table to help you choose appropriate components to install.

Optional Component	Description
Certificate Services	Provides authentication support, including secure e-mail, Web-based authentication, and smart card authentication.
Internet Information Services (IIS)	Provides support for Web site creation, configuration, and management, along with Network News Transfer Protocol (NNTP), FTP, and Simple Mail Transfer Protocol (SMTP).
Management and Monitoring Tools	Provides tools for network management and monitoring, specifically Network Monitor, a packet analyzer. Also includes the Simple Network Management Protocol (SNMP).
	Other management tools include support for client dialing and updating client phone books, and a utility for migrating from NDS to the Windows 2000 Active Directory services.
Message Queuing Services	Provides services that support the messaging needed by distributed applications, allowing these applications to function reliably in heterogeneous networks or when a computer is temporarily offline.
Microsoft Indexing Service	Provides indexing functions for documents stored on disk, allowing users to search for specific document text or properties.

Optional Component	Description
Microsoft Script Debugger	Provides support for script development.
Networking Services	Provides important support for networking, including the items in the following list:

COM Internet Services Proxy Supports distributed applications that use HTTP to communicate through IIS.

Domain Name System (DNS) Provides name resolution for clients running Windows 2000. With name resolution, users can access servers by name, instead of having to use IP addresses that are difficult to recognize and remember.

Dynamic Host Configuration Protocol (DHCP) Gives a server the ability to provide IP addresses dynamically to other servers on the network. With DHCP, you do not need to set and maintain static IP addresses on any intranet servers except for those providing DHCP, DNS, or WINS.

Internet Authentication Service Provides authentiction for dial-in users.

QoS Admission Control Service Allows you to control how applications are allotted network bandwidth. Important applications can be given more bandwidth, less important applications less bandwidth.

Simple TCP/IP Services Supports Character Generator, Daytime Discard, Echo, and Quote of the Day.

Site Server ILS Service Supports telephony applications, which help users access features such as caller ID, conference calls, video conferencing, and faxing. This support depends on IIS.

Windows Internet Naming Service Provides NetBIOS over TCP/IP name resolution for clients running Windows NT and earlier versions of Microsoft operating systems. With name resolution, users can access servers by name, instead of having to use IP addresses that are difficult to recognize and remember.

Note The Clients directory on the Windows 2000 Server installation CD-ROM contains two subdirectories. The WIN9X directory contains the directory service client for Windows 9*x* clients. The WIN9XIPP.CLI directory contains the Internet Printing client for Windows 9*x*. These services remove the WINS requirement from Windows 9*x* client computers.

Other Network File and Print Services	Provides file and print services for Macintosh, as well as print services for UNIX.

Optional Component	Description
Remote Installation Services	Provides services that allow you to set up new client computers remotely without having to visit each client. The target clients must support remote booting. On the server, a separate partition will be needed for Remote Installation Services.
Remote Storage	Provides an extension to your disk space by making removable media, such as tapes, more accessible. Infrequently used data can automatically be transferred to tape and retrieved when needed.
Terminal Services	Provides the ability to run client applications on the server so that client computers can function as terminals rather than independent systems. The server provides a multisession environment and runs the Windows-based programs being used on the clients. If you install Terminal Services, you must also install Terminal Services Licensing (to license Terminal Services' clients). However, temporary licenses can be issued for clients that allow you to use Terminal servers for up to 90 days.
Terminal Services Licensing	Provides the ability to register and track licenses for Terminal Services' clients. If you install Terminal Services, you must also install Terminal Services Licensing (to license Terminal Services' clients). However, temporary licenses can be issued for clients that allow you to use Terminal servers for up to 90 days.
Windows Media Services	Provides multimedia support, allowing you to deliver content using Advanced Streaming Format over an intranet or the Internet.

Lesson Summary

Before you begin to install Windows 2000 Server, you should gather any materials that you need, ensure that your hardware can support Windows 2000, and make decisions about how Windows 2000 Server should be installed. For example, you must ensure that your hardware meets the minimum hardware requirements and check all your hardware for compatibility with Windows 2000. You must identify how you want to partition your hard disk and what file system you should use for that partition. You must select a licensing mode, the type of network in which to participate, and the type of installation. You must also decide which optional components should be installed. Taking these steps can help to prepare you for the installation and to eliminate potential problems.

Lesson 2: Installing Windows 2000 Server

Once you have performed all the necessary steps to prepare for a Windows 2000 Server installation, you are ready to begin the Windows 2000 Setup process. This lesson focuses on performing a new installation of Windows 2000 Server. It begins with a discussion of the various installation programs and then describes the phases of the installation process.

After this lesson, you will be able to

- Determine which setup program you should use to install Windows 2000 Server
- Describe the three stages of the installation process
- Perform a new installation of Windows 2000 Server

Estimated lesson time: 30 minutes

Windows 2000 Server Setup Programs

Regardless of which method you use to install Windows 2000 Server, you must execute either Winnt.exe or Winnt32.exe. You can use the Setup.exe program to launch Winnt.exe or Winnt32.exe, or you can execute Winnt32.exe or Winnt.exe directly. For a clean installation on a computer running MS-DOS or Windows 3.*x*, run Winnt.exe from the MS-DOS command line. For a clean installation from Windows 95, Windows 98, or Windows NT Workstation, run Winnt32.exe. For a clean installation or upgrade from Windows NT Server 3.51 or 4.0, run Winnt32.exe. Several switches can be used with Winnt.exe and Winnt32.exe to customize how Windows 2000 Server is installed on your computer.

Windows 2000 Setup Program

The Windows 2000 Setup program, Setup.exe, is located in the root directory of the Windows 2000 Server installation CD-ROM. When you execute Setup.exe, the Microsoft Windows 2000 CD screen appears. From there, you can choose to install Windows 2000 Server, install add-on components, browse the CD, or exit the Setup program. If you select the Install Windows 2000 option, the Winnt.exe or the Winnt32.exe program runs, depending on which operating system you are currently running.

If Autorun is enabled on your system, the Windows 2000 CD screen will appear when you insert the Windows 2000 Server installation CD-ROM into your CD-ROM drive. Autorun calls Setup.exe, which checks the operating system. If Setup determines that the computer is running Windows NT Server 3.51, Windows NT Server 4.0, or an earlier version of Windows 2000 Server, you are prompted either to upgrade or install Windows 2000. If a newer version of Windows 2000 Server is installed on the computer, Setup.exe will not allow the installation of Windows 2000 Server to continue.

Winnt.exe Setup Program

Winnt.exe is commonly used for over-the-network installations that use an MS-DOS network client. Winnt.exe performs the following steps:

1. Creates a WIN_NT.~BT temporary directory on the system partition and copies Setup boot files into this directory.

2. Creates a WIN_NT.~LS temporary directory and copies the Windows 2000 files from the server into this directory.

3. Prompts users to restart their systems. After the computer restarts, the boot menu appears and installation continues.

Winnt.exe installs Windows 2000 Server and can be executed from an MS-DOS or a Windows 16-bit operating system command prompt.

Winnt.exe Switches

You can use the following switches to modify the behavior of the Winnt.exe Setup program:

```
WINNT [/s[:sourcepath]] [/t[:tempdrive]] [/u[:answer_file]]
[/udf:id[,UDF_file]][/r:folder] [/rx:folder] [/e:command] [/a]
```

These switches are described in detail in the following table:

Switch	Description
/s[:*sourcepath*]	Specifies the source location of the Windows 2000 files. The location must be a full path of the form x:*[path]* or a valid UNC.
/t[:*tempdrive*]	Directs Setup to place temporary files on the specified drive and to install Windows 2000 on that drive. If you do not specify a location, Setup attempts to locate a drive for you.

Switch	Description
/u[:*answer file*]	Performs an unattended Setup using an answer file (requires /s). The answer file provides answers to some or all of the prompts that the end user normally responds to during Setup.
/udf:id[,*UDF_file*]	Indicates an identifier (id) that Setup uses to specify how a Uniqueness Database File (UDF) modifies an answer file (see /u). The /udf parameter overrides values in the answer file, and the identifier determines which values in the UDF file are used. If no UDF_file is specified, Setup prompts you to insert a disk that contains the $Unique$.udb file.
/r[:*folder*]	Specifies an optional folder to be installed. The folder remains after Setup finishes.
/rx[:*folder*]	Specifies an optional folder to be copied. The folder is deleted after Setup finishes.
/e	Specifies a command to be executed at the end of GUI-mode Setup.
/a	Enables accessibility options.

Winnt32.exe Setup Program

Winnt32.exe is used to install Windows 2000 Server from an existing Windows 95, Windows 98, or Windows NT computer. It can be executed by double-clicking Winnt32.exe in the root of the source folder (such as \i386) on the Windows 2000 Server installation CD-ROM or in a network share location for over-the-network installations. You can also execute Winnt32.exe by using the run command from the Start Menu, which allows switches to be specified. In addition, the Winnt32 command can be run from a Windows 95, Windows 98, or Windows NT (all Windows 32-bit operating systems) command prompt.

If the Windows 2000 Server installation is initiated over the network, Winnt32.exe creates a WIN_NT.~LS temporary directory and copies the Windows 2000 Server files from the server into this directory. The temporary directory is created on the first partition that is large enough, unless otherwise specified by the /t switch. This is known as the Pre-Copy Phase.

WINNT32.EXE Switches

You can use the following switches to modify the behavior of the Winnt32.exe Setup program:

```
winnt32 [/s:sourcepath] [/tempdrive:drive_letter]
[/unattend[num]:
[answer_file]] [/copydir:folder_name]
[/copysource:folder_name]
[/cmd:command_line] [/debug[level]:[filename]]
[/udf:id[,UDF_file]]
[/syspart:drive_letter] [/checkupgradeonly] [/cmdcons]
[/m:folder_name]
[/makelocalsource] [/noreboot]
```

These switches are described in detail in the following table:

Switch	Description
/s:*sourcepath*	Specifies the source location of the Windows 2000 files. To simultaneously copy files from multiple servers, specify multiple /s sources. If you use multiple /s switches, the first specified server must be available or Setup will fail.
/tempdrive:*drive_letter*	Directs Setup to place temporary files on the specified partition and to install Windows 2000 on that partition.
/Unattend or /u	Upgrades your previous version of Windows 2000 in unattended Setup mode. All user settings are taken from the previous installation, so no user intervention is required during Setup.
	Using the /unattend switch to automate Setup affirms that you have read and accepted the End-User License Agreement (EULA) for Windows 2000. Before using this switch to install Windows 2000 on behalf of an organization other than your own, you must confirm that the end user has received, read, and accepted the terms of the Windows 2000 EULA. OEMs may not specify this key on machines being sold to end users.
/unattend[*num*][:*answer_file*]	Performs a fresh installation in unattended Setup mode. The answer file provides Setup with your custom specifications. Num is the number of seconds between the time that Setup finishes copying the files and when it restarts your computer. You can use num on any computer running Windows NT or Windows 2000. The *answer_file* placeholder is the name of the answer file.

Switch	Description
/copydir:*folder_name*	Creates an additional folder within the folder in which the Windows 2000 files are installed. For example, if the source folder contains a folder called Private_drivers that has modifications just for your site, you can type **/copydir:Private_drivers** to have Setup copy that folder to your installed Windows 2000 folder. So then the new folder location would be %systemroot%\Private_drivers. You can use /copydir to create as many additional folders as you want.
/copysource:*folder_name*	Creates a temporary additional folder within the folder in which the Windows 2000 files are installed. For example, if the source folder contains a folder called Private_drivers that has modifications just for your site, you can type **/copysource:Private_drivers** to have Setup copy that folder to your installed Windows 2000 folder and use its files during Setup. So then the temporary folder location would be %systemroot%\Private_drivers. Unlike the folders /copydir creates, /copysource folders are deleted after Setup completes.
/cmd:*command_line*	Instructs Setup to carry out a specific command before the final phase of Setup. This would occur after your computer has restarted twice and after Setup has collected the necessary configuration information, but before Setup is complete.
/debug[*level*][:*filename*]	Creates a debug log at the level specified, for example, /debug4:C:\Win2000.log. The default log file is %systemroot%\Winnt32.log, with the debug level set to 2. The log levels are as follows: 0-severe errors, 1-errors, 2-warnings, 3-information, and 4-detailed information for debugging. Each level includes the levels below it.
/udf:*id*[,*UDF_file*]	Indicates an identifier (*id*) that Setup uses to specify how a Uniqueness Database File (UDF) modifies an answer file (see the /unattend entry). The UDF overrides values in the answer file, and the identifier determines which values in the UDF are used. For example, /udf:RAS_user, Our_company.udb overrides settings specified for the identifier RAS_user in the Our_company.udb file. If no UDF is specified, Setup prompts the user to insert a disk that contains the $Unique$.udb file.
/syspart:*drive_letter*	Specifies that you can copy Setup startup files to a hard disk, mark the disk as active, and then install the disk into another computer. When you start that computer, it automatically starts with the next phase of the Setup. You must always use the /tempdrive parameter with the /syspart parameter.
	The /syspart switch for Winnt32.exe runs only from a computer that already has Windows NT 3.51, Windows NT 4.0, or Windows 2000 installed on it. It cannot be run from Windows 9*x*.

Switch	Description
/checkupgradeonly	Checks your computer for upgrade compatibility with Windows 2000. For Windows 95 or Windows 98 upgrades, Setup creates a report named Upgrade.txt in the Windows installation folder. For Windows NT 3.51 or 4.0 upgrades, it saves the report to the Winnt32.log in the installation folder.
/cmdcons	Adds a Recovery Console option to the operating system selection screen for repairing a failed installation. It is only used post-Setup.
/m:*folder_name*	Specifies that Setup copies replacement files from an alternate location. Instructs Setup to look in the alternate location first, and if files are present, use them instead of the files from the default location.
/makelocalsource	Instructs Setup to copy all installation source files to your local hard disk. Use /makelocalsource when installing from a CD to provide installation files when the CD is not available later in the installation.
/noreboot	Instructs Setup not to restart the computer after the file copy phase of winnt32 is completed so that you can execute another command.

The Installation Process

The Windows 2000 Server installation process includes three phases: the Pre-Copy Phase, Text mode, and GUI mode.

Pre-Copy Phase

During the Pre-Copy Phase, all of the files needed for the installation are copied to temporary directories on the local hard drive. When you use the Winnt.exe or Winnt32.exe command to initiate an installation over the network, all the files needed to complete the installation are copied over the network to a temporary directory named WIN_NT.~LS. Setup then continues, as it would if you were performing the installation from a local drive, moving on to the Text mode phase of the installation process and then to the GUI mode phase.

You can choose not to create the boot floppies by selecting the check box Copy All Setup Files From The Setup CD To The Hard Drive. The check box is under the Advanced Options button. When you select this option, a WIN_NT.~BT directory is created on the disk. This directory contains the files that would have been on the four boot floppies.

While the files are being copied into the WIN_NT.~LS directory, Windows 95, Windows 98, or Windows NT is still running. This means there is less down time during the upgrade.

Text Mode

In Text mode setup, Setup prompts you for information needed to complete the installation. After you accept the license agreement, you specify or create an installation partition and choose a file system. All files required for installation are copied from the temporary directory (or the CD-ROM) into the installation directory on the hard disk of the target computer.

Windows 2000 Server Licensing Agreement

The Windows 2000 Server Licensing Agreement takes up several pages. Use the Page Down key to move through the agreement, and then press F8 to agree. This appears before Text mode if you use Winnt32 or Autorun to start your setup.

Existing Installations

If Setup detects any existing Windows 2000 installations, it displays them in a list. You can select an installation and press R to repair it, or press Esc to continue.

Partitions

Setup displays all existing partitions and free space on the system. Using the Up and Down arrow keys you can select where you want to install Windows 2000 Server. At this point you can create and delete partitions. Press Enter to continue.

File Systems

Setup gives you the option of keeping the current file system intact or allows you to convert it to NTFS. If you do not want to change it, select the Leave Current File System Intact option, which is the default, and press Enter to continue.

Setup examines your hard disks and copies the files it needs for installation from the temporary directory to the installation directory. (Winnt is the default directory.)

GUI Mode

After completing the Text mode portion of Setup, the computer restarts and GUI mode begins. This phase allows you to select which optional components to install and allows you to select the administrator password.

GUI mode consists of three distinct stages:

1. Gathering Information About Your Computer

2. Installing Windows 2000 Server Networking

3. Completing Setup

Gathering Information About Your Computer

The Gathering Information About Your Computer stage is a series of dialog boxes that Windows 2000 uses to collect configuration information for setting up your system. During this stage, Windows 2000 security features are installed and devices are installed and configured.

Regional Settings

Windows 2000 displays the current (default) regional settings. You can add support for additional languages, change your location settings for the system, and configure the user account default settings as well.

Personalize Your Software

When configuring your system, you must enter the name that Windows 2000 Server is registered to. In addition, you can add the name of the organization, although this is optional.

Licensing Mode

You must select the Per Server or Per Seat licensing method. If you select Per Server, you must enter the number of Per Server licenses.

Computer Name and Administrator Password

You must enter a computer name (NetBIOS name of up to 15 characters) when you install Windows 2000. Note that the autogenerated name is 15 characters long. The name you enter must be different from other computer, workgroup, or domain names on the network. A default computer name is displayed. You can access the default name or type in a computer name.

You can also enter an Administrator password for the local Administrator user account. This password can be up to 127 characters long, or it can be left blank.

Optional Component Manager

The Optional Component Manager allows you to add or remove additional components during and after installation. For details about each of these components, see "Lesson 1: Preparing to Install Windows 2000 Server."

Date and Time Settings

During the installation process, you must select the appropriate time zone and adjust the date and time settings, if necessary, including automatic adjustments for daylight savings time.

Installing Windows 2000 Server Networking

When Setup completes the Gathering Information About Your Computer stage, it returns to the Windows 2000 Setup screen. Setup then examines the computer to detect installed network adapters. This can take several minutes.

Networking Settings

The Windows 2000 networking setup begins with a dialog box offering a choice between Typical settings (default) or Custom settings. Typical settings configure the system with the all the defaults: Client for Microsoft Networks, File and Print Sharing for Microsoft Networks, and Internet Protocol (TCP/IP) configured as a DHCP client.

Custom settings allows the configuration of the following three items:

- **Clients** The default client is Client For Microsoft Networks. You can add Gateway (and Client) Services for NetWare.

- **Services** The default service is File and Printer Sharing for Microsoft Networks. You can add SAP Agent and QoS Packet Scheduler. You can modify the settings for File and Printer Sharing for Microsoft Networks by highlighting the service and clicking Properties. This allows you to optimize server service settings and provide server service compatibility for LAN Manager 2.*x* clients.

- **Protocols** The default protocol is Internet Protocol (TCP/IP). You can add additional protocols, including NWLink IPX/SPX, NetBEUI, DLC, AppleTalk, Network Monitor Driver, and others. You can also modify the settings for a protocol (if applicable) by highlighting the protocol and clicking Properties.

Completing Setup

The Completing Setup stage performs the following actions and requires no user interaction. The following table provides an overview of the tasks performed by Setup during this stage.

Task	Description
Copying files	Setup copies any remaining files necessary to the installation directory such as accessories and bitmaps.
Configuring the computer	Setup creates your start menu, program groups, sets up the print spooler, printers, services, the administrator account, fonts, the Pagefile, and the registration of many dynamic-link libraries (DLLs).
Saving the configuration	Setup saves your configuration to the registry, creates the repair directory, and resets the Boot.ini.
Removing temporary files	Setup removes the temporary files and directories created and used during installation, such as the WIN_NT.~LS directory, and also compacts the system hives in the registry.

Exercise 1: Installing Windows 2000 Server

In this exercise, you install Windows 2000 Server on a computer with no formatted partitions. During installation, you use the Windows 2000 Server Setup program to create a partition on your hard disk, on which you install Windows 2000 Server as a stand-alone server in a workgroup.

▶ **Procedure 1: Creating Windows 2000 Server Setup diskettes**

Complete this procedure on a computer running MS-DOS or any version of Windows with access to the Bootdisk directory on the Windows 2000 Server installation CD-ROM.

If your computer is configured with a bootable CD-ROM drive, you can install Windows 2000 without using the Setup disks. To complete this exercise as outlined, bootable CD-ROM support must be disabled in the BIOS.

Important This procedure requires four formatted 1.44-MB disks. If you use diskettes that contain data, the data will be overwritten without warning.

1. Label the four blank, formatted 1.44-MB diskettes as follows:

   Windows 2000 Server Setup Disk #1

   Windows 2000 Server Setup Disk #2

   Windows 2000 Server Setup Disk #3

   Windows 2000 Server Setup Disk #4

2. Insert the Microsoft Windows 2000 Server CD-ROM into the CD-ROM drive.

3. If the Windows 2000 CD-ROM dialog box appears prompting you to install or upgrade to Windows 2000, click Exit.

4. Open a command prompt.

5. At the command prompt, change to your CD-ROM drive. For example, if your CD-ROM drive name is E, type **E:** and press Enter.

6. At the command prompt, change to the Bootdisk directory by typing **cd bootdisk** and pressing Enter.

7. If you are creating the setup boot diskettes from a computer running MS-DOS, a Windows 16-bit operating system or Windows 9x, type **makeboot a:** (where A: is the name of your floppy disk drive) and then press Enter. If you are creating the setup boot diskettes from a computer running Windows NT or Windows 2000, type **makebt32 a:** (where A: is the name of your floppy disk drive) and then press Enter.

   Windows 2000 displays a message indicating that this program creates the four setup disks for installing Windows 2000. It also indicates that four blank formatted high-density floppy disks are required.

8. Press any key to continue.

   Windows 2000 displays a message prompting you to insert the disk that will become the Windows 2000 Setup Boot Disk.

9. Insert the blank formatted diskette labeled Windows 2000 Server Setup Disk #1 into the floppy disk drive, and then press any key to continue.

   After Windows 2000 creates the disk image, it displays a message prompting you to insert the diskette labeled Windows 2000 Server Setup Disk #2.

10. Remove Disk #1, insert the blank formatted diskette labeled Windows 2000 Server Setup Disk #2 into the floppy disk drive, and then press any key to continue.

    After Windows 2000 creates the disk image, it displays a message prompting you to insert the diskette labeled Windows 2000 Server Setup Disk #3.

11. Remove Disk #2, insert the blank formatted diskette labeled Windows 2000 Server Setup Disk #3 into the floppy disk drive, and then press any key to continue.

    After Windows 2000 creates the disk image, it displays a message prompting you to insert the disk labeled Disk #4.

12. Remove Disk #3, insert the blank formatted diskette labeled Windows 2000 Server Setup Disk #4 into the floppy disk drive, and then press any key to continue.

    After Windows 2000 creates the disk image, it displays a message indicating that the imaging process is done.

13. At the command prompt, type **exit** and then press Enter.

14. Remove the disk from the floppy disk drive and the CD-ROM from the CD-ROM drive.

▶ **Procedure 2: Running the Windows 2000 Server Pre-Copy and Text mode Setup routine**

This procedure is completed on Computer 1. It is assumed for this procedure that Computer 1 has no operating system installed, the disk is not partitioned, and bootable CD-ROM support, if available, is disabled. To verify that Computer 1 meets all pre-installation requirements, please review "About This Book."

1. Insert the disk labeled Windows 2000 Server Setup Disk #1 into the floppy disk drive, insert the Windows 2000 Server CD-ROM into the CD-ROM drive, and restart Computer 1.

   After the computer starts, Windows 2000 Setup displays a brief message that your system configuration is being checked, and then the Windows 2000 Setup screen appears.

   Notice that the gray bar at the bottom of the screen indicates that the computer is being inspected and that the Windows 2000 Executive is loading, which is a minimal version of the Windows 2000 kernel.

2. When prompted, insert Setup Disk #2 into the floppy disk drive, and then press Enter.

   Notice that Setup indicates that it is loading the HAL, fonts, local specific data, bus drivers, and other software components to support your computer's motherboard, bus, and other hardware. Setup also loads the Windows 2000 Setup program files.

3. When prompted, insert Setup Disk #3 into the floppy disk drive, and then press Enter.

    Notice that Setup indicates that it is loading disk drive controller drivers. After the drive controllers load, the setup program initializes drivers appropriate to support access to your disk drives. Setup might pause several times during this process.

4. When prompted, insert Setup Disk #4 into the floppy disk drive, and then press Enter.

    Setup loads peripheral support drivers, like the floppy disk driver and file systems, and then it initializes the Windows 2000 Executive and loads the rest of the Windows 2000 Setup program.

    If you are installing the evaluation version of Windows 2000, a Setup notification screen appears informing you that you are about to install an evaluation version of Windows 2000.

5. Read the Setup Notification message, and then press Enter to continue.

    Setup displays the Welcome To Setup screen.

    Notice that, in addition to the initial installation of Windows 2000, you can use Windows 2000 Setup to repair or recover a damaged Windows 2000 installation.

6. Read the Welcome To Setup message, and then press Enter to begin the installation phase of Windows 2000 Setup.

    Setup displays the License Agreement screen.

7. Read the license agreement, pressing Page Down to scroll to the bottom of the screen.

8. Select I Accept The Agreement by pressing F8.

    Setup displays the Windows 2000 Server Setup screen, prompting you to select an area of free space or an existing partition on which to install Windows 2000. This stage of setup provides a way for you to create and delete partitions on your hard disk.

    If Computer 1 does not contain any disk partitions (as required for this exercise), you will notice that the hard disk listed on the screen contains an existing unformatted partition.

9. Make sure that the Unpartitioned space partition is highlighted, and then type **C**.

    Setup displays the Windows 2000 Setup screen, confirming that you've chosen to create a new partition in the unpartitioned space and informing you of the minimum and maximum sizes of the partition you might create.

10. Specify the size of the partition you want to create (2048 MB), and then press Enter to continue.

> **Note** Although you can create additional partitions from the remaining unpartitioned space during setup, it is recommended that you perform additional partitioning tasks after you install Windows 2000. To partition hard disks after installation, use the Disk Management snap-in.

Setup displays the Windows 2000 Setup screen, showing the new partition as C: New (Unformatted).

11. Make sure the new partition is highlighted, and press Enter.

You are prompted to select a file system for the partition.

12. Use the arrow keys to select Format The Partition Using The NTFS File System, and then press Enter.

The Setup program formats the partition with NTFS. After it formats the partition, Setup examines the hard disk for physical errors that might cause Setup to fail and then copies files to the hard disk. This process will take several minutes.

Eventually, Setup displays the Windows 2000 Server Setup screen. A red status bar counts down for 15 seconds before Setup restarts the computer.

13. Remove the Setup disk from the floppy disk drive.

> **Important** If your computer supports booting from the CD-ROM drive, and this feature was not disabled in the BIOS, the computer will boot from the Windows 2000 Server installation CD-ROM after Windows 2000 Setup restarts. This will cause Setup to start again from the beginning. If this happens, remove the CD-ROM and then restart the computer.

14. Setup copies additional files and then restarts your machine and loads the Windows 2000 Setup wizard.

▶ **Procedure 3: Running the GUI-mode and gathering information phase of Windows 2000 Server Setup**

This procedure begins the graphical portion of setup on Computer 1.

1. On the Welcome to the Windows 2000 Setup Wizard screen, click Next to begin gathering information about your computer.

Setup configures NTFS folder and file permissions for the operating system files, detects the hardware devices in the computer, and then installs and configures device drivers to support the detected hardware. This process takes several minutes.

2. On the Regional Settings page, make sure that the system locale, user locale, and keyboard layout are correct for your language and location, and then click Next.

Note You can modify regional settings after you install Windows 2000 by using Regional Options in Control Panel.

Setup displays the Personalize Your Software page, prompting you for your name and organization name. Setup uses your organization name to generate the default computer name. Many applications that you install later will use this information for product registration and document identification.

3. In the Name field, type your name; in the Organization field, type the name of an organization; and then click Next.

Note If the Your Product Key screen appears, enter the product key provided with Windows 2000 Server and then click Next.

Setup displays the Licensing Modes screen, prompting you to select a licensing mode. By default, the Per Server licensing mode is selected. Setup prompts you to enter the number of licenses you have purchased for this server.

4. Select the Per Server Number of concurrent connections radio button, type **5** for the number of concurrent connections, and then click Next.

Important Per Server number of concurrent connections and 5 concurrent connections are suggested values to be used to complete your self-study. You should use a legal number of concurrent connections based on the actual licenses that you own. You can also choose to use Per Seat instead of Per Server.

Setup displays the Computer Name And Administrator Password screen.

Notice that Setup uses your organization name to generate a suggested name for the computer.

5. In the Computer Name field, type **Server01**.

   Windows 2000 displays the computer name in all capital letters regardless of how it is entered.

   Warning To complete this exercise, your computer cannot be connected to a network.

   Throughout the rest of this self-paced training kit, the labs will refer to Server01. If you do not name your computer Server01, everywhere the materials reference Server01, you will have to substitute the name of your server.

6. In the Administrator Password field and the Confirm Password field, type **password** (all lower case) and then click Next. Passwords are case-sensitive, so make sure you type password in all lowercase letters.

   For the labs in this self-paced training kit, you will use password for the Administrator account. In a production environment, you should always use a complex password for the Administrator account (one that others cannot easily guess). Microsoft recommends mixing uppercase and lowercase letters, numbers, and symbols (for example, Lp6*g9).

   Setup displays the Windows 2000 Components screen, indicating which Windows 2000 system components Setup will install.

   You can install additional components after you install Windows 2000 by using Add/Remove Programs in Control Panel. Make sure to install only the components selected by default during setup. Later in your training, you will be installing additional components.

7. Click Next.

   If a modem is detected in the computer during setup, Setup displays the Modem Dialing Information page.

8. If the Modem Dialing Information screen appears, enter an area code or city code and click Next.

   The Date and Time Settings screen appears.

   Important Windows 2000 services perform many tasks whose successful completion depends on the computer's time and date settings. Be sure to select the correct time zone for your location to avoid problems in later labs.

9. Enter the correct date and time and time zone settings, and then click Next.

   The Network Settings screen appears and Setup installs networking components.

▸ **Procedure 4: Completing the installing Windows Networking Components phase of Windows 2000 Server Setup**

Networking is an integral part of Windows 2000 Server. There are many selections and configurations available. In this procedure, basic networking is configured. In a later exercise, you will install additional network components.

1. On the Networking Settings screen, make sure that Typical Settings is selected, and then click Next to begin installing Windows networking components.

   This setting installs networking components that are used to gain access to and share resources on a network and configures TCP/IP to automatically obtain an IP address from a DHCP server on the network.

   Setup displays the Workgroup or Computer Domain screen, prompting you to join either a workgroup or a domain.

2. On the Workgroup Or Computer Domain screen, make sure that the radio button No, This Computer Is Not On A Network Or Is On A Network Without A Domain is selected, and that the workgroup name is WORKGROUP, and then click Next.

   Setup displays the Installing Components screen, displaying the status as Setup installs and configures the remaining operating system components according to the options you specified. This will take several minutes.

   Setup then displays the Performing Final Tasks screen, which show the status as Setup finishes copying files, making and saving configuration changes, and deleting temporary files. Computers that do not exceed the minimum hardware requirements might take 30 minutes or more to complete this phase of installation.

   Setup then displays the Completing the Windows 2000 Setup Wizard screen.

3. Remove the Windows 2000 Server CD-ROM from the CD-ROM drive, and click Finish.

   Important If your computer supports booting from the CD-ROM drive and you did not remove the installation CD-ROM, and you didn't disable this feature in the BIOS, the computer might run setup again soon after Setup restarts the computer.

   Windows 2000 restarts and runs the newly installed version of Windows 2000 Server.

▶ **Procedure 5: Completing the hardware installation phase of Windows 2000 Server Setup**

During this final phase of installation, any Plug and Play hardware not detected in the previous phases of setup will be detected.

1. At the completion of the startup phase, log on by pressing Ctrl+Alt+Delete.

2. In the Enter Password dialog box, type **Administrator** in the User Name field, and type **password** in the Password field.

3. Click OK.

   If Windows 2000 detects hardware that was not detected during Setup, the Found New Hardware Wizard screen displays, indicating that Windows 2000 is installing the appropriate drivers.

4. If the Found New Hardware Wizard screen appears, verify that the Restart The Computer When I Click Finish check box is cleared and then click Finish to complete the Found New Hardware wizard.

   Windows 2000 displays the Microsoft Windows 2000 Configure Your Server dialog box. From this dialog box, you can configure a variety of advanced options and services.

5. Select the I Will Configure This Server Later radio button, and click Next.

6. From the next screen that appears, clear the Show This Screen At Startup check box.

7. Close the Configure Your Server screen.

▶ **Procedure 6: Adjusting the display settings**

Setup selects a default resolution that is compatible with the video adapter that Setup has detected. You can change the default settings now or at any time after you install Windows 2000.

Warning If you do not know the refresh frequency that your monitor supports with the color palette and screen area you selected, do not change the default setting. Setting the refresh frequency too high might damage your monitor.

---

1. If you wish to adjust your display settings to show more colors or a higher screen resolution, run Control Panel and select Display.

   The Display Properties dialog box appears.

2. Select the Settings tab to adjust your screen area and colors, and click OK.

   A Display Properties message box appears warning you that your settings will be applied and that if you don't respond to the message box that appears after the display settings are adjusted, the original display settings will be restored.

3. Click OK.

   If the display settings are valid, a Monitor Settings message box will appear.

4. Click Yes to make the changes permanent.

   You have now completed the Windows 2000 Server installation and are logged on as Administrator.

5. Close Control Panel.

Note To properly shutdown Windows NT Server, click the Start button, choose shutdown, and then follow the directions that appear.

Lesson Summary

To install Windows 2000 Server, you must run either Winnt.exe or Winnt32.exe. Winnt.exe is used on computers running MS-DOS or Windows 16-bit operating systems. Winnt32.exe is used on computers running Windows 32-bit operating systems (Windows 9x, Windows NT, or Windows 2000). You can use a number of parameters with Winnt.exe and Winnt32.exe to customize how Windows 2000 Server is installed on your computer. Once one of the Setup files is launched, the Windows 2000 Server installation begins. This process includes three phases: the Pre-Copy Phase, Text mode, and GUI mode. During the Pre-Copy Phase, all of the files needed for the installation are copied to temporary directories on the local hard drive. In Text mode setup, Setup prompts the user for information needed to complete the installation. The GUI mode allows you to select which optional components to install and to select the administrator password.

Lesson 3: Upgrading to Windows 2000 Server

The process for upgrading existing servers from Windows NT Server to Windows 2000 Server is primarily automated. During the upgrade, Windows 2000 Setup migrates the current settings of the operating system while requiring little administrator input during the process. This lesson focuses on three aspects of the upgrade process: upgrading to the Windows 2000 Server operating system, upgrading Windows NT domains, and consolidating domains.

After this lesson, you will be able to

- Upgrade a Windows NT computer to Windows 2000 Server

Estimated lesson time: 30 minutes

Upgrading to Windows 2000 Server

There is just one basic process for upgrading a member server. Once you begin the installation process, the Setup wizard will guide you through the upgrade. When prompted, select the Upgrade To Windows 2000 option. During the final stages of installation, Windows 2000 Server Setup will gather information, using preexisting settings from the previous operating system.

There are several reasons to choose to upgrade, assuming that your previous operating system is a version that allows upgrading. Configuration is simpler; your existing users, settings, groups, rights, and permissions are retained. In addition, files and applications do not need to be recopied to the disk after installation. (As with any major changes to the hard disk, however, you should plan on backing up the disk before running Setup.)

If you want to upgrade and then use the same applications as before, review the Windows 2000 Compatibility Guide at *http://www.microsoft.com* and read the Read1st.txt file and the Relnotes.doc file (in the root directory of the Windows 2000 Server installation CD-ROM). You can also install the Windows 2000 Support Tools, which are located in the \Support\Tools directory of the Windows 2000 Server installation CD-ROM. The Support Tools include the Windows 2000 Server Resource Kit Deployment Planning Guide. Review the "Testing Applications for Compatibility with Microsoft Windows 2000" chapter.

When you upgrade, you must consider whether to convert the file system on any FAT16 or FAT32 partitions that you might have to the NTFS file system. It is possible to install Windows 2000 Server and also allow the computer to sometimes run another operating system by setting up the computer as a dual-boot system. Using dual booting, however, presents complexities because of file system issues.

Upgrading Servers

Windows 2000 Server supports upgrades from Windows NT 3.51 Server, Windows NT Server 4.0, and earlier versions of Windows 2000 Server. If a computer is running versions of Windows NT older than Windows NT 3.51, upgrade to Windows NT Server 4.0 before upgrading to Windows 2000 Server.

Note Windows 2000 supports all service packs for Windows NT 3.51 and Windows NT 4.0. The upgrade of installed applications varies with the system.

Upgrade Methods

The easiest way to upgrade Windows NT Server is to insert the Windows 2000 Server installation CD-ROM into the computer's CD-ROM drive. You can also run Winnt32 from the CD-ROM.

Setup cannot upgrade the operating system from the boot floppies or from booting the CD-ROM. Winnt32 or Autorun must be used to upgrade Windows NT Server. Also, you can upgrade your system by running Winnt32.exe over the network.

Finding Windows NT Installations to Upgrade

To find Windows NT Server installations on the system, the C:\Boot.ini file is examined on *x*86-based systems.

Note Windows 2000 does not support RISC-based systems.

The setup process attempts to access the partition indicated by the Advanced RISC Computing (ARC) path in *<active partition>*:\Boot.ini for each installation it finds. The active partition is usually C:, so references to the drive containing Boot.ini will be C:. If setup can access the partition, it then examines the root directory by searching for the following items:

- **Directories** The setup process searches for System32, System32\Drivers, and System32\Config subfolders.

- **Files** Under the System32 subfolders, the setup process searches for Ntoskrnl.exe and Ntdll.dll.

After searching for directories and files, the setup process attempts to load portions of the registry to determine whether an attempt has been made to upgrade this installation and has failed. Setup also determines the type of the current Windows NT installation and finds the edition (Server or Workstation), version number of the Windows NT installation (either 3.1, 3.5, 3.51, or 4.0), and build number.

The system's current version and build number must be less than or equal to the version number to which the system will be upgraded. Also, the edition must be Server. Therefore, the Windows 2000 Server upgrade process upgrades only Windows NT Server 3.51 and Windows NT Server 4.0 systems.

Once each installation in C:\Boot.ini has been found and each entry has met the above criteria, setup presents a menu that lists the installations on the system that can be upgraded.

If a Windows NT Server installation does not appear in the list of possible installations to upgrade, it probably did not meet one of the above checks. At this point, it is possible to press F3 to exit from the upgrade and still boot into any version of Windows NT installed on the system to ensure that the installation meets the criteria.

Note If there are multiple C:\Boot.ini entries that point to the same Windows NT installation, the installation is listed in the upgrade selection menu only once.

Upgrading a Windows NT Domain

A critical task in upgrading your network to Windows 2000 Server is upgrading the Windows NT Server domain. Domains are an important feature of both Windows NT Server and Windows 2000 Server. A domain is a grouping of accounts and network resources under a single domain name and security boundary. It is necessary to have one or more domains if you want to use domain-based user accounts and other domain security features in Windows 2000 Server. (This was true for Windows NT Server as well.)

With Windows 2000, servers can have one of three roles in relation to domains: domain controllers, which contain matching copies of the user accounts and other Active Directory services data in a given domain; member servers, which belong to a domain but do not contain a copy of Active Directory services data; and stand-alone servers, which do not belong to a domain and instead belong to a workgroup. A domain must have at least one domain controller, and it should generally have multiple domain controllers, each one backing up the user accounts and other Active Directory services data for the others and helping provide logon support to users.

You should plan the roles that your servers will have within domains in Windows 2000 before running Setup; however, if adjustments are necessary to these roles, they can still be made after Setup.

There are several important points to remember about upgrading an existing Windows NT domain to Windows 2000 domain:

- You must use the NTFS file system on domain controllers.

- Any servers that have any partition formatted with FAT16 or FAT32 will lack local security. On FAT16 or FAT32 partitions, shared folders can be protected only with permissions set on the directories, not on individual files, and there is no access protection against local access to the partition.

- When upgrading the domain controllers in a Windows NT domain to Windows 2000, you must upgrade the PDC first.

The roles of the servers in a domain are named somewhat differently with Windows 2000 Server as compared to Windows NT Server. With Windows NT Server, the possible roles were PDC (limited to one per domain), BDC, member server, or stand-alone server. Windows 2000 has only one kind of domain controller (without a "primary" or "backup" designation) and also includes the roles of member server and stand-alone server. The following table illustrates how Windows 2000 Setup assigns server roles when you upgrade:

Role in Windows NT Domain	Role in Windows 2000 Domain
Primary domain controller	Domain controller
Backup domain controller	Your choice of domain controller or member server
Member server	Your choice of member server or stand-alone server
Stand-alone server	Your choice of member server (if a Windows 2000 domain exists) or stand-alone server

Upgrading a Windows NT domain involves several stages:

1. Planning for a Windows NT domain upgrade
2. Preparing for a Windows NT domain upgrade
3. Upgrading the PDC
4. Upgrading the BDCs
5. Upgrading member servers

Planning for a Windows NT Domain Upgrade

The main features to consider as part of a Windows 2000 upgrade planning are the following:

- **DNS domain name organization** Develop DNS structure for the root domain of an enterprise tree or multiple trees in a forest of disjointed DNS domain names. Once the root DNS domain is created, other subdomains can be added to build the tree. For example, microsoft.com is a root domain, and dev.microsoft.com and mktg.microsoft.com are subdomains.

- **Name space organization within large account domains** Determine how to use OUs to structure the people and project resources.

- **Domain consolidation** Rebalance administration and control of centrally managed and distributed network services by merging resource domains into a smaller number of Windows 2000 domains.

- **New machine accounts added for long-term organization** Determine the location of computer accounts in Windows 2000 OUs. This is an important part of deploying Windows 2000 computer security policies.

- **Deployment of advanced technologies** Deploy new advanced technologies such as PKI security for smart card logon and remote access authentication or IP security for secure data transfer over private intranet and public Internet communications.

Note For more information, see the "Windows 2000 Support Tools' Deployment and Planning Guide." The installation program for this guide and other support tools is located in the \support\tools directory on the Windows 2000 Server installation CD-ROM.

Preparing for a Windows NT Domain Upgrade

Whenever you make any major changes to the contents of the hard disks on your servers, you should back up the hard disks before upgrading any of them. Before upgrading, you should also consider disconnecting the network cable of a BDC in your existing Windows NT network. After upgrading your PDC to Windows 2000 Server, this disconnected system is available for promotion to a Windows NT PDC if needed. (In the course of an uneventful upgrade, you would not promote the Windows NT BDC to PDC, but instead continue the upgrade process, eventually reconnecting the disconnected server and upgrading it.)

In addition, for any computer that will be a domain controller in the Windows 2000 domain, you should make sure there is plenty of room on the disk, beyond the space needed for the operating system itself. When the user accounts database is upgraded to the format used by Windows 2000 Server, it can expand significantly.

Preparing to Upgrade the Domain Controller

Before upgrading a domain controller, there are a number of tasks that must be completed:

- Disable WINS by using the Services option in Control Panel in Windows NT Server 4.0 so that the WINS database can be converted during the upgrade process.

- Disable DHCP by using the Services option in Control Panel in Windows NT Server 4.0 so that the DHCP database can be converted during the upgrade process.

- Set up a test environment by creating test user accounts so that you can test the upgrade once it is complete. Create users and groups that are consistent with your implementation of Windows NT Server 4.0.

The following table describes items you might want to include in a test environment and how to implement them:

Item	Implementation
User and Group policies	Include both user and group policies that are easy to verify after the upgrade. An example is removing the Run command from the Start menu.
User profiles	Set up individual user profiles for the test users that are obvious and easy to verify, such as different background wallpaper.
Logon scripts	Use logon script commands that are easy to verify after the upgrade, such as mapping network drives with the net use command.

Note It is always a good idea to test any upgrade in a lab environment before implementing it in a production environment. To that end you may remove a BDC from the network and promote it to be a PDC in a private network. Then you can upgrade the PDC to Windows 2000 Server. If that is successful, you can bring that computer back to the production environment.

Upgrading the Primary Domain Controller

The first domain controller to be upgraded in a Windows NT domain must be the PDC. As you upgrade this server, you will be given the choices of creating a new domain or a child domain, and creating a new forest or a domain tree in an existing forest. For upgrading a domain of three to five servers, create a new domain and a new forest. You should also define the domain name space to set up the top-level name space for the organization. Other domains can be added to the tree as child domains.

During the upgrade, you have the opportunity to choose the location of three important files: the database containing user accounts and other Active Directory data, the log file, and the system volume file (SYSVOL). The database and the log file can be on any type of partition (FAT16, FAT32, or NTFS); the previous SAM database can expand significantly from the size it had with Windows NT Server, so allow plenty of room for it. (Initially, the log file will take up very little space.) The system volume file must be on an NTFS partition.

After the first server is upgraded to a Windows 2000 domain controller, it will be fully backward compatible. This means that in a multiple-server environment the domain controller appears as a Windows 2000 domain controller to Windows 2000 servers and clients but emulates a Windows NT 4.0 PDC to other servers and clients.

Upgrading the Backup Domain Controllers

After upgrading your PDC and ensuring that it is functioning to your satisfaction, upgrade any BDCs next. (If possible, it is best to begin the upgrades soon, rather than allowing a long delay.) Be sure that the first server upgraded (the former PDC) is running and available on the network as you upgrade other domain controllers. This server is used as a template for the other domain controllers to copy as they are upgraded.

Upgrade the BDCs one at a time, and ensure that each is backed up before upgrading. Start and test each server on the network to ensure that it is functioning to your satisfaction before upgrading another BDC.

When you have completely upgraded all servers to Windows 2000 domain controllers, you have the option of changing the domain from Mixed mode (where Windows NT domain controllers can exist in the domain) to Native mode (where only Windows 2000 domain controllers can exist in the domain). This is an important decision, because you cannot revert to Mixed mode after changing to native mode. Figure 2.2 shows the transition from a Windows NT domain to a Windows 2000 native mode domain.

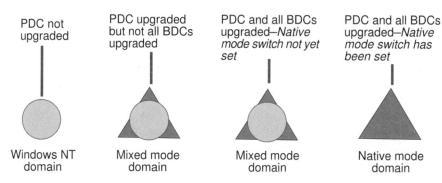

Figure 2.2 Transition from Windows NT domain to Windows 2000 Native mode domain

Mixed Mode

Mixed mode refers to a domain that contains both Windows 2000 and Windows NT 3.51/4.0 domain controllers. In Mixed mode the PDC is upgraded to Windows 2000 Server and one or more BDCs remain at version Windows NT Server 3.51/4.0. The Windows 2000 domain controller that was the PDC uses the Active Directory store to save objects. It is still fully backward compatible because it exposes the data as a flat store to down-level computers.

The PDC appears as a Windows 2000 domain controller to other Windows 2000 computers, and as a Windows NT 3.51/4.0 domain controller to computers that are not yet upgraded.

The domain still uses a single master replication with a Windows 2000 PDC; it is recognized as the domain master by the Windows NT Server 3.51/4.0 BDCs.

In Mixed mode the domain is limited by the functionality of the Windows NT 4.0 domain controllers. Some of the limitations on Windows 2000 operating in Mixed mode include the following:

- No group nesting is available.
- Non-Windows 2000 clients cannot benefit from transitive trust; they are limited to the limitations of pre-Windows 2000 trust relationships for access to resources.

Mixed mode is the default mode and is generally an interim step in the implementation of Windows 2000.

Native Mode

Once all domain controllers in a domain are upgraded, the domain can be moved from Mixed mode to Native mode. In Native mode all clients make use of Windows 2000 transitive trust. This means that a user can connect to any resource in the enterprise. Native mode also allows group nesting.

Note Moving to Native mode is a one-way move; once in Native mode, it is not possible to move the domain back to Mixed mode.

Upgrading Member Servers

Upgrade the member servers. Member servers in the domain can be upgraded in any order.

Domain Consolidation

Domain consolidation is a planning process for organizing domain resources to take advantage of new advanced features of the Windows 2000 Active Directory services. Domain reconfiguration is optional; it is not a requirement for deploying Windows 2000. Domain reconfiguration can take place over time as individual machines are upgraded and moved to different domains. Reconfiguration is also a fairly intensive and time-consuming administrator operation, as computers are moved to new domains and access control is verified or updated as needed.

There are two general ways to consolidate domains:

- Move user accounts from one domain to another to form a single larger domain.

- Move server computers from one resource domain into the OU of another domain.

One advantage to domain consolidation is that the number of master account domains can be reduced because each domain can be scaled to handle a much larger number of user, group, and computer accounts. Combining master account domains can reduce the number of server computers and interdomain trust accounts. However, moving users from one domain to another requires the creation of a new temporary password for the user account in the new domain. User passwords are not preserved when a user account is moved from one domain to another, although the SID for the user is.

Another advantage to domain consolidation is that the number of resource domains can be reduced by moving servers from many small domains into a combined resource domain. The domain controllers of the resource domains become member servers in the larger combined domain. This reduces the number of interdomain trust relationships between resource domains and account domains, saving system resources on domain controllers. Domain consolidation also makes it easier to redeploy server computers from one project or department to another.

Windows 2000 includes the following features that enable domain reconfiguration:

- Users and groups can be moved across domain boundaries and preserve security identity. The SID history is kept with the user account, and access tokens will contain both the new and the old SID to preserve access rights.

- Domain controllers can be demoted to a member server and moved to another domain.

- Security policies can be defined centrally and applied to many systems. These policies can grow in scope and change over time. They are used to deploy new technology, such as public key security and IP security. As new computers join a domain, they can automatically pick up the security policy in effect for the new domain.

- Computers can be moved to different domains by using remote administration tools.

- Access rights can be updated to reflect changes in organization or philosophy.

Lesson Summary

Upgrading from Windows NT Server to Windows 2000 Server is, for the most part, an automated process. The easiest way to upgrade Windows NT Server is to insert the Windows 2000 Server installation CD-ROM into the computer's CD-ROM drive. The Setup wizard will then guide you through the upgrade. However, an important aspect of upgrading to Windows 2000 is upgrading the domain, which involves a number of stages. First you must plan how you will upgrade the domain, including determining a domain name organization and deploying new technologies. Next you must prepare for that upgrade by completing such tasks as backing up files and disconnecting network cables. In addition, you must prepare to upgrade the domain controllers. The next step in upgrading the domain is to upgrade the PDC. This is followed by upgrading the BDCs and the member servers. When you've completed these steps, you should then consider consolidating your domain to take advantage of the new advanced features of the Windows 2000 Active Directory services.

Lesson 4: Troubleshooting a Windows 2000 Server Installation

Your installation of Windows 2000 Server should run to completion without any problems. However, this lesson covers some common issues that you might encounter during installation.

After this lesson, you will be able to

- Troubleshoot Windows 2000 installations

Estimated lesson time: 15 minutes

Troubleshooting Windows 2000 Server

When installing Windows 2000 Server, you might encounter problems caused by, for example, bad media or incompatible hardware. The following table lists some of these common installation problems and offers solutions to resolve them.

Problem	Solution
Media errors	If you are installing from a CD-ROM, use a different CD-ROM drive. If you still receive media errors, request a replacement CD by contacting Microsoft or your vendor.
Unsupported CD-ROM drive	Replace the CD-ROM drive with one that is supported, or if that is not possible, try another method of installation, such as installing over the network. After you have completed the installation, you can add the driver for the CD-ROM drive if it is available.
Insufficient disk space	Use the Setup program to create a partition by using existing free space on the hard disk. Delete and create partitions as needed to create a partition that is large enough for installation. Reformat an existing partition to create more space.
Failure of dependency service to start	Use the Windows 2000 Setup wizard, and return to the Network Settings dialog box and verify that you installed the correct protocol and network adapter. Verify that the network adapter has the proper configuration settings, such as transceiver type, and that the local computer name is unique on the network.

Problem	Solution
Inability to connect to the domain controller	Verify that the domain name is correct.
	Verify that the server running the DNS service and the domain controller are both running and online. If you cannot locate a domain controller, install into a workgroup and then join the domain after installation.
	Verify that the network adapter card and protocol settings are set correctly.
	If you are reinstalling Windows 2000 and using the same computer name, delete and then recreate the computer account.
Failure of Windows 2000 Server to install or start	Verify that Windows 2000 is detecting all of the hardware and that all of the hardware is on the HCL.

Lesson Summary

This lesson provides an overview of some of the common problems that can be encountered when installing Windows 2000 Server. Installation problems can be caused by bad media or incompatible hardware. In addition, there may not be enough room on any of the partitions to install Windows 2000 Server because you did not complete the preinstallation tasks. Other problems that might arise are the inability to connect to the domain controller or Windows 2000 Server might not install or start.

Review

The following questions are intended to reinforce key information presented in this chapter. If you are unable to answer a question, review the appropriate lesson and then try the question again. Answers to the questions can be found in Appendix A, "Questions and Answers."

1. If you are installing Microsoft Windows NT, in a dual-boot configuration on the same computer, which file system should you choose? Why?

2. Which licensing mode should you select if users in your organization require frequent access to multiple servers? Why?

3. You are installing Windows 2000 Server on a computer that will be a member server in an existing Windows 2000 domain. You want to add the computer to the domain during installation. What information do you need, and what computers must be available on the network, before you run the Setup program?

4. You are using a CD-ROM to install Windows 2000 Server on a computer that was previously running another operating system. There is not enough space on the hard disk to run both operating systems, so you have decided to repartition the hard disk and install a clean copy of Windows 2000 Server. Name two methods for repartitioning the hard disk.

5. You are installing Windows 2000 over the network. Before you install to a client computer, what must you do?

6. A client is running Windows NT 3.5 Server and is interested in upgrading to Windows 2000. From the list of choices, choose all possible upgrade paths:

   Upgrade to Windows NT 3.51 Workstation and then to Windows 2000 Server.

   Upgrade to Windows NT 4.0 Server and then to Windows 2000 Server.

   Upgrade directly to Windows 2000 Server.

   Run Convert.exe to modify any NTFS partitions for file system compatibility with Windows 2000, and then upgrade to Windows 2000 Server.

   Upgrade to Windows NT 3.51 Server and then to Windows 2000 Server.

7. In your current network environment, user disk space utilization has been a major issue. Describe three services in Windows 2000 Server to help you manage this issue.

C H A P T E R   3

Unattended Installations of Microsoft Windows 2000 Server

About This Chapter

To simplify the process of setting up Windows 2000 Server on multiple computers, you can automate your installations of the operating system and other server applications. To do this, you must create and use an answer file, which is a customized script that automatically answers the questions raised by Setup during installation. Once this file is created, you can run Setup from a command line, using the appropriate options for an unattended installation. This will allow you to install not only the Windows 2000 Server operating system, but server applications as well.

Before You Begin

To complete the lessons in this chapter, you must have

- Windows 2000 Server installed and running on Server01 as described in Chapter 2, Exercise 1.

- Computer 2 networked to Server01 and running a 32-bit version of Windows, either Windows 9*x* or Windows NT 3.51 or 4.0.

- Checked that Computer 2 meets the minimum hardware requirements as outlined in "About This Book."

- The Windows 2000 Server installation CD-ROM.

Lesson 1: Preparing for an Unattended Installation of Windows 2000 Server

When you perform an unattended installation of Windows 2000 Server, you create an answer file that supplies information to the setup routine. In addition, if you are going to install Windows 2000 Server on multiple computers over a network, you must create at least one set of distribution folders. This lesson describes the process of creating an answer file and setting up the distribution files necessary for a network installation.

After this lesson, you will be able to

- Create a customized answer file for an unattended installation

- Set up your distribution directory for a network installation of Windows 2000 Server

Estimated lesson time: 45 minutes

Creating the Answer File

The answer file is a customized script (usually saved as a .txt file) that allows you to run an unattended installation of Windows 2000 Server. The file, sometimes called the unattend file or the unattend script file, answers the questions that Setup normally prompts you for during installation. The \i386 directory of the Windows 2000 Server installation CD-ROM contains a sample answer file, Unattend.txt, that you can edit and use in your unattended installation. You can leave the name of the answer file as is, or you can change it according to the needs of your organization. For example, Comp1.txt, Install.txt, and Setup.txt are all valid names for an answer file, as long as those names are correctly specified in the Setup command. Being able to use different names allows you to build and use multiple answer files if you need to maintain different scripted installations for different parts of your organization.

Note that other programs, such as the Sysprep tool, which is used to facilitate the creation of a disk image of your Windows 2000 Server installation, also use answer files. (Sysprep is discussed in detail in Lesson 2.) The following table describes how the answer file can be named and when it is used:

Filename	When the file is used
<filename>.txt	When performing an unattended installation. You can use any name for the .txt file. Unattend.txt is the name of the sample answer file included with Windows 2000 Server.
Winnt.sif	When installing Windows 2000 Server from a bootable CD-ROM drive.
Sysprep.inf	When using the Sysprep tool to create a disk image of your Windows 2000 Server installation.

The same format that is used in Unattend.txt is used for the files shown in the preceding table. The answer file contains multiple optional sections that you modify to supply information about your installation requirements. The file supplies Setup with answers to all the questions you are asked when you install Windows 2000 Server manually. In addition, the answer file tells Setup how to interact with the distribution folders and files that you have created. For example, in the [Unattended] section there is an original equipment manufacturer (OEM) Preinstall entry that tells Setup whether to copy the OEM subfolders from the distribution folders to the target computer.

Answer File Format

An answer file consists of section headers, keys, and the values for each key. Most of the section headers are predefined, but some can be user defined. The following information is included in the Unattend.txt file. You can copy this file from the CD-ROM to writeable media, like a fixed disk, and then edit the file as necessary to meet the needs of your unattended installation. You can also rename the file.

```
Microsoft Windows 2000 Professional, Server, Advanced Server
and Datacenter
 (c) 1994 - 1999 Microsoft Corporation. All rights reserved.

Sample Unattended Setup Answer File

This file contains information about how to automate the
installation
or upgrade of Windows 2000 Professional and Windows 2000
Server so the
Setup program runs without requiring user input.
```

```
[Unattended]
Unattendmode = FullUnattended
OemPreinstall = NO
TargetPath = WINNT
Filesystem = LeaveAlone

[UserData]
FullName = "Your User Name"
OrgName = "Your Organization Name"
ComputerName = "COMPUTER_NAME"

[GuiUnattended]
Sets the Timezone to the Pacific Northwest
Sets the Admin Password to NULL
Turn AutoLogon ON and login once
TimeZone = "004"
AdminPassword = *
AutoLogon = Yes
AutoLogonCount = 1

For Server installs
[LicenseFilePrintData]
AutoMode = "PerServer"
AutoUsers = "5"

[GuiRunOnce]
List the programs that you want to launch when the machine
is logged on to for the first time

[Display]
BitsPerPel = 8
XResolution = 800
YResolution = 600
VRefresh = 70

[Networking]
When set to YES, setup will install default networking
components. The components to be set are
TCP/IP, File and Print Sharing, and the Client for Microsoft
Networks.
InstallDefaultComponents = YES

[Identification]
JoinWorkgroup = Workgroup
```

You do not need to specify all the possible keys in an answer file if the installation does not require them. Invalid key values generate errors or can cause incorrect behavior after setup.

The answer file is broken into sections. A section name is enclosed in brackets, as in the following example:

```
[UserData]
```

Sections contain keys and the corresponding values for those keys. Each key and value are separated by a space, an equal sign, and a space:

```
BitsPerPel = 8
```

Values that have spaces in them require double quotes around them:

```
OrgName = "Microsoft Corporation"
```

Some sections have no keys and merely contain a list of values:

```
[OEMBootFiles]
Txtsetup.oem
```

Comment lines start with a semicolon:

```
;Setup program runs without requiring user input.
```

Answer File Keys and Values

Every key in an answer file must have a value assigned to it; however, some keys are optional, and some keys have default values that are used if the key is omitted. Key values are strings of text, unless numeric is specified. If numeric is specified, the value is decimal unless otherwise noted.

Note Keys are not case sensitive; they can be uppercase or lowercase.

The Unattend.doc file has detailed information about the answer file keys and values. You can find Unattend.doc in the Deploy.cab file on the Windows 2000 Server installation CD-ROM, under the \Support\Tools folder. To extract or view the contents of the Deploy.cab file, use Windows Explorer. For more details about opening the Unattend.doc file, see the Sreadme.doc file on the Windows 2000 Server installation CD-ROM.

Important Running Setup.exe or 2000rkst.msi from the \Support\Tools folder installs the Windows 2000 Support Tools in Support.cab, but it does not extract the Unattend.doc file or any of the other compressed files in Deploy.cab.

Methods for Creating an Answer File

You can create an answer file by using Setup Manager or by creating the file manually.

Creating the Answer File by Using Setup Manager

To help you create or modify the answer file, an application called Setup Manager is available on the Windows 2000 Server installation CD-ROM in the Support\Tools\Deploy.cab file.

You can use Setup Manager to perform the following tasks:

- To specify the platform for the answer file (Windows 2000 Professional, Windows 2000 Server, Remote Operating System Installation, or Sysprep).

- To specify the level of automation for unattended Setup mode (Provide Defaults, Fully Automated, Hide Pages, Read Only, and GUI mode attended Setup).

- To specify default user name and organization information.

- To define one computer name or many computer names to support multiple unattended installations.

- To configure up to 99 automatic administrator logons to complete the setup process.

- To configure display settings.

- To configure network settings.

- To configure joining a workgroup or domain and automatically add a computer account to the domain.

- To create distribution folders.

- To add a custom logo and background files.

- To add files to the distribution folders.

- To add commands to the [GuiRunOnce] section of the answer file.

- To create Cmdlines.txt files.

- To specify code pages and other language-specific settings.

- To specify regional settings.

- To specify a time zone.

- To specify Telephony Application Programming Interface (TAPI) information.

- To customize browser and shell settings.

- To define the installation folder name. The boot partition (the partition containing the operating system files) is specified with the /t: or /tempdrive: switch.

- To add printers.

- To add mass storage device drivers and a custom HAL to be used during an unattended installation.

- To create a distribution folder and share for the distribution or specify that the unattended installation will run from the Windows 2000 Server CD-ROM.

With Setup Manager, you can add consistency to the process of creating or updating the answer file. However, you cannot use Setup Manager to specify all answer file settings, optional components, create Txtsetup.oem files, or create subfolders in the distribution folder.

After you use Setup Manager to create an answer file, add more settings by using a text editor. Refer to Unattend.doc and Readme.txt included in the Deploy.cab for a comprehensive list of available settings.

The following table describes the most commonly used Setup Manager specifications.

Parameter	Purpose
Upgrade option	Specifies whether to install Windows 2000 Professional or Windows 2000 Server.
Target computer name	Specifies the user name, organization name, and computer names to apply to the target computers.
Product ID	Specifies the product license number obtained from the product documentation.
Workgroup or domain	Specifies the name of the workgroup or domain to which the computer should be added.
Time zone	Specifies the time zone for the computer.
Network configuration information	Specifies the network adapter type and configuration information, including network protocols.

Creating the Answer File Manually

To create the answer file manually, you can use a text editor such as Notepad. In general, an answer file consists of section headers, parameters, and values for those parameters. Although most of the section headers are predefined, you can also define additional section headers. Note that it is not necessary to specify all the possible parameters in the answer file if the installation does not require them.

Appendix B, "Sample Answer Files for Unattended Setup," includes sample answer files that are appropriate for common installation configurations. You can customize the default answer file (Unattend.txt) that comes with Windows 2000 or write a new one based on the samples provided in this appendix.

Creating the Distribution Folders

To install Windows 2000 Server on multiple computers over a network, you must create at least one set of distribution folders. The distribution folders typically reside on a server to which the destination computers can connect. This allows users to install Windows 2000 Server by running Winnt.exe or Winnt32.exe on those computers. You can use one set of distribution folders and multiple answer files for different system implementations. Even if you intend to use disk imaging as your installation method, starting with distribution folders will help to provide consistent implementations for a variety of system types. In addition, distribution folders allow you to update future images by editing the files in the distribution folders to generate updated images without having to start from the beginning.

To help load balance the servers and to make the file-copy phase of Windows 2000 Setup faster, you can create distribution folders on multiple servers to support the installation process on computers that are running Windows 95, Windows 98, Windows NT, or Windows 2000. You can run Winnt32.exe with up to eight sets of distribution folders. Each set of distribution folders contains the Windows 2000 Server installation files as well as any device drivers and other files needed for installation.

To create a distribution folder manually, connect to the network server on which you want to create the distribution folder, and create a \W2kdist folder on the network share. To help differentiate between multiple distribution shares for the different editions of Windows 2000 (Windows 2000 Professional, Windows 2000 Server, and Windows 2000 Advanced Server), choose different names for each folder. If you need localized language versions of Windows 2000 to meet requirements for international branches of your organization, you can create separate distribution shares for each localized version. For each edition of Windows 2000, copy the contents of the \i386 folder to the distribution share created for it. For instance, if you are preparing a distribution for Windows 2000 Server, create and share a folder named \W2kdists and copy the \i386 directory on the Windows 2000 Server installation CD-ROM to it.

Note The distribution share to support a default installation of Windows 2000 Server requires approximately 313 megabytes (MB) of disk space.

You can also use Setup Manager to automatically create and share a distribution folder.

Structuring the Distribution Folder

This section provides detailed information about the folders and subfolders that make up the set of distribution folders. Figure 3.1 illustrates how these folders should be structured.

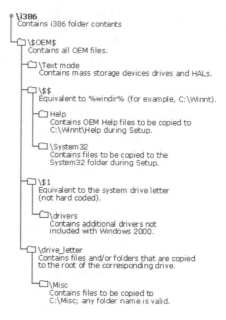

Figure 3.1 Example of a structure for the distribution folders

\i386 (On Windows 2000 Installation CD-ROM Copied to Distribution Share)

This is the primary distribution folder. It contains all the files required to install Windows 2000 Server. You copy the contents of this folder from the Windows 2000 Server installation CD-ROM to the root of the distribution share.

\OEM (On Distribution Share and Copied to WIN_NT.~LS)

The \$OEM$ subfolder is located directly beneath the primary distribution folder. During Setup you can automatically copy directories, standard Microsoft format 8.3 files, and any tools needed for your automated installation process to \$OEM$. Note that if you use the OEMFILESPATH key in the answer file, you can create the \$OEM$ subfolder outside of the distribution folder.

\OEM provides the necessary folder structure for supplemental files to be copied to the target computer during Setup. These files include drivers, utilities, applications, and any other files required to deploy Windows 2000 Server within your organization.

\OEM can contain the optional file Cmdlines.txt, which contains a list of commands to be run during the GUI mode phase of Setup. These commands can be used to install optional components, such as tools and utilities. Commands contained in Cmdlines.txt are run before the computer is logged on to the network.

As long as Setup finds \$OEM$ in the root of the distribution point, it will copy all the files found in this directory to the WIN_NT.~LS temporary directory created during the Text mode phase of Setup. During Setup, subfolders of \$OEM$ are copied to the corresponding location on the target computer. At Setup completion, OEM and all subfolders are deleted along with WIN_NT.~LS.

Note All folders described next are located on the distribution share below \OEM and are copied to various locations on the computer running Setup.

\OEM\textmode (Copied to WIN_NT.~BT)

The \OEM\textmode subfolder contains new or updated files for installing mass storage device drivers and HALs. These files can include OEM HALs, drivers for SCSI devices, and the Txtsetup.oem file, which directs the loading and installing of these components.

All files placed in the \OEM\textmode subfolder (HALs and drivers) must be listed in the [OEMBootFiles] section of the answer file.

\$OEM$\$$ (Copied to %windir% and Subfolders of %windir%)

The \$OEM$\$$ subfolder corresponds to the contents of the %windir% environment variable. The subfolder contains the operating system files (either new files or replacements for retail files) that are copied to the various subfolders when Windows 2000 is installed. The structure of this subfolder must match the structure of a standard Windows 2000 installation, where \$OEM$\$$ matches %windir%, \$OEM$\$$\System32 matches %windir%\System32, and so on. Each subfolder needs to contain the files that will be copied to the corresponding operating system folder on the target computer.

Note In Windows 2000, %systemroot% is equivalent to %windir%.

\$OEM$\$1 (Copied to $systemdrive$)

The \$OEM$\$1 subfolder, which is new for Windows 2000, points to the drive on which Windows 2000 is installed. $1 is equivalent to the %systemdrive% environment variable. For example, if you are installing Windows 2000 on the D: drive, \$OEM$\$1 points to the D: drive. This makes it possible to install Windows 2000 to drives other than the C: drive.

\$OEM$\$1\Drivers (Copied to $systemdrive$\Drivers and Subfolders of $systemdrive$\Drivers)

The \$OEM$\$1\Drivers subfolder, which is new for Windows 2000, allows you to place new or updated Plug and Play device drivers and their supporting files (catalog files and .INF installation files) in and below the Drivers subfolder. These folders and their contents are copied to the %systemdrive%\ Drivers folder on the target computer. Adding the OemPnPDriversPath parameter to your answer file will tell Windows 2000 where to look for the new or updated Plug and Play drivers. When searching for appropriate Plug and Play device drivers to install during Setup or afterward, Windows 2000 looks at the files in the folders you created as well as those originally included with the system. Note that you can replace Drivers with a name of your own choosing that follows the 8.3 MS-DOS naming convention.

Note The \$OEM$\$1\Drivers subfolder replaces the \Display and \Net subfolders used in Windows NT installation.

\$OEM\$\$1\Sysprep (Copied to %systemdrive%\Sysprep)

The \$OEM\$\$1\Sysprep subfolder contains the files needed to run the Sysprep utility. Sysprep.exe and Sysprepcl.exe must be in %systemdrive%\Sysprep folder for Sysprep to function properly.

Tip Add Sysprep.inf (created by Setup Manager or written manually) to the \$OEM\$\$1\Sysprep directory on the distribution share. Otherwise, a floppy disk containing the Sysprep.inf file is necessary to complete a Sysprep setup.

\$OEM\$\drive_letter

During Text mode, the structure of each \$OEM\$*drive_letter* subfolder is copied to the root of the corresponding drive in the target computer. For example, files that you place in the \$OEM\$\D subfolder are copied to the root of the D: drive. You can also create subfolders within these subfolders. For example, \$OEM\$\E\Misc causes Setup to create a \Misc subfolder on the E: drive.

Files that have to be renamed must be listed in the \$\$Rename.txt file. Note that the files in the distribution folders must have short file names (format 8.3).

Exercise 1: Preparing and Running an Automated Installation

In this exercise, you create and run an automated installation of Windows 2000 Server on Computer 2. To prepare for the automated installation, you use the Windows 2000 Server Setup Manager to create an answer file and a distribution share on Server01.

Warning Do not customize the desktop or any of the Windows 2000 applications on Server01. If you do, the steps in this exercise may not work. For example, this exercise is designed for the double-click behavior of the default desktop.

▸ **Procedure 1: Running Setup Manager**

Complete this procedure on a Server01 with the Windows 2000 Server installation CD-ROM inserted.

1. Create a folder named Deploy underneath C:\Program Files.

2. Using Windows Explorer, locate the \Support\Tools folder on the Windows 2000 Server installation CD-ROM.

3. Select the TOOLS folder in the Folders pane and then double-click the DEPLOY file in the right pane.

   The contents of the DEPLOY cab file appears.

4. From the Edit menu, choose Select All.

5. From the File menu, choose Extract.

   A Browse For Folder window appears.

6. Click on the + sign to the left of Local Disk (C:) to expand the C: drive.

7. Click on the + sign to the left of Program Files to expand the Program Files folder.

8. Click on the Deploy folder.

   The Deploy folder opens.

9. Click OK.

   A Copying message box appears momentarily as the files in the DEPLOY cab file are extracted to C:\Program Files\Deploy.

10. From the C:\Program Files\Deploy folder, double-click setupmgr.

    Setup Manager starts, and the Windows 2000 Setup Manager Wizard appears.

11. Read the descriptive text, and then click Next.

    The New Or Existing Answer File screen appears, and the Create A New Answer File radio button is selected.

12. Click Next.

    The Product To Install screen appears, and the Windows 2000 Unattended Installation radio button is selected.

13. Click Next.

    The Platform screen appears, and the Windows 2000 Professional radio button is selected.

14. Select the Windows 2000 Server radio button, and click Next.

    The User Interaction Level screen appears, and the Provide Defaults radio button is selected.

15. Select the Fully Automated radio button, read the Description text, and then click Next.

The License Agreement screen appears.

16. Read the text on this screen, select the I Accept The Terms Of The License Agreement check box, and then click Next.

The Customize The Software screen appears.

17. In the Name text box, type your name and press the Tab key.

18. In the Organization text box, type your organization name or **MSPress Self-Study** and click Next.

The Licensing Mode screen appears, and the Per Server radio button is selected.

19. Select the Per Seat radio button, and click Next.

The Computer Names screen appears.

20. Insert the Windows 2000 Training Supplemental CD-ROM into Server01, and click Import.

The Open window appears.

21. In the File Name drop-down list box, type *<cd-rom_drive:>\chapt03\ ex1\computer names.txt* and then click Open.

The Computer Names screen appears showing a list of computers to be installed.

22. Click Next.

The Administrator Password screen appears.

23. In the password text boxes, type **password**, and select the check box named When The Computer Starts, Automatically Log On As Administrator.

The Number of times to Auto Logon is set to 1.

24. Click Next.

The Display Settings screen appears.

25. Leave all text box values set to Use Windows Default, and click Next.

The Network Settings screen appears, and the Typical Settings radio button is selected.

26. Click Next.

    The Workgroup or Domain screen appears and the Workgroup radio button is selected.

    Server01 is currently configured as a member of a workgroup named WORKGROUP. Therefore, do not change the values appearing on the Workgroup or Domain screen. When the automated installation is run on Computer 2, it will become a member of the same workgroup. Later in your training, Server01 will become a domain controller and the computer you are preparing an answer file for will join that domain.

Note The answer file you are preparing now can be modified later to automatically join a domain and create computer accounts in the domain. These modifications are made by using either Setup Manager or a text editor.

---

27. Click Next.

    The Time Zone screen appears.

28. From the Time Zone drop-down list box, select your time zone and click Next.

    The Additional Settings screen appears, and the Yes, Edit The Additional Settings radio button is selected.

29. Click Next.

    The Telephony screen appears.

30. You may enter your country/region, area code or city code, and any other settings you require to dial out. If Computer 2 does not have dial-out access, you can ignore this screen and continue.

31. Click Next.

    The Regional Settings screen appears, and the Use The Default Regional Settings For The Windows Version You Are Installing radio button is selected.

32. Click Next.

    The Languages screen appears.

33. Select any additional language support you want to have available for the operation of Windows 2000 Server, and then click Next.

    The Browser and Shell Settings screen appears, and the Use Default Internet Explorer Settings radio button is selected.

34. Click Next.

The Installation Folder screen appears, and the A Folder Named Winnt radio button is selected.

35. Click Next.

The Install Printers screen appears.

36. Click Next.

The Run Once screen appears.

37. In the Command To Run text box, type **Notepad.exe** and click Add.

Typically, the Command To Run text box would contain a script or other executable program to further configure the user's environment. For the purpose of training, running Notepad is sufficient. Notice that if you added a printer on the previous screen, the AddPrinter command runs to add your printer to the list of installed printers.

38. Click Next.

The Distribution Folder screen appears.

39. Select the Yes, Create Or Modify A Distribution Folder radio button, and click Next.

The Distribution Folder Name screen appears, and the Create A New Distribution Folder radio button is selected.

The Distribution folder text box contains C:\win2000dist, and the Share As Text box contains win2000dist.

40. Click Next.

The Additional Mass Storage Drivers screen appears.

41. Read the screen, and click Next.

' The Hardware Abstraction Layer screen appears.

42. Read the screen, and click Next.

The Additional Commands screen appears.

43. Read the screen, and click Next.

Commands entered here are written to Cmdlines.txt. This file is created under the distribution folder in the OEM subfolder.

The OEM Branding screen appears.

44. Click Next.

The Additional Files Or Folders screen appears.

45. Browse the folders by clicking on them and reading the information that appears under Description.

    Click Next.

    The Answer File Name screen appears showing a path and file name located on the CD-ROM in the Location And File Name text box.

46. Verify that the path and file name to **C:\Win2000dist\Unattend.txt**, and click Next.

    The Location Of Setup Files screen appears, and the Copy The Files From CD radio button is selected.

47. Remove the Windows 2000 Server Training Supplemental CD-ROM, and insert the Windows 2000 Server installation CD-ROM.

    After the Windows 2000 Server installation CD-ROM is read, the Microsoft Windows 2000 CD screen appears.

48. Close the Microsoft Windows 2000 CD screen.

49. Click Next on the Location Of Setup Files screen.

    The Copying Files screen appears as the files are copied from the \i386 directory on the installation CD-ROM to C:\Win2000Dist.

50. Allow the file copy to complete before continuing to the next procedure.

    At the completion of Setup Manager's tasks, a Completing The Windows 2000 Setup Manager Wizard screen appears.

51. Read the screen, and then click Finish.

▶ **Procedure 2: Inspecting the distribution folder created by Setup Manager**

In this procedure you will inspect the folder structure created by Setup Manager, answer file (Unattend.txt), UDF file (Unattend.udf), and batch file (Unattend.bat).

1. Click Start and then Run.

   The Run dialog box appears.

2. In the Open text box, type **C:\Win2000dist** and click OK.

   The Win2000dist window appears.

3. Open another window to the following directory on the Windows 2000 installation CD-ROM: *<cd-rom drive>*:\i386.

   The i386 window appears.

4. Arrange the windows so that you can see both the win2000dist window and the i386 window.

5. What folder appears directly under the Win2000dist folder that does not appear in the i386 folder?

6. Examine the directory structure below oem, and review Figure 3.1 in the text. You will be asked a question about this structure in the "Review" section of this chapter.

7. Return to the Win2000dist folder, and locate the three Unattend files.

   Notice that two of the Unattend files do not appear with extensions.

8. To show file extensions for all files, select Tools and choose Folder Options.

   The Folder Options dialog box appears.

9. Click the View tab.

10. From the Advanced Settings box, clear the Hide File Extensions For Known File Types check box, and click OK.

11. Locate the Unattend files again.

    The Unattend files appear with their file extensions showing.

    Select Unattend.txt, and from the File menu, choose Open.

    Unattend.txt appears in Notepad.

12. Locate the [User Data] section and add an additional line named ProductID=<*your product ID*>. For the value of ProductID, type the Product Key provided with your copy of Windows 2000 Server.

13. Save and close Unattend.txt.

14. For an explanation of any sections in this file, refer to Unattend.doc located in the C:\Program Files\Deploy folder you created at the start of this exercise. Unattend.doc can be opened in Microsoft Wordpad, Microsoft Word, or any word processor capable of reading Microsoft Word files.

15. Close Unattend.doc.

16. From the Win2000dist window, select Unattend.udf; and from the File menu choose Open With.

    The Open With dialog box appears.

17. Select Notepad from the Choose The Program You Want To Use box, and click OK.

    Notice that the 12 computer names imported during the operation of Setup Manager appear here.

18. What is the purpose of the UDF file?

19. Close the UDF file.

20. From the Win2000dist window, select Unattend.bat; and from the File menu, choose Edit.

    The contents of the batch file appear in Notepad.

21. Notice that the batch file sets variables, and then the variables are used to run Winnt32 with switches. Notice also that you must specify the computer name when calling the batch file since a UDF file is involved in the setup routine.

22. Close the Unattend.bat window.

▶ **Procedure 3: Running an unattended setup of Windows 2000 Server from Computer 2**

Computer 2 must already be running a Windows 32-bit operating system, such as Windows 95 or Windows NT. In addition, Server01 must be connected to the same network as Computer 2. All requirements for the exercises are outlined in About This Book.

Please note that if the two computers are networked on an isolated network, you must perform one or more of the following steps before Computer 2 can properly communicate with Server01.

▪ If Computer 2 is running Windows 98, make sure it is configured to acquire an IP address from a DHCP server.

▪ If Computer 2 is running an operating system other than Windows 98, such as Windows 95 or Windows NT, complete the following steps:

    1. On Server01, type *ipconfig* at the command prompt to determine Server01's IP address.

    2. On Computer 2, manually specify an IP address between 169.254.0.0 and 169.254.255.255, but without using Server01's IP address, and then set the subnet mask to 255.255.0.0

Caution If Computer 2 is running Windows NT, the boot partition is C:\ and the operating system directory is Winnt, change the name of the installation directory in Unattend.txt. The directory name listed in Unattend.txt is found under the Unattended section, and the valuename is TargetPath. For example, change the value so that TargetPath=\WIN2000S.

1. From Computer 2, connect a drive letter (H: will be used throughout this exercise), to \\Server01\WIN2000dist. You can connect to Server01 by using the Administrator username and the password of "password."

   The connection might not work if you don't have a DHCP server available. If Computer2 is running Windows 98, configure it to acquire an IP address from a DHCP server. This way, when the DHCP server is not available, the Automatic Private IP Addressing (APIPA) feature of Windows 98 and Windows 2000 will ensure that your computer assigns itself an IP address.

   If Computer2 is running an operating system other than Windows 98, do the following:

   1. On Server01, type *ipconfig* at the command prompt to determine what the APIPA-assigned IP address is for Server01.

   2. On Computer2, manually specify an IP address in the form of 169.254.*x*.*x* (other than 169.254.0.0, 169.254.255.255, and the address assigned to Server01), then set the subnet mask to 255.255.0.0.

2. Open a command prompt, type **h:**, and press Enter.

   Caution If you have upgraded from Windows 9*x*, you might find that Setup can't find the .udf file. If this happens, open Unattend.bat on Server01 and specify the full path to the .udf file.

3. From the command prompt, type **H:\Unattend Server02**.

4. The Copying Installation Files screen appears as Windows 2000 Server runs an automated installation over the network.

   At the conclusion of this phase, a warning screen will inform you that the computer will be restarted.

   Note This pre-text mode phase of Setup can be completed using the \syspart switch with Winnt32.exe.

5. Allow the computer to restart.

Upon reboot, the Windows 2000 boot menu appears and Microsoft Windows 2000 Server setup continues to Text mode.

The computer reboots again, and the boot menu appears showing Windows 2000 Server.

Windows 2000 installation continues the graphical portion of setup. The Installing Devices And Installing Components screens take time to complete. The Performing Final Tasks screen appears where Windows 2000 Server completes the setup routine. When setup is completed, the Windows 2000 Setup screen announces that the computer will restart.

6. After the computer restarts, notice that it automatically logs on as Administrator as specified in Setup Manager. In this stage, the printer is installed and Notepad.exe runs.

7. Close Notepad.

The Windows 2000 Configure Your Server screen appears.

8. Select the I Will Configure This Server Later radio button, and click Next.

The Configure Your Server screen appears.

9. Clear the Show This Screen At Startup check box, and close the screen.

Caution If you are upgrading from Windows 9x, check to see if your partition is NTFS. If not, you will need to convert it. You can do this by typing convert c: /fs:ntfs at the command prompt.

Lesson Summary

Before you can perform an unattended installation of Windows 2000 Server, you must create an answer file, which is a customized script file that contains multiple optional sections that you modify to supply information about your installation requirements. The file supplies Setup with answers to all the questions you are asked when you install Windows 2000 Server manually. In addition, the answer file tells Setup how to interact with the distribution folders and files that you have created. You must create at least one set of distribution folders to install Windows 2000 Server over a network. Using Setup Manager can create a distribution folder and an answer file manually or automatically. To further customize the answer file, refer to the Unattend.doc file located on the Windows 2000 Server installation CD-ROM.

Lesson 2: Automating the Installation of Windows 2000 Server

Automated installations of Windows 2000 Server involve running Setup with an answer file. You can perform automated installations on multiple computers so that Setup can take place in an unattended fashion. The following installations can be automated:

- The core Windows 2000 Server operating system
- Any application that does not run as a service
- Additional language support for Windows 2000 Server through the installation of various language packs
- Service packs for Windows 2000 Server

This lesson focuses on unattended installations of the Windows 2000 Server operating system. To learn about unattended installations of other applications, see Lesson 3, "Automating the Installation of Server Applications."

After this lesson, you will be able to

- Perform an unattended installation of the Windows 2000 Server operating system

Estimated lesson time: 45 minutes

Performing an Unattended Installation

To perform an unattended installation of Windows 2000 Server, you must specify the answer file when you run Setup. There are three basic types of unattended installations that you can use to set up Windows 2000 Server: the bootable CD-ROM method, the Winnt.exe method, or the Winnt32.exe method.

Bootable CD-ROM

To start Windows 2000 Setup in unattended mode from the Windows 2000 Server installation CD-ROM, the following conditions must be met:

- The computer must support the El Torito Bootable CD-ROM (no emulation mode) format to boot from the CD-ROM drive.

- The answer file must be named Winnt.sif and be placed on a floppy disk to be inserted into the floppy drive as soon as the computer boots from the CD-ROM.

- The answer file must contain a [Data] section with the required keys specified.

Winnt.exe or Winnt32.exe

The following Winnt.exe command provides an example for implementing an unattended installation:

```
Winnt /s:Z:\i386 /u:Z:\unattend.txt /t:c
```

Note the use of the /u: command line switch, which indicates an unattended installation. The /t: switch indicates which drive Setup will copy the source files to continue the installation. Z:\i386 is the network location containing the Windows 2000 installation source files. The local computer must map the Z: drive to the network share containing the i386 subfolder before this example command line will work.

The following Winnt32.exe command provides an example similar to the previous Winnt example for implementing an unattended installation:

```
Winnt32 /s:Z:\i386 /unattend 10:Z:\unattend.txt /tempdrive:C
```

Winnt32.exe uses /unattend: rather then /u: for running an unattended setup. The number following the /unattend: switch indicates to the setup routine how long it should wait after copying files to automatically reboot the computer and continue setup. The num command works on Windows NT or Windows 2000 but is ignored on computers running Windows 9x.

Figure 3.2 shows the steps necessary to run the example unattended installation commands listed previously.

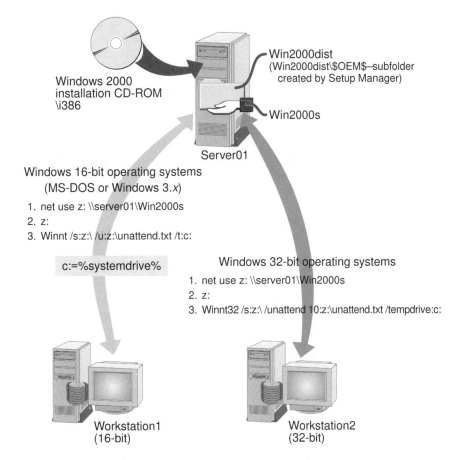

Figure 3.2 Initiating an unattended installation on computers running 16-bit and 32-bit operating systems

Automating the Installation of Windows 2000 Server

Several methods are available for creating an automated installation of Windows 2000 Server. The method you choose depends on the desired outcome. In certain situations, installation methods can be combined. For example, Syspart and Sysprep can be used together in certain setup installation scenarios.

In addition to the basic installation methods described above, you can use the following methods to perform automated installations of Windows 2000 Server:

- The Winnt32.exe Setup program along with the /syspart parameter
- The System Preparation Tool (Sysprep)
- Systems Management Server (SMS)
- Bootable CD-ROM

These methods either build on or replace the over-the-network unattended installation method described above. The following table provides details about when to use each installation method:

Installation Method	Use	Upgrade	Clean Installation
Syspart	Use Syspart for clean installations to computers that have dissimilar hardware.	No	Yes
Sysprep	Use Sysprep when the master computer and the target computers have identical or nearly identical hardware, including the HAL and mass storage devices.	No	Yes
SMS	Use SMS to perform managed upgrades of Windows 2000 Server to multiple systems, especially those that are geographically dispersed.	Yes	No
Bootable CD-ROM	Use the bootable CD-ROM method with a computer whose BIOS allows it to boot from the CD-ROM.	No	Yes
RIS (Remote Installation Service)	Use RIS with a computer that supports PXE or a bootable RIS diskette. Either method allows the computer to connect to a networked RIS Server during the initial boot process and receive an installation of Windows 2000 Professional. Pre-Boot Execution Environment (PXE) allows a computer that contains a PXE ROM to boot to the network server. The PXE ROM is either coded into the system BIOS or is located on a NIC as an option ROM.	Yes	Yes

Note As of the writing of this kit, RIS can roll out automated installations of Windows 2000 Professional only. It does not support automated installations of Windows 2000 Server. Future enhancement to RIS might allow roll-outs of Windows 2000 Server and other operating systems.

The preceding table also shows which installation methods can be used to perform upgrades or clean installations. Before you can automate the installation of Windows 2000 Server, you must decide if the installation will be an upgrade from Windows NT Server or a clean installation.

If you do perform a clean installation, note that because an automated installation is unattended, a clean installation can replace existing partitions or files on existing partitions. Application files and data files can still remain on partitions, although applications should be reinstalled to reregister them with the new operating system installation.

Using Syspart

Syspart is executed by including it as a parameter of the Winnt32.exe Setup program. Winnt32 with the Syspart switch is run on a reference computer to complete the first phase of installation. If the reference computer and the computers on which you will complete the installation of Windows 2000 Server do not have similar hardware, you can use the Syspart method. This method reduces deployment time by completing the file-copy phase of setup on the reference computer, thereby eliminating this step on the computers targeted for installation.

Syspart requires that you use two physical disks, with a primary partition on the target hard disk. However, the target hard disk does not need to be located in the master computer. It can be in another computer on a network, as long as it is a clean disk with no operating systems installed.

If you require a similar installation and operating system configuration on hardware types in which the HALs or mass storage controllers differ, you can use Syspart to create a master set of files with the necessary configuration information and driver support. This file set can then be used on dissimilar systems to properly detect the hardware and consistently configure the base operating system.

After the reference computer is running, connect to the distribution folder and run Setup by executing the Winnt32.exe program from the command prompt:

```
winnt32 /unattend:unattend.txt /s:install_source /
syspart:install_target /tempdrive:install_target /noreboot
```

After running the previous command where *install_target* equals D, the following structure is created on the D: drive (Figure 3.3):

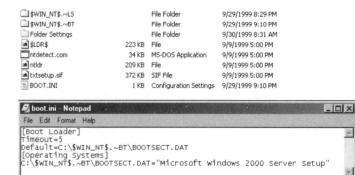

WIN_NT.~LS		File Folder	9/29/1999 8:29 PM
WIN_NT.~BT		File Folder	9/29/1999 9:10 PM
Folder Settings		File Folder	9/30/1999 8:31 AM
LDR	223 KB	File	9/9/1999 5:00 PM
ntdetect.com	34 KB	MS-DOS Application	9/9/1999 5:00 PM
ntldr	209 KB	File	9/9/1999 5:00 PM
txtsetup.sif	372 KB	SIF File	9/9/1999 5:00 PM
BOOT.INI	1 KB	Configuration Settings	9/29/1999 9:10 PM

```
boot.ini - Notepad
File  Edit  Format  Help
[Boot Loader]
Timeout=5
Default=C:\$WIN_NT$.~BT\BOOTSECT.DAT
[Operating Systems]
C:\$WIN_NT$.~BT\BOOTSECT.DAT="Microsoft Windows 2000 Server Setup"
```

Figure 3.3 The contents of the target computer's D: drive and Boot.ini after running Syspart

The following information provides more details about the parameters and values used when running the Winnt32.exe Setup program:

- The Unattend.txt value is the answer file used for an unattended setup. It provides answers to some or all of the prompts the end user normally responds to during Setup. Using an answer file is optional when creating the master file set.

- The *install_source* value is the location of the Windows 2000 Server files. Specify multiple /s command line switches if you want to install from multiple sources simultaneously. Figure 3.4 shows a file copy occurring from two sources. The first source is a network drive, the second source is a local CD-ROM drive. As the figure shows, up to eight install sources can be specified.

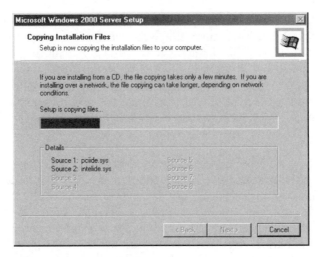

Figure 3.4 The Copy Installation Files screen showing two sources for file copy

- The /syspart and /tempdrive parameters must point to the same partition of a secondary hard disk. The Windows 2000 Server installation must take place on a primary partition of that secondary hard disk. Syspart will set the partition to active so that it is bootable.

- The /tempdrive parameter must be used for the Syspart installation to be successful. When you use the /tempdrive command line switch, make sure you have sufficient free disk space on your second partition to install both Windows 2000 Server and the installation files it places in WIN_NT.~LS.

- The *install_drive* value is the partition that contains the preinstallation of Windows 2000 Server. The files on this drive are shown in Figure 3-3.

Note Syspart will automatically mark the drive as active in preparation for moving it to the target computer.

Using Sysprep

Sysprep is a tool that facilitates creating a disk image of your Windows 2000 Server installation. Disk duplication is a good choice if you need to install an identical configuration on multiple computers. To use the Sysprep tool, you should install Windows 2000 Server on a reference computer. You should also install any other applications on the reference computer that you want installed on the target computers. Then run Sysprep followed by a third-party disk imaging utility. Sysprep prepares the hard disk on the master computer so that the disk imaging utility can transfer an image of the hard disk to the other computers. This method decreases deployment time dramatically compared to standard or scripted installations.

Tip Create a CD-ROM containing the disk image or move the image to a network location so that the image can be used to rapidly set up many identical or nearly identical computers.

To use Sysprep, the master computer and target computers must have identical HALs, Advanced Configuration and Power Interface (ACPI) support, and mass storage devices. Windows 2000 automatically detects plug and play devices, and Sysprep redetects and re-enumerates the devices on the system when the computer is turned on after Sysprep has run. This means the plug and play devices, such as network cards, modems, video adapters, and sound cards, do not have to be the same on the master and target computers. The major advantage of Sysprep installation is speed. The image can be packaged and compressed and only the files required for the given configuration are created as part of the image. Additional plug and play drivers that might be needed on other systems are also created. The image can also be copied to a CD-ROM to be distributed to remote sites that have slow links.

Note Because the master and target computers must have identical HALs, ACPI support, and mass storage devices, you might need to maintain multiple images for your environment.

Sysprep allows you to configure a master image containing the necessary components for a member server and then later configure the server and optionally promote it to a domain controller. This can be done manually or by running the commands in the [GuiRunOnce] section of the Sysprep.inf file. For more information about Sysprep.inf, see the Sysprep Files section later in this chapter.

If your environment includes multiple types of hardware-dependent systems, you can use Syspart in conjunction with Sysprep to create a master for each type. To do this, you install Windows 2000 on one computer of each type, and then use the Sysprep utility to help create images to be used on the remaining computers of each type. For more information about Sysprep, see the "Using Sysprep to Extend Disk Partitions" section later in this lesson.

Before you begin, choose a computer to use as a reference computer. The reference computer must have Windows NT Server or Windows 2000 Server installed.

Note Sysprep can also be used to create installations of Windows 2000 Professional.

The Sysprep Process

The following information provides an overview of the process of building a source computer to use for Sysprep duplication.

- **Installing Windows 2000** Windows 2000 Server should be installed on a computer with hardware similar to the intended target computers. The computer should not be joined to a domain while it is being built. In addition, the local administrator password should be kept blank.

- **Configuring the computer** You should be logged on as the administrator when you install and customize Windows 2000 Server and the associated applications. You might include IIS or install and configure other services.

- **Validating the image** You should run a client audit, based on your criteria, to verify that the image configuration is correct. Remove residual information, including anything left behind from audit and event logs.

- **Preparing the image for duplication** Once you are confident the computer is configured exactly the way you want, the system can be prepared for duplication. This is accomplished by running Sysprep with the optional Sysprep.inf file, which is described later in this section. When Sysprep has completed running, the computer will shut down automatically or will indicate that it is safe to be shut down.

- **Duplicating the installation** At this point, the computer hard disk is prepared to run plug and play detection, create a unique SID, and run the Mini-Setup wizard the next time the system is started. Before continuing the next stage of installation, the system is duplicated by using a third-party imaging utility such as Norton Utilities Ghost or PowerQuest Drive Image Pro 3.0. The next time Windows 2000 Server is booted from this hard disk, or from any duplicated hard disk created from this image, the system will detect and re-enumerate the plug and play devices, create a unique SID, and run the Mini-Setup wizard to complete the installation and configuration on the target computer.

Warning Components that depend on the Active Directory services cannot be duplicated. Local users and groups should not be created on the member server because new SIDs will not be assigned to these user and group accounts.

Sysprep Files

To use Sysprep, run Sysprep.exe manually or configure Setup to run Sysprep.exe automatically by using the [GuiRunOnce] section of the answer file. To run Sysprep, the files Sysprep.exe and Setupcl.exe must be located in a Sysprep folder at the root of the system drive (%systemdrive%\Sysprep\). To place the files in the correct location through Setup, you must add these files to your distribution folders under the OEM\$1\Sysprep\ subfolder.

The Sysprep files prepare the operating system for cloning and start the Mini-Setup wizard. An optional answer file, Sysprep.inf, can be included in the Sysprep folder. Sysprep.inf contains default parameters that can be used to provide consistent responses where appropriate. This limits the requirement for user input, thereby reducing potential user errors. Sysprep.inf can also be placed on a floppy disk to be placed in the floppy drive after the boot loader dialog appears. This provides more customized responses and further reduces the initial boot requirement for the end user. When the Mini-Setup wizard has successfully completed its tasks, the system will reboot one last time, the Sysprep folder and all its contents will be deleted, and the system will be ready for the user to log on.

The Sysprep files are defined in the following sections:

Sysprep.exe   Sysprep.exe has three optional parameters, which are described in the following table.

Parameter	Description
-quiet	Runs Sysprep without displaying onscreen messages.
-nosidgen	Runs Sysprep without regenerating SIDs that are already on the system. This is useful if you do not intend to clone the computer on which you are running Sysprep.
-reboot	Automatically reboots the computer after Sysprep shuts it down, eliminating the need for you to manually turn the computer back on. In addition, the -reboot parameter forces a system reboot after disk duplication is completed so that Mini-Setup (the version of Setup that runs when there is a duplicated image on the hard disk) will run automatically. The only time you will want to use this switch is if you are auditing the Sysprep process and want to make sure the Mini-Setup wizard is working properly.

Sysprep.inf   The Sysprep.inf file is an answer file used during the cloning process to provide unique configuration information for each of the target computers. It uses the same .ini-like file syntax and key names (for supported keys) as the Setup answer file (unattend.txt). Sysprep.inf needs to be placed in the %systemdrive%\Sysprep\ folder or on a floppy disk. If you use a floppy disk, immediately after the system boots and the boot loader appears, place the floppy disk in the drive; the system will look for an updated Sysprep.inf on a floppy disk drive. Note that if you do not include Sysprep.inf when running Sysprep, the Mini-Setup wizard will display all the available dialogs listed in the Mini-Setup wizard section later in this lesson.

If you use Sysprep.inf when creating the master computer and when running Sysprep, use the floppy disk method to provide an alternate Sysprep.inf. Locations specified for system files needed during Mini-Setup, such as OEMPnPDriversPath and InstallFilesPath, must remain the same for Sysprep.inf in the distribution folder and for Sysprep.inf on the floppy disk.

The following script is a sample of a Sysprep.inf file:

```
[Unattended]
;Prompt the user to accept the End Use License Agreement
(EULA).
OemSkipEula=No
;Use Sysprep's default and regenerate the page file for the
system
;to accommodate potential differences in available RAM.
KeepPageFile=0
;Provide the location for additional language support files
that
;may be needed in a global organization.
InstallFilesPath=%systemroot%\Sysprep\i386

[GuiUnattended]
;Specify a non-null administrator password.
;Any password supplied here will take effect only if the
original source
;for the image (master computer) specified a null password.
;Otherwise, the password used on the master computer will be
;the password used on this computer. This can be changed
only by
;logging on as Local Administrator and manually changing the
password.
AdminPassword=ABC123
;Set the time zone
TimeZone=20
;Skip the Welcome screen when the system boots
OemSkipWelcome=1
;Do not skip the regional options dialog so that the user
can indicate
;which regional options apply to her or him.
OemSkipRegional=No

[UserData]
;Prepopulate user information for the system
FullName="Authorized User"
OrgName="Organization Name"
ComputerName=XYZ_Computer1

[GUIRunOnce]
;Promote this computer to a Domain Controller on reboot
DCPromo

[Identification]
;Join the computer to the domain ITDOMAIN
JoinDomain=ITDOMAIN
```

```
[Networking]
;Bind the default protocols and services to the network
card(s) used
;in this computer.
InstallDefaultComponents=Yes
```

You can change the administrative password by using Sysprep.inf only if the existing administrative password is null. This is also true if you want to change the administrator password through the Sysprep GUI. For more information about the answer file sections and commands used with Sysprep.inf, see Appendix B, "Sample Answer Files for Unattended Setup."

Setupcl.exe   The Setupcl.exe file processes Sysprep.inf to determine pages for the Mini-Setup wizard and starts the Mini-Setup wizard.

Note The combination of Sysprep.exe and Setupcl.exe can be used to replace the Rollback.exe tool used in previous versions of Windows NT.

Mini-Setup Wizard

The Mini-Setup wizard starts the first time a computer boots from a disk that has been duplicated by using the Sysprep tool. The wizard gathers any information needed to further customize the target computer. If you do not use Sysprep.inf or if you leave some sections of the file blank, the Mini-Setup wizard will display screens for which no answers were provided in Sysprep.inf.

The screens that the Mini-Setup wizard can display include the following:

- EULA
- Regional options
- User name and company
- Computer name and administrator password
- Network settings
- Server licensing
- Time zone selection
- Finish/Restart

If you want to bypass these screens, you can specify certain parameters within the Sysprep.inf file. These parameters are listed in the following table.

Parameter	Value
EULA	[Unattended]
	OemSkipEula=Yes
Regional options	[RegionalSettings]
	LanguageGroup=1
	Language=00000409
User name and company	[UserData]
	FullName="User Name"
	OrgName="Organization Name"
Computer name and administrator password	[UserData]
	ComputerName=W2B32054
	[GuiUnattended]
	AdminPassword="password"
Network settings	[Networking]
	InstallDefaultComponents=Yes
TAPI settings	[TapiLocation]
	AreaCode=425
Time zone selection	OEMSkipRegional=1
	TimeZone=20
Finish/Restart	NA

Because Setup detects optimal settings for display devices, Display Settings is no longer a screen seen during Setup or during the Mini-Setup wizard. You can specify display settings either in the answer file used to create the master computer or in the Sysprep.inf file that will be used on the target computer. If the display settings are in the answer file used on the master computer, Sysprep will retain those settings unless Sysprep.inf contains different settings or a different video adapter or monitor type is detected that requires different settings from the master computer.

By using OemSkipEula = Yes, you are accepting the responsibility for agreeing to all licensing stipulations within the EULA on behalf of the user.

If you run Setup from the network and intend to use Sysprep, you need to configure your network adapters differently than how it is done by the InstallDefaultComponents option. You must provide the specific networking information in Sysprep.inf. If enabling DHCP on all adapters is sufficient and installing Microsoft Client for Microsoft Networks, TCP/IP, and File and Print Sharing for Microsoft Networks on all adapters is sufficient, there is nothing additional you need to specify in Sysprep.inf.

Running Sysprep

There are two ways to run the Sysprep utility: manually or automatically.

Running Sysprep Manually

After you install Windows 2000 Server, you can use Sysprep to prepare the system for transfer to other similarly configured computers. To run Sysprep manually, you must first install Windows 2000 Server, configure the system, and install the applications. Then run Sysprep without the -reboot command line switch. After the system shuts down, clone the image of the drive to the similarly configured computers.

Note You can find the Sysprep utility in Deploy.cab, which is located in the \Support\Tools directory of the Windows 2000 Server installation CD-ROM.

When users start up their cloned computers for the first time, the Mini-Setup wizard will run, allowing the users to customize their systems. You can also preassign all or part of the Sysprep configuration parameters by using Sysprep.inf. The Sysprep folder (which contains Sysprep.exe and Setupcl.exe) is automatically deleted after Sysprep Mini-Setup completes.

The following information provides an overview of how to prepare a Windows 2000 Server installation for duplication:

- **Preparing the Sysprep folder** A Sysprep folder must be created at the root of the drive. The Sysprep.exe, the Setupcl.exe, and if applicable, the Sysprep.inf files should be copied to the Sysprep folder.

- **Running the Sysprep utility** The Sysprep utility should be run from a command prompt within the Sysprep folder. One of the following commands should be used:

```
Sysprep
Sysprep -reboot
Sysprep /<optional parameter>
Sysprep /<optional parameter> -reboot
Sysprep /<optional parameter 1>.../<optional parameter X>
Sysprep /<optional parameter 1>.../<optional parameter X>
-reboot
```

- **Running Sysprep without the -reboot switch** When a message appears saying that the computer should be shut down, select the Shut Down command from the Start menu. A third-party disk-imaging utility can now be used to create an image of the installation.

- **Running Sysprep with the -reboot switch** The computer reboots automatically and the Mini-Setup wizard runs. The wizard's prompts should be verified. In addition, the system and other applications can be audited. When auditing is completed, Sysprep should be run again, without the -reboot command line switch. When a message appears saying that the computer should be shut down, select the Shut Down command from the Start menu. A third-party disk-imaging utility can now be used to create an image of the installation.

Note You can add a Cmdlines.txt file to the Sysprep folder to be processed by Setup. This file will run post-Setup commands, including those required for application installation.

Running Sysprep Automatically

The [GuiRunOnce] section of the answer file contains commands to be executed after Setup completes. You can use the [GuiRunOnce] section to create an installation that completes Setup, automatically logs on to the computer, runs Sysprep in quiet mode, and then shuts down the computer.

To run Sysprep automatically, the Sysprep files should be added to the distribution folders under OEM\$1\Sysprep\. This will ensure that the files are copied to the correct location on the system drive. In addition, the last command in the [GuiRunOnce] section of the answer file should be as follows:

```
%systemdrive%\Sysprep\Sysprep.exe -quiet
```

If multiple reboots are required, this command should be added as the last item run in the last [GuiRunOnce] section used.

If the computer has Advanced Power Management (APM) or ACPI support, Sysprep will automatically shut down the computer once this process has completed.

Using Sysprep to Extend Disk Partitions

Windows 2000 is designed to extend a partition in GUI mode. This new functionality allows you to create images that can be extended to take full advantage of hard disks that might have more space than the original hard disk on the master computer. In addition, it provides a way to reduce the image size needed by not requiring that the image take up a full hard disk. This maximizes the amount of hard disk space that can be used. Because Sysprep uses GUI mode, it can take advantage of this functionality.

If your imaging tools allow you to edit the image, you can delete the Pagefile.sys, Setupapi.log, and the Hyberfil.sys (if applicable) because these files will be re-created when the Mini-Setup wizard runs on the target computer. You must *not* delete these files on an active system because doing so can cause the system to function improperly. These files should be deleted, if desired, from the image only.

To extend a hard disk partition when using a third-party imaging product that supports NTFS, you should first configure the partition on the master computer hard disk to the minimum size required to install Windows 2000 Server with all the desired components and applications. This will help to reduce your overall image size requirements. You must also modify the answer file used to create the master image by including the FileSystem = ConvertNTFS option in the [Unattended] section. You should not include ExtendOemPartition here because you want to maintain the smallest possible image size. Then you can install Windows 2000 Server to the master computer and create an image of the drive. From there, you should place the image on the target computer where the target computer has the same size system partition as the master computer. After you reboot the target computer, the Mini-Setup wizard will begin and the partition will be extended almost instantaneously.

Using Systems Management Server

You can use Systems Management Server (SMS) to perform managed upgrades of Windows 2000 Server to multiple systems, especially those that are geographically dispersed. Note that SMS is used only for installations to computers that contain a previously installed operating system and are running the SMS client agent responsible for receiving software installation instructions. Before you use SMS to perform an upgrade, you should assess your existing network infrastructure, including bandwidth, hardware, and geographical constraints. The primary advantage of using SMS to upgrade is that you can maintain centralized control of the upgrade process. For example, you can control when upgrades take place (such as during or after training, after hardware verification, and after user data is backed up), which computers will be upgraded, and how you will apply network constraints.

SMS 2.0 contains package definition files (with an .sms extension) that allow you to import Windows 2000 Server installation routines into SMS 2.0 Package and Program settings. After importing the package definition, provide SMS with a data source for the Windows 2000 Server installation CD-ROM or an accessible network location containing the Windows 2000 Server distribution files.

Using a Bootable CD-ROM

You can use the bootable CD-ROM method to install Windows 2000 Server on a computer whose BIOS allows it to boot from a CD-ROM. This method is useful for computers at remote sites with slow links and no local information technology (IT) department. The bootable CD-ROM method runs Winnt32.exe, which allows for a fast installation.

Note You can use the bootable CD-ROM method only for clean installations. To perform upgrades, you must run Winnt32.exe from within the existing operating system.

To ensure maximum flexibility for setting up Windows 2000 Server, set the boot order in the BIOS as follows:

- **Network Adapter** for PXE-compliant read-only memory (ROM), this option can be used to support operating system installation from a RIS server.

- **CD-ROM** for bootable CD-ROM operating system installation.

- **Hard Disk** for Sysprep or Syspart prepared local disk-based operating system installation.

- **Floppy Disk** for floppy disk based operating system installation.

To use a bootable CD-ROM for a fully automated operating system installation, the following criteria must be met:

- Your computer's BIOS must support the El Torito Bootable CD-ROM (no emulation mode) format.

- The answer file must contain a [Data] section with the required keys.

- The answer file must be called Winnt.sif and be located on a floppy disk.

The following information provides an overview of how to install Windows 2000 Server by using a bootable CD-ROM drive:

- **Booting the system** After the Windows 2000 Server CD has been inserted into the CD-ROM drive, the system should be rebooted.

- **Loading the Winnt.sif file** After the system reboots, the blue Text mode screen for Windows 2000 Setup appears. The floppy disk that contains the Winnt.sif file should be inserted into the floppy drive. Once the computer reads the floppy drive, the floppy disk should be removed. Setup will now run from the CD-ROM drive as specified by the Winnt.sif file.

Note The bootable CD-ROM method requires that all necessary files be on the CD-ROM. Uniqueness Database Files (UDFs) cannot be used with this method. UDFs are not usable because a unique identifier is called for each installation when specifying a UDF file from Winnt.exe or Winnt32.exe.

Lesson Summary

There are four methods available for automating the installation of Windows 2000 Server. The first method is to run the Winnt32.exe command along with the Syspart parameter. This is the method you should use if the hardware on the target computers is not similar to the hardware on the master computer. If the hardware is similar, you can use the Sysprep utility to perform an unattended installation. Sysprep is a tool that facilitates creating a disk image of your Windows 2000 Server installation. A third option for automating installations is to use SMS to perform managed upgrades of Windows 2000 Server to multiple systems, especially those that are geographically dispersed. SMS is used only for installations to computers that contain a previously installed operating system and the appropriate SMS agent. Finally, one other method available for automated installations is the bootable CD-ROM. This method is useful for computers at remote sites with slow links and no local IT department.

Lesson 3: Automating the Installation of Server Applications

In addition to automating the installation of the Windows 2000 Server operating system, you can automate the installation of other applications that will reside on your target computers. You can use two methods to automate the installation of server applications: using the Cmdlines.txt file or using the answer file. The Cmdlines.txt file contains a list of commands that are executed during the GUI mode phase of the Windows 2000 installation. The answer file, which allows you to run an unattended installation of Windows 2000 Server, includes the [GuiRunOnce] section. You can add an application installation program or a batch file to this section to facilitate automated installation of server applications.

After this lesson, you will be able to

- Use the Cmdlines.txt file to perform an automated installation of server applications

- Use the [GuiRunOnce] section of the answer file to perform an automated installation of server applications

Estimated lesson time: 35 minutes

Using the Cmdlines.txt File

The Cmdlines.txt file contains the commands that are executed during the GUI mode phase of the installation process. Setup executes these commands when installing optional components, such as applications that need to be installed immediately after Windows 2000 Server is installed. If you plan to use Cmdlines.txt, you need to place the file in the \$OEM$ subfolder of the distribution folder. If you are using Sysprep, place Cmdlines.txt in the \$OEM$\$1\Sysprep subfolder.

You should use the Cmdlines.txt file in the following circumstances:

- When you are installing components from the \OEM subfolder of the distribution folders

- When the application you are installing does not configure itself for multiple users, such as Microsoft Office 95, or it is designed to be installed by one user and to replicate user-specific information

- When you want to log on as a service and you want your changes replicated to all users

The syntax for the Cmdlines.txt file is as follows:

```
[Commands]
"<command_1>"
"<command_2>"
        .
        .
"<command_x>"
```

The *<command_1>*, *<command_2>*, and *<command_x>* parameters are placeholders for the commands you want to run and in the order you want them to run when Setup is in the GUI mode and calls Cmdlines.txt. Note that all commands must be in quotation marks.

The Cmdlines.txt file runs as a service rather than as a logged-on user with network capability. Therefore, user-specific information is written to the default user registry, and all subsequently created users also get that information. In addition, Cmdlines.txt requires that you place the files necessary to run an application or utility in the distribution folders.

Using the Answer File

The [GuiRunOnce] section of the answer file contains a list of commands that are executed the first time a user logs on to the computer after Setup runs. For example, you would add the following command to the [GuiRunOnce] section to run Sysprep automatically and in quiet mode:

```
[GuiRunOnce]
Command()="%systemdrive%\Sysprep\Sysprep -quiet"
```

Note You need to run Sysprep from [GuiRunOnce] so that you replicate settings to all users.

A new capability of [GuiRunOnce] is to use environment variables, as illustrated in the example above. Fully qualified paths still work as well.

When using [GuiRunOnce] to initiate an installation, be aware that, if the application forces a reboot, you need to suppress the reboot. This is important because any time the system reboots, all previous RunOnce entries are lost. If the system reboots before completing entries previously listed in the RunOnce section, the remaining items will not be run.

If there is no way within the application to suppress a reboot, you can try repackaging the application into an MSI package or an SMS Installer package. VERITAS WinINSTALL LE is included with Windows 2000 Server, and the SMS Installer is included with SMS 2.0.

Another alternative is to place a command for a tool or application that forces a reboot at the end of a set of RunOnce commands. This also requires that before rebooting you add additional RunOnce entries to the registry so that after the reboot, Windows 2000 processes the next set of commands. You can have the first command that RunOnce executes be a registry edit command:

```
regedit /s <filename.reg>
```

The <*filename*.reg> placeholder is a registry file that is named or enumerated as needed to accomplish what is desired through multiple reboots. If multiple reboots are required, each <*filename*.reg> file should include as the first item a command to load the next set of RunOnce registry entries, until the final set of entries are made.

You can set the AutoAdminLogonCount parameter to log on automatically as administrator to the computer. An automatic logon supports the multiple reboots that might be required. (Up to 99 reboots are supported.) In addition, a local administrator password (AdminPassword) must be included in the answer file used to install Windows 2000.

Note If you are installing an application to multiple localized language versions of Windows 2000, it is recommended that you test the repackaged application on the localized versions to ensure it copies files to the correct locations and writes the required registry entries appropriately.

If an application requires a Microsoft Windows Explorer shell in order to be installed, you cannot use the [GuiRunOnce] section because the shell is not loaded when the Run and RunOnce commands are executed. Check with the application vendors to determine if they have an update or patch that can address this for the application setup. If not, you can repackage the application as an MSI package or use another means of distribution.

Applications that use the same type of installation mechanism might not run properly if a /wait command is not used. This happens when an application installation is running and starts another process. Although the setup routine is still running by initiating another process and closing an active one, the next routine listed in the RunOnce registry entries might start. Because more than one instance of the installation mechanism is running, the second application will usually fail.

Installing Applications

You can use two methods to install applications through the [GuiRunOnce] section of the answer file: using application installation programs and using a batch file.

Using Application Installation Programs

The preferred method for preinstalling an application is to use the installation routine supplied with the application. You can do this if the application you are preinstalling is able to run in quiet mode (without user intervention). Quiet mode usually requires a /q or /s command line switch. See the application help file or documentation for a list of command-line parameters supported by the installation mechanism.

The following command is an example of a line that you can place in the [GuiRunOnce] section to initiate the unattended installation of an application. Note that this command uses its own installation program:

```
<path to setup>\Setup.exe /q
```

Setup parameters vary between applications. For example, the /l parameter included in some applications is useful when you want to create a log file to monitor the installation. Some applications have commands that can keep them from rebooting automatically. This is useful in helping to control application installations with a minimal number of reboots.

Be sure that you check with the application vendor for information, instructions, tools, and best practices before you preinstall any application.

Note You must meet the licensing requirements for any application you install, regardless of how you install it.

Using a Batch File to Control How Multiple Applications Are Installed

If you want to control how multiple applications are installed, you can create a batch file that contains the individual installation commands and uses the Windows 2000 Start command with the /wait command line switch. The batch file can be run from the [GuiRunOnce] section of the answer file. Using a batch file ensures that your applications install sequentially and that each application is fully installed before the next application begins its installation routine.

The following information provides an overview of how to create the batch file, install the application, and then remove all references to the batch file after installation is complete:

- **Creating the batch file** The batch file should contain command lines similar to the following example:

```
Start /wait <path>\<setup file> <command line param-
eters>
Start /wait <path>\<setup file> <command line param-
eters>
Exit
```

where:

- The *<path>* placeholder is the path to the executable file that starts the installation. This path must be available during Setup.

- The *<setup file>* placeholder is the name of the executable file that starts the installation.

- The *<command line parameters>* placeholders are any available quiet-mode parameters appropriate for the application you want to install.

- **Copying the batch file** The batch file should be copied to the distribution folder or to another location that can be accessed during installation. If you intend to run Sysprep on the computer to which you are installing Windows 2000, you can copy the batch file to the Sysprep folder of your distribution folders. This will make the batch file local to the computer being installed. When the computer is powered on after Sysprep has been run and the Mini-Setup wizard has completed, the Sysprep folder and all its contents will be deleted. You do not have to delete the batch file through another process.

- **Adding the batch file to the answer file** An entry for the batch file should be added to the [GuiRunOnce] section of the answer file.

- **Copying the .lnk file to the source computer** The .lnk file should be copied from the source computer to the OEM\$1\documents and settings\all users\start menu\programs\startup folder. When the computer is restarted and runs in GUI mode, the application is installed and the .lnk file is deleted from the Startup Group.

Lesson Summary

You can use two methods to automate the installation of server applications. The first is to use the Cmdlines.txt file, which contains the commands that are executed during the GUI mode phase of the installation process. Setup executes these commands when installing optional components. The second is to modify the [GuiRunOnce] section of the answer file. This section contains a list of commands that are executed the first time a user logs on to the computer after Setup runs. If you plan to use the answer file to install applications, you can use the installation routine supplied with the application, or you can create a batch file that contains the individual installation commands.

Review

The following questions are intended to reinforce key information presented in this chapter. If you are unable to answer a question, review the appropriate lesson and then try the question again. Answers to the questions can be found in Appendix A, "Questions and Answers."

1. What is the purpose of using the /tempdrive: or /t: installation switches with Winnt32.exe or Winnt.exe, respectively?

2. You are asked to develop a strategy for rapidly installing Windows 2000 Server for one of your clients. You have assessed their environment and have determined that the following three categories of computers require Windows 2000 Server:

   - There are 30 unidentical computerconfigurations currently running Windows NT Server 4.0 that need to be upgraded to Windows 2000 Server.

   - There are 20 identical computers that need a new installation of Windows 2000 Server.

   - Remote sites will run a clean installation of Windows 2000 Server. You want to make sure that they install a standard image of Windows 2000 Server that is consistent with your local configuration of the operating system. You will provide them with hard disks that they will install in their servers.

   What are the steps for your installation strategy?

3. What is the purpose of the OEM folder and the subfolders created beneath it by Setup Manager?

4. How does Cmdlines.txt differ from [GuiRunOnce]?

5. How does Syspart differ from Sysprep?

CHAPTER 4

Microsoft Windows 2000 File Systems

About This Chapter

Windows 2000 supports the NT File System (NTFS) and two file allocation table (FAT) file systems, FAT16 and FAT32, for read and write data storage. Read-only support is provided by the CD-ROM File System (CDFS) and the Universal Disk Format (UDF). This chapter focuses on the Windows 2000 writable file systems.

The way volumes are structured and files are organized in NTFS is significantly different from FAT. NTFS version 5.0, the version of NTFS used by Windows 2000, includes several features that support the new functionality within Windows 2000, functionality that is not supported by FAT and only partially supported by NTFS in Windows NT 4.0. This chapter introduces you to the basics of disk management and then goes on to describe FAT and NTFS. The chapter also discusses file and folder security and how it is implemented in a FAT and NTFS environment.

Before You Begin

To complete the lessons in this chapter, you must have

- Met the requirements as outlined in "About This Book" so that Computer 1 contains 500 MB of unallocated (unpartitioned) disk space on the first disk (Disk 0).

- Completed the exercises in Chapter 2 and Chapter 3 so that both computers are running Windows 2000 Server and are configured as outlined in the exercises.

Lesson 1: Disk Management Basics

Before you can install Windows 2000 Server on a hard disk, the portion of the disk that Windows 2000 will use must be initialized with a storage type, partitioned, and formatted. If the system and boot partition will be separate, both the disk area to contain the system files and the disk area to contain the operating system must be partitioned and formatted. This lesson provides an overview of how to configure storage media and provides information about specific disk maintenance tasks.

After this lesson, you will be able to

- Describe disk management concepts
- Identify common disk management tasks
- Create and configure a dynamic disk

Estimated lesson time: 60 minutes

Setting Up a Hard Disk

Whether you are setting up the remaining free space on a hard disk on which you installed Windows 2000 or setting up a new hard disk, there are several tasks that must be performed to prepare the disk:

- **Initializing the disk with a storage type** Initialization defines the fundamental structure of a hard disk. Windows 2000 supports two types of disk storage structures: basic storage and dynamic storage.

- **Creating partitions or volumes** You must create partitions on a basic disk or create volumes on a dynamic disk.

- **Formatting the disk** After you create a partition or volume, you must format it with a specific file system—NTFS or one of the two FAT file systems: FAT16 or FAT32. The file system you choose affects disk operations. This includes how you control user access to data, how data is stored, hard disk capacity, and which operating systems can gain access to the data on the hard disk.

Storage, Partition, and Volume Types

Before you can decide how to perform the tasks for setting up a hard disk, you must understand the storage types, partition types, and volume types available in Windows 2000.

Storage Types

Windows 2000 supports two types of disk storage: basic storage and dynamic storage. A physical disk must be either basic or dynamic; you cannot use both storage types on one disk. You can, however, use both types of disk storage in a multidisk system, as shown in Figure 4.1.

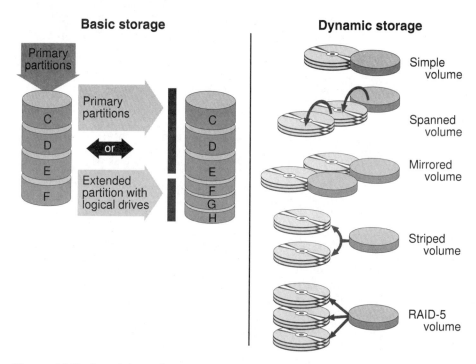

Figure 4.1 Basic and dynamic storage types

Note Windows 2000 storage types are distinct from hardware-level disk array configurations. A disk array is more commonly known as a redundant array of independent disks (RAID). Hardware-level RAID initially appears to Windows 2000 as unallocated space. This space is configured by Windows 2000 as either a basic or dynamic storage type.

Basic Storage

The traditional industry standard is basic storage. It dictates the division of a hard disk into partitions. A *partition* is a portion of the disk that functions as a physically separate unit of storage. Windows 2000 recognizes primary and extended partitions. A disk that is initialized for basic storage is called a *basic disk*. A basic disk can contain primary partitions, extended partitions, and logical drives. New disks added to a computer running Windows 2000 are basic disks.

Since basic storage is the traditional industry standard, MS-DOS, all versions of Microsoft Windows, Windows NT, and Windows 2000 support basic storage. For Windows 2000, basic storage is the default, so all disks are basic disks until you convert them to dynamic storage.

A basic disk is backward compatible with Windows NT volume sets, striped sets (RAID-0), mirrored volumes (RAID-1), and disk striping with parity (RAID-5).

Dynamic Storage

Only Windows 2000 supports dynamic storage. To support dynamic storage, a single partition is created that includes the entire disk. A disk that you initialize for dynamic storage is a *dynamic disk*.

Dynamic disks are divided into volumes, which can consist of a portion or portions of one or more physical disks. A dynamic disk can contain simple volumes, spanned volumes, striped volumes (RAID-0), mirrored volumes (RAID-1), and striped with parity volumes (RAID-5). You create a dynamic disk by upgrading a basic disk.

Dynamic storage does not have the restrictions of basic storage; for example, you can size and resize a dynamic disk without restarting Windows 2000.

Note Removable storage devices contain primary partitions only. You cannot create extended partitions, logical drives, or dynamic volumes on removable storage devices. You cannot mark a primary partition on a removable storage device active.

Partition Types (Basic Disks)

You can divide a basic disk into primary and extended partitions. Partitions function as physically separate storage units. This allows you to separate different types of information, such as user data on one partition and applications on another. A basic disk can contain up to four primary partitions, or up to three primary partitions and one extended partition, for a maximum of four partitions. Only one partition can be an extended partition, as shown in Figure 4.2.

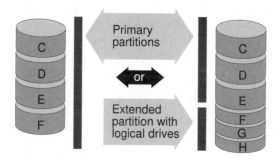

Figure 4.2 Partition types

Primary Partitions

Windows 2000 uses primary partitions to start the computer. One of these primary partitions is marked as the active partition. An *active partition* is where the hardware looks for the boot files to start the operating system. Only one partition on a single hard disk can be active at a time. Multiple primary partitions allow you to isolate different operating systems or types of data. To dual boot Windows 2000 with Microsoft Windows 95 or MS-DOS, the active partition must be formatted as FAT16 because Windows 95 cannot read a partition formatted as FAT32 or NTFS. To dual boot with Microsoft Windows 95 OSR2 (a later release of Windows 95 that contained enhancements, such as the ability to read partitions formatted with FAT32) or with Windows 98, the active partition must be formatted as FAT16 or FAT32.

Tip If the active partition is formatted with NTFS, Windows 9*x* can be started from a floppy diskette. The diskette contains a pointer to the FAT partition containing Windows 9*x*.

The Windows 2000 *system partition* (also called a system volume in Windows 2000 documentation) is the active partition that contains the hardware-specific files required to load the operating system. The Windows 2000 *boot partition* is the primary partition or logical drive where the operating system files are installed. The boot partition and the system partition can be the same partition. However, the system partition must be on the active partition, typically drive C, while the boot partition could be on another primary partition or on an extended partition.

Extended Partitions

An *extended partition* is created from free space. There can be only one extended partition on a hard disk, so it is important to include all remaining free space in the extended partition. Unlike primary partitions, you do not format extended partitions or assign drive letters to them. You divide extended partitions into segments. Each segment is a logical drive. You assign a drive letter to each logical drive and format it with a file system.

Volume Types (Dynamic Disks)

You can upgrade basic disks to dynamic storage and then create Windows 2000 volumes. Consider which volume type best suits your needs for efficient use of disk space, performance, and fault tolerance. *Fault tolerance* is the ability of a computer or operating system to respond to a catastrophic event without loss of data. In Windows 2000, RAID-1 and RAID-5 volumes are fault tolerant.

Simple Volume

A *simple volume* contains disk space from a single disk and is not fault tolerant. Simple volumes can be extended onto multiple regions (up to 32 regions) of the same disk. Simple volumes cannot provide fault tolerance. In fact, they become less fault tolerant than a nonextended disk because extending a simple volume increases the points of failure on the disk.

Spanned Volume

A *spanned volume* includes disk space from multiple disks (up to 32). Windows 2000 writes data to a spanned volume on the first disk, completely filling the space, and continues in this manner through each disk that you include in the spanned volume. A spanned volume is not fault tolerant. If any disk in a spanned volume fails, the data in the entire volume is lost.

Mirrored Volume

A *mirrored volume* consists of two identical copies of a simple volume, each on a separate hard disk. Mirrored volumes provide fault tolerance in the event of hard disk failure.

Striped Volume

A *striped volume* (RAID-0) combines areas of free space from multiple hard disks (up to 32) into one logical volume. In a striped volume, Windows 2000 optimizes performance by adding data to all disks at the same rate. If a disk in a striped volume fails, the data in the entire volume is lost. Therefore, like extending a simple volume or creating a spanned volume, RAID-0 is not fault tolerant.

RAID-5 Volume

A *RAID-5 volume* is a fault-tolerant striped volume. Windows 2000 adds a parity-information stripe to each disk partition in the volume. Windows 2000 uses the parity-information stripe to reconstruct data when a physical disk fails. A minimum of three hard disks is required in a RAID-5 volume.

Dynamic Disk and Dynamic Volume Limitations

Dynamic disks can be read only by computers running Windows 2000. Thus, dynamic disks cannot be used if you need to dual-boot another operating system that requires access to the disks configured for dynamic storage. Dynamic volumes are not supported on portable computers like laptop and notebook computers. Fault-tolerant configurations (RAID-1 and RAID-5) cannot be created locally on computers running Windows 2000 Professional.

File Systems

Windows 2000 provides read and write support for the NTFS, FAT16, and FAT32 file systems. Although NTFS and FAT partitions support basic and dynamic disks, you should use NTFS when you require a partition to have file-level and folder-level security, disk compression, disk quotas, or encryption. Only Windows 2000 and Windows NT can access data on a local hard disk that is formatted with NTFS. If you plan to promote a server to a domain controller, format the installation partition with NTFS. This is important because NTFS supports important server-based features such as the Active Directory services and RIS.

FAT16 and FAT32 allow access by, and compatibility with, other operating systems. To dual boot Windows 2000 and another operating system, format the system partition with either FAT16 or FAT32. FAT does not offer many of the features that are supported by NTFS, such as file-level security. Therefore, in most situations, you should format the hard disk with NTFS. The only reason to use FAT16 or FAT32 is for dual booting. Lesson 2 and Lesson 3 provide more information about FAT and NTFS.

Common Disk Management Tasks

The Disk Management snap-in (Figure 4.3) provides a central location for disk information and management tasks, such as creating and deleting partitions and volumes. With the proper permissions, you can manage disks locally and on remote computers.

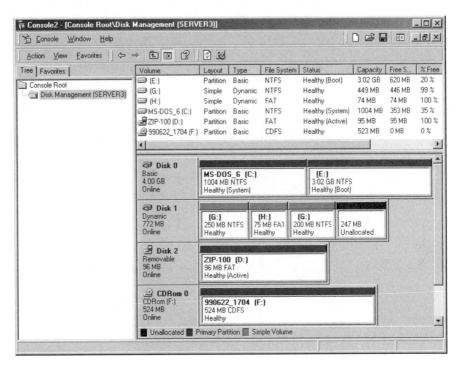

Figure 4.3 The Disk Management snap-in

You can create a custom MMC and add the Disk Management snap-in to it. The Disk Management snap-in is also included in the preconfigured Computer Management MMC on the Administrative Tools menu. The Disk Management snap-in provides shortcut menus to show you which tasks you can perform on the selected object, and it includes wizards to guide you through creating partitions and volumes and upgrading disks.

Use the Disk Management snap-in to configure and manage your network storage space. The Disk Management snap-in can display your storage system in either a graphical view or a list view. You can modify the display to suit your preferences by using the commands on the View menu.

In addition to monitoring disk information, other disk management tasks that you might need to perform include adding and removing hard disks and changing the disk storage type. Upgrading a disk to the dynamic storage type is shown in Figure 4.4.

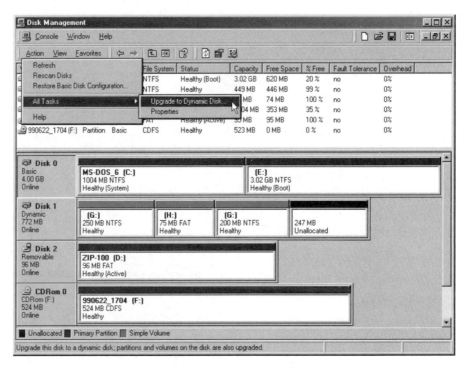

Figure 4.4 Upgrading a disk from basic to dynamic storage

Working with Simple Volumes

A simple volume contains disk space from a single disk. You can extend a simple volume to include unallocated space on the same disk. A simple volume is not fault tolerant; however, you can set up two simple volumes that are mirrored to one another. You can format a simple volume with NTFS, FAT16, or FAT32, but you can extend that volume only if it is formatted with NTFS.

You can create a simple volume by selecting Disk Management in the storage section of the Computer Management snap-in. On the dynamic disk where you want to create the volume, right-click the unallocated space and then click Create Volume. This launches the Create Volume wizard. The wizard walks you through the steps necessary to create a simple volume.

To extend an NTFS simple volume, right-click the simple volume you want to extend and click Extend Volume. This launches the Extend Volume wizard. Follow the instructions on your screen to use unallocated space on any dynamic disk to extend the existing volume. When you extend a simple volume to another disk, it becomes a spanned volume.

Working with Spanned Volumes

A spanned volume consists of disk space from multiple disks; spanned volumes enable you to use the total unallocated space on multiple disks more effectively. You can create spanned volumes only on dynamic disks, and you need at least two dynamic disks to create a spanned volume. Spanned volumes cannot be part of a mirror volume or striped volume and are not fault tolerant.

Combining Free Space to Create a Spanned Volume

You create spanned volumes by combining variously sized areas of free space from 2 to 32 disks into one large logical volume. The areas of free space that make up a spanned volume can be different sizes. Windows 2000 organizes spanned volumes so that data is stored in the space on one disk until it is full, and then, starting at the beginning of the next disk, data is stored in the space on the second disk. Windows 2000 continues this process in the same way on each subsequent disk up to a maximum of 32 disks.

By deleting smaller volumes and combining them into one spanned volume, you can free drive letters for other uses and create a large volume for file system use.

Note All dynamic disk configurations available in Windows 2000 can be configured to use different technology, manufacturer, or model controllers in a computer. For example, one dynamic disk in a spanned volume could be connected to an Integrated Device Electronics (IDE) controller while the other disk is connected to a small computer system interface (SCSI) controller.

Extending and Deleting

You can extend existing spanned volumes formatted with NTFS by adding free space. Disk Management formats the new area without affecting any existing files on the original volume. You cannot extend volumes formatted with FAT16 or FAT32.

You can extend spanned volumes on dynamic disks onto a maximum of 32 dynamic disks. After a volume is extended onto multiple disks (spanned), it cannot be part of a mirror volume or a striped volume. After a spanned volume is extended, no portion of it can be deleted without deleting the entire spanned volume. You cannot extend a system volume or a boot volume.

Working with Striped Volumes

Striped volumes offer the best performance of all the Windows 2000 Server disk management strategies. In a striped volume, data is written evenly across all physical disks in 64-kilobyte (KB) units. Because all the hard disks that belong to the striped volume perform the same functions as a single hard disk, Windows 2000 can issue and process concurrent I/O commands on all hard disks simultaneously. In this way, striped volumes can increase the speed of system I/O.

You create striped volumes by combining areas of free space from multiple disks (from 2 to 32) into one logical volume. With a striped volume, Windows 2000 writes data to multiple disks, similar to spanned volumes. However, on a striped volume, the operating system writes files across all disks so that data is added to all disks at the same rate. Like spanned volumes, striped volumes do not provide fault tolerance. If a disk in a striped volume fails, the data in the entire volume is lost.

You need at least two dynamic disks to create a striped volume, and you can create the striped volume onto a maximum of 32 disks. However, you cannot extend or mirror striped volumes. The Disk Management snap-in can be used to create a striped volume. On the dynamic disk where you want to create the striped volume, right-click the unallocated space and then click Create Volume. This launches the Create Volume wizard. The wizard will walk you through the process of creating a striped volume.

Adding Disks

When you install new disks in a computer running Windows 2000, they are added as basic storage.

Adding New Disks

To add a new disk, install or attach the new physical disk (or disks) and then click Rescan Disks on the Action menu of the Disk Management snap-in. You must use Rescan Disks every time that you remove or add disks to a computer. It should not be necessary to restart the computer when you add a new disk to your computer. However, you might need to restart the computer if Disk Management does not detect the new disk after you run Rescan Disks.

Adding a Disk That You Removed from Another Computer

The process of removing a disk from one computer and installing it into another computer is different from simply adding a new disk. After you remove the disk from the original computer and install it into the new computer, use Disk Management to add the disk. To do this, right-click the added disk and then click Import Foreign Disk. A wizard provides on-screen instructions.

Adding Multiple Disks That You Removed from Another Computer

The process of removing multiple disks from one computer and installing them into another computer is much the same as doing it for a single disk. To add multiple inherited disks, you must remove the disks from the original computer and install them in the new computer. Then use Disk Management to specify the disks from the group that you want to add.

When you move a dynamic disk to your computer from another computer running Windows 2000, you can see and use any existing volumes on that disk. However, if a volume on a foreign disk extends to multiple disks and you do not move all the disks for that volume, Disk Management will not show the portion of the volume that resides on the foreign disk.

Changing Storage Type

You can upgrade a disk from basic storage to dynamic storage at any time, with no loss of data. When you upgrade a basic disk to a dynamic disk, any existing partitions on the basic disk become simple volumes. Any existing mirrored, striped, or spanned volume sets created with Windows NT 4.0 become dynamic mirrored, striped, or spanned volumes, respectively. A Windows NT 4.0 stripe set with parity converts to a RAID-5 volume.

Any disks to be upgraded must contain at least 1 MB of unallocated space for the upgrade to succeed. Before you upgrade disks, close any programs that are running on those disks. The following table shows the results of converting a disk from basic storage to dynamic storage.

Basic disk organization	Dynamic disk organization
System partition	Simple volume (cannot be extended)
Boot partition	Simple volume (cannot be extended)
Primary partition	Simple volume
Extended partition	Simple volume for each logical drive and any remaining unallocated space
Logical drive	Simple volume
Volume set	Spanned volume
Stripe set	Striped volume
Mirror set	Mirrored volume
Stripe set with parity	RAID-5 volume

Note You should always back up the data on a disk before converting the storage type.

Upgrading Basic Disks to Dynamic Disks

To upgrade a basic disk to a dynamic disk, right-click the basic disk that you want to upgrade and then click Upgrade To Dynamic Disk. A wizard provides on-screen instructions. The upgrade process requires that you restart your computer.

After you upgrade a basic disk to a dynamic disk, you can create volumes with improved capabilities on the disk, but the disk cannot contain primary or extended partitions. Only Windows 2000 can access dynamic disks.

Reverting to a Basic Disk from a Dynamic Disk

You must remove all volumes from the dynamic disk, so that the entire disk is unallocated space, before you can change it back to a basic disk. To change a dynamic disk back to a basic disk, right-click the dynamic disk (all unallocated space) that you want to change back to a basic disk and then click Revert To Basic Disk.

Caution Converting a dynamic disk to a basic disk causes all data to be lost.

Viewing and Updating Information

The Properties dialog box for a selected disk or volume provides a concise view of all the pertinent properties.

Disk Properties

To view disk properties in Disk Management, right-click the name of a disk in the Graphical View window (don't click one of its volumes) and then click Properties. Figure 4.5 shows the disk properties screen.

Figure 4.5 The properties of disk 0 appearing in the Disk Management snap-in

The following table describes the information displayed in the Properties dialog box for a disk.

Category	Description
Disk	The number for the disk in the system, for example, Disk 0, Disk 1, Disk 2, and so on
Type	Type of storage (basic, dynamic, or removable)
Status	Online, offline, foreign, or unknown
Capacity	The total capacity for the disk
Unallocated Space	The amount of available unused space on the disk. This does not show free space on basic disk partitions or dynamic disk volumes.
Device Type	IDE, SCSI, or enhanced IDE (EIDE). Also shows the IDE channel (primary or secondary) on which an IDE disk resides and the port, target ID, and LUN number for SCSI disk identification
Hardware Vendor	The hardware vendor for the disk and the disk type
Adapter Name	The type of controller to which the disk is attached
Volumes contained on this disk	The volumes that exist on the disk and their total capacity

Volume Properties

To view volume properties in Disk Management, right-click a volume in the Graphical View window or in the Volume List window and then click Properties. Figure 4.6 shows the Properties dialog box for the local volume.

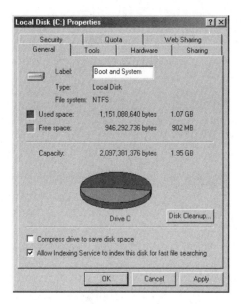

Figure 4.6 The Properties dialog box for the local volume

The following table describes the tabs in the Properties dialog box for a volume.

Tab	Description
General	Lists the volume label, type, file system, and used and free space. Click Disk Cleanup to delete unnecessary files. NTFS volumes list two options: (1) Compress drive to save disk space and (2) Allow Indexing Service to index this drive for fast file searching.
Tools	Provides a single location from which you can perform volume error checking, backup, and defragmentation tasks.
Web Sharing	Used to share specified folders through Internet Information Services (IIS). This tab appears only if IIS is installed on Windows 2000 Server or if Personal Web Server is installed on Windows 2000 Professional.
Sharing	Used to set network-shared volume parameters and permissions.
Hardware	Used to check properties of the physical disks installed on the system and to troubleshoot them.
Security	Used to set NTFS access permissions. This tab is available only for NTFS version 4.0 and 5.0 volumes. (Windows 2000 uses NTFS version 5.0.)
Quota	Used to set user quotas for NTFS 5.0 volumes.

Refresh and Rescan

When you are working with Disk Management, you might need to update the information in the display. The two commands for updating the display are Refresh and Rescan.

Refresh updates drive letter, file system, volume, and removable media information and determines whether unreadable volumes are now readable. To update drive letter, file system, and volume information, click Action and then click Refresh.

Rescan Disks updates hardware information. When Disk Management rescans disks, it scans all attached disks for disk configuration changes. It also updates information on removable media, CD-ROM drives, basic volumes, file systems, and drive letters. Rescanning disks can take several minutes, depending on the number of hardware devices installed. To update disk information, click Action and then click Rescan Disks.

Note If you are running the Computer Management snap-in, select the Disk Management node or any object within this node to start a refresh or rescan operation.

Managing Disks on a Remote Computer

As a member of the Administrators group, you can manage disks on a computer running Windows 2000 that is a member of the same workgroup, domain, or a trusted domain from any other computer running Windows 2000 in the network.

To manage one computer from another computer—remote management—create a Microsoft Management Console (MMC) that is focused on the remote computer. MMC is discussed in more detail in Chapter 5, "Administration and Management Tools."

Exercise 1: Configuring a Simple Disk and Converting It to a Dynamic Disk

This exercise requires that Windows 2000 Server has been installed as outlined in Chapter 2 and that unallocated disk space is available on Server01 as specified in "About This Book."

▶ Procedure 1: Installing FTP

On Server01, you will install FTP Server in order to complete steps in Procedure 2. See Chapter 14, Lesson 2: Administering a Web Environment, for details on this server service.

1. Insert the Windows 2000 Server CD-ROM into the CD-ROM drive.

2. Click the Start button, point to Settings, and then click Control Panel.

   Control Panel appears.

3. Double-click Add/Remove Programs.

   The Add/Remove Programs window appears.

4. In the left pane, click Add/Remove Windows Components.

   The Windows Components wizard appears.

5. In the Components box, click once on the Internet Information Services (IIS) and then click the Details button.

   The Internet Information Services (IIS) dialog box appears.

6. In the Subcomponents of Internet Information Services (IIS) box, select the File Transfer Protocol (FTP) Server check box.

7. Click OK.

   The Windows Components wizard appears.

8. Click Next.

   The Configuring Components screen appears as the configuration changes you requested are made. After a few minutes, the Completeing the Windows Components Wizard screen appears.

9. Click Finish.

   The Add/Remove Programs window appears.

10. Click Close.

    Control Panel appears.

11. Close Control Panel.

▶ **Procedure 2: Using the Disk Management snap-in**

On Server01, you create multiple primary partitions and an extended partition in the unallocated portion of Disk 0. To begin this procedure, log on to Server01 as Administrator with a password of "password."

1. Click the Start button, point to Programs, point to Administrative Tools, and then click Computer Management.

   The Computer Management snap-in appears.

2. From the left pane, expand the Storage node and then select Disk Management.

   The Volume List window (top) and the Graphical View window (bottom) appear in the right pane. Notice that Disk 0 displays a C: primary partition and the remainder of disk space unallocated.

3. Click on the unallocated space in the Graphical View.

4. On the Action menu, click All Tasks and then select Create Partition.

   The Create Partition wizard appears.

5. Read the information on the Welcome To The Create Partition wizard, and then click Next.

6. From the Select Partition Type screen, verify that the Primary Partition radio button is selected and then click Next.

7. From the Specify Partition Size screen, change the Amount Of Disk Space To Use value to 50 and click Next.

8. From the Assign Drive Letter Or Path screen, change the Assign a: drive letter to H: and click Next.

9. From the Format Partition screen, verify that Format This Partition With The Following Settings radio button is selected, click the Perform A Quick Format check box, and then click Next.

10. Review the information appearing on the Completing The Create Partition Wizard screen, and then click Finish.

    After Windows 2000 Server has completed the create partition request, an H: partition will appear in the Graphical View window.

11. If a System Change message box appears asking you to restart your computer, click Yes to restart the computer. Once the restart is complete, log on to the computer again as Administrator with a password of "password."

12. Following the previous steps in this procedure, create the following disk configurations in the unallocated disk space on Disk0. Use the table to replace values in the previous procedure:

Partition type	Size (MB)	Disk drive	Format
Primary	100	I	FAT32
Extended	Remaining unallocated space	N/A	N/A

13. Review the settings for drives H: and I: in the Volume View window. Notice that the free space appearing in the Graphical View window does not contain any drive letters. This area is the extended partition in which you will assign logical drives.

14. From the Graphical View window, click on the Free Space box in the extended partition.

15. On the Action menu, select All Tasks and then choose Create Logical Drive.

    The Create Partition wizard appears.

16. Read the information on the Welcome To The Create Partition Wizard screen, and then click Next.

17. From the Select Partition Type screen, verify that the Logical Drive radio button is selected and then click Next.

18. On the Specify Partition Size screen, change the Amount Of Disk Space To Use value to 150 and then click Next.

19. On the Assign Drive Letter or Path screen, select the Mount This Volume At An Empty Folder That Supports Drive Paths radio button and then click Browse.

    The Browse For Drive Path dialog box appears.

20. Expand the C:\ drive and then expand Inetpub.

21. Click on the ftproot subfolder, and then click OK.

    The Mount This Volume At An Empty Folder That Supports Drive Paths radio button shows the path: C:\Inetpub\ftproot.

22. Click Next.

23. From the Format Partition screen, quick format the partition for NTFS, change the volume label to FTPVol, and enable file and folder compression.

24. Click Next.

25. Review the information on the Completing The Create Partition Wizard screen, and then click Finish.

    Notice that because this procedure did not ask that you specify volume names, the I: and J: partitions show the volume names of NEW VOLUME (H:) and NEW VOLUME (I:) respectively.

26. To change the volume names, click on NEW VOLUME (H:) in the Volume View or Graphic View window.

27. From the Action menu, choose All Tasks and then Properties.

    The New Volume (H:) Properties dialog box appears.

28. In the Label text box, delete New Volume and then click OK.

29. Repeat the last three steps on NEW VOLUME (I:).

Your disk configuration for Disk0 should now be:

Drive/Path	Format	Type	Purpose
C:	NTFS	Primary	System (also the Boot partition, although this does not appear in the Disk Management MMC snap-in).
H:	NTFS	Primary	Unused
I:	FAT32	Primary	Unused
C:\InetPub\ftproot	NTFS	Extended	Files saved to c:\InetPub\ftproot are redirected to this disk partition.
N/A	N/A	Extended	Free space. (The amount of free space will vary based on the size of Disk0.)

30. To check that FTPVol is a partition available to C:\Inetpub\ftproot, open the Windows Explorer.

31. Expand My Computer from the left pane, and then expand C:\Inetpub.

Notice that ftproot appears as a drive icon. Any files stored on C:\Inetpub\ftproot are redirected to the FTPVol in the extended partition.

32. Close the Windows Explorer and close the Computer Management snap-in.

Lesson Summary

Before you can store data on a new hard disk, the disk must be initialized with a storage type, partitioned, and formatted. Windows 2000 supports basic storage and dynamic storage. A basic disk can contain primary partitions, extended partitions, and logical drives in the extended partition. For Windows 2000, basic storage is the default, so all disks are basic disks until you convert them to dynamic disks. Dynamic storage creates a single partition that includes the entire disk. You divide dynamic disks into volumes, which can consist of a portion or portions of one or more physical disks. The Disk Management snap-in provides a central location for disk information and management tasks, such as creating and deleting partitions and volumes. With the proper permissions, you can manage disks locally or on remote computers. In addition to monitoring disk information, other disk management tasks you might need to perform include adding and removing hard disks and changing the disk storage type.

Lesson 2: File Allocation Table (FAT)

Windows 2000 supports two versions of the FAT file system: FAT16 and FAT32. This lesson provides an overview of both file system versions and their use within the Windows 2000 operating system.

After this lesson, you will be able to

- Describe the Windows 2000 FAT16 file system
- Describe the Windows 2000 FAT32 file system

Estimated lesson time: 25 minutes

Introduction to the FAT File System

The FAT file system was designed when disks were smaller and folder structures were simple. To protect the file system, two copies of the file allocation table are stored on the volume. In the event that one copy of the table is corrupted, the other table is used. The file allocation table is stored in a specified byte offset so that the files needed to start the system can be located.

FAT16 works the same in Windows 2000 as it does in MS-DOS, Windows 3.*x*, Windows 95, and Windows 98. FAT32 works the same in Windows 2000 as it does in Windows 95 OSR2 and Windows 98. You can install Windows 2000 on an existing FAT primary partition or logical drive. When running Windows 2000, you can move or copy files between FAT and NTFS volumes.

You cannot use Windows 2000 with any compression or partitioning software that requires disk drivers to be loaded by MS-DOS. Therefore, you cannot use MS-DOS 6.0 DoubleSpace or MS-DOS 6.22 DriveSpace on a FAT primary partition or logical drive that you want to access when running Windows 2000.

The FAT16 File System

The FAT disk format is organized into sectors. Each sector can store 512 bytes of data. This is the smallest unit that is used when reading or writing to or from the disk.

Although the sector is the smallest unit used when transferring data to and from a FAT partition, the cluster (also called an allocation unit) is the smallest unit the operating system uses when allocating file storage space on a FAT partition. The size of the cluster varies from drive to drive, depending on the size of the partition. The default cluster size is determined by the partition size and can be as large as 64 KB.

The file allocation table identifies each cluster in the partition as one of the following:

- Unused

- Cluster in use by a file

- Bad cluster

- Last cluster in a file

Note Volumes less than 16 MB will usually be formatted for 12-bit FAT, but the exact size depends on the disk geometry. FAT12 was the original implementation of FAT. It is intended for very small media. By taking less space for each FAT entry, the space consumed by the FAT itself is smaller. Therefore, more space is available for data as opposed to on-disk file system structures. Currently, users might see FAT12 on very small or old media. For example, 3.5-inch floppies are FAT16, whereas 5.25-inch floppies are FAT12.

Figure 4.7 illustrates the structure of a FAT16 volume. The root folder contains an entry for each file and folder on the volume. The only difference between the root folder and other folders is that the root folder is on a specified location on the disk and has a fixed size of 512 table entries per disk drive. The number of entries on a floppy disk depends on the size of the disk.

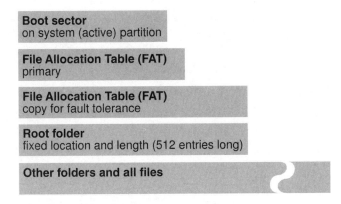

Figure 4.7 Structure of a FAT16 volume

Folders have a 32-byte entry for each file and folder contained in the folder. The following table lists the components of the file and folder entries:

Entry component	Bits
Name	8.3 format
Attribute	8
Create time	24
Create date	16
Last access date	16
Last modified time	16
Last modified date	16
Starting cluster number in FAT	16
File size	32

There is no organization to the FAT folder structure. Files are given the first available location on the volume. The starting cluster number is the address of the first cluster used by the file. Each cluster contains a pointer to the next cluster in the file or a hex indicator (0xFFFF) that this cluster is the end of the file.

The information in the folder is used by all operating systems that support the FAT file system. Windows NT operating systems can store additional time stamps in a FAT folder entry. These time stamps show when the file was created or last accessed; they are used principally by portable operating system interface standard (POSIX) applications.

Because all entries in a folder are the same size, the attribute byte for each entry in a folder describes what kind of entry it is. For example, one bit indicates that the entry is for a subfolder, and another bit marks the entry as a volume label. Normally, only the operating system controls the settings of these bits.

The attribute byte includes four bits that can be turned on or off by the user:

- Archive file
- System file
- Hidden file
- Read-only file

The FAT16 file system is included in Windows 2000 to support backward compatibility with previous Windows products. In addition, FAT16 offers widespread compatibility with many other non-Microsoft operating systems.

As in previous versions, the maximum FAT16 partition size in Windows 2000 is 4 gigabytes (GB). The default cluster size is determined by the size of the partition. The following table shows the default cluster sizes for FAT16 volumes:

Partition size	Sectors per cluster	Cluster size
0 MB–32 MB	1 partition sector size)	512 bytes (equivalent to the
33 MB–64 MB	2	1024 bytes
65 MB–128 MB	4	2048 bytes
129 MB–256 MB	8	4096 bytes
256 MB–512 MB	16	8192 bytes
512 MB–1024 MB	32	16 KB
1024 MB–2048 MB	64	32 KB
2048 MB–4096 MB	128	64 KB

You can specify a different cluster size if you use the Format utility with the /a:*size* switch from the command prompt to format the partition. However, default settings are strongly recommended for general use.

Note Disks that can support sector sizes greater than 512 bytes can create 128 KB and 256 KB clusters. However, the larger the cluster size the greater the potential for wasting disk space. Large cluster sizes are ideal for very large files like databases.

The FAT32 File System

The main benefit of FAT32 is its ability to support partitions larger than those handled by FAT16. FAT16 supports partitions up to 4 GB in size, while FAT32 supports partitions up to 2047 GB. However, Windows 2000 FAT32 implementations are limited to creating 32-GB volumes, although existing FAT32 volumes greater than 32 GB can be mounted. Except for this partition-formatting limit, the FAT32 on-disk format and features are the same on Windows 2000 as they are on Windows 95 OSR2 and Windows 98.

To maintain the greatest compatibility possible with existing programs, networks, and device drivers, FAT32 is implemented with as little change as possible to existing FAT16 architecture, internal data structures, application programming interfaces (APIs), and on-disk format.

However, because 4 bytes are now required in the table to store cluster values, many internal and on-disk data structures and published APIs have been revised or expanded. In some cases, existing APIs have been disabled to prevent legacy disk utilities from damaging the FAT32 drive. However, most programs will be unaffected by these changes. Existing FAT tools and drivers should continue to work on FAT32 partitions. MS-DOS operating system disk tools must be revised to support FAT32 drives.

FAT32 Partition Structure

The major benefit of FAT32 over FAT16 is the larger partition sizes it can support. FAT32 breaks the 4-GB partition limit by extending partition capac-ity. If you format a partition with FAT16, you have to specify at least a 32-KB cluster to support a 4-GB or larger partition.

The largest possible file for a FAT32 drive is 4 GB minus 2 bytes. FAT32 includes 4 bytes per cluster within the file allocation table. This differs from the FAT16 file system, which contains 2 bytes per cluster.

A FAT32 partition must have at least 65,527 clusters, and the partition cluster size cannot be increased. Figure 4.8 illustrates the structure of a FAT32 partition.

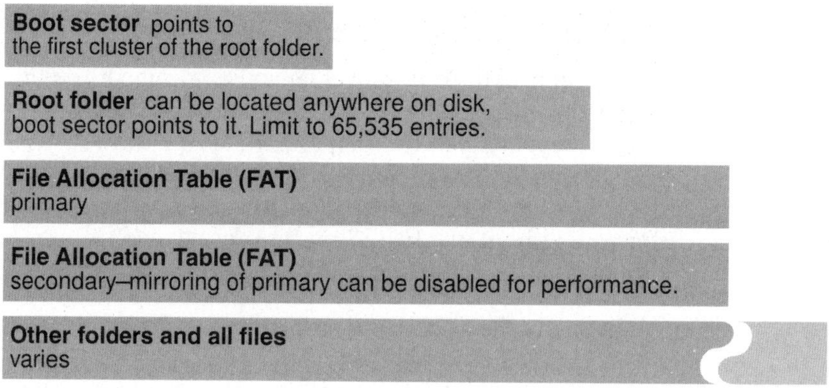

Boot sector points to
the first cluster of the root folder.

Root folder can be located anywhere on disk,
boot sector points to it. Limit to 65,535 entries.

File Allocation Table (FAT)
primary

File Allocation Table (FAT)
secondary—mirroring of primary can be disabled for performance.

Other folders and all files
varies

Figure 4.8 Structure of a FAT32 volume

FAT16 and FAT32 file systems do not scale well. As the volume gets bigger, the file allocation table gets bigger. One disadvantage of a large file allocation table is that it dramatically increases the amount of time it takes the operating system to compute how much free space is on the boot volume upon reboot.

The file allocation table is a packed list of 32-bit entries that have a one-to-one mapping with the data clusters. The folder structure of FAT32 is used in the same way that Windows 95 implements long file names. The only difference is the addition of the cluster high-word field in directory entries that access cluster numbers.

File System Limits

The maximum size of a FAT32 volume is limited by the maximum number of FAT entries, the number of sectors per cluster, and the 32-bit sector count in the partition record. (Sectors of 512 bytes each are assumed.)

The following table maps the maximum partition size possible per cluster size:

Cluster size	Maximum volume size
512 bytes	127.9 GB
1 KB	255.9 GB
2 KB	511.9 GB
4 KB	1023.9 GB or 1 Terabyte (TB)
8 KB	2047 GB (2 TB)
16 KB	2047 GB (2 TB)
32 KB	2047 GB (2 TB)

Keep in mind that Windows 2000 limits partition size to 32 GB but will mount larger FAT32 partitions created in other operating systems such as Windows 98.

Lesson Summary

The FAT file system was designed for small disks and simple folder structures. Windows 2000 supports two versions of the FAT file system: FAT16 and FAT32. A partition formatted with FAT16 is divided into 512 byte sectors and files are written to the disk in clusters, also known as allocation units. The default cluster size is determined by the partition size, and it can be as small as 4 KB, or 8 sectors, or as large as 64 KB, or 128 sectors. The main benefit of FAT32 is its ability to support partitions larger than those handled by FAT16. FAT16 supports partitions up to 4 GB in size, while FAT32 can handle partitions as large as 2047 GB in size. Windows 2000 will format a partition with FAT32 only up to 32 GB in size, but it can mount FAT32 partitions that are 2047 GB in size. FAT32 was implemented with as little change as possible to existing FAT16 architecture, internal data structures, application programming interfaces (APIs), and on-disk format.

Lesson 3: NT File System (NTFS)

Windows 2000 comes with a new version of NTFS. This newest version, NTFS version 5.0, provides performance, reliability, and compatibility not found in FAT. The NTFS data structures allow you to take advantage of new features in Windows 2000, such as Active Directory services, management software, and the storage features based on reparse points. NTFS includes security features required for file servers and high-end personal computers in a corporate environment, and it also includes data access control and owner-ship privileges important for data integrity.

After this lesson, you will be able to

- Describe the Windows 2000 NTFS file system

Estimated lesson time: 45 minutes

Introduction to NTFS

Microsoft recommends that you format all Windows 2000 partitions with NTFS, except multiple-boot configurations where non-Windows 2000 and non-Windows NT operating systems are necessary. Formatting your Windows 2000 partitions with NTFS instead of FAT allows you to use features available only on NTFS, including recoverability and compression. The recoverability designed into NTFS is such that a user should seldom have to run a disk repair program on an NTFS volume. NTFS guarantees the consistency of the volume by using standard transaction logging and recovery techniques. In addition, Windows 2000 supports compression on a folder or individual file basis for NTFS partitions. Files compressed on an NTFS partition can be read and written by any application running in Windows 2000 without first being decompressed by another program.

NTFS supports all Windows 2000 operating system features. It provides faster access speed than FAT and minimizes the number of disk accesses required to find a file. In addition, NTFS allows you to set local permissions on files and folders that specify which groups and users have access to them. This includes setting the level of access that is permitted. NTFS file and folder permissions apply both to users working at the computer where the file is stored and to users accessing the file over the network when the file is in a shared folder. With NTFS you can also set share rights that operate on shared folders in combination with file and folder permissions. FAT only supports share rights.

Tip Do not configure share folder rights on NTFS partitions. Instead, configure local NTFS permissions.

Features of Windows 2000

All the new features and enhancements in Windows 2000 are supported by the NTFS file system. This section outlines many of these features and how they relate to NTFS.

Reparse Points

Reparse points are new file system objects in NTFS used in Windows 2000. A *reparse point* is a file or a directory that has user-controlled data stored in the system-administered reparse attribute. The *reparse attribute* is used by file system filters to enhance the normal behavior of files or directories present in the underlying file system. Thus, a file or a directory that contains a reparse point acquires additional behavior not present in the underlying file system.

Reparse points enable layered file system filters to add user-controlled behavior to a file or to a directory. The underlying mechanism in a reparse point modifies the typical filename parsing process, forcing its restart with a new, user-controlled context. If the reparse point contains private reparse data, this reparse data is returned in an appropriate buffer and made available to all file system filters in the system.

Reparse tags are used to differentiate reparse points. When a file system object with a reparse point attribute is encountered during pathname resolution, it is passed back up the file system driver stack for an I/O reparse. The file system filter handles the I/O reparse, which includes identifying the reparse tag. File system drivers execute specific I/O functionality. These drivers use the reparse tag and a globally unique identifier (GUID) to identify I/O calls they are responsible for. Although the reparse tag itself is unique, the GUID provides additional identification.

When a user accesses a directory that has a directory junction reparse point attribute associated with it, a series of actions occur:

1. A user opens Windows 2000 Explorer and double-clicks on an NTFS directory in a Windows 2000 volume.

2. The call goes from User mode to Kernel mode where it reaches the file system object and encounters the matching reparse point attribute.

3. Each installable file system filter driver in the Windows 2000 I/O stack examines the tag associated with the reparse point. If there is a match, the associated file system filter driver intercepts the call. File system filters examine calls both inbound and outbound.

4. The NTFS directory junction filter driver intercepts the call and executes the enhanced functionality associated with the reparse point. In the case of a directory junction, the driver mounts another namespace.

5. The file system driver returns the call to the calling application. The file system driver mounts another namespace and returns a handle to the calling function.

Note If the directory junction is removed, the reparse point will not be present. Therefore, the call to open a directory will not be intercepted by one of the file system filter drivers in the I/O stack, resulting in normal behavior.

Windows 2000 allows the relative order of the file system stack to be altered. Using information stored in the registry, a filter can be placed above or below another filter. NTFS is always placed below the file system filters that require NTFS as a service and above the device drivers that are used by NTFS.

The Windows 2000 I/O subsystem builds the appropriate data structures to service requests and orchestrates the calling of the layers in turn. After a function has been processed by the stack, the Windows 2000 I/O subsystem examines the result of the operation and either issues further work requests or fails work requests that have been executing normally.

Two of the file system enhancements that reparse points provide include the following:

- **Hierarchical storage management** Unused files are automatically archived to less expensive media like tape or removable drive. When a user attempts to access a file that has been archived, the reparse point assists the operating system in locating the file on alternative media. To the user, the file does not appear to be archived.

- **Volume mount point** Allows the user to view multiple disk volumes as a single drive.

Native Structured Storage

Native Structured Storage (NSS) is a new function of Windows 2000. NSS allows ActiveX documents to be physically stored in the same multistream format that ActiveX uses to logically process structured storage. The NSS file system filter makes a file on the disk look like an OLE-structured storage file. The result is improved efficiency in the physical storage of ActiveX compound documents. Each of the embedded object's data now resides in its own stream within a file. Updating an object means that a new stream is created for the new object and that the original stream for the object is destroyed, causing the file system to reclaim the disk space. The NSS file system filter makes all of this appear transparent to an application. The NSS filter also allows an NSS file to be copied to a floppy, converting the file to the old file format and vice versa.

Windows 2000 requires a reparse point be placed on any file that uses NSS. A reparse point in a file performs the following functions:

- Indicates that the file has multiple streams
- Instructs a file system filter driver to translate the multiple streams into a single stream when the file is migrated to file systems that do not support NSS

Disk Quotas

Administrators can now limit the amount of disk space users can consume on a server. *Disk Quotas* is a powerful tool used to monitor and constrain disk space usage. Administrators can manage storage growth in distributed environments. Disk quotas, which are implemented in NTFS, are used in Windows 2000 on a per partition basis. Disk quotas are described in more detail in Chapter 13, "Monitoring and Optimization."

Sparse File Support

Sparse files allow programs to create very large files but to consume disk space only as needed. NTFS deallocates sparse data streams and maintains only non-sparse data as allocated. When a program accesses a sparse file, the file system yields allocated data as actual data and deallocated data as zeros.

A user-controlled file system attribute can be set to take advantage of the sparse file function in NTFS. With the sparse file attribute set, the file system can deallocate data from anywhere in the file and, when an application calls, yield the zero data by range instead of storing and returning the actual data. File system APIs allow for the file to be copied or backed as actual bits and sparse stream ranges. The net result is efficiency in file system storage and access.

A sparse file contains an attribute that causes the I/O subsystem to interpret the file's data based on allocated ranges. All meaningful or non-zero data is allocated, whereas all nonmeaningful data (large strings of data composed of zeros) is simply not allocated. When a sparse file is read, allocated data is returned as stored, and nonallocated data is returned, by default, as zeros in accordance with the C2 security requirement specification.

Sparse File Utilization

NTFS includes full sparse file support for both compressed and uncompressed files. Disk allocation is required for specified ranges only. NTFS handles read operations on sparse files by returning allocated data and sparse data defined by file map ranges. It is possible to read a sparse file as allocated data and range data without having to retrieve the entire data set. This is desirable for applications that want to efficiently handle sparse files in their operations. By default, NTFS returns the entire data set.

Data streams with an NTFS sparse attribute set have two allocation definitions. The first is the virtual *AllocatedLength*, which is rounded up to a cluster boundary greater than or equal to the size of the stream. The second is *TotalAllocatedLength*, which represents the actual disk clusters allocated to the stream. TotalAllocatedLength will always be less than or equal to the AllocatedLength.

An example of sparse file utilization is a scientific application that might require 1 TB of storage for data used in a matrix. Actual meaningful data in the matrix might account for only 1 MB. With the sparse file attribute set, the file system can deallocate from anywhere in the file and yield the zero data to calling applications by range, instead of storing and returning the actual data. The result is that file access requests are satisfied with the correct bits and disk space is managed efficiently. File system APIs allow the file to be copied or backed up as actual bits and sparse stream ranges. The net result is efficiency in file system storage and access.

Link Tracking and Object Identifiers

Windows 2000 provides a service that enables client applications to track link sources that have been moved locally or within a domain. Clients that subscribe to the link tracking service can maintain the integrity of their references, because the referenced objects can be moved transparently. *Link tracking* stores a file object identifier as part of its tracking information. This feature allows shortcuts to resolve the correct path of a folder or file after it has been moved.

The distributed link tracking service maintains file links if the link source file is moved from one NTFS version 5.0 volume to another within the same domain. File links are also maintained if the name of the machine that holds the link source is renamed, the network shares on the link source machine are changed, or the volume holding the link source file is moved to another machine within the same domain.

Change Journal

The *Change Journal* is a sparse stream that creates a persistent log to track file information about additions, deletions, and modifications for each NTFS volume. This is useful for applications that need to know what has occurred on a particular volume. File system indexing, replication managers, remote storage, and incremental backup applications are a few examples of applications that can benefit from the Change Journal.

With the Change Journal, only a small active range of the file uses any disk allocation. The active range initially begins at offset 0 in the stream and moves forward through the file. The Unique Sequence Number (USN) of a particular record represents its virtual offset in the stream. As the active range moves forward through the stream, earlier records are deallocated and become unavailable. The size of the active range in a sparse file can be adjusted.

The Change Journal is much more efficient than time stamps or file notifications for determining changes in a given namespace. A system administrator can view volume changes without resorting to namespace traversal.

Change Journal Awareness

The Change Journal will not affect a storage application unless it is specifically used by that application. The Change Journal operates in a bounded space. It is based on a sparse data stream that allows for deallocation from the front of a file. Therefore, change entries can be removed and any application that depends on these entries must be prepared to deal with this event. The Change Journal records data on a per volume basis. It is applicable only to NTFS used in Windows 2000 volumes.

Unique Sequence Number

The *USN Journal* provides a persistent log of all changes made to files on the volume. Applications can consult the USN Journal for information about the modifications made to a set of files. The USN Journal is more efficient than checking time stamps or registering for file notifications.

When a user, an administrator, or another domain controller updates a directory object, the directory object's controller assigns that change a USN. Each controller maintains its own update sequence numbers and applies each one incrementally to each directory change made to that controller's directory. In addition, each domain controller maintains a table of USNs it has received from every other controller in the domain.

When the domain controller writes the change into the directory, it also writes the USN of the change with the property. This is an atomic operation (a procedure that is considered one indivisible process), so when the controller writes the property change and the change's USN, it will either succeed completely or fail completely.

CD and DVD Support

Windows 2000 supports CDFS, UDF, and digital video disc (DVD) storage devices.

CD-ROM File System

Windows 2000 continues to provide read-only support for CDFS, which is ISO 9660 compliant. Windows 2000 also supports long filenames as listed in the ISO 9660 level two standards.

When creating a CD-ROM to be used under Windows 2000, the following standards must be followed:

- All directory names and filenames must be less than 32 characters.
- The directory tree cannot exceed eight levels from the root.
- File extensions are not mandatory.

Universal Disk Format

The *UDF*, which is new for Windows 2000, is a file system designed for interchanging data on DVD and CD. The primary intention of UDF is to support read-only DVD-ROM media. UDF is a standards-based file system that is ISO 13346 compliant.

The following table outlines the restrictions and requirements defined in the UDF specification:

Item	Requirement
Logical/Physical Sector Size	The logical and physical sector size for a specific volume will be the same.
Logical Block Size	The logical block size for a logical volume should be set to the logical sector size of the volume.
Volume Set Physical Sector Size	The physical sector size within all media of the same volume set should have the same physical sector size.

With UDF, multivolume support and multipartition support are optional. Media support is limited to rewrite, overwrite, and write once, read many (WORM) media only. Windows 2000 provides native read-only support for UDF. Rewrite, overwrite, and WORM capability must be provided by third-party applications.

DVD Support

One of the new storage devices that Windows 2000 supports is DVD. DVD has a capacity nearly 20 times that of a regular CD, so a user can store several video demos for a client presentation and still have room for other material.

Support for DVD from Microsoft is not limited to a new device driver to support DVD-ROM drives. Since DVD encompasses such a broad range of uses and technologies, DVD must be viewed in the context of the whole computer. DVD-ROM discs and devices provide cost-effective storage for large data files. In the future, DVD will allow for writeable devices, allowing a larger range of options.

Note The Microsoft Solution Developer Network (MSDN) library is now available on DVD-ROM.

On most PCs that have Microsoft DVD support, DVD will work as a storage device and, if the proper decoding hardware is present, will support full DVD playback.

Some components in the architecture will change based on advances in other hardware technologies, such as the advent of Accelerated Graphics Port (AGP) or improvements in the PCI bus. The only components that will always be present are the DVD-ROM driver, the UDF file system, the Windows Driver Model (WDM) Streaming class driver, and the DVD Splitter/Navigator.

DVD-ROM Class Driver

DVD-ROM has its own industry-defined command set. Support for this command set is provided in Windows 98 by an updated CD-ROM class driver. In Windows 2000, support is provided in a new WDM DVD-ROM device driver. The Windows 2000 driver provides the ability to read data sectors from a DVD-ROM drive.

Support for UDF is provided to ensure support for UDF-formatted DVD discs. Windows 2000 will provide UDF installable file systems similar to FAT16 and FAT32.

Copyright Protection

Copyright protection for DVD is provided by encrypting important sectors on a disc and then decrypting those sectors prior to decoding them. Microsoft will provide support for both software and hardware decrypters by using a software module that will enable authentication between the decoders and the DVD-ROM drives in a PC.

Regionalization

As part of the copyright protection scheme used for DVD, six worldwide regions have been set up by the DVD Consortium. Discs are playable on DVD devices in some or all of the regions according to regional codes set by the creators of the content. Microsoft will provide software that responds to the regional codes as required by the DVD Consortium and as part of the decryption licenses.

Structure of NTFS

This section discusses the main components of the NTFS structure: NTFS volume structure, Windows 2000 boot sector, Windows 2000 Master File Table and Metadata, and NTFS file attributes.

NTFS Volume Structure

NTFS uses clusters (also known as allocation units) made up of one or many sectors as the fundamental unit of disk allocation. However, the default cluster size depends on the partition size. In the Disk Management snap-in, a user can specify a cluster size up to 4 KB (4096 bytes). If the Format.com program is used to format the NTFS volume through the Command prompt, a user can specify any of the default cluster sizes shown in the following table.

Warning NTFS compression is not supported for cluster sizes greater than 4 KB.

The cluster sizes in this table are only recommendations. The sizes can be changed if necessary. However, changing disk cluster size requires that a partition be reformatted.

Volume size	Sectors per cluster	Cluster size
512 MB or less	1	512 bytes
513 MB-1024 MB	2	1 KB
1025 MB-2048 MB	4	2 KB
2049 MB-4096 MB	8	4 KB
4097 MB-8192 MB	16	8 KB
8193 MB-16,384 MB	32	16 KB
16,385 MB-32,768 MB	64	32 KB
> 32,768 MB	128	64 KB

Windows 2000 Boot Sector

The first information found on an NTFS volume is the boot sector. The boot sector starts at sector 0 and can be up to 16 sectors long. It consists of two structures:

- The BIOS Parameter Block, which contains information on the volume layout and file system structures.

- Code that describes how to find and load the startup files for the operating system being loaded. For Windows 2000 on *x*86-based computers, this code loads the file Ntldr.

Windows 2000 Master File Table and Metadata

When a volume is formatted with NTFS, a Master File Table (MFT) and Metadata are created.

NTFS uses MFT entries to define the files they correspond to. All information about a file, including its size, time and date stamps, permissions, and data content, is stored either within MFT entries or in space external to the MFT but described by the MFT entries.

NTFS creates a file record for each file and a directory record for each directory created on an NTFS volume. The MFT includes a separate file record for the MFT itself. These file and directory records are stored on the

MFT. NTFS allocates space for each MFT record based on the cluster size of the file. The attributes of the file are written to the allocated space in the MFT. Besides file attributes, each file record contains information about the position of the file record in the MFT.

Each file usually has one file record. However, if a file has a large number of attributes or becomes highly fragmented, it might need more than one file record. If this is the case, the first record for the file (the base file record) stores the location of the other file records required by the file. Small files and directories (typically 1500 bytes or smaller) are contained entirely within the file's MFT record.

Metadata are the files NTFS uses to implement the file system structure. NTFS reserves the first 16 records of the MFT for Metadata (approximately 1 MB). The remaining records of the MFT contain the file and directory records for each file and directory on the partition.

If the first MFT record is corrupted, NTFS reads the second record to find the MFT mirror file. The data segment locations for both $Mft and $MftMirr are recorded in the boot sector. A duplicate of the boot sector is located at the end of the partition.

NTFS File Attributes

Every allocated sector on an NTFS partition belongs to a file. Even the file system Metadata is part of a file. NTFS views each file (or folder) as a set of file attributes. Elements such as the file's name, its security information, and even its data are all file attributes.

An attribute type code and, optionally, an attribute name identify each attribute. When a file's attributes can fit within the MFT file record for that file, they are called *resident attributes*. Filename and time stamp information is always a resident attribute. When the information for a file is too large to fit in its MFT file record, some of the file attributes are nonresident. Nonresident attributes are allocated one or more clusters of disk space elsewhere in the volume. NTFS creates an Attribute List attribute to describe the location of all the attribute records.

Implementation of NTFS

When implementing NTFS, several factors should be taken into consideration: upgrading to Windows 2000, multibooting Windows 2000, and NTFS compatibility issues.

Upgrading to Windows 2000

An upgrade from Windows NT to Windows 2000 (when not multiple booting) results in the following:

- All volumes formatted with an earlier version of NTFS are upgraded to the NTFS version 5.0.

- All boot/system volumes formatted with FAT16 are converted to NTFS version 5.0.

- All volumes formatted with FAT16 that are not boot/system volumes are not converted.

Windows NT 4.0 Service Pack 4 or Later Conversion

When Windows 2000 is installed on a computer running Windows NT 4.0 with Service Pack (SP) 4 or later, the NTFS volumes are upgraded to NTFS version 5.0 the first time the new operating system is booted. Setup then installs a new NTFS driver so that all volumes can be accessed.

FAT Volume Conversion

Conversions from FAT to NTFS version 5.0 take place only if the user confirms it. Winnt32.exe started in attended mode will display a file system conversion page providing users an option to convert their existing FAT file system to NTFS. Installations or upgrades started with Winnt32.exe in unattended mode will convert or leave the file system alone, based on the value of the FileSystem value name in the answer file. Conversion will occur automatically if FileSystem = ConvertNTFS and will not be converted if FileSystem = LeaveAlone. When installing Windows 2000 Server, the option to convert FAT to NTFS will default to Yes. If the FileSystem value name does not exist, Setup will leave the file system alone.

If a user runs Setup by using Winnt.exe, boot floppies, or CD-ROM boot, the Text mode of the installation process allows the user to choose the file system.

This table outlines file system conversion information:

System	FAT to NTFS	NTFS to NTFS version 5.0
Windows NT 3.51 Workstation	Winnt32.exe will display the wizard page with the No option selected.	All mounted NTFS volumes will be upgraded to NTFS version 5.0. A warning will be displayed, and the user can cancel Setup or proceed.
Windows NT 3.51 Server (stand-alone/domain controller)	Winnt32.exe will display the wizard page with the Yes option selected.	All mounted NTFS volumes will be upgraded to NTFS version 5.0. A warning will be displayed, and the user can cancel Setup or proceed.
Windows NT 4.0 Workstation (pre-SP3)	Winnt32.exe will display the wizard page with the No option selected.	All mounted NTFS volumes will be upgraded to NTFS version 5.0. A warning will be displayed, and the user can cancel Setup or proceed.
Windows NT 4.0 Workstation (SP3)	Winnt32.exe will display the wizard page with the No option selected.	All mounted NTFS volumes will be upgraded to NTFS version 5.0. A warning will be displayed, and the user can cancel Setup or proceed.
Windows NT 4.0 Workstation (SP4 or later)	Winnt32.exe will display the wizard page with the No option selected.	All mounted NTFS volumes will be upgraded to NTFS version 5.0.
Windows NT 4.0 Server (pre-SP3—stand-alone/domain controller)	Winnt32.exe will display the wizard page with the Yes option selected.	All mounted NTFS volumes will be upgraded to NTFS used in Windows 2000. A warning will be displayed, and the user can cancel Setup or proceed.
Windows NT 4.0 Server (SP3—stand-alone/domain controller)	Winnt32.exe will display the wizard page with the Yes option selected.	All mounted NTFS volumes will be upgraded to NTFS version 5.0. A warning will be displayed, and the user can cancel Setup or proceed.
Windows NT 4.0 Server (SP4 or later—stand-alone/domain controller)	Winnt32.exe will display the wizard page with the Yes option selected.	All mounted NTFS volumes will be upgraded to NTFS version 5.0.
Windows 95	No conversion will take place. The file system will be left intact.	N/A
Windows 95 OSR2	No conversion will take place. The file system will be left intact.	N/A
Windows 98	No conversion will take place. The file system will be left intact.	N/A

Multibooting Windows 2000

The ability to access NTFS volumes when a user multiple boots Windows 2000 with earlier versions of Windows NT depends on which version of Windows NT is used. Network accessible NTFS volumes on file or print servers are not converted as a result of client computer upgrades to Windows 2000.

If a user multiple boots Windows 2000 and Windows NT 4.0 SP4, any basic (nondynamic) volumes formatted with NTFS used in Windows 2000 can be read.

If a user multiple boots Windows 2000 and a version of Windows NT that was released before Windows NT 4.0 SP4, the user cannot access the NTFS volumes with the earlier version of Windows NT. Configurations affected by this scenario include the following:

- Volumes on removable media

- Volumes used with multiple boot configurations

- Volumes shared within clustered configurations

NTFS Compatibility

If a user is running Windows NT 4.0 SP4, any basic (nondynamic) volumes formatted with NTFS used in Windows 2000 can be read.

The Windows NT 4.0 SP4 NTFS driver allows Windows NT 4.0 users to mount volumes formatted with NTFS 5.0. However, Windows NT 4.0 users cannot use any of the NTFS 5.0 features.

If another operating system is used in addition to Windows NT, the files on the NTFS volumes can be accessed only from Windows NT. A file system other than NTFS must be used for the system and boot partitions of the other operating system.

Ntfs.sys File System Driver

The new Ntfs.sys Windows NT 4.0 file system driver provides support for mounting volumes and dual-boot systems in mixed Windows NT environments. Because of these compatibility issues, dual booting between Windows NT 4.0 and Windows 2000 is not recommended. The Windows NT 4.0 SP4 NTFS driver is provided only to assist in evaluating and upgrading to Windows 2000.

Mounting Volumes

Windows NT 4.0 systems pre-SP4 are not able to mount NTFS 5.0 volumes. Windows 2000 automatically upgrades NTFS 4.0 volumes to NTFS version 5.0. When mounting an NTFS 5.0 volume under Windows NT 4.0 SP4, NTFS 5.0 features are unavailable.

Dual-Boot Systems

The new NTFS file system driver allows you to dual-boot between Windows NT 4.0 and Windows 2000 systems. To dual-boot Windows NT 4.0 and Windows 2000, install Windows NT 4.0 SP4 on the systems. However, since the on-disk NTFS data structures are different under Windows 2000, the Windows NT 4.0 disk utilities such as CHKDSK and AUTOCHK will not work. These utilities check the version stamp on the file system before performing their tasks. After installing Windows 2000, users must run the Windows 2000 version of the disk utilities.

Although the features are unavailable when mounting an NTFS 5.0 volume under Windows NT 4.0 SP4, most read and write operations can be done as normal if the operations do not make use of any NTFS 5.0 features.

Since files can be read and written on NTFS 5.0 volumes under Windows NT 4.0, Windows 2000 might need to perform clean-up operations on the volume after it was mounted on Windows NT 4.0. These clean-up operations ensure that the NTFS 5.0 data structures are consistent after a Windows NT 4.0 mount operation.

Disk Quotas

When running Windows NT 4.0, Windows 2000 disk quotas are ignored. This means that users can allocate more disk space than is allowed by their Windows 2000 quota.

If users violate their quotas under Windows NT 4.0, Windows 2000 will fail further disk allocations by those users. Users can still read and write data to existing files, but they cannot increase the size of the file. They can, however, delete files and shrink the size of files. This behavior lasts until the users reduce disk consumption below the assigned quotas. Once they are below quota, normal quota behavior resumes.

Note This is normal quota behavior any time the quota system is taken from a nontracking or tracking state to an enforced state. The same behavior will manifest itself when a system is upgraded from Windows NT 4.0 to Windows 2000 with quota enforcement.

Encryption

No operations, including open, read, write, copy and delete, can be done on encrypted files under Windows NT 4.0. Since encrypted files cannot be accessed on Windows NT 4.0, no clean-up operations are necessary under Windows 2000.

Sparse files

No operations, including open, read, write, copy and delete, can be done on sparse files under Windows NT 4.0. Since sparse files cannot be accessed on Windows NT 4.0, no clean-up operations are necessary under Windows 2000.

Object IDs

Full access to the object is available under Windows NT 4.0. Objects can be opened, read, written, copied, and deleted. If the user has deleted a file with an object ID on it, Windows 2000 must scan and clean up the orphaned entry in the index.

USN Journal

The USN Journal is ignored under Windows NT 4.0. No entries are logged when files are accessed.

Since the USN Journal is ignored under Windows NT 4.0, not all file changes are logged in the USN Journal. When Windows 2000 boots, the USN Journal parameters are reset to indicate that the Journal history is incomplete. Applications that use the USN Journal must respond appropriately to incomplete Journals. All further accesses under Windows 2000 will be logged, and the Journal can be trusted after the volume is mounted by Windows 2000. Note that a Journal query for valid USN ranges can be performed.

Reparse Points

No operations, including open, read, write, copy and delete, can be done on reparse points under Windows NT 4.0. Since reparse points cannot be accessed on Windows NT 4.0, no clean-up operations are necessary under Windows 2000.

Lesson Summary

NTFS 5.0 supports all Windows 2000 operating system features, including reparse points, NSS, and disk quotas. NTFS also supports the CDFS, the UDF, and DVD storage devices. NTFS uses clusters made up of multiple sectors as the fundamental unit of disk allocation. However, with NTFS, the default cluster size depends on the partition size. The first information found on an NTFS partition is the boot sector. The boot sector starts at sector 0 and can be up to 16 sectors long. When a volume is formatted with NTFS, an MFT and Metadata are created. Every allocated sector on an NTFS volume belongs to a file. Even the file system Metadata is part of a file. NTFS views each file (or folder) as a set of file attributes. When implementing NTFS, several factors should be taken into consideration: upgrading to Windows 2000, multibooting Windows 2000, and NTFS compatibility issues.

Lesson 4: File System Security

Sharing folders is the only way to make folders and their contents available over the network. Shared folders provide a way to secure file resources; they can be used on FAT16 and FAT32 partitions, as well as on NTFS partitions. But NTFS supports more than just shared folders. NTFS permissions can be used to specify which users and groups can gain access to files and folders and what they can do with their content. However, NTFS permissions are not available on volumes that are formatted with FAT.

After this lesson, you will be able to

- Share folders and assign permissions to those shares
- Assign NTFS permissions to files and folders

Estimated lesson time: 35 minutes

Shared Folders

Shared folders are used to provide network users with access to file resources. When a folder is shared, users can connect to the folder over the network and gain access to the files it contains. However, to gain access to the files, users must have permissions to access the shared folders.

Shared Folder Permissions

A shared folder can contain applications, data, or users' personal data (called home folders). Each type of data can require different shared folder permissions.

Shared folder permissions have the following characteristics in common:

- Shared folder permissions apply to folders, not individual files. Since you can apply shared folder permissions only to the entire shared folder and not to individual files or subfolders in the shared folder, shared folder permissions provide less detailed security than NTFS permissions.

- Shared folder permissions do not restrict access to users who gain access to the folder at the computer where the folder is stored. They apply only to users who connect to the folder over the network.

- Shared folder permissions are the only way to secure network resources on a FAT volume. NTFS permissions are not available on FAT volumes.

- The default shared folder permission is Full Control, and it is assigned to the Everyone group when you share the folder.

A shared folder appears in Microsoft Windows Explorer as an icon of a hand holding the shared folder (Figure 4.9).

download

Figure 4.9 Shared folders in Windows Explorer

To control how users gain access to a shared folder, you must assign shared folder permissions. The following table explains what each of the shared folder permissions allows a user to do. The permissions are presented from most restrictive to least restrictive.

Permission	Description
Read	Users can display folder names, filenames, file data and attributes; run program files; and change folders within the shared folder.
Change	Users can create folders, add files to folders, change data in files, append data to files, change file attributes, delete folders and files, and perform actions permitted by the Read permission.
Full Control	Users can change file permissions, take ownership of files, and perform all tasks permitted by the Change permission.

You can allow or deny shared folder permissions to individual users or to user groups. Generally, it is best to assign permissions to a group rather than to individual users. You should deny permissions only when it is necessary to override permissions that are otherwise applied. For example, it might be necessary to deny permissions to a specific user who belongs to a group that has been granted permissions. If you deny a shared folder permission to a user, the user will not have that permission.

Applying Shared Folder Permissions

Applying shared permissions to user accounts and groups affects access to a shared folder. Denying permission takes precedence over the permissions that you allow.

Multiple Permissions

A user can be a member of multiple groups, each with different permissions that provide different levels of access to a shared folder. When you assign a permission to a user for a shared folder and that user is a member of a group to which you assigned a different permission, the user's effective permissions are the combination of the user and group permissions. For example, if a user has Read permission and is a member of a group with Change permission, the user's effective permission is Change, which includes Read.

Deny Overrides Other Permissions

Denied permissions take precedence over any permissions that you otherwise allow for user accounts and groups. If you deny a shared folder permission to a user, the user will not have that permission, even if you allow the permission for a group of which the user is a member.

NTFS Permissions

Shared folder permissions are sufficient to gain access to files and folders on a FAT volume but are not the best solution for NTFS partition. On a FAT partition, users can gain access to a shared folder in which they have permissions, as well as to all of the folder's contents. When users gain access to a shared folder on an NTFS partition, you should use either share rights or NTFS permissions but not both. NTFS permissions are preferred since permissions can be set on both files and folders. If share rights are configured for a folder and NTFS permissions are configured for folder or files within a folder, the most restrictive rights will become the user's effective rights to the resource. This significantly increases the complexity of resolving access permissions for network resources.

Copying or Moving Shared Folders

When you copy a shared folder, the original shared folder is still shared, but the copy is not shared. When you move a shared folder, it is no longer shared.

Guidelines for Shared Folder Permissions

The following list provides some general guidelines for managing your shared folders and assigning shared folder permissions:

- Determine which groups need access to each resource and the level of access they require. Document the groups and their permissions for each resource.

- Assign permissions to groups instead of user accounts to simplify access administration.

- Assign to a resource the most restrictive permissions that still allow users to perform required tasks. For example, if users need only to read information in a folder, and they will never delete or create files, assign the Read permission.

- Organize resources so that folders with the same security requirements are located within a folder. For example, if users require Read permission for several application folders, store the application folders within the same folder. Then share this folder instead of sharing each individual application folder.

- Use intuitive share names so that users can easily recognize and locate resources, and use share names that all client operating systems can use.

Note MS-DOS, Windows 3.x, and WFW clients read up to 8.3 format share names; consequently, longer share names are not advisable in mixed environments.

Microsoft Windows 2000 provides 8.3-character equivalent names, but the resulting names might not be intuitive to users. For example, a Windows 2000 folder named Accountants Database would appear as Account~1 on client computers running MS-DOS, Windows 3.x, and Windows for Workgroups.

Sharing Folders

You can share resources with others by sharing folders containing those resources. To share a folder, you must be a member of one of several privileged groups, depending on the role of the computer where the shared folder resides. When you share a folder you can control access to the folder by limiting the number of users who can simultaneously gain access to it. You can also control access to the folder and its contents by assigning permissions to selected users and groups. Once you have shared a folder, users must connect to the shared folder and must have the appropriate permissions to gain access to it. After you have shared a folder, you may want to modify it. You can stop sharing it, change its share name, and change user and group permissions to gain access to it.

Requirements for Sharing Folders

In Windows 2000, members of the built-in Administrators, Server Operators, and Power Users groups are able to share folders. Which groups can share folders on which machines depends on whether the computers belong to workgroups or domains and on the type of computers on which the shared folders reside:

- In a Windows 2000 domain, the Administrators group and Server Operators group can share folders residing on any machines in the domain. The Power Users group is a local group and can only share folders residing on the stand-alone server or on the computer running Windows 2000 Professional where the group is located.

- In a Windows 2000 workgroup, the Administrators group and Power Users group can share folders on the Windows 2000 Server stand-alone server or the computer running Windows 2000 Professional on which the group exists.

- Users that are granted the Create Permanent Shared Objects user right can also create shares on the computer where this right is assigned.

Note If the folder to be shared resides on an NTFS volume, users must also have at least the Read permission for that folder.

Administrative Shared Folders

Windows 2000 automatically shares folders for administrative purposes. These shares are appended with a dollar sign ($). The $ hides the shared folder from users who browse the computer. The root of each volume, the system root folder, and the location of the printer drivers are all hidden shared folders that you can gain access to across the network.

The following table describes the purpose of the administrative shared folders that Windows 2000 automatically generates:

Share	Purpose
C$, D$, E$, and so on	The root of each volume on a fixed disk is automatically shared, and the share name is the drive letter appended with a dollar sign ($). When you connect to this folder, you have access to the entire volume. You use the administrative shares to connect remotely to the computer to perform administrative tasks. Windows 2000 assigns the Full Control permission to the Administrators group. Removable drives like CD-ROM drives are not assigned the hidden share drive letter.
Admin$	The system root folder, which is C:\Winnt by default, is shared as Admin$. Administrators can gain access to this shared folder to administer Windows 2000 without knowing which folder it is installed in. Only members of Administrators have access to this share. Windows 2000 assigns the Full Control permission to the Administrators group.
Print$	When you install the first shared printer, the %systemroot%\System32\Spool\Drivers folder is shared as Print$. This folder provides access to printer driver files for clients. Only members of Administrators, Server Operators, and Print Operators have the Full Control permission. The Everyone group has the Read permission.

Hidden shared folders are not limited to those that the system automatically creates. You can share additional folders and append a $ to the share name. Only users who know the folder name can gain access to it, if they have also been granted the proper permissions.

Sharing a Folder

When you share a folder, you can give it a share name, provide comments to describe the folder and its content, limit the number of users who have access to the folder, assign permissions, and share the same folder multiple times. To share a folder, right-click the folder you want to share and then click Properties. The share properties are set on the Sharing tab of the Properties dialog box (Figure 4.10).

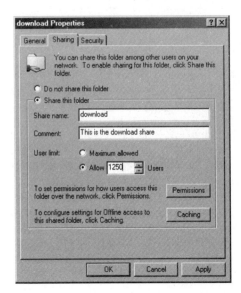

Figure 4.10 Sharing tab of a folder's Properties dialog box

The following table provides a description of the options on the Sharing tab:

Option	Description
Do Not Share This Folder	The option you should select if you do not want to share this folder. When this option is selected, all other options are grayed out.
Share This Folder	The option you should select if you want to share this folder. When this option is selected, all other options are active.
Share Name	The name that users from remote locations use to make a connection to the shared folder. You must enter a share name.
Comment	An optional description for the share name. The comment appears in addition to the share name when users at client computers browse the server for shared folders. This comment can be used to identify contents of the shared folder.
User Limit	The number of users who can concurrently connect to the shared folder. The Maximum Allowed option allows Windows 2000 Server to support an unlimited number of connections. However, the number of Client Access Licenses (CALs) that you purchased limits the connections.
Permissions	The shared folder permissions that apply only when the folder is accessed over the network. By default, the Everyone group is assigned Full Control for all new shared folders.

Option	Description
Caching	The settings to configure if and how files within the shared folder are cached locally when accessed by others.
New Share	The option that allows you to create a new share.
Remove Share	The option that allows you to remove a share. This option appears only after the folder has been shared more than once.

After you share a folder, the next step is to specify which users have access to the shared folder. This is done by assigning shared folder permissions to selected user accounts and groups. You can assign permissions by clicking the Permission button on the Sharing tab of the shared folder's Properties dialog box. From there, you can select the user accounts and groups to which you want to assign permissions.

Modifying Shared Folders

You can modify the properties of a shared folder. For example, you can stop sharing a folder, modify the share name, or modify shared folder permissions. To modify a shared folder, open the Properties dialog box for that folder. The following table provides the steps you should take to perform specific modifications:

Modification	Action
Stop sharing a folder	Click the option Do Not Share This Folder.
Modify the share name	First, stop sharing the folder by clicking the option Do Not Share This Folder. Click the Apply button to apply the change, and then click the option Share This Folder. Enter the new share name in the Share Name text box.
Modify shared folder permissions	Click the Permissions button. In the Permissions dialog box, click Add or Remove. To add a group or user account, select that group or use in the Select Users, Computers, Or Groups dialog box, which opens when you click Add.
Share folder multiple times	Click the New Share button to share a folder with an additional shared folder name. Do so to consolidate multiple shared folders into one while allowing users to continue to use the same shared folder name that they used before you consolidated the folders.
Remove a share name	Click the Remove Share button. This option appears only after the folder has been shared more than once.

Note If you stop sharing a folder while a user has a file open, the user might lose data. If you click the Do Not Share This Folder option and a user has a connection to the shared folder, Windows 2000 displays a dialog box notifying you that a user has a connection to the shared folder.

NTFS Permissions

NTFS permissions are a set of standard permissions that allow or deny access for each user or group. They provide security for resources by allowing administrators and users to control who can gain access to individual files and folders and to specify the kind of access users can gain. NTFS security is effective whether a file or folder is accessed interactively at a computer or over a network.

Windows NT provides the following standard NTFS permissions:

- **NTFS folder permissions** Use these permissions to secure access to individual folders on NTFS formatted volumes.

- **NTFS file permissions** Use these permissions to secure access to individual files on NTFS formatted volumes.

Assigning NTFS Permissions

When new files and folders are created, rules and priorities are associated with the ways permissions are assigned, combined, and inherited.

NTFS Full Control Permission

The Full Control permission grants all permissions to access a resource. It is assigned as follows by default:

- When a user creates a file or folder, he or she becomes the Creator Owner and is assigned the Full Control permission.

- When a volume is formatted with NTFS, Full Control is assigned to the Everyone group at the root of the drive.

- When a FAT16 or FAT32 partition is converted to NTFS, Full Control is assigned to the Everyone group on all resources on that volume.

Multiple NTFS Permissions

Permissions to files and folders can be assigned to users and groups. It is possible for users to have multiple permissions assigned to them: those assigned to his or her user account and those assigned to groups the user is a member of. A user's effective permissions are the combination of NTFS permissions assigned to the individual user and the NTFS permissions assigned to all the groups the user belongs to. For example, if a user has Write permission to a folder and is also a member of a group with Read permission to the same folder, the user has both Read and Write permission for that folder.

NTFS file permissions take priority over NTFS folder permissions. For example, if a user is assigned the Write permission to a folder and the Modify permission to a file in that folder, the user can both write to and modify the file. This is also true when a user has not been assigned access to a folder. A user can always gain access to the files for which he or she has permissions by using the full universal naming convention (UNC) or path to open the file from its application. For example, a user has no permissions for a folder that contains a file for which the user has Change permission. The user can open the file from the file's appropriate application by typing the full UNC or path to the file.

Denying a permission for a user or group blocks that permission from the user, even if the permission has been granted to a group the user belongs to. For example, the Everyone group is assigned Full Control permission for a file for which a user has been denied Delete permission. The user will be able to read and modify the file, but will not be able to delete it.

Permission Inheritance

There are rules associated with the priority of file and folder permissions as you move down a directory tree from the parent folder to the subfolder and files. By default, permissions assigned to the parent folder are inherited and propagate to subfolders and files contained within the parent folder. However, inheritance can be prevented. When NTFS permissions are assigned or changed for a folder, permissions are assigned for the folder itself, for any existing files and subfolders, as well as for any new files and subfolders that might be created in the folder. A file or folder can be prevented from inheriting permissions from the parent folder, and permissions can be assigned explicitly to the file or folder. Also, permissions that have been inherited can be changed or removed.

Guidelines for Assigning NTFS Permissions

Administrators and the owner of a file or folder control which users and groups have permissions to the file or folder and what the permissions are. Use the following guidelines when assigning NTFS permissions:

- To simplify administration, group resources into application, data, and home folders. Doing so provides three benefits:

  - Permissions are assigned only to folders, not to individual files.

  - Backup is less complex because it is typically a lower priority to back up application files.

  - All home folders are in one location.

- Use NTFS permissions to control access to files and folders. Assign the minimum level of permission required. This reduces the possibility of users accidentally modifying or deleting important documents and application files.

- Whenever possible, assign permissions to groups rather than individual user accounts. Create groups according to the access they require for resources, and then assign the appropriate permissions to the group. Only when necessary, assign permissions to individual user accounts.

- When assigning permissions to home folders, centralize home folders on a network volume separate from applications and the operating system to streamline backing up data and administration.

- When assigning permissions to working data or application folders, remove the default Full Control permission from the Everyone group. Assign Read & Execute permission to the Users and Administrators groups. This prevents application files from being accidentally deleted or damaged by users or viruses. Administrators and users responsible for upgrading troubleshooting application software can be assigned Full Control permission, can complete their tasks, and then be assigned Read & Execute again.

- When assigning permission to public data folders, assign Read and Write to the Users group, and Full Control to Creator Owner. This gives users the ability to delete and modify only the files and folders they create, as well as the ability to read documents created by other users.

- In general, it is better not to assign permissions than to deny permissions. Deny permissions only when it is essential to deny specific access to a specific user account or group.

- Encourage and educate users to assign permissions to the files and folders they create and own. Provide them with guidelines for assigning appropriate permissions to the resources they control.

Configuring NTFS Permissions

The owners of files and folders can assign permissions to user accounts and groups. Administrators can also assign permissions to these resources.

To assign or modify NTFS permissions for a file or folder, open the Properties dialog box for that file or folder. NTFS permissions are configured on the Security tab of the Properties dialog box. The following table provides a description of the options on the Security tab:

Option	Description
Name	Lists the user accounts and groups with permissions for the file or folder. Click the user account or group to assign or change permissions, or to remove from the list.
Permissions	The permissions that you can allow or deny for the user account or group: Select the Allow check box to allow permission. Select the Deny check box to deny permission.
Add	Click this button to open the Select Users, Groups, or Computers dialog box where you can select user accounts and groups to add to the Name list.
Remove	Click this button to remove the selected user account or group and the associated permissions from the file or folder.
Allow Inheritable Permissions From To Propagate To This Object	By default, this option is selected for folders, which means subfolders inherit permissions assigned to their parent folder. Files are assigned this option, which means that files within a folder automatically receive the permissions assigned to their parent folder.
Advanced	Opens the Access Control Settings dialog box. From here you can configure special access permissions, auditing capability, and ownership control for files and folders.

Assigning Special Access Permissions

In general, the standard NTFS permissions provide all the permissions necessary to secure data. However, there are instances where the standard permissions do not provide the special access that might be needed. To create special access, use special NTFS permissions. Like standard permissions, special access permissions are either allowed or denied.

Note When special access permissions are assigned to a user or group, the permissions are indicated as Special on the Access Control Settings dialog box.

Special access permissions provide a finer degree of control for assigning access to resources. There are 13 special access permissions that, when combined, constitute the standard NTFS permissions, such as Read & Execute, Modify, and Full Control. For example, the standard NTFS Read permission includes the Read data, Read attributes, and Read extended attributes permissions.

Assigning special access permissions to folders and files requires three tasks:

- Configuring more granular permissions
- Transferring ownership
- Auditing access

Changing Permissions

File and folder owners and other users with Full Control permissions can assign or change permissions. You can grant network administrators the ability to change permissions on a file or folder without giving them Full Control over the file or folder. In this way, the administrator can assign permissions but not have permission to delete a file or folder or write to it. To give network administrators the ability to change permissions, grant the Change Permissions special access permission on the file or folder to the network administrators' group account.

If a member of the Administrators group takes ownership, the Administrators group becomes the owner and any member can access and change the permissions for the file or folder.

Transferring Ownership

In addition to changing permissions, ownership can be transferred. There are several way to transfer ownership:

- The current owner can assign the Full Control standard permission or the Take Ownership special access permission to other users, allowing those users to take ownership.

- An administrator can take ownership of any folder or file under his or her administrative control. For example, if an employee leaves the company, an administrator can take ownership of the employee's files and change the permissions so that others can access the files or folders.

- When assigned to a volume or folder, special access permissions are initially applied only where specified in the Apply Onto drop-down menu, which is discussed in more detail later in this lesson.

To transfer or take ownership of a file or folder, click the Owner tab in the Access Control Settings dialog box. The current owner of the file or folder is shown in the Current Owner Of This Item text box. You can select a new owner from the Change Owner To list. You can also select the Replace Owner On Subdirectories And Objects check box to change ownership for all subfolders and files contained within the folder.

Setting Special Access Permissions

To set special access permissions, access the Properties dialog box for a file or folder and click Advanced on the Security tab. In the Access Control Settings dialog box, click the Permissions tab, and then click Add to add a new user or group and modify the special access rights. Click View/Edit to modify the special access rights of an existing user or group. From here you can configure the options that allow you to set special access permissions. These options are described in the following table:

Option	Description
Name	The user account or group name. To select a different user account or group, click Change.
Apply Onto	The level of the folder hierarchy at which the special NTFS permissions are inherited. The default is This Folder, Subfolders, and Files.
Permissions	The individual special access permissions. To allow or deny an individual NTFS permission, select the Allow or Deny check box, respectively.
Apply These Permissions To Objects And/Or Containers Within This Container Only	This check box is available to folders and subfolders. Folders that are lower in the folder hierarchy can inherit the modified individual NTFS permissions from this folder. This option does not apply to files. Select this check box to prevent permissions inheritance. Click to clear this check box to propagate the modified individual NTFS permissions down the folder hierarchy.

Option	Description
Reset Permission On All Child Objects And Enable Propagation Of Inheritable permissions	This check box is only available to the partition.
	From a partition, permissions on all folders, subfolders, and files can be reset.
	Select this check box to reset all permissions for folders and files located on the partition to the settings designated for the partition. This option also enables the Apply These Permissions To Objects And/or Containers Within This Container Only check box. This check box is described in the previous row.
Clear all	Clear all selected permissions and the level of folder hierarchy selected to inherit permissions.

The following table provides an overview of the options available in the Apply Onto drop-down menu:

Option	Objects that permissions apply to
This Folder Only	Only to the folder.
This Folder, Subfolders, And Files	The folder, subfolder, and files. New files and folders created in this folder will inherit the permissions.
This Folder And Subfolders	The folder and subfolders. New files and folders created in this folder and subfolder will inherit the permissions.
This Folder And Files	The folder and files. New files and folders created in this folder will inherit the permissions.
Subfolders And Files Only	The subfolders and files. New files and folders created in the subfolder will inherit the permissions.
Subfolders Only	The subfolders. New folders created in the subfolder will inherit the permissions.
Files Only	Only to the files.

Copying and Moving Files and Folders

NTFS allows you to copy and move files and folders.

Copying Files and Folders

To copy files and folders within or between NTFS volumes, a user must have been granted Create Files/Write Data and Create Folders/Append Data permissions for the destination folder. The user who performs the copy will become the owner of the new file or folder.

When files or folders are copied, permissions will be inherited or lost, depending on where the file or folder is copied to:

- When a folder or file is moved within an NTFS partition, the folder or file retains its permissions.

- When a folder or file is copied within or between NTFS partitions, or moved to another partition, the folder or file inherits the permissions of the destination folder.

- When folders or files are copied to FAT16 or FAT32 volumes, the folders and files lose their NTFS permissions because FAT16 and FAT32 volumes do not support NTFS permissions.

Moving Files and Folders

To move files and folders between NTFS partitions requires the Create Files/Write Data and Create Folders/Append Data permissions for the destination folder or file and the Delete permission for the source folder or file. The Delete permission is required to move a folder or file because the folder or file is deleted from the source folder after it is moved to the destination folder. When a folder or file is moved to another partition, the user who performed the move will become Creator Owner.

Moving folders or files within and between NTFS volumes can affect the original permissions. The following table describes the results of what can occur when moving a file or folder:

Action	Result
Intra-volume move (within the same volume)	The folder or file retains the original permissions that are set for folder or file.
Inter-volume move (across different volumes)	The folder or file inherits the permissions that are set for the destination folder.

When folders or files are moved to FAT16 or FAT32 volumes, the folders and files lose their NTFS permissions because FAT16 and FAT32 volumes do not support NTFS permissions.

Note After you learn how to create users and groups in a later chapter, you will apply share rights and NTFS permissions to the users and groups you created.

Troubleshooting NTFS Permissions

The following table describes common permission problems and provides solutions:

Problem	Solution
A user cannot gain access to a file or folder.	Check the permissions assigned to the user account and to groups the user is a member of. If the user or a group that the user is a member of has been denied access to the file or folder, the user has no access to the resource. If the file or folder was copied within an NTFS partition, or copied or moved to another NTFS partition, the permissions may have changed by inheriting new permissions from the destination folder. If both share rights and NTFS permissions are configured for a folder, the most restrictive rights apply. Therefore, set the share rights to Everyone Full Control and control access exclusively through NTFS permissions.
A user account is added to a group to give that user access to a file or folder, but the user still cannot gain access to the file or folder.	An access token is created every time a user logs on and is authenticated by a computer running Windows NT or Windows 2000. The access token contains information about the groups the user belongs to. For the access token to be updated to include the new group, the user must log off and then log on again, or close all connections to the computer and then make new connections.
A user deletes a file, although that user does not have permission to delete the file.	Assign all permissions at the folder level, not at the file level. To deny users access, group files in a separate folder and then assign that folder restricted access. If this problem is unavoidable, do not assign Full Control permission for a folder. Instead, assign all the permissions, that is, Modify, Read & Execute, List Folder Contents, Read, and Write. This assigns all the abilities for the Full Control permission for the folder and its contents, except that users cannot delete files in the folder.

Lesson Summary

Folders can be shared so that users can connect to a folder over the network and gain access to the files it contains. However, to gain access to the files, users must have permissions to access the shared folders. Shared folder permissions apply to folders, not individual files. When you share a folder, you can give it a share name, provide comments to describe the folder and its content, limit the number of users who have access to the folder, assign permissions, and share the same folder multiple times. Shared folder permissions are the only way to secure network resources on a FAT partition. NTFS permissions are not available on FAT volumes. NTFS permissions are a set of standard permissions that allow or deny access for each user or group. By default, permissions assigned to the partition and parent folder are inherited and propagate to subfolders and files contained within the parent folder. The owner of a file or folder and administrators control which users and groups have permissions to the file or folder and what the permissions are. The owners of files and folders can assign permissions to user accounts and groups. Administrators can also assign permissions to these resources.

Review

The following questions are intended to reinforce key information presented in this chapter. If you are unable to answer a question, review the appropriate lesson and then try the question again. Answers to the questions can be found in Appendix A, "Questions and Answers."

1. You install a new 10-GB disk drive that you want to divide into five equal 2-GB sections. What are your options?

2. You are trying to create a striped volume on your Windows 2000 Server to improve performance. You confirm that you have enough unallocated disk space on two disks in your computer, but when you right-click an area of unallocated space on a disk, your only option is to create a partition. What is the problem, and how would you resolve it?

3. You dual boot your computer with Windows 98 and Windows 2000. You upgrade Disk 1, which you are using to archive files, from basic storage to dynamic storage. The next time you try to access your files on Disk 1 from Windows 98, you are unable to read the files. Why?

4. What is the default permission when a partition is formatted with NTFS? Who has access to the volume?

5. If a user has Write permission for a folder and is also a member of a group with Read permission for the folder, what are the user's effective permissions for the folder?

6. What happens to permissions that are assigned to a file when the file is moved from one folder to another folder on the same NTFS partition? What happens when the file is moved to a folder on another NTFS partition?

7. If an employee leaves the company, what must you do to transfer ownership of his or her files and folders to another employee?

8. What is the best way to secure files and folders that you share on NTFS partitions?

C H A P T E R   5

Advanced File Systems

About This Chapter

This chapter introduces you to the distributed file system (Dfs) and the File Replication Service (FRS). Dfs allows system administrators to make it easier for users to access and manage files that are physically distributed across a network. With Dfs, you can make files distributed across multiple servers appear to users as if they reside in one place on the network. Users no longer need to know and specify the actual physical location of files in order to access them. Dfs uses FRS to automatically synchronize content between assigned replicas. The Microsoft Active Directory Sites And Services snap-in uses FRS to replicate topology and global catalog information across domain controllers.

Before You Begin

To complete the lessons in this chapter, you must have

- Completed all previous exercises so that both computers are running Microsoft Windows 2000 Server and are configured as outlined in the exercises.

Lesson 1: Distributed File System

Dfs for Windows 2000 Server provides users with convenient access to shared folders that are distributed throughout a network. A single Dfs shared folder serves as an access point to other shared folders in the network.

After this lesson, you will be able to

- Configure a stand-alone Dfs root
- Configure a Dfs link
- Configure a fault tolerant Dfs root

Estimated lesson time: 35 minutes

Dfs Overview

Dfs is a single, logical, hierarchical file system. It organizes shared folders on different computers in a network to provide a logical tree structure for file system resources. Figure 5.1 shows how Dfs can organize resources that reside on different components of a network.

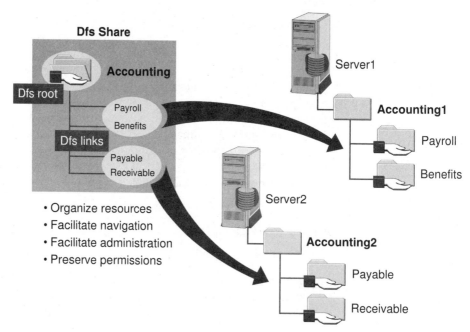

Figure 5.1 An example of a Dfs share

Because the Dfs tree is a single point of reference, regardless of the actual location of the underlying resources, users can easily gain access to network resources. As Figure 5.1 demonstrates, accounting file system resources from multiple servers are organized in one logical Dfs root named Accounting.

A user who navigates a Dfs-managed shared folder does not need to know the name of the server on which the folder is shared. This simplifies network access because users no longer need to locate the server where a specific resource resides. After connecting to a Dfs root, users can browse and gain access to all resources below the root, regardless of the location of the server on which the resource resides. In the example above, users needing access to accounting file resources would be able to find them in this one location.

A Dfs share uses a tree structure containing a root and Dfs links. To create a Dfs share, you must first create a Dfs root. Each Dfs root can have multiple Dfs links beneath it, each of which points to a shared folder on the network. The Dfs links of the Dfs root represent shared folders (*<computer_name>\ <share_name>*) that can be physically located on different file servers.

The following table describes the advantages of using Dfs:

Function	Advantages
Network administration	Dfs simplifies network administration. If a server fails, you can move a Dfs link from one server to another without users being aware of the change. All that is required to move a Dfs link is to modify the Dfs folder to refer to the new server location of the shared folders. Users continue to use the same Dfs path for the Dfs link.
Namespace	Clients access file resources by using a single namespace (the Dfs root), as opposed to mapping logical drive letters throughout the enterprise.
Memory overhead	Windows 2000 and Windows NT 4.0 clients use no additional memory because Dfs support is integrated with the Microsoft client redirector for both Windows 2000 and Windows NT 4.0. The Dfs Service for Microsoft Network Client must be installed on top of the Windows 9*x*-based Microsoft client redirector for this Windows 32-bit client to access a Dfs share. Without this service installed, Windows 9*x* clients can access standard shares that are Dfs links of a Dfs root share.
Server replacement	Administrators can replace file servers without affecting the namespace used by network clients simply by updating the path for the new server in the Distributed File System snap-in.

Function	Advantages
Load balancing and fault tolerance	Dfs provides a level of load balancing and fault tolerance since clients randomly select a physical server to connect to from the list of alternates returned by the Dfs server.
Extensibility	The Dfs namespace can be extended at any time to incorporate additional disk space or new business requirements.
Network permissions	Dfs preserves network permissions. No additional permissions or security are required because Dfs volumes use existing Windows 2000 file and directory permissions. ACLs on Windows 2000 fault tolerant replicas are replicated.
Client caching	Dfs clients cache frequently used network resources without experiencing delays locating servers. The first access to a new area of the Dfs tree will incur a slight performance loss (analogous to performing a Net Use command). Caching this data eliminates any performance penalty for subsequent accesses until the client is rebooted or the cache expires.
Internet Information Services (IIS) integration	Dfs works with IIS. Links made to other pages stored in Dfs will not have to be updated if the initial page is physically moved from one server to another, provided an administrator reconfigures Dfs accordingly. If the server hosting an Internet page is removed and the page is republished someplace else, the links on that page will not have to be reconfigured.

Limits of Dfs

The following table details the limitations of Dfs:

Description	Limit
Maximum number of characters per file path	260
Maximum number of alternates per volume	32
Maximum number of Dfs roots per server	1
Maximum number of Dfs roots per domain	Unlimited
Maximum number of volumes hosted in a domain or enterprise	Limited by system resources. Six thousand have been successfully tested in stand-alone roots.

Note The white paper "Distributed File System: A Logical View of Physical Storage" includes details about alternatives and other aspects of Dfs. See the Supplemental Course Materials CD (\chapt05\articles\Dfs New.doc) that accompanies this book.

Types of Dfs Roots

The Dfs Service is auto-installed with the installation of Windows 2000 Server. The service can be paused, stopped, and started but not removed from the operating system.

Two types of Dfs roots can be configured on Windows 2000 Servers: stand-alone Dfs roots and domain Dfs roots (sometimes called fault tolerant Dfs roots).

Stand-Alone Dfs Roots

The following characteristics are common to stand-alone Dfs roots:

- Stand-alone Dfs information is stored in the local registry.

- A stand-alone Dfs root permits a single level of Dfs links.

- When using the Distributed File System snap-in to connect to existing stand-alone Dfs roots, all servers known to the browse list are retrieved since there is no unique NetBIOS name registered by Dfs-enabled servers.

- Stand-alone Dfs roots can be located on all supported file systems, although locating resources on NTFS formatted partitions is recommended.

- Stand-alone Dfs roots offer no replication or backup; consequently, the Dfs root represents a single point of failure. You can create a replica from a stand-alone Dfs link; however, file replication services are not available.

Domain Dfs Roots

The following characteristics are common to Dfs fault-tolerant roots:

- In a domain Dfs root, multiple servers hand out referrals for the Dfs namespace. Fault tolerant Dfs roots use Active Directory services to store Dfs tree topology and remove the root as a single point of failure.

- A fault tolerant Dfs root is stored in Active Directory services and replicated to every participating Dfs root server. Changes to a Dfs tree are automatically synchronized with Active Directory services. This ensures that you can always restore a Dfs tree topology if the Dfs root is offline for any reason. You can also implement fault tolerance at the file and content level by assigning alternate resources to a Dfs volume. Any branch node on the Dfs tree can be serviced by a set of replicated resources. If a client connection to one alternate resource fails for any reason, the Dfs client attempts to connect to another. The Dfs client cycles through the alternates until an available one is found.

- Fault-tolerant roots must be located on NTFS version 5.0 formatted partitions.

- The list of domains and servers is populated by querying the global catalog for all fault-tolerant Dfs roots (ObjectClass = ftDfs).

- Dfs replication topology uses the existing Active Directory replication topology.

Configuring Dfs

Windows 2000 allows you to configure stand-alone Dfs roots, Dfs links, and domain Dfs roots.

Configuring a Stand-Alone Dfs Root

Stand-alone Dfs stores the Dfs topology on a single computer. This type of Dfs provides no fault tolerance if the computer that stores the Dfs topology or any of the shared folders that Dfs uses fails.

A stand-alone Dfs root is physically located on the server users initially connect to. The first step in setting up stand-alone Dfs is to create the Dfs root.

To create a stand-alone Dfs root, use the Distributed File System snap-in to start the New Dfs Root wizard. Figure 5.2 shows the Select The Dfs Root Type screen with the Create A Stand-Alone Dfs Root radio button selected.

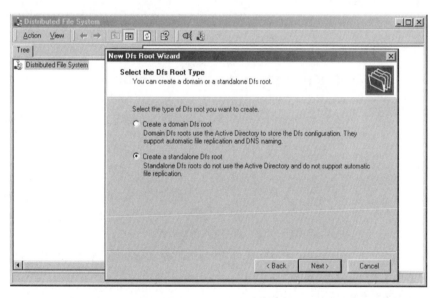

Figure 5.2 Creating a stand-alone Dfs root from the Distributed File System snap-in

The following table describes the screens within the wizard and what actions you can take to configure the new Dfs root:

Screen	Actions
Select The Dfs Root Type	Select the Create A Stand-Alone Dfs Root option (Figure 5.2).
Specify The Host Server For The Dfs Root	Enter the initial connection point for all resources in the Dfs tree. You can create a Dfs root on any computer running Windows 2000 Server.
Specify The Dfs Share	Enter a shared folder to host the Dfs root. You can choose an existing shared folder or create a new share.
Name The Dfs Root	Enter a descriptive name in the Comment text box for the Dfs root.
Completing The New Root wizard	Review the settings for the Host Server, Root Share, and Root Name text boxes. Click Back if changes are necessary or click Finish to complete the setup process.

Configuring a Domain Dfs Root

Domain Dfs writes the Dfs topology to the Active Directory store. This type of Dfs allows Dfs links to point to multiple identical shared folders (also called replicas) for fault tolerance. In addition, it supports DNS, multiple levels of child volumes, and file replication.

To create a fault-tolerant Dfs root, use the Distributed File System tool to start the New Dfs Root wizard.

Configuring New Dfs Links

Users can browse folders under a Dfs root without knowing where the referenced resources are physically located. After you create a Dfs root, you can create Dfs links (also known as child nodes).

To create a Dfs link, open the Distributed File System snap-in, and click the Dfs root to which you will attach a Dfs link. On the Action menu, click New Dfs Link. The Create A New Dfs Link dialog box appears, as shown in Figure 5.3.

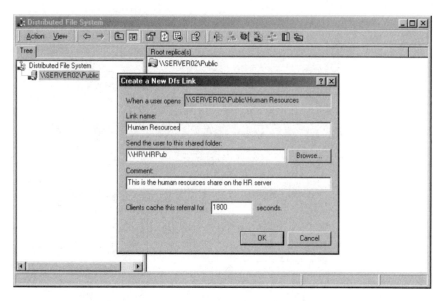

Figure 5.3 Creating a New Dfs Link off a public Dfs root for a human resources share

The following table describes the option in the dialog box:

Option	Description
Link Name	The name below the Dfs root that users will see when they connect to Dfs.
Send the user to this shared folder	The UNC name for the actual location of the shared folder the Dfs link refers to. Note that the Dfs host server must be able to access any shared folders referred to in a Dfs link.
Comment	Additional information (optional) to help keep track of the shared folder (for example, the actual name of the shared folder).
Clients cache this Dfs referral for *x* seconds	Length of time for which clients cache a referral to a Dfs link. After the referral time expires, a client queries the Dfs server about the location of the Dfs link, even if the client has previously established a connection with the Dfs link.

The Dfs link will appear below the Dfs root volume in the Distributed File System tool and will appear to a Dfs enabled client as a folder below the Dfs root. Figure 5.4 shows the appearance of a Dfs root named \\Server02\Public and a Dfs link on another server.

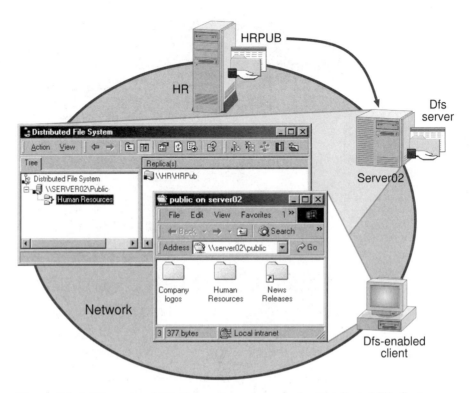

Figure 5.4 A Dfs root and Dfs link as they appear in the Distributed File System snap-in and how they appear on a Dfs-enabled client

Exercise 1: Creating a Dfs Root and Dfs Link

In this practice, you configure shares, create a stand-alone Dfs root, and then create Dfs links.

▶ **Procedure 1: Creating directories and shares**

In this procedure, you will create or use existing folders and create shares for the folders. You can use any method you prefer to create folders and shares or follow the steps in procedure 1.

1. Log on to Server01 as Administrator with a password of "password."

2. Open My Computer on the desktop.

   The My Computer window appears.

3. Open Local Disk (H:).

4. From the File menu, select New and then Folder.

   A folder named New Folder appears in the Local Disk (H:) window, and the blinking cursor appears inside the New Folder box.

5. Rename the folder "Public."

6. Select the Public folder, and from the File menu choose Sharing.

   The Public Properties dialog box appears.

7. Select the Share This Folder radio button, and in the Comment text box, type **Dfs root share**.

8. Click OK.

   The Public folder appears with a hand underneath the folder.

9. Repeat the last seven steps to create the folders and shares listed in the following table, using default permissions.

   Be aware that in some cases, the folders will be created on drive letters other than H:, and in one case a share will be created on Server02 to a folder that already exists.

Computer name	Drive	Folder	Share name	Purpose/ Comment
Server02	C:	\Inetpub\wwwroot	internal	Internal Web content
Server01	H:	\Press	Press	Current press releases
Server01	C:	\Inetpub\ftproot	ftproot	FTP root directory mapped partition
Server01	I:	\dev\TechDocs	TechDocs	Technical documents area
Server01	C:	\Public\Press	PressRepl	Current press releases replica

▶ **Procedure 2: Creating a stand-alone Dfs root on Server01**

In this procedure, you create a stand-alone Dfs root to host the shares created in procedure 1.

1. Click the Start button, point to Programs, point to Administrative Tools, and then click Distributed File System.

   The Distributed File System snap-in appears.

2. Read the message displayed in the right pane.

3. On the Action menu, click New Dfs Root.

   The New Dfs Root Wizard appears.

4. Read the information on the Welcome To The New Dfs Root Wizard, and then click Next.

5. On the Select The Dfs Root Type screen, notice that there are two types of Dfs you can create:

   A domain Dfs root that writes the Dfs tree topology to the Active Directory store and supports DNS, and file replication.

   A stand-alone Dfs root that does not use Active Directory services and does not support automatic file replication.

   Because you have not configured a domain controller at this point in your training, you will create a stand-alone Dfs root.

6. Select the Create A Stand-Alone Dfs Root radio button, and then click Next.

7. On the Specify The Host Server For The Dfs Root screen, confirm that SERVER01 is displayed, and then click Next.

   On the Specify The Dfs Root Share screen, you will specify a share you created in procedure 1.

   Notice that you can use an existing share for the Dfs root, or the wizard can create a new shared folder for you.

8. Verify that the Use An Existing Share radio button is selected, and then from the drop-down menu, select Public.

9. Click Next.

10. In the Comment text box appearing on the Name The Dfs Root screen, type **Public access share** and then click Next.

11. Review the settings appearing on the Completing The New Dfs Root Wizard screen, and then click Finish.

The Distributed File System snap-in appears and the Dfs root is configured on SERVER01 to Public.

▶ **Procedure 3: Creating Dfs links**

In the following procedure, you will create Dfs links below the \\SERVER01\Public Dfs root.

1. In the left pane of the Distributed File System snap-in, select \\SERVER01\Public.

2. Click on the Action menu, and notice that New Root Replica and Replication Policy are not available.

3. Click New Dfs Link.

The Create A New Dfs Link dialog box appears.

4. In the Link Name text box, type **intranet**.

5. Click Browse.

The Browse For Folder window appears.

6. Expand the + sign to the left of Computers Near Me.

7. Expand the + sign to the left of Server02, and then click internal and click OK.

The Send The User To This Shared Folder text box contains \\Server02\internal.

8. In the Comment text box, type **Internal Web content** and click OK.

9. Always begin this step by clicking on \\SERVER01\Public in the Distributed File System snap-in, and then repeat steps 3–8 to create new Dfs links using information in the following table:

Link name	Send the user to this shared folder	Comment
news	\\Server01\Press	Current Press Releases
ftp	\\Server01\ftproot	FTP Root Directory
tech	\\Server01\TechDocs	Technical Documents Area

Note Rather than browsing for a share, you can enter the server and share name using standard UNC syntax.

▸ **Procedure 4: Creating a Dfs Replica**

In the following procedure, you will create a replica of the News Dfs link. This Dfs link points to the H:\Press folder shared as Press, and the replica will be stored on C:\Public\Press folder, which is shared as PressRepl.

Note Because you created a stand-alone Dfs link, files must be manually copied or synchronized between the two folders. File replication services are not available for replicas created on a stand-alone Dfs link.

1. Select the News link in the left pane of the Distributed File System snap-in.

2. On the Action menu, click New Replica.

   The Add A New Replica dialog box appears.

3. In the Send The User To This Shared Folder text box, type **\\SERVER01\PressRepl**. Notice that no replication policy can be configured for this replica.

4. Click OK.

   In the right pane both the \\SERVER01\Press and \\SERVER01\PressRepl shares appear.

▸ **Procedure 5: Accessing the Dfs on Server01**

In this procedure, you will use the batch file provided with this course to copy files to Dfs links created in the previous procedures. After the files are copied, you will access the files through Windows Explorer.

Important The batch file included with this course will work properly only if both servers are running, the shares are created exactly as specified in this exercise, and the Administrator account password is "password" on both computers.

1. Insert the Windows 2000 Server Training Supplemental CD-ROM into the CD-ROM drive in Server01.

2. Open the CD-ROM drive from My Computer.

3. Open the \chapt05\ex1 folder

4. Click on the ex1copy.bat file, and from the File menu click Open.

   A command window will open as files are copied to the Dfs links, and then the command window will close.

   Complete all of the remaining steps in this procedure from Server02.

5. To access the stand-alone Dfs root on Server01 from Server02, open My Network Places and then open Computers Near Me.

    The Computers Near Me windows appears showing all computers in the workgroup.

6. Click on Server01, and from the File menu click Open.

    All shares and the Dfs root (Public) appear along with other objects on Server01. Notice that the Public folder appears like any share on Server01.

7. Click on the Public folder, and from the File menu click Open.

    The four Dfs links created in a previous procedure appear.

8. Open each folder and verify that the following files are present:

Folder	File(s)
ftp	dirmap.htm, dirmap.txt
intranet	Q240126 - Best Practices for Using Sysprep with NTFS Volumes.htm
news	press.wri
tech	Dfsnew.doc, RFS 1777.txt

    Note that the intranet folder will contain additional files since this folder points to a directory created during the installation of Windows 2000 Server.

9. Which folder represents a location on a server other than Server01?

10. Which folder represents a mounted drive to a previously empty folder?

11. Earlier in this exercise, you created a replica of the Press Dfs link. The name of that replica is \\SERVER01\PressRepl. This Dfs link is a shared folder by the name of PressRepl and is located in C:\Public\Press. If you examine the contents of this directory, you will notice that it is empty. However, when you view the News Dfs link, you will notice that there is a file named Press.wri. Why is the PressRepl Dfs replica empty?

Tip You can use the Distributed File System snap-in to check the status of the Dfs links and to open a window to the contents of the link.

Lesson Summary

Dfs provides a convenient way for users to access shared folders that are distributed throughout a network. A single Dfs shared folder, called a Dfs root, serves as an access point to other shared folders in the network, called Dfs links. Dfs organizes shared folders on different computers in a network into a single, logical, hierarchical file system. Dfs facilitates network navigation and administration while preserving network permissions. Two types of Dfs roots can be configured on Windows 2000 Servers: stand-alone Dfs roots and domain Dfs roots. Stand-alone Dfs stores the Dfs topology on a single computer. This type of Dfs provides no fault tolerance if the computer that stores the Dfs topology or any of the shared folders that Dfs uses fail. Domain Dfs writes the Dfs topology to the Active Directory store. This type of Dfs allows Dfs links to point to multiple identical shared folders and supports file replication for fault tolerance. In addition, it supports DNS and multiple levels of Dfs links. Dfs uses the FRS to replicate data in domain Dfs roots and domain Dfs links. When changes are made to a Dfs link that is part of a domain Dfs root, the changes are automatically replicated to other replica members.

Lesson 2: File Replication Service

FRS is the file replication service in Windows 2000 Server. It is used to copy and maintain files on multiple servers simultaneously and to replicate the Windows 2000 system volume (SYSVOL) on all domain controllers. In addition it can be configured to replicate data for domain Dfs roots.

After this lesson, you will be able to

- Describe what data can be replicated by FRS
- Configure replication for domain Dfs roots
- Describe the replication process in the Active Directory services and FRS

Estimated lesson time: 25 minutes

FRS Replication

FRS is installed automatically on all Windows 2000 Servers. It is configured to start automatically on all domain controllers and manually on all stand-alone and member servers. Although Active Directory replication and the FRS are independent of each other, they share a common replication topology, terminology, and methodology. In fact, the Active Directory store uses FRS to synchronize the directory among all domain controllers.

Each Windows 2000 domain has one or more servers that serve as domain controllers. Each domain controller stores a complete copy of Active Directory store for its domain and is involved in managing changes and updates to the directory.

Within a site, Active Directory services automatically generates a ring topology for replication among domain controllers in the same domain. The topology defines the path for directory updates to flow from one domain controller to another until all domain controllers receive the directory updates.

The ring structure ensures that there are at least two replication paths from one domain controller to another; if one domain controller is down temporarily, replication still continues to all other domain controllers.

Active Directory services uses multimaster replication, in which no one domain controller is the master; instead, all domain controllers within a domain are equivalent.

Active Directory services periodically analyzes the replication topology within a site to ensure that it is still efficient. If you add or remove a domain controller from the network or a site, Active Directory services reconfigures the topology to reflect the change.

Sites and Replication

A site is made up of one or more IP subnets that identify a group of well-connected computers. Only those subnets that share fast and reliable network connections of at least 512 kilobits per second (Kbps) should be combined.

Domain structure and site structure are maintained separately in Active Directory services. A single domain can include multiple sites, and a single site can include multiple domains or parts of multiple domains, as shown in Figure 5.5.

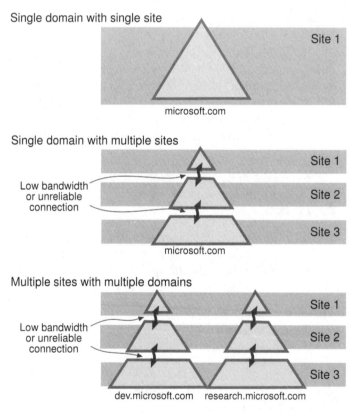

Figure 5.5 A single domain with a single site, a single domain with multiple sites, and multiple sites with multiple domains

There are two types of replication: intra-site replication and inter-site replication.

Intra-Site Replication

Intra-site replication has the following characteristics:

- Intra-site replication occurs between domain controllers within a site.
- Replicated data is not compressed.
- The default replication interval is 5 minutes.
- Replication is *trigger-based,* that is, notification and pull.

Inter-Site Replication

Inter-site replication has the following characteristics:

- Inter-site replication occurs between domain controllers in different sites.
- You can specify the time when inter-site replication should occur. The default replication interval is 3 hours.
- You can specify the network transport for use in inter-site replication.
- Inter-site replication is compressed, regardless of the transport used.
- Inter-site replication compression reduces the data on the network by 88 to 90 percent.

One disadvantage to inter-site replication is that it is not configured automatically; it must be configured by an administrator.

Knowledge Consistency Checker

Within a site, a process called the Knowledge Consistency Checker (KCC) generates a ring topology for replication among domain controllers in the same domain. The generated topology defines paths for directory updates to flow from one domain controller to another until all domain controllers have received the directory updates.

This ring structure guarantees that there are at least two replication paths from one domain controller to another, ensuring that if one domain controller is temporarily down, replication will continue to all other domain controllers. In addition, the ring structure is created such that an update takes, at most, three "hops" from the domain controller where it originates to any other domain controller in the site.

The KCC periodically analyzes the replication topology within a site to ensure that the replication topology is efficient. If a domain controller is added or removed from the network or a site, the KCC reconfigures the topology to reflect the change.

Note Administrators can make modifications to the replication topology, including changing the schedule for inter-site replication, to meet the requirements of an organization.

Unique Sequence Numbers

When a directory object is updated at a domain controller, either through a change that a user or administrator makes or by replication from another domain controller, the domain controller assigns the change a Unique Sequence Number (USN). Each domain controller maintains its own USNs and applies USNs incrementally to each directory change made at the domain controller.

When the domain controller writes the change into the directory, it also writes the USN of the change with the property.

Each domain controller maintains a table of the USNs that it receives from every other domain controller in the domain, and the table lists the highest USN that is received from each domain controller. Each domain controller then periodically notifies the other domain controllers in the domain that it has received changes and sends its current USN. Each domain controller that receives this message checks its USN table for the last USN that it received from the sending domain controller. If there are changes and the domain controller has not received them, it requests that only the changes be sent.

Using USNs eliminates the need for precise timestamps for changes and for time to be synchronized precisely among domain controllers within a domain. However, timestamps are still applied to directory changes for tie breaking.

The use of USNs also simplifies recovery after a failure. When a domain controller is running again after a failure, it restarts replication by asking each of the other domain controllers for changed USNs greater than the last USN in the table for that domain controller. Because the table is updated automatically as the change is applied, interrupted replication cycles pick up exactly where they left off, with no loss or duplication of updates.

Implementing FRS

Implementation of FRS consists of several phases: replicating SYSVOL, replicating domain Dfs roots, and configuring FRS for inter-site replication.

Replicating SYSVOL

Changes to the %systemroot%\SYSVOL directory on any domain controller are automatically replicated to the other domain controllers within the site. The replication topology and process is separate but identical to Active Directory replication. When an administrator adds, removes, or modifies the contents of %systemroot%\SYSVOL folder on any domain controller, those changes will be replicated to the other domain controllers within the site automatically.

The default folder structure is as follows:

- %systemroot%\SYSVOL\Sysvol*domain_name*\Policies
- %systemroot%\SYSVOL\Sysvol*domain_name*\Scripts

Any files and folders added to %systemroot%\SYSVOL\Sysvol*domain_name* are automatically replicated.

Replicating Dfs Fault Tolerant Roots

Dfs uses FRS to replicate data in domain Dfs links. When changes are made to a domain Dfs link that is part of a domain Dfs root, the changes are automatically replicated to other replica members.

Dfs and file replication support the following features:

- Multimaster replication replicates modified files and modified ACLs when a file is closed.
- Files can be modified on any replica member.
- Only Windows 2000 NTFS volumes have the potential to replicate. Other shares can be published as alternates, but no replication occurs.
- Replication is journal based.
- Replication is Remote Procedure Call (RPC) based.
- FRS topology follows Active Directory replication topology.

The process of Dfs replication consists of a number of steps:

1. A file changes. This is noted when a user closes a file.

2. NTFS makes an entry in the NTFS Change Log.

3. FRS monitors the NTFS journal for changes to Dfs links.

4. FRS makes an entry into its own journal.

5. FRS generates a staging file of the file change.

6. FRS holds on to changes until scheduled to replicate.

7. The destination pulls the staging file and applies the new files.

Adding Replica Dfs Root Servers

Each Dfs root or link can reference a replicated set of shared resources. Dfs clients will automatically select the nearest replica based on site topology information.

To add Dfs replica servers to a Dfs domain root or link, right-click the Dfs root in the Distributed File System Manager tool, click New, and then click Root Replica. Enter the UNC path for the replica server and share.

Enabling Dfs Replication

Dfs replication is disabled by default. To enable replication, right-click the Dfs root or Dfs link in the Distributed File System snap-in, and then select Replication Policy. Highlight every server in the replica set that you want to participate in FRS replication, and click the Enable button. Servers that do not participate in replication will have to be synchronized manually.

Configuring FRS for Inter-Site Replication

You can configure inter-site replication by using the Active Directory Sites and Services snap-in. To configure the FRS settings, you must create a new site link for the inter-site transport protocol listed in the console tree. Once you've created the site link, right-click the site link object and click Properties. The Properties dialog box opens. You can now configure the inter-site replication as necessary.

Lesson Summary

FRS is the automatic file replication service in Windows 2000 Server. It copies and maintains files on multiple servers. There are two types of replication: intra-site replication and inter-site replication. Sites are defined as one or more subnets that identify a group of well-connected computers. Within a site, a process called KCC automatically generates a ring topology for replication among domain controllers in the same domain. Implementing FRS consists of several phases, including replicating SYSVOL, replicating domain Dfs roots, and configuring FRS.

Note Domain Dfs roots and FRS will be installed in the next chapter after Active Directory services are running.

Review

The following questions are intended to reinforce key information presented in this chapter. If you are unable to answer a question, review the appropriate lesson and then try the question again. Answers to the questions can be found in Appendix A, "Questions and Answers."

1. How does a mounted drive to an empty folder differ from a Dfs root?

2. In Exercise 1, you were asked to notice that New Root Replica and Replication Policy were not available options in the Distributed File System snap-in. Explain why these options are not available.

3. Why doesn't Dfs directly provide a security infrastructure?

4. How is the KCC involved in maintaining Active Directory store synchronization between domain controllers?

5. What data does the FRS replicate?

C H A P T E R   6

Active Directory Services

About This Chapter

In Chapter 1, "Introduction to Microsoft Windows 2000," you were introduced to the basic concepts of Microsoft Active Directory services. This included a discussion of several Active Directory features, such as scalability and open standards support, and continued with a discussion of the logical and physical structures of the Active Directory store. Chapter 6 provides more details about Active Directory concepts and Active Directory architecture. The chapter then describes how to plan for the implementation of Active Directory services in your Microsoft Windows 2000 environment and how to perform that implementation. Finally, the chapter discusses the administration of Active Directory services once it has been implemented in a Windows 2000 environment.

Before You Begin

To complete the lessons in this chapter, you must have

- Windows 2000 Server installed and running on Server01 as described in Chapter 2, Exercise 1.
- Computer 2 networked to Server01 and be running Windows 2000 Server, as described in Chapter 3, Exercise 1.
- The Windows 2000 Server installation CD-ROM.

Lesson 1: Overview of Active Directory Services

Active Directory services is the directory service included with Windows 2000 Server. It extends the functionality of previous Windows-based directory services and adds new features. Active Directory services is secure, distributed, partitioned, and replicated. It is designed to work well in any size installation, from a single server with a few hundred objects to thousands of servers with millions of objects. Active Directory services adds many new features that make it easy to navigate and manage large amounts of information, saving time for both administrators and end users.

After this lesson, you will be able to

- Describe the concepts and architecture of Active Directory services

Estimated lesson time: 40 minutes

Introduction to Active Directory Services

Active Directory services is completely integrated with Windows 2000 Server and offers the hierarchical view, extensibility, scalability, and distributed security required by all business customers. Active Directory services allows administrators, developers, and end users to gain access to a directory service that is seamlessly integrated with both Internet and intranet environments. Active Directory services is a critical part of the distributed system. It allows administrators and end users to use the directory service as a source of information as well as an administrative service.

Active Directory services integrates the Internet concept of namespace with the operating system's directory service. A *namespace* is a structured collection of information in which names can be used to symbolically represent another type of information, such as a host name representing an IP address, and in which specific rules are established that determine how names can be created and used. The integration of the concept of namespace with the directory services allows enterprises to unify and manage the multiple namespaces that now exist in the heterogeneous software and hardware environments of corporate networks. Active Directory services uses the Lightweight Directory Access Protocol (LDAP) as its core protocol and can work across operating system boundaries, integrating multiple namespaces. It can manage application-specific directories, as well as other NOS-based directories, to provide a general-purpose directory that can reduce the administrative burden and costs associated with maintaining multiple namespaces.

Active Directory services is not an X.500 directory. Instead, it uses LDAP as the access protocol and supports the X.500 information model without requiring systems to host the entire X.500 overhead. The result is a high level of interoperability that supports real-world heterogeneous networks.

Note For information on how LDAP uses X.500, see the Supplemental Course Materials CD-ROM (\chapt01\articles\RFC 1777.txt) that accompanies this book.

Active Directory services allows a single point of administration for all published resources, such as files, peripheral devices, host connections, databases, Web access, users, services, and other objects. It uses the Internet Domain Name System (DNS) as its locator service, organizes objects in domains into a hierarchy of organizational units (OUs), and allows multiple domains to be connected to a tree structure. Administration is further simplified because there is no primary domain controller (PDC)/backup domain controller (BDC) structure, as was implemented in Windows NT Server. Instead, Active Directory services uses domain controllers only, and all domain controllers are peers. An administrator can make changes to any domain controller, and the updates will be replicated to all other domain controllers.

Note For further information about Active Directory features, concepts, and architecture, see the Supplemental Course Materials CD-ROM that accompanies this book. The \chapt06\articles folder includes three articles that expand on this material: Managing the Active Directory.doc, Active_Directory_Technical_Summary.doc, and Active_Directory_DS_Strategy.doc.

Understanding Active Directory Concepts

There are several new concepts introduced with Active Directory services. Some of these concepts might be familiar, while others have meanings that differ from traditional usage. This section describes several of these concepts, including extensible schema, the global catalog, namespace, and naming conventions.

Extensible Schema

The Active Directory schema contains a formal definition of the contents and structure of the Active Directory store, including all attributes, classes, and class properties. For each object class, the *schema* defines what attributes an instance of the class must have, what additional attributes it can have, and what object class can be a parent of the current object class.

Installing Active Directory services on the first domain controller in a network creates a default schema. The default schema contains definitions of commonly used objects and properties, such as users, computers, printers, and groups. The default schema also contains definitions of objects and properties that Active Directory services uses internally to function.

The Active Directory schema is extensible, which means that you can define new directory object types and attributes and new attributes for existing objects. The schema is implemented and stored within the Active Directory store itself (in the global catalog) and can be updated dynamically. Therefore, an application can extend the schema with new attributes and classes, and it can use the extensions immediately.

Extending the Schema

Extending the Active Directory schema is an advanced operation intended to be performed by experienced programmers and system administrators. Before modifying the schema, see Windows 2000 Server Help and the *Active Directory Programmer's Guide* at *http://msdn.microsoft.com/developer/windows2000/ adsi/actdirguide.asp*. If this URL doesn't access the Active Directory Programmer's Guide, visit *http://msdn.microsoft.com* and search for the title *Active Directory Programmer's Guide*. The *Active Directory Programmer's Guide* includes detailed information about each method of extending Active Directory schema as well as sample scripts and examples of programming code.

Warning Extending the schema is a highly sensitive operation, with implications potentially throughout your network. Schema extension is best handled programmatically and only when absolutely necessary. Improper schema modifications can impair or disable Windows 2000 Server and possibly your entire network.

Global Catalog

The *global catalog* is the central repository of information about objects in a domain tree (a collection of domains that form a domain hierarchy) or forest (a collection of domain trees that are part of different hierarchies). Active Directory services generates the contents of the global catalog from the domains that are part of the directory via the normal replication process. The Active Directory replication system automatically builds the global catalog and generates the replication topology.

The global catalog is a service as well as a physical storage location that contains a replica of selected attributes of every object in the Active Directory store. The process of partial replication allows many common queries to be resolved from the global catalog without requiring a lookup in the source domain. By default, the attributes stored in the global catalog are those most frequently used in search operations (such as a user's first and last names, login name, and so forth) and those necessary to locate a full replica of the object. Consequently, you can use the global catalog to locate objects anywhere in the network without replicating all domain information between domain controllers.

Note You can use the Active Directory Schema snap-in to define which attributes are included in the global catalog replication process. This snap-in is contained in %systemroot%\system32 and is named Schmmgmt.msc. Caution should be exercised when using this tool. Only experienced programmers or advanced administrators who understand the schema and how it functions should use this tool.

When you are installing Active Directory services on the first domain controller, that domain controller is, by default, a global catalog server. A global catalog server is a domain controller that stores a copy of the global catalog. The configuration of the initial global catalog server should have the capacity to support several hundred thousand to one million objects, with the potential for growth.

Additional domain controllers can also be designated as global catalog servers by using the Active Directory Sites and Services snap-in. When considering which domain controllers to designate as global catalog servers, you should base the decision on the ability of the network structure to handle replication and query traffic. The more global catalog servers, the greater the replication traffic. However, the availability of additional servers can provide quicker responses to user inquiries. It is recommended that every major site in the enterprise have a global catalog server.

Namespace

Active Directory services, like all directory services, is primarily a namespace. A namespace is any bounded area in which a name can be resolved. Name resolution is the process of translating a name into some object or information that the name represents. The Active Directory namespace is based on the DNS naming scheme, which allows for interoperability with Internet technologies. An example namespace is shown in Figure 6.1.

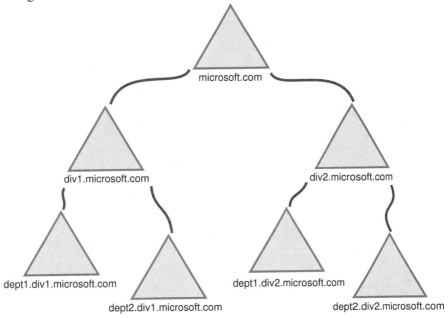

Figure 6.1 Namespace diagram of a sample domain

Using a common namespace allows you to unify and manage multiple hardware and software environments in your network. There are two types of namespaces:

- **Contiguous namespace** The name of the child object in an object hierarchy always contains the name of the parent domain. A tree is a contiguous namespace.

- **Disjointed namespace** The names of a parent object and a child of the same parent object are not directly related to each other. A forest is a disjointed namespace.

Naming Conventions

Every object in the Active Directory store is identified with a name. Active Directory services uses a variety of naming conventions: distinguished names, relative distinguished names, globally unique identifiers, and user principal names. Active Directory services is an LDAP-compliant directory service, which means that all access to directory objects occurs through LDAP. LDAP requires that names of directory objects are Request for Comments (RFC)–compliant, which defines the standard for object names in an LDAP directory service.

Distinguished Name

Objects are located within Active Directory domains according to a hierarchical path, which includes the labels of the Active Directory domain name and each level of container objects. Every object in the Active Directory store has a *distinguished name* (DN). The DN uniquely identifies an object and contains sufficient information for a client to retrieve the object from the directory. The DN includes the name of the domain that holds the object, as well as the complete path through the container hierarchy to the object.

The following example is a DN that identifies the James Smith user object in the microsoft.com domain:

    CN=James Smith, CN=Users, DC=Microsoft, DC=COM

The delimiters and values used in the DN for James Smith are identified in the following table:

LDAP Delimiter	Value	Represents
DC	COM	Domain component
DC	Microsoft	Domain component
CN	Users	Common name
CN	James Smith	Common name

Note that the Active Directory snap-in tools do not display the LDAP abbreviations (O=, DC=, CN=). These abbreviations are shown only to illustrate how LDAP recognizes the portions of the distinguished name. Some of the naming attributes described in the RFCs, such as O= for Organization Name and C= for Country Name, are not used in Active Directory services, although they are recognized by LDAP.

Note To read more about distinguished names, see the Supplemental Course Materials CD-ROM (\chapt06\articles\rfc1779.txt) that accompanies this book.

Relative Distinguished Name

In Active Directory services, you can search for an object even if you don't know the exact DN or if the DN has changed. This can be accomplished by querying an object's attributes. One of an object's attributes is its *relative distinguished name* (RDN), which is a part of the full DN name. In the preceding example, the RDN of the James Smith user object is CN=James Smith. The RDN of the parent object is CN=Users.

Active Directory services allows duplicate RDNs for objects, but no two objects with the same RDN can exist within the same OU. For example, if an OU contains a James Smith user account, you could not add another James Smith user to it. However, if the OU contains two smaller OUs, such as Managers and Sales, the Managers OU can contain a James Smith user account and the Sales OU can contain a James Smith user account because each of these accounts would have a different DN.

Globally Unique Identifier

In addition to its distinguished name, every object in the Active Directory store has a unique identity. Objects might be moved or renamed, but their identity never changes. The identity of an object is defined by a *globally unique identifier* (GUID), a 128-bit number that is assigned by the Directory System Agent (DSA) when the object is created. Unlike a distinguished name or a relative distinguished name, a GUID never changes, even if you move or rename the object. Applications can store the GUID of an object and be assured of retrieving that object regardless of its current DN.

In Windows NT, domain resources were associated to a security identifier (SID), which was generated within the domain. This meant that the SID was guaranteed to be unique only within the domain. A GUID is unique across all domains; you can move objects from domain to domain, and they will still have a unique identifier.

The GUID is stored in an attribute, objectGUID, that is present on every object. The objectGUID attribute is protected so that it cannot be altered or removed. When you store a reference to an Active Directory object in an external store (for example, a Microsoft SQL Server database), the objectGUID value should be used. Figure 6.2 shows the properties of the objectGUID attribute.

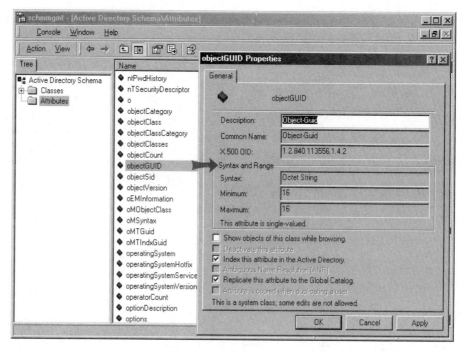

Figure 6.2 The objectGUID attribute as it appears in the Active Directory Schema Management snap-in

User Principal Name

A *user principal name* (UPN) is a friendly name that is shorter than the DN and easier to remember. The UPN consists of a shorthand name that represents the user and usually the DNS name of the domain where the user object resides. The UPN format is the user name, the "@" character, plus a user principal name suffix. For example, user James Smith in the microsoft.com tree might have a UPN of username@microsoft.com. The user principal name is independent of the distinguished name of the user object, so a user object can be moved or renamed without affecting the user logon name. The user principal name is an attribute (userPrincipalName) of the security principal object.

Active Directory Architecture

The structure of Active Directory services can be broken into several primary architectural components: the data model, schema, security model, and administration model.

Data Model

The Active Directory data model is derived from the X.500 data model. The directory holds objects that represent various components of the network, and each of the objects is described by attributes. The collection of objects that can be stored in the directory is defined in the schema.

Schema

The Active Directory schema is implemented as a set of object class instances stored in the directory. The schema can be updated dynamically. That is, an application can extend the schema with new attributes and classes and can use the extensions immediately. Schema updates are accomplished by creating or modifying the schema objects stored in the directory. Like every object in the Active Directory store, schema objects are protected by access control lists (ACLs), so only authorized users may alter the schema.

Security Model

The directory is part of the Windows 2000 Trusted Computing Base and is a full participant in the Windows 2000 security infrastructure. The *Trusted Computing Base* is the set of operating system components responsible for enforcing the security policies of the operating system. ACLs protect all objects in the Active Directory store. The Windows 2000 access validation routines use the ACL to validate any attempt to access an object or attribute in the Active Directory store.

Administration Model

Authorized users perform administration in Active Directory services. A user is authorized by a higher authority to perform a specified set of actions on a specified set of object instances and object classes in some identified subtree of the directory. This is called delegated administration. Delegated administration allows granular control over who can do what and enables delegation of authority without granting elevated privileges.

The DSA is the process that manages the directory's physical storage. Clients use one of the supported interfaces to connect to the DSA and then search for read and write directory objects and their attributes. The DSA provides client isolation from the physical storage format of the directory data. This provides convenient access while enhancing system security.

Access to Active Directory services

Access to Active Directory services is via wire protocols. Wire protocols define the formats of messages and interactions of client and server. Various application programming interfaces (APIs) give developers access to these protocols.

Protocol Support

Active Directory services supports the following protocols:

- **LDAP** The Active Directory core protocol is the LDAP. LDAP version 2 and version 3 are supported.

- **MAPI-RPC** Active Directory services supports the remote procedure call (RPC) interfaces supporting the Messaging Application Program Interface (MAPI) interfaces.

- **X.500** The Active Directory information model is derived from the X.500 information model. X.500 defines several wire protocols that Active Directory services does not implement, in part because of their dependence on the OSI network protocol:

    - Directory Access Protocol (DAP)

    - Directory System Protocol (DSP)

    - Directory Information Shadowing Protocol (DISP)

    - Directory Operational Binding Management Protocol (DOP)

Application Programming Interfaces

Active Directory services provides powerful, flexible, and easy-to-use APIs. The availability of a rich set of APIs for the directory service encourages the development of applications and tools that make use of the directory's services.

Active Directory Service Interfaces

To make it easier to write directory-enabled applications that access Active Directory services and other LDAP-enabled directories, Microsoft developed

Active Directory Service Interfaces (ADSI). ADSI is a set of extensible, easy-to-use programming interfaces that can be used to write applications to access and manage the following:

- Active Directory services

- Any LDAP-based directory

- Other directory services in a customer's network, including Novell Directory Services (NDS)

ADSI is part of the Open Directory Services Interfaces (ODSI) and Windows Open Services Architecture (WOSA). ADSI objects are available for Windows NT 4.0, Novell NetWare 3.*x* and 4.*x*, and Active Directory services, as well as any other directory service that supports the LDAP protocol.

ADSI extracts the capabilities of directory services from different network providers to present a single set of directory service interfaces for managing network resources. This greatly simplifies the development of distributed applications as well as the administration of distributed systems. Developers and administrators use this single set of directory service interfaces to enumerate and manage the resources in a directory service, no matter which network environment contains the resource. Thus, ADSI makes it easier to perform common administrative tasks, such as adding new users, managing printers, and locating resources throughout the distributed computing environment. ADSI also makes it easy for developers to make their applications directory-enabled.

ADSI objects are designed to meet the needs of three main audiences:

- **Developers** Typically, this audience will use ADSI with a compiled language such as C++, although Microsoft Visual Basic can be used for prototyping the application. For example, a developer could write an application to manage multiple directories, network printing, back up databases, and so on.

- **System administrators** Typically, this audience will access ADSI through a scripting language, such as Microsoft Visual Basic, although C/C++ can also be used to enhance performance. For example, with Active Directory services an administrator could write a script to add 100 new users to the system and establish them as members of selected security groups.

- **Users** Like the system administrators, this audience will access ADSI through a scripting language. For example, a user might write a script to locate all print jobs in a group of print queues and display the status of each.

LDAP C API

The LDAP C API provides a lowest common denominator solution for developers who need their applications to work on many different client types. Similarly, existing LDAP applications will run against Active Directory services with little or no modification beyond extending the application to support object types unique to Active Directory services. Developers of LDAP applications are encouraged to migrate to ADSI, which supports any LDAP-enabled directory services.

Windows Messaging API

Active Directory services provides support for MAPI so that legacy MAPI applications will continue to work with Active Directory services. However, developers of new applications are encouraged to use ADSI to build their directory-enabled applications.

Virtual Containers

Active Directory services supports virtual containers, which allow any LDAP-compliant directory to be accessed transparently via Active Directory services. The virtual container is implemented via location information stored in the Active Directory store. The location information describes where in the Active Directory store the foreign directory should appear and contains the DNS name of a server holding a copy of the actual directory and the DN at which to begin search operations in the foreign DS.

Directory Service Architecture

Active Directory functionality can be illustrated as a layered architecture in which the layers represent the server processes that provide directory services to client applications (see Figure 6.3). The Active Directory architecture consists of three service layers and several interfaces and protocols that work together to provide directory services. The three service layers (DSA, Database Layer, and Extensible Storage Engine) accommodate the different types of information that are required to locate records in the directory database. Above the service layers in this architecture are the protocols and APIs that enable communication between clients and the directory service.

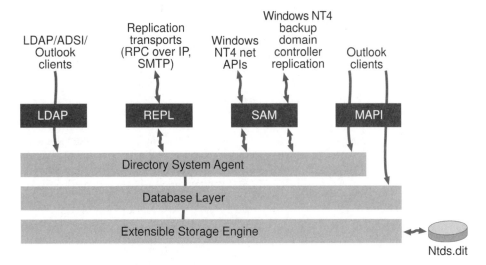

Figure 6.3 Active Directory services architecture

Active Directory services architecture includes the following key service components:

- **Directory System Agent (DSA)** Builds a hierarchy from the parent-child relationships stored in the directory. Provides APIs for directory access calls.

- **Database Layer** Provides an abstraction layer between applications and the database. Calls from applications are never made directly to the database; they go through the database layer.

- **Extensible Storage Engine (ESE)** Communicates directly with individual records in the directory data store on the basis of the object's RDN attribute.

- **Data store (the database file Ntds.dit)** This file is manipulated only by the Extensible Storage Engine (ESE) database engine. You can administer the file by using the Ntdsutil tool.

Note Ntdsutil.exe is installed in %systemroot%\system32 when Windows 2000 Server is installed.

The Interfaces

Clients obtain access to Active Directory services by using mechanisms that are supported by the DSA. The following table provides a description of each of these mechanisms:

Interface	Description
LDAP	Provides the API for LDAP clients and exposes the ADSI so that additional applications can be written that can talk to the Active Directory services. Clients that support LDAP use it to connect to the directory system agent. Active Directory services supports LDAP version 3 and LDAP version 2. Windows 2000 clients, as well as Windows 9x clients that have the Active Directory client components installed, use LDAP version 3 to connect to the DSA. ADSI is a means of abstracting the LDAP API; however, only LDAP is used by Active Directory services.
REPL	Used by the replication service to facilitate Active Directory replication via RPC over IP or Simple Mail Transport Protocol (SMTP), a part of the TCP/IP protocol suite. SMTP can be used only for intersite replication (between sites); RPC over IP replication is used for both intrasite and intersite replication.
SAM	Provides down-level compatibility to facilitate communication between Windows 2000 and Windows NT 4.0 domains. Windows clients that use Windows NT 4.0 or earlier use the SAM interface to connect to the DSA. Replication from backup domain controllers in a mixed-mode domain goes through the SAM interface as well.
MAPI	Legacy MAPI clients, such as Microsoft Outlook messaging and collaboration client, connect to the DSA by using the MAPI RPC address book provider interface.

Directory System Agent

The DSA is the Active Directory process that runs on each domain controller and manages all the directory service functions. This process manages the directory's physical storage. Clients use one of the supported interfaces to connect to the DSA and then search for read and write directory objects and their attributes. The DSA provides client isolation from the physical storage format of the directory data.

The DSA provides access to the store, which is the database file containing directory information located on a hard disk. DSA is an X.500 term that describes the server-side process that creates an instance of a directory service, that is, applications binding to a DSA.

The DSA layer exposes interfaces to support the following set of core operations:

Object Identification

Every object in the Active Directory store has a permanent GUID associated with a string form of the object name. The object name is not permanent; it can be changed. All permanent references to the object are kept in terms of the GUID; the object name is used for hierarchy navigation and for display. The DSA maintains the GUID association with an object when the object's DN changes.

Transaction Processing

Transactions are processed automatically. A write request either commits, and all of its effects are durable, or it fails before completion and has no effect. Transactions are written synchronously to the transaction log file and then to the database.

Schema Enforcement of Updates

The duplication and synchronization of directory information is known as *multimaster replication*. In a multimaster system, a change to a schema object in one replica might conflict with existing objects in that replica and also with objects in other replicas. The schema is a formal definition of every object class that can be created in the directory, the attributes of each object class, and the possible parents for every object class. In Windows 2000, schema change is a *single-master operation*, which means that any change you make on the master is updated on all other replicas. Replicated updates do not perform any schema checks. Making the replicas of an object consistent with one another is the primary goal; making them consistent with a changing schema is secondary.

Access Control Enforcement

The DSA enforces security limitations in the directory. The DSA layer reads SIDs on the access token.

Support for Replication

The DSA contains the hooks for replication notifications. All object updates ultimately must go through the appropriate function for the directory service to work properly.

Referrals

DSA manages the directory hierarchy information (referred to as knowledge), that it receives from the database layer. DSA is responsible for cross-references of Active Directory domain objects up and down the hierarchy and also out to other domain hierarchies.

Database Layer

The database layer provides an object view of database information by applying schema semantics to database records, thereby isolating the upper layers of the directory service from the underlying database system. The database layer is an internal interface that is not exposed to the public. No database access calls are made directly to the ESE; instead, all database access is routed through the database layer.

Active Directory services provides a hierarchical namespace. Each object is uniquely identified in the database by its individual naming attribute, called the RDN. The RDN and the chain of successive parent object names make up the object's DN. The database stores the RDN for each object as well as a reference to the parent object. The database layer follows these parent references and concatenates the successive RDNs to form DNs.

A major function of the database layer is to translate each DN into an integer structure called the DN tag, which is used for all internal accesses. The database layer guarantees the uniqueness of the DN tag for each database record.

All data that describes an object is held as a set of attributes, which are stored as columns in the database. The database layer is responsible for the creation, retrieval, and deletion of individual records, attributes within records, and values within attributes. To carry out these functions, the database layer uses the schema cache (an in-memory structure in the DSA) to get information about the attributes that it needs.

Extensible Storage Engine

Active Directory services is implemented on top of an Indexed Sequential Access Method (ISAM) table manager. An earlier version of this table manager, called the JET database, is used by Microsoft Exchange Server version 5.5 client-server messaging and groupware, the File Replication Service, the security configuration editor, the certificate server, Windows Internet Name Service (WINS), and various other Windows components. Windows 2000 has a new and improved version of the JET database, the ESE.

The ESE (Esent.dll) implements a transacted database system that uses log files to ensure that committed transactions are indeed safe. Thus, the directory service uses both data files (Ntds.dit) and log files. By default, Esent.dll and Ntds.dit are stored in the %systemroot%\system32 folder.

The ESE stores all Active Directory objects. The ESE can support a database of up to 16 TB in size, which can theoretically hold many millions of objects per domain.

The ESE is well suited to the storage needs of Active Directory services:

- The ESE update operations are transacted for stability and integrity across system failures.
- The ESE handles sparse rows well, that is, rows in which many of the properties do not have values.

Active Directory services comes with a predefined schema that defines all the attributes required and allowed for a given object. The ESE reserves storage only for the space used—that is, only for the attributes assigned to an object, not for all possible attributes. For example, if a user object already has 50 attributes defined in the schema and you create a user with only four attributes; storage space is allocated only for those four attributes. If more attributes are added later, more storage is allocated for them.

Also, the ESE is able to store attributes that can have multiple values. For example, the database can store multiple phone numbers for a single user without requiring a different phone number attribute for each phone number.

Active Directory services is a functional superset of the Exchange Server directory service; it offers additional functionality, such as rename-safe objects, a dynamically extensible schema, and per-attribute replication and reconciliation. Esent.dll implements the search and retrieval functionality of the underlying database.

Lesson Summary

Active Directory services offers the hierarchical view, extensibility, scalability, and distributed security required by all business customers. Active Directory services integrates the Internet concept of namespace with the operating system's directory service. It uses the LDAP as its core protocol and can work across operating system boundaries, integrating multiple namespaces. The Active Directory schema contains a formal definition of the contents and structure of the Active Directory store, including all attributes, classes, and class properties. The global catalog, which is the central repository of information about objects in a tree or a forest, is a service and a physical storage location that contains a replica of selected attributes of every object in the Active Directory store. Active Directory services, like all directory services, is primarily a namespace, and every object in the Active Directory store is identified with a name. The structure of Active Directory services can be broken into several primary architectural components, namely the data model, schema, security model, and administration model. Access to Active Directory services is via wire protocols that define the formats of messages and interactions of client and server. Active Directory architecture consists of three service layers and several interfaces and protocols that work together to provide directory services.

Lesson 2: Planning Active Directory Implementation

Before you implement a Windows 2000 network environment, you should first consider how to implement Active Directory services. Your planning should take into account the business structure and operation of your organization, such as physical office locations, future growth and reorganization, and access to network resources. There are several aspects of the Active Directory implementation that are part of the planning process. First, you must plan the DNS namespace. The namespace includes a domain hierarchy, the global catalog, trust relationships, and replication. In addition, the namespace includes OUs, which must also be considered in the planning process. In a single domain, users and resources can be organized by using a hierarchy of OUs to reflect the structure of the company. Finally, the planning process for the Active Directory implementation must include a plan to establish sites that can effectively facilitate the management of replication and logon traffic over links in your enterprise.

After this lesson, you will be able to

- Plan a namespace, a site, and organizational units in preparation for an Active Directory implementation

Estimated lesson time: 75 minutes

Planning a Namespace

Similar to DNS, the Active Directory namespace is the top-level fully qualified domain name for a company consisting of Windows 2000 domains, domain controllers, OUs, trust relationships, and domain trees. One of the decisions you will need to make when implementing Active Directory services is whether the internal namespace (inside the firewall) or the external namespace (outside the firewall) will be the same or separate. Simply put, will the Active Directory namespace match the DNS namespace (typically the Internet domain name) that might already be defined for your organization?

For example, the existing, external DNS namespace for your company might be microsoft.com. You can choose an Active Directory namespace that matches microsoft.com, or you can choose a different internal namespace. Each has its advantages and disadvantages, as will be discussed later in this lesson.

Note This is not to say that DNS is an external namespace only. The point is that, if the namespaces are separate, Active Directory services will be administered separately from the external namespace.

Internal and External Namespaces

A namespace is the top-level Active Directory domain name for an organization. To implement Active Directory services, there are primarily two choices for namespace design. The Active Directory namespace can be either the same or separate from the established, registered external DNS namespace.

This section provides two scenarios, one in which the namespaces are the same and another in which they are different. In the first scenario, where the internal and external namespaces are the same, the same top-level domain appears on both sides of the firewall. Private users of the corporate network and public users of the Internet see microsoft.com. In the second scenario, in which the internal and external namespaces are separate, the top-level domain name inside the firewall is different from the top-level registered DNS domain name seen by the Internet. The internal namespace is expedia.com, and the external namespace is microsoft.com.

Scenario 1: Same Internal and External Namespaces

In this scenario, the company uses the same name for the internal and external namespaces. microsoft.com is used both inside and outside the company. To implement this scenario, the following requirements must be met:

- Clients on the company's internal, private network must be able to access both internal and external servers (both sides of the firewall).

- Clients accessing resources from the outside must not be able to access internal company resources or resolve names.

For this scenario to work, two separate DNS zones must exist. One zone will exist outside the firewall, providing name resolution for public resources. This zone is not configured to resolve internal resources, thereby making internal company resources unreachable to external clients.

The challenge in this configuration is making publicly available resources accessible to internal clients, since the external DNS zone is not configured to resolve internal resources. One suggestion is to duplicate the external zone on an internal DNS for internal clients to resolve resources. If a proxy is being used, the proxy client should be configured to treat microsoft.com as an internal resource.

Advantages

Using the same name for an internal and external namespace has the following advantages:

- The tree name, microsoft.com, is consistent both on the private network and on the public Internet.

- This scenario extends the idea of a single logon name to the public Internet, allowing users to use the same logon name both internally and externally. For example, username@microsoft.com would serve as both the logon and e-mail ID.

Disadvantages

Using the same name for an internal and external namespace has the following disadvantages:

- The configuration is more complex. Proxy clients must be configured to know the difference between internal and external resources.

- Care must be taken not to publish internal resources on the public Internet.

- There will be duplication of efforts in managing resources. For example, maintaining duplicate zone records for internal and external name resolution.

- Even though the namespace is the same, users will get a different view of internal and external resources.

Scenario 2: Separate Internal and External Namespaces

In this scenario, the company uses separate internal and external namespaces. As a result, the names are different on either side of the firewall. Separate names are used inside and outside the corporation. microsoft.com is the name that the Internet community sees and uses. expedia.com is the name that the private network sees and uses. The two namespaces must be registered with the Internet DNS. Registering both names prevents duplication of the internal name by another public network. If the internal name is not reserved and is used by another organization, internal clients cannot distinguish between the internal name and the publicly registered DNS namespace.

Two zones will be established. One zone will resolve microsoft.com and the other zone will resolve expedia.com. Clients can clearly distinguish between internal and external resources.

Advantages

Using the separate names for internal and external namespaces has the following advantages:

- Based on different domain names, the difference between internal and external resources is clear.

- There is no overlap or duplication of effort, resulting in a more easily managed environment.

- Configuration of proxy clients is simpler since exclusion lists need to contain only expedia.com when identifying external resources.

Disadvantages

Using the separate names for internal and external namespaces has the following disadvantages:

- Logon names are different from e-mail names. For example, if someone logs on as username@microsoft.com but his e-mail address is username@expedia.com, he must remember and maintain separate user names.

- Multiple names must be registered with an Internet DNS.

Tip In this scenario, logon names are different by default. An administrator can use the Microsoft Management Console (MMC) to change the UPN suffix properties of users so that the user logon will match the e-mail address of the user.

Defining a Namespace Architecture

In addition to determining whether or not to use similar or separate internal and external namespaces, other variables will affect the overall namespace architecture. Of major consideration is the impact that replication traffic will have over wide area network (WAN) links. Additionally, organizations and their structure change constantly. Besides having the ability to create a Windows 2000 forest, administrators must be able to change the namespace structure without great expense and by being as unobtrusive as possible. The goal is to have a namespace architecture that is scalable, can adapt to change, can distinguish between internal and external resources, and can protect company data at the same time.

The namespace architecture should represent the structure of the organization but simultaneously provide the administrative granularity required to manage an enterprise-wide, global network based on Active Directory services. Additionally, the design must be scalable and extensible to accommodate organizational changes and shifts in management.

One way to accomplish this is to have three layers of domains:

- Root domain
- First-layer domain
- Second-layer domain

This structure provides a granular replication topology and the ability to limit the scope of administrators as necessary.

Root Domain

A *root domain* is the first domain in the namespace, like expedia.com. The root domain in Active Directory services maps to the company namespace. All internal domains are a part of this domain, creating a contiguous, jointed namespace in the form of a domain tree. Additionally, servers containing the namespace root will not exist on the public side of the firewall and therefore will not be visible to the Internet.

First-Layer Domains

The objective at this layer in the model is to create domain names that don't change, even in the event of internal company reorganization. The easiest way to do this is to name domains at this level based on continental, geographical, or political boundaries, for example, noamer.expedia.com or europe.microsoft.com. Additionally, this will help minimize directory service replication, since a user in North America does not have to exist in Active Directory services of a server located in Europe. However, global catalog servers still make it possible for a user in North America to find a resource in Europe as needed.

The trust relationships between the root and all first-layer domains make resources available to all branches of the domain tree. Therefore, a user in noamer.expedia.com can access a resource in europe.microsoft.com.

Domain names at this layer should be at least three characters long so that they do not conflict with the ISO 3166 standard. This is the standard that specifies two-character country codes for second-layer domains and OUs.

Note For a review of ISO 3166 two-letter country codes, see the Supplemental Course Materials CD-ROM (\chapt06\articles\ iso3166.txt) that accompanies this book. For the most current information on country codes, access an Internet search engine and enter the keyword ISO3166 or ISO +3166.

The assumption is that the first-layer domain is stable and does not change.

The following table provides suggested naming conventions:

Domain	Definition
CORPIT	Company IT Headquarters
NOAMER	United States of America and Canada
SOAMER	Mexico, Central America, and South America
NOPAC	Hong Kong and sites north of Hong Kong (Japan, China, Korea, Taiwan)
SOPAC	Sites south of Hong Kong, including the India subcontinent over to but not including Afghanistan
EUROPE	Austria, Belgium, Switzerland, Czech Republic, Denmark, Spain, Finland, Greece, Croatia, Hungary, Ireland, Italy, Holland, Norway, Poland, Portugal, Romania, Russia, Sweden, Slovakia, Slovenia
MEAST	United Arab Emirates, Israel, Saudi Arabia, Turkey
AFRICA	Africa
PARTNERS	Business partners and companies to which work is outsourced
JVT	Joint ventures

Important These naming conventions are merely suggestions that do not conflict with the ISO 3166 naming standard. Organizations can choose any naming convention that suits their policies and needs.

Second-Layer Domains

Ideally, domains at this layer should be countries only and branch off of their corresponding first-layer domains. The benefit of this method is that child-level domains can be created below the second-layer domains.

Use the same naming convention when creating OUs within a domain. This allows an OU to be promoted to a domain, if necessary, with minimal user impact.

When naming sites internal to the United States, the ISO 3166 standard is *not* used. Instead use the two-letter postal codes when naming locations. The only exception to this rule is California, which conflicts with the ISO code for Canada. So, use CALIF when creating domains for California.

For example, usa.noamer.microsoft.com is a second-layer domain, and ny.usa.noamer.microsoft.com is a child-level domain.

Planning Organizational Units

OUs should reflect the details of the organization's business structure. Create OUs to delegate administrative control over smaller groups of users, groups, and resources. The administrative control granted can be complete (creating users, changing passwords, managing account policies, and so on) or limited (as minor as maintaining print queues). Because top-level OUs can hold additional levels of OUs, one can extend the level of detail as far as necessary. Organize these objects into a logical structure that maps to the way you work and organize your business.

OUs eliminate the need to provide users with administrative access at the domain level to perform tasks such as creating computer accounts and setting passwords. One can now give users administrative control at the OU level, thereby freeing domain administrators from these tasks. OUs add a level of security by allowing restricted visibility (through the use of ACLs) of published resources; users can view only those objects they have been granted access to.

OUs inherit security policies from the parent domain and parent OU unless they are specifically disabled.

Creating the OU Structure

It is a good idea to begin your OU design by creating an OU structure for the first domain in the namespace. Use that domain and OU structure as a model for any domains added to the enterprise. Additionally, the OU structure created should be able to facilitate future reorganizations with minimal object movement.

Any time an OU is created, it is important to determine who will be able to view and control certain objects and what level of administration each administrator will have over the objects. In addition, it is necessary to determine which administrators will be granted global access to certain OUs and objects, which administrators will be restricted, and what will be the extent of that restriction.

OU Design Guidelines

Use the following guidelines when creating OUs for your enterprise:

- Create OUs to delegate administration.

- Create a logical and meaningful OU structure that allows OU administrators to complete their tasks efficiently.

- Create OUs to apply security policies.

- Create OUs to provide or restrict visibility of published resources from certain users.

- Create OU structures that are relatively static. OUs also give the namespace flexibility to adapt to changing needs of the enterprise.

- Avoid allocating too many child objects to any OU.

As you begin to design the OU structure, remember to create OU and object names that are hierarchical, uniform, static, and general enough to use in any domain in the enterprise. Try to keep any OU from having too many child objects, because it could cause bottlenecks during search and navigation queries.

One method to creating the OU structure for the first domain is to name the top-level OUs, which become headers that define the more detailed OUs and objects beneath them. Another approach to creating a consistent OU structure is to start by determining the natural hierarchy of the objects. Once you have the detailed objects separated hierarchically into groups, they can be labeled with appropriate top-level OU names.

If there are multiple domains in the design, determine whether the OU structure can be used across all domains. If not, rethink the design.

Structure the OU Hierarchy

It is crucial to determine what concept will be used as a base for the OU hierarchy. Many organizations base their domain structure on a model that mirrors their business. The following categories provide different ways to classify your OU hierarchy.

Administration or Object-Based OUs

When the OU structure is based on the administrative model, this benefits all administrators who own the OUs. In Active Directory services, you can create OUs based on objects, such as users, computers, applications, groups, printers, security policies, and more. When administration-based OUs are created in a logical and meaningful manner, it helps administrators do their jobs quickly and easily. Under most circumstances, this would be the best way to organize OUs because it will ensure the least number of changes.

Geographical-Based OUs

You can create OUs that contain all business functions in each geographical location. Again, this will tend to be a stable structure over time. However, if you envision major changes in the company's organizational structure, consider a different basis for an OU design.

Business Function-Based OUs

If it makes sense for the organization, OUs can be created that are based on various business functions within the organization, such as marketing, IT, and operations. These functions are likely to be stable even if the specific organizations that perform them are not.

Department-Based OUs

Another approach is to create OUs that mirror a department's cost center association. This method will map to the current organization but will tend to be quite unstable as the enterprise undergoes reorganizations.

Project-Based OUs

Use this type of OU model to align a cost center with a project rather than with a department. Some organizations' business is project-driven, for example, software developers, the airline industry, and more. This is why an organization might want to create project-based OUs. This is not typically a recommended OU structure because it is not considered static. Typically, this type of OU will be a child of other more stable OUs. Remember to determine who will administer this OU.

Planning a Site

Up to this point in the lesson, you have considered the logical structure of the domain and OU. Attention to the physical design is also critical to a successful implementation of a Windows 2000 Server network supporting Active Directory services. The physical design of a Windows 2000 Server–based network is demarcated by site. A site is a combination of one or more IP subnets connected by a high-speed link. Often, a site has the same boundaries as a local area network (LAN) or a very high-bandwidth WAN like an OC3 SONET (155 Mbps) or T3 (45 Mbps) WAN.

The Active Directory replication engine allows you to differentiate between replication that takes place over a local network connection and replication that takes place over a low-bandwidth WAN connection. Network traffic within a site will generally be greater than traffic between sites. How you set up your sites affects Windows 2000 in two key ways:

- **Workstation logon** When a user logs on, Active Directory services–enabled clients will try to find a domain controller in the same site as the user's computer to service the user's logon request and subsequent requests for network information.

- **Directory replication** The schedule and path for replication of a domain's directory can be configured differently for intersite replication, as opposed to replication within a site. Generally, set replication between sites tends to be less frequent than replication within a site.

In Active Directory services, sites are not part of the namespace. When browsing the logical namespace, you will see computers and users grouped into domains and OUs—not sites. The site structure is kept in a separate part of the directory. Sites contain only computer objects and connection objects used to configure intersite replication.

Properly planned sites ensure that network links are not saturated by replication traffic, that Active Directory services stays current, and that client computers access resources which are closest to them.

When planning how to group subnets into sites, consider the connection speed between the subnets. Use the following guidelines when planning to combine subnets into sites:

- Combine only those subnets that share fast, inexpensive, and reliable network connections. "Fast" network connections have at least 512 Kbps of unused bandwidth that can be dedicated to replication traffic. It is prudent to consider much higher bandwidth connections only for a single site.

- Configure your sites so that replication occurs at times that will not interfere with network performance.

Domain structure and site structure are maintained separately in Active Directory services. A single domain can span multiple sites, and a single site can include multiple domains or parts of multiple domains (Figure 6.4).

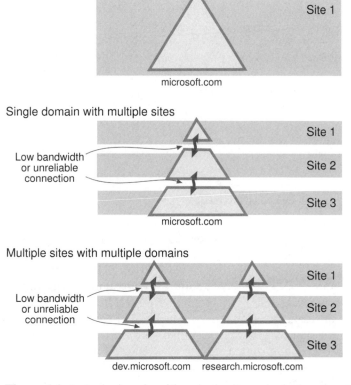

Figure 6.4 A single domain with a single site, a single domain with multiple sites, and multiple sites with multiple domains

Optimizing Workstation Logon Traffic

When planning sites, consider which domain controllers that workstations on each subnet should use. To have a particular workstation log on to a specific set of domain controllers, define the sites so that only those domain controllers are in the same site as that workstation.

Optimizing Directory Replication

When planning sites, consider where the domain controllers will be located. Because each domain controller must participate in directory replication with the other domain controllers in its domain, you must configure sites so that replication occurs at times or intervals that will not interfere with network performance.

The following table shows when to implement sites in branch offices based on the size of the branch office.

Workstations	Create a Site?	Notes
One to five	No	Users are authenticated across a slow link. The slow link will not be subjected to domain replication traffic.
More than five	Yes	Locate domain controllers locally to speed up authentication of users in the local site. Replication traffic can be set to occur on slow links at off peak times and at less frequent intervals.

Lesson Summary

When preparing for the implementation of Active Directory services, you should carefully plan how you will structure the namespace, the OUs, and the sites. You will need to determine if the internal namespace and the external namespace will be the same or separate. If the namespace is the same, the same top-level domain name appears on both sides of the firewall. If the namespaces are different, the top-level domain name inside the firewall is different from the top-level domain name outside the firewall. In addition to the namespace, you must plan your OUs. The OUs should reflect the details of the organization's business structure and map to the way you work and organize your business. Your sites must also be carefully planned before you implement Active Directory services. When planning a site, combine only those subnets that share high-bandwidth, inexpensive, and reliable network connections. Sites should be configured so that replication occurs at times that will not interfere with network performance.

Lesson 3: Implementing Active Directory Services

This lesson covers information about installing Active Directory services onto a Windows 2000 Server computer. This includes a review of the Active Directory Installation wizard. In addition, the lesson discusses the database and shared system volume created during the installation of Active Directory services. Finally, the lesson describes the Ntds.dit file and domain modes.

After this lesson, you will be able to

- Install Active Directory services on a Windows 2000 Server computer

Estimated lesson time: 30 minutes

The Active Directory Installation Wizard

The Active Directory Installation wizard is used to perform the following tasks:

- Adding a domain controller to an existing domain
- Creating the first domain controller of a new domain
- Creating a new child domain
- Creating a new domain tree

To launch the Active Directory Installation wizard, run Configure Your Server, which is located on the Administrative Tools menu of the Start menu, and then select the Active Directory link. From there you can run the Active Directory Installation wizard. You can also start the wizard by running the dcpromo.exe utility from the Run window or from a command prompt. Either of these procedures will run the Active Directory Installation wizard on a stand-alone server and step you through the process of installing Active Directory services on the computer and creating a new domain controller.

As you install Active Directory services, you can choose either to add the new domain controller to an existing domain or create the first domain controller for a new domain (Figure 6.5).

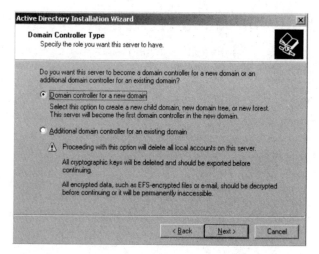

Figure 6.5 The Domain Controller Type screen in the Active Directory Installation wizard

Adding a Domain Controller to an Existing Domain

If you choose to add a domain controller to an existing domain, you create a peer domain controller. Peer domain controllers are created for redundancy and to reduce the load on the existing domain controllers.

Creating the First Domain Controller for a New Domain

If you choose to create the first domain controller for a new domain, not only will you be creating a new domain controller, but also a new domain. Domains should be created to partition information, which enables you to scale Active Directory services to meet the needs of very large organizations.

When you create a new domain, you can select whether to create a new child domain or a new domain tree. When you create a child domain, the new domain is added as a child domain in an existing domain. When you create a new domain tree, the new domain is not part of an existing domain. At this point, you can create a new forest of domain trees or join an existing forest.

Domain controller for a new domain

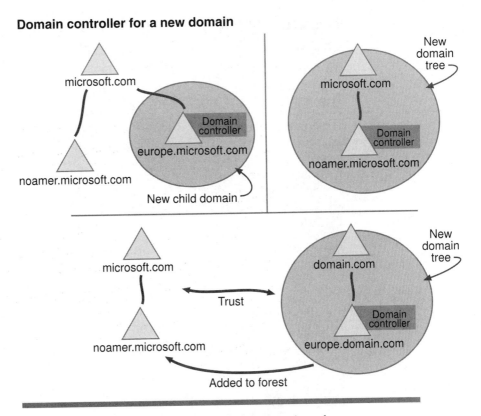

Additional domain controller for an existing domain

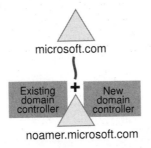

Figure 6.6 A graphical representation of the different domain controller type.

Caution Running dcpromo.exe on a domain controller allows you to remove Active Directory services from the domain controller and demote it to a stand-alone server. If you remove Active Directory services from all domain controllers in a domain, you also delete the directory database for the domain, and the domain no longer exists.

The Database and Shared System Volume

When you install Active Directory services, the database, the database log files, and the shared system volume are automatically created.

The Active Directory Database

The database is the directory for the new domain. The default location for the database and database log files is %systemroot%\Ntds. However, you can specify a different location during the Active Directory installation. For best performance, place the database and the log file on separate hard disks. Consider placing the database on a hardware-level redundant array of independent disks (RAID) implementation such as RAID-5 or RAID-10 (mirrored and striped disks) for fault tolerance and performance.

The directory database is actually stored in a file named Ntds.dit. The Ntds.dit file contains all of the information stored in the Active Directory store. It is an ESE database that contains the entire schema, the global catalog, and all the objects stored on that domain controller. During the promotion process, Ntds.dit is copied from the %systemroot%\System32 directory into the designated directory. Active Directory services is then started from the new copy of the file, and if there are other domain controllers present, the replication process updates this file from other domain controllers.

The Shared System Volume

The shared system volume is a folder structure that exists on all Windows 2000 domain controllers. It stores scripts and some of the group policy objects for the current domain as well as the enterprise. The default location for the shared system volume is %systemroot%\Sysvol. The shared system volume must be located on a partition or volume formatted with NTFS 5.0.

Replication of the shared system volume occurs on the same schedule as Active Directory replication. As a result, you may not notice file replication to or from the newly created system volume until two replication periods have elapsed (typically, 10 minutes). This is because the first file replication period updates the configuration of other system volumes so that they are aware of the newly created system volume.

Domain Modes

There are two domain modes: Mixed mode and Native mode.

Mixed Mode

When you first install or upgrade a domain controller to Windows 2000 Server, the domain controller runs in Mixed mode. Mixed mode allows the domain controller to interact with any domain controllers in the domain that are running Windows NT 3.51 or 4.0 (down-level domain controllers). In addition, any clients using NTLM and the directory service in Windows NT 3.51 and Windows NT 4.0 need Mixed mode to authenticate to the network. They also need WINS for name resolution. These down-level clients will usually authenticate to the Windows 2000 Server computers before a down-level Windows NT Server computer answers their logon request. Also, a Windows 2000 Server computer always wins an election to become the master browser. This combined behavior places additional stress on the Windows 2000 Server domain controllers.

Native Mode

When all the domain controllers in the domain run Windows 2000 Server, and you do not plan to add any more down-level domain controllers to the domain, you can switch the domain from Mixed mode to Native mode.

Several things happen during the conversion from Mixed mode to Native mode:

- Support for down-level replication ceases. Since down-level replication is gone, you can no longer have any domain controllers in your domain that are not running Windows 2000 Server.

- You can no longer add new down-level domain controllers to the domain.

- The server that served as the primary domain controller during migration is no longer the domain master; all domain controllers begin acting as peers.

Note The change from Mixed mode to Native mode is one way only; you cannot change from Native mode to Mixed mode.

Exercise 1: Installing Active Directory services

In this exercise, you will make your stand-alone server, Server01 into the first domain controller in an Active Directory tree. The installation will install and configure DNS to support name resolution. In a later chapter, you will learn more about DNS and other network services, such as the Dynamic Host Configuration Protocol (DHCP). Complete all procedures in this exercise on Server01.

▶ **Procedure 1: Promoting a stand-alone server to a domain controller**

In this exercise, you run dcpromo.exe to install Active Directory services and DNS on your stand-alone server (Server01), making it a domain controller and a DNS server in a new domain.

1. Start Server01 and log on as Administrator with a password of "password."

2. If the Windows 2000 Configure Server page opens, close it because the dcpromo.exe program will be used instead to accomplish the tasks in this procedure.

3. Insert the Windows 2000 Server installation CD-ROM in Server01.

   The installation CD-ROM is required to install the DNS service during the operation of dcpromo.exe.

4. If the Windows 2000 CD wizard appears, click Exit to close the screen.

5. Click Start and then click Run.

6. In the Run dialog box, type **dcpromo.exe** and click OK.

   The Active Directory Installation wizard appears.

7. Click Next.

   The Domain Controller Type screen appears.

8. Select Domain Controller For A New Domain, and then click Next.

   The Create Tree Or Child Domain screen appears.

9. Verify that the Create A New Domain Tree radio button is selected, and then click Next.

   The Create Or Join Forest screen appears.

10. Select the Create A New Forest Of Domain Trees radio button, and then click Next.

    The New Domain Name screen appears.

11. In the Full DNS Name For The New Domain box, type **microsoft.com**, and click Next.

    After a few moments, the NetBIOS Domain Name screen appears.

12. Verify that MICROSOFT appears in the Domain NetBIOS Name text box, and then click Next.

    The Database And Log Locations screen appears.

13. Verify that C:\Winnt\Ntds is the location of both the database and the log, and then click Next.

    The Shared System Volume screen appears.

14. Read the information on the Shared System Volume screen, and then verify that the SYSVOL location is C:\WINNT\SYSVOL.

15. Click Next.

    An Active Directory Installation Wizard message box appears, stating that a DNS for microsoft.com could not be found.

16. Click OK.

    Dcpromo did not find an available DNS for microsoft.com, so the Configure DNS screen appears.

17. Verify that the Yes, Install And Configure DNS On The Computer (Recommended) radio button is selected, and click Next.

    The Permissions screen appears.

18. Initially, the domain controller will be run in Mixed mode, so verify that the Permissions Compatible With Pre-Windows 2000 Servers radio button is selected, and click Next.

    The Directory Services Restore Mode Administrator Password screen appears.

19. Read this screen, then type **password** in both text boxes, and click Next.

    The Summary screen appears, listing the options you selected.

20. Review the contents of the Summary screen, and then click Next.

    The Configuring Active Directory progress indicator appears as Active Directory services is installed on the server.

    This process will take several minutes. While you are waiting, verify that you have inserted the Windows 2000 Server installation CD-ROM into Server01 in preparation for the DNS service installation.

20. When the Completing The Active Directory Installation Wizard screen appears, remove the CD-ROM, click Finish and then click Restart Now.

   It will take longer for Windows 2000 Server to start the first time as a domain controller.

▶ **Procedure 2: Viewing your domain**

In this procedure, you view your domain.

1. Log on to Server01 as Administrator with a password of "password."

2. Double-click My Network Places.

   The My Network Places window appears.

3. Double-click Entire Network, and then click the link on the left side of the window that says, You May Also View The Entire Contents Of The Network.

4. Double-click Microsoft Windows Network.

   Notice that the network Microsoft appears.

5. Close My Network Places.

▶ **Procedure 3: Using Active Directory Manager**

In this procedure, you use Active Directory Users And Computers to view your domain.

1. Click Start, point to Programs, point to Administrative Tools, and then click Active Directory Users And Computers.

   The Active Directory Users And Computers snap-in appears.

2. In the console tree, click on the + sign to the left of microsoft.com.

3. Examine each of the containers below microsoft.com. Do not modify any information that you see in these nodes.

   What selections are listed under microsoft.com and what is their purpose? Hint, choose the properties of each container in the console tree to view their purpose.

4. Close Active Directory Users And Computers snap-in.

Exercise 2: Joining Server02 to the Domain

In this exercise, Server02 will join the microsoft.com domain. Because DHCP is not in use at this point in your training, you will manually configure IP address information on Server01 and Server02. When Server02 joins the domain, a computer account in the domain will be created for Server02. This computer account will appear in the Active Directory store. Both computers will be used to complete this exercise.

▶ ### Procedure 1: Manually configuring IP addressing and joining Server02 to the micorosft.com domain

1. On Server01 and Server02, log on as Administrator with a password of "password."

2. On Server01, click Start, point to Settings and then click Network And Dial-Up Connections.

   The Network And Dial-Up Connections window appears.

3. Click Local Area Connection and from the File menu, click Properties.

   The Local Area Connection Properties dialog box appears.

4. In the Components Checked Are Used By This Connection box, click Internet Protocol (TCP/IP).

5. Click Properties.

   The Internet Protocol (TCP/IP) Properties dialog box appears.

6. Click the Use The Following IP Address radio button.

7. In the IP Address box, type **10.10.10.1**.

8. In the Subnet Mask box, verify that 255.0.0.0 appears.

9. Click the Use The Following DNS Server Addresses radio button.

10. In the preferred DNS Server box, type **10.10.10.1**.

11. Click OK.

12. The Local Area Connection Properties dialog box appears.

13. Click OK.

14. On Server02, click Start, point to Settings and then click Network And Dial-Up Connections.

15. The Network And Dial-Up Connections window appears.

16. Click Local Area Connection and from the File menu, click Properties.

   The Local Area Connection Properties dialog box appears.

17. In the Components Checked Are Used By This Connection box, click Internet Protocol (TCP/IP).

18. Click Properties.

    The Internet Protocol (TCP/IP) Properties dialog box appears.

19. Click the Use The Following IP Address radio button.

20. In the IP Address box, type **10.10.10.2**.

21. In the Subnet Mask box, verify that 255.0.0.0 appears.

22. Click the Use The Following DNS Server Addresses radio button.

23. In the Preferred DNS Server box, type **10.10.10.1**.

24. Click OK.

    The Local Area Connection Properties dialog box appears.

25. Click OK.

26. Select Network Identification on the Advanced menu of the Network And Dial-Up Connections window.

27. Click the Network Identification tab, and then click Properties.

    The Identification Changes dialog box appears.

28. Select the Domain radio button, type **microsoft**, and then click OK.

    The Domain Username And Password dialog box appears.

29. In the Name text box, type **administrator,** and in the Password text box, type **password**. Then click OK.

    After a few moments, a Network Identification message box will appear, welcoming you to the domain.

30. Click OK.

    The Network Identification message box will state that the computer must be restarted for the changes to take effect.

31. Click OK.

    The System Properties dialog box appears.

32. Click OK.

    The System Settings Change message box will state the computer must be restarted for the changes to take effect.

33. Click Yes to restart Server02.

34. From Server02, log on to the microsoft.com domain as Administrator with a password of "password."

35. If the Configure Your Server screen appears, clear the Show This Screen At Startup check box and close the screen.

Exercise 3: Installing and Examining the Contents of Adminpak.msi

In this exercise, you will first list the tools installed under the Administrative Tools group and then you will install Adminpak.msi to determine the additional tools installed by this administrative tools installation routine. Complete all procedures in this exercise on Server01.

▸ **Procedure 1: Adjusting start menu settings and reviewing new tools installed under Administrative tools**

In this procedure you will disable the feature that shows only the most used menu items under the Start button.

1. On Server01, log on as Administrator with a password of "password."

2. Click the Start button, point to Settings, and then click Taskbar And Start menu.

    The Taskbar And Start Menu Properties dialog box appears.

3. Clear the Use Personalized Menus check box, and then click OK.

4. Click the Start button, point to Programs, and then point to Administrative Tools.

    Notice that all installed Administrative Tools applications appear under Administrative Tools rather than just the most recently used applications.

    When Server01 was a stand-alone server, all the applications appeared under Administrative Tools except those specific to Active Directory services, domain, and DNS maintenance. Using your mouse, point to each of the applications listed below to see the screen hint, and then write a description in the space provided.

    Active Directory Domains and Trusts

    Active Directory Sites and Services

    Active Directory Users and Computers

    DNS

▸ **Procedure 2: Installing additional administration tools**

In this procedure you will install the Windows 2000 Administrative Pack on Server01. These tools can also be installed on Windows 2000 Professional to facilitate remote administration of Windows 2000 Servers.

1. Click the Start menu, and then click Run.

   The Run dialog box appears.

2. Type **adminpak.msi**.

   Adminpak.msi is located in C:\WINNT\system32, which is in the search path. Therefore, there is no need to type the path to this Microsoft installer file.

3. Click OK.

   After a moment, the Windows 2000 Administration Tools Setup wizard appears.

4. Read the information on the screen, and then click Next.

   The Setup Options screen appears.

5. Click the Install All Of The Administrative Tools radio button, and then click Next.

   The Installation Progress screen appears as the administrative tools are installed.

6. When the Completing The Windows 2000 Administration Tools Setup Wizard screen appears, click Finish to complete the installation.

7. Notice the additional tools installed under Administrative Tools. To determine the purpose of each tool, place the mouse pointer over each new tool and a tool hint will appear.

Exercise 4: Changing from Stand-Alone Dfs to Domain Dfs

In Chapter 3, you installed stand-alone Microsoft distributed file system (Dfs). In this exercise, you will delete the stand-alone Dfs, create a domain Dfs, and create a Dfs root replica since you are now running a domain controller. You will use Server01 and Server02 to complete the procedures in this exercise.

▸ **Procedure 1: Deleting the stand-alone Dfs root**

Only one Dfs root can exist on a server. Therefore the stand-alone Dfs must first be deleted on Server01.

1. Click the Start button, point to Programs, and then point to Administrative Tools.

2. From the Administrative tools group, click Distributed File System.

   The Distributed File System snap-in appears.

3. In the console tree, click \\SERVER01\Public.

4. Click the Action menu, and then click Delete Dfs Root.

   A Distributed File System message box appears stating that deleting the Dfs root disables the ability to access the Dfs again. This procedure does not delete the shares that were linked to the Dfs root.

5. Click Yes.

▶ Procedure 2: Creating a domain Dfs

The domain Dfs will be configured similarly to the stand-alone Dfs, but it will provide file replication to the Dfs link replicas. Complete this procedure on Server01.

1. In the console tree of the Distributed File System snap-in, click Distributed File System.

2. Click the Action menu, and then click New Dfs Root.

   The New Dfs Root wizard appears.

3. Click Next.

   The Select The Dfs Root Type screen appears.

4. Select the Create A Domain Dfs Root radio button, and then click Next.

   The Select The Host Domain For The Dfs Root screen appears, and microsoft.com appears in the Domain Name text box and in the Trusting Domains box.

5. Click Next.

   The Specify The Host Server For The Dfs Root Screen appears.

6. Notice that server01.microsoft.com is shown in the Server Name text box.

   If Server01 was still hosting the stand-alone Dfs, its name would not be written in the Server Name text box. This is intentional because a server can only host a single Dfs root.

7. Click Next.

   The Specify The Dfs Root Share screen appears.

8. Verify that the Use An Existing Share radio button is selected, and then from the drop-down list box, select Public.

9. Click Next.

10. In the Comment text box appearing on the Name The Dfs Root screen, type **Public access share** and then click Next.

11. Review the settings appearing on the Completing The New Dfs Root Wizard screen. Notice that the host server is SERVER01.microsoft.com. When you created a stand-alone Dfs root, the host server name was SERVER01.

12. Click Finish.

    The Distributed File System Manager snap-in appears, and the Dfs root is configured on Server01.microsoft.com and appears as \\microsoft.com\Public.

▸ Procedure 3: Creating a Dfs root replica

In the following procedure, you will create a Dfs root replica of \\SERVER01\Public on Server02. Server02 was made part of the microsoft.com domain in Exercise 2.

1. On Server01, select \\microsoft.com\Public from the console tree of the Distributed File System snap-in.

   The \\SERVER01\Public Dfs root appears in the right pane.

2. Click the Action menu, and then click New Root Replica.

   The Specify The Host Server For The Dfs Root screen appears.

3. In the Server Name text box, type **Server02** and then click Next.

   A Domain Dfs root can be replicated to another server (domain controller or member server) in the domain.

   The Specify The Dfs Root Share screen appears.

4. Select the Create A New Share radio button.

5. In the Path To Share text box, type **c:\publicrepl**.

6. In the Share Name text box, type **pubrepl**.

7. Click Finish.

   The distributed file system message box appears stating that \\Server02\c$\publicrepl does not exist.

8. Click Yes to create the folder.

▶ **Procedure 4: Enabling FRS for the Dfs root replica**

In this procedure you will enable a replication policy so that the Dfs root is automatically synchronized with its replica.

1. On Server01, select \\microsoft.com\Public from the console tree of the Distributed File System snap-in.

   The \\SERVER01\Public Dfs root and the \\SERVER02\pubrepl appear in the right pane.

2. Click the Action menu, and then click Replication Policy.

   The Replication Policy dialog box appears.

3. Click \\SERVER01\Public, and then click Set Master.

4. Click \\SERVER02\pubrepl, and then click Enable to enable replication.

5. Click OK to close the Replication Policy dialog box.

▶ **Procedure 5: Creating Dfs links**

In this procedure you will recreate the Dfs links that you created in Chapter 3, Exercise 1, Procedure 3.

1. On Server01, select \\microsoft.com\Public from the console tree of the Distributed File System snap-in.

   The \\SERVER01\Public Dfs root and the \\SERVER02\pubrepl appear in the right pane.

2. Click the Action menu, and then click New Dfs Link.

   The Create A New Dfs Link dialog box appears.

3. In the Link Name text box, type **intranet**.

4. In the Send The User To This Shared Folder text box, type **\\Server02\internal**.

5. In the Comment text box, type **Internal web content** and click OK.

6. Repeat steps 3–8 to create new Dfs links using information in the following table:

Link name	Send the user to this shared folder	Comment
news	\\Server01\Press	Current Press Releases
ftp	\\Server01\ftproot	FTP Root Directory
tech	\\Server01\TechDocs	Technical Documents Area

7. On Server02, open C:\Publicrepl (the Dfs root replica) and you will see new folder replicas appearing below the Dfs root.

Lesson Summary

The Active Directory Installation wizard is used to install Active Directory services onto a Windows 2000 Server computer. The Active Directory Installation wizard is also used to add a domain controller to an existing domain, create the first domain controller in a new domain, create a new child domain, or create a new domain tree. When you install Active Directory services, the database, the database log files, and the shared system volume are automatically created. The directory database is stored in a file named Ntds.dit. The Ntds.dit file contains the Active Directory store. The shared system volume is a folder structure that exists on all Windows 2000 domain controllers. It stores scripts and some of the group policy objects for both the current domain as well as the enterprise. There are two domain modes: Mixed mode and Native mode. When you first install or upgrade a domain controller to Windows 2000 Server, the domain controller runs in Mixed mode. When all the domain controllers in the domain run Windows 2000 Server, and you do not plan to add any more down-level domain controllers to the domain, you can switch the domain from Mixed mode to Native mode.

Lesson 4: Administering Active Directory Services

Once you have installed Active Directory services, you are ready to create and manage the objects that are stored within the directory service. This lesson describes the process of creating OUs and adding objects to those units. The lesson then provides details about how to manage those objects so that you can find, modify, and delete objects as necessary. Finally, this lesson covers how to control access to the objects, which includes managing Active Directory permissions and delegating administrative control of objects.

After this lesson, you will be able to

- Create OUs and their objects
- Find, modify, move, and delete the objects that you created
- Control access to Active Directory objects

Estimated lesson time: 50 minutes

Creating Organizational Units and Their Objects

Active Directory objects represent network resources. Each object is a distinct, named set of attributes that represents a specific network resource. When you add new resources to your network, such as user accounts, groups, or printers, you create new Active Directory objects that represent these resources.

Before objects are added to Active Directory services, you should create the OUs that will contain those objects.

Creating Organizational Units

You can create an OU under a domain, under the Domain Controller object, or within another OU. Once you create an OU, you can add objects to the OU.

To create OUs, you must have the required permissions to add OUs in the parent OU, domain, or Domain Controller node where you want to create the OU. By default, members of the Administrators group have the permissions to create OUs. You cannot create OUs within the majority of default containers, such as Computers or Users.

OUs are created to facilitate network administration. Your OU structure should be based on your particular administrative needs. If necessary, you can easily change your OU structure or move objects between OUs.

You should create an OU for any of the following reasons:

- To delegate administrative control to other users or administrators.

- To group objects that require similar administrative tasks. Grouping objects allows the administrators to locate similar network resources easily and perform their administrative tasks. For example, they can group all user objects for temporary employees in the same OU.

- To restrict visibility of network resources in the Active Directory store. Users can view only objects to which you have given them access. Permissions can easily be changed for an OU to restrict access to confidential network information.

You can create an OU in the Active Directory Users and Computers snap-in by selecting the domain or existing OU where you want to create the new OU. From there, click the Action menu, point to New, and then click Organizational Unit (Figure 6.7). Enter the name of the new OU in the Name text box, and click OK.

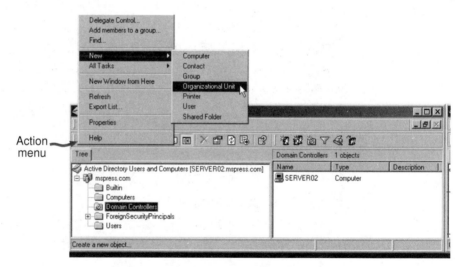

Figure 6.7 Creating an OU in the Active Directory Users and Computers snap-in

Adding Objects to Organizational Units

To add objects to OUs, you must have the required permissions to create objects within the OU where you want to create the object. By default, members of the Administrators group have the permissions to add objects to OUs. The objects available to create are dictated by the rules of the schema, wizard, or snap-in you use. When you create an object, sometimes not all attributes are available for definition. Often, to completely define all the object attributes, you must modify the object after you create it.

Note Object attributes (also referred to as properties) in the schema are categories of information that define the characteristics for all instances of a defined object type. All instances of a certain object type have the same attributes. The attribute values of any object instance make it unique. For example, all instances of a user object have a First Name attribute; however, the value for the First Name attribute can be any name, such as Linda or Max.

You can create object instances in the Active Directory Users and Computers snap-in. Select the OU that you want to add the object to, click the Action menu, point to New, and then click the name of the object type that you want to add. Enter the appropriate information in the dialog box(es) that appears.

Description of Active Directory Objects

Adding new resources to your network creates new Active Directory objects that represent these resources. The following table describes the most common object types that you can add to Active Directory services:

Icon	Object	Description
	Computer	A computer object represents a computer on the network. For Windows NT Workstation and Windows NT Server computers, this is the machine account. The object contains information about a computer that is a member of the domain.
	Contact	A contact object is an account that does not have any security permissions. You cannot log on to the network as a contact. Contacts are typically used to represent external users for the purpose of e-mail.
	Group	A group object can contain users, computers, and other groups. Groups simplify the management of large numbers of objects.

Icon	Object	Description
	Printer	A printer object is a network printer that has been published in the directory. The object is actually a pointer to a printer on a computer. You must manually publish a printer on a computer that is not in Active Directory services.
	User	A user object is a security principal in the directory. The information in this object allows a user to log on to Windows 2000. The information also includes many optional fields, such as first name, last name, display name, and e-mail address.
	Shared Folder	A shared folder object is a network share that has published in the directory. The object is

actually a   pointer to the shared folder. It
contains the address of   the data, rather than the
data itself. Shared folders   exist in a computer's
registry. When you publish a   shared folder in Active
Directory services, you

are creating an object that contains a pointer to the shared folder.

Exercise 5: Creating an Organizational Unit and Its Objects

In this practice, you create part of the organizational structure of a domain by creating an OU. You then create three user accounts that you use in a later practice.

▶ **Procedure 1: Creating instances of OU and user objects**

In this procedure you will create two OUs and three User objects.

1. Log on to Server01 as Administrator with a password of "password."

2. Open Active Directory Users And Computers.

   To ensure that you are creating a new OU in the correct location, you must first select the location.

3. In the console tree, click microsoft.com.

4. Click the Action menu, point to New, and then click Organizational Unit.

   The New Object - Organizational Unit dialog box appears.

   Notice that the only required information is the name. The dialog box indicates the location where the object will be created. This should be microsoft.com/.

5. In the Name box, type **Sales** and then click OK.

   The Sales OU appears in the console tree.

6. Under microsoft.com, create another OU, called Servers.

7. In the console tree, click Users.

8. Click the Action menu, point to New, and then click User.

   Notice that the New Object - User dialog box shows that the new user account is being created in the User folder of microsoft.com/Users.

Note User objects can be created in any OU. In this procedure, you will create most user objects in the Users OU; however, this is not a requirement for creating these objects.

9. Create a new user account with the following information:

Text box name	Type
First name	Jane
Last name	Doe
User logon name:	Jane_Doe

10. Click Next.

11. Leave the password fields blank, do not change the default settings for this user account, and click Next.

    The summary screen appears showing the full name and user logon name for Jane Doe.

12. Click Finish.

13. Click Jane_Doe in the right pane of the Active Directory Users And Computers snap-in.

14. Click the Action menu and then click Properties.

    The Jane Doe Properties dialog box appears.

15. On the General tab of the Jane Doe Properties dialog box, in the Telephone Number text box, type 555-1234.

16. Click OK.

17. Create the following user accounts under the Users object.

Text box name	Type
First name	John
Last name	Smith
User logon name:	John_Smith

Text box name	Type
First name	Bob
Last name	Train
User logon name:	Bob_Train

You will be working with these user accounts in the next chapter.

Managing Active Directory Objects

The process of managing Active Directory objects involves several different tasks, such as locating objects, modifying and deleting objects, and moving objects. To modify, delete, or move objects, you must have the required permissions for the object and the OU to which you move the object. By default, members of the Administrators group have the required permissions.

Locating Objects

The global catalog contains a partial replica of the entire directory, so it stores information about every object in a domain tree or forest. As a result, a user can find information regardless of which domain in the tree or forest contains the data. The contents of the global catalog are automatically generated by Active Directory services from the domains that make up the directory.

To locate Active Directory objects, open the Active Directory Users And Computers snap-in located in the Administrative Tools folder. Then right-click a domain or OU in the console tree, and click Find. The Find dialog box appears.

Note If you access the context menu of a shared folder object and then click Find, the Windows Explorer search function is launched, and you can search the share for files and folders.

The Find dialog box provides options that allow you to search the global catalog so that you can locate user accounts, groups, and printers (see Figure 6.8).

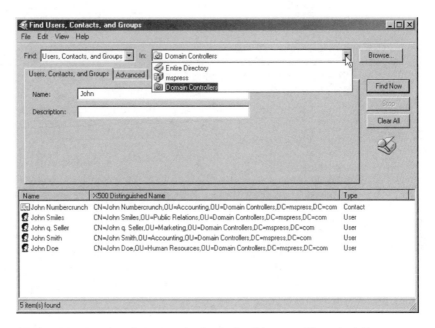

Figure 6.8 The Find dialog box in the Active Directory Users And Computers snap-in.

As Figure 6.8 illustrates, the Find dialog box can be broken into several distinct sections: the main window, the object tab, the Advanced tab, and the results window. The object tab in Figure 6.8 is Users, Contacts, and Groups.

The Main Window

The main window of the Find tool contains a set of menus, buttons, and drop-down menu. Although most of these options are self-explanatory and offer standard functionality, the Find drop-down menu and the In drop-down menu (shown in Figure 6.8) are unique to the Active Directory Find dialog box and are discussed in more detail below. In addition, the main window contains two tabs: the object tab and the Advanced tab, both of which are also discussed later in this section.

The Find Drop-Down Menu

The Find drop-down menu contains the type of objects that you can include in your search.

You must select one of the available options to perform your search. By default, the Users, Contacts, And Groups is selected.

Note The title of the dialog box varies according to the type of search selected from the Find drop-down menu. For example, if Organizational Units is selected, the dialog box title will read Find Organizational Units.

The In Drop-Down Menu

The In drop-down menu contains the location that you want to search, which can be the entire Active Directory store, a specific domain, or an OU. You must select one of these options. By default, the domain you are in is selected.

Users, Contacts, and Groups Tab

The Users, Contacts, And Groups tab is selected when you open the Find dialog box. The tab contains the Name text box and the Description text box. The name of the object is entered into the Name text box, and the contents of the object's description are entered into the Description text box. You can enter information into either one of the text boxes or into both text boxes. The search is based on the combination of both. You can also use wild cards in either text box to conduct a search.

Advanced Tab

The Advanced tab provides you with advanced search features that you can use in conjunction with the object tab or use by themselves. The search results are based on a combination of the information entered on both tabs. If nothing is added the text boxes on the Users, Contacts, And Groups tab, the search results will be based only on the information entered on the Advanced tab.

The following table provides a detailed description of the fields on the Advanced tab:

Field	Description
Field	A list of the attributes for which you can search on the object type that you select.
Condition	The methods that are available to further define the search for an attribute. The options are Starts With, Ends With, Is (Exactly), Is Not, Present, or Not Present.
Value	The value for the condition of the Field (attribute) value that you are using to search the directory. You can search for an object by using an attribute of the object only if you enter a value for the attribute. For example, if the Field value you select is First Name and the Condition value is Starts With, the Value text box would contain an R if you're looking for users whose first name starts with R.
Search Criteria	The box that lists each search criteria that you have defined. After you have defined the search criteria in the Field, Condition, and Value fields, click Add. The search criteria are added to the window. You can add or remove search criteria to narrow or widen your search.

Results Window

The results window opens at the bottom of the main window and displays the results of your search after you click Find Now, which is located on the main window. You can add or delete columns appearing in the Results window from the View menu Choose Columns option.

Modifying Attribute Values and Deleting Objects

You can modify the attribute values of an object to change or add information. Modifying an object changes the value of an attribute associated with the object.

Note Do not confuse modifying an object's attribute values with adding, deleting, or modifying objects or attributes in the schema. Schema modifications are permanent and are replicated to all domain controllers in the forest.

To modify the values of an attribute, open the Active Directory Users And Computers snap-in, and select an instance of an object. From the Action menu click Properties. In the Properties dialog box, make the necessary changes to the attribute values. You should modify objects when the values of the attributes change; for example, modify a user object to change the name, location, or e-mail for that user.

To maintain security, delete objects when they are no longer needed. To delete objects, open the Active Directory Users And Computers snap-in and select the object instance you want to delete. From the Action menu, click Delete.

Moving Objects

It is possible to move objects from one location in the Active Directory store to another location, such as from one OU to another, to reflect changes within the organization. You should move objects from one location to another when organizational or administrative functions change; for example, an employee moves from one department to another. To move an object, open the Active Directory Users And Computers snap-in, and select the object you want to move. From the Action menu, click Move and select the new location for the object.

Exercise 6: Managing Active Directory Objects

In this exercise you will first search for a user object that you created in the last exercise and then move the object to a new location.

▸ **Procedure 1: Finding a user account in the domain**

In this procedure you will locate a user with a first name of Jane. Jane was promoted to a position in the sales department, so her user object will be moved to the Sales OU. You know most of her phone number, and you know her first name.

1. Log on to Server01 as Administrator with a password of "password."

2. Open Active Directory Users And Computers.

3. In the console tree, click on microsoft.com.

4. Click the Action menu and then click Find.

   The Find Users, Contacts, And Groups dialog box appears.

5. Verify that Users, Contacts, And Groups is selected in the Find drop-down list box, and then click Find Now.

   Notice how all Users and Groups are located, regardless of their location.

6. Click Clear All, and then click OK to acknowledge that you want to clear the search results.

7. In the In drop-down list box, verify that the microsoft domain appears.

8. In the Name text box, type **Jane**.

9. Click the Advanced tab.

10. Click Field, point to User, and then click Telephone Number.

Note If you don't see Telephone Number listed, click the arrow at the bottom of the list to scroll down to Telephone Number.

Starts With appears in the Condition text box.

11. In the Value text box, type **555-12** and then click Add.

12. Click the View menu, and then click Choose Columns.

The Choose Columns dialog box appears.

13. From the Columns Shown box, click Description and then click Remove.

14. From the Columns Available box, scroll down and click X500 Distinguished Name and then click Add.

15. Click OK to close the Choose Columns dialog box.

The Find Users, Contacts, And Groups dialog box displays Jane Doe with an object type value of User and an X.500 distinguished name value of CN=Jane Doe,CN=Users,DC=microsoft,DC=com.

The distinguished name tells you that user Jane Doe is located in the Users container in the microsoft.com domain.

16. Close the Find Users, Contacts, And Groups dialog box.

▶ **Procedure 2: Moving an Object in Active Directory Users and Computers**

In this procedure you will move the Jane Doe user object from the Users container to the Sales container.

1. In the Active Directory Users And Computers snap-in, click on the Users OU in the console tree.

All User and Security Group objects appear in the right pane.

2. Click the Jane Doe user object in the right pane.

3. Click the Action menu and then click Move.

   The Move window appears.

4. Click the Sales OU and then click OK.

   Jane Doe is moved from the Users OU to the Sales OU.

5. Click on the Sales OU in the console tree.

   The Jane Doe user object appears in the right pane.

6. Close the Active Directory Users and Computers snap-in.

Controlling Access to Active Directory Objects

Windows 2000 uses an object-based security model to implement access control for all Active Directory objects. This security model is similar to the one that Windows 2000 uses to implement NTFS security. Every Active Directory object has a security descriptor that defines who has the permissions to gain access to the object and what type of access is allowed. Windows 2000 uses these security descriptors to control access to objects.

To reduce administrative overhead, you can group objects with identical security requirements into the same OU and then assign access permissions to the entire OU and all objects in it.

Managing Active Directory Permissions

Active Directory permissions provide security for resources by allowing you to control who can gain access to object instances or object attributes and the type of access that you will allow.

Active Directory Security

Use Active Directory permissions to determine who has the permissions to gain access to the object and what type of access is allowed. An administrator or the object owner must assign permissions to the object before users can gain access to the object. Windows 2000 stores a list of user access permissions, called the ACL, for every Active Directory object. The ACL for an object lists who can access the object and the specific actions each user can perform on the object.

You can use permissions to assign administrative privileges to a specific user or group for an OU, a hierarchy of OUs, or a single object, without assigning administrative permissions for controlling other Active Directory objects.

Object Permissions

The object type determines which permissions you can select. Permissions vary for different object types. For example, you can assign the Reset Password permission for a user object but not for a computer object.

A user can be a member of multiple groups, each with different permissions that provide different levels of access to objects. When you assign a permission to a user for access to an object and that user is a member of a group that has been assigned a different permission for that object, the user's effective permissions are the combination of the user and group permissions. For example, if a user is granted the write account expiration data (Write accountExpires) permission to user objects and is a member of a group with read account expiration data (Read accountExpires) permission, the user's effective permission is read and write account expiration data.

You can allow or deny permissions. Denied permissions take precedence over any allowed permissions for users and groups. If you deny permission to a user to gain access to an object, the user will not have that permission, even if you allow the permission for a group the user is a member of. You should deny permissions only when it is necessary to deny permissions to a specific user who is a member of a group with allowed permissions.

Note Always ensure that all objects have at least one user with the Full Control permission. Failure to do so might result in some objects being inaccessible to the person who is using the Active Directory Users And Computers snap-in, even an administrator.

Assigning Active Directory Permissions

You can use the Active Directory Users And Computers snap-in to set permissions for objects and attributes of objects. The Security tab of the Properties dialog box for the object allows you to assign permissions.

Note If you do not see the Security tab for an object, from the View menu click Advanced Features.

Standard permissions are sufficient for most administrative tasks. However, you might need to view the special permissions. To view special permissions, click Advanced. On the Permissions tab, click the entry you want to view, and then click View/Edit. To view the permissions for specific attributes, click the Properties tab of the Permission Entry dialog box.

Note Avoid assigning permissions for specific attributes of objects because this can complicate system administration. Errors can result, such as Active Directory objects not being visible.

Permissions Inheritance

Similar to other permissions inheritance in Windows 2000, permissions inheritance in Active Directory services minimizes the number of times you need to assign permissions for objects. When you assign permissions, you can apply the permissions to subobjects (child objects), a feature that propagates the permissions to all the subobjects for a given object. This feature is called permissions inheritance.

You can prevent permissions inheritance so that a child object does not inherit permissions from its parent object by deselecting the check box Allow Inheritable Permissions From Parent To Propagate To This Object. When you prevent inheritance, only the permissions that you explicitly assign to the object apply. You use the Security tab in the Properties dialog box to prevent permissions inheritance.

When you prevent permissions inheritance, Windows 2000 Server allows you to do the following:

- Copy previously inherited permissions to the object. The new explicit permissions for the object are a copy of the permissions that it previously inherited from its parent object. Then, according to your needs, you can make any necessary changes to the permissions.

- Remove previously inherited permissions from the object. Windows 2000 removes any previously inherited permissions. No permissions exist for the object. Then, according to your needs, you can assign any permissions for the object.

Delegating Administrative Control of Objects

You can delegate administrative control of objects to individuals so that they can perform administrative tasks on the objects. There are different ways to delegate control of objects, and there are also guidelines for delegating control. After you determine who to assign control to, use the Delegation Of Control wizard to delegate control of objects.

You delegate administrative control of objects by assigning permissions to the object to allow users or groups of users to administer the objects. An administrator can delegate the following types of control:

- Assigning permissions to a user or group to create or modify objects in a specific OU

- Assigning permissions to a user or group to modify specific permissions for the attributes of an object, such as assigning the permission to reset passwords on a user account object

Because tracking permissions at the OU level is easier than tracking permissions on objects or object attributes, the most common method of delegating administrative control is to assign permissions at the OU level. Assigning permissions at the OU level allows you to delegate administrative control for the objects contained in the OU. Use the Delegation Of Control wizard to assign permissions at the OU level.

For example, you can delegate administrative control by assigning Full Control for an OU to the appropriate manager, only within his or her area of responsibility. By delegating control of the OU to the manager, you can decentralize administrative operations and issues. This reduces your administration time and costs by distributing administrative control closer to its point of service.

To help you delegate administrative control, follow these guidelines:

- Assign control at the OU level whenever possible. Assigning control at the OU level allows for easier tracking of permission assignments. Tracking permission assignments becomes more complex for objects and object attributes.

- Use the Delegation Of Control wizard. The wizard assigns permissions to a number of objects, including OU object instances and other built-in objects like the Users object and the Subnets object. The Subnets object is part of the Active Directory Sites And Services snap-in. The wizard simplifies the process of assigning object permissions by stepping you through the process.

- Track the delegation of permission assignments. Tracking assignments allows you to maintain records to easily review security settings.

- Follow business requirements. Follow any guidelines your organization has in place for delegating control.

Delegation Of Control Wizard

The Delegation Of Control wizard steps you through the process of assigning permissions at the OU level. For more specialized permissions, you must manually assign permissions.

To use the Delegation Of Control wizard, open the Active Directory Users And Computers snap-in and select the OU for which you want to delegate control. On the Action menu, click Delegate Control to start the wizard (Figure 6.9).

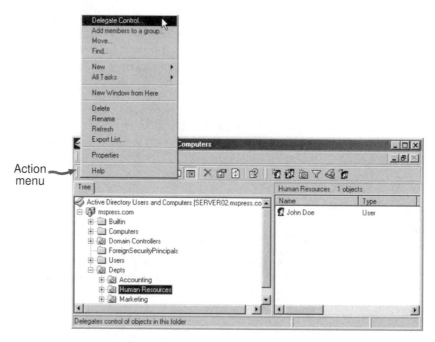

Figure 6.9 Navigating to the Delegate Control Wizard

Guidelines for Administering Active Directory Services

The following list provides best practices for administering Active Directory services:

- In larger organizations, coordinate your Active Directory structure with other administrators. You can move objects later, but this might create extra work.

- When you create Active Directory objects, such as users, complete all attributes that are important to your organization. Completing the attributes gives you more flexibility when you search for objects.

- Use deny permissions sparingly. If you assign permissions correctly, you should not need to deny permissions. In most cases, denied permissions indicate mistakes that were made in assigning group membership.

- Always ensure that at least one user has Full Control for each Active Directory object. Failure to do so might result in objects being inaccessible.

- Ensure that delegated users take responsibility and can be held account-able. You gain nothing if you delegate administrative control without ensuring future accountability. As an administrator, you are ultimately responsible for all the administrative changes made. If the users to whom you delegate responsibility are not performing the administrative tasks, you will need to assume responsibility for their failure.

- Provide training for users who have control of objects. Ensure that the users to whom you delegate responsibility understand their responsibilities and know how to perform the administrative tasks.

Lesson Summary

After Active Directory services has been installed, you can create and manage the objects stored within the directory. Before objects are added to Active Directory services, you should create the OUs that will contain those objects. You can create an OU at the domain level, under the Domain Controllers level, or within another OU, but you must have the required permissions to create OUs in the existing OU, domain, or domain controller. To add object instances to OUs, you must have the required permissions to create objects within the OU where you want to create the object. The process of managing Active Directory objects involves several different tasks, such as locating objects, modifying and deleting objects, and moving objects. These tasks can be performed in the Active Directory Users And Computers snap-in, which is located in the Administrative Tools folder. Another aspect of Active Directory administration is controlling access to Active Directory objects. Active Directory permissions provide security for resources by allowing you to control who can gain access to individual objects or object attributes and the type of access that you will allow. In addition, you can delegate administrative control of objects to individuals so that they can perform administrative tasks on the objects.

Review

The following questions are intended to reinforce key information presented in this chapter. If you are unable to answer a question, review the appropriate lesson and then try the question again. Answers to the questions can be found in Appendix A, "Questions and Answers."

1. What is Ntds.dit, and what is its purpose?

2. What is the one SYSVOL location requirement?

3. What is the function of SYSVOL, and what is the one disk requirement for SYSVOL?

4. What is the difference between an attribute and an attribute value? Give examples.

5. What is the difference between modifying an object and modifying the attribute values of an object instance?

6. You want to allow the manager of the sales department to create, modify, and delete only user accounts for sales personnel. How can you accomplish this?

7. What is the global catalog, and what is its purpose?

CHAPTER 7

Administering Microsoft Windows 2000 Server

About This Chapter

This chapter introduces you to Microsoft Windows 2000 Server administration. The first lesson discusses the Microsoft Management Console (MMC), which is the primary tool used to administer Windows 2000 and other Microsoft products like the BackOffice suite. The rest of the chapter focuses on the specific administrative tasks involved with implementing user accounts, group accounts, and group policies.

Before You Begin

To complete the lessons in this chapter, you must have

- A computer that has Windows 2000 Server installed and operating.
- Microsoft Active Directory services installed and operating.
- Completed all the exercises in the previous chapters.

Lesson 1: Using the Microsoft Management Console

One of the primary administrative tools you use to manage Windows 2000 is the MMC. The MMC provides a standardized method to create, save, and open administrative tools. It unifies and simplifies day-to-day management tasks. The MMC does not provide management functions itself, but it is the program that hosts management applications called snap-ins, which you use to perform one or more administrative tasks.

After this lesson, you will be able to

- Describe the function and components of MMC, including snap-ins and console options

- Create a custom MMC console

Estimated lesson time: 45 minutes

The MMC Environment

MMC is a common console framework for management applications. MMC consoles can run on Windows 2000, Windows NT 4.0, Windows 98, and Windows 95.

The MMC itself does not provide management capability but does provide a common environment for *snap-ins*, the tools that support the actual management functionality. The MMC environment provides seamless integration among the various snap-ins, even those provided by different vendors. Administrators can create tools that include multiple snap-ins and then save the tools for later use or to share with other administrators.

The MMC allows you to do the following:

- **Perform most administrative tasks by using only the MMC** Being able to use one interface instead of numerous interfaces saves time.

- **Centralize administration** You can use MMC consoles to perform the majority of your administrative tasks from one computer.

- **Use most snap-ins for remote administration** Not all snap-ins are available for remote administration, so Windows 2000 prompts you with a dialog box when you can use the snap-in for remote administration.

- **Build a customized console** MMC provides for the creation of specialized consoles containing all or part of multiple snap-ins. These custom consoles can then be distributed to support groups in order to delegate administrative tasks.

Note MMC 1.1 did not support more than one snap-in, while MMC 1.2 in Windows 2000 supports multiple snap-ins in a single console window.

The MMC Window

At first glance, an MMC user interface looks and feels much like a version of Windows Explorer. The components of an MMC console are contained in the MMC window. This window has several menus and a toolbar that provides commands to open, create, and save MMC consoles. The menu and toolbar are called the *main menu bar* and the *main toolbar*. In addition, there is a status bar at the bottom of the window and a description bar along the top of the details pane. The parent window contains the child windows, which are the actual MMC consoles.

The MMC, as shown in Figure 7.1, can be configured to contain powerful management tools. MMC is also designed to offer a scaled-down view that is much less complex to less-experienced administrators.

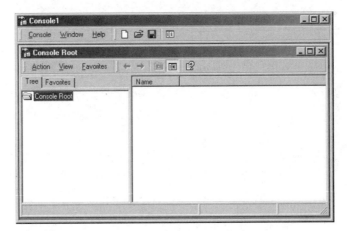

Figure 7.1 The MMC window

MMC Consoles

An MMC console is a set of one or more snap-ins. Consoles are saved as files that use an .msc extension. Each console file is represented as a child window in the MMC interface. An MMC console file contains the console tree, which displays the hierarchical organization of multiple snap-ins contained within the file. All the settings for the snap-ins contained in the console are saved and are restored when the file is opened, even if the console file is opened on a different computer or network.

Console Window

A console window (child window), which is an interface to an MMC console file, offers many differing views. Each console window includes a command bar, a console tree (left pane), and a detail pane (right pane). The console window in the background of Figure 7.2 shows three snap-ins, and the foreground window is a child window of the Computer Management console.

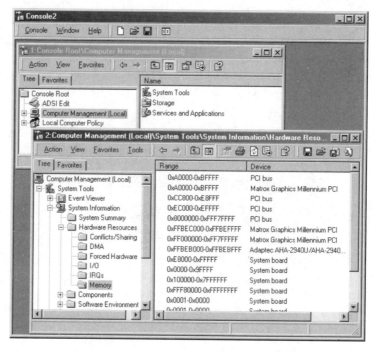

Figure 7.2 An MMC console containing multiple snap-ins, and a child window

The command bar contains both pull-down menus and buttons. The following table describes the console window menus.

Menu	Description
Action	Create, delete, and modify the items that are managed by the snap-in. Specific functions vary depending on the active snap-in.
View	Configure the snap-in display.
Favorites	Organize snap-ins or nodes of snap-ins, or manage folders that contain MMC objects. These components then appear under the Favorites tab. The Favorites tab is behind the Tree tab in Figures 7.1 and 7.2.

Note Additional pull-down menu items will appear for some objects in the console tree. For example, Figure 7.2 shows that when the System Information node is selected from the console tree, a Tools pull-down menu appears.

The console tree, also referred to as the scope pane, organizes snap-ins that are part of an MMC console. This organization allows you to locate a specific snap-in easily. Items that you add to the console tree appear under the console root. The console tree displays the tool's namespace and the tree-formatted listing of all visible nodes, each of which represents a manageable object, task, or view. The console tree might not be visible in all views.

Each detail pane, also referred to as the results pane, displays the results of selecting a node in the console tree. In many cases, it is a list of a folder's contents, but in other cases, it is a management related view, which can be Web-based or ActiveX control-based.

Types of MMC Consoles

There are two types of MMC consoles: customized and preconfigured.

Customized MMC Consoles

You can combine one or more snap-ins or parts of snap-ins to create customized MMC consoles, which can then be used to centralize and combine administrative tasks. MMC allows administrators to perform the following tasks:

- Saving the customized MMC to use again

- Distributing to and sharing the customized MMC with other administrators

- Using the customized MMC from any computer to centralize and unify administrative tasks

Although you can use many of the preconfigured MMC consoles for administrative tasks, sometimes you will need to create your own custom MMC consoles. You can combine multiple preconfigured snap-ins with third-party snap-ins provided by independent software vendors (ISVs) that perform related tasks to create custom MMC consoles. Creating custom MMC consoles allows you to meet your administrative requirements by combining snap-ins that you use to perform common administrative tasks. By creating a custom MMC console, you do not have to switch between different programs or different preconfigured MMC consoles because all the snap-ins you need to perform your job are located in the custom MMC console.

By default, Windows 2000 saves customized MMC files in the My Administrative Tools folder with an .msc file extension. If the My Administrative Tools folder does not exist, Windows 2000 creates it. Windows 2000 saves the My Administrative Tools folder contents separately for each user.

Note For more information about creating MMC consoles, see the Supplemental Course Materials CD-ROM (\chapt07\articles\microsoft management console.doc) that accompanies this book.

Preconfigured MMC Consoles

When Windows 2000 is installed, preconfigured MMC consoles are also installed. These MMC consoles contain commonly used snap-ins that are used to perform administrative tasks. Preconfigured MMC consoles cannot be modified nor can additional snap-ins be added.

Preconfigured MMC consoles contain only one snap-in that provides the functionality to perform a related set of administrative tasks. The consoles function in user mode, which means that you cannot modify them, save them, or add additional snap-ins. User mode operation is indicated by the absence of the MMC console pull-down menus (Console, Window, and Help) and the absence of the MMC toolbar objects. Also, MMC consoles are sometimes added when you install additional components. For example, when you install the Domain Name System (DNS) service, Windows 2000 also installs the DNS console.

Note To select preconfigured MMC consoles, click the Start button, point to Programs, and then click Administrative Tools.

Which MMC consoles are installed on a computer varies depending on which Windows 2000 operating system is running and which Windows 2000 components are installed. Windows 2000 Server and Windows 2000 Professional have different preconfigured MMC consoles that appear on the Administrative Tools menu. The preconfigured MMC consoles included in Windows 2000 Server can be added to Windows 2000 Professional to enable remote administration of server functions. A convenient way to add all the Windows 2000 Server administrative tools is by running Adminpak.msi from the Windows 2000 Server installation CD-ROM.

Snap-Ins

Each MMC console is made up of a collection of smaller tools called snap-ins. *Snap-ins* are applications designed to work in MMC. One snap-in represents one unit of management functionality. A snap-in is the smallest unit of console extension. A snap-in extends the MMC console by adding and enabling management capability and functionality. You can use snap-ins to perform a variety of administrative tasks. There are two types of snap-ins: stand-alone and extension. Figure 7.3 shows the Add/Remove Snap-In dialog box, which is accessed from the MMC console menu. Both types of snap-ins are added from this dialog box.

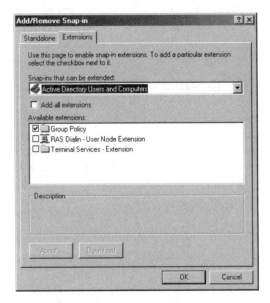

Figure 7.3 The Add/Remove Snap-In dialog box showing how snap-in extensions are adjusted from the Extensions tab

Stand-Alone Snap-Ins

Stand-alone snap-ins are usually referred to simply as snap-ins. Use stand-alone snap-ins to perform Windows 2000 administrative tasks. Each snap-in provides one function or a related set of functions. Windows 2000 Server comes with standard snap-ins. Windows 2000 Professional includes a smaller set of standard snap-ins.

Extension Snap-Ins

Extension snap-ins are usually referred to as extensions. They provide additional administrative functionality to another snap-in. Extensions are designed to work with one or more stand-alone snap-ins, based on the function of the stand-alone snap-in. When you add an extension, Windows 2000 displays only extensions that are compatible with the stand-alone snap-in. Windows 2000 places the extensions into the appropriate location within the stand-alone snap-in. Some snap-ins, such as Event Viewer, can act as a snap-in or an extension.

Extensions can provide a variety of functionality. Some actually extend the console namespace. For example, a snap-in that provides system information about computers would add that system information to the namespace under each computer in the namespace. Other extensions simply extend context menus or specific wizards.

Many snap-ins offer stand-alone functionality while extending the functionality of other snap-ins. For example, the Event Log snap-in will read the event logs of computers. If the Computer Management object exists in the console, Event Log automatically extends each instance of a Computer Management object and provides the event logs for the computer. Alternatively, the event log can also operate in Stand-alone mode, in which case it does not appear as a node below the Computer Management node.

Console Options

An MMC console holds snap-ins that perform specific tasks. Console options determine how an MMC console operates. By using console options, you can create MMC consoles for other administrators to use from their computers to perform specific tasks. The Console mode determines the MMC console functionality for the person who is using a saved MMC console. There are two available Console modes: author mode and user mode.

Author Mode

When you save an MMC console in author mode, you enable full access to all MMC functionality, which includes modifying the MMC console. An MMC console that has been saved in author mode allows users to do the following:

- Add or remove snap-ins
- Create new windows
- View all portions of the console tree
- Save MMC consoles

Note By default, all new MMC consoles are saved in author mode.

User Mode

If you plan to distribute an MMC console to other administrators, you should usually save the MMC console in user mode. When you set an MMC console to user mode, users cannot add snap-ins to, remove snap-ins from, or save the MMC console.

There are three types of user modes. Each type provides a different level of access and functionality. The following table describes when to use each user mode.

Type of user mode	Description
Full Access	Allows users to navigate between snap-ins, open new windows, and gain access to all portions of the console tree.
Limited Access, Multiple Windows	Prevents users from opening new windows or gaining access to a portion of the console tree, but allows them to view multiple windows in the console.
Limited Access, Single Window	Prevents users from opening new windows or gaining access to a portion of the console tree, and allows them to view only one window in the console.

Exercise 1: Navigating and Creating a Custom MMC

In this exercise, you use one of the MMC consoles included with Windows 2000 Server. Then you create a customized MMC console.

▶ Procedure 1: Using an existing MMC console

In this procedure, you use MMC consoles that ship with Windows 2000 Server. Complete this exercise from Server01.

1. Log on as Administrator with a password of "password."

2. Click the Start button, point to Programs, point to Administrative Tools, and then click Event Viewer.

   Windows 2000 displays the Event Viewer console, which gives you access to the contents of the Event Log service files on your computer. You use Event Viewer to monitor various hardware and software activities.

   Notice that a number of logs are listed. The logs always appearing when Windows 2000 Server is installed are the Application log, Security log, and System log. Additional logs appear as additional services are added. You should see the Directory Service log because Server01 is configured to run Active Directory services, a DNS Server log because it is configured to run as a DNS server, and a File Replication Service log because Server01 is running FRS.

3. Close the Event Viewer console.

▶ Procedure 2: Creating and manipulating a customized MMC console

In this procedure, you create and customize an MMC console. You use this console to confirm the last time your computer was started. You also add a snap-in with extensions.

1. Click the Start button, and then click Run.

2. In the Open text box, type **mmc** and then click OK.

   MMC starts and displays an empty console.

3. Maximize the Console1 window by clicking the Maximize button.

4. Maximize the Console Root window by clicking the Maximize button in the child window.

5. Click the Console menu, and then choose Options to view the currently configured options.

   MMC displays the Options dialog box.

6. In what mode is the console running?

7. Verify that the Console Mode drop-down list box is in author mode, and then click OK.

8. Click the Console menu, and then click Save.

   The Save As dialog box appears.

   Notice that the default location for customized consoles is the Administrative Tools folder. This maps to the Administrative Tools Program Group for the currently logged on user. You can see this by clicking the down arrow to the far right of the Save In: drop-down list box.

9. In the File Name text box, type **All Events** and then click Save.

   The name of your console appears in the MMC title bar.

10. To confirm that the console was saved in the correct location, click the Console menu and then click Exit.

11. Click the Start button, point to Programs, point to Administrative Tools, and then click All Events.msc.

   The All Events console, which you saved previously, appears.

12. Click the Console menu, and then click Add/Remove Snap-In.

   The Add/Remove Snap-In dialog box appears with the Stand-Alone tab active. Notice that there are currently no loaded snap-ins.

13. In the Add/Remove Snap-In dialog box, click Add.

   The Add Stand Alone Snap-In dialog box appears.

14. In the Add Stand Alone Snap-In dialog box, scroll down to find and select Event Viewer and then click Add.

   The Select Computer dialog box appears, allowing you to specify which computer you want to administer.

   Notice that you can add Event Viewer for the local computer you are working on, or if your local computer is part of a network, you can also add Event Viewer for a remote computer.

15. In the Select Computer dialog box, verify that the Local Computer: (the computer this console is running on) radio button is selected and then click Finish.

16. In the Add Stand-Alone Snap-In dialog box, click Close; and in the Add/Remove Snap-In dialog box, click OK.

    Event Viewer (Local) now appears in the console tree.

    Tip To see the entire folder name, drag the border between the console panes to the right.

17. In the console tree of the All Events console, expand the Event Viewer (Local) node and then click System.

    The most recent system events are shown in the results pane.

18. Double-click the most recent event listed as Information in the Type column and listed as eventlog in the Source column.

    The Event Log service started as part of your system startup. The date and time represents the approximate time your system was started.

19. Click OK to close the Event Properties dialog box.

20. Click the Console menu, and then click Exit to close the All Events console.

    A Microsoft Management Console dialog box appears, asking if you want to save the console settings to All Events.

21. Click No.

22. Click the Start button, and then click Run.

23. In the Open box, type **mmc** and then click OK.

24. Maximize the Console1 and Console Root windows.

25. Click the Console menu, and then click Add/Remove Snap-In.

    The Add/Remove Snap-In dialog box appears with the Stand-Alone tab active. You will add a snap-in to the console root.

26. Click Add.

    All snap-ins that are listed here are stand-alone snap-ins.

27. In the Add Stand Alone Snap-In dialog box, click Computer Management and then click Add.

    The Computer Management dialog box appears.

28. Verify that Local Computer: (the computer this console is running on) radio button is selected, and then click Finish.

29. Click Close.

   Computer Management appears in the list of snap-ins that have been added.

30. In the Add/Remove Snap-In dialog box, click OK.

   The Computer Management snap-in appears under the Console Root.

31. Expand the Computer Management node, review the available functions, and then expand the System Tools node.

   Note Do not use any of the tools at this point.

   Notice that several extensions are available, including Device Manager and System Information. You can restrict the functionality of a snap-in by removing extensions.

32. Click the Console menu, and then click Add/Remove Snap-In.

   The Add/Remove Snap-In dialog box appears.

33. Click Computer Management (Local), and then click the Extensions tab.

   A list of available extensions contained in the Computer Management snap-in appears.

34. Clear the Add All Extensions check box, and then in the Available Extensions box, clear the Device Manager Extension check box, scroll down the list and then clear the System Information Extension check box.

35. Click OK.

   The console window appears.

36. Expand Computer Management, and then expand System Tools to confirm that Device Manager and System Information have been removed.

   Note Do not use any of the tools at this point.
   ---

37. Click the Console menu, and then click Options.

   The Options dialog box appears.

38. From the Console Mode drop-down list box, select User Mode - Limited Access single window.

39. Click the Do Not Save Changes To This Console check box, and then click OK.

40. Close the console.

    MMC displays a message prompting for confirmation to save console settings.

41. Click Yes.

    The Save As dialog box appears.

42. In the File Name text box, type **ComputerMgmt Restricted** and then click Save.

43. Click the Start menu, point to Programs, point to Administrative Tools, and then click ComputerMgmt Restricted.

    Notice that the custom console opens in a single window.

44. Close the custom console.

    Notice that the Save This Console message box does not appear.

Lesson Summary

One of the primary administrative tools you use to manage Windows 2000 Server is the MMC, which provides a standardized method to create, save, and open administrative tools. These tools, called MMC consoles, hold one or more snap-ins, which are management applications used to perform administrative tasks. By default, Windows 2000 saves custom MMC console files with the .msc extension in the Administrative Tools folder. Every MMC console has a console tree, which displays the hierarchical organization of the snap-ins contained in that console, and a details pane, which lists the contents of the active snap-in. There are two types of snap-ins: stand-alone and extension. A stand-alone snap-in provides one function or a related set of functions. An extension snap-in adds administrative functionality to a stand-alone snap-in. Each console can be configured to operate in one of two modes: user mode or author mode. User mode prevents other users from adding or removing snap-ins to the console or saving the console. Author mode enables full access to all MMC functionality. Consoles can be customized and distributed to users running in the network.

Lesson 2: Administering User Accounts

User accounts must be created to give users the ability to log on to a domain to access network resources or to log on to a computer to access resources on that computer. A *user account* is a user's unique credentials. It is a record that defines a user to Windows 2000. This includes the user name and password, if required, for the user to log on, the groups the user account has membership in, and the rights and permissions the user has for using the computer and network and for accessing resources. Each person who regularly uses the network is assigned a user account.

After this lesson, you will be able to

- Describe the role and purpose of user accounts
- Plan and create user accounts
- Administer user accounts, including setting account properties

Estimated lesson time: 60 minutes

Windows 2000 User Accounts

A user account provides a user with the ability to log on to the domain to gain access to network resources or to log on to a computer to gain access to resources on that computer. Each person who regularly uses the network should have a user account.

Windows 2000 supports two types of user accounts: domain and local. With a domain user account, a user can log on to the domain to gain access to network resources. With a local user account, a user can log on to a specific computer to gain access to resources on that computer.

Windows 2000 also provides built-in user accounts, which are used to perform administrative tasks or to gain access to network resources.

Domain User Accounts

Domain user accounts allow users to log on to the domain and gain access to resources anywhere on the network. The user provides his or her password and user name during the logon process. By using this information, Windows 2000 authenticates the user and then builds an access token that contains information about the user and security settings. The access token identifies the user to computers running Windows 2000 on which the user tries to gain access to resources. Windows 2000 provides the access token for the duration of the logon session.

You create a domain user account in an organizational unit (OU) in a replica of the Active Directory store (called the directory) on a domain controller. The domain controller replicates the new user account information to all domain controllers in the domain.

After Windows 2000 replicates the new user account information, all the domain controllers in the domain tree can authenticate the user during the logon process.

Note It can take a few minutes to replicate the domain user account information to all the domain controllers. This delay might prevent a user from immediately logging on by using the newly created domain user account. Replication of Active Directory information within a site (intrasite replication) occurs automatically every five minutes.

Local User Accounts

Local user accounts allow users to log on to and gain access to resources on only the computer where you create the local user account. When you create a local user account, Windows 2000 creates the account in that computer's security database only. Windows 2000 does not replicate local user account information to domain controllers. After the local user account is created, the computer uses its local security database to authenticate the local user account, which allows the user to log on to that computer.

Built-In User Accounts

Windows 2000 automatically creates accounts called built-in accounts. Two commonly used built-in accounts are Administrator and Guest. The operating system will not allow built-in accounts to be deleted or the built-in Administrator account to be disabled. However, built-in accounts can be renamed.

Administrator

Use the built-in Administrator account to manage the overall computer and domain configuration, such as creating and modifying user accounts and groups, managing security policies, creating printers, and assigning permissions and rights to user accounts to gain access to resources.

If you are the administrator, you should create a user account that you use to perform nonadministrative tasks. Use the Administrator account only when you perform administrative tasks. For convenience, use the run as command to run in the context of a more privileged account while logged on with a lesser privileged account. For example, to run MMC as an administrator while logged on with standard user rights, run the following command:

```
runas user:<domain_name>\<administrator_account> mmc
```

If the Administrator account in the microsoft.com domain is named Administrator, the following command can be used to start the MMC as Administrator:

```
runas /user:microsoft\administrator mmc
```

Tip Rename the built-in Administrator account to provide a greater degree of security. Use a name that does not identify it as the Administrator account. This makes it difficult for unauthorized users to break into the Administrator account because they do not know which user account it is. For additional security, after you rename the built-in Administrator account, create another account named Administrator that has no rights to the system. This will frustrate a hacker's attempt to use the Administrator account to access the system.

Guest

Use the built-in Guest account to give occasional users the ability to log on and gain access to resources. For example, an employee who needs access to resources for a short time can use the Guest account.

Note The Guest account is disabled by default. Enable the Guest account only in low-security networks and always assign it a password.

Planning New User Accounts

You can streamline the process of creating user accounts by planning and organizing the information for the user accounts. You should plan the following three areas:

- Naming conventions for user accounts
- Requirements for passwords
- Account options, such as logon hours, the computers from which users can log on, and account expiration

Naming Conventions

The naming convention establishes how users are identified in the domain. A consistent naming convention will help you and your users remember user logon names and locate them in lists.

The following table summarizes several points to consider in determining a naming convention for your organization:

Consideration	Explanation
Unique user logon names	User logon names for domain user accounts must be unique to the Directory. Domain user account names must be unique within the OU where you create the domain user account. Local user account names must be unique on the computer where you create the local user account.
20 characters maximum	User logon names can contain up to 20 uppercase or lowercase characters; the field accepts more than 20 characters, but Windows 2000 recognizes only the first 20.
Invalid characters	The following characters are invalid: " / \ [ ] : ;	= , + * ? < >
User logon names are not case sensitive	You can use a combination of special and alphanumeric characters to help uniquely identify user accounts. User logon names are not case sensitive, but Windows 2000 preserves the case.
Employees with duplicate names	If two users are named John Doe, you can use the first name and the last initial and then add letters from the last name to differentiate the duplicate names. In this example, one user account logon name could be Johnd and the other Johndo. Another possibility would be to number each useR logon name, for example, Johnd1 and Johnd2.
Type of employee	In some organizations, it is useful to identify temporary employees by their user account. For example, to identify temporary employees, you can use a T and a dash in front of the user's logon name: T-Johnd. Or you might use a parenthetical phrase, such as John Doe (Temp).
Service account naming conventions	Many background services require user accounts in order to operate. Consider appending the name of the user account with an abbreviated generic name such as svc for service or a service type name such as exc for a background account used by Microsoft Exchange services.

Password Requirements

To protect access to the domain or a computer, every user account should have a password. Consider the following guidelines for passwords:

- Always assign a password for the Administrator account to prevent unauthorized access to the account.

- Determine whether the administrator or the users will control passwords. You can assign unique passwords for the user accounts and prevent users from changing them, or you can allow users to enter their own passwords the first time they log on. In most cases, users should control their passwords.

- Use passwords that are hard to guess. For example, avoid using passwords with an obvious association, such as a family member's name.

- Passwords can be up to 128 characters; a minimum length of eight characters is recommended.

- Use both uppercase and lowercase letters, numerals, and valid nonalphanumeric characters. The table above lists the invalid nonalphanumeric characters.

Account Options

You should assess the hours when a user can log on to the network and the computers from which a user can log on, and you should determine if temporary user accounts need to expire. To determine account options, consider the following information.

Logon Hours

Set logon hours to control when a user can log on to the domain. Restricting logon hours limits the hours that users can explore the network. By default, Windows 2000 permits access for all hours on all days. You might want to allow users to log on only during working hours. Setting logon hours reduces the amount of time that the account is open to unauthorized access.

Computers from Which Users Can Log On

Determine the computers that users can log on from. By default, users can log on to the domain by using any computer in the domain. For security, require users to log on to the domain only from their own computers. This prevents users from gaining access to sensitive information stored on other computers.

Note If you have disabled NetBIOS over Transmission Control Protocol/ Internet Protocol (TCP/IP), Windows 2000 is unable to determine which computer you are logging on from, and therefore you cannot restrict users to specific computers. This is because this feature restricts access by computer name rather than Message Authentication Code address.

Account Expiration

Determine whether a user account should expire. If so, set an expiration date on the user account to ensure that the account is disabled when the user should no longer have access to the network. As a good security practice, you should set user accounts for temporary employees to expire when their contract ends.

Creating User Accounts

You can create two types of user accounts: domain and local.

Creating Domain User Accounts

Use the Active Directory Users And Computers snap-in to create a new domain user account. When you create a domain user account, it is always created on the first available domain controller contacted by MMC, and then the account is replicated to all domain controllers.

Tip You can rapidly create many user accounts by creating and running scripts through the Windows Script Host (WSH). For information on WSH, open Windows 2000 Server Help and locate the book titled *Automating Administrative Tasks* and the chapter titled "Windows Script Host."

Active Directory Users And Computers Snap-In

The Active Directory Users And Computers snap-in allows you to create domain user accounts (Figure 7.4).

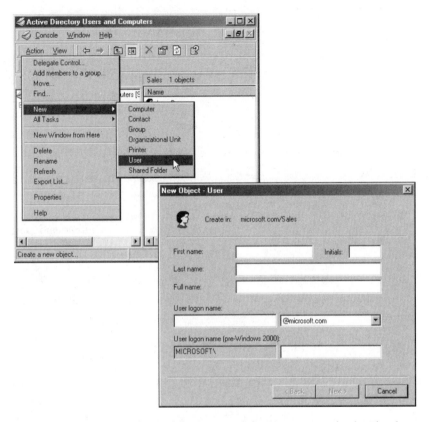

Figure 7.4 The Active Directory Users And Computers snap-in showing how to navigate to the New Object - User dialog box

You must select the OU to create the new account in. You can create the domain user account in the default Users OU or in an OU or in OUs that you create to hold domain user accounts.

To create a domain user account, open the Active Directory Users And Computers snap-in and select the Users OU. In the Action menu, point to New and then point to Users (Figure 7.4). Enter the user information in the New Object - User dialog box.

When you create the domain user account, User Logon Name defaults to the domain in which you are creating the domain user account, as shown in Figure 7.4. However, you can select any domain in which you have permissions to create domain user accounts.

The following table describes the domain user account options:

Option	Description
First Name	The user's first name. This, Initials, or Last Name is required.
Last Name	The user's last name. This, Initials, or First Name is required.
Full Name	The user's full name. Windows 2000 completes this option if you enter information in First Name or Last Name. Windows 2000 displays this name in the OU where the user account is located in the Directory.
User Logon Name	The user's unique logon name, based on your naming conventions. This is required and must be unique within the directory.
User Logon Name (pre-Windows 2000)	The user's unique logon name used to log on from down-level clients, such as Windows NT 4.0 or Windows NT 3.51. This is required and must be unique within the domain.

Setting Password Requirements

When you are adding a new user account, you can enter a password for the user. In the New Object - User dialog box, click Next to open a second New Object - User dialog box. This screen contains password settings. In this dialog box, you set the password requirements for the domain user account. You do not have to enter a password for the user. If you don't enter a password, the user will be able to log on to the domain without a password.

The following table describes the password options:

Option	Description
Password	The password used to authenticate the user. For greater security, you should always assign a password. Notice that you do not see the password. It is represented as asterisks when you type it.
Confirm Password	Confirm the password by typing it a second time to make sure you typed it correctly. This is required if you assign a password.
User Must Change Password At Next Logon	Select this check box if you want the user to change his or her password the first time he or she logs on. This ensures that the user is the only person who knows the password.

Option	Description
User Cannot Change Password	Select this check box if you have more than one person using the same domain user account (such as Guest) or to maintain control over user account passwords. This feature is commonly used for background service account password control.
Password Never Expires	Select this check box if the password should never change, for example, for a domain user account that will be used by a program or a Windows 2000 service. The Password Never Expires setting overrides the User Must Change Password At Next Logon setting. If both check boxes are selected, Windows 2000 will automatically clear the User Must Change Password At Next Logon check box.
Account Is Disabled	Select this check box to prevent use of this user account, for example, for a new employee who has not yet started.

Note Always require new users to change their passwords the first time they log on. This will force users to use passwords that only they know. For added security on networks, create random initial passwords for all new user accounts by combining letters and numbers. Creating a random initial password will help keep the user account secure.

Exercise 2: Modifying Domain User Account Properties

In Exercise 5, Procedure 1 of the previous chapter, you created three user accounts. In this exercise, you use the Active Directory Users And Computers snap-in to manipulate the properties of the Jane_Doe, John_Smith, and Bob_Train user accounts. Complete all the procedures in the exercise from Server01.

▶ Procedure 1: Manipulating user accounts

In this procedure, you modify user account properties. You configure the Logon Hours, Account Expiration, and password restriction settings for several of the user accounts that you created in the previous chapter. You add these user accounts to the Print Operators group so that the accounts can log on locally to the domain controller. You then test the Logon Hours restrictions, the password restrictions, and the Account Expiration Settings.

1. Log on to Server01 as Administrator with a password of "password."

2. Click Start, point to programs, point to Administrative Tools, and then click Active Directory Users And Computers.

   The Active Directory Users And Computers snap-in appears.

3. Expand the microsoft.com node in the left pane.

   The console tree appears.

4. Select the Users folder.

5. In the details pane, double-click the Bob Train user.

   The Bob Train Properties dialog box appears with the General tab active.

   Notice that on the General tab, you specify a number of user account properties in addition to first and last name. Text box values like Office and Telephone Number are especially useful for locating users.

6. Click the Account tab, and then click Logon Hours.

   The Logon Hours For Bob Train dialog box appears.

   Notice that Bob is permitted to logon at any time.

7. To restrict Bob's logon hours, click the start time of the first period during which you want to prevent the user from logging on and then drag the pointer to the end time for the period. For this procedure, locate the current day and hour of the day and deny logon for the next three hours.

   Important You must complete this entire exercise in the next three hours for this account restriction to work properly. Otherwise, extend the account restriction to the time when you plan to complete the exercise.

   A frame outlines the blocks for all the selected hours, and the time restriction appears in the bottom left of the Logon Hours For Bob Train dialog box.

8. Click the Logon Denied radio button.

   The outlined area is now a white block, indicating that the user will not be permitted to log on during those hours.

   Tip To select the same block of time for all days in the week, in the row labeled All click the gray block that represents the start time, and then drag the pointer to the end time. To select an entire day, click the gray block that is labeled with the name of day.

   ---

9. Click OK to close the Logon Hours For Bob Train dialog box.

10. In the Bob Train Properties dialog box, click OK to apply your settings.

11. In the details pane, double-click John Smith.

    The John Smith Properties dialog box appears with the General tab active.

12. Click the Account tab.

13. When will the account expire?

14. In the Account expires section, click the End Of radio button and then set the date to today's date.

15. Click OK to apply your changes.

16. Click the Sales folder in the console tree.

    The Jane Doe account appears in the details pane.

17. Double click the Jane Doe account.

    The Jane Doe Properties dialog box appears with the General tab active.

18. Click the Account tab.

19. In the Account options box, click the User Must Change Password At Next Logon check box.

20. Click OK to close the Jane Doe Properties dialog box.

21. Close the Active Directory Users And Computers snap-in.

22. Click Start and then click Shut Down.

    The Shut Down Windows dialog box appears.

23. Select Log Off Administrator from the drop-down list box, and click OK.

    Windows 2000 logs off the Administrator account and displays the Welcome To Windows message box.

24. Press Ctrl+Alt+Delete, and continue to Procedure 2.

▶ **Procedure 2: Attempting to log on to Server01 with a user account**

In this procedure, you attempt to use the Jane Doe (Jane_Doe) user account to log on to Server01.

1. In the User Name text box, log on as Jane_Doe with no password.

   The Logon Message message box appears, indicating that your password has expired and must be changed.

2. Click OK.

   The Change Password dialog box appears, and the cursor is in the Old Password text box.

3. Press the tab key since the Jane_Doe account was not assigned a password.

4. In the New Password text box and the Confirm New Password text box, type **student** and then click OK.

   The Change Password message box appears, indicating that your password was changed.

5. Click OK to close the Change Password message box.

   Were you able to log on successfully? Why or why not?

6. Click OK to close the message box.

▸ **Procedure 3: Granting local logon access to user accounts**

There are several ways to allow regular users to log on locally at a domain controller. In this procedure, you add the three users you created in the previous chapter to the Print Operators group, because this group has the right to log on to a domain controller.

Note A group is a collection of user accounts. Groups simplify administration by allowing you to assign permissions to a group of users rather than having to assign permissions to each individual user account. You will learn more about groups later in this chapter.

---

1. Log on as Administrator with a password of "password."

2. Open Active Directory Users And Computers, and in the console tree, expand the Sales OU.

3. In the details pane, double-click the Jane Doe user account.

   The Jane Doe Properties dialog box appears with the General tab active.

4. Click the Member Of tab.

5. Click Add.

   The Select Groups dialog box appears.

6. Scroll down in the top box to locate and click Print Operators.

7. Click Add, and then click OK to close the Select Groups dialog box.

8. Click OK to close the Jane Doe Properties dialog box.

   In the next steps, you will use a simpler method to add both the Bob Train and John Smith accounts to the Print Operators group.

9. In the console tree, click the Users folder.

10. In the details pane, click once on Bob Train, press and hold down the Ctrl key, and click once on John Smith.

11. Click the Action menu, and then click Add Members To Group.

    The Select Group dialog box appears.

12. Scroll down to locate and double-click Print Operators.

    An Active Directory message box appears stating that the Add To Group operation completed successfully.

13. Click OK.

14. Close Active Directory Users And Computers and log off.

15. Attempt to log on as Jane_Doe with a password of "student."

    Notice that you are now able to log on locally with the Jane_Doe user account.

16. Attempt to log on as Bob_Train with no password.

    Notice that you were not able to log on because of an account restriction. In Procedure 1 you restricted Bob's logon hours.

17. Attempt to log on as John_Smith with no password.

    Notice that you are allowed to logon as the John_Smith user account. In Procedure 1 you set John's account expiration to the end of the day. If you try to log on as John Smith tomorrow, logon will fail because of an account restriction.

18. Log off of Server01.

Creating Local User Accounts

A local user account allows a user to log on and access resources only on the computer for which you create the account. Use the Local Users And Groups snap-in to create local user accounts (Figure 7.5).

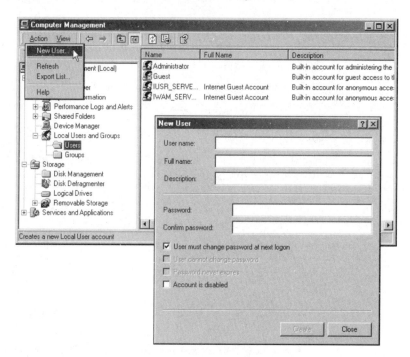

Figure 7.5 The Local Users And Groups snap-in and the New User dialog box

You can create local user accounts only on computers running Windows 2000 Professional and on stand-alone servers or member servers running Windows 2000 Server. Local user accounts are not stored in the directory for the domain; they are stored in the security database of the computer where you create them.

Modifying Properties for User Accounts

A set of default properties is associated with each domain user account and local user account created. Domain user accounts contain more properties than local user accounts. Local user account properties represent a subset of domain user account properties.

Properties that are defined for a domain user account can be used to search for users in the Active Directory store. For this reason, detailed property definitions for domain user accounts should be used. For example, a user knows a person's first name and telephone number and wants to find the person's last name. The user can use the telephone number to search for the last name.

The following properties should be configured for each domain user account based on the business requirements of each user:

- Personal properties, including General, Address, Telephones, and Organization properties
- Account properties
- Logon Hours properties
- Log On To properties

One way to modify a domain user account is to open the Active Directory Users And Computers snap-in and double-click the user object whose properties you want to modify.

One way to modify a local user account is to open the Computer Management snap-in and select Local Users And Groups. Double-click the user object whose properties you want to modify.

The Properties Dialog Box

The Properties dialog box for each user account contains a set of tabs that allows users to configure various properties for a specific user. All the tabs described below apply to domain user accounts. Only the General, Dial-In, Member Of, and Profile tabs apply to local user accounts.

Personal Properties Tabs

The personal properties tabs include the General, Address, Telephones, and Organization tabs. Completing the attributes on each of these tabs enables users and administrators to locate other users in Active Directory services.

The following table describes the personal properties tabs:

Tab	Description
General	Use this tab to document the user's name, description, office location, telephone, e-mail name, and home page information.
Address	Use this tab to document the user's street address, post office box, city, state or province, zip code, and country.
Telephones	Use this tab to document the user's home, pager, mobile, fax, and IP telephone numbers, and to add comments.
Organization	Use this tab to document the user's title, department, company manager, and direct reports.

Account Tab

The Account tab allows you to define a user's logon name and set other account options for the user account. Some of these options were set as default when the user object was created in the Active Directory store. You can modify these properties as well as configure the additional properties.

Profile Tab

User profiles automatically create and maintain the desktop settings for each user's work environment on the local computer. The Profile tab allows you to set a path to the network share where the user profiles are to be stored. In addition, you can assign a logon script and home folder for the user account.

Published Certificates Tab

A *certificate* is a collection of data used for authentication and secure exchange of information on nonsecured networks, such as the Internet. A certificate securely binds a public encryption key to the entity that holds the corresponding private encryption key. The Published Certificates tab allows you to create a list of X.509 certificates for the user account.

Member Of Tab

Groups are used to consolidate administrative tasks. For example, assign NTFS permissions to a group and then add users to the group. Each group member is affected by the rights assignment. The Member Of tab allows you to document the groups the user belongs to.

Dial-In Tab

The Dial-In tab allows you to control how a user can make a dial-in connection to the network from a remote location. To gain access to the network, the user dials in to a computer running the Windows 2000 Remote Access Service (RAS).

Note In addition to configuring dial-in settings and having RAS on the server the user is dialing in to, you must also set up a dial-up connection for the server on the client computer. Set up a dial-up connection by using the Network Connection wizard, which you can access from Network Connections in My Computer.

The following table describes the required options for setting up security for a dial-up connection:

Option	Description
Allow Access	Specifies whether to enable dial-in settings.
Deny Access	Specifies whether to disable dial-in settings.
Verify Caller-ID	The telephone number that the user must dial in to.
No Callback	Specifies that the RAS server will not call the user back. This allows a user to call from any phone number. This is the default and is designed for a low-security environment or where other dial-in security methods are implemented.
Set By Caller (Routing and Remote Access Service only)	Specifies that the user provide the telephone number for the RAS server to call back. This allows a user to call from any phone number, and the RAS server calls the user back. This calling information can be logged. Use this feature for a medium-security environment.
Always Callback To	Specifies that the RAS server calls back the user. The RAS server uses the specified telephone number. The user must be at the specified telephone number to make a connection to the server. This reduces the risk of an unauthorized person dialing in because the number is preconfigured. Use this option in a high-security environment.

Object Tab

The Object tab provides the fully qualified domain name of the object. It also provides additional information, such as the object class, the create and modified dates, the original Unique Sequence Number (USN), and the current USN. The USNs are used to track changes to objects in the Active Directory store.

Security Tab

The Security tab is used to set permissions on the user object in the Active Directory store. You can allow or deny specific permissions to groups or users within the domain. You can also configure advanced permissions, and you can allow or prevent the inheritance of permissions from the parent object to the user object in the Active Directory tree.

Terminal Services Tabs

The Terminal Services tabs contain information about the user that is specific to Terminal Services. Terminal Services allows a user to log on from a computer terminal and run a Windows 2000 session on the terminal. The information on the Terminal Services tabs includes when users can log on, under what conditions, and how specific desktop settings are stored. The Terminal Services tabs are the Environment, Sessions, Remote Control, and Terminal Services Profile tabs.

Environment Tab

The Environment tab contains settings for creating the client working environment. If a starting program is specified, it opens automatically whenever the user connects to a Terminal server. It is the only application that can be used by the user. When the application is closed, the connection to the Terminal server closes.

You can also set the user account so that Terminal Services can automatically connect local client drives and printers at logon. When the client logs on to the server, the local drives and printers are detected and the appropriate printer driver is installed on the Terminal server. If multiple printers are connected, you can also default all print jobs to the main client printer.

Sessions Tab

The Sessions tab of the Terminal Services extension provides settings for limiting the length of sessions based on their current state (active, idle, or disconnected). You can also specify what action to take when a session has reached a time limit.

The following table describes several options on the Sessions tab:

Time-out setting	Description
End A Disconnected Session	Specifies the maximum duration that a disconnected session is retained. The session will be reset and can no longer be reconnected once the time limit has expired.
Active Session Limit	Specifies the maximum connection duration. When the time limit is reached, the session will be either disconnected, leaving the session active on the server, or reset.
Idle Session Limit	Specifies the maximum idle time (time without connection activity) allowed before the session is disconnected or reset. The session is disconnected or reset when the interval elapses without any activity at the connection.

Remote Control Tab

The Remote Control tab allows you to configure Terminal Services' remote control settings. You can monitor the actions of a client logged on to a Terminal server by using remote control from another session. Remote control allows you to either observe or actively control a client session. If you choose to actively control a client session, you will be able to input keyboard and mouse actions to the session. You can warn a client that you want to remotely control the session by choosing to display a message on the client that asks permission to view or take part in the session. You can use either Local Users And Groups (for local users) or Active Directory Users And Computers (for domain users) to enable remote control for a user account.

Note This feature does not allow you to run remote control for non-terminal connections. Tools like Systems Management Server (SMS) provide a remote control facility to access network connected computers running Windows.

Terminal Services Profile Tab

The Terminal Services Profile tab allows you to assign a profile to a user to apply to Terminal sessions. Administrators can then create user profiles tailored to the Terminal Services environment. The Terminal Services profile can be used to restrict access to applications by removing them from the user's Start menu. Administrators can also create and store network connections to printers and other resources for use during user sessions.

You can specify a path to a home directory to be used for Terminal sessions. This directory can be either a local directory or a network share. You can also specify whether a user has access to Terminal Services. If the Allow Logon To Terminal Server option is left disabled, the user is not allowed to log on to any Terminal servers.

Administering User Accounts

Administering user accounts goes beyond creating user accounts for new users. It involves modifying user accounts as well as setting up user profiles and home directories. This section explains how to perform each of these tasks.

Managing User Profiles

A user profile is a collection of folders and data that stores your current desktop environment and application settings as well as personal data. A user profile also contains all the network connections that are established when logging on to a computer, such as Start menu items and mapped drives to network servers. User profiles maintain consistency in your desktop environment by providing the same desktop environment you had the last time you logged on to the computer.

Windows 2000 creates a local user profile the first time you log on at a computer. After logging on for the first time, Windows 2000 stores the user profile on that computer.

User profiles operate in the following manner:

- When you log on to a client computer running Windows 2000, you always receive your individual desktop settings and connections, regardless of how many users share your computer.

- The first time you log on to a client computer running Windows 2000, Windows 2000 copies the local Default User folder profile to the %systemdrive%\Documents and Settings\<user_logon_name> folder (typically C:\Documents and Settings\<user_logon_name>), where user_logon_name is your Windows 2000 user account name.

- If the computer where you are logging on was updated from Windows 95 or Windows 98 with profiles enabled or from Windows NT to Windows 2000 Professional, the profile folder remains in %systemroot%\profiles rather than being created in the Documents And Settings folder.

- A user profile folder contains many files and folders for storing user information. For example, the My Documents folder provides a place to store personal files. My Documents is the default location for the File Open and Save As application commands. By default, Windows 2000 creates a My Documents icon on the desktop. This makes it easier to locate your personal documents.

Note You can change the target directory for My Documents by accessing the properties of the My Documents icon on the desktop.

- The simplest way to modify your user profile is by changing desktop settings, for example, when you establish a new network connection or add a file to My Documents. Then when you log off, Windows 2000 incorporates the changes into your profile. The next time you log on, the new network connection and the file are present.

Note You should have users store their documents in My Documents rather than in home directories. Windows 2000 automatically sets up My Documents, and it is the default location for storing data for Microsoft applications. Using folder redirection and offline folders, which you will learn about later, My Documents can be set to a network location and made available to users whether or not they are connected to the network.

Roaming User Profiles

To support users who work at multiple computers, you can set up roaming user profiles (RUPs). A *roaming user profile* is one that you set up on a network server so that the profile is available to you no matter where you log on in the domain. When a user logs on, Windows 2000 copies the roaming user profile from the network server to the client computer running Windows 2000 at which the user logs on. Consequently, the user always receives his or her individual desktop settings and connections. This is in contrast to a local user profile, which resides on one client computer only.

When a user logs on, Windows 2000 applies the roaming user profile settings to that computer. The first time that a user logs on at a computer, Windows 2000 copies all documents to the local computer. Thereafter, when the user logs on to the computer, Windows 2000 compares the locally stored user profile files and the RUP files. It copies only the files that have changed since the last time the user logged on at the computer. Since Windows 2000 only copies the files that have changed, the logon process is shorter.

When a user logs off, Windows 2000 copies changes that were made to the local copy of the RUP back to the server where it is stored.

Creating Customized Roaming User Profiles

You can also customize and assign a preconfigured RUP that you assign to all user accounts, as well as make roaming user profiles read-only. You can create a customized RUP by configuring the desktop environment for the user and then copying the customized profile to the user's RUP location.

You use customized RUPs for the following reasons:

- To provide users with the work environment they need to perform their jobs and to remove connections and applications that the user does not require.

- To provide a standard desktop environment for multiple users with similar job responsibilities. These users require the same network resources.

- To simplify troubleshooting. Technical support would know the exact baseline setup of the desktops and could easily find a deviation or a problem.

Note You can customize local user profiles, but this is not recommended. Customizing local user profiles is inefficient because they reside only on the client computer the user logs on to. Therefore, you would have to customize the user profile at each client computer a user logs on to.

Using Mandatory Profiles

A mandatory profile is a read-only RUP. When the user logs off, Windows 2000 does not save any changes the user made during the session. The next time the user logs on, the profile is the same as the last time he or she logged on.

You can assign one mandatory profile to multiple users who require the same desktop settings, such as bank tellers. This means that by changing one profile, you change the desktop environment for several users.

A hidden file in the profile called Ntuser.dat contains that section of the Windows 2000 system settings that applies to the individual user account and contains the user environment settings, such as desktop appearance. This is the file you make read-only by changing its name to Ntuser.man.

Setting Up a Roaming User Profile

When you set up an RUP on a server, the next time that the user logs on to a computer in the domain, Windows 2000 copies the local user profile to the RUP path on the server. When the user logs on thereafter, the RUP copies the profile from the server to the computer.

You should set up RUPs on a file server that you frequently back up so that you have copies of the RUPs. To improve logon performance for a busy network, place the RUP folders on a member server rather than on a domain controller. Copying RUPs between the server and client computers can use a lot of system resources, such as bandwidth and computer processing. If the profiles are on the domain controller, this can delay the authentication of users by the domain controller.

Tip To further improve performance and profile availability, consider configuring a Domain Dfs root for user profiles and configuring FRS so that the profiles are replicated to multiple available locations on the network.

To set up an RUP, you must create a shared folder on a server and use a path with the following format: \\<*server*>\<*share*>. Use an intuitive name for the shared folder, such as Profiles. On the Profile tab in the Properties dialog box for the user account, provide the path to the shared folder in the Profile Path box (\\<*server*>\<*share*>\<*logon_name*>).

You can type the variable %username% instead of the user's logon name. When you use this variable, Windows 2000 automatically replaces the variable with the user account name for the RUP.

Assigning a Customized Roaming User Profile

You can customize an RUP and assign it to multiple users, who will then have the same settings and connections when they log on. Before you can customize and assign an RUP, you must first create a user profile template, which contains the customized desktop settings that you want the users to have. A template is created by configuring a desktop exactly as you want it to appear for the users who will be assigned this profile. No special tools are required to create this template.

After you have created your user profile template, log on as Administrator and copy the user profile template to an RUP folder on the server. This folder must be accessible to all users who will be assigned this profile. The Control Panel System application can be used to copy the profile template to a shared network location, as shown in Figure 7.6. Notice that the profile is assigned to the built-in Users group in the domain.

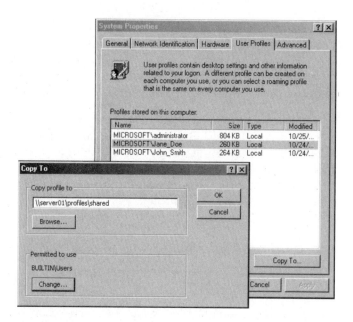

Figure 7.6 Copying the Jane_Doe profile template to a subfolder (shared) of the \\server01\profiles share

To complete the process, assign the profile to the appropriate users by using the Active Directory Users And Computers snap-in. After opening the snap-in, access the Profile tab in the Properties Of A User Account, and assign a path to the profile in the Profile path text box.

Since changes to the template profile affect all users who are assigned the profile, you should make the profile mandatory. To make the profile a mandatory (read-only) user profile, change the extension on the Ntuser file in the profile folder on the server from .dat to .man.

Note The Ntuser.dat file is a hidden file. You must either use the attrib command line utility to remove the hidden attribute or enable viewing of hidden files through Windows 2000 Explorer.

Modifying User Accounts

Company needs and changes might require you to modify user accounts. For example, you might need to rename an existing user account for a new employee so that this employee can have the same permissions and network access as his or her predecessor. Other modifications are based on personnel changes or personal information, such as disabling, enabling, and deleting a user account. You might also need to reset a user's password or unlock a user account.

Note You can modify a user account by changing the user account object in the Active Directory store. To complete the tasks for modifying user accounts successfully, creating roaming user profiles and assigning home directories, you must have permission to administer the OU in which the user accounts reside.

Disabling, Enabling, Renaming, and Deleting User Accounts

Following are modifications you make to user accounts that affect the accounts' functionality:

- **Disabling and enabling a user account** You disable a user account when a user does not need an account for an extended period but will need it again. For example, if John took a two-month leave of absence, you would disable his user account when he left. When he returned, you would enable his user account so that he could log on to the network again.

- **Renaming a user account** You rename a user account when you want to retain all rights, permissions, group memberships, and most properties for the user account and reassign it to a different user. For example, if there is a new company accountant, rename the account by changing the first, last, and user logon names to those of the new accountant.

- **Deleting a user account** Delete a user account when an employee leaves the company and you are not going to rename the user account. By deleting these user accounts, you do not have unused accounts in Active Directory services.

The procedures for disabling, enabling, renaming, and deleting user accounts are similar for domain and local accounts. For domain user accounts, use the Active Directory Users And Computers snap-in. Select the user account, and click on action in the Action menu. For local user accounts, use the Local Users And Groups extension from the console tree in the Computer Management snap-in.

Note If a user account is enabled, the Action menu displays the Disable Account command. If a user account is disabled, the Action menu displays the Enable Account command.

Resetting Passwords and Unlocking User Accounts

If a user cannot log on to the domain or to a local computer, you might need to reset the user's password or unlock the user's account. To perform these tasks, you must have administrative privileges for the OU in which the user account resides.

Resetting Passwords

If a user forgets her or his password, you need to reset the password.

Note You do not need to know the old password to reset a password.

To reset a user's password, open the Active Directory Users And Computers snap-in and select the user object. On the Action menu, click Reset Password. In the Reset Password dialog box, enter a password and select User Must Change Password At Next Logon to force the user to change his or her password the next time that the user logs on.

Unlocking User Accounts

A Windows 2000 group policy locks out a user account when the user violates the policy, for example, the user exceeding the limit that a group policy allows for bad logon attempts. When a user account is locked out, Windows 2000 displays an error message.

To unlock a user's account, open the Active Directory Users And Computers snap-in and right-click the user object. Click Properties and select the Account tab. Clear The Account Is Locked Out check box.

Creating Home Folders

In addition to the My Documents folder, Windows 2000 provides you with the means to create a home folder for the user. A home folder is an additional one that you can provide for users to store personal documents, and for older applications, it is sometimes the default folder for saving documents. You can store a home folder on a client computer or in a shared folder on a file server. Because a home folder is not part of an RUP, its size does not affect network traffic during logon. You can locate all users' home folders in a central location on a network server.

Storing all home folders on a file server provides the following advantages:

- Users can gain access to their home folders from any client computer on the network.

- Backing up and administering user documents is centralized.

- Home folders are accessible from a client computer running any Microsoft operating system (including MS-DOS, Windows 95, Windows 98, and Windows 2000).

Note You should store home folders on an NT file system (NTFS) volume so that you can use NTFS permissions to secure user documents. If you store home folders on a file allocation table (FAT) volume, you can restrict home folder access only by using shared folder permissions.

To create a home folder on a network file server, you must perform the following three tasks:

- **Creating and sharing a folder** Create and share a folder in which to store all home folders on a network server. The home folder for each user will reside below the shared folder.

- **Changing the Full Control permission** For the shared folder, remove the default permission Full Control from the Everyone group and assign Full Control to the Users group. This ensures that only users with domain user accounts can gain access to the shared folder.

- **Providing the home folder path** Provide the path to the user's home folder in the Home folder section on the Profile tab of the Properties dialog box for the user account (Figure 7.7). Since the home folder is on a network server, click Connect and specify a drive letter to use to connect. As a result, when the user logs on to the network, the driver letter you assign will appear in My Computer. In the To text box, a UNC name appears in the form of \\<*server*>\<*share*>\<*user_logon_name*>. You can use the %username% variable as the user's logon name to automatically name and create each user's home folder the same as the user logon name.

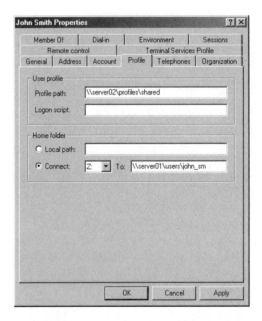

Figure 7.7 The Profile tab appearing in the properties of a user account. Both a profile path and a network accessible home folder path are specified

---

Note If you use %username% to name a folder on an NTFS volume, the user and the built-in local Administrators group is assigned the NTFS Full Control permission. All other permissions are removed for the folder, including those for the Everyone Special group.

You can further enhance the home folder feature by redirecting the user's My Documents pointer to the location of her or his home directory.

Exercise 3: Creating a Roaming Profile and Assigning a Home Folder

In this exercise, you use the Jane_Doe user accounts to create a profile. You then log on as Jane Doe to create a local profile for the account. Then you log on as Administrator and use the System application in Control Panel to verify that the profile for Jane Doe was created. In Procedure 2, you use the Jane_Doe profile to create and test an RUP from a second computer. In Procedure 3, you create and test a home folder for Jane_Doe.

▶ Procedure 1: Creating a user profile template

In this procedure, you define and test a local user profile. You will use Server01 to create the user profile template. Typically, a computer running Windows 2000 Professional would be used to create a user profile template. However, this kit assumes that you are running Windows 2000 Server only to complete these procedures.

1. If you are logged on as Administrator on Server01, log off.

2. Log on to the microsoft.com domain as Jane_Doe with a password of "student."

    If this was the first time that you logged on using the Jane_Doe account, a local user profile is created for her with default settings. This local profile will be customized and then assigned to other users.

3. Double-click the My Computer icon on the desktop.

    The My Computer window appears.

4. Click and drag the Local Disk (C:) icon to the desktop.

    A Shortcut message box appears stating that this item cannot be copied or moved but a shortcut can be created.

5. Click Yes to create a shortcut to the C: drive.

6. Close the My Computer window.

7. Click Start, point to Settings, click Control Panel, and then double-click Display.

    The Display Properties dialog box appears.

8. Click the Appearance tab.

    Notice the current color scheme.

9. In the Scheme box, select a different color scheme and then click OK.

    The desktop changes to the new color scheme.

10. Close Control Panel.

11. Log off as Jane_Doe, and then log on as Administrator with a password of "password."

12. Click Start, point to Settings, click Control Panel, and then double-click System.

13. Click the User Profiles tab.

    Notice that there are multiple user profiles stored on Server01. These profiles represent all user accounts that have logged on to Server01.

14. Do not close the System application since you will need it to complete the next procedure.

▸ **Procedure 2: Defining and assigning a mandatory roaming profile**

In this procedure, you create a roaming profile from the Jane_Doe user profile and assign it to the John Smith user account. For simplicity, you will complete all steps in this procedure from Server01. If you are running Server02, you can optionally log on from this computer to test the RUP.

Note This procedure assumes knowledge of how to create and share a folder. If you are not sure how to do this, revisit Chapter 5, Exercise 1.

---

1. On the C:\ drive, create a folder named Profiles.

2. Share the C:\Profiles folder as Profiles.

3. Open the Profiles folder, and create a subfolder named Shared.

    Close the Profiles window.

4. Locate the System Properties dialog box. The System application was opened in the previous procedure.

5. Click the User Profiles tab.

6. Under Profiles Stored On This Computer, select MICROSOFT\Jane_Doe.

7. Click Copy To.

    The Copy To dialog box appears.

8. In the Copy Profile to text box, type **\\server01\profiles\shared**.

9. Under Permitted to use, click Change.

    The Select User Or Group dialog box appears.

10. In the Name column, click Users and then click OK.

    BUILTIN\Users appears in the Permitted To Use section.

11. Click OK to return to the System Properties dialog box.

    A Confirm Copy message box appears, stating that the
    \\server01\profiles\shared folder already exists and that the current
    contents will be deleted. This appears because you already created the
    folder for the profile.

12. Click Yes.

13. Click OK to return to Control Panel.

14. Open the Active Directory Users And Computers snap-in.

15. Expand microsoft.com, and then click the Users folder.

16. In the details pane, double-click the John Smith user account.

    The John Smith Properties dialog box appears.

17. In an earlier exercise, you set an account expiration for the John Smith
    account. To remove this expiration, click the Account tab and select
    Never in the Account Expires section.

18. Click the Profile tab.

19. In the Profile path box, type **\\server01\profiles\shared** and click OK.

    Close Active Directory Users And Computers snap-in.

    Because you are using a centralized profile that could be assigned to
    other users, the next step is to configure the profile as mandatory.

20. Double-click My Computer on the desktop.

21. Double-click Local Disk (C:).

22. Double-click Profiles.

23. Double-click Shared.

    Notice that User Profile folders appear.

24. Click the Tools menu, and then click Folder Options.

    The Folder Options dialog box appears.

25. Click the View tab.

26. Select the Show Hidden Files And Folders radio button, and clear the
    Hide File Extensions For Known File Types check box.

27. Click OK.

    The Shared window appears, showing hidden files and folders. Notice that Ntuser.dat appears.

28. Select Ntuser.dat.

29. Click the File menu and then click Rename.

    The Ntuser.dat file name box is highlighted and can be edited.

30. Change the extension so that the file name is ntuser.man, and then press Enter.

31. Close the Shared window and close Control Panel.

32. Log off as Administrator and log on as John_Smith with no password.

    The John_Smith desktop appears. Notice that the John_Smith user is using the color scheme you assigned to the user profile template and that the shortcut to Local Disk (C:) appears on the desktop.

33. To test the mandatory profile, delete the Connect To The Internet shortcut on the desktop.

34. Log off and log on again as John_Smith with no password.

    Notice that the Connect to the Internet shortcut appears on the desktop. This happens because you assigned a mandatory profile to the John_Smith user account.

▶ **Procedure 3: Assigning a Home folder to a user**

In this procedure you will assign John_Smith a home folder.

1. Log off as John_Smith and log on as Administrator with a password of "password."

2. Create a folder on the C: drive named HomeDirs.

3. Share this folder as HomeDirs.

4. Open the Active Directory User And Computers snap-in.

5. Access the properties of the John Smith user account, and click the Profile tab.

6. In the Home Folder section, click the Connect radio button.

7. Verify that Z: appears in the drop-down list box to the right of Connect.

8. In the To text box, type **\\server01\HomeDirs\%username%** and then click OK.

9. Close the Active Directory Users And Computers snap-in.

10. Find and click the HomeDirs folder in Windows Explorer.

11. Click the File menu and then click Properties.

    The HomeDirs Properties dialog box appears.

12. Click the Security tab.

    Notice that the Everyone group is granted Full Control of this directory.

13. Click Add.

    The Select Users, Computers, Or Groups dialog box appears.

14. Select Users and then click Add.

15. Click OK.

    The HomeDirs Properties dialog box appears showing both the Everyone Special group and the MICROSOFT\Users group. Notice that the Users group is assigned Read & Execute, List Folder Contents, and Read permissions.

16. Clear the Allow Inheritable Permissions From Parent To Propagate To This Object check box.

    A Security message box appears.

17. Read this message box, and then click Remove.

    Notice that the Everyone Special group no longer has rights to the HomeDirs folder.

18. Click Add.

    The Select Users, Computers, Or Groups dialog box appears.

19. Select Administrators and then click Add.

20. Click OK.

    The HomeDirs Properties dialog box appears showing both the MICROSOFT\Users group and the MICROSOFT\Administrators group.

21. Verify that the Administrators (MICROSOFT\Administrators) group is highlighted.

22. In the Permissions box, click the Allow check box in the Full Control row.

    All check boxes are selected.

23. Click OK.

24. Double-click the HomeDirs folder.

25. Click John_Smith.

26. Click the File menu and then click Properties.

   The John_Smith Properties dialog box appears.

27. Click the Security tab.

   Notice that Administrators and John Smith are granted full control of this directory. These assignments were automatically granted when you stipulated that the John_Smith user account use the \\server01\HomeDirs\%username% folder as a home folder.

28. Click OK, and then close Windows Explorer.

29. Log off as administrator and log on as John_Smith with no password.

30. Double-click My Computer.

   Notice that a new network drive icon appears that is pointing to the John_Smith folder on \\server01\HomeDirs with a drive assignment of Z:.

31. Close the My Computer window, and log off.

Lesson Summary

A user account provides a user with the ability to log on to the domain to gain access to network resources or to log on to a computer to gain access to resources on that computer. Windows 2000 provides different types of user accounts: domain user accounts and local user accounts. Windows 2000 also provides built-in user accounts, which you use to perform administrative tasks or to gain access to network resources. Before you begin creating user accounts, you should plan the naming convention for those accounts, the password requirements, and account options, such as logon hours. Use the Active Directory Users And Computers snap-in to create a new domain user account. Use the Local Users And Groups snap-in to create local user accounts. A set of default properties is associated with each domain user account and local user account created. You can modify those properties by using the Properties dialog box for the individual user account. Administering user accounts involves modifying user accounts, as well as managing user profiles and home directories. A user profile is a collection of folders and data that stores the user's current desktop environment and application settings as well as personal data. A home folder is a folder that you can provide for users to store personal documents, and for older applications, it is sometimes the default folder for saving documents.

Lesson 3: Administering Group Accounts

This lesson introduces you to groups and how they are implemented in a Windows 2000 environment. You will learn what groups are and how they are used to simplify user account administration. The chapter also reviews the types of groups and presents the skills and knowledge necessary to implement groups into a domain as well as to implement local groups and built-in groups.

After this lesson, you will be able to

- Implement groups into a domain
- Implement local groups and built-in groups

Estimated lesson time: 60 minutes

Introduction to Groups

A *group* is a collection of user accounts. Groups simplify administration by allowing you to assign permissions and rights to a group of users rather than having to assign permissions to each individual user account. Users can be members of more than one group.

When you assign permissions, you give users the capability to gain access to specific resources and you define the type of access they have. For example, if several users needed to read the same file, you would add their user accounts to a group. Then you would give that group permission to read the file. Rights allow users to perform system tasks, such as changing the time on a computer, backing up or restoring files, or logging on locally.

In addition to user accounts, you can add contacts, computers, and other groups to a group. By adding computers to a group, you can simplify the process of granting a system task on one computer access to a resource on another computer.

Implementing Groups into a Domain

Before you implement groups into a domain, you should have a basic understanding of group types, group scopes, and group membership. From there, you can create the groups, add members to the groups, or change the group scope. You can even delete a group.

Note In much of the Windows 2000 documentation, groups that are implemented into a domain are usually referred to simply as groups, whereas other groups in Windows 2000 are specifically referred to as local groups or built-in groups, both of which are discussed later in this lesson. At the same time, the term *group* is often used in a generic sense, referring to any type of group that can be implemented in Windows 2000.

Types of Groups

Sometimes you create groups for security, such as assigning permissions. At other times you use them for reasons unrelated to security, such as sending e-mail messages. To facilitate this, Windows 2000 Server includes two group types: security and distribution. The group type determines how you use the group. Both types of groups are contained in the Active Directory store, which allows you to use them anywhere in your network.

Security Groups

The Windows 2000 operating system uses only security groups, which you use to assign permissions to gain access to resources. Programs designed to search the Active Directory store can also use security groups for reasons unrelated to security, such as sending e-mail messages to a number of users at the same time. Thus, a security group has all the capabilities of a distribution group.

Distribution Groups

Applications use distribution groups as lists for functions unrelated to security. Use distribution groups when the only function of the group isn't security related, such as sending e-mail messages to a group of users at the same time. You cannot use distribution groups to assign permissions.

Note Only programs that are designed to work with Active Directory services can use distribution groups. For example, future versions of Microsoft Exchange Server will be able to use distribution groups as distribution lists for sending e-mail messages.

Group Scopes

When you create a group, you must select a group type and group scope (Figure 7.8). Group scopes allow you to use groups in different ways to assign permissions.

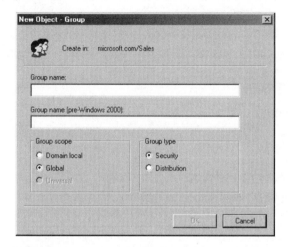

Figure 7.8 The New Object - Group dialog box opened from Active Directory Users And Computers in the Sales OU

The scope of a group determines where in the network you are able to use the group. The three group scopes are domain local, global, and universal.

Domain Local Groups

Domain local groups are most often used to assign permissions to resources. A domain local group has the following characteristics:

- **Open membership** You can add members from any domain.

- **Access to resources in one domain** You can use a domain local group to assign permissions to gain access only to resources that are located in the same domain where you create the domain local group.

Global Groups

Global groups are most often used to organize users who share similar network access requirements. A global group has the following characteristics:

- **Limited membership** You can add members only from the domain in which you create the global group.

- **Access to resources in any domain** You can use a global group to assign permissions to gain access to resources that are located in any domain.

Universal Groups

Universal groups are most often used to assign permissions to related resources in multiple domains. A universal security group has the following characteristics:

- **Open membership** You can add members from any domain.

- **Access to resources in any domain** You can use a universal group to assign permissions to gain access to resources that are located in any domain.

- **Available in Native mode only** Universal security groups are not available in Mixed mode. The full feature set of Windows 2000 is available only in Native mode. Notice in Figure 7.8 that the Universal group is not available because the server is running in Mixed mode and the Group Type shows the Security radio button selected. Universal distribution groups are allowed in Mixed mode.

Group Membership

The group scope determines the membership of the group. Membership rules define which members a group can contain. Group members include user accounts and other groups. The following table describes group membership rules:

Group scope	In Mixed-mode scope can contain	In Native-mode scope can contain
Domain local	User accounts, computer accounts, and global groups from any domain	User accounts, computer accounts, global groups, and universal groups from any domain, as well as other domain local groups from the same domain
Global	User accounts from the same domain, and computer accounts	User accounts, computer accounts, and global groups from the same domain
Universal	Not available in Mixed mode, unless the Group Type is Distribution	User accounts, computer accounts, global groups, and universal groups from any domain

Domain local and global groups can be converted to universal groups. A successful conversion requires that Active Directory services is operating in Native mode and the domain local or global group does not contain other group members of the same scope. For instance, a global group containing another global group cannot be converted to a universal group.

Note Distribution groups running in Mixed mode follow the same membership rules as security groups running in Native mode.

Group Nesting

Adding groups to other groups (referred to as nesting groups) can reduce the number of times permissions need to be assigned. You should create a hierarchy of groups based on the business needs of the members. Windows 2000 allows for unlimited levels of nesting in Native mode.

For example, you can create a group for each region in your organization and then add managers from each region into their own group. You can then add each regional group to another group called Worldwide Managers. When all managers in the network need access to a resource, assign permissions to the Worldwide Managers group. Because the Worldwide Managers group contains all members of the regional groups through nesting, all managers in the network can access the required resource. This strategy allows for easy hierarchical assignment of permissions and, at the same time, enables decentralized tracking of group membership.

When adding groups to other groups, try to minimize levels of nesting. Nesting reduces the number of times you assign permissions. However, tracking permissions becomes more complex with multiple levels of nesting. One level of nesting is the most effective to use because it reduces the number of times you need to assign permissions and allows you to track permissions easily.

In addition, you should document group membership to keep track of permission assignments. Consider a scenario in which one administrator adds temporary employees to a group created for employees assigned to a project. Not knowing there are temporary employees in the project group, another administrator adds the project group to a group that has access to confidential company information. The temporary employees now have access to confidential company information, which is not acceptable.

Effectively nesting groups in a multiple domain environment will reduce network traffic between domains and simplify administration in a domain tree. To efficiently use nesting, you need to understand the membership rules of groups.

When nesting groups, consider which groups initiate less cross-domain replication. For example, Windows 2000 replicates only a global group and not its membership list. In addition, you need to consider the Domain Operation mode of your domain tree:

- In Mixed mode, only one type of nesting is available; global groups from any domain can be members of domain local groups. Universal security groups do not exist in Mixed mode.

- In Native mode, all the group membership rules are available and Windows 2000 permits multiple levels of nesting.

Group Strategies

To use groups effectively, you need to determine how you will use groups and which types of groups you will use in certain situations.

Using Global and Domain Local Groups

Global and domain local group implementation guidelines are identical to the group strategy recommendations for a Windows NT 3.*x* or 4.0 domain. When you plan to use global and domain local groups, consider the following guidelines:

- Identify users with common job responsibilities, and add the user accounts to a global group. For example, in an accounting department, add user accounts for all accountants to a global group called Accounting.

- Identify what resources or group of resources, such as related files, users need access to, and then create a domain local group for that resource. For example, if you have a number of color printers in your company, create a domain local group called Color Printers.

- Identify all global groups that share the same access needs for resources, and make them members of the appropriate domain local group. For example, add the global groups Accounting, Sales, and Management to the domain local group Color Printers.

- Assign the required permissions to the domain local group. For example, assign the necessary permissions to use color printers to the Color Printers group.

Figure 7.9 illustrates the strategy for using global and domain local groups: place user accounts into global groups, create a domain local group for a group of resources to be shared in common, place the global groups into the domain local group, and then assign permissions to the domain local group. This strategy gives you the most flexibility for growth and reduces permissions assignments.

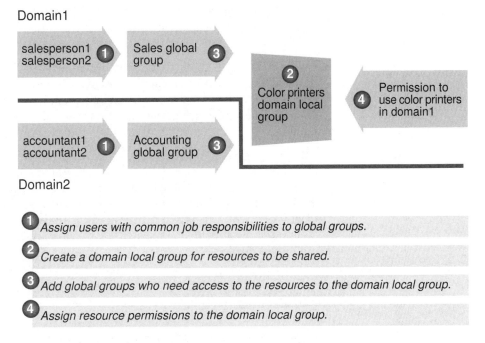

Figure 7.9 Planning a group strategy

In addition, placing user accounts in domain local groups and assigning permissions to the domain local groups does not allow you to assign permissions for resources outside of the domain. This strategy reduces the flexibility when your network grows.

Despite the advantage of using this strategy, placing user accounts in global groups and assigning permissions to the global groups can complicate administration when you are using multiple domains. If global groups from multiple domains require the same permissions, you have to assign permissions for each global group.

Using Universal Groups

Universal groups is a new feature in Windows 2000. When you plan to use universal groups, consider the following guidelines:

- Use universal groups to give users access to resources that are located in more than one domain. Unlike domain local groups, you can assign permissions to universal groups for resources in any domain in your network. For example, if executives need access to printers throughout your network, you can create a universal group for this purpose and assign it permissions for using printers on print servers in all domains.

- Use universal groups only when their membership is static. In a domain tree, universal groups can cause excessive network traffic between domain controllers whenever you change membership for the universal group, because changes to the membership of universal groups might be replicated to a large number of domain controllers.

- Add global groups from several domains to a universal group, and then assign permissions for access to a resource to the universal group. This allows you to use a universal group in the same way as domain local groups to assign permissions for resources. However, unlike a domain local group, you can assign permissions to a universal group to give users access to a resource that is located in a domain other than where the group was created.

Implementing Groups

After you assess user needs and have a group plan in place, you are ready to implement your groups. Before you implement your group strategy, consider the following guidelines:

- Determine the required group scope based on how you want to use the group. For example, use global groups to group user accounts. Use domain local groups or universal groups to assign permissions to a resource. Assign global groups to domain local groups and universal groups.

- Avoid adding users to universal groups since adding and removing users from universal groups will increase replication traffic.

- Determine if you have the necessary permissions to create a group in the appropriate domain. Members of the Administrators group or the Account Operators group in a domain, by default, have the necessary permissions to create groups. An administrator can give a user the permission to create groups in the domain or in a single OU.

- Determine the name of the group. Make the name intuitive, especially if administrators from other domains search for it in Active Directory services. If there are parallel groups in multiple domains, make sure that the names are also parallel. For example, if there is a group for managers in each domain, these groups should use a similar naming scheme, such as Managers USA and Managers Australia.

Creating Groups

Use the Active Directory Users And Computers snap-in to create and delete groups. When you create groups, create them in the Users OU or in an OU that you have created specifically for groups. As your organization grows and changes, you might discover there are groups that you no longer need. Be sure that you delete groups when you no longer need them. This will help you maintain security so that you do not accidentally assign permissions for accessing resources to groups that you no longer need.

To create a group, start the Active Directory Users And Computers snap-in and select the Users OU. From the Action menu, point to New, and then click Group to open the New Object - Group dialog box (Figure 7.8). The following table describes the information you need to provide in the New Object - Group dialog box.

Option	Description
Group Name	The name of the new group. The name must be unique in the domain where you create the group.
Group Name (preWindows 2000)	The down-level name of the group. This is filled in automatically for you based on the name you type in.
Group Scope	The group scope. Click Domain Local, Global, or Universal. Note that the Universal group scope is grayed out unless the Distribution group type is selected or you are running in native mode.
Group Type	The type of group. Click Distribution or Security.

Administering Groups

You can administer a group by using the Active Directory Users And Computers snap-in. The snap-in allows you to perform a number of administrative tasks, including adding members to a group, changing the group scope, or deleting a group.

Adding Members to a Group

After you create a group, you add members. Members of groups can include user accounts, contacts, other groups, and computers. You can add a computer to a group to give one computer access to a shared resource on another computer, for example, for remote backup.

To add members to a group, double-click the appropriate group. In the Properties dialog box, click the Members tab, and then click Add. The Select Users, Contacts, Or Computers dialog box appears, as shown in Figure 7.10.

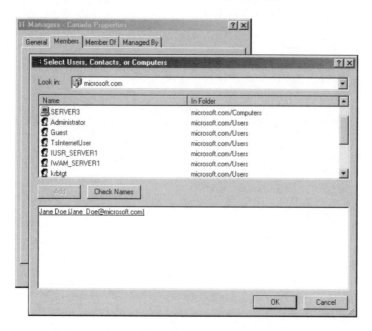

Figure 7.10 The Select Users, Contacts, Or Computers dialog box

---

Note If your domain is in Mixed mode, you will not always be able to add groups to your new group, depending on the group scope of the group you are creating.

In the Look In drop-down list box, you can select a domain from which to display user accounts, contacts, computers, and groups, or you can select Entire Directory to view user accounts and groups from anywhere in the Active Directory store. Now select the user account or group that you want to add, and then click Add.

Note If there are multiple user accounts or groups that you want to add, you can repeat the process of selecting them one at a time and then click Add, or you can hold down the Shift or Ctrl key to select multiple user accounts or groups all at once. The Shift key allows you to select a consecutive range of accounts, while the Ctrl key allows you to pick some accounts and skip others. Click Add after you have selected all the accounts you wish to add.

Clicking Add lists the accounts you have selected in the Name box. Once you review the accounts to make sure they are the accounts you wish to add to the group, click OK to add the members.

Changing the Group Scope

As your network changes, you might need to change a group scope. For example, you might want to change an existing domain local group to a universal group when you need to allow users to gain access to resources in other domains. You change the scope of a group on the General tab of the Properties dialog box for the group.

Note You can change the scope of a group only in Native-mode domains. Changing a group scope is not allowed in Mixed-mode domains. In addition, Windows 2000 does not permit changing the scope of a universal group because all other groups have more restrictive membership and scope than universal groups.

You can make the following changes to a group scope:

- **Change a global group to a universal group** You can do this only if the global group is not a member of another global group.

- **Change a domain local group to a universal group** You can do this only if the domain local group you are converting does not contain another domain local group.

Deleting a Group

Each group you create has a unique, nonreusable identifier, called the security ID (SID). Windows 2000 uses the SID to identify the group and the permissions that are assigned to it. When you delete a group, Windows 2000 does not use the SID again, even if you create a new group with the same name as the group you deleted. Therefore, you cannot restore access to resources by re-creating the group.

When you delete a group, you delete only the group and remove the permissions and rights that are associated with it. Deleting a group does not delete the user accounts that are members of the group. To delete a group, right-click the group, and then click Delete.

Implementing Local Groups

A local group can contain user accounts on a computer and can be assigned to resources on that computer. Use local groups to assign permissions to resources residing on the computer on which the local group is created. Windows 2000 creates local groups in the local security database. There are two types of local groups: domain and non-domain.

Following are some guidelines for using local groups:

- Domain local groups are created in the Active Directory store and are used by all domain controllers within the domain. A domain local group can be assigned to any resource running on domain controllers in the domain.

- Non-domain local groups are created on stand-alone servers, member servers, and computers running Windows 2000 Professional. However, these local groups can be used only on the computer where the local group is created. Therefore, do not use non-domain local groups on computers that are part of a domain. Using non-domain local groups prevents you from centralizing group administration. Non-domain local groups do not appear in the Active Directory store. They must be managed separately for each computer.

- You can assign permissions to non-domain local groups for access only to the resources on the computer where you create the local groups.

Non-domain local groups can contain local user accounts from the computer where you create the local groups. In addition, non-domain local groups cannot be a member of any other group.

Creating Local Groups

Use the Computer Management snap-in to create non-domain local groups. You create local groups in the Groups folder (Figure 7.11). To create a local group, expand Local Users And Groups in the console tree and select Groups. From the Action menu, click New Group. Enter a name and description for the group.

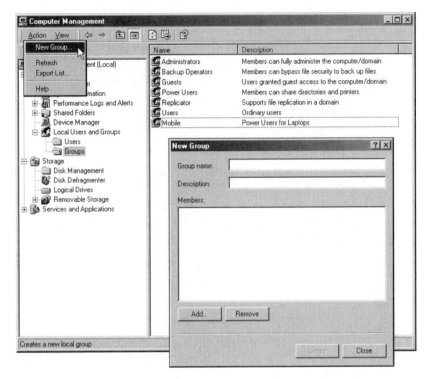

Figure 7.11 Creating a new local group on a computer running Windows 2000 Professional

The following table describes the options presented in the New Group dialog box:

Option	Description
Group Name	A unique name for the local group. This is the only required entry. Use any character except for the backslash (\). The name can contain up to 256 characters; however, very long names will not display in some windows.
Description	A description of the group.
Add	Adds a user to the list of members.
Remove	Removes a user from the list of members.
Create	Creates the group.

You can add members to a local group while you create the group or after you create the local group.

Built-In Groups

Windows 2000 has four categories of built-in groups: global, domain local, local, and system. Built-in groups have a predetermined set of user rights or group membership. Windows 2000 creates these groups for you so that you don't have to create groups and assign rights and permissions for commonly used functions.

Built-In Global Groups

Windows 2000 creates built-in global groups to group common types of user accounts. By default, Windows 2000 automatically adds members to some built-in global groups. You can add user accounts to these built-in groups to provide additional users with the privileges and permissions that you assign to the built-in group.

When you create a domain, Windows 2000 creates built-in global groups in the Active Directory store. You assign rights by either adding the global groups to domain local groups or explicitly assigning user rights or permissions to the built-in global groups.

The Users OU contains the built-in global groups in a domain. The following table describes the default membership of the most commonly used built-in global groups:

Global group	Description
Domain Users	Windows 2000 automatically adds Domain Users to the Users built-in local group. By default, the Administrator account is initially a member, and Windows 2000 automatically makes each new domain user account a member.
Domain Admins	Windows 2000 automatically adds Domain Admins to the Administrators domain local group so that members of Domain Admins can perform administrative tasks on any computer anywhere in the domain. By default, the Administrator account is a member.
Domain Guests	Windows 2000 automatically adds Domain Guests to the Guests domain local group. By default, the Guest account is a member and this account is disabled.
Enterprise Admins	You can add user accounts to Enterprise Admins for users who should have administrative control for the entire network. By default, the Enterprise Admins global group is a member of the Administrators built-in local group. By default, the Administrator account is a member.

Note Members of a group and groups with which a group is a member are viewable from the Members and Member Of tabs in the properties of each group.

Built-In Domain Local Groups

Windows 2000 creates built-in local groups in the domain to provide users with user rights and permissions to perform tasks on domain controllers and in the Active Directory store. A built-in local group performs the same way that a domain local group functions. The only difference is that a built-in local group cannot be deleted.

Built-in local groups in the domain give predefined rights and permissions to user accounts when you add user accounts or global groups as members. The following table describes the most commonly used built-in local groups in the domain and the capabilities that the members have.

Domain local group	Description
Account Operators	Members can create, delete, and modify user accounts and groups; members cannot modify the Administrators group or any of the Operators groups.
Server Operators	Members can share disk resources and back up and restore files on a domain controller.
Print Operators	Members can set up and manage network printers on domain controllers.
Administrators	Members can perform all administrative tasks on all domain controllers and the domain itself. By default, the Administrator user account, the Domain Admins group, and the Enterprise Admins group are members.
Guests	Members can perform only tasks for which you have granted rights and gain access only to resources for which you have assigned permissions; members cannot make permanent changes to their desktop environment. By default, the Guest user account and the Domain Guests domain local group are members. Some services automatically add users to this account when they are installed. For example, Microsoft Internet Information Services (IIS) adds anonymous user accounts to the Guests built-in group.

Domain local group	Description
Backup Operators	Members can back up and restore all domain controllers by using Windows Backup.
Users	Members can perform only tasks for which you have granted rights and gain access only to resources for which you have assigned permissions. By default, the Domain Users group, the Authenticated Users special group, and the INTERACTIVE special group are members. The system groups are maintained by Windows 2000 and cannot be removed from the system. Use the Users built-in local group to assign permissions and rights that every user with a user account in your domain should have.

Built-In Local Groups

All stand-alone servers, member servers, and computers running Windows 2000 Professional have built-in local groups. Built-in local groups give rights to perform system tasks on a single computer, such as backing up and restoring files, changing the system time, and administering system resources. Windows 2000 places the built-in local groups into the Groups folder in the Computer Management snap-in. Like built-in groups in the domain, built-in non-domain local groups cannot be deleted.

The following table describes the capabilities that members of the most commonly used built-in local groups have:

Local group	Description
Users	Members can perform only tasks for which you have specifically granted rights and can gain access only to resources for which you have assigned permissions. By default, Windows 2000 adds local user accounts that you create on the computer to the Users group. When a member server or a computer running Windows 2000 Professional joins a domain, Windows 2000 adds the Domain Users global group, the Authenticated Users special group, and the INTERACTIVE special group to the local Users group.
Administrators	Members can perform all administrative tasks on the computer. By default, the built-in Administrator user account for the computer is a member. When a member server or a computer running Windows 2000 Workstation joins a domain, Windows 2000 adds the Domain Admins group to the local Administrators group.

Local group	Description
Guests	Members can perform only tasks for which you have specifically granted rights and gain access only to resources for which you have assigned permissions; members cannot make permanent changes to their desktop environment. By default, the built-in Guest account for the computer is a member. This account is disabled during installation. When a member server or a computer running Windows 2000 Professional joins a domain, no groups from the domain are added to this group.
Backup Operators	Members can use Windows Backup to back up and restore the computer.
Power Users	Members can create and modify local user accounts on the computer and share resources.
Replicator	Members can use this to configure file replication services.

Built-In System Groups

Built-in system groups, known as special groups in Windows NT, exist on all computers running Windows 2000. System groups do not have specific memberships you can modify, but they can represent different users at different times, depending on how a user gains access to a computer or resource. You do not see system groups when you administer groups, but they are available for use when you assign rights and permissions to resources. Windows 2000 bases system group membership on how the computer is accessed, not on who uses the computer. The following table describes the most commonly used built-in system groups.

System group	Description
Everyone	Includes all users who access the computer. Be careful if you assign permissions to the Everyone group and enable the Guest account. Windows 2000 will authenticate a user who does not have a valid user account as Guest. The user automatically gets all rights and permissions you have assigned to the Everyone group.
Authenticated Users	Includes all users with a valid user account on the computer or in Active Directory services. Use the Authenticated Users group instead of the Everyone group to prevent anonymous access to a resource.

System group	Description
Creator Owner	Includes the user account for the user who created or took ownership of a resource. If a member of the Administrators group creates a resource, the Administrators group is the owner of the resource.
Network	Includes any user with a current connection from another computer on the network to a shared resource on the computer.
Interactive	Includes the user account for the user who is logged on at the computer. Members of the Interactive group gain access to resources on the computer at which they are physically located. They log on and gain access to resources by "interacting" with the computer.
Anonymous Logon	Includes any user account that Windows 2000 did not authenticate.
Dialup	Includes any user who currently has a dial-up connection.

Exercise 4: Changing the Domain Mode

In this exercise, you use the Active Directory Users And Computers snap-in to change your domain mode.

▶ **Procedure 1: Changing from Mixed mode to Native mode**

The default operation for Windows 2000 Server is Mixed mode. To take advantage of all features relating to groups in Windows 2000 Server, your domain must be in Native mode. Complete this exercise from Server01.

1. Log on to Server01 as Administrator with a password of "password."

2. Open the Active Directory Users And Computers snap-in.

3. In the console tree, select your domain, click the Action menu, and then click Properties.

    The microsoft.com Properties dialog box appears.

    Notice that your domain is currently in Mixed mode. Also notice the warning about changing the domain mode.

4. Click Change Mode.

   An Active Directory message box displays, warning you that this change is irreversible.

   Click Yes.

   The microsoft.com Properties dialog box shows that you changed the domain to Native mode.

5. Click OK to close the microsoft.com Properties dialog box.

   An Active Directory message box appears indicating that the operation was successful and telling you that it could take 15 minutes or more for this information to replicate to all domain controllers.

6. Click OK.

7. Keep the Active Directory Users And Computers snap-in open since you will use it in the next exercise.

Exercise 5: Creating Groups

In this exercise, you create a security global group. You then add members to the group. To add members to the group, you add two user accounts, Jane Doe and John Smith, that you created previously. Next you create a domain local group which you use to assign permissions to gain access to the sales reports. Finally, you provide access to the sales reports for the members of the security global group by adding the security global group to the domain local group. Complete this exercise on Server01.

▶ **Procedure 1: Creating a global group,
adding members, and organizing user accounts**

In this procedure, you create a security global group, add members to the group, and then move a user from one OU to another.

1. Verify that the Active Directory Users And Computers snap-in is opened and has the focus.

2. In the console tree, click the Sales OU.

   In the details pane, the Jane Doe user account appears.

3. Click the Action menu, point to New, and then click Group.

   The New Object - Group dialog box appears.

   Notice that the Universal group scope is available when the Security group type is selected. This is available because you are running Active Directory services in Native mode.

4. Verify that the Global radio button is selected and that the Security radio button is selected.

5. Type **Sales** in the Group Name text box, and then click OK.

   The group appears in the details pane of the Sales OU.

6. In the details pane, double-click Sales.

   The Sales Properties dialog box displays the properties of the group.

7. Click the Members tab.

8. Click Add.

   The Select Users, Contacts, Computers, Or Groups dialog box appears and the Look In drop-down list box shows microsoft.com.

9. In the list, select Jane_Doe, press and hold down the Ctrl key and then click John_Smith.

   Both user accounts are selected. Notice that Jane Doe is in the microsoft.com/Sales OU and John Smith is in the microsoft.com/Users OU.

10. Click Add.

    Jane Doe and John Smith are now members of the Sales security global group.

11. Click OK.

12. Click OK again to close the Sales Properties dialog box.

    For organizational purposes, you have decided to move John Smith to the Sales OU.

13. Click on the Users OU.

14. Click the John Smith user account in the details pane.

15. Click Action and then click Move.

    The Move window appears.

16. Click the Sales OU in the Move window, and then click OK.

    The John Smith user account disappears from the details pane of the Users OU.

17. In the console tree, click the Sales OU.

    John Smith, Jane Doe, and the Sales global security group appear in the details pane.

18. Double-click the Sales global group. The Sales Properties dialog box appears.

19. Click the Members tab.

   Notice that the John Smith user account remains a member of the group but that the Active Directory Folder is now set to microsoft.com/Sales.

20. Click OK.

21. Remain in the Sales OU, and continue to the next procedure.

▶ **Procedure 2: Creating and using a domain local group**

In this procedure, you create a domain local group that you use to assign permissions to gain access to sales reports. Because you use the group to assign permissions, you make it a domain local group. You then add members to the group by adding the security global group you created in Procedure 1.

1. Click in the details pane so that the Sales global group is no longer selected.

2. Click the Action menu, point to New, and then click Group.

   The New Object - Group dialog box appears.

3. In the Group Name text box, enter Reports.

4. For Group type, confirm that Security is selected, and for Group Scope, click Domain Local.

5. Click OK.

   The domain local group appears in the details pane of the Sales OU.

6. In the details pane of the Sales OU, double-click Reports.

   The Reports Properties dialog box displays the properties of the group.

7. Click the Members tab.

8. Click Add.

   The Select Users, Contacts, Computers, Or Groups dialog box appears.

9. Click the down arrow to the right of the Look In drop-down list box, select Entire Directory.

   User accounts and groups from all domains and locations of each user account or group appear.

10. Above the list of user accounts, groups, and computers, click the Name column.

    The Name column is sorted alphabetically by name (in descending order).

11. Click the Name column again to sort the list in ascending order.

12. Click Sales, click Add, and then click OK.

    The Sales group is now a member of the Reports domain local group.

13. Click OK.

14. Close the Active Directory Users And Computers snap-in.

▶ **Procedure 3: Implementing NTFS security**

In Chapter 4, you learned about NTFS permissions. In this procedure, you will assign NTFS permissions to the local group you created in the last procedure and then you will test access to the sales folder. Complete this exercise from Server01.

1. Create a folder on the C: drive named Dept.

2. Share the Dept folder as Dept, and in the Comment text box, type **Department share**.

    There is no need to set permissions on the share since the Dept folder is created on an NTFS volume.

3. Create a subfolder below the Dept folder, and name it **Sales**.

4. Click the Sales folder.

5. Click the File menu and then click Properties.

    The Sales Properties dialog box appears.

6. Click the Security tab.

    Notice that the Everyone system group is granted full control to this folder.

7. Clear the Allows Inheritable Permissions From Parent To Propagate To This Object check box.

    The Security message box appears instructing you on your options.

8. Click Remove.

    The Sales Properties dialog box appears.

9. Click Add.

    The Select Users, Computers, Or Group dialog box appears.

10. Select Entire Directory in the Look In drop-down list box.

11. Select the Reports domain local group, and then click Add.

12. Click OK.

    In the Sales Properties dialog box, the Reports local group is granted Read & Execute, List Folder Contents, and Read permissions.

13. Click the Write check box, and click OK.

14. Close the Dept window, and log off as Administrator.

15. Log on as Jane_Doe with a password of "student" and access the C:\Dept\Sales folder from My Computer.

16. Click the File menu, point to New and then click Text Document.

    The New Text Document file appears in the Sales window.

17. Double-click the New Text Document.

    New Text Document - Notepad appears.

18. Type a few letters, and then close Notepad.

    A message box appears asking if you want to save the changes.

19. Click Yes.

20. Close the Sales window.

21. Log off as Jane_Doe, and then log on as Bob_Train with no password.

    If you are unable to logon as Bob Train, check to see if you are logging on during a time when you configured Bob Train not to be able to log on. You configured this in an earlier exercise in this chapter.

22. Attempt to access the C:\Dept\Sales folder.

    A Dept message box appears stating that access is denied.

    Access is not allowed for the Bob Train user account since he is not a member of the global group Sales which was made a member of the domain local group, Reports. Notice also that local access is not allowed. This is because NTFS permissions restricts both network and local access.

23. Click OK and close the Dept window.

24. Log off as Bob Train.

Lesson Summary

A group is a collection of user accounts, contacts, computers, and other groups. There are two types of groups in Windows 2000: security groups and distribution groups. The Windows 2000 operating system uses only security groups, which you use to assign permissions to gain access to resources. Applications use distribution groups as lists for nonsecurity-related functions. In addition to being defined by type, a group is also defined by its scope. There are three group scopes: global, domain local, and universal. Domain local security groups are most often used to assign permissions to resources, while global groups are most often used to organize users who share similar network access requirements. Universal groups are most often used to assign permissions to related resources in multiple domains. The group scope determines the membership of the group. Membership rules consist of the members that a group can contain and the groups of which a group can be a member. When you're ready to create your group in a domain, use the Active Directory Users And Computers snap-in. The snap-in also allows you to administer groups, which includes adding members to a group, changing the scope of a group, and deleting a group. To create a non-domain local group, use the Computer Management snap-in.

Lesson 4: Administering Group Policies

Group policies provide a facility for further refining and centralizing management of a user's desktop environment. Group policies can be used to control the programs that are available to users, the programs that appear on a user's desktop, and the Start menu options.

Typically, you will not set group policies; rather group policy administrators configure and administer them. Group policies are typically set for the entire domain or network and are used to enforce corporate policies. However, even if you do not administer group policies, they affect the user accounts, groups, computers, and OUs that you administer. You should be aware of what group policies are and be familiar with the different types of group policies.

After this lesson, you will be able to

- Explain the structure of group policies, including group policy objects, containers, and templates

- Explain the hierarchy of applying group policies, including the rule of inheritance and methods for modifying inheritance of policies

- Use the Active Directory Users And Computers snap-in to create a group policy object and modify the settings in that object

- Use the Group Policy snap-in to specify group policy settings for computers and users

Estimated lesson time: 90 minutes

Introduction to Group Policies

Group policies are a set of configuration settings that a group policy administrator applies to one or more objects in the Active Directory store. A group policy administrator uses group policies to control the work environments for users in a domain. Group policies can also control the work environment of users with accounts that are located in a specific OU. In addition, group policies can be set at the site level, using the Active Directory Sites And Services snap-in.

A group policy consists of settings that govern how an object and its child objects behave. Group policies allow a group policy administrator to provide users with a fully populated desktop environment. This environment can include a customized Start menu, applications that are automatically set up, and restricted access to files, folders, and Microsoft Windows 2000 system settings. Group policies can also affect rights that are granted to user accounts and groups.

Conflicts can exist between group policies and local needs, such as when a policy restricts a user's ability to gain access to a resource that the user needs to perform his or her job. When this occurs, you must work with the group policy administrator to resolve the conflict. For example, if a group policy that is applied at the domain level prevents users in your network from gaining access to an application that they need to perform their jobs, contact the group policy administrator to correct the situation.

There is an exception to always having to contact the group policy administrator; you can unlock a user account that a group policy locked out. However, be aware that you should not perform tasks that a group policy overrides if the group policy overrides profile settings.

Benefits of Group Policy

Total cost of ownership (TCO) is the cost involved in administering distributed personal computer networks. Recent studies on TCO cite lost user productivity as one of the major costs to corporations. Lost productivity is often due to user error, such as modifying system configuration files and thereby rendering the computer unusable, or it is attributed to the confusing array of unessential applications and features available to the user.

You can lower your network's TCO by using group policies to create a managed desktop environment tailored to the user's job responsibilities and experience level.

Securing a User's Environment

As an administrator in a high-security network, you might want to create a locked down environment on a computer. By implementing appropriate group policy settings for specific users, combined with NTFS permissions, mandatory profiles, and other Windows 2000 security features, you can prevent users from installing software and accessing unauthorized programs or data. You can also prevent users from deleting files that are important to the proper functioning of their applications or operating system.

Enhancing a User's Environment

You can use group policy to enhance a user's environment by doing the following:

- Automatically delivering applications to a user's Start menu
- Enabling application distribution so that users can easily find applications on the network and install them

- Delivering files or shortcuts to useful places on the network or to a specific folder on a user's computer

- Automating the execution of tasks or programs when a user logs on or off and when a computer starts or shuts down

- Redirect folders to network locations to increase data reliability

Note For more information about group policies, see the Supplemental Course Materials CD-ROM (\chapt07\articles\Outline for Group Policy Design Readiness White Paper 3.doc and \chapt07\articles\ GroupPolicyWhitePaperBeta3.doc) that accompanies this book.

Types of Group Policies

Group policies influence a variety of network components and Active Directory objects. The following table describes the types of group policies:

Type of group policy	Description
Software Settings	Affects the applications to which users can gain access. These policies make application installations automatic in two ways:
	Application assignment The group policy installs or upgrades applications automatically on the client computers or provides the user with a connection to an application, which she or he cannot delete.
	Application publication The group policy administrator publishes applications via Active Directory services. The applications then appear in the list of components that a user can install by using Add/Remove Programs in Control Panel. Users can uninstall these applications.
Scripts	Allows group policy administrators to specify scripts and batch files to run at specified times, such as during system startup or system shutdown, or when a user logs on or logs off. Scripts automate repetitive tasks, such as mapping network drives.
Security Settings	Allows group policy administrators to restrict user access to files and folders, configure account restrictions (such as how many incorrect passwords a user can enter before Windows 2000 locks out the user account), set local policy (such as user rights and auditing), control service operation, restrict registry and Event Log access, set public key access, and configure IP security (IPSec) policy.

Type of group policy	Description
Administrative Templates	Includes registry-based group policies, which you use to mandate registry settings that govern the behavior and appearance of the desktop, including the operating system components and applications.
Remote Installation Services (RIS)	Controls RIS installation options presented to the user when running the Client Installation wizard.
Folder Redirection	Allows you to redirect Windows 2000 special folders from their default user profile location to an alternate location on the network, where they can be centrally managed.

Group Policy Structure

Group policies are collections of configuration settings that can be applied to one or more objects in the Active Directory store. These settings are contained within a group policy object (GPO). *Group policy objects* store group policy information in two locations: containers and templates.

Group Policy Objects

A GPO contains group policy settings for sites, domains, and OUs. Group policy objects contain properties that are written to the Active Directory store in an object called the *group policy container* (GPC). In addition, GPOs store group policy information in a folder structure called the *group policy template* (GPT). The underlying structure of the GPO is, for the most part, hidden from the administrator.

One or more GPOs can be applied to a site, domain, or OU. Multiple containers in the Active Directory store can be associated with the same GPO, and a single container can have more than one GPO associated with it. Filtering the scope of the GPO is accomplished through membership in security groups.

Group policy data that is small in size and changes infrequently is stored in GPCs. Group policy data that is large and can change frequently is stored in the GPT.

Local Group Policy Objects

A local GPO exists on every Windows 2000 computer and, by default, only security settings are configured. The local GPO is stored in the %systemroot%\System32\GroupPolicy folder, and it has the following ACL permissions:

- Administrators: Full Control

- SYSTEM: Full Control

- Authenticated Users: Read & Execute, List Folder Contents, and Read

Note SYSTEM and Authenticated Users are system groups.

Group Policy Containers

A GPC is an Active Directory object that stores GPO properties and includes subcontainers for computer and user group policy information. The GPC contains version information to ensure that the information contained within the GPC is synchronized with the GPT information. The GPC also contains status information that indicates whether the GPO is enabled or disabled.

The GPC stores the Windows 2000 class store information for application deployment. The *class store* is a server-based repository for all applications, interfaces, and APIs that provide application publishing and assigning functions.

Group Policy Templates

The GPT is a folder structure in the %systemroot%\SYSVOL\sysvol\ <*domain_name*>\Policies folder of domain controllers. The GPT is the container where policy settings for administrative templates, security settings, script files, and software settings are stored.

GPT Structure

When a GPO is created, the corresponding GPT folder structure is created. The folder name given to the GPT is the GUID of the GPO that was created. For example, if a GPO is created that is associated with a domain called microsoft.com, the resulting GPT folder would be named as follows:

```
%systemroot%\SYSVOL\sysvol\microsoft.com\Policies\
{45265FA6-554F-4F74-97CC-61B4663DAE61}
```

Note The above GUID is an example.

GPT Contents

Typically the default contents of the GPT are the User and Machine subfolders and a Gpt.ini file. As you create and modify policies, additional folders are created. The specific folder structure depends on the group policies that you set. The following table describes some of the subfolders that are often contained in the GPT structure:

Subfolder	Contents
\Adm	The .adm template files that are associated with a specific GPT. The .adm files are text files that are processed by Windows 2000 to apply changes to the registry.
\User	A Registry.pol file with the registry settings to apply to users.
\User\Applications	The advertisement files (.aas files) used by the Microsoft Windows Installer for software packages published to users.
\User\Documents & Settings	Any files to deploy to the user's desktop as part of this GPT.
\User\Scripts	The Logon and Logoff subfolders.
\User\Scripts\Logon	The scripts and related files for logon scripting.
\User\Scripts\Logoff	The scripts and related files for logoff scripting.
\Machine	A Registry.pol file with the registry setting to apply to computers.
\Machine\ Applications	The advertisement files (.aas files) used by the Windows Installer for packages published to computers.
\Machine\Documents & Settings	Any files to deploy to all desktops for all users who log on to this computer as part of this GPT.
\Machine\Microsoft\ WindowsNT\SecEdit	The GptTmpl.ini Security Editor file.
\Machine\Scripts	The Startup and Shutdown subfolders.
\Machine\Scripts\ Startup	The scripts and related files for startup scripting.
\Machine\Scripts\ Shutdown	The scripts and related files for shutdown scripting.

Gpt.ini File

The root folder of each GPT contains a file called Gpt.ini. The following entries can be included in this file:

- **Version=*x*** Where *x* represents the version number of the GPO. The version number begins at 0 when you first create the GPO and then is automatically incremented by 1 each time you modify the GPO.

- **Disabled=*y*** Where *y* is either 0 or 1 and refers only to the local GPO. This switch indicates whether the local GPO is enabled or disabled. The Gpt.ini file defines whether the local GPO is disabled or enabled; for all other GPOs, this information is stored in the GPC contained in the Active Directory store.

Registry.pol File

The Registry.pol file in the User subfolder is downloaded and applied to the HKEY_CURRENT_USER section of the registry when the user logs on. The Registry.pol file in the Machine subfolder is downloaded and applied to the HKEY_LOCAL_MACHINE section of the registry during the boot process of the computer.

The format of the Registry.pol files differs from those created by using the System Policy Editor for Windows 95, Windows 98, or Windows NT 4.0. Files created by using the earlier version of the System Policy Editor cannot be applied to Windows 2000 computers, and files created with the Windows 2000 Group Policy snap-in cannot be applied to Windows 95, Windows 98, or Windows NT 4.0 computers.

Applying Group Policies

Before you can create group policies, you must create the group policy objects. From there you can edit group policies, manage permissions, and manage inheritance.

Creating a GPO

The first step in creating a group policy is to create or open a GPO. You can create a group policy object for a domain or an OU by using the Active Directory Users And Computers snap-in. You can create a group policy object for a site by using the Active Directory Sites And Services snap-in. In both cases, the process is the same.

To create a group policy object, open the properties for the site, domain, or OU object. In the Properties dialog box, select the Group Policy tab. Click New and enter a name for the object. Figure 7.12 shows how to create a GPO.

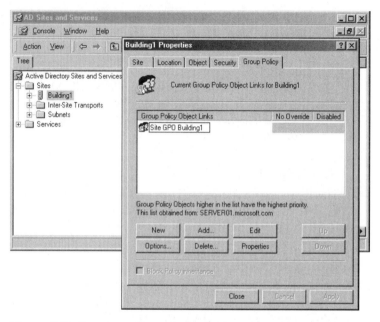

Figure 7.12 Creating a Group Policy Object for a Site named Building1

Note You can also add an existing GPO by clicking Add and selecting GPOs from sites, domains, and OUs.

Using the Group Policy Snap-In

The Group Policy snap-in is the administrator's primary tool for defining and controlling how programs, network resources, and the operating system behave for users and computers in an organization. In an Active Directory services environment, group policies are applied to users or computers on the basis of their membership in sites, domains, or OUs.

Once you have created a GPO, you can use the Group Policy snap-in to specify group policy settings for computers and user accounts. Figure 7.13 shows the Group Policy snap-in.

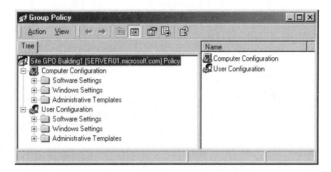

Figure 7.13 The Group Policy snap-in that appears by clicking the Edit button as shown in Figure 7.12

Group Policy Snap-In Interface

The Group Policy snap-in includes the Computer Configuration node and the User Configuration node. Each node displays the following extensions:

- Software Settings
- Windows Settings
- Administrative Templates

Computer Configuration

The Computer Configuration node's folders contain settings you can use to customize the user's environment or enforce lockdown policies for computers on the network. Computer Configuration policies apply when the operating system initializes. If you assign user policies to computers, the user policies apply to every user who logs on to the computer, regardless of the OU to which the user belongs.

User Configuration

The User Configuration node's folders contain settings that you can use to customize the user's environment or enforce lockdown policies for users on the network. These settings include all user-specific policies, such as desktop appearance, application settings, logon and logoff scripts, and assigned and published applications. User Configuration policies apply when the user logs on to the computer.

Using the Group Policy Snap-In

Each instance of the Group Policy snap-in is specific to a GPO. You can add a GPO-specific Group Policy snap-in to an MMC console to use as a stand-alone tool. This allows you to add a snap-in for each GPO that you want to administer. You can also open the Group Policy snap-in for a particular GPO through the site, domain, or OU where the GPO is located. Finally, you can edit the local GPO by using Gpedit.msc.

Creating an MMC Console

By using an MMC console, you can create a tool that contains a Group Policy snap-in for each GPO you want to administer. After you open the MMC interface, add Group Policy as a stand-alone snap-in. When you add the snap-in, you must select the GPO associated with that snap-in. You can add the local GPO, which is the default setting, or you can browse for GPOs that are in sites, domains, or OUs (Figure 7.14). You can also browse for the local GPO on any computers in your domain. Once you've added a Group Policy snap-in for each GPO you are going to administer, save the MMC console as an .msc file. You can then open the file at any time to administer the GPOs you added to the console. You can also add or delete GPOs as necessary.

Figure 7.14 Browsing for all group policies created in the microsoft.com domain

Editing a GPO in Sites, Domains, and OUs

To create and edit a GPO, open the Group Policy snap-in for a specific GPO from a site, domain, or OU. For sites, use the Active Directory Sites And Services snap-in. For domains and OUs, use the Active Directory Users And Computers snap-in. Open the Properties dialog box for the site, domain, or OU, and select the Group Policy tab. Select the GPO you want to administer, and click Edit. This launches the Group Policy snap-in for that specific object. This navigation is shown in Figures 7.12 and 7.13. At this point, you can edit the GPO as necessary.

Using Gpedit.msc

You can edit the local GPO by using Gpedit.msc. From the Run command, type **gpedit.msc** and click OK. This launches the Group Policy snap-in for the GPO on the local computer. From there, you can edit the GPO as necessary.

You can perform remote group policy administration by using the gpcomputer: *<computername>* parameter or the gpobject parameter with Gpedit.msc. The *computername* variable used with gpcomputer can be either a NetBIOS name or a DNS name. To view and configure the domain GPO for Server01 in the microsoft.com domain, you can type:

```
gpedit.msc /gpcomputer:"server01"
```

or

```
gpedit.msc /gpcomputer:"server01.microsoft.com"
```

The gpcomputer parameter is designed to display the domain GPO. The gpobject parameter requires an ADSI path and can open any GPO created in the Active Directory store. For example, to open a GPO with a GUID of 45265FA6-554F-4F74-97CC-61B4663DAE61 in the microsoft.com domain, you can type:

```
gpedit.msc /gpobject:"LDAP://CN={45265FA6-554F-4F74-97CC-
61B4663DAE61},CN=Policies,CN=System,DC=microsoft,DC=com"
```

GPO Permissions

When you create a GPO, a set of groups is added to the object and each of those groups is configured with a set of properties. By default, Domain Admins, Enterprise Admins, and System groups are granted Read, Write, Create All Child Objects, and Delete All Child Objects permissions to the GPO. The Creator Owner system group is also assigned special permissions to manage child objects within the GPO. The Authenticated Users system group is given Read And Apply Group Policy access. Note that by default, only the Authenticated Users group is granted the Apply Group Policy attribute. Except for the Authenticated Users group, members of the other groups can edit the GPO. The policy settings contained in the GPO do not apply to members of a group that has been denied the Apply Group Policy permission (Deny).

Administrators can specify which groups of users and computers have Apply Group Policy access to the object. Groups that have Apply Group Policy and Read access to the GPO receive the configured group policy settings contained in the object.

The following table lists a GPO's default groups and their properties:

Security group	Default settings
Authenticated Users	Read, Apply Group Policy (AGP)
Creator Owner	Special oObject and Attribute permissions assigned to child objects and properties within the GPO
Domain Admins	Read, Write, Create All Child Objects, Delete All Child Objects
Enterprise Admins	Read, Write, Create All Child Objects, Delete All Child Objects
System	Read, Write, Create All Child Objects, Delete All Child Objects

Administrators are also authenticated users, which means that they have the Apply Group Policy attribute set. If this is not desired, administrators have two choices:

- Remove Authenticated Users from the list, and add another security group with the Apply Group Policy attribute set to Allow. This new group should contain all the users that the GPO is intended to affect.

- Set the Apply Group Policy attribute to Deny for the Domain Admins and Enterprise Admins groups and possibly the Creator Owner group. This will prevent the GPO from being applied to members of those groups. Remember that a permission set to Deny always takes precedence over Allow. Therefore, even if a user is a member of another group that has been granted the Apply Group Policy permission, the user will still be denied.

To edit a GPO, the user must have both Read and Write access to the object. A GPO cannot be opened in Read-Only mode. In other words, if you can open the Group Policy snap-in, you can edit the Group Policy object that appears in the namespace. Moreover, the changes occur during the edit; there is no Save or Activate step. An administrator might want to unlink a GPO from any site, domain, or OU during the edit, or he or she might want to leave it linked, but disable both the User and Computer nodes.

You cannot use security groups to apply (or prevent from applying) only some of the settings in a Group Policy object—except in the cases of Folder Redirection and Software Installation, which have additional ACLs set at the GPO level to further refine behavior based on security group membership.

To edit a GPO, the user must be one of the following:

- An administrator
- A Creator Owner
- A user with delegated access to the Group Policy object

You can modify the permissions on a GPO by opening the Properties dialog box for the site, domain, or OU that contains the GPO and then selecting the Group Policy tab. Select the GPO, click Properties, and select the Security tab, as shown in Figure 7.15.

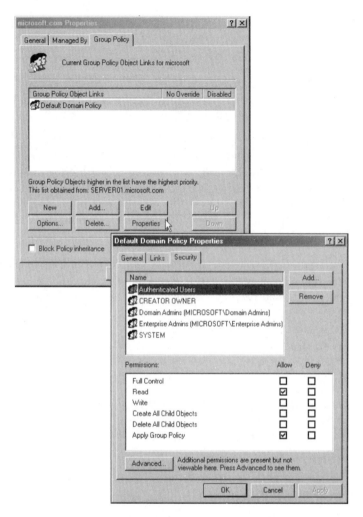

Figure 7.15 Accessing the security settings of the microsoft.com Default Domain Policy GPO

From there, you can modify the basic permissions or click the Advanced button to modify advanced permissions.

Order of Inheritance

In general, a group policy is passed down from parent to child containers. If you have assigned a specific group policy to a high-level parent container, that group policy applies to all containers beneath the parent container, including the user and computer objects in each container. However, if you explicitly specify a group policy setting for a child container, the child container's group policy setting overrides the parent container's setting.

If a parent OU has policy settings that are not configured, the child OU doesn't inherit them. Policy settings that are disabled are inherited as disabled. Also, if a policy is configured for a parent OU and the same policy is not configured for a child OU, the child inherits the parent's policy setting.

If a parent policy and a child policy are compatible, the child inherits the parent policy and the child's setting is also applied. Policies are inherited as long as they are compatible. For example, if the parent's policy causes a certain folder to be placed on the desktop and the child's setting calls for an additional folder, the user sees both folders.

If a policy configured for a parent OU is incompatible with the same policy configured for a child OU, the child does not inherit the policy setting from the parent. The setting in the child is applied.

You can use the Active Directory Users And Computers snap-in to configure inheritance for domains and OUs. Open the Properties dialog box for the domain or OU, and select the Group Policy tab. In addition, you can configure inheritance for sites by using the Active Directory Sites And Services snap-in. Open the Properties dialog box for the specific site, and select the Group Policy tab. There are two options you can use to configure inheritance: the Block Policy Inheritance check box and the No Override check box.

Block Policy Inheritance

You can block inheritance of policies at the domain or OU levels by using the Block Policy Inheritance check box. This check box is located on the first tab of each GPO's Properties dialog box. Block policy inheritance is not available to a site policy since a site is at the top of the GPO hierarchy. If this option is selected for a child-level group policy object, the child does not inherit any policies from a parent-level group policy object.

No Override

The No Override check box forces all child policy containers to inherit the parent's policies even if those policies conflict with the child's policies, and even if Block Inheritance has been set for the child. This check box and the check box described next are located by clicking the Options button on the GPO's Properties dialog box.

Disabled

The Disabled check box turns off the GPO so that it is removed from operation. However, it is still associated with the container where it is specified. This option is commonly used to change settings in a policy without affecting users. When the modifications are complete, clearing this check box applies the GPO to all users who are assigned the Apply Group Policy permission.

Deleting the Default Domain Policy

By default, the Default Domain Policy GPO cannot be deleted by any administrator. This is to prevent the accidental deletion of this GPO, which contains important and required settings for the domain. If the Default Domain Policy should not be applied, for example, because the policies have been set in other GPOs, select the Disable Computer Configuration settings, and the Disable User Configuration settings check boxes in the properties of the Default Domain Policy. You can also select the Block Policy Inheritance check box for a GPO lower in the hierarchy so that the Default Domain Policy does not apply. This will work as long as the parent GPO is not configured for the No Override link option.

Support for Windows 95, Windows 98, and Windows NT 4.0

The Group Policy snap-in does not provide client support for Windows 95, Windows 98, and Windows NT computers.

Support for Windows NT 4.0 clients is provided by fully supporting the Windows NT 4.0 style administrative templates (.adm files) and by providing the Windows NT 4.0 System Policy Editor (Poledit.exe) files. Windows 95 and Windows 98 clients still need to be managed by using the Windows 9*x* System Policy Editor.

Client computers that are running Windows 95 and Windows 98 need to have the Config.pol file created on the client computer's operating system copied to the domain's network logon share. Windows NT 4.0 clients use the Ntconfig.pol file, which they read from the network logon share. In a Windows NT Server network, the logon share is named Netlogon and is located in the %systemroot%\System32\Repl\Import\Scripts folder. The network logon share for Windows 2000 is located in the %systemroot%\SYSVOL\Sysvol\ <*DomainName.com*>\Scripts folder and is shared as Netlogon. Windows 95, Windows 98, and Windows NT client computers will look to this share for their respective .pol file.

For information about installing the System Policy Editor, see Windows 2000 Server Help. The System Policy Editor is included with Windows 2000 Server but not with Windows 2000 Professional. The Windows 2000 Optional

Administrative Tools package (Adminpak.msi), which includes the System Policy Editor, comes on the Windows 2000 Server CD-ROM for installation onto computers running Windows 2000 Professional. Adminpak.msi does not place a program item in the Administrative Tools program group. To run the Windows NT policy editor, type **poledit** in the Run dialog box.

Administering Group Policies

Once you have set up your group policy objects and, if desired, configured an MMC console that contains a Group Policy snap-in for each of the GPOs, you are ready to administer the group policies.

Managing Software Settings

Use the Group Policy snap-in to centrally manage software distribution. Software can be installed, assigned, published, updated, repaired, and uninstalled for groups of users and computers.

Before using the Group Policy snap-in to deploy software, Microsoft Windows Installer (.msi) packages must be acquired for the applications. Packages can be acquired in the following ways:

- The software vendor or developer may supply the Windows Installer packages for their applications. For example, Microsoft products will provide Windows Installer packages. Third-party software installation tool vendors will supply developers with the Windows Installer package-authoring tools for authoring or creating native Windows Installer packages for their software.

- The administrator can use a repackaging tool to create a repackaged Windows Installer package for the application. Third-party software installation tool vendors can supply administrators with the Windows Installer repackaging tools they need to repackage their existing software.

Assigning and Publishing Applications

You can assign applications to users and computers, and you can publish applications to users.

Assigning to users

When you assign an application to a user, the application is advertised to the user the next time that user logs onto a workstation. The application advertisement follows the user regardless of which physical computer he or she actually uses. This application is installed the first time the user activates the application on the computer, either by selecting the application on the Start menu or by activating a document associated with the application.

Assigning to Computers

When you assign an application to the computer, the application is advertised and the installation is performed when it is safe to do so. Typically, this happens when the computer starts up so that there are no competing processes on the computer.

Publishing to Users

When you publish the application to users, the application does not appear installed on the users' computers. No shortcuts are visible on the desktop or Start menu, and no changes are made to the local registry on the users' computers. Instead, published applications store their advertisement attributes in the Active Directory store. Then, information such as the application's name and file associations is exposed to the users in the Active Directory container. The application is then available for the user to install by using Add/Remove Programs in Control Panel or by clicking a file associated with the application (such as an .xls file for Microsoft Excel).

Assigning and Publishing Applications

To assign or publish an application, create a shared folder and copy the application files and package files (.msi files) to the shared folder. Assign the following permissions to the shared folder:

- Everyone = Read
- Administrators = Full Control

To assign or publish an application, open the Group Policy snap-in for the appropriate GPO and select the Software Settings\Software installation subfolder from either Computer Configuration or User Configuration. From the Action menu, select New and then select Package. Browse to the network share that was created, and select the package to be assigned. The Deploy Application dialog box appears. Select the deployment method.

Click Assigned: Deployed To All Users At Logon, or click Published: Users Install Via Add/Remove Programs wizard, and then click OK. The name of the application to be assigned or published, along with additional properties for the application, appears in the details pane.

The following table describes how applications are deployed:

If the application is	In this node	It appears in
Assigned	User Configuration	The Start menu for all users in the site, domain, or OU
	Computer Configuration	The Start menu for all computers in the site, domain, or OU
Published	User Configuration	The Add/Remove Programs wizard for all users in the site, domain, or OU

Managing Scripts

Windows 2000 group policy allows considerable flexibility when assigning scripts. You can assign startup and shutdown scripts to computers, which Windows 2000 processes when it starts up and shuts down. You can also assign logon and logoff scripts to users, which Windows 2000 processes when the user logs on and logs off.

Windows 2000 executes scripts in the following way:

- When you assign multiple logon and logoff or startup and shutdown scripts to a user or computer, Windows 2000 executes the scripts from top to bottom. You can determine the order of execution for multiple scripts in the Properties dialog box.

- When a computer is shut down, Windows 2000 first processes logoff scripts and then shutdown scripts. By default, the timeout value for processing scripts is two minutes. If the logoff and shutdown scripts require more than two minutes to process, you must adjust the timeout value with a software policy.

Note Windows 2000 stores scripts in the Scripts folder of the GPT.

The Group Policy snap-in in Windows 2000 allows considerable flexibility when assigning scripts. Administrators can assign both startup and shutdown scripts to computers as well as logon and logoff scripts to users. Scripts are scheduled to run upon a specific event through the Scripts (Startup/Shutdown) extension for Computers and the Scripts (Logon/Logoff) extension for Users. As their names imply, the scripts process when the operating system starts up or shuts down or when the user logs on or logs off.

The scripts that can be used include Windows NT batch files (.bat or .cmd), VBScript (.vbs), or JScript (.js) with Windows Scripting Host.

To assign scripts, double-click the appropriate scripts icon (Startup, Shutdown, Logon, or Logoff) and click Add. Browse to the script you want implemented. Once the script is selected, enter any command line parameters for the script.

Multiple Scripts

Multiple Logon/Logoff or Startup/Shutdown scripts can be assigned to a user or computer. Use the Up and Down buttons in the Properties dialog box to determine the order of execution when using multiple scripts. The scripts will execute in order from top to bottom.

Show Files

Clicking the Show Files button will open a window that displays the contents of the appropriate scripts folder. This allows the scripts and associated files that exist for this GPO to be viewed.

Managing Security Settings

Computer security policy covers different areas of policy, administrative rights, and user permissions.

There are two types of security policies defined in Windows 2000:

- Domain security policy
- Computer security policy (also known as local policy)

A computer that is not part of a Windows 2000 domain is affected only by computer security policy. A computer that is a member of a Windows 2000 domain has the computer security policy applied first, followed by the domain security policy.

Windows 2000 provides the infrastructure to define and manage these security policies centrally and distribute the enforcement to all machines in the domain. The security infrastructure can be separated into a number of configurable categories:

- **Account Policies** This category allows you to configure security settings for password policy, lockout policy, and Kerberos policy in Windows 2000 domains.

- **Local Policies** This category allows you to configure security settings for audit policy, user rights assignment, and security options. Local policy allows you to configure who has local or network access to the computer and whether or how local events are audited.

- **Event Log** This category allows you to configure security settings for the Application, Security, and System event logs. You can access these logs by using the Event Viewer.

- **Restricted Groups** This category allows you to configure who should and should not belong to a restricted group, as well as which groups a restricted group should belong to. These settings allow administrators to enforce security policies regarding sensitive groups, such as Enterprise Administrators or Payroll. For example, it may be decided that only Joe and Mary should be members of the Enterprise Administrators group. Restricted groups can be used to enforce that policy. If a third user is added to the group (for example, to accomplish some task in an emergency situation), the next time policy is enforced, that third user is automatically removed from the Enterprise Administrators group. Policies are reapplied every 90 minutes by default. So the third user would have Enterprise Administrator privileges for a maximum of 90 minutes.

- **System Services** This category allows you to configure the startup mode and security options (security descriptors) for system services such as network services, file and print services, telephone and fax services, Internet and intranet services, and so on.

- **Registry** This category allows you to configure security settings for registry keys including access control, audit, and ownership. When you apply security on registry keys, the Security Settings extension follows the same inheritance model as that used for all tree-structured hierarchies in Windows 2000 (such as the Active Directory store and NTFS). Microsoft recommends that you use the inheritance capabilities to specify security only at top-level objects and redefine security only for those child objects that require it. This approach greatly simplifies your security structure and reduces the administrative overhead that results from a needlessly complex access control structure.

- **File System** This category allows you to configure security settings for file-system objects, including access control, audit, and ownership.

- **Public Key Policies** This category allows you to configure encrypted data recovery agents, auto-enrollment policy, domain roots, and trusted certificate authorities.

- **IP Security Policies on Active Directory services** This category allows you to configure IP security on a network.

A set of predefined security configuration templates are stored in %systemroot%\Security\Templates. These predefined security configurations can be used as the basis for security settings and then edited according to your organization's needs.

Security configurations are stored as .inf files in a text format called the Security Descriptor Definition Language (SDDL). When a security configuration is assigned or edited, the configuration file is processed and the corresponding changes are made to the associated computers or user accounts.

Managing Administrative Templates

In Windows 2000, the Administrative Templates extension in the Group Policy snap-in uses an administrative template (.adm) file to specify the registry settings that can be modified through the Group Policy snap-in. Each policy lists the policy settings that are applied to the selected site, domain, or organizational unit.

The policies listed under Administrative Templates represent registry-based group policy settings. Administrative Templates govern a variety of behaviors for the Windows 2000 operating system and its components and applications. These settings are written to the HKEY_CURRENT_USER (HKCU) or HKEY_LOCAL_MACHINE (HKLM) portion of the registry database, as appropriate.

The .adm file is a Unicode text file. (Unicode support for .adm files is new to Windows 2000). The file specifies a hierarchy of categories and subcategories that together define how the options are displayed. It also indicates the registry locations where changes should be made for a particular selection, specifies any options or restrictions (in values) associated with the selection, and in some cases, specifies a default value to use if a selection is activated.

The Explain tab of each policy's Properties page contains details on the policy settings within the .adm file. Figure 7.16 shows the Explain tab for a System policy.

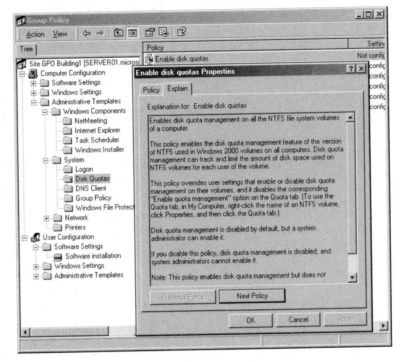

Figure 7.16 The Explain tab for the Enable Disk Quotas system property

The Administrative Templates nodes of the Group Policy snap-in can be extended by using custom .adm files.

Persistent Registry Settings

Windows NT 4.0 registry settings remain in effect until they are explicitly reversed. This behavior is called "tattooing." Windows 2000 registry settings, by contrast, are cleaned and rewritten each time policy changes. Be aware of this behavior if you are familiar with Windows NT 4.0 registry configuration using policies.

Managing Folder Redirection

The Folder Redirection extension allows you to redirect any of the following special folders in a user profile to an alternate location (such as a network share):

- Application Data
- Desktop
- My Documents

- My Documents\My Pictures
- Start Menu

For example, you could redirect a user's My Documents folder to \\<*server*>\ <*share*>\%username%. By redirecting the My Documents folder, you can provide the following advantages:

- Ensure that users' documents are available when they roam from one computer to another.

- Reduce the time it takes to log on to and log off from the network. In Windows NT 4.0, the My Documents folder is part of the Roaming User Profile (RUP). This means that the My Documents folder and its contents are copied back and forth between the client computer and the server when users log on and log off. Relocating the My Documents folder outside of the user profile can significantly decrease that time.

- Store user data on the network (rather than on the local computer). The data can then be centrally managed and protected with network backup procedures and Domain Dfs.

- Make users' network-based My Documents folder available to users when they are disconnected from the corporate network by using Offline Folder technologies.

By default, the Folder Redirection extension is not included with the Group Policy snap-in. To use Folder Redirection, you should create an MMC console that includes a Group Policy snap-in for each GPO that you support. Where appropriate, add the Folder Redirection extension to the Group Policy snap-in.

Exercise 6: Creating a Group Policy Object and Setting a Policy

In this exercise, you create a GPO named Domain Policy for your domain. Then you use the Group Policy snap-in to modify security settings of the GPO to give Domain Users the right to log on locally at the domain controllers. Complete this exercise on Server01.

Procedure 1: Creating a GPO

▶ In this procedure, you create a GPO at the domain level.

1. Log on to the domain as Administrator with a password of "password."

2. Click Start, point to Programs, point to Administrative Tools, and then click Active Directory Users And Computers.

   The Active Directory Users And Computers snap-in appears.

3. Click microsoft.com in the console tree, click the Action menu, and then click Properties.

   The microsoft.com Properties dialog box appears.

4. Click the Group Policy tab, and then click Add.

   The Add A Group Policy Object Link dialog box appears.

5. Click the All tab.

   Notice that there is a Default Domain Policy listed. You could use this GPO and modify it as you wish, but for the purpose of this procedure you will create a new GPO for the domain.

6. Click the middle button of the three buttons on the toolbar.

   A new GPO named New Group Policy Object appears in the Group Policy Objects list.

7. Name the new GPO **Domain Policy**, and then click OK.

   The Domain Policy GPO is listed in the Group Policy Object Links column.

8. Click ok to close the Group Policy Properties dialog box.

9. Leave the Active Directory Users And Computers snap-in open.

▸ Procedure 2: Modifying security settings

In this procedure, you use the Group Policy Editor to modify security settings in order to give the Domain Users group the right to log on locally to Server01.

1. In the console tree, expand microsoft.com.

2. Click the Domain Controllers container.

3. Click the Action menu and then click Properties.

   The Domain Controllers Properties dialog box appears.

4. Click the Group Policy tab.

   In the Group Policy Object Links list, verify that Default Domain Controllers Policy is highlighted, and then click Edit.

5. The Group Policy snap-in appears and displays the Default Domain Controller Policy console tree.

6. In the console tree, verify that the Computer Configuration node is expanded.

   The Computer Configuration policies appear.

7. Expand Windows Settings below the Computer Configuration node.

The Windows Settings policies appear.

8. Expand Security Settings below the Windows Settings node.

The Security Settings policies appear.

9. Expand Local Policies below the Security Settings object.

The Local Policies appear.

10. Click User Rights Assignment below the Local Policies object.

A list of User Rights Assignment attributes appears in the details pane.

11. Double-click Log On Locally in the details pane.

The Log On Locally dialog box appears.

Notice that a number of user and group objects are granted this policy setting.

12. Click Add.

The Add User Or Group dialog box appears.

13. Click Browse.

The Select Users Or Groups dialog box appears.

14. In the Name list, select Domain Users, click Add, and then click OK.

Tip If you are having trouble locating the Domain Users group, simply type **Domain Users** and the Windows type-down feature will locate the group for you.

15. Click OK again.

Domain Users appears in the list of users and groups with the right to log on locally.

16. Click OK, and then close the Group Policy snap-in.

17. Click OK to close the Domain Controllers Properties dialog box.

18. Leave the Active Directory Users And Computers snap-in running since you will use it in the next exercise.

All domain users are now able to logon locally to Server01.

Exercise 7: Modifying Software Policies

In this exercise, you create and then modify the Sales OU group policy by removing the Search item and Run item from the Start menu. You also disable the Lock Workstation policy. You then view the effects of these software policy modifications. In the last part of this exercise, you prevent the Sales OU from overriding the group policy of its parent container, the domain. Complete this exercise on Server01.

▶ Procedure 1: Modifying software policies

In this procedure, you create and then modify software policies for the Sales OU. You created the Sales OU in an earlier chapter.

1. In the Active Directory Users And Computers snap-in expand microsoft.com.

2. In the console tree, click Sales, click the Action menu, and then click Properties.

   The Sales Properties dialog box appears.

3. Click the Group Policy tab.

4. Click Add.

   The Add A Group Policy Object Link dialog box appears.

5. Select the All tab, and then click the middle button of the three buttons on the toolbar.

   A new GPO appears under Group Policy Objects Associated With This Container.

6. Name the new GPO **SalesSoftware**, and then click OK.

   You are returned to the Group Policy tab of the Sales Properties dialog box.

7. With SalesSoftware highlighted, click Edit.

   The Group Policy snap-in appears.

8. Locate and expand Administrative templates under User Configuration.

9. In the console tree, click Start Menu & Task Bar.

   The policies available for this category appear in the details pane.

10. In the details pane, double-click Remove Search Menu From Start Menu.

    The Remove Search Menu From Start Menu Properties dialog box appears.

11. Click Explain to read about this policy.

12. Click the Policy tab, and then click the Enabled radio button.

13. Click OK.

14. Repeat steps 10 through 13 to enable the Remove Run Menu From Start Menu policy.

15. In the console tree, double-click System and then click Logon/Logoff.

    The policies available for this category appear in the details pane.

16. In the details pane, enable the Disable Lock Computer policy.

17. Close the Group Policy snap-in, and then close the Sales Properties dialog box.

18. Close the Active Directory Users And Computers snap-in.

▸ **Procedure 2: Testing software policies**

In this procedure, you view the effects of the software policies implemented in the previous procedure.

Important From the completion of exercises in this chapter and in Chapter 6, "Active Directory Services," you should have two user accounts in the Sales OU, Jane Doe, and John Smith.

---

1. Log off of Server01 as Administrator.

2. Press Ctrl+Alt+Delete.

3. The Windows NT Security dialog box appears.

    Notice that the Shutdown button is not available. This is controlled by the Shutdown Without Logon policy. Note that Windows 2000 Server does not make this button available by default.

4. Log on to Server01 as Jane_Doe with a password of "student."

5. Click the Start menu.

    Notice that the Search and Run menu items do not appear on the Start menu.

▶ **Procedure 3: Preventing group policy override**

In this exercise, you prevent the Sales OU from overriding the group policy of its parent container.

1. Log on as Administrator with a password of "password."

2. Click Start, point to Programs, point to Administrative Tools, and then click the Active Directory Users And Computers snap-in.

   The Active Directory Users And Computers snap-in window appears.

3. Expand microsoft.com.

4. Click Sales, click the Action menu, and then click Properties.

   The Sales Properties dialog box appears.

5. Click the Group Policy tab.

6. Verify that SalesSoftware is highlighted in the Group Policy Objects Link list, and then click Options.

7. Click the No Override: Prevents Other Group Policy Objects From Overriding Policy Set In This One check box, and then click OK.

8. Click OK again, and then close the Active Directory Users And Computers snap-in.

Lesson Summary

Group policies are a set of configuration settings that apply to one or more objects in the Active Directory store. They can be used to control the work environments for users in a site, for a domain, or for users associated with a specific OU. There are many types of group policies, including software settings, scripts, security settings, administrative templates, and folder redirection. The group policy structure is made up of group policy objects, containers, and templates. Before you can create group policies, you must create the group policy objects. From there, you can edit group policies by using the Group Policy snap-in or manage permissions by using the Active Directory Users And Computers snap-in. Administering group policies includes managing software settings, scripts, security settings, administrative templates, and folder redirection.

Review

The following questions are intended to reinforce key information presented in this chapter. If you are unable to answer a question, review the appropriate lesson and then try the question again. Answers to the questions can be found in Appendix A, "Questions and Answers."

1. When you use the Administrative Tools program group to open an MMC console provided with Windows 2000 Server, can you add snap-ins to it? Why or why not?

2. You receive a call from a member of the Help Desk support team. She tells you that a number of users are complaining of a window that appears every time they log on. The support person tells you there is nothing in the Startup menu. Additionally, she has closed the window and shut down and restarted the computer, but the window still appears at logon. What is the most likely cause of this issue, and how can you resolve it?

3. When should you use security groups instead of distribution groups?

4. What are the implications of changing the domain mode from Mixed mode to Native mode?

5. By default, in what order is group policy implemented through the Active Directory store hierarchy? How can you control this behavior?

6. What is a GPO, GPC, and GPT?

C H A P T E R   8

Administering Print Services

About This Chapter

This chapter introduces you to setting up and configuring network printers
so that users can print over the network. You will also learn about Active
Directory–based printing and how to connect to network printers. This
chapter also provides information about how to troubleshoot common
printing problems associated with setting up network printers.

Before You Begin

To complete the lessons in this chapter, you must have

- A computer that has Microsoft Windows 2000 Server installed and operating.
- Active Directory services installed and operating.
- Completed all the exercises in the previous chapters.

Note You do not need a printer to complete the exercises in this chapter.

Lesson 1: Introduction to Windows 2000 Printing

Microsoft Windows 2000 Server is designed for network printing. Using a variety of platforms, applications send print jobs to printers attached to a Windows 2000 print server or connected to the network by internal network adapters, external network adapters (print server devices), or another server. By using a computer that is running Windows 2000 Server as your network print server, you can print from any supported operating system that your networked computers use. This lesson introduces you to network printing by first reviewing the terminology used in print services and providing guidelines for setting up a network printing environment. This lesson also reviews the issues involved in local and remote printing and with print devices that are either attached through the network or directly to the computer.

After this lesson, you will be able to

- Define the terms used in Windows 2000 printing

- Define the requirements and guidelines for a network printing environment

- Describe the different printing scenarios for local and remote printing for print devices attached to the network and for print devices attached directly to the computer

Estimated lesson time: 35 minutes

Terminology

Before you set up printing, you should be familiar with Windows 2000 printing terminology to understand how the different components fit together, as shown in Figure 8.1.

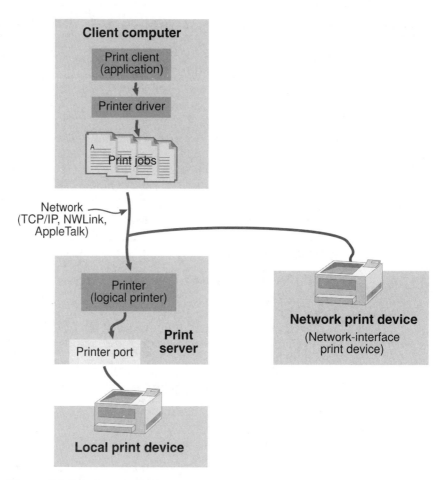

Figure 8.1 Printing terminology

If you are new to Windows 2000, you might find some of the printing terminology to be different from what you expected (although printing terminology
has not changed significantly from that used in Microsoft Windows NT
Server). The following list defines a few Windows 2000 printing terms:

- **Printer** A printer is the software interface between the operating system
  and the print device. The printer defines where a document will go to reach
  the print device (that is, to a local port, a port for a network connection, or
  a file), when it will go, and how various other aspects of the printing
  process will be handled. When users make connections to printers, they
  use printer names, which point to one or more print devices.

- **Print device** A print device is the hardware device that produces printed documents. Windows 2000 supports the following print devices:

  - *Local print devices* are those that are connected to a physical port on the print server. A local print device is connected to the computer by a local interface, such as a parallel, serial RS-232/422/IRDA, USB, or SCSI port.

  - *Network print devices* are those that are connected to a print server through the network instead of a physical port. Network print devices, also called *network-interface print devices,* require their own network interface cards and have their own network address or they are attached to an external network adapter. A networked printer is a node on the network; computers send print jobs to it through a network adapter, which might be built in.

- **Print server** A print server is the computer on which the printers associated with local and network print devices reside. The print server receives and processes documents from client computers. You set up and share network printers on print servers.

- **Printer driver** A printer driver is one or more files containing information that Windows 2000 requires to convert print commands into a specific printer language, such as PostScript. This conversion makes it possible for a print device to print a document. A printer driver is specific to each print device model.

Requirements for Network Printing

The requirements for setting up printing on a Windows 2000 network include the following:

- At least one computer to operate as the print server. If the print server will manage many heavily used printers, Microsoft recommends a dedicated print server. The computer can run either of the following:

  - Windows 2000 Server, which can handle a large number of connections and supports client computers running MS-DOS, Windows, Macintosh, UNIX, and NetWare client redirectors and printing services.

  - Windows 2000 Professional, which is limited to 10 concurrent connections from other computers for file and print services. It does not support Macintosh computers or NetWare clients but does support MS-DOS, Windows, and UNIX computers.

- Sufficient random access memory (RAM) to process documents. If a print server manages a large number of printers or many large documents, the server might require additional RAM beyond what Windows 2000 requires for other tasks. If a print server does not have sufficient RAM for its workload, printing performance deteriorates.

- Sufficient disk space on the print server to ensure that Windows 2000 can store documents and other printable data sent to the print server until the print server sends the data to the print device. This is critical when documents are large or likely to accumulate. For example, if 10 users send large documents to print at the same time, the print server must have enough disk space to hold all the spooled documents in the print queue until the print server sends them to the print device. If there is not enough space to hold all the documents, users will get error messages and be unable to print.

Note Spooled print jobs can be significantly larger than the actual data the print application reads. This is because print jobs are sent through the printer device driver to prepare the data for the printer.

Guidelines for a Network Printing Environment

Before you set up network printing, develop a network-wide printing strategy to meet users' printing needs without unnecessary duplication of resources or delays in printing. The following table provides some guidelines for developing a network printing strategy:

Guideline	Explanation
Determine users' printing requirements.	Determine the number of users who print and the printing workload. For example, 15 people in a billing department who print invoices continually will have a larger printing workload and might require more printers, print devices, and possibly more print servers than 15 software developers who do all their work online.
Determine company's printing requirements.	Determine the printing needs of your company. This includes the number and types of print devices required. In addition, consider the type of workload each print device will handle. Do not use a personal print device for network printing.

Guideline	Explanation
Determine the number of print servers required. your	Determine the number of print servers your network requires to handle the number and types of printers network will have.
Determine where to locate print devices.	Determine where you will locate the print devices. In a routed network, consider placing the print servers and print devices on the same network with the client computers that will use them. Additionally, it should be easy for users to pick up their printed

documents.

Printing Configurations

Several combinations of clients, servers, and print devices are possible with Windows 2000, depending on whether the print device is remote or nonremote. A remote print device is accessed through a print server. A nonremote print device receives data directly from the computer. The combination of clients, servers, and print devices also depends on whether the print device is networked or directly attached to the computer.

The following figures show four basic printing configurations. The thin lines represent physical connections, such as network or parallel cables, and the arrows represent the logical print data flow.

Figure 8.2 shows the simplest configuration, a nonremote, local print device. The print device is plugged into the parallel port of the computer that runs the application. The printer driver and job queue are on that computer, which sends print data directly to the print device.

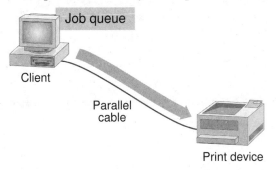

Figure 8.2 A nonremote, local print device

Figure 8.3 shows a small group of computers sharing a network print device. This is a peer-to-peer network, where each computer has equal access to the print device and there is no central control of printing or security. Each computer has its own job queue and cannot see the documents queued on the print device by other computers. If printing halts, the error message does not appear on every client. This is acceptable for small organizations where the users are in frequent contact, but it becomes less manageable as traffic increases. Contention among computers submitting documents might cause the print device to time out or reject print jobs.

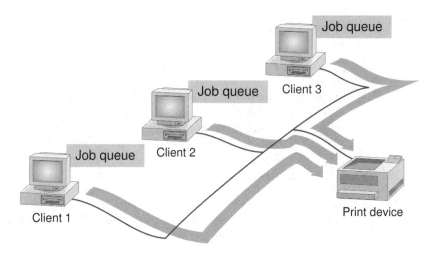

Figure 8.3 A nonremote, network print device

Figure 8.4 illustrates a network configuration using a central print server. Many clients share access to the print device through the server, which is locally connected to the print device. The job queue resides on the server and is visible to each client.

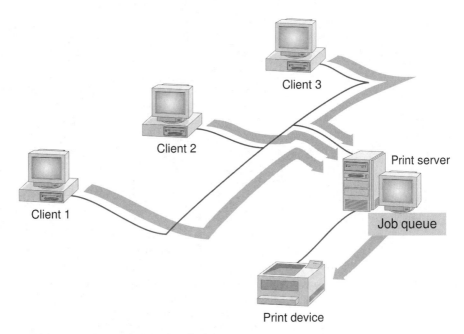

Figure 8.4 Remote, local print device

Printing is controlled by the server administrator. The administrator defines and enforces a security plan for the network, maintains the printer software, and downloads it to clients when they connect to the printer share. When a client connects to a network print queue, the client checks for new printer drivers on the print server and updates older printer drivers on the client.

Clients might also be connected to other print devices, and the print server often has several attached print devices. However, the number of parallel ports on the print server limits the number of print devices that can be directly attached to it.

Figure 8.5 shows several clients sharing a print device in a domain managed by a computer that is running Windows 2000 Server; the print device is connected to the server over the network, allowing one print server to manage several print devices.

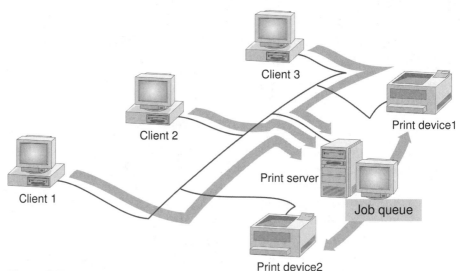

Figure 8.5 Remote, network print devices

To create and share printers, use the Add Printer wizard on the print server. The Add Printer wizard is located in the Printers folder, which you can access on the Start menu by clicking Settings and then clicking Printers. Regardless of where the print devices are located, the printer software must be located on the print server. If the print device is directly attached, the wizard detects it and then attempts to configure the printer software. If the print device is attached elsewhere on the network, you must create a port for it when you configure the printer software. You can also use the Add Printer wizard to connect to remote print devices. When doing so, remember the following:

- *Creating a printer* means installing the print device either directly on a print server or on the network, and then configuring the printer software that controls the print device on the print server. Run the Add Printer wizard, and click the Local Computer option. You must name the printer, install the printer driver, and specify a port.

- *Connecting to a printer* means connecting to the share on the computer that created the printer. To connect to a printer, run the Add Printer wizard and click the Network Printer option. If the printer driver for the client platform exists on the print server, installing it is not necessary because Windows 2000 downloads it automatically. This includes printer drivers for Windows 95, Windows 98, and all versions of Windows NT. Otherwise, you will be prompted to install the printer software.

Lesson Summary

A printer is the software interface between the operating system and the print device. A print device is the hardware device that produces printed documents. A print server is the computer on which the printers associated with local and network print devices reside. A printer driver is one or more files containing information that Windows 2000 requires to convert print commands into a specific printer language. You should also be familiar with the requirements for network printing, which include at least one computer to operate as the print server, sufficient RAM, and sufficient disk space. You should also determine the users' print requirements, the company's requirements, the number of print servers required, and where to locate print devices. Several combinations of clients, servers, and print devices are possible with Windows 2000, depending on whether the print device is local or remote and whether it is networked or directly attached to the computer.

Lesson 2: Setting Up Network Printers

Setting up and sharing a network printer makes it possible for multiple users to print to it. You can set up a printer for a print device connected directly to the print server, or you can set up a printer for a print device connected to the print server over the network. In larger organizations, most printers point to network print devices.

After this lesson, you will be able to

- Identify the requirements for setting up a network printer and network printing resources
- Add and share a new printer for a local print device or a network print device
- Share an existing printer

Estimated lesson time: 35 minutes

Installing a Local Print Device

The steps for adding a printer for a local print device or for a network print device are similar. To install a local print device, use the Add Printer wizard on the print server. When prompted, select Local Printer rather than Network Printer, as shown in Figure 8.6.

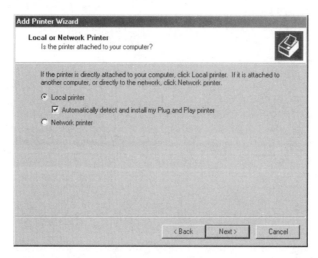

Figure 8.6 The Local Or Network Printer screen appearing in the Add Printer wizard

The wizard guides you through the remaining steps necessary to add a printer for a print device connected to the print server. The number of local print devices you can connect to a print server through physical ports depends on your hardware configuration.

Installing a Network Print Device

In larger companies, most print devices are network print devices. These print devices offer several advantages. You do not need to place print devices near the print server. In addition, network connections transfer data more quickly than printer cable connections.

You add a printer for a network print device by using the Add Printer wizard. The main difference between adding a printer for a local print device and adding a printer for a network print device is that for a typical network print device, you provide additional port and network protocol information.

The default network protocol for Windows 2000 is Transmission Control Protocol/Internet Protocol (TCP/IP), which many network print devices use. For TCP/IP, you provide additional port information by using the Add Standard TCP/IP Printer Port wizard, which is accessed through the Add Printer wizard. See Windows 2000 Server Help for more details about installing a TCP/IP print device onto your network.

Sharing an Existing Printer

If the printing demands on your network increase and your network has an existing, unshared printer for a print device, you can share it so that users can print to the print device.

When you share a printer, consider the following guidelines:

- You need to assign the printer a share name, which appears in My Network Places. Use an intuitive name to help users when they are browsing for a printer.

- You can add printer drivers for Windows 95, Windows 98, all versions of Windows NT, and Windows 2000.

- You can choose to publish the printer in Active Directory services so that users can search for the printer.

To share an existing printer, open the Printers window, open the Properties dialog box for that printer, and then select the Sharing tab (Figure 8.7). The Sharing tab provides a simple interface for sharing the printer.

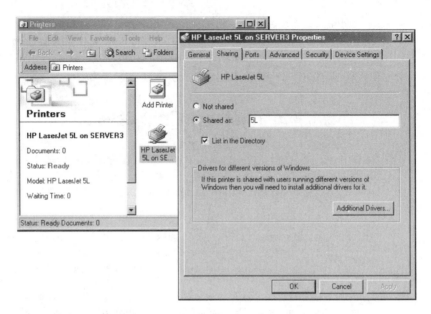

Figure 8.7 The Sharing tab in the Properties dialog box for a printer

After you have shared the printer, Windows 2000 displays an open hand under the printer icon, indicating that the printer is shared.

Exercise 1: Installing and Configuring Print Sharing and Setting the Printer for Offline Operation

In this exercise, you use the Add Printer wizard to add a local printer to your computer and share it. This exercise does not require you to have a print device because the printer will be taken offline to avoid error messages that would otherwise appear in later exercises. Complete this exercise on Server01.

▶ Procedure 1: Adding a local printer and configuring print sharing

1. Log on to the domain as administrator with a password of "password."

2. Click the Start button, point to Settings, and then click Printers.

   The Printers window appears. A Fax icon appears in the Printers window. During a typical installation of Windows 2000 Server, the Fax Service is installed.

3. Double-click Add Printer.

   The Add Printer wizard appears.

4. Click Next.

   The Local Or Network Printer screen appears, and you are prompted for the location of the printer. Because you are creating the printer on the computer at which you are sitting and not on a different computer, this printer is referred to as a local printer.

5. Verify that the Local Printer radio button is selected, clear the Automatically Detect And Install My Plug And Play Printer check box, and then click Next.

   The Select The Printer Port screen appears.

6. Click the Create A New Port radio button.

   The Type drop-down list box appears.

7. Click the arrow to the right of the Type drop-down list box.

   Notice that Local Port and Standard TCP/IP Port are the available options.

   The port types that will be available other than local port depend on the installed network protocols. In this case, TCP/IP is installed, so this protocol-based port is available.

8. Click the Use The Following Port radio button, and then verify that LPT1: is highlighted.

   For this exercise, assume that the print device you are adding is directly attached to your computer and using the LPT1 port.

9. Click Next.

   The wizard prompts you for the printer manufacturer and model. You will add an HP LaserJet 5Si printer.

   Tip The list of printers is sorted in alphabetical order. If you cannot find a printer name, make sure you are looking in the correct location.
   ---

10. Under Manufacturers, click HP; under Printers, click HP LaserJet 5Si; and then click Next.

    The Name Your Printer screen appears. In the Printer Name box, Windows 2000 defaults to the printer name HP LaserJet 5Si. For this exercise, do not change this name.

11. Verify that the Yes radio button is selected for the Do You Want Your Windows-Based Programs To Use This Printer As The Default Printer? radio button.

12. Click Next.

    The Printer Sharing screen appears, prompting you for printer sharing information.

13. Verify that the Share As radio button is selected.

    Notice that you can assign a shared printer name even though you already supplied a printer name. The shared printer name is used to identify a printer on the network and must conform to a naming convention. This shared name is different from the printer name you entered previously. The printer name is a description that will appear with the printer's icon in the Printers system folder and in Active Directory services. The share name is kept short for compatibility with other operating systems like Windows 3.*x*.

14. In the Share As text box, type **Printer1** and then click Next.

    The Location And Comment screen appears.

    Note Windows 2000 displays the values you enter for the Location and Comment text boxes when a user searches the Active Directory store for a printer. Entering this information is optional, but doing so helps users locate the printer.

    ---

15. In the Location text box, type **Building 520, Floor 18, Office 1831**; in the Comment text box, type **Black and White Output Laser Printer - High Volume**; and then click Next.

    The Print Test Page screen appears.

    Notice that you can print a test page to confirm that your printer is set up properly. You can also install additional drivers for other versions of Microsoft Windows.

16. Click the No radio button, and click Next.

    The Completing The Add Printer Wizard screen appears and provides a summary of your installation choices.

17. Confirm the summary of your installation choices, and then click Finish.

    If necessary, Windows 2000 displays the Files Needed dialog box, prompting you for the location of the Windows 2000 Server distribution files.

18. If the Files Needed dialog box appears, insert the Windows 2000 Server Installation CD-ROM and wait for about 10 seconds. If the Files Needed dialog box doesn't appear, read the information following step 20.

19. If Windows displays the Windows 2000 CD-ROM window, close it.

20. Click OK to close the Insert Disk dialog box.

    Windows 2000 copies the printer files, and an icon for the HP LaserJet 5Si printer appears in the Printers window.

    Notice that Windows 2000 displays an open hand under the printer icon. This indicates the printer is shared. Also notice the check mark next to the printer, which indicates the printer is the default printer for the print server.

21. Keep the Printers window open since you will need it to complete the next exercise.

▶ **Procedure 2: Taking a printer offline and printing a test document**

In this exercise, you take the printer you created offline. Taking a printer offline causes documents you send to this printer to be held on the computer while the print device is unavailable. Doing this will prevent error messages about unavailable print devices from occurring in later exercises. Otherwise, Windows 2000 will display such error messages when it attempts to send documents to a print device that is not connected to the computer.

1. In the Printers window, click the HP LaserJet 5Si icon.

2. Click the File menu, and then click Use Printer Offline.

    Notice that Windows 2000 changes the icon to reflect that the printer is not available and the text in the left pane of the Printers window indicates the status of the printer is Use Printer Offline.

3. In the Printers window, double-click the HP LaserJet 5Si icon.

    Notice that the list of documents to be sent to the print device is empty.

4. Click the Start button, point to Programs, point to Accessories, and then click Notepad.

5. In Notepad, type any sample text that you want.

6. Arrange Notepad and the HP LaserJet 5Si window so that you can see the contents of each.

Tip Access the context menu of the taskbar, and click Tile Windows Horizontally.

---

7. In Notepad, click the File menu, and then click Print.

   The Print dialog box appears, allowing you to select the printer and print options.

   The Print dialog box displays the location and comment information you entered when you created the printer, and it shows that the printer is currently offline. You can also use the Find Printer button on the dialog box to search the Active Directory store for a printer.

   Notice that HP LaserJet 5Si is selected as the printer. This printer is automatically selected because the HP LaserJet 5Si is the default printer for the print server.

8. Click Print.

   Notepad briefly displays a message stating that the document is printing on your computer. On a fast computer, you might not be able to see this message.

   In the HP LaserJet 5Si - Use Printer Offline window, you will see the document waiting to be sent to the print device. The document is held in the print queue because you took the printer offline. If the printer was online, the document would be sent to the print device.

9. Close Notepad, and click No when prompted to save changes to your document.

10. Select the document in the HP LaserJet 5Si_Use Printer Offline window, click the Printer menu, and then click Cancel All Documents.

    A Printer message box appears asking if you are sure you want to cancel all documents for HP LaserJet 5Si.

11. Click Yes.

    The document is removed.

12. Close the HP LaserJet 5Si - Use Printer Offline window.

13. Close the Printers window.

Lesson Summary

The steps for adding a printer for a local print device or for a network print device are similar. In both cases, use the Add Printer wizard on the print server. The Add Printer wizard starts with the Welcome To The Add Printer Wizard screen. The wizard guides you through the steps to add a printer for a print device. The default network protocol for Windows 2000 is TCP/IP, which many network print devices use. In addition, if the printing demands on your network increase and your network has an existing, nonshared printer for a print device, you can share it so that users can print to the print device.

Lesson 3: Administering Network Printers

In this lesson, you will learn about setting up and administering network printers. This includes managing printers and documents, using a Web browser to administer printers, setting up a printer pool, setting up priorities between printers, and troubleshooting common printing problems.

After this lesson, you will be able to

- Access printers and assign permissions
- Manage printers and documents
- Use a Web browser to administer printers
- Set up a printer pool
- Set priorities between printers

Estimated lesson time: 90 minutes

Accessing Printers

You can gain access to printers for administration by using either the Printers window on the Start menu or the Find feature in the Active Directory Users And Computers snap-in. The Printers window allows you to perform all administrative tasks; however, you cannot perform some tasks from the Active Directory Users And Computers snap-in. For example, you cannot use the snap-in to take a printer offline. To take a printer offline, you must access the specific printer through the Printers window.

Microsoft Windows 2000 allows you to control printer usage and administration by assigning permissions through the Security tab of the printer Properties dialog box (Figure 8.8). By using printer permissions, you can control who can use a printer. You can also assign printer permissions to control who can administer a printer and the level of administration, which can include managing printers and managing documents.

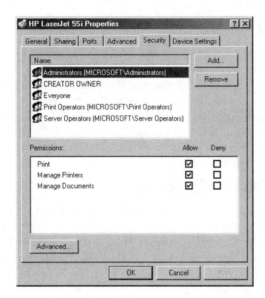

Figure 8.8 The default permissions assigned to a printer as seen in the HP LaserJet 5Si Properties dialog box with the Security tab active

For security reasons, you might need to limit user access to certain printers. You can also use printer permissions to delegate responsibilities for specific printers to users who are not administrators. Windows 2000 provides three levels of printer permissions: Print, Manage Documents, and Manage Printers, as shown in the Permissions box in Figure 8.8.

You can allow or deny printer permissions. As with group policy and NTFS permissions, denied permissions always override allowed permissions. For example, if you select the Everyone system group appearing in Figure 8.8 and then click the Deny check box next to Manage Documents, no one can manage documents, even if you granted this permission to another user account or group. This is because all user accounts are members of the Everyone system group.

By default, Windows 2000 assigns the Print permission for each printer to the Everyone system group, allowing all users to send documents to the printer. You can also assign printer permissions to users or groups. You can change the default printer permissions that Windows 2000 assigned, or those that you previously assigned, for any user or group.

Managing Printers

Managing printers includes assigning forms to paper trays and setting a separator page. In addition, you can pause, resume, and cancel all print jobs in a printer queue or a specific document if a problem occurs on a print device. If a print device is faulty or you add print devices to your network, you might need to redirect documents to a different printer. In addition, you might need to change who has ultimate administrative responsibility for printers, which involves changing ownership.

Assigning Forms to Paper Trays

If a print device has multiple trays that regularly hold different paper sizes, you can assign a form to a specific tray. A form defines a paper size. Users can then select the paper size from within their application. When the user prints a document, Windows 2000 automatically routes the print job to the paper tray that holds the correct form. Examples of forms include Legal, Letter, A4, and Executive.

To assign a form to a paper tray, select the printer in the Printers folder and then select Properties from the File menu. In the Properties dialog box for the printer, click the Device Settings tab as shown in Figure 8.9. From here, you can assign a form.

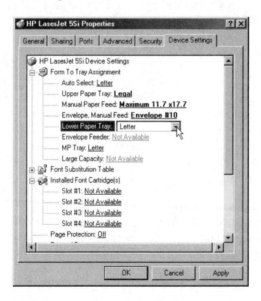

Figure 8.9 The Device Settings for an HP LaserJet 5Si

After you have set up a paper tray, users specify the paper size from within applications. Windows 2000 knows which paper tray the form is located in.

Note that Figure 8.9 shows some features grayed out. This is because the feature is not installed or not available on the printer. The features that appear under the Device Settings tab are determined by the device driver for the print device. For example, an HP LaserJet 5L personal laser printer has only two possible paper inputs: the automatic paper feed (called the Paper Input Bin) and the manual paper feed. Notice that in Figure 8.9, the device settings shows seven possible paper input locations and many other features not available in every print device.

Setting a Separator Page

A separator page is a file that contains print device commands. Separator pages have two functions:

- To identify and separate printed documents.

- To switch between print modes. Some print devices can switch between print modes that take advantage of different device features. You can use separator pages to specify the correct page description language. For example, you can specify PostScript or Printer Control Language (PCL) for a print device that can switch between different print modes but cannot automatically detect which language a print job uses.

Windows 2000 includes four separator page files. They are located in the %systemroot%\System32 folder. The following table lists the file name and describes the function for each of the included separator page files:

File name	Function
Pcl.sep	Switches the print mode to PCL for HP-series print devices and prints a page before each document
Pscript.sep	Switches the print mode to PostScript for HP-series print devices but does not print a page before each document
Sysprint.sep	Prints a page before each document. Compatible with PostScript print devices
Sysprtj.sep	A version of Sysprint.sep that uses Japanese characters

You can build your own custom separator pages by creating a .sep file that contains legal printer commands. Or you can customize the existing .sep files to meet your needs. Refer to the documentation with your printer for commands that are legal for your printer.

Once you have decided to use a separator page and have chosen an appropriate one, click the Advanced tab in the printer's Properties dialog box, then click the Separator Page button. From the Separator Page dialog box, you can type in the name of the separator page to use or browse for it. Once the separator page is configured, it will print at the beginning of each print job.

Pausing, Resuming, and Canceling Documents

Pausing and resuming a printer or canceling all documents on a printer might be necessary if there is a printing problem.

There are two places within the Printers window to pause, resume, or cancel all documents. First select the name of the print device, and then click the File menu. From there, you can either click Pause Printing or Cancel All Documents or click Open in the File menu and then select the appropriate command.

The following table describes the tasks you can perform when you manage printers, how to perform the tasks, and examples of situations in which you might perform these tasks:

Task	Action	Example
To pause printing	Click Pause Printing. A check mark, indicating that the printer is paused, appears next to the Pause Printing command.	Pause the printer if there is a problem with the printer or print device until you fix the problem.
To resume printing	Click Pause Printing again. The check mark next to the Pause Printing command disappears, which indicates the printer is active.	Resume printing after you fix a problem with a printer or print device.
To cancel all documents	Click Cancel All Documents. All documents are deleted from the printer.	Cancel all documents to clear a print queue after old documents that no longer need to print have accumulated.

Note You can also pause a printer by taking the printer offline. When you take a printer offline, documents stay in the print queue, even when the print server is shut down and then restarted. To take a printer offline, open the window for the specific printer, and on the Printer menu, click Use Printer Offline.

Redirecting Documents to a Different Printer

You can redirect documents to a different printer. For example, if a printer is connected to a faulty print device, redirect the documents so that users do not need to resubmit them. You can redirect all print jobs for a printer, but you cannot redirect specific documents. The new printer must use the same printer driver as the current printer.

You can redirect documents by opening the Properties dialog box for the specific printer. Select the Ports tab, and add a port.

If another print device is available for the current print server, you can continue to use the same printer and configure the printer to use the other print device. To configure a printer to use another local or network print device that uses the same printer driver, select the appropriate port on the print server and cancel the selection of the current port. Any currently printing documents cannot be redirected to another printer.

Taking Ownership of a Printer

By default, the user who installs the printer owns it. If that user can no longer administer the printer—for example, if the current owner leaves the company—another owner should take ownership to administer that printer.

The following users can take ownership of a printer:

- A user or a member of a group who has the Manage Printers permission for the printer.

- Members of the Administrators, Print Operators, Server Operators, and Power Users groups. By default, these groups have the Manage Printers permission, which allows them to take ownership.

Taking ownership of a printer is an advanced security feature that can be accessed from the Advanced button located under the Security tab of a printer's Properties dialog box. Ownership of a printer cannot be assigned by one user to another user. However, an administrator can assign ownership to the Administrators group.

Auditing can be used to track who successfully and unsuccessfully attempts to take ownership of a printer. Auditing, like taking ownership, is an advanced security feature that can be accessed from the Advanced button located under the Security tab of a printer's Properties dialog box.

Managing Documents

In addition to managing printers, Windows 2000 allows you to manage documents. Managing documents includes pausing, resuming, restarting, and canceling a document if there is a printing problem. In addition, you can set who should be notified when a print job is finished, the priority level (which allows a critical document to print before other documents), and a specific time for a document to print.

Pausing, Restarting, and Canceling a Document

If there is a printing problem with a specific document, you can pause and resume printing of the document. Additionally, you can restart or cancel a document. You must have the Manage Documents permission for the appropriate printer to perform these actions. Because the creator of a document has the default permissions to manage that document, users can perform any of these actions on their own documents.

To manage a document, open the window for the printer and select the document. Click the Document menu, and then click the appropriate command to pause, resume, restart, or cancel a document.

The following table describes the tasks you might perform when you manage individual documents, how to perform the tasks, and examples of situations in which you might perform these tasks.

Task	Action	Example
To pause printing a document	Select the document for which you want to pause printing, and then click Pause. (The status changes to Paused.)	Pause printing when there is a problem with the document.
To resume printing a document	Select the document for which you want to resume printing, and then click Resume. (The status changes to Printing.)	Resume printing after you fix a problem with a paused document.
To restart printing a document	Select the document for which you want to restart printing, and then click Restart. Restart causes printing to start from the beginning of the document.	Restart printing of a partially printed document after you fix a problem with the document or the print device.
To cancel printing a document	Select the document for which you want to cancel printing, and then click Cancel. You can also cancel a document by pressing the Delete key.	When a document has the wrong printer settings or is no longer needed, delete it before it prints.

Setting Notification, Priority, and Printing Time

You can control print jobs by setting the notification, priority, and printing time. To perform these document management tasks; you must have the Manage Documents permission for the appropriate printer.

You set the notification, priority, and printing time for a document on the General tab of the Properties dialog box for the document. To open the Properties dialog box for a document, open the printer in the Printers folder. Select the document, and then click Properties in the Document menu.

The following table describes the tasks you might perform when you control print jobs, how to perform the tasks, and examples of situations in which you might perform these tasks:

Task	Action	Example
Set a notification	In the Notify dialog box, type the logon name of the user who should receive the notification. By default, Windows 2000 enters the name of the user who printed the document.	Change the print notification when someone other than the user who printed the document needs to retrieve it.
Change a document priority	Move the Priority slider to the priority you want. The highest priority is 99, and the lowest is 1.	Change a priority so that a critical document prints before the other documents.
Schedule print times	To restrict print times, click Only From in the Schedule section, and then set the hours between which you want the document to print.	Set the print time for a large document so that it will print during off hours, such as late at night.

Administering Printers from a Web Browser

Windows 2000 enables you to manage printers from any computer running a Web browser, regardless of whether the computer is running Windows 2000 or has the correct printer driver installed. With any of the more common Internet browsers executing on any type of client platform, users can view Web pages that display the status of a Windows 2000 print server and its connected printers. All management tasks you perform with Windows 2000 management tools are the same when you use a Web browser. The difference in administering with a Web browser is the interface, which is a Web-based interface. For a Windows 2000 Server print server to support Web pages, the computer on which the printer resides must have Microsoft Internet Information Services (IIS) installed. For a Windows 2000 Professional print server to support Web pages, the computer must be configured with the Microsoft Peer Web Server (PWS).

When IIS is installed, a Printers virtual directory is created under the Default Web site as shown in Figure 8.10. This virtual directory points to the %systemroot%\web\printers folder.

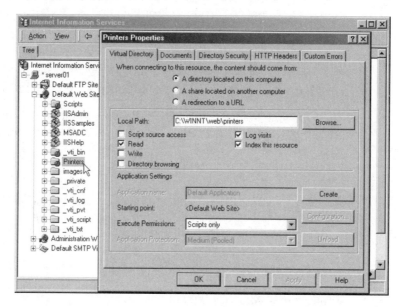

Figure 8.10 The Virtual Directoy tab of the Printers Properties dialog box

Using a Web Browser to Manage Printers

Using a Web browser to manage printers has several advantages:

- It allows you to administer printers from any computer running a Web browser, regardless of whether the computer is running Windows 2000 or has the correct printer driver installed.

- It allows you to customize the interface. For example, you can create your own Web page containing a floor plan with the locations of the printers and the links to the printers.

- It provides a summary page listing the status of all printers on a print server.

- It can report real-time print device data, such as whether the print device is in power saving mode, if the printer driver makes such information available. This information is not available from the Printers window.

Accessing Printers Using a Web Browser

If you want to gain access to all printers on a print server by using a
Web browser, open the Web browser and use the following address:
http://<print_server>/printers.

If you want to gain access to a specific printer without first viewing a list of
all printers, use *http://<print_server>/<share>*. Figure 8.11 shows the Web
page that appears when accessing the Printer1 share on Server01. Notice that
after typing *http://Server01/printer1*, the address appearing in the address
field is redirected via active server pages (ASP) to *http://server01/printers/
ipp_0004.asp?eprinter=Printer1&view=q&page=1139*.

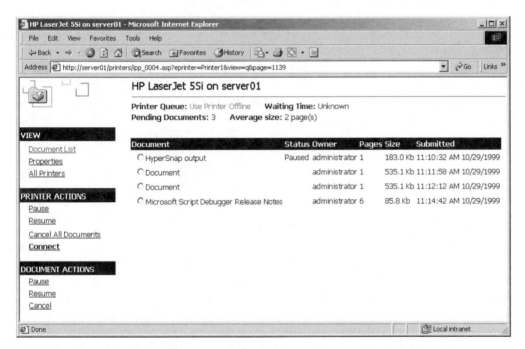

Figure 8.11 The document list Web page appearing for printer HP LaserJet 5Si on Server01

Setting Up a Printer Pool

A printer pool is one printer that is connected to multiple print devices through multiple ports on a print server. The print devices can be local or network print devices. Print devices should be identical; however, you can use print devices that are not identical but use the same printer driver. Figure 8.12 shows a printer pool to three print devices.

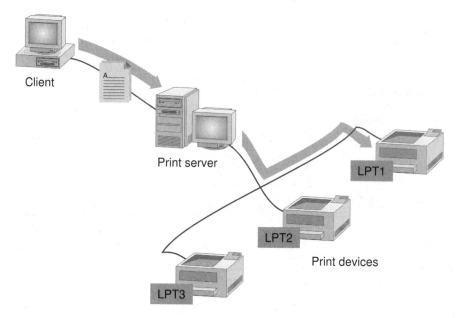

Figure 8.12 Printing to a printer pool containing three print devices

When you create a printer pool, users can print documents without having to find out which print device is available—the printer checks for an available port. Printer pooling is configured from the Ports tab of the printer's Properties dialog box. Once there, check the Enable Printer Pooling check box at the bottom of the page, then select or create the ports containing print devices that will be part of the pool.

Note When you set up a printer pool, place the print devices in the same physical area so that users can easily locate their documents. If you don't place the physical devices in the same area, the downside is that users won't know exactly where their print jobs have printed. The upside to this approach is that users will get additional exercise.

A printer pool has the following advantages:

- In a network with a high volume of printing, it decreases the time that documents wait on the print server.

- It simplifies administration because you can administer multiple print devices from a single printer.

Before you create a printer pool, make sure that you connect the print devices to the print server or to the network.

Setting Priorities Between Printers

Setting priorities between printers makes it possible to set priorities between groups of documents that all print to the same print device. Multiple printers pointing to the same print device allows users to send critical documents to a high priority printer and noncritical documents to a lower priority printer. The critical documents always print first.

To set priorities between printers, point two or more printers to the same print device—that is, the same port. The port can be either a physical port on the print server or a port that points to a network print device. Set a different priority for each printer that is connected to the print device, and then have different groups of users print to different printers, or have users send different types of documents to different printers.

Troubleshooting Common Printing Problems

When you detect a printing problem, always verify that the print device is plugged in, powered on, and connected to the print server. For a network print device, verify there is a network connection between the print device and the print server.

To determine the cause of a problem, first try printing from a different program to verify the problem is with the printer and not with the program. If the problem is with the printer, ask the following questions:

- Can other users print normally to this printer and print device?

- Does the print server use the correct printer driver for the print device?

- Is the print server operational and is there enough disk space for spooling?

- Does the client computer have the correct printer driver?

- Is the Print Spooler service and Remote Procedure Call (RPC) service running on the print server?

Print Server Properties

If you suspect there is a problem with the print server, you can access the properties of the print server from the Printers window. Once there, click the File menu and choose Server Properties. From the Print Server Properties dialog box, you can configure forms, port settings, installed printer drivers, and advanced properties such as the spool folder.

By default, the spool folder points to %systemroot%\System32\spool\PRINTERS. For a high-volume print server, consider moving the spool folder to a partition other than the boot partition. If the boot partition fills to capacity with print jobs, printing will stop and, more importantly, the operating system will become unstable.

Reviewing Common Printing Problems

Certain printing problems are common to most network printing environments. The following table describes some of these common printing problems, as well as some possible causes and solutions:

Problem	Possible cause	Solution
A user receives an Access Denied message when trying to configure a printer from an application (for example, earlier versions of Microsoft Excel).	The user does not have the appropriate permissions to change printer configurations.	Change the user's permissions, or configure the printer for the user.
The document does not print completely or comes out garbled.	The printer driver is incorrect.	Install the correct printer driver.
The hard disk starts thrashing on the print server, and the document does not reach the print device.	There is insufficient hard disk space for spooling.	Create more free space on the print server hard disk or change the spool folder location to a partition with free space.
Test page does not print. You have confirmed that the print device is connected and turned on.	The selected port is not correct.	Configure the printer for the correct port. For a printer that uses a network print device, make sure that the network address is correct.
Users report an error message that asks them to install a printer driver when they print to a print server running Windows 2000.	Printer drivers for the client computers are not not installed on the print server.	On the print server, add the appropriate printer drivers for the client computers. Use the client computer operating system CD-ROM or a printer driver from the vendor.

Problem	Possible cause	Solution
Documents from one client computer do not print, but documents from other client computers do.	The client computer is connected to the wrong printer.	On the client computer, remove the printer, and then add the correct printer.
Documents print correctly on some print devices in a printer pool but not on all of them.	The print devices in the printer pool are not identical.	Verify that all print devices in the printer pool are identical or that they use the same printer driver. Remove inappropriate devices.
Documents do not print in the right priority.	The printing priorities between the printers are set incorrectly.	Adjust the printing priorities for the printers associated with the print device.

Lesson Summary

You can gain access to printers for administration by using either the Printers window, the Active Directory Users And Computers snap-in, or a Web browser. Microsoft Windows 2000 allows you to control printer usage and administration by assigning permissions. Managing printers includes assigning forms to paper trays and setting a separator page. In addition, you can pause, resume, and cancel the documents in the print queue if a problem occurs on a print device. In addition to managing printers, Windows 2000 allows you to manage documents. Managing documents includes pausing, resuming, restarting, and canceling a document if there is a printing problem. Windows 2000 enables you to manage printers from any computer running a Web browser, regardless of whether the computer is running Windows 2000 or has the correct printer driver installed. Windows 2000 also allows you to set up a printer pool to connect multiple print devices. You can also set priorities between printers to prioritize groups of documents that print on the same print device. In addition to reviewing administration of network printing, this lesson also reviewed troubleshooting common printing problems, such as documents not printing or users being denied access to print devices.

Lesson 4: Printing and Active Directory Services

A directory service needs to make it easy for users to find printers. In Windows 2000, the print subsystem is tightly integrated with Active Directory services, making it possible to search across a domain for printers at different locations.

After this lesson, you will be able to

- Describe how printing is integrated in Active Directory services

Estimated lesson time: 20 minutes

Overview of Printing and Active Directory Services

Active Directory services is a distributed database shared by the domain controllers in a network. Information about printer queues, sites, names, and addresses is kept in the Active Directory store. This information must be sent by individual print servers, which is why it is important to keep the printer information contained in the Active Directory store up-to-date.

Pertinent characteristics of the relationship between print servers and Active Directory services include the following:

- Each print server is responsible for publishing its own printers in the Active Directory store.

- The print server does not have an affinity to any specific domain controller. It dynamically finds a domain controller in the appropriate domain.

- When a printer is updated on the print server, the changes are automatically propagated through Active Directory services to the Active Directory store.

- Printers are published in the Active Directory store as printQueue objects. The published printQueue object contains a subset of the information stored on the print server for a printer.

By default, printing is integrated with Active Directory services to work without administrative intervention. You need to make changes only if the default behavior is not acceptable. The default behavior includes the following:

- Any printer shared by a print server is published in Active Directory services. Administrative access to the host computer is still required to install and share a printer.

- The printQueue object is placed in the print server's computer object in the Active Directory store.

Note The printer does not appear below the Computer object in the Active Directory Users And Computers snap-in. Instead, using the Find command in the Active Directory Users And Computers snap-in, the result will display the printer associated with a server.

- When any change occurs in the printer's configuration, the Active Directory object is updated. All the configuration information is re-sent to the Active Directory store even if some of it has remained unchanged.

- If a print server disappears from the network, its printers are removed from Active Directory services.

Publishing Windows 2000 Printers

You can publish only printers that are shared. Printer publishing is controlled by the List In The Directory check box on the printer's Sharing tab (Figure 8.7).

The Add Printer wizard does not let you change this setting when you create a printer. Printers that are added by using the Add Printer wizard are published by default. If you do not want a printer published in the Active Directory service, clear the List In The Directory check box on the Sharing tab of the printer's Properties dialog box.

Note A print device connected to a universal serial bus (USB) port will likely be detected and as a consequence a printer will be installed for it automatically. In this case, you must manually share and publish the printer by using the Sharing tab.

The printer is placed in the print server's computer object in Active Directory services. Once it has been placed in Active Directory services, the object can be moved or renamed from the Find Printers dialog box. This dialog box can be accessed from the Active Directory Users And Computers snap-in. Once the snap-in is opened, click the Action menu and then choose Find. From the Find drop-down list box, choose printers and then click Find Now. Figure 8.13 shows how to access the move feature in the Find Printers dialog box.

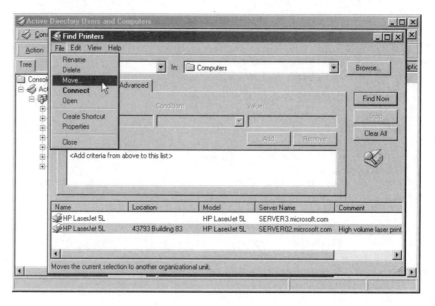

Figure 8.13 The Find Printers dialog box showing how to move a printer

Publishing Mechanism

The print server sends data asynchronously to Active Directory services. Initially it sends the data after a one-second delay. If this fails, the server retries after a longer period and continues until it reaches a delay of 2 hours. At this point, the server retries at this interval until it is successful. During this pending phase, the message "The Directory operation is still in progress" is displayed on the Sharing tab of the printer's Properties dialog box.

The printer is published to a random domain controller, so a query might not show the printer until it has been replicated to all the domain controllers. For local domain controllers on the same site, the maximum delay is approximately 30 minutes, but the typical delay is 5 to 10 minutes. For intersite searches, the delay depends on the replication strategy of your organization.

Pruning Orphans

When a printer is deleted from a print server, the corresponding Active Directory object is removed. A program called an orphan pruner accomplishes this by running on each domain controller to periodically check for orphaned printer objects. If a printer does not exist, the object is deleted. The orphan pruner looks only at print servers in the same site as the domain controller on which it is running.

The orphan pruner is controlled by several policy settings. By default, if the orphan pruner cannot see a printer three times in a row at 8-hour intervals, it assumes the entry is no longer valid and deletes it.

However, there can be circumstances where the printer is no longer available, such as when the print server is being rebuilt or is powered off, so the print objects are removed because the Active Directory store must reflect only the print devices currently available. Once the server comes back up, its printers need to be republished. To cover this situation, a print server verifies that its printers are published when it restarts and the spooler starts up. You can force a restart by issuing the net stop spooler and net start spooler commands. Alternatively, you can use the Check Published State group policy. The Check Published State group policy is found in the Group Policy snap-in in the Printers folder under the Computer Configuration node.

Supporting Windows NT Printers

Printers that are on print servers running Windows NT 4.0 or Windows NT 3.51 can be published in Active Directory services by using the Active Directory Users And Computers snap-in. Once in the snap-in, a printer object is created in an organizational unit (OU), container, or domain node in much the same way that a user or group object is created. Alternately, you can use the Pubprn.vbs script, which is provided in the System32 folder. Pubprn.vbs is a Windows Script Host (WSH) file and requires two parameters. The print server computer name or UNC name (\\<*computername*>\<*sharename*>) is the first parameter. The second parameter is the ADSI path to which you want the information published in the directory. You can publish all printers on a server or specify single printers to be published. For example, to publish a single shared printer \\Server03\5L running on a Windows NT Server to the Sales OU in the microsoft.com domain using Pubprn.vbs, open a command prompt and type:

```
cscript %systemroot%\system32\pubprn.vbs \\server03\5L
"LDAP://OU=Sales,DC=microsoft,DC=com"
```

Note You cannot use this command to publish printers running a Windows 2000 print server.

Group Policy Settings

Active Directory services includes a set of group policies that apply to Windows 2000 printing. The policies are located in the Computer Configuration node of the Group Policy snap-in, under Administration Templates. For a description of each of these policies, open the Properties dialog box for a specific property and select the Explain tab.

Printer Location Tracking

Printer location tracking in Windows 2000 allows users to search for and find printers at their location or another specified location, according to attributes assigned to printers. Location tracking lets you design a location scheme and assign computers and printers to locations in your scheme. Location tracking overrides the standard method of locating and associating users and printers, which uses the IP address and subnet mask of a computer to estimate its physical location and proximity to other computers. The group policy Pre-Populate Printer Search Location Text is used to enable printer location tracking for a group of computers. For more information about printer location tracking and procedures for setting it up, see Windows 2000 Server Help.

Lesson Summary

In Windows 2000, the print subsystem is tightly integrated with Active Directory services, making it possible to search across a domain for printers at different locations. By default, the printing is integrated with Active Directory services so that it can work without administrative intervention. Any printer shared by a print server is published in Active Directory services. The printQueue object is placed in the print server's computer object in Active Directory services. When any change occurs in the printer's configuration, the Active Directory object is updated. If a print server disappears from the network, its printers are removed from the Active Directory store. You can publish only printers that are shared. Printer publishing is controlled by the List In The Directory check box on the Sharing tab of the printer's Properties dialog box. In addition, printers that are on print servers running Windows NT 3.51 or Windows NT 4.0 can be published in the Active Directory store by using the Active Directory Users aAnd Computers snap-in or the Pubprn.vbs WSH file. Active Directory services also includes a set of group policies that apply to Windows 2000 printing.

Lesson 5: Connecting to Network Printers

After you have set up the print server with all required printer drivers for the shared printers, users on client computers running Windows 95, Windows 98, Windows NT, and Windows 2000 can easily make a connection and start printing. For most Windows-based client computers, the client computer automatically downloads the printer when the user makes a connection to the printer, as long as the appropriate printer drivers are on the print server.

Other client computers able to access a share or print to an IP address can use printers configured for sharing on a Windows 2000 Server print server. The connect-to-printer capability is available only in Windows 95, Windows 98, Windows NT, and Windows 2000 computers.

After this lesson, you will be able to

- Make a connection to a network printer by using the Add Printer wizard or a Web browser

- Describe how printer drivers are downloaded

Estimated lesson time: 15 minutes

Using the Add Printer Wizard

When you add and share a printer, by default, all users can make a connection to that printer and print documents. The method used to make a connection to a printer depends on the client computer. Client computers running Windows 95, Windows 98, Windows NT, or Windows 2000 can use the Add Printer wizard, although the Add Printer wizard in Windows 2000 provides more features than in the earlier versions. This is the same wizard you use to add and share a printer. The options available in the Add Printer wizard that allow you to locate and connect to a printer vary depending on the operating system the client computer is running.

Client computers running Windows 2000 can also use a Web browser to make a connection to the printer.

Client Computers Running Windows 2000

By using the Add Printer wizard on client computers running Windows 2000, you can make a connection to a printer with any of the following methods:

- **Searching Active Directory services** You can find the printer by using Active Directory services search capabilities. You can search either the entire Active Directory store or just a portion of it. You can also narrow the search by providing features of the printer, such as color printing. An easy way to search is by clicking Start, pointing to Search, and then clicking the For Printers option.

- **Using the universal naming convention (UNC) name** You can use the UNC name (\\<*print_server*>\<*share*>) to make connections, which can be a quick method to use.

- **Browsing the network for the printer** You can browse for a printer by clicking Browse.

Client Computers Running Windows 95, Windows 98, or Windows NT

On client computers running Windows 95, Windows 98, or Windows NT, the Add Printer wizard allows you to enter a UNC name or to browse Network Neighborhood to locate the printer.

Note You can also make a connection to a printer by using the Run command on the Start menu. Type the UNC name of the printer in the Open text box, and click OK.

Client Computers Running Other Microsoft Operating Systems

Users at client computers running Windows 3.*x* and Windows for Workgroups use Print Manager instead of the Add Printer wizard to make a connection to a printer.

Users at any Windows-based client computer can make a connection to a network printer by using the following command:

```
net use lpt<x>: \\<print_server>\<share>
```

Note that *x* is the number of the printer port.

The net use command is the only method available for making a connection to a network printer from client computers running MS-DOS or OS/2 with Microsoft LAN Manager client software installed.

Automatic printer driver download upon connection is not available for these operating systems. Use the local computer operating system's driver installation procedure to install a printer driver for these clients.

Using a Web Browser

If you are using a computer running Windows 2000, you can make a connection to a printer through your corporate intranet. You can type a Uniform Resource Locator (URL) in your Web browser, and you do not have to use the Add Printer wizard. In the address field of the Web browser, type the *http://<print_server>/<share>* URL of the printer and then click the Connect link on the page that appears. Figure 8.14 shows the Web page that is displayed at the conclusion of the printer connection.

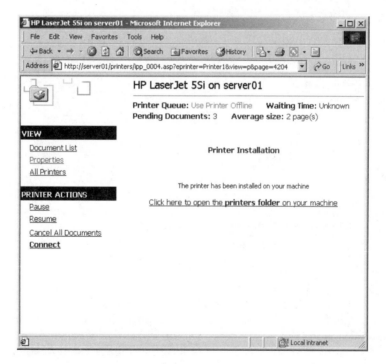

Figure 8.14 Connecting and installing a printer through a Web browser

After you make a connection, Windows 2000 automatically copies the correct printer drivers to the client computer.

There are two URLs you can use to make a connection to a printer by using a Web browser:

- *http://<print_server>/printers* The Web page lists all the shared printers on the print server that you have permission to use. The page includes information about the printers, including the printer name, status of print jobs, location, model, and any comments entered when the printers were installed. This information helps you select the correct printer for your needs. You must have permission to use the printer.

- *http://<print_server>/<share>* You provide the intranet path for a specific printer. You must have permission to use the printer.

You can customize the Web page that is used for printer connections. For example, you might want to display a floor plan that shows the location of print devices to which users can connect.

For a Windows 2000 print server to accept print requests containing URLs, it must be configured in one of the following ways:

- Windows 2000 Server software with Microsoft IIS installed

- Windows 2000 Professional with Microsoft PWS installed

Downloading Printer Drivers

When users at client computers running Windows 95, Windows 98, Windows NT, or Windows 2000 make the first connection to a printer on the print server, the client computer automatically downloads the printer driver. The print server must have a copy of the printer driver installed. Additional printer drivers are installed from the Additional Drivers button under the Sharing tab of the printer's Properties dialog box.

Printer drivers are platform specific. Therefore, if you will be providing connect and download printer driver support for multiple Windows NT platforms, make sure to install the platform-specific driver. For example, to support both Alpha-based and x86-based Windows NT client computers, install both drivers on the print server. The Windows 2000 printer drivers are not compatible with Windows NT printer drivers. Therefore, if you are running an x86-based Windows 2000 print server and plan to support x86-based Windows NT clients, make sure to install the x86-based Windows NT printer drivers. In the Additional Drivers window, the x86-based printer drivers list Intel under the Environment column. However, these drivers work for non-Intel x86-based platforms as well.

Client computers running Windows 2000 and Windows NT verify that they have the current printer driver each time they print. If they do not have the current printer driver, they download it. For these client computers, you only need to update printer drivers on the print server. Client computers running Windows 95 or Windows 98 do not check for updated printer drivers. You must manually install updated printer drivers on these clients.

Lesson Summary

Clients running Windows 95, Windows 98, Windows NT, and Windows 2000 can use the Add Printer wizard to connect to a printer. Windows 95, Windows 98, and Windows NT computers can use UNC names or browse Network Neighborhood. Computers running Windows 3.*x* and Windows for Workgroups use Print Manager to connect to a printer. Any Windows or MS-DOS computer can use the net use command to connect to a printer. Windows 2000 computers can search Active Directory services, use a UNC name, and browse the network for the printer. Windows 2000 computers can also make a connection through a Web browser. When users at client computers running Windows 95,Windows 98, Windows NT, or Windows 2000 make the first connection to a printer on the print server, the client computer automatically downloads the printer driver from the print server.

Review

The following questions are intended to reinforce key information presented in this chapter. If you are unable to answer a question, review the appropriate lesson and then try the question again. Answers to the questions can be found in Appendix A, "Questions and Answers."

1. Explain the difference between a print device and a printer.

2. You are told by a colleague never to remove the Everyone system group from the permissions of a printer or no one will be able to manage the printer or its documents. Why is this statement incorrect? How could you configure this undesirable behavior?

3. You have configured two Windows 2000 print servers on your network. When a user connects to one from Windows 95, printing is automatic. When the same user connects to the same print server for a different printer, she gets prompted to install a driver. Why is this happening?

4. In an environment where many users print to the same print device, how can you help reduce the likelihood of users picking up the wrong documents?

5. Can you redirect a single document?

6. A user needs to print a very large document. How can the user print the job after hours without being present while the document prints?

C H A P T E R   9

Network Protocols and Services

About This Chapter

This chapter introduces the network protocols supported by Microsoft Windows 2000, including the Transmission Control Protocol/Internet Protocol (TCP/IP) suite, NWLink, AppleTalk, and others. This chapter also discusses how to implement TCP/IP and network services such as the Dynamic Host Configuration Protocol (DHCP) Service, the Windows Internet Naming Service (WINS), and the Domain Name System (DNS).

Before You Begin

To complete the lessons in this chapter, you must have

- A computer that has Windows 2000 Server installed and operating.
- Completed the exercises in the previous chapters.

Lesson 1: Network Protocols

Protocols are specifications for standardized packets of data that make it possible for networks to share information. The packets of information are moved up and down the protocol stack and across the transmission media. Windows 2000 supports many different protocols. This lesson introduces you to the primary network protocols supported by Windows 2000.

After this lesson, you will be able to

- Describe the primary network protocols supported by Windows 2000

Estimated lesson time: 15 minutes

Introduction to Network Protocols

A *protocol* is a set of rules and conventions for sending information over a network. Among the protocols supported by Windows 2000 is TCP/IP, which Windows 2000 relies on for logon, file and print services, replication of information between domain controllers, and other common functions. In addition to TCP/IP, the primary network protocols that Windows 2000 supports include the following:

- Asynchronous Transfer Mode (ATM)
- Internetwork Packet Exchange/Sequenced Packet Exchange (IPX/SPX)
- NetBIOS Enhanced User Interface (NetBEUI)
- AppleTalk
- Data Link Control (DLC)
- Infrared Data Association (IrDA)

Note Systems Network Architecture (SNA) protocols are not included in Windows 2000. SNA protocols are available through Microsoft SNA Server. SNA Server is a separate product that supports interoperability with IBM midrange and mainframe computers.

Protocol Binding Order

Protocols can be added or deleted at will and selectively bound to all network interfaces that are present in the server. Protocol binding order is determined by the order in which the protocols were initially installed, although it can be changed at any time on a per-interface basis, allowing a greater degree of control. For example, the first interface could have TCP/IP and IPX/SPX both bound with TCP/IP having precedence, whereas the second interface could still have both protocols bound while the IPX/SPX protocol has precedence. Additionally, network services can be selectively enabled or disabled on a per-adapter or per-protocol basis or any combination thereof. This selectivity gives system administrators extremely fine control over networking configuration and allows extremely secure configurations (such as disabling all network services on public interfaces connected directly to the Internet) to be constructed with minimal difficulty.

TCP/IP

The TCP/IP suite of protocols has been adopted by Microsoft as the strategic enterprise transport protocol for Windows 2000. The Windows 2000 TCP/IP suite is designed to make it easy to integrate Microsoft enterprise networks into large-scale corporate, government, and public networks, and to provide the ability to operate over those networks in a secure manner. TCP/IP is discussed in greater detail in Lesson 2.

ATM

The Asynchronous Transfer Mode (ATM) protocol is an advanced implementation of packet switching that is ideal for voice, video, and data communications. ATM is a high-speed networking technology that transmits data in cells of a fixed length. It is composed of a number of related technologies including software, hardware, and connection-oriented media. A cell is a fixed-length packet containing 53 bytes of information, as shown in Figure 9.1.

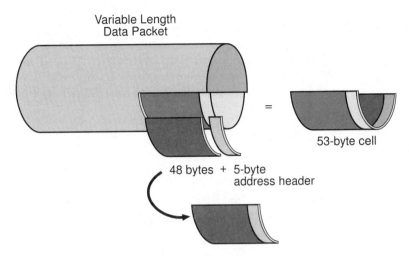

Figure 9.1 A 1000-byte data packet broken down into 53-byte cells

Since the number of bytes—and consequently the transit time—of a cell is constant, cells can be switched at a constant interval.

An ATM endpoint establishes a connection or virtual circuit before sending any data on the network. It then sends cells along this path toward the destination. This virtual circuit is a direct path from one endpoint to another. While establishing the connection, the ATM endpoint also negotiates a Quality of Service (QoS) contract for the transmission. This contract spells out the bandwidth, maximum delay, acceptable variance, and other parameters the virtual circuit (VC) provides, and it extends from one endpoint to the other. Since the virtual circuit is connection oriented, data arrives at the receiving end in proper order and with the specified service levels. ATM is an excellent compromise for the transmission of both voice and data on a network. ATM provides a guaranteed QoS on a local area network (LAN), a wide area network (WAN), and a public internetwork.

The Windows 2000 architecture uses the following components to support ATM: LAN Emulation, IP over ATM, ATM over xDSL, and native ATM access through Microsoft Windows Sockets (Winsock) 2.0.

LAN Emulation

LAN Emulation (LANE) is a method by which protocols that understand only connectionless media can communicate over ATM. It allows ATM to utilize both legacy networks and applications. Traditional LAN-aware applications and protocols can communicate over an ATM network without modification.

LANE consists of two primary components: the LANE client (Atmlane.sys) and the LANE services. The LANE client is located in the %systemroot%\system32\drivers folder. It allows LAN protocols and LAN-aware applications to function as if they were communicating with a traditional LAN. The LANE client communicates LAN commands to the network protocols and native ATM commands to the ATM protocol layer. The LANE services are a group of ATM components, usually located on a switch that supports LAN emulation.

IP over ATM

IP over ATM is a group of services that is used for communicating over an ATM network and which can be used as an alternative to LAN emulation. IP over ATM uses the connection-oriented properties of ATM to overcome the connectionless nature of IP. It functions in a manner similar to LANE. A central IP server (called an ATMARP server) maintains a database of IP and ATM addresses, and provides configuration and broadcast services. These broadcast services are necessary because ATM is a nonbroadcast protocol. IP over ATM services do not reside in one place and are not usually on an ATM switch. All the IP over ATM services are provided with Windows 2000.

In effect, IP over ATM is a small layer between the ATM protocol and the TCP/IP protocols. The client emulates standard IP to the TCP/IP protocol at its top edge and uses native ATM commands to the ATM protocol layers underneath.

IP over ATM is handled by two primary components: the Address Resolution Protocol (ARP) server (Atmarps.sys) and the ARP client (Atmarpc.sys). The ARP server is composed of an ATMARP server and Multicast Address Resolution Service (MARS). The ATMARP server provides services that emulate standard IP functions, while MARS provides broadcast and multicast services. Both services maintain IP address databases.

ATM over xDSL

Digital Subscriber Line (xDSL) technology is a means by which plain old telephone service (POTS) can be used to send digital data over a pair of copper wires to the central station of a telephone company. To connect many

DSL users to an ATM backbone network, the DSL data is sent to a Digital Subscriber Line Access Multiplexer (DSLAM). The far side of the DSLAM connects to an ATM network that provides gigabit data rates. At the other end of each transmission, a DSLAM demultiplexes the signals and forwards them to appropriate individual DSL connections.

ATM over xDSL offers high-speed network access from the home and small office environment. Many types of DSL, including asymmetric digital subscriber line (ADSL) and very high digital subscriber line (VDSL), are being developed in these areas. These technologies use the *local loop,* the copper wires for ADSL or fiber optic cable for VDSL, that connect the local central office in a user's neighborhood to the user's data jack. In many areas, this local loop connects directly to an ATM core network run by a telephone company.

ATM over xDSL service preserves the high-speed characteristics and QoS guarantees available in the core ATM network without changing protocols. This creates the potential for an end-to-end ATM network to the residence or small office.

ATM Access through Winsock 2.0 and Native ATM Access

ATM support for Winsock 2.0 is available through the Windows Sockets ATM Service Provider. As a result, applications that use TCP as their transport protocol can use Winsock 2.0 directly to gain access to ATM-based networks.

Applications that use native ATM can create virtual circuits and access QoS guarantees. This capability is supplied by a connection-oriented service added to version 5.0 of the Network Driver Interface Service (NDIS). The connection-oriented service in NDIS 5.0 is called *CoNDIS.*

NWLink

NWLink is Microsoft's implementation of the Novell NetWare IPX/SPX protocol. NWLink is most commonly used in environments where clients running Microsoft operating systems are used to access resources on NetWare servers, or where clients running NetWare are used to access resources on computers running Microsoft operating systems. NWLink does not allow a computer running Windows 2000 to directly access files or printers shared on a NetWare server, or to act as a file or print server to a NetWare client. To access files or printers on a NetWare server, the Client Service for NetWare (CSNW) in Windows 2000 Professional or the Gateway Service for NetWare (GSNW) in Windows 2000 Server must be used.

GSNW acts as a redirector for a computer running Windows 2000 Server where it is installed and as a gateway for other client computers. The gateway function allows a computer running Windows 2000 Server to share NetWare resources (folders and printers) as if they are located on the Windows 2000 server. As a result, client computers that are able to access shares on the Windows 2000 Server computer can use the shares made available through GSNW. GSNW is a low-performance access solution; it allows a single user connection provides gateway access to resources on the NetWare server.

NWLink is useful if there are NetWare client/server applications running that use Winsock or NetBIOS over IPX/SPX protocols. In addition, NetWare NetBIOS Link (NWNBLink) contains Microsoft enhancements to NetBIOS. The NWNBLink component is used to format NetBIOS-level requests and pass them to the NWLink component for transmission on the network.

Setting the Frame Type

The frame type defines the way in which the network adapter, in a computer running Windows 2000, formats data to be sent over a network. To communicate between a computer running Windows 2000 and NetWare servers, you need to configure NWLink on the computer running Windows 2000 with the same frame type as that used by the NetWare servers.

The following table lists the topologies and frame types supported by NWLink.

Topology	Supported frame type
Ethernet	Ethernet II, 802.3, 802.2, and Sub Network Access Protocol (SNAP), which defaults to 802.2
Token ring	802.5 and SNAP
Fiber Distributed Data Interface (FDDI)	802.2 and 802.3

On Ethernet networks, the standard frame type for NetWare 2.2 and NetWare 3.11 is 802.3. Starting with NetWare 3.12, the default frame type was changed to 802.2.

You can choose to automatically detect or manually configure the frame type. However, the frame type is automatically detected when NWLink is loaded. If multiple frame types are detected in addition to the 802.2 frame type, NWLink defaults to the 802.2 frame type.

If the frame type is manually configured, a computer running Windows 2000 can use multiple frame types simultaneously.

You can configure the frame type by using the NWLink IPX/SPX/NetBIOS-Compatible Transport Protocol Properties dialog box. For more information, see Windows 2000 Help.

NetBEUI

NetBEUI was originally developed as a protocol for small departmental LANs of 20 to 200 computers. NetBEUI is not routable because it doesn't have a network layer. Because of this limitation, you must connect computers running Windows 2000 and NetBEUI by using bridges instead of routers. In addition, NetBEUI is broadcast-based, which means it relies on broadcasts for many of its functions, such as name registration and discovery, and so it creates more broadcast traffic than other protocols. NetBEUI is included with Windows 2000 Server and Windows 2000 Professional primarily as a legacy protocol to support workstations that have not been upgraded to Windows 2000.

NetBEUI provides compatibility with existing LANs that use the NetBEUI protocol. NetBEUI provides computers running Windows 2000 with the following capabilities:

- Connection-oriented and connectionless communication between computers

- Self-configuration and self-tuning

- Error protection

- Small memory overhead

Note A Windows 2000 network running Active Directory services cannot use NWLink or NetBEUI as the primary protocol. Only TCP/IP is supported for access to Active Directory services.

AppleTalk

AppleTalk is a protocol suite developed by Apple Computer Corporation for communication between Macintosh computers. Windows 2000 includes support for AppleTalk, which allows computers running Windows 2000 Server and Apple Macintosh clients to share files and printers. AppleTalk also allows Windows 2000 to be a router and a dial-up server.

For the AppleTalk protocol to function properly, a Windows 2000 Server computer must be configured with Windows 2000 Services for Macintosh and must be available on the network.

DLC

The DLC protocol was developed for IBM mainframe communications. It was not designed to be a primary protocol for network use between personal computers. However, DLC is used to print to Hewlett-Packard printers that are connected directly to networks. Network-attached printers use the DLC protocol because the received frames are easy to disassemble and because DLC functionality can easily be coded into read-only memory (ROM). The usefulness of DLC is limited because it doesn't directly interface with the Transport Driver Interface layer. DLC should be installed only on network machines that perform tasks such as sending data to a network Hewlett-Packard printer. Clients sending print jobs to a network print device through a Windows 2000 print server do not need the DLC protocol installed.

Only the print server communicating directly with the print device requires the DLC protocol to be installed. Once the DLC protocol is installed on a computer running Windows 2000 Server, a new printer port type will be available. Figure 9.2 shows the new port type appearing in the Printer Ports dialog box. This dialog box is accessed from the Ports tab in the Properties dialog box of a printer.

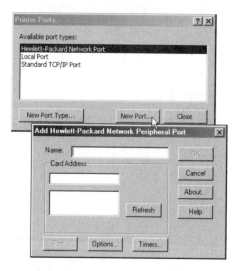

Figure 9.2 The dialog box used to configure a new DLC-based Hewlett-Packard network printer

The network adapter card MAC (Media Access Control) address of DLC-enabled printers or print servers appears in the larger box below Card Address in Figure 9.2. Make sure that the DLC-enabled network print device is connected to the network, turned on, and configured for DLC operation.

After you have configured a Windows 2000 Server computer to perform the role of print server for the DLC-enabled network print device, client computers can connect to the printer share on the Windows 2000 Server. If print jobs are appearing on the DLC-enabled print device that were not sent through the Windows 2000 Server print server, client computers might be running the DLC protocol and printing directly to the DLC-enabled network print device. Use Network Monitor or another network analyzer to determine which computers on the network are running the DLC protocol.

Note All Hewlett-Packard JetDirect cards currently support the TCP/IP suite and should be added by using the standard TCP/IP port. Only older Hewlett-Packard JetDirect cards that do not support TCP/IP require the Hewlett-Packard network port that uses the DLC protocol.

IrDA

IrDA is a group of short-range, high-speed, bidirectional wireless infrared protocols. IrDA allows a variety of devices to communicate with each other, such as cameras, printers, portable computers, desktop computers, and personal digital assistants (PDAs). The IrDA protocol stack is accessed by using NDIS connectionless drivers.

Lesson Summary

A protocol is a set of rules and conventions for sending information over a network. Windows 2000 supports a number of protocols, including TCP/IP. The TCP/IP suite of protocols has been adopted by Microsoft as the strategic enterprise transport protocol for Windows 2000. TCP/IP can be transported over a number of networks based on media access technologies such as Ethernet, Token Ring, and ATM. Media access is only part of what ATM provides. ATM is a group of technologies (hardware and software) that together provide for connection-oriented communication that is ideal for voice, video, and data communications. NWLink is a Microsoft-compatible IPX/SPX protocol for Windows 2000. NetBEUI is also included with Windows 2000 Server and Windows 2000 Professional, although it is primarily a legacy protocol used to support workstations that have not been upgraded to Windows 2000. In addition, Windows 2000 includes support for AppleTalk, which allows Windows 2000 to be a router and a dial-up server. DLC was developed for IBM mainframe communications; however, older models of Hewlett-Packard printers connected directly to networks use DLC. IrDA is a group of short-range, high-speed, bidirectional wireless infrared protocols.

Lesson 2: Transmission Control Protocol/ Internet Protocol

TCP/IP provides communication across networks that contain computers with various hardware architectures and operating systems. Microsoft's implementation of TCP/IP enables enterprise networking and connectivity on computers running Windows 2000.

After this lesson, you will be able to

- Describe the TCP/IP protocol suite and the TCP/IP utilities that ship with Windows 2000
- Configure TCP/IP

Estimated lesson time: 60 minutes

Overview of the TCP/IP Suite

TCP/IP is an industry-standard suite of protocols that enables enterprise networking and connectivity on Windows 2000–based computers. Adding TCP/IP to a Windows 2000 configuration offers the following advantages:

- A routable networking protocol supported by most operating systems. Most large networks rely on TCP/IP.

- A technology for connecting dissimilar systems. You can use many standard connectivity utilities to access and transfer data between dissimilar systems. Windows 2000 includes several of these standard utilities.

- A robust, scalable, cross-platform client/server framework. TCP/IP supports the Winsock interface, which is ideal for developing client/ server applications for Winsock-compliant stacks.

- A method of gaining access to Internet resources.

The TCP/IP suite of protocols provides a set of standards for how computers communicate and how networks are interconnected. The TCP/IP suite of protocols maps to a four-layer conceptual model: network interface, Internet, transport, and application (Figure 9.3).

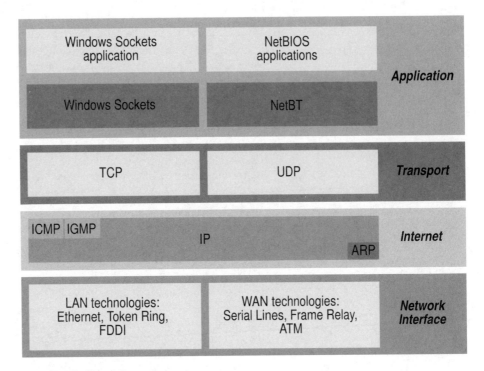

Network Interface Layer

At the base of the model is the network interface layer. This layer puts frames on the wire and pulls frames off the wire.

Internet Layer

Internet-layer protocols encapsulate packets in Internet datagrams and run all the necessary routing algorithms. The four Internet layer protocols are Internet Protocol (IP), Address Resolution Protocol (ARP), Internet Control Message Protocol (ICMP), and Internet Group Management Protocol (IGMP). The following table describes these four protocols.

Protocol	Description
IP	Provides connectionless packet delivery for all other protocols in the suite. Does not guarantee packet arrival or correct packet sequence.
ARP	Provides IP address mapping to the MAC sublayer address to acquire the physical MAC control address of the destination. IP broadcasts a special ARP inquiry packet containing the IP address of the destination system. The system that owns the IP address replies by sending its physical address to the requester. The MAC sublayer communicates directly with the network adapter card and is responsible for delivering error-free data between two computers on a network.
ICMP	Provides special communication between hosts, allowing them to share status and error information. Higher-level protocols use this information to recover from transmission problems. Network administrators use this information to detect network trouble. The ping utility uses ICMP packets to determine whether a particular IP device on a network is functional.
IGMP	Provides multicasting, which is a limited form of broadcasting, to communicate and manage information between all member devices in a multicast group. IGMP informs neighboring multicast routers of the host group memberships present on a particular network. Windows 2000 supports multicast capabilities, such as Windows 2000 Server NetShow Services, that allow developers to create multicast programs.

Transport Layer

Transport layer protocols provide communication sessions between computers. The desired method of data delivery determines the transport protocol. The two transport layer protocols are Transmission Control Protocol (TCP) and User Datagram Protocol (UDP). The following table describes these two protocols.

Protocol	Description
TCP	Provides connection-oriented, reliable communications for applications that typically transfer large amounts of data at one time or that require an acknowledgment for data received. TCP guarantees the delivery of packets, ensures proper sequencing of data, and provides a checksum feature that validates both the packet header and its data for accuracy.
UDP	Provides connectionless communications and does not guarantee that packets will be delivered. Applications that use UDP typically transfer small amounts of data at one time. Reliable delivery is the responsibility of the application.

Application Layer

At the top of the model is the application layer, in which applications gain access to the network. There are many standard TCP/IP utilities and services in the application layer, such as FTP, Telnet, Simple Network Management Protocol (SNMP), DNS, and so on.

TCP/IP provides two interfaces for network applications to use the services of the TCP/IP protocol stack: Winsock and the NetBIOS over TCP/IP (NetBT) interface. The following table describes these two interfaces.

Interface	Description
Winsock	Serves as the standard interface between socket-based applications and TCP/IP protocols.
NetBT	Serves as the standard interface for NetBIOS services, including name, datagram, and session services. It also provides a standard interface between NetBIOS-based applications and TCP/IP protocols.

Note For more information about TCP/IP and TCP/IP implementation, see the Supplemental Course Materials CD-ROM (\chapt09\articles\tcpip2000.doc) that accompanies this book.

Configuring TCP/IP to Use a Static IP Address

By default, client computers running Microsoft Windows 2000, Windows NT, Windows 95, or Windows 98 obtain TCP/IP configuration information automatically from the Dynamic Host Configuration Protocol (DHCP) Service. However, even in a DHCP-enabled environment, you should assign a static IP address to selected network computers. For example, a computer running the DHCP Service cannot be a DHCP client, so it must have a static IP address. If the DHCP Service is not available, you must also configure TCP/IP to use a static IP address.

Note In a small private network where a DHCP server is not available, you can use the Windows 2000 Server feature called Automatic Private IP Addressing (APIPA) to automatically assign IP addresses for you. This feature is described later in this lesson.

For each network adapter card that uses TCP/IP in a computer, you can configure an IP address, subnet mask, and default gateway, as shown in Figure 9.4.

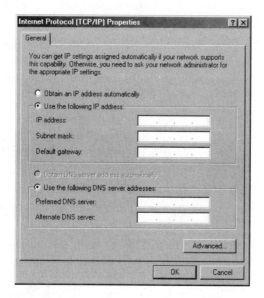

Figure 9.4 Configuring a static TCP/IP address in the Internet Protocol (TCP/IP) Properties dialog box

The following table describes the options used in configuring a static TCP/IP address.

Option	Description
IP Address	A logical 32-bit address that identifies a TCP/IP host. Each network adapter card in a computer running TCP/IP requires a unique IP address, such as 192.168.0.108. Each address has two parts: a network ID, which identifies all hosts on the same physical network, and a host ID, which identifies a host on the network. In this example, the network ID is 192.168.0, and the host ID is 108.
Subnet Mask	A network in a multiple-network environment that uses IP addresses derived from a single network ID. Subnets divide a large network into multiple physical networks connected with routers. A subnet mask blocks out part of the IP address so that TCP/IP can distinguish the network ID from the host ID. When TCP/IP hosts try to communicate, the subnet mask determines whether the destination host is on a local or remote network. To communicate within a local network, computers must have the same subnet mask.

Option	Description
Default Gateway	The intermediate device on a local network that stores network IDs of other networks in the enterprise or on the Internet. To communicate with a host on another network, configure an IP address for the default gateway. TCP/IP sends packets for remote networks to the default gateway (if no other route is configured), which forwards the packets to other gateways until the packet is delivered to a gateway connected to the specified destination.

You can open the Internet Protocol (TCP/IP) Properties dialog box by first opening the Properties dialog box for My Network Places, opening the Properties dialog box for the appropriate network adapter card, and then opening the Internet Protocol (TCP/IP) Properties dialog box for the Internet Protocol (TCP/IP) component.

Caution IP communications can fail if duplicate IP addresses exist on a network. Therefore, you should always check with the network administrator to obtain a valid static IP address.

Configuring TCP/IP to Obtain an IP Address Automatically

If a server running the DHCP Service is available on the network, it can automatically assign TCP/IP configuration information to the DHCP client. You can then configure any clients running MS-DOS, Windows 3.*x*, Windows for Workgroups, Windows 95, Windows 98, Windows NT, or Windows 2000 to obtain TCP/IP configuration information automatically from the DHCP Service. Using DHCP to configure TCP/IP automatically on client computers can simplify administration and ensure correct configuration information. To use the DHCP Service to provide clients with TCP/IP configuration information automatically, however, you must first configure a computer as a DHCP client.

To configure a DHCP client, open the Internet Protocol (TCP/IP) Properties dialog box and click Obtain An IP Address Automatically. (DHCP is described in more detail in Lesson 3, "Dynamic Host Configuration Protocol Service.")

Using Automatic Private IP Addressing

The Windows 2000 implementation of TCP/IP supports a new mechanism for automatic address assignment of IP addresses for simple LAN-based network configurations. This addressing mechanism is an extension of dynamic IP address assignment for LAN adapters, enabling configuration of IP addresses without using static IP address assignment or installing the DHCP Service.

For the Automatic Private IP Addressing (APIPA) feature to function properly on a computer running Windows 2000, you must configure a network LAN adapter for TCP/IP and click Obtain An IP Address Automatically in the Internet Protocol (TCP/IP) Properties dialog box.

The following steps outline how APIPA assigns an IP address:

1. Windows 2000 TCP/IP attempts to find a DHCP server on the attached network to obtain a dynamically assigned IP address.

2. In the absence of a DHCP server during startup (for example, if the server is down for maintenance or repairs), the client cannot obtain an IP address.

3. APIPA generates an IP address in the form of 169.254.$x.y$ (where $x.y$ is the client's unique identifier) and a subnet mask of 255.255.0.0. If the address is in use, APIPA selects another IP address and, if necessary, reselects addresses up to 10 times.

Note The Internet Assigned Numbers Authority (IANA) has reserved 169.254.0.0 through 169.254.255.255 for Automatic Private IP Addressing. As a result, APIPA provides an address that is guaranteed not to conflict with routable addresses.

After the computer generates the address, it broadcasts to this address and then assigns the address to itself if no other computer responds. The computer continues to use this address until it detects and receives configuration information from a DHCP server. This allows two computers to be plugged into a LAN hub, to restart without any IP address configuration, and to use TCP/IP for local network access.

Note Windows 98 also supports APIPA.

Although APIPA can assign a TCP/IP address to DHCP clients automatically, it does not generate all the information that is typically provided by DHCP, such as the address of a default gateway. Consequently, computers enabled with APIPA can communicate only with computers on the same subnet that also have addresses of the form 169.254.*x.y*.

Disabling Automatic Private IP Addressing

By default, the Automatic Private IP Addressing feature is enabled. However, you can disable this feature by adding the IPAutoconfigurationEnabled value to the HKEY_LOCAL_MACHINE\SYSTEM\CurrentControlSet\Services\ Tcpip\Parameters\Interfaces*Adapter_GUID* subkey of the registry and setting its value to zero.

The IPAutoconfigurationEnabled entry takes a REG_DWORD value. To disable APIPA, specify a value of 0 for the entry. To enable APIPA, specify a value of 1, which is the default state when IPAutoconfigurationEnabled is omitted from the registry.

Troubleshooting TCP/IP

Windows 2000 offers several utilities to assist you in troubleshooting TCP/IP. The following table describes the Windows 2000 utilities you can use to troubleshoot TCP/IP.

Option	Description
Ping	Verifies configurations and tests connections
Arp	Displays locally resolved IP addresses as physical addresses
Ipconfig	Displays the current TCP/IP configuration
Nbtstat	Displays statistics and connections using NetBIOS over TCP/IP
Netstat	Displays TCP/IP protocol statistics and connections
Route	Displays or modifies the local routing table
Hostname	Prints the name of the host on which the command is issued
Tracert	Checks the route to a remote system

Testing TCP/IP Connectivity

Windows 2000 also provides a number of common TCP/IP utilities. These tools are described in the following table.

Option	Description
FTP	Provides bidirectional file transfer between a computer running Windows 2000 and any TCP/IP host running FTP. Windows 2000 Server ships can serve as an FTP client or server.
Trivial File Transfer Protocol (TFTP)	Provides bidirectional file transfer between a computer running Windows 2000 and a TCP/IP host running TFTP.
Telnet	Provides terminal emulation to a TCP/IP host running Telnet. Windows 2000 Server ships can serve as a Telnet client.
Remote Copy Protocol (RCP)	Copies files between a client and a host that support RCP (for example, a computer running Windows 2000 and a UNIX host).
Remote shell (RSH)	Runs commands on a UNIX host.
Remote execution (REXEC)	Runs a process on a remote computer.
Finger	Retrieves system information from a remote computer that supports TCP/IP and the finger utility.

After configuring TCP/IP and restarting the computer, you should use the ipconfig and ping command-prompt utilities to test the configuration and connections to other TCP/IP hosts and networks. Such testing helps to verify that TCP/IP is functioning properly.

Using Ipconfig

You can use the ipconfig utility to verify the TCP/IP configuration parameters on a host. This helps to determine whether the configuration is initialized or whether a duplicate IP address exists. Use the ipconfig command with the /all switch to verify all configuration information.

Tip Type **ipconfig /all | more** to prevent the ipconfig output from scrolling off the screen; to scroll down and view additional output, press the Spacebar. Type **ipconfig /all > ipconfig.txt** to write the screen output to a file named ipconfig.txt. You can then view this file with an ASCII text editor such as Notepad.

Executing the ipconfig /all command provides the following results:

- If a configuration has initialized, the ipconfig utility displays the IP address and subnet mask, and, if it is assigned, the default gateway.

- If a duplicate IP address exists, the ipconfig utility indicates that the IP address is configured; however, the subnet mask is 0.0.0.0.

- If the computer is unable to obtain an IP address from a server running the DHCP Service on the network, the ipconfig utility displays the IP address provided by APIPA.

Using Ping

After you have verified the TCP/IP configuration, use the ping utility to test connectivity. The ping utility is a diagnostic tool you can use to test TCP/IP configurations and diagnose connection failures. Use the ping utility to determine whether a particular TCP/IP host is available and functional. To test connectivity, use the ping command with the following syntax:

```
ping <IP_address>
```

Using Ipconfig and Ping

You can use a combination of the ipconfig and ping commands to verify a computer's configuration and test router connections. The following steps show how to use the tools:

1. The ipconfig command is used to verify that the TCP/IP configuration has been initialized.

2. The ping command is used against the loopback address (127.0.0.1) to verify that TCP/IP is correctly installed and bound to your network adapter card.

3. The ping command is used with the IP address of the local computer to verify that the computer is not a duplicate of another IP address on the network.

4. The ping command is used with the IP address of the default gateway to verify that the default gateway is operational and that the computer can communicate with the local network.

5. The ping command is used with the IP address of a remote host to verify that the computer can communicate through a router.

Note Typically, if you ping the remote host (step 5) and the ping command is successful, steps 1 through 4 are successful by default. If the ping command is not successful, ping the IP address of another remote host before completing the entire diagnostic process because the current host might be turned off.

Exercise 1: Configuring and Testing TCP/IP

In this exercise, you use two TCP/IP utilities to verify the protocol configuration of Server01. Then you configure Server01 to use a static IP address and verify its new configuration. Next you configure Server01 to obtain an IP address automatically, and then you test the APIPA feature in Windows 2000. Complete this exercise on Server01.

Important The DHCP Service should not be running anywhere on your network. In addition, this exercise requires that you assign IP addresses that might not be valid in the network. If your network is part of a larger network in which DHCP is running, isolate your network from the larger network.

▸ **Procedure 1: Verifying a computer's TCP/IP configuration**

In this procedure, you use two TCP/IP utilities, ipconfig and ping, to verify your computer's static configuration.

1. Log on to Server01 as Administrator with a password of "password."

2. Open a command prompt.

3. At the command prompt, type **ipconfig /all | more** and then press Enter. (The vertical line between the words "all" and "more" is the dashed line typically located on the \ key.)

   The Windows 2000 IP Configuration utility displays the TCP/IP configuration of the adapter or adapters configured on your computer.

4. Press the Spacebar as necessary to display the heading *<adapter type>* adapter Local Area Connection. Use the information displayed on the screen to complete the missing values in the following table. Some values entered in the table were set through configuration procedures in earlier exercises.

Local Area Connection setting	Value
Host Name	SERVER01
Primary DNS Suffix	microsoft.com
DNS Servers	10.10.10.1
Description	
Physical Address	
DHCP Enabled	No
Subnet Mask	255.0.0.0
Default Gateway	none

5. Press the Spacebar as necessary to return to the command prompt.

6. To verify that the IP address is working and configured for your adapter, type **ping 127.0.0.1** and then press Enter.

   This IP address is called the *loop-back address* and is used to verify that the TCP/IP stack is functioning properly.

   A response similar to the following indicates a successful ping:

   ```
   Pinging 127.0.0.1 with 32 bytes of data:
   Reply from 127.0.0.1: bytes=32 time<10ms TTL=128
   Reply from 127.0.0.1: bytes=32 time<10ms TTL=128
   Reply from 127.0.0.1: bytes=32 time<10ms TTL=128
   Reply from 127.0.0.1: bytes=32 time<10ms TTL=128
   Ping statistics for 127.0.0.1:
   Packets: Sent = 4, Received = 4, Lost = 0 <0% loss>,
   Approximate round trip times in milliseconds:
   Minimum = 0ms, Maximum = 0ms, Average = 0ms
   ```

7. Minimize the command prompt. You will be using it in a later procedure.

▸ **Procedure 2: Configuring TCP/IP to automatically obtain an IP address**

In this procedure, you configure TCP/IP to automatically obtain an IP address. You then test the configuration to verify that APIPA has provided the appropriate IP addressing information. Complete this procedure on Server01 and Server 02.

1. Click Start, point to Settings, and then click Network And Dial-Up Connections.

   The Network And Dial-Up Connections window appears.

2. Click Local Area Connection, click the File menu, and then click Properties.

   The Local Area Connection Properties dialog box appears, displaying the network adapter in use and the network components used in this connection.

3. Click Internet Protocol (TCP/IP), and then verify that the check box to the left of the entry is selected.

4. Click Properties.

   The Internet Protocol (TCP/IP) Properties dialog box appears.

5. Click the Obtain An IP Address Automatically radio button.

6. Click the Obtain DNS Server Address Automatically radio button.

7. Click OK to close the Internet Protocol (TCP/IP) Properties dialog box.

8. Click OK to close the Local Area Connection Properties dialog box.

9. Minimize the Network And Dial-Up Connections window.

10. At the command prompt, type **ipconfig /all | more** and then press Enter.

11. Pressing the Spacebar as necessary, find the current TCP/IP settings for your *<adapter type>* adapter Local Area Connection and enter them in the following table. Some entries have been filled in for you.

Setting	Value
Autoconfiguration Enabled	Yes
IP Address	
Subnet Mask	
DHCP Enabled	Yes
Default Gateway	None – requires manual configuration or DHCP
DNS Servers	None – requires manual configuration or DHCP

Notice that the IP address and subnet mask assigned to you through APIPA are different than the values you specified for manual configuration. Notice also that the IP address is now labeled Autoconfiguration IP Address and that DHCP is enabled. DHCP is enabled because you specified that the IP address should be obtained automatically.

12. Press the Spacebar as necessary to finish scrolling through the configuration information.

13. To verify that TCP/IP is working and bound to your adapter, type **ping 127.0.0.1** and then press Enter.

    The internal loop-back address test displays four replies if TCP/IP is bound to the adapter.

14. Exit the command prompt, and close the Network And Dial-Up Connections window.

Lesson Summary

Microsoft's implementation of TCP/IP enables networking and connectivity. The TCP/IP suite maps to a four-layer conceptual model: network interface, Internet, transport, and application. By default, client computers running Windows 2000 obtain TCP/IP configuration automatically from DHCP, although some computers require a static IP address. For each network adapter card that uses TCP/IP, you can configure an IP address, subnet mask, and default gateway. In addition, the Windows 2000 implementation of TCP/IP supports APIPA, which provides automatic address assignment of IP addresses for simple LAN-based network configurations. APIPA enables a configuration of IP addresses without using static IP address assignments or installing the DHCP Service. Windows 2000 also includes utilities you can use to troubleshoot TCP/IP and test connectivity. Ping and ipconfig are two common troubleshooting utilities, and FTP and telnet are two service utilities.

Lesson 3: Dynamic Host Configuration Protocol Service

The DHCP Service in Windows 2000 centralizes and manages the allocation of TCP/IP configuration information by assigning IP addresses and other TCP/IP configuration information automatically to computers that are setup as DHCP clients. Implementing the DHCP Service can eliminate many of the configuration problems associated with configuring TCP/IP manually. This lesson discusses the skills necessary and provides information to install and configure the DHCP Service. It also discusses the DHCP lease process.

After this lesson, you will be able to

- Install the DHCP Service

- Create a scope for the DHCP Service and configure a range of addresses and a reservation for a DHCP scope

- Back up and restore the DHCP database

Estimated lesson time: 70 minutes

Introduction to DHCP

DHCP is a TCP/IP standard for simplifying the management of IP configuration. DHCP is an extension of the Bootstrap Protocol (BOOTP), which is based on the User Datagram Protocol/Internet Protocol (UDP/IP). BOOTP enables a booting host to configure itself dynamically.

Each time a DHCP client starts, it requests IP addressing information from a DHCP server. This addressing information includes the following:

- An IP address

- A subnet mask

- Optional values, such as a default gateway address, a DNS server address, or a WINS server address

When a DHCP server receives a request for an IP address, it selects IP addressing information from a pool of addresses defined in its database and offers the IP addressing information to the DHCP client. If the client accepts the offer, the DHCP server leases the IP addressing information to the client for a specified period.

Manual versus automatic TCP/IP configuration

To understand why the DHCP Service is beneficial for configuring TCP/IP on clients, contrast the manual method of configuring TCP/IP with the automatic method using DHCP, as shown in the following table.

Configuring TCP/IP manually	Configuring TCP/IP using DHCP
Users can pick an IP address at random rather than obtaining a valid IP address from the network administrator. Using incorrect addresses can lead to network problems that can be difficult to trace to the source.	Users no longer need to acquire IP addressing information from an administrator to configure TCP/IP. The DHCP Service supplies all the necessary configuration information to all the DHCP clients.
Typing in the IP address, subnet mask, or default gateway can lead to problems ranging from difficulty communicating, if the default gateway or subnet mask is incorrect, to problems associated with a duplicate IP address.	Valid IP addressing information ensures correct configuration, which eliminates most difficult-to-trace network problems.
There is administrative overhead for networks if you frequently move computers from one subnet to another. For example, you must change the IP address and default gateway address for a client to communicate from a new location.	Having servers running the DHCP Service on each subnet eliminates the overhead associated with having to manually reconfigure IP addresses, subnet masks, and default gateways when you move computers from one subnet to another. Note that a single DHCP server can support IP address allocation for multiple networks.

The DHCP Lease Process

The DHCP Service allocates IP addressing information to client computers. The allocation of IP addressing information is called a *DHCP lease*. The DHCP lease process occurs when one of the following events occurs:

- TCP/IP is initialized for the first time on a DHCP client.

- A client requests a specific IP address and is denied, possibly because the DHCP server dropped the lease.

- A client previously leased an IP address but released the IP address and requires a new one. A DHCP lease can be manually released by typing **ipconfig /release** at a command prompt.

DHCP uses a four-phase process to lease IP addressing information to a DHCP client for a specific period: DHCPDISCOVER, DHCPOFFER, DHCPREQUEST, and DHCPACK (Figure 9.5).

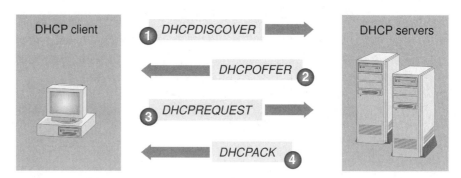

Figure 9.5 The DHCP lease process

DHCPDISCOVER

The first step in the DHCP lease process is DHCPDISCOVER. To begin the DHCP lease process, a client initializes a limited version of TCP/IP and broadcasts a DHCPDISCOVER message requesting the location of a DHCP server and IP addressing information. Because the client does not know the IP address of a DHCP server, the client uses 0.0.0.0 as the source address and 255.255.255.255 as the destination address. The DHCPDISCOVER message contains the client's hardware address and computer name so that the DHCP servers can determine which client sent the request.

DHCPOFFER

The second step in the DHCP lease process is DHCPOFFER. All DHCP servers that receive the IP lease request and have a valid client configuration broadcast a DHCPOFFER message that includes the following information:

- The client's hardware address
- An offered IP address
- A subnet mask
- The length of the lease
- A server identifier (the IP address of the offering DHCP server)

The DHCP server sends a broadcasted message because the client does not yet have an IP address. The DHCP client selects the IP address from the first offer that it receives. The DHCP server issuing the IP address reserves the address so that it cannot be offered to another DHCP client.

DHCPREQUEST

The third step in the DHCP lease process occurs after the client receives a DHCPOFFER from at least one DHCP server and selects an IP address. The client broadcasts a DHCPREQUEST message to all DHCP servers, indicating that it has accepted an offer. The DHCPREQUEST message includes the server identifier (IP address) of the server whose offer it accepted. All other DHCP servers then retract their offers and retain their IP addresses for the next IP lease request.

DHCPACK

The final step in a successful DHCP lease process occurs when the DHCP server issuing the accepted offer broadcasts a successful acknowledgment to the client in the form of a DHCPACK message. This message contains a valid lease for an IP address and possibly other configuration information.

When the DHCP client receives the acknowledgment, TCP/IP is completely initialized and the client is considered a bound DHCP client. Once bound, the client can use TCP/IP to communicate on the network.

DHCPNACK

If the DHCPREQUEST is not successful, the DHCP server broadcasts a negative acknowledgement (DHCPNACK). A DHCP server broadcasts a DHCPNACK if one of the following conditions are met:

- The client is trying to lease its previous IP address, and the IP address is no longer available.

- The IP address is invalid because the client computer has been moved to a different subnet.

When the client receives an unsuccessful acknowledgment, it resumes the DHCP lease process.

Note If a computer has multiple network adapters bound to TCP/IP, the DHCP process occurs separately over each adapter. The DHCP Service assigns a unique and valid IP address to each adapter in the computer bound to TCP/IP.

IP Lease Renewal and Release

All DHCP clients attempt to renew their lease when 50 percent of the lease time has expired. To renew its lease, a DHCP client sends a DHCPREQUEST message directly to the DHCP server from which it obtained the lease. If the DHCP server is available, it renews the lease and sends the client a DHCPACK message with the new lease time and any updated configuration parameters. The client updates its configuration when it receives the acknowledgment.

Note Each time a DHCP client restarts, it attempts to lease the same IP address from the original DHCP server. If the lease request is unsuccessful and lease time is still available, the DHCP client continues to use the same IP address until the next attempt to renew the lease.

If a DHCP client cannot renew its lease with the original DHCP server at the 50 percent interval, the client broadcasts a DHCPREQUEST to contact any available DHCP server when 87.5 percent of the lease time has expired. Any DHCP server can respond with a DHCPACK message (renewing the lease) or a DHCPNACK message (forcing the DHCP client to reinitialize and obtain a lease for a different IP address).

If the lease expires or a DHCPNACK message is received, the DHCP client must immediately discontinue using that IP address. The DHCP client then begins the DHCP lease process to lease a new IP address.

Using Ipconfig to Renew a Lease

Use the ipconfig command with the /renew switch to send a DHCPREQUEST message to the DHCP server to receive updated options and lease time. If the DHCP server is unavailable, the client continues using the current DHCP-supplied configuration options.

Using Ipconfig to Release a Lease

You can use the ipconfig command with the /release switch to cause a DHCP client to send a DHCPRELEASE message to the DHCP server and to release its lease. This is useful when you are moving a client to a different network and the client will not require its previous lease. TCP/IP communications with the client stops after you issue this command.

Microsoft DHCP clients do not initiate DHCPRELEASE messages when shutting down. If a client remains shut down for the length of its lease (and the lease is not renewed), the DHCP server might assign that client's IP address to a different client after the lease expires. A client has a better chance of receiving the same IP address during initialization if it does not send a DHCPRELEASE message.

Note For more information about DHCP and DHCP implementation, see the Supplemental Course Materials CD-ROM (\chapt09\articles\DHCP2000.doc) that accompanies this book.

Installing and Configuring the DHCP Service

To implement DHCP, you must install and configure the DHCP Service on at least one computer running Windows 2000 Server within the TCP/IP network. The computer can be configured as a domain controller or as a stand-alone server. In addition, for DHCP to function properly, you must manually configure the TCP/IP settings for the server and set up the clients for dynamic address configuration.

Requirements for a Server Running the DHCP Service

A DHCP server requires a computer running Windows 2000 Server that is configured with the following:

- A static IP address, subnet mask, default gateway (if necessary), and other TCP/IP parameters. A DHCP server cannot be a DHCP client.

- The DHCP Service.

- An activated DHCP scope. A scope is a range of IP addresses that are available for lease or assignment to clients. Once the scope is created, it must be activated.

- An authorization. The DHCP server must be authorized with Active Directory services.

Requirements for DHCP Clients

A DHCP client requires a computer that is DHCP-enabled and running any of the following supported operating systems:

- Windows 2000
- Windows NT Server 3.51 or later
- Windows NT Workstation 3.51 or later
- Windows 98
- Windows 95
- Windows for Workgroups 3.11 running Microsoft TCP/IP-32
- Microsoft Network Client 3.0 for Microsoft MS-DOS with the real-mode TCP/IP driver
- LAN Manager version 2.2c for MS-DOS (LAN Manager 2.2c for OS/2 is not supported.)

Installing the DHCP Service

The first step in implementing DHCP is to install the DHCP Service. Before you install the DHCP Service, you should specify a static IP address, subnet mask, and default gateway address for the network adapter bound to TCP/IP in the computer designated as the DHCP server.

To install the DHCP Service, use the Add/Remove Programs utility in Control Panel. The DHCP Service starts automatically during installation and must be running to communicate with DHCP clients.

The DHCP Snap-In

You can use the DHCP snap-in, shown in Figure 9.6, for all DHCP management and configuration tasks. The DHCP snap-in provides access to detailed information about the DHCP scopes and options. The snap-in also allows you to create and modify scopes, view address leases, create and modify client reservations, and configure server, scope, and client reservation options.

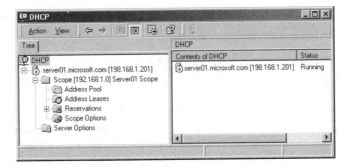

Figure 9.6 The DHCP snap-in

You can access the DHCP snap-in as a stand-alone MMC console or through the Computer Management snap-in. The DHCP snap-in can be installed by running Adminpak.msi or by installing the DHCP Service. Before the DHCP Service is installed, the DHCP snap-in is used to manage remote servers running the DHCP Service.

Creating a DHCP Scope

After you have installed the DHCP Service and it is running, the next step is to create a scope. The scope must be created before a DHCP server can lease an address to DHCP clients. A scope is a pool of valid IP addresses available for lease to DHCP clients.

When creating a DHCP scope, consider the following guidelines:

- You must create at least one scope for every DHCP server.

- You must exclude static IP addresses from the scope.

- You can create multiple scopes on a DHCP server to centralize administration and to assign IP addresses specific to a subnet. You can assign only one scope to a specific subnet.

- DHCP servers do not share scope information. As a result, when you create scopes on multiple DHCP servers, ensure that the same IP addresses do not exist in more than one scope to prevent duplicate IP addressing.

To create a scope, use the DHCP snap-in. The following table describes some of the parameters that you can specify when creating a new scope:

Parameter	Description
Name	The name of the scope.
Description	An optional description for the scope.
Start IP Address	The starting IP address of the range of addresses that can be assigned to a DHCP client from this scope.
End IP Address	The ending IP address of the range of addresses that can be assigned to a DHCP client from this scope.
Subnet Mask	The subnet mask to assign to DHCP clients. You can specify the subnet mask by bit length or by the actual subnet mask.
Start IP Address (for excluded range)	The starting IP address of the range to exclude from the pool of addresses. The addresses in this exclusion will not be assigned to DHCP clients. Use this feature if you have static IP addresses configured on non-DCHP clients. (Assigning an excluded range is optional.)
End IP Address (for excluded range)	The ending IP address of the range to exclude from the pool of addresses. The addresses in this exclusion will not be assigned to DHCP clients. Use this feature if you have static IP addresses configured on non-DCHP clients. (Assigning an excluded range is optional.)
Lease Duration	The number of days, hours, and minutes that a DHCP client lease is available before it must be renewed.

Once you have created the scope, you must activate it to make it available for lease assignments. To activate a scope, select the scope and then select Activate from the Action menu.

Note You must delete and re-create a scope to specify a new subnet mask or range of IP addresses.

Configuring a DHCP Scope

Once you have created the DHCP scope, you can configure options for DHCP clients. There are three levels of scope options: server, scope, and client.

Server Options

Server options are available to all DHCP clients. Use server options when all clients on all subnets require the same configuration information. For example, you might want all clients configured to use the same WINS server. Server options are always used, unless scope or client options are configured. To configure server options, select Server Options and then select Configure Options from the Action menu.

Scope Options

Scope options are available only to clients who lease an address from the specific scope. For example, if you have a different scope for each subnet, you can define a unique default gateway address for each subnet. Scope options override server options. To configure scope options, select Scope Options from the specific scope and then select Configure Options from the Action menu.

Client Options

Client options are available to specific clients with reserved DHCP address leases. Client options are always used before scope or server options. To configure client options, select the specific client reservation and then select Configure Options from the Action menu.

Configuring DHCP Options

The following table describes some of the options available when you configure the DHCP server, scope, or client reservation. The Properties dialog box for the server, scope, or client reservation includes all the options supported by Microsoft DHCP.

Option	Description
003 Router	The IP address of a router, such as the default gateway address. A locally defined default gateway on a client takes precedence over the DHCP option. To make sure that router information is sent to a client computer, verify that the Default Gateway text box on the client computer is empty (Figure 9.4).
006 DNS Servers	The IP address of a DNS server. A locally defined DNS on a client takes precedence over the DHCP option. Make sure the Obtain DNS Server Address Automatically radio button is selected on the client computer (Figure 9.4).
015 DNS Domain Name	The DNS domain name for client resolutions.

Option	Description
044 WINS/NBNS Servers	The IP address of a WINS/NBNS server available to clients. If a WINS server address is configured manually on a client, that configuration overrides the values configured for this option.
046 WINS/NBT Node Type	The type of network basic input/output system (NetBIOS) over TCP/IP name resolution to be used by the client. Options are 1 = B-node (broadcast), 2 = P-node (peer), 4 = M-node (mixed), and 8 = H-node (hybrid).
047 NetBIOS Scope ID	The local NetBIOS over TCP/IP scope ID. NetBIOS over TCP/IP communicate only with other NetBIOS hosts that are using the same scope ID.

The following table describes the available value types used when configuring the DHCP options.

Value type	Description
IP Address	The IP address of a server, for example, 003 Routers.
Long	A 32-bit numeric value, for example, 035 ARP Cache Timeout.
String Value	A string of characters, for example, 015 Domain Name.
Word	A 16-bit numeric value of specific block sizes, for example, 022 Max DG Reassembly Size.
Byte	A numeric value consisting of a single byte, for example, 046 WINS/NBT Node Type.
Binary	A binary value, for example, 043 Vendor-Specific Information.

Configuring a Client Reservation

For some DHCP clients, it is important that the same IP address be reassigned when their lease expires. For example, client computers that run TCP/IP server services might rely on a static IP address configuration to be identified by other clients on the network. For clients running server services, you can configure the DHCP service so that it always assigns the same IP address to them. This is called a client reservation and is created by using the New Reservation dialog box shown in Figure 9.7.

Figure 9.7 Using the New Reservation dialog box to add a client reservation

Clients using static host name resolution might also require that critical servers maintain their IP address configuration. For example, if a server with a host name of SRV187 is on a network containing clients that accomplish name resolution using a static HOSTS or LMHOSTS file, SRV187 should be set up with a client reservation. Setting up the reservation ensures that SRV187 always leases the same IP address from the DHCP server. Non-WINS-enabled clients on the network must use the LMHOSTS file to resolve NetBIOS computer names. Non-DNS-enabled clients on the network must use the HOSTS file to resolve IP host names. Since the LMHOSTS and HOSTS files are static files containing name-to-IP-address mappings, name resolution using these files will fail if the IP address of SRV187 changes.

To configure a client reservation, select Reservations under the specific scope and then select New Reservation from the Action menu. Be certain to type in the correct IP address and MAC address when you configure the reservation. If you type the value for MAC Address incorrectly, it will not match the value sent by the DHCP client, and the DHCP Service will assign the client any available IP address instead of the IP address reserved for that client. If you replace the NIC in the client receiving a reservation, be sure to reconfigure the reservation to match the new MAC address.

Authorizing the DHCP Server

A DHCP server must be authorized in Active Directory services before it can assign IP addresses. Authorization is a security precaution that ensures that only authorized DHCP servers run on your network. To authorize a DHCP server, select the domain from the DHCP snap-in tree and then select Authorize from the Action menu.

Exercise 2: Installing and configuring the DHCP Service

In this exercise, you install and configure the DHCP Service on Server01. You create a scope and configure a small range of addresses for the scope. As with the previous exercise, make sure that Server01 is on an isolated network so that it doesn't conflict with IP addressing in a larger network. You will complete some procedures on Server01 and other procedures on Server02.

▶ **Procedure 1: Reconfiguring TCP/IP to use a static IP address on Server01**

In this procedure, you configure Server01 to use a static IP address; this is a prerequisite for installing the DHCP Service.

1. Log on to Server01 as Administrator with a password of "password."

2. Click Start, point to Settings, and then click Network And Dial-Up Connections.

   The Network And Dial-Up Connections window appears.

3. Click Local Area Connection, click the File menu, and then click Properties.

   The Local Area Connection Properties dialog box appears, displaying the network adapter in use and the network components used in this connection.

4. Click Internet Protocol (TCP/IP), and verify that the check box to the left of the entry is selected.

5. Click Properties.

   The Internet Protocol (TCP/IP) Properties dialog box appears.

6. Click the Use The Following IP Address radio button.

7. In the IP address box, type 192.168.1.201, press Tab, and verify that in the Subnet mask box 255.255.255.0 appears.

8. Click OK.

   A Microsoft TCP/IP message box appears stating that the DNS server list is empty and that the local IP address will be used since DNS was installed on the computer.

9. Click OK to accept the message.

10. Click OK to close the Local Area Connection Properties dialog box.

11. Minimize the Network And Dial-Up Connections window.

▸ **Procedure 2: Determining the physical address of a computer**

In this procedure, you determine the physical address of Server02. You will use this physical address (the MAC address) in a later procedure to configure a DHCP reservation.

1. Verify that Server02 is connected to the same isolated network as Server01, and then log on to Server02 in the Microsoft domain as Administrator with a password of "password."

2. Open a command prompt, and type **ipconfig /all | more** to determine the physical address (MAC address) of the *<adapter type>* adapter Local Area Network on Server02.

Note If Server02 was configured with a valid IP address that Server01 could reach, you could ping the IP address from Server01, type **arp -a**, and then press Enter to determine from Server01 the MAC address of the network adapter in Server02.

---

3. Record the physical address of Server02 in the line provided.

The physical address is the hardware address or the MAC address. It is the address permanently burned into your network adapter, and it should look something like 00-50-04-B4-3A-23.

MAC address:

4. Minimize the command prompt on Server02.

▸ **Procedure 3: Installing the DHCP service**

In this procedure, you install the DHCP Service on Server01.

1. On Server01, click Start, point to Programs, and then point to Administrative Tools.

Notice that DHCP is listed in the list of Administrative Tools. The DHCP snap-in is present because you installed Adminpak.msi in an earlier chapter exercise. This is only the DHCP snap-in; DHCP is not installed on Server01.

2. Point to Settings on the Start menu, and then click Control Panel.

3. Double-click Add/Remove Programs.

The Add/Remove Programs window appears.

4. Click Add/Remote Windows Components in the left frame.

   The Windows Components wizard appears.

5. In the Components box, click Networking Services, but do not click or change the status of the check box to the left of this option.

   Note The Networking Services check box is already selected because some networking services have already been installed on Server01.

6. Click Details.

   The Networking Services dialog box appears.

   In the Subcomponents Of Networking Services box, select the Dynamic Host Configuration Protocol (DHCP) check box.

7. Click OK.

   The Windows Components screen appears.

8. Click Next.

   The Configuring Components screen makes the configuration changes you requested. A File Copy box appears as DHCP files are copied into the operating system folders.

   The Completing The Windows Components Wizard screen appears.

9. Click Finish.

10. Close the Add/Remove Programs window.

11. Close Control Panel.

▶ **Procedure 4: Creating and configuring a DHCP scope**

In this procedure, you create and configure a DHCP scope on Server01.

1. Click Start, point to Programs, point to Administrative Tools, and then click DHCP.

   The DHCP snap-in appears.

2. Maximize the DHCP snap-in.

3. In the console tree, double-click Server01.microsoft.com[192.168.1.201].

   A Configure The DHCP Server message appears in the details pane.

4. Read the message appearing in the details pane.

5. Click the Action menu, and then click New Scope.

   The New Scope wizard appears.

6. Click Next.

   The Scope Name screen appears.

7. In the Name text box, type **Server01 Scope**.

8. In the Description text box, type **Training network**, and then click Next.

   The IP Address Range screen appears.

9. Type **192.168.1.70** in the Start box, and type **192.168.1.90** in the End box.

   Notice that the subnet mask is set to a standard Class C address, 255.255.255.0, and that 24 bits are enabled; all bits in the first three octets in binary are set to 1.

10. Click Next.

    The Add Exclusions screen appears.

11. In the Start Address box, type **192.168.1.76**.

12. In the End Address box, type **192.168.1.80**.

13. Click Add.

    Notice that 192.168.1.76 to 192.168.1.80 appears in the Excluded Addresses box.

14. Click Next.

    The Lease Duration screen appears. Read the information on this page, and notice that the default lease duration is 8 days.

15. Click Next to accept the default lease duration.

    The Configure DHCP Options screen appears, asking if you would like to configure the most common DHCP options now.

16. Click the No, I Will Configure These Options Later radio button, and then click Next.

    The Completing The New Scope Wizard screen appears.

17. Read the instructions on this screen, and then click Finish.

    An icon representing the new scope appears in DHCP Manager.

    The red arrow pointing down indicates that the scope is not activated. You will activate the scope in a later procedure.

▶   **Procedure 5: Adding a reservation to a DHCP scope**

In this procedure, you use the physical address of Server02 that you determined in Procedure 2 to add a reservation to a DHCP scope.

1. From the DHCP snap-in running on Server01, click Scope [192.168.1.0] Server01 Scope in the console tree.

   The scope contents appear in the details pane.

2. In the console tree, click Reservations and read the message appearing in the details pane.

3. Click the Action menu, and then click New Reservation.

   The New Reservation dialog box appears.

4. In the Reservation Name text box, type **Server02**.

5. In the IP Address box, notice the first three octets are entered for you. In the fourth octet position, type **76**. The entire box should read: 192.168.1.76.

6. In the MAC Address box, type the physical address you determined in Procedure 2. Do not type in the dashes.

   For example, for the physical address 00-50-04-B4-3A-23, you would type 005004B43A23 in the MAC Address text box.

7. In the Description text box, type **Reservation made by: *<your name>***.

   Notice that DHCP, BOOTP, or both types of clients can be configured to use this reservation. A BOOTP client could be a device like a legacy terminal or router. This type of client request is answered by the DHCP server, and additional configuration information can be downloaded. Dynamic BOOTP scopes are also supported. For more information on these configuration options, see the section in the DHCP online help file titled "Supporting BOOTP Clients."

8. Under Supported types, select the DHCP Only radio button and then click Add.

   Another New Reservation dialog box appears.

9. Click Close.

10. Notice that the reservation appears in the details pane.

11. In the console tree, click Scope [192.168.1.0] Server01 Scope.

12. Click the Action menu, and then click Activate.

    Notice that the red down arrow to the right of the scope's name disappears. Notice also that the down arrow for server01.microsoft.com [192.168.1.201] still remains.

13. In the console tree, click server01.microsoft.com [192.168.1.201].

14. Click the Action menu, and then click Authorize to authorize this DHCP server in the Active Directory store.

15. Press the F5 key to refresh the display.

    When a green up arrow appears next to server01.microsoft.com [192.168.1.201], the DHCP Service has been authorized.

▶ **Procedure 6: Configuring scope options**

In this procedure, you configure DHCP so that the preferred DNS Server and DNS domain name is sent to the DHCP client upon registration. This procedure is similar to setting server options, which apply to all DHCP clients using this server, and setting individual client options.

1. In the console tree, expand server01.microsoft.com [192.168.1.201], expand Scope [192.168.1.0] Server Scope, and click Scope Options.

2. Click the Action menu, and then click Configure Options.

    The Scope Options dialog box appears.

3. Select the 006 DNS Servers check box.

    Options under Data Entry appears.

4. In the Server Name text box, type **Server01** and then click Resolve.

    The IP address 198.168.1.201 appears in the IP Address box.

5. Click Add.

6. Scroll down in the Available Options box to find 015 DNS Domain Name.

7. Select the 015 DNS Domain Name check box.

8. In the String value box, type **microsoft.com** and then click OK.

    DNS data will now be downloaded to DHCP client computers within this scope.

9. Leave the DHCP snap-in open; you will be using it in the next procedure.

▶ **Procedure 7: Testing DHCP**

In this procedure, you test the DHCP Service to verify that the IP address information you specified in the client reservation appears on Server02 and that the address lease appears on Server01.

1. On Server02, verify that the Internet Protocol (TCP/IP) Properties dialog box shows the Obtain An IP Address Automatically and the Obtain DNS Server Address Automatically radio buttons selected.

   If you are not sure how to complete this step, return to "Exercise 1: Configuring and Testing TCP/IP" to review Procedure 3.

2. On Server02, restore the command prompt, type **ipconfig /renew**, and then press Enter.

   After a few moments, the client reservation 192.168.1.76 is assigned to Server02.

3. At the command prompt, type **ipconfig /all | more** and then press Enter.

   Notice that DHCP information has been sent to the client computer. You will see a DHCP-assigned IP address, subnet mask, DNS server address, and DNS domain name. Additional information such as the default gateway are commonly sent to the DHCP client.

4. To test that Server02 can communicate with Server01, type **ping server01**.

   Notice that the server name is resolved to server01.microsoft.com and its IP address. This resolution is possible because the DNS information from Server01 was sent to Server02 in the DHCP data.

5. On Server01 in the DHCP snap-in, click Addresses Leases in the console tree.

   Notice that server02.microsoft.com appears with an IP address of 192.168.1.76. Notice also that the lease expiration reads Reservation (Active). This is because a reserved address does not expire. A DHCP client without a reservation would show a date and time of expiration in the Lease Expiration column.

6. Close the DHCP snap-in on Server01, and close the command prompt on Server02.

Backing Up and Restoring the DHCP Database

You can edit the registry to specify the interval at which Windows 2000 backs up the DHCP database. In addition, you can manually restore the DHCP database by editing the registry.

Backing Up the DHCP Database

By default, Windows 2000 backs up the DHCP database every 60 minutes. Windows 2000 stores the backup copies of the file in the %systemroot%\System32\Dhcp\Backup\Jet\new folder.

You can change the default backup interval by changing the value, representing the number of minutes between backups, of the BackupInterval entry located in the registry under the following key:

```
HKEY_LOCAL_MACHINE\SYSTEM\CurrentControlSet\Services\
DHCPServer\Parameters
```

Restoring the DHCP Database

By default, the DHCP Service restores a corrupt DHCP database automatically when you restart the DHCP Service. However, you can also manually restore the DHCP database file.

To manually restore the DHCP database, edit the registry, set the value for the RestoreFlag entry to 1, and then restart the DHCP Service. The RestoreFlag entry is located in the registry under the following subkey:

```
HKEY_LOCAL_MACHINE\SYSTEM\CurrentControlSet\Services\
DHCPServer\Parameters
```

Note After the DHCP Service successfully restores the database, the server automatically changes the RestoreFlag parameter to the default value of 0.

You can also restore the DHCP database file manually by copying the contents of the %systemroot%\System32\Dhcp\Backup\Jet new folder to the %systemroot%\System32\Dhcp folder and then restarting the DHCP Service.

The following table describes some of the files stored in the %systemroot%\ System32\Dhcp directory:

File	Description
Dhcp.mdb	The DHCP database file.
Tmp.edb	A temporary file the DHCP Service creates for temporary database information while the DHCP Service is running.
J50.log and J50*.log	Log files, including all transactions done with the database. The DHCP Service uses these files to recover data if necessary.

Important Do not tamper with or remove these files.

Lesson Summary

The DHCP Service in Windows 2000 centralizes and manages the allocation of TCP/IP configuration information by assigning IP addresses automatically to computers configured as DHCP clients. Each time a DHCP client starts, it requests IP addressing information from a DHCP server, including an IP address, a subnet mask, and optional values such as a default gateway. DHCP uses a four-phase process to lease IP addressing information to a DHCP client for a specific period of time: DHCPDISCOVER, DHCPOFFER, DHCPREQUEST, and DHCPACK. To implement DHCP, you must install and configure the DHCP Service on at least one computer running Windows 2000 Server within the TCP/IP network. In addition, you must create and activate a DHCP scope, which is a range of IP addresses available for lease to clients. You must also authorize the domain in Active Directory services. Once you have created the DHCP scope, you can configure options for DHCP clients. There are three levels of scope options: server, scope, and client. For some DHCP clients, you can create client reservations so that the DHCP service always assigns the same IP address to them. You can edit the registry to specify the interval at which Windows 2000 backs up the DHCP database. In addition, you can manually restore the DHCP database by editing the registry.

Lesson 4: Windows Internet Naming Service

This lesson explains the purpose and function of WINS and name registration. It also covers the WINS server and client configuration, support for non-WINS clients, and how to use the DHCP snap-in to configure WINS on a DHCP client computer.

After this lesson, you will be able to

- Explain the purpose and function of the WINS process, including name registration, renewal and name release, and name query
- Implement WINS in a Windows 2000 environment

Estimated lesson time: 35 minutes

Introduction to WINS

In a mixed network environment, down-level clients, such as computers running Windows 98 or Windows NT 4.0, use Network Basic Input/Output System (NetBIOS) names to communicate. As a result, a Microsoft Windows 2000 network with down-level clients requires a means of resolving NetBIOS names to IP addresses. WINS is an enhanced NetBIOS name server that registers NetBIOS computer names and resolves them to IP addresses. WINS also provides a dynamic database that maintains mapping of computer names to IP addresses.

Note For more information about WINS, see the Supplemental Course Materials CD (\chapt09\articles\WINS2000.doc) that accompanies this book.

The WINS Name Resolution Process

The WINS name resolution process allows WINS clients to register their name and IP address with WINS servers. WINS clients can query the WINS servers to locate and communicate with other resources on the network.

The following steps outline the WINS name resolution process:

1. Every time a WINS client starts, it registers its NetBIOS name/IP address mapping with a designated WINS server. It then queries the WINS server for computer name resolution.

   Note A WINS client automatically updates the WINS database whenever its IP addressing information changes, for example, when dynamic addressing through the DHCP Service results in a new IP address for a computer that moved from one subnet to another.

2. When a WINS client initiates a NetBIOS command to communicate with another network resource, it sends the name query request directly to the WINS server instead of broadcasting the request on the local network.

3. The WINS server finds a NetBIOS name/IP address mapping for the destination resource in this database, and it returns the IP address to the WINS client.

Name Registration

Each WINS client is configured with the IP address of a primary WINS server and, optionally, a secondary WINS server. When a client starts, it registers its NetBIOS name and IP address by sending a name registration request directly to the configured WINS server.

If the WINS server is available and another WINS client has not registered the name already, the WINS server returns a successful registration message to the client. This message includes the amount of time that the NetBIOS name is registered to the client, specified as the Time to Live (TTL). In addition, the WINS server stores the client's NetBIOS name/IP address mapping in its database.

When a Name Is Already Registered

When a name is already registered in the WINS database, the WINS server sends a name query request to the currently registered owner of the name. The WINS server sends the request three times at 500-millisecond intervals. If the registered computer is a multihomed computer, which means it has more than one network adapter card bound to TCP/IP and has an IP address for each network adapter card, the WINS server tries each IP address it has for the computer until it receives a response or until it has tried all the IP addresses.

If the current registered owner responds successfully to the WINS server, the WINS server sends a negative name registration response to the WINS client that is attempting to register the name. However, if the current registered owner does not respond to the WINS server, the WINS server sends a successful name registration response to the WINS client that is attempting to register the name.

When the WINS Server Is Unavailable

A WINS client makes three attempts to find the primary WINS server. If the client fails after the third attempt, it sends the name registration request to the secondary WINS server (if one is configured for the client). If neither server is available, the client generates three B-node broadcasts on the local network. If the NetBIOS name is found on the local network, the name is resolved to an IP address.

Name Renewal

A WINS server registers all NetBIOS names on a temporary basis so that other computers can use the same name later if the original owner stops using it. Since client name registrations with a WINS server are temporary, a WINS client must renew its name or the lease will expire.

To continue using the same NetBIOS name, a client must renew its lease before the lease expires. If a client does not renew its lease, the WINS server makes the lease available for another WINS client.

A WINS client first attempts to refresh its lease after one-eighth of the TTL interval has expired. If the WINS client does not receive a name refresh response, it continues attempting to refresh its lease every two minutes, until half of the TTL interval has expired.

When half of the TTL interval has expired, the WINS client attempts to refresh its lease with a secondary WINS server, if one is configured. When switching to a secondary WINS server, the WINS client attempts to refresh its lease as if it were the first refresh attempt—every one-eighth of the TTL interval until successful or until half the TTL interval has expired (four tries). The WINS client then reverts to the primary WINS server.

When a WINS server receives the name refresh request, it sends the client a name refresh response with a new TTL. After a client successfully refreshes its lease once, it attempts to refresh its lease when half the TTL interval has expired.

Name Release

When a WINS client's name is no longer in use, the client sends a message to the WINS server to release the name. When you shut down a WINS client properly, the client sends a name release request directly to the WINS server for each registered name. The request includes the client's IP address and the NetBIOS name.

When the WINS server receives the name release request, it checks its database for the specified name. If the WINS server encounters a database error, or if a different IP address maps the registered name, it sends a negative name release to the WINS client. Otherwise, the WINS server sends a positive name release, and then the server designates the specified name as released in its database. The name release response contains the released NetBIOS name and a TTL value of 0.

Name Query

After a WINS client has registered its NetBIOS name and IP address with a WINS server, it can communicate with other hosts by obtaining the IP address of other NetBIOS-based computers from the WINS server.

By default, a WINS client attempts to resolve another host's NetBIOS name to an IP address in the following manner:

1. The client checks its NetBIOS name cache for the NetBIOS name/IP address mapping of the destination computer.

2. If the client cannot resolve the name from its cache, it sends a name query request directly to its primary WINS server.

3. If the primary WINS server is unavailable, the client resends the request two more times before switching to the secondary WINS server.

4. If either WINS server, primary or secondary, resolves the name, it sends a response to the client with the IP address for the requested NetBIOS name.

5. If no WINS server can resolve the name, the client receives a message saying that the requested name does not exist and initiates a network broadcast.

Note All WINS communications use directed datagrams over UDP port 137 (NetBIOS Name Service).

Implementing WINS

To implement WINS, you must install and configure WINS on a computer running Windows 2000 Server. In addition, you must configure selected options on computers that participate as WINS clients.

WINS Server Configuration

A WINS server requires a computer running Windows 2000 Server; however, the server does not have to be a domain controller. In addition, the server must be configured with WINS and assigned a static IP address, subnet mask, and default gateway.

The WINS server can also include the following configurations:

- A static mapping for all non-WINS clients to allow communication with WINS clients on remote networks
- WINS support through the DHCP Service

WINS Client Configuration

A WINS client must be running one of the following operating systems:

- Windows 2000
- Windows NT Server 3.5 or later
- Windows NT Workstation 3.5 or later
- Windows 98
- Windows 95
- Windows for Workgroups version 3.11 running Microsoft TCP/IP-32
- Microsoft Network Client version 3.0 for Microsoft MS-DOS with the real-mode TCP/IP driver
- LAN Manager version 2.2c for MS-DOS (LAN Manager version 2.2c for OS/2 is not supported.)

A WINS client also requires the IP address of a primary WINS server, and, optionally, the IP address of a secondary WINS server.

WINS Installation

The WINS Service is not installed as part of the default Windows 2000 Server installation. You must add the service, as outlined below. To install the WINS Service, use the Add/Remove Programs utility in Control Panel.

After you install the WINS Service on the Windows 2000 Server computer, you should configure its TCP/IP properties so that the computer points to itself. You do this on the WINS tab of the Advanced TCP/IP Settings dialog box.

The WINS Snap-In

You can use the WINS snap-in, shown in Figure 9.8, for all management and configuration tasks of the WINS server. The WINS snap-in provides access to detailed information about the WINS servers on a network. The snap-in also allows you to view the contents of the WINS database and search for specific entries.

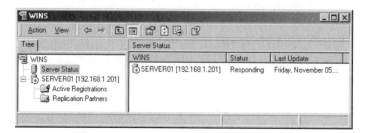

Figure 9.8 The WINS snap-in

You can access the WINS snap-in as a stand-alone MMC console or through the Computer Management snap-in, under Services And Applications. WINS must be installed before you can use the Windows 2000 snap-in.

Support for Non-WINS Clients

In a WINS environment, you can provide support for non-WINS clients by using static mappings and configuring a WINS proxy agent.

Static Mappings

On a network that includes non-WINS clients, you can configure a static NetBIOS name/IP address mapping for each non-WINS client. This ensures that WINS clients can resolve the NetBIOS names of the non-WINS clients.

Note If you have DHCP clients that require a static mapping, you must reserve an IP address for the DHCP client so that its IP address is always the same.

To configure a static entry for non-WINS clients, select Active Registrations and then select New Static Mapping from the Action menu. When you create a static mapping, you can specify a NetBIOS scope. A NetBIOS scope is an optional extension to a computer name that you can use to group computers in a network.

There are five types of static mappings that you can create when you add a new static mapping. These types of static mappings are described in the following table.

Option	Description
Unique	A unique name that maps to a single IP address.
Group	A name that maps to a group. When adding an entry to a group by using the WINS snap-in, enter the computer name and IP address. The IP addresses of group members are not stored in the WINS database, so there is no limit to the number of members you can add.
Domain Name	A NetBIOS name/IP address mapping with 0x1C as the 16th byte. A domain group stores up to 25 addresses for members. For registrations after the 25th address, WINS overwrites a replica address or, if none is present, overwrites the oldest registration.
Internet Group	User-defined groups that you use to group resources, such as printers, for reference and browsing. An Internet group can store up to 25 addresses for members. A dynamic member, however, does not replace a static member that you add by using the WINS snap-in or by importing the LMHOSTS file.
Multihomed	A unique name that can have more than one address. Use this option for computers with multiple network adapter cards. You can register up to 25 multihomed addresses. For registrations after the 25th address, WINS overwrites a replica address or, if none is present, it overwrites the oldest registration.

Note The WINS snap-in adds a static mapping to the WINS database when you click OK. If you enter incorrect information for a static mapping, you must delete that mapping and then create a new one.

Configuring a WINS Proxy Agent

A WINS proxy agent extends the name resolution capabilities of the WINS server to non-WINS clients by listening for broadcast name registrations and broadcast resolution requests and then forwarding them to a WINS server.

- **NetBIOS name registration** When a non-WINS client broadcasts a name registration request, the WINS proxy agent forwards the request to the WINS server to verify that no other WINS client has registered that name. The NetBIOS name does not get registered, only verified.

- **NetBIOS name resolution** When a WINS proxy agent detects a name resolution broadcast, it checks its NetBIOS name cache and attempts to resolve the name. If the name is not in cache, the request is sent to a WINS server. The WINS server sends the WINS proxy agent the IP address for the requested NetBIOS name. The WINS proxy agent returns this information to the non-WINS client.

To configure a WINS proxy agent, edit the registry on a WINS-enabled client by setting the value for the EnableProxy entry to 1, and then restart the computer. The EnableProxy entry is located in the registry under the subkey HKEY_LOCAL_MACHINE\SYSTEM\CurrentControlSet\Services\ NetBT\Parameters.

DHCP Server Configuration

If a computer is a DHCP client, you can configure WINS support by using the DHCP snap-in. The snap-in allows you to add and configure the DHCP scope option 044 WINS/NBNS Servers and configure the address of primary and secondary servers (Figure 9.9).

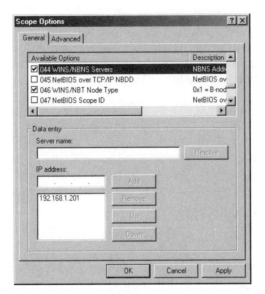

Figure 9.9 The Scope Options dialog box in the DHCP snap-in

When the DHCP client leases or renews an address lease, it receives this DHCP scope option, and the client is configured for WINS support.

Note If you configure a client computer with IP addresses for a primary and secondary WINS server, those values take precedence over the same parameters provided by a DHCP server.

You also can configure the 046 WINS/NBT Node Type option to set the node type. Node types include B-node, P-node, M-node, and H-node.

Note For more information about node types, see RFC 1001 and RFC 1002. An RFC (Request for Comment) is a document in which a standard, a protocol, or other information pertaining to the operation of the Internet is published. The RFC is actually issued after discussion and serves as the standard. You can find the text of each RFC that is cited in this book (as well as much associated discussion material) on the Internet. Use your Web browser to search for the RFC of interest. In this case, search for "RFC 1001" and then search for "RFC 1002." (Earlier chapters included RFCs so that you could see how they are structured.)

Exercise 3: Installing and Configuring WINS

In this exercise, you will install WINS on Server01. After the installation, additional settings will be configured for the DHCP Service to support WINS. Make sure the Windows 2000 Server installation CD is running on Server01.

Note WINS is required only for legacy support. In your small training network and in a homogeneous network of Windows 2000 clients and servers, WINS is not necessary because all computers running Windows 2000 use DNS for name resolution. This exercise is intended to teach you how to perform a basic installation and configuration of WINS.

▶ Procedure 1: Installing WINS

In this procedure, you install WINS on Server01.

1. Log on to Server01 as Administrator with a password of "password."

2. Click Start, point to Settings, and then click Control Panel.

3. Double-click Add/Remove Programs.

   The Add/Remove Programs window appears.

4. Click Add/Remote Windows Components in the left frame.

   The Windows Components wizard appears.

5. In the Components box, click Networking Services, but do not click or change the status of the check box to the left of this option.

6. Click Details.

   The Networking Services dialog box appears.

   In the Subcomponents Of Networking Services box, select the Windows Internet Naming Service (WINS) check box.

7. Click OK.

   The Windows Components screen appears.

8. Click Next.

   The Configuring Components screen makes the configuration changes you requested. A File Copy box will appear as WINS files are copied into the operating system folders.

   The Completing The Windows Components Wizard screen appears.

9. Click Finish.

10. Close the Add/Remove Programs window.

11. Close Control Panel.

▶ **Procedure 2: Configuring DHCP to support WINS**

In this procedure, you configure WINS settings in the DHCP snap-in on Server01. To give you practice with setting server options, you will use the Server Options node. These settings could also be configured as Scope options if you want them to apply only to a specific scope or even to a specific DHCP client.

1. Open the DHCP snap-in on Server01.

2. In the console tree, click Server Options.

3. Read the message appearing in the details pane.

4. Click the Action menu, and then choose Configure Options.

   The Server Options dialog box appears.

5. Scroll down to 044 WINS/NBNS Servers, and then click this check box.

6. In the Server name text box, type **Server01** and then click Resolve.

   Server01's IP address, 192.168.1.201, appears in the IP Address box.

7. Click Add.

8. In the Available Options box, scroll down to 046 WINS/NBT Node Type and then click this check box.

9. In the Byte text box, type **8** so that the text box entry reads: 0x8.

   0x8 sets the node type to h-node. Node type determines how WINS resolution occurs at a client computer. H-node instructs the client to check with the WINS server (p-node point-to-point communications with name server) first and then sends out a b-node broadcast if necessary.

10. Click OK.

    The two server options appear in the details pane.

11. Close the DHCP snap-in.

▶ **Procedure 3: Testing WINS settings (optional)**

In this procedure, you release and renew the DHCP lease on Server02. Then you load the WINS snap-in on Server01 to verify the registration of Server02 in the WINS database.

Note If you just started Server02, skip to step 4. The first three steps are only necessary to update the DHCP lease.

1. On Server02, open a command prompt.

2. Type **ipconfig /release**, and then press Enter.

    A message appears stating that the IP address successfully released for the adapter "Local Area Connection."

3. Type **ipconfig /renew**, and then press Enter.

    The IP configuration is displayed as the lease is renewed.

4. Type **ipconfig /all | more**, and then press Enter.

5. Press Enter as necessary so that you can see the settings for *<adapter type>* adapter Local Area Connection.

6. Notice that Node Type is set to Hybrid. Hybrid is equivalent to h-node. Also notice that the primary WINS server is set to 192.168.1.201. This is the IP address of Server01.

7. Close the command prompt on Server02.

8. On Server01, click Start, point to Programs, point to Administrative Tools, and then click WINS.

    The WINS snap-in appears.

9. Maximize the WINS snap-in.

10. Expand SERVER01 [192.168.1.201], and then click Active Registrations.

11. Read the message appearing in the details pane.

12. Click the Action menu, and then click Find By Name.

    The Find By Name dialog box appears.

13. In the Find Names Beginning With text box, type **Ser** and then click Find Now.

    Under Record Name, Server02 appears with three entries. These three entries are the services that broadcast the name of Server02 onto the network. The first entry, 00h, is the NetBIOS computer name. 03h is used for sending and receiving broadcast messages. 20h is used for share access by other computers on the network.

14. Close the WINS snap-in.

Lesson Summary

Name registration is an important part of the name resolution process. Each WINS client is configured with the IP address of a primary WINS server and, optionally, a secondary WINS server. Each time a WINS client starts, it registers its NetBIOS name and IP address by sending a name registration request directly to the configured WINS server. A WINS server registers all NetBIOS names on a temporary basis, so a WINS client must renew its name or the lease will expire. When a WINS server receives the name refresh request, it sends the client a name refresh response with a new TTL. In addition, when a WINS client's name is no longer in use, the client sends a message to the WINS server to release the name. When the WINS server receives the name release request, it checks its database for the specified name. If the WINS server finds the correct NetBIOS name/IP address mapping in its database, it sends a positive name release, and then the server designates the specified name as released in its database. To implement WINS, you must install and configure WINS on a computer running Window 2000 Server. In addition to installing WINS, you must configure selected options on computers that participate as WINS clients. The WINS snap-in provides access to detailed information about the WINS servers on a network and allows you to view the contents of the WINS database and search for specific entries.

Lesson 5: Domain Name System

DNS is a distributed database used in TCP/IP networks to translate computer names (host names) to IP addresses. This lesson introduces you to DNS and name resolution. It also discusses the skills necessary and provides information to install and configure the DNS service.

After this lesson, you will be able to

- Explain the function of DNS and its components, and explain the name resolution process

- Install and configure the DNS service, including Dynamic DNS and the DHCP Service for DNS

- Configure a DNS client

- Troubleshoot the DNS service

Estimated lesson time: 90 minutes

Introduction to DNS

DNS is most commonly associated with the Internet. However, private networks use DNS extensively to resolve computer host names and to locate computers within their local networks and the Internet. DNS name resolution is different than the name resolution provided by WINS. WINS resolves NetBIOS names to IP addresses, while DNS resolves IP host names to IP addresses. IP host names resolved using DNS or other means, provide the following benefits:

- IP host names are user-friendly, which means they are easier to remember than IP addresses.

- IP host names remain more constant than IP addresses. An IP address for a server can change, but the server name remains the same.

- IP host names allow users to connect to local servers by using the same naming convention as the Internet.

Note For more information on DNS, see RFC 1034 and RFC 1035. Use your Web browser to search for "RFC 1034" and "RFC 1035." You can also find information about DNS and DNS implementation on the Supplemental Course Materials CD (\chapt09\articles\w2kDNS.doc) that accompanies this book.

Domain Namespace

Domain namespace is the naming scheme that provides the hierarchical structure for the DNS database. Each node represents a partition of the DNS database. These nodes are referred to as domains.

The DNS database is indexed by name; therefore, each domain must have a name. As you add domains to the hierarchy, the name of the parent domain is appended to its child domain (called a subdomain). Consequently, a domain's name identifies its position in the hierarchy. For example, in Figure 9.10 the domain name sales.microsoft.com identifies the sales domain as a subdomain of the microsoft domain and microsoft as a subdomain of the com domain.

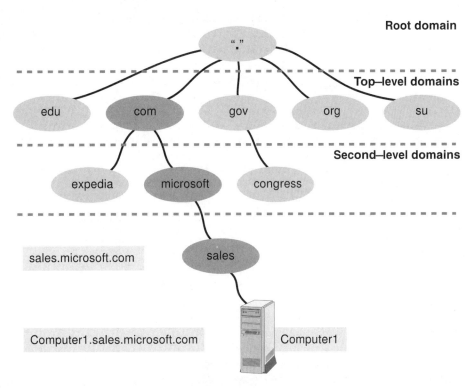

Figure 9.10 Hierarchical structure of a domain namespace

As Figure 9.10 illustrates, the hierarchical structure of the domain namespace consists of a root domain, top-level domains, second-level domains, and host names.

Note The term domain, in the context of DNS, has a slightly different meaning than it does when used in the Microsoft Windows 2000 directory services. A Windows 2000 domain is a grouping of computers and devices that are administered as a unit. In DNS, a domain is a node that represents a partition in the DNS database.

Root Domain

The root domain is at the top of the hierarchy and is represented as a period (.). The Internet root domain is managed by several organizations, including Network Solutions, Inc.

Top-Level Domains

Top-level domains are two-character or three-character name codes. Top-level domains are categorized by organization type or geographic location. The following table provides some examples of top-level domain names.

Top-level domain	Description
gov	Government organizations
com	Commercial organizations
edu	Educational institutions
org	Noncommercial organizations
au	Country code of Australia

Top-level domains can contain second-level domains and host names.

Second-Level Domains

Organizations such as Network Solutions, Inc. assign and register second-level domains to individuals and organizations for the Internet. A second-level domain can contain both hosts and subdomains. For example, microsoft.com can contain computers such as ftp.microsoft.com and subdomains such as dev.microsoft.com. The subdomain dev.microsoft.com can contain hosts such as printerserver1.dev.microsoft.com.

Host Names

Host names refer to specific computers on the Internet or a private network. For example, in Figure 9.10, Computer1 is a host name. A host name is the leftmost portion of a fully qualified domain name (FQDN), which describes the exact position of a host within the domain hierarchy. In Figure 9.10, Computer1.sales.microsoft.com. (including the end period, which represents the root domain) is an FQDN.

DNS uses a host's FQDN to resolve a name to an IP address.

Note The host name does not have to be the same as the computer name. By default, TCP/IP Setup uses the computer name for the host name, replacing illegal characters, such as the underscore (_), with a hyphen (-). For accepted domain naming conventions, see RFC 1035.

Domain Naming Guidelines

When you create a domain namespace, consider the following domain guidelines and standard naming conventions:

- Limit the number of domain levels. Typically, DNS host entries should be three or four levels down the DNS hierarchy and no more than five levels down the hierarchy. As the number of levels increases, so do the administrative tasks.

- Use unique names. Each subdomain must have a unique name within its parent domain to ensure that the name is unique throughout the DNS namespace.

- Use simple names. Simple and precise domain names are easier for users to remember and enable users to search intuitively and locate Web sites or other computers on the Internet or an intranet.

- Avoid lengthy domain names. Domain names can be up to 63 characters, including the periods. The total length of an FQDN cannot exceed 255 characters. Case-sensitive naming is not supported.

- Use standard DNS characters and Unicode characters:

    - Windows 2000 supports the following standard DNS characters: A through Z, a through z, 0 through 9, and the hyphen (-), as defined in RFC 1035.

    - The DNS Service also supports the Unicode character set. The Unicode character set, which includes additional characters not found in the American Standard Code for Information Exchange (ASCII) character set, is required for languages such as French, German, and Spanish.

Note Use Unicode characters only if all servers running the DNS service in your environment support Unicode. For more information on the Unicode character set, read RFC 2044 by searching for "RFC 2044" with your Web browser.

Zones

A zone represents a discrete portion of the domain namespace. Zones provide a way to partition the domain namespace into manageable sections.

Multiple zones in a domain namespace are used to distribute administrative tasks to different groups. For example, Figure 9.11 depicts the microsoft.com domain namespace divided into two zones. The two zones allow one administrator to manage the microsoft and sales domains and another administrator to manage the development domain.

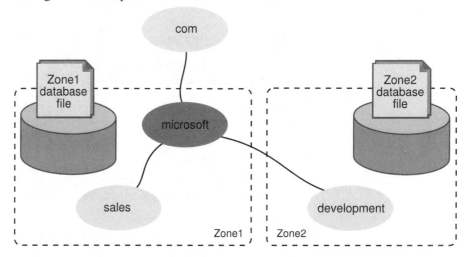

Figure 9.11 Domain namespace divided into zones

A zone must encompass a contiguous domain namespace. For example, as Figure 9.11 shows, you can create a zone for sales.microsoft.com and the parent domain microsoft.com because these zones are contiguous. However, you cannot create a zone that consists of only the sales.microsoft.com domain and the development.microsoft.com domain because these two domains are not contiguous.

The name-to-IP-address mappings for a zone are stored in the zone database file. Each zone is anchored to a specific domain, referred to as the zone's root domain. The zone database file does not necessarily contain information for all subdomains of the zone's root domain, only those subdomains within the zone.

In Figure 9.11, the root domain for Zone1 is microsoft, and its zone file contains the name-to-IP-address mappings for the microsoft and sales domains. The root domain for Zone2 is development, and its zone file contains the name-to-IP-address mappings for the development domain only. The zone file for Zone1 does not contain the name-to-IP address mappings for the development domain, although development is a subdomain of the microsoft domain.

Name Servers

A DNS name server stores the zone database file. Name servers can store data for one zone or multiple zones. A name server is said to have authority for the domain namespace that the zone encompasses.

There must be at least one name server for a zone. However, a zone can have multiple name servers associated with it. One of these servers contains the master zone database file, which is also referred to as the primary zone database file, for that zone. Changes to a zone, such as adding domains or hosts, are performed on the server that contains the primary zone database file. Any other name servers associated with the zone act as a backup to the name server containing the primary zone database file. These name servers contain a secondary zone database file.

Multiple name servers provide several advantages:

- **Performing zone transfers** The additional name servers obtain a copy of the zone database file from the name server that contains the primary database zone file. This is called a zone transfer. These name servers periodically query the name server containing the primary zone database file for updated zone data.

- **Providing redundancy** If the name server containing the primary zone database file fails, the additional name servers can provide service.

- **Improving access speed for remote locations** If a number of clients are in remote locations, use additional name servers to reduce query traffic across slow WAN links.

- **Reducing loads** The additional name servers reduce the load on the name server containing the primary zone database file. Windows 2000 also supports directory-integrated zone storage by using the Active Directory database. Zones stored this way are located in the Active Directory tree under the domain object container. Each directory-integrated zone is stored in a DNS zone container object identified by the name you choose for the zone when you create it.

Overview of the Name Resolution Process

Name resolution is the process of resolving names to IP addresses. Name resolution is similar to looking up a name in a telephone book, where the name is associated with a telephone number. For example, when you connect to the Microsoft Web site, you use the name www.microsoft.com. DNS resolves www.microsoft.com to its associated IP address. The mapping of names to IP addresses is stored in the DNS distributed database.

DNS name servers resolve forward and reverse lookup queries. A forward lookup query resolves a name to an IP address. A reverse lookup query resolves an IP address to a name. A name server can resolve a query only for a zone for which it has authority. If a name server cannot resolve the query, it passes the query to other name servers that can resolve the query. The name server caches the query results to reduce the DNS traffic on the network.

Forward Lookup Query

The DNS Service uses a client/server model for name resolution. To resolve a forward lookup query, a client passes a query to a local name server. The local name server either resolves the query or queries another name server for resolution.

Figure 9.12 illustrates the process of a client querying a name server for an IP address of www.microsoft.com. The numbers in the figures are described in the steps that follow the diagram.

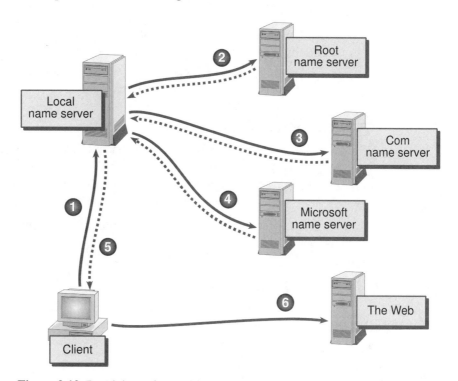

Figure 9.12 Resolving a forward lookup query

1. The client passes a forward lookup query for www.microsoft.com to its local name server.

2. The local name server checks its zone database file to determine whether it contains the name-to-IP address-mapping for the client query. Because the local name server does not have authority for the microsoft.com domain, it passes the query to one of the DNS root servers, requesting resolution of the host name. The root name server sends back a referral to the com name servers.

3. The local name server sends a request to a com name server, which responds with a referral to the Microsoft name servers.

4. The local name server sends a request to the Microsoft name server. The Microsoft name server receives the request. Because the Microsoft name server has authority for that portion of the domain namespace, it returns the IP address for www.microsoft.com to the local name server.

5. The local name server sends the IP address for www.microsoft.com to the client.

6. The name resolution is complete, and the client can now access www.microsoft.com by its IP address.

Name Server Caching

When a name server is processing a query, it might be required to send out several queries to find the answer. With each query, the name server discovers other name servers that have authority for a portion of the domain namespace. The name server caches these query results to reduce network traffic.

When a name server receives a query result, the following actions take place:

1. The name server caches the query result for a specified amount of time, referred to as TTL. The zone that provided the query results specifies the TTL. TTL is configured by using the DNS snap-in. The default value is 60 minutes.

2. Once the name server caches the query result, TTL starts counting down from its original value.

3. When TTL expires, the name server deletes the query result from its cache.

Caching query results enable the name server to quickly resolve other queries to the same portion of the domain namespace.

Note Use shorter TTL values to help ensure that data about the domain namespace is more current across the network. Although shorter TTL values increase the load on name servers and longer TTL values decrease the time required to resolve information, the client will not receive the updated information until the TTL expires and a new query to that portion of the domain namespace is resolved.

Reverse Lookup Query

A reverse lookup query maps an IP address to a name. Troubleshooting tools, such as the nslookup command-line utility, use reverse lookup queries to report back host names. Additionally, certain applications implement security based on the ability to connect to names, not IP addresses.

Because the DNS distributed database is indexed by name and not by IP address, a reverse lookup query would require an exhaustive search of every domain name. To solve this problem, a special second-level domain called in-addr.arpa was created.

The in-addr.arpa domain follows the same hierarchical naming scheme as the rest of the domain namespace; however, it is based on IP addresses, not domain names, using the following guidelines:

- Subdomains are named after the numbers in the dotted-decimal representation of IP addresses.

- The order of the IP address octets is reversed.

- Companies administer subdomains of the in-addr.arpa domain based on their assigned IP addresses and subnet mask.

For example, a company that has an assigned IP address range of 169.254.16.0 to 169.254.16.255 with a subnet mask of 255.255.255.0 has authority over the 16.254.169.in-addr.arpa domain.

Installing the DNS Service

To implement DNS, you must configure the server and then install the DNS service. The DNS server must be configured with a static IP address. In addition, you should configure the TCP/IP properties so that the DNS settings point back to the server. You can install the DNS service anytime after or during the installation of Windows 2000 Server.

The DNS installation process does the following:

- Installs the DNS snap-in, and adds a shortcut to Administrative Tools on the Start menu. The DNS snap-in is used to manage local and remote DNS name servers.

- Adds the following key for the DNS Service to the registry:

    HKEY_LOCAL_MACHINE\System\CurrentControlSet\Services\DNS

- Creates the %systemroot%\System32\DNS folder, which contains the DNS database files.

Generally, you will not need to edit the DNS database files. However, you might use them to troubleshoot DNS. The DNS service provides a set of sample files, which are added to the %systemroot%\System32\DNS\Samples folder after you have installed the DNS service.

> **Note** The %systemroot%\System32\DNS\Samples folder includes the BOOT file. The BOOT file is not defined in an RFC and is not needed for RFC compliance. However, the BOOT file is a part of the Berkeley Internet Name Daemon (BIND)–specific implementation of DNS. If you are migrating from a BIND DNS server, copying the BOOT file allows easy migration of your existing configuration.

Configuring the DNS Service

Once the DNS service is installed, you are ready to configure and manage the service.

The DNS Snap-In

You can use the DNS snap-in, shown in Figure 9.13, for all configuration and management tasks of the DNS server. The DNS snap-in allows you to configure forward lookup zones and reverse lookup zones, add resource records to the zone database file, and configure the DNS service for Dynamic DNS (DDNS), which enables automatic updates to your zone files by other servers or services.

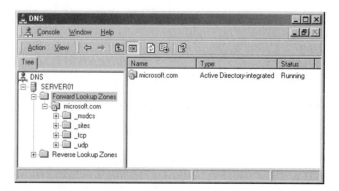

Figure 9.13 The DNS snap-in

You can access the DNS snap-in as a stand-alone MMC console or through the Computer Management snap-in, under Services And Applications. The DNS snap-in can be installed by running Adminpak.msi or by installing the DNS service. Before the DNS service is installed, the DNS snap-in is used to manage remote servers running the DNS service.

Creating Forward Lookup Zones

A forward lookup zone enables forward lookup queries. On name servers, you must configure at least one forward lookup zone for the DNS Service to work.

To create a new forward lookup zone, select the Forward Lookup Zone folder and then select New Zone from the Action menu. The New Zone wizard guides you through the process of creating a new forward lookup zone. The wizard presents the following configuration options: Zone Type, Zone Name, and Zone File.

Zone Type

There are three types of zones that you can configure:

- **Active Directory–integrated** An Active Directory–integrated zone is the master copy of a new zone. The zone uses Active Directory services to store and replicate zone files. This option provides secure updates and integrated storage. Standard zone transfers do not occur with Active Directory–integrated zones. Instead, the zone database file is replicated when Active Directory store replication occurs.

- **Standard primary** A standard primary zone is the master copy of a new zone and is stored in a standard text file. You administer and maintain a primary zone on the computer at which you create the zone. This option facilitates the exchange of DNS data with other DNS servers that use text-based storage methods.

- **Standard secondary** A standard secondary zone is a replica of an existing zone. Secondary zones are read-only and are stored in standard text files. A primary zone must be configured in order to create a secondary zone. When creating a secondary zone, you must specify the DNS server, called the master server, which transfers zone information to the name server containing the standard secondary zone. You create a secondary zone to provide redundancy and to reduce the load on the name server containing the primary zone database file.

Zone Name

Typically, a zone is named after the highest domain in the hierarchy that the zone encompasses—that is, the root domain for the zone. For example, for a zone that encompasses both microsoft.com and sales.microsoft.com, the zone name would be microsoft.com.

Zone File

The zone file refers to the database file name, which defaults to the zone name with a .dns extension. For example, if your zone name is microsoft.com, the default zone database file name is microsoft.com.dns.

When migrating a zone from another server, you can import the existing zone file. You must place the existing file in the %systemroot%\System32\DNS folder on the target computer before creating the new zone. There are two zone transfer methods for zone transfer: full-zone transfer (AXFR) and incremental-zone transfer (IXFR). AXFR is the standard way of transferring zone information, and it is essentially a zone file copy. Windows 2000 supports AXFR, but it also supports IXFR, which uses less bandwidth since only zone changes are replicated.

Creating Reverse Lookup Zones

A reverse lookup zone enables reverse lookup queries. Reverse lookup zones are not required. However, a reverse lookup zone is required to run troubleshooting tools, such as nslookup, and to record a name instead of an IP address in Microsoft Internet Information Services (IIS) log files.

To create a new reverse lookup zone, select the Reverse Lookup Zones folder and then select New Zone. The New Zone wizard guides you through the process of creating a reverse lookup zone. The wizard presents the following configuration options: Zone Type, Reverse Lookup Zone, and Zone File.

Zone Type

The zone types are the same as the zone type options available when creating a forward lookup zone: Active Directory–integrated, standard primary, and standard secondary.

Reverse Lookup Zone

Enter your network ID or the name of the reverse lookup zone. If you use a zero in the network ID, it will appear in the zone name. For example, network ID 169 would create zone 169.in-addr.arpa, and network ID 169.0 would create zone 0.169.in-addr.arpa.

Zone File

The network ID and subnet mask determine the default zone file name. DNS reverses the IP octets and adds the in-addr.arpa suffix. For example, the reverse lookup zone for the 169.254 network becomes 254.169.in-addr.arpa.dns.

When migrating a zone from another server, you can import the existing zone file. You must place the existing file in the %systemroot%\System32\DNS directory on the target computer before creating the new zone.

Adding Resource Records

Once you create your zones, you can use the DNS snap-in to add resource records. Resource records are entries in the zone database file. Each resource record identifies a particular resource within the database. To add a resource record, select the zone to which you want to add the record and then select Other New Record from the Action menu. When the Resource Record Type dialog box appears, you can create records for any of the record types listed in the Select A Resource Record Type list.

There are many types of resource records. When a zone is created, DNS automatically adds two resource records: the Start of Authority (SOA) and the Name Server (NS) records. An SOA record identifies which name server is the authoritative source of information for data within this domain. The first record in the zone database file must be the SOA record. An NS record lists the name servers that are assigned to a particular domain. Both of these record types can be configured in the Properties dialog box for the specific forward lookup zone.

For a list of the other types of resource records, along with a description of each type, open the Resource Record Type dialog box and view the record types listed in the Select A Resource Record Type list. When you select a record type, a description for that record type appears at the bottom of the dialog box.

Note For more information on resource records, see RFC 1034, RFC 2052, and RFC 2065. Use your Web browser to search for "RFC 1034," "RFC 2052," and "RFC 2065." For more information on how DNS works, read *DNS and BIND* by Paul Albitz and Cricket Liu, published by O'Reilly and Associates, Inc. (1998)

Configuring Dynamic DNS

The DNS Service includes a dynamic update capability called Dynamic DNS (DDNS). With DNS, when there are changes to the domain for which a name server has authority, you must manually update the zone database file on the primary name server. With DDNS, name servers and clients within a network automatically update the zone database files.

Dynamic Updates

You can configure a list of authorized servers to initiate dynamic updates. This list can include secondary name servers, domain controllers, and other servers that perform network registration for clients, such as servers running the DHCP Service or WINS.

The update sequence consists of the following steps:

1. A client, using an SOA query, locates the primary DNS server and zone authoritative for the record to be registered.

2. The client sends to the located DNS server an assertion or prerequisite-only update to verify an existing registration. If the registration does not exist, the client sends the appropriate dynamic update package to register the record.

3. If the update fails, the client attempts to register the record with the other primary DNS server if the authoritative zone is multimaster. If all primary DNS servers fail to process the dynamic update, it is repeated after 5 minutes, and if it fails again, after another 10 minutes. If registration still fails, the described pattern of the registration attempts are repeated 50 minutes after the last retry.

Every computer running Windows 2000 attempts the registration of its A and PTR records. An A record, also known as the host record, provides the name-to-address mapping, and the PTR record, also known as the pointer record, provides the address-to-name mapping for the computer sending the registration. The service that actually generates the DNS dynamic updates is the DHCP client. The DHCP client service runs on every Windows 2000 computer, regardless of whether or not it is configured as a DHCP client.

DDNS and DHCP

DDNS interacts with the DHCP Service to maintain synchronized name-to-IP-address mappings for network hosts. By default, the DHCP Service allows clients to add their own A (host) records to the zone, and the DHCP Service adds the PTR (pointer) record to the zone. The DHCP Service cleans up both the A records and PTR records in the zone when the lease expires.

To configure a zone for DDNS, use the DNS snap-in. Select the appropriate zone, and then select Properties from the Action menu. On the General tab of the Properties dialog box, select Yes from the Allow Dynamic Updates drop-down list.

To configure the server to send dynamic updates, use the DHCP snap-in to configure the DHCP server to point to the appropriate DNS servers.

Note For more information on Dynamic DNS, read RFC 2136 and RFC 2137. Use your Web browser to search for "RFC 2136" and "RFC 2137." You can also find information about DDNS on the Supplemental Course Materials CD-ROM (\chapt09\articles\w2kDNS.doc) that accompanies this book.

Exercise 4: Configuring the DNS Service

In this exercise, you delete and re-create a forward lookup zone, create a reverse lookup zone, configure Dynamic DNS, and test your DNS Server. You will use both Server01 and Server02 to complete this exercise.

Note In Chapter 6, "Exercise 1: Installing Active Directory Services," DNS was installed automatically because Server01, as a stand-alone server, was not using a DNS for name resolution. Installing DNS is similar to installing DHCP and WINS—DNS is a component of Networking Services. If you wish, navigate to the details of Networking Services to verify that DNS is installed.

▸ **Procedure 1: Confirming a forward lookup zone and creating a reverse lookup zone**

In this procedure, you delete the Active Directory–integrated forward lookup zone type created as a result of the DNS installation. You then create standard primary forward and reverse lookup zones.

1. Log on to Server01 as Administrator with a password of "password."

2. Click Start, point to Programs, point to Administrative Tools, and then click DNS.

   The DNS snap-in appears.

3. Maximize the DNS snap-in.

4. In the console tree, expand SERVER01 and then expand the Forward Lookup Zones folder.

5. Select the microsoft.com container.

6. Click the Action menu, and then click Delete.

7. A message appears asking whether you are sure you want to delete. Click OK.

   A DNS warning message appears.

8. Read the DNS warning message, and then click Yes.

9. Click the Action menu, and then click New Zone.

   The New Zone wizard appears.

10. Click Next.

    The Zone Type screen appears.

11. Ensure that the Standard Primary radio button is selected, and then click Next.

    The Zone Name screen appears.

12. Type microsoft.com, and then click Next.

13. The Zone File screen appears.

14. Ensure that the Create A New File With This File Name radio button is selected and that the name of the file to be created is microsoft.com.dns.

15. Click Next.

    The Completing The New Zone Wizard screen appears.

16. Review the information on this screen, and then click Finish.

    The DNS snap-in appears.

17. Click microsoft.com in the console tree.

    Notice that Start of Authority (SOA), Name Server (NS), and the Host (A) records are generated.

    Server01 is now able to resolve host names to IP addresses using the Standard Primary lookup zone file.

18. In the console tree, click the Reverse Lookup Zones container.

19. Click the Action menu, and then click New Zone.

    The New Zone wizard appears.

20. Click Next.

    The Zone Type screen appears.

21. Ensure that the Standard Primary radio button is selected, and then click Next.

    The Reverse Lookup Zone screen appears.

22. Ensure that The Network ID radio button is selected and type 192.168.1 in the Network ID box.

    The Reverse Lookup Zone Name text box at the bottom of the screen now contains 1.168.192.in-addr.arpa.

23. Click Next.

    The Zone File screen appears.

24. Ensure that the Create A New File With This File Name radio button is selected and that the name of the file to be created is 1.168.192.in-addr.arpa.dns.

25. Click Next.

    The Completing The New Zone Wizard screen appears.

26. Review the information on the screen, and then click Finish.

    The DNS Service on Server01 is now capable of providing host names when given a host address in its subnet.

Note After creating a DNS, DNS configuration information is commonly added to the DHCP Service. You completed this procedure in the DHCP exercise earlier in this chapter.

▶ **Procedure 2: Configuring dynamic DNS service**

In this procedure, you configure the DNS Service to allow dynamic updates. Complete this procedure using the DNS snap-in on Server01.

1. In the console tree, select the microsoft.com container. This folder is located under the Forward Lookup Zones folder.

2. Click the Action menu, and then click Properties.

    The microsoft.com Properties dialog box appears.

3. In the Allow Dynamic Updates drop-down list box, select Yes, and then click OK.

    This part of the procedure configured Dynamic DNS for the forward lookup zone.

4. In the console tree, select the 192.168.1.x Subnet container.

5. Click the Action menu, and then click Properties.

   The 192.168.1.x Subnet Properties dialog box appears.

6. In the Allow Dynamic Updates drop-down list box, select Yes, and then click OK.

   This part of the procedure configured Dynamic DNS for the reverse lookup zone.

7. Minimize the DNS snap-in.

▶ **Procedure 3: Testing and further configuring DNS**

In this procedure, you confirm that the DNS Service is working properly and you further configure the DNS using the DNS snap-in.

1. On Server01, restore the minimized DNS snap-in.

2. In the console tree, click SERVER01.

3. Click the Action menu, and then click Properties.

   The SERVER01 Properties dialog box appears.

4. Click the Monitoring tab.

5. Under Select A Test Type, select the A Simple Query Against This DNS Server, and the A Recursive Query To Other DNS Servers check boxes.

6. Click Test Now.

   In the Test Results box, you will see PASS in both columns. If you are on a stand-alone server, you will see FAIL in the Recursive Query column.

7. Click OK.

   The DNS snap-in appears.

8. In the console tree, click Reverse Lookup Zones.

9. Click 192.168.1.x Subnet.

   Notice that this reverse lookup zone contains two records, the SOA and the NS records, as shown in the details pane.

10. In the console tree, click 192.168.1.x Subnet.

11. Click the Action menu, and then click New Pointer.

    The New Resource Record dialog box appears.

12. In the Host IP Number box, type **201** in the highlighted fourth octet.

13. In the Host Name text box, type **server01.microsoft.com**. (Make sure to include the period after the word com.)

14. Click OK.

    A Pointer record appears in the details pane.

15. Close the DNS snap-in.

16. Open a command prompt on Server01 or Server02.

17. At the command prompt, type **nslookup** and then press Enter.

    From Server01, the default server is listed as localhost and the address is listed as 127.0.0.1.

    From Server02, the default server is listed as server01.microsoft.com and the address is listed as 192.168.1.201.

    Both listings are pointing to server01.microsoft.com. The listing appearing at the command prompt on Server01 is the server's loop-back address.

18. Type **ls microsoft.com**.

    Notice that the NS and A records are displayed as a result of this DNS query.

19. Type **exit**, and then press Enter.

    Close the command prompt.

Configuring a DNS Client

Once you install and configure the DNS service on computers running Windows 2000 Server, you can configure your Windows 2000 DNS clients. You must ensure that TCP/IP is installed on the client before you can configure the client to use the DNS Service. Once TCP/IP is installed on the client, open the Internet Protocol (TCP/IP) Properties dialog box (Figure 9.4). From there, you can configure automatic DNS address acquisition (provided by a DHCP server) or specify the IP addresses of a preferred and alternate DNS. You can configure more advanced settings for DNS by first clicking the Advanced button. From the Advanced TCP/IP Settings dialog box (Figure 9.14), click the DNS tab to configure DNS settings. You will need to supply the IP address or addresses of the DNS servers. These should be listed in order of use. You can also specify DNS settings that assist in resolving host names not specified by their FQDN, and you can configure DDNS registration settings from this dialog box.

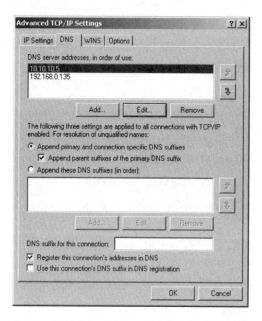

Figure 9.14 The Advanced TCP/IP Settings dialog box showing two DNS addresses in order of use, name resolution properties, and automatic registration settings

Troubleshooting the DNS Service

You can troubleshoot name servers by using the monitoring and logging options in the DNS snap-in or by using the nslookup command-line utility.

Monitoring the DNS Server

The DNS snap-in allows you to monitor the DNS Service. Select the name server, and then select Properties from the Action menu. In the Properties dialog box, select the Monitoring tab. You can test the name server by performing two types of queries:

- **Simple query** Select this type of query to perform a simple query test of the DNS server. This is a local test that uses the DNS client on this computer to query the name server.

- **Recursive query** Select this type of query to perform a more complex, recursive query test of the name server. This query tests the name server by forwarding a recursive query to another name server.

Setting Logging Options

The DNS snap-in allows you to set additional logging options for debugging purposes. Open the Properties dialog box for the name server, and select the Logging tab. You can select from 11 options: Query, Notify, Update, Questions, Answers, Send, Receive, UDP, TCP, Full Packets, and Write Through. Information from any of the selected options is saved to the log file.

Using Nslookup

The nslookup command-line utility is the primary diagnostic tool for the DNS service, and it is installed when the TCP/IP protocol is installed. Use nslookup to view any resource record and to direct queries to any name server, including UNIX DNS implementations.

Nslookup has two modes: interactive and noninteractive.

- When you require more than one piece of data, use interactive mode. To run interactive mode, type **nslookup** at the command prompt. To exit interactive mode, type **exit**.

- When you require a single piece of data, use noninteractive mode. Type the nslookup syntax at the command line, and the data is returned. The syntax for nslookup is as follows:

```
nslookup [-option ...] [computer-to-find | - [server]]
```

The following table describes the optional parameters for nslookup.

Syntax	Description
-option...	Specifies one or more nslookup commands. For a list of commands, type a question mark (?) in interactive mode to open Help.
computer-to-find	If the computer to find is an IP address, nslookup returns the host name. If the computer to find is a name, nslookup returns an IP address. If the computer to find is a name and does not have a trailing period, the default DNS domain name is appended to the name. To look up a computer outside the current DNS domain, append a period to the name.
server	Use this server as the DNS name server. If the server is omitted, the currently configured default name server is used.

Lesson Summary

DNS is a distributed database used in TCP/IP networks to translate computer names to IP addresses. The domain namespace is the naming scheme that provides the hierarchical structure for the DNS database. The hierarchical structure of the domain namespace consists of a root domain, top-level domains, second-level domains, and host names. Zones provide a way to partition the domain namespace into manageable sections. A zone must encompass a contiguous domain namespace. A DNS name server stores the zone database file and can be authoritative for more than one zone. Name resolution is the process of resolving names to IP addresses. DNS name servers resolve forward and reverse lookup queries. A forward lookup query resolves a name to an IP address. A reverse lookup query resolves an IP address to a name. To implement DNS, you must install the DNS Service and then configure the server by using the DNS snap-in. You can use the DNS snap-in to configure forward lookup zones and reverse lookup zones, add resource records to the zone database file, and configure the DNS Service for DDNS, which enables automatic updates to your zone files by other servers or services. Along with setting up DNS on a Windows 2000 Server computer, you must configure the Windows 2000 client. To configure a DNS client, TCP/IP must be installed and the appropriate DNS settings must be selected in the Internet Protocol (TCP/IP) Properties dialog box. Once DNS is set up in your network, you can troubleshoot the DNS service by using the monitoring and logging options in the DNS snap-in and by using the nslookup command-line utility.

Review

The following questions are intended to reinforce key information presented in this chapter. If you are unable to answer a question, review the appropriate lesson and then try the question again. Answers to the questions can be found in Appendix A, "Questions and Answers."

1. Your computer receives its TCP/IP configuration information from a DHCP server in the network. After DHCP information is received, you can connect to any host on your own subnet, but you cannot connect to or successfully ping any host on a remote subnet. You checked the DHCP Service to ensure that the router information specified for your address scope is correct. What is the likely cause of the problem and how would you fix it?

2. You installed NWLink IPX/SPX and GSNW. After installing these components, you cannot communicate with one of the NetWare servers on your network. You have no trouble accessing this NetWare server from your client computer running Windows 2000 Professional, NWLink IPX/SPX, and CSNW. You must communicate with this NetWare server from your Windows 2000 Server because the NetWare server contains resources you must make available to users running the Microsoft Network Client. What is the likely cause of the problem?

3. You notice that access to network resources seems slower on your computer running Windows 2000 Server than from another identical computer running Windows 2000 Server on the same network. The only difference you can determine is that the slower Windows 2000 Server computer is running multiple protocols. How could network protocol binding order potentially resolve this problem?

4. When do DHCP clients attempt to renew their leases?

5. Why might you create multiple scopes on a DHCP server?

6. How can you manually restore the DHCP database?

7. What are the configuration requirements for a WINS server?

8. Why would you want to have multiple name servers?

9. Why do you create forward and reverse lookup zones?

10. What is the difference between Dynamic DNS and DNS?

CHAPTER 10

Routing and Remote Access Service

About This Chapter

The Routing and Remote Access Service (RRAS) provides integrated multiprotocol routing and virtual private network (VPN) server services for Microsoft Windows 2000 Server computers. The service was first introduced in Windows NT Server 4.0 to provide services and components that turned the computer into a mid-range dynamic software router. This chapter introduces you to how RRAS is implemented in Windows 2000. The chapter also covers features of the service, how remote access and virtual private networks are implemented, and tools available in Windows 2000 to administer RRAS.

Before You Begin

To complete the lessons in this chapter, you must have

- Server01 and Server02 running Windows 2000 Server.

- An installed and configured modem in Server01. The installation of Windows 2000 Server may have automatically detected your modem. If not, use the Add/Remote Hardware application in Control Panel to install the software to support your modem.

- Completed the exercises in the previous chapters.

Lesson 1: Introduction to the Routing and Remote Access Service

Multiprotocol routing support for the Windows NT family of operating systems began with Windows NT 3.51 Service Pack 2, which included components for the Routing Information Protocol (RIP) for IP, RIP for IPX, and the Service Advertising Protocol (SAP) for IPX. Windows NT 4.0 also includes these components. In June 1996, Microsoft released RRAS for Windows NT 4.0, a component that replaced the Windows NT 4.0 remote access service, RIP for IP, RIP for IPX, and SAP for IPX services with a single integrated service providing both remote access and multiprotocol routing. This lesson focuses on how RRAS is implemented in Windows 2000. It discusses installation and configuration, as well authentication and authorization.

After this lesson, you will be able to

- Describe RRAS in Windows 2000

- Use the Routing And Remote Access snap-in to configure and enable RRAS

Estimated lesson time: 30 minutes

Windows 2000 Routing and Remote Access Service

RRAS for Windows 2000 Server continues the evolution of multiprotocol routing and remote access services for the Microsoft Windows platform. When RRAS was implemented in Windows NT 4.0, it added support for the following features:

- RIP version 2 for IP (RIP for IP version 1 is still supported)

- Open Shortest Path First (OSPF) routing protocol for IP

- Demand-dial routing (routing over persistent or on-demand WAN links such as analog phone lines)

- Internet Control Message Protocol (ICMP) router discovery

- Remote Authentication Dial-In User Service (RADIUS) client to benefit from the services provided by a RADIUS server

- RADIUS server for providing centralized authentication, authorization, accounting, and remote access policy to dial-up and VPN remote access clients (included with the Windows NT 4.0 Option Pack)

- IP and IPX packet filtering for protocol-level security

- A graphical user interface (GUI) administrative program called Routing and RAS Admin and a command-line utility called Routemon

Windows 2000 builds on RRAS in Windows NT 4.0 and adds the following features:

- Internet Group Management Protocol (IGMP) and support for multicast boundaries

- Network address translation with addressing and name resolution components that simplify the connection of a small office/home office (SOHO) network to the Internet

- Integrated AppleTalk routing

- Layer 2 Tunneling Protocol (L2TP) over IP Security (IPSec) support for VPN connections

- Improved administration and management tools. (The graphical user interface program is the Routing And Remote Access snap-in. The command-line utility is netsh (Net Shell).)

- Improved IAS

RRAS is fully integrated with the Windows 2000 Server operating system. RRAS works with a wide variety of hardware platforms and hundreds of network adapters; the result is a lower cost solution than many midrange dedicated router or remote access server products.

RRAS is extensible with application programming interfaces (APIs) that third-party developers can use to create custom networking solutions and that vendors can use to participate in the growing business of open internetworking.

The combined features of Windows 2000 RRAS allow a Windows 2000 Server computer to function as a multiprotocol router, a demand-dial router, and a remote access server.

Multiprotocol Router

The computer running RRAS can route IP, IPX, and AppleTalk simultaneously. All routable protocols and routing protocols are configured from the same administrative utility.

Demand-Dial Router

A computer running RRAS can route IP and IPX over on-demand or persistent WAN links, such as analog telephone lines or Integrated Services Digital Network (ISDN), or over VPN connections by using either PPTP or L2TP over IPSec.

Remote Access Server

A computer running RRAS can act as a remote access server providing remote access connectivity to dial-up or VPN remote access clients that use IP, IPX, AppleTalk, or NetBEUI. The combination of routing and remote access services on the same computer creates a Windows 2000 remote access router.

Combining Routing and Remote Access

Before RRAS was implemented in Windows NT, the routing services and remote access services worked separately. However, the two services have been combined because of the Point-to-Point Protocol (PPP), which is the protocol suite that is commonly used to negotiate point-to-point connections for remote access clients. PPP provides link parameter negotiation, the exchange of authentication credentials, and network layer protocol negotiation. For example, when you dial an Internet service provider (ISP) via PPP, you agree to the size of the packets you are sending and how they are framed (link negotiation), you log on by using a user name and password (authentication), and you obtain an IP address (network layer negotiation).

Demand-dial routing connections also use PPP to provide the same kinds of services as remote access connections (link negotiation, authentication, and network layer negotiation). Therefore, the integration of routing (which includes demand-dial routing) and remote access is done to leverage the PPP client/server infrastructure available for the remote access components.

The PPP infrastructure of Windows 2000 Server includes support for the following types of access:

- Dial-up remote access (over dial-up equipment such as analog telephone lines, and ISDN) as either the client or server

- VPN remote access as either the client or server

- On-demand or persistent dial-up demand-dial routing (over dial-up equipment such as analog telephone lines, and ISDN) as either the calling router or the answering router

- On-demand or persistent VPN demand-dial routing as either the calling router or the answering router

LAN and WAN Support

RRAS can run over any of the LAN and WAN network adapters supported by Windows 2000 Server, including cards from Eicon, Cisco, SysKonnect, Allied, and US Robotics. For more information about supported network adapter cards, see the Windows 2000 Hardware Compatibility List at *http://www.microsoft.com*.

Installation and Configuration

Unlike RRAS for Windows NT 4.0 and most network services of Windows 2000, you do not elect to install or uninstall RRAS through Add/Remove Programs in Control Panel. Windows 2000 RRAS is automatically installed in a disabled state.

You can use the Routing And Remote Access snap-in to enable and configure RRAS. By default, a local Windows 2000 Server is listed as a RRAS server as shown in Figure 10.1.

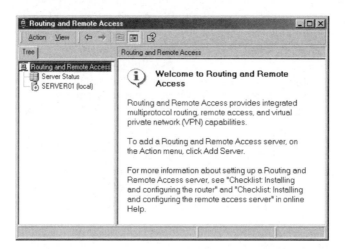

Figure 10.1 Routing And Remote Access snap-in showing the local server, SERVER01, as a RRAS server in a disabled state

You can add additional computers by selecting either the root of the console tree or the Server Status node (Figure 10.1) and then selecting Add Server from the Action menu. Once the server is added in the console tree, select the server that you want to enable and then select Configure And Enable Routing And Remote Access from the Action menu. Follow the instructions in the Routing And Remote Access Server Setup wizard.

Once the wizard has finished, the remote access router is enabled and configured based on your selections in the wizard. To do further configuration, use the Routing And Remote Access snap-in or the netsh command-line utility.

Note If you type **?** after entering the netsh command mode, the help information may scroll beyond the window size. If it does, you can scroll the command-prompt window, maximize the window, or run in full-screen mode.

Note that each computer on the intranet served by the RRAS server should use a private IP address in one of the following blocks of addresses:

Network address blocks	Address class
10.0.0.0 – 10.255.255.255	A
172.16.0.0 – 172.31.255.255	B
192.168.0.0 – 192.168.255.255	C

The Internet Assigned Numbers Authority (IANA) has specifically reserved these addresses for private network use. See RFC 1918 for more information.

Exercise 1: Enabling RRAS and Examining a Basic Configuration

RRAS is in a disabled state on Server01. In this exercise you will enable RRAS and then examine the default configuration of RRAS. In later exercises, you will reconfigure RRAS to meet a more complex set of routing and remote access requirements. Complete this exercise on Server01.

▶ **Procedure 1: Enabling RRAS**

Completing this procedure enables RRAS on Server01. Before starting this procedure, verify that a modem is installed in Server01 and that it is recognized by the operating system. You can verify this by using the Add/Remove Hardware application in Control Panel.

1. Log on to Server01 as administrator with a password of "password."

2. Click Start, point to Programs, point to Administrative Tools and then click Routing And Remote Access.

   The Routing And Remote Access snap-in appears and Server01(local) is highlighted.

3. Maximize the Routing And Remote Access snap-in and read the message appearing in the details pane.

4. Click the Action menu and then click Configure And Enable Routing And Remote Access.

The Routing And Remote Access Server Setup wizard appears.

5. Click Next.

The Common Configurations screen appears. Notice that there are five paths that you can follow in configuring an RRAS server. In the next step, you will examine these various options before configuring the RRAS server to act as a RAS server.

6. Verify that the Internet Connection Server radio button is selected and click Next.

The Internet Connection Server Setup screen appears. Notice that the RRAS server is configured in one of two ways in order to provide all computers on the network with access to the Internet. The first method, Internet Connection Sharing (ICS), instructs you to use the Network and Dial-Up Connections folder in order to configure this option. The properties of each dial-up connection contain a Sharing tab where this feature is configured. The second method, Network Address Translation (NAT), is configured from this wizard. NAT allows you to configure the server to send and receive packets from the Internet on behalf of other client computers on the intranet. Only the hardware on the RRAS server that connects to the Internet requires an IP address that is valid and legal on the Internet.

7. Click Back.

The Common Configurations screen appears. Read but do not complete the navigation procedures in this paragraph. Select the Remote Access Server radio button to configure the RRAS server for RAS dial-in access. Select the Virtual Private Network (VPN) server radio button to configure the server for VPN (PPTP and L2TP) access. VPN allows remote access clients to connect to a public network like the Internet, and then establishes a secure remote access connection to the RRAS server. Select the Network Router radio button to configure the RRAS server so that packets can be transmitted between networks. Select the Manually Configured Server radio button to use the Routing And Remote Access snap-in to configure the RRAS server.

Note An RRAS server can be configured for a combination of options appearing on the Common Configurations screen. The purpose of this screen is to help you get started with RRAS. Further configuration is completed using the Routing And Remote Access snap-in or the Net Shell utility.

---

8. Select the Manually Configured Server radio button and then click Next.

   The Completing The Routing And Remote Access Server Setup Wizard screen appears.

9. Click Finish.

   A Routing And Remote Access message box appears stating that the Routing and Remote Access Service has been installed. You are asked whether the service should be started.

10. Click Yes.

    The Starting Routing And Remote Access and Completing Initialization message boxes appear.

▶ Procedure 2: Examining a default RRAS configuration

In this procedure, you examine default remote access and router settings. This procedure is completed in the Routing And Remote Access snap-in. The purpose of this procedure is to introduce you to the features appearing in the Routing And Remote Access snap-in before you learn more about these features by studying the remaining lessons in this chapter.

Caution Do not change any settings while examining the default configuration.

---

1. In the console tree, expand Server01 (local).

   Notice that a green up arrow appears to the left Server01 (local). This means that RRAS is configured and enabled on the computer.

2. Click the Action menu.

   Notice that Disable Routing And Remote Access is now available because the RRAS server is enabled and configured.

3. Click Properties.

   The Server01 (Local) Properties dialog box appears.

   Notice that the default settings appearing on the General tab show that the server has been configured as both a LAN and demand-dial routing router and as a remote access server.

4. Click the Security tab.

   Notice that the Authentication Provider and the Accounting Provider uses Windows 2000 for both functions.

5. Click the Authentication Methods button.

Notice that MS-CHAP and MS-CHAP version 2 are selected. For troubleshooting authentication problems, you can check the Allow Remote Systems To Connect Without Authentication check box. Other authentication methods are selected based on the needs of the dial-up client and your security requirements.

6. Click Cancel and then click the IP tab.

Notice that the Enable IP Routing check box and the Allow IP-Based Remote Access And Demand-Dial Connections check box are selected. IP routing allows dial-up clients to access the entire network. If you want dial-up clients to access resources on the RRAS server only, clear this check box. The Allow IP-Based Remote Access And Demand-Dial Connections option allows RRAS to send IPCP to negotiate the use of IP over the remote access or demand-dial interface. Notice also that the IP tab is used to configure either IP address allocation via DHCP or a static pool configured on the RRAS server.

7. Click the PPP tab.

From this tab you configure global PPP support settings for remote access clients. These options will be discussed in Lesson 3, "Remote Access."

8. Click the Event Logging tab.

From here, you configure the amount of information you want to collect about RRAS events occurring on the server. For troubleshooting, click the Log The Maximum Amount Of Information radio button and select the Enable Point-To-Point Protocol (PPP) Logging check box. To optimize the server's performance, click the Disable Event Logging radio button.

9. Click Cancel.

10. In the console tree, click Routing Interfaces.

The list of router interfaces appears in the details pane. The Loopback interface is the local protocol stack on the RRAS server. Local Area Connection is the network interface card in the RRAS server connected to your network. Internal is the routing function in RRAS. If routing is disabled, then Internal has an Operational Status of Non-operational.

11. In the console tree, click Ports.

    Notice that your modem or WAN device is listed in the details pane. Also notice that the default settings for VPN is 5 PPTP miniports and 5 L2TP miniports. The Parallel Device(s) appearing in the details pane is available to support direct cable connections between two computers. If you have a single LPT port designated as LPT1, then the name of this connection is Direct Parallel (LPT1). If a remote client has connected to a port but performance is poor or you are troubleshooting the connection, select the port in which the client is connected, and from the Action menu, click Status. This shows you network registration, statistics, and error information about the connection.

12. Verify that Ports is selected in the console tree, click the Action menu, and then click Properties.

    The Ports Properties dialog box appears. From this dialog box, you configure the number of ports allowed for each port type (only applicable to VPN connections), and decide if connections on this port type are inbound only or inbound and outbound. You also configure the telephone number for the device. This feature is used if the Called-Station-ID is configured for remote access policy, the dial-up hardware and driver software do not support caller ID, or if you use multi-link with the bandwidth allocation protocol (BAP) enabled. If you are configuring a VPN port, enter the IP address of the port rather than a telephone number.

13. Click Cancel.

14. In the console tree, click Remote Access Clients.

    If a remote client is connected to the RRAS server, the details pane shows the connected user, call duration, and number of ports allocated to the call (multilink).

15. In the console tree, expand IP Routing and then click General.

    Notice that the information appearing in the details pane looks similar to the information appearing in the details pane of Routing Interfaces.

16. Click the Action menu and then click New Routing Protocol.

    The New Routing Protocol dialog box appears.

    Notice that there are three protocols appearing by default: NAT, OSPF, and RIP version 2. These protocols will be discussed in Lesson 2, "Features of RRAS."

17. Click Cancel.

18. Click Internal in the details pane and then click the Action menu.

    Notice that many options for monitoring the interface are available under the Action menu. The Properties option is used to configure general router settings in the RRAS server.

    Examine the properties of the Internal interface and the Local Area Connection interface and then return to the Routing And Remote Access snap-in console.

    The Static Routes node in the console tree is used to view and configure additional routes to other networks. This tool is the graphical equivalent of the Route command-line utility.

    The DHCP Relay Agent node allows DHCP request and response messages to be sent from one network to another. This feature allows a single server running the DHCP service to provide IP address configuration information to DHCP (modified BOOTP) and BOOTP-enabled clients on other networks accessible by the router.

    The IGMP node allows you to configure Internet Group Messaging Protocol settings.

19. In the console tree, click Remote Access Logging.

    Note If you are using a RADIUS server for authentication and logging, the Remote Access Logging folder does not appear in RRAS.

    Local File appears in the details pane and the description column shows the path to the LogFiles folder.

20. Double-click Local File in the details pane.

    The Local File Properties dialog box appears.

    The Settings tab and the Local File tab are used to configure logging. Use the information under the Settings tab to configure the amount of information you want to log about remote access authentication, administration, and status.

21. Click the Local File tab.

    Use the information under the Local File tab to configure the log file format, when new logs are generated, and where the logs are stored. Moving the log file directory (folder) to another partition other than the boot partition is advised.

22. Click Cancel.

23. In the console tree, click Remote Access Policies.

    The default remote access policy, Allow Access If Dial-In Permission Is Enabled, appears in the details pane.

24. Double-click Allow Access If Dial-In Permission Is Enabled.

    The Allow Access If Dial-In Permission Is Enabled Properties dialog box appears.

25. Click the Edit button.

    The Time Of Day Constraints dialog box appears.

    Notice that Dial-In permission is allowed around the clock.

26. Click Cancel.

    Notice that the Deny Remote Access Permission radio button is selected. This means that unless this profile is overridden on a per-user basis, users depending on access based on a profile will always be denied access.

27. Click the Add button.

    The Select Attribute dialog box appears.

    This dialog box lists the various connection attributes that can be associated with this profile. Users who meet the conditions specified in the profile are either allowed or denied access.

28. Click Cancel.

29. Click Edit Profile and explore the various tabs and settings available for editing the profile. Notice that many of the settings configured for the profile can also be set separately from the profile in the Routing And Remote Access snap-in.

30. Click Cancel.

31. Click Cancel again to close the Allow Access If Dial-In Permission Is Enabled Properties box.

32. Minimize the Routing And Remote Access snap-in; you will be using it in the next exercise.

    This procedure provided an exploration of the Routing And Remote Access snap-in. The rest of the chapter explores RRAS features.

Note RRAS can also be configured from the command prompt by using the netsh utility (Net Shell) rather than using the Routing And Remote Access snap-in.

Disabling RRAS

Although the Windows 2000 interface is not designed to allow you to easily remove RRAS, you can disable it by using the Routing And Remote Access snap-in. In the console tree, select the computer that you want to disable and then select Disable Routing And Remote Access from the Action menu. Disabling the service removes all Routing and Remote Access registry settings.

You can also refresh the configuration of RRAS by first disabling the server and then enabling it.

Note If you disable RRAS, all current configurations for the service, including routing protocol configuration and demand-dial interfaces, are removed and all currently connected clients are disconnected.

Authentication and Authorization

The distinction between authentication and authorization is important for understanding how connection attempts are either accepted or denied:

- **Authentication** Authentication is the verification of the credentials of the connection attempt. This process consists of sending the credentials from the remote access client to the remote access server in either a clear text or encrypted form that uses an authentication protocol.

- **Authorization** Authorization is the verification that the connection attempt is allowed. Authorization occurs after successful authentication.

For a connection attempt to be accepted, the connection must be both authenticated and authorized. It is possible for the connection attempt to be authenticated through the use of valid credentials, but not authorized. In this case, the connection attempt is denied.

If the remote access server is configured for Windows authentication, Windows 2000 security verifies the credentials for authentication and the dial-up properties of the user account, and locally stored remote access policies authorize the connection. If the connection attempt is both authenticated and authorized, the connection attempt is accepted.

If the remote access server is configured for Remote Authentication Dial-In User Service (RADIUS) authentication, the credentials of the connection attempt are passed to the RADIUS server for authentication and authorization. If the connection attempt is both authenticated and authorized, the RADIUS server sends an accept message back to the remote access server and the connection attempt is accepted. If the connection attempt is either not authenticated or not authorized, the RADIUS server sends a reject message back to the RAS server and the connection process is denied.

If the RADIUS server is a Windows 2000–based computer running the Internet Authentication Service (IAS), the IAS server performs authentication through Windows 2000 security and authorization through the dial-up properties of the user account and the remote access policies stored on the IAS server.

The configuration of the RRAS authentication provider is done from the Security tab from the properties of a remote access router in the Routing And Remote Access snap-in (Figure 10.2) or by using the netsh command-line utility.

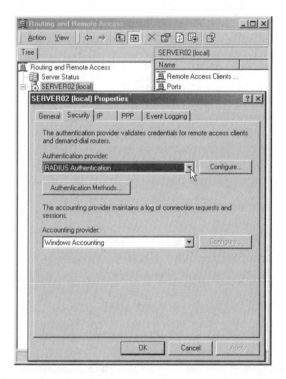

Figure 10.2 Properties of RRAS server Server02 with the RADIUS authentication provider selected

Lesson Summary

RRAS for Windows 2000 Server continues the evolution of multiprotocol routing and remote access services for the Microsoft Windows platform. RRAS is integrated with the Windows 2000 Server operating system and works with a wide variety of hardware platforms and hundreds of network adapters. The combined features of Windows 2000 RRAS allows a Windows 2000 Server computer to function as a multiprotocol router, a demand-dial router, and a remote access server. RRAS uses PPP to negotiate point-to-point connections for remote access clients. PPP provides link parameter negotiation, the exchange of authentication credentials, and network layer protocol negotiation. You can use the Routing And Remote Access snap-in to enable and configure RRAS or to disable the service. For a connection attempt to be accepted, the connection must be both authenticated and authorized.

Lesson 2: Features of the Routing and Remote Access Service

RRAS for Windows 2000 includes a wide variety of features that support unicast and multicast IP routing, IPX routing, AppleTalk routing, remote access, and VPN support.

After this lesson, you will be able to

- Describe the primary features of Windows 2000 RRAS

Estimated lesson time: 25 minutes

Unicast IP Support

Windows 2000 provides extensive support for unicast IP routing (routing to a unicast destination IP address) by using the unicast IP routing protocols and features of the Windows 2000 Router. Unicasting is where two computers establish a two-way, point-to-point connection in order to exchange data. Unicast IP routing is where a router or routers forward packets between a two-way, point-to-point connection. Your implementation of unicast routing can be simple or complex depending on the size of your IP internetwork, the use of Dynamic Host Configuration Protocol (DHCP) to allocate IP address configuration, connectivity to the Internet, the presence of non-Microsoft or legacy hosts on your internetwork, and other factors.

The following table describes the various components of Unicast IP routing.

Feature	Description
Static IP routing	With this inherent function of the TCP/IP protocol for Windows 2000, you can manage static routes by using the Routing And Remote Access snap-in or netsh. The routemon utility is not supported in Windows 2000.
RIP versions 1 and 2	A distance-vector routing protocol commonly used in small and medium IP internetworks.
OSPF	A link-state routing protocol commonly used in medium to large IP internetworks. This protocol is significantly more efficient then RIP because more sophisticated algorithms are used to find the best route between two points.

Feature	Description
DHCP Relay Agent	An agent that relays DHCP messages between DHCP clients and DHCP servers on different network segments. This allows a DHCP server to service many network scopes. See RFC1542 for more information.
Network address translation (NAT)	A network address translator component that creates a translated connection between privately addressed networks and the Internet. This allows addressing on an internal network that is not legal on the Internet but is still able to access the Internet.
IP packet filtering	The ability to define what traffic is allowed into and out of each interface based on filters defined by the values of source and destination IP addresses, TCP and UDP port numbers, ICMP types and codes, and IP protocol numbers. This is an important security feature.
ICMP router discovery	The ability to periodically advertise and respond to host router solicitations to support ICMP router discovery by hosts on a network segment.

IP Multicast Support

Windows 2000 supports the sending, receiving, and forwarding of IP multicast traffic. Multicast traffic is sent to a single host but is processed by multiple hosts who listen for this type of traffic destined for a single host. This is commonly used for delivering real-time data to multiple users, such as when delivering a distributed media presentation. The IP multicast components of RRAS allow you to send and receive IP multicast traffic from remote access clients and multicast-enabled portions of the Internet or a private intranet.

The following table describes the various components of IP multicast routing.

Feature	Description
Multicast forwarding	With this inherent function of the TCP/IP protocol for Windows 2000, you can view the multicast forwarding table by using the Routing And Remote Access snap-in or you can use the netsh command-line utility.
IGMP versions 1 and 2	The TCP/IP protocol to track multicast group membership on attached network segments.

Feature	Description
Specific forwarding and routing	When you use the IGMP routing protocol and configure interfaces for IGMP Router mode and IGMP Proxy mode, the Windows 2000 router can support multicast forwarding and routing for specific configurations.
Multicast boundaries	Multicast boundaries (barriers to the forwarding of IP multicast traffic) can be based on the IP multicast group address, the Time-To-Live (TTL) in the IP header, or on the maximum amount of multicast traffic in kilobytes per second.

IPX Support

The Windows 2000 Server Router is a fully functional IPX router supporting RIP for IPX, the primary routing protocol used in IPX internetworks; Novell NetWare SAP for IPX, a protocol for the collection and distribution of service names and addresses; and NetBIOS over IPX broadcast forwarding.

The following table describes the various components of IPX routing.

Feature	Description
IPX packet filtering	The ability to define what traffic is allowed into and out of each interface based on filters defined by the values of source and destination IPX network, node, socket numbers, and packet type.
RIP for IPX	A distance-vector-based routing protocol commonly used on IPX internetworks. RRAS also allows you to configure static IPX routes and RIP route filters.
SAP for IPX	SAP is a distance-vector-based advertising protocol commonly used on IPX internetworks to advertise services and their locations. RRAS also provides the ability to configure static SAP services and SAP service filters. SAP service filters reduce unneeded SAP traffic from being sent of RRAS connection.
NetBIOS over IPX	NetBIOS over IPX is used by Microsoft networking components to support file and printer sharing components. RRAS can also forward NetBIOS over IPX broadcasts and configure static NetBIOS names.

AppleTalk

Windows 2000 RRAS can operate as an AppleTalk router by forwarding AppleTalk packets and supporting the use of the Routing Table Maintenance Protocol (RTMP). Windows 2000 supports an AppleTalk protocol stack and AppleTalk routing software so that the Windows 2000–based server can connect to and provide routing for AppleTalk-based Macintosh networks.

Most large AppleTalk networks, like any large network, are not single physical networks in which all computers are attached to the same network cabling system. Instead, they are AppleTalk internets, which are smaller, physical networks connected by routers.

A Windows 2000–based server can provide routing and seed routing support. RRAS does not limit the number of network adapters on a computer that can support an AppleTalk network, which consists of multiple smaller physical networks connected by routers.

Demand-Dial Routing

Windows 2000 provides support for demand-dial routing, the routing of packets over point-to-point links such as analog telephone lines and ISDN. Demand-dial routing allows you to connect to the Internet, to connect branch offices, or to implement router-to-router VPN connections.

IP and IPX traffic can be forwarded over demand-dial interfaces over persistent or on-demand WAN links. For on-demand connections, RRAS automatically creates a PPP connection to the configured endpoint when traffic matching a static route is received.

Remote Access

RRAS enables a computer to be a remote access server, accepting remote access connections (dial-in) from remote access clients that use traditional dial-up technologies such as analog phone lines and ISDN. Remote access is discussed in detail in Lesson 3, "Remote Access."

VPN Server

RRAS enables a computer to be a VPN server, supporting both PPTP and L2TP over IPSec and accepting both remote access and router-to-router (demand-dial) VPN connections from remote access clients and calling routers. VPN is discussed in detail in Lesson 4, "Virtual Private Networks."

RADIUS Client-Server

The Internet Authentication Service (IAS) in Windows 2000 is the Microsoft implementation of a RADIUS server. IAS performs centralized authentication, authorization, auditing, and accounting (AAAA) of connections for dial-up and VPN remote access and demand-dial connections, and it can be used in conjunction with Windows 2000 RRAS. IAS enables the use of a single or multiple vendor network of remote access or VPN equipment.

Internet service providers (ISPs) and corporations maintaining remote access service for their employees are faced with the increasing challenge of managing all remote access from a single point of administration—regardless of the type of remote access equipment employed. The RADIUS standard supports this functionality in a homogeneous or heterogeneous environment. RADIUS is a client-server protocol, which enables remote access equipment acting as RADIUS clients to submit authentication and accounting requests to a RADIUS server.

The RADIUS server has access to user account information and can check remote access authentication credentials. If the user's credentials are authentic and the connection attempt is authorized, the RADIUS server authorizes the user's access based on specified conditions and logs the remote access connections as accounting events.

RADIUS supports remote access user authentication and authorization and allows accounting data to be maintained in a central location, rather than on each network access server (NAS). Users connect to a RADIUS-compliant NAS computer, such as a Windows 2000–based computer that is running RRAS, which in turn forwards authentication requests to the centralized IAS server.

SNMP MIB Support

Windows 2000 and RRAS provide Simple Network Management Protocol (SNMP) agent functionality with support for Internet MIB II (as documented in RFC 1213). Network Management Stations (NMS), such as HP OpenView, can compile the MIB to manage IP network layer events relating to Windows 2000 remote access router functions. The computer running RRAS must also be running the SNMP service, also called the SNMP agent, in order to be managed by an NMS. Beyond Internet MIB II, support for RRAS additional MIB enhancements that can be compiled on the NMS to support RRAS include:

- IP Forwarding Table MIB
- Microsoft RIP version 2 for Internet Protocol MIB
- Wellfleet-Series7-MIB for OSPF
- Microsoft BOOTP for Internet Protocol MIB
- Microsoft IPX MIB
- Microsoft RIP and SAP for IPX MIB
- Internet Group Management Protocol MIB
- IP Multicast Routing MIB

Note MIB support is also provided for Windows 2000 operating system functions, legacy LAN Manager MIB functions, and the WINS, DHCP, IIS services. IPX is also supported by the SNMP service; however, TCP/IP must be installed to allow for IPX SNMP support.

API Support for Third-Party Components

RRAS has fully published API sets for unicast and multicast routing protocol and administration utility support. Routing protocol developers can write additional routing protocols and interfaces directly into RRAS architecture. Other software vendors can also use RRAS administration APIs to provide their own management utilities.

Lesson Summary

RRAS for Windows 2000 includes a wide variety of features. Windows 2000 supports unicast IP routing (routing to a unicast destination IP address); it also supports the sending, receiving, and forwarding of IP multicast traffic, and can act as a fully functional IPX router. In addition, RRAS supports AppleTalk, demand-dial routing, remote access, and VPN. A Windows 2000 Server computer can also act as a RADIUS server and can provide SNMP agent functionality. Finally, RRAS has fully published API sets for unicast and multicast routing protocol and administration utility support.

Lesson 3: Remote Access

Windows 2000 remote access technology allows remote clients to connect to corporate networks or the Internet. This lesson provides an overview of remote access and discusses dial-up remote access connections, remote access security, and managing remote access. This lesson focuses on the Remote Access Service part of RRAS. Hereafter, the acronym RAS will be used to refer to the Remote Access Service component of RRAS.

After this lesson, you will be able to

- Describe how remote access works, including dial-up remote access connections and remote access security

- Manage remote access, including the management of users, addresses, access, and authentication

Estimated lesson time: 35 minutes

Overview of Remote Access

In Windows 2000 RAS, remote access clients are either connected to only the remote access server's resources (point-to-point remote access connectivity), or they are connected to the RAS server's resources and the resources in the network to which the remote access server is attached (point-to-LAN remote access connectivity). The latter type of connection type allows remote access clients to access resources as if they were physically attached to the network.

A Windows 2000 remote access server provides two remote access connection methods:

- **Dial-up remote access** With dial-up remote access, a remote access client uses the telecommunications infrastructure to create a temporary physical circuit or a virtual circuit to a port on a remote access server. Once the physical or virtual circuit is created, the rest of the connection parameters can be negotiated.

- **VPN remote access** With virtual private network remote access, a VPN client uses an IP internetwork to create a virtual point-to-point connection with a RAS server acting as the VPN server. Once the virtual point-to-point connection is created, the rest of the connection parameters can be negotiated.

Note This lesson focuses primarily on dial-up remote access; however, many topics also apply to VPN remote access. For a complete understanding of VPNs, read this lesson and then review Lesson 4, "Virtual Private Networks."

Dial-Up Remote Access Connections

A dial-up remote access connection consists of a remote access client, a remote access server, and a WAN infrastructure (Figure 10.3).

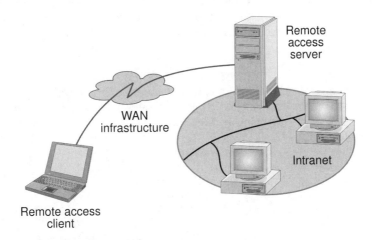

Figure 10.3 Elements of a dial-up remote access connection

Remote Access Client

Windows 2000, Windows NT 3.5 or later, Windows 98, Windows 95, Windows for Workgroups, MS-DOS, and Microsoft LAN Manager remote access clients can all connect to a Windows 2000 remote access server. Almost any third-party Point-to-Point Protocol (PPP) remote access clients—including UNIX and Apple Macintosh clients—can connect to a Windows 2000 remote access server.

The Microsoft remote access client is also capable of dialing into a Serial Line Interface Protocol (SLIP) server. SLIP is a legacy dial-in protocol that does not provide the security, performance, or reliability of PPP. A Windows 2000 RAS server does not support SLIP dial-up (dial-in) connections.

Remote Access Service Server

The Windows 2000 remote access server accepts dial-up connections and forwards packets between remote access clients and the network to which the remote access server is attached.

Dial-Up Equipment and WAN Infrastructure

The physical or logical connection between the remote access server and the remote access client is facilitated by dial-up equipment installed at the remote access client, the remote access server, and the telecommunications infrastructure. The nature of the dial-up equipment and telecommunications infrastructure varies depending on the type of connection being made.

Public Switched Telephone Network

The Public Switched Telephone Network (PSTN), also known as Plain Old Telephone Service (POTS), is the analog telephone system designed to carry the minimal frequencies to distinguish human voices. Because the PSTN was not designed for data transmissions, there are limits to the maximum bit rate that a PSTN connection can support. Dial-up equipment consists of an analog modem for the remote access client and the remote access server. For large organizations, the remote access server is attached to a modem bank containing up to hundreds of modems. With analog modems at both the remote access server and the remote access client, the maximum bit rate supported by PSTN connections is 33,600 bits per second, or 33.6 kilobits per second (Kbps).

Figure 10.4 illustrates a PSTN connection.

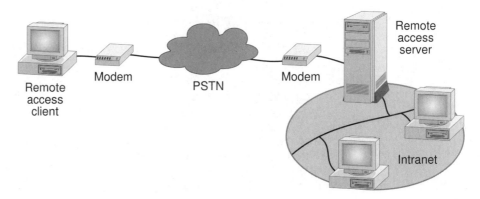

Figure 10.4 Dial-up equipment and WAN infrastructure for PSTN connections

Digital Links and V.90

The maximum bit rate of the PSTN is a function of the range of frequencies passed by PSTN switches and the signal-to-noise ratio of the connection. The modern-day analog telephone system is analog only on the *local loop,* the set of wires that connects the customer to the central office PSTN switch. Once the analog signal reaches the PSTN switch, it is converted to a digital signal. The analog-to-digital conversion introduces noise on the connection known as *quantization* noise.

When a RAS server is connected to a central office through a digital switch based on T-Carrier or ISDN rather than an analog PSTN switch, there is no analog-to-digital conversion when the remote access server sends information to the remote access client. As a result, there is no quantization noise in the downstream path to the remote access client, and therefore, there is a higher signal-to-noise ratio and a higher maximum bit rate.

With this new technology, called V.90, remote access clients can send data at 33.6 Kbps and receive data at 56 Kbps. In North America, the maximum receive bit rate is 53 Kbps due to Federal Communications Commission (FCC) rules.

To obtain V.90 speeds, the following conditions must be met:

- The remote access client must be using a V.90 modem.

- The RAS server must be using a V.90 digital switch and must be using a digita link to connect to the PSTN, such as T-Carrier or ISDN.

- There cannot be any analog-to-digital conversions in the path from the RAS server to the remote access client.

Figure 10.5 illustrates a V.90-based PSTN connection.

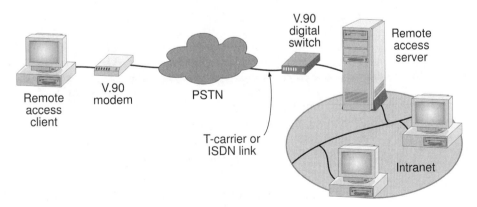

Figure 10.5 Dial-up equipment and WAN infrastructure for V.90 connections

Integrated Services Digital Network

ISDN is a set of international specifications for digital replacement of the PSTN. ISDN provides a single digital network to handle voice, data, fax, and other services over existing local loop wiring. ISDN behaves like an analog telephone line except that it is a digital technology at higher data rates with a much lower connection time. ISDN offers multiple channels; each channel operates at 64 Kbps and because the network is digital end-to-end there are no analog-to-digital conversions.

Dial-up equipment consists of an ISDN adapter for the remote access client and the remote access server. Remote access clients typically use Basic Rate ISDN (BRI) with two 64-Kbps channels, and large organizations typically use Primary Rate ISDN (PRI) with 23 64-Kbps channels. Figure 10.6 illustrates an ISDN connection.

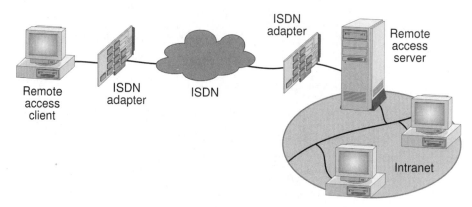

Figure 10.6 Dial-up equipment and WAN infrastructure for ISDN connections

X.25

X.25 is an international standard for sending data across public packet switching networks. Windows 2000 remote access supports X.25 in two ways:

- The remote access client supports the use of X.25 smart cards, which can connect directly to the X.25 data network and use the X.25 protocol to establish connections and send and receive data. The remote access client also supports dialing into a packet assembler/disassembler (PAD) of an X.25 carrier by using an analog modem.

- The Windows 2000 remote access server supports only direct connections to X.25 networks by using an X.25 smart card.

For more information about the configuration of X.25 and PADs, see Windows 2000 Server Help. Figure 10.7 illustrates an X.25 connection.

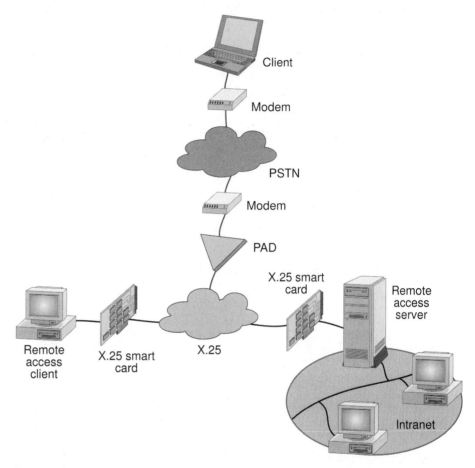

Figure 10.7 Dial-up equipment and WAN infrastructure for X.25 connections

---

Note X.25 smart cards are adapters that use the X.25 protocol and can directly connect to an X.25 public data network. X.25 smart cards are not related to smart cards used for authentication and secure communications.

ATM over ADSL

Asymmetric Digital Subscriber Line (ADSL) is a new local loop technology for small business and residential customers. Although ADSL provides higher bit rates than PSTN and ISDN connections, the bit rate is not the same in the upstream and downstream directions. Typical ADSL connections offer 64 Kbps from the customer and 1.544 megabits per second (Mbps) to the customer. The asymmetric nature of the connection fits well with typical Internet use. Most Internet users receive a lot more information than they send.

ADSL equipment can appear to Windows 2000 as either an Ethernet interface or a dial-up interface. When an ADSL adapter appears as an Ethernet interface, the ADSL connection operates in the same way as an Ethernet connection to the Internet.

When an ADSL adapter appears as a dial-up interface, ADSL provides a physical connection, and the individual LAN protocol packets are sent by using Asynchronous Transfer Mode (ATM). An ATM adapter with an ADSL port is installed in both the remote access client and remote access server.

Figure 10.8 illustrates an ATM over ADSL connection.

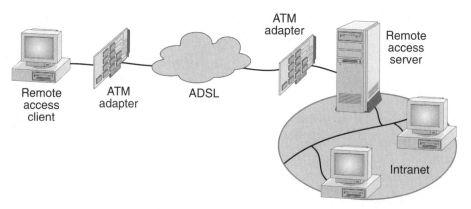

Figure 10.8 Dial-up equipment and WAN infrastructure for ATM over ADSL connections

Remote Access Protocols

Remote access protocols control the establishment of connections and the transmission of data over WAN links. The operating system and LAN protocols used on remote access clients and servers dictate which remote access protocol your clients can use.

There are three types of remote access protocols supported by Windows 2000 remote access:

- Point-to-Point Protocol (PPP) is an industry-standard set of protocols providing the best security, multi-protocol support, and interoperability.

- Serial Line Internet Protocol (SLIP) is used by older remote access servers. A Windows 2000 RAS server does not support SLIP dial-up connections.

- Microsoft remote access protocol, also known as Asynchronous NetBEUI (AsyBEUI), is a remote access protocol used by legacy remote access clients running Microsoft operating systems, such as Windows NT 3.1, Windows for Workgroups, MS-DOS, and LAN Manager.

LAN Protocols

LAN protocols are the protocols used by the remote access client to access resources on the network connected to the RAS server. Windows 2000 remote access supports TCP/IP, IPX, AppleTalk, and NetBEUI.

Remote Access Security

Windows 2000 remote access offers a wide range of security features, including secure user authentication, mutual authentication, data encryption, callback, caller ID, and remote access account lockout.

Secure User Authentication

Secure user authentication is obtained through the encrypted exchange of user credentials. This is possible through the use of the PPP remote access protocol along with one of the following authentication protocols:

- Extensible Authentication Protocol (EAP)

- Microsoft Challenge Handshake Authentication Protocol (MS-CHAP) version 1 and version 2

- Challenge Handshake Authentication Protocol (CHAP)

- Shiva Password Authentication Protocol (SPAP)

The RAS server can be configured to require a secure authentication method. If the remote access client cannot perform the required secure authentication, the connection is denied.

Mutual Authentication

Mutual authentication is obtained by authenticating both ends of the connection through the encrypted exchange of user credentials. This is possible through the use of PPP along with EAP-Transport Level Security (EAP-TLS) or MS-CHAP version 2. During mutual authentication, the remote access client authenticates itself to the RAS server, and then the RAS server authenticates itself to the remote access client.

It is possible for a RAS server not to request authentication from the remote access client. However, in the case of a Windows 2000 remote access client configured for only EAP-TLS or MS-CHAP version 2, the remote access client forces the mutual authentication of the client and server. If the RAS server does not respond to the authentication request, the connection is terminated by the client.

Data Encryption

Data encryption encrypts the data sent between the remote access client and the RAS server. Remote access data encryption provides data encryption only on the communications link between the remote access client and the RAS server. If end-to-end encryption is needed, use IPSec to create an encrypted end-to-end connection after the remote access connection has been made.

Note IPSec can also be used for encrypting a Layer 2 Tunneling Protocol (L2TP) VPN connection. For more information, see Lesson 4.

Data encryption on a remote access connection is based on a secret encryption key known to the RAS server and remote access client. This shared secret key is generated during the user authentication process.

Data encryption is possible over dial-up remote access links when using PPP along with EAP-TLS or MS-CHAP. The RAS server can be configured to require data encryption. If the remote access client cannot perform the required encryption, the connection attempt is rejected.

Windows 2000, Windows NT 4.0, Windows 98, and Windows 95 remote access clients and remote access servers support the Microsoft Point-to-Point Encryption Protocol (MPPE). MPPE uses the Rivest-Shamir-Adleman (RSA) RC4 stream cipher and 40-bit, 56-bit, or 128-bit secret keys. MPPE keys are generated from the EAP-TLS and MS-CHAP user authentication processes.

Callback

With callback, the RAS server calls the remote access client after the user credentials have been verified. Callback can be configured on the server to call the remote access client back at a number specified by the user of the remote access client during the time of the call. This allows a traveling user to dial in and have the RAS server call back the remote access client at the current location, saving telephone charges. Callback can also be configured to always call back the remote access client at a specific phone number, which is the secure form of callback.

Caller ID

Caller ID can be used to verify that the incoming call is coming from a specified phone number. Caller ID is configured as part of the dial-in properties of the user account. If the caller ID number of the incoming connection for that user does not match the configured caller ID, the connection is denied.

Caller ID requires that the caller's telephone line, the phone system, the RAS server's telephone line, and the Windows 2000 driver for the dial-up equipment all support caller ID. If caller ID is configured for a user account and the caller ID is not being passed from the caller to the RAS server, then the connection is denied.

Caller ID is a feature designed to provide a higher degree of security for networks that support telecommuters. The disadvantage of configuring caller ID is that the user must always dial-in from the same telephone line. This is the same disadvantage of callback configured to a specific telephone number.

Remote Access Account Lockout

The remote access account lockout feature is used to specify how many times a remote access authentication can fail against a valid user account before the user is denied remote access. Remote access account lockout is especially important for VPN connections over the Internet. Malicious users on the Internet can attempt to access an organization's intranet by sending credentials (valid user name and a guessed password) during the VPN connection authentication process. When using a dictionary attack, the user sends hundreds or thousands of credentials by using a list of passwords based on common words or phrases. With remote access account lockout enabled, a dictionary attack is thwarted after a specified number of failed attempts.

The remote access account lockout feature does not distinguish between malicious users who attempt to access your intranet and authentic users who attempt remote access but have forgotten their current passwords. Users who have forgotten their current password typically try several passwords. Depending on the number of attempts and the MaxDenials setting, they may have their accounts locked out.

If you enable the remote access account lockout feature, a malicious user can deliberately force an account to be locked out by attempting multiple authentications with the user account until the account is locked out, thereby preventing the authentic user from being able to log on.

As the network administrator, you must decide on two remote access account lockout variables:

- **The number of failed attempts before future attempts are denied** After each failed attempt, a failed attempts counter for the user account is incremented. If the counter reaches the configured maximum, future attempts to connect are denied. A successful authentication resets the failed attempts counter when its value is less than the configured maximum. In other words, the failed attempts counter does not accumulate beyond a successful authentication.

- **How often the failed attempts counter is reset** You must periodically reset the failed attempts counter to prevent inadvertent lockouts due to normal mistakes by users when typing in their passwords.

Managing Remote Access

When managing remote access, you must take into consideration a variety of factors, such as where user account data is to be stored, how addresses are assigned to remote access clients, and who is allowed to create remote access connections. Remote access management includes managing users, addresses, access, and authentication.

Managing Users

Rather than maintaining separate user accounts for the same user on separate servers and trying to keep the accounts simultaneously current, most administrators set up a master account database in the Active Directory store or on a RADIUS server. This allows the RAS server to send the authentication credentials to a central authenticating device.

Managing Addresses

For PPP connections, IP, IPX, and AppleTalk, addressing information must be allocated to remote access clients during the establishment of the connection. The Windows 2000 RAS server must be configured to allocate IP addresses, IPX network and node addresses, or AppleTalk network and node addresses.

Managing Access

In Windows 2000, remote access connections are accepted based on the dial-in properties of a user account and the remote access policies. A remote access policy is a set of conditions and connection parameters that define the characteristics of the incoming connection and the set of constraints imposed on it. Remote access policies can be used to impose connection parameters such as maximum session time, idle disconnect time, required secure authentication methods, required encryption, and so on.

With multiple remote access policies, different sets of conditions can be applied to different remote access clients, or different requirements can be applied to the same remote access client based on the parameters of the connection attempt. For example, multiple remote access policies can be used to meet the following conditions:

- Allow or deny connections if the user account belongs to a specific group.

- Define different days and times for different user accounts based on group membership.

- Configure different authentication methods for dial-up and VPN remote access clients.

- Configure different authentication or encryption settings for PPTP or L2TP connections.

- Configure different maximum session times for different user accounts based on group membership.

- Send network access server–specific RADIUS attributes to a RADIUS client.

When you have multiple Windows 2000 remote access servers or VPN servers on which you want to use a centralized set of remote access policies, you can configure a Windows 2000 computer with the Internet Authentication Service (IAS) and then configure each remote access or VPN server as a RADIUS client to the IAS server computer.

Windows 2000 RRAS and Windows 2000 IAS both use remote access policies to determine whether to accept or reject connection attempts. For Windows 2000 RRAS, remote access policies are administered through the Routing And Remote Access snap-in. For Windows 2000 IAS servers, remote access policies are administered through the Internet Authentication Service snap-in.

With remote access policies, you can grant remote access by configuring individual user account or by configuring specific remote access policies.

Access by User Account

The user account for a stand-alone or Active Directory–based server contains a set of dial-in properties that are used when allowing or denying a connection attempt made by a user. For a stand-alone server, you can set the dial-in properties on the Dial-In tab of the user account properties in the Local Users And Groups snap-in. For an Active Directory–based server, you can set the dial-in properties on the Dial-In tab of the user account properties in the Active Directory Users And Computers snap-in as shown in Figure 10.9.

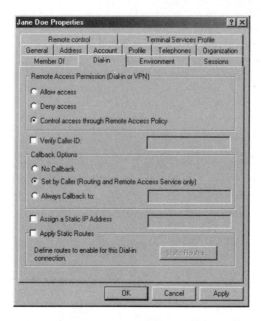

Figure 10.9 Dial-in settings for Active Directory services user Jane Doe

The Dial-In tab includes several options: Remote Access Permission (Dial-In or VPN), Verify Caller ID, Callback Options, Assign A Static IP Address, and Apply Static Routes.

Note For a user account in a Windows NT 4.0 domain or a Windows 2000 Mixed-mode domain, only the Allow Access option and the Deny Access option in the Remote Access Permission (Dial-In or VPN) section and the options in the Callback Options section are available.

Remote Access Permission (Dial-In or VPN)

You use this property to set remote access to be explicitly allowed, denied, or determined through remote access policies. If access is explicitly allowed, remote access policy conditions, user account properties, or profile properties can still deny the connection attempt. The Control access through Remote Access Policy option is available only on user accounts in a Windows 2000 Native-mode domain or for local accounts on remote access servers running stand-alone Windows 2000 computers.

By default, the Administrator and Guest accounts on a stand-alone remote access server or in a Windows 2000 Native-mode domain are set to Control access through Remote Access Policy and for a Windows 2000 Mixed-mode domain are set to Deny access. New accounts created on a stand-alone RAS server or in a Windows 2000 Native-mode domain are set to Control access through Remote Access Policy. New accounts created in a Windows 2000 Mixed-mode domain are set to Deny access.

Verify Caller ID

If this property is enabled, the server verifies the caller's phone number. If the caller's phone number does not match the configured phone number, the connection attempt is denied.

Caller ID must be supported by the caller, the phone system between the caller, and the remote access server. Caller ID on the remote access server consists of call answering equipment that supports the passing of caller ID information and the appropriate driver inside Windows 2000 that supports the passing of caller ID information to the remote access server.

If you configure a caller ID telephone number for a user and you do not have support for the passing of caller ID information from the caller to the remote access server, the connection attempt is denied.

Callback Options

If this property is enabled, the server calls the caller back during the connection establishment at a telephone number set by the caller or a specific telephone number set by the network administrator.

If the Windows 2000 Routing and Remote Access service server is a stand-alone server or a member of a Windows 2000 native domain, the callback number can be of unlimited size. If a Windows 2000 Routing and Remote Access service server is a member of a Windows NT 4.0 domain or a Windows 2000 mixed domain, the callback number can only be 128 characters long. Callback numbers may be long for international calling, or calling using additional codes such as telephone card numbers.

Assign a Static IP Address

If this property is enabled, you can assign a specific IP address to a user when a connection is made.

Apply Static Routes

If this property is enabled, you can define a series of static IP routes that are added to the routing table of the remote access server when a connection is made. This setting is designed for user accounts that Windows 2000 routers use for demand-dial routing.

Access by Policy

The access by policy administrative model is intended for Windows 2000 RAS servers that are either stand-alone servers or members of a Windows 2000 Native-mode domain. To manage remote access by policy, select the Control Access Through Remote Access Policy radio button (on the Dial-In tab of the user's Properties dialog box) on all user accounts (see Figure 10.9) , and then define the new remote access policies that allow or deny access based on your needs. Remote access policy is configured through RRAS or a RADIUS authentication provider. Figure 10.10 shows the Remote Access Policy node in the Routing And Remote Access snap-in.

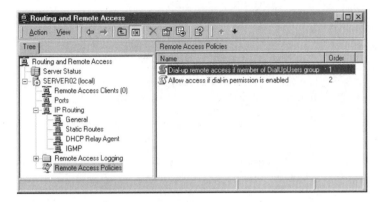

Figure 10.10 Remote Access Policies node in the Routing And Remote Access snap-in with two policies appearing in the details pane

The Remote Access Policies node appears in the Routing And Remote Access snap-in when the authentication provider is set to Windows Authentication. When the authentication provider is set to RADIUS Authentication (see Figure 10.2), the Remote Access Policies node does not appear in the Routing And Remote Access snap-in. Instead, policies are configured from the RADIUS authentication provider interface.

If the remote access server computer is a member of a Windows NT 4.0 domain or a Windows 2000 Mixed-mode domain and you want to manage access by policy, select the Allow Access radio button (on the Dial-In tab of the user's Properties dialog box) on all user accounts. Then remove the default policy called Allow Access If Dial-In Permission Is Enabled, and create a new policy that allows or denies access. A connection that does not match any configured remote access policy is denied, even if the Allow Access radio button is selected on the user account.

A typical use of policy-based access is to allow access through group membership. For example, create a Windows 2000 group with a name such as DialUpUsers, whose members are those users who are allowed to create dial-up remote access connections.

To create a remote access server that allows only dial-up remote access connections, create a new remote access policy with a descriptive name, such as Dial-Up Remote Access If Member Of DialUpUsers group, assign the DialUpUsers group to the policy, and then delete the default remote access policy called Allow Access If Dial-In Permission Is Enabled.

Accepting a connection attempt

When a user attempts a connection, the connection attempt is accepted or rejected based on the following logic:

1. The first policy in the ordered list of remote access policies is checked. If there are no policies, reject the connection attempt.

2. If all the conditions of the policy do not match the connection attempt, go to next policy. If there are no more policies, reject the connection attempt.

3. If all the conditions of the policy match the connection attempt, check the remote access permission setting for the user attempting the connection.

   - If Deny Access is selected, reject the connection attempt.

   - If Allow Access is selected, apply the user account properties and profile properties.

     - If the connection attempt does not match the settings of the user account properties and profile properties, reject the connection attempt.

     - If the connection attempt matches the settings of the user account properties and profile properties, accept the connection attempt.

   - If Control Access Through Remote Access Policy is selected, check the remote access permission setting of the policy.

     - If Deny Remote Access Permission is selected, reject the connection attempt.

     - If Grant Remote Access Permission is selected, apply the user account properties and profile properties.

   - If the connection attempt does not match the settings of the user account properties and profile properties, reject the connection attempt.

   - If the connection attempt matches the settings of the user account properties and profile properties, accept the connection attempt.

Figure 10.11 shows the logic of remote access policies and user account settings.

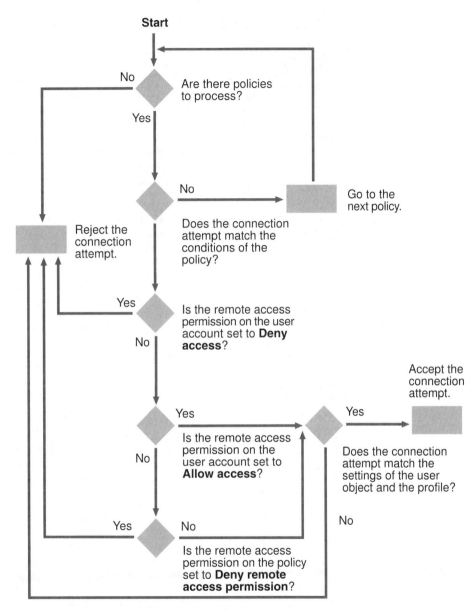

Figure 10.11 Using remote access policies and user account settings to accept a connection attempt

Managing Account Lockout

Changing settings in the Windows 2000 registry on the computer that provides authentication services configures the account lockout feature. If the RAS server is configured for Windows authentication, modify the registry on the RAS server computer. If the RAS server is configured for RADIUS authentication and Windows 2000 IAS is being used, modify the registry on the IAS server computer.

To enable account lockout, you must set the MaxDenials entry in the registry (HKEY_LOCAL_MACHINE\SYSTEM\CurrentControlSet\Services\ RemoteAccess\Parameters\AccountLockout) to 1 or greater. MaxDenials is the maximum number of failed attempts before the account is locked out. By default, MaxDenials is set to 0, which means that account lockout is disabled. The AccountLockout key is created when RRAS is enabled.

To modify the amount of time before the failed attempts counter is reset, you must set the ResetTime (Mins) entry in the registry (HKEY_LOCAL_MACHINE\ SYSTEM\CurrentControlSet\Services\RemoteAccess\Parameters\ AccountLockout) to the required number of minutes. By default, ResetTime (Mins) is set to a hex value of b40, or 2,880 minutes (48 hours) in decimal.

To manually reset a user account that has been locked out before the failed attempts counter is automatically reset, delete the following registry subkey that corresponds to the user's account name: HKEY_LOCAL_MACHINE\ SYSTEM\CurrentControlSet\Services\RemoteAccess\Parameters\ AccountLockout\<*domain_name:user_name*>.

Note The remote access account lockout feature is not related to the Account is locked out setting on the Account tab of the user account properties or related to the administration of account lockout policies in Windows 2000 group policies.

Managing Authentication

The remote access server can be configured to use either Windows or RADIUS as an authentication provider. Figure 10.2 shows where this option is selected in the Routing And Remote Access snap-in.

Windows Authentication

If Windows is selected as the authentication provider, then the user credentials sent by users attempting remote access connections are authenticated through normal Windows authentication mechanisms.

If the remote access server is a member server in a Mixed-mode or Native-mode Windows 2000 domain and is configured for Windows authentication, the computer account of the RAS server computer must be a member of the RAS and IAS Servers security group. Configuring membership can be completed by a domain administrator by using the Active Directory Users And Computers snap-in to add the computer to the RAS And IAS Servers security group in the Users container. The netsh command-line utility can also be used to add the server to this group. For example, to add a server named RAS1 to the microsoft.com domain RAS And IAS Servers security group, open a command prompt and enter the Net Shell Command mode by typing **netsh**. Once in Net Shell Command mode, type **add registeredserver domain=microsoft.com server=ras1**. If the user installing RRAS is a domain administrator, the computer account is automatically added to the RAS and IAS Servers security group during the installation of RRAS.

RADIUS Authentication

If RADIUS is selected and configured as the authentication provider on the remote access server, user credentials and parameters of the connection request are sent as a series of RADIUS request messages to a RADIUS server, such as a computer running Windows 2000 Server and IAS.

The RADIUS server receives a user-connection request from the RAS server and authenticates the client against its authentication database. A RADIUS server can also maintain a central storage database of other relevant user properties. In addition to the simple yes or no response to an authentication request, RADIUS can inform the RAS server of other applicable connection parameters for this user, such as maximum session time, static IP address assignment, and so on.

RADIUS can respond to authentication requests based upon its own database, or it can be a front end to another database server, such as a generic Open Database Connectivity (ODBC) server or a Windows 2000 domain controller. The latter server could be located on the same machine as the RADIUS server, or could be centralized elsewhere. In addition, a RADIUS server can act as a proxy client to a remote RADIUS server.

The RADIUS protocol is described in RFC 2138 and RFC 2139. For more information about RAS server authentication scenarios and the RAS server as a RADIUS client, see Windows 2000 Server Help.

Note When configured for Windows authentication, both RRAS and IAS use the same process to provide authentication and authorization of incoming connection requests.

Windows and Radius Accounting

You can also select Windows Accounting, RADIUS Accounting, or None on the Security tab of the Properties dialog box for the remote access server. A remote access server running Windows 2000 supports the logging of accounting information for remote access server connections in local logging files when Windows Accounting is enabled. This logging is separate from the events recorded in the system event log. Accounting logging is especially useful for troubleshooting remote access policy issues. The accounting information is stored in a configurable log file or files stored in the %systemroot%\System32\LogFiles folder. The log files are saved in IAS 1.0 or Open Database Connectivity (ODBC) format, meaning that any ODBC-compliant database program can read the log file directly for analysis.

A remote access server running Windows 2000 also supports the logging of accounting information for remote access serve connections at a RADIUS server when RADIUS authentication and accounting are enabled. This logging is separate from the events recorded in the system event log. If your RADIUS server is a Windows 2000 computer running IAS, then accounting information is logged in log files stored on the IAS server.

Exercise 2: Configuring and Monitoring a RAS Connection

This exercise should be completed on Server01 and Server02.

▶ **Procedure 1: Allowing and denying dial-in access**

In this procedure, you will selectively allow or deny remote access to user accounts. Complete this procedure on Server01.

1. Open the Active Directory Users And Computers snap-in.

    The Active Directory Users And Computers snap-in appears.

2. Click the Sales OU in the console tree.

    The objects in the Sales OU appear in the details pane.

3. Double-click Jane Doe.

    The Jane Doe Properties dialog box appears.

4. Click the Dial-in tab.

    The dial-in settings for Jane Doe appear.

5. Click the Allow Access radio button and then click OK.

6. Double-click John Smith in the details pane and then click the Dial-In tab.

    The dial-in settings for John Smith appear.

7. Verify that the Control Access Through Remote Access Policy radio button is selected and then click OK.

8. Click the Users container in the console tree.

   The objects in the Users container appear in the details pane.

9. Access the dial-in properties for Bob Train.

10. Click the Deny Access radio button and then click OK.

11. Close Active Directory Users And Computers.

▶ **Procedure 2: Enabling accounting and configuring logging on the RRAS server**

In this procedure, you configure the RRAS server for Windows account logging and event logging. Complete this procedure on Server01.

1. Restore the Routing And Remote Access snap-in.

2. Click Remote Access Logging in the console tree.

3. In the details pane, double-click Local File.

   The Local File Properties dialog box appears.

4. Click the Log Authentication Requests (For Example, Access-Accept Or Access-Reject) – Recommended check box.

5. Click OK.

6. Click Server01 (Local) in the console tree.

7. Click the Action menu and choose Properties.

   The Server01 (Local) Properties dialog box appears.

8. Click the Event Logging tab.

9. Click the Log The Maximum Amount Of Information radio button and check the Enable Point-To-Point Protocol (PPP) Logging check box.

10. Click OK.

    The Routing And Remote Access message box appears asking to restart the router.

11. Click Yes.

    A number of message boxes appear as routing and remote access is stopped and restarted.

▸ **Procedure 3: Configuring a dial-up client and accessing the RRAS server (optional)**

In this procedure, you configure Server02 to act as a dial-up client. There must be a modem in Server02 in order for you to complete this exercise.

1. Before starting Server02, disconnect the network cable.

2. Start Server02.

3. At the logon screen, change the Logon To drop-down list box to SERVER02 (This Computer) then log on as Administrator with a password of "password."

4. Click Start, point to Settings, then click Network And Dial-up Connections.

   The Network And Dial-up Connections window appears. Notice that Local Area Connection contains a red "X." You disconnected Local Area Connection before starting this procedure.

5. Double-click Make New Connection.

   The Network Connection wizard appears.

6. Click Next.

   The Network Connection Type screen appears.

7. Verify that the Dial-Up To Private Network radio button is selected and then click Next.

   The Phone Number To Dial screen appears.

8. If you are able to dial up the RRAS server, type in the telephone number that the RRAS server modem is connected to. If you are unable to complete this connection, type any telephone number in this text box.

9. Click Next.

   The Connection Availability screen appears.

10. Click Next.

    The Internet Connection Sharing screen appears.

11. Click Next.

    The Completing The Network Connection Wizard screen appears and the connection appears with the default name of Dial-Up Connection.

12. Click Finish.

    The Connect Dial-Up Connection dialog box appears.

13. If you are unable to dial up the RRAS server, click Cancel. Screen shots will be provided in the next optional procedure to allow you to see what appears in RRAS when a connection is established. If you are able to dial up the RRAS server, complete the remaining steps.

14. In the User Name text box, type **Bob_Train** (there is an underscore between the first and last name), and then click the Dial button.

    The Error Connecting To Dial-Up Connection message box appears stating that this user account does not have permission to dial in. The Bob Train user account was assigned the Deny Access Remote Access permission.

15. In the User Name text box, type **Jane_Doe** (there is an underscore between the first and last name), and in the password box type **student** and then click the Dial button.

    The Connecting Dial-Up Connection message box appears on Server02 and the connection is verified, authenticated, and registered.

    The Connection Complete message box appears on Server02.

16. Click the Do Not Display The Message Again check box and then click OK.

    The Jane Doe account successfully connected to the RAS server because Allow Access was configured for the properties of the user account.

17. In the Network And Dial-Up Connection window, double-click Dial-Up Connection.

    The Dial-Up Connection Status dialog box appears.

18. Click the Disconnect button.

19. Double-click Dial-Up Connection.

20. In the User name text box, type **John_Smith** (there is an underscore between the first and last name), and then click the Dial button.

    The Error Connecting To Dial-Up Connection message box appears stating that this user account does not have permission to dial in. The John Smith user account was assigned the Control access through Remote Access Policy setting.

21. On Server01, restore the Routing And Remote Access snap-in.

22. Click the Remote Access Policies node in the console tree.

23. Double-click the Allow Access If Dial-In Permission Is Enabled policy in the details pane.

    The Allow Access If Dial-In Permission Is Enabled Properties dialog box appears.

24. In the If A User Matches The Conditions section, select the Grant Remote Access Permission radio button and then click OK.

25. Return to Server02.

26. In the User Name text box click the Dial button to attempt another logon as John_Smith.

    The Connecting Dial-Up Connection appears on Server02 and the connection is verified, authenticated, and registered. The default remote access policy now grants access to all user accounts that have the Control Access Through Remote Access Policy radio button (on the Dial-In tab) selected.

▶ **Procedure 4: Monitoring the remote access connection (optional)**

If you were able to connect to the remote access server, you can complete this procedure. If you weren't able to connect to the remote access server, important screen shots are provided in this procedure. Complete this procedure from Server01.

1. Restore the Routing And Remote Access snap-in.

2. Click Remote Access Clients (1) in the console tree.

    MICROSOFT\John_Smith appears in the User Name column. Notice that the connection duration and the number of ports connected also appears (Figure 10.12).

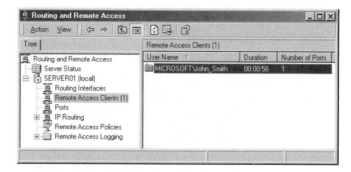

Figure 10.12 User Name column showing connection duration and number of ports connected

3. Double-click MICROSOFT\John_Smith appearing in the details pane.

    The Status dialog box appears (Figure 10.13).

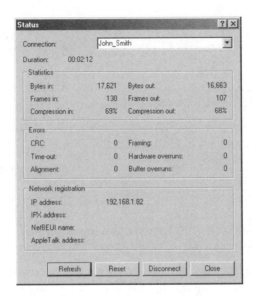

Figure 10.13 User Status dialog box showing TCP/IP

Notice that the only protocol registered for this connection is TCP/IP. This is because all values are blank under Network Registration except for IP address. The IP address appearing was allocated by DHCP since the default setting for the RAS server is to use DHCP to supply the network address to remote access clients. You can verify this information from the DHCP snap-in on Server01.

From the details pane you can also send a message to the selected remote access client or all connected clients, and disconnect a remote access client.

4. Close the Status dialog box.

5. Click Start, then click Run.

6. In the Open text box, type **c:\winnt\system32\logfiles\iaslog.log,** then click OK.

   The Accounting log is displayed in Notepad. If you were unable to complete this exercise, open the iaslog.log file on the Windows 2000 Supplemental Training CD-ROM. You can find this file in the \Chapt10\ex2 folder. Only two lines from the last two connections made by the John Smith user account are included in this file.

   For information on how to interpret this log, open the IAS Help file and search for the title, IAS-Formatted Log Files. For a more readable format with less information, consider setting logging to the database-compatible file format.

7. Close Notepad.

8. To view the results of event logging, open the Event Viewer from the Administrative Tools program group.

   The Event Viewer snap-in appears and the contents of the System Log appear in the details pane.

9. Locate and double-click a system log event with a Source of RemoteAccess and an Event ID of 20015.

   A remote access connection event appears, showing you who connected and to what port.

10. Click OK.

11. Locate and double-click a system log event with a Source of RemoteAccess and an Event ID of 20187.

    A remote access connection event appears, showing you that a remote access authentication attempt failed and the username of the failed attempt.

12. Click OK, then close the Event Viewer snap-in.

Lesson Summary

Windows 2000 remote access provides two different types of remote access connectivity: dial-up remote access and VPN remote access. A dial-up remote access connection consists of a remote access client, a remote access server, and a WAN infrastructure. Remote access protocols control the connection establishment and transmission of data over WAN links. There are three types of remote access protocols supported by Windows 2000: PPP, SLIP, and Asynchronous NetBEUI. Windows 2000 remote access supports the following LAN protocols: TCP/IP, IPX, AppleTalk, and NetBEUI. Windows 2000 remote access offers a wide range of security features, including secure user authentication, mutual authentication, data encryption, callback, caller ID, and remote access account lockout. Remote access management includes managing users, addresses, access, and authentication.

Lesson 4: Virtual Private Networks

A virtual private network (VPN) is an extension of the private network that encompasses encapsulated, encrypted, and authenticated links across shared or public networks. A VPN mimics the properties of a dedicated private network, allowing data to be transferred between two computers across an internetwork, such as the Internet. Point-to-point connections can be simulated through the use of tunneling, and LAN connectivity can be simulated through the use of virtual LANs (VLANs). This lesson introduces you to VPNs and tunneling basics. It explains how to manage the RAS server for VPNs and covers how to troubleshoot common VPN problems.

After this lesson, you will be able to

- Describe the basic characteristics of VPNs and tunneling, including the most common tunneling protocols
- Manage VPN servers
- Troubleshoot VPNs

Estimated lesson time: 45 minutes

Introduction to Virtual Private Networks

VPNs allow users working at home or on the road to connect securely to a remote corporate server by using the routing infrastructure provided by a public internetwork such as the Internet. From the user's perspective, the VPN is a point-to-point connection between the user's computer and a corporate server. The nature of the internetwork is irrelevant because it appears as if the data is being sent over a dedicated private link.

VPN technology also allows a corporation to connect with its branch offices or with other companies over a public internetwork while maintaining secure communications. A VPN connection across the Internet logically operates as a dedicated WAN link.

The secure connection across the internetwork appears to the user as a virtual network interface providing private network communication over a public internetwork. Rather than having a remote user make a long distance call (or toll free call) to a corporate or outsourced NAS, the user calls the local ISP. Using the connection to the local ISP, a VPN is created between the dial-up user and the corporate VPN server across the Internet.

Note For more information about virtual private networking, see the Supplemental Course Materials CD-ROM (\chapt10\articles\VPNoverview.doc) that accompanies this book.

Connecting Networks over the Internet

When connecting to networks over the Internet, branch offices can use either dedicated lines or dial-up lines.

Dedicated Lines

Rather than using an expensive long-haul dedicated circuit between the branch office and the corporate hub, both the branch office and the corporate hub routers connect to the Internet through the use of a local dedicated circuit and local ISP. Utilizing the local ISP connections, a VPN is created between the branch office router and corporate hub router across the Internet.

Dial-Up Lines

Rather than having a router at the branch office make a long distance call to a corporate or outsourced Network Access Server (NAS), the router at the branch office calls its local ISP. From the connection to the local ISP, a VPN is created between the branch office router to the corporate hub router across the Internet. The corporate hub router, acting as a VPN server, must be connected to a local ISP via a dedicated line. The VPN server must be listening 24 hours a day for incoming VPN traffic.

Note Whether the branch offices use dedicated lines or dial-up lines, the transfer of data through the VPN is distance insensitive since only local physical links are being used.

Connecting Computers over an Intranet

In some corporate internetworks, the data of certain departments is so sensitive that the department's LAN is physically disconnected from the rest of the corporate internetwork. While this protects the department's data, it also creates information accessibility problems for users that are not physically connected to the separate LAN.

VPNs allow the department's LAN to be physically connected to the corporate internetwork but separated by a VPN server. Note that the VPN server is not acting as a router between the corporate internetwork and the department LAN. Users on the corporate internetwork who have the appropriate credentials (based on a need-to-know policy within the company) can establish a VPN with the VPN server and gain access to the protected resources of the department. Additionally, all communication across the VPN can be encrypted for confidentiality. For users without proper credentials, the department LAN is essentially hidden from view.

Tunneling Basics

Tunneling, also known as encapsulation, is a method of using an internetwork infrastructure to transfer a payload. The payload may be the frames (or packets) of another protocol. Instead of sending the frame as produced by the originating node, the frame is encapsulated with an additional header. The additional header provides routing information so that the encapsulated payload can traverse the intermediate internetwork. The encapsulated packets are then routed between tunnel endpoints over the transit internetwork. Once the encapsulated frames reach their destination on the transit internetwork, the frame is de-encapsulated and forwarded to its final destination.

This entire process (the encapsulation and transmission of packets) is known as tunneling. The logical path through which the encapsulated packets travel the transit internetwork is called a *tunnel*.

Tunnel Maintenance and Data Transfer

The collective functionality of a tunnel maintenance protocol and tunnel data transfer protocol is known as a tunneling protocol. In order for a tunnel to be established, both the tunnel client and the tunnel server must be using the same tunneling protocol. Examples of tunneling protocols are PPTP and L2TP, which are discussed in more detail later in this lesson.

Tunnel Maintenance Protocol

A tunnel maintenance protocol is used as the mechanism to manage the tunnel. For some tunneling technologies, such as PPTP and L2TP, a tunnel is similar to a session: both endpoints of the tunnel must agree to the tunnel and be aware of its presence. However, unlike a session, a tunnel does not guarantee reliable data delivery. Data transferred across the tunnel is typically sent by a datagram-based protocol such as UDP when L2TP is used or TCP for tunnel management and a modified Generic Routing Encapsulation (GRE) protocol when PPTP is used.

Creating the Tunnel

A tunnel must be created before data transfer occurs. The tunnel creation is initiated by one end of the tunnel, the tunnel client. At the other end of the tunnel the tunnel server receives the connection request.

To create the tunnel, a connection creation process similar to a PPP connection is performed. The tunnel server requests that the tunnel client authenticate itself. Once validated by the tunnel server, the tunnel connection is granted and data transfer across the tunnel can begin.

Tunnel creation messages are sent by the tunnel client to the internetwork address of the tunnel server. Using the Internet as an example, the tunnel client sends tunnel creation messages from its InterNIC-compliant IP address to the InterNIC-compliant address of the tunnel server on the Internet. If the tunnel client is a dial-up Internet user, the tunnel client uses the IP address as allocated by the ISP as a source IP address and the IP address of the tunnel server as the destination IP address.

Maintaining the Tunnel

For some tunneling technologies, such PPTP and L2TP, once the tunnel has been created, it must be maintained. Both ends of the tunnel must be aware of the state of the other end of the tunnel in case of a connection fault. Tunnel maintenance is typically performed through a keep-alive process that periodically polls the other end of the tunnel when no data is being transferred.

Terminating the Tunnel

Certain tunneling technologies allow either end of the tunnel to gracefully terminate the tunnel through an exchange of tunnel termination messages.

Tunnel Data Transfer Protocol

Once the tunnel is established, tunneled data can be sent. A tunnel data transfer protocol encapsulates the data to be transferred across the tunnel. When the tunnel client sends a tunneled payload to the tunnel server, the tunnel client appends a tunnel data transfer protocol header onto the payload. The resulting encapsulated payload is sent across the transit internetwork and routed to the tunnel server.

The tunnel server accepts the packets, removes the tunnel data transfer protocol header, and forwards the payload appropriately. Information sent between the tunnel server and the tunnel client behaves similarly.

Tunnel Types

There are two basic types of tunnels: voluntary tunnels and compulsory tunnels. Depending upon the client configuration, compulsory tunnels consist of either static or dynamic compulsory tunnels.

Voluntary Tunnels

Voluntary tunnels are configured and created through a conscious action by the user at the tunnel client computer. The user's computer is a tunnel endpoint and acts as the tunnel client.

Voluntary tunneling occurs when the client workstation volunteers to create the tunnel to the target tunnel server. Since the client is acting as a tunnel client, the appropriate tunneling protocol must be installed on the client computer. Voluntary tunneling can occur in either of the following cases:

- The client already has a connection to the transit internetwork that can provide routing of encapsulated payloads between the client computer and its chosen tunnel server.

- The client may have to establish a connection (via dial-up) to the transit internetwork before the client can set up a tunnel. This is the more common case. The best example of this case is the dial-up Internet user. Internet users must dial their ISP and obtain an Internet connection before a tunnel over the Internet can be created.

Compulsory Tunnels

Compulsory tunnels are configured and created automatically for users without their knowledge or intervention. With compulsory tunnels, the user's computer is not a tunnel endpoint. Another device between the user's computer and the tunnel server is the tunnel endpoint and acts as the tunnel client.

If a client computer does not have a tunneling protocol installed and tunneling is still desired, then it is possible for another computer or network device to create the tunnel on the client computer's behalf. This is a functionality referred to as *access concentrator*. In order to carry out its function, the access concentrator must have the appropriate tunneling protocol installed and be capable of establishing the tunnel when the client computer connects.

When connecting through the Internet, the client computer calls a tunneling-enabled NAS at the ISP. For example, a corporation may have contracted with an ISP to assemble a nationwide set of access concentrators. These access concentrators can establish tunnels across the Internet to a tunnel server connected to the corporation's private network. This configuration is known as compulsory tunneling because the client is compelled to use the tunnel created by the access concentrator. Once the initial connection is made, all network traffic to and from the client is automatically sent through the tunnel.

With compulsory tunneling, the client computer makes a single PPP connection, and when a client dials into the NAS, a tunnel is created and all traffic is automatically routed through the tunnel.

The decision by the access concentrator to tunnel a dial-up client to a specific tunnel server can be based on statically configured information at the access concentrator or by dynamically consulting a user database.

Static Compulsory Tunnels

Static tunnel configurations typically require either dedicated equipment (automatic tunnels) or manual configuration (realm-based tunnels).

Automatic tunneling is where all dial-in clients to the access concentrator are automatically tunneled to a specific tunnel server. This requires dedicated local access lines and network access equipment, with its associated costs. For example, users might be required to call a specific telephone number in order to connect to an access concentrator that automatically tunnels all connections to a particular tunnel server.

In realm-based tunneling schemes, the access concentrator examines a portion of the user's name (called a realm) to decide where to tunnel the traffic associated with that user. For example, users in the microsoft.com realm (logging on as user@microsoft.com) would be tunneled to one destination, while users in the domain.com realm (logging on as user@domain.com) would be tunneled elsewhere. Realm-based tunneling is relatively simple to implement, does not require dedicated equipment, and has low overhead after initial configuration. However, configuration changes may be expensive and time-consuming. In addition, all traffic for all users of the same realm is tunneled to the same destination. Realm-based tunneling does not allow any further granularity of tunnel server designation.

Dynamic Compulsory Tunnels

With dynamic compulsory tunneling, the choice of tunnel destination is made on a per-user basis at the time the user connects to the access concentrator. Users from the same realm may be tunneled to different destinations depending upon parameters such as user name, called or calling phone number, department, location, and even the time of day. Dynamic tunnels offer the greatest flexibility of any compulsory tunneling scheme.

Dynamic tunneling also permits the access concentrator to be a multi-use NAS, allowing the connection of tunneling clients and ordinary (non-tunneled) Internet clients. A dedicated access concentrator or telephone line is not required. In order for the access concentrator to determine whether or not to tunnel a particular dial-up client, it must consult a database.

While each access concentrator can store its own database of user information, this solution does not scale well administratively. A better solution is to store the user information in a centrally administered location and have the access concentrator consult the central database as needed (when dial-up clients call). RADIUS, for example, can provide this type of solution.

VPN Protocols

The primary protocols used by Windows 2000 for VPN access are PPTP, L2TP, IPSEC, and IP-IP. These protocols may work together or independently of each other.

PPTP

Point-to-Point Tunneling Protocol (PPTP), an extension of PPP, encapsulates PPP frames into IP datagrams for transmission over an IP internetwork such as the Internet. PPTP can also be used in private LAN-to-LAN networking.

PPTP uses a TCP connection for tunnel maintenance and uses modified GRE encapsulated PPP frames for tunneled data. The payloads of the encapsulated PPP frames can be encrypted and compressed.

PPTP was created by the PPTP forum consisting of Microsoft Corporation, Ascend Communications, 3COM, ECI Telematics, and US Robotics.

PPTP tunnels must be authenticated by using the same authentication mechanisms as PPP connections (PAP, MS-CHAP, CHAP, and EAP). PPTP inherits encryption and compression of PPP payloads from PPP. In Windows 2000, PPP encryption can be used only when the authentication protocol is EAP-TLS or MSCHAP. PPP encryption provides confidentiality between the endpoints of the tunnel only. If stronger security or end-to-end security is needed, IPSEC can be used. Figure 10.14 shows a fully constructed PPTP packet.

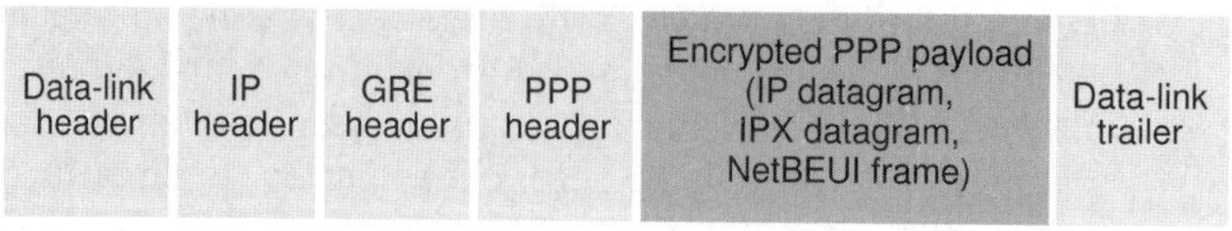

Data-link header	IP header	GRE header	PPP header	Encrypted PPP payload (IP datagram, IPX datagram, NetBEUI frame)	Data-link trailer

Figure 10.14 PPTP packet showing the encrypted data being sent, including header and trailer information

L2TP

Layer 2 Tunneling Protocol (L2TP) is a combination of PPTP and Layer 2 Forwarding (L2F), a technology proposed by Cisco Corporation. L2TP is a hybrid of the best features in PPTP and L2F.

L2TP is a network protocol that encapsulates PPP frames to be sent over IP, X.25, Frame Relay, or ATM networks. When utilizing IP as its datagram transport, L2TP can be used as a tunneling protocol over the Internet. L2TP can also be used in private LAN-to-LAN networking.

Note L2TP in Windows 2000 runs only over an IP network. It does not run in Native mode over X.25, Frame Relay, or ATM networks.

L2TP uses UDP and a series of L2TP messages for tunnel maintenance. L2TP also uses UDP to send L2TP-encapsulated PPP frames as the tunneled data. The payloads of encapsulated PPP frames can be both encrypted and compressed. Microsoft chose IPSec instead of PPP encryption for L2TP. However, it is possible for other implementations of L2TP to use PPP encryption. Figure 10.15 shows an L2TP packet prepared to be sent using IPSec authentication and encryption settings over a point-to-point WAN connection, such as a dial-up line. The processing steps are shown in the figure. Steps 1–4 show normal processing prior to IPSec encapsulation. Steps 5–7 show IPSec processing. The remaining steps are necessary in order to send the packet on the network to its final destination.

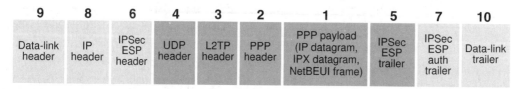

Figure 10.15 L2TP packet showing encrypted data with IPSec authentication, an additional IP header, and data-link header and trailer information

L2TP is very similar to PPTP in function. An L2TP tunnel is created between an L2TP client and an L2TP server. The client may already be attached to an IP internetwork (such as a LAN) that can reach the tunnel server, or a client may have to dial into a NAS to establish IP connectivity (for dial-up Internet users).

Creation of L2TP tunnels must be authenticated by using the same authentication mechanisms as PPP connections (PAP, MS-CHAP, CHAP, and EAP). L2TP inherits PPP compression but not encryption. PPP encryption is not used because it does not meet the security requirements of L2TP. PPP encryption could provide confidentiality but would not provide per packet authentication, integrity, or replay protection. Data encryption is provided by IPSec. Using PPP connection encryption with an IPSec encrypted payload, increases processing overhead with little to no added benefit.

PPTP versus L2TP

Both PPTP and L2TP use PPP for point-to-point WAN connections, to provide an initial envelope for the data and then append additional headers for transport through the transit internetwork. However, there are some differences between PPTP and L2TP:

- PPTP requires that the transit internetwork be an IP internetwork. L2TP requires only that the tunnel media provide packet oriented point-to-point connectivity. L2TP can be run over IP (using UDP), Frame Relay PVCs, X.25 VCs or ATM VCs.

- L2TP provides header compression capability. When header compression is enabled, L2TP operates with 4 bytes of overhead, compared to 6 bytes for PPTP.

- L2TP also provides tunnel authentication, while PPTP does not. However, when either PPTP or L2TP is run over IPSec, it provides tunnel authentication, making Layer 2 tunnel authentication unnecessary.

- PPTP uses PPP encryption and L2TP does not. Microsoft's L2TP requires IPSec for encryption.

IPSec

IPSec, a layer 3 tunneling protocol, is a series of standards that support the secured transfer of information across an IP internetwork. IPSec Encapsulating Security Payload (ESP) Tunnel mode supports the encapsulation and encryption of entire IP datagrams for secure transfer across a private or public IP internetwork.

With IPSec ESP Tunnel mode, a complete IP datagram is encapsulated and encrypted with ESP. The result is then encapsulated—using a plaintext IP header—and sent on the transit internetwork (Figure 10.15).

Upon receipt of the encrypted datagram, the tunnel server processes and discards the clear text IP header and authenticates and decrypts the ESP and IP packet. The IP packet is then processed normally. Normal processing may include routing the packet to its final destination.

ESP Tunnel Mode versus Transport Mode

The main difference between ESP Tunnel mode and ESP Transport mode is the former has an encapsulated IP header. Because of this IP header, when the packet exits the tunnel (IPSec encapsulation and encryption is removed) it can be routed to its final destination. By using ESP Transport mode, the packet is always decrypted by the time it reaches its final destination.

IPSec ESP Tunnel Mode Packet Structure

IPSec ESP Tunnel mode is performed through multiple layers of encapsulation. Figure 10.15 refers to these steps:

- **First Layer of Encapsulation** The initial IP datagram is appended with an ESP trailer and then encrypted (step 5 in Figure 10.15).

- **Second Layer of Encapsulation** The encrypted payload is encapsulated with an ESP header and an ESP Authentication trailer. The ESP Authentication trailer contains the Integrity Check Value (ICV), a cryptographic checksum that is used to authenticate and verify the integrity of the payload (steps 6 and 7).

- **Third Layer of Encapsulation** The IPSec packet is encapsulated with a final IP header containing the source and destination IP addresses of the tunnel endpoints (step 8).

- **Data Link Layer of Encapsulation** To be sent on a LAN or WAN link, the IP datagram is finally encapsulated with a header and trailer for the data link layer technology of the outgoing physical interface (steps 9 and 10).

IPSec Tunnel mode is an OSI layer 3 (network layer) tunneling technique. Unlike L2TP and PPTP, IPSec Tunnel mode does not rely on PPP for authentication or security. In addition, it cannot be used as a Windows 2000 Router interface as IP-IP can. Because IPSec Tunnel mode cannot be a router interface, it cannot support routing protocols or dial on demand. Instead, IPSec Tunnel mode can be used based on packet filters for each route. The packet filters define the IPSec tunnel destination.

IP-IP

IP-IP, or IP in IP, is a simple OSI layer 3 (network layer) tunneling technique. A virtual network is created by encapsulating an IP packet with an additional IP header. The primary use of IP-IP is for tunneling multicast traffic over sections of a network that does not support multicast routing. The IP-IP packet structure consists of the outer IP header, the tunnel header, the inner IP header, and the IP payload.

The IP payload includes everything above IP. This could be TCP, UDP, or ICMP headers, and data. A limited form of tunnel maintenance is achieved by using standard ICMP messages. ICMP messages allow the tunnel to do tunnel MTU discovery and detect congestion and routing failures.

Managing Virtual Private Networking

In lesson 3, you learned how to manage remote access. In many ways, the management of VPNs is similar to managing remote access. Virtual private networking must be managed just like any other network resource, and VPN security issues must be managed carefully, particularly with Internet VPN connections.

Managing Users

Because it is not practical to have separate user accounts on separate servers for the same user, most administrators set up a master account database at a domain controller or on a RADIUS server. This allows the VPN server to send the authentication credentials to a central authenticating device. The same user account is used for both dial-in remote access and VPN-based remote access.

Managing Addresses and Name Servers

The VPN server must have IP addresses available in order to assign them to the VPN server's virtual interface and to VPN clients during the IP Control Protocol (IPCP) negotiation phase of the connection process. The IP address assigned to the VPN client is assigned to the virtual interface of the VPN client.

For Windows 2000–based VPN servers, the IP addresses assigned to VPN clients are obtained through DHCP by default. You can also configure a static IP address pool. The VPN server must also be configured with name resolution servers, typically DNS and WINS server addresses, to assign to the VPN client during IPCP negotiation.

Managing Access

For Windows 2000, configure the dial-in properties on user accounts and remote access policies to manage access for dial-up networking and VPN connections.

Access by User Account

If you are managing remote access on a user basis, select the Allow Access radio button on the Dial-In tab of the user's Properties dialog box for those user accounts that are allowed to create VPN connections. If the VPN server is allowing only VPN connections, delete the default remote access policy called Allow Access If Dial-In Permission Is Enabled. Then create a new remote access policy with a descriptive name, such as VPN Access If Allowed By User Account.

Caution After deleting the default policy, a dial-up client that does not match at least one of the policy configurations you create will be denied access.

If the VPN server is also allowing dial-up remote access services, do not delete the default policy, but move it so that it is the last policy to be evaluated.

Access by Group Membership

If you are managing remote access on a group basis, select the Control access through remote access policy radio button on all user accounts. Create a Windows 2000 group with members who are allowed to create VPN connections. If the VPN server allows only VPN connections, delete the default remote access policy called Allow Access If Dial-In Permission Is Enabled. Next, create a new remote access policy with a descriptive name such as VPN Access If Member Of VPN-Allowed Group, and then assign the Windows 2000 group to the policy.

If the VPN server also allows dial-up networking remote access services, do not delete the default policy; instead move it so that it is the last policy to be evaluated.

Managing Authentication

The VPN server can be configured to use either Windows or RADIUS as an authentication provider. If Windows is selected as the authentication provider, the user credentials sent by users attempting VPN connections are authenticated using Windows authentication mechanisms and remote access policy configured through the Routing And Remote Access snap-in.

If RADIUS is selected and configured as the authentication provider on the VPN server, user credentials and parameters of the connection request are sent as a series of RADIUS request messages to a RADIUS server.

The RADIUS server receives a user-connection request from the VPN server and authenticates the user by using its authentication database. A RADIUS server can also maintain a central storage database of other relevant user properties. In addition to a yes or no response to an authentication request, RADIUS can inform the VPN server of other applicable connection profile data for users, such as maximum session time, static IP address assignment, and so on. An IAS RADIUS server stores remote access profile information for clients that use the RADIUS server as the authentication provider. If RADIUS authentication is configured for a RAS server, the Remote Access Policies node disappears from the Routing And Remote Access snap-in console tree; remote access policy is then configured in IAS.

RADIUS can respond to authentication requests based on its own database, or it can be a front end to another database server, such as a generic Open Database Connectivity (ODBC) server or a Windows 2000 domain controller. The latter can be located on the same computer as the RADIUS server, or elsewhere. In addition, a RADIUS server can act as a proxy client to a remote RADIUS server.

Troubleshooting

Troubleshooting VPNs is a combination of troubleshooting IP connectivity, remote access connection establishment, routing, and IPSec. A firm understanding of all of these topics is required.

The following sections outline common VPN problems and the troubleshooting tools provided with Windows 2000. VPN problems typically fall into the following categories:

- Connection attempt is rejected when it should be accepted.

- Connection attempt is accepted when it should be rejected.

- Unable to reach locations beyond the VPN server.

- Unable to establish a tunnel.

Connection Attempt is Rejected When it Should Be Accepted

Verify the following information in order to troubleshoot this problem:

- Verify that the host name or IP address of the VPN server is reachable by using the ping command. If a host name is being used, verify that it is resolved to its correct IP address.

- Verify that RRAS is running on the VPN server.

- Verify that all of the PPTP or L2TP ports on the VPN server are not already being used. If necessary, change the number of PPTP to L2TP ports to allow more concurrent connections. Ports are added and configured from the Ports node in the Routing And Remote Access snap-in.

- Verify that the tunneling protocol of the VPN client is supported by the VPN server. You can do this by checking the Port Properties on the RAS server.

- Remote access VPN clients are set to the Automatic server type by default, which means that they will try to establish a PPTP tunnel first, then try an L2TP over IPSec tunnel. If the server type is set to either Point-to-Point Tunneling Protocol (PPTP) or Layer 2 Tunneling Protocol (L2TP), verify that the selected tunneling protocol is supported by the VPN server.

- A Windows 2000 computer running RRAS is a PPTP and L2TP server with five L2TP ports and five PPTP ports by default (appearing in the details pane of the Ports node in the Routing And Remote Access snap-in). To create a PPTP-only server, set the number of L2TP ports to 0.

  To create an L2TP-only server, set the number of PPTP ports to 1, because the number of PPTP ports cannot be set to 0, and then clear the Remote Access Connection (Inbound Only) and the Demand Dial Routing Connections (Inbound And Outbound) check boxes. These settings are configured from the properties of the Ports node. On the client computer, change the type of VPN server from automatic to Layer-2 Tunneling Protocol (L2TP).

- Verify that the VPN client and the VPN server are enabled to use at least one common authentication method.

- For PPTP connections, test whether a PPTP connection can be made without encryption. If so, check the encryption settings on the VPN client and VPN server.

- For L2TP over IPSec connections, test whether a L2TP connection can be made without encryption (without IPSec). If so, check the L2TP over IPSec encryption settings on the VPN client and VPN server.

To disable IPSec on the client computer, access the properties of the VPN connection. Click the Networking tab and then access the properties of Internet Protocol (TCP/IP). Next, click the Advanced button and then the Options tab. Finally, access the properties of the IP Security option. From the IP Security dialog box, you can configure the client to not use IPSEC.

To disable IPSec on the server, access the properties of the local area network adapter. From there, access the properties of Internet Protocol (TCP/IP) and then follow the navigation procedure outlined for the client connection. This procedure can also be followed for the client computer if the client computer contains a Local Area Connection option in the Network And Dial-up Connections window.

- Verify that the parameters of the connection have permission through remote access policies. Remote access policy is configured through the Routing And Remote Access snap-in or through the RADIUS server, depending on the authentication provider.

In order for the connection to be established, the parameters of the connection attempt must meet the following conditions:

- Match all of the conditions of at least one remote access policy.

- Be granted remote access permission either through the remote access permission of the user object (set to Allow Access) or through a combination of the user object settings and remote access policy. In the latter case, the Control Access Through Remote Access Policy option in the User Object properties is selected and the Grant Remote Access Permission option is selected in the properties of the remote access policy.

- Match all the settings of the profile.

- Match all the settings of the dial-in properties of the user object. Verify that the settings of the remote access policy profile are not in conflict with properties of the routing and remote access server.

If the settings of the profile of the matching remote access policy are in conflict with the settings of the VPN server, the connection attempt is rejected. For example, if the matching remote access policy profile specifies that the EAP-TLS authentication protocol must be used and EAP-TLS is not enabled on the VPN server, the VPN server rejects the connection attempt.

- Verify that the VPN client's credentials consisting of user name, password, and domain name are correct and can be validated by the VPN server.

- If the VPN server is configured with a static IP address pool, verify that there are enough addresses in the pool. If all the addresses in the static pool have been allocated to connected VPN clients, the VPN server is unable to allocate an IP address and the connection attempt is rejected.

- Verify the configuration of the authentication provider. For a VPN server that is a member server in a mixed or native Windows 2000 domain configured for Windows NT authentication, verify that the machine account of the VPN server computer is a member of the RAS and IAS Servers security group.

- For remote access VPN connections, verify that remote access is enabled on the VPN server.

- For remote access VPN connections, verify that the PPTP and/or L2TP ports are enabled for inbound remote access requests.

- For remote client VPNs, verify that the LAN protocols used by the VPN client are enabled for remote access.

- For router-to-router VPN connections, verify that routing is enabled and LAN and demand-dial routing is selected on the VPN server. This option can be configured from the General tab of the RRAS server's Properties dialog box.

- For router-to-router VPN connections, verify that the PPTP and L2TP ports are enabled for inbound and outbound demand-dial routing connections. This option can be configured from the properties of the Ports node.

Connection Attempt is Accepted When it Should Be Rejected

Verify that the parameters of the connection do not have permission through remote access policies.

In order for the connection to be rejected, the parameters of the connection attempt must be denied remote access permission through one of the following methods:

- The remote access permission of the user object is set to Deny Access.

- The remote access permission of the user object is set to Control Access Through Remote Access Policy and the first remote access policy that matches the parameters of the connection attempt is set to Deny Remote Access Permission.

Unable to Reach Locations beyond the VPN Server

Verify the following information in order to troubleshoot this problem:

- For remote client VPNs, verify that the Entire network option is selected for LAN protocols being used by the VPN clients.

- Verify the IP address pool of the VPN server.

  - If the VPN server is configured to use a static IP address pool, verify that the route to the range of addresses defined by the static IP address pool is reachable by the hosts and routers of the intranet. If not, an IP route consisting of the VPN server static IP address pool (IP Address, Subnet Mask) must be added to the routers of the intranet. If the route is not added, remote access clients will not receive traffic from resources on the intranet. A route for the network can be implemented through static routing entries or through a routing protocol such as RIP or OSPF.

  - If the VPN server is configured to use DHCP for IP address allocation and no DHCP server is available, a route to 169.254.0.0/16 (subnet mask 255.255.0.0) must be added to the routers of the intranet. When the VPN server is configured to use DHCP and no DHCP server is found, the VPN server allocates addresses from the AutoNet address range of 169.254.0.0/16. To check this address allocation on the client computer, access the properties of the active connection.

  - If the static IP address pool is a range of IP addresses that is a subset of the range of IP addresses for the network to which the VPN server is attached, verify that the range of IP addresses in the static IP address pool are not assigned to other TCP/IP nodes either statically or through DHCP.

  - For router-to-router VPNs, verify that the router-to-router VPN connection is being interpreted by the VPN server as a router-to-router VPN connection rather than as a remote access connection.

  - If the user name of the calling router's credentials appears under Dial-In Clients in the Routing And Remote Access Manager, then the VPN server has interpreted the calling router as a remote access client. Verify that the user name in the calling router's credentials matches the name of a demand-dial interface on the VPN server.

Unable to Establish Tunnel

Verify the following information in order to troubleshoot this problem:

- Verify that you are connecting to the correct address. Try to use the IP address of the server interface closest to you. This is the address of the interface that has the route back to you. If you are using DNS to resolve the IP address, the correct address may not be in use. Using the wrong address will cause the PPTP session to reset.

- Verify that packet filtering on a router interface between the VPN client and the VPN server is not preventing the forwarding of tunnel maintenance traffic or tunneled data.

  - On a Windows 2000 VPN server, IP packet filtering can be configured from the advanced TCP/IP properties and from the Routing And Remote Access snap-in. Check both places for filters that may be excluding VPN traffic.

  - Verify that packet filtering on other routers in the path are not blocking the needed protocols.

  - Verify the configuration of tunneling protocols:

    - **PPTP** Pass TCP port 1723 and IP protocol ID 47 for the control session and GRE.

    - **L2TP** Pass UDP port 1701.

    - **IPSec** Pass protocol ID 50 and 51 for IPSEC Authentication header and ESP encapsulating security payload.

    - **IP-IP** Pass IP protocol ID 4.

- Verify that the WinSock Proxy client is not currently running on the VPN client. When the WinSock Proxy client is active, WinSock API calls, such as those used to create tunnels and send tunneled data, are intercepted and forwarded to a configured proxy server.

Lesson Summary

A VPN mimics the properties of a dedicated private network, allowing data to be transferred between two computers across an internetwork, such as the Internet. Branch offices can use two different methods to connect to a network over the internet: using dedicated lines or dial-up lines. VPNs use tunneling to transfer data. Tunneling is a method of using an internetwork infrastructure to transfer a payload. A tunneling protocol is made up of a tunnel maintenance protocol and a tunnel data transfer protocol. There are two basic types of tunnels: voluntary tunnels and compulsory tunnels. The primary protocols used by Windows 2000 for VPN access are PPTP, L2TP, IPSec, and IP-IP. When managing VPNs, you must manage users, addresses and name servers, access, authentication, and encryption. If you cannot establish a VPN connection, you must troubleshoot the problem. Troubleshooting VPNs is a combination of troubleshooting IP connectivity, remote access connection establishment, routing, and IPSec.

Lesson 5: RRAS Tools

Windows 2000 includes a set of tools that you can use to manage and trouble-shoot RRAS. These tools include the Routing And Remote Access snap-in, the netsh command-line utility, authentication and accounting logging, event logging, and tracing.

After this lesson, you will be able to

- Use the Windows 2000 tools that are provided to administer and trouble-shoot RRAS

Estimated lesson time: 30 minutes

Routing And Remote Access Snap-In

The Routing And Remote Access snap-in allows you to perform a variety of management tasks, such as enabling RRAS, managing routing interfaces, configuring IPX routing, creating a static IP address pool, configuring remote access policies, and so on. For more information about the Routing And Remote Access snap-in, open the snap-in and then click the Help button (Figure 10.16).

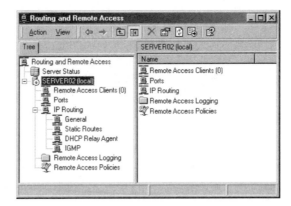

Figure 10.16 Routing And Remote Access snap-in

The Routing And Remote Access snap-in is available from the Administrative Tools folder and is the primary management utility for configuring Windows 2000 local and remote access servers and routers.

Net Shell Command-Line Utility

Net Shell is a command-line and scripting utility for Windows 2000 networking components for local or remote computers. The Net Shell utility is named Netsh.exe and is installed in %systemroot%\system32 when Windows 2000 is installed. Netsh also allows you to save a configuration script in a text file for archival purposes or for configuring other servers.

Netsh can support multiple Windows 2000 components through the addition of netsh helper DLLs. A netsh helper DLL extends its functionality by providing additional commands to monitor or configure a specific Windows 2000 networking component. For example, Ippromon.dll is a helper for using the dhcp, dnsproxy, igmp, nat, ospf, dhcp relay, and rip commands. Each netsh helper DLL provides a context (a group of commands for a specific networking component). Within each context, subcontexts can exist. For example, within the routing context, the subcontexts ip and ipx exist to group IP routing and IPX routing commands together.

Note All command-line options beginning with a minus sign are run outside of the Shell mode. Once in Shell mode, commands are carried out without specifying netsh or a command starting with a minus sign.

Netsh command-line options include the following:

- **–a** *<AliasFile>* Specifies that an alias file can be used. An alias file contains a list of netsh commands and an aliased version so that the aliased command line can be used in place of the netsh command. Alias files can be used to map commands to the appropriate netsh command that might be more familiar in other platforms.

- **–c** *<Context>* Specifies the context of the command corresponding to an installed helper DLL. For example:

  ```
  netsh -c routing
  ```

  places you in the context of the routing helper.

- **Command** Specifies which Netsh command to carry out. Commands can be run both inside and outside of Shell mode. For example:

  ```
  netsh show helper
  ```

  shows the helpers installed at the root of the shell. After entering the shell by typing **netsh**, the command for showing helper DLLs at the root of netsh is:

  ```
  show helper
  ```

- **–f** *<ScriptFile>* Specifies that all of the netsh commands in the script file be run. For example:

  ```
  netsh -f config.txt
  ```

  runs all commands in a file named config.txt.

- **–r** *<RemoteComputerName or IP_address>* Specifies that netsh commands are run on the remote computer specified by its name or IP address. For example:

  ```
  netsh -r RRAS2
  ```

  places Net Shell in command mode for a RRAS server named RRAS2. The command prompt is changed to:

  ```
  [RRAS2] netsh>
  ```

Commands can be abbreviated to the shortest unambiguous string. For example, while in the command shell, typing the command **ro ip sh int** is equivalent to typing **routing ip show interface**. Netsh commands can be either global or context specific. Global commands can be issued in any context and are used for general netsh functions. Context-specific commands vary according to context.

The following table lists the netsh global commands.

Command	Description
..	Moves up one context level.
? or help	Displays command-line Help.
add helper	Adds a netsh helper DLL.
delete helper	Removes a netsh helper DLL.
show helper	Displays the installed netsh helper DLLs.
online	Sets the current mode to online.
offline	Sets the current mode to offline.
set mode	Sets the current mode to online or offline.
show mode	Displays the current mode.
flush	Discards any changes in Offline mode.
commit	Commits changes made in Offline mode.
set machine	Configures the computer on which the netsh commands are carried out.

Command	Description
show machine	Displays the computer on which the netsh commands are carried out.
Exec	Executes a script file containing netsh commands.
quit or bye or exit	Exits netsh.
add alias	Adds an alias to an existing command.
delete alias	Deletes an alias from an existing command.
show alias	Displays all defined aliases.
dump	Dumps or appends configuration to a text file.
popd	A scripting command that pops a context from the stack.
pushd	A scripting command that pushes the current context on the stack.

Netsh has the following command modes:

- **Online** In Online mode, commands issued at a netsh command prompt are carried out immediately.

- **Offline** In Offline mode, commands issued at a netsh command prompt are accumulated and carried out as a batch by issuing the commit global command. Accumulated commands can be discarded by issuing the flush global command.

You can also run a script (a text file with a list of netsh commands) by using either the -f command-line option or by typing the exec global command while in the netsh shell.

To create a script of the current configuration, type the global dump command. The dump command generates the current running configuration in terms of netsh commands. You can then use the script created by this command that you configure a new server or to reconfigure the existing server. If you are making extensive changes to the configuration of a component, it is recommended to begin the configuration session with the dump command, in case you need to restore the configuration before you make changes.

For RRAS, netsh has the following contexts:

- **ras** Use commands in the ras context to configure remote access configuration.

- **aaaa** Use commands in the aaaa context to configure the AAAA component used by both Routing and Remote Access and Internet Authentication Service. AAAA stores the configuration setting of the IAS server.

- **routing** Use commands in the routing context to configure IP and IPX routing.

- **interface** Use commands in the interface context to configure demand-dial interfaces.

For more information about context-specific commands, see Windows 2000 Server Help and the help provided by the netsh command.

Authentication and Accounting Logging

RRAS supports the logging of authentication and accounting information for PPP-based connection attempts when Windows authentication or accounting is enabled. This logging is separate from the events recorded in the system event log. You can use the information that is logged to track remote access usage and authentication attempts. Authentication and accounting logging is especially useful for troubleshooting remote access policy issues. For each authentication attempt, the name of the remote access policy that either accepted or rejected the connection attempt is recorded.

The authentication and accounting information is stored in a configurable log file or files stored in the %systemroot%\System32\LogFiles folder. Log files are saved in IAS 1.0 or database format, meaning that any database program can read the log file directly for analysis.

You can configure the type of activity to log (accounting or authentication activity) and log file settings, including an alternate storage location, from the properties of the Remote Access Logging folder in either the Routing And Remote Access snap-in or the Internet Authentication Service snap-in. The logging location is based on the settings configured for the authentication and logging provider used by RRAS.

Event Logging

The Windows 2000 Router performs extensive error logging in the system event log. You can use information in the event logs to troubleshoot routing or remote access processes.

The following four levels of logging are available

- Log errors only
- Log errors and warnings
- Log the maximum amount of information
- Disable event logging

For example, if an Open Shortest Path First (OSPF) router is unable to establish an adjacency on an interface, you can take the following steps:

1. Disable OSPF on the interface.
2. Change the level of logging for OSPF to log the maximum amount of information.
3. Enable OSPF on the interface.
4. Examine the system event log for information about the OSPF adjacency process.
5. Change the level of logging for OSPF to log errors only.

You can then troubleshoot the adjacency problem by analyzing the OSPF entries in the system event log.

The level of event logging can be set from various places within the Routing And Remote Access snap-in. For example, logging can be set for a specific computer on the Event Logging tab of that computer's properties. You can also set logging in the General Properties dialog box for IP Routing (on the General tab).

Logging consumes system resources and should be used sparingly to help identify network problems. After the event has been logged or the problem is identified, you should immediately reset logging to log errors only.

When logging the maximum amount of information, the logging information can be complex and very detailed. Some of this information is useful only to Microsoft Product Support Services engineers or to network administrators who are very experienced with Windows 2000 routing.

Tracing

Windows 2000 RRAS has an extensive tracing capability that you can use to troubleshoot complex network problems. Tracing records internal component variables, function calls, and interactions. Separate routing and remote access components can be independently enabled to log tracing information to files (file tracing). You must enable the tracing function by changing settings in the Windows 2000 registry.

Caution Do not use a registry editor to edit the registry directly unless you have no alternative. Registry editors bypass the standard safeguards provided by administrative tools. These safeguards prevent you from entering conflicting settings or settings that are likely to degrade performance or damage your system. Editing the registry directly can have serious, unexpected consequences that can prevent the system from starting and require that you reinstall Windows 2000. To configure or customize Windows 2000, use the programs in Control Panel or snap-ins whenever possible.

You can enable tracing for each routing protocol by setting the registry values described later in this section. You can also enable and disable tracing for routing protocols while the router is running. Each installed routing protocol or component is capable of tracing and appears as a key (such as OSPF and RIPV2).

Tracing consumes system resources and should be used sparingly to help identify network problems. After the trace is captured or the problem is identified, you should immediately disable tracing. Do not leave tracing enabled on multiprocessor computers.

Tracing information can be complex and very detailed. Most of the time this information is useful only to Microsoft support engineers or to network administrators who are very experienced with Windows 2000 routing.

File Tracing

To enable file tracing for each component (represented as Component below), you must set the value of the EnableFileTracing registry entry in HKEY_LOCAL_MACHINE\SOFTWARE\Microsoft\Tracing\Component to 1. The default value is 0.

To set the location of the trace file for each component, you must set the value of the FileDirectory registry entry. The location of the log file is entered as a path. The file name for the log file is the name of the component for which tracing is enabled. By default, log files are placed in the %systemroot%\ Tracing folder.

To set the level of file tracing for each component, you must set the value of the FileTracingMask registry entry. The tracing level can be from 0 to 0xffff0000. By default, the level of file tracing is set to 0xffff0000, the maximum level of tracing.

To set the maximum size of a log file, you must set the value of the MaxFileSize registry entry. You can change the size of the log file by setting different values for MaxFileSize. The default value is 10000 (64 KB).

Lesson Summary

Windows 2000 includes a set of tools that allows you to manage and trouble-shoot RRAS. The Routing And Remote Access snap-in allows you to perform a variety of management tasks, such as enabling RRAS, managing routing interfaces, configuring IPX routing, creating a static IP address pool, configuring remote access policies, and so on. Netsh is a command-line and scripting utility for Windows 2000 networking components for local or remote computers. RRAS also supports the logging of authentication and accounting information for PPP-based connection attempts when Windows authentication or accounting is enabled. In addition, the Windows 2000 Router performs extensive error logging in the system event log. You can use information in the event logs to troubleshoot routing or remote access processes. Windows 2000 RRAS also has an extensive tracing capability that you can use to troubleshoot complex network problems.

Review

The following questions are intended to reinforce key information presented in this chapter. If you are unable to answer a question, review the appropriate lesson and then try the question again. Answers to the questions can be found in Appendix A, "Questions and Answers."

1. What is the purpose of demand-dial routing?

2. What authentication providers are available in RRAS and how are they different from authentication methods?

3. What is the purpose of VPN and what two VPN technologies are supported in Windows 2000 RRAS?

4. If a remote access client begins to connect to the RAS server but the connection is dropped, what troubleshooting steps will help you to solve this error?

5. How is the remote access permission of Deny Access (in Mixed mode or Native mode), similar in function to the Native-mode domain default remote access policy?

6. You need to configure 10 RRAS servers for a client. All 10 servers will have identical RRAS configurations. What is the most efficient way to complete this configuration?

CHAPTER 11

Microsoft Windows 2000 Security

About This Chapter

Microsoft Windows 2000 introduces a comprehensive public key infrastructure (PKI) to the Windows platform. PKI extends the Windows-based public key (PK) cryptographic services introduced over the past few years, providing an integrated set of services and administrative tools for creating, deploying, and managing PK-based applications. This chapter describes the Windows 2000 PKI, discusses the primary public key technologies that are supported by Windows 2000, and provides an overview of the Kerberos and IPSec protocols in Windows 2000. Finally, the chapter introduces you to Windows 2000 security configuration tools and to auditing, a tool you can use to maintain network security.

Note Windows 2000 security is a sophisticated and comprehensive set of services. Although this chapter introduces you to Windows 2000 security, it cannot address it in depth. We recommend that you refer to Windows 2000 Help and the Microsoft Web site (*http://www.microsoft.com*) to supplement the material in this chapter. In addition, a set of white papers is provided with this kit. These supplemental documents contain detailed information about Windows 2000 security. See the Supplemental Course Materials CD-ROM (\chapt11\articles\) that accompanies this book.

Before You Begin

To complete the lessons in this chapter, you must have

- A computer that has Windows 2000 Server installed and operating.
- Completed the exercises in the previous chapters.

Lesson 1: Public Key Infrastructure

Public key cryptography is a critical technology for e-commerce, intranets, extranets, and other Web-enabled applications. However, to take advantage of the benefits of public key cryptography, a supporting infrastructure is needed. The Windows 2000 operating system includes a native public key infrastructure (PKI) that is designed from the ground up to take full advantage of the Windows 2000 security architecture. This lesson provides an overview of the Windows 2000 PKI and includes discussions about security properties, cryptography, certificates, and Microsoft Certificate Services.

After this lesson, you will be able to

- Describe the fundamental concepts of public key cryptography and the Windows 2000 implementation of PKI
- Process certificate requests and add certificate authorities (CAs)
- Install Microsoft Certificate Services

Estimated lesson time: 35 minutes

Security Properties

Computer security includes everything from the physical computing environment to the software environment. In a software environment, security should provide four functions: authentication, integrity, confidentiality, and anti-replay.

Authentication

Authentication is the process of reliably determining the genuine identity of the communicating computer (host) or user. Authentication is based on cryptography; it ensures that an attacker eavesdropping on the network cannot gain the information needed to impersonate a valid user or entity. It allows a communicating entity to prove its identity to another entity before unprotected data is sent across the network. Without strong authentication, any data and the host it is sent from is suspect.

Integrity

Integrity is the correctness of data as it was originally sent. Integrity services protect data from unauthorized modification in transit. Without data integrity, any data and the host it is sent from is suspect.

Confidentiality

Confidentiality ensures that data is disclosed only to intended recipients.

Anti-Replay

Anti-replay, also called *replay prevention,* ensures that datagrams are not retransmitted. Each datagram sent is unique. This uniqueness prevents attacks in which a message is intercepted and stored, then re-used later to attempt illegal access to information.

Cryptography

Cryptography is a set of mathematical techniques for encrypting and decrypting data so it can be transmitted securely and not be interpreted by unauthorized parties. Cryptography uses keys in conjunction with algorithms to secure data. A *key* is a value used to encrypt or decrypt information. Even if the algorithm is publicly known, security is not compromised because the data cannot be read without the key. For example, the algorithm of a combination lock is common knowledge: the dials are moved in a specific order to open the lock. However, the key to the lock—the numbers of the combination code—is secret and known only to the person with the combination. In other words, the key provides the security, not the algorithm. The algorithm provides the infrastructure in which the key is applied. Security systems can be based on public key or secret key cryptography, which are described later in this lesson.

There are a number of well-known cryptographic algorithms, each supporting different security operations. The following table describes several well-known cryptographic algorithms:

Algorithm	Description
Rivest, Shamir, Adleman (RSA)	A general purpose algorithm that can support digital signatures, distributed authentication, secret key agreement via public key, and bulk data encryption without prior shared secrets.
Digital Signature Standard (DSA)	A public key algorithm used for producing digital signatures.
Diffie-Hellman	A public key cryptography algorithm that allows two communicating entities to agree on a shared key without requiring encryption during the key generation.

Algorithm	Description
Hash Message Authentication Code (HMAC)	A secret key algorithm that provides integrity, authentication, and anti-replay. HMAC uses hash functions combined with a secret key. A hash, also known as a message digest, is used to create and verify a digital signature.
HMAC-Message Digest function 5 (MD5)	A hash function that produces a 128-bit value known as a digital signature. This signature is used for authentication, integrity, and anti-replay.
HMAC-Secure Hash Algorithm (SHA)	A hash function that produces a 160-bit digital signature and that is used for authentication, integrity, and anti-replay.
Data Encryption Standard-Cipher Chaining (DES-CBC)	A secret key algorithm used for confidentiality. A random number is generated and used with the secret key to Block encrypt data.

Public Key Cryptography

Public key cryptography is an asymmetric scheme that uses a pair of keys for encryption. It is called asymmetric because it uses two encryption keys that are mathematically related. These related keys are called the public and private key pair. To use public key encryption, an object (such as a user) must generate a public and private key pair. The object will have only one private key (its own) but may obtain multiple public keys that pair to other private keys. Objects obtain public keys in one of two ways:

- The owner of the private key sends the receiver the matching public key.

- The receiver obtains the key from a directory service such as the Active Directory service or Domain Name System (DNS).

A public and private key pair are typically used for two purposes: data encryption and digital message signing.

Data Encryption

Data encryption provides confidentiality by ensuring that only the intended recipient is able to decrypt and view the original data. When secure data must be transmitted, the sender obtains the recipient's public key. The sender then uses the recipient's public key to encrypt data and then send it. When the recipient receives the data, the recipient uses his or her own private key to decrypt the data. Encryption is only secure if the sender uses the recipient's public key for encryption. If a sender uses his or her private key to encrypt data, anyone can capture the data and decrypt it by obtaining the sender's public key.

Digital Message Signing

Digital signing provides authentication and integrity but does not provide confidentiality. Digital signing allows a recipient to be certain of the identity of the sender and verifies the content has not been modified during transit. This is to prevent the originator of a message from attempting to send a message under the guise of another identity.

When a sender signs a message, a message digest is created. A message digest is a representation of the message and is similar to a cyclic redundancy check (CRC). The sender uses his or her private key to encrypt the message digest. When the recipient receives the message, the recipient obtains the sender's public key to decrypt the message digest. The recipient then creates a message digest from the message and compares the message digest to the decrypted message digest. If the message digests match, integrity is guaranteed (Figure 11.1).

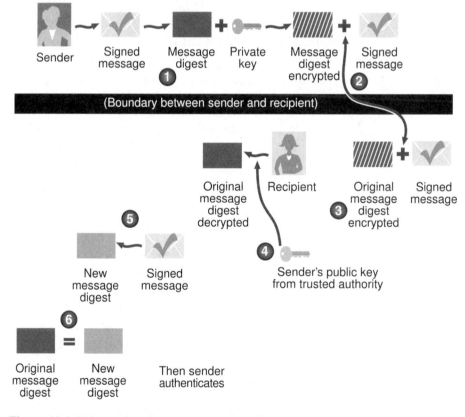

Figure 11.1 Using a signed message, message digest and the PKI to verify authenticity of sender

Authentication is provided through the key pair. Since the message digest was encrypted by using the sender's private key (and only the sender's public key will decrypt the message digest), the recipient can be certain that the message came from the owner of the key pair. The recipient, however, must have a mechanism for ensuring that the key pair belongs to the intended sender and not someone impersonating the sender. This is done through a certificate issued by a trusted third party, which confirms the identity of the owner of the public key. The trusted third party is known as a Certificate Authority (CA), which will be discussed later in the lesson.

Secret Keys

A *secret key* (also known as *shared secret* or *shared secret key*) is used in much the same way as a public key; however, there is only one key that provides security. Secret keys are generally used only for a particular session or for a short period of time before being discarded. This process holds an advantage over public keys. For example, if an unauthorized person became aware of the key, that person may be able to gain access to a session. However, the unauthorized person would not be able to impersonate either the user or computer outside of the session, and would not have access to other resources with the secret key.

In order to get the shared secret key to both parties, there must exist a mechanism for doing so without compromising security. If the key was sent over the network, an eavesdropper would have easy access to the key.

Note An *eavesdropper* is someone using a network-monitoring tool to capture packets on the network.

Secret Key Exchange

A common solution to providing the secret key to both parties is using public keys. Public keys make it possible to encrypt the secret key as it is sent across the network. Public keys ensure confidentiality, authentication, and integrity; therefore, security is not compromised when a secret key is sent.

For example, if Bruce wants to send data to Max by using a secret key, Bruce and Max will each generate half of the secret key. Bruce will obtain Max's public key to encrypt his half of the secret key and send it to Max. Likewise, Max will obtain Bruce's public key to encrypt his half of the secret key and send it to Bruce. Bruce and Max then combine the halves of the secret key to generate the shared secret key to be used for encrypting the data to be sent (Figure 11.2). This secret key negotiation and the use of the secret key to encrypt the data provide authenticity, integrity, and confidentiality.

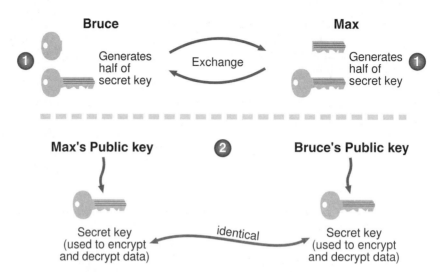

Figure 11.2 Secret key exchange where Bruce and Max each generate half of a secret key to create a shared secret key

Data Encryption

In order to provide confidentiality, the data must be encrypted by using the shared secret key. Because there is only one key known to both the sender and the receiver, encryption is a straightforward process. The sender encrypts the data with the shared secret key and the receiver decrypts it with the shared secret key. Since no other entity on the network has knowledge of the secret key, the data is safe from attack. The sender and the receiver generally discard shared secret keys once the session has been terminated.

Certificates

Public key encryption assumes that the identity of the key pair owner is established beyond doubt. A *digital certificate*, also referred to simply as a *certificate*, is a set of data that completely identifies an entity. A trusted Certificate Authority (CA) issues certificates after the authority has verified the entity's identity. The CA provides a trusted third party for both communicating parties.

For example, if Tucker wants to send authenticated data to Max, Tucker sends his public key to Max. A trusted CA certifies Tucker's public key, thus certifying Tucker's identity. Because Max trusts the CA, he trusts Tucker.

This process is similar to that of a notary public. A person signs a document in front of a notary public and provides proof of identity. The notary public is a trusted entity so that anyone examining the document can be sure that the signature is authentic. Likewise, when the sender of a message signs the message with a private key, the recipient of the message can use the sender's public key, signed by a trusted CA, to verify that the sender is legitimate. Since the trusted CA certifies the public key, the recipient can be sure that the sender is the assumed sender. A trusted CA may be a third-party provider of certificates such as VeriSign or Microsoft Certificate Services.

A user, for example, can obtain a digital certificate for use with e-mail. The digital certificate includes the public key and information about the user. When the user sends e-mail, the e-mail includes a digital signature that uses the private key. The recipient obtains the public key and determines whether or not the sender of the mail message is the assumed sender. A private key is never sent to the recipient.

X.509

The term *X.509* refers to the International Telecommunication Union-Telecommunication (ITU-T) standard for certificate syntax and format. The Windows 2000 certificate–based processes use the X.509 standard. Because it is possible to use certificates for different applications (for example, secure e-mail, file system encryption), each certificate has different information contained within it. However, certificates should, at a minimum, contain the following attributes:

- Version
- Serial number
- Signature algorithm ID
- Issuer name
- Validity period
- Subject (user) name
- Subject public key information
- Issuer unique identifier
- Subject unique identifier
- Extensions
- Signature on the above fields

Certificate Revocation Lists

Certificates, like most real-world forms of identification, can expire and become invalid. The CA can also revoke them for other reasons. In order to handle the existence of invalid certificates, the CA maintains a certificate revocation list (CRL). The CRL is available to network users to determine the validity of any given certificate.

CA Hierarchy

Rather than having one trusted CA provide authentication for the entire Internet or intranet, it is possible to have CAs certify other CAs. This hierarchical structure, called chaining, allows users to trust a single CA rather than having to trust all CAs. This chaining of CAs provides several benefits:

- **Flexibility** It is easy to move, revoke, or chain CA's without affecting other parts of the organization.

- **Distributed Administration** Administrators can be responsible for their own sites.

- **Security Policies** Security policies can be different at each CA site.

The CA at the top of the chain is referred to as the root CA. CAs below the root are referred to as intermediate, subordinate, or issuing CAs.

Microsoft Certificate Services

Microsoft Certificate Services enables an organization to manage the issuance, renewal, and revocation of digital certificates without having to rely on external certificate authorities. In addition, Certificate Services allows an organization to fully control the policies associated with issuing, managing, and revoking certificates, as well as the format and contents of the certificates themselves. In addition, Certificate Services logs all transactions, enabling the administrator to track, audit, and manage certificate requests.

Certificate Services Features

Microsoft Certificate Services has a number of features that make it valuable to organizations that do not choose to rely upon external certificate authorities and who require a flexible tool that can be adapted to the needs of their organization.

Policy Independence

In order to obtain a certificate, requesters must meet certain criteria. This criteria is defined in certificate policies. For example, one policy may grant commercial certificates only if applicants present their identification in person. Another policy may grant credentials based on e-mail requests.

Policies are implemented in policy components that can be written in Java, Visual Basic, or Microsoft C/C++. The default policy for Certificate Services allows users to request certificates through an HTML page.

Transport Independence

Certificate Services can request and distribute certificates through any transport mechanism. That is, it can accept certificate requests from an applicant and post certificates to the applicant through Hypertext Transfer Protocol (HTTP), remote procedure call (RPC), disk file, or custom transport.

Adherence to Standards

Microsoft Certificate Services can perform the following services:

- Accept standard Public Key Cryptography Standards (PKCS) #10 requests.
- Support PKCS #7 cryptographically signed data.
- Issue X.509 version 1.0 and 3.0 certificates.

Support for additional certificate formats can be added to Certificate Services. Certificate Services includes an LDAP component so that Certificate Services can integrate with the Active Directory service.

Key Management

The security of a certification system depends on the protection of private keys. The design of Certificate Services ensures that individuals cannot access private key information without authorization. Certificate Services relies on Microsoft CryptoAPI to provide key management functionality and other cryptographic capabilities for building a secure store, with certificates kept in a certificate store.

Certificate Services Architecture

Certificate Services architectural elements include the server engine that handles certificate requests and other modules that perform tasks by communicating with the server engine. Figure 11.3 illustrates how the components communicate with the server engine.

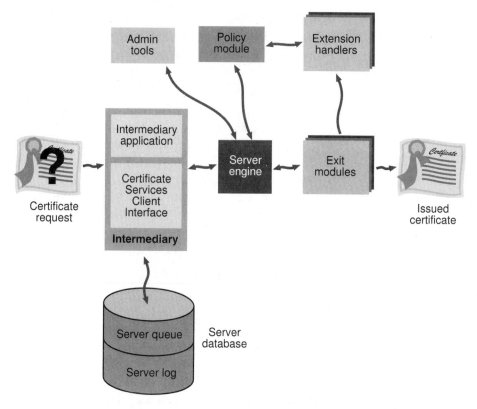

Figure 11.3 Server engine and other components of Certificate Services

Server Engine

The server engine is the core component of Certificate Services. The engine acts as a broker for all requests it receives from the entry modules, driving the flow of information between components during the processing of a request and generation of a certificate. At each processing stage, the engine interacts with the various modules to ensure appropriate action is taken based on the state of the request.

Intermediary

The intermediary is the architectural component that receives new certificate requests from clients and submits them to the server engine. The intermediary is composed of two parts: the intermediary application that performs actions on behalf of clients and the Certificate Services Client Interface that handles communications between the intermediary application and the server engine.

Intermediary applications can be written to handle certificate requests from different types of clients, across multiple transports, or according to policy-specific criteria. Microsoft Internet Information Services (IIS) is an intermediary application that provides support for clients over HTTP. Intermediaries can also check on the status of a previously submitted request and obtain the Certificate Services' configuration information.

Server Database

Certificate Services includes a server database that maintains status information and a log of all issued certificates and certificate revocation lists (CRLs). The database is composed of two parts: the server log and the server queue.

Server Log

The server log stores all certificates and CRLs issued by the server so that administrators can track, audit, and archive server activity. In addition, the server log is used by the server engine to store pending revocations before publishing them in the CRL. The server log also stores recent certificate requests for a configurable period in case a problem is encountered when a certificate is issued.

Server Queue

The server queue maintains status information (receipt, parsing, authorization, signing, and dispatch) as the server processes a certificate request.

Policy Module

The policy module contains the set of rules governing issuance, renewal, and revocation of certificates. All requests received by the server engine are passed to the policy module for validation. Policy modules are also used to parse any supplemental information provided within a request and set properties on the certificate accordingly.

Extension Handlers

Extension handlers work in tandem with the policy module to set custom extensions on a certificate. Each extension handler acts as a template for the custom extensions that should appear in a certificate. The policy module must load the appropriate extension handler when it is needed.

Exit Modules

Exit modules publish completed certificates and CRLs through any number of transports or protocols. By default, the server notifies each exit module installed on the server whenever a certificate or CRL is published.

Certificate Services provides a Component Object Model (COM) interface for writing custom exit modules for different transports and protocols or for custom delivery options. For example, an LDAP exit module might be used to publish only client certificates in a directory service and not server certificates. In this case, the exit module can use the COM interface to determine the type of certificate that the server is issuing and filter out any that are not client certificates.

Processing Certificate Requests

Certificate Services provides services for processing certificate requests and issuing digital certificates (Figure 11.4).

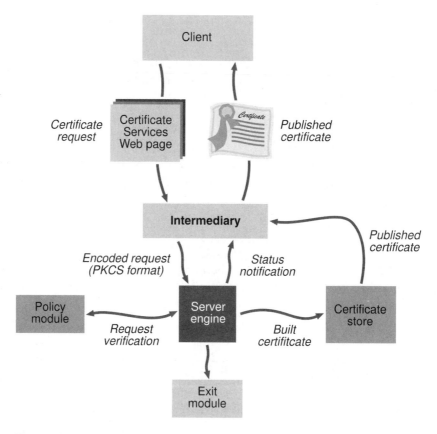

Figure 11.4 Processing certificate requests

Certificate Services performs the following steps when processing a certificate request:

1. The certificate request is sent by the client to an intermediary application. The intermediary application formats it into a PKCS #10 format request and submits it to the server engine.

2. The server engine calls the policy module, which queries request properties, decides whether or not the request is authorized, and sets optional certificate properties.

3. If the request is approved, the server engine takes the request and builds a complete certificate.

4. The server engine stores the completed certificate in the certificate store and notifies the intermediary application of the request status. If the exit module has so requested, the server engine notifies it of a certificate issuance event. This allows the exit module to perform further operations, such as publishing the certificate to a directory service.

5. The intermediary gets the published certificate from the certificate store and passes it back to the client.

Enrolling Certificates

The process of obtaining a digital certificate is called *certificate enrollment*. This process begins with a client submitting a certificate request and ends with the installation of the issued certificate in the client application.

The enrollment control and its forms are accessed through the Certificate Services Enrollment Page. This page is available from the Certificate Services Web page at *http://server_name/certsrv/*.

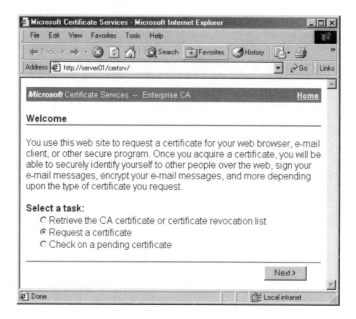

Figure 11.5 Enrollment control form for Server01 configured as an Enterprise CA

CA Certificates

In the process of issuing a digital certificate, the CA validates the identity of the individual requesting the certificate and then signs the certificate with its own private key.

A client application, such as Microsoft Internet Explorer, checks the CA signature before accepting a certificate. If the CA signature is not valid or if it comes from an unknown source, Internet Explorer warns the user by displaying a security message and may prevent the user from accepting the certificate.

Note If Internet Explorer is set to the low security level, it will not warn the user of invalid certificates. This setting is appropriate for highly trusted intranet environments and is inappropriate for Internet access.

In addition to the server and client authentication certificates issued by Certificate Services, there are certificates that identify CAs.

The CA certificate is a signature certificate that contains a public key used to verify digital signatures. It identifies the CA that issues authentication certificates to the servers and clients that request these certificates. Clients use the CA certificate of the CA issuing the server certificate to validate the server certificate. Servers use the CA certificate of the CA issuing the client certificate to validate the client certificate.

A self-signed CA certificate is also called a root certificate because it is the certificate for the root CA. The root CA must sign its own CA certificate because by definition there is no higher certifying authority to sign its CA certificate.

Distribution and Installation of CA Certificates

CA certificates are not requested and issued in the same manner as server and client authentication certificates. Server and client authentication certificates are unique for each requesting server and client, and are not shared—they must be generated and issued by a CA upon demand. In contrast, the CA certificate does not require issuance upon demand. Instead, it is created once and then made readily available to all servers or clients who request certificates from the CA.

A commonly used technique for distributing CA certificates is to place them in a location known and accessible to anyone who requests certificates from the CA.

Installing Certificate Services

You can install Certificate Services by using the Add/Remove Programs utility in Control Panel or optionally during the installation of Windows 2000 Server. Administrators familiar with creating CAs can choose a custom setup by using the advanced options available when installing Certificate Services. Those unfamiliar with creating CAs can select the default settings.

Certificate Authority Type

The CA type allows selection of how the CA will be utilized in a CA hierarchy and whether or not the CA will rely upon Active Directory services. The following certificate authority types are available:

- **Enterprise Root CA** This CA becomes the root CA for the hierarchy and requires Active Directory services.

- **Enterprise Subordinate CA** This CA becomes a subordinate CA to an Enterprise Root CA. It requires Active Directory services. It will request a certificate from the Enterprise Root CA.

- **Stand-alone Root CA** This CA becomes the root CA for the hierarchy but does not require Active Directory services.

- **Stand-alone Subordinate CA** This CA becomes a subordinate CA to a Stand-alone Root CA. It does not require Active Directory services. It requests a certificate from the Stand-alone Root CA.

When installing the Certificate Services as an Enterprise CA, Certificate Services copies the certificates into Active Directory services. Security support providers such as Kerberos can query Active Directory services to get the certificate, which contains the public key.

CA Information

You must supply information about the initial CA that is created when you install Certificate Services. This information includes the CA name and other necessary information. None of this information can be changed after the CA setup is complete.

Advanced Configuration

The advanced configuration contains options for the type of cryptography algorithms to be used for the CA that you are creating. The advanced configuration options include the name of the cryptographic provider, the hash algorithm, the option to use existing public keys and private keys, and the key length.

Administering Certificate Services

The main tool used to administer Certificate Services is the Certification Authority snap-in (Figure 11.6).

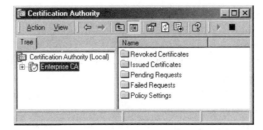

Figure 11.6 Certification Authority snap-in for an Enterprise CA

The snap-in allows you to perform a variety of administrative tasks:

- Start or stop the CA service
- Set security permissions and delegate control of a CA
- View a CA certificate
- Back up a CA
- Restore a CA from a backup copy
- Renew a root CA
- Renew a subordinate CA
- Manage certificate revocation
- Manage certificate requests
- Manage certificate templates
- Change policy settings
- Map certificate to user accounts
- Modify the Policy Module or Exit Module

You can use the Certification Authority snap-in to administer a certification authority on the local computer or on a another computer. The snap-in is installed when Certificate Services are installed or when installing the Administration Pack (Adminpak.msi).

Certutil.exe is a command-line utility used for administering certificate services. Running certutil without any command-line switches displays summary information about the local certificate authority. Certutil is used to dump and display CA configuration information, configure Certificate Services, back up and restore CA components, and verify certificates, key pairs, and certificate chains.

If you need to set security for the CA Web pages, you should use the Internet Information Services snap-in. Expand the Default Web Site from the console tree and then select CertSrv. From the Action menu, select Properties. On the Directory Security tab, under Anonymous access and authentication control, click Edit. In the Authentication Methods dialog box, configure the security settings for the CA Web pages.

Exercise 1: Installing and Configuring Certificate Services

In this exercise you install an Enterprise Root CA and use this CA to issue, install, and revoke certificates. Note that the secure way to configure Certification Services is to create a root CA that only issues certificates to subordinate CA types. The subordinate CA types then issue certificates for specific purposes such as application services and authentication. Using a root CA for this purpose is not secure because if the root CA security is breached, all certificates issued are compromised. However, for the purpose of learning how to install and configure certificate services, a root CA can be used.

▶ Procedure 1: Installing Certificate Services and configuring the Certificate Authority

In this procedure, you install Certificate Services on Server01. Server01 acts as an Enterprise Root CA.

1. Log on to Server01 as Administrator with a password of "password."

2. Click Start, point to Settings and then click Control Panel.

   Control Panel appears.

3. Double-click the Add/Remove Programs application.

   The Add/Remove Programs window appears.

4. In the left pane, click the Add/Remove Windows components icon.

   The Windows Components wizard appears.

5. Click the Certificate Services check box.

   A Microsoft Certificate Services message box appears stating that once Certificate Services is installed, the computer cannot be renamed and it cannot join or be removed from a domain.

6. Click Yes.

7. On the Windows Components screen, click Details.

   The Certificate Services window appears.

   Notice that Certificate Services subcomponents include both the service used to create a certificate authority and a Web enrollment form for submitting requests and retrieving certificates from the computer running as a CA.

8. Click OK.

9. On the Windows Components screen, click Next.

   The Certification Authority Type screen appears.

10. Select each radio button and read the text appearing in the Description box.

    Notice that the Enterprise CA types can only be used if Active Directory services is running. The stand-alone CA types run independently of Active Directory services. Thus, they can be used in the presence or absence of Active Directory services. If Active Directory services is present, the stand-alone CA types will use it. Subordinate CA types are dependent on the presence of a CA higher up in the CA hierarchy.

11. Click the Enterprise Root CA radio button and click the Advanced Options check box.

12. Click Next.

    The Public and Private Key Pair screen appears.

    Notice that there are a number of Cryptographic Service Providers (CSPs), each having one or more associated hash algorithms used to generate key pairs. From this screen you can also specify the key length or use existing keys installed on the computer, import keys, and view certificates.

13. In the CSP list box, verify that Microsoft Base Cryptographic Provider v1.0 is selected. In the Hash Algorithm list box, verify that the SHA-1 hash algorithm is selected. In the Key Length drop-down list box, verify that Default is selected. Click Next.

    The CA Identifying Information screen appears.

14. Type the information in the table into the text boxes on the CA Identifying Information screen.

Label	Value to type
CA name	Enterprise CA
Organization	Microsoft Corporation
Organizational unit	Microsoft Press
City	Redmond
State or province	Washington
E-mail	ca-mp@microsoft.com
CA description	Root CA for self-study training only

Notice that this certificate is configured to be valid for two years.

15. Click Next.

The Data Storage Location screen appears.

Notice that the certificate database and log file folder, CertLog, is stored on the boot partition. If disk capacity on the boot partition is limited, consider specifying another secure partition for the certificate database and log folder.

The Store configuration information in a shared folder is not necessary if Active Directory services is running and the computer operating as the certificate authority is a member of a domain. Configuration information about the CA is automatically published to the Active Directory store.

16. Click Next.

A Microsoft Certificate Services message box appears stating that Internet Information Services is running on the computer and warning you that it must be stopped in order for you to be able to continue.

17. Click OK.

The Configuring Components screen appears as the software is installed and configured, and then the Completing the Windows Components Wizard screen appears.

18. Click Finish and then on the Add/Remove Programs window, click Close.

19. Close Control Panel.

▶ **Procedure 2: Running Certificate Services**

In this procedure you will generate, install, and revoke a certificate on Server01. You will use the Certificate Enrollment URL and the Certificate Authority snap-in to complete this procedure.

1. Open Certification Authority from the Administrative Tools program group.

   The Certification Authority snap-in appears.

2. In the console tree, expand the Enterprise CA node.

3. In the console tree, select the Issued Certificates folder and then minimize the Certification Authority snap-in.

4. Click the Start menu and then choose run.

   The Run dialog box appears.

5. In the Open text box, type **http://server01/certsrv** and then click OK.

   The Internet Connection wizard appears.

6. Click the I Want To Setup My Internet Connection Manually, or I Want To Connect Through A Local Area Network (LAN) radio button.

7. Click Next.

   The Setting Up Your Internet Connection screen appears.

8. Click the I Connect Through A Local Area Network (LAN) radio button.

9. Click Next.

   The Local Area Network Internet Configuration screen appears.

10. Clear the Automatic Discovery Of Proxy Server (Recommended) check box.

11. Click Next.

   The Set Up Your Internet Mail Account screen appears.

12. Click the No radio button and then click Next.

   The Completing The Internet Connection wizard appears.

13. Click Finish.

   Internet Explorer appears and displays the certificate services enrollment page.

14. Read the information on this page and then verify that the Request A Certificate radio button is selected.

15. Click Next.

   The Choose Request Type page appears and the User Certificate Request radio button is selected.

16. Click Next.

   The User Certificate – Identifying Information page appears.

17. Click More Options.

   Notice that the CSP selected was the CSP type you specified during installation of Certificate Services.

18. Click Submit.

   The Certificate Issued page appears.

19. Minimize Internet Explorer and restore the Certification Authority snap-in.

   The Certification Authority snap-in appears and one certificate is listed in the details pane. If you don't see the certificate request, press F5 to refresh the details pane.

20. Double click the certificate appearing in the details pane.

   The Certificate dialog box appears with three tabs.

21. Click the Details tab.

22. In the top box below the Show drop-down list box, click Issuer.

   Notice that the information appearing in the bottom box is the information you typed into the CA Identifying Information screen.

23. Click OK.

24. Minimize the Certification Authority snap-in and restore Internet Explorer.

25. Click the Install This Certificate hyperlink.

   The Certificate Installed page appears stating that you have successfully installed a certificate.

26. Close Internet Explorer.

27. Restore the Certification Authority snap-in and select the certificate in the details pane.

28. Click the Action Menu, point to All Tasks and then click Revoke Certificate.

   The Certificate Revocation dialog box appears.

29. In the Reason Code drop-down list box choose Key Compromise and then click Yes.

30. In the console tree, click the Revoked Certificates folder.

    The revoked certificate appears in the details pane.

31. Click the Action menu, point to All Tasks and then click Publish.

    The Certificate Revocation List dialog box appears stating that the previous list is still valid.

32. Click Yes.

33. Close the Certification Authority snap-in.

34. Click the Start menu, and then click Run.

    The URL to the Certsrv directory appears.

35. Click OK.

    Internet Explorer appears and displays the certificate services enrollment page.

36. Click the Retrieve The CA Certificate Or Certificate Revocation List radio button and then click next.

37. Click the Download Latest Certificate Revocation List hyperlink.

    The File Download dialog box appears.

38. Click the Open This File From Its Current Location radio button and then click OK.

    The Certificate Revocation List dialog box appears.

39. Click the Revocation List tab.

40. In the Revoked Certificates box, click the item that appears.

    In the Revocation entry box, the Serial number of the revoked certificate, the date of revocation, and the reason for revocation appear.

41. Click OK.

42. Close Internet Explorer.

Lesson Summary

Windows 2000 includes a native PKI that is designed to take full advantage of the Windows 2000 security architecture. Public key cryptography is an asymmetric scheme that uses a pair of keys for encryption. To use public key encryption, a user must generate a public and private key pair. Public key encryption uses digital certificates to completely identify the key pair owner. The Windows 2000 certificate-based processes use the X.509 standard. Certificate Services enables an organization to manage the issuance, renewal, and revocation of digital certificates without having to rely on external CAs. Certificate Services supports policy independence, transport independence, adherence to standards, and key management. Certificate Services architectural elements include the server engine that handles certificate requests and other modules that perform tasks by communicating with the server engine. Certificate Services provides services for processing certificate requests and issuing digital certificates. You can install Certificate Services by using the Add/Remove Programs utility in Control Panel or optionally during Windows 2000 Server installation. The tools used to administer Certificate Services once it is installed are the Certification Authority snap-in, the Certutil utility, and the Certificate Services enrollment Web page.

Lesson 2: Public Key Technologies

Windows 2000 extends security by supporting a number of technologies that are based on public key security, including the Secure Channel authentication package, smart cards, Authenticode, the Encrypting File System (EFS), and Internet Protocol Security (IPSec). This lesson reviews each of these technologies and explains how they fit into the PKI framework.

After this lesson, you will be able to

- Describe the primary public key–based components of Windows 2000 security

Estimated lesson time: 35 minutes

Secure Channel Authentication Package

In Windows 2000, a Secure Channel (SChannel) authentication package is located below the Security Support Provider Interface (SSPI) as shown in Figure 11.7.

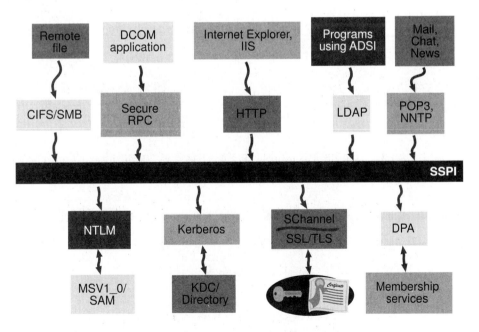

Figure 11.7 Authentication Services architecture in Windows 2000

The SChannel authentication package implements the Secure Sockets Layer (SSL) 3.0 protocol and the Transport Layer Security (TLS) 1.0 protocol. SSL and TLS are flexible security protocols that can be layered on top of other transport protocols. They rely on PK-based authentication technology and use PK-based key negotiation to generate a unique encryption key for each client/ server session. They are most commonly associated with Web-based applications and the HTTP protocol (referred to as HTTPS).

The TLS protocol is based on the SSL 3.0 protocol and moves forward as the Internet Engineering Task Force (IETF) standard. The differences between TLS 1.0 and SSL 3.0 are not significant, but they are enough that TLS 1.0 and SSL 3.0 cannot interoperate. TLS 1.0, however, does have a negotiation mechanism whereby TLS can back down to and use SSL 3.0. Therefore, a client that supports only SSL 3.0 can still communicate with a server that supports TLS 1.0.

Both the SSL and TLS protocols provide secure data communication through data encryption and decryption, client authentication, and optional server authentication. Both are typically used to send and receive private communication across the Internet by using public key cryptography as its authentication method.

The SSL/TLS protocol is implemented by an SChannel provider (such as IIS, Proxy Server, and Exchange), and by client applications that transit the Internet (such as Internet Explorer and Outlook e-mail clients). Applications request the services of SSL and TLS through the SSPI API.

The benefits of SSL and TLS include the following:

- Authentication that assures the client that data is sent to the correct server and that the server is secure

- Encryption that assures that nothing other than the secure target server can read the data

- Data integrity that assures that the transferred data has not been altered

Smart Cards

Smart cards, which are the size of credit cards, can be used to store a user's public key, private key, and certificate. Smart cards are a secure way to protect and control a user's keys, instead of storing them on a computer. A user's keys and certificates move with the user. Security-critical computations are performed by the smart card, instead of exposing a user's private key to the computer. In addition, smart cards enhance software-only solutions, such as logon and secure e-mail.

To use a smart card, a computer must have a smart card reader. A smart card is an ISO 7816–compatible device that contains an embedded microprocessor, an RSA or equivalent cryptography coprocessor, and local storage. The local storage includes the following:

- 6 to 24 KB ROM for the smart card operating system and applications
- 128 to 512 bytes of RAM for run-time data
- 1 to 16 KB EEPROM for user data

Smart Card Logon

Windows 2000 introduces PK-based smart card logon as an alternative to passwords for domain authentication. This relies on a PC/SC Workgroup-compliant smart card infrastructure, first introduced for Windows NT and Windows 95 in December 1997, and RSA-capable smart cards with supporting CryptoAPI cryptographic service providers (CSPs). The authentication process makes use of the PKINIT protocol to integrate PK-based authentication with the Windows 2000 Kerberos access-control system.

During operation, the system recognizes a smart card insertion event as an alternative to the standard Ctrl+Alt+Del secure attention sequence to initiate a logon. The user is then prompted for the smart card PIN code, which controls access to operations with the private key stored on the smart card. In this system, the smart card also contains a copy of the user's certificate (issued by an enterprise CA). This allows the user to roam within the domain.

Authenticode

The growing use of the Internet has led to an increased reliance on downloaded active content, such as Windows-based applications, ActiveX controls, and Java applets. The result has been a heightened concern for the safety of such downloads, since they often occur as a side effect of Web scripts without any specific user notification. In response to these concerns, Microsoft introduced Authenticode digital signature technology in 1996 and introduced significant enhancements of it in 1997.

Authenticode technology, a security feature in Microsoft Internet Explorer, assures accountability and authenticity for software components on the Internet. Authenticode verifies that the software hasn't been tampered with and identifies the publisher of the software. Users can decide on a case-by-case basis what code to download, based on their experience with and trust in a software publisher. By signing their code, developers can build an increasingly trusting relationship with their users.

Authenticode technology allows software publishers to digitally sign any form of active content, including multiple-file archives. These signatures may be used to verify both the publishers of the content and the content integrity at download time. This verification infrastructure scales to the worldwide base of users of Windows by relying on a hierarchical CA structure in which a small number of commercial CAs issue software-publishing certificates. For enterprise needs, the Windows 2000 PKI allows you to issue Authenticode certificates to internal developers or contractors and allows any employee to verify the origin and integrity of downloaded applications.

Encrypting File System

EFS is an extension to the NTFS file system that provides strong data protection and encryption for files and folders. The encryption technology is based on use of public keys and runs as an integrated system service, making it easy to manage, difficult to attack, and transparent to the user. This is particularly useful for securing data on computers that may be vulnerable to theft, such as mobile computers.

The encrypting user's public key is used in the encryption process, ensuring data privacy. Decryption is denied to any user without the corresponding private key. A special recovery key is also generated for each encrypted file. This key is for emergency use by a qualified administrator in the event that an employee leaves or a private key is lost.

Encryption and decryption is done transparently during the I/O process. EFS imposes no discernible performance penalty during the encryption/decryption process.

EFS also supports encryption and decryption of files stored on remote NTFS volumes. However, EFS addresses only the encryption and decryption of stored data. Although encrypted files can be exported, data is transferred over the network in a clear (unencrypted) format by default. Windows 2000 provides network protocols such as SSL, TLS, and IPSec to encrypt data during transfer over the network.

Data Protection

EFS uses a combination of the user's public and private keys as well as a randomly generated file encryption key (FEK). The FEK is a 128-bit key for North America and a 40-bit key for international releases. Windows 2000 uses the Data Encryption Standard X (DESX) algorithm to encrypt files.

Data Recovery

The Encrypted Data Recovery Policy (EDRP) is used to specify who can recover data in case a user's private key is lost. An EDRP is automatically generated on stand-alone computers to minimize administration. Computers that are members of a domain receive the EDRP from the domain policy. For security, recovery is limited to the encrypted data; it is not possible to recover the users' keys.

Encrypted Backup and Restoration

Because members of the Backup Operators group do not have the keys necessary for decryption, encrypted data is read and stored in the backup as an opaque stream of data.

Fault Tolerance

Encryption and decryption are sensitive operations because failure could result in data loss. Therefore, EFS makes all operations automatic. If an operation cannot be completed, it is completely undone. For example, if a computer loses power during an encryption operation, EFS undoes the operation on restart so that the file is in a consistent state.

Once a file is encrypted, the processes of encryption and decryption are automatic and transparent to users and applications whenever the file is used. It is possible to perform encryption one file at a time or one folder at a time.

You can encrypt a file or folder in Windows Explorer and from the command prompt.

Note It is not possible to use NTFS compression and encryption on the same file. Compression and encryption are mutually exclusive.

EFS Encryption

EFS encrypts, decrypts, and recovers files. Figure 11.8 provides an overview of the encryption process. The numbered steps shown in the illustration are described below.

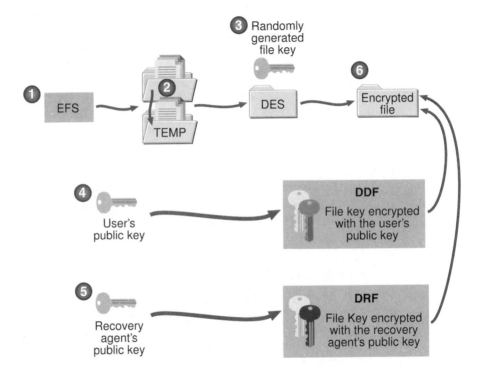

Figure 11.8 EFS encryption process

When a user encrypts a file in EFS, the following process occurs:

1. The EFS service opens the file for exclusive access.

2. All data streams in the file are copied to a temporary file.

3. A file key is randomly generated and used to encrypt the file according to the DES encryption scheme.

4. A Data Decryption Field (DDF) is created that contains the file key, which is encrypted with the user's public key.

5. A Data Recovery Field (DRF) is created that contains the file key, this time encrypted with the recovery agent's public key. The recovery agent's public key is obtained from the Encrypted Data Recovery Policy (EDRP).

6. The EFS server writes the encrypted data, along with the DDF and DRF, back to the file.

EFS Decryption

The decryption process uses the DDF, created during encryption, to decrypt a file. Figure 11.9 provides an overview of the decryption process. The numbered steps shown in the illustration are described below.

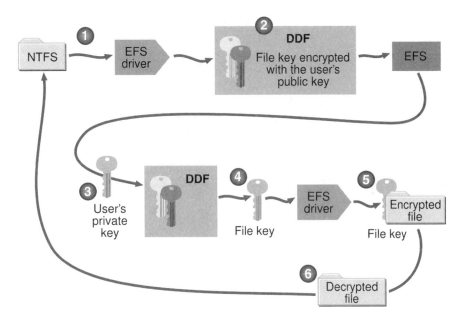

Figure 11.9 EFS decryption process

When a file is decrypted in EFS, the following process occurs:

1. When an application accesses an encrypted file, NTFS recognizes the file as encrypted and sends a request to the EFS driver.

2. The EFS driver retrieves the DDF and passes it to the EFS service.

3. The EFS service decrypts the DDF with the user's private key to obtain the file key.

4. The EFS service passes the file key back to the EFS driver.

5. The EFS driver uses the file key to decrypt the file.

6. The EFS driver returns the decrypted data to NTFS, which then completes the file request, and sends the data to the requesting application.

EFS Recovery

The EFS recovery is much the same as the decryption process. Figure 11.10 provides an overview of the recovery process. The numbered steps shown in the illustration are described below.

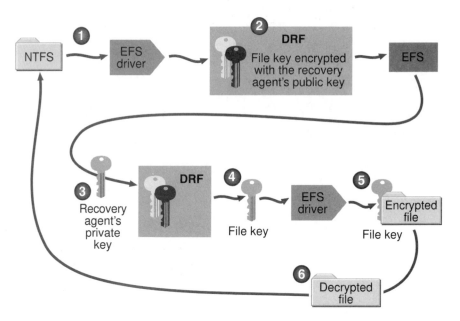

Figure 11.10 EFS recovery process

When a file is recovered in EFS, the following process occurs:

1. NTFS sends a request to the EFS driver.

2. The EFS driver retrieves the DRF and passes it to the EFS service.

3. The EFS service recovers the DRF by using the recovery agent's private key to obtain the file key.

4. The EFS service passes the file key back to the EFS driver.

5. The EFS driver uses the file key to recover the file.

6. The EFS driver returns the recovered data to NTFS, which then completes the file request, and sends the data to the requesting application.

Cipher Command-Line Utility

The cipher command-line utility allows you to encrypt and decrypt files from a command prompt. The command uses the following syntax:

```
cipher [/e| /d] [/s:dir] [/a][/i] [/f] [/q] [/h] [/k] [path-
name [...]]
```

If no parameters are used, the cipher command displays the encryption state of the current folder and any files it contains. Spaces must be put in between multiple parameters. The following table provides a description of each parameter.

Parameter	Description
/e	Encrypts the specified folders. Folders are marked so that files added to the folder later will be encrypted.
/d	Decrypts the specified folders. Folders are marked so that files added to the folder later will not be encrypted.
/s:*dir*	Performs the selected operation on folders in the specified folder and all subfolders.
/a	Performs the selected operation on files with the specified names. If there is no matching file, this parameter is ignored.
/I	Continues performing the specified operation even after errors have occurred. By default, cipher stops when an error is encountered.
/f	Forces the encryption or decryption of all specified objects. By default, files that have already been encrypted or decrypted are skipped.
/q	Reports only the most essential information.
/h	Displays files with hidden or system attributes. By default, these files are not encrypted or decrypted.
/k	Creates a new file encryption certificate on the computer where CIPHER is run. This switch causes all other switches to be ignored. Therefore, run /k exclusive of the other switches.
pathname	Specifies a pattern, file, or folder. You can use multiple filenames and wildcards.

Examples

To encrypt the C:\My Documents directory, type **cipher /e "My Documents"** at the C: command prompt.

To encrypt all files on the C: drive with the word "test" in the filename, type **cipher /e /s *test*** at the C: command prompt

Exercise 2: Configuring and Using File Encryption

In this exercise you configure a data recovery policy in the domain, and then encrypt a folder. Complete this exercise on Server01.

Note For additional practice, open the \chapt11\articles\efs-wp.doc on the Windows 2000 Training Supplemental CD-ROM and complete examples 2-7 (starting on page 12).

▶ **Procedure 1: Configuring a data recovery policy for the domain**

Recovery policy is configured by default when the first domain controller is installed. As a result, a self-signed certificate assigns the domain administrator as the recovery agent. In this procedure, you manually add the administrator as the recovery agent before using EFS.

1. Log on to Server01 as administrator with a password of "password."

2. Click Run, verify that the URL for the Certificate Services enrollment page (*http://server01/certsrv/*) appears and then click OK.

   Internet Explorer appears and it is displaying the Certificate Services enrollment page.

3. Verify that the Request A Certificate radio button is selected and then click Next.

   The Choose Request Type page appears.

4. Click the Advanced Request radio button and then click Next.

   The Advanced Certificate Requests page appears.

5. Verify that the Submit A Certificate Request To This CA Using A Form radio button is selected and then click Next.

   The Advanced Certificate Requests form page appears.

6. From the Certificate Template drop-down list box select EFS Recovery Agent.

7. Click Submit.

The Certificate Issued page appears.

8. Click the Install This Certificate hyperlink.

A Certificate Installed page appears.

9. Close Internet Explorer.

Note You can complete all of the preceding steps in this procedure from the Group Policy snap-in. In step 19 of this procedure, you choose Create rather than Add. The Create option creates the certificate and then allows you to assign the certificate to the group policy.

---

10. Open the Active Directory Users And Computers snap-in from the Administrative Tools group.

11. Expand the console tree and then select the microsoft.com node.

12. Click the Action menu and then click Properties.

13. The microsoft.com Properties dialog box appears.

14. Click the Group Policy tab and then click Edit.

The Group Policy snap-in appears.

15. Under the Computer Configuration node, expand the Windows Settings container.

16. Under the Windows Settings container, expand the Security Settings node.

17. Under the Security Settings node, expand the Public Key Policies container.

18. Under the Public Key Policies container, expand the Encrypted Data Recovery Agents container.

19. Click the Action menu, and then click Add.

The Add Recovery Agent wizard appears.

20. Click Next.

The Select Recovery Agents screen appears.

21. Read the Select Recovery Agents screen and then click Browse Directory.

The Find Users, Contacts, And Groups dialog box appears.

22. Click Find Now.

23. In the list of Users And Groups, double-click Administrator.

The Select Recover Agents screen appears.

24. Click Next.

The Completing The Add Recovery Agent wizard appears.

25. Click Finish.

Administrator appears in the details pane of the Group Policy snap-in.

26. Click the entry in the details pane.

27. Click the Action menu and then click Properties.

The Administrator Properties dialog box appears.

Notice that all purposes are enabled for this certificate. The only purpose currently available for this certificate is File Recovery.

28. Click OK.

29. Close the Group Policy snap-in.

The microsoft.com Properties dialog box appears.

30. Click OK.

The Active Directory Users And Computers snap-in appears.

31. Click the View menu and then click Advanced Features.

32. In the console tree, click the Users container.

33. In the details pane, click Administrator.

34. Click the Action menu and then click Properties.

The Administrator Properties dialog box appears.

35. Click the Published Certificates tab.

The list of X.509 certificates published to this user account appears.

Notice that two certificates were published to the Administrator account and were issued by the Administrator account. The certificate listed as File Recovery under the Intended Purpose column is used to recover files encrypted with EFS if the original private key is lost or otherwise invalid.

36. Click OK.

37. Close the Active Directory Users And Computers snap-in.

▶ **Procedure 2: Encrypting a folder using EFS**

In this procedure, you encrypt a folder using the Windows Explorer on Server01.

1. On the desktop, double-click My Computer.

   The My Computer window appears.

2. Double-click the Local Disk (C:) drive.

   The Local Disk (C:) window appears.

3. Double-click the Document And Settings folder.

   The Document And Settings window appears.

4. Double-click the Administrator folder.

   The Administrator window appears.

5. Click once on the My Documents folder.

6. Click the File menu and then click Properties.

   The My Documents Properties dialog box appears.

7. Click the Advanced button.

   The Advanced Attributes dialog box appears.

8. Click the Encrypt Contents To Secure Data check box and then click OK.

   The My Documents Properties dialog box appears.

9. Click OK.

   The Confirm Attribute Changes dialog box appears.

10. Click the Apply Changes To This Folder, Subfolders And Files radio button.

11. Click OK.

   The My Documents Properties dialog box appears and then the Applying Attributes status message box appears. When the operation has completed, the My Documents Properties dialog box closes.

12. The Administrator window appears.

   Notice that the Attributes for the selected My Documents folder is Encrypted.

13. Close the Administrator window.

IP Security

In the previous chapter, an overview of IPSec was provided in the discussion of tunneling protocols. This chapter continues with the discussion of IPSec, providing more details about how IPSec is used to support public key security.

IPSec in Windows 2000 is designed to protect sensitive data on a TCP/IP network. IPSec is useful when the network between two communicating computers is not secure. It provides confidentiality, integrity, and authentication of IP traffic for each packet traversing the network.

When using IPSec, the two computers communicating over the network first agree on the highest common security policy; then each handles the IP Security at its respective end. Before sending data across the network, the computer initiating communication transparently encrypts the data by using IP Security. The destination computer transparently decrypts the data before passing it to the destination process. Because the data is passed down to and encrypted at the IP protocol level, separate security packages are not required for each protocol in the TCP/IP suite.

Using IPSec to encrypt all IP network traffic ensures that any TCP/IP-based communication is secure from network eavesdropping. Any routers or switches that are in the path between the communicating computers can simply forward the encrypted IP packets.

Note To ensure full compatibility with previous versions of Windows, a computer running Windows 2000 configured for IPSec sends the data without encryption to pre-Windows 2000 computers.

IPSec Policies

With Windows 2000 IPSec, you can create policies that define the type and level of security to be used during network communication.

Negotiation Policies

Negotiation policies determine the security services used during network communication. The security protocol chosen for negotiation policies is the basis for the security services. For example, if the IP Authentication Header protocol is chosen, integrity, authentication, and anti-replay services will be provided—but not confidentiality.

It is possible to set multiple security methods for each negotiation policy. If the first method is not acceptable for the security association, the service continues through an ordered list until it finds a policy it can use to establish the association. If the negotiation is not successful, the communication is established without IPSec.

IP Filters

IP filters direct actions based on the destination of an IP packet, what IP protocol is in effect, and the related ports that the protocol uses. Each IP packet is checked against the IP filter, and if a match is found, the properties of the associated security policy are used to send the communication. Filters need to be configured for both incoming and outgoing traffic.

Security Policies

Security policies are used to configure IPSec attributes. These policies are made up of associated negotiation policies and IP filters, and are associated with domain controller policies. Security policies define the type and level of security to use for any given IP network communication. An IP security policy can be assigned to the default domain policy, the default local policy, or a customized domain policy.

A computer logging onto a domain automatically obtains the properties of the default domain and local policies, including the IPSec policy assigned to the domain policy.

IPSec Components

The Windows 2000 installation process installs the services, protocols, and drivers necessary for IPSec:

- IPSec Policy Agent service
- Internet Security Association and Key Management Protocol (ISAKMP)
- Oakley Key Management protocol
- IPSec driver

The ISAKMP and Oakly Key Management protocols are collectively referred to as ISAKMP/Oakley (IKE) protocols.

IPSec Policy Agent Service

During system initialization, the IPSec Policy Agent service retrieves IPSec polices from the Active Directory service. The IPSec Policy Agent service passes the policy information to the IPSec network driver and the ISAKMP/ Oakley protocols. The IPSec Policy Agent service does not store policies locally; instead, it must retrieve them from the Active Directory store. The IPSec Policy Agent service also starts both the ISAKMP/Oakley (IKE) protocols and the IPSec driver.

ISAKMP/Oakley IKE Protocols

Using the information in the IPSec policy, the ISAKMP/Oakley (IKE) protocols negotiate and establish a Security Association (SA) between computers. The Kerberos service authenticates the identities of the communicating computers. Finally, the ISAKMP/Oakley (IKE) protocols send the SA and key information to the IPSec driver.

IPSec Driver

This driver examines all IP packets for a match with an IP filter. If a match is found, the IPSec driver holds the packets in a queue while the ISAKMP/ Oakley (IKE) protocols generate the necessary SA and key to secure the packet. After the IPSec driver receives the information from the ISAKMP/ Oakley (IKE) protocols, the driver encrypts the IP packets and sends them to the destination computer.

Example of IPSec Communication

In this example, User 1 on Computer A is sending data to User 2 on Computer B. IP Security has been implemented for both computers. Figure 11.11 provides an overview of the IPSec communication process. The numbered steps in the illustration are described below.

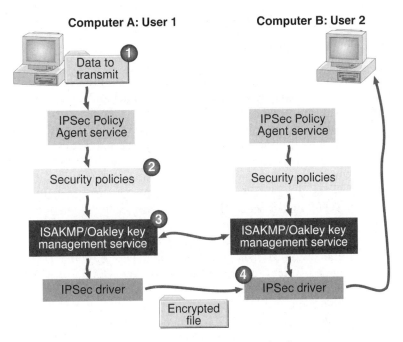

Figure 11.11 An example of the IPSec communication process

At the user level, the process of securing the IP packets is transparent and works as follows:

1. User 1 launches an application that communicates on the network by using TCP/IP to send data to User 2. The security policies assigned to Computer A and Computer B determine the level of security for the network communication.

2. The IPSec Policy Agent service retrieves the policies and passes them to the ISAKMP/Oakley (IKE) protocols and IPSec driver.

3. The ISAKMP/Oakley (IKE) protocols on each computer use the negotiation policies associated with the assigned security policy to establish the key and a common negotiation method, or Security Association (SA). The results of the policy negotiation are passed between the two computers to the IPSec driver, which uses the key to encrypt the data.

4. Finally, the IPSec driver sends the encrypted data to Computer B. The IPSec driver on Computer B decrypts the data and passes it on to the receiving application.

Lesson Summary

Windows 2000 extends security by supporting a number technologies that are based on public key security, including the SChannel authentication package, smart cards, Authenticode, the Encrypting File System (EFS), and Internet Protocol Security (IPSec). The SChannel authentication package implements SSL 3.0 and the TLS 1.0. SSL and TLS are flexible security protocols that can be layered on top of other transport protocols. Smart Cards are credit-card-sized devices that can be used to store a user's public key, private key, and certificate. Smart cards are a secure way to protect and control a user's keys, instead of storing them on a computer. Authenticode technology allows software publishers to digitally sign any form of active content, including multiple-file archives. These signatures can be used to verify both the publishers of the content and the content integrity at download time. EFS is an extension to the NTFS file system that provides strong data protection and encryption for files and folders. The encryption technology is based on the use of public keys and runs as an integrated system service. IPSec in Windows 2000 is designed to protect sensitive data on a TCP/IP network. IPSec is useful when the network between two communicating computers is not secure. It provides confidentiality, integrity, and authentication of IP traffic per packet.

Lesson 3: The Kerberos Protocol in Windows 2000

A standard process within computer security is to include a function that requires users to prove that they are who they claim to be. This affirmation of identity is accomplished when the user supplies the correct password for the user account. For example, when User1 attempts to connect to a server to access a file, the server must be sure that it is really User1 sending the request. Traditionally, the server assumes that it is User1 because the correct password was supplied when the connection was established. Stronger security is accomplished by having a trusted third party verify the identity of the user. This is a core function of the Kerberos authentication protocol.

After this lesson, you will be able to

- Describe the Kerberos protocol and how it works in Windows 2000

Estimated lesson time: 35 minutes

Overview of the Kerberos Protocol

The Kerberos protocol is the default authentication provider in Windows 2000 and the primary security protocol. It allows users to use a single logon to access all resources. The Kerberos protocol verifies both the identity of the user and the integrity of the session data. This is accomplished by having a Kerberos service installed on each domain controller and a Kerberos client installed on all computers running Windows 2000.

Note The Active Directory client for Windows 95 and Windows 98 allows users to log on by using the Kerberos V5 authentication protocol.

When the Kerberos authentication protocol is used, a trusted Kerberos service on a server verifies the user's identity. Before connecting to the server the user requests a ticket from the Kerberos service, called the Kerberos Key Distribution Center service, to confirm the user's identity. The user then sends this ticket to the target server. Because the server trusts the Kerberos service to vouch for user identities, the server accepts the ticket as proof of the authenticity of the user.

When using the Kerberos authentication protocol, users can no longer log on and then access resources simply by providing a valid user ID and the correct password. Instead of trusting the source, the resource must contact the Kerberos service to obtain a ticket that vouches for the user. The Kerberos service operates as a trusted third party to generate session keys and grant tickets for specific client/server sessions.

When the Kerberos service issues a ticket, it contains the following components:

- Session key
- Name of the user to whom the session key was issued
- Expiration period of the ticket
- Any additional data fields or settings that may be required

The expiration period of a ticket is defined by the domain policy. If a ticket expires during an active session, the Kerberos service notifies the client and the server to refresh the ticket. The Kerberos service then generates a new session key and the session is resumed.

Kerberos Protocol Terms

To better understand the Kerberos protocol, you should review the following terms used to describe the various components of Kerberos.

Principal

A *principal* is a uniquely named user, client, or server that participates in a network communication.

Realm

A *realm* is an authentication boundary, which can be compared to a Windows 2000 domain. Each organization wishing to run a Kerberos server establishes its own realm. A Windows 2000 domain is a Kerberos realm but is named domain to maintain naming conventions established previously for Windows NT.

Secret Key

A *secret key* is an encryption key that is shared by a client or a server and a trusted third party to encrypt the information that is to be moved between them. In the case of Kerberos, the trusted third party is the Kerberos service. In the case of a principal, the secret key is typically based upon a hash or encryption of the principal's password. Secret keys are never transmitted on the network; only the encrypted information is transmitted.

Session Key

The *session key* is a temporary encryption key used between two principals, with a lifetime limited to the duration of a single login session. The session key is exchanged between the communication partners and is therefore known as a shared secret. The session key is always sent encrypted.

Authenticator

An *authenticator* is a record that is used to verify that a request actually originated from the principal. An authenticator contains information that verifies the identity of the sender and the time the request was initiated. This information is encrypted with the shared session key that is known only by the communicating principals. An authenticator is typically sent along with a ticket to allow the receiver to verify that the intended client recently initiated a request.

Key Distribution Center

The *key distribution center* (KDC) provides two functions: the authentication server (AS) and the ticket granting service (TGS). The TGS distributes tickets to clients that wish to connect to services on the network. However, before a client can use the TGS to obtain tickets, it must first obtain a special ticket (the ticket granting ticket [TGT]) from the AS.

Privilege Attribute Certificate

The *privilege attribute certificate* (PAC) is a structure that contains the user's security ID (SID).

Tickets

In a basic Kerberos exchange, the client will contact the TGS and request a ticket for the target server before contacting the target server. A *ticket* is a record that allows a client to authenticate itself to a server; it is simply a certificate issued by the Kerberos service. The ticket is encrypted so that only the target server is able to decrypt and read it. Tickets contain the identity of the requesting client, the timestamp, the servers session key, the lifetime of the ticket, and other information (such as the PAC) that will help verify the identity of the client to the target server. Tickets are reusable within their life span, which is usually 8 hours.

Ticket Granting Tickets

One method for using Kerberos is to simply request a ticket for each target server from the TGS portion of the Kerberos service whenever the user wants to access the specified target server. Using this method, the response from the request would contain a session key and other information that is encrypted with the user's secret key. This method results in a component of the user's secret key being exposed on the network every time a new ticket request is made.

In Windows 2000, Kerberos protects the secret key by initially authenticating the user and then requesting a ticket granting ticket (TGT). A *ticket granting ticket* is a request for a ticket and a random session key to be used with the TGS portion of the Kerberos service. After obtaining the ticket, the user can contact a service at any time; the requested ticket does not come from the AS, but from the TGS. The reply is encrypted not with the user's secret key, but with the session key that the AS provided for use with the TGS.

Features of the Kerberos Protocol

The Kerberos protocol has several advantages over traditional challenge/ response authentication systems.

Mature Open Standard

The Windows 2000 implementation of the Kerberos protocol complies with RFC 1510 and RFC 1964. It can interoperate with other implementations of Kerberos that also comply with the RFCs. Therefore, Kerberos clients on other platforms, such as UNIX, can be authenticated by Windows 2000. In some cases, however, implementation-dependent values will not exist or will be unavailable. In the absence of required data, the Windows 2000 Kerberos service attempts to match the principal name in the ticket either to a Windows 2000 user account or to a default account created for this purpose.

Faster Connection Authentication

When using the Kerberos protocol, servers do not need to do pass-through authentication. A server running Windows 2000 can verify the client credentials by using the client-supplied ticket, without having to query the Kerberos service. This is because the client will have already obtained a Kerberos ticket from a domain controller, which the server can then use to build the client's access token. Since the server is required to do less work when establishing a connection, it can more easily accommodate a large number of simultaneous connection requests.

Mutual Authentication

The Kerberos protocol provides mutual authentication of both the client and server. The Windows NTLM authentication protocol provides only client authentication, and it assumes that all servers are trusted. It does not verify the identity of the server that a client connects to. The assumption that all servers can be trusted is no longer valid. Mutual authentication of both client and server is an important foundation for secure networks.

Delegation of Authentication

Delegation of authentication allows a user to connect to an application server, which in turn can connect to one or more additional servers on the client's behalf, by using the client's credentials.

Transitive Trusts

Authentication credentials issued by one Kerberos service are accepted by all Kerberos services within the domain.

Kerberos Authentication Process

The Kerberos authentication process involves the client computer negotiating exchanges between the target server and the KDC. Figure 11.12 provides an overview of the authentication process. The numbered steps in the diagram are described below.

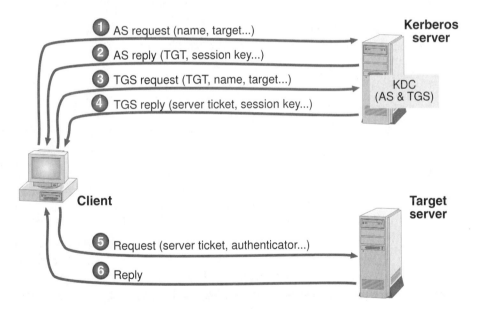

Kerberos server

1 AS request (name, target...)

2 AS reply (TGT, session key...)

3 TGS request (TGT, name, target...)

4 TGS reply (server ticket, session key...)

KDC (AS & TGS)

Client

Target server

5 Request (server ticket, authenticator...)

6 Reply

Figure 11.12 Kerberos authentication process

The Kerberos authentication process works as follows:

1. The client sends an initial AS request to the AS portion of the Kerberos service. The AS includes the client's principal name and the principal name of the target server for which it is requesting a ticket.

2. The Kerberos service generates an AS reply and sends it to the client. The reply contains the following:

   - A TGT for the TGS portion of the Kerberos service. The TGT is encrypted with the TGS secret key. The TGT contains the user's SID. By encrypting the TGT with the TGS secret key, the client is unable to change the SID properties.

   - A session key for exchanges with the TGS portion of the Kerberos service. The session key is encrypted with the client's secret key. The client's secret key is a computation of the client's password. It is similar to the session key used in NTLM challenge/response. The encryption here makes it difficult for someone to steal the session key.

3. The client generates and sends a TGS request that contains the client's and target server's principal names, realms, and the TGT that identifies the client.

4. The TGS portion of the Kerberos service generates and sends a TGS reply to the client. This reply contains a ticket for the target server. The ticket is encrypted with the server's secret key. The server's secret key is a computation of the password generated when the server joined the domain. The reply also includes other information, including the session key.

5. The client extracts the session key for the target server and generates a request for the server. This request contains the target server and an authenticator encrypted with the session key. The client sends this request to the target server by using an established transport path.

6. The target server decrypts the ticket by using its secret key to obtain the session key. The server then uses the session key to decrypt the authenticator to verify the client. If the client has requested mutual authentication, the target server generates a reply encrypted with the session key and send it to the client. Mutual authentication not only authenticates the client to the target server, but also authenticates the target server to the client.

Note The AS and TGS exchanges with the Kerberos service operate over User Datagram Protocol (UDP) port 88. The exchanges between the client and target server are dependent on the protocol in use between the two principals.

Kerberos Delegation

Occasionally, it is necessary for an application server to connect to another server on behalf of a client. Like impersonation, delegation is used to ensure that proper security permissions are applied against the application server's request.

The Kerberos authentication protocol supports delegated authentication. This type of authentication is used when a client transaction involves multiple servers. In this case, each of the verifying servers obtains another ticket and authenticates the ticket to the requested server on behalf of the client. There is no restriction on the number of consecutive servers that can delegate authentication. This is different than impersonation, in that the server accesses remote resources on the behalf of the client instead of local resources.

Figure 11.13 provides an overview of the Kerberos delegation process. The numbered steps in the diagram are described below.

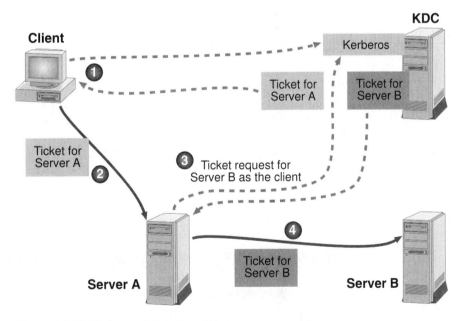

Figure 11.13 Kerberos delegation process

The following steps describe the access of resources involving two servers:

1. The client requests and receives a ticket for target Server A from the Kerberos service.

2. The client sends the ticket directly to Server A.

3. Server A sends a request, impersonating the client, to the Kerberos service for a ticket for target Server B. The Kerberos service responds with a ticket that allows the client to access Server B.

4. Server A can then send the ticket to Server B, accessing Server B as the client.

Kerberos Logon Processes

The addition of Kerberos as an authentication package in Windows 2000 affects various aspects of the logon process. However, the portions of the logon process that run before an authentication package becomes involved remain unchanged in Windows 2000.

Local Interactive Logon

When a local interactive logon occurs, the user logs on with a user account that exists on the local computer rather than with a domain user account. Figure 11.14 provides an overview of the local interactive logon process in Windows 2000. The numbered steps in the diagram are described below.

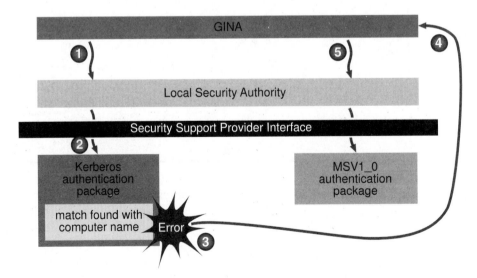

Figure 11.14 Local interactive logon process

For local user accounts, the following occurs in Windows 2000:

1. When the Graphical Identification and Authentication DLL (GINA) receives the logon request, it forwards the request to the Local Security Authority (LSA). This request specifies Kerberos as the authentication package to use because this is the default package in Windows 2000.

2. LSA processes the request and sends it to the Kerberos authentication package.

3. When Kerberos receives the logon request. Kerberos returns an error because it is used only when authenticating logon requests for domain user accounts, not local user accounts.

4. LSA receives the error and returns an error to the GINA.

5. The GINA resubmits the logon request to LSA specifying the "MSV1_0" authentication package. The logon process then occurs as it would for a local interactive logon under Windows NT 4.0.

Domain Interactive Logon

The exchange that occurs when a user logs on to Windows 2000 with a domain user account is similar to the basic Kerberos exchange. Figure 11.15 provides an overview of this logon process. The number steps in the diagram are described below.

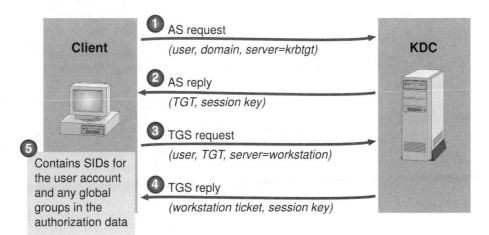

Figure 11.15 Domain interactive logon process

The domain interactive logon process occurs as follows:

1. When the logon request reaches the LSA, it passes the request to the Kerberos authentication package. The client sends an initial AS request to the Kerberos service, providing the user name and domain name. This is a request for authentication and a TGT. The request is made by using the principal name of krbtgt@*<domain_name>*, where *<domain_name>* is the name of the domain in which the user account is located. The first domain controller in the domain automatically generates the krbtgt@*<domain_name>* account.

2. The Kerberos service generates an AS reply containing a TGT (encrypted with the Kerberos secret key) and a session key for the TGS exchanges (encrypted with the client's secret key). This response is sent back to the client. The authorization data portion of the TGT contains the SID for the user account and SIDs for any global groups to which the user belongs. The SIDs are returned to the LSA for inclusion in the user's access token. The SIDs are copied by the Kerberos service from the TGT into subsequent tickets obtained from the Kerberos service.

3. The client then generates and sends a TGS request containing the client's principal name and realm, the TGT to identify the client, and the local workstation name as the target server. This is done to request access to the local computer for the user.

4. The Kerberos service generates and sends a TGS reply. This reply contains a ticket for the workstation and other information, including the session key (encrypted by using the session key from the TGT). Also included in the authorization data portion of the TGS reply are the SIDs for the user account and any global groups copied by the Kerberos service from the original TGT.

5. The Kerberos authentication package returns the list of SIDs to the LSA.

Windows 2000 services use the Kernel Mode Security Support Provider Interface (SSPI) to perform authentication. Instead of communicating directly with the Kerberos authentication package, both services access Kerberos through an authentication package built into LSA. This authentication package is called the Negotiate package.

During startup, both the Server and Workstation services initialize their interface with the Negotiate package in LSA by using SSPI. During this process, the server service obtains a credential handle for its default credentials.

The network communication occurs in two segments: protocol negotiation and session setup. Before a user can establish a session with the server, the client computer and the server must agree on the security protocol to use by determining which version of security they both support. Once the client has been authenticated and has a ticket, it can establish a session with the server.

Kerberos Public Key Support

Windows 2000 extends the functionality of Kerberos to allow it to interact with the Active Directory service. Windows 2000 includes extensions to the Kerberos V5 authentication protocol to support public key–based authentication. The public key extensions allow clients to request an initial TGT by using a private key. The Kerberos service verifies such a request by using the user's public key that is obtained from the user's X.509 certificate published to the Active Directory store. In order to obtain a ticket, the user's X.509 certificate must be stored in their user object. If the Kerberos service finds the certificate, the Kerberos service issues a ticket for the client and the standard Kerberos procedure is followed thereafter. This replaces the secret key that is known only to the principal and the KDC. Smart cards, for example, use public key extensions provided by Kerberos.

Lesson Summary

Kerberos is the default authentication provider in Windows 2000 and the primary security protocol. To better understand the Kerberos protocol, you should be familiar with the terms common to Kerberos, including principal, realm, secret key, session key, authenticator, KDC, AS, TGS, PAC, ticket, and TGT. The Kerberos authentication process involves the client computer negotiating exchanges between the target server and the KDC. The Kerberos authentication protocol supports delegated authentication. When a local interactive logon occurs, the user logs on with a user account that exists on the local computer rather than with a domain user account. The exchange that occurs when a user logs on to Windows 2000 with a domain user account is similar to the basic Kerberos exchange. Windows 2000 services use the Kernel Mode SSPI to perform authentication. In addition, Windows 2000 extends the functionality of Kerberos to allow it to interact with Active Directory services. Windows 2000 includes extensions to the Kerberos V5 authentication protocol to support public key–based authentication.

Lesson 4: Security Configuration Tools

Windows 2000 provides a set of security configuration tools that are designed to reduce the costs associated with security configuration and analysis of Windows 2000 networks. These tools are MMC snap-ins that allow you to configure Windows 2000 security settings and perform periodic analyses of the system to ensure that the configuration remains intact or to make necessary changes over time. Security settings include security policies (account and local policies), access control (services, files, and the registry), event logs, group membership (restricted groups), IPSec security policies, and public key policies. The security configuration tools include three snap-ins: the Security Configuration And Analysis snap-in, the Security Templates snap-in, and the Group Policy snap-in.

After this lesson, you will be able to

- Understand how the security configuration tools are used to configure security settings and analyze system security in your Windows 2000 network

Estimated lesson time: 30 minutes

Security Configuration And Analysis Snap-In

The Security Configuration And Analysis snap-in allows you to configure and analyze local system security.

Security Configuration

The Security Configuration And Analysis snap-in can also be used to directly configure local system security. You can import security templates created with the Security Templates snap-in, and apply these templates to the group policy object (GPO) for the local computer. This immediately configures the system security with the levels specified in the template.

Security Analysis

The state of the operating system and applications on a computer is dynamic. For example, security levels may be required to change temporarily to enable immediate resolution of an administration or network issue; this change can often go unreversed. This means that a computer may no longer meet the requirements for enterprise security.

Regular analysis enables an administrator to track and ensure an adequate level of security on each computer as part of an enterprise risk management program. Analysis is highly specified; information about all system aspects related to security is provided in the results. This enables an administrator to tune the security levels and, most importantly, detect any security flaws that may occur in the system over time.

The Security Configuration And Analysis snap-in enables quick review of security analysis results. Recommendations are presented along with current system settings, and icons or remarks are used to highlight any areas where current settings do not match the proposed level of security. The Security Configuration And Analysis snap-in also allows you to resolve any discrepancies revealed by analysis.

If frequent analysis of a large number of computers is required, as in a domain-based infrastructure, the Secedit command-line tool may be used as a method of batch analysis. However, analysis results still must be viewed by using the Security Configuration And Analysis snap-in. For more information about the Secedit utility, see Windows 2000 Help.

Using the Security Configuration And Analysis Snap-In

The Security Configuration And Analysis snap-in (Figure 11.16) reviews and analyzes your system security settings and recommends modifications to the current system settings. Administrators can use the snap-in to adjust the security policy and detect security flaws that arise in the system.

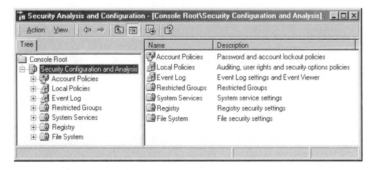

Figure 11.16 Security Configuration And Analysis snap-in

The Security Configuration And Analysis snap-in allows you to perform a variety of tasks:

- Set a working database
- Import a security template
- Analyze system security
- Review security analysis results
- Configure system security
- Edit the base security configuration
- Export a security template

For details about how to perform each of these tasks, see Windows 2000 Help.

Security Templates Snap-In

A security template is a physical representation of a security configuration; it is a file where a group of security settings may be stored. Windows 2000 includes a set of security templates, each based on the role of a computer. The templates range from security settings for low security domain clients to highly secure domain controllers. They can be used as provided, modified, or serve as a basis for creating custom security templates.

Using the Security Templates Snap-In

The Security Templates snap-in (Figure 11.17) is a tool for creating and assigning security templates for one or more computers.

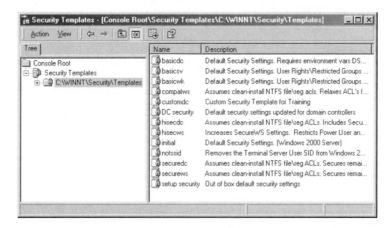

Figure 11.17 Security Templates snap-in

A security template is a physical file representation of a security configuration, and can be applied to a local computer or imported to a Group Policy Object (GPO) in the Active Directory service. When you import a security template to a GPO, Group Policy processes the template and makes the corresponding changes to the members of that GPO, which may be users or computers.

The Security Templates snap-in allows you to perform a variety of tasks:

- Customize a predefined security template
- Define a security template
- Delete a security template
- Refresh the security template list
- Set a description for a security template

Exercise 3: Creating and Using the Security Analysis And Configuration Snap-In

In this exercise you create a custom snap-in containing the Security Analysis And Configuration snap-in and the Security Templates snap-in. You then customize a template and open a new database using the custom template. You will then analyze the security settings of Server01 against the template and then you will apply the template's configuration to the security settings of Server01. Complete this exercise on Server01.

▶ **Procedure 1: Creating a Security Analysis And Configuration snap-in**

You will run the MMC and add the Security Analysis And Configuration snap-in. MMC version 1.2, included with Windows 2000, allows you to add multiple snap-ins to an existing console. For the purpose of clarity, you will create a new console rather than adding to an existing console running other snap-ins.

1. Log on to Server01 as administrator with a password of "password."
2. Click Start and then click Run.

   The Run dialog box appears.
3. In the Open text box, type **mmc** and then click OK.

   An empty MMC console opens and is named Console1.
4. Click the Console menu and then click Add/Remove Snap-in.

   The Add/Remove Snap-in dialog box appears.

5. Click the Add button.

   The Add Standalone snap-in window appears.

6. Scroll down and click Security Configuration And Analysis and then click the Add button.

7. Click Close.

   The Add/Remove Snap-in dialog box appears.

8. Click OK.

9. Click the Console menu and then click Save.

   The Save As dialog box appears.

10. In the File Name text box, type **Security** and then click Save.

▶ **Procedure 2: Adding and configuring security using the Security Template snap-in to the Security console**

Before analyzing Server01 and applying new security settings, you install the Security Template snap-in to the Security console.

1. Click the Console menu and then choose Add/Remove Snap-in.

   The Add/Remove Snap-in dialog box appears.

2. Click the Add button.

   The Add Standalone Snap-in window appears.

3. Scroll down and click Security Templates and then click the Add button.

4. Click Close.

   The Add/Remove Snap-in dialog box appears.

5. Click OK.

6. Click the Console menu and then click Save.

7. Expand the Security Templates node then expand the C:\WINNT\Security\Templates folder.

   All of the defined templates appear in the console tree and in the details pane.

8. Expand the securedc.

   This is an incremental security template usually used after a basic security template is applied. For the purpose of this exercise, this template is sufficient.

9. Expand the Account Policies node and then click Password Policy.

   Password policy settings appear in the details pane.

10. In the details pane, double-click Minimum Password Length.

    The Template Security Policy Setting dialog box appears.

11. In the Password Must Be At Least box, change the value to **5** characters and then click OK.

12. In the console tree, click securedc.

13. Click the Action menu and then click Save As.

    The Save As window appears.

14. In the File Name text box, type **customdc** and then click Save.

15. In the console tree, click customdc.

16. Click the Action menu and click Set Description.

    The Security Template Description box appears.

17. In the Description box, type **Custom Security Template for Training** and click OK.

18. In the console tree, click the C:\WINNT\Security\Templates folder.

    Notice in the details pane that customdc now has a description associated with it.

19. Read the other template descriptions to familiarize yourself with the templates included with Windows 2000 Server.

▶ **Procedure 3: Creating a new security database**

In this procedure you create a new security database.

1. In the console tree, click Security Configuration And Analysis and read the text in the details pane.

2. Click the Action menu and then click Open Database.

   The Open Database dialog box appears.

3. In the File Name text box, type **training** and then click Open.

   The Import Template dialog box appears.

4. Click customdc.inf and then click Open.

   This is the custom template you created in the previous procedure.

▶ **Procedure 4: Analyzing current security settings**

In this procedure you analyze the current settings of Server01 against the custom template you created in Procedure 2.

1. In the console tree, verify that the Security Configuration And Analysis node is selected.

2. Click the Action menu and then click Analyze Computer Now.

   The Perform Analysis dialog box appears an it is shows the path and name of the error log as C:\Documents and Settings\Administrator\Local Settings\Temp\training.log.

3. Click OK.

   The Analyzing System Security status box appears as various aspect of Server01's security configuration are checked against the template.

4. When the analysis is complete, expand the Security Configuration And Analysis node.

5. Expand the Account Policies node and then click the Password Policy node.

   In the details pane, both template settings and the computer's settings are displayed for each policy. Discrepancies appear with a red circle with a white "X" in the center. Consistencies appear with a white circle and a green check mark in the center. If there is no flag or check mark, the security setting is not specified in the template.

6. In the console tree, click the Security Configuration And Analysis node.

7. Click the Action menu and then click Configure Computer Now.

   The Configure System dialog box appears.

8. Click OK.

9. Click the Action menu and then click Analyze Computer Now.

   The Perform Analysis dialog box appears.

10. Click OK.

11. Review the policy settings to verify that the Database Settings column is equivalent to the Computer Setting column.

12. Close the Security snap-in.

    The Microsoft Management Console message box appears.

13. Click Yes.

14. If a Save Security Templates window appears, click Yes.

Group Policy Snap-In

Security settings define the security-relevant behavior of the system. Through the use of GPOs in Active Directory services, administrators can centrally apply the security levels required to protect enterprise systems.

When determining settings for a GPO that contains multiple computers, the organizational and functional character of that given site, domain, or organizational unit (OU) must be considered. For example, the security levels necessary for an OU containing computers in a sales department would be very different from that for an OU containing finance department computers.

The Group Policy snap-in allows you to configure security centrally in the Active Directory store. A Security Settings folder is located on the Computer Configuration node and the User Configuration node. The security settings allow group policy administrators to set policies that can restrict user access to files and folders, set how many incorrect passwords a user can enter before the user is locked out, and control user rights, such as which users are able to log on at a domain server. For details about how to use the Group Policy snap-in and how to administer group policies, see Chapter 7, Lesson 4, "Administering Group Policies."

Lesson Summary

Windows 2000 provides a set of security configuration tools that allow you to configure Windows 2000 security settings and perform periodic analyses of the system to ensure that the configuration remains intact or to make necessary changes over time. The Security Configuration And Analysis snap-in allows you to configure and analyze local system security. It reviews and analyzes your system security settings and recommends modifications to the current system settings. The Security Templates snap-in allows you to create and assign security templates for one or more computers. The Group Policy snap-in allows you to configure security centrally in the Active Directory store.

Lesson 5: Microsoft Windows 2000 Auditing

In this lesson, you will learn about Windows 2000 auditing, which is a tool for maintaining network security. Auditing allows you to track user activities and system-wide events. In addition, you will learn about audit policies and what you need to consider before you set up a policy. You will also learn how to set up auditing on resources and how to maintain security logs.

After this lesson, you will be able to

- Plan an audit strategy and determine which events to audit

- Set up auditing on Active Directory objects and on files, folders, and printers

- Use Event Viewer to view a log and locate events

Estimated lesson time: 75 minutes

Overview of Windows 2000 Auditing

Auditing in Microsoft Windows 2000 is the process of tracking both user activities and Windows 2000 activities, called events, on a computer. Through auditing, you can specify that Windows 2000 writes a record of an event to the security log. The security log maintains a record of valid and invalid logon attempts and events related to creating, opening, or deleting files or other objects. An audit entry in the security log contains the following information:

- The action that was performed

- The user who performed the action

- The success or failure of the event and when the event occurred

Using an Audit Policy

An audit policy defines the types of security events that Windows 2000 records in the security log on each computer. The security log allows you to track the events that you specify.

Windows 2000 writes events to the security log on the computer where the event occurs. For example, you can configure auditing so that any time someone tries to log on to the domain by using a domain user account and the logon attempt fails, Windows 2000 writes an event to the security log on the domain controller. The event is recorded on the domain controller rather than on the computer at which the logon attempt was made, because it is the domain controller that attempted to and could not authenticate the logon attempt.

You can set up an audit policy for a computer to do the following:

- Track the success and failure of events, such as logon attempts by users, an attempt by a particular user to read a specific file, changes to a user account or to group memberships, and changes to your security settings.

- Eliminate or minimize the risk of unauthorized use of resources.

You can use Event Viewer to view events that Windows 2000 has recorded in the security log. You can also archive log files to track trends over time—for example, to determine the use of printers or files or to verify attempts at unauthorized use of resources.

Planning an Audit Policy

When you plan an audit policy, you must determine the computers on which to set up auditing. Auditing is turned off by default. As you are determining which computers to audit, you must also plan what to audit on each computer. Windows 2000 records audited events on each computer separately.

The types of events that you can audit include the following:

- Access to files and folders

- Users logging on and off

- Shutting down and restarting a computer running Windows 2000 Server

- Changes to user accounts and groups

- Attempts to make changes to Active Directory objects

After you have determined the types of events to audit, you must determine whether to audit the success and/or failure of events. Tracking successful events can tell you how often Windows 2000 users or services gain access to specific files, printers, or other objects. You can use this information for resource planning. Tracking failed events can alert you to possible security breaches. For example, if you notice a lot of failed logon attempts by a certain user account, especially if these attempts are occurring outside normal business hours, an unauthorized person might be attempting to break into your system.

Consider the following guidelines in determining your audit policy:

- Determine if you need to track trends of system usage. If so, plan to archive event logs. Archiving these logs allows you to view how usage changes over time and allows you to plan to increase system resources before they become a problem.

- Review security logs frequently. You should set a schedule and regularly review security logs because configuring auditing alone does not alert you to security breaches.

- Define an audit policy that is useful and manageable. Always audit sensitive and confidential data. Audit only those events that will provide you with meaningful information about your network environment. This minimizes usage of server resources and makes essential information easier to locate. Auditing too many types of events can create excess overhead for Windows 2000.

- Audit resource access by the Everyone group instead of the Users group. This ensures that you audit anyone who can connect to the network, not just the users for whom you create user accounts in the domain.

Implementing an Audit Policy

Auditing is a powerful tool for tracking events that occur on computers in your organization. To implement auditing, you must consider auditing requirements and set the audit policy. After you set an audit policy on a computer, you can implement auditing on files, folders, printers, and Active Directory objects.

Configuring Auditing

You can implement an audit policy based on the role of the computer in the Windows 2000 network. Auditing is configured differently for the following types of computers running Windows 2000:

- For member or stand-alone servers or computers running Windows 2000 Professional, an audit policy is set for each individual computer. For example, to audit user access to a file on a member server, you set the audit policy on that computer.

- For domain controllers, an audit policy is set for all domain controllers in the domain. To audit events that occur on domain controllers, such as changes to Active Directory objects, you configure a group policy for the domain, which applies to all domain controllers.

Note The types of events that you can audit on a domain controller are identical to those you can audit on a computer that is not a domain controller. The procedure is similar as well, but you use a group policy for the domain to control auditing for domain controllers.

Auditing Requirements

The requirements to set up and administer auditing are as follows:

- You must have the Manage Auditing And Security Log permission for the computer where you want to configure an audit policy or review an audit log. Windows 2000 grants these rights to the Administrators group by default.

- The files and folders to be audited must be on NTFS volumes.

Setting Up Auditing

Setting up auditing is a two-part process:

- **Setting the audit policy** The audit policy enables auditing of objects but does not activate auditing of specific objects.

- **Enabling auditing of specific resources** You identify the specific events to audit for files, folders, printers, and Active Directory objects. Windows 2000 then tracks and logs the specified events.

Setting an Audit Policy

The first step in implementing an audit policy is selecting the types of events that Windows 2000 audits. For each event that you can audit, the configuration settings indicate whether to track successful or failed attempts. You can set audit policies by using the Group Policy snap-in.

The following table describes the types of events that Windows 2000 can audit.

Event	Description
Account logon events	A domain controller received a request to validate a user account.
Account management	An administrator created, changed, or deleted a user account or group. A user account was renamed, disabled, or enabled, or a password was set or changed.
Directory service access	A user gained access to an Active Directory object. You must configure specific Active Directory objects for auditing to log this type of event.
Logon events	A user logged on or logged off, or a user made or canceled a network connection to the computer.
Object access	A user gained access to a file, folder, or printer. You must configure specific files, folders, or printers for auditing. Directory service access is auditing a user's access to specific Active Directory objects. Object access is auditing a user's access to files, folders, and printers.
Policy change	A change was made to the user security options, user rights, or audit policies.
Privilege use	A user exercised a right, such as changing the system time. (This does not include rights that are related to logging on and logging off.)
Process tracking	A program performed an action. This information is generally useful only for programmers who want to track details of program execution.
System	A user restarted or shut down the computer, or an event occurred that affects Windows 2000 security or the security log. (For example, the audit log is full and Windows 2000 discards entries.)

To set an audit policy on a computer that is not a domain controller, create a custom MMC console and add the Group Policy snap-in. In the console tree, select Audit Policy from the Computer Configuration node, as shown in Figure 11.18. The console displays the current audit policy settings in the details pane.

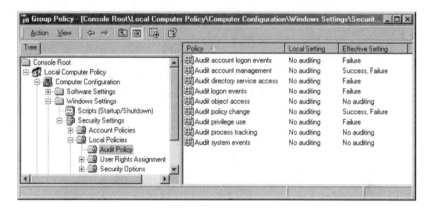

Figure 11.18 Group Policy snap-in with the Audit Policy folder selected

Changes that you make to your computer's audit policy take effect when one of the following events occurs:

- You initiate policy propagation by typing **secedit /RefreshPolicy machine_policy** at the command prompt and then pressing Enter.

- You restart your computer. Windows 2000 applies changes that you made to your audit policy the next time that you restart your computer.

- Policy propagation occurs. Policy propagation is a process that applies policy settings, including audit policy settings, to your computer. Automatic policy propagation occurs at regular, configurable intervals. By default, policy propagation occurs every eight hours.

Auditing Access to Files and Folders

If security breaches are an issue for your organization, you can set up auditing for files and folders on NTFS partitions. To audit user access to files and folders, you must first enable the Audit object access policy, which includes files and folders.

Once you have set your audit policy to audit object access, you enable auditing for specific files and folders and specify which types of access, by which users or groups, to audit. To enable auditing for a specific file or folder, open the Properties dialog box for that file or folder, select the Security tab, and then click Advanced. Select the Auditing tab and configure auditing for the selected file or folder.

Auditing Access to Active Directory Objects

To audit Active Directory object access, you must configure an audit policy and then set auditing for specific objects, such as users, computers, organizational units (OUs), or groups by specifying which types of access and access by which users to audit.

To enable auditing of access to Active Directory objects, enable the Audit directory services access policy in the Group Policy snap-in.

To enable auditing for specific Active Directory objects, open the Active Directory Users And Computers snap-in and select Advanced Features from the View menu. Open the Properties dialog box for the object that you want to audit. On the Security tab, click Advanced. Select the Auditing tab and configure auditing for that object.

Auditing Access to Printers

You can audit access to printers in order to track access to sensitive printers. To audit access to printers, enable the Audit Object Access policy, which includes printers. Then enable auditing for specific printers, and specify which types of access and access by which users to audit. After you select the printer, you use the same steps that you use to set up auditing on files and folders.

To set up auditing on a printer, open the Properties dialog box for the printer that you want to audit. On the Security tab, click Advanced. Select the Auditing tab and configure auditing for the printer.

Using Event Viewer

You can use Event Viewer to perform a variety of tasks, including viewing the audit logs that are generated as a result of setting audit policies and auditing events. You can also use Event Viewer to view the contents of security log files and find specific events within log files.

Windows 2000 Logs

You can use Event Viewer to view information contained in Windows 2000 logs. By default there are three logs available to view in Event Viewer. These logs are described in the following table.

Log	Description
Application log	Contains errors, warnings, or information that programs, such as a database program or an e-mail program, generate. The program developer presets which events to record.
Security log	Contains information about the success or failure of audited events. The events that Windows 2000 records are a result of your audit policy.
System log	Contains errors, warnings, and information that Windows 2000 generates. Windows 2000 presets which events to record.

Note If additional services are installed, they might add their own event log. For example, the Domain Name System (DNS) service logs DNS events in the DNS Server log.

Viewing the Security Log

The Security log contains information about events that are monitored by an audit policy, such as failed and successful logon attempts. You can view the Security log in the Event Viewer snap-in, as shown in Figure 11-19.

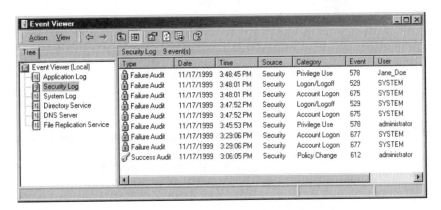

Figure 11.19 Event Viewer snap-in with the Security Log selected

In the details pane, Event Viewer displays a list of log entries and summary information for each item.

Successful events appear with a key icon, and unsuccessful events appear with a lock icon. Other important information includes the date and time that the event occurred, the category of the event, and the user who generated the event. The category indicates the type of event, such as object access, account management, directory service access, or logon events.

Windows 2000 records events in the Security log on the computer at which the event occurred. You can view these events from any computer as long as you have administrative privileges for the computer where the events occurred. To view the security log on a remote computer, point Event Viewer to a remote computer when you add this snap-in to a console.

Locating Events

When you first start Event Viewer, it automatically displays all events that are recorded in the selected log. To change what appears in the log, you can locate selected events by using the Filter command. You can also search for specific events by using the Find command. To filter or find events, start Event Viewer, and click Filter or click Find on the View menu.

Managing Audit Logs

You can track trends in Windows 2000 by archiving event logs and comparing logs from different periods. Viewing trends helps you determine resource use and plan for growth. If unauthorized use of resources is a concern, you can also use logs to determine patterns of usage. Windows 2000 allows you to control the size of the logs and to specify the action that Windows 2000 takes when a log becomes full.

You can configure the properties of each individual audit log. To configure the settings for logs, select the log in Event Viewer, and then display the Properties dialog box for the log.

Use the Properties dialog box for each type of audit log to control the size of each log, which can be from 64 KB to 4,194,240 KB (4 GB). The default size is 512 KB. You can also use the log properties to control the action that Windows 2000 takes when the log fills up.

Tip Use the Security Configuration And Analysis snap-in to configure settings for Event Viewer.

Archiving Logs

Archiving security logs allows you to maintain a history of security-related events. Many companies have policies on keeping archive logs for a specified period to track security-related information over time. If you want to save the log file, clear all events, or open a log file, select the log from the Event Viewer console tree and then select the appropriate option from the Action menu.

Lesson Summary

Auditing in Microsoft Windows 2000 is the process of tracking both user activities and Windows 2000 activities, called events, on a computer. Through auditing, you can specify that Windows 2000 writes a record of an event to the Security log. An audit policy defines the types of security events that Windows 2000 records in the Security log on each computer. The Security log allows you to track the events that you specify. When you plan an audit policy you must determine the computers on which to set up auditing. As you are determining which computers to audit, you must also plan what to audit on each computer. To implement auditing, you need to consider auditing requirements and set the audit policy. After you set an audit policy on a computer, you can implement auditing on files, folders, printers, and Active Directory objects. You can use Event Viewer to view the audit logs that are generated as a result of setting the audit policy and auditing events. You can also use Event Viewer to view the contents of Security log files and find specific events within log files.

Review

The following questions are intended to reinforce key information presented in this chapter. If you are unable to answer a question, review the appropriate lesson and then try the question again. Answers to the questions can be found in Appendix A, "Questions and Answers."

1. Which key is associated with the creation of digital signatures, the public key or the private key? Explain your answer.

2. What security credential(s) will be in use if you are supporting client computers running Windows 2000 and Windows NT that authenticate to servers running Windows 2000 Server, and Windows NT Server?

3. How can a security template be used to facilitate configuration and analysis of security settings?

4. Where is the Certificate Services Enrollment page and what is its purpose?

5. What steps must you follow to enable auditing of specific file objects on domain controllers in a domain where Group Policy is enabled?

C H A P T E R   1 2

Reliability and Availability

About This Chapter

Two of the top requirements for a business operating system are high reliability and availability. In the context of an operating system, *reliability* refers to how consistently a server runs applications and services, while *availability* refers to the amount of time a system can be used. Reliability is increased by reducing the potential causes of system failure. Availability is increased by addressing the causes of downtime. In other words, reliable and available systems resist failure and are easy to restart after they've been shut down. This chapter focuses on maintaining hardware devices and drivers, backing up data, and implementing disaster protection. In addition, the chapter reviews several approaches to disaster recovery to assist you should your system fail.

Before You Begin

To complete the lessons in this chapter, you must have

- Server01 running Microsoft Windows 2000 Server as a domain controller.
- Completed the exercises in the previous chapters.

Lesson 1: Managing Hardware Devices and Drivers

Hardware includes any physical device connected to your computer and controlled by its microprocessor. For a device to work properly with Windows 2000, a device driver must be loaded onto the computer. A *device driver* is a program that allows a specific device to communicate with Windows 2000. Although a device might be installed on your system, Windows 2000 cannot use the device until an appropriate driver is installed and configured. This lesson provides an overview of hardware and describes how to manage devices and their drivers. It also describes the tools necessary to add, remove, and configure these devices and their drivers.

After this lesson, you will be able to

- Manage hardware devices and drivers by using the Add/Remove Hardware wizard and the Device Manager snap-in, by configuring driver signing options and hardware profiles, and by using event logs to monitor reliability and availability

- Apply service pack updates

Estimated lesson time: 40 minutes

Hardware Overview

Hardware includes any devices that were connected to your computer when it was manufactured, as well as peripheral equipment added later. For example, your system's hardware can include modems, disk drives, drive controllers, CD-ROM drives, printers, network adapters, keyboards, monitors, and display adapter cards.

These devices, which might or might not be Plug and Play compliant, are connected to the computer in several ways. Some devices, such as network adapters and sound cards, are connected to expansion slots inside the computer. Other devices, such as printers and scanners, are connected to ports on the outside of the computer, while some devices, known as PC cards, connect only to PC Card slots on a portable computer.

Each device has its own unique device driver, which is typically supplied by the device manufacturer. Many of these device drivers are included on the Windows 2000 installation CD-ROM.

Hardware Types

Windows 2000 classifies devices by hardware type. Hardware types include such things as display adapter cards, keyboards, CD-ROM drives, ports, and printers. When you use the Device Manager snap-in (Figure 12.1) or the Add/Remove Hardware wizard, you see a list of the hardware types installed on your computer.

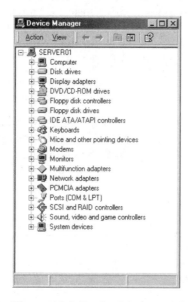

Figure 12.1 Device Manager snap-in for the local computer

Hardware types are further categorized according to individual devices. For example, the modem hardware type includes over 200 modems you can install and use with Windows 2000.

Devices can also be classified according to the way they are connected to your computer. Most devices are permanently connected to your computer and are typically installed only once. They are available every time you turn on your computer unless you disable or uninstall them. Permanently connected devices include the following:

- Sound cards
- Video display cards
- Modems
- Hard disks

Other devices are designed to be connected and disconnected from your computer as you need them. You can plug or insert these types of devices into the appropriate port or expansion slot, and Windows 2000 will recognize the device and configure it without restarting your computer. Likewise, when you disconnect these types of devices, you need to inform Windows 2000 only that you are ejecting, removing, or unplugging it. You do not need to shut down or restart your computer. Devices designed to be connected and disconnected include the following:

- PC Cards that connect to portable computers

- Hardware that connects to a universal serial bus (USB) or an IEEE 1394 bus

- Docking stations that support hot docking and undocking of portable computers

- Hardware that connects to serial or parallel ports

For a comprehensive list of the devices supported by Windows 2000, see the Microsoft Windows Hardware Compatibility List (HCL) by performing a search on the keyword HCL at the Microsoft Web site (*http://www.microsoft.com*).

Plug and Play Overview

A *Plug and Play* device adheres to a set of specifications developed by the IEEE and computer and software manufacturers such as Intel, Compaq Corporation, Microsoft Corporation, and Phoenix Technologies. These specifications allow a computer to automatically detect and configure a device and install the appropriate device drivers. With Windows 2000, it is simple to install a PnP device. Just connect it to the computer and provide an external power source if necessary, and Windows 2000 does the rest by installing any necessary drivers, updating the system, and allocating system resources.

For example, you can dock a portable computer and connect to a network without changing the configuration. Later, you can undock that same computer and use a modem to connect to the network, again without making any manual changes to the operating system configuration. Windows 2000 automatically adjusts the device driver state to match a changed hardware configuration.

With Plug and Play, you can be confident that any new devices will work together properly and that your computer will restart correctly after you install or uninstall hardware. Windows 2000 also recognizes any new hardware when you start your computer and loads any drivers that the hardware device needs.

When you install or uninstall a hardware device, Plug and Play works with the Windows 2000 Power Options utility to manage the power requirements of your hardware and peripherals, shutting them down or conserving power when you are not using them. And if you are working in another program when you install or uninstall a device, Plug and Play lets you know it is about to change your computer configuration and warns you to save your work.

If something does go wrong, the Event Log service records the information in the System log.

Plug and Play Device Driver Support

Windows 2000 installs a Plug and Play device and its driver automatically. However, if you choose to install an older driver or legacy hardware device, you might have limited Plug and Play support or none at all.

Using a Plug and Play driver to install a non–Plug and Play device might provide some Plug and Play support. Although the system cannot recognize the hardware and load the appropriate drivers on its own, Plug and Play can oversee the installation by allocating resources, interacting with the Power Options utility in Control Panel, and recording any issues in the System log.

Generally, you cannot install non–Plug and Play hardware without performing some manual setup. Use the Add/Remove Hardware wizard or the Device Manager snap-in to change configuration settings for legacy hardware.

Installing Devices

Installing a new device typically involves three steps:

1. Connecting the device to your computer

2. Loading the appropriate device drivers for the device

3. Configuring device properties and settings

To ensure the device functions properly, you should follow the device manufacturer's installation instructions. This might require you to shut down and unplug your computer, and then connect the device to the appropriate port or insert it into the appropriate slot.

If the device is Plug and Play or is a necessary startup device like the hard disk, this detection happens automatically. However, for some older devices, you might have to restart your computer after you have connected one of them to your computer. Windows 2000 then attempts to detect your new device.

If the device is not Plug and Play, you might have to use the Add/Remove Hardware wizard in Control Panel to tell Windows 2000 what type of device you are installing. After the device is detected or you have identified the device by using the Add/Remove Hardware wizard, Windows 2000 might ask you to insert the Windows 2000 installation CD-ROM or the manufacturer's floppy disk or CD-ROM so that it can load the proper device drivers.

Once the device drivers are loaded onto your system, Windows 2000 configures the properties and settings for the device. Although you can manually configure device properties and settings, you should let Windows 2000 do it. When you manually configure properties and settings, the settings become fixed, which means Windows 2000 cannot modify them in the future if a problem arises or there is a conflict with another device.

To install the device, connect it to the appropriate port or slot on your computer according to the device manufacturer's instructions. You might need to start or restart your computer. You must be logged on as an administrator or a member of the Administrators group to complete this procedure. However, if a user with administrator privileges has already loaded the drivers for a device, you can install the device without administrator privileges. Note also that network policy settings might prevent you from completing this procedure if your computer is connected to a network.

In a situation where you need to restart your computer, Windows 2000 should detect the device and start the Found New Hardware wizard. When installing a device, such as installing a sound card into a motherboard slot, shut down Windows and turn off and unplug the computer. Remove the computer cover and install the device in the appropriate slot. Replace the computer cover, and then plug in and turn on the computer.

If your device does not install properly, you might have an older, non–Plug and Play device. Follow the instructions on the screen (if prompted) to choose a destination path to install drivers for the device.

If the device is a small computer system interface (SCSI) device, connect it to the SCSI controller port on your computer according to the device manufacturer's instructions. Restart your computer. You need to be sure the device number for the SCSI device is not used by another SCSI device and that the device is properly terminated. To change the device number, see the device manufacturer's instructions.

Note Personal Computer Memory Card International Association (PCMCIA) SCSI controller cards and other devices might not require a reboot after installation. As always, refer to the manufacturer's instructions when installing hardware. Use the information provided in this chapter as a general guideline to hardware installation.

If the device is a USB or IEEE 1394 device, plug it into any USB or IEEE port on your computer. Follow the instructions that appear on your screen. You do not need to shut down or turn off your computer when you install or plug in a USB or IEEE 1394 device. Although USB and IEEE 1394 are similar technologies, you cannot interchange USB connections with IEEE 1394 connections.

Uninstalling Devices

You can usually uninstall a Plug and Play device by disconnecting or removing the device. Some devices might require you to turn off the computer first. To ensure that you do this properly, consult the device manufacturer's installation and removal instructions.

You can use either the Add/Remove Hardware wizard or Device Manager snap-in to notify Windows 2000 that you want to uninstall a non–Plug and Play device. After you notify Windows 2000 that you are uninstalling a device, you must physically disconnect or remove the device from your computer. For example, if the device is connected to a port on the outside of your computer, you would shut down your computer, disconnect the device from the port, and then unplug the power cord, if there is one for the device.

Instead of uninstalling a Plug and Play device that you might attach again, like a modem, you can disable a device. When you disable a device, the physical device stays connected to your computer, but Windows 2000 updates the system registry so that the device drivers are no longer loaded when you start your computer. When you enable the device, the drivers are available again. Disabling devices is useful if you want to have more than one hardware configuration (hardware profile) for your computer. Multiple hardware profiles are common for mobile computers that operate both on and off of a docking station.

Note The Device Manager snap-in does not remove device drivers from your hard disk. If you want to do this, use the Add/Remove Hardware wizard and select the Uninstall A Device Removal Task option. Additionally, consult the hardware manufacturer's documentation to determine the best way to remove device drivers.

Tools for Managing Devices and Drivers

Several tools are available for managing hardware devices and their drivers. Most of these tools can be accessed through the Hardware tab of the System Properties dialog box. To open the System Properties dialog box, open Control Panel and then open the System application or hold down the Windows flag key and press the Break key. When the System Properties dialog box appears, select the Hardware tab (Figure 12.2).

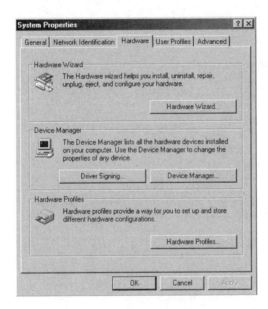

Figure 12.2 System Properties dialog box showing the Hardware tab

From here, you can open the Add/Remove Hardware wizard, the Device Manager snap-in, the Driver Signing Options dialog box, and the Hardware Profiles dialog box. In addition to the tools you can access through the System Properties dialog box, you can use Event Viewer logs to troubleshoot hardware configurations.

Add/Remove Hardware Wizard

The Add/Remove Hardware wizard allows you to add new hardware, unplug or remove hardware from your computer, or troubleshoot hardware-related problems (Figure 12.3).

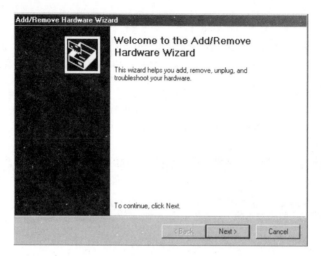

Figure 12.3 Opening screen of the Add/Remove Hardware wizard

In addition to being able to open the wizard from the Hardware tab of the System Properties dialog box, you can open it from Control Panel by selecting Add/Remove Hardware. Once you have opened the wizard, follow the steps in the wizard to add, remove, unplug, or troubleshoot your hardware.

Note To use the Add/Remove Hardware wizard, you must be logged on to or running in the context of an account with administrator privileges. Use the Runas command-line utility to run in the security context of another user account. If your computer is connected to a network, network policy settings might prevent you from using the Add/Remove Hardware wizard.

The Device Manager Snap-In

Device Manager is an MMC snap-in that provides you with a graphical view of the hardware that is installed on your computer (Figure 12.1).

In addition to being able to open the Device Manager snap-in from the Hardware tab of the System Properties dialog box, you can open the tool from the Computer Management MMC or create a custom MMC containing the Device Manager snap-in. Once you open Device Manager, you can use it to change the way your hardware is configured as well as the way your hardware interacts with your computer's microprocessor.

The Device Manager snap-in allows you to perform the following tasks:

- Determine whether the hardware on your computer is working properly
- Change hardware configuration settings
- Identify the device drivers loaded for each device, and obtain information about each device driver
- Change advanced settings and properties for devices
- Install updated device drivers
- Disable, enable, and uninstall devices
- Identify Ldevice conflicts and manually configure resource settings
- Print a System Resource Report of the devices installed on your computer

Typically Device Manager is used to check hardware status and update device drivers. Advanced users who have a thorough understanding of computer hardware also use Device Manager's diagnostic features to resolve device conflicts and change resource settings.

Important Changing resource settings improperly can disable your hardware and cause your computer to malfunction or be inoperable. Only users who have expert knowledge of computer hardware and hardware configurations should change resource settings.

Ordinarily, you will not need to use the Device Manager snap-in to change resource settings because resources are allocated automatically by Windows 2000 during hardware setup. In addition, Device Manager can be used to manage devices on a local computer only. Device Manager works in read-only mode on a remote computer.

Note To use the Device Manager snap-in, you must be logged on to or running in the security context of a user account with administrator privileges. If your computer is connected to a network, network policy settings might prevent you from using the snap-in.

Driver Signing

The Driver Signing function allows Windows 2000 to notify users whether or not a driver they are installing has passed the Microsoft certification process (Figure 12.4). Driver Signing attaches an encrypted digital signature to a code file that has passed the Windows Hardware Quality Labs (WHQL) tests.

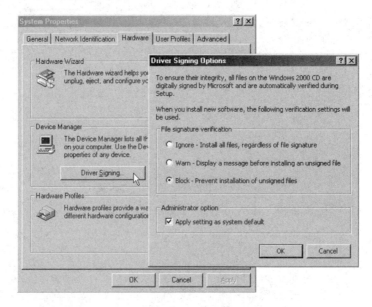

Figure 12.4 Driver Signing Options dialog box

Microsoft digitally signs drivers as part of WHQL testing if the driver runs on Windows 2000 operating systems. The digital signature is associated with individual driver packages and recognized by Windows 2000. This certification process proves to users that the drivers they employ are identical to those Microsoft has tested and notifies them if a driver file has been changed after the driver was put on the HCL.

Driver Signing allows for three responses:

- **Ignore** Allows all files to be installed, whether they've been signed or not.

- **Warn** Notifies the user if a driver that's being installed hasn't been signed, and gives the user a chance to say "no" to the installation. Warn also gives the user the option to install unsigned versions of a protected driver file.

- **Block** Prevents all unsigned drivers from being installed.

Windows 2000 ships with the Warn mode set as the default.

Driver Signing doesn't affect the code itself. Rather, Microsoft signs the binary driver code that passes the WHQL tests. Microsoft then produces a catalog file that contains the code and a cryptographic digital signature. The resulting binary file is constructed in such a way that the code can't be altered without the catalog file's signature becoming invalid.

Note For more information on digital signatures and cryptography, see Chapter 11.

Specifically, a hash (encryption) of the driver binary and relevant information are stored in a catalog (.cat) file, and the .cat file is signed with the Microsoft digital signature. The binary itself is not touched; only a .cat file is created for each driver package. The relationship between the driver package and its .cat file is referenced in the driver's .inf file and maintained by the system after the driver is installed.

Vendors wishing to have drivers tested and signed can find information on driver signing at *http://www.microsoft.com/hwdev/*. Only signed drivers are published on the Windows Update Web site at *http://windowsupdate.microsoft.com/default.htm*.

Note If you are logged on to or running in the context of an account with administrator privileges, select the Apply Setting As System Default check box (Figure 12.4) to apply the selected setting as the default for all users who log on to the computer. Driver Signing options can also be specified in Group Policy by specifying the Unsigned Driver Installation Behavior security setting.

Hardware Profiles

A hardware profile is a set of instructions that tells Windows 2000 which devices to start when you start your computer or what settings to use for each device. When you first install Windows 2000, a hardware profile named Profile 1 (Current) is created. The default profile name varies for mobile computers. A common name given to mobile computers, by default, is Undocked Profile (Current), as shown in Figure 12.5.

Figure 12.5 Hardware Profiles dialog box

By default, every device installed on your computer at the time you install Windows 2000 is enabled in the default hardware profile.

Hardware profiles are especially useful if you have a portable computer. Most portable computers are used in a variety of locations, and hardware profiles let you change which devices your computer uses when you move it from location to location. For example, you might have one profile named Docking Station Configuration for using your portable computer at a docking station with hardware components such as a CD-ROM drive and a network adapter. And you might have a second profile named Undocked Configuration for using your portable computer in a hotel or on an airplane, when you are not using a network adapter or CD-ROM but you are using a modem and portable printer.

You can manage hardware profiles by opening System in Control Panel, clicking the Hardware tab, and clicking Hardware Profiles. If there is more than one hardware profile, you can designate a default profile that will be used every time you start your computer. You can also have Windows 2000 ask you which profile to use every time you start your computer. Once you create a hardware profile, you can use Device Manager to disable and enable devices in the profile. When you disable a device in a hardware profile, the device drivers for the device are not loaded when you start your computer.

Note You must be logged on to or running in the context of an account with administrator privileges on the local computer to create, copy, rename, or delete hardware profiles.

The profile created when Windows 2000 is installed (installation profile) provides a model for you to create new hardware profiles. To make a hardware profile appear after it is created, access the properties of the profile and select the Always Include This Profile As An Option When Windows Starts check box.

Event Logs

Careful monitoring of the System log generated by the Event Log service can help you predict and identify the sources of system problems. For example, if log warnings show that a disk driver can read or write to a sector only after several retries, the sector is likely to go bad eventually.

The Application and System logs can confirm problems with software. If a program crashes, the Application log can provide a record of activity leading up to the event.

The following suggestions might help you use event logs to diagnose problems:

- **Archive logs in log format** The binary data associated with an event is saved if you archive the log in log format (.evt), but it is discarded if you archive data in text (.txt) or comma-delimited (.csv) format. The binary data might help a developer or technical support specialist identify the source of a problem.

- **Note event IDs** These numbers match a text description in a message file. The numbers can be used by product support representatives to understand what occurred in the system.

- **Address hardware problems** If you suspect a hardware component is the source of system problems, filter the System log to show only those events generated by the component.

- **Address system problems** If a particular event seems related to system problems, try searching Event Log to find other instances of the same event or to judge the frequency of an error.

Note For more information about using event logs, see the Supplemental Course Materials CD-ROM (\chapt12\articles\Monitoring Reliability.doc) that accompanies this book.

Installing Service Packs

Windows 2000 makes it easier for administrators to add service packs. In Windows NT, Windows 95 and Windows 98, service packs are installed separately, after the operating system is installed. Windows 2000 supports service pack slipstreaming, which means the service pack is applied directly to the operating system's distribution share during installation.

Windows 2000 also eliminates the need to reinstall components applied before a service pack was installed. This makes it much easier to install service packs on existing systems. In the past, when service packs were installed, many previously installed components had to be reinstalled. For example, when a service pack is applied to Windows NT 4.0, services installed previously, such as IPX or RAS, have to be reinstalled. To address the problems that existed with Windows NT 4.0 service packs, Windows 2000 provides service pack slipstreaming and post-setup installation of service packs.

Service Pack Slipstreaming

Service pack slipstreaming refers to a service pack being applied to Windows 2000 distribution files on a CD-ROM or on a network share. When Windows 2000 is installed from either source, the appropriate files from the service pack are installed without you having to manually apply the service pack after the installation.

To apply a new service pack, use update.exe with the -s:*distribution_folder* switch, where *distribution_folder* is the name of the folder that contains the Windows 2000 installation files. This copies the updated service pack files over the existing Windows 2000 files. Some of the key files that are replaced include the following:

- A new layout.inf, dosnet.inf, and txtsetup.sif that contains updated checksums for all the service pack files. These files need additional entries if additional files are added.

- A new driver.cab if the drivers in the cabinet file are changed.

Post-Setup Installation of a Service Pack

A service pack is applied on an existing Windows 2000 system by running update.exe and updating the system to Windows 2000 plus the service pack. When the system state changes (for example, services are added or removed), the base system is told that a service pack was installed, what files were replaced or updated by the service pack, and where the service pack was installed from. This means that the correct files are copied from the service pack distribution location (the network share, CD-ROM, or Web site) and from the Windows 2000 installation source (network share or CD-ROM). This eliminates the need to reapply a service pack when the system state changes.

Once the service pack is applied, if the system state changes (for example, an RAS is added after the service pack is applied), Windows 2000 installs the correct files, whether those files originate from the Windows 2000 CD-ROM or from the service pack. Again, this eliminates the need to reapply the service pack whenever the system state changes.

Lesson Summary

Hardware includes any physical device connected to your computer and controlled by your computer's microprocessor. A device driver allows a specific device to communicate with Windows 2000. Windows 2000 classifies devices by hardware type. A Plug and Play device adheres to a set of specifications that allow a computer to automatically detect and configure a device and install the appropriate device drivers. Installing a new device typically involves three steps: connecting the device to your computer, loading the appropriate device drivers for the device, and configuring device properties and settings. You can usually uninstall a Plug and Play device by disconnecting or removing the device. You can use either the Add/Remove Hardware wizard or Device Manager snap-in to notify Windows 2000 that you want to uninstall a non–Plug and Play device. Several tools are available for managing hardware devices and their drivers. From the Hardware tab of the System Properties dialog box, you can open the Add/Remove Hardware wizard, the Device Manager snap-in, the Driver Signing Options dialog box, and the Hardware Profiles dialog box. In addition to the tools you can access through the System Properties dialog box, Event Log can be used to troubleshoot hardware configurations. Service pack updates can be seamlessly integrated into the network so that new Windows 2000 installations apply the service pack updates as part of the setup routine. Changes to existing Windows 2000 configurations automatically apply the service pack updates.

Lesson 2: Backing Up Data

The goal of all backup jobs is to ensure that lost data can be recovered efficiently and quickly. A backup job is a single process of backing up data. Regularly backing up data on server hard disks and client computer hard disks prevents data loss due to disk drive failures, power outages, virus infections, and other such incidents. If data loss occurs and you have carefully planned and performed regular backup jobs, you can restore the lost data, whether the lost data is a single file or an entire hard disk.

After this lesson, you will be able to

- Back up data at a computer and over the network
- Schedule a backup job
- Set backup options for Windows Backup

Estimated lesson time: 60 minutes

Introduction to Windows Backup

Windows 2000 provides Windows Backup (Figure 12.6), which is a tool that allows you to easily back up and restore data. To launch Windows Backup, on the Start menu, point to Programs, point to Accessories, point to System Tools, and then click Backup; or, on the Start menu, click Run, type **ntbackup**, and then click OK.

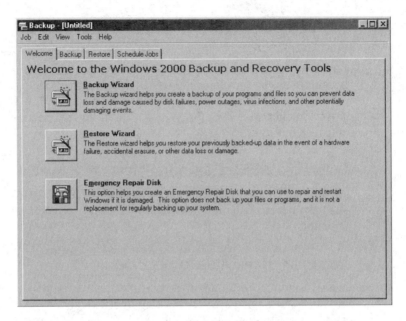

Figure 12.6 Welcome tab of the Backup dialog box

You can use Backup to back up data manually or to schedule unattended backup jobs on a regular basis. You can back up data to a file or to a tape. Files can be stored on hard disks, removable disks (such as Iomega Zip drives and Jaz drives), recordable compact discs, optical drives, and tapes.

To successfully back up and restore data on a computer running Windows 2000, you must have the appropriate permissions and user rights, as outlined below:

- All users can back up their own files and folders. They can also back up files for which they have the Read, Read and Execute, Modify, or Full Control permission.

- All users can restore files and folders for which they have the Write, Modify, or Full Control permission.

- Members of the Administrators, Backup Operators, and Server Operators groups can back up and restore all files (regardless of the assigned permissions). By default, members of these groups have the Backup Files And Directories and Restore Files And Directories user rights.

Planning Issues for Windows Backup

You should plan your backup jobs to fit the needs of your company. The primary goal of backing up data is to be able to restore it if necessary, so any backup plan you develop should include how to restore data. You should be able to quickly and successfully restore critical lost data. There is no single correct backup plan for all networks. The following sections cover issues to consider in formulating your backup plan.

Determine Which Files and Folders to Back Up

Always back up critical files and folders that your company needs to operate, such as sales and financial records, the registry for each server, and the Active Directory store.

Determine How Often to Back Up

If data is critical for company operations, back it up daily. If users create or modify reports once a week, backing up the reports weekly is sufficient. You need to back up data only as often as it changes. For example, there is no need to do daily backups on files that rarely change, such as monthly reports.

Determine Which Target Media to Use for Storing Backup Data

With Windows Backup, you can back up to the following removable media:

- **Files** You can store the files on a removable media device, such as an Iomega Zip drive, or on a network location, such as a file server. The file created contains the files and folders you have selected to backup. The file has a .bkf extension. Users can back up their personal data to a network server.

- **Tape** A less expensive medium than other removable media, a tape is more convenient for large backup jobs because of its high storage capacity. However, tapes have a limited life and can deteriorate. Be sure to check the tape manufacturer's recommendations for usage.

Note If you use a removable media device to back up and restore data, be sure to verify that the device is supported on the Windows 2000 HCL.

Determine Whether to Perform Network or Local Backup Jobs

A network backup can contain data from multiple network computers. This allows you to consolidate backup data from multiple computers to a single removable backup media. A network backup also allows one administrator to back up the entire network. Whether you perform a network or local backup job depends on the data that must be backed up. For example, you can back up the registry and the Active Directory store only at the computer from which you are performing the backup.

If you decide to perform local backups, they must be performed at each computer, including servers and client computers. There are several things to consider in performing local backups. First you must move from computer to computer so that you can perform a backup at each computer, or you must rely on users to back up their own computers. Typically most users fail to back up their data on a regular basis. A second consideration with local backups is the number of removable storage media devices available. If you use removable storage media devices, such as tape drives, you must have one for each computer, or you must move the tape drive from computer to computer so that you can perform a local backup on each computer.

You can also choose to use a combination of network and local backup jobs. Do this when critical data resides on client computers and servers and you do not have a removable storage media device for each computer. In this situation, users perform a local backup and store their backup files on a server. You then back up the server.

Setting Backup Options

Windows Backup allows you to change the default settings for all backup and restore jobs. These default settings are on the tabs in the Options dialog box (Figure 12.7). To access the Options dialog box, select Options from the Tools menu.

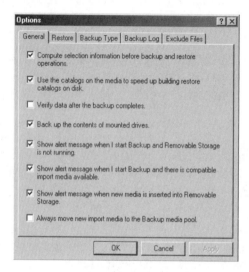

Figure 12.7 General tab of the Options dialog box

The following list provides an overview of the Windows default backup settings on the tabs in the Options dialog box:

- **General tab** Settings affect data verification, the status information for backup and restore jobs, alert messages, and what is backed up. You should select the Verify Data After The Backup Completes check box because it is critical that your backup data is not corrupted.

- **Restore tab** Settings affect what happens when the file to restore is identical to an existing file.

- **Backup Type tab** Settings affect the default backup type when you perform a backup job. The options you select depend on how often you back up, how quickly you want to restore, and how much storage space you have. Backup types are discussed in more detail below.

- **Backup Log tab** Settings affect the amount of information included in the backup log.

- **Exclude Files tab** Settings affect which files are excluded from backup jobs.

You can modify some default settings in the Backup wizard for a specific backup job. For example, the default backup type is normal, but you can change it to another backup type in the Backup wizard. However, the next time you run the Backup wizard, the default backup type (normal) is selected.

Backup Types

Windows Backup provides five backup types that define what data is backed up: normal, copy, differential, incremental, and daily. You can set the default backup types on the Backup Types tab of the Options dialog box (Figure 12.8).

Figure 12.8 Backup Types tab of the Options dialog box

Some backup types use backup markers, also known as archive attributes, which mark a file as having changed. When a file changes, an attribute is set on the file that indicates the file has changed since the last backup. Backing up the file clears or resets the attribute.

Normal

During a normal backup, known as a full backup, all selected files and folders are backed up. A normal backup does not rely on markers to determine which files to back up, but it does clear the archive attribute from all files. Normal backups speed up the restore process because the backup files are the most current and you do not need to restore multiple backup jobs. However, they are the most time consuming and require the most storage capacity of any backup type.

Copy

During a copy backup, all selected files and folders are backed up. It neither looks for nor clears markers. If you do not want to clear markers and affect other backup types, use a copy backup. For example, use a copy backup between a normal and an incremental backup to create an archival snapshot of network data.

Differential

During a differential backup, only selected files and folders that have a marker are backed up. Because a differential backup does not clear markers, if you did two differential backups in a row on a file, the file would be backed up each time. This backup type is moderately fast at backing up and restoring data. To perform a full restore by using a differential backup, the last normal backup session should be followed by the last differential backup session.

Incremental

During an incremental backup, only selected files and folders that have a marker are backed up. An incremental backup clears markers. Because it clears markers, if you did two incremental backups in a row on a file and nothing changed in the file, the file would not be backed up the second time. This backup type is very fast at backing up data and slow at restoring data. To perform a full restore using an incremental backup, the last normal backup session is followed by all incremental backup sessions up to the very last incremental backup session.

Daily

During a daily backup, all selected files and folders that have changed during the day are backed up. A daily backup neither looks for nor clears markers. If you want to back up all files and folders that change during the day without affecting a backup schedule, use a daily backup.

Setting Backup Types for Specific Jobs

You can set the backup type for a specific backup job when you are running the Backup wizard (Figure 12.9). The Backup wizard is described later in this lesson.

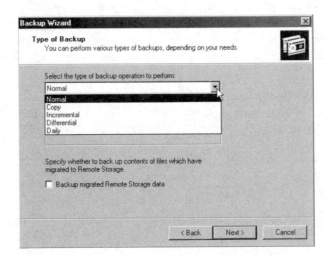

Figure 12.9 Setting the backup type for a specific backup job

You can also set the backup type for a specific backup job when you perform a backup without using the Backup wizard. On the Backup tab of the Windows Backup utility, click Start Backup. In the Backup Job Information screen that appears after you start the backup process, click Advanced. When the Advanced Backup Options dialog box appears, select the backup type from the drop-down list.

Combining Backup Types

An effective backup strategy is likely to combine different backup types. Some backup types require more time to back up data but less time to restore data. Conversely, other backup types require less time to back up data but more time to restore data. If you combine backup types, markers (archive attribute) are critical. Incremental and differential backup types check for and rely on the markers.

The following information provides examples of combining different backup types:

- **Normal and differential backups** On Monday a normal backup is performed, and on Tuesday through Friday differential backups are performed. Differential backups do not clear markers, which means that each backup includes all changes since Monday. If data becomes corrupted on Friday, you need to restore only the normal backup from Monday and the differential backup from Thursday. This strategy takes more time to back up but less time to restore.

- **Normal and incremental backups** On Monday a normal backup is performed, and on Tuesday through Friday incremental backups are performed. Incremental backups clear markers, which means that each backup includes only the files that changed since the previous backup. If data becomes corrupt on Friday, you need to restore the normal backup from Monday and all incremental backups, from Tuesday through Friday. This strategy takes less time to back up but more time to restore.

- **Normal, differential, and copy backups** These backups use the same strategy as the normal and incremental backups, except that on Wednesday, you perform a copy backup. Copy backups include all selected files and do not clear markers or interrupt the usual backup schedule. Therefore, each differential backup includes all changes since Monday. The copy backup type done on Wednesday is not part of the Friday restore. Copy backups are helpful when you need to create a snapshot of your data but you don't want to affect your scheduled backup.

Backing Up Data

After you have planned your backup, including planning the backup type to use and when to perform backup jobs, the next step is to prepare to back up your data. There are certain preliminary tasks that must be completed before you can back up your data. After you have completed the preliminary tasks, you can perform the backup.

Performing Preliminary Tasks

One task you must do before each backup job is ensure that the files you want to back up are closed. You should send a notification to users to close files before you begin backing up data. Windows Backup does not back up files locked open by applications. You can use e-mail or the Send Console Message dialog box in the Computer Management snap-in to send administrative messages to users. You can access the Send Console Message dialog box by right-clicking Computer Management in the Computer Management snap-in and select All Tasks.

Note Many third-party backup programs create image backups of open files.

If you use a removable media device, make sure the following preliminary tasks are completed:

- The backup device is attached to a computer on the network and is turned on. If you are backing up to tape, you must attach the tape device to the computer on which you run Windows Backup.

- The media device is listed on the Windows 2000 HCL.

- The media is loaded in the media device. For example, if you are using a tape drive, ensure that a tape is loaded in the tape drive.

Selecting Files and Folders to Back Up

After you have completed the preliminary tasks, you can perform the backup by using the Backup wizard. To start the Backup wizard, open Backup and click the Backup Wizard button on the Welcome tab.

The first step of setting up a backup is to specify what to back up (Figure 12.10).

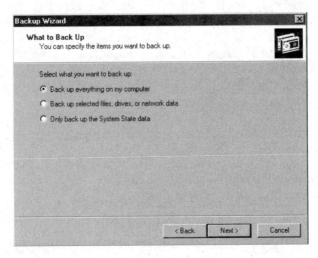

Figure 12.10 What To Back Up screen of the Backup wizard

You must select one of the following options:

- **Back Up Everything On My Computer** Backs up all files on the computer on which you are running Windows Backup, except those files that Windows Backup excludes by default, such as certain power management files.

- **Back Up Selected Files, Drives, Or Network Data** Backs up selected files and folders. This includes files and folders on the computer from which you run Windows Backup and any shared file or folder on the network. When you click this option, the Backup wizard provides a hierarchical view of the computer and the network (through My Network Places).

- **Only Back Up The System State Data** Backs up the registry, the Active Directory store, the SYSVOL folder, the COM+ Class Registration database, system startup files, and the Certificate Services (if Certificate Services are installed). The Active Directory store and the SYSVOL folder is available only at a domain controller. Use this option to create a copy of the Active Directory store, which contains all domain objects and their attributes. Back up the Certificate Services and stop the Certificate Services before running this option. Windows Backup will fail if the Certificate Services are running. You should keep the Certificate Services backup file created by backing up the Certificate Services with your backup. All system state data relevant to your computer is backed up or restored. You cannot back up or restore individual components of the system state data because of the dependencies among the system state components.

Specifying Backup Destination and Media Settings

After you select what you want to back up, provide information about the backup media. The following table describes the information you must provide for the backup media options:

Option	Description
Backup Media Type	The target medium to use, such as a tape or file. A file can be located on any disk-based media, including a hard disk, a shared network folder, or a removable disk, such as an Iomega Zip drive.
Backup Media Or File Name	The location where Windows Backup will store the data. For a tape, enter the tape name. For a file, enter the path for the backup file.

After you provide the media information, the Backup wizard displays the wizard settings and the opportunity to do either of the following:

- **Start the backup** If you click Finish, the backup process begins, and the Backup wizard displays status information about the backup job in the Backup Progress dialog box.

- **Specify advanced backup options** If you click Advanced, the Backup wizard allows you to select the advanced backup settings. The advanced backup settings are described in the following section.

Note When the backup process is complete, you can choose to review the backup report, which is the backup log. A backup log is a text file that records backup operations and is stored on the hard disk of the computer on which you are running Windows Backup.

Specifying Advanced Backup Settings

When you specify advanced backup settings, you are changing the default backup settings for the current backup job only. The following table describes the advanced options you can configure:

Advanced option	Description
Select The Type Of Backup Operation To Perform	Allows you to choose the backup type for this backup job. Select one of the following options: Normal, Copy, Incremental, Differential, and Daily.
Backup Migrated Remote Storage Data	Backs up data that Hierarchical Storage Manager (HSM) has moved to remote storage.
Verify Data After Backup	Confirms that files are correctly backed up. Windows Backup compares the backup data and the source data to verify that they are the same. Microsoft recommends that you select this option.
Use Hardware Compression, If Available	Enables hardware compression for tape devices that support it. If your tape device does not support hardware compression, this option is unavailable.
If The Archive Media Already Contains Backups	Specifies whether to append or replace the existing backup on the backup media. Choose Append to store multiple backup jobs on a storage device, or choose Replace if you do not need to save previous backup jobs and you only want to save the most recent backup data.

Advanced option	Description
Allow Only The Owner And The Administrator Access To The Backup Data And To Any Backups Appended To The Media	Allows you to restrict who can gain access to the completed backup file or tape. This option is available only if you choose to replace an existing backup on a backup media, rather than appending to the backup media. If you back up the registry or the Active Directory store, click this option to prevent others from getting copies of the backup job.
Backup Label	Allows you to specify a name and description for the backup job. The name and description appear in the backup log. You can change the name and description to a more intuitive name (for example, Sales-normal backup September 14, 2000).
Media Label	Allows you to specify the name of the backup media (for example, the tape name). The first time you back up to a new media or overwrite an existing backup job, you can specify the name, such as Active Directory store backup.
When To Back Up	Allows you to specify Now or Later. If you choose later, you specify the job name and start date. You can also set the schedule.

Depending on whether you choose to back up now or later, the Backup wizard provides you with the opportunity to do either of the following:

- If you choose to finish the backup process, the Backup wizard displays the Completing The Backup Wizard settings and then presents the option to finish and immediately start the backup. During the backup, the wizard displays status information about the backup job.

- If you choose to back up later, you are shown additional dialog boxes to schedule the backup process to occur later, as described in the next section.

Scheduling Backup Jobs

Scheduling a backup job means you can have an unattended backup job occur at a later time, for example, when users are not at work and files are closed. You can also schedule backup jobs to occur at regular intervals. Windows 2000 supports this scheduling functionality by integrating Windows Backup with the Task Scheduler service.

To schedule a backup, click the Later radio button on the When To Back Up screen of the Backup wizard. Task Scheduler presents the Set Account Information dialog box, prompting you for your password. The user account must have the appropriate user rights and permissions to perform backup jobs.

Note If the Task Scheduler service is not running or not set to start automatically, Windows 2000 displays a dialog box prompting you to start the service. Click OK, and the Set Account Information dialog box appears.

In the Schedule Job dialog box, you can set the date, time, and number of occurrences for the backup job to repeat, such as every Friday at 10:00 P.M. You can also display all the scheduled tasks for the computer by selecting the Show Multiple Schedules check box. This helps to prevent you from scheduling multiple tasks on the same computer at the same time.

By clicking the Advanced button, you can also schedule how long the backup can last and for how many days, weeks, months, or years you want this schedule to continue.

After you have scheduled the backup job and completed the Backup wizard, Windows Backup places the backup job on the calendar on the Schedule Jobs tab in Windows Backup. The backup job automatically starts at the time you specified.

Tip If the computer targeted for backup is running Certificate Services, you can schedule Certificate Services to stop before the backup begins. At the conclusion of the backup, configure the Task Scheduler to restart the Certificate Service. The easiest way to configure this is to stop and start Certificate Services and initiate the backup routine in a single command file. The command file is then scheduled to run through the Task Scheduler. This procedure is described near the conclusion of Exercise 1 in this chapter.

Exercise 1: Backing Up Files

In this exercise you use the Backup wizard to back up some files to your hard disk. You then create a backup job to perform a backup operation at a later time by using Task Scheduler. Complete this exercise on Server01.

▶ **Procedure 1: Creating, running, and verifying a backup job**

In this procedure, you start Windows Backup and use the Backup wizard to back up files to the local disk on Server01

1. Log on to Server01 as administrator with a password of "password."

2. Click Start, and then click Run.

   The Run dialog box appears.

3. In the Open text box, type **ntbackup** and then click OK.

   The Backup - [Untitled] dialog box appears.

4. Read the descriptions appearing for the three options under the Welcome tab, and then click Backup wizard.

   The Backup wizard starts and displays the Welcome To The Windows 2000 Backup And Recovery Tools screen.

5. Click Next.

   The What To Back Up screen appears, prompting you to choose the scope of the backup job.

6. Click the Back Up Selected Files, Drives, Or Network Data radio button, and then click Next.

   The Items To Back Up screen appears, prompting you to select the local and network drives, folders, and files to be backed up.

7. Expand My Computer.

8. Click once on the words System State. (Do not select the checkbox to the left of System State.)

   Notice that in the details pane, the Active Directory store, Boot files, Registry settings, COM+ Class Registration database, SYSVOL folder and Certificate services database are backed up.

9. In the left pane, expand C: and then click on the letter C. Do not select the check box to the left of C:.

10. In the details pane, scroll down and select the Boot.ini check box and then click Next.

The Where To Store The Backup screen appears.

> **Note** If there is no tape drive connected to your computer, the Backup Media Type drop-down list box will be gray because File is the only backup media type available.

11. In the Backup Media Or File Name text box, type **c:\ backup1.bkf** and then click Next.

> **Note** You would normally back up data to a tape or a file stored on another hard disk, removable disks (such as Iomega Zip and Jaz drives), or recordable compact discs or optical drives. However, for simplicity the backup here is performed on the same drive on which the file is located.

The Completing The Backup Wizard screen appears showing the details of the backup job to be conducted and allowing you to continue or further configure the job.

12. Click the Advanced button to specify additional backup options.

The Type Of Backup screen appears.

13. Look at the backup types listed in the Select The Type Of Backup Operation To Perform drop-down list box.

These backup types were described in the text preceding this exercise.

14. Verify that Normal is selected.

15. Verify that the Backup Migrated Remote Storage Data check box is cleared.

This option supports HSM features in Windows 2000 Server.

16. Click Next.

The How To Backup screen appears, prompting you to specify whether or not to verify the backed up data after the backup job.

17. Select the Verify Data After Backup check box, and then click Next.

The Media Options page appears, prompting you to specify whether to append this backup job to existing media or overwrite existing backup data on the destination media.

18. Click the Replace The Data On The Media With This Backup radio button.

   Notice the Allow Only The Owner And The Administrator Access To The Backup Data And Any Backups Appended To This Media check box. This option provides greater security because when it is selected, only the backup owner and the Administrator can recover a backup job. Verify that this option is not checked.

19. Click Next.

   The Backup Label screen appears, prompting you to supply a label for the backup job and for the backup media.

   Notice that Windows Backup generates a backup label and media label by using the current date and time.

20. In the Backup Label text box, type **Boot.ini backup set created on** *<date>* (where *<date>* is today's date and time).

21. Leave the Media Label text box as is, and click Next.

   The When To Back Up screen appears, prompting you to choose whether to run the backup job now or schedule this backup job.

22. Verify that the Now radio button is selected, and then click Next.

   The Completing The Backup Wizard screen appears.

23. Click Finish to start the backup job.

   Windows Backup briefly displays the Selection Information dialog box, indicating the estimated amount of data for, and the time to complete, the backup job.

   Then Windows Backup displays the Backup Progress dialog box, providing the status of the backup operation, statistics on estimated and actual amount of data being processed, the time that has elapsed, and the estimated time that remains for the backup operation.

24. When the Backup Progress dialog box indicates the backup is complete, click the Report button.

   Notepad starts and displays the backup report.

   The backup report contains key details about the backup operation, such as the time it started and how many files were backed up.

25. Examine the report, and when you are finished, close Notepad.

26. In the Backup Progress dialog box, click Close.

   The Backup - [Untitled] dialog box appears with the Welcome tab active.

▶ **Procedure 2: Creating, running, and verifying an unattended backup job**

In this procedure, you create a backup job to perform a backup operation at a later time by using Task Scheduler.

1. On the Welcome tab, click Backup Wizard.

   The Backup wizard starts and displays the Welcome To The Windows 2000 Backup And Recovery Tools screen.

2. Click Next.

   The What To Back Up screen appears, prompting you to choose the scope of the backup job.

3. Click the Back Up Selected Files, Drives, Or Network Data radio button, and then click Next.

   The Items To Back Up screen appears, prompting you to select the local and network drives, folders, and files to be backed up.

4. Expand My Computer, expand drive C, and then select the Inetpub check box.

5. Click Next.

   The Where To Store The Backup screen appears, prompting you to select the destination for your backup data.

6. In the Backup Media Or File Name text box, type **C:\ backup2.bkf** and then click Next.

   The Completing The Backup Wizard screen appears.

7. Click the Advanced button to specify additional backup options.

   The Type Of Backup screen appears, prompting you to select a backup type for this backup job.

8. Verify that in the Type Of Backup Operation To Perform drop-down list box, Normal is selected.

9. Click Next.

   The How To Backup screen appears, prompting you to specify whether to verify the backed up data after the backup job.

10. Select the Verify Data After Backup check box, and then click Next.

    The Media Options screen appears, prompting you to specify whether to append this backup job to existing media or overwrite existing backup data on the destination media.

11. Click the Replace The Data On The Media With This Backup radio button.

12. Verify that the Allow Only The Owner And The Administrator Access To The Backup Data And Any Backups Appended To This Media check box is not selected, and then click Next.

    The Backup Label screen appears, prompting you to supply a label for the backup job and for the backup media.

13. In the Backup Label text box, type **Inetpub backup set created on** **<date>** (where *<date>* is today's date and time).

14. Leave the Media Label text box as is, and click Next.

    The When To Backup screen appears, prompting you to choose whether to run the backup job now or schedule this backup job.

15. Click the Later radio button.

    The Set Account Information dialog box appears, prompting you for the password for the MICROSOFT\administrator account. (If the Task Scheduler service isn't set to start automatically, you might first see a dialog box asking whether you want to start the Task Scheduler. Click OK, and then the Set Account Information dialog box appears.)

    Because the Task Scheduler service automatically runs applications within the security context of a valid user for the computer or domain, you are prompted for the name and password with which the scheduled backup job will run. For scheduled backup jobs, you should supply a user account that is a member of the Backup Operators group with permission to gain access to all the folders and files to be backed up.

    For simplicity, you will use the Administrator account to run the scheduled backup job.

16. Verify that MICROSOFT\administrator appears in the Run As text box, and then in the Password and Confirm Password text boxes, type **password**.

17. Click OK.

18. In the Job Name text box, type **Inetpub Backup** and then click the Set Schedule button.

    The Schedule Job dialog box appears, prompting you to select the start time and schedule options for the backup job.

19. In the Schedule Task drop-down list box select Daily Is Selected, and in the Start Time box enter a time five minutes from the present time.

20. Click the Advanced button.

    The Advanced Schedule Options dialog box appears.

21. Click the End Date check box, and in the drop-down list box select tomorrow's date and then click OK.

The Schedule Job dialog box appears.

22. Click OK.

The When To Backup screen appears.

23. Click Next.

The Completing The Backup Wizard screen appears, displaying the options and settings you selected for this backup job.

24. Click Finish to start the backup job.

The Backup - [Untitled] dialog box appears with the Welcome tab active.

25. Close the Backup - [Untitled] dialog box.

When it is time for the backup job to begin, Windows Backup starts and performs the requested backup operation.

26. Start Windows Explorer, click drive C, and verify that Backup2.bkf exists.

▶ **Procedure 3: Viewing and configuring tasks**

In this procedure, you view the scheduled backup task and create a new task.

1. Click Start, point to Programs, point to Accessories, point to System Tools, and then click Scheduled Tasks.

The Scheduled Tasks window appears.

Notice that the Inetpub Backup task appears.

2. Double-click Inetpub Backup.

The Inetpub Backup dialog box appears.

Notice the text in the Run text box. This is the ntbackup command with the parameters created by the Backup wizard to back up Inetpub.

If you need to stop a service, such as Certificate Services, before running a backup routine, you can create a batch file (.cmd or .bat) that stops the service, runs the backup routine, and then restarts the service. The command to stop Certificate Services is:

```
net stop "certificate services"
```

The command to restart Certificate Services is:

```
net start "certificate services"
```

3. Click the Schedule tab.

   Notice that this is the schedule you created using the Backup wizard.

4. Click OK to close the Inetpub Backup dialog box.

   The Scheduled Tasks window appears.

5. Click the File menu, and then click Delete.

   The Confirm File Delete message box appears asking whether you want to delete the scheduled task.

6. Click Yes.

7. Close the Scheduled Tasks window.

Lesson Summary

Windows Backup is a tool that allows you to easily back up and restore data. You can use Windows Backup to back up data manually or to schedule unattended backup jobs on a regular basis. You should plan your backup jobs to fit the needs of your company. Windows Backup allows you to change the default settings for all backup and restore jobs. It provides five backup types that define what data is backed up: normal, copy, differential, incremental, and daily. Before you back up data, you must ensure the files that you want to back up are closed and, if applicable, you must prepare any removable media devices. After you have completed the preliminary tasks, you can perform the backup by using the Backup wizard. The Backup wizard allows you to select which files and folders to back up and to specify the backup destination and media settings. The wizard also allows you to specify advanced settings for your current backup job and to schedule backup jobs.

Lesson 3: Implementing Disaster Protection

A *computer disaster* is any event that renders a computer unable to start. This can include the destruction of the master boot record stored on a system device, the deletion of one or more operating system files, destruction of a computer's physical system device, or destruction of the computer itself. The term *disaster protection* refers to any effort to prevent computer disasters and minimize downtime in the event of system failure. You can achieve a level of disaster protection by configuring an uninterruptible power supply (UPS) and implementing fault-tolerant disk configurations.

After this lesson, you will be able to

- Configure a UPS to provide power if a local power source fails
- Implement disk fault tolerance

Estimated lesson time: 40 minutes

Configuring an Uninterruptible Power Supply

Disaster recovery is the restoration of a computer so that you can log on and access system resources after a computer disaster has occurred. One common type of computer disaster is the loss of local power, which can result in damaged or lost data on a server or client computer. While companies usually protect servers against this type of disaster, you might also consider providing protection for client computers against power loss, depending on the reliability of your local power supply.

An *uninterruptible power supply* provides power if the local power fails and usually is rated to provide a specific amount of power for a specific period of time. In general, a UPS should provide power long enough for you to shut down a computer in an orderly way by quitting processes and closing sessions.

Note Before purchasing a UPS for use with Windows 2000, determine whether the proposed device is on the Windows 2000 HCL.

Configuring Options for the UPS Service

Use the UPS tab of Power Options Properties dialog box to configure the UPS service. You can access this dialog box by selecting Power Options in Control Panel. To configure the UPS service, you must specify the following information:

- The COM port to which the UPS device is connected

- The conditions that trigger the UPS device to send a signal, such as a power failure, low battery power, and remote shutdown by the UPS device

- The time interval for maintaining battery power, recharging the battery, and sending warning messages after power failure

Note The configuration options for the UPS service can vary depending on the specific UPS device attached to your computer. For details about possible settings, see the manufacturer's documentation included with the UPS device.

Testing a UPS Configuration

After you have configured the UPS service for your computer, test the configuration to ensure that your computer is protected from power failures. You can simulate a power failure by disconnecting the main power supply to the UPS device. During the test, the computer and peripherals connected to the UPS device should remain operational, messages should display, and events should be logged.

Note You should not use a production computer to test the UPS configuration. You should use a spare computer or test computer. If you use a production computer, you could lose some of the data on the computer and possibly have to reinstall Windows 2000. Remember, when a computer suddenly stops, data can be lost or corrupted. The reason for having a UPS is to allow a graceful shutdown of the computers rather than an abrupt stop.

In addition, you should wait until the UPS battery reaches a low level to verify that an orderly shutdown occurs. Then, restore the main power source to the UPS device and check the event log to ensure that all actions were logged and there were no errors.

Note Some UPS manufacturers provide their own UPS software to take advantage of the unique features of their UPS devices.

Implementing Disk Fault Tolerance

Fault tolerance is the ability of a computer or operating system to respond to a catastrophic event, such as a power outage or hardware failure, so that no data is lost and that work in progress is not corrupted. Fully fault-tolerant systems using fault-tolerant disk arrays prevent the loss of data.

Although the data is available and current in a fault-tolerant system, you should still make backups to protect the information on hard disks from erroneous deletions, fire, theft, or other disasters. Disk fault tolerance is not an alternative to a backup strategy with offsite storage, which is the best insurance for recovering lost or damaged data.

If you experience the loss of a hard disk due to mechanical or electrical failure and have not implemented fault tolerance, your only option for recovering the data on the failed drive is to replace the hard disk and restore your data from a backup. However, the loss of access to the data while you replace the hard disk and restore your data can translate into lost time and money.

RAID Implementations

To maintain access to data during the loss of a single hard disk, Windows 2000 Server provides a software implementation of a fault tolerance technology known as redundant array of independent disks (RAID). RAID provides fault tolerance by implementing data redundancy. With data redundancy, a computer writes data to more than one disk, which protects the data in the event of a single hard disk failure.

You can implement RAID fault tolerance as either a software or hardware solution.

Software Implementations of RAID

Windows 2000 Server supports two software implementations of RAID: mirrored volumes (RAID 1) and striped volumes with parity (RAID 5), otherwise known as RAID-5 volumes. However, you can create new RAID volumes only on Windows 2000 dynamic disks.

With software implementations of RAID, there is no fault tolerance following a failure until the fault is repaired. If a second fault occurs before the data lost from the first fault is regenerated, you can recover the data only by restoring it from a backup.

Note When you upgrade Windows NT 4.0 to Windows 2000, any existing mirror sets or stripe sets with parity are retained. Windows 2000 provides limited support for these fault tolerance sets, allowing you to manage and delete them.

Hardware Implementations of RAID

In a hardware solution, the disk controller interface handles the creation and regeneration of redundant information. Some hardware vendors implement RAID data protection directly in their hardware, as with disk array controller cards. Because these methods are vendor specific and bypass the fault tolerance software drivers of the operating system, they offer performance improvements over software implementations of RAID. In addition, hardware implementations of RAID usually include extra features, such as additional fault-tolerant RAID configurations, hot swapping of failed hard disks, hot sparing for online failover, and dedicated cache memory for improved performance.

Note The level of RAID supported in a hardware implementation is dependent on the hardware manufacturer.

Consider the following when deciding whether to use a software or hardware implementation of RAID:

- Hardware fault tolerance is more expensive than software fault tolerance.

- Hardware fault tolerance generally provides faster disk I/O than software fault tolerance.

- Hardware fault tolerance solutions might limit equipment options to a single vendor.

- Hardware fault tolerance solutions might implement hot swapping of hard disks to allow for replacement of a failed hard disk without shutting down the computer and hot sparing so that a failed disk is automatically replaced by an online spare.

Mirrored Volumes

A mirrored volume uses the Windows 2000 Server fault tolerance driver (Ftdisk.sys) to write the same data to a volume on each of two physical disks simultaneously, as shown in Figure 12.11. Each volume is considered a member of the mirrored volume. Implementing a mirrored volume helps to ensure the survival of data in the event that one member of the mirrored volume fails.

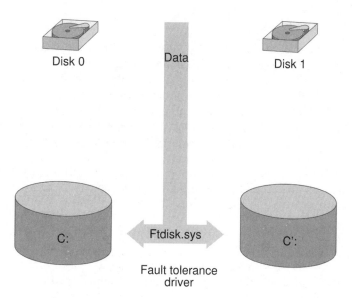

Figure 12.11 Mirrored volume

A mirrored volume can contain any partition, including the boot or system partition; however, both disks in a mirrored volume must be Windows 2000 dynamic disks.

Mirrored volumes can be striped across multiple disks. This configuration is often referred to as RAID 10, RAID 1 mirroring and RAID 0 striping. Unlike RAID 0, RAID 10 is a fault-tolerant RAID configuration because each disk in the stripe is also mirrored. RAID 10 improves disk I/O by performing read and write operations across the stripe.

Performance on Mirrored Volumes

Mirrored volumes can enhance read performance because the fault tolerance driver reads from both members of the volume at once. There can be a slight decrease in write performance because the fault tolerance driver must write to both members. When one member of a mirrored volume fails, performance returns to normal because the fault tolerance driver works with only a single partition.

Because disk space usage is only 50 percent (two members for one set of data), mirrored volumes can be expensive.

Caution Deleting a mirrored volume will delete all the information stored on that volume.

Disk Duplexing

If the same disk controller controls both physical disks in a mirrored volume and the disk controller fails, neither member of the mirrored volume is accessible. You can install a second controller in the computer so that each disk in the mirrored volume has its own controller. This arrangement, called *disk duplexing*, can protect the mirrored volume against both controller failure and hard disk failure. Some hardware implementations of disk duplexing use two or more channels on a single disk controller card.

Disk duplexing reduces bus traffic and potentially improves read performance. Disk duplexing is a hardware enhancement to a Windows 2000 mirrored volume and requires no additional software configuration.

RAID-5 Volumes

Windows 2000 Server also supports fault tolerance through striped volumes with parity (RAID 5). Parity is a mathematical method of determining the number of odd and even bits in a number or series of numbers, which can be used to reconstruct data if one number in a sequence of numbers is lost.

In a RAID-5 volume, Windows 2000 achieves fault tolerance by adding a parity-information stripe to each disk partition in the volume, as shown in Figure 12.12. If a single disk fails, Windows 2000 can use the data and parity information on the remaining disks to reconstruct the data that was on the failed disk.

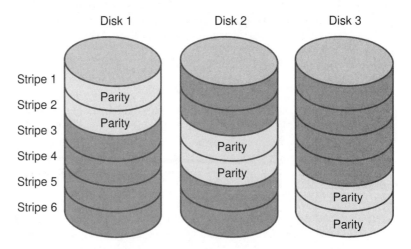

Figure 12.12 Raid-5 parity-information stripes

Because of the parity calculation, write operations on a RAID-5 volume are slower than on a mirrored volume. However, RAID-5 volumes provide better read performance than mirrored volumes, especially with multiple controllers, because data is distributed among multiple drives. If a disk fails, however, the read performance on a RAID-5 volume slows while Windows 2000 Server reconstructs the data for the failed disk by using parity information.

RAID-5 volumes have a cost advantage over mirrored volumes because disk usage is optimized. The more disks you have in the RAID-5 volume, the less the cost of the redundant data stripe. The following table shows how the amount of space required for the data stripe decreases with the addition of 2-gigabyte (GB) disks to the RAID-5 volume:

Number of disks	Disk space used	Available disk space	Redundancy
3	6 GB	4 GB	33 percent
4	8 GB	6 GB	25 percent
5	10 GB	8 GB	20 percent

There are some restrictions that RAID-5 volumes implement in software. First, RAID-5 volumes involve a minimum of three drives and a maximum of 32 drives. Second, a software-level RAID-5 volume cannot contain the boot or system partition.

The Windows 2000 operating system is not aware of RAID implementations in hardware. Therefore, the restrictions that apply to software-level RAID do not apply to hardware-level RAID configurations.

Mirrored Volumes versus RAID-5 Volumes

Mirrored volumes and RAID-5 volumes provide different levels of fault tolerance. Deciding which option to implement depends on the level of protection you require and the cost of hardware. The major differences between mirrored volumes (RAID 1) and RAID-5 volumes are performance and cost. The following table describes some differences between software-level RAID 1 and RAID 5.

Mirrored volumes RAID 1	Striped volumes with parity RAID 5
Supports FAT and NTFS	Supports FAT and NTFS
Can protect system or boot partition	Cannot protect system or boot partition
Requires 2 hard disks	Requires a minimum of 3 hard disks and allows a maximum of 32 hard disks
Has a higher cost per megabyte	Has a lower cost per megabyte
50 percent utilization	33 percent minimum utilization
Has good write performance	Has moderate write performance
Has good read performance	Has excellent read performance
Uses less system memory	Requires more system memory

Generally, mirrored volumes offer read and write performance comparable to that of single disks. RAID-5 volumes offer better read performance than mirrored volumes, especially with multiple controllers, because data is distributed among multiple drives. However, the need to calculate parity information requires more computer memory, which can slow write performance.

Mirroring uses only 50 percent of the available disk space, so it is more expensive in cost per megabyte (MB) than disks without mirroring. RAID 5 uses 33 percent of the available disk space for parity information when you use the minimum number of hard disks (three). With RAID 5, disk utilization improves as you increase the number of hard disks.

Implementing RAID Systems

The software-level fault tolerance features of Windows 2000 Server are available only on Windows 2000 dynamic disks. In Windows 2000 Server, you create software-level mirrored and RAID-5 volumes by using the Create Volume wizard in the Computer Management snap-in.

To create a volume by using the Create Volume wizard, access the Disk Management folder in the Computer Management snap-in. When you select the Disk Management folder, the details pane of the Computer Management window displays a text view of the physical disks in your computer and a graphical view (Figure 12.13).

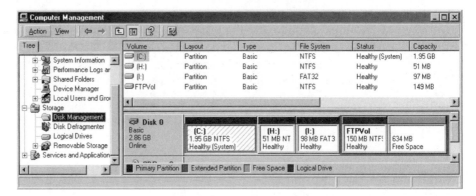

Figure 12.13 Disk Management folder of the Computer Management snap-in

In the details pane, select an area of unallocated space, and then from the Action menu point to All Tasks and then click Create Volume. Follow the steps in the Create Volume wizard to create a volume.

Note Windows 2000 Advanced Server and Windows 2000 Data Center support server clustering for an even higher level of fault tolerance. Clustering is beyond the scope of this course.

Lesson Summary

You can achieve a level of disaster protection by configuring a UPS and by implementing disk fault tolerance. A UPS provides power in case the local power fails. In general, a UPS should provide power long enough to warn users connected to the server and perform an orderly shut down. You can configure the UPS service on the UPS tab of the Power Options Properties dialog box. After you have configured the UPS service for your computer, you should test the configuration to ensure that your computer is protected from power failures. In addition to UPS for power protection, fault-tolerant RAID provides an additional level of data protection. You can use fault-tolerant RAID configurations to implement disk fault tolerance as either a software or hardware solution. A software-level mirrored volume uses the Windows 2000 Server fault tolerance driver (Ftdisk.sys) to write the same data to a volume on each of two physical disks simultaneously. Windows 2000 Server also supports fault tolerance through software-level striped volumes with parity (RAID 5). In a RAID-5 volume, Windows 2000 achieves fault tolerance by adding a parity-information stripe to each disk partition in the volume.

Generally, mirrored volumes offer read and write performance comparable to that of single disks. RAID-5 volumes offer better read performance than mirrored volumes. RAID implementations benefit from using multiple controllers (disk duplexing) because disk I/O is distributed among multiple data channels to increase performance and fault tolerance. You create software-level mirrored and RAID-5 volumes by using the Create Volume wizard in the Computer Management snap-in.

Lesson 4: Recovering from a Disaster

Reliability and availability are in part affected by your system's ability to recover from a disaster. Disaster recovery allows you to restore a computer so that you can log on and access system resources after a computer disaster has occurred. This lesson provides information on repairing a Windows 2000 installation, restoring data, and recovering a RAID-5 or mirrored volume.

Note For more information about Windows 2000 reliability and availability, see the Supplemental Course Materials CD-ROM (\chapt12\articles\ Win2000Reliability.doc) that accompanies this book.

After this lesson, you will be able to

- Use Safe mode, the Recovery Console, and the Emergency Repair Disk to repair a Windows 2000 installation
- Restore data that has been backed up
- Recover a RAID-5 or RAID-1 volume

Estimated lesson time: 60 minutes

Repairing the Windows 2000 Installation

Windows 2000 has several features that allow you to repair a system that does not start or load Windows 2000. These features are useful if some of your system files become corrupted or are accidentally erased, or if you have in-stalled software or device drivers that cause your system to not work properly. Windows 2000 includes three methods that allow you to repair a system: Safe mode, the Recovery Console, and the Emergency Repair Disk (ERD).

Note You can also reinstall Windows 2000 over a damaged Windows 2000 system or install Windows 2000 into a separate folder. This may be time consuming, but it is useful if the emergency repair process does not solve your problem. If you reinstall Windows 2000, you might lose changes that have been made to your system, such as service pack upgrades.

Safe mode

Safe mode lets you start your system with a minimal set of device drivers and services. For example, if newly installed device drivers or software are preventing your computer from starting, you might be able to start you computer in Safe mode and then remove the software or device drivers from your system. Safe mode does not work in all circumstances, especially if your system files are corrupted or missing or your hard disk is damaged or has failed.

In Safe mode, Windows 2000 uses default settings (VGA monitor, Microsoft mouse driver, and the minimum device drivers required to start Windows). If a symptom does not reappear when you start in Safe mode, you can eliminate the default settings and minimum device drivers as possible causes of the problem.

You can choose one of the following options when you start Safe mode:

- **Safe Mode** Starts Windows 2000 and uses only basic files and drivers (mouse, except serial mice; monitor; keyboard; mass storage; base video; default system services; and no network connections). If your computer does not start successfully by using Safe mode, you might need to use the ERD to repair your system.

- **Safe Mode With Networking** Starts Windows 2000 with only basic files and drivers, plus network connections.

- **Safe Mode With Command Prompt** Starts Windows 2000 with only basic files and drivers. After logging on, the command prompt is displayed instead of the Windows desktop, Start menu, and Taskbar.

- **Enable Boot Logging** Starts Windows 2000 while logging all the installed drivers and services that were loaded (or not loaded) by the system to a file. This file is called ntbtlog.txt and is located in the %systemroot% directory. Safe mode, Safe mode with Networking, and Safe mode with Command Prompt add to the boot log a list of all the drivers and services that are loaded. The boot log is useful in determining the exact cause of system startup problems.

- **Enable VGA Mode** Starts Windows 2000 with the basic VGA driver. This mode is useful when you have installed a new driver for your video card that is causing Windows 2000 to not start properly. The basic video driver is always used when you start Windows 2000 in Safe mode (either Safe mode, Safe mode with Networking, or Safe mode with Command Prompt).

- **Last Known Good Configuration** Starts Windows 2000 with the registry information that Windows saved at the last shutdown. Use this option only in cases of incorrect configuration. Last Known Good Configuration does not solve problems caused by corrupted, incompatible, or missing drivers or files. Also, any changes made since the last successful startup will be lost.

- **Directory Service Restore Mode** Used to restore the SYSVOL directory and Active Directory services on a domain controller. This option is available only on domain controllers.

- **Debugging Mode** Starts Windows 2000 while sending debug information through a serial cable to another computer. This is an important mode for software developers.

If you are using or have used Remote Install Services to install Windows 2000 on your computer, you might see additional options related to restoring or recovering your system through Remote Install Services.

To start Windows 2000 in Safe mode, restart your computer. Press F8 when you see the message Starting Windows 2000. Use the arrow keys to highlight the appropriate Safe mode option, and then press Enter.

Safe mode helps you diagnose problems. If a symptom does not reappear when you start in Safe mode, you can eliminate the default settings and minimum device drivers as possible causes. If a newly added device or a changed driver is causing problems, you can use Safe mode to remove the device or reverse the change.

Recovery Console

The Recovery Console is a text-mode command interpreter that is separate from the Windows 2000 command prompt and allows the system administrator to gain access to the hard disk of a computer running Windows 2000, regardless of the file system (NTFS or FAT) used, for basic troubleshooting and system maintenance. Since starting Windows 2000 is not a prerequisite for using the Recovery Console, it can help you recover when your Windows 2000–based computer does not start properly or at all.

The Recovery Console allows you to obtain limited access to NTFS, FAT16, and FAT32 volumes without starting the graphical interface. The Recovery Console allows administrators and Microsoft Product Support Services technicians to start and stop services and repair the system in a very granular way. It can also be used to repair the master boot record and boot sector and to format volumes. The Recovery Console prevents unauthorized access to volumes by requiring the user to enter the system administrator password.

Starting the Recovery Console

To start the Recovery Console, start the computer from the Windows 2000 installation CD-ROM or the Windows 2000 Setup floppy disks. If you do not have Setup floppy disks and your computer cannot start from the Windows 2000 installation CD-ROM, use another computer and the Makeboot.exe or Makebt32.exe utility to create the Setup floppy disks.

If the Recovery Console was installed on the local hard disk, it can also be accessed from the Windows 2000 startup menu. However, if the master boot record or the system volume boot sector has been damaged, you need to start the computer by using either the Windows 2000 Setup floppy disks or the Windows 2000 installation CD-ROM to access the Recovery Console.

To add the Recovery Console to existing installations of Windows 2000, on the Start menu, click Run, and then type *<cdrom>*:**\I386\Winnt32.exe /cmdcons**, where *<cdrom>* is the drive letter of the CD-ROM drive.

The installation of the Recovery Console requires approximately 7 MB of disk space on the system partition.

Important You cannot preinstall the Recovery Console on a computer that contains a mirrored volume. First break the mirror, and then install the Recovery Console. After the Recovery Console is installed, you can reestablish the mirrored volume.

If the Recovery Console is not installed, run Windows 2000 Setup. Press Enter at the Setup Notification screen. Press R to repair a Windows 2000 installation, and then press C to use the Recovery Console.

Certain installations and configurations can affect how you use the Recovery Console:

- If there is more than one installation of Windows 2000 or Windows NT 4.0 or earlier, they are shown in the Recovery Console Startup menu.

- Mirrored volumes appear twice in the Recovery Console Startup menu, but each entry has the same drive letter, so they are actually the same drive.

- Changes made with the Recovery Console to mirrored volumes are mirrored.

To access the disk by using the Recovery Console, press the number key representing the Windows 2000 installation that you want to repair, and then press Enter. The Recovery Console then prompts you for the administrator password. If you press Enter without typing a number, the Recovery Console exits and restarts the computer.

Note To use the Recovery Console, you must know the password for the local Administrator account. If you do not have the correct password, Recovery Console does not allow access to the computer. If an incorrect password is entered three times, the Recovery Console quits and restarts the computer. However, you can use either the Group Policy snap-in or the Security Configuration And Analysis snap-in to enable automatic administrative logon. This setting is contained in the Security Options node, and the value name is Recovery Console: Allow automatic administrative logon.

Once the password has been validated, you have full access to the Recovery Console but limited access to the hard disk. You can access the following partitions and folders on your computer:

- %systemroot% and subfolders of the Windows 2000 installation in which you are currently logged on

- The root of all partitions, including %systemdrive%, the CD-ROM, and floppy drive with some restrictions (Floppy drive restrictions are outlined later in this lesson.)

Note With the set command enabled, you can copy files to removable media, disable the file copy prompt, use wild cards with the Copy command, and access all paths on the system. The Set command is an optional Recovery Console command that can be enabled by using either the Group Policy snap-in or the Security Configuration And Analysis snap-in.

The Recovery Console prevents access to other folders such as Program Files or Documents And Settings, as well as to folders containing other installations of Windows 2000. However, you can use the logon command to access an alternate installation. Alternatively, you can gain access to other installation folders by restarting the Recovery Console, choosing the number representing that installation, and then entering the administrator password for that installation.

You cannot copy a file from the local hard disk to a floppy disk, but you can copy a file from a floppy disk or a CD-ROM to any hard disk, and from a hard disk to another hard disk. However, with the set command enabled, you can copy files to a floppy disk. The Recovery Console displays an Access Is Denied error message when it detects invalid commands.

Important The set command makes use of Recovery Console environment variables to enable disk write access to floppy disks as well as enable other options. To enable the user to modify the restricted default Recovery Console environment variables, a policy setting must be made.

The Recovery Console buffers previously entered commands and makes them available to the user with the up and down arrow keys. To edit a previously entered command, use Backspace to move the cursor to the point of the edit and retype the remainder of the command. At any point, you can quit the Recovery Console and restart the computer by typing **exit** at the command prompt.

Note that the Recovery Console might not map disk volumes with the same drive letters they have in Windows 2000. If you are having trouble copying files from one location to another, use the Map command from the Recovery Console to make sure that the drive mappings for both the source and the target locations are correct.

Tip You can use the Help command to list the commands supported by the Recovery Console. In addition, the /? switch works with every Recovery Console command to display a help screen that includes a description of the command, its syntax, a definition of its parameters, and other useful information.

Emergency Repair Disk

If your system does not start and using Safe mode or the Recovery Console has not helped, you can try using the ERD. Backup includes a wizard to help you create an ERD. If a system failure occurs, first start the system by using the Windows 2000 installation CD-ROM or the Windows 2000 Setup floppy disks, which can be created by running Makeboot.exe or Makebt32.exe from the Bootdisk folder of the Windows 2000 installation CD-ROM. In Text mode, type **r** to enter recovery options and type **r** again to enter Emergency Repair. Then use the ERD to restore core system files. Note that you cannot repair all disk problems by using the ERD.

Make sure to create an ERD when your computer is functioning well so that you are prepared if you need to repair system files. You can use the ERD to fix problems that might be preventing you from starting your computer. This includes problems with your registry, system files, partition boot sector, and startup environment. However, the ERD does not back up data or programs and is not a replacement for regular system backups.

The Windows 2000 ERD, unlike the ERD used with Windows NT, does not contain a copy of the registry files. The backup registry files are in the folder %systemroot%\Repair as they are in Windows NT. However, these files are from the original installation of Windows 2000. In the event of a problem, they can be used to return your computer to a usable state.

When you back up system state data, a copy of your registry files is placed in the folder %systemroot%\Repair\Regback. If your registry files become corrupted or are accidentally erased, use the files in this folder to repair your registry without performing a full restore of the system state data. This method is recommended for advanced users only and can also be accomplished by using the Recovery Console commands.

Creating the Emergency Repair Disk

When the ERD is created, the files described in the following table are copied from %systemroot%\Repair to a floppy disk.

File Name	Contents
Autoexec.nt	A copy of %systemroot%\System32\Autoexec.nt, which is used to initialize the MS-DOS environment.
Config.nt	A copy of %systemroot%\System32\Config.nt, which is used to initialize the MS-DOS environment.
Setup.log	A log of which files were installed and of Cyclic Redundancy Check (CRC) information for use during the emergency repair process. This file has the read-only, system, and hidden attributes, and it is not visible unless you have configured My Computer to show all files or used the dir /a, dir /as or dir /ah command-line commands.

Create the ERD after Windows 2000 is installed. Re-create the ERD after each service pack, system date, or updated driver is installed. Be sure to make a copy of your current ERD and store it in a secure location, perhaps off site.

Emergency Repair Process

If you have prepared an ERD, you can use it to help repair system files after starting the computer by using either the Windows 2000 installation CD-ROM or the Windows 2000 Setup floppy disks. However, the Windows 2000 installation CD-ROM is required for replacing any damaged files.

The ERD must include current configuration information. Make sure that you have an ERD for each installation of Windows 2000 on your computer, and never use an ERD from another computer.

When you start the emergency repair process, you will be asked to choose one of the following options:

- **Manual Repair** To choose from a list of repair options, press M. It is recommended that only advanced users or administrators choose this option. Using it, you can repair system files, boot sector problems, and startup environment problems.

- **Fast Repair** To perform all repair options, press F. This is the easier option to use and does not require user input. If you choose this option, the emergency recovery process attempts to repair problems related to system files, the boot sector on your system disk, and your startup environment (if your computer has more than one operating system installed). This option also checks and repairs the registry files by loading and unloading each registry key. If a key is not successfully checked, it is automatically copied from the repair directory to the folder %systemroot%\System32\Config.

If you select Manual Repair, the registry files are not checked. If you select Fast Repair and the folder %systemroot%\Repair is accessible, the registry files are checked. If the folder %systemroot%\Repair is inaccessible (for example, due to file system corruption), the registry files are not checked.

Manual Repair allows you to select from the following three options:

- **Inspect Startup Environment** Inspect Startup Environment verifies that the Windows 2000 files in the system partition are correct. If any of the files needed to start Windows 2000 are missing or corrupted, Repair replaces them from the Windows 2000 installation CD-ROM. These include Ntldr and Ntdetect.com. If Boot.ini is missing, it is re-created.

- **Verify Windows 2000 System Files** Verify Windows 2000 System Files uses a checksum to verify that each installed file is good and matches the file that was installed from the Windows 2000 installation CD-ROM. If the recovery process determines that a file on the disk does not match what was installed, it displays a message that identifies the file and asks if you want to replace it. The emergency repair process also verifies that startup files, such as Ntldr and Ntoskrnl.exe, are present and valid.

- **Inspect Boot Sector** Inspect Boot Sector verifies that the boot sector on the system partition still references Ntldr. The Emergency Repair Process can only replace the boot sector for the system partition on the first hard disk. The Emergency Repair Process can also repair the boot sector for the system partition on the startup disk.

Note If the boot sector is infected with a virus, boot the computer using an antivirus boot diskette. Instruct the antivirus program to inspect and cure the boot sector. An antivirus program for inspecting the boot sector is included on the Windows 2000 Server Installation CD-ROM in the \3RDPARTY\ CA_ANTIV folder. This program might not be included on the Windows 2000 Server installation CD-ROM included with this training kit.

If the Emergency Repair Process Does Not Fix Your System

If you have performed the emergency repair process and the computer still does not operate normally, you can perform an in-place upgrade over the existing installation. This is a last resort before reinstalling the operating system. However, note that the time required to perform an upgrade is similar to the time it takes to reinstall the operating system.

Note If you perform an in-place upgrade of your Windows 2000 existing installation, you might lose some customized settings of your system files.

Restoring Data

The ability to restore corrupt or lost data is critical to all corporations and is the goal of all backup jobs. To ensure that you can successfully restore data, you should follow certain guidelines, such as keeping thorough documentation on all of your backup jobs. In addition, you must select the backup sets, files, and folders to restore. You can also specify additional settings based on your restore requirements. Windows Backup provides a Restore wizard to help you restore data, or you can restore data without using the wizard.

Preparing to Restore Data

When critical data is lost, you need to restore the data quickly. Use the following guidelines to prepare for restoring data:

- Base your restore strategy on the backup type you used for the backup. If time is critical when you are restoring data, your restore strategy must ensure that the backup types you choose for backups expedite the restore process. For example, use normal and differential backups so that you need to restore only the last normal backup and the last differential backup.

- Perform a trial restore periodically to verify that Windows Backup is backing up your files correctly. A trial restore can uncover hardware problems that do not show up with backup file verifications. Restore the data to an alternate location, and then compare the restored data to the data on the original hard disk.

- Keep documentation for each backup job. Create and print a detailed Backup log for each backup job. A detailed backup log contains a record of all files and folders that were backed up. By using the Backup log, you can quickly locate which piece of media contains the files you need to restore without having to load the catalogs. A *catalog* is an index of the files and folders from a backup job that Windows 2000 automatically creates and stores with the backup job on the computer running Windows Backup.

- Keep a record of multiple backup jobs in a calendar format that shows the days on which you perform the backup jobs. For each job, note the backup type and identify the storage used, such as a tape number or removable disk name. Then, if you need to restore data, you can easily review several weeks' worth of backup jobs to select which type to use.

Selecting Backup Sets, Files, and Folders to Restore

The first step in restoring data is to select the data to restore. You can select individual files and folders, an entire backup job, or a backup set. A *backup set* is a collection of files or folders from one volume that you back up during a backup job. If you back up two volumes on a hard disk during a backup job, the job has two backup sets. You can select the data to restore in the catalog.

To restore data, use the Restore wizard, which you access through Windows Backup. After you run the wizard, the initial settings for the restore process are displayed in the Completing The Restore Wizard screen. At this time, you can perform one of the following actions:

- Finish the restore process by clicking the Finish button. If you choose to finish the restore job, the Restore wizard requests verification for the source of the restore media and then performs the restore. During the restore process, the Restore wizard displays status information about the restore.

- Specify advanced restore options by clicking the Advanced button.

Specifying Advanced Restore Settings

The advanced settings in the Restore wizard vary, depending on the types of backup media from which you are restoring. After you have finished the Restore wizard, Windows Backup does the following:

- Prompts you to verify your selection of the source media to use to restore data. After the verification, Windows Backup starts the restore process.

- Displays status information about the restore process. As with a backup process, you can choose to view the report (restore log) of the restore. It contains information about the restore, such as the number of files that have been restored and the duration of the restore process.

The following table describes the advanced restore options.

Option	Description
Restore Files To	The target location for the data you are restoring. You can choose from the following options: **Original Location** Replaces corrupted or lost data. **Alternate Location** Restores an older version of a file or does a practice restore. **Single Folder** Consolidates the files from a tree structure into a single folder. For example, use this option if you want copies of specific files but do not want to restore the hierarchical structure of the files. If you select either an alternate location or a single folder, you must provide the path.
When Restoring A File That Is Already On My Computer	The options for whether or not to overwrite existing files. You can choose from the following options: **Do Not Replace The File On My Disk (Recommended)** Prevents accidental overwriting of existing data. This option is the default. **Replace The File On My Disk Only If The File On Disk Is Older Than The Backup Copy** Verifies that the most recent copy exists on the computer. **Always Replace The File On My Computer** Windows Backup does not provide a confirmation message if it encounters a duplicate file name during the restore operation.

Option	Description
Advanced Restore Options	The options for whether or not to restore security or special system files. You can choose from the following options:
	Restore Security Applies the original permissions to files you are restoring to an NTFS volume. Security settings include access permissions, audit entries, and ownership. This option is available only if you have backed up data from an NTFS volume and are restoring to an NTFS volume.
	Restore Removable Storage Database Restores the configuration database for Removable Storage Management (RSM) devices and the media pool settings. The database is located in %systemroot%\system32\remotestorage.
	Restore Junction Points, And Restore File And Folder Data Under Junction Points To The Original Location Restores junction points on your hard disk as well as the data the junction points refer to. If you have any mounted drives and you want to restore the data that mounted drives point to, you should select this check box. If you do not select this check box, the junction point will be restored but the data your junction point refers to might not be accessible.

Exercise 2: Restoring Data

In this exercise, you delete the Inetpub folder and then run a restore routine to restore the Inetpub folder. Complete this exercise on Server01.

▶ Procedure 1: Deleting critical data

In this procedure, you intentionally delete Boot.ini. Typically, deleting critical files is an accident or a result of hardware failure.

1. Double-click My Computer, and then double-click Local Disk (C:).

   The Local Disk (C:) window appears.

2. Maximize the window.

3. Click the Tools menu, and then click Folder Options.

   The Folder Options dialog box appears.

4. Click the View tab.

5. Clear the Hide Protected Operating System Files (Recommended) check box.

   A Warning message box appears stating that you are about to show critical hidden and system files.

6. Click Yes.

The Folder Options dialog box appears.

7. Click OK.

More files appear in the Local Disk (C:) window.

8. Click once on boot.ini.

9. Click the File menu, and then click Delete.

A Confirm File Delete message box appears asking if you are sure you want to delete this critical file.

10. Click Yes.

The boot.ini file is now gone. While you could recover it from the Recycle Bin, you will use the restore program in the next procedure to recover the file backed up in Exercise 1.

11. Keep the Local Disk (C:) window maximized; it will be used in the next procedure.

▶ **Procedure 2: Restoring critical data**

In this procedure, you recover boot.ini from a backup set.

1. In the Local Disk (C:) window, double-click Backup1.bkf.

The Backup - [Untitled] dialog box appears.

2. Click the Restore Wizard button.

The Welcome To The Restore Wizard screen appears.

3. Click Next.

The What To Restore screen appears, prompting you to select the backup media from which you wish to restore files.

Notice that the only media from which you can restore is a file and the backup files are listed according to the media label specified.

4. Under the What To Restore box, expand the first backup job you created in Exercise 1.

Notice that drive C appears as the first folder in the backup file. Windows Backup creates a separate backup set for each volume backed up. All folders and files backed up from a single volume appear under the drive letter for the volume.

5. Expand drive C.

   The Backup File Name dialog box appears with C:\ Backup1.bkf in the Catalog Backup File text box.

   If c:\Backup2.bkf appears, change the name to C:\Backup1.bkf.

6. Click OK.

7. When you are returned to the What To Restore screen, click on C:.

   Boot.ini appears in the Name column.

8. In the Name column, click the Boot.ini check box and then click Next.

   The Completing The Restore Wizard screen appears, prompting you to start the restore operation and use the default restore settings.

9. Click the Advanced button.

   The Where To Restore screen appears, prompting you for a target location to restore files.

10. Click the drop-down list box to review the restore location options.

11. Verify that Original location is selected, and click Next.

12. The How To Restore screen appears, prompting you to specify how to process duplicate files during the restore job.

13. Verify that the Do Not Replace The File On My Disk (Recommended) radio button is selected, and then click Next.

14. The Advanced Restore Options screen appears, prompting you to select security options for the restore job.

15. Verify that the Restore Security check box is selected, clear the Restore Junction Points, Not The Folders And File Data They Reference check box, and then click Next.

    The Completing The Restore Wizard screen appears, displaying a summary of the restore options you selected.

16. Click Finish to begin the restore process.

    Windows Backup displays the Enter Backup File Name dialog box, prompting you to supply or verify the name of the backup file that contains the folders and files to be restored.

17. Verify that C:\ Backup1.bkf is entered in the Restore From Backup File text box, and then click OK.

    The Selection Information dialog box appears.

    The Restore Progress dialog box appears, providing the status of the restore operation, statistics on estimated and actual amount of data being processed, the time that has elapsed, and the estimated time that remains for the restore operation.

18. When the Restore Progress dialog box indicates that the restore is complete, click the Report button.

    Notepad starts and displays the report. Notice that the details about the restore operation are appended to the Backup log. This provides a centralized location from which to view all status information for this backup and restore operation.

19. Examine the report, and then close Notepad.

20. In the Restore Progress dialog box, click Close.

    Backup [Untitled] dialog box appears with the Welcome tab active.

21. Close the Backup [Untitled] dialog box.

    The Local Disk (C:) window appears.

22. Notice that boot.ini has been restored.

23. Close the Local Disk (C:) window.

Recovering a Mirrored or RAID-5 Volume

This section provides information about recovering from a mirrored volume failure and repairing a RAID-5 volume.

Recovering from a Mirrored Volume Failure

In a mirrored volume, the computer saves data to each member simultaneously. If one member fails, the functional member continues to operate.

To replace the failed member, you must first "remove" the failed disk from the mirrored volume. Using the Computer Management snap-in, you can isolate the working member as a separate volume. Then you can replace the failed disk with a functional disk.

To re-create the mirrored volume after replacing the failed disk, click the working partition in the Computer Management window, and then click Add Mirror. The computer then presents the option to mirror this partition to the replacement disk.

In Figure 12.14, drive D on disk 0 is mirrored on disk 1. Drive D on disk 1 is the secondary member of the mirrored volume.

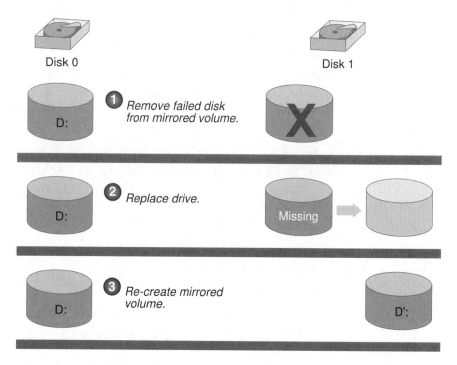

Figure 12.14 Replacing a failed disk in a mirrored volume

If the primary member of a mirrored volume, including the boot partition, fails, use a boot disk to start the computer and access the functioning member. The Boot.ini file on the boot disk must include the Advanced RISC Computing (ARC) path pointing to the mirrored partition. It is recommended that you create and test a boot disk immediately after implementing a mirrored volume.

Note Replacing a failed member is not the only reason to remove a mirrored volume. You might also remove one member of a mirrored volume to reclaim the disk space for other purposes.

Repairing a RAID-5 Volume

If a member of a RAID-5 volume fails, the computer continues to operate with access to all data. However, as data is requested, the Windows 2000 Server fault tolerance driver uses the data and parity bits on the remaining members to regenerate the missing data in RAM. During this regeneration, computer performance decreases.

To restore the computer's level of performance, you can replace the failed drive and then repair the RAID-5 volume. The fault tolerance driver reads the parity information from the parity information stripes on the remaining members, and then re-creates the data contained on the missing member. When complete, the fault tolerance driver writes the data to the new member.

Lesson Summary

Disaster recovery allows you to restore a computer so that you can log on and access system resources after a computer disaster has occurred. Windows 2000 includes three methods that allow you to repair a system: Safe mode, the Recovery Console, and the Emergency Repair Disk. Safe mode lets you start your system with a minimal set of device drivers and services. The Recovery Console is a text-mode command interpreter that is separate from the Windows 2000 command prompt and allows the system administrator to gain access to the hard disk of a computer running Windows 2000. The Emergency Repair Disk allows you to restore core system files. In addition to repairing a system, you should be able to restore data. Windows Backup provides a Restore wizard to help you restore data, or you can restore data without using the wizard. Also, if you have set up your system with disk fault tolerance, you can recover from a mirrored volume failure or repair a RAID-5 volume.

Review

The following questions are intended to reinforce key information presented in this chapter. If you are unable to answer a question, review the appropriate lesson and then try the question again. Answers to the questions can be found in Appendix A, "Questions and Answers."

1. You have configured a computer to boot Windows 2000 Server as the default operating system, and Windows NT 4.0 Server as the optional operating system. After modifying the attributes of files on %systemdrive% and deleting some of the files, the computer does not display Windows NT 4.0 Server as an operating system to start. Windows 2000 Server starts up properly. The problem is caused because you deleted a file. What is the name of the file, and what can you do to recover from this error?

2. You have created three hardware profiles for your mobile computer: Docked, Undocked On The Network, and Undocked At Home. When you reboot the computer, the first two hardware profiles appear, but the third one does not. What is the most likely reason that the Undocked At Home profile is not appearing?

3. Why would the Use Hardware Compression, If Available check box be unavailable in the Backup wizard?

4. You performed a normal backup on Monday. For the remaining days of the week, you only want to back up files and folders that have changed since the previous day. What backup type do you select?

5. How can you test the configuration of the UPS service on a computer?

CHAPTER 13

Monitoring and Optimization

About This Chapter

Microsoft Windows 2000 provides a set of tools and services that allows you to monitor and optimize your system. For example, you can use the Disk Defragmenter snap-in to locate and consolidate fragmented files and folders on local volumes, and you can use Network Monitor to view and detect problems on the network. This chapter discusses many of the tools and services that allow you to monitor, troubleshoot, and fine-tune your system, including those that can be used to optimize disk performance and your network.

Before You Begin

To complete the lessons in this chapter, you must have

- Server01 running Windows 2000 Server.
- Completed the exercises in the previous chapters.

Lesson 1: Disk Monitoring and Optimization

Windows 2000 includes several tools that you can use to diagnose disk problems, improve performance, and compress data, such as Check Disk, the Disk Defragmenter snap-in, data compression, and disk quotas. This lesson discusses each of these tools and shows how the tools are used. Lesson 2 explores disk monitoring in the context of system performance monitoring.

After this lesson, you will be able to

- Use Check Disk, the Disk Defragmenter snap-in, data compression, and disk quotas to optimize disk performance

Estimated lesson time: 40 minutes

Check Disk

The Check Disk tool, also referred to as the Error-checking tool, allows you to check for file system errors and bad sectors on your hard disk. To use Check Disk, open the Properties dialog box for the specific disk you want to check. You can open the Properties dialog box from Windows Explorer or from My Computer. On the Tools tab, click Check Now to open the Check Disk dialog box and select the appropriate options (Figure 13.1).

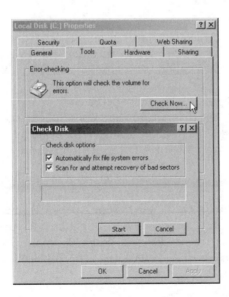

Figure 13.1 Check Disk dialog box, accessed through the Tools tab of the Properties dialog box

All running applications or open files on the disk being checked must be closed in order for the Check Disk process to be able to automatically fix file system errors. If any open files or applications are running, a message box appears informing you that exclusive access to the drive could not be obtained and asking if you want to reschedule disk checking for the next time your start your computer.

If a volume is formatted with NT file system (NTFS), Windows 2000 logs all file transactions, replaces bad clusters automatically, and stores copies of key information for all files on the NTFS volume.

Disk Defragmenter Snap-In

Windows 2000 saves files and folders in the first available space on a hard disk and not necessarily in an area of contiguous space. This leads to file and folder fragmentation. When your hard disk contains a lot of fragmented files and folders, your computer takes longer to gain access to them because it requires several additional reads to collect the various pieces. Creating new files and folders also takes longer because the available free space on the hard disk is scattered. Your computer must save a new file or folder in various locations on the hard disk.

Defragmenting Disks

The process of finding and consolidating fragmented files and folders is called *defragmenting*. The Disk Defragmenter snap-in is used to locate fragmented files and folders and then defragment them. It does this by moving the pieces of each file or folder to one location so that each file or folder occupies a single area of contiguous space on the hard disk. Consequently, your system can gain access to and save files and folders more efficiently. By consolidating files and folders, the Disk Defragmenter snap-in also consolidates free space, making it less likely that new files will be fragmented. Disk Defragmenter defragments FAT16, FAT32, and NTFS volumes.

You can access the Disk Defragmenter snap-in through the Computer Management snap-in or by creating a custom console containing the Disk Defragmenter snap-in. When the Disk Defragmenter is selected, the detail window is split into three areas, as shown in Figure 13.2. You can also access the Disk Defragmenter snap-in through Windows Explorer or My Computer by opening the Properties dialog box for the specific drive. On the Tools tab, click Defragment Now.

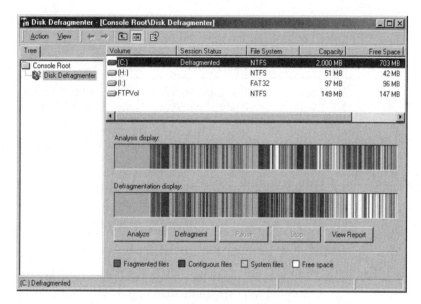

Figure 13.2 The Disk Defragmenter snap-in, accessed through a custom console

The upper portion of the window lists the volumes you can analyze and defragment. The middle portion is a graphic representation of how fragmented the selected volume is. The lower portion is a dynamic representation of the volume that is continuously updated during defragmentation. The display colors indicate the condition of the volume.

- Red indicates fragmented files.

- Dark blue indicates contiguous (nonfragmented) files.

- White indicates free space on the volume.

- Green indicates system files, which Disk Defragmenter cannot move.

By comparing the Analysis display band to the Defragmentation display band during defragmentation and at its conclusion, you can quickly see the improvement in the volume.

To analyze or defragment a volume, you can choose one of the options described in the following table.

Option	Description
Analyze	Click this button to analyze the disk for fragmentation. After the analysis, the Analysis display band provides a graphical representation of how fragmented the volume is.
Defragment	Click this button to defragment the disk. After defragmentation, the Defragmentation display band provides a graphical representation of the defragmented volume.

Using Disk Defragmenter Effectively

The following list provides guidelines for using the Disk Defragmenter snap-in.

- Run Disk Defragmenter when the computer will receive the least usage. During defragmentation, data is moved around on the hard disk. The defragmentation process is CPU intensive and will adversely affect access time to other disk-based resources.

- Recommend users defragment their local hard disks at least once a month to prevent accumulation of fragmented files.

- Analyze the target volume before you install large applications, and then defragment the volume if necessary. Installations are completed more quickly when the target medium has adequate contiguous free space. Additionally, gaining access to the application after it is installed is faster.

- When you delete a large number of files or folders, your hard disk might become excessively fragmented, so be sure to analyze it afterwards. Generally, you should defragment hard disks on busy file servers more often than those on single-user client computers.

- Consider using a disk defragmentation utility that allows you to perform a regularly scheduled network-wide defragmentation from a central location. Executive Software created the manual Disk Defragmenter included with Windows 2000 and manufactures an automated, more feature-rich version of this utility as a separate product called Diskeeper.

Note For more information about Executive Software Diskeeper 5.0, visit their Web site at *http://www.execsoft.com.*

Data Compression

Data compression enables you to compress files and folders on NTFS volumes. Compressed files and folders occupy less space on an NTFS-formatted volume, which enables you to store more data. The compression state for each file and folder on an NTFS volume is set to either compressed or uncompressed.

Using Compressed Files and Folders

Compressed files can be read by and written to any Windows-based or MS-DOS-based application without first being uncompressed by another program. When an application, such as Microsoft Word for Windows, or an operating system command, such as copy, requests access to a compressed file, NTFS automatically uncompresses the file before making it available. When you close or explicitly save a file, NTFS compresses it again.

NTFS allocates disk space based on the uncompressed file size. If you copy a compressed file to an NTFS volume with enough space for the compressed file, but not enough space for the uncompressed file, you will get an error message stating there is not enough disk space for the file. The file will not be copied to the volume.

Compressing Files and Folders

You can set the compression state of folders and files in Windows Explorer or by using the compact command-line utility. For information on compact utility syntax, go to a command prompt and type **compact /?**.

To compress a file or folder, open the Properties dialog box for the specific file or folder. On the General tab, click Advanced. In the Advanced Attributes dialog box, select the Compress Contents To Save Disk Space check box, as shown in Figure 13.3. Note that NTFS encryption and compression are mutually exclusive. If you choose the Encrypt Contents To Secure Data check box, you cannot compress that folder or file.

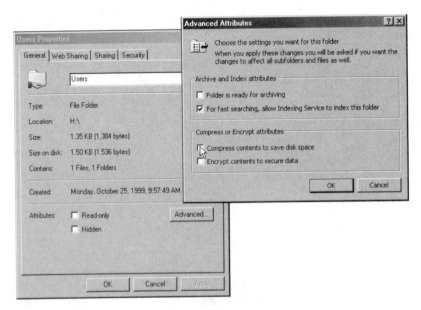

Figure 13.3 Advanced Attributes dialog box

You can also set compression on the entire drive. To do so, open the Properties dialog box for the specific drive. On the General tab, select the Compress Drive To Save Disk Space check box.

To change the compression state for a file or folder, you must have Write permission for it.

The compression flag on a folder does not reflect the compression state of the files in that folder and its subfolders. A folder can be marked so that files added afterward will be compressed, yet all of the files currently in that folder remain uncompressed. Alternatively, a folder not marked with the compression flag can contain compressed files. When you select the folder compression option and then click Apply or OK in the Properties dialog box, Windows 2000 displays the Confirm Attribute Changes dialog box, which has the two additional options. These options are described in the following table.

Option	Description
Apply changes to this folder only	Compresses only the files in the folder you have selected
Apply changes to this folder, subfolders and files	Compresses the files in the folder, marks subfolders with the compression flag, and compresses files that are contained within it and added to it subsequently

Note Windows 2000 does not support NTFS compression for cluster sizes larger than 4 kilobytes (KB) because compression on large clusters causes performance degradation. If you select a larger cluster size when you format an NTFS volume, compression is not available for that volume.

Selecting an Alternate Display Color for Compressed Files and Folders

Windows Explorer makes it easy for you to determine quickly if a file or folder is compressed by allowing you to select a different display color for compressed files and folders to distinguish them from uncompressed files and folders.

To set an alternative display color for compressed files and folders, select Folder Options from the Tools menu. On the View tab, select the Display Compressed Files And Folders With Alternate Color check box.

Copying and Moving Compressed Files and Folders

There are rules that determine whether the compression state of files and folders is retained when you copy or move them within and between NTFS and FAT volumes. The following sections describe how Windows 2000 treats the compression state of a file or folder when you copy or move a compressed file or folder within or between NTFS volumes or between NTFS and FAT volumes.

Copying a File Within an NTFS Volume

When you copy a file within an NTFS volume, the file inherits the compression state of the target folder. For example, if you copy a compressed file to an uncompressed folder, the file is automatically uncompressed.

Moving a File or Folder Within an NTFS Volume

When you move a file or folder within an NTFS volume, the file or folder retains its original compression state. For example, if you move a compressed file to an uncompressed folder, the file remains compressed.

Copying a File or Folder Between NTFS Volumes

When you copy a file or folder between NTFS volumes, the file or folder inherits the compression state of the target folder.

Moving a File or Folder Between NTFS Volumes

When you move a file or folder between NTFS volumes, the file or folder inherits the compression state of the target folder. Because Windows 2000 treats a move as a copy and then a delete, the files inherit the compression state of the target folder.

Moving or Copying a File or Folder to a FAT Volume

Windows 2000 supports compression for NTFS files only. Because of this, when you move or copy a compressed NTFS file or folder to a FAT volume, Windows 2000 automatically uncompresses the file or folder.

Moving or Copying a Compressed File or Folder to a Floppy Disk

When you move or copy a compressed NTFS file or folder to a floppy disk, Windows 2000 automatically uncompresses the file or folder.

Note When you copy a compressed NTFS file, Windows 2000 uncompresses the file, copies the file, and then if the target folder is marked for compression, compresses the file again as a new file. This might cause performance degradation.

Using NTFS Compression

The following is a list of best practices for using compression on NTFS volumes.

- Because some file types compress more than others, select file types to compress based on the anticipated resulting file size. For example, because Windows bitmap files contain more redundant data than application-executable files, this file type compresses to a smaller size. Bitmaps often compress to less than a quarter of their original file size, whereas application files rarely compress to less than 75 percent of their original size.

- Do not store compressed files, such as PKZIP files, in a compressed folder. Windows 2000 will attempt to compress the file, wasting system time and yielding no additional disk space.

- To make it easier to locate compressed data, use a different display color for compressed folders and files.

- Compress static data rather than data that changes frequently. Compressing and uncompressing files incurs some system overhead. By choosing to compress files that are infrequently accessed, you minimize the amount of system time dedicated to compression and uncompression activities.

- NTFS compression can cause performance degradation when you copy and move files. When a compressed file is copied to another folder marked for compression, it is uncompressed, copied, and then compressed again as a new file.

Disk Quotas

You can use disk quotas to manage storage growth in distributed environments. Disk quotas allow you to allocate disk space usage to users based on the files and folders that they own. You can set disk quotas, quota thresholds, and quota limits for all users and for individual users. You can also monitor the amount of hard disk space users have used and the amount they have left against their quota.

Managing Disk Quotas

Windows 2000 disk quotas track and control disk usage on a per-user, per-volume basis. Windows 2000 tracks disk quotas for each volume, even if the volumes are on the same hard disk. Because quotas are tracked on a per-user basis, every user's disk space is tracked regardless of the folder in which the user stores files. Third-party disk quota management tools provide granular quota management capabilities like tracking disk usage on per-user, per-folder basis.

The following list describes several important characteristics of Windows 2000 disk quotas.

- Windows 2000 calculates disk space usage for users based on the files and folders they own. When a user copies or saves a new file to an NTFS volume or takes ownership of a file on an NTFS volume, Windows 2000 charges the disk space for the file against the user's quota limit.

- Windows 2000 ignores compression when it calculates hard disk space usage. Users are charged for each uncompressed byte, regardless of how much hard disk space is actually used. In part, this charge is made because file compression produces different degrees of compression for different types of files. Different file types that are the same size when uncompressed might end up to be very different sizes when they are compressed.

- When you enable disk quotas, the free space Windows 2000 reports to applications for the volume is the amount of space remaining within the user's disk quota limit. For example, a user whose files occupy 50 megabytes (MB) of an assigned disk quota limit of 100 MB will show 50 MB of free space even if the volume contains several gigabytes of free space.

Note Disk quotas can be applied only to Windows 2000 NTFS volumes.

You can use disk quotas to monitor and control hard disk space usage. System administrators can perform the following tasks:

- Set a disk quota limit to specify the amount of disk space for each user.

- Set a disk quota warning to specify when Windows 2000 should log an event, indicating that the user is nearing his or her limit.

- Enforce disk quota limits and either deny users access if they exceed their limit or allow them continued access.

- Log an event when a user exceeds a specified disk space threshold. For example, a threshold might be when users exceed their quota limit or when they exceed their warning level.

After you enable disk quotas for a volume, Windows 2000 collects disk usage data for all users who own files and folders on the volume. This allows you to monitor volume usage on a per-user basis. By default, only members of the Administrators group can view and change quota settings. However, you can allow users to view quota settings.

Setting Disk Quotas

You can enable disk quotas and enforce disk quota warnings and limits for all users or for individual users. To enable disk quotas, open the Properties dialog box of a particular disk, click the Quota tab, and configure the disk quota options (Figure 13.4).

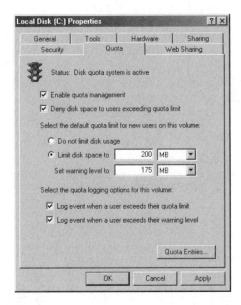

Figure 13.4 Quota tab of a disk's Properties dialog box

The options on the Quota tab are described in the following table.

Option	Description
Enable Quota Management	Select this check box to enable disk quota management.
Deny Disk Space To Users Exceeding Quota Limit	Select this check box so that when users exceed their hard disk space allocation, they receive an "out of disk space" message and cannot write to the volume.
Do Not Limit Disk Usage	Click this option when you do not want to limit the amount of hard disk space for users.
Limit Disk Space To	Configure the amount of disk space that users can use.
Set Warning Level To	Configure the amount of disk space that a user can fill before Windows 2000 logs an event, indicating that a user is nearing his or her limit.
Quota Entries	Click this button to open the Quota Entries for a dialog box, where you can add a new entry, delete an entry, and view the per-user quota information.

To enforce identical quota limits for all users, enter the appropriate values in the Limit Disk Space To text box and the Set Warning Level To text box, and then select the Deny Disk Space To Users Exceeding Quota Limit check box.

Windows 2000 monitors usage and will not allow users to create files or folders on the volume when they exceed the limit.

Determining the Status of Disk Quotas

You can determine the status of disk quotas in the Properties dialog box for a disk by checking the traffic light icon and reading the status message to its right (Figure 13.4). The traffic light colors and the status they indicate are as follows:

- A red traffic light indicates that disk quotas are disabled.
- A yellow traffic light indicates that Windows 2000 is rebuilding disk quota information.
- A green traffic light indicates that the disk quota system is active.

Enforcing Disk Quotas

To enforce different quota limits for one or more specific users, click the Quota Entries button to open the Quota Entries For dialog box. Configure the disk space limit and the warning level for each individual user.

You can use the Quota Entries For <volume_name> dialog box to monitor usage for all users who have copied, saved, or taken ownership of files and folders on the volume. Windows 2000 scans the volume and monitor the amount of disk space in use by each user. The Quota Entries For <volume_name> dialog box allows you to view the following information:

- The amount of hard disk space that each user uses
- Users who are over their quota-warning threshold, which is signified by a yellow triangle
- Users who are over their quota limit, which is signified by a red circle
- The warning threshold and the disk quota limit for each user

Volume usage is tracked for all users owning files on a volume where the Disk quota system is active. Existing users owning files are limited to the default disk quotas unless you modify the user quota setting using the Quota Entries For *<volume_name>* dialog box. Users not owning files on the volume will not appear in the Quota Entries For *<volume_name>* dialog box but can also be added manually. By default, quota limits are not applied to the Administrators local group.

Best Uses of Disk Quotas

The following is a list of guidelines for using disk quotas:

- If you enable disk quota settings on the volume where Windows 2000 is installed and your user account has a disk quota limit, log on as Administrator to install additional Windows 2000 components and applications. When you do so, Windows 2000 will not charge the disk space you use to install applications against the disk quota allowance for your user account.

- You can monitor hard disk usage and generate hard disk usage information without preventing users from saving data. To do so, clear the Deny Disk Space To Users Exceeding Quota Limit check box when you enable disk quotas.

- Set more restrictive default limits for all user accounts, and then modify the limits from the Quota Entries For *<volume_name>* dialog box to allow more disk space to users who work with large files.

- Generally, you should set disk quotas on shared volumes to limit storage for users. Set disk quotas on public folders and network servers to ensure that users share hard disk space appropriately. When storage resources are scarce, you may want to set disk quotas on all shared hard disk space.

- Delete disk quota entries users who no longer store their files on a volume. You can delete quota entries for a user account only after all files that the user owns have been removed from the volume or another user has taken ownership of the files.

- Before you can delete a quota entry for a user account, all files that the user owns must be removed from the volume or another user must take ownership of the files. An efficient way to remove a user's files or take ownership of them for this purpose is to delete the user account in the Quota Entries For *<volume_name>* dialog box. The Disk Quota management system will display the Disk Quota dialog box. From this dialog box you can take ownership, delete, or move the files.

Exercise 1: Implementing Disk Quotas

In this exercise, you configure default quota management settings to limit the amount of data users can store on drive C of Server01. Drive C on Server01 contains the HomeDirs share you created for user John Smith to store his files. Next you configure a custom quota setting for a user account. You increase the amount of data the user may store on drive C to 20 MB with a warning level set to 16. Finally, you turn off quota management for drive C. Complete this exercise on Server01.

▸ Procedure 1: Configuring quota management settings

In this procedure, you configure the quota management settings for drive C to limit the data that users can store on the volume.

1. Log on to Server01 as Administrator with a password of "password."

2. On the desktop, double-click My Computer.

3. Click the Local Disk (C:) icon, click the File menu, and then click Properties.

   Windows 2000 displays the Local Disk (C:) Properties dialog box with the General tab active.

4. Click the Quota tab.

   Notice that disk quotas are disabled by default.

5. On the Quota tab, click the Enable Quota Management check box.

6. Click the Limit Disk Space To radio button.

7. Type **10** in the Limit Disk Space To text box, and then type **6** in the Set Warning Level To text box.

   Notice the default unit size is KB.

8. Change the unit sizes to MB, and then click the Apply button.

   A Disk Quota dialog box appears, warning you that the volume will be rescanned to update disk usage statistics if you enable quotas.

9. Click OK to enable disk quotas.

10. Do not close the Local Disk (C:) Properties dialog box; you will use it in the next procedure.

▸ Procedure 2: Creating a custom quota setting for a user

In this procedure, you configure a custom quota setting for the John Smith user account.

1. On the Quota tab of the Local Disk (C:) Properties dialog box, click the Quota Entries button.

   Windows 2000 displays the Quota Entries For Local Disk (C:) dialog box. Notice that the user accounts you created, the NT AUTHORITY\ SYSTEM, and the BUILTIN\Administrators group are listed. The user accounts you created are added because all three accounts (Jane_Doe, John_Smith, and Bob_Train) own files on the volume.

2. In the Quota Entries For Local Disk (C:) dialog box, double-click the row containing John Smith.

   The Quota Settings For John Smith dialog box appears.

3. Increase the amount of data that John Smith can store on drive C by changing the value in the Limit Disk Space To box to 20 MB and changing the value in the Set Warning Level To box to 16 MB.

4. Click OK to return to the Quota Entries For Local Disk (C:) dialog box.

5. Close the Quota Entries For Local Disk (C:) dialog box.

6. Leave the Local Disk (C:) Properties dialog box open since you will be using it in the next procedure.

▸ Procedure 3: Disabling quota management

In this procedure, you disable quota management settings for drive C.

1. On the Quota tab, clear the Enable Quota Management check box.

   Notice that all quota settings for drive C are no longer available.

2. Click Apply.

   A Disk Quota message box appears, warning that if you disable quotas, the volume will be rescanned if you enable them later.

3. Click OK to close the Disk Quota dialog box.

4. Click OK to close the Local Disk (C:) Properties dialog box.

5. Close the My Computer window.

Lesson Summary

Windows 2000 includes several tools you can use to diagnose disk problems, improve performance, or compress data. The Check Disk tool, also referred to as the Error-checking tool, allows you to check for file system errors and bad sectors on a disk. The Disk Defragmenter snap-in allows you to locate fragmented files and folders and then defragment them. It does this by moving the pieces of each file or folder to one location so that each file or folder occupies a single area contiguous space on the hard disk. Data compression enables you to compress files and folders on NTFS volumes. Compressed files can be read and written to by any Windows-based or MS-DOS–based application without first being uncompressed by another program. Disk quotas allow you to allocate disk space usage to users based on the files and folders they own. You can set disk quotas, quota thresholds, and quota limits for all users and individual users. Disk quotas track and control disk usage on a per-user, per-volume basis.

Lesson 2: Simple Network Management Protocol Service

To meet the challenges of designing an effective network management platform for heterogeneous TCP/IP-based networks, the Simple Network Management Protocol (SNMP) was defined in 1988 and approved as an Internet standard in 1990 by the Internet Activities Board (IAB). SNMP allows you to monitor and communicate status information from SNMP agents to a network management station (NMS). This lesson provides the background and conceptual material necessary to understand and implement SNMP within the context of Windows 2000.

After this lesson, you will be able to

- Understand the purpose and function of the SNMP service

Estimated lesson time: 35 minutes

Overview of SNMP

SNMP is a network management standard widely used with TCP/IP networks and, more recently, with Internetwork Packet Exchange (IPX) networks. SNMP provides a method of managing network nodes (servers, workstations, routers, bridges, and hubs) from a centrally located NMS.

To perform its management services, SNMP uses a distributed architecture of management systems and agents, as shown in Figure 13.5. The centrally located host, which is running network management software, is referred to as an NMS, or an SNMP manager. Managed network nodes are referred to as SNMP agents.

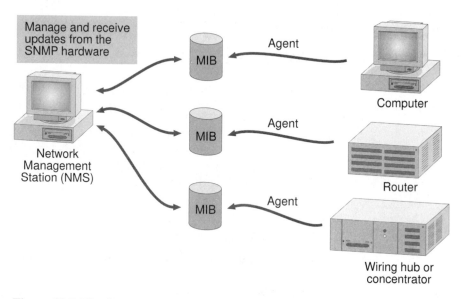

Figure 13.5 Distributed architecture used by SNMP

The agent reports hardware status and configuration information to a database called a Management Information Base (MIB). The MIB defines the hardware and software information in the host that should be collected by the SNMP agent. The SNMP agent communicates with the NMS to provide device-monitoring functions.

Network management is critical for resource management and auditing. SNMP can be used in several ways:

- **To configure remote devices** You can configure information so that it can be sent to each networked host from the NMS.

- **To monitor network performance** You can track the speed of processing and network throughput and collect information about the success of data transmissions.

- **To detect network faults or inappropriate access** You can configure trigger alarms on network devices that alert you to the occurrence of specific events. When an alarm is triggered, the device forwards an event message via a trap to the NMS. The following are common types of events for which an alarm can be configured:

    - The shutdown or restart of a device

    - The detection of a link failure on a router

    - The inappropriate access to a network mode

- **To audit network usage** You can monitor overall network usage to identify user or group access or types of usage for network devices or services. This information can be used to generate direct billing of individual or group accounts or to justify current network costs or planned expenditures.

The Windows 2000 implementation of the SNMP agent is a 32-bit service that supports computers running TCP/IP and IPX protocols. Windows 2000 implements SNMP versions 1 and 2C. These versions are based on industry standards that define how network management information is structured, stored, and communicated between agents and management systems for TCP/IP-based networks.

To use the information that the Windows 2000 SNMP service provides, you must have at least one NMS. The Windows 2000 SNMP service provides only the SNMP agent; it does not include SNMP management software. You can use a third-party SNMP management software application on the host to act as the management system.

Note A number of software manufacturers design network management systems to run on UNIX or Windows NT/2000 operating systems.

Management Systems and Agents

The NMS does not have to run on the same computer as the SNMP agents. The NMS can request the following information from SNMP agents:

- Network protocol identification and statistics
- Dynamic identification of devices attached to the network (a process referred to as discovery)
- Hardware and software configuration data
- Device performance and usage statistics
- Device error and event messages
- Program and application usage statistics

The management system can also send a configuration request to the agent that requests the agent to change a local parameter; however, this is a rare occurrence because most client parameters have read-only access.

SNMP agents provide SNMP managers with information about activities that occur at the Internet Protocol (IP) network layer and respond to management system requests for information. Any computer running SNMP agent software, such as the Windows 2000 SNMP service, is an SNMP agent. The agent service can be configured to determine what statistics are to be tracked and what management systems are authorized to request information.

In general, agents do not originate messages; they only respond to messages. The exception is an alarm message triggered by a specific event. An alarm message is known as a *trap message*. A *trap* is an alarm-triggering event on an agent computer, such as a system reboot or illegal access. Traps and trap messages provide a rudimentary form of security by notifying the management system whenever such an event occurs.

Management Information Base

A *Management Information Base (MIB)* is a container of objects, each of which represents a particular type of information. This collection of objects contains information required by a management system. For example, one MIB object can represent the number of active sessions on an agent; another can represent the amount of available hard drive space on the agent. All the information a management system might request from an agent is stored in various MIBs.

A MIB defines the following values for each object it contains:

- Name and identifier.
- Defined data type.
- A textual description of the object.
- An index method used for complex data-type objects (usually described as a multidimensional array or as tabular data). Complex data refers to such items as the list of network interfaces configured into the system, the routing table, or the Address Resolution Protocol (ARP) table.
- Read/write permissions.

Each object in a MIB has a unique identifier that contains the following information:

- Type (counter, string, gauge, or address)
- Access level (read or read/write)
- Size restriction
- Range information

The Windows 2000 SNMP service supports the Internet MIB II; LAN Manager MIB II; Host Resources MIB; and Microsoft proprietary MIBs, such as the WINS, DHCP, and IIS MIBs.

SNMP Messages

Both agents and management systems use SNMP messages to inspect and communicate information about managed objects. SNMP messages are sent via the User Datagram Protocol (UDP). IP is used to route messages between the management system and host. By default, UDP port 161 is used to listen for SNMP messages and port 162 is used to listen for SNMP traps.

When an NMS sends requests to a network device, the agent program on the device receives the requests and retrieves the requested information from the MIBs. The agent sends the requested information back to the initiating NMS. An SNMP agent sends information when a trap event occurs or when it responds to a request for information from a management system.

The management system and agent programs use the following types of messages:

- **GET** The basic SNMP request message. Sent by an NMS, it requests information about a single MIB entry on an agent—for example, the amount of free disk space.

- **GET-NEXT** An extended type of request message that can be used to browse the entire hierarchy of management objects. When it processes a GET-NEXT request for a particular object, the agent returns the identity and value of the object that logically follows the previous information that was sent. The GET-NEXT request is useful mostly for dynamic tables, such as an internal IP route table.

- **SET** A message that can be used to send and assign an updated MIB value to the agent when write access is permitted.

- **GET-BULK** A request that the data transferred by the agent be as large as possible within the given restraints of message size. This minimizes the number of protocol exchanges required to retrieve a large amount of management information.

- **NOTIFY** An unsolicited message sent by an agent to a management system when the agent detects a certain type of event; also called a trap message. For example, a trap message might be sent when a system restart occurs. The NMS that receives the trap message is referred to as the trap destination.

Figure 13.6 is an example of how management systems and agents communicate information.

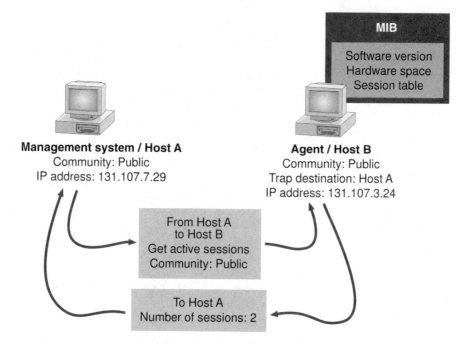

Figure 13.6 SNMP manager and agent interaction

The communication process is as follows:

1. A management system forms an SNMP message that contains an information request (GET), the name of the community to which the management system belongs, and the destination of the message—the agent's IP address (131.107.3.24).

2. The SNMP message is sent to the agent.

3. The agent receives the packet and decodes it. The community name (Public) is verified as acceptable.

4. The SNMP service calls the appropriate subagent to retrieve the session information requested from the MIB.

5. The SNMP takes the session information from the subagent and forms a return SNMP message that contains the number of active sessions and the destination—the management system's IP address (131.107.7.29).

6. The SNMP message is sent to the management system.

Defining SNMP Communities

You can assign groups of hosts to SNMP communities for limited security checking of agents and management systems or for administration. Communities are identified by community names that you assign. A host can belong to multiple communities at the same time, but an agent does not accept a request from a management system outside its list of acceptable community names.

You can define communities logically to take advantage of the basic authentication service provided by SNMP. Figure 13.7 shows an example of two communities, Public and Public 2:

- Agent 1 can send traps and other messages to Manager 2 because they are both members of the Public 2 community.

- Agent 2, Agent 3, and Agent 4 can send traps and messages to Manager 1 because they are all members, by default, of the Public community.

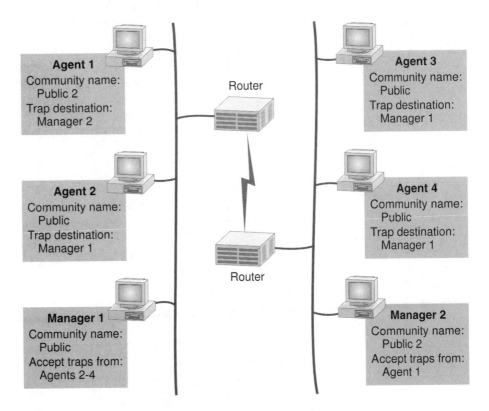

Figure 13.7 Example of two communities: Public and Public 2

Community names are managed by configuring SNMP security properties, which are described later in this lesson.

Note There is no relationship between community names and domain or workgroup names. Community names represent a shared password for groups of network hosts, and they should be selected and changed as you would change any password. Deciding which hosts belong to the same community is generally determined by physical proximity.

Installing and Configuring the SNMP Service

The SNMP agent is not installed by default on Windows 2000 Server. It is installed from the Control Panel Add/Remove Windows Programs application. From the Add/Remove Programs window, choose Add/Remove Windows Components, and from the Windows Components wizard that appears, choose Management And Monitoring Tools. The Management And Monitoring Tools item contains Simple Network Management Protocol, which is the SNMP agent. This agent is listed as SNMP Service after it is installed.

Once the SNMP service is installed, you can configure the SNMP services through the Services node of the Computer Management snap-in or through the Services snap-in in the Administrative Tools program group. In the Services node, select SNMP Service from the details pane, and then select Properties from the Action menu. The SNMP Service Properties dialog box appears, as shown in Figure 13.8.

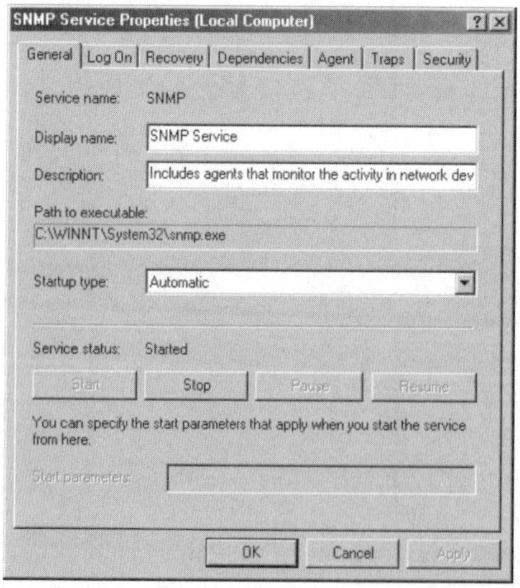

Figure 13.8 SNMP Service Properties dialog box

Note The SNMP Trap Service is also installed when SNMP is installed. The trap service passes traps from a local or remote computer to a trap destination, typically an NMS, running on the local computer.

SNMP Service Properties

You can use the General, Log On, and Recovery tabs in the SNMP Service Properties dialog box to configure how the SNMP service starts, logs on to the system, and recovers from an abnormal program termination of the service or operating system. Other services listed in the Computer Management snap-in contain these four tabs for service configuration. The General tab allows you to start or stop the service. You can also specify a display name, description, startup type, and start parameters. Another tab called the Dependencies tab provides a list of those services (if any) that depend on the SNMP service and those that the SNMP service depends on. By default, the SNMP service depends on Event Log.

Windows 2000 SNMP Agent Properties

The SNMP agent provides the related management system with information on activities that occur at the IP network layer. The SNMP service sends agent information in response to an SNMP request or in an SNMP trap message.

You can configure the agent properties on the Agent tab of the SNMP Service Properties dialog box. The Agent tab lists the services you can select. These services are described in the following table.

Agent Service	Conditions for selecting this service
Physical	The computer manages physical devices, such as a hard disk partition.
Applications	The computer uses any applications that send data via TCP/IP. This service should always be enabled.
Datalink and subnetwork	The computer manages a bridge.
Internet	The computer is an IP gateway (router).
End-to-end	The computer is an IP host. This service should always be enabled.

The Agent tab also allows you to configure the name of the person to contact, such as the network administrator, and the location of the contact person. An NMS might require this information when communicating with the SNMP agent.

Trap Properties

SNMP traps can be used for limited security checking. When configured for an agent, the SNMP service generates trap messages any time specific events occur. These messages are sent to a trap destination, typically an NMS. For example, an agent can be configured to initiate an authentication trap if a request for information is sent by an unrecognized management system. Trap messages can also be generated for events such as host system startup or shutdown.

You can configure trap destinations on the Traps tab of SNMP Service Properties dialog box. Trap destinations consist of the computer name or the IP or IPX address of the management system. The trap destination must be a network-enabled host running SNMP management software. Trap destinations can be configured by a user, but the events (such as a system reboot) that generate a trap message are internally defined by the SNMP agent.

Security Properties

You can configure SNMP security on the Security tab of the SNMP Service Properties dialog box. The following list describes the options you can configure on the Security tab.

- **Send authentication traps** When an SNMP agent receives a request that does not contain a valid community name or the host sending the message is not on the list of acceptable hosts, the agent can send an authentication trap message to one or more trap destinations (management systems). The trap message indicates that the SNMP request failed authentication. This is a default setting.

- **Accepted community names** The SNMP service requires the configuration of at least one default community name. The name Public is generally used as the community name because it is universally accepted in all SNMP implementations. You can delete or change the default community name or add multiple community names. The Public SNMP community name is not secure because it is so widely used. Therefore, consider removing this name. If the SNMP agent receives a request from a community that is not on this list, it generates an authentication trap. If no community names are defined, the SNMP agent denies all incoming SNMP requests.

- **Community Rights** You can select permission levels that determine how an agent processes SNMP requests from the various communities. For example, you can configure the permissions level to block the SNMP agent from processing any request from a specific community.

- **Accept SNMP packets from any host** In this context, the source host and list of acceptable hosts refer to the source SNMP management system and the list of other acceptable management systems. When this option is enabled, no SNMP packets are rejected on the basis of the name or address of the source host or on the basis of the list of acceptable hosts. This option is enabled by default.

- **Only accept SNMP packets from these hosts** This option provides limited security. When the option is enabled, only SNMP packets received from the hosts on a list of allowed hosts are accepted. The SNMP agent rejects messages from other hosts and sends an authentication trap. Limiting access only to hosts on a list provides a higher level of security than limiting access to specific communities, because a community name can encompass a large group of hosts.

Troubleshooting SNMP

This section contains methods for determining the cause of SNMP-related communication problems. Run normal workloads during your testing to gain realistic feedback.

Event Viewer

SNMP error handling has been improved in Windows 2000. Manual configuration of SNMP error-logging parameters has been replaced with improved error handling that is integrated with Event Viewer. Use Event Viewer if you suspect a problem with the SNMP service.

WINS Service

When querying WINS server MIBs, you might need to increase the SNMP time-out period on the SNMP management system. If some WINS queries work and others time out, increase the time-out period.

IPX Addresses

If you enter an IPX address as a trap destination when installing SNMP service, you might receive an Error 3 error message when you restart your computer. This occurs when the IPX address has been entered incorrectly—by using a comma or hyphen to separate a network number from a Media Access Control (MAC) address. For example, SNMP management software might normally accept an address like 00008022,0002C0-F7AABD. However, the Windows 2000 SNMP service does not recognize an address with a comma or hyphen between the network number and MAC address.

The address used for an IPX trap destination must follow the IETF defined 8.12 format for the network number and MAC address: xxxxxxxx.yyyyyyyyyyyy, where xxxxxxxx is the network number and yyyyyyyyyyyy is the MAC address.

SNMP Service Files

For your convenience and assistance in troubleshooting, the following table contains a list of the SNMP-associated files provided as part of the Microsoft Windows 2000 SNMP service.

File	Description
Wsnmp32.dll, Mgmtapi.dll	Windows 2000–based SNMP manager APIs. These APIs listen for manager requests and send the requests to SNMP agents and receive responses from them.
*.dll	Extension agent DLLs such as Inetmib1.dll for IIS, and Dhcpmib.dll for DHCP. These extension agents support the proprietary MIBs for these products.
Mib.bin	Installed with the SNMP service and used by the Management API (Mgmtapi.dll). The file maps text-based object names to numerical OIDobject identifiers.
Snmp.exe	SNMP agent service; a master (proxy) agent. This program accepts manager program requests and forwards the requests to the appropriate extension-subagent DLL for processing.
Snmptrap.exe	A background process. The program receives SNMP traps from the SNMP agent and forwards them to the SNMP Management API on the management console. The program starts only when the SNMP manager API receives a manager request for traps.

Figure 13.9 shows how the various SNMP files work together to communicate to and from an NMS.

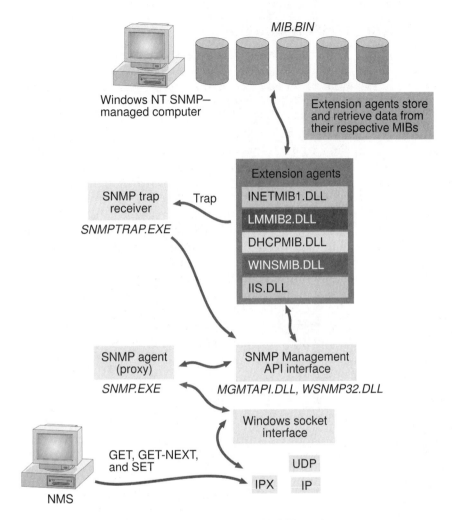

Figure 13.9 Communication to and from the SNMP service

Lesson Summary

SNMP is a network management standard that provides a method of managing network devices such as servers, workstations, routers, bridges, and hubs from a centrally located host. To perform its management services, SNMP uses a distributed architecture of management systems and agents. The SNMP management system, commonly knows as an NMS, can request the information from managed computers (SNMP agents). SNMP agents provide the NMS with information about activities that occur at the IP network layer and respond to management system requests for information. SNMP uses a MIB as a container for objects; each container represents a particular type of information. Both agents and NMS use SNMP messages to inspect and communicate information about managed objects. You can assign groups of hosts to SNMP communities for limited security checking of agents and NMS or for administration. Communities are identified by community names that you assign. For additional security, you can specify the IP address or host name of network management system(s) in which the SNMP agent should communicate. You can configure the SNMP service through the Services node of the Computer Management snap-in or through the Services snap-in in the Administrative Tools program group. The SNMP Service Properties dialog box allows you to configure the various properties of the SNMP service.

Lesson 3: Performance Console

Windows 2000 provides two utilities for monitoring resource usage on your computer: the System Monitor snap-in and the Performance Logs And Alerts snap-in, both of which are pre-installed on the Performance console. The System Monitor snap-in allows you to track resource use and network throughput. The Performance Logs And Alerts snap-in allows you to collect performance data from local or remote computers.

After this lesson, you will be able to

- Use the Performance console snap-ins—System Monitor and Performance Logs And Alerts—to monitor resource usage on your computer

Estimated lesson time: 40 minutes

Introduction to the Performance Console

The Performance console is a built-in utility you can access through the Administrative Tools program group. The Performance console is an MMC console that contains two pre-installed snap-ins: System Monitor and Performance Logs And Alerts (Figure 13.10).

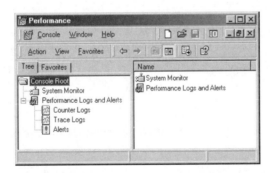

Figure 13.10 System Monitor snap-in and the Performance Logs And Alerts snap-in in the Performance MMC console

With System Monitor, you can collect and view real-time data about memory, disk, processor, network, and other activity in graph, histogram, or report form. Through Performance Logs And Alerts, you can configure logs to record performance data and set system alerts to notify you when a specified counter's value is above or below a defined threshold.

Monitoring system performance is an important part of maintaining and administering your Windows 2000 Server installation. You can use performance data for the following:

- To understand your workload and its effect on your system's resources

- To observe changes and trends in workloads and resource usage so that you can plan for future upgrades

- To test configuration changes or other tuning efforts by monitoring the results

- To diagnose problems and target components or processes for optimization

The System Monitor snap-in and the Performance Logs And Alerts snap-in provide detailed data about the resources used by specific components of the operating system and by server programs that have been designed to collect performance data. The graphs provide a display for performance-monitoring data; logs provide recording capabilities for the data; and alerts send notification to users by means of the Messenger service when a counter value reaches, rises above, or falls below a defined threshold.

Microsoft technical support often uses the results of performance monitoring to diagnose problems. Therefore, Microsoft recommends that you monitor system performance as part of your administrative routine.

System Monitor Snap-In

In Windows 2000, Performance Monitor has been replaced by System Monitor. With System Monitor, you can measure the performance of your own computer or other computers on a network. System Monitor allows you to perform the following tasks:

- Collect and view real-time performance data on a local computer or from remote computers

- View data collected either currently or previously in a counter log

- Present data in a printable graph, histogram, or report view

- Incorporate System Monitor functionality into Microsoft Word or other applications in the Microsoft Office suite by means of *Automation*

- Create HTML pages from performance views

- Create reusable monitoring configurations that can be installed on other computers that use MMC

With System Monitor, you can collect and view extensive data about the usage of hardware resources and the activity of system services on computers you administer. You can define the data you want the graph to collect in the following ways:

- **Type of data** To select the data to be collected, you can specify one or more counter instances of performance monitor objects. Some objects (such as the memory object) provide system resource counters; others provide counters on the operation of applications (for example, system services or Microsoft BackOffice applications).

- **Source of data** System Monitor can collect data from your local computer or from other computers on the network where you have permission. (By default, administrative permission is required.) In addition, you can include real-time data or data collected previously and saved in counter logs.

- **Sampling parameters** System Monitor supports manual, on-demand sampling or automatic sampling based on the time interval you specify. When viewing logged data, you can also choose starting and stopping times so that you can view data spanning a specific time range.

System Monitor Interface

When you open the Performance console, the graph view and a toolbar appear by default and the graph area is blank. After you add counters to the graph, System Monitor begins charting counter values in this graph area (Figure 13.11). The console tree is hidden in Figure 13.11 for clarity.

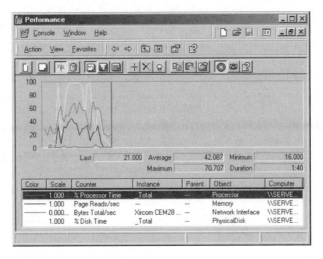

Figure 13.11 System Monitor snap-in charting counter values in graph view

As Figure 13.11 illustrates, there are three main areas in the System Monitor interface: the graph area, the legend, and the value bar.

Graph Area

You can choose to have data updated automatically or on demand. For updating on demand, use the Update Data button (camera toolbar icon) to start and stop the collection intervals. Click the Clear Display button (the second toolbar icon from the left) to remove all data from the display. To add counters to the graph, click the Add button (plus sign toolbar icon) and select the counters from the Add Counters dialog box.

The movement of the timer bar (vertical line in Figure 13.11) across the graph indicates the passing of each update interval. Regardless of the update interval, the view will show up to 100 samples. System Monitor compresses log data as necessary to fit it in the display. To see the compressed data in a log, click the Properties button (the fourth toolbar icon from the right), click the Source tab, select a log file, and then select a shorter time range. Shorter time ranges contain less data, so it is less likely that data points will be eliminated.

You can also define the following attributes of the graph:

- Type of display, with options for graph, histogram, or report
- Background color of the detail pane and of the data display area
- Size, type, and style of font used to show text in the display
- Color, width, and style of line used to chart data

To draw attention to a particular counter's data, use the highlighting feature. To do so, press Ctrl+H or click the Highlight button (light bulb toolbar icon), on the toolbar. When highlighting is in effect, the bar or line representing data for the selected counter changes color to white for most background colors (including the default color) or black for white or light-colored backgrounds.

Note Default key settings in Microsoft Word may conflict with the Ctrl+H combination used for System Monitor highlighting. You might need to change these to support highlighting when the System Monitor control, %systemroot%\System32\Sysmon.ocx, is used in Microsoft Word.

Legend

The names and associated information for the counters you select are shown in the legend, the set of columns beneath the graph. The legend displays the following information:

- **Object** An *object* is a logical collection of counters associated with a resource or service that can be monitored.

- **Counter** A *counter* is a data item associated with an object. For each counter selected, System Monitor presents a value corresponding to a particular aspect of the performance defined for the object.

- **Instance** An *object instance* is a term used to distinguish between multiple occurrences of the same counter on a computer. Note that by default counter instances are listed by name and numerical index. This index appears after the instance name, represented by a pound sign (#) and a number. This index makes it easier to monitor multiple instances, for example, when you are monitoring threads of a process. To turn off the index display, click the Properties button and clear the Allow Duplicate Counter Instances check box.

You can sort entries in ascending or descending order by object, counter, instance, or computer by clicking the appropriate column name in the counter legend. For example, to sort all counters by name, click Counter.

Note To match a line in a graph with the counter it is charting values for, double-click a position in the graph line. The counter will be selected in the legend. If chart lines are close together, try to find a point in the graph where they diverge. Otherwise, System Monitor might not be able to pinpoint the value you are interested in.

Value Bar

The value bar is located beneath the graph area and above the legend. The value bar contains the Last, Average, Minimum, and Maximum values for the counter currently selected. The values are calculated over the time period and number of samples displayed in the graph, not over the time that has elapsed since monitoring was started. The Duration value in the value bar indicates the total elapsed time displayed in the graph (based on the update interval).

Monitoring System and Network Performance

Network activity can influence the performance not only of your network components but of your system as a whole. You should monitor other resources along with network activity, such as disk, memory, and processor activity. System Monitor enables you to track network and system activity by using a single tool.

You should use the following counters as part of your normal monitoring configuration:

- Cache\Data Map Hits %
- Cache\Fast Reads/sec
- Cache\Lazy Write Pages/sec
- Logical Disk\% Disk Space
- Memory\Available Bytes
- Memory\Nonpaged Pool Allocs
- Memory\Nonpaged Pool Bytes
- Memory\Paged Pool Allocs
- Memory\Paged Pool Bytes
- Processor(_Total)\% Processor Time
- System\Context Switches/sec
- System\Processor Queue Length
- Processor(_Total)\Interrupts/sec

Monitoring network activity with System Monitor involves examining performance data at each network layer, as defined in the Open Systems Interconnect (OSI) model. System Monitor provides performance objects for collection of data that reflects transmission rates, packet queue lengths, and other network performance data.

Note Because of the overhead of the protocol headers, actual transmission rates might differ from the rates specified for the wire or line in use.

The following table provides information about the network layers and their associated performance objects.

OSI layer	Performance objects
Application, Presentation Session	Browser, Server, Redirector, and Server Work Queues NBT Connection. (NBT is an abbreviation for NetBT, which means NetBIOS over TCP/IP; NetBIOS stands for network basic input/output system.)
Transport	Protocol objects: TCP for the Transmission Control Protocol; UDP for the User Datagram Protocol, NetBEUI for NetBIOS, AppleTalk (installed by protocol).
Network	Network Segment (installed when you install the Network Monitor driver), IP for the Internet Protocol, NWLink IPX/SPX for the Microsoft implementation of Internetwork Packet Exchange/Sequenced Packet Exchange (IPX/SPX). NWLink performance objects display only zeros for counters that report on frame activity. On systems running Windows NT 4.0, installing the Network Monitor Agent also installs the Network Segment counters.
Data Link, Physical	Network Interface. These counters are maintained by the driver and can report inaccurate or zero values because of problems with implementation of counters by the driver.

When monitoring performance data for your network, you should begin with the lowest-level components and work your way up. Monitor the objects over periods ranging from days to weeks to a month. Using this data, determine a *performance baseline,* the level of performance you expect under typical workloads and usage. A performance baseline gives you a point from which to compare performance over time to identify growth trends, changing demands, or the emergence of a bottleneck. If performance within the baseline range becomes unsatisfactory, tune the network.

As with other resources, establish a baseline for network performance. When performance data is incompatible with your baseline values, investigate the cause. Abnormal network counter values on a server often indicate problems with the server's memory, processor, or disks. For that reason, the best approach to monitoring a server is to watch network counters in conjunction with Processor\% Processor Time, PhysicalDisk\% Disk Time, and Memory\Pages/sec.

For example, if a dramatic increase in Pages/sec is accompanied by a decrease in Bytes Total/sec handled by a server, the computer is probably running short of physical memory for network operations. Most network resources, including network adapters and protocol software, use unpaged memory. If a computer is paging excessively, it could be because most of its physical memory has been allocated to network activities, leaving a small amount of memory for processes that use paged memory. To verify this situation, check the computer's system event log for entries indicating that it has run out of paged or unpaged memory. Also monitor the unpaged pool memory and overall memory counters.

Disk Objects and the Diskperf Utility

Two primary disk objects contain counters in System Monitor, the PhysicalDisk, and LogicalDisk objects. The physical disk performance counters are enabled and the logical disk performance counters are disabled by default on Windows 2000 Server. The logical disk performance counters are enabled using the Diskperf command line utility. Use the diskperf -yv command to enable Logical Disk performance counters.

After this command is run, the computer must be rebooted. On reboot, the logical disk and physical disk performance counters will start. These counters are contained in the System Monitor–PhysicalDisk and LogicalDisk objects respectively.

There is a small performance cost for running these counters. If you are not monitoring disk performance, type **diskperf -n** to disable both disk objects and their counters.

You can selectively enable or disable both physical and logical disk performance counters using Diskperf.

Performance Logs and Alerts Snap-In

With Performance Logs And Alerts, you can collect performance data automatically from local or remote computers. You can view logged counter data by using System Monitor, or you can export the data to spreadsheet programs or databases for analysis and report generation. Note that, because logging runs as a service, data collection can occur regardless of whether any user is logged on to the computer being monitored.

The Performance Logs And Alerts snap-in allows you to perform the following tasks:

- Collect data in a comma-delimited or tab-separated format for easy import to spreadsheet programs. A binary log-file format is also provided for circular logging or for logging instances such as threads or processes that might begin after the log starts collecting data. (Circular logging is the process of continuously logging data to a single file, overwriting previous data with new data.)

- View counter data during collection and after collection has stopped.

- Define start and stop times, file names, file sizes, and other parameters for automatic log generation.

- Manage multiple logging sessions from a single console window.

- Set an alert on a counter, thereby stipulating that a message be sent, a program be run, or a log be started when the selected counter's value exceeds or falls below a specified setting.

Similar to System Monitor, Performance Logs And Alerts supports the following: 1) defining performance objects, performance counters, and object instances and 2) setting sampling intervals for monitoring data about hardware resources and system services. Performance Logs And Alerts also offers these other options related to recording performance data:

- Starting and stopping logging—either manually on demand or automatically based on a user-defined schedule.

- Creating trace logs. Using the default system data provider or another provider, trace logs record data when certain activities such as disk I/O operations or page faults occur. When the event occurs, the provider sends the data to the Performance Logs And Alerts service. This recording and sending data differs from the operation of counter logs; when counter logs are in use, the service obtains data from the system when the update interval has elapsed, rather than waiting for a specific event. A parsing tool is required to interpret the trace log output. Developers can create such a tool using application programming interfaces (APIs) provided on the Microsoft Web site, *http://msdn.microsoft.com/*.

- Defining a program that runs when a log is stopped.

- Configuring additional settings for automatic logging, such as automatic file renaming, and setting parameters for stopping and starting a log based on the elapsed time or the file size.

Note You can work with data from a log file while the service is collecting data and has the log file locked. For example, Microsoft Excel can import an active log file, but it will open a read-only version of the locked log.

Performance Logs And Alerts Interface

In Performance Logs And Alerts, you can define settings for counter logs, trace logs, and alerts. The details pane of the console window shows logs and alerts that you have created (Figure 13.12).

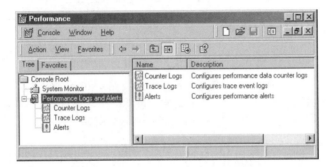

Figure 13.12 Logs and alerts in the Performance Logs And Alerts snap-in

You can define multiple logs or alerts to run simultaneously. Each log or alert is a saved configuration that you define. If you have configured the log for automatic starting and stopping, a single log can generate many individual log data files. For example, if you were generating a log file for each day's activity, one file would close at 11:59 P.M. today, and a new file would open at 12:00 A.M. tomorrow.

The following table explains the query summary information provided by the columns in the details pane.

Column	Description
Name	This is the name of the log or alert. Think of this as a "friendly name" describing the type of data you are collecting or the condition you are monitoring. One log can generate multiple log files. Note that a sample log file, named System Overview, has been predefined for counter logging. You can start logging by using this file or by defining your own settings as appropriate.
Comment	This can be any descriptive information about the log or alert.

Column	Description
Log File Type	This is the log-file format you define. For alert, the type will always be alerts; for trace logs, it will always be sequential. For logs, this can be binary, binary circular, text-CSV (for comma-delimited text), or text-TSV (for tab-delimited text).
Log File Name	This is the path and base file name you defined for the files generated by this log. The base file name is used for automatically naming new files.

To see the parameters defined for each log, select the log name in the details pane and then select Properties from the Action menu. In the dialog box that appears, you can choose how to name your log files, when logging is scheduled to occur, and what performance objects and counters you want to monitor in your log.

If a log is currently running and collecting data (based on the schedule you defined for the log or alert), a green data icon appears next to the log or alert. If a red icon appears, the log or alert has been defined but is not currently running.

Note You can configure more than one type of log to run at a time. One log can generate multiple log files if the restart option is selected or if you start and stop the log multiple times. However, you will not see these individual log files listed in the console window. Use Windows Explorer to view a listing of these files.

Lesson Summary

The Performance tool in the Administrative Tools program group contains two utilities for monitoring resource usage on your computer: the System Monitor snap-in and the Performance Logs And Alerts snap-in. System Monitor allows you to measure the performance of your own computer or other computers on a network. With System Monitor, you can collect and view extensive data about the usage of hardware resources and the activity of system services on computers you administer. There are three main areas in the System Monitor interface: the graph area, the legend, and the value bar. System Monitor provides performance objects for collection of data that reflects transmission rates, packet queue lengths, and other network performance data. Each object is a logical collection of counters. For each counter selected, System Monitor presents a value corresponding to a particular aspect of the performance defined for the performance object. With Performance Logs And Alerts, you can collect performance data automatically from local or remote computers. Similar to System Monitor, Performance Logs And Alerts allows you to define performance objects, performance counters, and object instances and set sampling intervals for monitoring data about hardware resources and system services. In Performance Logs And Alerts, you define settings for counter logs, trace logs, and alerts. The details pane of the console window shows logs and alerts that you have created.

Lesson 4: Network Monitor

Unlike System Monitor, which is used to monitor anything from hardware to software, Network Monitor focuses exclusively on network activity. Network Monitor allows you to view network activity and detect problems on a network. For example, you can use Network Monitor to diagnose hardware and software problems when two or more computers cannot communicate. You can also copy a log of network activity into a file and then send the file to a professional network analyst or support organization. Network application developers can use Network Monitor to monitor and debug network applications as they are developed.

After this lesson, you will be able to

- Use Network Monitor to capture and display network frames

Estimated lesson time: 35 minutes

Overview of Network Monitor

Network Monitor tracks network throughput in terms of captured network traffic. Network Monitor monitors traffic only on the local network segment. To monitor remote traffic, you must use the version of Network Monitor that ships with Microsoft Systems Management Server (SMS) version 1.2 or 2.0.

Network Monitor monitors the network data stream, which consists of all information transferred over a network at any given time. Prior to transmission, this information is divided by the network software into smaller pieces, called frames or packets. Each frame contains the following information:

- The source address of the computer that sent the message

- The destination address of the computer that received the frame

- Headers from each protocol used to send the frame

- The data or a portion of the information being sent

- A trailer that usually contains a CRC to verify frame integrity

The process by which Network Monitor copies frames is referred to as *capturing*. You can use Network Monitor to capture all local network traffic or you can single out a subset of frames to be captured. You can also make a capture respond to events on your network. For example, you can make the network start an executable file when Network Monitor detects a particular set of conditions on the network. This is similar to the system Alerts feature in the Performance Logs And Alerts snap-in.

After you have captured data, you can view it in the Network Monitor user interface. Network Monitor does much of the data analysis for you by translating the raw capture data into its logical frame structure.

For security, Windows 2000 Network Monitor captures only those frames, including broadcast and multicast frames, sent to or from the local computer. Network Monitor also displays overall network segment statistics for broadcast frames, multicast frames, network use, total bytes received per second, and total frames received per second.

To help protect your network from unauthorized use of Network Monitor installations, Network Monitor can detect other installations of Network Monitor that are running on the local segment of your network. Network Monitor also detects all instances of the Network Monitor driver being used remotely (by either Network Monitor from Systems Management Server or the Network Segment object in System Monitor) to capture data on your network.

When Network Monitor detects other Network Monitor installations running on the network, it displays the following information:

- The name of the computer
- The name of the user logged on at the computer
- The state of Network Monitor on the remote computer (running, capturing, or transmitting)
- The adapter address of the remote computer
- The version number of Network Monitor on the remote computer

In some instances, your network architecture might prevent one installation of Network Monitor from detecting another. For example, if an installation is separated from yours by a router that does not forward multicasts, your installation cannot detect that installation.

Network Monitor uses a network driver interface specification (NDIS) feature to copy all frames it detects to its capture buffer, a resizable storage area in memory. The default size is 1 MB; however, you can adjust the size manually as needed. The buffer is a memory-mapped file and occupies disk space.

Note Because Network Monitor uses the local-only mode of NDIS instead of promiscuous mode (in which the network adapter passes on all frames sent on the network), you can use Network Monitor even if your network adapter does not support promiscuous mode. Networking performance is not affected when you use an NDIS driver to capture frames. (Putting the network adapter in promiscuous mode can add 30 percent or more to the load on the CPU.)

Installing Network Monitor Tools

Network Monitor Tools include both the Network Monitor console and the Network Monitor driver. These tools are not installed by default on Windows 2000 Server. You can install them from the Control Panel Add/Remove Windows Programs application. From the Add/Remove Programs window, choose Add/Remove Windows Components and from the Windows Components wizard that appears, choose Management And Monitoring Tools. The Management And Monitoring Tools item contains Network Monitor Tools. Once installed, the Network Monitor console appears in the Administrative Tools program group and Network Monitor Driver is listed in the Local Area Connection Properties dialog box.

Capturing Frame Data

To capture frame data, Network Monitor and the Network Monitor driver must be installed on your Windows 2000 computer. The Network Monitor driver (also called the Network Monitor agent) enables Network Monitor to receive frames from a network adapter and allows the Network Monitor provided with SMS to capture and display frames from a remote computer, including those with a dial-up network connection. When the user of a computer running SMS Network Monitor connects remotely to a computer on which the Network Monitor driver has been installed, and that user initiates a capture, network statistics are captured locally on the computer running the network monitor driver and the data from the capture is viewed from the managing computer.

Note Network Monitor drivers for other Windows operating systems other than Windows 2000 are provided with SMS. When you install Network Monitor on a Windows 2000 computer, the Network Monitor driver is automatically installed.

To capture data, open Network Monitor and select Start from the Capture menu. As frames are captured from the network, statistics about the frames are displayed in the Network Monitor Capture window, as shown in Figure 13.13.

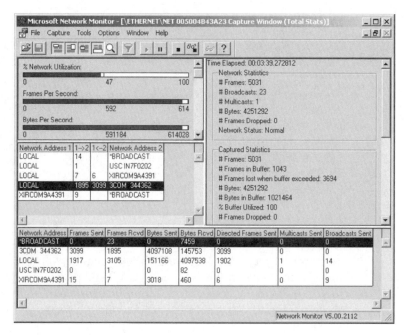

Figure 13.13 Capture window of the Network Monitor interface

Network Monitor displays session statistics from the first 100 unique network sessions it detects. To reset statistics and see information on the next 100 network sessions detected, select Clear Statistics from the Capture menu.

Using Capture Filters

A capture filter functions like a database query. You can use it to specify the types of network information you want to monitor. For example, to see only a specific subset of computers or protocols, you can create an address database, use the database to add addresses to your filter, and then save the filter to a file. By filtering frames, you save both buffer resources and time. Later, if necessary, you can load the capture filter file and use the filter again.

To design a capture filter, specify decision statements in the Capture Filter dialog box (Figure 13.14).

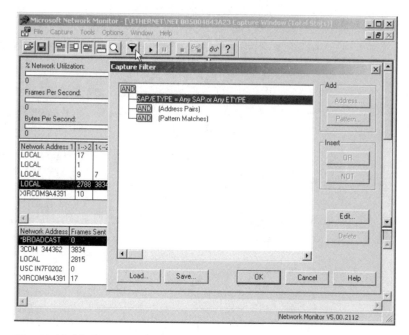

Figure 13.14 Capture Filter dialog box

To open the Capture Filter dialog box, select Filter from the Capture menu, click the funnel toolbar icon (Figure 13.14), or press F8. The dialog box displays the filter's decision tree, which is a graphical representation of a filter's logic. When you include or exclude information from your capture specifications, the decision tree reflects these specifications.

Filtering by Protocol

To capture frames that use a specific protocol, specify the protocol on the SAP/ETYPE= line of the capture filter. For example, to capture only IP frames, disable all protocols and then enable IP ETYPE 0x800 and IP SAP 0x6. By default, all the protocols that Network Monitor supports are enabled.

Filtering by Address

To capture frames from specific computers on your network, specify one or more address pairs in a capture filter. You can monitor up to four specific address pairs simultaneously.

An address pair consists of the following:

- The addresses of the two computers between which you want to monitor traffic between

- Arrows that specify the traffic direction you want to monitor

- The INCLUDE or EXCLUDE keyword, indicating how Network Monitor should respond to a frame that meets a filter's specifications

Regardless of the sequence in which statements appear in the Capture Filter dialog box, EXCLUDE statements are evaluated first. Therefore, if a frame meets the criteria specified in an EXCLUDE statement in a filter containing both an EXCLUDE and INCLUDE statement, that frame is discarded. Network Monitor does not test that frame by INCLUDE statements to see if it also meets that criterion.

Filtering by Data Pattern

By specifying a pattern match in a capture filter, you can:

- Limit a capture to only those frames containing a specific pattern of ASCII or hexadecimal data

- Specify how many bytes (offsets) into the frame the pattern must occur

When you filter based on a pattern match at a specific point in the data, you must specify where the pattern occurs in the frame (how many bytes from the beginning or end). If your network medium uses variable-sized frames, specify to begin counting in for a pattern match from the end of the topology header.

Displaying Captured Data

To simplify data analysis, Network Monitor interprets raw data collected during the capture and displays it in the Capture window. To display captured information in the Capture window, click Stop And View on the Capture menu while the capture is running. You can also display the Capture window by opening a file with the .cap extension. If you have stopped a capture, you can view the data in the Capture window by selecting Display Captured Data from the Capture menu, clicking the glasses toolbar icon, or pressing F12.

Figure 13.15 shows the key elements in the Capture window.

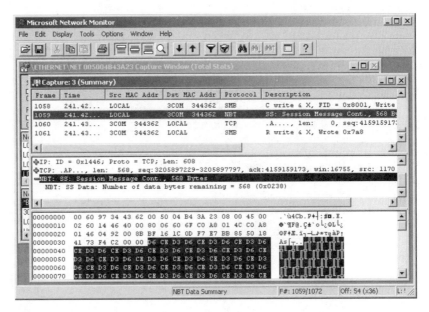

Figure 13.15 Capture window in Network Monitor

Using Display Filters

You can use a display filter to determine which frames to display. Like a capture filter, a display filter functions like a database query, allowing you to single out specific types of information. But because a display filter operates on data that has already been captured, it does not affect the contents of the Network Monitor capture buffer.

You can filter a frame by the following information:

- The source or destination address of the frame

- The protocols used to send the frame

- The properties and values contained in the frame (A property is a data field within a protocol header. A protocol's properties indicate the purpose of the protocol.)

The capture window must have the focus in Network Monitor for the Display Filter dialog box to appear. Figure 13.16 shows the Display Filter dialog box, which is accessed from the Display menu, by pressing F8, or by clicking the funnel toolbar icon.

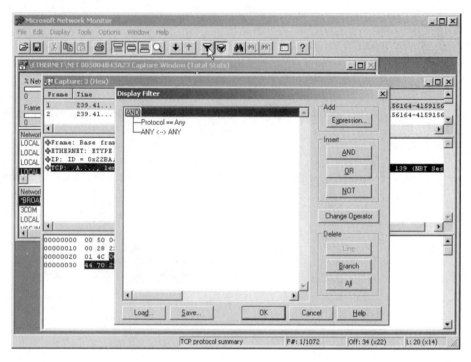

Figure 13.16 Display Filter dialog box

To design a display filter, specify decision statements in the Display Filter dialog box. Information in the Display Filter dialog box is in the form of a decision tree, which is a graphical representation of a filter's logic. When you modify display filter specifications, the decision tree reflects these modifications. You must click OK to save the specified decision statement and add it to the decision tree before adding another decision statement.

Although capture filters are limited to four address filter expressions, display filters are not. With display filters, you can also use AND, OR, and NOT logic. When you display captured data, all available information about the captured frames appears in the Frame Viewer window. To display only those frames sent by a specific protocol, edit the Protocol line in the Display Filter dialog box.

Protocol properties are information that defines a protocol's purpose. Because the purpose of protocols varies, properties differ from one protocol to another. Suppose, for example, that you have captured a large number of frames that use the SMB protocol, but you want to examine only those frames in which the SMB protocol was used to create a directory on your computer. In this instance, you can single out frames where the SMB command property is equal to the Make Directory command.

When you display captured data, all addresses from which information was captured appear in the Frame Viewer window. To display only those frames originating from a specific computer, edit the ANY < – > ANY line in the Display Filter dialog box.

Network Monitor Performance Issues

Network Monitor creates a memory-mapped file for its capture buffer. For best results, make sure you create a capture buffer large enough to accommodate the traffic you need.

In addition, although you cannot adjust the frame size, you can store only part of the frame, thereby reducing the amount of wasted capture buffer space. For example, if you are interested only in the data in the frame header, set the frame size (in bytes) to the size of the header frame. Network Monitor discards the frame data as it stores frames in the capture buffer, thereby using less capture buffer space.

Running Network Monitor in the background is a way to reduce the amount of system resources necessary to operate the program. To run Network Monitor in the background, choose Dedicated Capture Mode from the Capture menu. This is one strategy to reduce resource use if network packets are being dropped rather than captured.

Lesson Summary

Network Monitor allows you to view and detect problems on networks. It tracks network throughput in terms of captured network traffic. Network Monitor monitors the network data stream on the local segment, which consists of all information transferred over the network segment at any given time. To capture frame data, Network Monitor and the Network Monitor driver must be installed on your Windows 2000 computer. The Network Monitor driver enables Network Monitor to receive frames from a network adapter. A capture filter functions like a database query. You can use it to specify the types of network information you want to monitor. To simplify data analysis, Network Monitor interprets raw data collected during the capture and displays it in the Frame Viewer window. You can use a display filter to specify what information you want to view in the Frame Viewer window. Like a capture filter, a display filter functions like a database query, allowing you to single out specific types of information.

Lesson 5: Task Manager

Windows Task Manager provides summary information about computer performance as well as about programs and processes running on the computer. By using Task Manager, you can end programs or processes, start programs, and view a dynamic display of your computer's performance.

After this lesson, you will be able to

- Use Task Manager to manage applications and tasks
- Use Task Manager to view computer performance

Estimated lesson time: 20 minutes

Overview of Task Manager

Task Manager provides information about programs and processes running on your computer. It also displays the most commonly used performance measures for processes.

You can use Task Manager to monitor key indicators of your computer's performance. You can quickly see the status of programs that are running and end programs that have stopped responding. You can also assess the activity of running processes by viewing many critical data points, and you can see graphs and data on CPU and memory usage.

To open Task Manager, right-click an empty space on the taskbar and then click Task Manager. You can also open Task Manager by pressing Ctrl+Alt+Delete and then clicking the Task Manager button. The Task Manager interface contains three tabs: Applications, Processes, and Performance. You can change the display options for each tab by selecting the option you want from the View menu. Many of the View menu options are specific to the selected tab.

To update Task Manager data, click Refresh Now on the View menu. You can also change the frequency at which the data is automatically updated. On the View menu, click Update Speed and then click the option that you want. To temporarily freeze the data displayed by Task Manager, click Update Speed on the View menu and then click Paused.

Applications Tab

The Applications tab shows the status of the programs running on your computer (Figure 13.17). On this tab, you can start a new program (New Task button), end a program (End Task button), or switch to another program (Switch To button).

Figure 13.17 Applications tab of Task Manager

Using Task Manager to start a program is identical to using the Run command on the Start menu. If a program stops responding, press Ctrl+Alt+Delete to start Task Manager, select the program that is not responding, and then click End Task. Any data entered or changes made that were not saved will be lost.

Processes Tab

The Processes tab shows information about the processes running on your computer (Figure 13.18). For example, you can display information on CPU and memory usage, page faults, handle count, and a number of other parameters.

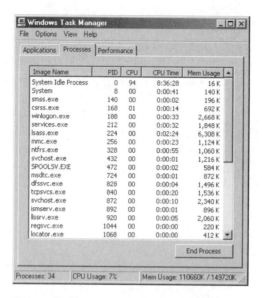

Figure 13.18 Processes tab of Task Manager

On the Processes tab, you can sort the list of processes and display other process counters. For a description of each type of counter that you can monitor, see Task Manager Help. To see the available process counters, click the Processes tab and then choose Select Columns from the View menu.

You can also end a process on the Processes tab. However, be careful when ending a process. If you end an application, you will lose unsaved data. If you end a system service, some part of the system might not function properly.

Note Task Manager does not allow you to end a process that is critical to the operation of Windows 2000. Utilities on the Windows 2000 Resource Kit will allow you to end critical processes. However, this procedure is likely to cause operating system instability.

You can end a process plus all processes directly or indirectly created by it. Right-click the process you want to end, and then click End Process Tree. For example, if you end the process tree for an e-mail program such as Microsoft Outlook 98, you will also end related processes such as mapisp32.exe and the MAPI spooler.

The Processes tab also allows you to assign a process to a processor by using the Set Affinity command. However, this command is available only on multiprocessor computers. Using the Set Affinity command limits the execution of the process to the selected processors and could decrease overall performance. In addition, the Process tab allows you to change the priority of a running program. Changing the priority of a process can make it run faster or slower, depending on whether you raise or lower the priority, and it can also adversely affect the performance of other processes. If you have installed a debugger, the debug command can be launched directly from the context menu of a running process appearing under the Processes tab.

Performance Tab

The Performance tab displays a dynamic overview of your computer's performance (Figure 13.19). This view includes graphs for CPU and memory usage; totals for the number of handles, threads, and processes running on the computer; and totals, in kilobytes, for physical, kernel, and commit memory.

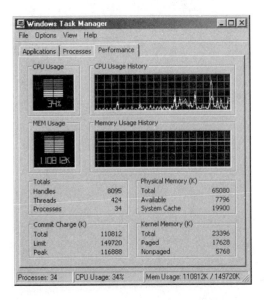

Figure 13.19 Performance tab of Task Manager

If you select the Show Kernel Times option from the View menu, a red line is added to the CPU Usage graph and to the CPU Usage History graph. The red lines indicate the amount of CPU resources consumed by kernel operations.

Lesson Summary

Task Manager provides information about programs and processes running on your computer. It also displays the most commonly used performance measures for processes. The Task Manager interface contains three tabs: Applications, Processes, and Performance. The Applications tab shows the status of the programs running on your computer. The Processes tab shows information about the processes running on your computer. The Performance tab displays a dynamic overview of your computer's performance.

Review

The following questions are intended to reinforce key information presented in this chapter. If you are unable to answer a question, review the appropriate lesson and then try the question again. Answers to the questions can be found in Appendix A, "Questions and Answers."

1. You have used the Compact utility to compress the files contained in the Users subfolders on an NTFS partition. You have enabled the Folder Option, Display Compressed Files And Folders With Alternate Color. A week later you use Windows Explorer to see if files are being compressed. To your surprise, user account subfolders, located directly under the Users folder created after you ran the compress utility, are not compressed. Why did this happen and how can you fix it?

2. Your department has recently archived several GB of data from a computer running Windows 2000 Server to CD-ROMs. As users have added files to the server, you have noticed that the server has been taking longer than usual to gain access to the hard disk. How can you decrease disk access time for the server?

3. You are the administrator for a computer running Windows 2000 Server that is used to store user's home folders and roaming user profiles. You want to restrict users to 25 MB of available storage for their home folder while monitoring, but not limiting, the disk space used for the roaming user profiles. How should you configure the volumes on the server?

4. You notice that a new server is not performing as well as you expected. You need to obtain summary information on a server's performance, and then you want to use a utility to obtain detailed reports of performance bottlenecks. After you have resolved the performance problem, what should you do to track the performance of the server as more users begin to access the server?

5. You want to filter out all network traffic except for traffic between two computers, and you also want to locate specific data within the packets. Which Network Monitor filter features should you specify?

6. You goal is to make sure that only two network management stations in your organization are able to communicate with the SNMP agents. What measures can you take when configuring the SNMP service to enhance security?

CHAPTER 14

Microsoft Windows 2000 Application Servers

About This Chapter

Microsoft Windows 2000 Server supports a number of services that extend the functionality of the Windows 2000 operating system. This chapter focuses on several of these services, including Internet Information Services (IIS), Telnet services, and Terminal Services. The chapter also provides the information necessary to implement each of these services into a Windows 2000 environment and administer that service once it is implemented.

Before You Begin

To complete the lessons in this chapter, you must have

- Server01 and Server02 running Windows 2000 Server.
- Completed the exercises in the previous chapters.

Lesson 1: Exploring Microsoft Internet Information Services 5.0 Features

Windows 2000 Server includes an updated version of IIS (version 5.0). IIS runs as an enterprise service within Windows 2000 and uses other services provided by Windows 2000, such as security and Active Directory services. IIS 5.0 improves the Web server's reliability, performance, management, security, and application services. Many of these improvements result from the way IIS 5.0 incorporates new operating system features in Windows 2000. This lesson provides an overview of IIS 5.0 and explains how to install IIS and configure a Web environment.

After this lesson, you will be able to

- Install IIS 5.0 and configure a Web environment

Estimated lesson time: 40 minutes

Introduction to Microsoft IIS 5.0

While IIS 4.0 focused on security, administration, programmability, and support for Internet standards, IIS 5.0 builds on these capabilities to deliver the type of Web sites required in an increasingly intranet- and Internet-centric business environment. In particular, IIS 5.0 has been improved in the following four areas: reliability and performance, management, security, and application environment.

Reliability and Performance

IIS 5.0 performs better and is more reliable than previous versions of the product for a number of reasons. Internally, the speed of the IIS 5.0 engine has been increased through coding refinements. The new Reliable Restart feature lets system administrators quickly restart the server. Beyond these inherent capabilities, this version introduces features you can use to improve the speed and reliability of Web sites.

One of the more significant improvements in IIS 5.0 is the addition of application protection through support for pooled, out-of-process applications. To better control resource consumption, new throttling features (based on the new job object feature of Windows 2000) make it easier for administrators to allocate the amount of CPU bandwidth available to processes, as well as the amount of network bandwidth available to sites. In addition, the new Socket Pooling feature allows multiple sites sharing a port also to share a set of sockets.

Application Protection

Most operating systems view a process as a unit of work in a system. Services and applications are processes that run in memory areas allocated by the operating system to each process. In IIS 5.0, application protection refers to the way in which the operating system guards each application process from other processes in memory. In earlier versions of IIS, all Internet Server API (ISAPI) applications (including ASP technology) shared the resources and memory of the IIS server process. Although this provided fast performance, unstable components could cause the IIS server to hang or crash, which made it more difficult to develop and debug new components. In addition, in-process components could not be unloaded unless the server was restarted—which meant that modifying existing components would affect all sites that shared the same IIS server, whether they were directly affected by the upgrade or not.

As a first step toward addressing these issues, IIS 4.0 allowed applications to run either in the same IIS server process (Inetinfo.exe) or out-of-process, that is in a process separate from the IIS server process. The DLLHost.exe acts as a surrogate application to the IIS server process to manage each out-of-process application. Out-of-process applications are run separately from one another which is memory intensive and less efficient than running in-process. In IIS 5.0, there is a third option: applications can be run in a pooled process separate from the IIS server process. This approach allows related applications to be run together without adversely affecting the IIS server process. These three options provide varying levels of protection, each of which impacts performance. Greater isolation comes at the cost of slower performance.

Reliable Restart

In the event of a system failure, it's clearly important to be able to get IIS back to an operational state as quickly as possible. In the past, rebooting was an acceptable, although not optimal, way to restart IIS. To reliably restart IIS, an administrator needed to start up four separate services after every stoppage, and was required to have specialized knowledge, such as which services to start and in what order. To avoid this, Windows 2000 includes IIS Reliable Restart, which is a faster, easier, more flexible one-step restart process.

Socket Pooling

IIS 5.0 increases performance by adding the ability to optimize access to your Web site. A socket is a protocol identifier for a particular node on a network. The socket consists of a node address and a port number, which identifies the service. For example, port 80 on an Internet node represents the World Wide Web HTTP service on a Web server.

In IIS 4.0, each Web site is bound to a different IP address, which means that each site has its own socket that is not shared with sites bound to other IP addresses. Each sockets is created when the site starts, and consumes significant non-paged memory (RAM). This memory consumption limits the number of sites bound to IP addresses that can be created on a single machine.

For IIS 5.0, this process has been modified so that sites bound to different IP addresses but sharing the same port number can now share the same set of sockets. The end result is that more sites can be bound to an IP address on the same machine than in IIS 4.0. In IIS 5.0, these shared sockets are used flexibly among all of the started sites, thus reducing resource consumption.

Multisite Hosting

To improve the scalability of IIS, Windows 2000 Server supports the ability to host multiple Web sites on a single server. This can save the time and money required within a company that wants to host different sites for different departments, or for an ISP hosting multiple sites for different customers.

The key to hosting multiple sites on a single server is the ability to distinguish between them. This can be done in several ways, each using the Web site's identification. Each Web site has a unique, three-part identity it uses to receive and to respond to requests: a port number, an IP address, and a host header name. With IIS 5.0, companies can host multiple Web sites on a single server by using one of three techniques: assigning different ports, assigning different IP addresses, or assigning different host header names. Each Web site can share two out of three unique characteristics and still be identified as a unique site.

Note IIS 4.0 also allows you to host multiple Web sites on a single server.

Process Throttling

If you run multiple Web sites that primarily use HTML pages on one computer, or if you have other applications running on the same computer as your Web server, you can limit how much processor time a Web site's applications are permitted to use. This can help ensure that processor time is available to other Web sites or applications unrelated to IIS.

Bandwidth Throttling

If the network or Internet connection used by your Web server is also used by other services such as e-mail or news, you may want to limit the bandwidth used by your Web server in order to free up bandwidth for other services. Bandwidth Throttling is an improved feature in IIS 5.0 that allows administrators to regulate the amount of server bandwidth each site uses by throttling the available bandwidth for the net card. For example, this allows an ISP to guarantee a predetermined amount of bandwidth to each site.

Note IIS 4.0 allows you to throttle bandwidth on a per-Web site basis.

Management

While IIS 4.0 introduced a significant number of new technologies, a core design goal for IIS 5.0 was to make the Web server easier for managers to use. For example, some administrators found IIS 4.0 difficult to install. With IIS 5.0, the installation process is built right into Windows 2000 Server Setup. In addition, to make it easier to configure security settings, there are three new security wizards. This release also includes improved command-line administration scripts as well as additional built-in management scripts.

Setup and Upgrade Integration

The setup process for IIS 5.0 is integrated with Windows 2000 Server setup, and IIS 5.0 installs by default as a windows component of Windows 2000 Server. In the Windows Components wizard, it is listed as Internet Information Services (IIS). During operating system setup, a wizard helps you either to install a new copy of IIS 5.0 or to upgrade an older version.

IIS creates a default Web site, an Administration Web site, and a Default SMTP Virtual Server when you install Windows 2000 Server. You can add or remove IIS or select additional components, such as the Network News Transfer Protocol (NNTP) Service, by using the Add/Remove Programs application in Control Panel. Then from Add/Remove Programs, start the Windows Components wizard, and click the Details button of the Internet Information Services (IIS) component.

Centralized Administration

IIS 5.0 is managed by using the Internet Information Services snap-in (Figure 14.1), which is integrated with other administrative functions of Windows 2000. (In previous releases this tool was called Internet Service Manager.) You can access the Internet Information Services snap-in through the Internet Information Services snap-in, which is located in the Administrative Tools program group. The Internet Information Services snap-in is also located in the Computer Management snap-in under Services and Applications.

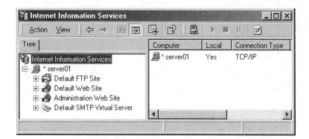

Figure 14.1 Internet Information Services snap-in

The browser-based administration tool, Internet Services Manager (HTML), is no longer available in the Administrative Tools program group, but it is still available to let you remotely administer IIS over an HTTP or HTTPS connection, depending on how you have the Administration Web site configured for security. You can run Internet Services Manager (HTML) by selecting the Administration Web Site node in the console tree of the Internet Information Services snap-in and then clicking Browse from the Action menu. Or you can access it directly by specifying the server name, the TCP port number assigned to the site, and the administration Web site address as shown in the Address field in Figure 14.2.

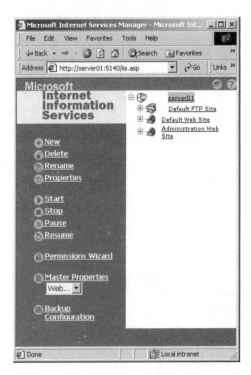

Figure 14.2 Administering IIS on Server01 from a remote computer

---

Note The TCP port number assigned to the administration site is randomly selected and is between 2,000 and 9,999. View the Administration Web site Properties dialog box under the Web Site tab to determine or change the port number assigned to the site.

Browsers other than Microsoft Internet Explorer can be used to access the administration Web site, but basic authentication must be enabled if the browser does not support NTLM authentication and you don't want to enable anonymous access. In addition, you can use Terminal Services to remotely administer IIS by using the Internet Information Services snap-in.

Delegated Administration

To help distribute the workload of administrative tasks, administrators can add administration accounts to the Operators group. Members of the Operators group have limited administration privileges on Web sites. For example, an ISP that hosts sites for a number of different companies can assign delegates from each company as the operators for each company's Web site. Operators can administer properties that affect only their respective sites. They do not have access to properties that affect IIS, the Windows server computer hosting IIS, or the network. This lets an IT or ISP administrator who hosts multiple Web sites on a single server delegate the day-to-day management of the Web site without giving up total administrative control.

Process Accounting

Process Accounting (sometimes referred to as CPU Usage Logging, CPU Accounting, or Job Object Accounting) is a new feature in IIS 5.0 that lets administrators monitor and log how Web sites use CPU resources on the server. Processes Accounting adds fields to the W3C Extended log file to record information about how Web sites use CPU resources on the server. ISPs can use this information to determine which sites are using disproportionately high CPU resources or that may have malfunctioning scripts or Common Gateway Interface (CGI) processes. IT managers can use this information to charge back the cost of hosting a Web site or application to the appropriate division within a company or to determine how to adjust process throttling to control resource utilization.

To enable process accounting on a site using the Internet Information Services snap-in, open the site's property page and from the properties of the W3C Extended Log File Format, choose the Extended Properties tab. In the Internet Service Manager (HTML), follow the same navigation and then choose the Extended Properties link. Figure 14.3 shows the Extended Logging Properties dialog box and the Extended Logging Options Web page.

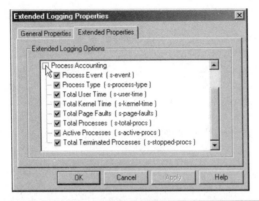

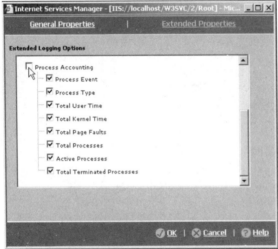

Figure 14.3 Enabling process accounting through the Extended Logging Properties dialog box or through the Extended Logging Options Web page

Improved Command-Line Administration Scripts

IIS 5.0 ships with scripts that can be executed from the command line to automate the management of common Web server tasks. These scripts are located in the \Inetpub\Scripts folder. Administration scripts automate some of the most common administrative tasks. You can use them to create and control Web sites, applications, directories, and more. Administrators can also create custom scripts that automate the management of IIS. Windows Script Host (WSH) is used to run the .vbs administration scripts included in IIS 5.0.

Backing Up and Restoring IIS

The Internet Information Services snap-in includes options that allow you to back up and restore your IIS configuration so that you can save the IIS 5.0 metabase settings to make it easy to return to a safe, known state. By using this method, you can back up and restore your Web server configuration, but not your content files or those settings that remain in the registry.

To back up and restore your Web server configuration, select the IIS computer in Internet Information Services snap-in, and then select the Backup/Restore Configuration option from the Action menu. The Configuration Backup/Restore dialog box appears (Figure 14.4), which allows you to create a backup, restore a backup, or delete a backup that has already been created.

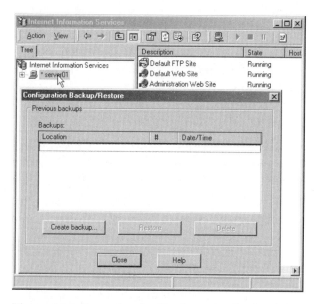

Figure 14.4 Accessing the Configuration Backup/Restore dialog box for Server01

Custom Error Messages

When a user attempts to connect to a Web site and an HTTP error occurs, a generic message is sent back to the client browser with a brief description of what happened during the attempt to establish a connection. As with IIS 4.0, with IIS 5.0 you can send more informative error messages to clients that encounter an ASP or HTML error on your site. You can use the custom error messages that IIS 5.0 provides or create you own.

In IIS 5.0, the custom error messages are stored in %systemroot%\Help\ iisHelp\common folder. In IIS 4.0 custom error messages are stored in the %systemroot%\Help\common folder. The prefix of the custom error message file is the name of the error, and the extension is .htm. If the error message contains a period, such as error 403.3, the corresponding custom message file name contains a hyphen, e.g., 403-3.htm.

Support for FrontPage Server Extensions

Windows 2000 Server allows administrators to use FrontPage Web authoring and management features to deploy and manage Web sites. With FrontPage Server Extensions, administrators can view and manage a Web site in a graphical interface. In addition, authors can create, edit, and post Web pages to IIS remotely. The FrontPage Server Extensions snap-in allows you to administer the FrontPage Server Extensions and FrontPage-extended Web sites.

Unlike previous versions of IIS, FrontPage Web is enabled by default. You can access the FrontPage Extensions snap-in from the Server Extensions Administrator MMC or from the Internet Information Services snap-in. The following two setup features in the FrontPage Server Extensions snap-in are important for initially configuring and checking the extensions:

- **Configuring an existing Web server to use the server extensions** Once a Web site is configured to use server extensions, Web applications that depend on server extensions, like FrontPage, can operate against the Web site.

- **Checking server extension security** This feature allows you to check the security of any Web site or a single Web site running Server Extensions.

In the Internet Information Services snap-in, configuring an existing Web server for server extensions is accomplished by selecting a Web site and then, from the Action menu, pointing to New and clicking the Server Extensions Web option. To check server extension security of all Web sites, choose Internet Information Services in the console tree and then from the Action menu, point to All Tasks and click Check Server Extensions. To check server extensions on a single site, select the site from the console tree, and follow the same navigation procedure as you did to check all sites.

Web Distributed Authoring and Versioning

The Web is a great medium for publishing documents, but until now it hasn't been easy for organizations to use the Internet to let users collaborate on documents. That's because while it is easy to read documents stored on a Web site, it has not been easy for users to make changes to those documents. To address this need, IIS 5.0 has added full support for Web Distributed Authoring and Versioning (WebDAV).

By setting up a WebDAV directory on your Web server, you can let users share documents over the Internet or an intranet. WebDAV in IIS 5.0 takes advantage of the security and file access features provided by Windows 2000, so you can lock and unlock resources to let multiple people read a file, while only one person at a time can modify the file. WebDAV is discussed in more detail in Lesson 2, "Administering A Web Environment."

Distributed File System

IIS 5.0 makes use of the Windows 2000 *distributed file system* (Dfs). Dfs is a means for uniting files on different computers into a single namespace. Dfs lets system administrators build a single, hierarchical view of multiple file servers and file server shares on the network, making it easier for users to access and manage files that are physically distributed across a network. With Dfs, you can make files that are distributed across multiple servers appear to users as if they reside in one place on the network. Users no longer need to know and specify the actual physical location of files in order to access them.

Note For more information on Dfs, see Chapter 5, Lesson 1.

HTTP Compression

HTTP compression allows faster transmission of pages between a Web server and compression-enabled clients. This is useful in situations where bandwidth is limited. Depending on the content you're hosting, your storage space, and the connection speed of your typical Web site visitor, HTTP compression can provide faster transmission of pages between your Web server and compression-enabled browsers.

In the Internet Information Services snap-in, HTTP Compression is enabled from the master properties of the Internet Information Services node. On the Internet Information Services Properties dialog box, click the Edit button for the WWW Service and then choose the Service tab (Figure 14.5).

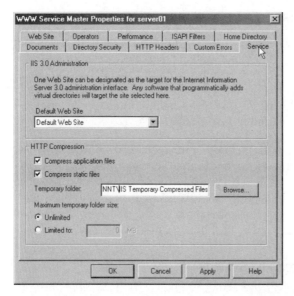

Figure 14.5 WWW Service Master Properties for Server01 as seen from the Internet Information Services snap-in

From the Internet Information Service (HTML) home page, click the Service option under Master Properties. View the service properties and configure compression (Figure 14.6).

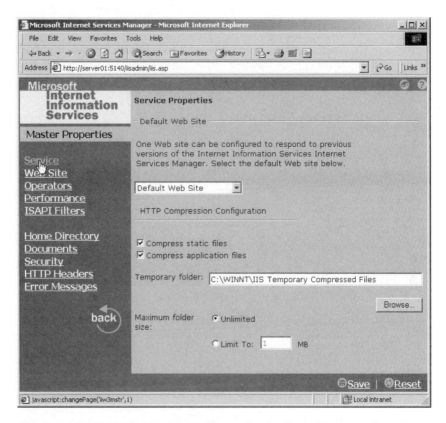

Figure 14.6 WWW Service Master Properties for Server01 as seen from Internet Services Manager (HTML) page

FTP and FTP Restart

The FTP service, an industry standard protocol used to publish information to a Web server, is integrated into Windows 2000 Server. In IIS 5.0, the FTP Restart protocol is also supported by Windows 2000 Server. It provides a faster and smoother way to download information from the Internet. If an interruption occurs during data transfer from an FTP site, the download can continue where it left off, without having to download the entire file again.

Note This feature is available only to FTP clients that support the FTP restart function. The FTP client initiates the REST command to connect and continue a failed download.

Security

Security features, which are an important area of improvement in IIS 5.0, take advantage of the Internet-standard security features that are fully integrated with Windows 2000.

Security Standards

The security protocols supported in IIS 5.0 are described in the following table.

Security	Protocol description
Fortezza	Support for the U.S. government security standard called Fortezza is new in IIS 5.0. Fortezza satisfies the Defense Message System security architecture with a cryptographic mechanism that provides message confidentiality, integrity, authentication, non-repudiation, and access control to messages, components, and systems. These features are implemented both with server and browser software and with PCMCIA card hardware.
Secure Sockets Layer (SSL) 3.0	SSL security protocols are used widely by Internet browsers and servers for authentication, message integrity, and confidentiality. You can configure your Web server's SSL security features to verify the integrity of your content, verify the identity of users, and encrypt network transmissions. SSL relies upon certificates. Microsoft Certificate Services can be used to issue certificates. See Chapter 11, Lesson 1 "Public Key Infrastructure" for additional information on certificates and Certificate Services.
Transport Layer Security (TLS)	TLS is based on SSL. It provides for cryptographic user authentication and provides a way for independent programmers to write TLS-enabled code that can exchange cryptographic information with another process without a programmer needing to be familiar with another programmer's code. In addition, TLS is intended to provide a framework that can be used by new public key and bulk encryption methods as they emerge. TLS also focuses on improving performance by reducing network traffic and providing an optional session caching scheme that can reduce the number of connections that need to be established from scratch.
PKCS #7	This protocol describes the format of encrypted data such as digital signatures or digital envelopes. Both of these are involved in the certificate features of IIS.
PKCS #10	This protocol describes the format of requests for certificates that are submitted to certification authorities.

Security	Protocol description
Basic authentication	Basic Authentication is a part of the HTTP 1.0 specification. It sends passwords over networks in Base64-encoded format. The Basic Authentication method is a widely used, industry-standard method for collecting user name and password information. The advantage of Basic Authentication is that it is part of the HTTP specification, and is supported by most browsers. The disadvantage is that Web browsers using Basic Authentication transmit passwords in an unencrypted form. By monitoring communications on your network, someone could easily intercept and decipher these passwords by using publicly available tools. Therefore, Basic Authentication is not recommended unless you are confident that the connection between the user and your Web server is secure, with a direct cable connection, a dedicated line, or a secure intranet.
Digest authentication	A new feature of IIS 5.0, Digest Authentication offers the same features as Basic Authentication but involves a different method for transmitting the authentication credentials. The authentication credentials pass through a one-way process, often referred to as *hashing*. The result of this process is called a *hash*, or *message digest*, and the original text cannot be deciphered from the hash. The server generates additional information that is added to the password before hashing so no one can capture the password hash and use it to impersonate the true client. This is a shared secret password methodology. This a clear advantage over Basic Authentication, in which the password can be intercepted and used by an unauthorized person. Digest Authentication is structured to be usable across proxy servers and other firewall applications and is available to WebDAV. Because Digest Authentication is a new HTTP 1.1 feature, not all browsers support it. If a non-compliant browser makes a request on a server that requires Digest Authentication, the server will reject the request and send the client an error message. Digest Authentication is supported only for Windows 2000 domains, and Internet Explorer version 5 or later is one of the few browsers that supports this feature.
Integrated Windows Authentication	This authentication method provides NTLM (Windows NT Challenge/Response) authentication for older versions of Internet Explorer 3.0 that use it to cryptographically authenticate with IIS. Integrated Windows Authentication also provides Web sites and new versions of Internet Explorer with Kerberos v5 authentication. Integrated Windows Authentication is only used if Anonymous access is disabled or denied as a result of NTFS permissions restrictions. Integrated Windows Authentication is not supported over Proxy server connections.

Security Mechanisms

IIS 5.0 uses five basic security mechanisms: authentication, certificates, access control, encryption, and auditing.

Authentication

Authentication allows you to confirm the identity of anyone requesting access to your Web sites. IIS supports the following types of authentication for HTTP and FTP services:

- Anonymous FTP and HTTP authentication

- Basic FTP and HTTP authentication

- Digest authentication for Windows 2000 Domains and browsers supporting this HTTP 1.1 authentication method

- Integrated Windows authentication (HTTP only)

Certificates

To complete the authentication process, you need a mechanism for verifying user identities. Certificates are digital identification documents that allow both servers and clients to authenticate each other. They are required for the server and client's browser to set up an SSL connection over which encrypted information can be sent. Server certificates usually contain information about your company and the organization that issued the certificate. Client certificates usually contain identifying information about the user and the organization that issued the certificate.

Access Control

After verifying the identity of a user, you'll want to control their access to resources on your server. IIS 5.0 uses two layers of access control: Web permissions and NTFS permissions. Web permissions apply to all HTTP clients and define access to server resources. NTFS permissions define what level of access individual user accounts have to folders and files on the server.

Encryption

Once you've controlled access to information, you need to protect that information as it passes over the Internet. You can let users exchange private information, such as credit card numbers or phone numbers, with your server in a secure way by using encryption. Encryption scrambles the information before it is sent, and decryption unscrambles it after it is received. The foundation for this encryption is the SSL 3.0 protocol and the emerging TLS 1.0 protocol, which provides a secure way of establishing an encrypted communication link with users. SSL confirms the authenticity of your Web site and, optionally, the identity of users accessing restricted Web sites.

Auditing

The last step to ensuring security is to regularly monitor your site's usage. Administrators can use security auditing techniques to monitor a broad range of user and Web server security activity. Auditing consists of creating auditing policies for directory and file access or server events, and monitoring the security logs to detect any access attempts by unauthorized persons. For more information on auditing, read Chapter 13, Lesson 5 "Windows 2000 Auditing."

Security Wizards

To make it simpler to establish and maintain security settings, IIS 5.0 includes three new security task wizards: the Web Server Certificate wizard, the Permissions wizard, and the Certificate Trust Lists wizard.

The Certificate wizard simplifies certificate administration tasks, such as creating certificate requests and managing the certificate life cycle. The Web Server Certificate wizard is started from the Server Certificate button on the properties of a Web site in the Internet Information Services snap-in.

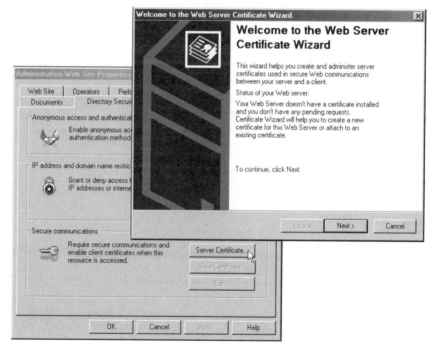

Figure 14.7 Starting the Web Server Certificate wizard on the Properties page of the Administration Web site

Note Using Internet Information Services (HTML) to create a Web server certificate is similar to using the Internet Information Services snap-in; however, there is no HTML-based wizard to walk you through the configuration process.

SSL security is an increasingly common requirement for Web sites that provide e-commerce and access to sensitive business information. The new wizard makes it easy to set up SSL-enabled Web sites on a Windows 2000 Server computer. In addition, this wizard makes it easier to establish and maintain SSL encryption and client certificate authentication.

The Permissions wizard walks administrators through the tasks of setting up permissions and authenticated access on an IIS Web site, making it much easier to set up and manage a Web site that requires authenticated access to its content.

The Permissions wizard is started from the Internet Information Services snap-in. Select either a Web site or FTP site. From the Action menu, point to All Tasks and then click Permissions wizard. Figure 14.8 shows the Permissions Wizard screen started from the Internet Information Services snap-in.

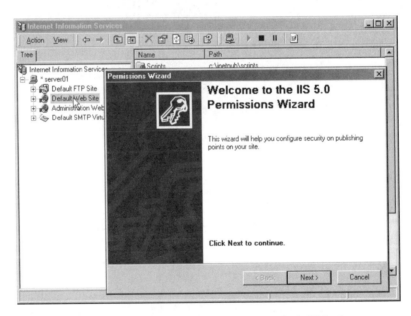

Figure 14.8 Permissions Wizard screen for the Default Web site

The Permissions wizard can also be started from Internet Services Manager (HTML) by selecting a Web or FTP site from the home page and then clicking the Permissions Wizard link in the left frame of the home page, as shown in Figure 14.9.

Figure 14.9 HTML-based Permissions Wizard screen for the Default Web site

The Permissions wizard provides two top-level options:

- Inherited security settings applied to the parent site or virtual directory
- Security settings based on a template

Two templates are available for configuring security: the Public Web Site template and the Secure Web Site template. The Public Web Site template applies security settings that are cross-browser compatible and provide access to the site regardless of whether the user has a Windows 2000 account for the network being accessed. The Secure Web Site template applies security settings that only users with Windows 2000 user accounts can access.

The Certificate Trust List wizard allows administrators to configure certificate trust lists (CTLs). A CTL is a list of trusted certification authorities (CAs) for a particular directory. CTLs are especially useful for ISPs that have several Web sites on their server and who need to have a different list of approved CAs for each site. CTLs are available only at the Web site level and are not available for FTP sites.

After a Server Certificate is configured for the site, the Certificate Trust List wizard is run from the properties of a Web site in the Internet Information Services snap-in. On the Directory Security tab of the Properties dialog box, click the Edit button under Secure Communications to display the Secure Communications dialog box. From this dialog box, select the Enable certificate trust list check box and then click New. The Certificate Trust List wizard appears (Figure 14.10).

Figure 14.10 Navigating to the Certificate Trust List wizard after enabling CTL

You can also enable and configure CTL from the Internet Service Manager (HTML), but there is no corresponding HTML-based wizard. Additionally, you cannot edit the certificates through the HTML interface, but you can edit the certificates from the Internet Information Services snap-in.

Application Environment

IIS 5.0 includes performance enhancements that make it easier to develop Web-enabled applications. The Active Server Pages (ASP) technology within IIS, combined with the data access and component services within Windows 2000 Server, provide a well-rounded application environment.

With this release, enhanced flow control and error handling, Windows Script Host Components, and other improvements make ASP easier to use for script writers and Web application developers. In addition, features such as scriptless ASP, ASP self-tuning, and performance-enhanced objects, as well as improvements within the Windows 2000 operating system, can increase the speed of ASP applications.

ASP is a server-side scripting environment that you can use to create and run dynamic, interactive Web server applications. With ASP, you can combine HTML pages, script commands, and Component Object Model (COM) components to create interactive Web pages or Web-based applications that are easy to deploy and modify. There are a number of new ASP features in IIS 5.0, such as new flow control capabilities and error handling features that make it easier to write and control the behavior of Web applications. Other new features, such as scriptless ASP processing, improve the performance of ASP pages.

Component Services

IIS 5.0 and the Component Services (COM+) included in Windows 2000 Server work together to form a basic architecture for building Web applications. In IIS version 4.0, Microsoft Transaction Server (MTS) provided transaction support. In IIS 5.0 and Windows 2000, Component Services provides all the transaction support of MTS, in addition to a number of other component development and deployment features. IIS uses the functionality provided by Component Services to perform the following tasks:

- Isolate applications into distinct processes

- Manage communication between COM components (including the ASP built-in objects)

- Coordinate transaction processing for transactional ASP applications

Active Directory Services

Active Directory services in Windows 2000 Server is used to store and manage information about networked resources. By providing a centralized store for essential information, Active Directory services simplifies network management, makes it easier for users to find resources, and makes it easier for developers to write applications.

Microsoft Active Directory Service Interfaces (ADSI) is a COM-based directory service model that allows ADSI-compliant client applications to access a wide variety of distinct directory protocols, including Active Directory services, LDAP, and NDS, while using a single, standard set of interfaces. ADSI shields the client application from the implementation and operational details of the underlying data store or protocol.

IIS stores most Internet site configuration information in the IIS metabase. IIS exposes a low-level DCOM interface that allows applications to gain access to and manipulate the metabase. To make it easy to access the metabase, IIS also includes an ADSI provider that wraps most of the functionality provided by the DCOM interface, and exposes it to any ADSI-compliant client applications.

Note For more information about the new features in IIS 5.0, see the Supplemental Course Materials CD-ROM (\chapt14\articles\IISover.doc) that accompanies this book.

Installing IIS 5.0

Internet Information Services 5.0 is a component of the Windows 2000 operating system. Installation and removal of IIS is accomplished in one of three ways: when installing or upgrading Windows 2000, by using the Add/Remove Programs utility in Control Panel, or by using an unattended.txt file during an unattended installation.

When performing a clean installation of Windows 2000 Server, IIS is installed by default. You can remove IIS or select IIS components to be added or removed by using the Add/Remove Programs utility.

When you upgrade from a previous version of Windows 95, Windows 98, or Windows NT to Windows 2000, Setup attempts to detect previous version of IIS, Peer Web Services, or Personal Web Server. If one of these programs is detected, IIS 5.0 is installed. You cannot prevent an upgrade to IIS 5.0 if a previous version of IIS, Peer Web Services, or Personal Web Server is detected. However, IIS 5.0 will not be installed if these legacy services are not detected.

When installing IIS 5.0, either as an upgrade or as a clean install, Setup verifies that the TCP/IP protocol suite is installed. If Setup does not find TCP/IP installed, it automatically installs the protocol suite and configures it to use DHCP.

During the IIS installation, the Default Web site, Administration Web site, Default SMTP Virtual Server, and Default FTP site are created. Managing the Web sites and the FTP site are discussed in more detail in Lesson 2 "Administering a Web Environment."

Note The Default SMTP Virtual Server is beyond the scope of this training. SMTP provides e-mail message delivery support to intranet- and Internet-enabled applications.

Setting Up a Web Environment

Whether your site is on an intranet or the Internet, the principles of providing content are the same. You place your Web files in folders on your server so that users can establish an HTTP connection and view your files with a Web browser. But beyond simply storing files on your server, you must manage how your site is deployed, and more importantly, how your site evolves.

Getting Started

You should set up your Web sites by indicating which folders contain the documents that you want to publish. The Web server cannot publish documents that are not within these specified folders. So, the first step in deploying a Web site should be to first determine how you want your files organized. You then use the Internet Information Services snap-in, or the Internet Services Manager (HTML) interface to identify which folders (called directories in the snap-in and HTML interface), are part of the site.

If you want to get started right away without having to create a special folder structure and your files are all located on the same hard disk of the computer running IIS, you can publish your documents immediately by copying your Web files into the default home folder. Intranet users can then access these files by using any of the following URLs:

- *http://<computer_name/file_name>*
- *http://<FQDN/file_name>*
- *http://<IP_address/file_name>*

Where *computer_name*, *FQDN*, and *IP_address* identify the Web server.

Note In the following section, the words *folder* and *folders* are replaced by the words *directory* and *directories* because the latter are used in the Internet Information Services interface.

Defining Home Directories

Each Web site and FTP site must have one home directory. The home directory is the central location for your published pages. It contains a home page (typically named index.htm, index.html, default.asp, default.htm, or default.html) that welcomes Web browser users and contains links to other pages in your site. More than one default document can be specified for a single site. IIS displays the first default document it finds. The home directory is mapped to your site's domain name or to your server name. For example, if your site's Internet domain name is www.microsoft.com and your home directory is C:\Website\Microsoft, browsers use the URL *http://www.microsoft.com* to access files in your home directory. On an intranet, if your server name is AcctServer, browsers can use the URL *http://acctserver* to access files in your home directory.

A default home directory is created when you install IIS and when you create a new Web site. If you are setting up both a Web site and an FTP site on the same computer, you must specify a different home directory for each service (WWW and FTP). The default home directory for the WWW service is \InetPub\Wwwroot. The default home directory for the FTP service is \InetPub\Ftproot. You can choose a different directory as your home directory.

You can use the Internet Information Services snap-in to change the home directory. Select a Web site or FTP site and open its Properties dialog box. Click the Home Directory tab, and then specify where your home directory is located (Figure 14.11).

Figure 14.11 Home Directory tab of the Default Web Site Properties dialog box

If you select a directory on a network share, you may need to enter a user name and password to access the resource. It is recommend that you use the IUSR_*computername* account. If you use an account that has administration permissions on the server, clients can gain access to server operations. This seriously jeopardizes the security of your network.

Notice that the home directory can reside on the computer running IIS, on a share, or be can be redirected to a URL hosted by another Web site. The share option provides transparent support for Dfs.

Creating Virtual Directories

You can create a virtual directory to publish from a directory not contained within your home directory. A virtual directory is one that is not contained in the home directory but appears to client browsers as though it were.

A virtual directory has an alias, a name that Web browsers use to access that directory. Because an alias is usually shorter than the path name of the directory, it is more convenient for users to type. An alias also is more secure; users do not know where your files are physically located on the server and cannot use that information to modify your files. Aliases also make it easier for you to move directories in your site. Rather than change the URL for the directory, you can simply change the mapping between the alias and the physical location of the directory.

For a simple Web site, you may not need to add virtual directories. You can instead place all of your files in the site's home directory. If you have a complex site or want to specify different URLs for different parts of your site, you can add virtual directories as needed.

The Internet Information Services snap-in or the Internet Services Manger (HTML) allows you to create a virtual directory. In the Internet Information Services snap-in, select the Web site or FTP site to which you want to add a virtual directory. From the Action menu, click New and then click Virtual Directory. The Virtual Directory Creation wizard walks you through the process of creating a virtual directory (Figure 14.12).

Figure 14.12 Creating a virtual directory for the Default Web site using the Virtual Directory Creation wizard

In Internet Services Manager (HTML), the same link used to create a new site is also used to publish your content to a virtual directory or a directory. After selecting a site in Internet Services Manager (HTML) and clicking New link in the left frame, the IIS New Site wizard appears. On the next screen in the wizard, you select the Virtual Directory radio button to publish a new virtual directory.

Reroute Requests with Redirects

When a browser requests a page on your Web site, the Web server locates the page identified by the URL and returns it to the browser. When you move a page on your Web site, you can't always correct all of the links that refer to the old URL of the page. To make sure that browsers can find the page at the new URL, you instruct the Web server to give the browser the new URL. The browser uses the new URL to request the page again. This process is called *redirecting a browser request* or *redirecting to another URL*. Redirecting a request for a page is similar to using a forwarding address with a postal service. The forwarding address ensures that letters and packages addressed to your original residence are delivered to your new residence.

Redirecting a URL is useful when you are updating your Web site and want to make a portion of the site temporarily unavailable, or when you have changed the name of a virtual directory and want links to files in the original virtual directory to access the same files in the new virtual directory.

You can use the Internet Information Services snap-in to redirect requests to a Web site, a virtual directory, or another directory. Select the Web site, virtual directory, or directory and open its Properties dialog box. For a Web site, use the Home Directory tab; for a virtual directory, use the Virtual Directory tab; for a directory, use the Directory tab. Select the A Redirection To A URL option, and type the URL of the destination in the Redirect To text box.

Other Tools

Often, it may be useful to dynamically alter Web content after the content has been requested, but before it is returned to the browser. IIS includes two features that provide this functionality: server-side includes (SSI) and the ASP scripting environment.

Using SSI, you can carry out a whole host of Web site management activities from adding dynamic time-stamping to running a special shell command each time a file is requested. SSI commands, called *directives*, are added to Web pages at design time. When a page is requested, the Web server parses out all the directives it finds in a Web page and then executes them. A commonly used SSI directive inserts, or includes, the contents of a file into a Web page. For example, if you are required to continually update a Web page advertisement, you could use SSI to include the advertisement's HTML source into the Web page. To update the advertisement, you need only modify the file containing advertisement's HTML source. You do not have to know a scripting language to use SSI; simply follow the correct directive syntax.

ASP is a server-side scripting environment that you can use to dynamically alter Web content. Although ASP is primarily designed for Web application development, it has many features that can be used to make Web sites easier to manage. For example, with ASP you can track users visiting a Web site, or you can customize Web content based on browser capabilities. However, unlike SSI, ASP requires you to use a scripting language such as VBScript or JScript.

Using ASP to Manage Web Site Content

Windows 2000 includes Microsoft ASP, a server-side scripting environment that you can use to automate and centralize many of your Web site management tasks.

Scripting

A *script* is a series of instructions and commands that you can use to programmatically alter the content of your Web pages. If you have ever visited an online store that enabled you to search for items and check product availability, then you have undoubtedly encountered some type of script.

There are two kinds of scripting: client-side and server-side. Client-side scripts run on the Web browser and are embedded in a Web page between HTML <SCRIPT> and </SCRIPT> tags. If you view the HTML source for a highly dynamic Web page, you will most likely discover a client-side script.

Server-side scripts run exclusively on the Web server and are most often used to modify Web pages before they are delivered to the browser. Server-side scripts can instruct the Web server to perform an action such as process user input or log how often a user visits your Web site. You can think of server-side scripts as affecting how the Web server assembles a Web page before it's sent to the browser. Server-side scripts can greatly facilitate your management of Web content by processing data and automatically updating Web pages.

ASP Overview

Just as you might write a custom macro to automate repetitive spreadsheet or word processing tasks, you can create a server-side script to automatically perform difficult or repetitive Web management tasks. Imagine that you need to update a Web site consisting of several dozen pages containing identical formatting information (bylines, company logos, copyright information, and so on). Normally, such work is time consuming and requires that you update (and test) each page manually. However, you can use ASP to automate such work.

ASP is a powerful, server-side scripting environment that you can use to write scripts with only a standard text editor, such as Notepad. For example, using ASP you could create a central file that contains information common to all of the pages of a Web site. While designing the Web site, you could add a one-line script command to each page that inserts the contents of the central file. Whenever you need to update your site's navigation menu, for example, you need only update the central file; changes would automatically appear the next time a user reloads and views the Web content.

ASP uses *delimiters* to differentiate script commands from regular text and HTML. Specifically, <% and %> delimiters enclose script commands that are to be executed by the server, as opposed to < and > delimiters used by HTML to denote tags that are to be parsed by a Web browser.

The following example illustrates how ASP works:

```
<%
author = "Max"
department = "Quality Assurance"
%>

This page was updated <B>today</B>, by <%= author %> from
the <%= department %> Department.
```

When viewed in a Web browser, a page containing this script appears as follows:

```
This page was updated today, by Max from the Quality Assur-
ance Department.
```

However, a user viewing the source for this page from a Web browser would see only the following text and HTML:

```
This page was updated <B>today</B>, by Max from the Quality
Assurance Department.
```

The script runs on the server (that is, commands within the <% and %> delimiters are executed on the server) and returns only HTML to a user's browser.

At a minimum, all ASP files must have an .ASP extension and contain script commands written in a scripting language such as Microsoft Visual Basic Scripting Edition (VBScript) or Microsoft JScript. If you are new to scripting and need to learn the fundamentals, visit the Microsoft Windows Script Technologies Web site at *http://msdn.microsoft.com/scripting/*.

Exercise 1: Accessing the Administration Web Site

In this exercise you use the Internet Information Services snap-in to configure the Administration Web site. You configure access to this sensitive area of the Web server. You then run Internet Service Manager (HTML) to test access capability to the site. Complete this exercise on Server01.

▶ **Procedure 1: Configuring the Administration Web site with the Internet Information Services snap-in**

In this procedure you use the Internet Informations Services snap-in to configure the Administration Web site.

1. Log on to Server01 as Administrator with a password of "password."

2. Click the Start button, point to Programs, point to Administrative Tools, and click Internet Services Manager.

   The Internet Information Services snap-in appears.

3. In the console tree, expand * server01

   Four containers appears under * server01: Default FTP site, Default Web site, Administration Web site, and Default SMTP Virtual Server.

4. In the console tree, expand Administration Web site.

   Notice that two virtual directories, IISAdmin and IISHelp, appear.

5. In the console tree, click on Administration Web site.

6. Click the Action menu and then click Properties.

   The Administration Web Site Properties dialog box appears.

7. With the Web Site tab active, record the TCP Port value appearing in the TCP Port text box.

   This random value between 2000–9999 is referred to in this exercise as a variable with a name of *tcp_port*.

8. Under the Enable Logging check box, verify that W3C Extended Log File Format is selected and then click the Properties button.

   The Extended Logging Properties dialog box appears. Notice that the log file is stored in the %WinDir%\System32\LogFiles, which is equivalent to %SystemRoot%\System32\LogFiles.

9. Click the Extended Properties tab.

10. Scroll down to the bottom of the Extended Logging Options box and then select the Process Accounting check box.

11. Click OK to close the Extended Logging Properties dialog box.

The Administration Web Site Properties dialog box appears.

12. Click the Directory Security tab.

13. In the Anonymous Access And Authentication Control region of the screen, click the Edit button.

The Authentication Methods dialog box appears.

Notice that Anonymous access is not available to the Administration Web site, Basic authentication is not enabled, and that Integrated Windows authentication is enabled.

This configuration means that a browser client connecting to the Administration Web site must be able to authenticate using either secure NTLM or Kerberos authentication. The type of Integrated Windows authentication method used is browser dependent.

14. Select the Digest Authentication For Windows Domain Servers check box.

An IIS WWW Configuration message box appears and explains that only Windows 2000 domain accounts can be used and that passwords will be stored as encrypted clear text.

15. Click Yes.

This provides additional security in your Windows 2000 domain. You will only be using Windows 2000 domain user accounts to access the Administration Web site.

16. Click OK to close the Authentication Methods dialog box.

The Administration Web Site Properties dialog box appears.

17. In the IP Address And Domain Name Restrictions region of the screen, click the Edit button.

The IP Address and Domain Name Restrictions dialog box appears.

Notice that the Denied Access radio button is selected and that only the local loopback address, 127.0.0.1 is granted access to this area.

18. Click the Granted Access radio button so that you can access the Administration Web site from any computer in your training network.

For additional security, consider adding specific IP addresses, a scope of IP addresses, or computers within a specific domain that can access the Administration Web site. This last option is resource intensive and not recommended for most implementations of IIS 5.0.

19. Click OK.

20. Click OK to close the Administration Web Site Properties dialog box.

    The Inheritance Overrides dialog box appears and explains that the Child node, IISAdmin, defines the value of "Authentication Methods." You will override the currently configured value in favor of the value you configured for the Administration Web Site node.

21. In the Child Nodes box, click IISAdmin and then click OK.

    The Inheritance Overrides dialog box appears again for the IISHelp Child node.

22. Click IISHelp and click OK.

23. Close Internet Information Services snap-in.

▶ **Procedure 2: Accessing the Administration Web site from Internet Service Manager (HTML)**

In this procedure you attempt to access the Administration Web site with the new settings you configured in the previous procedure.

Note The *tcp_port* variable in this procedure must be replaced with the value you obtained from the previous procedure.

---

1. On Server01, click the Start button and then click Run.

    The Run dialog box appears.

2. In the Open text box, type ***http://server01:<tcp_port>*** and then click OK.

    Internet Explorer starts and a Microsoft Internet Explorer text box appears and explains that you are not running a secure connection for Web-based administration.

    This means that while authentication information between the browser and the Administration Web site is secure, data transmission after the connection is established is not secure.

3. Click OK.

    Internet Explorer shows the Internet Services Manager (HTML) interface.

4. Explore the three Web sites appearing in the main window of the interface. Use the links in the left frame to explore the features discussed in this lesson.

5. Close Internet Explorer.

▶ Procedure 3: Configuring SSL access to the Administration Web site

In this procedure, you apply the SSL protocol to the Administration Web site to establish secure communications when operating on this site. To do this, you issue your own server certificate using Server01 and Certificate Services.

Note You installed Certificate Services in Chapter 11, "Exercise 1: Installing and Configuring Certificate Services."

1. On Server01, open Internet Services Manager.

   The Internet Information Services snap-in appears.

2. In the console tree, expand * server01.

3. Click on the Administration Web site.

4. Click the Action menu and then click Properties.

   The Administration Web Site Properties dialog box appears.

5. Click the Directory Security tab.

6. In the Secure communications region of the screen, click Server Certificate.

   The Welcome to the Web Server Certificate wizard appears.

7. Read the information on this screen and then click Next.

   The IIS Certificate wizard appears.

8. Confirm that the Create A New Certificate radio button is selected and then click Next.

   The Delayed or Immediate Request screen appears.

9. Click the Send The Request Immediately To An Online Certification Authority radio button and then click Next.

   The Name and Security Settings screen appears.

   Notice that the default name given to this certificate is Administration Web site and that the bit length is set to 512 bits.

10. Click Next.

    The Organization Information screen appears.

11. In the Organization drop-down list box, type **Microsoft Corporation** and in the Organizational Unit drop-down list box, type **Microsoft Press**.

12. Click Next.

    The Your Site's Common Name screen appears.

13. In the Common Name text box, type **server01.microsoft.com**. and then click next.

    The Geographical Information screen appears.

14. Do not change the value in the Country/Region drop-down list box.

15. In the State/Province drop-down list box, type **Washington** and in the City/Locality drop-down list box, type **Redmond**.

16. Click Next.

    The Choose a Certification Authority screen appears and server01.microsoft.com\Enterprise CA appears in the Certification Authorities drop-down list box.

17. Click Next.

    The Certificate Request Submission screen appears.

18. Read through the summary information on this screen and then click Next.

    After a few moments, the Completing the Web Server Certificate Wizard screen appears.

19. Click Finish.

    The Administration Web Site Properties dialog box appears. Notice that under the Secure communications region of the screen, the View Certificate and Edit buttons are now available.

20. In the Secure communications region of the screen, click the Edit button.

    The Secure Communications dialog box appears.

21. Click the Require Secure Channel (SSL) check box.

22. Verify that the Ignore Client Certificates radio button is selected and then Click OK.

    The Administration Web Site Properties dialog box appears.

23. Click the Web Site tab.

24. In the SSL Port field, type **5000**.

25. Click OK.

26. Close the Internet Information Services snap-in.

▶ **Procedure 4: Testing access to the secured Administration Web site**

In this procedure you test access to the Administration Web site now that a server certificate and SSL has been configured for the site.

1. On Server01, click the Start button and then click Run.

   The Run dialog box appears.

2. In the Open text box, type ***http://server01:<tcp_port>*** and then click OK.

   The *tcp_port* variable in this procedure must be replaced with the value you obtained in Procedure 1.

   Internet Explorer starts and a message appears, explaining that the page must be viewed over a secure channel.

3. In the Internet Explorer Address drop-down list box, type **https:// server01.microsoft.com:5000** and then click Go. The 5000 value is the *SSL_port* value you entered on the Web Site tab.

   A Security Alert message box appears stating that you are about to view information over a secure connection.

4. Click the In The Future Do Not Show This Warning check box and then click OK.

   The Enter Network Password dialog box appears.

5. In the User Name text box, type Administrator, in the Password text box, type "password," and in the Domain text box, type **microsoft**.

6. Select the Save This Password In Your Password List check box and then click OK.

   The Internet Services Manager (HTML) interface appears. Notice that there is a lock icon on the bottom right corner of the status bar.

7. Place the mouse pointer on top of the lock icon.

   Notice that a tip states: "SSL secured (56 Bit)." 128-bit encryption is available from the Secure Communications dialog box for the properties of the site. In the previous procedure, you configured SSL for the connection but you did not require 128-bit encryption.

8. Double-click the lock icon.

   The Certificate dialog box appears.

9. Review the information under the tabs of the Certificate dialog box.

   From the Certificate dialog box you can run the Certificate Import wizard to copy certificate information from the local computer to a certificate store.

10. Click OK.

11. Close the Internet Services Manager (HTML) interface.

Lesson Summary

IIS 5.0 introduces improvements in reliability and performance, management, security, and application environment. IIS also introduces features you can use to improve the speed and reliability of Web sites, such as the addition of application protection through support for pooled, out-of-process applications. In addition, IIS 5.0 makes the Web server easier for managers to use. For example, the installation process is built right into Windows 2000 Server Setup. And, to make it easier to configure security settings, there are three new security wizards. Security features are an important area of improvement in IIS 5.0, which takes advantage of the Internet-standard security features that are fully integrated with Windows 2000. IIS 5.0 also adds performance enhancements to make it easier to debug and deploy Web-enabled applications. Installation and removal of IIS is accomplished in one of three ways: when installing or upgrading Windows 2000, by using the Add/Remove Programs utility in Control Panel, or by using an unattended.txt file during an unattended installation. When IIS is installed, a Default Web site, Administration Web site and Default SMTP Virtual Server are created. You should set up your Web sites by indicating which directories contain the documents that you want to publish. Each Web or FTP site must have one home directory. To publish from any directory not contained within your home directory, you can create a virtual directory. Windows 2000 includes Microsoft ASP, a server-side scripting environment that you can use to automate and centralize many of your Web site management tasks.

Lesson 2: Administering a Web Environment

When IIS is installed, a default Web site is created, allowing you to quickly and easily implement a Web environment. However, you can modify that Web environment to meet your specific needs. In addition, you can implement WebDAV, which allows you to share documents over the Internet or an intranet. This lesson covers several aspects of administering a Web environment: Web site management, FTP site management, and WebDAV publishing. Administering Web and FTP sites is very similar and, as a result, are discussed together. This is followed by a discussion of WebDAV publishing.

After this lesson, you will be able to

- Administer Web and FTP sites

- Manage WebDAV publishing

Estimated lesson time: 35 minutes

Administering Web and FTP Sites

Originally, each domain name, such as www.microsoft.com, represented an individual computer. With IIS 5.0, multiple Web sites or FTP sites can be hosted simultaneously on a single computer running Windows 2000 Server. Each Web site can host one or more domain names. Because each site mimics the appearance of an individual computer, sites are sometimes referred to as *virtual servers.*

Web Sites and FTP Sites

Whether your system is on an intranet or the Internet, you can create multiple Web sites and FTP sites on a single computer running Windows 2000 in one of three ways:

- Append port numbers to the IP address

- Use multiple IP addresses, each having its own network adapter card

- Assign multiple domain names and IP addresses to one network adapter card by using host header names

The example in Figure 14.13 illustrates an intranet scenario where the system administrator has installed Windows 2000 Server with IIS on the company's server, resulting in one default Web site: *http://CompanyServer*. The system administrator then creates two additional Web sites, one for each of two departments: marketing and human resources.

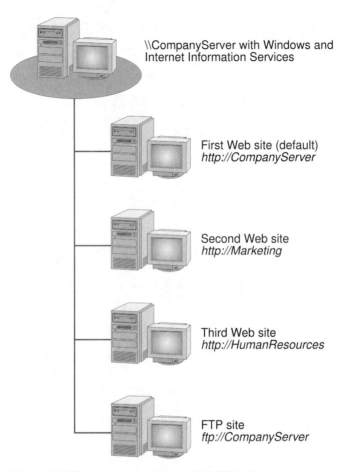

Figure 14.13 An intranet with multiple Web sites

Though hosted on the same computer, CompanyServer, Marketing, and HumanResources each appears to be a unique Web site. These departmental sites have the same security options as they would if they existed on separate computers because each site has its own access and administration permission settings. In addition, the administrative tasks can be distributed to members of each department.

Note When creating a very large number of sites, be sure to consider computer hardware and network limitations and upgrade these resources as necessary.

Properties and Inheritance of Properties on Sites

Properties are values that can be set on your Web site. For example, you can use the Internet Information Services snap-in to change the TCP port assigned to the default Web site from the default value of 80 to another port number. Properties for a site are displayed in the Properties dialog box (Figure 14.14) for that site and stored in a database called the metabase.

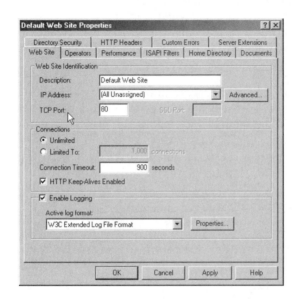

Figure 14.14 Properties dialog box for the default Web site

During the installation of IIS, default values were assigned to the various properties. You can use the default settings in IIS, or you can customize these settings to suit your Web publishing needs. You may be able to provide additional value, better performance, and improved security by making adjustments to the default settings.

Note In Exercise 1 in this chapter you adjusted the properties of the Administration Web site to increase security to this sensitive area.

Properties can be set on the site level, directory level, or on the file level. Settings on higher levels (such as the site level) are automatically used, or inherited, by the lower levels (such as the directory level) but can still be edited individually at the lower level as well. Once a property has been changed on an individual site, directory, or file, later changes to the master defaults will not automatically override the individual setting. Instead, you will receive a warning message asking whether you want to change the individual site, directory, or file setting to match the new defaults.

Some properties have a value that takes the form of a list. For instance, the value of the default document can be a list of documents to be loaded when users do not specify a file in a URL. Custom error messages, TCP/IP access control, script mappings, and MIME mappings are other examples of properties stored in a list format. Although these lists have multiple entries, IIS treats the entire list as a single property. If you edit a list on a directory and then make a global change on the site level, the list at the directory level is completely replaced with the new list from the site level; the lists are not merged. Also, properties with list values display their lists only at the master level, or on a site or directory that has been changed from the default value. List values are not displayed if they are the inherited defaults.

Master properties, server extensions, bandwidth throttling, and MIME mapping for a site's services are viewed from the properties of a computer node appearing in the Internet Information Services snap-in or in the Internet Services Manager (HTML) interface. Figure 14.15 shows the WWW Service master properties accessed from the first Edit button appearing in the Properties screen of a computer node.

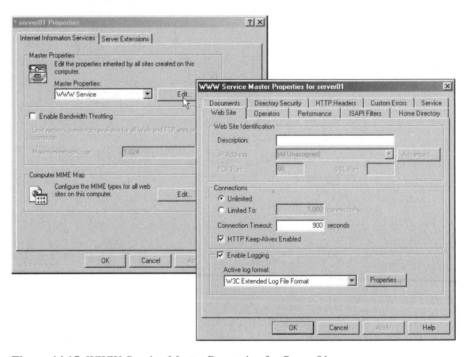

Figure 14.15 WWW Service Master Properties for Server01

On the Internet Services Manager (HTML) interface there is a Master Properties link and drop-down list box on the left frame of the home page (Figure 14.2).

Internet Server API (ISAPI) filters are displayed in a list format, but are not treated as a list. If you add filters at the site level, the new filters are merged with the list of filters from the master level. If two filters have the same priority setting, the filter from the master level is loaded before the filter from the site level. Installed ISAPI filters and their priority are viewed from the ISAPI Filters tab contained in the WWW Service Master Properties, and on the properties page of each Web site.

If the default property values need to be modified and you are creating several Web or FTP sites, you can edit the default values so that each site you create inherits your custom values.

Operators Group

Operators are a special group of users who have limited administrative privileges on individual Web sites. Members of the Operators group can administer properties that affect only their respective sites. They do not have access to properties that affect IIS, the Windows server computer hosting IIS, or the network.

For example, an ISP who hosts sites for a number of different companies can assign delegates from each company as the operators for each company's Web site. This method of distributed server administration has the following advantages:

- Each member of the Operators group can act as the site administrator and can change or reconfigure the Web site as necessary. For example, the operator can set Web site access permissions, enable logging, change the default document or footer, set content expiration, and enable content ratings features.

- The Web site operator is not permitted to change the identification of Web sites, configure the anonymous user name or password, throttle bandwidth, create virtual directories or change their paths, or change application isolation.

- Because members of the Operators group have more limited privileges than Web site administrators, they are unable to remotely browse the file system and therefore cannot set properties on directories and files, unless a UNC path is used.

Administering Sites Remotely

Because it may not always be convenient to perform administrative tasks on the computer running IIS, two remote administration options are available. If you are connecting to your server over the Internet or through a proxy server, you can use the browser-based Internet Services Manager (HTML) to change properties on your site. If you are on an intranet, you can use either the Internet Services Manager (HTML) or the Internet Information Services snap-in. Although Internet Services Manager (HTML) offers many of the same features as the snap-in, property changes that require coordination with Windows utilities, such as certificate mapping, cannot be made with Internet Services Manager (HTML).

Note In previous releases the Internet Information Services snap-in was called the Internet Services Manager. The Internet Information Services snap-in appears on the Administrative Tools menu as Internet Services Manager.

Internet Services Manager (HTML) uses a Web site listed as Administration Web site to access IIS properties. When IIS is installed, a port number between 2,000 and 9,999 is randomly selected and assigned to this Web site. The site responds to Web browser requests for all domain names installed on the computer, provided the port number is appended to the address. If Basic authentication is used, the administrator will be asked for a user name and password when the site is reached. Only members of the Administrators group and Operators group can use the site.

Note Although the HTML version of Internet Services Manager (HTML) has much of the same functionality of the Internet Information Services snap-in, the HTML version is designed along the lines of a Web page. Accessing context menus on interface objects is not supported. Many of the familiar toolbar buttons or tab headings are displayed as links in the left frame. Because of these differences, instructions in the documentation may not always precisely describe the steps performed in Internet Services Manager (HTML).

You can also use Terminal Services over a network connection (such as LAN, PPTP, or dial-up) to remotely administer IIS. Terminal Services does not require you to install Microsoft Management Console (MMC) or the Internet Information Services snap-in on the remote computer.

The IIS 5.0 online documentation is available for you to use when you are performing remote administration tasks. To reach the documentation, start the Administration Web site and then click the book icon in the top right corner of the home page. This link opens a new window to the following URL *http:// <servername>/iishelp/iis/misc/default.asp*, where *<servername>* is an identifying name (IP address, computer name, or FQDN) of the computer running IIS.

The IIS documentation search function is dependent on the Indexing Service. The Indexing Service is installed in Windows 2000 Server by default but is set to manual startup. The Indexing Service is configured from the Computer Management snap-in under the Services and Applications node. So that the IIS 5.0 documentation is indexed for searches, add the physical path to the iisHelp folder to the Web Directories folder for the Indexing Service. After configuring the Indexing Service, startup can be set to Automatic by using the Services snap-in.

Note The Indexing Service can be processor intensive, particularly if a significant amount of material must be indexed. Consider running Indexing Service functions on a computer with enough resources to accommodate this function.

FTP Restart

FTP Restart addresses the problem of losing a network connection while down-loading files. Clients that support FTP Restart need only re-establish their FTP connection, and the file transfer automatically picks up where it left off.

Note The IIS 5.0 implementation of FTP Restart is not enabled when using FTP to download wildcard requests (MGET), uploading files to a server (PUT), or downloading files larger than 4 gigabytes.

Managing Sites

The process of managing sites includes a number of tasks, such as starting and stopping sites, adding sites, naming sites, and restarting IIS.

Starting and Stopping Sites

By default, sites start automatically when your computer restarts. Stopping a site stops Internet services and unloads Internet services from your computer's memory. Pausing a site prevents Internet services from accepting new connections but does not affect requests that are already being processed. Starting a site restarts or resumes Internet services.

To start, stop, or pause a site, use the Internet Information Services snap-in. Select the site you want to start, stop, or pause, and then click the Start Item, Stop Item, or Pause Item button on the toolbar.

Note If a site stops unexpectedly, the Internet Information Services snap-in may not correctly indicate the state of the server. Before restarting, click Stop, and then click Start to restart the site.

Adding Sites

You can add new sites to a computer by launching the Web Site Creation wizard, the FTP Site Creation wizard, or the SMTP Virtual Server wizard in the Internet Information Services snap-in. Select the computer or a site, click the Action menu, click New, and then click Web Site, FTP Site, or SMTP Virtual Server to launch the corresponding wizard.

Note The SMTP Virtual Server wizard is beyond the scope of this training kit and is therefore not explained any further.

Follow the on-screen directions to assign identification information to your new site. You must provide the port address and the home directory path. If you are adding additional sites to a single IP address by using host headers, you must assign a host header name.

Note The All Unassigned option in the Enter the IP address to use for this Web Site drop-down list of the Web Site Creation wizard (or in the IP Address drop-down list in the FTP Site Creation wizard) refers to IP addresses that are assigned to a computer but not assigned to a specific site. The default Web site uses all of the IP addresses that are not assigned to other sites. Only one site can be set to use unassigned IP addresses.

Naming Web Sites

Each Web site (virtual server) has a descriptive name and can support one or more host header names. Host header names make it possible to host multiple domain names on one computer. Not all browsers support the use of host header names. Internet Explorer 3.0, Netscape Navigator 2.0, and later versions of both browsers support the use of host header names; earlier versions of the browsers do not.

If a visitor attempts to connect to your site with an older browser that does not support host headers, the visitor is directed to the default Web site assigned to that IP address (if a default site is enabled), which may not necessarily be the site requested. Also, if a request from any browser is received for a site that is currently stopped, the visitor receives the default Web site instead. For this reason, carefully consider what the default Web site displays. Typically, ISPs display their own home page as the default, and not one of their customers' Web sites. This prevents requests for a stopped site from reaching the wrong site. Additionally, the default site can include a script that supports the use of host header names for older browsers.

You can use the Internet Information Services snap-in to name a site. Select the Web site and open its Properties dialog box. On the Web Site tab, type a descriptive name for the site in the Description box (Figure 14.14).

Stop, Start, Restart, or Reboot in IIS

In IIS 5.0, you can stop, start, or reset (restart option) all of your Internet services or reboot the server from within the Internet Information Services snap-in. The stop, start, and restart functions makes it less likely that you will need to reboot the server when applications misbehave or become unavailable.

The restart function conveniently stops and starts internet services, effectively resetting the service. To restart IIS, select the Computer node in the console tree, click the Action menu, and then select Restart IIS. Figure 14.16 shows the resulting Stop/Start/Reboot dialog box.

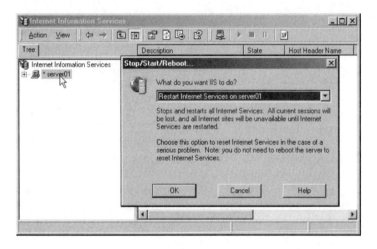

Figure 14.16 Restarting Internet Services on Server01

The drop-down list box shown in Figure 14.16 also contains start and stop IIS options and the Reboot Server option.

Important Restarting will stop all Drwtsn32.exe, Mtx.exe, and Dllhost.exe processes in order to restart Internet services. You cannot stop or start IIS or reboot the server by using browser-based Internet Services Manager (HTML). However, both the snap-in and the HTML interface can be used to individually start, stop, pause, and resume individual sites.

You should use the Internet Information Services snap-in to restart Internet services, not the Services snap-in in Computer Management. Because several Internet services run in one process, Internet services shut down and restart differently from other Windows services.

Backing Up and Restoring IIS

You can back up your IIS configuration so that it is easy to return to a previous state. The steps to restore a configuration differ depending upon whether you removed and reinstalled IIS.

You can use the Internet Information Services snap-in to back up your IIS configuration. Select the Computer node in the console tree, click the Action menu, and then select Backup/Restore Configuration.

This backup method will provide a way to restore only your IIS settings, not your content files. In addition, this method will not work if you re-install your operating system, and Backup files cannot be used to restore an IIS configuration on other Windows 2000 computers.

Note You can back up IIS using the Internet Services Manager (HTML) interface, but you must use the Internet Information Services snap-in to restore your configuration. The Backup Configuration link appears in the left pane of the Internet Services Manager (HTML) interface (Figure 14.2).

To restore your IIS configuration in the Internet Information Services snap-in, select the Computer node in the console tree, click the Action menu, and then click Backup/Restore Configuration. Select a backup file and click the Restore button. When asked whether to restore your configuration settings, click Yes.

Managing WebDAV Publishing

WebDAV extends the HTTP/1.1 protocol to allow clients to publish, lock, and manage resources on the Web. Integrated into IIS, WebDAV allows clients to do the following:

- Manipulate resources in a WebDAV publishing directory on your server. For example, with this feature, users with the apporpriate permissions can copy and move files around in a WebDAV directory.

- Modify properties associated with certain resources. For example, a user can write to and retrieve a file's property information.

- Lock and unlock resources so that multiple users can read a file concurrently, but only one person at a time can modify the file.

- Search the content and properties of files in a WebDAV directory.

Setting up a WebDAV publishing directory on your server is as straightforward as setting up a virtual directory. Once you have set up your publishing directory, users with the appropriate permissions can publish documents to the server and manipulate files in the directory.

WebDAV Clients

You can access a WebDAV publishing directory through one of the Microsoft products described in the following list, or through any other client that supports the industry standard WebDAV protocol.

- Windows 2000 connects to a WebDAV server through the Add Network Place wizard and displays the contents of a WebDAV directory as if it were part of the same file system on your local computer. Once connected, you can drag and drop files, retrieve and modify file properties, and do many other file-system tasks.

  For example, if you create a virtual directory named WebDAV under the Default Web site on server01.microsoft.com, you can access it from the following address: *http://server01.microsoft.com/webdav/*.

- Internet Explorer 5 connects to a WebDAV directory and lets you do the same file-system tasks as you can through Windows 2000.

  Make sure to enable the Directory Browsing permission in the properties of the virtual directory in order to access the virtual directory using Internet Explorer 5.

- Office 2000 creates, publishes, edits, and saves documents directly into a WebDAV directory through any application in Office 2000.

Searching in WebDAV

Once connected to a WebDAV directory, you can quickly search the files on that directory for content as well as properties. For example, you can search for all files that contain the word table or for all files written by Fred.

Integrated Security

Because WebDAV is integrated with Windows 2000 and IIS 5.0, it borrows the security features offered by both. These features include the IIS permissions specified in the Internet Information Services snap-in and the discretionary access control lists (DACLs) in the NTFS file system.

Because clients with proper permissions can write to a WebDAV directory, it is vital that you can control who is accessing your directory at all times. To help control access, IIS 5.0 has reinforced Integrated Windows authentication by building in support for the Kerberos 5 authentication protocol. By selecting Integrated Windows authentication, you can make sure that only clients with permission can access and write to the WebDAV directory on your intranet.

In addition, IIS 5.0 introduces a new type of authentication called Digest authentication. Created for Windows domain servers, this type of authentication offers tighter security for passwords and for transmitting information across the Internet.

Creating a Publishing Directory

To set up a publishing directory, create a physical directory below Inetpub. For example, if you call the directory WebDAV, the path to this directory might be C:\Inetpub\WebDAV.

You can actually put this directory anywhere, except under the Wwwroot directory. (Wwwroot is an exception because its default DACLs are different from those on other directories).

In the Internet Information Services snap-in, create a new Web site or use an existing site and then create a virtual directory beneath it. Type **WebDAV**, or any other convenient name, as the alias for this virtual directory, and link it to the physical directory you just created. Grant Read, Write, and Browsing access permissions for the virtual directory.

You are granting users the right to publish documents on this virtual directory and to see a list of the files in it. Although not recommended for security reasons, you can grant the same access to your entire Web site and allow clients to publish to your entire Web server.

Note Granting Write access does not enable clients to modify Active Server Pages (ASP) or any other script-mapped files. To allow these files to be modified, you must grant Write permission and Script source access after creating the virtual directory.

Once you finish setting up a WebDAV virtual directory, you can allow clients to publish to it.

Managing WebDAV Security

To protect your server and its content, you must coordinate three different aspects of security into an integrated whole: authenticating clients, controlling access, and denying service.

Authenticating Clients

IIS 5.0 offers the following levels of authentication:

- **Anonymous** Anonymous access grants anyone access to the directory, and therefore, you should turn it off for a WebDAV directory. Without controlling who has access, your directory could be vandalized by unknown clients.

- **Basic** Basic authentication sends passwords over the connection in clear text. Because clear text can easily be intercepted and read, you should turn on Basic authentication only if you encrypt data through SSL.

- **Integrated Windows** Integrated Windows authentication works best when you are setting up a WebDAV directory on an intranet.

- **Digest** Digest authentication is the best choice for publishing information on a server over the Internet and through firewalls.

The best way to configure a WebDAV directory depends on the kind of publishing you want to do. When you create a virtual directory through IIS 5.0, Anonymous and Integrated Windows authentication are both turned on. Although this default configuration works well for clients connecting to your server, reading content on a Web page, and running scripts, it does not work well with clients publishing to a directory and manipulating files in that directory.

Controlling Access

You can control access to your WebDAV directory by coordinating IIS 5.0 and Windows 2000 permissions.

Setting Up Web Permissions

How you configure Web permissions is based on the purpose of the material you are publishing.

- **Read, Write, Directory Browsing enabled** Turning on these permissions lets clients see a list of resources, modify them (except for those resources without Write permission), publish their own resources, and manipulate files.

- **Write enabled, Read and Directory Browsing disabled** If you want clients to publish private information on the directory, but do not want others to see what has been published, set Write permission, but do not set Read or Directory browsing permission. This configuration works well if clients are submitting ballots or performance reviews. Note that disabling Directory Browsing permission denies access to browser clients attempting to access the WebDAV directory.

- **Read and Write enabled, Directory Browsing disabled** Set this configuration if you want to rely on obscuring file names as a security method. However, be aware that "security by obscurity" is a low-level precautionary method, because a vandal could easily guess file names by trial and error.

- **Index This Resource enabled** Be sure to enable Indexing Service if you plan to let clients search directory resources.

Controlling Access with DACLs

When setting up a WebDAV publishing directory on an NTFS file system drive, Windows 2000 Server gives everyone Full Control by default. Change this level of permission so that everyone has Read permission only. Then grant Write permission to certain individuals or groups.

Protecting Script Code

If you have script files in your publishing directory that you do not want to expose to clients, you can easily deny access to these files by making sure Script source access is not granted. Scripts include files with extensions that appear in the Applications Mapping list. All other executable files will be treated as static HTML files, including files with .exe extensions, unless Scripts and Executables is enabled for the directory.

To prevent .exe files from being downloaded and treated as if they were HTML files, select the Scripts and Executables option from the Execute Permissions drop-down list, which is located on the Virtual Directory tab of the publishing directory's Properties dialog box (Figure 14.17).

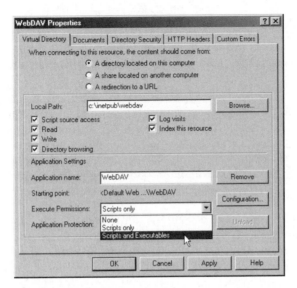

Figure 14.17 Selecting the Scripts and Executables option from the Execute Permissions drop-down list box

This level of permission makes all executable files subject to the Script source access setting. In other words, if Script source access is selected, clients with Read permission can see all executables, and clients with Write permission can edit them, as well as run them. This configuration is a security risk because programs can then be published to the directory and run against the site.

With the following permissions, clients can write to an executable file that does not appear in the Application Mapping:

- Write permission
- Execute Permissions set to Scripts only

With the following permissions, clients can also write to an executable file:

- Script source access granted
- Execute Permissions set to Scripts and Executables

Denying Service

Dragging and dropping extremely large files into a WebDAV directory could take up a large amount of disk space. To limit this amount, consider setting quotas on disk usage.

Publishing and Managing Files

Users can connect to a WebDAV publishing directory, publish documents by dragging them from their computers to the publishing directory, and manipulate files in the directory.

Note Even if users connect from behind a firewall, they can still publish on a WebDAV directory if they have the correct permissions and if the firewall is configured to allow publishing.

From a Windows 2000 computer, you can connect to a WebDAV publishing directory on another server through My Network Places.

You can also connect to a WebDAV directory through Internet Explorer 5 on the Windows 2000, Windows NT 4.0, Windows 98, or Windows 95 operating systems. Once connected, you can manipulate files and publish to that directory just as you could after connecting through Windows 2000. In addition you can create, publish, or save documents in a WebDAV directory through any Office 2000 application.

Lesson Summary

Multiple Web site or FTP sites can be hosted simultaneously on a single computer running Windows 2000 Server. This gives the appearance of being several computers. Each Web site can host one or more domain names. The process of managing sites includes a number of tasks, such as starting and stopping sites, adding sites, naming sites, and restarting IIS. You can back up your IIS configuration so that it is easy to return to a previous state, and you can administer IIS remotely. WebDAV extends the HTTP/1.1 protocol to allow clients to publish, lock, and manage resources on the Web. Once connected to a WebDAV directory, you can quickly search the files on that directory for content as well as properties. You can place a WebDAV directory anywhere you want, except under the Wwwroot directory. You can protect your server and content by coordinating different aspects of security (authenticating clients, controlling access, and denying service) into an integrated whole. Once you have created a WebDAV publishing directory, you can configure your directory to allow users to search for content and file properties. From Windows 2000, you can connect to a WebDAV publishing directory on another server. You can connect to a WebDAV directory through Internet Explorer 5 on the Windows 2000, Windows NT 4.0, Windows 98, or Windows 95 operating systems.

Lesson 3: Configuring and Running Telnet Services

In Windows 2000, Telnet provides user support for the Telnet protocol, a part of the TCP/IP suite. Telnet is a remote access protocol that you can use to log on to a remote computer, network device, or private TCP/IP network. Telnet Server and Telnet Client work together to allow users to communicate with a remote computer. In Windows 2000, Telnet Server is installed as a service, simply named Telnet. The Telnet service allows users of a Telnet client to log on to the computer running the Telnet service and run character-mode applications on that computer. The Telnet service acts as a gateway through which computers running the Telnet client can communicate with each other. The Telnet client allows users to connect to a remote computer and interact with that computer through a terminal window.

After this lesson, you will be able to

- Set up the Windows 2000 Telnet service to allow a computer running the Telnet client to access it

- Use the Microsoft Telnet Client to connect to the Telnet service

Estimated lesson time: 25 minutes

Telnet Service

Windows 2000 Telnet Service allows users of a Telnet client to connect to the computer running the Telnet service and use command-line commands on the computer as if they were sitting in front of it. Telnet clients can connect to a server, log on to that server, and run character-mode applications. The Telnet service also acts as a gateway for Telnet clients to communicate with each other. A computer running the Telnet service can support a maximum of 63 Telnet client computers at any given time.

Telnet Server Connection Licensing

Two Telnet service connection licenses are provided with each installation of Windows 2000 Server. This limits Telnet service to two connecting Telnet clients at a time. If you need additional licenses, use Telnet services from the Windows Services for UNIX add-on pack.

Telnet Authentication

You can use your local Windows 2000 user name and password or domain account information to access the Telnet server. The security scheme is integrated into Windows 2000 security. If you do not use the NT LAN Manager (NTLM) authentication option, the user name and password are sent to the Telnet server as plain text.

If you are using NTLM authentication, the client uses the Windows 2000 security context for authentication and the user is not prompted for a user name and password. The user name and password are encrypted.

Note If the User Must Change Password At Next Logon option is set for a user, the user cannot log on to the Telnet service when NTLM authentication is used. The user must log on to the server directly and change the password, and then log on through the Telnet client.

Starting and Stopping Telnet Server

In a Windows 2000 Server default installation, the Telnet service is set to manual startup. You can use the Services snap-in or the Computer Management snap-in to start, stop, or configure the Telnet service for automatic startup. Figure 14.18 shows the Telnet Properties dialog box for the Telnet service.

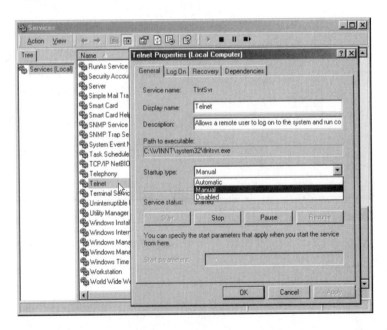

Figure 14.18 Telnet Properties page showing the Startup type options for this server service

In the Computer Management snap-in, Telnet is a service located under the Services and Applications node. Select Services from the console tree, and then select Telnet from the list of services in the details pane.

You can also start or stop the Telnet service from a command prompt. To start Telnet Server, type **net start tlntsvr** or **net start telnet** at the command prompt, and then press Enter. To stop Telnet Server, type **net stop tlntsvr** or **net stop telnet** at the command prompt, and then press Enter.

Telnet Server Admin Utility

You can use the Telnet Server Admin utility to start, stop, or get information about Telnet Server. You can also use it to get a list of current users, terminate a user's session, or change Telnet Server registry settings.

Caution Incorrectly editing the registry may severely damage your system. Before making changes to the registry, it is strongly recommended that you back up any valuable data on the computer.

To open the Telnet Server Admin utility, click the Telnet Administration Tool in the Administrative Tools program group or click Start, click Run, type **tlntadmn**, and then click OK. If you cannot open the Telnet Server Admin utility, you may need to install the Administration Tools pack (Adminpak.msi).

The following table lists the Telnet Server Administration utility options.

Option	Name	Description
0	Quit this application	Ends the Telnet Server Admin utility session.
1	List the current users	Gives a list of the current users, including the user name, domain, remote computer address, session ID, and log time.
2	Terminate a user session	Terminates a selected user's session.
3	Display/change registry settings	Provides a list of registry settings that you can change. See the following table.
4	Start the service	Starts the Telnet Server service.
5	Stop the service	Stops the Telnet Server service.

Registry changes made using the Telnet Server Admin utility modifies settings stored in the following registry key on the Telnet server computer: HKEY_LOCAL_MACHINE\SOFTWARE\Microsoft\TelnetServer\1.0. This registration location is shown in Figure 14.19.

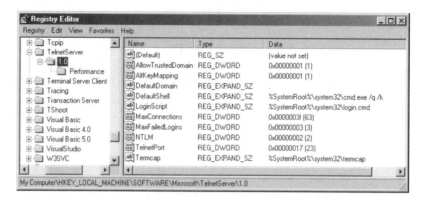

Figure 14.19 Telnet Server registry settings that can be modified by using the Telnet Server Admin utility

The following table lists the Telnet Server registry settings that you can change:

Option	Name	Description	Default Value
0	Exit this menu	Exits this menu and returns to the original Telnet Server Administration utility options.	N/A
1	AllowTrustedDomain	Changes the current value of the trusted domain.	1
2	AltKeyMapping	Changes the current value.	1
3	DefaultDomain	Sets the default domain name.	. (a period means the current domain of the Telnet server)

Option	Name	Description	Default Value
4	DefaultShell	Displays the path location for the shell installation.	%systemroot%\System32\ Cmd.exe /q /k. The /q switch disables echo and the /k switch carries out a command but does not close the command window.
5	LogonScript	Displays the path location and name for the Telnet service global client login script file. By default this file maps the Telnet client to their home directory if one is specified in the user's profile.	%systemroot%\System32\ login.cmd
6	MaxFailedLogins	Displays the maximum number of failed attempts to log on before a connection is terminated.	3
7	NTLM	Displays the current number of allowed NTLM authenticated logons.	2
8	TelnetPort	Displays the default Telnet Server port.	23

Note The Termcap registry setting specifies the location of the Termcap (Terminal Capabilities) file, which is used by a number of terminal client utilities to determine how to move the cursor during a terminal session.

When you change the default domain account, the setting takes effect only after the Telnet service is restarted. You must be logged on as a member of the Administrators group to use the Telnet Server Administration utility.

Troubleshooting

The following table provides information about a few common problems you might encounter when running Telnet Server.

Error message	Cause	Solution
Invalid input	The entered value was not acceptable.	Review the range of the optional values and re-enter your choice.
Failed to open the registry key	The Telnet server must be running to open a registry key. This error indicates that it is not currently running.	Start Telnet service.
Failed to query the registry value	The Telnet server must be running to query a registry value. This error indicates that it is not currently running.	Start Telnet service.

Telnet Client

You can use Microsoft Telnet Client to connect to a remote computer running the Telnet service or other Telnet server software. Once you have made this connection, you can communicate with the Telnet server. The type of session you conduct depends on how the Telnet software is configured. Communication, games, system administration, and local logon simulations are some typical uses of Telnet.

The Telnet client uses the Telnet protocol, part of the TCP/IP suite of protocols, to connect to a remote computer over a network. The Telnet client software allows a computer to connect to a remote server. You can use the Telnet client provided with Windows 2000 to connect to a remote computer, log on to the remote computer, and interact with it as if you were sitting in front of it.

Users of previous versions of Microsoft's Telnet client may notice a few changes in the version included with Windows 2000. The most obvious change is that Microsoft Telnet Client is now a command-line application rather than a Windows application. As a command-line application, Microsoft Telnet Client will seem very familiar to users of UNIX-based Telnet clients.

An important new feature found in Microsoft Telnet Client is NTLM authentication support. Using this feature, a computer using Microsoft Telnet Client can log on to a Windows 2000 computer running the Telnet service by using NTLM authentication.

Note Telnet session logging is not supported in Microsoft Telnet Client.

Using Telnet

To open Telnet, click Start, click Run, and then type **telnet**. You can also type **telnet** at the command prompt. To use Telnet, you must have the TCP/IP protocol installed and configured on your computer and you must have a user account established on a remote host.

To display help for Telnet, type **help** at the Microsoft Telnet command prompt. To connect to a site, type **connect** *<computer_name>* where *<computer_name>* is the IP address or host name of the computer running the Telnet service.

Exercise 2: Configuring and Connecting to the Telnet Service

In this exercise you configure the Telnet service to start on Server01. Then, you connect to the Telnet service from Server01 and verify the connection. Complete this exercise from Server01.

Note If you are running Server02, you may complete Procedure 2 from Server02.

▶ **Procedure 1: Enabling and configuring the Telnet service**

In this procedure, you configure the Telnet service for automatic startup and then start the Telnet service.

1. Log on to Server01 as Administrator with a password of "password."

2. Click the Start button, point to Programs, point to Administrative Tools and then click Services.

   The Services console appears.

3. In the details pane, scroll down and double-click Telnet.

   The Telnet Properties (Local Computer) dialog box appears.

4. Change the Startup Type drop-down list box from Manual to Automatic.

5. Under Service status, click the Start button.

   A Service Control status box appears briefly as the Telnet service starts.

6. Click OK to close the Telnet Properties (Local Computer) dialog box.

7. Close the Services console.

▶ **Procedure 2: Using the Microsoft Telnet Client**

In this procedure you connect to the Telnet service from the Microsoft Telnet Client. You may complete this procedure on either Server01 or Server02. Completing the procedure from Server02 provides remote access to Server01. However, for the purpose of training, running these commands from Server01 is adequate. If you complete this procedure from Server02, log on as Administrator before starting.

1. Click the Start button, and then click Run.

   The Run dialog box appears.

2. In the Open text box, type **telnet** and then click OK.

   The Microsoft Telnet command prompt appears.

3. Type **help** or **?** to see a list of available commands.

   A list of supported commands appears.

4. Type **open server01**.

   A Welcome to Microsoft Telnet Server message appears.

   Note You can use abbreviations for the commands you enter. For example, **o server01** is equivalent to **open server01**.

   ---

5. Any commands that you can run from the command line on Server01 can be run from the Telnet shell.

6. Leave the Telnet session active while you complete the next procedure.

▶ **Procedure 3: Running the Telnet Server Administration tool**

In this procedure you monitor the Telnet service for Telnet client connections and then disconnect the connected Telnet client using the Telnet Server Administrator.

1. Click the Start button, and then click Run.

   The Run dialog box appears.

2. In the Open text box, type **tlntadmn** and then click OK.

   The Telnet Server Admin utility command window appears.

3. Type **1** to list the current users.

   Statistics on the administrator user appear.

4. Type **2** to terminate a user session.

   A message appears instructing you to enter a user's session ID to terminate.

5. Type **1**; this is the session ID of the connected user.

   A list of command options reappear.

6. Return to the Microsoft Telnet client window on Server01 or Server02.

   Notice that the connection with the host was lost.

7. Press any key to continue.

   You are returned to the Microsoft Telnet Client command window.

8. Type **q** or **quit** to close the Microsoft Telnet Client command window.

9. Return to the Telnet Server Administrator command window.

10. Type **0** to close the Telnet Server Administrator.

Lesson Summary

The Telnet service and a Telnet client work together to allow users to communicate with a remote computer. The Windows 2000 Telnet service allows users of the Microsoft Telnet Client to remotely connect to the computer and use command-line applications on the computer as if they were sitting in front of it. You can use the Services snap-in, the Computer Management snap-in, or the command prompt to start or stop the Telnet service. In addition, you can use the Telnet Server Admin utility to start, stop, or get information about the Telnet service. You can also use it to get a list of current users, terminate a user's session, or change Telnet service registry settings. Microsoft Telnet Client allows you to connect to a remote computer running Telnet server software. NTLM authentication is supported when a Microsoft Telnet Client connects to the Microsoft Telnet service. Telnet provides user support for the Telnet protocol, a remote access protocol you can use to log on to a remote computer, network device, or private network.

Lesson 4: Installing and Configuring Terminal Services

Terminal Services provides access to Windows 2000 and the latest Windows-based applications for client computers. It also provides access to your desktop and installed applications anywhere, from any supported client. Terminal Services is a built-in feature of Windows 2000 that allows IT managers and system administrators who want to increase flexibility in application deployment, control computer management costs, and remotely administer network resources.

After this lesson, you will be able to

- Deploy Terminal Services in a Windows 2000 environment

Estimated lesson time: 40 minutes

Overview of Terminal Services

Terminal Services running on a Windows 2000 Server enables all client application execution, data processing, and data storage to occur on the server. It provides remote access to a server desktop through terminal emulation software. The terminal emulation software can run on a number of client hardware devices, such as a personal computer, Windows CE-based Handheld PC (H/PC), or terminal.

With Terminal Services, the terminal emulation software sends keystrokes and mouse movements to the server. Terminal Services does all the data manipulation locally and passes back the display. This approach allows remote control of servers and centralized application management, minimizing network bandwidth requirements between the server and client.

Users can gain access to Terminal Services over any TCP/IP connection including Remote Access, Ethernet, the Internet, wireless, wide area network (WAN), or virtual private network (VPN). The user experience is limited only by the slowest link in the connection, and the security of the link is governed by the TCP/IP deployment in the data center.

Terminal Services provides remote administration of network resources, a uniform experience to users in branch offices in remote locations, or a graphical interface to line of business applications on text-based computers.

Terminal Services is a built-in feature of Windows 2000. You can enable Terminal Services in one of two modes: Remote Administration and Application Server.

Remote Administration

Remote Administration gives system administrators a powerful method for remotely administering each Windows 2000 Server computer over any TCP/IP connection. You can administer file and print sharing, edit the registry from another computer on the network, or perform any task as if you were sitting at the console. You can use Remote Administration mode to manage servers not normally compatible with the Application Server mode of Terminal Services, such as servers running the Cluster service.

Remote Administration mode installs only the remote access components of Terminal Services. It does not install application sharing components. This means that you can use Remote Administration with very little overhead on mission critical servers. Terminal Services allows a maximum of two concurrent Remote Administration connections. No additional licensing is required for those connections, and you do not need a license server.

Note For more information about remote administration, see the Supplemental Course Materials CD-ROM (\chapt14\articles\TSRemote.doc) that accompanies this book.

Application Server

In Application Server mode, you can deploy and manage applications from a central location, saving administrators development and deployment time as well as the time and effort required for maintenance and upgrade. After an application is deployed in Terminal Services, many clients can connect—through a Remote Access connection, LAN, or WAN, and from many different types of clients.

You can install applications directly at the Terminal server, or you can use remote installation. For example, you can use Group Policy and Active Directory services to publish Windows Installer application packages to a Terminal server or a group of Terminal servers. Applications can be installed only by an Administrator on a per server basis and only if the appropriate Group Policy setting is enabled.

Client licensing is required when deploying a Terminal server as an application server. Each client computer, regardless of the protocol used to connect to Terminal server, must have the Terminal Services Client Access License as well as the Windows 2000 Client Access License.

Note For information about optimizing applications for Windows 2000 Terminal Services, see the Supplemental Course Materials CD-ROM (\chapt14\articles\TSAppDev.doc) that accompanies this book.

Tools for Administration

To help you install Terminal Services for Windows 2000, additional administration tools are added to the Administrative Tools folder, including Terminal Services Client Creator, Terminal Services Manager, Terminal Services Configuration, and Terminal Services Licensing.

Note Terminal Services Licensing is installed only if Application Server mode is selected or if Adminpak.msi is installed.

Terminal Services Client Creator

Use this tool to create floppy disks for installing the Terminal Services Client software on Windows for Workgroups, Windows 95, Windows 98, and Windows NT platforms.

Terminal Services Manager

With this tool, you can manage all Windows 2000 servers running Terminal Services. Administrators can view current users, servers, and processes. Additionally, administrators can send messages to specific users, use the Remote Control feature, and terminate processes. Figure 14.20 shows the Terminal Services Manager console running inside a terminal services session.

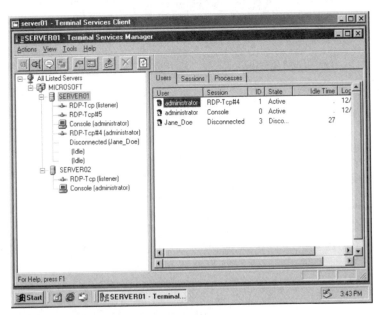

Figure 14.20 Running Terminal Services Manager to manage Terminal Services running on Server01

Terminal Services Configuration

This tool allows you to manage your Remote Desktop Protocol (RDP) configuration. Modifying options in this tool are global, unless you choose to inherit information from the same options located in the user configuration. Available options include setting connection encryption, logon settings, time-outs, initial programs run on successful logon, remote control options, Windows printer mapping, LPT port mapping, clipboard mapping, and applying these options to a specific LAN adapter.

Terminal Services Licensing

With this tool, you store and track Windows 2000 Terminal Services client access licenses. It can be installed either during installation of Terminal Services or later. When clients log on to Terminal Services, Terminal Services validates the client license. If a client does not have a license or requires a replacement license, Terminal Services requests one from the license server. The license server provides a license from its pool of available licenses, and Terminal Services passes the license to the client. If there are no available licenses, the license server grants a temporary license for the client. After it is granted, each client license is associated with a particular computer or terminal.

Note For more information about Terminal Services administration tools, see the Supplemental Course Materials CD-ROM (\chapt14\articles\TSsol.doc) that accompanies this book.

Terminal Services Licensing Components

Terminal Services has its own method for licensing clients that log on to Terminal servers. This method is separate from the licensing method for Windows 2000 Server clients. Terminal Services licensing includes four components: the Microsoft Clearinghouse, a license server, a Terminal server, and client licenses.

Microsoft Clearinghouse

The Microsoft Clearinghouse is the database that Microsoft maintains to activate license servers and to issue client license key packs to the license servers that request them. The Clearinghouse stores information about all activated license servers and client license key packs that have been issued. You can access the Clearinghouse through the Licensing wizard in the Terminal Services Licensing snap-in.

License Server

A license server stores all Terminal Services client licenses that have been installed for a Terminal server and tracks the licenses that have been issued to client computers or terminals. A Terminal server must be able to connect to an activated license server before clients can be issued licenses. One activated license server can serve multiple Terminal servers.

Terminal Server

A Terminal server is the computer on which Terminal Services is enabled and running. It provides clients access to Windows-based applications running entirely on the server and supports multiple client sessions on the server. When clients log on to a Terminal server, the server validates the client license. If a client does not have a license, the Terminal server requests one for the client from the license server.

Client Licenses

Each client computer or terminal that connects to a Terminal server must have a valid client license. The client license is stored locally and presented to the Terminal server each time the client connects to the server. The server validates the license, and then allows the client to connect.

Note For more information about Terminal Services licensing, see the Supplemental Course Materials CD-ROM (\chapt14\articles\TSLicensing.doc) that accompanies this book.

Administering the License Server

Deploying Terminal Services license server includes setting up the license server, enabling the server, activating the server, and installing the licenses.

Setting Up a License Server

A license server is required by Terminal Services when running in Application Server mode. The Terminal Services Licensing service is a low-impact service that stores the client licenses that have been issued for a Terminal server and tracks the licenses that have been issued to client computers or terminals.

The license server must be activated through the Microsoft Clearinghouse and loaded with Client Access Licenses for distribution from the Clearinghouse. The license server is accessed by the Terminal servers only to issue a new license, and need only be administered to obtain licenses from the Clearinghouse.

Enabling a License Server

You can enable the Terminal Services Licensing service on your computer when you run Windows 2000 Server Setup. In a production environment it is recommended that you enable Terminal Services on a member server or stand-alone server, and that you install the license server on a different computer. Terminal Services is resource intensive.

There are two types of license servers: a domain license server and an enterprise license server. Before installing the license server, consider which of the following two types of license servers you require:

- **Domain license server** Appropriate if you want to maintain a separate license server for each domain. If you have workgroups or Windows NT 4.0 domains, a domain license server is the only type that you can install. Terminal servers can access domain license servers only if they are in the same domain as the license server. By default, a license server is installed as a domain license server.

- **Enterprise license server** Can serve Terminal servers in any domain within a site, but the domain must be a Windows 2000 domain. It can serve only Terminal servers in the same site. This type of license server is appropriate if you have many domains. Enterprise license servers can only be installed by using Add/Remove Programs. They cannot be installed during Windows 2000 Setup.

When deciding where on your physical network to deploy your license server, consider how a Terminal server discovers and communicates with a license server. Upon enabling Terminal Services, the Terminal server begins polling the domain and Active Directory services looking for a license server. (In a workgroup environment, the Terminal server broadcasts to all the servers in the workgroup on the same subnet.)

Note In Windows 2000 domains, the domain license server must be installed on a domain controller. In workgroups or Windows NT 4.0 domains, the domain license server can be installed on any server. If you are planning to eventually migrate from a Workgroup or Windows NT 4.0 domain to a Windows 2000 domain, you might want to install the license server on a computer that can be promoted to a Windows 2000 domain controller.

To activate the license server quickly and to access the Microsoft Clearinghouse through the Internet, install the server on a computer that has Internet access.

You must enable a Windows 2000 license server within 90 days of enabling Windows 2000 Terminal Services. If you have not enabled the license service when this period ends, your Windows 2000 Terminal Services will fail to operate.

Activating a License Server

A license server must be activated in order to identify the server and allow it to issue client licenses to your Terminal servers. You can activate a license server by using the Licensing wizard.

There are four methods to activate your license server:

- Internet
- Web-based
- Fax
- Telephone

If the computer running the Terminal Services Licensing snap-in is connected to the Internet, the Internet activation method is the quickest and easiest method. The Licensing wizard directs you to the secure Microsoft Internet site where license servers are activated. When you activate the license server, Microsoft provides the server with a digital certificate that validates server ownership and identity. Using this certificate, a license server can make subsequent transactions with Microsoft and receive client access licenses for your Terminal servers.

If your license server does not have Internet connectivity but you do have the ability to access the World Wide Web from a browser on another computer, you can activate your license server by means of the Web-based activation method. The Licensing wizard directs you to the secure Microsoft Web site to obtain a certificate for the license server.

Alternate methods for activating a license server include faxing your information to or calling the Customer Support Center (CSC) nearest you. The Licensing wizard also guides you through these steps. You can locate the appropriate telephone or fax number to call by using the Licensing wizard. If you use the fax activation method, your confirmed request is returned by fax from Microsoft. If you use the telephone activation method, your request is completed with a customer service representative over the telephone.

You are required to activate a license server only once. While waiting to complete the activation process, your license server can issue temporary licenses for clients that allow them to use Terminal servers for up to 90 days.

The digital certificate that uniquely identifies your license server is stored in the form of a License Server ID. Place a copy of this number in a safe location. To view this number after your license server has been activated, highlight the license server and select Properties from the View menu. Set your communication method to World Wide Web and click OK. Then select Install Licenses from the Action menu and click Next. The License Server ID is listed in the center of the Licensing Wizard screen.

Installing Licenses

Terminal Services licenses must be installed on your license server in order for the Internet Connector setting to be enabled or for non-Windows 2000 clients to permanently access a Windows 2000 Terminal server. To obtain Windows 2000 Terminal Services Client Access licenses or Internet Connector licenses, purchase them through your standard software procurement method. After you purchase them you can then install the licenses by using the Licensing wizard.

After you have installed your licenses, your license server can begin deploying the licenses. Clients with 90-day temporary licenses will be upgraded to a Terminal Services Client Access license the next time they log on (unless the number of client access licenses installed has exceeded by the number of outstanding temporary licenses).

Deploying to Client Computers

Client computers or terminals connect to a Terminal server by using a small client program installed on disk or in firmware. The choice of which client platform to use depends on the current installed base and individual user need. At a minimum, ensure that every client computer or terminal that you expect to connect to a Terminal server is physically capable of hosting the client software and connecting over the network.

Windows-based client computers connecting to Terminal Services should have at least an 80386 microprocessor running at 33 MHz (though a 486/66 is recommended), a 16-bit VGA video card, and the Microsoft TCP/IP stack. The Terminal Services client runs on Windows for Workgroups 3.11, Windows 95, Windows 98, and Windows NT 3.51 or later, and Windows 2000.

The Terminal Services client takes up only about 500 KB of disk space and typically uses approximately 4 MB of RAM when running. If client bitmap caching is enabled, another 10 MB of disk space might be used. For best performance, a computer running the Terminal Services client should have a total of 8 MB of physical RAM or more under Windows for Workgroups 3.11 or Windows 95, 24 MB or more for Windows 98, and 32 MB or more for Windows 2000.

Note A Terminal Services client for Windows CE devices can be found on the Windows 2000 Server installation CD-ROM in the \Valueadd\msft\mgmt\mstsc_hpc folder.

The RDP client software is installed by default as a subcomponent of Terminal Services. The various clients are installed in the directory %systemroot%\system32\clients\tsclient

There are two ways to deploy the client:

- Create a file share to do the installation over the network.
- Select Terminal Services Client Creator from the Administrative Tools menu, and make a client image that can be installed with a floppy disk.

Note The Terminal Services client requires TCP/IP to connect to the server, but Terminal Services itself can use IPX to gain access to Novell servers if necessary.

Client Configurations

You can optimize Terminal Services by following these recommendations:

- Disable the Active Desktop.
- Disable smooth scrolling.
- Minimize the use of graphics and animation, including animated graphics, screen savers, blinking cursors, and the animated Microsoft Office Assistant. Place shortcuts on the desktop and keep the Programs submenu as flat as possible. Avoid using bitmaps in wallpaper; in Display Properties set Wallpaper to None on the Background tab, and select a single color from the Appearance tab.
- Enable file sharing on client computers and share drives with easily identifiable names like "drivec." Be aware of the security implications involved.
- Avoid the use of MS-DOS or Win16 (16-bit) applications where possible.
- Configure the Terminal server to return the user's logon name rather than the computer name to applications that make use of a NetBIOS function that calls for the computer name.
- Train users to use Terminal Services hot key sequences. There are a few important differences in the hot key sequences used in a Terminal Services client session than in a Windows 2000 session.

Upgrading to Terminal Services

The approach you take to upgrade to Terminal Services depends upon your existing Terminal Services setup.

WinFrame with or without MetaFrame

There is no direct upgrade path from WinFrame to Terminal Services. In this case you first have to upgrade to Microsoft Terminal Server 4.0 and then upgrade to Windows 2000.

Terminal Server 4.0 without MetaFrame

With Terminal Server 4.0 installed, there is a direct upgrade path to Terminal Services. When you install Windows 2000, the server recognizes the Terminal Server 4.0 edition, automatically performs the upgrade, and automatically enables Terminal Services in Application Server mode. Note that you might need to reinstall existing applications if you enable Terminal Services in Application Server mode.

Terminal Server 4.0 with MetaFrame

With MetaFrame for Terminal Server 4.0 installed, you first install Windows 2000 with Terminal Services, then you install the latest version of MetaFrame for Windows 2000.

Windows NT without Terminal Services

When you install Windows 2000, select Terminal Services in Remote Administration or Application mode, to enable Terminal Services.

Installing and Configuring Applications

A Windows 2000 server that is configured to run Terminal Services in Application Server mode provides multiple concurrent user connections to any number of applications.

It is recommended that applications be added or removed by using the Add/Remove Programs function under Control Panel. This process automatically manages the Terminal Services installation requirements. It is also possible to install the application directly by putting the server into Install mode.

To put the Terminal Server in Install mode, type **change user /install**. After the software installation is complete, type **change user /execute** to return the Terminal Server to execute mode.

The change user commands are not necessary when using Add/Remove Programs because Add/Remove Programs takes care of this process in the background. Add/Remove Programs is preferred because there is always the possibility of error or omission when using the command lines. If an application is installed without using Add/Remove Programs and without using the command line to set the Install mode, the application should be removed and reinstalled.

Only administrators are allowed to install applications on a Terminal Services application server.

Deploying Applications through Group Policy

Deploying applications through Active Directory services and Group Policy by using Windows Installer is a very flexible application deployment method. It allows applications to be installed and managed in a number of different ways. The three main ways you can deploy applications when using Windows Installer:

- Install on a local computer by the user.

- Assign by the system administrator from the domain controller to a user or a computer.

- Publish by the system administrator from the domain controller for a user.

Before an application can be installed using Windows Installer, an .MSI installation package must be available for the application.

Deploying Applications from a Domain Controller

To deploy an application from a domain controller, a system administrator needs to assign a .MSI-based application to a computer. Application servers cannot assign or publish applications to users.

Transform files are required if the original application installation package did not install all of the necessary components of the application to the local disk. Transform files allow you to select what, if anything, needs to be installed during the installation.

A system administrator can also install an application from a remote session or the console of an application server. A typical installation is initiated by using the following command:

```
Msiexec/I ApplicationName.MSI
TRANSFORMS=TransformFileName.MST ALLUSERS=1
```

The installation of an application in a multi-user environment is quite different from an installation to an individual user. Application server software installation must not jeopardize the system that is running, and the installation must be configured to allow concurrent users. For these reasons, only administrators can install applications, and users are not able to install anything.

It is the responsibility of the system administrator to decide which applications are needed and to ensure that applications are locally installed and available before allowing remote user connections.

Exercise 3: Installing and Configuring Terminal Services and Terminal Services Licensing

In this exercise you install Windows 2000 Terminal Services, and then run remote administration from Server02 to Server01. Next, you install Terminal Services Licensing and then establish a terminal session from Server02 to Server01.

▸ **Procedure 1: Installing Terminal Services and running Remote Administration**

In this procedure, you install Terminal Services to run in Remote Administration mode on Server01. You then run a remote administration session from Server02. Make sure that the Windows 2000 Server installation CD-ROM is inserted in the CD-ROM drive on Server01.

1. Log on to Server01 as Administrator with a password of "password."

2. Click the Start menu, point to Settings and click Control Panel.

3. In Control Panel, double-click Add/Remove Programs.

   The Add/Remove Programs dialog box appears.

4. In the left frame, click Add/Remove Windows Components.

   After a few moments, the Windows Components wizard appears.

5. Scroll down and select the Terminal Services check box and click Next.

   The Terminal Services Setup screen appears.

6. Read the information on this screen, verify that the Remote Administration Mode radio button is selected and then click Next.

   The Configuring Components screen appears as Windows 2000 configures and installs components. After a few minutes, the Completing the Windows Components Wizard screen appears.

7. Click Finish.

   The Add/Remove Programs dialog box appears.

8. Click Close and then close Control Panel.

   A System Setting Change message box appears, informing you that you must restart the computer before the settings will take effect.

9. Click Yes to restart the computer.

10. After Server01 restarts, do not log on. You will log on from Server02 using Terminal Services remote administration.

11. From Server02, logon to Server01 as Administrator with a password of "password." Make sure you are logging on to the MICROSOFT domain.

12. Click the Start menu and then click Run.

    The Run dialog box appears.

13. In the Open text box, type **\\server01\c$\Program Files\terminal services client** and then click OK.

    The Terminal Services Client window appears.

14. Double-click the Conman icon.

    Client Connection Manager appears.

15. Click the first toolbar icon.

    The Client Connection Manager wizard starts.

16. Click Next.

    The Create A Connection screen appears.

17. In the Connection Name text box, type **Server01 Remote Administration**.

18. In the Server name or IP Address text box, type **Server01** and click Next.

    The Automatic Logon screen appears.

19. Click the Logon Automatically With This Information check box.

20. In the User Name text box, type **administrator**.

21. In the Password text box, type **password**.

22. In the Domain text box, type **microsoft** and click Next.

    The Screen options screen appears.

23. Select a resolution that the monitor on Server02 can support. If you don't know what resolution it supports, choose the 640 x 480 radio button.

24. Click Next.

    The Connection Properties screen appears.

25. Click the Enable Data Compression and Cache Bitmaps check boxes and click Next.

    The Starting A Program screen appears.

26. Click Next.

    The Icon And Program Group screen appears.

27. Click Next.

    The Completing The Client Connection Manager Wizard screen appears.

28. Click Finish.

    The Client Connection Manager appears with the new connection you created.

29. Double-click the Server01 Remote Administration icon.

    A Connecting box appears. Then a terminal window opens whose title bar is SERVER01 – Terminal Services Client (Server01 Remote Administration).

30. In the Log On To Windows dialog box, type **password** and click OK.

    You are now able to remotely administer Server01 from Server02. Notice that on the Server01 monitor, the computer is not logged on but you are logged on to Server01 from Server02.

31. Close the SERVER01 – Terminal Services Client (Server01 Remote Administration) terminal window appearing on Server02.

    A Disconnect Windows Session message box appears stating that you are about to disconnect from Server01 but that you can return to this session later and continue to run programs started in this terminal session.

32. Click OK.

33. Close the Client Connection Manager and close the Terminal Services Client window.

▸ **Procedure 2: Installing Terminal Services Licensing**

In this procedure, you install Terminal Services Licensing on Server01 to serve the license requirements of Application Server mode. Make sure that the Windows 2000 Server installation CD-ROM is inserted in the CD-ROM drive on Server01.

Note In a production environment, it is advisable to install licensing services on a computer that is not also running Terminal services in Application Server mode.

---

1. Log on to Server01 as Administrator with a password of **password**.

2. Click the Start menu, point to Settings and then click Control Panel.

3. In Control Panel, double-click Add/Remove Programs.

   The Add/Remove Programs dialog box appears.

4. In the left frame, click Add/Remove Windows Components.

   After a few moments, the Windows Components wizard appears.

5. Scroll down and select the Terminal Services Licensing check box and then click Next.

   The Terminal Services Setup screen appears.

6. Select the Application Server Mode radio button and then click Next.

   The Terminal Services Setup screen appears and informs you that Windows 2000 Administration Tools may not work properly after the installation of Terminal services in Application Server mode.

7. Click Next.

   The Terminal Services Licensing Setup screen appears.

8. Click the Your Entire Enterprise radio button.

   Notice that the license server database will be stored in C:\WINNT\ System32\LServer.

9. Click Next.

   The Configuring Components screen appears as Windows 2000 configures and installs components. After a few minutes, the Completing the Windows Components Wizard screen appears.

10. Click Finish.

    The Add/Remove Programs dialog box appears.

11. Click Close and then close Control Panel.

   A System Setting Change message box appears, informing you that you must restart the computer before the settings will take effect.

12. Click Yes to restart the computer.

13. Log on to Server01 as Administrator with a password of "password."

14. Click the Start menu, point to Programs, point to Administrative Tools, and then click Terminal Services Licensing.

   The Terminal Services Licensing snap-in appears and the Terminal Services Licensing Manager status box appears as Terminal services are located. Once Server01 is found, it appears in the details pane with a status of Not Activated.

15. In the details pane, click SERVER01.

16. Click the Action menu and then click Activate Server.

   The Licensing wizard appears.

17. Click Next.

   The Connection Method screen appears.

18. In the Connection Method drop-down list box, select Telephone and then click Next.

   The Country/Region Selection screen appears.

19. Select a country and then click Next.

20. Without entering a license server ID, click Next.

   A Licensing Wizard message box appears explaining that the license server ID entered is not valid or was not entered.

21. Click OK.

22. On the License Server Activation screen, click Cancel.

23. Close the Terminal Services Licensing snap-in.

   The Terminal Services Licensing component is installed and you will be able to use Terminal Services in Application Server mode for 90 days. Before 90 days have passed, you must activate the server using the Terminal Services Licensing snap-in and information provided to you by Microsoft Corporation.

▶ **Procedure 3: Preparing an application for Terminal Services Application mode operation**

In this procedure, you uninstall the Windows 2000 Administration Tools and then reinstall them to ensure that they run properly from a terminal session. Make sure that the Windows 2000 Server installation CD-ROM is inserted in the CD-ROM drive on Server01 and that you are logged on as Administrator on Server01.

1. On Server01, click the Start menu, point to Settings and then click Control Panel.

2. In Control Panel, double-click Add/Remove Programs.

    The Add/Remove Programs dialog box appears.

3. In the Currently Installed Programs box, click Windows 2000 Administration Tools and then click the Remove button.

    The Add/Remove Programs message box appears asking you if you want to remove the Windows 2000 Administration Tools from your computer.

4. Click Yes.

    A Windows Installer status box appears and then the Windows 2000 Administration Tools status box appears as the tools are removed.

    The Add/Remove Programs dialog box no longer contains the Windows 2000 Administration Tools.

5. In the left frame, click Add New Programs.

6. From the main window, click CD or Floppy.

    The Install Program From Floppy Disk or CD-ROM screen appears.

7. Click Next.

    The Run Installation Program screen appears.

8. In the Open text box, type *<cd-rom>*:**\i386\adminpak.msi** where *<cd-rom>* is the drive letter of your CD-ROM drive.

9. Click Next.

    The Windows Installer status box appears and then the Windows 2000 Administration Tools Installation status box appears. After a few moments, the Windows 2000 Administration Tools Setup wizard appears.

10. Click Next.

    The Installation Progress screen appears as installation proceeds.

    After a few minutes, the Completing the Windows 2000 Administration Tools Setup wizard appears.

11. Click Finish.

    The After Installation screen appears.

12. Click Next.

    The Finish Admin Install screen appears.

13. Read the text on this screen and then click Finish.

    The Add/Remove Programs dialog box appears.

14. Click the Close button.

15. Close Control Panel.

▶ **Procedure 4: Connecting to Terminal Services in Application mode and running Terminal Services tools**

In this procedure you install the terminal services client on Server02 and then run a terminal screen from Server02 to Server01. Inside the terminal session running on Server02 you monitor the session using tools installed on Server01. Server01 and Server02 should be logged on as Administrator to the MICROSOFT domain.

1. On Server01 click the Start menu and then click Run.

   The Run dialog box appears.

2. In the Open text box, type **C:\winnt\system32\clients** and then click OK.

   The Clients window appears.

3. Click the Tsclient folder.

4. Click the File menu and then click Sharing.

   The Tsclient Properties dialog box appears with the Sharing tab active.

5. Click the Share This Folder radio button.

   Tsclient appears in the Share Name text box.

6. Click OK.

7. Close the Clients window.

8. On Server02 click the Start menu and then click Run.

   The Run dialog box appears.

9. In the Open text box, type **\\server01\tsclient** and then click OK.

   The Tsclient On Server01 window appears.

10. Double-click the win32 folder.

11. Double-click the disks folder.

12. Double-click the disk1 folder.

13. Double-click the setup icon.

    The Terminal Services Client Setup screen appears.

14. Click Continue.

    The Name And Organization Information dialog box appears.

15. Enter your name and then click OK.

    The Confirm Name And Organization Information message box appears.

16. Click OK.

    A License Agreement message box appears.

17. Click the I Agree button.

    The Terminal Services Client Setup dialog box appears.

    Notice that the client software will be installed below the Program Files folder.

18. Click the large button to install the Terminal Services Client software.

    The Terminal Services Client Setup message box appears asking if you want this installation routine to apply to all users of this computer.

19. Click Yes.

    The installation progresses and then the Terminal Service Client Setup message box appears stating that the installation was successful.

20. Click OK.

21. Close the Disk1 window.

22. On Server02 click the Start menu, point to Programs, point to Terminal Services Client and then click the Terminal Services Client icon.

    The Terminal Services Client dialog box appears.

23. In the Server drop-down list box, type **Server01**.

24. Leave the Screen area at 640 x 480, verify that the Enable Disk Compression check box is selected and select the Cache Bitmaps To Disk check box.

25. Click the Connect button.

    The Server01 – Terminal Services Client window appears.

26. In the Log On To Windows dialog box, type **Jane_Doe** with a password of **student** and then click OK.

    Notice that the Jane_Doe personal profile appears which is indicated by the custom color scheme.

27. From within the terminal session, click the Start menu, point to Programs, point to Administrative Tools, and then click Terminal Services Manager.

    The SERVER01 – Terminal Services Manager snap-in starts inside of the terminal session.

28. In the console tree, click SERVER01.

29. In the details pane, click Jane_Doe.

30. Click the Actions menu and then click Status.

    Status information about the Jane_Doe session appears.

31. Click the Close button.

32. Click the Actions menu and then click Send Message.

    The Send Message dialog box appears.

33. In the top Message title box, type **Message from the Administrator** and in the bottom Message box, type **Terminal Services will be shutting down for maintenance in a few minutes. Please close your session.**

34. Click OK.

    A message box from the Administrator appears in the terminal session.

35. Click OK.

36. Close the SERVER01 – Terminal Services Manager snap-in and then close the SERVER01 – Terminal Services Client window.

    The Disconnect Windows Session message box appears.

37. Read the message and then click OK.

38. Shut down Server02 and Server01.

Lesson Summary

Terminal Services running on a Windows 2000 Server enables all client application execution, data processing, and data storage to occur on the server. It provides remote access to a server desktop through terminal emulation software. You can enable Terminal Services in one of two modes: Remote Administration and Application Server. Remote Administration gives system administrators a powerful method for remotely administering each Windows 2000 server over any TCP/IP connection. In Application Server mode, you can deploy and manage applications from a central location, saving administrators development and deployment time as well as the time and effort required for maintenance and upgrade. Terminal Services licensing includes four components: the Microsoft Clearinghouse, a license server, a Terminal server, and client licenses. Deploying Terminal Services license server includes setting up the license server, enabling the server, activating the server, and installing the licenses. Every client computer or terminal that you expect to connect to a Terminal server must be physically capable of hosting the client software and connecting over the network. A Windows 2000 server that is configured to run Terminal Services in Application Server mode provides multiple concurrent user connections to any number of applications. You can deploy applications through Active Directory services and Group Policy, and you can deploy applications from a domain controller. When you install Terminal Services for Windows 2000, additional administration tools are added to the Administrative Tools folder, including Terminal Services Client Creator, Terminal Services Manager, Terminal Services Configuration, and Terminal Services Licensing.

Review

The following questions are intended to reinforce key information presented in this chapter. If you are unable to answer a question, review the appropriate lesson and then try the question again. Answers to the questions can be found in Appendix A, "Questions and Answers."

1. Compare a virtual directory to a Dfs root.

2. You are accessing the IIS 5.0 documentation from Internet Services Manager (HTML). All of the documentation appears and you are able to access information via the Index tab. Under the Index tab, you find the phrase Process Accounting. However, when you perform a search on this phrase, the Web browser reports that your search phrase cannot be found. What is the most likely reason that this is happening?

3. You have created a virtual directory for the purpose of WebDAV publishing. The home directory of the Web site is accessible from Internet Explorer 5 but when you attempt to access the virtual directory for WebDAV publishing, access is denied. Name two reasons why this may happen and how you can solve this access problem.

4. Why is it important that the Microsoft Telnet Client and the Microsoft Telnet service support NTLM authentication?

5. If Terminal Services is not licensed, what features of Terminal Services will work and for how long?

Preparation for MCP Exam 70-215

Installing Windows 2000 Server

Whenever you install or upgrade to Microsoft Windows 2000 Server, regardless of the type of installation, there are several steps that you should take, such as making certain that the computer meets the minimum hardware requirements and that the hardware is supported by Windows 2000 Server. You should also perform such tasks as backing up files, uncompressing drives, disabling disk mirroring, and checking the boot sector for viruses. After you've completed all these preliminary tasks, you can then perform a clean installation of Windows 2000 Server or upgrade from certain versions of Microsoft Windows NT Server and earlier versions of Windows 2000 Server. You can also perform unattended installations of Windows 2000 Server, which simplifies the process of setting up Windows 2000 Server on multiple computers.

Tested Skills and Suggested Practices

The skills that you need to successfully master the Installing Windows 2000 Server objective domain on the *Installing, Configuring, and Administering Microsoft Windows 2000 Server* exam include:

- **Performing an attended installation of Windows 2000 Server.**

    - Practice 1: Prepare for a Windows 2000 Server installation by determining whether your computer has the minimum hardware requirements necessary to install and operate Windows 2000 Server. Be sure to evaluate the processor, the amount of free hard disk space, and memory.

    - Practice 2: Verify that your computer's hardware is listed on the Hardware Compatibility List (HCL). You can find the most current HCL at *http:// www.microsoft.com/hcl/default.asp.*

▪ Practice 3: Perform a clean installation of Windows 2000 Server by using the Setup Boot disks. If you don't have these disks, you can create a set by running the MAKEBOOT.EXE utility or the MAKEBT32.EXE utility, which are located in the Bootdisk folder of the Windows 2000 Server installation CD-ROM. You should perform this practice on a computer that is not in a production environment and does not contain any critical files. You should be able to partition and format the hard disk during the installation process without having to worry about loss of data.

▪ **Performing an unattended installation of Windows 2000 Server.**

  ▪ Practice 1: Use Notepad or another text editor to create an answer file that allows you to run an unattended installation of Windows 2000 Server. You can use the Unattend.txt answer file that is included on the Windows 2000 Server installation CD-ROM and modify it as necessary, or you can create a new answer file. Also try creating an answer file by using the Setup Manager wizard.

  ▪ Practice 2: Perform an unattended installation on a computer that is running a Windows 32-bit operating system. From a command prompt, launch the WINNT32.EXE installation program located on the Windows 2000 Server installation CD-ROM. Be certain to use the appropriate switches to define the type of installation and specify the answer file that you created in Practice 1. You should perform this practice on a computer that is not in a production environment and does not contain any critical files. You should be able to partition and format the hard disk during the installation process without having to worry about loss of data. You can perform the unattended installation on the same computer on which you performed the attended installation.

▪ **Upgrading a server from Microsoft Windows NT Server 4 to Windows 2000 Server.**

  ▪ Practice 1: If you are using a different computer than was used in the previous practices, determine whether your computer has the minimum hardware requirements necessary to install and operate Windows 2000 Server. Be sure to evaluate the processor, the amount of free hard disk space, and memory.

  ▪ Practice 2: If you're performing this practice on a different computer than you previously used, verify that your computer's hardware is listed on the HCL. You can find the most current HCL at *http://www.microsoft.com/hcl/default.asp*.

  ▪ Practice 3: Perform an upgrade from Windows NT 4 to Windows 2000 Server. The easiest way to upgrade Windows NT Server 4 to Windows 2000 Server is to insert the Windows 2000 Server installation CD-ROM into the computer's CD-ROM drive. You can also run WINNT32.EXE from the CD-ROM.

Further Reading

This section lists supplemental readings by objective. Study these sources thoroughly before taking exam 70-215.

Objective 1.1

Microsoft Corporation. *Windows 2000 Server Resource Kit*. Volume: *Microsoft Windows 2000 Server Deployment Planning Guide*. Redmond, Washington: Microsoft Press, 2000. (This book can be downloaded for free at *http://www.microsoft.com/windows2000/library/resources/reskit/dpg/default.asp*.) Review Chapter 13, "Automating Server Installation and Upgrade." This chapter includes a discussion about using a bootable CD-ROM. Also review Chapter 15, "Preparing Member Servers for Upgrade or New Installation." This chapter includes information about minimum hardware requirements, pre-installation tasks, and performing an installation.

Microsoft Corporation. *MCSE Training Kit: Microsoft Windows 2000 Server*. Redmond, Washington: Microsoft Press, 2000. Review Lessons 1 and 2 in Chapter 2, "Installing and Configuring Microsoft Windows 2000 Server."

Microsoft Corporation. "Step-by-Step Guide to a Common Infrastructure for Windows 2000 Server Deployment - Part 1: Installing a Windows 2000 Server as a Domain Controller." (This Step-by-Step guide can be downloaded for free at *http://www.microsoft.com/windows2000/library/planning/walkthroughs/default.asp*.) This document includes information about hardware requirements, server configuration, and server installation.

Objective 1.2

"Deploying Microsoft Windows 2000 Professional and Microsoft Office 2000 Using Sysprep." (This article, which is titled "Automating the Deployment of Windows 2000 Professional and Office 2000" on the downloaded version can be downloaded for free at *http://www.microsoft.com/windows2000/library/planning/incremental/sysprep.asp*.) Although this article focuses on Windows 2000 Professional and Microsoft Office 2000, it provides a good overview of using the Sysprep tool.

"Microsoft Windows 2000 Guide to Unattended Setup." The document filename is Unattend.doc, and it can be found on the Windows 2000 Server installation CD-ROM. The file is part of the Deploy.cab file in the \Support\Tools folder. In Windows 98 or Windows 2000, use Windows Explorer to extract this document. In Windows 95 and earlier, or in MS-DOS, use the Extract command to access the file. This document provides information about the answer file, its parameters, and its syntax. The document also provides sample Sysprep.inf files.

Microsoft Corporation. *Windows 2000 Server Resource Kit*. Volume: *Microsoft Windows 2000 Server Deployment Planning Guide*. Redmond, Washington: Microsoft

Press, 2000. (This book can be downloaded for free at *http://www.microsoft.com/ windows2000/library/resources/reskit/dpg/default.asp*.) Review Chapter 13, "Automating Server Installation and Upgrade," and Chapter 14, "Using Systems Management Server to Deploy Windows 2000."

Microsoft Corporation. *MCSE Training Kit: Microsoft Windows 2000 Server*. Redmond, Washington: Microsoft Press, 2000. Review Lessons 1 and 2 in Chapter 3, "Unattended Installations of Microsoft Windows 2000 Server."

Objective 1.3

Microsoft Corporation. *Windows 2000 Server Resource Kit*. Volume: *Microsoft Windows 2000 Server Deployment Planning Guide*. Redmond, Washington: Microsoft Press, 2000. (This book can be downloaded for free at *http://www.microsoft.com/ windows2000/library/resources/reskit/dpg/default.asp*.) Review Chapter 13, "Automating Server Installation and Upgrade," and Chapter 15, "Upgrading and Installing Member Servers."

Microsoft Corporation. *MCSE Training Kit: Microsoft Windows 2000 Server*. Redmond, Washington: Microsoft Press, 2000. Review Lesson 3 in Chapter 2, "Installing and Configuring Microsoft Windows 2000 Server."

Objective 1.4

"Making Deployment Easier in Windows 2000." (This white paper can be downloaded for free at *http://www.microsoft.com/TechNet/win2000/easydep.asp*.) This paper includes a short section about installing service packs.

Microsoft Corporation. *MCSE Training Kit: Microsoft Windows 2000 Server*. Redmond, Washington: Microsoft Press, 2000. Review Lesson 1 in Chapter 12, "Reliability and Availability." This lesson includes a section that specifically discusses the installation of service packs. See "Installing Service Packs."

Objective 1.5

Microsoft Corporation. *Windows 2000 Server Resource Kit*. Volume: *Automating the Deployment of Windows 2000 Professional and Office 2000*. Redmond, Washington: Microsoft Press, 2000. (Several chapters from this book, including the three listed below, can be downloaded for free at *http://www.microsoft.com/windows2000/library/ resources/reskit/samplechapters/default.asp*.) Review Chapter 1, "Disk Concepts and Troubleshooting"; Chapter 14, "Troubleshooting Strategies"; and Chapter 15, "Startup Process."

Microsoft Corporation. *MCSE Training Kit: Microsoft Windows 2000 Server*. Redmond, Washington: Microsoft Press, 2000. Review Lesson 4 in Chapter 2, "Installing and Configuring Microsoft Windows 2000 Server."

OBJECTIVE 1.1

Perform an attended installation of Windows 2000 Server.

Before you can install Windows 2000 Server, you must gather information and make decisions about how you want to install the operating system. First, you must verify that your computer meets the minimum hardware requirements and that all hardware is compatible with Windows 2000 Server. You can determine compatibility by reviewing the **HCL**. You should identify how you will partition the hard disk and choose the appropriate file system. Windows 2000 Server Setup allows you to install Windows 2000 Server onto an existing **partition** or to create a partition and then install Windows 2000 onto the new one. The partition can be formatted with either the **NTFS file system** or the **file allocation table (FAT)** 16 or 32 file system. During installation, you will have to select a licensing mode, choose the type of network group (**workgroup** or **domain**) that your computer will join, and determine whether to perform a new installation or upgrade an existing installation. You must also determine the installation method and which optional components to install.

Regardless of which method you use to install Windows 2000 Server, you must launch either the WINNT.EXE or the WINNT32.EXE installation program. Use WINNT.EXE for a clean installation on a computer running MS-DOS or Windows 3.*x*, and use WINNT32.EXE for a clean installation on a computer running Windows 95, Windows 98, or Windows NT Workstation. For a clean installation or upgrade from Windows NT Server 3.51 or 4, use WINNT32.EXE. Once you launch one of these two programs, the installation process begins. The installation process can be divided into three distinct phases: **Pre-Copy**, **Text Mode**, and **GUI Mode**. During the Pre-Copy phase, all the files needed for the installation are copied to temporary folders on the local hard drive. During the Text Mode phase, you are prompted for the information necessary to complete the installation. During the GUI Mode phase, Setup gathers information about your computer, installs Windows 2000 Server networking, and completes the installation process.

To answer the questions in this objective, you should be familiar with the various tasks that you need to perform in order to prepare for a Windows 2000 Server installation. You should also have a working knowledge of the Windows 2000 Setup programs as well as an understanding of each phase of the installation process. In addition, you should understand the differences among the various installation methods and know how to use each one in order to install Windows 2000 Server.

Objective 1.1 Questions

70-215.01.01.001

You are preparing to install a new installation of Windows 2000 Server on four computers. On which computer or computers can you install Windows 2000 Server without modifying the hardware? (Choose all that apply.)

Examine the four computers shown in the image below.

Computer Name	A	B	C	D
Processor configuration	5 Pentium III's, each 500 MHz	2 Pentium III's, each 500 MHz	1 Pentium 166 MHz	1 Pentium 100 MHz
RAM	2 GB	512 MB	128 MB	32 MB
Free hard disk space	10 GB	620 MB	2 GB	10 GB
Partition type	FAT32	FAT16	FAT16	NTFS

A. Computer A

B. Computer B

C. Computer C

D. Computer D

70-215.01.01.002

You are performing an installation of Windows 2000 Server on a new Pentium III 500-MHz computer with 256 MB of RAM, one 10-GB hard disk, a CD-ROM drive, and a floppy drive. No operating system has been loaded on the computer, and the hard disk has not been formatted.

You want to accomplish the following goals:

- You want to format the hard disk during the installation process, rather than before installation.

- You do not want to load any other operating system onto the computer prior to the Windows 2000 Server installation.

- You want to start the installation process by booting off the floppy drive.

Using your Windows 2000 Server installation CD, you create Windows 2000 Server boot disks on a neighboring system that already has a version of Windows installed. You then install Windows 2000 Server on the new computer by using your new boot disks.

Which result or results does your installation achieve? (Choose all that apply.)

A. You can format the hard disk during installation, rather than before installation.

B. You do not have to load another operating system onto the drive before installing Windows 2000.

C. You can start the installation process by booting off the floppy drive.

D. The installation does not meet any of the required results.

70-215.01.01.003

You are installing Windows 2000 Server on a computer and must ensure that the server has the following functionality:

- The computer must be able to support the use of Simple Network Management Protocol (SNMP) to monitor network traffic.

- The computer must provide support for Smart Card authentication.

- The computer must provide for script development from Windows 2000 Server.

- The computer must provide for remote installation of clients so that you can perform unattended installations on client computers.

You install the following components:

- Certificate Services

- Internet Information Services

- Management and Monitoring Tools

- Indexing Services

- Script Debugger

- Remote Storage

- Windows Media Services

Which functionality is available given the above optional components on the Windows 2000 Server computer? (Choose all that apply.)

A. The computer supports the use of SNMP to monitor network traffic.

B. The computer can provide for Smart Card authentication.

C. The computer can provide script development tools.

D. The computer can provide for remote installations on client computers.

E. The installation does not allow any of the desired functionality.

70-215.01.01.004

You are installing Windows 2000 Server on a computer and must ensure that the server has the following functionality:

- The computer must be able to support the use of SNMP to monitor network traffic.

- The computer must provide support for Smart Card authentication.

- The computer must provide for script development from Windows 2000 Server.

- The computer must provide for remote installation of clients so that you can perform unattended installations on client computers.

You install the following components:

- Internet Information Services

- Management and Monitoring Tools

- Indexing Services

- Script Debugger

- Remote Storage

- Windows Media Services

Which functionality is available given the above optional components on the Windows 2000 Server computer? (Choose all that apply.)

A. The computer supports the use of SNMP to monitor network traffic.

B. The computer can provide for Smart Card authentication.

C. The computer can provide script development tools.

D. The computer can provide for remote installations on client computers.

E. The installation does not allow any of the desired functionality.

Objective 1.1 Answers

70-215.01.01.001

▶ **Correct Answers: C**

A. **Incorrect:** You cannot install Windows 2000 Server on Computer A because Windows 2000 Server supports only four processors, and Computer A has five processors. To support five processors, you must install Windows 2000 Advanced Server. However, Computer A does meet the minimum hardware requirements for RAM and hard disk space, and Windows 2000 Server can be installed on a FAT32 partition.

B. **Incorrect:** You cannot install Windows 2000 Server on Computer B because you need at least 1 GB of free hard disk space, and Computer B has only 620 MB of free hard disk space. However, Computer B does meet the minimum hardware requirements for processors and RAM, and Windows 2000 Server will support two processors and can be installed on a FAT16 partition.

C. **Correct:** Computer C meets the minimum hardware requirements for a Windows 2000 Server installation. The processor must be at least a Pentium 133-MHz, and the computer must have at least 128 MB of RAM, although 256 MB is recommended for most network environments. Computer C has a 166-MHz processor and 128 MB of RAM. In addition, Windows 2000 Server requires at least 671 MB of free hard disk space, and Computer C has 2 GB. Windows 2000 Server can be installed on a FAT16, FAT32, or NTFS partition.

D. **Incorrect:** You cannot install Windows 2000 Server on Computer D because you need at least a Pentium 133-MHz processor and Computer D has only a 100-MHz processor. In addition, Windows 2000 Server requires 64 MB of RAM, and Computer D has only 32 MB. However, Computer D does meet the minimum hardware requirements for free hard disk space, and Windows 2000 Server can be installed on an NTFS partition.

70-215.01.01.002

▶ **Correct Answers: A, B, and C**

   A. **Correct:** The Windows 2000 Setup boot disks allow you to format the hard disk during the installation process. The hard disk does not have to be formatted prior to installation. If you are installing Windows 2000 Server on a computer with no previous operating system, and you are using an MS-DOS boot floppy disk (performing an over-the-network installation), you have to format the drive first. However, if you are using the Windows 2000 Setup boot disks to start Setup, you can format the drive during Setup.

   B. **Correct:** No previous operating system needs to be loaded on the computer in order to use the Setup boot disks. The Setup boot disks are required if you are installing Windows 2000 Server on an *x*86-based computer that is not running MS-DOS or a Windows operating system and does not support the bootable CD-ROM format.

   C. **Correct:** You can start the Windows 2000 Server installation process by inserting the first Windows 2000 Setup boot disk into the floppy drive (drive A:) and then turning on your computer. Setup starts automatically. As files are loaded from the Setup boot disks, the bar at the bottom of the screen displays the components that are being loaded.

   D. **Incorrect:** The installation meets all the required results.

70-215.01.01.003

▶ **Correct Answers: A, B, and C**

   A. **Correct:** SNMP is included with the installation of Management and Monitoring Tools. The tools are software components that include utilities for network management and monitoring, along with services that support client dialing and the updating of client phone books. SNMP is a network protocol used to manage TCP/IP networks. In Windows, the SNMP service is used to provide status information about a host on a TCP/IP network.

   B. **Correct:** Smart Card authentication is supported through the installation of Certificate Services. Certificate Services provides authentication support, including secure e-mail, Web-based authentication, and Smart Card authentication. A Smart Card is a credit card-sized device used to securely store public and private keys, passwords, and other types of personal information. To use a Smart Card, you need a Smart Card reader attached to the computer and a Personal Identification Number (PIN) for the Smart Card. In Windows 2000, Smart Cards can be used to enable certificate-based authentication and single sign-on to the enterprise.

   C. **Correct:** Script Debugger provides support for script development. You can use Script Debugger to test scripts written in Microsoft VBScript and Microsoft JScript, as well as applications written in Java. You can also debug scripts in other languages that support host-independent debugging, such as REXX or PerlScript. You can use Script Debugger to view the source code of the script that you are debugging, control execution line by line through the scripts, view and alter variable and property values, set breakpoints and view the call stack, and switch between threads of execution.

D. **Incorrect:** To enable Windows 2000 Server to perform remote installations on client computers, you must install Remote Installation Services (RIS). Remote Installation Services allows you to set up new client computers remotely without having to visit each client. The target client computers must support remote booting. On the server, a separate partition will be needed for Remote Installation Services.

E. **Incorrect:** The installation provides all the required functionality except remote installations on client computers.

70-215.01.01.004

▶ **Correct Answers: A and C**

A. **Correct:** SNMP is included with the installation of the Management and Monitoring Tools. The tools are software components that include utilities for network management and monitoring, along with services that support client dialing and the updating of client phone books. SNMP is a network protocol used to manage TCP/IP networks. In Windows, the SNMP service is used to provide status information about a host on a TCP/IP network.

B. **Incorrect:** The computer cannot support Smart Card authentication. Smart Card authentication is supported through the installation of Certificate Services. Certificate Services provides authentication support, including secure e-mail, Web-based authentication, and Smart Card authentication. A Smart Card is a credit card-sized device used to securely store public and private keys, passwords, and other types of personal information. To use a Smart Card, you need a Smart Card reader attached to the computer and a Personal Identification Number (PIN) for the Smart Card. In Windows 2000, Smart Cards can be used to enable certificate-based authentication and single sign-on to the enterprise.

C. **Correct:** Script Debugger provides support for script development. You can use Script Debugger to test scripts written in VBScript and JScript, as well as applications written in Java. You can also debug scripts in other languages that support host-independent debugging, such as REXX or PerlScript. You can use Script Debugger to view the source code of the script that you are debugging, control execution line by line through the scripts, view and alter variable and property values, set breakpoints and view the call stack, and switch between threads of execution.

D. **Incorrect:** To enable Windows 2000 Server to perform remote installations on client computers, you must install Remote Installation Services (RIS). Remote Installation Services allows you to set up new client computers remotely without having to visit each client. The target client computers must support remote booting. On the server, a separate partition will be needed for Remote Installation Services.

E. **Incorrect:** The installation can provide support for SNMP and script development tools, but it cannot support the other required functionality.

OBJECTIVE 1.2

Perform an unattended installation of Windows 2000 Server.

Windows 2000 Server Setup allows you to automate the installation of the operating system and other server applications. To automate an installation, you must create and use an **answer file**, which is a customized script that automatically answers the questions raised by Setup during installation. The answer file is usually saved as a .txt file, and is sometimes called the unattend file or the unattend script file. When the answer file is saved as a .txt file, you can use any name for the file. Being able to use different names allows you to build and use multiple answer files. However, when installing Windows 2000 Server from a bootable CD-ROM drive, you must name the answer file Winnt.sif, and when you use an answer file in conjunction with the Sysprep tool, you must name the answer file Sysprep.inf. The answer file consists of section headers, keys, and the values for each key. Every key in an answer file must have a value assigned to it; however, some keys are optional, and some keys have default values that are used if the key is omitted. You can create an answer file automatically by using the Setup Manager wizard or manually by using a text editor such as Notepad.

To perform an unattended installation of Windows 2000 Server, you must specify the answer file when you run Setup. There are three basic types of unattended installations that you can use to set up Windows 2000 Server: the bootable CD-ROM method, the WINNT.EXE method, and the WINNT32.EXE method. In addition to the basic types of unattended installation, several methods are available for creating an automated installation of Windows 2000 Server:

- The WINNT32.EXE Setup program along with the /syspart parameter

- The System Preparation Tool (Sysprep)

- Systems Management Server (SMS)

- Bootable CD-ROM

The method you choose depends on the desired outcome. These methods either build on or replace the over-the-network installations that use WINNT.EXE or WINNT32.EXE. You should use the syspart parameter for clean installations to computers that have dissimilar hardware; however, use Sysprep when the master computer and the target computers have identical or nearly identical hardware. Use SMS to perform managed upgrades of Windows 2000 Server to multiple systems, and use the bootable CD-ROM method for computers at remote sites with slow links.

To answer the questions in this objective, you should know how to use the Setup Manager wizard to prepare for a Windows 2000 Server installation and to create an answer file. You should also know how to create an answer file manually by using a text editor such as Notepad. And you should be familiar with the various methods that you can use to perform unattended installations and create automated installations.

Objective 1.2 Questions

70-215.01.02.001

You are creating an automated installation of Windows 2000 Server.

You want to accomplish the following goals:

- You want to configure customized network settings.

- You want to create a subfolder in the distribution folder.

- You want to specify that the Internet Information Services (IIS) system component be installed.

- You want to specify the default user name and organization name.

You plan to use the Setup Manager wizard to create a fully automated installation and specify the settings above.

Which result or results does your solution achieve? (Choose all that apply.)

A. You can configure customized network settings.

B. You can create a subfolder in the distribution folder.

C. You can specify that the Internet Information Services (IIS) system component be installed.

D. You can specify the default user name and organization information.

E. Your solution does not achieve any of the required results.

70-215.01.02.002

You are creating an automated installation of Windows 2000 Server.

You want to accomplish the following goals:

- You want to configure customized network settings.

- You want to specify the default user name and organization name.

- You want to specify that the Internet Information Services (IIS) system component be installed.

You decide to use Notepad to create the answer file that will be used in the automated installation.

Which result or results does your solution achieve? (Choose all that apply.)

A. You can configure customized network settings.

B. You can specify the default user name and organization name.

C. You can specify that the Internet Information Services (IIS) system component be installed.

D. Your solution does not achieve any of the required results.

70-215.01.02.003

You create an answer file for an unattended installation of Windows 2000 Server, and you now want to install Windows 2000 Server on a computer that has a bootable CD-ROM drive. You plan to install the software via the CD-ROM, so you change the BIOS to boot from the CD-ROM. How should you install Windows 2000 Server on this computer?

A. Ensure that the answer file has a [Data] section that specifies the required keys. Save the answer file as a Winnt.sif file, and copy the file to a floppy diskette. Insert the diskette into the floppy drive as soon as the computer boots from the CD-ROM.

B. Ensure that the answer file has a [Data] section that specifies the required keys. Save the answer file as a Winnt.txt file, and copy the file to a floppy diskette. Insert the diskette into the floppy drive as soon as the computer boots from the CD-ROM.

C. Ensure that the answer file has a [Winnt] section that specifies the required keys. Save the answer file as a Winnt.sif file, and copy the file to a floppy diskette. Insert the diskette into the floppy drive as soon as the computer boots from the CD-ROM.

D. Ensure that the answer file has a [Winnt] section that specifies the required keys. Save the answer file as a Sysprep.inf file, and copy the file to a floppy diskette. Insert the diskette into the floppy drive as soon as the computer boots from the CD-ROM.

Objective 1.2 Answers

70-215.01.02.001

▶ **Correct Answers: A and D**

A. **Correct:** The Setup Manager wizard allows you to create or modify the answer file, which can include network configuration settings. The answer file is a customized script that allows you to run an unattended installation of Windows 2000 Server. The file is usually saved as a .txt file and is sometimes called the unattend file or the unattend script file. The script answers the questions that Setup normally prompts you for during installation. Setup Manager is available on the Windows 2000 Server installation CD-ROM in the Support\Tools\Deploy.cab file. By using the Setup Manager wizard, you can configure the answer file to perform a number of tasks, including configuring network settings. After you use the Setup Manager wizard to create an answer file, you can add more settings by using a text editor. Refer to the Unattend.doc file in Deploy.cab for a comprehensive list of available settings.

B. **Incorrect:** Although the Setup Manager wizard will allow you to create a distribution folder and add files to the folder, you cannot use Setup Manager to create subfolders in the distribution folder.

C. **Incorrect:** You cannot use the Setup Manager wizard to specify system components, such as the Internet Information Services (IIS) system component. However, you can specify system components by manually updating the [Components] section of the answer file.

D. **Correct:** The Setup Manager wizard allows you to specify the default user name and organization information.

E. **Incorrect:** The solution allows you to configure network settings and specify the default user name and organization information, but it does not allow you to create a subfolder in the distribution folder or specify the IIS component.

70-215.01.02.002

▶ **Correct Answers: A, B, and C**

A. **Correct:** The answer file allows you to specify network configuration settings. The answer file is a customized script that allows you to run an unattended installation of Windows 2000 Server. The file is usually saved as a .txt file and is sometimes called the unattend file or the unattend script file. The script answers the questions that Setup normally prompts you for during installation. You can use a text editor such as Notepad to create the answer file manually. In general, the answer file consists of section headers, parameters, and values for those parameters. Although most section headers are pre-defined, you can define additional section headers. Notepad allows you to create an answer file that performs all the tasks that can be performed by an answer file that is created by the Setup Manager wizard, such as configuring network settings and specifying the default user name and organization information. In addition, a text editor allows you to create an answer file that performs other tasks, such as specifying IIS system components.

B. **Correct:** The answer file allows you to specify the default user name and organization name in the [UserData] section.

C. **Correct:** The answer file allows you to specify system components, such as the IIS component, in the [Components] section.

D. **Incorrect:** The proposed solution allows you to configure network settings, create the distribution folder, add files to that folder, and specify the IIS system component.

70-215.01.02.003

▶ **Correct Answers: A**

A. **Correct:** The [Data] section is an optional section that is required only when performing an unattended installation by booting directly from the Windows 2000 installation CD-ROM. The [Data] section can contain four keys and their values: AutoPartition, MsDosInitiated, UnattendedInstall, and UseBIOSToBoot. To start Windows 2000 Setup in unattended mode from the Windows 2000 Server installation CD-ROM, the computer must support the El Torito Bootable CD-ROM (no emulation mode) format. In addition, the answer file must be named Winnt.sif and be placed on a floppy disk to be inserted into the floppy drive as soon as the computer boots from the CD-ROM drive.

B. **Incorrect:** You must name the answer file Winnt.sif, not Winnt.txt. A .txt file is used for regular unattended installations of Windows 2000 Server, not when installing Windows 2000 from a bootable CD-ROM drive or when using the Sysprep tool to prepare a hard disk for creating a disk image of your Windows 2000 Server installation. You can use any name for the .txt file.

C. **Incorrect:** The answer file must have a [Data] section that specifies the required keys, not a [Winnt] section.

D. **Incorrect:** The answer file must have a [Data] section that specifies the required keys, not a [Winnt] section. In addition, you must name the answer file Winnt.sif, not Sysprep.inf. Sysprep.inf is the name of the answer file that is used when using the Sysprep tool to prepare a hard disk for creating a disk image of your Windows 2000 Server installation.

O B J E C T I V E   1 . 3

Upgrade a server from Microsoft Windows NT 4.

Before you can run Windows 2000 Server Setup, you need to determine whether to perform an **upgrade** or a clean **installation**. Upgrading is the process of setting up Windows 2000 Server in a directory that currently contains certain versions of Windows operating systems. Installing is the process of placing the operating system in a new directory, wiping out the previous operating system, or installing Windows 2000 Server on a disk or a partition with no previous operating system. You can upgrade to Windows 2000 Server from Windows NT Server 3.51, Windows NT Server 4, Windows NT 4 Terminal Server, and earlier versions of Windows 2000 Server. For all other operating systems, you must perform a clean installation. Upgrading, in contrast to performing a clean installation, allows you to retain existing users, settings, groups, and permissions. In addition, files and applications do not need to be recopied to the disk after Windows 2000 Server is set up. During the upgrade, Windows 2000 Setup migrates the current settings of the operating system while requiring little administrator input during the process.

You can use several methods to upgrade a computer to Windows 2000 Server. The easiest way to perform an upgrade is to insert the Windows 2000 Server installation CD-ROM into the CD-ROM drive. When the current operating system reads the CD-ROM, you are prompted with a message box that asks you whether you want to upgrade to Windows 2000 Server. Once you begin the installation process, the Setup wizard guides you through the upgrade. You can also initiate an upgrade by running the WINNT32.EXE file from the CD-ROM or over the network; however, you cannot perform an upgrade from the boot floppy disks or from booting the CD-ROM. When you perform an upgrade, you must determine whether to convert any FAT16 or FAT32 partitions to NTFS. In addition, you should review the Windows 2000 Compatibility Guide at *http://www.microsoft.com* if you want to upgrade your system and use the same applications as before.

To answer the questions in this objective, you should know which operating systems can be upgraded to Windows 2000 Server and which operating systems require a clean installation. In addition, you should know what methods can be used to perform an upgrade, and you should have a clear understanding of the differences between performing an upgrade and performing a clean installation.

Objective 1.3 Questions

70-215.01.03.001

You are preparing to set up Windows 2000 Server on four computers, but you want to perform upgrades rather than clean installations. Which computer or computers can be upgraded to Windows 2000 Server without any modifications? (Choose all that apply.)

Examine the four computers shown in the image below.

Computer Name	A	B	C	D
Processor configuration	3 Pentium III's, each 500 MHz	5 Pentium III's, each 600 MHz	1 Pentium 166 MHz	4 Pentium III's, each 350 MHz
RAM	2 GB	512 MB	64 MB	3.5 GB
Free hard disk space	10 GB	620 MB	2 GB	10 GB
Operating system	Windows NT 4 Server	Windows NT 4 Server	Windows 95	Windows NT 4 Server
Partition type	NTFS	NTFS	FAT16	NTFS

A. Computer A

B. Computer B

C. Computer C

D. Computer D

70-215.01.03.002

You are preparing to set up Windows 2000 Server on four computers, but you want to perform upgrades rather than clean installations. Which computer or computers can be upgraded to Windows 2000 Server without any modifications? (Choose all that apply.)

Examine the four computers shown in the image below.

Computer Name	A	B	C	D
Processor configuration	1 Pentium 100 MHz	1 Pentium 166 MHz	1 Pentium 166 MHz	1 Pentium III 350 MHz
RAM	128 MB	64 MB	128 MB	128 MB
Free hard disk space	10 GB	2 GB	2 GB	10 GB
Operating system	Windows NT 4 Server	Windows 98	Windows NT 3.51 Server	Windows NT 4 Server
Partition type	NTFS	NTFS	FAT16	NTFS

A. Computer A

B. Computer B

C. Computer C

D. Computer D

70-215.01.03.003

You are preparing to set up Windows 2000 Server on four computers, but you want to perform upgrades rather than clean installations. Which computer or computers can be upgraded to Windows 2000 Server without any modifications? (Choose all that apply.)

Examine the four computers shown in the image below.

Computer Name	A	B	C	D
Processor configuration	1 Pentium 100 MHz	1 Pentium 166 MHz	1 Pentium 166 MHz	1 Pentium III 350 MHz
RAM	128 MB	128 MB	64 MB	128 MB
Free hard disk space	10 GB	2 GB	2 GB	10 GB
Operating system	Windows NT 4 Server	Windows NT 4 Server	Windows 2000 Professional	Windows 98
Partition type	NTFS	FAT32	FAT16	NTFS

A. Computer A

B. Computer B

C. Computer C

D. Computer D

Objective 1.3 Answers

70-215.01.03.001

▶ **Correct Answers: A and D**

A. **Correct:** Computer A meets the minimum hardware requirements for a Windows 2000 Server instal-lation. The processor must be at least a Pentium 133 MHz, and the computer must have at least 64 MB of RAM, although 128 MB is recommended for most network environments. Computer A has a 500-MHz processor and 2 GB of RAM. In addition, Windows 2000 Server requires at least 1 GB of free hard disk space, and Computer A has 10 GB. Windows 2000 Server can be installed on a FAT16, FAT32, or NTFS partition. You can upgrade this computer to Windows 2000 Server because the cur-rent operating system is Windows NT 4 Server. You can upgrade to Windows 2000 Server from a computer configured with Windows NT Server 3.51, Windows NT Server 4, Windows NT Terminal Server, or an earlier version of Windows 2000 Server.

B. **Incorrect:** You cannot perform an upgrade or a clean installation on Computer B because you need at least 1 GB of free hard disk space, and Computer B has only 620 MB of free hard disk space. In addi-tion, Windows 2000 will support only four processors, and Computer B has five processors. However, Computer B does meet the minimum hardware requirements for RAM, and Windows 2000 Server can be installed on an NTFS partition. If this computer met the minimum hardware requirements, you would be able to upgrade to Windows 2000 Server because the current operating system is Windows NT 4 Server.

C. **Incorrect:** You cannot perform an upgrade on Computer C because it is configured with Windows 95. You can upgrade to Windows 2000 Server only from a computer configured with Windows NT Server 3.51, Windows NT Server 4, Windows NT Terminal Server, and an earlier ver-sion of Windows 2000 Server. However, you can perform a clean installation on Computer C because it meets the minimum hardware requirements.

D. **Correct:** Computer D meets the minimum hardware requirements for a Windows 2000 Server instal-lation. The processor must be at least a Pentium 133 MHz, and the computer must have at least 64 MB of RAM, although 128 MB is recommended for most network environments. Computer D has a 350-MHz processor and 3.5 GB of RAM. In addition, Windows 2000 Server requires at least 1 GB of free hard disk space, and Computer D has 10 GB. Windows 2000 Server can be installed on a FAT16, FAT32, or NTFS partition. You can upgrade this computer to Windows 2000 Server because the cur-rent operating system is Windows NT 4 Server.

70-215.01.03.002

▶ **Correct Answers: C and D**

A. **Incorrect:** You cannot perform an upgrade or a clean installation on Computer A because you need at least a 133-MHz processor, and Computer A has only a 100-MHz processor. However, Computer A does meet the minimum hardware requirements for RAM and free hard disk space, and Windows 2000 Server can be installed on an NTFS partition. If this computer met the minimum hardware requirements, you would be able to upgrade to Windows 2000 Server because the current operating system is Windows NT 4 Server.

B. **Incorrect:** You cannot perform an upgrade on Computer B because it is configured with Windows 98. You can upgrade to Windows 2000 Server only from a computer configured with Windows NT Server 3.51, Windows NT Server 4, Windows NT Terminal Server, or an earlier version of Windows 2000 Server. However, you can perform a clean installation on Computer B because it meets the minimum hardware requirements.

C. **Correct:** Computer C meets the minimum hardware requirements for a Windows 2000 Server installation. The processor must be at least a Pentium 133-MHz, and the computer must have at least 128 MB of RAM, although 256 MB is recommended for most network environments. Computer C has a 166-MHz processor and 128 MB of RAM. In addition, Windows 2000 Server requires at least 1 GB of free hard disk space, and Computer C has 2 GB. Windows 2000 Server can be installed on a FAT16, FAT32, or NTFS partition. You can upgrade this computer to Windows 2000 Server because the current operating system is Windows NT 3.51 Server. You can upgrade to Windows 2000 Server from a computer configured with Windows NT Server 3.51, Windows NT Server 4, Windows NT Terminal Server, or an earlier version of Windows 2000 Server.

D. **Correct:** Computer D meets the minimum hardware requirements for a Windows 2000 Server installation. The processor must be at least a Pentium 133 MHz, and the computer must have at least 64 MB of RAM, although 128 MB is recommended for most network environments. Computer D has a 350-MHz processor and 128 MB of RAM. In addition, Windows 2000 Server requires at least 1 GB of free hard disk space, and Computer D has 10 GB. Windows 2000 Server can be installed on a FAT16, FAT32, or NTFS partition. You can upgrade this computer to Windows 2000 Server because the current operating system is Windows NT 4 Server.

70-215.01.03.003

▶ **Correct Answers: B**

A. **Incorrect:** You cannot perform an upgrade or a clean installation on Computer A because you need at least a 133-MHz processor, and Computer A has only a 100-MHz processor. However, Computer A does meet the minimum hardware requirements for RAM and free hard disk space, and Windows 2000 Server can be installed on an NTFS partition. If this computer met the minimum hardware requirements, you would be able to upgrade to Windows 2000 Server because the current operating system is Windows NT 4 Server.

B. **Correct:** Computer B meets the minimum hardware requirements for a Windows 2000 Server installation. The processor must be at least a Pentium 133-MHz, and the computer must have at least 128 MB of RAM, although 256 MB is recommended for most network environments. Computer B has a 166-MHz processor and 128 MB of RAM. In addition, Windows 2000 Server requires at least 1 GB of free hard disk space, and Computer B has 2 GB. Windows 2000 Server can be installed on a FAT16, FAT32, or NTFS partition. You can upgrade this computer to Windows 2000 Server because the current operating system is Windows NT 4 Server. You can upgrade to Windows 2000 Server from a computer configured with Windows NT Server 3.51, Windows NT Server 4, Windows NT Terminal Server, or an earlier version of Windows 2000 Server.

C. **Incorrect:** You cannot perform an upgrade on Computer C because it is configured with Windows 2000 Professional. You can upgrade to Windows 2000 Server only from a computer configured with Windows NT Server 3.51, Windows NT Server 4, Windows NT Terminal Server, or an earlier version of Windows 2000 Server. However, you can perform a clean installation on Computer C because it meets the minimum hardware requirements.

D. **Incorrect:** You cannot perform an upgrade on Computer D because it is configured with Windows 98. You can upgrade to Windows 2000 Server only from a computer configured with Windows NT Server 3.51, Windows NT Server 4, Windows NT Terminal Server, or an earlier version of Windows 2000 Server. However, you can perform a clean installation on Computer D because it meets the minimum hardware requirements.

OBJECTIVE 1.4

Deploy service packs.

Windows 2000 supports service pack **slipstreaming**, which allows **service packs** to be applied directly to the operating system's distribution share during installation. With slipstreaming, service packs are applied to Windows 2000 distribution files on a network share. When Windows 2000 is installed from a source that has been updated through slipstreaming, the appropriate files from the service pack are installed automatically; you don't have to manually apply the service pack after the installation. To apply a new service pack, use the UPDATE command along with the -s:*<distribution_folder>* switch, where *<distribution_folder>* is the location containing the operating system files. The updated service pack files are copied over the existing Windows 2000 files in your distribution folder. Windows 2000 also eliminates the need to reinstall components applied before a service pack was installed, which makes it easier to install service packs on existing systems.

When a service pack is installed, the updated service pack files are applied to the Windows 2000 installation. In addition, a new log file (Svcpack.log) is created. The log remembers what has been overwritten and which system files have come from where. If the system state data changes, such as when services are added or removed, the base system is told that a service pack was installed, what files were replaced or updated by the service pack, and from which location the service pack was installed. As a result, if you install a service or a component after you install a service pack, the component will know whether to look for the service pack, the distribution folder, or the Windows 2000 installation CD-ROM again in order to install the service successfully. (If all the sources are available, this will happen transparently.) In general, this eliminates the need to completely reapply the service pack every time you add a component. If the system state data changes, Windows 2000 installs the correct files, whether those files originate from the Windows 2000 installation source or from the service pack installation source.

To answer the questions in this objective, you must be familiar with adding service packs, applying service pack slipstreaming, and changing system state data after a service pack is applied. You should also know how to use the UPDATE command along with the appropriate parameters to add a new service pack and apply slipstreaming.

Objective 1.4 Questions

70-215.01.04.001

You are applying a service pack to your Windows 2000 Server distribution share. You must ensure that the service pack files are installed over the existing Windows 2000 files so that you do not have to reinstall any components. How should you apply the service pack?

A. Apply the service pack by using the UPDATE command without using any switches.

B. Apply the service pack by using the UPDATE command along with the /sp switch.

C. Apply the service pack by using the UPDATE command along with the -s:*<distribution_folder>* switch.

D. Apply the service pack by using the UPDATE command along with the /overwrite switch.

70-215.01.04.002

You applied a service pack to your Windows 2000 Server distribution share, and you then applied the updated operating system to the servers that installed Windows 2000 Server from that share. You must now add Remote Access Service (RAS) to one of your servers. How should you update the RAS component on the server so that the service pack is applied to that component?

A. Reapply the service pack by using the UPDATE command, without using any switches.

B. Reapply the service pack by using the UPDATE command along with the -s:*<distribution_folder>* switch.

C. Use the Add/Remove Programs utility to remove the service pack, and then reinstall the service pack by using the UPDATE command.

D. Do not take any further action. The RAS component will automatically use the correct files, whether they originate from the Windows 2000 installation source or from the service pack.

70-215.01.04.003

You are applying a service pack to a Windows 2000 Server distribution share, and you will then apply the service pack to the servers that installed Windows 2000 Server from that share.

You want to accomplish the following goals:

- You want the service pack files to be copied over the existing Windows 2000 files in your distribution share.

- You want to be able to use all existing components on the Windows 2000 Server computers after the service pack is applied.

- You want to be able to install additional components to the Windows 2000 Server computers without having to reapply the service pack.

You install the service pack on the installation share by using the UPDATE command along with the -s:*<distribution_folder>* switch.

Which result or results does your installation achieve? (Choose all that apply.)

A. The service pack files are copied over the existing Windows 2000 files.

B. You can use all existing Windows 2000 components after the service pack is installed.

C. You can install additional Windows 2000 components without reinstalling the service pack.

D. The installation does not meet any of the required results.

Objective 1.4 Answers

70-215.01.04.001

▶ **Correct Answers: C**

A. **Incorrect:** Although you should use the UPDATE command, you must also use the -s:*<distribution_folder>* switch to copy the updated service pack files over the existing Windows 2000 files.

B. **Incorrect:** Although you should use the UPDATE command, you must also use the -s:*<distribution_folder>* switch to copy the updated service pack files over the existing Windows 2000 files. The UPDATE command does not include an /sp switch.

C. **Correct:** The UPDATE command, when used with the -s:*<distribution_folder>* switch, implements service pack slipstreaming, which refers to a service pack being applied to the Windows 2000 distribution files on a network share. The -s:*<distribution_folder>* switch copies updated service pack files over the existing Windows 2000 files. Some of the key files that are replaced include layout.inf, dosnet.inf, txtsetup.sif, and a new driver.cab file if the drivers in the cabinet are changed. Slipstreaming eliminates the need to reinstall components applied before a service pack was installed.

D. **Incorrect:** Although you should use the UPDATE command, you must also use the -s:*<distribution_folder>* switch to copy the updated service pack files over the existing Windows 2000 files. The UPDATE command does not include an /overwrite switch.

70-215.01.04.002

▶ **Correct Answers: D**

A. **Incorrect:** You do not need to reapply the service pack. The RAS component will automatically use the correct files, whether they originate from the Windows 2000 installation source or from the service pack.

B. **Incorrect:** You do not need to reapply the service pack. The RAS component will automatically use the correct files, whether they originate from the Windows 2000 installation source or from the service pack.

C. **Incorrect:** You do not need to remove the service pack and then reinstall it. The RAS component will automatically use the correct files, whether they originate from the Windows 2000 installation source or from the service pack.

D. **Correct:** If a service pack is applied to the distribution share and RAS is then installed on one of the servers (which changes the system state data), Windows 2000 installs the correct files, eliminating the need to reapply the service pack whenever the system state data changes. When system state data changes after a service pack is applied, the base system is told that a service pack was installed, what files were replaced or updated by the service pack, and from which location the service pack was installed. As a result, the correct files are copied from the service pack distribution location and from the Windows 2000 installation source, eliminating the need to reapply a service pack when the system state data changes.

70-215.01.04.003

▶ **Correct Answers: A, B, and C**

A. **Correct:** The UPDATE command, when used with the -s:*<distribution_folder>* switch, implements service pack slipstreaming, which refers to a service pack being applied to the Windows 2000 distribution files on a network share. The -s:*<distribution_folder>* switch copies updated service pack files over the existing Windows 2000 files. Some of the key files that are replaced include layout.inf, dosnet.inf, txtsetup.sif, and a new driver.cab file if the drivers in the cabinet are changed.

B. **Correct:** Windows 2000 support for service packs eliminates the need to reinstall components applied before a service pack is installed.

C. **Correct:** If a service pack is applied and additional components are then installed (which changes the system state data), Windows 2000 installs the correct files, eliminating the need to reapply the service pack whenever the system state data changes. When system state data changes after a service pack is applied, the base system is told that a service pack was installed, what files were replaced or updated by the service pack, and from which location the service pack was installed. As a result, the correct files are copied from the service pack distribution location and from the Windows 2000 installation source. This process eliminates the need to reapply a service pack when the system state data changes.

D. **Incorrect:** The installation meets all the required results.

Troubleshoot failed installations.

Most of the Windows 2000 Server installation process is automated and should run to completion without any problems. However, if problems occur, it becomes necessary to troubleshoot the problem in order to determine what actions should be taken to proceed with the installation. For example, it is possible to encounter problems caused by bad media or incompatible hardware.

To answer the questions in this objective, you should be familiar with the following issues that can occur when installing Windows 2000 Server:

- Media errors

- Unsupported CD-ROM drive

- Insufficient disk space

- Failure of dependency service to start

- Inability to connect to the domain controller

- Failure of Windows 2000 Server to install or start

For each type of problem, you should know what solution to implement in order to complete the installation and ensure that Windows 2000 Server is installed and operating properly. In addition to these issues, you should become familiar with any other types of problems that might occur during installation and know how to resolve them as quickly and efficiently as possible.

Objective 1.5 Questions

70-215.01.05.001

During the installation of Windows 2000 Server via a bootable CD-ROM drive, you receive a media error. You shut down the computer and restart the installation, but you receive the same error. How should you troubleshoot this problem? (Choose two.)

A. Replace the CD-ROM drive in the computer.

B. Shut down the computer and restart the installation.

C. Contact Microsoft to obtain a copy of the Windows 2000 Server CD.

D. Create more free hard disk space on the hard drive by deleting unnecessary files.

70-215.01.05.002

After the installation of Windows 2000 Server, you cannot get Windows 2000 to initialize. How should you troubleshoot this problem?

A. Verify that the domain name is correct.

B. Use the Windows 2000 Setup wizard to verify that you installed the correct protocol and network adapter.

C. Ensure that all hardware in the computer is on the Windows 2000 HCL.

D. Create more free hard disk space on the hard drive by deleting unnecessary files.

70-215.01.05.003

During the installation of Windows 2000 Server, you cannot get the dependency service to start. How should you troubleshoot this problem?

A. Replace the CD-ROM drive in the computer.

B. Ensure that all hardware in the computer is on the Windows 2000 HCL.

C. Create more free hard disk space on the hard drive by deleting unnecessary files.

D. Use the Windows 2000 Setup wizard to verify that the network settings are correct.

Objective 1.5 Answers

70-215.01.05.001

▶ **Correct Answers: A and C**

A. **Correct:** If you receive a media error, it might mean that your CD-ROM drive is malfunctioning. If this happens, you can try replacing the existing CD-ROM drive, using a different CD-ROM drive if a second is installed on the computer, or installing a new drive in the computer. By using a different CD-ROM drive, you can determine whether the drive is the likely cause of the problem. If you use a different drive and still receive a media error, you should request a replacement Windows 2000 Server installation CD-ROM from Microsoft or from the vendor where you bought Windows 2000 Server.

B. **Incorrect:** If there is a problem with the media, shutting down the computer and restarting the installation is not likely to fix the problem. If the CD-ROM drive or Windows 2000 Server installation CD-ROM is not working, it will most likely continue to malfunction after you restart your computer.

C. **Correct:** A CD-ROM can sometimes malfunction, in which case it must be replaced. If you suspect that your Windows 2000 Server installation CD-ROM has problems, request a replacement from Microsoft or the vendor where you purchased Windows 2000 Server. However, before requesting a new CD-ROM, try using a different CD-ROM drive to ensure that the drive is not the cause of the problem.

D. **Incorrect:** Freeing hard disk space will not solve the problem of a media error. You should free disk space if you receive an error that says that there is insufficient disk space. A media error is unrelated to insufficient disk space.

70-215.01.05.002

▶ **Correct Answers: C**

A. **Incorrect:** You should verify whether the domain name is correct if your computer is unable to connect to the domain controller, not if Windows 2000 fails to initialize. Windows 2000 cannot connect to the domain controller until after it starts up, so if the operating system fails to initialize, the problem is occurring before it attempts to connect to the domain controller.

B. **Incorrect:** You should verify that you installed the correct protocol and network adapter if you encounter a failure of a dependency service to start, not if Windows 2000 fails to initialize. Dependency services start after Windows 2000 initializes, so if the operating system fails to start up, the problem is occurring before the dependency services start.

C. **Correct:** If Windows 2000 Server does not install or start, it is possible that a piece of hardware is not supported by the operating system. If you run into this problem, verify that all the hardware is on the Hardware Compatibility List (HCL). The HCL is a list of devices supported by Windows 2000. A device not supported by Windows 2000 Server can cause many problems, including the inability of Windows 2000 Server to install or start.

D. **Incorrect:** You should free disk space if you receive an error that says that there is insufficient disk space, not if Windows 2000 fails to initialize.

70-215.01.05.003

▶ **Correct Answers: D**

A. **Incorrect:** You should consider replacing the CD-ROM drive if you receive a media error when using that drive, not when a dependency service fails to start. The failure of a dependency service to start is usually caused by a failed network connection.

B. **Incorrect:** You should ensure that all hardware is on the Windows 2000 HCL if Windows 2000 Server fails to install or start, not if a dependency service fails to start. The HCL is a list of devices that are supported by Windows 2000 Server. A dependency service can fail to start even if all hardware on the computer is supported.

C. **Incorrect:** You should free disk space if you receive an error that says that there is insufficient disk space, not if a dependency service fails to start.

D. **Correct:** Failure of a dependency service, such as the File Replication Service (FRS), can be a result of a failed network connection. Therefore, you should use the Windows 2000 Setup wizard to verify that you installed the correct protocol and network adapter. You should verify that the network adapter has the proper configuration settings, such as the transceiver type, and that the local computer name is unique on the network.

Installing, Configuring, and Troubleshooting Access to Resources

Managing access to various resources is a significant responsibility in Windows 2000 Server administration. For example, you might be using a Windows 2000 Server computer as a print server, in which case you must be familiar with the various components that make up network printing, such as the **printer driver** and the **print device**. However, accessing resources does not always refer to devices that are not on the server. The administration of Windows 2000 Server includes managing files, folders, and shared folders, so you must be familiar with how folders and shares are structured and how they are accessed and secured. Your Windows 2000 Server computer might also host Web and FTP sites, so you must be able to administer Internet Information Services (IIS) and set up a Web environment. The Installing, Configuring, and Troubleshooting Access to Resources domain covers a wide range of resources, and understanding how to manage these resources is critical to your ability to effectively administer a Windows 2000 Server computer.

Tested Skills and Suggested Practices

The skills that you need to successfully master the Installing, Configuring, and Troubleshooting Access to Resources domain on the *Installing, Configuring, and Administering Microsoft Windows 2000 Server* exam include:

- **Setting up printing on a Windows 2000 Server computer.**

  - Practice 1: Add a local printer to the computer. You do not need to have a print device connected to the printer in order to complete this practice. The printer can be taken off line to avoid generating any errors. If a print device is connected to your printer, configure a printer for that device; otherwise, you can configure a printer for an HP LaserJet 5Si printer, for example, or any other printer that you choose. When you're adding the printer, be sure to share the printer and create a name for the printer share.

▪ Practice 2: Take the printer off line by opening the window for that printer and selecting the appropriate option. Leave the window open. Create a test document in Microsoft Notepad or another program and send the document to the printer. Notice that the document appears in the printer's window. The document will be held in the queue while it waits to be sent to the print device. Close Notepad without saving the document.

▪ Practice 3: Change the status of the document in the printer's window by first pausing the document and then restarting it. Notice that the status changes in the status column. If a print device is connected to the computer, return the printer to being on line, and allow the document to be printed. Otherwise, cancel the document.

■ **Managing files and folders on an NTFS volume.**

▪ Practice 1: In Windows Explorer, create a test folder and subfolders, and add test documents to the folders. Do not change any of the default properties for the folders or files. Share the folder, and then view the share permissions. Add a test users account to the share permissions. If necessary, create the user account in the Active Directory Users And Computers snap-in. Once you've added the user to the share permissions, modify the permissions for that user.

▪ Practice 2: On the shared folder, configure NTFS permissions for the test user account. Modify the permissions for the user. Once you've configured the permissions, view the NTFS permissions for one of the subfolders in the share. Notice that the test user account has propagated to the subfolder. On one of the files in the share, remove the test user account from the NTFS permissions, and configure the permissions so that they cannot be inherited from a parent object.

▪ Practice 3: Create a standalone Dfs root on your computer. Configure the root with several Dfs links. Although Dfs allows you to link to other computers, for this exercise you can link to folders on the same computer. After you've created the root and links, check the status of each one. A green arrow should appear at each folder icon. Select a replica path for one of the shared folders (in the right pane of the Distributed File System snap-in), and open the window for that share to view the contents of the folder.

■ **Setting up and administering a Web environment.**

▪ Practice 1: Use the Internet Information Services snap-in to add a Web site to your IIS configuration. Configure the properties for the site, including directory security and performance. Add a test user to the Web Site Operators group. Also add an FTP site, and configure those properties as well.

▪ Practice 2: For the new Web site and FTP site that you created, stop the service and then restart it. Also pause the service for each site. Refresh each site, and then delete the new sites.

- Practice 3: Set up Web-based Distributed Authoring and Versioning (WebDAV) publishing on your computer. To set up the publishing directory, you must create a physical directory. You can place this directory below the Inetpub folder or anywhere else except under the Wwwroot folder. Try configuring security, which includes coordinating three components: authenticating clients, controlling access, and denying service.

Further Reading

This section lists supplemental readings by objective. Study these sources thoroughly before taking exam 70-215.

Objective 2.1

"File and Print Services Technical Overview." (This white paper can be downloaded for free at *http://www.microsoft.com/TechNet/win2000/fileprin.asp.*) The paper includes an overview of Windows 2000 printing.

"General Services for UNIX version 2.0 White Paper." (This white paper can be downloaded for free at *http://www.microsoft.com/windows2000/sfu/sfu2wp.asp.*)

"Interoperability Capabilities." (This white paper can be downloaded for free at *http://www.microsoft.com/windows2000/guide/server/features/interop.asp.*)

"Introduction to Services for UNIX." (This white paper can be downloaded for free at *http://www.microsoft.com/windows2000/sfu/sfuwp.asp.*)

Microsoft Corporation. *Windows 2000 Server Resource Kit.* Volume: *Microsoft Windows 2000 Server Internetworking Guide.* Redmond, Washington: Microsoft Press, 2000. Review Chapter 10, "Interoperability with IBM Host Systems"; Chapter 11, "Services for UNIX"; Chapter 12, "Interoperability with NetWare"; and Chapter 13, "Services for Macintosh."

Microsoft Corporation. *Windows 2000 Server Resource Kit.* Volume: *Microsoft Windows 2000 Server Operations Guide.* Redmond, Washington: Microsoft Press, 2000. Review Chapter 4, "Network Printing."

Microsoft Corporation. *MCSE Training Kit: Microsoft Windows 2000 Server.* Redmond, Washington: Microsoft Press, 2000. Review Lesson 1 in Chapter 9, "Network Protocols and Services."

Objective 2.2

"File and Print Services Technical Overview." (This white paper can be downloaded for free at *http://www.microsoft.com/TechNet/win2000/fileprin.asp.*) The paper includes an overview of Windows 2000 printing.

Microsoft Corporation. *Windows 2000 Server Resource Kit.* Volume: *Microsoft Windows 2000 Server Operations Guide.* Redmond, Washington: Microsoft Press, 2000. Review Chapter 4, "Network Printing."

Microsoft Corporation. *MCSE Training Kit: Microsoft Windows 2000 Server*. Redmond, Washington: Microsoft Press, 2000. Review Lessons 1, 2, 3, 4, and 5 in Chapter 8, "Administering Print Services."

Objective 2.3

"*Distributed File System.*" (This white paper can be downloaded for free at *http://www.microsoft.com/windows2000/library/howitworks/fileandprint/dfsnew.asp.*)

"*File and Print Services Technical Overview.*" (This white paper can be downloaded for free at *http://www.microsoft.com/TechNet/win2000/fileprin.asp.*) The paper includes an overview of Windows 2000 file services.

Microsoft Corporation. *Windows 2000 Server Resource Kit*. Volume: *Microsoft Windows 2000 Server Distributed Systems Guide*. Redmond, Washington: Microsoft Press, 2000. Review Chapter 17, "Distributed File System."

Microsoft Corporation. *Windows 2000 Server Resource Kit*. Volume: *Microsoft Windows 2000 Server Operations Guide*. Redmond, Washington: Microsoft Press, 2000. Review Chapter 3, "File Systems."

Microsoft Corporation. *MCSE Training Kit: Microsoft Windows 2000 Server*. Redmond, Washington: Microsoft Press, 2000. Review Lessons 1, 2, 3, and 4 in Chapter 4, "Microsoft Windows 2000 File Systems." Also review Lessons 1 and 2 in Chapter 5, "Advanced File Systems."

Objective 2.4

"*Internet Information Services 5.0 Technical Overview.*" (This white paper can be downloaded for free at *http://www.microsoft.com/windows2000/library/howitworks/iis/iis5techoverview.asp.*) The paper includes an extensive look at security provisions and introduces new security protocols supported by IIS 5.0, including Transport Layer Security and Digest Authentication.

"*Internet Information Services Features.*" (This white paper can be downloaded for free at *http://www.microsoft.com/WINDOWS2000/guide/server/features/web.asp.*)

Microsoft Corporation. *Windows 2000 Server Resource Kit*. Volume: *Microsoft Internet Information Services 5.0 Resource Guide*. Redmond, Washington: Microsoft Press, 2000. Review Chapter 5, "Monitoring and Tuning Your Server," and Chapter 9, "Security."

Microsoft Corporation. *MCSE Training Kit: Microsoft Windows 2000 Server*. Redmond, Washington: Microsoft Press, 2000. Review Lessons 1 and 2 in Chapter 14, "Microsoft Windows Application Servers."

Morey, Jim. "*IIS 4.0 and 5.0 Authentication Methods Chart.*" (This paper can be downloaded for free at *http://www.microsoft.com/technet/iis/authmeth.asp.*)

Install and configure network services for interoperability.

Interoperability is essential in today's increasingly heterogeneous computing environment. Windows 2000 Server provides a number of network services that support interoperability with non-Windows operating systems. Microsoft SNA Server is the Microsoft solution for integrating Windows 2000–based networks and intranets with IBM SNA or TCP/IP-based mainframe, midrange, and AS/400 host systems. Using SNA Server, you can provide Microsoft and non-Microsoft-based clients with secure access to IBM host data, applications, and network services. By providing core interoperability components, Windows Services for UNIX offers the means to integrate Windows into an existing UNIX environment and to migrate existing UNIX scripts into the Windows environment. Windows 2000 also provides protocols and services that allow you to integrate Windows 2000 networks with Novell NetWare networks. These protocols and services include NWLink, which is the Windows 2000 implementation of the Internet Packet Exchange/Sequenced Packet Exchange (IPX/SPX) protocol, as well as Gateway Service for NetWare and Client Service for NetWare, both of which work with NWLink to provide access to NetWare file, print, and directory services. In addition, Windows 2000 supports the AppleTalk protocol and Windows 2000 Services for Macintosh (also called AppleTalk network integration), which provide a powerful integration platform for Macintosh and Windows 2000 internetworking.

To answer the questions in this objective, you should be familiar with the various kinds of services included in Windows 2000 Server that support interoperability with non-Windows operating systems. You should know how to install these services on your Windows 2000 Server computer, and you should know how to configure the services and the protocols that support them.

Objective 2.1 Questions

70-215.02.01.001

Your Windows 2000 network contains 4 Windows 2000 Server computers and 100 client computers configured with Windows 2000 Professional, Windows NT Workstation, Windows 98, and Windows 95. One of the Windows 2000 Server computers is configured as a print server. You are adding two NetWare 5.0 servers to your network, one to act as a file server and the other to act as a print server.

You want to accomplish the following goals:

- The Windows client computers must use TCP/IP as their only network protocol.

- All Windows 2000 computers must be able to access files on the NetWare servers and be able to print to the NetWare print server.

- The two NetWare servers must be able to print to the Windows 2000 print server.

You install the Gateway Service for NetWare service and the File and Print Services for NetWare service on the Windows 2000 Server computers.

Which result or results does your installation achieve? (Choose all that apply.)

A. The Windows client computers can use TCP/IP as their only network protocol.

B. All Windows 2000 computers can access files on the NetWare servers and print to the NetWare print server.

C. The two NetWare servers can print to the Windows 2000 print server.

D. The proposed solution does not provide any of the required results.

70-215.02.01.002

You are adding a Windows 2000 Server computer to an AppleTalk network. A print device is directly connected to one of the communication ports on the computer.

You want to meet the following requirements:

- Computers on the AppleTalk network must be able to print to the print device connected to the Windows 2000 Server computer.

- Computers on the AppleTalk network must be able to access files on the Windows 2000 Server computer.

- The Windows 2000 Server computer must be able to act as a router for the AppleTalk network.

You configure the Windows 2000 Server computer with the File Services for Macintosh service, and you install authentication files on the Macintosh clients. You then configure the file server for Macintosh users, configure Macintosh-accessible volumes, and set security on the volumes.

Which result or results does the proposed solution achieve?

A. Computers on the AppleTalk network can print to the print device connected to the Windows 2000 Server computer.

B. Computers on the AppleTalk network can access files on the Windows 2000 Server computer.

C. The Windows 2000 Server computer can act as a router for the AppleTalk network.

D. The proposed solution does not provide any of the required results.

70-215.02.01.003

You are adding a Windows 2000 Server computer to an AppleTalk network. A print device is directly connected to one of the communication ports on the computer.

You want to meet the following requirements:

- Computers on the AppleTalk network must be able to print to the print device connected to the Windows 2000 Server computer.

- Computers on the AppleTalk network must be able to access files on the Windows 2000 Server computer.

- The Windows 2000 Server computer must be able to act as a router for the AppleTalk network.

You configure the Windows 2000 Server computer with the File Services for Macintosh service, and you install authentication files on the Macintosh clients. You then configure the file server for Macintosh users, configure Macintosh-accessible volumes, and set security on the volumes. You then configure the Windows 2000 Server computer with the Print Services for Macintosh service and create a new printer for the Macintosh clients.

Which result or results does the proposed solution achieve?

A. Computers on the AppleTalk network can print to the print device connected to the Windows 2000 Server computer.

B. Computers on the AppleTalk network can access files on the Windows 2000 Server computer.

C. The Windows 2000 Server computer can act as a router for the AppleTalk network.

D. The proposed solution does not provide any of the required results.

Objective 2.1 Answers

70-215.02.01.001

▶ **Correct Answers: A, B, and C**

A. **Correct:** When Gateway Service for NetWare is installed on a Windows 2000 Server computer, NWLink is also installed. NWLink is the Windows 2000 implementation of the IPX/SPX protocol, which can be used for connectivity between Windows 2000 computers and NetWare computers. NWLink also provides the functionality of NetBIOS and the Routing Information Protocol (RIP). Together, Gateway Service for NetWare and NWLink allow the Windows 2000 Server computers to connect to the NetWare computers while providing protocol isolation for IPX. As a result, you do not have to route IPX throughout your entire network. The Windows 2000 Professional computers can use TCP/IP to connect to the Windows 2000 Server computers and from there access resources on the NetWare computers through the Gateway Service for NetWare connection established between the Windows 2000 Server computer and the NetWare computers.

B. **Correct:** When Gateway Service for NetWare is installed on a Windows 2000 Server computer, multiple Windows 2000 Professional, Windows NT Workstation, Windows 98, and Windows 95 client computers can access NetWare file, print, and directory services. Because the gateway provides a single access point to NetWare services, you do not need to install and maintain NetWare client software (such as Client Service for NetWare) on each of your client computers. Gateway Service for NetWare also supports direct access to NetWare services from the Windows 2000 Server computers, in the same way that Client Service for NetWare can support direct access from client computers. A Windows 2000 Server gateway can be used to communicate with only one NetWare server at a time. Simultaneous connections are not supported.

C. **Correct:** A print server that is running Windows 2000 Server can process print jobs from NetWare print clients if File and Print Services for NetWare is installed. NWLink is installed automatically with File and Print Services for NetWare if it is not already installed. NetWare connectivity over TCP/IP is not supported. With File and Print Services for NetWare, the Windows 2000 print server appears to the NetWare client as a NetWare 3.*x*–compatible file and print server. File and Print Services for NetWare presents the same dialog boxes to the client that a NetWare server uses to process a print job from a client. The printers on the Windows 2000 print server are displayed and searched in the same manner as NetWare print queues.

D. **Incorrect:** The proposed solution provides all the required results.

70-215.02.01.002

▶ **Correct Answers: B and C**

A. **Incorrect:** Computers on the AppleTalk network cannot print to the print device because you have not configured the Windows 2000 Server computer with Print Services for Macintosh. Print Services for Macintosh allows you to configure a Windows 2000 Server computer to provide printing services. A Macintosh client can access any print device connected to a communication port of a Windows 2000 Server computer or connected over the network. In addition, Windows 2000 clients can use the server to gain access to the PostScript printers that are connected to AppleTalk networks. Print Services for Macintosh requires the AppleTalk protocol, which is installed automatically when you install the service.

B. **Correct:** File Services for Macintosh provides Macintosh users with access to files that are stored on Windows 2000 Server computers. The file server is accessible over TCP/IP networks as well as AppleTalk networks. Although the AppleTalk protocol is installed automatically when you install File Services for Macintosh, the protocol is not required if the computer is configured with TCP/IP. When both protocols are installed on the Macintosh client and the Windows 2000 Server computer, the client attempts to start a connection by using TCP/IP. If the server has multiple IP addresses, the list of all IP addresses is sent to the client. Even though the Windows 2000 file system differs from that of the Macintosh file system, both Windows 2000 clients and Macintosh clients can use the files that are stored on the Windows 2000 Server computer.

C. **Correct:** A Windows 2000 Server computer can act as a router for an AppleTalk network if the server is configured with the AppleTalk protocol. AppleTalk is installed automatically when you install File Services for Macintosh or Print Services for Macintosh, or you can install the protocol without installing either of the services. Windows 2000 supports the AppleTalk protocol stack and AppleTalk routing software so that the Windows 2000 Server computer can connect to and provide routing for AppleTalk networks. AppleTalk is a protocol suite developed by Apple Computer Corporation for communication among Macintosh computers and is based on the AppleTalk protocol architecture.

In addition to installing File Services for Macintosh, you must install authentication files on the Macintosh client. You must also configure the file server for the Macintosh clients. This process includes setting logon security and creating a new logon message for the Macintosh users. You must also set session limits and make new extension associations for Intel-based and Macintosh files. To install and configure the file server, you must also configure the Macintosh-accessible volumes, which includes creating the volume and setting permissions and security options on the volumes. A Macintosh-accessible volume is a folder on a computer running Windows 2000 Server that is made available to Macintosh clients. Once the volume has been created and a share has been created for users of Intel-based computers, both types of users can exchange files.

D. **Incorrect:** The proposed solution allows computers on the AppleTalk network to access files on the Windows 2000 Server computer and allows the Windows 2000 Server computer to act as a router for the AppleTalk network. However, the proposed solution does not allow computers on the AppleTalk network to print to the print device connected to the Windows 2000 Server computer.

70-215.02.01.003

▶ **Correct Answers: A, B, and C**

A. **Correct:** Print Services for Macintosh allows you to configure a Windows 2000 Server computer to provide printing services. A Macintosh client can access any print device connected to a communication port of a Windows 2000 Server computer or connected over the network. In addition, Windows 2000 clients can use the server to gain access to the PostScript printers that are connected to AppleTalk networks. Print Services for Macintosh requires the AppleTalk protocol, which is installed automatically when you install the service. Once the computer is configured with Print Services for Macintosh, you can create a printer specifically for the Macintosh clients.

B. **Correct:** File Services for Macintosh provides Macintosh users with access to files that are stored on Windows 2000 Server computers. The file server is accessible over TCP/IP networks as well as AppleTalk networks. Although the AppleTalk protocol is installed automatically when you install File Services for Macintosh, the protocol is not required if the computer is configured with TCP/IP. When both protocols are installed on the Macintosh client and the Windows 2000 Server computer, the client attempts to start a connection by using TCP/IP. If the server has multiple IP addresses, the list of all IP addresses is sent to the client. Even though the Windows 2000 file system differs from that of the Macintosh file system, both Windows 2000 clients and Macintosh clients can use the files that are stored on the Windows 2000 Server computer.

In addition to installing File Services for Macintosh, you must install authentication files on the Macintosh client. In addition, you must configure the file server for the Macintosh clients. This process includes setting logon security and creating a new logon message for the Macintosh users. You must also set session limits and make new extension associations for Intel-based and Macintosh files. To install and configure the file server, you must also configure the Macintosh-accessible volumes, which includes creating the volumes and setting permissions and security options on the volumes. A Macintosh-accessible volume is a folder on a computer running Windows 2000 Server that is made available to Macintosh clients. Once the volume has been created and a share created for users of Intel-based computers, both types of users can exchange files.

C. **Correct:** A Windows 2000 Server computer can act as a router for an AppleTalk network if the server is configured with the AppleTalk protocol. AppleTalk is installed automatically when you install File Services for Macintosh or Print Services for Macintosh, or you can install the protocol without installing either of the services. Windows 2000 supports the AppleTalk protocol stack and AppleTalk routing software so that the Windows 2000 Server computer can connect to and provide routing for AppleTalk networks.

D. **Incorrect:** The proposed solution provides all the required results.

Monitor, configure, troubleshoot, and control access to printers.

Windows 2000 printing is made up of a number of components that allow a user to print data from an application. When a user requests that a document be printed, the data is sent from the application to the **printer driver**, which is one or more files containing information that Windows 2000 requires to convert print commands into a specific language. The printer driver resides on the computer from which the print job originates. From the printer driver, the print job is then sent to the **printer**. A printer is a software interface between the operating system and the **print device**. The printer defines where a document will go to reach the print device. In a networked environment, a printer usually resides on a **print server**, which is a computer that receives and processes documents from client computers. A print server manages a queue of print jobs for a shared print device. Finally, the print job is sent to the print device. A print device is the hardware device that produces the printed documents.

Several combinations of client computers, print servers, and print devices are possible with Windows 2000. A print device can be **local**, which means that it receives data directly from the computer that is requesting the print job, or it can be **remote**, which means that the print job is sent to the print device by way of a print server. Windows 2000 print configurations can also be determined by whether the print devices are **networked** or are **directly attached** to a computer. A networked print device is a node on the network; computers send print jobs to the network adapter, which might be built into the print device. A directly attached print device is connected to the computer by a local interface, such as a parallel, serial, or universal serial bus (USB) port.

Note The documentation varies with regard to the terminology used to define the possible printing configurations. For example, in some cases, a local print device is considered one that is connected directly to the computer, in contrast with a network print device, which is one that is connected to the network. In addition, a nonremote print device is one that receives data directly from the computer from which the print job originates, in contrast with a remote print device that is accessed through the print server. However, the terminology that is used in this Readiness Review, as defined in the previous paragraph, is most consistent with the industry standard, and the following questions adhere to that standard.

To answer the questions in this objective, you should have a very thorough knowledge of the various components that make up Windows 2000 printing and understand how client computers, print servers, and print devices can be arranged in various configurations. You should also be aware of the requirements necessary for setting up printing in a Windows 2000 network and what steps should be taken to set up and administer printing. In addition, you should be able to troubleshoot problems should any arise.

Objective 2.2 Questions

70-215.02.02.001

You are connecting a Hewlett-Packard 5SI print device directly to a Windows 2000 network. The print device uses a legacy JetDirect card that does not support TCP/IP. Which protocol should be configured on the print server in order to communicate with the print device?

A. Data Link Control (DLC)

B. Asynchronous Transfer Mode (ATM)

C. NetBIOS Enhanced User Interface (NetBEUI)

D. NWLink

70-215.02.02.002

You are installing a Hewlett-Packard 5SI print device in the office of the accounting department of your organization. The printer is connected to a network hub, and the print jobs will be managed by a Windows 2000 print server. Which type of print device are you installing?

A. Local, directly attached print device

B. Local, networked print device

C. Remote, directly attached print device

D. Remote, networked print device

70-215.02.02.003

You are configuring a printer, but you would like to take the printer off line first so that print jobs sent to the printer will still be queued after you have completed the configuration. How can you take the printer off line?

A. By turning off the print device

B. By modifying the printer's properties

C. By accessing the specific printer through the Printers window

D. By using the Active Directory Users And Computers snap-in

70-215.02.02.004

You send a print job to a printer on a print server, and the print server's hard disk starts thrashing. The system is spending most of its time swapping pages in and out of virtual memory rather than executing the print job. What is a likely cause of the problem?

A. The client computer is connected to the wrong printer.

B. The hard disk space on the server's hard disk is insufficient.

C. There are no printer drivers for the client computer on the print server.

D. You do not have the appropriate permission to print to the printer.

70-215.02.02.005

You try to configure a printer, but you receive an Access Denied message. What is the most likely cause of the problem?

A. The client computer is connected to the wrong printer.

B. The hard disk space on the server's hard drive is insufficient.

C. There are no printer drivers for the client computer on the print server.

D. You do not have the appropriate permission to change printer configurations.

Objective 2.2 Answers

70-215.02.02.001

▶ **Correct Answers: A**

A. **Correct:** The DLC protocol was developed for IBM mainframe communications; however, DLC can be used to print to some Hewlett-Packard printers that are connected directly to the network and that use older JetDirect cards that support DLC but do not support TCP/IP. Network-attached printers may use the DLC protocol because the received frames are easy to disassemble and because DLC functionality can easily be coded into read-only memory (ROM). Clients sending print jobs to a network print device through a Windows 2000 print server do not need the DLC protocol installed. Only the print server communicating directly with the print device requires DLC. After you have configured a Windows 2000 Server computer to perform the role of print server for the DLC-enabled network print device, client computers can connect to the printer share on the print server.

B. **Incorrect:** The ATM protocol is an advanced implementation of packet switching that is ideal for voice, video, and data communication. ATM is a high-speed networking technology that transmits data in cells of a fixed length. It comprises a number of related technologies, including software, hardware, and connection-oriented media. ATM is an excellent compromise for the transmission of both voice and data on a network. It provides a guaranteed Quality of Service (QoS) on a local area network, a wide area network, and a public internetwork. However, you would not configure the print server with ATM in order to communicate with the print device. Many of the older JetDirect cards use DLC, not ATM.

C. **Incorrect:** NetBEUI was originally developed as a protocol for small departmental local area networks of 20 to 200 computers. NetBEUI is not routable because it does not have a network layer. As a result, you must connect computers running Windows 2000 and NetBEUI by using bridges instead of routers. In addition, NetBEUI is broadcast-based and relies on broadcasts for many of its functions, such as name registration and discovery. NetBEUI is included with Windows 2000 primarily as a legacy protocol to support workstations that have not been upgraded to Windows 2000. However, you would not configure the print server with NetBEUI in order to communicate with the print device. Many of the older JetDirect cards use DLC, not NetBEUI.

D. **Incorrect:** NWLink is Microsoft's implementation of the Novell IPX/SPX protocol. NWLink is most commonly used in environments where clients running Microsoft operating systems are used to access resources on NetWare servers, or where clients running NetWare are used to access resources on computers running Microsoft operating systems. NWLink can also function either as a protocol that connects computers running Windows 2000, Windows NT, Windows for Workgroups 3.11, Windows 95, and Windows 98 or as a protocol that connects computers running MS-DOS, when used in combination with a redirector. Additionally, NWLink functions as an alternative transport protocol for servers running Microsoft Exchange Server, Microsoft SQL Server, and Microsoft SNA Server. However, you would not configure the print server with NetWare in order to communicate with the print device. Many of the older JetDirect cards use DLC, not NetWare.

70-215.02.02.002

▶ **Correct Answers: D**

A. **Incorrect:** A local print device is one that receives data directly from the computer that is sending the print job, and a directly attached print device is one that is connected to the computer by a local interface, such as a parallel, serial RS-232/422/IRDA, or USB port.

B. **Incorrect:** A local print device is one that receives data directly from the computer that is sending the print job, and a networked print device is a node on a network and receives jobs through its network adapter card.

C. **Incorrect:** A remote print device is one that receives print jobs from a print server, and a directly attached print device is one that is connected to the computer by a local interface, such as a parallel, serial RS-232/422/IRDA, or USB port.

D. **Correct:** A remote print device is one that receives print jobs from a print server, in contrast with a local print device, which receives data directly from the computer that is sending the print job. A networked print device is a node on a network and receives jobs through its network adapter card, in contrast with a directly attached print device, which is connected to the computer by a local interface, such as a parallel, serial RS-232/422/IRDA, or USB port.

70-215.02.02.003

▶ **Correct Answers: C**

A. **Incorrect:** You cannot take a printer off line by turning off a print device. In addition, you risk losing print jobs that are in the queue. Jobs that have already spooled and have been sent to the printer might be either partially printed or lost.

B. **Incorrect:** You cannot take a printer off line by modifying a printer's properties. A printer's properties allow you to perform a number of tasks, such as sharing the printer, configuring ports, specifying advanced settings, setting security, and configuring device settings.

C. **Correct:** You can take a printer off line in one of two ways. The first way is simply to open the Printers window, highlight the specific printer, and then select the Use Printer Offline option from the File menu. You can also take a printer off line by opening the window for the specific printer and then selecting the Use Printer Offline option from the Printer menu. When you take a printer off line, documents stay in the print queue, even when the print server is shut down and then restarted.

D. **Incorrect:** You can access a printer for administration by using the Find feature in the Active Directory Users And Computers snap-in. The snap-in allows you to open a window for a specific printer. However, you cannot perform all the tasks in this window that you can when you access the printer through the Printers window. For example, you cannot use the Active Directory Users And Computers snap-in to take a printer off line. To do this, you must access the specific printer through the Printers window.

70-215.02.02.004

▶ **Correct Answers: B**

A. **Incorrect:** If the client computer is connected to the wrong printer, documents from your computer will not print or will print to another print device. If documents from another client computer will print correctly, the print server and print device are operating correctly, and the problem is most likely that your computer is connected to the wrong printer. However, a client computer connected to the wrong printer will not cause the hard disk to start thrashing.

B. **Correct:** A print server must have sufficient hard disk space to ensure that Windows 2000 can store documents and other printable data sent to the print server until the print server sends the data to the print device. This is critical when documents are large or likely to accumulate. If there is not enough space to hold all the documents, users will get error messages and be unable to print. In general, spooled print jobs can be significantly larger than the actual data that the print application reads because print jobs are sent through the printer driver to prepare the data for the print device. If the hard disk starts thrashing, create more free space on the print server hard disk or change the spool folder location to a partition with plenty of free space.

C. **Incorrect:** If the printer driver for the client computer is not installed on the print server, you will receive an error message asking you to install a printer driver. The print job will never be sent to the print server, so the print server's hard disk will not start thrashing as a result of that print job.

D. **Incorrect:** If you do not have the appropriate permission to print to the printer, you will receive an Access Denied message when trying to print to the printer. The print job will never be sent to the print server, so the print server's hard disk will not start thrashing as a result of that print job.

70-215.02.02.005

▶ **Correct Answers: D**

A. **Incorrect:** If the client computer is connected to the wrong printer, documents from your computer will not print or will print to the wrong print device. If documents from another client computer will print correctly, the print server and print device are operating correctly, and the problem is most likely that your computer is connected to the wrong printer. However, a client computer connected to the wrong printer is unrelated to whether you can successfully configure the printer.

B. **Incorrect:** If there is insufficient hard disk space on the print server, the hard disk starts thrashing when too many documents or documents that are too large are sent to the print spooler. However, the amount of hard disk space on the print server's hard disk is unrelated to whether you can configure the printer.

C. **Incorrect:** If the printer driver for the client computer was not installed on the print server, you receive an error message asking you to install a printer driver. You do not receive an Access Denied message.

D. **Correct:** If you try to configure a printer, but you receive an Access Denied message, you do not have the appropriate permissions to change the printer configuration. Windows 2000 allows you to control printer usage and administration by assigning permissions through the Security tab of the printer's Properties dialog box. By using printer permissions, you can control who can use a printer and who can administer a printer and the level of administration, which can include managing printers and managing documents. You can also use printer permissions to delegate responsibilities for specific printers to users who are not administrators. Windows 2000 provides three levels of printer permissions: Print, Manage Documents, and Manage Printers. You can allow or deny printer permissions. Denied permissions always override allowed permissions.

O B J E C T I V E   2 . 3

Monitor, configure, troubleshoot, and control access to files, folders, and shared folders.

When you prepare a hard disk for a Windows 2000 installation, you must initialize the disk with a storage type, create **partitions** or **volumes** on the disk, and format the disk with a file system. Windows 2000 supports the **NTFS** and the **FAT** 16 and 32 file systems. The FAT file system was designed when disks were smaller and folder structures were simpler. Two copies of the file allocation table are stored on the volume in case one copy becomes corrupted. NTFS volumes are structured differently than FAT volumes. When a volume is formatted with NTFS, a **Master File Table (MFT)** and **Metadata** are created. Windows 2000 uses NTFS version 5.0, which includes several features that support new functionality within Windows 2000, functionality that is not supported by FAT and only partially supported by earlier versions of NTFS. In addition, NTFS version 5.0 provides performance, reliability, and compatibility not found in FAT. NTFS provides faster access speed than FAT and minimizes the number of disk accesses required to find a file.

In order to make folders and their contents available over the network, you must **share** those folders. Shared folders provide a way to secure file resources; they can be used on either FAT partitions or NTFS partitions. When a folder is shared, users can connect to the folder over the network and gain access to the files contained in the folder as long as users have permissions to access that folder. Shared folder permissions are sufficient to gain access to files and folders on a FAT volume but are not the best solution for an NTFS volume. On a FAT volume, user access is controlled at the share level only, and users with permissions to access that share have access to all files and folders within the share. However, NTFS permissions allow or deny access to users and groups for each folder and file within a shared folder. NTFS security is effective whether a file or folder is accessed interactively at a computer or over a network. When configuring user access to a share on an NTFS volume, you should use either share permissions or NTFS permissions, but not both. NTFS permissions are preferred because permissions can be set for individual files and folders. If permissions are configured on a share and NTFS permissions are configured on folders or files within that share, the most restrictive rights will become the user's effective rights to the resource.

To answer the questions in this objective, you should have a good understanding of how to prepare a hard disk for a Windows 2000 installation, and you should be familiar with the differences between NTFS and FAT. You should also know how to set up shared folders and how to manage share permissions and NTFS permissions. In addition, you should have a good understanding of the **distributed file system (Dfs)** and how to implement Dfs roots and links, and you should be familiar with how the **File Replication Service (FRS)** is implemented in Windows 2000.

Objective 2.3 Questions

70-215.02.03.001

Users are unable to connect to a Dfs link from their client computers. In the past, they have had no problem connecting to the link, and they can still connect to other links that are configured under the same Dfs root that contains the nonworking link. You open the Distributed File System snap-in on the Windows 2000 Server computer that is hosting the domain Dfs root. You check the status of the Dfs link, and a red circle with a white X appears on the Dfs link folder and on the replica path for the shared folder. What are the most likely causes of the problem? (Choose all that apply.)

A. The shared folder has been retired, or the permissions on the shared folder have been modified.

B. The name of the server on which the shared folder resides has been changed, or the shared folder name has been changed.

C. The Dfs service has been stopped, or the Dfs root has been deleted.

D. The server that is hosting the Dfs root has been configured with a second domain Dfs root, or the server has been configured with a standalone Dfs root in addition to the existing Dfs root.

70-215.02.03.002

You are the administrator of a Windows 2000 Server computer that is configured with a 10-GB FAT32 partition on its only hard disk. The partition includes the AccountingDept folder, which contains documents specific to the accounting department. You create two user groups: the Accounting group and the AccountAdmin group. The Accounting group includes all members of the accounting department. The AccountAdmin group includes about 10 members of the accounting department who manage accounting-related documents.

You want to accomplish the following goals:

- Only the Accounting group should have read-only access to content in the AccountingDept folder.

- Only the AccountAdmin group should have full control over content in the AccountingDept folder.

- Only the Accounting group and the AccountAdmin group should have full control over specified files in the AccountingDept folder.

You share the AccountingDept folder and implement share-level security by granting Read permission to the Accounting group and by granting Full Control permission to the AccountAdmin group. Then you remove the Everyone group from the folder's share permissions.

Which result or results does your installation achieve?

A. Only the Accounting group will have read-only access to content in the AccountingDept folder.

B. Only the AccountAdmin group will have full control over content in the AccountingDept folder.

C. Only the Accounting group and the AccountAdmin group will have full control over specified files in the AccountingDept folder.

D. The proposed solution does not meet any of the required results.

70-215.02.03.003

You are the administrator of a Windows 2000 Server computer that is configured with a 10-GB FAT32 partition on its only hard disk. The partition includes the AccountingDept folder, which contains documents specific to the accounting department. You create two user groups: the Accounting group and the AccountAdmin group. The Accounting group includes all members of the Accounting department. The AccountAdmin group includes about 10 members of the Accounting department who manage accounting-related documents.

You want to accomplish the following goals:

- Only the Accounting group should have read-only access to content in the AccountingDept folder.

- Only the AccountAdmin group should have full control over content in the AccountingDept folder.

- Only the Accounting group and the AccountAdmin group should have full control over specified files in the AccountingDept folder.

You convert the FAT32 partition to an NTFS partition and share the AccountingDept folder. You implement share-level security for the AccountingDept folder by granting Read permission to the Accounting group and by granting Full Control permission to the AccountAdmin group. You implement NTFS permissions on the specified files within the AccountingDept folder, granting full control to members of the Accounting group and the AccountAdmin group and removing the Everyone group.

Which result or results does your installation achieve?

A. Only the Accounting group will have read-only access to content in the AccountingDept folder.

B. Only the AccountAdmin group will have full control over content in the AccountingDept folder.

C. Only the Accounting group and the AccountAdmin group will have full control over specified files in the AccountingDept folder.

D. The proposed solution does not meet any of the required results.

70-215.02.03.004

You are the administrator of a Windows 2000 Server computer that is configured with a 10-GB FAT32 partition on its only hard disk. The partition includes the AccountingDept folder, which contains documents specific to the accounting department. You create two user groups: the Accounting group and the AccountAdmin group. The Accounting group includes all members of the Accounting department. The AccountAdmin group includes about 10 members of the Accounting department who manage accounting-related documents.

You want to accomplish the following goals:

- Only the Accounting group should have read-only access to content in the AccountingDept folder.

- Only the AccountAdmin group should have full control over content in the AccountingDept folder.

- Only the Accounting group and the AccountAdmin group should have full control over specified files in the AccountingDept folder.

You convert the FAT32 partition to an NTFS partition and share the AccountingDept folder. You implement NTFS security on all files and folders in the AccountingDept folder by granting Read permission to the Accounting group and by granting Full Control permission to the AccountAdmin group. Then you remove the Everyone group from the NTFS file and folder permissions and ensure that the security settings propagate to all files and folders within the share. Finally you implement NTFS permissions on the specified files within the AccountingDept folder, granting full control to members of the Accounting group and the AccountAdmin group and removing the Everyone group, and you configure the files' security so that they do not inherit permissions from the parent object.

Which result or results does your installation achieve?

A. Only the Accounting group will have read-only access to content in the AccountingDept folder.

B. Only the AccountAdmin group will have full control over content in the AccountingDept folder.

C. Only the Accounting group and the AccountAdmin group will have full control over specified files in the AccountingDept folder.

D. The proposed solution does not meet any of the required results.

Objective 2.3 Answers

70-215.02.03.001

▶ **Correct Answers: B**

A. **Incorrect:** A red circle with a white X on the Dfs link indicates that the link cannot be negotiated because of a bad link or lack of transport. A red circle with a white X on a replica path indicates that the shared folder cannot be found because the share or its server is off line or unreachable as a result of a bad link or no transport. Whenever you are maintaining Dfs roots and their links, particularly as you build up an extensive distributed Dfs namespace, it is always possible that some of the underlying shared folders might be retired or permissions on the shared folders might be modified. If the Dfs link is not modified to reflect these changes, the link will point to a shared folder that is now nonexistent, and users will be unable to connect to that shared folder through the link. You can use the Distributed File System snap-in to check the status of individual shared folders as well as check the links that specify them in the Dfs namespace. By checking the status, you are verifying that Dfs can see both the server and the shared folders and that the shared folders are valid. Your operational plan for maintaining Dfs should include the periodic running of the Check Status function on shared folders.

B. **Correct:** If the name of the server or the shared folder changes and the Dfs link is not modified, the link will point to a shared folder that is now nonexistent, and users will be unable to connect to that shared folder through the link.

C. **Incorrect:** If the Dfs service is stopped, the Dfs root and its links are no longer available, and the Dfs links are deleted from beneath the Dfs root in the Distributed File System snap-in. As a result, users will not be able to access the Dfs root or its links. Because users are able to make these connections, except for the nonworking Dfs link, the Dfs service must still be running. In addition, if the Dfs root had been deleted, users would not be able to connect to any of the Dfs links because they would be deleted as well.

D. **Incorrect:** Only one Dfs root can be configured on a server at a time, so a second Dfs root or a standalone Dfs root cannot exist if another Dfs root already exists.

70-215.02.03.002

▶ **Correct Answers: A and B**

A. **Correct:** A shared folder is used to provide network users with access to file resources. When a folder is shared, users can connect to the folder over the network and gain access to the files that it contains. If you grant Read permission to the members of the Accounting group, these users will be granted read-only access to all content within the shared folder, including subfolders and all files. Read permission allows users to display folder names, filenames, file data, and file attributes; run program files; and change folders within the shared folders. Share-level permissions can be applied only to the shared folder as a whole, and not to individual files or subfolders in the shared folder. Shared folder permissions do not restrict access to users who access the folder at the computer where the folder is stored. They apply only to users who connect to the shared folder over the network. Shared folder permissions are the only way to secure network resources on a FAT volume. NTFS permissions are not available on FAT volumes. By default, the Everyone group is granted Full Control permission to a shared folder. As a result, you must remove the Everyone group if you want to restrict access to the share; otherwise, all users on the network will have full control over all content in the shared folder except those users who are specifically allowed or denied specific permissions.

B. **Correct:** If you grant Full Control permission to the members of the Accounting group, these users will have full control over all content within the shared folder, including subfolders and all files. Full Control permission allows users to change file permissions, take ownership of files, create folders, add files to folders, change data in files, append data to files, change file attributes, delete folders and files, and perform all actions permitted by the Read permission.

C. **Incorrect:** The groups cannot be granted full control over specified files because FAT does not support NTFS permissions, and NTFS permissions are necessary to grant permissions on specific files or subfolders within the shared folder. Shared folder permissions apply to the shared folder as a whole, not to individual files.

D. **Incorrect:** The proposed solution grants read-only access to the Accounting group and full control to the AccountAdmin group, but the solution does not provide the Accounting group with full control over specific files.

70-215.02.03.003

▶ **Correct Answers: D**

   A. **Incorrect:** A shared folder is used to provide network users with access to file resources. When a folder is shared, users can connect to the folder over the network and gain access to the files that it contains. However, although the Accounting group has been granted Read permission to the shared folder, all other network users will have full control over the content because the Everyone group was not removed from the share permissions. By default, the Everyone group is granted Full Control permission to a shared folder. If you grant Read permission to the members of the Accounting group, these users will be granted read-only access to all content within the shared folder, including subfolders and all files. Read permission allows users to display folder names, filenames, file data, and file attributes; run program files; and change folders within the shared folders. However, Full Control permission allows users to change file permissions, take ownership of files, create folders, add files to folders, change data in files, append data to files, change file attributes, delete folders and files, and perform all actions permitted by the Read permission. Users who are members of the Accounting group are also, by default, members of the Everyone group. When multiple permissions are granted to a resource, the most restrictive permissions apply.

   B. **Incorrect:** Although the AccountAdmin group has been granted Full Control permission to the shared folder, all other network users will have full control over the content because the Everyone group was not removed from the share permissions. By default, the Everyone group is granted Full Control permission to a shared folder. As a result, you must remove the Everyone group if you want to restrict access to the share; otherwise, all users on the network will have full control over all content in the shared folder except those users who are specifically allowed or denied specific permissions.

   C. **Incorrect:** Although the AccountAdmin group will have full control over the specified files, the Accounting group will not because the Accounting group was granted read-only access at the share level. If share rights are configured for a shared folder and NTFS permissions are configured for folders or files within that shared folder, the most restrictive rights become the user's effective rights. So even though the Accounting group has been granted full control over the files, it still has read-only access to those files. Another problem is that the Everyone group has full control over the entire folder, so the AccountAdmin and Accounting groups are not the only ones who will have full control over the specified files. In general, you should use either share permissions or NTFS permissions, but not both. Using both significantly increases the complexity of resolving access permissions for network resources. NTFS permissions are preferred because they can be set on both files and folders.

   D. **Correct:** The proposed solution fails to meet any of the requirements because the Everyone group was not removed from the share permission, which granted all network users full control over all content in the shared folder. In addition, the solution fails because Read permission was granted to the Accounting group at a share level, but Full Control permission was granted to the group for individual files, and the share-level Read permission overrides the NTFS-level Full Control permission for those files.

70-215.02.03.004

► **Correct Answers: A, B, and C**

A. **Correct:** A shared folder is used to provide network users with access to file resources. When a folder is shared, users can connect to the folder over the network and gain access to the files that it contains. NTFS permissions control access to individual files and folders within the share. NTFS security is effective whether a file or folder is accessed interactively at a computer or over the network. When a FAT partition is converted to NTFS, the Full Control permission is assigned to the Everyone group on all resources on that volume. By removing the Everyone group from the NTFS permissions, you limit access to shared resources to those users who have been granted the necessary permissions. NTFS permissions allow you to restrict who can gain access to individual files and folders and what kind of access users can gain. In this case, the Accounting group has been granted Read permission, which allows members of this group to list folder contents, read data, read attributes, read extended attributes, read permissions, and synchronize the folder.

B. **Correct:** The AccountAdmin group has been granted the Full Control permission, which allows members of the group to traverse folder contents, execute files, create files, write data, create folders, append data, write attributes, write extended attributes, delete subfolders and files, change permissions, take ownership, and perform all of the functions included in the Read permission.

C. **Correct:** NTFS permissions allow you to control access to individual files. If you grant Full Control permission to both groups, only the members of these two groups will have access to the specific files. Initially, the files will have inherited the NTFS permissions from their parent folder, which means that the Accounting group will have been granted the Read permission, the AccountAdmin group will have been granted the Full Control permission, and the Everyone group will have already been removed. You will have to remove the Accounting group and the AccountAdmin group, add them back in, grant each group the appropriate permission, and then configure the permissions to prevent the files from inheriting permissions from the parent objects. As a result, members of the Accounting group will have full control over the specific files but will continue to have read-only access to the other content in the shared folder.

D. **Incorrect:** The proposed solution meets all the required results.

O B J E C T I V E   2 . 4

Monitor, configure, troubleshoot, and control access to Web sites.

Microsoft Internet Information Services (IIS) version 5.0 runs as an enterprise service within Windows 2000 and uses other services provided by Windows 2000, such as security and Active Directory. You can manage IIS by using the Internet Information Services snap-in, which is integrated with other administrative functions of Windows 2000. You can also manage IIS by using Internet Services Manager (HTML), a browser-based administrative tool that allows you to administer IIS remotely. In addition, IIS administrators can delegate administrative tasks for specific Web sites by adding user accounts to the **Web Site Operators group** of a specific site. Members of Web Site Operators have limited administrative privileges for that site. They can administer properties that affect only their respective sites. They cannot access properties that affect IIS, the Windows server hosting IIS, or the network.

When IIS is installed, a default Web site is created, which allows you to implement a Web environment quickly and easily. However, you can create multiple Web sites and FTP sites on a single computer running Windows 2000. During the installation of IIS, default values are assigned to various properties on a site. You can use the default settings, or you can customize these settings to suit your needs. Properties can be set on the site level, folder level, or file level. Settings on higher levels (such as the site level) are automatically inherited by the lower level (such as the folder level), but the lower level can be modified individually. If the default property values need to be modified and you are creating server Web or FTP sites, you can edit the default values so that each site you create inherits your custom values.

To answer the questions in this objective, you should be familiar with the various features in IIS 5.0 and know what tools are used to administer the Web environment and how to use those tools. You should also be familiar with the various security protocols that are supported by IIS 5.0. In addition, you should know how to delegate administrative responsibilities for specific sites, set up a Web environment, and administer that environment.

Objective 2.4 Questions

70-215.02.04.001

You are setting up security on an Internet Information Services (IIS) 5.0 Web server.

You must meet the following security requirements:

- You must use an authentication method that supports Microsoft Internet Explorer 2.0 or later.

- You must use an authentication method that hashes the password so the original texts cannot be read.

- You must provide Windows NT Challenge/Response (NTLM) authentication.

- You must provide an authentication method that is part of the HyperText Transfer Protocol (HTTP) specification.

The proposed solution is to use Digest Authentication.

What does the proposed solution provide?

A. The proposed solution provides an authentication method that supports Internet Explorer 2.0 or later.

B. The proposed solution provides an authentication method that hashes the passwords.

C. The proposed solution provides NTLM authentication.

D. The proposed solution provides an authentication method that is part of the HTTP specifications.

70-215.02.04.002

You are setting up security on an Internet Information Services (IIS) 5.0 Web server.

You must meet the following security requirements:

- You must use an authentication method that supports Microsoft Internet Explorer 2.0 or later.

- You must use an authentication method that hashes the password so the original texts cannot be read.

- You must provide Windows NT Challenge/Response (NTLM) authentication.

- You must provide an authentication method that is part of the HTTP specification.

The proposed solution is to use Integrated Windows Authentication.

What does the proposed solution provide?

A. The proposed solution provides an authentication method that supports Internet Explorer 2.0 or later.

B. The proposed solution provides an authentication method that hashes the passwords.

C. The proposed solution provides NTLM authentication.

D. The proposed solution provides an authentication method that is part of the HTTP specifications.

70-215.02.04.003

You are setting up security on an Internet Information Services (IIS) 5.0 Web server.

You must meet the following security requirements:

- You must use an authentication method that supports Microsoft Internet Explorer 2.0 or later.

- You must use an authentication method that hashes the password so the original texts cannot be read.

- You must provide Windows NT Challenge/Response (NTLM) authentication.

- You must provide an authentication method that is part of the HTTP specification.

The proposed solution is to use Basic Authentication.

What does the proposed solution provide?

A. The proposed solution provides an authentication method that supports Internet Explorer 2.0 or later.

B. The proposed solution provides an authentication method that hashes the passwords.

C. The proposed solution provides NTLM authentication.

D. The proposed solution provides an authentication method that is part of the HTTP specifications.

70-215.02.04.004

You have been given the responsibility of managing an Internet Information Services (IIS) 5.0 Web site, but you have encountered several problems administering the site. You can enable content rating, enable logging, and set content expiration, but you cannot change the Web site's identity, configure bandwidth throttling, or create virtual directories. How should an administrator configure the server so that you can perform all these administrative tasks?

A. By configuring share-level security on the Inetpub folder so that you have full control over the folder's contents

B. By configuring NTFS security on the Inetpub folder so that you have full control over the folder's contents

C. By adding you to the local Administrators group on the server

D. By adding you to the Web Site Operators group for the Web site

Objective 2.4 Answers

70-215.02.04.001

▶ **Correct Answers: B and D**

A. **Incorrect:** Because Digest Authentication is a new HTTP 1.1 feature, not all browsers support it. Digest Authentication is supported only for Windows 2000 domains, and Internet Explorer 5.0 or later is one of the few browsers that support it. If a noncompliant browser makes a request on a server that requires Digest Authentication, the server will reject the request and send the client an error message. In order to use Digest Authentication in Windows 2000, the server must have access to an Active Directory server that is set up for Digest Authentication. If the server running IIS is not an Active Directory server or does not have access to the Active Directory, this authentication will not work.

B. **Correct:** Digest Authentication offers the same features as Basic Authentication but involves a different method for transmitting the authentication credentials. The credentials pass through a one-way process, which is referred to as *hashing*. The result of the process is called a hash, or message digest, and the original text cannot be deciphered from the hash. The server generates additional information that is added to the password before hashing so that no one can capture the password hash and use it to impersonate the true client. This shared secret password methodology has an advantage over Basic Authentication, in which the password can be intercepted and used by an unauthorized person.

C. **Incorrect:** Digest Authentication does not provide NTLM authentication. Integrated Windows Authentication provides NTLM authentication for older versions of Internet Explorer that use it to cryptographically authenticate with IIS.

D. **Correct:** Digest Authentication is a new HTTP 1.1 feature. It is the latest authentication standard of the World Wide Web Consortium (W3C), the organization that sets standards for the Web and HTML. IIS 5.0 complies with the HTTP 1.1 standard, including features such as PUT and DELETE, the ability to customize HTTP error messages, and support for custom HTTP headers.

70-215.02.04.002

▶ **Correct Answers: A, B, and C**

A. **Correct:** Integrated Windows Authentication provides NTLM authentication for Internet Explorer 2.0 or later. Integrated Windows Authentication also provides Web sites and new versions of Internet Explorer with Kerberos authentication. Integrated Windows Authentication is used only if Anonymous access is disabled or denied as a result of NTFS permission restrictions. Integrated Windows Authentication is not supported over proxy server connections.

B. **Correct:** Integrated Windows Authentication uses a hashing technology for a secure exchange with the user's browser in order to establish the user's identity. Information already stored on the user's computer, from a domain logon, is used in the exchange, so the user does not need to enter this information. If the initial authentication attempt fails, the user will see a dialog box pop up in the browser asking for user information. If this attempt fails, no other attempts will be made and the method will fail.

C. **Correct:** Integrated Windows Authentication provides NTLM authentication for Internet Explorer 2.0 or later. NTLM is more secure than Basic Authentication. In Integrated Windows Authentication, the browser attempts to use the current user's credentials from a domain logon. If those credentials are rejected, Integrated Windows Authentication will prompt the user for a user name and password. The user's password is not passed from the client to the server in clear text. If a user has logged on as a domain user on a local computer, the user won't have to be authenticated again when accessing a network computer in that domain. The user is not prompted for a user name and password for each HTTP request; rather, the user is prompted only when the cached credentials do not have sufficient permissions to access a specific page or file.

D. **Incorrect:** Integrated Windows Authentication is not part of the HTTP specification. Basic Authentication is part of the HTTP 1.0 specification, and Digest Authentication is part of the HTTP 1.1 specification. HTTP specifications are set by the World Wide Web Consortium (W3C), the organization that sets standards for the Web and HTML. IIS 5.0 complies with the HTTP 1.1 standard, including features such as PUT and DELETE, the ability to customize HTTP error messages, and support for custom HTTP headers.

70-215.02.04.003

▶ **Correct Answers: A and D**

A. **Correct:** Most browsers support Basic Authentication. Basic Authentication sends passwords over networks in Base64-encoded format. This authentication is a widely used, industry-standard method for collecting user name and password information. However, passwords are transmitted in an unencrypted form. By monitoring communications on your network, someone could easily intercept and decipher these passwords by using publicly available tools. Basic Authentication should be used only if the connection between the user and your Web server is secure, with a direct cable connection, a dedicated line, or a secure intranet.

B. **Incorrect:** Basic Authentication does not use a hashing technology for a secure exchange with the user's browser in order to establish the user's identity. Basic authentication results in the transmission of passwords across the network in an unencrypted form. A determined computer vandal equipped with a network monitoring tool could intercept user names and passwords.

C. **Incorrect:** Basic Authentication does not provide NTLM authentication. Integrated Windows Authentication provides NTLM authentication for Internet Explorer 2.0 or later. NTLM is more secure than Basic Authentication.

D. **Correct:** Basic Authentication is part of the HTTP 1.0 specification, unlike Digest Authentication, which is part of the HTTP 1.1 specification. HTTP specifications are set by the World Wide Web Consortium (W3C), the organization that sets standards for the Web and HTML. IIS 5.0 complies with the HTTP 1.1 standard, including features such as PUT and DELETE, the ability to customize HTTP error messages, and support for custom HTTP headers.

70-215.02.04.004

▶ **Correct Answers: C**

A. **Incorrect:** By default, the Inetpub folder is not shared, so you cannot configure share-level security on that folder. If the folder were shared and you were granted the Full Control permission on the share, you would be able to access and manipulate the folders and files within the share. For example, you could modify the contents of the DEFAULT.HTM file in the root folder of a Web site. However, you would not be able to perform the specified administrative tasks necessary to manage the site. To do that, you must be added to the local Administrators group, whose members have total control over the system.

B. **Incorrect:** If you were granted Full Control permission through NTFS security, you would be able to access and manipulate the folders and files within the share. For example, you could modify the contents of the DEFAULT.HTM file in the root folder of a Web site. However, you would not be able to perform the specified administrative tasks necessary to manage the site. To do that, you must be added to the local Administrators group, whose members have total control over the system.

C. **Correct:** The local Administrators group has total control over the system. For a specific computer, the users in the local administrator security group have full rights and permissions for that computer. The full-privilege Administrators group is used for local administration activities, such as managing Internet Information Services. By default, the Administrators group is added to the Web Site Operators group. As a result, members of Administrators can perform all the tasks that can be performed by members of Web Site Operators, which include enabling content rating, enabling logging, and setting content expiration. In addition, members of the Administrators group can change the Web site's identity, configure bandwidth throttling, or create virtual directories. Members have access to properties that affect IIS and the Windows 2000 Server computer hosting IIS.

D. **Incorrect:** Judging by the types of tasks you can and cannot perform, we can assume that you are probably already a member of the Web Site Operators group. Members of Web Site Operators are a special group of users who have limited administrative privileges on individual Web sites. Members can administer properties that affect only their respective sites. They do not have access to properties that affect IIS, the Windows 2000 Server computer hosting IIS, or the network. Members of Web Site Operators can act as the site administrator and can change or reconfigure the Web site as necessary. However, members are not permitted to change the identification of Web sites, configure the anonymous user name or password, throttle bandwidth, create virtual directories or change their paths, or change application isolation.

Configuring and Troubleshooting Hardware Devices and Drivers

Hardware includes any physical device connected to your computer and controlled by its microprocessor. Hardware includes devices that were connected to your computer when it was manufactured, as well as peripheral equipment added later. For example, your system's hardware can include modems, disk drives, drive controllers, CD-ROM drives, print devices, network adapters, keyboards, monitors, and display adapters. For a device to work properly with Windows 2000, a **device driver** must be loaded onto the computer. A device driver is a program that allows a specific device to communicate with Microsoft Windows 2000. Although a device might be installed on your computer, Windows 2000 cannot use the device until an appropriate driver is installed and configured. The management of devices on your system includes installing, configuring, and removing the actual devices as well as the device drivers. In addition, you must be able to update device drivers, configure driver signing options, manage hardware profiles, and monitor the performance of hardware devices and their drivers.

Tested Skills and Suggested Practices

The skills that you need to successfully master the Configuring and Troubleshooting Hardware Devices and Drivers domain on the *Installing, Configuring, and Administering Microsoft Windows 2000 Server* exam include:

- **Configuring hardware devices.**

    - Practice 1: Select a device on your computer that is not critical to your current operations, such as a modem. Use Device Manager to disable the device. Notice how Device Manager refreshes the list of devices and how a red X appears over the device. Now enable the device and watch how the list of devices is refreshed.

- ▪ Practice 2: Use Device Manager to access the device's properties. Click the Troubleshooter button to launch Hardware Troubleshooter in Windows 2000 Help. Note that you can launch Hardware Troubleshooter even though the hardware is functioning properly. Run through some of the steps in Hardware Troubleshooter by selecting available options, and then clicking Next.

- ▪ Practice 3: From Control Panel, launch the Add/Remove Hardware wizard to uninstall a Plug and Play device that is not critical to your operation. Select a device that you know is supported by Windows 2000 and for which the device driver can be easily reinstalled. Do not physically remove or disconnect the device from your computer. Open Device Manager, and notice that the device you uninstalled is no longer listed. Scan the devices for hardware changes. Windows 2000 finds the device and reinstalls it on your computer, and the device is added to the list in Device Manager.

- ▪ **Configuring Driver Signing options.**

  - ▪ Practice 1: From Control Panel, launch the System utility and open Driver Signing. Notice that three options can be configured: Ignore, Warn, and Block. Warn is selected by default. Do not change this option unless you plan to change it back or unless you want to block the installation of unsigned files or allow unsigned files to be installed without warning the user. Close the Driver Signing Options dialog box, and then close the System Properties dialog box.

  - ▪ Practice 2: Open a command prompt, and launch the File Signature Verification tool by typing **sigverif**. Click the Advanced button to open the Advanced File Signature Verification Settings dialog box. Review the options on the Search tab and the Logging tab, and then close the dialog box. Click Start to check for any system files that are not digitally signed. When the search is complete, open the Advanced File Signature Verification Settings dialog box, and open the Logging tab to view the log.

- ▪ **Updating device drivers.**

  - ▪ Practice 1: Select a device on your computer that is not critical to your current operations. Use Device Manager to access the device's properties and update the device driver. If the device is working properly, the Upgrade Device Driver wizard should find a suitable driver already installed. Click Cancel to keep the currently installed driver.

  - ▪ Practice 2: Once you cancel the Upgrade Device Driver wizard, click the Driver Details button to view information about the device driver. Notice that the driver information includes a list of driver files and other information about the driver. Close The Driver File Details dialog box, and return to the Driver tab of the Properties dialog box. Notice that the information on the table includes the name of the digital signer.

Further Reading

This section lists supplemental readings by objective. Study these sources thoroughly before taking exam 70-215.

Objective 3.1

Microsoft Corporation. *Windows 2000 Server Resource Kit*. Volume: *Microsoft Windows 2000 Server Operations Guide*. Review Chapter 14, "Troubleshooting."

"Plug and Play." (This white paper can be downloaded for free at *http://www.microsoft.com/windows2000/library/howitworks/hardware/plugnplay.asp*.)

Microsoft Corporation. *MCSE Training Kit: Microsoft Windows 2000 Server*. Redmond, Washington: Microsoft Press, 2000. Review Lesson 1 in Chapter 12, "Reliability and Availability."

"Troubleshooting Tools and Strategies." (This article can be downloaded for free at *http://www.microsoft.com/windows2000/library/resources/reskit/samplechapters/pref/pref_tts_juhe.asp*.) This document is taken from the *Windows 2000 Professional Resource Kit* and provides useful information about hardware devices, their drivers, and driver signing.

Willis, Will, David Watts, and Tillman Strahan. *Windows 2000 System Administration Handbook*. Upper Saddle River, New Jersey: Prentice-Hall Professional Technical Reference, 2000. Chapter 5, "Using the Windows Control Panel." (This document can be downloaded for free at *http://microsoft.com/technet/win2000/usingthe.asp*.) This document includes a discussion about the Add/Remove Hardware wizard and about hardware profiles.

Objective 3.2

"Driver Signing Set to 'Warn' During Windows 2000 Setup." (This article can be downloaded for free at *http://support.microsoft.com/support/kb/articles/Q216/7/54.asp*.)

"How to Set the Driver Signing Policy for Windows 2000 Unattended Setup." (This article can be downloaded for free at *http://support.microsoft.com/support/kb/articles/Q236/0/29.asp*.)

Microsoft Corporation. *MCSE Training Kit: Microsoft Windows 2000 Server*. Redmond, Washington: Microsoft Press, 2000. Review Lesson 1 in Chapter 12, "Reliability and Availability."

"Troubleshooting Tools and Strategies." (This article can be downloaded for free at *http://www.microsoft.com/windows2000/library/resources/reskit/samplechapters/pref/pref_tts_juhe.asp*.) This document is taken from the *Windows 2000 Professional Resource Kit* and provides useful information about hardware devices, their drivers, and driver signing.

Willis, Will, David Watts, and Tillman Strahan. *Windows 2000 System Administration Handbook*. Upper Saddle River, New Jersey: Prentice-Hall Professional Technical Reference, 2000. Chapter 5, "Using the Windows Control Panel." (This document can be downloaded for free at *http://microsoft.com/technet/win2000/usingthe.asp*.) This document includes a discussion about the Add/Remove Hardware wizard and about hardware profiles.

"Windows 2000 Code Signing: Digitally Signed Drivers." (This article can be downloaded for free at *http://support.microsoft.com/support/kb/articles/Q224/4/04.asp*.)

Objective 3.3

"Finding Hardware Device Drivers that Are Compatible with Windows 2000." (This article can be downloaded for free at *http://www.microsoft.com/WINDOWS2000/upgrade/compat/driverissue.asp*.)

Microsoft Corporation. *Windows 2000 Server Resource Kit*. Volume: *Microsoft Windows 2000 Server Operations Guide*. Review Chapter 14, "Troubleshooting."

Microsoft Corporation. *MCSE Training Kit: Microsoft Windows 2000 Server*. Redmond, Washington: Microsoft Press, 2000. Review Lesson 1 in Chapter 12, "Reliability and Availability."

"Troubleshooting Tools and Strategies." (This article can be downloaded for free at *http://www.microsoft.com/windows2000/library/resources/reskit/samplechapters/pref/pref_tts_juhe.asp*.) This document is taken from the *Windows 2000 Professional Resource Kit* and provides useful information about hardware devices, their drivers, and driver signing.

Willis, Will, David Watts, and Tillman Strahan. *Windows 2000 System Administration Handbook*. Upper Saddle River, New Jersey: Prentice-Hall Professional Technical Reference, 2000. Chapter 5, "Using the Windows Control Panel." (This document can be downloaded for free at *http://microsoft.com/technet/win2000/usingthe.asp*.) This document includes a discussion about the Add/Remove Hardware wizard and about hardware profiles.

Objective 3.4

"Finding Hardware Device Drivers that Are Compatible with Windows 2000." (This article can be downloaded for free at *http://www.microsoft.com/WINDOWS2000/ upgrade/compat/driverissue.asp.*)

Microsoft Corporation. *Windows 2000 Server Resource Kit.* Volume: *Microsoft Windows 2000 Server Operations Guide.* Review Chapter 14, "Troubleshooting."

Microsoft Corporation. *MCSE Training Kit: Microsoft Windows 2000 Server.* Redmond, Washington: Microsoft Press, 2000. Review Lesson 1 in Chapter 12, "Reliability and Availability."

"Troubleshooting Tools and Strategies." (This article can be downloaded for free at *http://www.microsoft.com/windows2000/library/resources/reskit/samplechapters/pref/ pref_tts_juhe.asp.*) This document is taken from the *Windows 2000 Professional Resource Kit* and provides useful information about hardware devices, their drivers, and driver signing.

Willis, Will, David Watts, and Tillman Strahan. *Windows 2000 System Administration Handbook.* Upper Saddle River, New Jersey: Prentice-Hall Professional Technical Reference, 2000. Chapter 5, "Using the Windows Control Panel." (This document can be downloaded for free at *http://microsoft.com/technet/win2000/usingthe.asp.*) This document includes a discussion about the Add/Remove Hardware wizard and about hardware profiles.

OBJECTIVE 3.1

Configure hardware devices.

Windows 2000 supports a number of types of hardware devices that can be connected to the computer in different ways. Some devices, such as network adapters and audio adapters, are connected to expansion slots inside the computer. Other devices, such as printers and scanners, are connected to ports on the outside of the computer. And other devices, known as PC cards, connect only to the PC card slots on a portable computer. Many systems now contain hardware devices that are **Plug and Play** compliant. Plug and Play refers to a set of specifications developed by the Institute of Electronic and Electrical Engineers (IEEE) and computer and software manufacturers that allows a computer to automatically detect and configure a device and install the appropriate device drivers. Windows 2000 fully supports Plug and Play technology, allowing you to easily add and remove hardware devices from your computer without having to manually load and configure the device drivers. All devices connected to your computer, whether or not they are Plug and Play compliant, have their own unique device drivers, which are typically supplied by the device manufacturers. Many of these device drivers are included on the Windows 2000 Server installation CD-ROM.

Windows 2000 classifies devices by hardware types, which include such categories as disk drives, display adapters, keyboards, modems, and monitors. When you use the Device Manager snap-in or the Add/Remove Hardware wizard in Control Panel, you can see a list of the hardware types installed on your computer. Hardware types are further categorized according to individual devices. For example, the modem hardware type includes over 200 modems that you can install and use with Windows 2000. Devices are also classified according to how they are connected to your computer. Most devices are permanently connected to your computer. As a result, they are usually installed only once. Permanently connected devices can include sound cards, video display cards, modems, or hard disks. However, some devices are designed to be connected and disconnected from your computer, such as PC cards or hardware that connects to USB, serial, or parallel ports. You can plug or insert these types of devices into the appropriate port or expansion slot, and Windows 2000 will recognize the device and configure it without restarting your computer.

To answer the questions in this objective, you should first have a good overview of the various types of hardware devices that can be connected to a computer. You should know how to use the Device Manager snap-in and the Add/Remove Hardware wizard to install, view, remove, and troubleshoot devices. You should also know how to use the Driver Signing functionality within Windows 2000 and how to add and configure hardware profiles.

Objective 3.1 Questions

70-215.03.01.001

You have a Pentium III 350-MHz laptop computer with a modem and a network card installed. The modem should be available only when you are not connected to the network. You create a new hardware profile named Network and plan to configure the profile so that the modem is disabled when you are connected to the network. However, after you restart your computer, you discover that you are not presented with a menu of available profiles to select. How should you configure hardware profiles so that the menu will effectively appear at startup and allow you to configure separate modem settings under the two profiles?

Examine the Hardware Profiles dialog box shown in the image below to view the hardware profiles.

A. Remove the Network profile.

B. Make the Network profile the default profile.

C. Select the Wait Until I Select A Hardware Profile radio button.

D. Create a new hardware profile called Modem, and ensure that the modem is enabled in the profile.

70-215.03.01.002

You have a Pentium III 366-MHz laptop computer with a built-in modem on your motherboard. You want to configure the computer so that the modem will not be available when you are connected to the network. You duplicate the only existing hardware profile, name the new version "Docked Profile," and configure Windows 2000 so that it will not start until you select a profile. Then you restart your computer and select the new profile. What should you do next?

A. Use Device Manager to remove the modem.

B. Use Device Manager to disable the modem.

C. Use the Add/Remove Hardware wizard to uninstall the modem.

D. Use the Add/Remove Hardware wizard to disable the modem.

Objective 3.1 Answers

70-215.03.01.001

▶ **Correct Answers: C**

   A. **Incorrect:** You should not remove the Network profile. If you remove this profile, Windows 2000 will use only the original profile, which does not disable the modem. As a result, you will have to create another profile that can be used to disable the modem.

   B. **Incorrect:** If you make the Network profile the default hardware profile, you still will not be presented with the Hardware Profile/Configuration Recovery menu during startup. Windows 2000 will automatically select the Network profile, and you will not be able to configure separate docked (Network) and undocked (Roaming User) settings. When Windows 2000 Server starts, it selects, by default, the first hardware profile that appears in the list of available hardware profiles. Normally, you have 30 seconds (or the number of seconds configured) to choose a hardware profile. In this scenario, however, the setting of 0 seconds prevents the Hardware Profile/Configuration Recovery menu from appearing at all. If you discover that the modem is always available, it is because the original hardware profile is automatically being selected each time you start the computer. This means that you are not seeing the prompt in time to choose a profile. However, if you select the Wait Until I Select A Hardware Profile radio button, Windows 2000 will not start until you select a profile. This will allow you to select whichever profile you want, without needing to be concerned about missing the prompt.

   C. **Correct:** The Wait Until I Select A Hardware Profile radio button allows you to select which hardware profile to use when you start Windows 2000 Server. If this option is not selected, Windows 2000 normally uses the default profile after 30 seconds. However, in this scenario, the default delay period of 30 seconds has been changed to 0 seconds. This will result in Windows 2000 automatically choosing the default Roaming User profile, without presenting the Hardware Profile/Configuration Recovery menu at startup. The default profile is the first profile to appear in the list of hardware profiles. Selecting the Wait Until I Select A Hardware Profile radio button is not required for you to choose between profiles; however, if you are likely to miss the hardware profile prompt when you start Windows 2000, you should select this option to ensure that you are always prompted to select a hardware profile.

D. **Incorrect:** You do not need to create a new hardware profile.

70-215.03.01.002

▶ **Correct Answers: B**

A. **Incorrect:** When you use Device Manager to remove the modem, you are uninstalling the device but not removing the device drivers from your hard disk. You should then physically remove or disconnect the device from your computer, which you cannot do with a built-in modem. If you do not physically remove the device, Windows 2000 will detect it the next time you start the operating system and reinstall it, and you will have to uninstall it again. It is better to disable the modem rather than uninstall it. That way, you can keep the device connected to the computer and simply log on with the applicable hardware profile, rather than uninstall the modem each time you connect to the network.

B. **Correct:** Once you create a hardware profile, you can use Device Manager to disable and enable a device in a profile. When you disable a device, the device drivers for the device are not loaded when you start the computer. This is preferable to removing a device, which means that you plan to uninstall the device from your system. Device Manager is an MMC snap-in that provides you with a graphical view of the hardware that is installed on your computer. Device Manager allows you to change the way your hardware interacts with your computer's microprocessor. Any hardware configuration changes that you make are implemented in the current hardware profile.

C. **Incorrect:** When you use the Add/Remove Hardware wizard to uninstall the modem, you are telling Windows 2000 that the device is going to be removed from the computer. You should then physically remove or disconnect the device from your computer, which you cannot do with a built-in modem. If you do not physically remove the device, Windows 2000 will detect it the next time you start the operating system and reinstall it if it can locate the device drivers, or you will be prompted for the location of the device drivers. Either you will have to cancel the installation, or you will have to uninstall the device again. It is better to use Device Manager to disable the modem rather than remove it. That way, you can keep the device connected to the computer and simply log on with the original hardware profile, and you do not have to be concerned about Windows 2000 attempting to reinstall the device.

D. **Incorrect:** You cannot use the Add/Remove Hardware wizard to disable the modem. You must use Device Manager.

Configure Driver Signing options.

Driver Signing is a multifaceted process that allows Windows 2000 to notify users whether the drivers that they are installing have passed the Microsoft certification processes. In Driver Signing, device drivers are verified through a series of tests administered by the **Windows Hardware Quality Lab (WHQL)**. Drivers that earn this certification are more robust and cause fewer problems with Windows 2000. Driver Signing attaches an encrypted digital signature to a code file that has passed the WHQL tests. The system files provided with Windows 2000 include this signature, indicating that the files are original and unaltered and that they have been approved by Microsoft for use with Windows 2000.

Windows 2000 can warn or prevent users from installing unsigned code. If a file has not been digitally signed and resides in one of the device driver classes, a message alerts the user, offering the option of whether to continue. You can configure Driver Signing to respond in one of three ways: Ignore, Warn, or Block. Ignore allows all files to be installed, whether or not they've been installed. Warn notifies the user if a driver being installed has not been signed. Block prevents all unsigned drivers from being installed. All drivers included with Windows 2000 are digitally signed by Microsoft. To ensure that device drivers are compatible with Windows 2000, look for vendors offering drivers signed by Microsoft.

To answer the questions in this objective, you should be familiar with the basic principles behind Driver Signing and know how to configure the Driver Signing options. You should also know how to use the File Signature Verification tool and be able to view the log that the tool can generate.

Objective 3.2 Questions

70-215.03.02.001

You are adding a legacy SCSI controller to your Windows 2000 Server computer. The device driver for the controller is not signed, and you have been unable to install the SCSI adapter. How can you configure the computer so that you can install the unsigned driver?

A. Use Device Manager to access the device's Properties dialog box to modify the device's properties.

B. Use the System Information snap-in in the Computer Management console to access the device's Properties dialog box to modify the device's properties.

C. Set the Driver Signing option to Warn.

D. Set the Driver Signing option to Block.

70-215.03.02.002

You must add a DVD-ROM drive to your Windows 2000 Server computer, but the drive's adapter is not on the Hardware Compatibility List (HCL). You try to install the adapter's driver, but Windows 2000 prevents the installation. How should you add the drive?

A. Set the Driver Signing option to Block, and use Device Manager to access the device's Properties dialog box to install the driver.

B. Set the Driver Signing option to Block, and use the System Information snap-in in the Computer Management console to access the device's Properties dialog box to install the driver.

C. Set the Driver Signing option to Warn or Ignore, and use Device Manager to access the device's Properties dialog box to install the driver.

D. Set the Driver Signing option to Warn or Ignore, and use the System Information snap-in in the Computer Management console to access the device's Properties dialog box to install the driver.

70-215.03.02.003

Your company decides that all drivers on Windows 2000 Server computers must now be signed, so you have to check all current Windows 2000 Server computers and update any unsigned drivers. Which tool should you use to check your Windows 2000 Server computers?

A. Add/Remove Hardware wizard in Control Panel

B. System Information snap-in in the Computer Management console

C. Driver Signing, which is accessed through the Systems utility in Control Panel

D. The File Signature Verification utility, which is accessed by typing **sigverif** at a command prompt

70-215.03.02.004

You have 25 Microsoft Windows NT Server 4.0 computers with identical configurations. Each computer contains an audio adapter that is not on the Windows 2000 Hardware Compatibility List (HCL). You upgrade one of the computers to Windows 2000 Server and run an unsigned driver for the sound card without any problems. You want to set up the other servers so that you can install the driver without receiving a warning message. How should you configure the computer?

A. Use the System Information snap-in in the Computer Management console to access Driver Signing, and set the Driver Signing option to Block on each computer.

B. Use the System Information snap-in in the Computer Management console to access Driver Signing, and set the Driver Signing option to Ignore on each computer.

C. Use the System utility in Control Panel to access Driver Signing, and set the Driver Signing option to Ignore on each computer.

D. Use the System utility in Control Panel to access Driver Signing, and set the Driver Signing option to Block on each of the computers.

Objective 3.2 Answers

70-215.03.02.001

▶ **Correct Answers: C**

A. **Incorrect:** Device Manager is an MMC snap-in that provides you with a graphical view of the hardware that is installed on your computer. Device Manager allows you to change the way your hardware interacts with your computer's microprocessor. Although you can use Device Manager to access a device's properties, modifying those properties will not allow you to install an unsigned driver.

B. **Incorrect:** You cannot use the System Information snap-in to access the device's properties or modify them. You should use Device Manager to access the device's properties. However, modifying the device's properties will not allow you to install an unsigned driver.

C. **Correct:** Driver Signing allows you to configure one of three options: Ignore, Warn, and Block. The Ignore option allows all files to be installed, whether or not they have been signed. The Warn option notifies the user if a driver that's being installed has not been signed and gives the user a chance to cancel the installation. The Block option prevents all unsigned drivers from being installed. Because Windows 2000 is preventing the installation of the device driver, it is likely that the Driver Signing option has been set to Block, so you must change the option to Warn or Ignore.

D. **Incorrect:** You should not set the Driver Signing option to Block. Block prevents all unsigned drivers from being installed. You should set the option to Warn or Ignore.

70-215.03.02.002

▶ **Correct Answers: C**

A. **Incorrect:** You should not set the Driver Signing option to Block. Block prevents all unsigned drivers from being installed. However, if you set the option to Warn or Ignore, you can use Device Manager to install the driver.

B. **Incorrect:** You should not set the Driver Signing option to Block. Block prevents all unsigned drivers from being installed. You should set the option to Warn or Ignore. However, you cannot use the System Information snap-in to access the device's properties or install the driver. System Information collects and displays your system configuration information. It provides specific information about your computer when you are troubleshooting your configuration. You should use Device Manager to install the driver.

C. **Correct:** Driver Signing allows you to configure one of three options: Ignore, Warn, and Block. The Ignore option allows all files to be installed, whether or not they have been signed. The Warn option notifies the user if a driver that is being installed has not been signed and gives the user a chance to cancel the installation. The Block option prevents all unsigned drivers from being installed. Because Windows 2000 is preventing the installation of the device driver, it is likely that the Driver Signing option has been set to Block, so you must change the option to Warn or Ignore. Once you set the option, you can use the Device Manager snap-in to access the device's properties and install the driver. Device Manager provides you with a graphical view of the hardware that is installed on your computer. You can use Device Manager to verify that your hardware is working properly, configure hardware settings, identify device drivers, and install updated device drivers. You can also disable, enable, and uninstall devices.

D. **Incorrect:** Although you should set the Driver Signing option to Warn or Ignore, you cannot use the System Information snap-in to access the device's properties or install the driver. You should use Device Manager.

70-215.03.02.003

▶ **Correct Answers: D**

A. **Incorrect:** The Add/Remove Hardware wizard allows you to add new hardware, unplug or remove hardware from your computer, or troubleshoot hardware-related problems. When you launch the Add/Remove Hardware wizard, you are given a choice of hardware-related tasks. You can choose to add or troubleshoot a device, or you can uninstall or unplug a device. Choose the first option if you are adding a new device to your computer or are having problems getting a device to work. Choose the second option if you want to uninstall a device or prepare the computer to unplug a device. The Add/Remove Hardware wizard does not allow you to verify whether any unsigned drivers are installed.

B. **Incorrect:** The System Information snap-in collects and displays your system configuration information. It provides specific information about your computer when you are troubleshooting your configuration. System Information displays a comprehensive view of your hardware, system components, and the software environment, including driver information. The software environment displays a snapshot of the software loaded in computer memory. This information can be used to see if a process is still running or to check version information. However, System Information does not allow you to verify whether any unsigned drivers are installed.

C. **Incorrect:** Driver Signing is a Windows 2000 function that can be configured to notify users if they try to install a driver that has not passed the Microsoft certification process, to prevent unsigned drivers from being installed, or to allow all drivers to be installed, without notifying the users. Driver Signing attaches an encrypted digital signature to a code file that has passed the Windows Hardware Quality Labs (WHQL) tests. Microsoft digitally signs drivers as part of the WHQL testing if the driver runs on the Windows 2000 operating system. However, Driver Signing does not allow you to verify whether any unsigned drivers are already installed.

D. **Correct:** The File Signature Verification utility allows you to check for files that have not been digitally signed. By default, the File Signature Verification utility searches for unsigned system files in the *%systemroot%* folder and saves the search results to the SIGVERIF.TXT log file. However, you can configure the utility to search for any type of unsigned file in any folder and that folder's subfolders. You can also turn off logging or change the name of the logging file. Normally, the File Signature Verification utility overwrites the existing log file when conducting a search, but you can configure the tool to append the existing log file rather than overwrite it. The log records the name of the files scanned, date modified, version, status, catalog, and who signed the file. You can start the File Signature Verification utility by clicking Start, clicking Run, and then typing **sigverif**.

70-215.03.02.004

▶ **Correct Answers: C**

A. **Incorrect:** You cannot use the System Information snap-in to access Driver Signing. The System Information snap-in collects and displays your system configuration information. It provides specific information about your computer when you are troubleshooting your configuration. System Information displays a comprehensive view of your hardware, system components, and the software environment, including driver information. Even if you could access Driver Signing from System Information, you should set the Driver Signing option to Ignore, not Block. The Block option prevents all unsigned drivers from being installed.

B. **Incorrect:** You cannot use the System Information snap-in to access Driver Signing. However, you should set the Driver Signing option to Ignore. The Ignore option allows all files to be installed, whether or not they have been signed.

C. **Correct:** Driver Signing is a Windows 2000 function that can be configured to notify users whether the drivers that they are installing have passed the Microsoft certification processes. Driver Signing allows you to configure one of three options: Ignore, Warn, and Block. The Ignore option allows all files to be installed, whether or not they have been signed. The Warn option notifies the user if a driver that is being installed has not been signed and gives the user a chance to cancel the installation. The Block option prevents all unsigned drivers from being installed.

D. **Incorrect:** You should set the Driver Signing option to Ignore, not Block.

O B J E C T I V E   3 . 3

Update device drivers.

A device driver is a program that allows a specific device, such as a modem, a network adapter, or a printer, to communicate with Windows 2000. Although a device might be installed on your system, Windows 2000 cannot use the device until you have installed and configured the appropriate driver. Device drivers load automatically when a computer is started unless the device is disabled. Once the device drivers are loaded, Windows 2000 configures the properties and settings for the device. Although you can manually configure device properties and settings, you should allow Windows 2000 to do this automatically whenever possible. When you install a Plug and Play device, Windows 2000 automatically configures the device so that it will work properly with other devices that are installed on your computer.

You can usually uninstall a Plug and Play device by disconnecting or removing the device. To uninstall a non–Plug and Play device, you can use the Add/Remove Hardware wizard or Device Manager to notify Windows 2000. After you notify Windows 2000, you must physically disconnect or remove the device from your computer. If you do not remove the device, it will be detected when you restart Windows 2000 Server. When you use Device Manager to uninstall a device, the device driver remains on your hard disk. If you want to remove the driver, you should use the Add/Remove Hardware wizard or consult the device's documentation. Instead of uninstalling a device that you might need to reattach, such as a modem, you can disable the device. When you disable a device, the physical device stays connected to your computer, but Windows 2000 updates the registry so that the device drivers are no longer loaded when you start the computer. The drivers are available again when you enable the device.

To answer the questions in this objective, you should have a thorough understanding of how hardware devices and device drivers are installed and uninstalled on your computer. In addition, you should know how to use the Device Manager snap-in to access a device's properties and update the driver for that device.

Objective 3.3 Questions

70-215.03.03.001

You must update a driver for a USB camera on your Windows 2000 Server computer. How can you best update the driver?

A. Use Device Manager to disable the camera, and then restart your computer.

B. Use Device Manager to scan the camera for hardware changes.

C. Use the Add/Remove Hardware wizard in Control Panel to remove the camera, and then restart the computer.

D. Use Device Manager to access the camera's Properties dialog box to update the driver.

70-215.03.03.002

You must update a driver for a 56K modem in your Windows 2000 Server computer. How can you best update the driver?

A. Use the Phone And Modem Options utility in Control Panel to update the driver.

B. Use Device Manager to scan the modem for hardware changes.

C. Use the Add/Remove Hardware wizard in Control Panel to remove the modem, and then restart the computer.

D. Use Device Manager to access the modem's Properties dialog box to update the driver.

70-215.03.03.003

An external Plug and Play–compliant modem is connected to your computer, but it is turned off. You turn on the computer and boot up Windows 2000 Server. After Windows 2000 Server starts up you turn on the modem and try to connect to an ISP, but you receive an error message stating that the modem is not present. You view the modem in Device Manager, which shows that the device is working properly. What should you do to make Windows 2000 recognize the modem?

A. Use Device Manager to scan the modem for hardware changes.

B. Use Device Manager to access the modem's Properties dialog box to update the driver.

C. Use the Phone And Modem Options utility in Control Panel to scan the modem for hardware changes.

D. Use the Phone And Modem Options utility in Control Panel to update the driver.

Objective 3.3 Answers

70-215.03.03.001

► **Correct Answers: D**

A. **Incorrect:** Disabling the camera will not update the device driver. When you disable a device, Windows 2000 updates the registry so that the device drivers are no longer loaded when you start your computer. The device drivers are available again when you enable the device. Disabling a device is useful if you want to have more than one hardware configuration for your computer or if you have a portable computer and you use it at a docking station. You should use Device Manager to update the device driver, not disable the device.

B. **Incorrect:** Scanning the camera will not update the device driver. The Scan For Hardware Changes option in Device Manager is used to scan for Plug and Play–compliant hardware connected to your computer. It will not reinstall a Plug and Play device if it detects a device and its driver, and it will not update the driver. If you scan the camera, Device Manager will most likely not find any hardware changes.

C. **Incorrect:** You can use the Add/Remove Hardware wizard to update the device driver, although it is not the most efficient method. If you use the Add/Remove Hardware wizard to uninstall the camera and its device drivers, you would need to connect the camera to the computer and restart the computer to allow Windows 2000 to detect the camera. If device drivers are found on your hard disk, which is possible even though you specified removing the device drivers, the hardware is reinstalled and the existing drivers are used. If no device drivers are found, you will be prompted for the source of the device driver. At this point, you can provide the updated driver. However, it is simpler to use Device Manager to access the device's properties and update the driver from there, without having to uninstall or reinstall hardware.

D. **Correct:** Device Manager is an MMC snap-in that provides you with a graphical view of the hardware that is installed on your computer. Device Manager allows you to change the way your hardware interacts with your computer's microprocessor. You can use Device Manager to access a device's properties. From there, you can install an updated device driver. To install the updated driver, click the Update Driver button on the Drivers tab of the device's Properties dialog box. This will launch the Update Device Driver wizard, which will step you through the process of updating the driver. During this process, you will be prompted for the source of the new driver. Be certain that you have the driver ready when you launch the wizard.

70-215.03.03.002

▶ **Correct Answers: D**

A. **Incorrect:** The Phone And Modem Options utility in Control Panel allows you to configure your tele-phone dialing rules and modem properties. However, these properties are not the same properties that you would access through Device Manager. The modem properties that you can access through the Phone And Modem Options utility address such issues as speaker volume, port speed, diagnostics, and initialization commands. You cannot update the device driver through the Phone And Modem Options utility.

B. **Incorrect:** Scanning the modem will not update the device driver. The Scan For Hardware Changes option in Device Manager is used to scan for Plug and Play–compliant hardware connected to your computer. It will not reinstall a Plug and Play device if it detects a device and its driver, and it will not update the driver. If you scan the modem, Device Manager will most likely not find any hardware changes to the modem.

C. **Incorrect:** It is possible that you can use the Add/Remove Hardware wizard to update the device driver, although it is not the most efficient method. If you use the Add/Remove Hardware wizard to uninstall the modem and its device drivers and you leave the modem connected to the computer when you restart the computer, Windows 2000 should automatically detect the modem. If device drivers are found on your hard disk, which is possible even though you specified removing the device drivers, the hardware is reinstalled and the existing drivers are used. If no device drivers are found, you will be prompted for the source of the device driver. At this point, you can provide the updated driver. How-ever, it is easier simply to use Device Manager to access the device's properties and update the driver from there, without having to uninstall or reinstall hardware.

D. **Correct:** Device Manager is an MMC snap-in that provides you with a graphical view of the hard-ware that is installed on your computer. Device Manager allows you to change the way your hardware interacts with your computer's microprocessor. You can use Device Manager to access a device's properties. From there, you can install an updated device driver. To install the updated driver, click the Update Driver button on the Drivers tab of the device's Properties dialog box. This will launch the Update Device Driver wizard, which will step you through the process of updating the driver. During this process, you will be prompted for the source of the new driver. Be certain that you are prepared to supply the driver when you launch the wizard.

70-215.03.03.003

▶ **Correct Answers: A**

A. **Correct:** The Scan For Hardware Changes option in Device Manager is used to scan for Plug and Play–compliant hardware connected to your computer. It will update the list of hardware devices that are connected to the computer. In some cases, you might find that if you start your computer with an external device turned off, Windows 2000 interprets this to mean that the modem is not present during startup. As a result, you must refresh the list of hardware devices after you turn on the modem so that Windows 2000 can see that the device is present.

B. **Incorrect:** Device Manager is an MMC snap-in that provides you with a graphical view of the hardware that is installed on your computer. Device Manager allows you to change the way your hardware interacts with your computer's microprocessor. You can use Device Manager to access a device's properties and update the device driver. If you perform the update process, whether using the existing driver or installing a new one, Device Manager will scan for hardware changes when you complete the update and, as a result, will see that the device is present. However, rather than update the driver unnecessarily, it is easier to simply scan for hardware changes and not update the driver.

C. **Incorrect:** The Phone And Modem Options utility in Control Panel allows you to configure your telephone dialing rules and modem properties. However, these properties are not the same properties that you would access through Device Manager. The modem properties that you can access through the Phone And Modem Options utility address such issues as speaker volume, port speed, diagnostics, and initialization commands. You cannot use the Phone And Modem Options utility to scan the modem for hardware changes.

D. **Incorrect:** You cannot use the Phone And Modem Options utility to update the device driver.

O B J E C T I V E   3 . 4

Troubleshoot problems with hardware.

Problems can arise when hardware is used with incompatible software, when hardware is configured incorrectly, when cables and other connections are not working properly, or as a result of other hardware-related issues. Often problems arise with hardware that is not on the **Hardware Compatibility List (HCL)**. The HCL is a compilation of computers and system hardware that have been extensively tested with Windows 2000 for stability and compatibility. To avoid problems, make sure that you are using a device make and mode that is listed on the HCL. If your hardware components are listed on the HCL and you are still having problems, check that the physical connections are secure and that your hardware is configured correctly.

Windows 2000 provides several tools that allow you to manage hardware devices and their drivers. The Add/Remove Hardware wizard allows you to add new hardware, unplug or remove hardware from your computer, or troubleshoot hardware-related problems. The Device Manager snap-in allows you to perform a number of hardware-related tasks, which include determining whether the hardware is working properly, changing configuration settings, installing updated drivers, and disabling, enabling, and uninstalling devices. The Driver Signing function allows you to configure Windows 2000 to accept or reject unsigned drivers, and the File Signature Verification utility allows you to check for any system files that have not been digitally signed.

To answer the questions in this objective, you should be familiar with the HCL, including how to access the most current version of the list and how to use the list to verify that hardware on your computer is supported by Windows 2000. You should have a basic understanding of the differences between Plug and Play devices and non–Plug and Play devices, and you should know how to install devices, including connecting devices to your computer, loading the appropriate drivers, and configuring device properties and settings. You should also know how to configure Driver Signing and be able to search for system files that have not been digitally signed.

Objective 3.4 Questions

70-215.03.04.001

You just installed Windows 2000 Server on a Pentium III 550-MHz computer with 128 MB of RAM and a 6-GB hard drive. You view Device Manager and notice that there is a yellow question mark next to one of the audio controllers. You decide to install an updated driver that shipped with the controller; however, the driver is not signed. You try to install the driver, but Windows 2000 prevents the installation. How should you install the driver?

A. Set the Driver Signing option to Block, and use Device Manager to open the controller's Properties dialog box and launch the Update Device Driver wizard to install the new driver.

B. Set the Driver Signing option to Ignore, and use Device Manager to open the controller's Properties dialog box and launch the Update Device Driver wizard to install the new driver.

C. Set the Driver Signing option to Warn, and use Device Manager to scan the controller for hardware changes to install the new driver.

D. Set the Driver Signing option to Block, and use Device Manager to scan the controller for hardware changes to install the new driver.

70-215.03.04.002

You just installed Windows 2000 Server on a Pentium III 550-MHz computer with 128 MB of RAM and a 6-GB hard drive. You view Device Manager and notice that there is a yellow question mark next to a USB camera. The camera is Plug and Play–compliant and is listed on the Hardware Compatibility List (HCL). You want to use the camera, but you prefer not to restart your computer. What is the first step you should take to address the problem?

A. Use Device Manager to disable the device driver, and then scan the devices for hardware changes.

B. Use Device Manager to uninstall the camera, and then scan the devices for hardware changes.

C. Use the Add/Remove Hardware wizard to uninstall the device, and then scan the devices for hardware changes.

D. Use the Add/Remove Hardware wizard to uninstall the device and its driver, and then unplug the device to update the driver.

70-215.03.04.003

You configure your Windows 2000 Server as a multihomed computer so that one network adapter can connect to the Internet through a cable modem and the other network adapter can connect to the local network, which uses the IPX/SPX protocol. The network adapter that connects to the cable modem is a 10-Mbps adapter, and the network adapter that connects to the network is a 100-Mbps Ethernet card. You are able to access the Internet, but you cannot access the network. How can you resolve the connectivity problem to the network?

Examine the adapter configurations shown in the image below.

10MBPS Realtek adapter	
Protocols	TCP/IP AppleTalk Network Monitor Driver NWLink IPX/SPX
Client services	Client for Microsoft Networks
	File and Print Sharing for Microsoft Networks

10MBPS Realtek adapter	
Protocols	TCP/IP
Client services	Client for Microsoft Networks
	File and Print Sharing for Microsoft Networks

A. Add the NWLink protocol to the 100-Mbps network adapter.

B. Remove the NWLink protocol from the 10-Mbps network adapter.

C. Remove the TCP/IP protocol from the 10-Mbps network adapter.

D. Add the AppleTalk protocol to the 100-Mbps network adapter.

Objective 3.4 Answers

70-215.03.04.001

▶ **Correct Answers: B**

A. **Incorrect:** If the Driver Signing option is set to Block, unsigned drivers cannot be installed. However, if the option were set to Warn or Ignore, you could use Device Manager to install the new device driver.

B. **Correct:** Driver Signing is a Windows 2000 function that can be configured to notify users whether the drivers that they are installing have passed the Microsoft certification processes. Driver Signing allows you to configure one of three options: Ignore, Warn, and Block. Ignore allows all files to be installed, whether or not they have been signed. Warn notifies the user if a driver that's being installed has not been signed and gives the user a chance to cancel the installation. Block prevents all unsigned drivers from being installed. Once you set the Driver Signing option to Ignore or Warn, you can use Device Manager to install the device driver. Device Manager is an MMC snap-in that provides you with a graphical view of the hardware that is installed on your computer. Device Manager allows you to change the way your hardware interacts with your computer's microprocessor. You can use Device Manager to access a device's properties and update the device driver.

C. **Incorrect:** If you set the Driver Signing option to Warn, you can still install an unsigned driver. However, scanning the hardware does not allow you to install the updated driver. The Scan For Hardware Changes option in Device Manager is used to scan for Plug and Play–compliant hardware connected to your computer. It will update the list of hardware devices that are connected to the computer.

D. **Incorrect:** If the Driver Signing option is set to Block, unsigned drivers cannot be installed. In addition, scanning the hardware does not allow you to install the driver.

70-215.03.04.002

▶ **Correct Answers: B**

A. **Incorrect:** You can use Device Manager to disable and enable a device. When you disable a device, the device drivers for the device are not loaded when you start the computer. However, if you then scan for hardware changes the device will remain disabled, and you still cannot use the device. You need to uninstall the device before you scan for hardware changes, not disable it.

B. **Correct:** Device Manager is an MMC snap-in that provides you with a graphical view of the hardware that is installed on your computer. Device Manager allows you to change the way your hardware interacts with your computer's microprocessor. You can use Device Manager to uninstall the camera. Once the camera has been uninstalled, you can use Device Manager to scan devices for hardware changes. The Scan For Hardware Changes option in Device Manager is used to scan for Plug and Play–compliant hardware connected to your computer. It will update the list of hardware devices that are connected to the computer. When you scan for hardware changes, Windows 2000 finds the camera and reinstalls the device. You should reinstall a Plug and Play device only if that device is not working properly or if it has stopped working.

C. **Incorrect:** You cannot use the Add/Remove Hardware wizard to scan for hardware changes. When you use the Add/Remove Hardware wizard to uninstall a device, you are notifying Windows 2000 that you want to uninstall the individual device from your system. You should then physically remove or disconnect the device from your computer. If you unplug the camera from the USB port, and then scan for hardware changes, the camera will disappear from Device Manager, and you still will not be able to use it. However, if you plug the device back in, Windows 2000 should automatically detect it and install it. If Windows 2000 fails to install the device automatically, you can use Device Manager to scan for hardware changes, which should then reinstall the camera. Even though the Add/Remove Hardware wizard can probably be used to accomplish the same results as using Device Manager to uninstall the device and then scan for hardware changes, it is much simpler to use Device Manager than to go through the process of using the Add/Remove Hardware wizard and physically unplugging and then plugging in the device.

D. **Incorrect:** You do not need to uninstall the camera and its driver and unplug the camera to update the driver. In addition, updating the driver may not be necessary in this case. You should first uninstall the device and then scan the devices for hardware changes, which is the easiest first step you can take to try to address the problem.

70-215.03.04.003

▶ **Correct Answers: A**

A. **Correct:** The 100-Mbps network adapter must be configured with IPX/SPX because that is the protocol used by the network. A network adapter must be configured with the same protocol that is being used on the network. NWLink is Microsoft's implementation of the Novell NetWare IPX/SPX protocol. NWLink is most commonly used in environments where clients running Microsoft operating systems are used to access resource on NetWare servers, or where clients running NetWare are used to access resources on computers running Microsoft operating systems.

B. **Incorrect:** Removing NWLink from the 10-Mbps network adapter will not affect the computer's ability to communicate with the network or with the Internet. The Internet uses TCP/IP for all communications, so a network adapter communicating with the Internet must be configured with TCP/IP. NWLink is not necessary on this adapter.

C. **Incorrect:** If you remove TCP/IP from the 10-Mbps network adapter, you would not be able to communicate with the Internet. The Internet uses TCP/IP for all communications, so a network adapter communicating with the Internet must be configured with TCP/IP.

D. **Incorrect:** Adding AppleTalk to the 100-Mbps network adapter will not allow you to communicate with the network. Because the network uses IPX/SPX for its communications, the network adapter must be configured with NWLink, which is Microsoft's implementation of IPX/SPX.

OBJECTIVE DOMAIN 4

Managing, Monitoring, and Optimizing System Performance, Reliability, and Availability

An important function in administering a Microsoft Windows 2000 Server computer is to ensure system performance, reliability, and availability. This administrative responsibility includes monitoring and optimizing system resources as well as managing processes, which can involve setting priorities on the processes or starting and stopping them. You must also be able to manage and optimize disk performance, system state data, user data, and any other component of Windows 2000 Server that affects performance, reliability, and availability. In addition, you must be able to recover system state data and user data. Windows 2000 Server includes a variety of tools and services that allow you to monitor and optimize your system. These tools include System Monitor, Performance Logs And Alerts, and Network Monitor. Several tools, such as Disk Defragmenter and Check Disk, are also available to diagnose disk problems, improve disk performance, and compress data. In addition, Windows 2000 Server provides two tools that allow you to recover this data: Windows Backup and the Recovery Console. You can also use Safe Mode to troubleshoot system restoration. Safe Mode is a method of starting Windows 2000 Server that uses basic files and drivers only. By optimizing system performance, reliability, and availability, you can ensure that the Windows 2000 Server computer consistently runs applications and services, that you've addressed the causes of downtime, and that your system resists failures and is easy to restart after it has been shut down.

Tested Skills and Suggested Practices

The skills that you need to successfully master the Managing, Monitoring, and Optimizing System Performance, Reliability, and Availability domain on the *Installing, Configuring, and Administering Microsoft Windows 2000 Server* exam include:

- **Monitoring usage of system resources.**

  - Practice 1: Use the Performance console to collect and view data about your system's performance. First collect and view real-time data by using the System Monitor snap-in. Be certain to add a variety of counters so that you can monitor memory, disk, processor, and other system activity. Next use Performance Logs And Alerts to configure logs to record performance data. Again, use a variety of counters. When the logs have finished collecting data, use System Monitor to view their contents.

  - Practice 2: If your computer is connected to a network, use Network Monitor to capture and display packets that the computer receives from the network. You might have to install Network Monitor the first time you want to use it. Experiment with the different types of displays and window options. Capture several frames and compare the differences among the frames.

  - Practice 3: Use Task Manager to view information about applications and processes currently running on your computer. From the Applications tab, select an application and then go to that application's process. Select different columns on the Processes tab and view their values in the table. Use the Performance tab to monitor real-time performance data about your computer. Be sure to display information about kernel usage.

- **Monitoring and optimizing disk performance.**

  - Practice 1: Use the Check Disk tool to check for file system errors on your computer. Try accessing the tool through the disk's properties, and then try using the tool at a command prompt. Select different options when optimizing the disk. Remember that all running applications or open files on the disk being checked must be closed for the Check Disk process to be able to automatically fix file system errors.

  - Practice 2: Use the Disk Defragmenter snap-in in Computer Management to defragment a disk. Analyze the disk before you defragment it. If you have not defragmented your disk before or it has been a while since it was defragmented, the process could be time-consuming, so plan accordingly. You should run Disk Defragmenter when the computer will receive the least usage. The defragmentation process needs some free disk space to defragment a disk, so be certain to try this on a disk that has plenty of free space.

- Practice 3: Enable data compression on a folder that contains subfolders and different types of files. Data compression can affect performance, so select a folder that is not used very much and that is not too large. Try accessing different files in the folder once you have enabled compression. Remember that you cannot enable compression on a folder that is encrypted. Select an alternative display color for compressed files and folders. When you are through, you can disable compression on the folder.

- Practice 4: Configure disk quotas for a user on your computer. You might have to create a fictitious user account to experiment with disk quotas. Set the limits low so that you can easily test how quotas work. After you have set the quotas, try saving too much data to the volume that has been configured with the quota. If necessary, turn off the quotas when you are finished.

- **Backing up and restoring data.**

  - Practice 1: Back up a set of selected files and folders on your computer. Use a folder that contains files that you can delete. Do not back up too much data. You want to keep the amount of data small so that you are not waiting too long for the process to be completed. If you like, you can back up the data to a floppy disk if the files are small enough.

  - Practice 2: Delete several files from the folder that you backed up in Practice 1. When finished, do a restore of the backup job. After the restore is complete, view the folder on your computer to ensure that the files you deleted have been restored.

  - Practice 3: Schedule a backup job similar to the one you performed in Practice 1. When the job is complete, delete some of the files from that folder, and then restore the folder. Ensure that the files you deleted have been restored.

  - Practice 4: Back up the system state data on your computer. The volume of data will be much too large to put on a floppy disk, so use a tape drive or other storage device that has plenty of room. For purposes of this practice, you can use the same hard disk that is running Windows 2000 if there is enough room.

Further Reading

This section lists supplemental readings by objective. Study these sources thoroughly before taking exam 70-215.

Objective 4.1

"How to Create a Log Using System Monitor in Windows 2000." (This article can be downloaded for free at *http://support.microsoft.com/support/kb/articles/Q248/3/45.ASP*.)

Microsoft Corporation. *Windows 2000 Server Resource Kit*. Volume: *Microsoft Windows 2000 Server Operations Guide*. Redmond, Washington: Microsoft Press, 2000. Review Chapter 5, "Overview of Performance Monitoring."

Microsoft Corporation. *Windows 2000 Server Resource Kit*. Volume: *Microsoft Windows 2000 Server TCP/IP Core Networking Guide*. Redmond, Washington: Microsoft Press, 2000. Review Chapter 10, "Simple Network Management Protocol."

Microsoft Corporation. *MCSE Training Kit: Microsoft Windows 2000 Server*. Redmond, Washington: Microsoft Press, 2000. Review Lessons 2, 3, 4, and 5 in Chapter 13, "Monitoring and Optimization."

Objective 4.2

Microsoft Corporation. *Windows 2000 Server Resource Kit*. Volume: *Microsoft Windows 2000 Server Operations Guide*. Redmond, Washington: Microsoft Press, 2000. Review Chapter 5, "Overview of Performance Monitoring." Also review Chapter 7, "Analyzing Processor Activity."

Microsoft Corporation. *MCSE Training Kit: Microsoft Windows 2000 Server*. Redmond, Washington: Microsoft Press, 2000. Review Lesson 5 in Chapter 13, "Monitoring and Optimization."

Objective 4.3

"Managing Windows 2000 Disks, Backup and Restore." (This article can be downloaded for free at *http://www.microsoft.com/technet/win2000/disbare.asp*.)

Microsoft Corporation. *Windows 2000 Server Resource Kit*. Volume: *Microsoft Windows 2000 Server Deployment Planning Guide*. Redmond, Washington: Microsoft Press, 2000. (This book can be downloaded for free at *http://www.microsoft.com/windows2000/library/resources/reskit/dpg/default.asp*.) Review Chapter 19, "Determining Windows 2000 Storage Strategies."

Microsoft Corporation. *Windows 2000 Server Resource Kit*. Volume: *Microsoft Windows 2000 Server Operations Guide*. Redmond, Washington: Microsoft Press, 2000. Review Chapter 2, "Data Storage and Management"; Chapter 8, "Examining and Tuning Disk Performance"; and Chapter 11, "Planning a Reliable Configuration."

Microsoft Corporation. *MCSE Training Kit: Microsoft Windows 2000 Server*. Redmond, Washington: Microsoft Press, 2000. Review Lesson 3 in Chapter 12, "Implementing Disk Fault Tolerance." Also review Lesson 1 in Chapter 13, "Monitoring and Optimization."

"Troubleshooting Tools and Strategies." (This article can be downloaded for free at *http://www.microsoft.com/windows2000/library/resources/reskit/samplechapters/pref/pref_tts_juhe.asp*.) Although this document is taken from the *Windows 2000 Professional Resource Kit*, it provides useful information about maintenance tools specific to disk performance.

Objective 4.4

Microsoft Corporation. *Windows 2000 Server Resource Kit*. Volume: *Microsoft Windows 2000 Server Operations Guide*. Redmond, Washington: Microsoft Press, 2000. (Several chapters from this book, including Chapter 13, can be downloaded for free at *http://www.microsoft.com/windows2000/library/resources/reskit/samplechapters/default.asp*.) Review Chapter 12, "Backup," and Chapter 13, "Repair, Recovery, and Restore."

Microsoft Corporation. *Windows 2000 Server Resource Kit*. Volume: *Microsoft Windows 2000 Server Deployment Planning Guide*. Redmond, Washington: Microsoft Press, 2000. (This book can be downloaded for free at *http://www.microsoft.com/windows2000/library/resources/reskit/dpg/default.asp*.) Review Chapter 24, "Applying Change and Configuration Management." This chapter includes a discussion on maintaining user data and settings on a network.

Microsoft Corporation. *Windows 2000 Server Resource Kit*. Volume: *Microsoft Windows 2000 Server Distributed Systems Guide*. Redmond, Washington: Microsoft Press, 2000. Review Chapter 9, "Active Directory Backup and Restore"; Chapter 21, "Introduction to Desktop Management"; and Chapter 25, "User Data Management Issues."

Microsoft Corporation. *MCSE Training Kit: Microsoft Windows 2000 Server*. Redmond, Washington: Microsoft Press, 2000. Review Lesson 2 in Chapter 12, "Reliability and Availability."

"Step-by-Step Guide to User Data and User Settings." (This article can be downloaded for free at *http://www.microsoft.com/windows2000/library/planning/management/userdata.asp*.)

"Windows 2000 Server Disaster Recovery Guidelines." (This article can be downloaded for free at *http://www.microsoft.com/TechNet/win2000/recovery.asp*.)

Objective 4.5

Microsoft Corporation. *Windows 2000 Server Resource Kit*. Volume: *Microsoft Windows 2000 Server Operations Guide*. Redmond, Washington: Microsoft Press, 2000. (Several chapters from this book, including Chapter 13, can be downloaded for free at *http://www.microsoft.com/windows2000/library/resources/reskit/samplechapters/default.asp*.) Review Chapter 12, "Backup," and Chapter 13, "Repair, Recovery, and Restore."

Microsoft Corporation. *Windows 2000 Server Resource Kit*. Volume: *Microsoft Windows 2000 Server Deployment Planning Guide*. (This book can be downloaded for free at *http://www.microsoft.com/windows2000/library/resources/reskit/dpg/default.asp*.) Review Chapter 24, "Applying Change and Configuration Management." This chapter includes a discussion on maintaining user data and settings on a network.

Microsoft Corporation. *Windows 2000 Server Resource Kit*. Volume: *Microsoft Windows 2000 Server Distributed Systems Guide*. Redmond, Washington: Microsoft Press, 2000. Review Chapter 9, "Active Directory Backup and Restore"; Chapter 21, "Introduction to Desktop Management"; and Chapter 25, "User Data Management Issues."

Microsoft Corporation. *MCSE Training Kit: Microsoft Windows 2000 Server*. Redmond, Washington: Microsoft Press, 2000. Review Lessons 2 and 4 in Chapter 12, "Reliability and Availability."

"Step-by-Step Guide to User Data and User Settings." (This article can be downloaded for free at *http://www.microsoft.com/windows2000/library/planning/management/userdata.asp*.)

"Windows 2000 Server Disaster Recovery Guidelines." (This white paper can be downloaded for free at *http://www.microsoft.com/TechNet/win2000/recovery.asp*.)

O B J E C T I V E 4 . 1

Monitor and optimize usage of system resources.

The first step in optimizing your system resources is to be able to monitor those resources. Monitoring is a necessary part of preventive maintenance for your system. Through monitoring, you obtain performance data that is useful in diagnosing system problems and in planning for the growth in demand for system resources. From the data you collect by monitoring your system, you can optimize system resources to improve performance, availability, and reliability.

Microsoft Windows 2000 Server provides a set of tools and services that allows you to monitor and optimize your system. For example, you can use System Monitor to collect and view real-time data about memory, disk, processor, network, and other system activity, and you can use Performance Logs And Alerts to configure logs to record performance data and set system alerts to notify you when the value of a specified **counter** is above or below a defined threshold. Unlike System Monitor, Network Monitor focuses exclusively on network activity, allowing you to view and detect problems on the network. The **Simple Network Management Protocol (SNMP)** service allows you to configure your computers as **SNMP agents** in order to communicate with **SNMP management systems** so that those agents can be managed centrally from the management system. Another tool is Task Manager, which provides summary information about computer performance as well as about programs and processes running on the computer.

To answer the questions in this objective, you should be very familiar with the tools and services that are available to monitor and optimize your system. You should understand how these tools differ in terms of their purpose and the types of information that they can access, and how they are similar. You should also be familiar with the kinds of steps you can take to optimize your system based on the results you find by monitoring that system.

Objective 4.1 Questions

70-215.04.01.001

Your Windows 2000 network consists of two Windows 2000 Server computers and 50 Windows 2000 Professional computers. The servers are named Server01 and Server02. The network uses the IPX/SPX protocol. You want be able to configure remote devices, monitor network traffic, and audit network usage from Server01. How should you configure the network? (Choose all that apply.)

A. Configure each computer, except Server01, with the Windows 2000 SNMP service.

B. Install Active Directory directory service on Server01.

C. Convert the network from the IPX/SPX protocol to TCP/IP.

D. Install third-party SNMP management software on Server01.

70-215.04.01.002

You want to monitor the following information on your Windows 2000 Server computer:

- Physical memory

- CPU usage

- Virtual memory usage

- CPU resources used by kernel operations

You access the Performance tab in Task Manager and select Show Kernel Times from the View menu.

What does the proposed solution provide? (Choose all that apply.)

A. Physical memory will be monitored.

B. CPU usage will be monitored.

C. Virtual memory usage will be monitored.

D. CPU resources used by kernel operations will be monitored.

E. The proposed solution will not meet any of the results.

70-215.04.01.003

You want to monitor the following real-time data on your Windows 2000 Server computer:

- Processor activity in kernel mode

- Processor activity in user mode

- Available physical memory, in bytes

- Average number of bytes transferred to or from the disk

Which tool should you use?

A. The Performance tab of Task Manager

B. The Processes tab of Task Manager

C. The System Monitor snap-in in the Performance console

D. The Performance Logs And Alerts snap-in in the Performance console

Objective 4.1 Answers

70-215.04.01.001

▶ **Correct Answers: A and D**

A. **Correct:** Simple Network Management Protocol (SNMP) is a network management standard used on TCP/IP and IPX networks. SNMP provides a method for managing nodes from a centrally located host by using a distributed architecture of management systems and agents. SNMP agents (the network nodes) provide SNMP management systems with information about activities that occur at the Internet Protocol (IP) or IPX network layer and respond to management system requests for information. Any computer that is running SNMP agent software, such as the Windows 2000 SNMP service, is an SNMP agent. The agent service can be configured to determine what statistics are to be tracked and what management systems are authorized to request information. The SNMP service is not installed by default on Windows 2000 computers, so each of these computers must be configured with the agent software. However, the SNMP management system does not have to run on the same computer as the SNMP agents, so Server01 does not need the agent installed.

B. **Incorrect:** Active Directory stores information about objects on a network and makes this information available to user and network administrators. Active Directory provides administrators with an intuitive hierarchical view of the network and a single point of administration for all network objects. However, unlike SNMP, Active Directory does not allow administrators to configure remote devices, monitor network performance, detect network faults or inappropriate access, or audit network usage.

C. **Incorrect:** It is not necessary to convert the network to TCP/IP to configure remote devices, monitor network traffic, and audit network usage from Server01. You can use SNMP to manage the computers, and SNMP can be used in an IPX network as well as a TCP/IP network. However, TCP/IP is generally considered a more efficient network protocol than IPX/SPX, so unless there is some underlying reason why you should maintain an IPX/SPX network, you might consider switching to a TCP/IP network, which is the default network protocol installed on Windows 2000 computers.

D. **Correct:** SNMP management software is necessary to use the information that the Windows 2000 SNMP service provides. The SNMP management system can request information from the SNMP agents, including network protocol identification and statistics, hardware and software configuration data, device performance and usage statistics, device error and event messages, program and application usage statistics, and dynamic identification of devices attached to the network. SNMP agents provide SNMP managers with information about activities that occur at the IP network layer. You must have at least one computer configured with the management system software. The Windows 2000 SNMP service provides only the SNMP agent; it does not include management software. You can use a third-party SNMP management application on the host to act as the management system.

70-215.04.01.002

▶ **Correct Answers: A, B, C, and D**

A. **Correct:** Task Manager provides information about programs and processes running on your computer. It also displays the most commonly used performance measures for processes. These performance measures are displayed on the Performance tab. One of the measures that you can monitor is physical memory. Task Manager provides three measures, in kilobytes, of physical memory: total memory, available memory, and system cache. Available memory refers to the amount of physical memory available to processes. It includes zeroed, free, and standby memory. Total memory is the amount of random access memory (RAM) installed on the computer. System cache is the amount of physical memory released to the file cache on demand.

B. **Correct:** The Performance tab of Task Manager allows you to monitor CPU usage. CPU usage refers to the percentage of time the processor is running a thread other than the Idle thread.

C. **Correct:** The Performance tab of Task Manager allows you to monitor memory usage. Memory usage refers to the amount, in kilobytes, of virtual memory used.

D. **Correct:** The Performance tab of Task Manager allows you to monitor CPU resources used by kernel operations. This is the measure of time that applications are using operating system services. The remaining time, known as user mode, is spent running threads within the application code. By default, Task Manager does not monitor kernel mode usage. To monitor kernel mode usage, you must select the Show Kernel Mode option from the View menu. A red line is added to the CPU Usage graph and to the CPU Usage History graph. The red lines indicate the amount of CPU resources consumed by kernel operations.

E. **Incorrect:** The proposed solution allows you to monitor all the required information.

70-215.04.01.003

▶ **Correct Answers: C**

A. **Incorrect:** Task Manager provides information about programs and processes running on your computer. It also displays the most commonly used performance measures for processes. These performance measures are displayed on the Performance tab. One of the measures that you can monitor is CPU usage. CPU usage refers to the percentage of time the processor is running a thread other than the Idle thread. By default, CPU usage displays user mode and kernel mode processor activity, with no distinction between the two. You can refine the display so that it shows kernel operations in red. The remaining time in the display is user mode operations. You cannot display these operations separately, as you can in System Manager. Task Manager also provides information about physical memory; however, these numbers are displayed in kilobytes, not bytes, and Task Manager does not display information about the number of bytes transferred to or from the disk.

B. **Incorrect:** The Processes tab in Task Manager shows information about the processes running on your computer, such as CPU and memory usage. The information displayed is on a per-process basis and does not include systemwide details, such as total processor activity in kernel mode and user mode, available physical memory, or the number of bytes transferred to or from the disk.

C. **Correct:** System Monitor allows you to collect and view real-time performance data on local or remote computers. This data can include extensive information about the usage of hardware resources and activity of system services. To display performance information in System Monitor, you must add counters to the graph area. A counter is a data item associated with an object. An object is a logical collection of counters associated with a resource or services that can be monitored. For each counter selected, System Monitor presents a value corresponding to a particular aspect of the performance defined for the object. To monitor the required information, you must add four counters to System Monitor: %Privileged Time, %User Time, Available Bytes, and Avg. Disk Bytes/Transfer. %Privileged Time is found under the Processor object and refers to the percentage of nonidle processor time spent in kernel mode (also called privileged mode). %User Time, also under the Processor object, is the percentage of nonidle processor time spent in user mode. Available Bytes, which is a counter in the Memory object, is the amount of physical memory, in bytes, available to processes running on the computer. Avg. Disk Bytes/Transfer is available in the PhysicalDisk object and measures the average number of bytes transferred to or from the disk during write or read operations.

D. **Incorrect:** Although you can capture the required information by using the Performance Logs And Alerts snap-in, you cannot view real-time data because the data is captured in log files, which are viewed after all the information has been collected. With Performance Logs And Alerts, you can collect performance data automatically from local or remote computers. You can view logged counter data by using System Monitor, or you can export the data to spreadsheet programs or databases for analysis and report generation. Because logging runs as a service, data collection can occur regardless of whether any user is logged on to the computer being monitored.

O B J E C T I V E   4 . 2

Manage processes.

Processor activity is one of the most important aspects of system performance that you should monitor. A busy processor might be efficiently handling all the work on your computer, or it might be overwhelmed. You must examine processor activity to distinguish the difference. Processor activity refers to the **processes** that are running on your computer at a given time. In Windows 2000, a process is an object consisting of an executable program, a set of virtual memory addresses, and the **threads**. A thread is the basic entity to which the operating system allocates CPU time. A thread can execute any part of the application's code, including a part currently being executed by another thread. All threads of a process share the virtual address space, global variables, and operating-system resources of the process.

Windows 2000 Server provides a number of tools that can be used to monitor and manage processes. Two important tools are Task Manager and the Performance console. The Processes tab in Task Manager allows you to view a list of running processes and measures of their performance. The list includes all processes that run in their own address space, including all applications and system services. In addition to viewing processes, you can end a process and all processes directly or indirectly created by it if all the processes in the process tree are still running. You can also set the base priority for each process. The Performance console is another tool you can use to monitor processes. The Performance console contains the System Monitor snap-in and the Performance Logs And Alerts snap-in. System Monitor allows you to collect and view real-time data about the usage of hardware resources and the activity of system services, including information about the processes and threads running on your computer. Performance Logs And Alerts allows you to configure logs to record performance data and set system alerts to notify you when a specified counter value is above or below a defined threshold. Windows 2000 also provides Process Viewer (pviewer), which is included in the Windows 2000 Support Tools. Process Viewer provides more detail on each process than Task Manager provides, and Process Viewer shows each thread running within each process. Another tool is Task List (or tlist), which is a command-line utility. When you type **tlist /t** at the command prompt, you get a hierarchical arrangement of all running processes. This is the only way to show which processes are parents or children of other processes.

To answer the questions in this objective, you should know how to use the two main tools that allow you to monitor and administer processes on your Windows 2000 Server computer: Task Manager and the Performance console, which includes the System Monitor snap-in and the Performance Logs And Alerts snap-in.

Objective 4.2 Questions

70-215.04.02.001

You have Outlook 2000, Word 2000, and two MS-DOS applications running on your Windows 2000 Server computer. One of the MS-DOS applications stops responding. How can you verify the status of the application and terminate the application if it has hung?

A. Use the Applications tab of the Task Manager.

B. Use the Processes tab of the Task Manager.

C. Use the System utility in Control Panel.

D. Use the Add/Remove Programs utility in Control Panel.

70-215.04.02.002

You must display information on how several processes that are running on your Windows 2000 Server computer are using system resources. You want to see how each process is affecting CPU usage, memory usage, and page faults. How can you use Task Manager to view this information?

A. Use the Applications tab.

B. Use the Processes tab.

C. Use the Performance tab.

D. You cannot use Task Manager to view specific processes.

70-215.04.02.003

You are editing a document in Microsoft Word. Three other applications are running in the background, and the performance of Word seems sluggish. You want to improve performance in Word, but you need to keep the other programs running. You have already optimized performance for applications in the System utility. What more could you do to give Word more processor time relative to the other background applications?

A. On the Processes tab in Task Manager, change the base priority of the WINWORD.EXE process to High.

B. On the Applications tab in Task Manager, change the update speed of the Microsoft Word application to High.

C. In System Monitor, add the Priority Base counter for the WINWORD.EXE process, and then change the Base Priority value of the WINWORD.EXE process to High.

D. In System Monitor, add the Priority Base counters for the WINWORD.EXE threads, and then change the Base Priority values of the WINWORD.EXE threads to High.

Objective 4.2 Answers

70-215.04.02.001

▶ **Correct Answers: A**

A. **Correct:** Task Manager provides information about programs and processes running on your computer. It also displays the most commonly used performance measures for processes. The Applications tab shows the status of the programs running on your computer. On this tab, you can start a new program, end a program, or switch to another program. When you use the Applications tab to end a program, you are provided with the opportunity to save any unsaved data if possible.

B. **Incorrect:** The Processes tab does not show the status of an application, although it does provide information about the processes running on your computer. You can end an application by ending the process or processes associated with that application; however, terminating a process can cause undesired results, such as loss of data or system instability. The process is not given the chance to save its state or data before it is terminated.

C. **Incorrect:** The System utility allows you to configure system properties related to network identification, user profiles, performance, environment variables, and startup and recovers. You can also use the System utility to open the Add/Remove Hardware wizard, Driver Signing, Device Manager, and Hardware Profiles. However, you cannot use the System utility to verify the status of an application or end an application.

D. **Incorrect:** The Add/Remove Programs utility allows you to manage programs on your computer. It prompts you through the steps necessary to add a new program or to change or remove an existing program. You can also use the Add/Remove Programs utility to install Windows 2000 components that you did not include in the original installation. However, you cannot use the utility to verify the status of an application or end an application.

70-215.04.02.002

▶ **Correct Answers: B**

A. **Incorrect:** The Applications tab shows the status of the programs running on your computer. On this tab, you can start a new program, end a program, or switch to another program. However, you cannot use the Applications tab to view information about the processes running on your computer.

B. **Correct:** Task Manager provides information about programs and processes running on your computer. It also displays the most commonly used performance measures for processes. The Processes tab displays a list of running processes and measures of their performance, such as CPU time, memory usage, and page faults. You can sort the list of processes and select which process counters are displayed. You can also end a process. However, if you end an application, you could lose unsaved data, and if you end a system service, some part of the system might not function properly.

C. **Incorrect:** The Performance tab displays the most commonly used performance measures for processes, including CPU usage and memory usage. However, these measures are based on all the processes that are currently running. You cannot measure individual processes. In addition, the Performance tab does not provide information about page faults.

D. **Incorrect:** The Processes tab of Task Manager allows you to view the required information about each process that is running on the computer.

70-215.04.02.003

▶ **Correct Answers: A**

A. **Correct:** Task Manager provides information about programs and processes running on your computer. It also displays the most commonly used performance measures for processes. The Processes tab displays a list of running processes and measures of their performance. One of these measures is Base Priorities. The base priority of a process determines the order in which a process is scheduled for processing, relative to other processes. The base priority is set by the process code, not the operating system. The operating system sets and changes the dynamic priorities of threads in the process within the range of the base. The Processes tab allows you to change the Base Priority value of a process, but it does not monitor threads. Base priorities changed through Task Manager are effective only as long as the process runs. The change in priority is effective at the next Task Manager update; you do not need to restart the process.

B. **Incorrect:** The Update Speed option controls the rate at which Task Manager updates its counts. By default, the update speed is set to Normal, which means that data is updated once per second. The Update Speed option applies to all tabs in Task Manager; you cannot set the update speed on a specific tab. In addition, you cannot use the Update Speed option to set the priority of a process.

C. **Incorrect:** System Monitor allows you to collect and view real-time performance data on local or remote computers. This data can include extensive information about the usage of hardware resources and activity of system services. You can use System Monitor to view and record the base priorities of threads and processes, but you cannot use System Monitor to set those priorities.

D. **Incorrect:** You can use System Monitor to view and record the base priorities of threads and processes, but you cannot use System Monitor to set those priorities.

O B J E C T I V E   4 . 3

Optimize disk performance.

Your computers' hard disks handle the storage and movement of programs and data on your system. As a result, the disks have a powerful influence on a system's overall responsiveness. You need to observe many factors in determining the performance of a disk system, including the level of utilization, the rate of throughput, the amount of disk space available, and whether a queue is developing for the disk systems. You should also monitor other types of activity that arise from disk operations, such as interrupts generated by the disk system and paging activity, because of their influence on other resources, such as processor and memory. Many of these factors are related. For example, if utilization is high, transfer rates (throughput) might peak and a queue might begin to form. These conditions might result in increased response time and cause performance to slow. Although disk space does not directly affect the disk's transfer rate, disk space, when extremely low, can influence response time because applications that read and write data cannot do so as efficiently.

Windows 2000 provides a number of tools that you can use to diagnose disk problems, improve performance, and compress data. The Performance console provides disk-specific counters that enable you to measure disk activity and throughput. Check Disk allows you to check for file system errors and bad sectors on your hard disk. You can use the Disk Defragmenter snap-in to locate fragmented files or folders and then defragment them by moving pieces of each file or folder to one location so that each file or folder occupies a single area of contiguous space on the hard disk. Data compression allows you to compress files and folders on NTFS volumes. Compressed files and folders occupy less space on an NTFS volume. You can use disk quotas to manage storage growth in distributed environments. Disk quotas allow you to allocate disk space usage to users based on the files and folders that they own. You can also monitor the amount of hard disk space users have used and the amount they have left against their quotas.

To answer the questions in this objective, you should have a good understanding of how hard disks are configured and how to support the different types of partitions, volumes, and file systems. You should know how to use the various tools that are available to diagnose disk problems and optimize performance, and you should know how to implement data compression, disk quotas, and disk fault tolerance.

Objective 4.3 Questions

70-215.04.03.001

Your network consists of one Windows 2000 Server computer and 10 Windows 2000 Professional computers connected to a 100Base-T network with Category 5 UTP cable. The network has been running for six months. The Windows 2000 Server computer is a SQL Server 7.0 server, a Microsoft Internet Information Services (IIS) server, and a file and print server. The computer's performance has steadily declined since the network was implemented, and it now takes two to three times longer for the Windows 2000 Professional users to access data on the server than it used to. Nothing has changed in the network configuration, and the hard disk on the Windows 2000 Server computer contains ample free space. How can you improve performance on the hard disk?

A. Run Check Disk.

B. Run Disk Defragmenter.

C. Implement data compression.

D. Implement disk quotas.

70-215.04.03.002

You must optimize a Windows 2000 Server computer so that applications always run at a higher priority than background services. How should you configure the server?

A. Use the Processes tab in Task Manager to select the processes associated with each application, and then set the base priority to High for each of those processes.

B. Use the Applications tab in Task Manager to select each running application, and then set the update speed to High.

C. Use the System Information snap-in in Computer Management to access the running tasks, and optimize performance for applications rather than background services.

D. Use the System utility in Control Panel to access performance options, and optimize performance for applications rather than background services.

70-215.04.03.003

You must implement disaster protection on your Windows 2000 Server computer. The server contains five hard disks. You plan to implement RAID-1 or RAID-5 disk fault tolerance.

You want to achieve the following results:

- You must maximize disk space.

- You must be able to recover information if a hard disk fails in your computer.

- You must protect the boot volume.

- You must optimize write operations on your hard disk configuration.

You implement a RAID-5 configuration on your server.

Which result or results does your implementation achieve? (Choose all that apply.)

A. Disk space is maximized.

B. Recovery is possible if a single hard disk fails.

C. The boot volume is protected.

D. Write operations are optimized with respect to all fault-tolerant solutions.

70-215.04.03.004

You must implement disaster protection on your Windows 2000 Server computer. The server contains five hard disks. You plan to implement RAID-1 or RAID-5 disk fault tolerance.

You want to achieve the following results:

- You must maximize disk utilization.

- You must be able to recover information if a hard disk fails in your computer.

- You must protect the boot volume.

- You must optimize write operations on your hard disk configuration.

You implement a RAID-1 configuration on your server.

Which result or results does your implementation achieve? (Choose all that apply.)

A. Disk utilization is maximized.

B. Recovery is possible if a single hard disk fails.

C. The boot volume is protected.

D. Write operations are optimized with respect to all fault-tolerant solutions.

Objective 4.3 Answers

70-215.04.03.001

▶ **Correct Answers: B**

A. **Incorrect:** The Check Disk tool, also referred to as the Error-Checking tool, allows you to check for file system errors and bad sectors on your hard disk. You can scan for and repair problems such as bad blocks, lost clusters, or directory errors. Check Disk allows you to automatically fix file system errors and scan for and attempt recovery of bad sectors. However, running Check Disk does not necessarily affect performance. Check Disk does not identify or fix the kind of errors that users are reporting in the scenario. Although Check Disk can fix disk errors, fixing these errors will not help users access data more quickly.

B. **Correct:** When Windows 2000 saves data to a hard disk, files and folders are added to the first available space on the disk and not necessarily in an area of contiguous space. This process leads to file and folder fragmentation. When a hard disk contains a lot of fragmented files and folders, your computer takes longer to gain access to them because it requires several additional reads to collect the various pieces. Creating new files and folders also takes longer because the available free space on the hard disk is scattered. The Disk Defragmenter snap-in allows you to locate fragmented files and folders and then defragment them by moving the pieces of each file and folder to one location so that each file or folder occupies a single area of contiguous space on the hard disk. Consequently, your system accesses and saves files and folders more efficiently. By consolidating files and folders, Disk Defragmenter also consolidates free space, making it less likely that new files will be fragmented.

C. **Incorrect:** Data compression enables you to compress files and folders on NTFS volumes. Compressed files and folders occupy less space on an NTFS-formatted volume. The compression state for each file and folder on an NTFS volume is set to either compressed or uncompressed. Enabling data compression on the hard disk will not improve performance. In fact, NTFS compression will usually cause performance degradation when you access, copy, or move files.

D. **Incorrect:** Disk quotas allow you to manage storage growth in distributed environments. You can use disk quotas to allocate disk space usage to users based on the files and folders that they own. You can set disk quotas, quota thresholds, and quota limits for all users and for individual users. Because quotas are tracked on a per-user basis, every user's disk space is tracked regardless of the folder in which the user stores files. Enabling disk quotas causes a slight increase in server overhead and a slight decrease in file server performance.

70-215.04.03.002

▶ **Correct Answers: D**

A. **Incorrect:** Task Manager provides information about programs and processes running on your computer. It also displays the most commonly used performance measures for processes. The Processes tab displays a list of running processes and measures of their performance. One of these measures is Base Priorities. The base priority of a process determines the order in which a process is scheduled for processing, relative to other processes. The base priority is set by the process code, not the operating system. The operating system sets and changes the dynamic priorities of threads in the process within the range of the base. The Processes tab allows you to change the Base Priority value of a process; however, base priorities changed through Task Manager are effective only as long as the process runs. In addition, you can change process priority only for applications that are currently running, not for applications that might run on your system in the future. Also note that changing priorities might destabilize the system. Increasing the priority of a process might prevent other processes, including system services, from running.

B. **Incorrect:** The Applications tab shows the status of the programs running on your computer. On this tab, you can start a new program, end a program, or switch to another program. The Update Speed option controls the rate at which Task Manager updates its counts. By default, the update speed is set to Normal, which means that data is updated once per second. The Update Speed option applies to all tabs in Task Manager; you cannot set the update speed on a specific tab or specific application, and you cannot use the Update Speed option to set the priority of a process.

C. **Incorrect:** System Information collects and displays your system configuration information. It provides specific information about your computer when you are troubleshooting your configuration. However, you cannot use System Information to configure your Windows 2000 Server computer so that applications always run at a higher priority than background services.

D. **Correct:** Performance options control how applications use memory, which can affect the speed of your computer. Performance options allow you to set application response options and configure the paging file. You can use the application response options to optimize performance for applications or background services. By default, Windows 2000 Server is optimized for background services, in contrast with Windows 2000 Professional, which is optimized for applications. Windows 2000 Professional is configured to assign variable, short quanta (time slices) to applications and to boost applications in the foreground. In contrast, Windows 2000 Server is configured to assign long, fixed quanta without any foreground boost to support the efficiency of background services. Foreground boost is a mechanism that increases the priority of a foreground application. You can simulate the behavior of one type of operating system when the other type of system is installed—that is, you can optimize the performance for background services on a Windows 2000 Professional computer to simulate Windows 2000 Server, or vice versa.

70-215.04.03.003

▶ **Correct Answers: A and B**

A. **Correct:** A RAID-5 volume utilizes disk space more efficiently than a mirrored (RAID-1) volume, especially when a larger number of disks are used. A mirrored volume provides an identical twin of the selected volume. All data written to the mirrored volume is written to both volumes, which results in a disk capacity of only 50 percent. In a RAID-5 volume, the space required for storing the parity information is equivalent to 1/*<number of disks>*, so a 5-disk array uses 1/5 (20 percent) of its capacity for parity information, and a 10-disk array uses 1/10 (10 percent) of its capacity for parity information. With RAID-5, disk utilization improves as you increase the number of hard disks.

B. **Correct:** Windows 2000 Server supports fault tolerance through striped volumes with parity (RAID-5). Parity is a mathematical method of determining the number of odd and even bits in a number or series of numbers, which can be used to reconstruct data if one number in a sequence of numbers is lost. In a RAID-5 volume, Windows 2000 achieves fault tolerance by adding a parity-information stripe to each disk partition in the volume. If a single disk fails, Windows 2000 can use the data and parity information on the remaining disks to reconstruct the data that was on the failed disk. As a result, none of the data is lost.

C. **Incorrect:** A RAID-5 volume cannot protect the boot volume. Neither the system volume nor the boot volume can be on a RAID-5 volume.

D. **Incorrect:** Because of the parity calculation, write operations on a RAID-5 volume are slower than on a mirrored volume. RAID-5 volumes are not well suited for any write-intensive workload because a single write is likely to generate a disk read of the parity and two writes (to update data and parity information). Consequently, it is better to use mirrored volumes when using applications that require high-speed data collection from a process. This type of application requires continuous high-speed disk writes, which do not work well with the asymmetrical I/O balance inherent in RAID-5 volumes and the extra I/Os required to write the parity stripe. In addition, mirrored volumes should be used in transaction processing database applications in which records are continually updated and when applications require large sequential data transfers to disk.

70-215.04.03.004

► **Correct Answers: B, C, and D**

A. **Incorrect:** A mirrored (RAID-1) volume provides an identical twin of the selected volume. All data written to the mirrored volume is written to both volumes, which results in a disk capacity of only 50 percent. In terms of space utilization, mirrored volumes are less efficient than RAID-5 volumes. The space requirements for a mirrored volume are higher than for a RAID-5 volume because the data is duplicated. In a RAID-5 volume, the space required for storing the parity information is equivalent to 1/<*number of disks*>, so a 5-disk array uses 1/5 (20 percent) of its capacity for parity information, and a 10-disk array uses 1/10 (10 percent) of its capacity for parity information. With RAID-5, disk utilization improves as you increase the number of hard disks.

B. **Correct:** A mirrored volume created in Windows 2000 Server uses the driver DMIO.SYS to write the same data to a volume on each of two physical disks. Each volume is considered a member of the mirrored volume. Implementing a mirrored volume helps to ensure the survival of data in the event that one member of the mirrored volume fails. If there is a read failure on one of the disks, data is read from the other disk. If there is a write failure on one of the disks, the remaining disk is used for all accesses. Recovery from a disk failure is very rapid. Mirrored volumes offer the fastest data recovery, with the least impact on system performance, because the shadow volume contains all the data. No data recomputation is needed to restore the system.

C. **Correct:** A mirrored volume can contain any partition, including the boot or system volume.

D. **Correct:** Disk write operations are less efficient in mirrored volumes than in single disks because data must be written to both disks. However, the penalty is not 100 percent. In many situations, a user-mode application is not affected by the extra disk update. In addition, a mirrored volume has better write performance than a RAID-5 volume. In RAID-5, the need to calculate parity information requires more computer memory, which can slow write performance, but mirrored volumes tend to provide good overall performance.

Manage and optimize availability of system state data and user data.

One of the primary administrative tasks that is part of managing **system state data** is to back up the data to ensure that you have current, reliable copies of the data in the event of a disaster. In Windows 2000 Server, system state data comprises the registry, the COM+ Class Registration database, system startup files, performance counter configuration information, and the Certificate Services database if the computer is a certificate server. If the computer is a domain controller, the system state data includes Active Directory and the Sysvol folder, and if the computer is running the Cluster service, the system state data includes resource registry checkpoints and the quorum resource recovery log, which contains the most recent cluster database information. Also, if you are running Domain Name Service (DNS) on a domain controller, the Active Directory portion of the system state data also contains all of the DNS zone information (DS integrated and non-DS integrated). System state data backup includes all system state data; you cannot choose to back up individual components because of dependencies among the components. When you back up system state data, a copy of your registry files is also saved in the *%systemroot%*\Repair\Regback folder. If your registry files become corrupted or are accidentally erased, you can use these files to repair the registry without performing a full restore of the system state data.

User data management makes it possible for data to follow users whether they are on line and connected to the network or off line working in a standalone state. The user's data follows the user because Windows 2000 can store the data in specified network locations while making the data appear local to the user. You can configure which files and folders are available manually, set them up on a per-user basis, or configure them through Group Policy. User data management ensures that the items that users create, such as personal files and documents, are easily accessible and readily available to the user. You can increase a user's access to data and his or her personal environment by storing that information on network servers as well as in synchronized off line locations on the local hard disk. If users take their work home or on the road, they still have access to their files. The network files that a user works with when on line are automatically cached on that user's computer and available when he or she is off line.

To answer the questions in this objective, you must know how to use Windows Backup to back up system state data. You should also be familiar with the various functionality, services, and tools that support the management of user data, including Active Directory, Group Policy, roaming user profiles, offline folders and files, disk quotas, and security settings.

Objective 4.4 Questions

70-215.04.04.001

You are the administrator of a Windows 2000 Server computer that is configured as a domain controller. You must back up the following information:

- Registry

- SYSVOL folder

- Certificate Services

- COM+ Class Registration database

- Memory Page File

You use Windows Backup to back up only the system state data. Assume that the default options for excluded files have not been changed.

Which files will be backed up on the computer? (Choose all that apply.)

A. Registry

B. SYSVOL folder

C. Certificate Services

D. COM+ Class Registration database

E. Memory Page File

70-215.04.04.002

You are the administrator of a Windows 2000 Server computer that is configured as a member server. You must back up the following information:

- Registry
- SYSVOL folder
- Certificate Services
- COM+ Class Registration database
- Memory Page File

You use Windows Backup to back up only the system state data. Assume that the default options for excluded files have not been changed.

Which files will be backed up on the computer? (Choose all that apply.)

A. Registry

B. SYSVOL folder

C. Certificate Services

D. COM+ Class Registration database

E. Memory Page File

70-215.04.04.003

You are the administrator of a Windows 2000 Server computer that is configured as a member server. You must back up the following information:

- Registry
- SYSVOL folder
- Certificate Services
- COM+ Class Registration database
- Memory Page File

You use Windows Backup to back up everything on your computer. Assume that the default options for excluded files have not been changed.

Which files will be backed up on the computer? (Choose all that apply.)

A. Registry

B. SYSVOL folder

C. Certificate Services

D. COM+ Class Registration database

E. Memory Page File

Objective 4.4 Answers

70-215.04.04.001

▶ **Correct Answers: A, B, C, and D**

A. **Correct:** Windows Backup is a tool that allows you to easily back up or restore data on your Windows 2000 Server computer. When you run the Backup wizard, you can choose to back up everything on the computer; back up selected files, drives, or network data; or back up only the system state data. You can back up system state data to a disk, a tape, or a network share while the domain controller is on line. The system state data includes the registry. When you back up system state data, a copy of the registry is placed in the *%systemroot%*\Repair\Regback folder. If your registry files become corrupted or are accidentally erased, use the files in this folder to repair your registry without performing a full restore of the system state data.

B. **Correct:** When a Windows 2000 Server computer is set up as a domain controller, the system state data includes the SYSVOL folder. As a result, the folder is backed up when you perform a backup of the system state data.

C. **Correct:** When a Windows 2000 Server computer is configured with Certificate Services, the system state data includes the Certificate Services files. As a result, these files are backed up when you perform a backup of the system state data.

D. **Correct:** The system state data includes the COM+ Class Registration database. As a result, the database is backed up when you perform a backup of the system state data.

E. **Incorrect:** The system state data does not include the Memory Page File, PAGEFILE.SYS. In addition, the Memory Page File is excluded by default from a backup job that backs up everything on your computer.

70-215.04.04.002

▶ **Correct Answers: A, C, and D**

A. **Correct:** Windows Backup is a tool that allows you to easily back up or restore data on your Windows 2000 Server computer. When you run the Backup wizard, you can choose to back up everything on the computer; back up selected files, drives, or network data; or back up only the system state data. You can back up system state data to a disk, tape, or network share while the domain controller is on line. The system state data includes the registry. When you back up system state data, a copy of the registry is placed in the *%systemroot%*\Repair\Regback folder. If your registry files become corrupted or are accidentally erased, use the files in this folder to repair your registry without performing a full restore of the system state data.

B. **Incorrect:** The SYSVOL folder exists only on Windows 2000 Server computers that are configured as domain controllers; consequently, the folder is included in the system state data only when the computer is a domain controller. Because the computer in this scenario is a member server, the SYSVOL folder does not exist and therefore cannot be backed up.

C. **Correct:** When a Windows 2000 Server computer is configured with Certificate Services, the system state data includes the Certificate Services files. As a result, these files are backed up when you perform a backup of the system state data.

D. **Correct:** The system state data includes the COM+ Class Registration database. As a result, the database is backed up when you perform a backup of the system state data.

E. **Incorrect:** The system state data does not include the Memory Page File, PAGEFILE.SYS. In addition, the Memory Page File is excluded by default from a backup job that backs up everything on your computer.

70-215.04.04.003

▶ **Correct Answers: A, C, and D**

A. **Correct:** Windows Backup is a tool that allows you to easily back up or restore data on your Windows 2000 Server computer. When you run the Backup wizard, you can choose to back up everything on the computer; back up selected files, drives, or network data; or back up only the system state data. When you choose to back up everything on your computer, all files are backed up except those that are excluded by default, such as certain power management files. A full backup includes system state data, and system state data includes the registry. When you back up system state data, a copy of the registry is placed in the *%systemroot%*\Repair\Regback folder. If your registry files become corrupted or are accidentally erased, use the files in this folder to repair your registry without performing a full restore of the system state data.

B. **Incorrect:** A full backup includes the system state data. However, the SYSVOL folder exists only on Windows 2000 Server computers that are configured as domain controllers; consequently, the folder is included in the system state data only when the computer is a domain controller. Because the computer in this scenario is a member server, the SYSVOL folder does not exist and therefore cannot be backed up.

C. **Correct:** When a Windows 2000 Server computer is configured with Certificate Services, the system state data includes the Certificate Services files. As a result, these files are backed up when you perform a full backup, which includes the system state data.

D. **Correct:** The system state data includes the COM+ Class Registration database. As a result, the database is backed up when you perform a full backup, which includes the system state data.

E. **Incorrect:** The Memory Page File is excluded by default from a backup job that backs up everything on your computer.

OBJECTIVE 4.5

Recover system state data and user data.

The recovery of system state data and user state data is dependent on your ability to access your Windows 2000 Server computer in the event of a disaster and recover any data that might be lost or corrupted. Part of this recovery includes your ability to access the operating system if you cannot start up Windows 2000 Server as you normally would. In this case, you might have to use the Safe Mode functionality in Windows 2000 to access the operating system or use the Recovery Console to perform administrative tasks. Safe Mode is a function within Windows 2000 that allows you to start the operating system with a minimal set of device drivers and services. For example, if newly installed device drivers or software are preventing your computer from starting, you may be able to start your computer in Safe Mode and then remove the software or device drivers from your system. Safe Mode will not work in all circumstances, especially if your system files are corrupted or missing or your hard disk is damaged or has failed. The Recovery Console is a command-line interface that allows you to repair system problems by using a limited set of command-line commands. You can use the Recovery Console to start and stop services, read and write data on a local drive, repair a master boot record (MBR), or format drives.

In addition to accessing the operating system, you should be able to recover lost or corrupted data. When critical data is lost, you need to restore that data quickly. You should base your restore on the backup type that you used for the backup. If time is critical when you are restoring data, your restore strategy must ensure that the backup types expedite the restore process. You should perform a trial restore periodically to verify that Windows Backup is backing up your files correctly. In addition, you should maintain documentation for each backup job, and for multiple backup jobs you should keep a record in a calendar format that shows the days on which you perform the backup jobs. When it is necessary to perform a restore, you must select the backup sets, files, and folders to restore. You can also specify additional settings based on the restore requirements. The first step in restoring data is to select the data to restore. You can select individual files and folders, an entire backup job, or a backup set. A backup set is a collection of files and folders from one volume that you back up during a backup job.

If you back up two volumes on a hard disk during a backup job, the job has two backup sets. Although you can select individual files and folders to restore, you cannot restore individual components of the system state data because of the dependencies among the system state components. However, you can restore the system state data to an alternative location. To restore data, use the Restore wizard, which you can access by using Windows Backup.

To answer the questions in this objective, you should know how to prepare to restore data, which includes being familiar with the various guidelines that should be followed. You should also know how to use the Restore wizard to restore specific files and folders, backup jobs, and backup sets.

Objective 4.5 Questions

70-215.04.05.001

You install a new audio adapter and its unsigned driver in your Windows 2000 Server computer. When you restart the computer, the system hangs and you cannot log in to Windows 2000. You decide to use one of the advanced startup options to open Windows 2000 Server and remove the device driver. Which advanced startup option should you use?

A. Safe Mode

B. Debugging Mode

C. Enable VGA Mode

D. Last Known Good Configuration

70-215.04.05.002

You manage documents on a Windows 2000 Server computer that is used as a file server for various word processing and spreadsheet documents. On Friday, you backed up the C:\Documents And Settings\Username\My Documents folder, the D:\Spreadsheet folder, the D:\Accounts folder, and the C:\Custom folder. On Monday, you discover that the files in the folders are now corrupt.

You have the following permissions to the folders:

- Full Control permission on C:\Documents And Settings\Username\My Documents

- Modify permission on D:\Spreadsheet

- Read permission on D:\Accounts

- Read permission on C:\Custom

Which folder or folders can you restore? (Choose all that apply.)

A. C:\Documents And Settings\Username\My Documents

B. D:\Spreadsheet

C. D:\Accounts

D. C:\Custom

E. You cannot restore any of the folders.

70-215.04.05.003

You install a new audio adapter and its unsigned driver in your Windows 2000 Server computer. Then you restart the computer and successfully log in. After the login is complete and the desktop initializes, you notice that the system intermittently freezes for brief periods. Eventually, you are able to shut down. You decide to restart the computer and use one of the advanced startup options to open Windows 2000 Server and remove the device driver. Which advanced startup option should you use?

A. Safe Mode

B. Debugging Mode

C. Enable VGA Mode

D. Last Known Good Configuration

70-215.04.05.004

You manage documents on a Windows 2000 Server computer that is used as a file server for various word processing and spreadsheet documents. On Friday, you backed up the C:\Documents And Settings\ Username\My Documents folder, the D:\Spreadsheet folder, the D:\Accounts folder, and the C:\Custom folder. On Monday, you discover that the files in the folders are now corrupt. You are also concerned that some of the system state data might be corrupt.

You are a member of the Backup Operators group, and you have the following permissions on the folders:

- Full Control permission on C:\Documents And Settings\Username\My Documents

- Modify permission on D:\Spreadsheet

- Read permission on D:\Accounts

- Read permission on C:\Custom

Which folder or folders can you restore? (Choose all that apply.)

A. C:\Documents And Settings\Username\My Documents

B. D:\Spreadsheet

C. D:\Accounts

D. C:\Custom

E. System state data

Objective 4.5 Answers

70-215.04.05.001

▶ **Correct Answers: D**

A. **Incorrect:** The Safe Mode option starts Windows 2000 and uses only basic files and drivers (mouse, monitor, keyboard, mass storage, base video, default system services, and no network connections). However, you should try to use the Last Known Good Configuration option before you use the Safe Mode option. The Last Known Good Configuration option preserves your last effective configuration, before system settings were changed as a result of the device driver installation. Because you did not log on to the computer, changes will not have been made in the registry, and the last known good configuration settings will refer to the state of the operating system before your problem appeared. As a result, you will not need to reinstall the old driver or reboot the computer for changes to take effect.

B. **Incorrect:** The Debugging Mode option starts Windows 2000 while sending debug information through a serial cable to another computer. The Debugging Mode option starts Windows 2000 in Kernel Debug mode, which allows a debugger to access the kernel for troubleshooting and system analysis. This is an important mode for software developers, but it is not necessary to use this mode to open Windows 2000, which is what you need to do to uninstall the device driver.

C. **Incorrect:** The Enable VGA Mode option starts Windows 2000 with the basic VGA driver. This mode is useful when you have installed a new driver for your video adapter that is causing Windows 2000 to not start properly. Because you want to remove only the device driver for the audio adapter, it is not necessary to use the Enable VGA mode. In addition, this mode, like the Safe Mode option, uses a basic configuration to start Windows 2000. You should first try the Last Known Good Configuration option so that you can preserve your last effective configuration, before system settings are changed as a result of the device driver installation.

D. **Correct:** The Last Known Good Configuration option starts Windows 2000 by using the settings (registry information) that Windows 2000 saved at the last shutdown. These settings do not yet reflect the changes that resulted from installing the device driver. Use the Last Known Good Configuration option only in cases of incorrect configuration. All system setting changes made after the last successful startup are lost, which means that the settings that were changed as a result of installing the device driver would be lost and you would be returned to your last effective configuration. If you were able to log on to the computer and successfully shut down, the Last Known Good Configuration option would not help because the configuration changes would already have been made to the registry. Using this option in this case would merely return you to your problematic configuration.

70-215.04.05.002

▶ **Correct Answers: A and B**

A. **Correct:** You can use Windows Backup to restore any files and folders that you create. In addition, you can restore any files and folders for which you have been granted the Modify permission or the Full Control permission. You can also restore data if you are a member of the Administrators group or the Backup Operators group.

B. **Correct:** You can restore any files and folders for which you have been granted the Modify permission.

C. **Incorrect:** You cannot restore files or folders for which you have been granted the Read permission.

D. **Incorrect:** You cannot restore files or folders for which you have been granted the Read permission.

E. **Incorrect:** You can restore any files and folders for which you have been granted the Modify permission or the Full Control permission, but you cannot modify them if you have been granted the Read permission.

70-215.04.05.003

▶ **Correct Answers: A**

A. **Correct:** The Safe Mode option starts Windows 2000 and uses only basic files and drivers (mouse, monitor, keyboard, mass storage, base video, default system services, and no network connections). If you were able to log on and shut down from the computer, you should use the Safe Mode option rather than the Last Known Good Configuration option because a configuration from which you can shut down constitutes a good configuration. Consequently, the current configuration in this case is the last known good configuration, and selecting the Last Known Good Configuration would simply re-create the conditions of your computer problem. If, on the other hand, you had not been able to log on and shut down, you should have first tried the Last Known Good Configuration option because this would return you to the configuration before the problem appeared.

B. **Incorrect:** The Debugging Mode option starts Windows 2000 while sending debug information through a serial cable to another computer. The Debugging Mode option starts Windows 2000 in kernel debug mode, which allows a debugger to access the kernel for troubleshooting and system analysis. This is an important mode for software developers, but it is not necessary to use this mode to open Windows 2000, which is what you need to do to uninstall the device driver.

C. **Incorrect:** The Enable VGA Mode option starts Windows 2000 with the basic VGA driver. This mode is useful when you have installed a new driver for your video adapter that is causing Windows 2000 to not start properly. Because the problem with your computer is most likely caused by the device driver for the audio adapter, it is not necessary to use the Enable VGA mode.

D. **Incorrect:** The Last Known Good Configuration option starts Windows 2000 by using the settings (registry information) that Windows 2000 saved at the last shutdown. Because you were able to log on and shut down from the computer, using this option will not help. Configuration changes have been made to the registry, and the Last Known Good Configuration option will merely return you to the problematic configuration that existed after you logged on the last time. If you had not been able to log on and shut down, however, the Last Known Good Configuration option would revert the changes that were made as a result of installing the faulty device driver, and you would be returned to the state your configuration was in before the problem appeared.

70-215.04.05.004

▶ **Correct Answers: A, B, C, and D**

A. **Correct:** You can use Windows Backup to restore any files and folders that you create. In addition, you can restore any files and folders for which you have been granted the Modify permission or Full Control permission. You can also restore data if you are a member of the Administrators group or the Backup Operators group.

B. **Correct:** You can restore any files and folders for which you have been granted the Modify permission.

C. **Correct:** Although you cannot restore files or folders for which you have been granted the Read permission, you can restore these files and folders if you are a member of the Backup Operators group.

D. **Correct:** Although you cannot restore files or folders for which you have been granted the Read permission, you can restore these files and folders if you are a member of the Backup Operators group.

E. **Incorrect:** To restore the system state data, the person performing the procedure must be a Local Administrator.

Managing, Configuring, and Troubleshooting Storage Use

Storage management in Microsoft Windows 2000 Server includes a number of skills and practices. A key component in this type of management is the ability to monitor, configure, and troubleshoot disks and volumes. All disks used by Windows 2000 must be initialized with a storage type, partitioned, and formatted. You can initialize a hard disk as a **basic disk** or a **dynamic disk**. A basic disk is a physical disk that contains primary partitions and extended partitions with logical drives. Dynamic disks do not use partitions or logical drives. They can contain only dynamic volumes and can be accessed only by Windows 2000. A partition or volume must be formatted with **NTFS** or with the **FAT16** or **FAT32** file system. A system can also be configured to support **fault tolerance** through the use of multiple hard disks. Once you have configured a computer's hard disks, you can monitor their performance to optimize how the disks are used or to troubleshoot problems that might arise as a result of that usage. Storage management in Windows 2000 can also include adding new disks, replacing disks, modifying disk properties, administering removable storage media and robotic storage libraries, and administering remote storage. In addition, you can enable data **compression** on files and folders in NTFS volumes or use **disk quotas** to allocate disk space to users based on the files and folders that they own. Another important skill in storage management is the ability to recover from disk failures. If you have set up your system to support fault tolerance, you should be able to replace a failed disk without losing any data.

Tested Skills and Suggested Practices

The skills that you need to successfully master the Managing, Configuring, and Troubleshooting Storage Use domain on the *Installing, Configuring, and Administering Microsoft Windows 2000 Server* exam include:

- **Monitoring and configuring disks and volumes.**

    - Practice 1: Use the Disk Management snap-in to view the hard disk configuration on your computer. Note the disk type, layout, file system, and status. Open the properties for each disk on the computer, and then view the individual tabs to see how the disk is configured. Notice that the Tools tab allows you to open several tools that are used to optimize the disk and back up data.

    - Practice 2: On an unallocated hard disk in your computer, initialize the disk as a basic disk and create several partitions and logical drives. Configure at least one partition with FAT. After the partitions and logical drives are created, format the FAT partition with NTFS. Try changing the drive letter of at least one partition. Now upgrade the disk to a dynamic disk. Notice that the partitions and logical drives are changed to dynamic volumes.

    - Practice 3: If you have at least three unallocated disks on your computer, configure them as dynamic disks and then set up each of the different types of volumes: simple, spanned, striped, mirrored, and RAID-5. If you have only two disks that you can work with, set up all but the RAID-5 volume. After the disks are configured, read and write similar data to each volume and see whether you notice any differences in performance. Make sure that the files you use are large enough to provide a clear demonstration.

    - Practice 4: Use disk-specific counters in the Performance console to monitor disk performance. You can create log files in the Performance Logs And Alerts snap-in and then view the logs in the System Monitor snap-in.

- **Configuring data compression.**

    - Practice 1: Use Windows Explorer to select a folder that does not contain any critical data, and enable data compression on that folder. Because a folder cannot be both encrypted and compressed, you must select a folder in which encryption does not need to be enabled. Apply compression to the folder and any subfolders that exist within the folder.

    - Practice 2: In Windows Explorer, change the folder options so that compressed files and folders are displayed in alternative colors. After you've set the option, view the folder and notice that any compressed folders or files are displayed in a color different from files and folders that are not compressed.

■ Practice 3: Try accessing data from and saving data to the compressed folder. Use files that are large enough to demonstrate differences in performance. Now disable compression and access and save the same data. Notice the difference in access speeds.

■ **Monitoring and configuring disk quotas.**

■ Practice 1: Open the properties of a volume for which you want to enable disk quotas. You can access the properties through the Disk Management snap-in or through Windows Explorer. Enable quota management, and then configure a default disk quota limit and a warning level that are relatively small so that you can test the configuration. You might want to establish a test user account that you can use to test the limit. Log off Windows 2000 Server and log back on as the test user. (Remember that a user must be granted special rights to log on locally to a domain controller.) Save a file to the volume that is smaller than the warning limit. Save another file that causes the warning level to be exceeded but does not exceed the limit. Finally, save a file that causes the limit to be exceeded. Delete the three files.

■ Practice 2: Repeat Practice 1, but this time configure disk quotas to log an event when a user exceeds the warning level and when a user exceeds the quota limit. After the test user has saved or tried to save files, view the event log for those specific events.

■ Practice 3: Configure a default disk quota limit and a warning level that are relatively small. Then configure a quota limit and a warning level for the test user that are higher than the default limits. The warning level for the test user should be higher than the default disk quota limit. Log off Windows 2000 Server and log back on as the test user. Save a file to the volume that exceeds the size of the default disk quota limit. The test user should have no problem saving the file. Now save a file that causes the warning level to be exceeded but does not exceed the disk quota limit for the user. Save another file that causes the limit to be exceeded. View the event logs.

Further Reading

This section lists supplemental readings by objective. Study these sources thoroughly before taking the 70-215 exam.

Objective 5.1

"Managing Windows 2000 Disks, Backup, and Restore." (This article can be downloaded for free at *http://www.microsoft.com/technet/win2000/disbare.asp.*)

Microsoft Corporation. *Windows 2000 Server Resource Kit.* Volume: *Microsoft Windows 2000 Server Deployment Planning Guide.* Redmond, Washington: Microsoft Press, 2000. (This book can be downloaded for free at *http://www.microsoft.com/windows2000/library/resources/reskit/dpg/default.asp.*) Review Chapter 19, "Determining Windows 2000 Storage Strategies."

Microsoft Corporation. *Windows 2000 Server Resource Kit.* Volume: *Microsoft Windows 2000 Server Operations Guide.* Redmond, Washington: Microsoft Press, 2000. Review Chapter 1, "Disk Concepts and Troubleshooting"; Chapter 2, "Data Storage and Management"; Chapter 3, "File Systems"; Chapter 8, "Examining and Tuning Disk Performance"; and Chapter 11, "Planning a Reliable Configuration."

Microsoft Corporation. *MCSE Training Kit: Microsoft Windows 2000 Server.* Redmond, Washington: Microsoft Press, 2000. Review Lessons 1, 2, and 3 in Chapter 4, "Microsoft Windows 2000 File Systems"; Lesson 3 in Chapter 12, "Reliability and Availability"; and Lesson 1 in Chapter 13, "Monitoring and Optimization."

"Troubleshooting Tools and Strategies." (This article can be downloaded for free at *http://www.microsoft.com/windows2000/library/resources/reskit/samplechapters/pref/pref_tts_juhe.asp.*) This document is taken from the *Windows 2000 Professional Resource Kit*, and it provides useful information about maintenance tools specific to disk performance.

Objective 5.2

"Best Practices for NTFS Compression in Windows 2000 and Windows NT 4.0." (This article can be downloaded for free at *http://support.microsoft.com/support/kb/articles/Q251/1/86.ASP.*)

Microsoft Corporation. *Windows 2000 Server Resource Kit.* Volume: *Microsoft Windows 2000 Server Operations Guide.* Redmond, Washington: Microsoft Press, 2000. Review Chapter 3, "File Systems."

Microsoft Corporation. *MCSE Training Kit: Microsoft Windows 2000 Server.* Redmond, Washington: Microsoft Press, 2000. Review Lesson 1 in Chapter 13, "Monitoring and Optimization."

Objective 5.3

"Disk Quotas." (This article can be downloaded for free at *http://msdn.microsoft.com/library/psdk/winbase/fsys_4lv7.htm*.)

"How to Enable Disk Quotas in Windows 2000." (This article can be downloaded for free at *http://support.microsoft.com/support/kb/articles/Q183/3/22.asp*.)

Microsoft Corporation. *Windows 2000 Server Resource Kit*. Volume: *Microsoft Windows 2000 Server Deployment Planning Guide*. Redmond, Washington: Microsoft Press, 2000. (This book can be downloaded for free at *http://www.microsoft.com/windows2000/library/resources/reskit/dpg/default.asp*.) Review Chapter 24, "Applying Change and Configuration Management."

Microsoft Corporation. *Windows 2000 Server Resource Kit*. Volume: *Microsoft Windows 2000 Server Operations Guide*. Redmond, Washington: Microsoft Press, 2000. Review Chapter 2, "Data Storage and Management."

Microsoft Corporation. *MCSE Training Kit: Microsoft Windows 2000 Server*. Redmond, Washington: Microsoft Press, 2000. Review Lesson 1 in Chapter 13, "Monitoring and Optimization."

Objective 5.4

"Description of the Windows 2000 Recovery Console." (This article can be downloaded for free at *http://support.microsoft.com/support/kb/articles/Q229/7/16.asp*.)

Microsoft Corporation. *Windows 2000 Server Resource Kit*. Volume: *Microsoft Windows 2000 Server Operations Guide*. Redmond, Washington: Microsoft Press, 2000. (Portions of this book, including the following chapter, can be downloaded for free at *http://www.microsoft.com/TechNet/win2000/win2ksrv/reskit/sopch13.asp*.) Review Chapter 13, "Repair, Recovery, and Restore."

Microsoft Corporation. *MCSE Training Kit: Microsoft Windows 2000 Server*. Redmond, Washington: Microsoft Press, 2000. Review Lesson 4 in Chapter 12, "Reliability and Availability."

O B J E C T I V E   5 . 1

Monitor, configure, and troubleshoot disks and volumes.

Your computer's disks and volumes handle the storage and movement of programs and data on your system, giving it a powerful influence on your system's overall responsiveness. As a result, disk management is an integral part of managing your Windows 2000 configuration. Disk management includes creating, deleting, altering, and maintaining storage volumes in your system. Before you can install Windows 2000 Server on a hard disk, the portion of the disk that Windows 2000 will use must be initialized with a storage type, partitioned, and formatted. After Windows 2000 Server has been installed, most disk management tasks can be performed by using the Disk Management snap-in in Computer Management. Disk Management is a graphical tool that provides a central location for disk information so that you can manage disks and volumes. Disk Management allows you to view and modify a volume's properties; assign, change, or remove a drive letter; create a mounted drive; format a volume; delete a volume; and manage **simple**, **spanned**, **striped**, **mirrored**, and **RAID-5** volumes. You can also manage disks on a remote computer, change a disk's storage type, restore disk configuration information, manage new disks, and perform a number of other tasks related to disk and volume maintenance. In addition, Disk Management allows you to check a volume's status. If there is a problem with a disk, you can use the status to help troubleshoot the problem.

Another tool that can be integral to the management of your system's disks and volumes is the Performance console, which provides disk-specific counters that enable you to measure disk activity and throughput, and instructs you on strategies to improve disk performance. You must be able to observe many factors to determine the performance of a disk system. These factors include the level of utilization, the rate of throughput, the amount of disk space available, and whether a queue is developing for the disk system. You should also monitor other types of activity that arise from the disk operations, such as interrupts generated by the disk system and paging activity, because of their influence on other resources, such as the processor and memory. For example, if utilization is high, throughput might peak and a queue might begin to form, which would result in an increased response time and slower performance. Windows 2000 includes counters that monitor the activity of physical disks and logical volumes.

To answer the questions in this objective, you should be familiar with the various components that make up the system of disks and volumes. You should know how to initialize a disk with a storage type, partition the disk, and format it with FAT or NTFS. You should know how to perform the various tasks necessary to configure and administer disks and volumes, and you should know how to monitor those disks and volumes to optimize disk performance and troubleshoot any problems that can occur.

Objective 5.1 Questions

70-215.05.01.001

You are the administrator of a Windows 2000 Server computer that contains three hard disks and one disk controller. Currently, the disks are configured with four volumes. The server must support a large database that will be accessed simultaneously by network users. Which volume will support the fastest write operations to the database?

Examine the Disk Management detail pane shown in the image below to view disk configuration information.

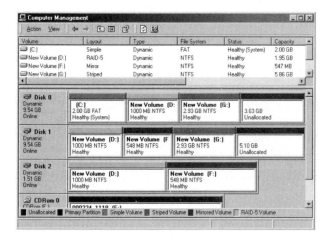

A. Volume C:

B. Volume D:

C. Volume F:

D. Volume G:

70-215.05.01.002

You are the administrator of a Windows 2000 Server computer that contains three hard disks and one disk controller. Currently, the disks are configured with four volumes. You will be storing about 600 MB of data on the server, and you want to ensure that the data will not be lost if one of the hard disks fails. Which volume should you use?

Examine the Disk Management detail pane shown in the image below to view disk configuration information.

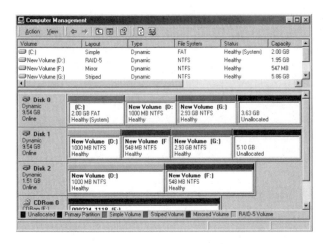

A. Volume C:

B. Volume D:

C. Volume F:

D. Volume G:

70-215.05.01.003

You are the administrator of a Windows 2000 Server computer that contains three hard disks and one disk controller. Currently, the disks are configured with four volumes. You want to use the unallocated space on Disk 0 and Disk 1 to create one more volume. How can you configure that volume? (Choose all that apply.)

Examine the Disk Management detail pane shown in the image below to view disk configuration information.

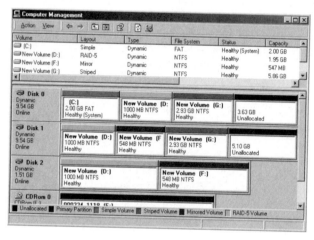

A. As a 7-GB RAID-1 volume

B. As a 3.5-GB RAID-1 volume

C. As a 3.5-GB RAID-5 volume

D. As a 7-GB simple volume

E. As a 7-GB striped volume

Objective 5.1 Answers

70-215.05.01.001

► **Correct Answers: D**

A. **Incorrect:** Volume C: is a simple volume. A simple volume contains disk space from a single disk and is not fault tolerant. Simple volumes can be created on dynamic disks only, and when you have only one dynamic disk, the only type of volume that you can create is a simple volume. When formatted with NTFS, simple volumes can be extended onto multiple regions of the same disk; however, they become less fault tolerant because extending a simple volume increases the points of failure on the disk. Although a simple volume can support fast write operations, striped volumes are faster because I/O requests are distributed across disks.

B. **Incorrect:** Volume D: is a RAID-5 volume. A RAID-5 volume is a fault-tolerant striped volume. Windows 2000 adds a parity-information stripe to each disk partition in the volume. Windows 2000 uses the parity-information stripe to reconstruct data when a physical disk fails. RAID-5 requires a minimum of 3 disks and a maximum of 32 disks. RAID-5 volumes are well-suited for large sequential reads, such as in database mining; however, the volumes are not well suited for any write-intensive workload because a single write is likely to generate a disk read of the parity and two writes, one to update the parity information and one to update the data. In addition, the need to calculate parity information requires more computer memory, which can slow write performance.

C. **Incorrect:** Volume F: is a mirrored volume. A mirrored volume is made up of two identical copies of a simple volume, each on a separate disk. All data written to the mirrored volume is written to both volumes, which provides fault tolerance but results in disk capacity of only 50 percent. Write performance is less efficient than on a simple volume because data must be written to both disks. However, when one member of a mirrored volume fails, performance returns to that of a simple volume because the fault tolerance driver works with only a single partition. Performance will also be that of a simple disk if each disk resides on its own disk controller. Even if performance can be matched to that of a simple disk, write operations still are not as fast as they are on striped volumes.

D. **Correct:** Volume G: is a striped volume. A striped volume combines areas of free space from multiple hard disks (up to 32) into one logical volume. A striped volume is not fault tolerant; if a disk in a striped volume fails, the data in the entire volume is lost. In a striped volume, Windows 2000 optimizes performance by adding data to all disks at the same rate. Striped volumes are composed of stripes of data of equal size written across each disk in the volume. Striped volumes improve I/O performance by distributing I/O requests across disks. Access to the data on a striped volume is usually faster than access to the same data would be on a single disk because the I/O is spread across more than one disk. Windows 2000 can be seeking on more than one disk at the same time, and can have simultaneous read or write operations occurring.

70-215.05.01.002

▶ **Correct Answers: B**

A. **Incorrect:** Volume C: is a simple volume. A simple volume contains disk space from a single disk and is not fault tolerant. Simple volumes can be created on dynamic disks only, and when you have only one dynamic disk, the only type of volume that you can create is a simple volume. Simple volumes can be extended onto multiple regions of the same disk; however, they become less fault tolerant because extending a simple volume increases the points of failure on the disk. Increasing the size of a simple volume to include space on other hard disks of the same computer creates a spanned volume, but spanned volumes, like simple volumes, do not support fault tolerance.

B. **Correct:** Volume D: is a RAID-5 volume. A RAID-5 volume is a fault-tolerant striped volume. It requires a minimum of 3 disks and a maximum of 32 disks. Windows 2000 adds a parity-information stripe to each disk partition in the volume. Windows 2000 uses the parity-information stripe to reconstruct data when a physical disk fails. If one of the disks fails, none of the data is lost. When a read operation requires data from the failed disk, the system reads all the remaining good data stripes in the stripe and the parity stripe. Each data stripe is subtracted from the parity stripe. The result is the missing data stripe. When the system needs to write a data stripe to a disk that has failed, it reads the other data stripes and backs them out of the parity stripe, leaving the missing data stripe. The modifications needed to the parity stripe can now be calculated and made. Because the data stripe is unavailable, it is not written; only the parity stripe is written. The parity stripe isn't needed for a read unless there is a failure in a data stripe. When the failed disk contains a parity stripe, the system does not compute or write the parity stripe when there is a change in the data stripe.

C. **Incorrect:** Volume F: is a mirrored volume. A mirrored volume is made up of two identical copies of a simple volume, each on a separate disk. All data written to the mirrored volume is written to both volumes, which provides fault tolerance but results in disk capacity of only 50 percent. If there is a read failure from one of the disks, data can be read from the other disk of the mirrored volume. If there is a write failure to one of the disks, the remaining disk is used for all write operations. Although a mirror volume can be used to ensure that data will not be lost in case one of the hard disks fails, volume F: contains only 548 MB of space, and you need at least 600 MB.

D. **Incorrect:** Volume G: is a striped volume. A striped volume combines areas of free space from multiple hard disks (up to 32) into one logical volume. Striped volumes are composed of stripes of data of equal size written across each disk in the volume. Striped volumes improve I/O performance by distributing I/O requests across disks. However, a striped volume is not fault tolerant; if a disk in a striped volume fails, the data in the entire volume is lost.

70-215.05.01.003

▶ **Correct Answers: B and E**

A. **Incorrect:** Although a RAID-1 (mirrored) volume can be created from the unallocated space, it can be only 3.63 GB. The size of the volume is limited to the size of the unallocated space on the disk that has the least amount of space. In other words, the volume can be only 3.63 GB because that is how much unallocated space remains on Disk 0, and Disk 0 has the least amount of unallocated space of the two disks. (Disk 1 has 5.10 GB of unallocated space.) You cannot add together the amounts of unallocated space from the two disks. A mirrored volume does not span the two disks; the two disks are a copy of one another.

B. **Correct:** A RAID-1 volume, also referred to as a mirrored volume, is made up of two identical copies of a simple volume, each on a separate disk. All data written to the mirrored volume is written to both volumes, which provides fault tolerance but results in disk capacity of only 50 percent. If there is a read failure from one of the disks, data can be read from the other disk of the mirrored volume. If there is a write failure to one of the disks, the remaining disk is used for all write operations. Because Disk 0 has 3.63 GB of unallocated space, and because it is the disk that contains the least amount of available space, you can create a mirrored volume up to 3.63 GB in size. The size of the volume is limited to the size of the unallocated space on the disk that has the least amount of space. The unused area that you select for the shadow volume cannot be smaller than the original volume. If the area that you select for the shadow volume is larger than the original, the extra space on the shadow disk can be configured as another volume.

C. **Incorrect:** A RAID-5 volume is a fault-tolerant striped volume. Windows 2000 adds a parity-information stripe to each disk partition in the volume. Windows 2000 uses the parity-information stripe to reconstruct data when a physical disk fails. If one of the disks fails, none of the data is lost. A RAID-5 volume requires a minimum of 3 disks and a maximum of 32 disks. Because you are using only 2 disks to create the new volume, you cannot create a RAID-5 volume.

D. **Incorrect:** A simple volume contains disk space from a single disk and is not fault tolerant. Simple volumes can be created on dynamic disks only, and when you have only one dynamic disk, the only type of volume that you can create is a simple volume. You cannot create a simple volume across two different disks. Increasing the size of a simple volume to include space on other hard disks of the same computer creates a spanned volume.

E. **Correct:** You can create a striped volume that is as large as 8.73 GB in size, the total amount of unallocated space on the two disks. A striped volume combines areas of free space from multiple hard disks (up to 32) into one logical volume. The physical disks in a striped volume do not need to be identical, but there must be unused space available on each disk. Striped volumes do not contain redundant information. Therefore, the cost per megabyte is identical to that for the same amount of storage configured from a contiguous area on a single disk. Striped volumes are composed of stripes of data of equal size written across each disk in the volume. Striped volumes improve I/O performance by distributing I/O requests across disks. However, a striped volume is not fault tolerant; if a disk in a striped volume fails, the data in the entire volume is lost.

O B J E C T I V E   5 . 2

Configure data compression.

Data compression in Windows 2000 allows you to compress files and folders on NTFS volumes. Compressed files and folders occupy less space on the volume. As a result, compression allows you to store more data. Files compressed on an NTFS volume can be read and written by any Windows-based application without first being decompressed by another program. Decompression occurs automatically when the file is read. The file is compressed again when it is closed or saved. Only NTFS can read the compressed form of the data. When an application, such as Microsoft Word, or an operating system command, such as COPY, requests access to a compressed file, NTFS automatically uncompresses the file before making it available. When the file is closed or saved, NTFS automatically compresses it again. The compression state for each file and folder on an NTFS volume is set to either compressed or uncompressed. The compression state of a folder does not reflect the compression state of the files in that folder. For example, a folder might be compressed, yet some or all of the files within that folder could be decompressed if they were moved from a compressed folder or if you selectively decompressed some of the files in the folder.

Data compression can cause performance degradation because a compressed NTFS file is decompressed, copied, and then recompressed as a new file, even when copied inside the same computer. In network transfers, the file is decompressed, which affects network saturation and transfer speed. Heavily loaded servers with considerable write traffic are poor candidates for data compression, whereas read-only, read-mostly, or lightly loaded servers might not experience significant performance degradation. Programs that use transaction logging and constantly write to a database or log should not store their files on a compressed volume. If a program is modifying data through mapped sections in a compressed file, it can produce dirty pages faster than the mapped writer can write them. The two measures that you can use to gauge the performance of NTFS data compression are size and speed. You can tell how well compression works by comparing the uncompressed file and folder sizes to the compressed sizes. In general, to minimize the amount of system time dedicated to compression and uncompression activities, you should compress static data rather than data that changes frequently.

To answer the questions in this objective, you should know how to change the compression state of a file or a folder on an NTFS volume and you should know how performance can be affected by the type of data being compressed. You should also know how to select a different display color for compressed files and folders. In addition, you should be familiar with what happens to compressed files and folders when you copy or move them.

Objective 5.2 Questions

70-215.05.02.001

You have a Windows 2000 Server computer with a 20-GB hard disk. The disk is partitioned and formatted with NTFS. The C:\Download folder (along with its contents) is the only compressed folder on the disk. You must copy the C:\Download\Accounting subfolder and its contents to the C:\Backup folder. Currently, the C:\Backup folder does not contain an Accounting subfolder. What will be the compression state of the Accounting subfolder and its contents in their new location when you copy them to C:\Backup?

A. The Accounting subfolder and its contents will remain compressed.

B. The C:\Backup folder will inherit the compression state of the C:\Download folder.

C. The Accounting subfolder and its contents will be uncompressed.

D. The Accounting subfolder will be uncompressed, but the files within the Accounting subfolder will remain compressed.

70-215.05.02.002

You have a Windows 2000 Server computer with a 20-GB hard disk. The disk is partitioned and formatted with NTFS. The C:\Download folder (along with its contents) is the only compressed folder on the disk. You must move the C:\Download\Accounting subfolder and its contents to the C:\Backup folder. Currently, the C:\Backup folder does not contain an Accounting subfolder. What will be the compression state of the Accounting subfolder and its contents when you move them to C:\Backup?

A. The Accounting subfolder and its contents will remain compressed.

B. The C:\Backup folder will inherit the compression state of the C:\Download folder.

C. The Accounting subfolder and its contents will be uncompressed.

D. The Accounting subfolder will be uncompressed, but the files within the Accounting subfolder will remain compressed.

70-215.05.02.003

You have a Windows 2000 Server computer with a 20-GB hard disk. The disk includes an NTFS volume (C:) and a FAT32 volume (D:). The C:\Download folder (along with its contents) is compressed. You must move the C:\Download\Accounting subfolder and its contents to the D:\Backup folder. Currently, the D:\Backup folder does not contain an Accounting subfolder. What will be the compression state of the Accounting subfolder and its contents when you move them to D:\Backup?

A. The Accounting subfolder and its contents will remain compressed.

B. The D:\Backup folder will inherit the compression state of the C:\Download folder.

C. The Accounting subfolder and its contents will be uncompressed.

D. The Accounting subfolder will be uncompressed, but the files within the Accounting subfolder will remain compressed.

70-215.05.02.004

You have a Windows 2000 Server computer with a 20-GB hard disk. The disk includes two NTFS volumes (C: and D:). The C:\Download folder (along with its contents) is the only compressed folder on the disk. You must move the C:\Download\Accounting subfolder and its contents to the D:\Backup folder. Currently, the D:\Backup folder does not contain an Accounting subfolder. What will be the compression state of the Accounting subfolder and its contents when you move them to D:\Backup?

A. The Accounting subfolder and its contents will remain compressed.

B. The D:\Backup folder will inherit the compression state of the C:\Download folder.

C. The Accounting subfolder and its contents will be uncompressed.

D. The Accounting subfolder will be uncompressed, but the files within the Accounting subfolder will remain compressed.

Objective 5.2 Answers

70-215.05.02.001

▶ **Correct Answers: C**

A. **Incorrect:** The Accounting subfolder and its contents will be uncompressed. When you move a compressed file or folder to another folder, the file or folder remains compressed after the move, regardless of the compression state of the folder that it was moved to. However, when you copy a compressed file or folder, the file or folder inherits the compression state of the target folder.

B. **Incorrect:** The compression state of the C:\Backup folder will not change.

C. **Correct:** Moving and copying files and folders in disk volumes can change their compression state. The compression state of these files and folders, and the file system in which they were created, can affect them while they are being moved or copied. The compression state of an NTFS file or folder is controlled by its compression attribute. When you copy files and folders to another folder within an NTFS volume, the files and folders will take on the compression attribute of the target folder (assuming that there isn't already a pre-existing file or folder of the same name in the target folder).

D. **Incorrect:** The Accounting subfolder as well as its contents will inherit the compression state of the C:\Backup folder.

70-215.05.02.002

▶ **Correct Answers: A**

A. **Correct:** Moving and copying files and folders in disk volumes can change their compression state. The compression state of these files and folders, and the file system in which they were created, can affect them while they are being moved or copied. The compression state of an NTFS file or folder is controlled by its compression attribute. When you move a compressed file or folder to another folder within the same volume, the file or folder remains compressed after the move, regardless of the compression state of the folder that it was moved to. When you move an uncompressed file or folder to another folder, the file or folder remains uncompressed after the move, regardless of the compression state of the folder it was moved to.

B. **Incorrect:** The compression state of the C:\Backup folder will not change.

C. **Incorrect:** The Accounting subfolder and its contents will remain compressed after the move. When you copy a file or folder, the file or folder takes on the compression attribute of the target folder. However, when you move a file or folder, the file or folder inherits the compression state of the target folder.

D. **Incorrect:** The Accounting subfolder as well as its contents will remain compressed after the move.

70-215.05.02.003

▶ **Correct Answers: C**

A. **Incorrect:** Any compressed files or folders moved or copied from an NTFS volume to a FAT volume are automatically uncompressed.

B. **Incorrect:** Because the Backup folder resides on a FAT volume, the folder and its contents cannot be compressed. However, if the Backup folder resided on an NTFS volume, the compression state of the D:\Backup folder would not change.

C. **Correct:** Moving and copying files and folders between disk volumes can change their compression state. The compression state of these files and folders, and the file system in which they were created, can affect them while they are being moved or copied. The compression state of an NTFS file or folder is controlled by its compression attribute. Windows 2000 supports compression for NTFS volumes only. As a result, any compressed files or folders moved or copied from an NTFS volume to a FAT volume are automatically uncompressed. However, even if the Backup folder resided on an NTFS volume, the Accounting subfolder and its contents would inherit the compression state of the target folder. When you move a file or folder between NTFS volumes, the file or folder inherits the compression state of the target folder because Windows 2000 treats the move as a COPY and then a DELETE.

D. **Incorrect:** Any compressed files or folders moved or copied from an NTFS volume to a FAT volume are automatically uncompressed.

70-215.05.02.004

▶ **Correct Answers: C**

A. **Incorrect:** When you move or copy a file or folder between NTFS volumes, the file or folder inherits the compression state of the target folder.

B. **Incorrect:** The compression state of the D:\Backup folder will not change.

C. **Correct:** Moving and copying files and folders between disk volumes can change their compression state. The compression state of these files and folders, and the file system in which they were created, can impact the way that they are affected while being moved or copied. The compression state of an NTFS file or folder is controlled by its compression attribute. When you move a file or folder between NTFS volumes, the file or folder inherits the compression state of the target folder. This is because Windows 2000 treats a move to another volume as a COPY and then a DELETE, and a copy inherits the compression state of the target folder.

D. **Incorrect:** The Accounting subfolder as well as its contents will inherit the compression state of the D:\Backup folder.

OBJECTIVE 5.3

Monitor and configure disk quotas.

Windows 2000 supports disk quotas for volumes formatted with NTFS. Disk quotas allow you to manage storage growth in distributed environments. You can use disk quotas to allocate disk space to users based on the files and folders that they own. You can enable or disable disk quotas on a volume, prevent users from saving new data when their quotas are exceeded, set the default disk quota warning level and limit, and view disk quota information for each user. You can also monitor the amount of hard disk space users have used and the amount that they have left against their quota. Disk quotas are tracked independently for different volumes, even if the volumes are different partitions on the same physical drive. When you enable disk quotas, you can set both the disk quota limit and the disk quota warning level. The limit specifies the amount of disk space that is allocated to a user. The warning level specifies when a user is nearing the limit.

Disk quotas are transparent to the users. Windows 2000 tracks and controls disk usage on a per-user, per-volume basis. It tracks disk quotas for each volume, even if the volumes are on the same hard disk. Every user's disk space is tracked regardless of the folder in which the user stores files. When a user asks how much space is free on a disk, the system reports only the user's available quota allowance. If the user exceeds this allowance, the system indicates that the disk is full. Windows 2000 calculates disk space usage for users based on the files and folders that they own. Windows 2000 ignores compression when it calculates hard disk space usage. When you enable disk quotas on a volume that already contains files, the disk space used by all users who have copied, saved, or taken ownership of files on the volume up to that point is calculated. The quota limit and warning level are then applied to all current users and to all new users. The free space that Windows 2000 reports to applications for the volume is the amount of space remaining within the user's disk quota limit.

To answer the questions in this objective, you should be able to enable or disable disk quotas, and you should be able to perform all configuration tasks related to managing disk quotas, such as setting the default disk quota warning level and limit. You should also be able to log events when users exceed their disk space limits and warning levels.

Objective 5.3 Questions

70-215.05.03.001

You are setting up a Windows 2000 Server computer. Users will be storing data on one of the NTFS volumes (C:) on the computer, and you want to implement disk quotas on that volume before users begin accessing it.

You want to achieve the following results:

- You must enforce the disk quota limit for all users.

- You must ensure that no user exceeds 5 MB of storage.

- You must log an event to the system log when a user exceeds 4 MB of storage.

How should you configure disk quotas on the C: volume? (Choose all that apply.)

Examine the Local Disk (C:) Properties dialog box shown in the image below to view the disk quota configuration options.

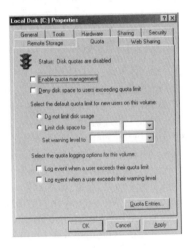

A. Enable quota management.

B. Deny disk space to users exceeding the quota limit.

C. Select the Do Not Limit Disk Usage option button.

D. Set the disk quota limit to 4 MB, and set the warning level to 5 MB.

E. Set the disk quota limit to 5 MB, and set the warning level to 4 MB.

F. Log an event when a user exceeds the disk quota limit.

G. Log an event when a user exceeds the warning level.

70-215.05.03.002

You are setting up a Windows 2000 Server computer that will be used by 50 network users. These users will be storing data on one of the NTFS volumes (C:) on the computer, and you want to implement disk quotas on that volume before users begin accessing it. The volume contains 100 GB of unused space that will be used only to store user data.

You want to achieve the following results:

- You must enforce a disk quota limit for each user so that available storage on the C: volume is divided equally among the 50 users.

- You must warn a user when that user's storage level exceeds 90 percent of his or her available storage.

- You must log an event to the system log when a user exceeds the default disk quota limit.

- You must log an event to the system log when a user exceeds the default warning level.

You configure disk quotas for the C: volume, as shown in the exhibit.

Which result or results does the configuration achieve? (Choose all that apply.)

Examine the Local Disk (C:) Properties dialog box shown in the image below to view disk quota configuration information.

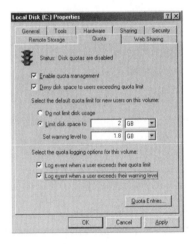

A. A disk quota limit is enforced for each user, and the available storage is divided equally among the 50 users.

B. A user will be warned when that user's storage level exceeds 90 percent of his or her available storage.

C. An event will be logged when a user exceeds the disk quota limit.

D. An event will be logged when a user exceeds the warning level.

E. The solution does not achieve any of the required results.

70-215.05.03.003

You are setting up a Windows 2000 Server computer that will be used by 50 network users. These users will be storing data on one of the NTFS volumes (C:) on the computer, and you want to implement disk quotas on that volume before users begin accessing it. The volume contains 100 GB of unused space that will be used only to store user data.

You want to achieve the following results:

- You must enforce a disk quota limit for each user so that available storage on the C: volume is divided equally among the 50 users.

- You must warn a user when that user's storage level exceeds 90 percent of his or her available storage.

- You must log an event to the system log when a user exceeds the default disk quota limit.

- You must log an event to the system log when a user exceeds the default warning level.

You configure disk quotas for the C: volume, as shown in the exhibit.

Which result or results does the configuration achieve? (Choose all that apply.)

Examine the Local Disk (C:) Properties dialog box shown in the image below to view disk quota configuration information.

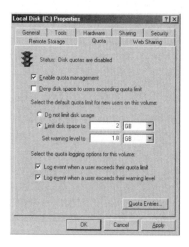

A. A disk quota limit is enforced for each user, and the available storage is divided equally among the 50 users.

B. A user will be warned when that user's storage level exceeds 90 percent of his or her available storage.

C. An event will be logged when a user exceeds the default disk quota limit.

D. An event will be logged when a user exceeds the default warning level.

E. The solution does not achieve any of the required results.

Objective 5.3 Answers

70-215.05.03.001

▶ **Correct Answers: A, B, E, and G**

A. **Correct:** Before you can configure disk quotas on your system, you must enable disk quotas by selecting the Enable Quota Management check box. Enabling disk quotas allows Windows 2000 to track and control disk usage on a per-user, per-volume basis. The disk space of every user on a volume is tracked regardless of the folder in which the user stores files. Disk quotas are based on file ownership. If a user moves files from one folder to another on the same volume, the volume space usage does not change; if the user copies the files to a different folder on the same volume, the volume space usage doubles. You must enable disk quotas before you can deny disk space to users, set the default quota limit, or log quota-related events.

B. **Correct:** When you enable disk quotas and set the default quota limit, Windows 2000 tracks disk usage for each user on that volume. However, disk quotas do not control disk usage unless you select the Deny Disk Space To Users Exceeding Quota Limit check box. When you select this option, users are prevented from storing more data on the volume than their quotas allow. When users try to exceed their quota limits, they receive an insufficient disk space error message and cannot write additional data to the volume without deleting or moving files. Individual programs determine their own error handling for this condition. To the program, the disk appears to be full. By leaving the option cleared, you can allow users to exceed their limit, which is useful when you do not want to deny users access to a volume, but want to track disk space use on a per-user basis.

C. **Incorrect:** If you select this option, users will be able to use as much disk space as is available on the volume. Although their disk usage will still be monitored, no limits will be placed on the usage, and no events will be logged regardless of how much disk space they use.

D. **Incorrect:** You must set the disk quota limit to 5 MB, and the warning level to 4 MB.

E. **Correct:** When you set the disk quota limit to 5 MB, Windows 2000 tracks whether a user exceeds that limit. If the Deny Disk Space To Users Exceeding Quota Limit option is selected in addition to setting the disk quota limit to 5 MB, the user is prevented from storing more than 5 MB of data on that volume. If the Log Event When A User Exceeds Their Quota Limit option is selected in addition to setting the disk quota limit to 5 MB, an event is logged to the system log if a user exceeds 5 MB of storage on the volume. When you set the warning level to 4 MB, Windows 2000 tracks whether a user exceeds that level. The user will not receive a warning if that user exceeds the limit; however, if the Log Event When A User Exceeds Their Warning Level option is selected in addition to setting the warning level to 4 MB, an event is logged to the system log if a user exceeds 4 MB of storage.

F. **Incorrect:** Although you can log an event to the system log if the user exceeds the disk quota limit, logging this event is not part of the required results. Consequently, you should not select the Log Event When A User Exceeds Their Quota Limit check box.

G. **Correct:** When you select the Log Event When A User Exceeds Their Warning Level check box, an event is logged to the system log if a user exceeds the warning level.

70-215.05.03.002

▶ **Correct Answers: A, C, and D**

A. **Correct:** A disk quota limit is enforced by taking two steps. The first step is to select the Deny Disk Space To Users Exceeding Quota Limit check box. When you select this option, users are prevented from storing more data on the volume than their quotas allow. When users try to exceed their quota limits, they receive an insufficient disk space error message and cannot write additional data to the volume without deleting or moving files. Individual programs determine their own error handling for this condition. To the program, the disk appears to be full. The second step is to select the Limit Disk Space To option button and set the limit to 2 GB, which would be the number of GB that each of 50 users can use if there are 100 GB of unused space available. When you set the disk quota limit to 2 GB, Windows 2000 tracks whether a user exceeds that limit. If you set the limit and select the Deny Disk Space To Users Exceeding Quota Limit check box, users are prevented from exceeding their limits. If you were to set the disk quota limit without selecting the Deny Disk Space To Users Exceeding Quota Limit check box, users would be able to exceed their limit, although Windows 2000 would still track disk space use on a per-user basis and track whether users exceed their limits.

B. **Incorrect:** You can configure disk quotas to track warning levels by setting the warning level to the required amount. If you want to monitor when a user's storage level exceeds 90 percent, you must set the warning level to 1.8 GB, which is 90 percent of 2 GB. If the Log Event When A User Exceeds Their Warning Level option is selected in addition to setting the warning level to 1.8 GB, an event is logged to the system log if a user exceeds 1.8 GB of storage. Although Windows 2000 will track the warning level and log an event if it is exceeded, the user will not receive a warning when that level is exceeded.

C. **Correct:** When you select the Log Event When A User Exceeds Their Quota Limit check box, an event is logged to the system log if a user exceeds the disk quota limit. In addition to selecting this check box, you must select the Limit Disk Space To check box and define a disk quota limit. In this case, an event is logged when a user exceeds 2 GB of storage.

D. **Correct:** When you select the Log Event When A User Exceeds Their Warning Level check box, an event is logged to the system log if a user exceeds the warning level. In addition to selecting this check box, you must define a disk quota warning level. In this case, an event is logged when a user exceeds 1.8 GB of storage.

E. **Incorrect:** A disk quota limit is enforced for each user, and the available storage is divided equally among the 50 users. In addition, an event is logged when a user exceeds the disk quota limit or the warning level. However, a user will not be warned when that user's storage level exceeds 90 percent of his or her available storage.

70-215.05.03.003

▶ **Correct Answers: C and D**

A. **Incorrect:** When you select the Limit Disk Space To option button and set the limit to 2 GB, Windows 2000 tracks whether a user exceeds that limit. The 2 GB is the number of GB that each of 50 users can use if there are 100 GB of unused space available. However, the user will not be prevented from exceeding this limit. To limit disk usage, you must also select the Deny Disk Space To Users Exceeding Quota Limit check box. When you select this option, users are prevented from storing more data on the volume than their quotas allow. When users try to exceed their quota limits, they receive an insufficient disk space error message and cannot write additional data to the volume without deleting or moving files. Individual programs determine their own error handling for this condition. To the program, the disk appears to be full. When you set the disk quota limit without selecting the Deny Disk Space To Users Exceeding Quota Limit check box, users can exceed their limit, although Windows 2000 still tracks disk space use on a per-user basis and tracks whether users exceed their limits.

B. **Incorrect:** You can configure disk quotas to track warning levels by setting the warning level to the required amount. If you want to monitor when a user's storage level exceeds 90 percent, you must set the warning level to 1.8 GB, which is 90 percent of 2 GB. If the Log Event When A User Exceeds Their Warning Level option is selected in addition to setting the warning level to 1.8 GB, an event is logged to the system log if a user exceeds 1.8 GB of storage. Although Windows 2000 will track the warning level and log an event if it is exceeded, the user will not receive a warning when that level is exceeded.

C. **Correct:** When you select the Log Event When A User Exceeds Their Quota Limit check box, an event is logged to the system log if a user exceeds the disk quota limit. In addition to selecting this check box, you must select the Limit Disk Space To check box and define a disk quota limit. In this case, an event is logged when a user exceeds 2 GB of storage.

D. **Correct:** When you select the Log Event When A User Exceeds Their Warning Level check box, an event is logged to the system log if a user exceeds the warning level. In addition to selecting this check box, you must define a disk quota warning level. In this case, an event is logged when a user exceeds 1.8 GB of storage.

E. **Incorrect:** An event is logged when a user exceeds the disk quota limit or the warning level. However, the disk quota limit will not be enforced for each user, and a user will not be warned when that user's storage level exceeds 90 percent of his or her available storage.

OBJECTIVE 5.4

Recover from disk failures.

When a system is configured with **fault-tolerant** disk arrays, Windows 2000 can respond to catastrophic events so that no data is lost and work in progress is not corrupted. Windows 2000 Server provides a software implementation of a fault tolerance technology known as **redundant array of independent disks (RAID)**. RAID provides fault tolerance by implementing data redundancy. With data redundancy, a computer writes data to more than one disk, which protects the data in the event of a single hard disk failure. The process of error detection and recovery for Windows 2000 fault-tolerant volumes is similar for both mirrored (RAID-1) and RAID-5 volumes. During system initialization, if the system cannot locate a partition in a mirrored volume or RAID-5 volume, Windows 2000 logs a severe error in the event log, marks the volume as Failed Redundancy, and uses the remaining portions of the volume to allow the system to continue to work normally. Users accessing resources over the network are usually not affected, except that they may see a deterioration in performance. If a disk fails, you should back up data immediately because the volume is no longer fault tolerant. You should replace the failed disk and begin the recovery of the volume as soon as possible.

When a member of a mirrored or RAID-5 volume fails, it becomes an orphan. Windows 2000 determines that the orphan can no longer be used and directs reading and writing all new data to the remaining members of the volume. A mirrored volume provides fault tolerance by duplicating data on two disks. If one disk fails, the functional disk continues to operate. You can continue running in a configuration that is not fault tolerant, although you should replace the disk and reconstruct the mirror as soon as possible. When a member of a mirrored volume fails, you must break the mirrored volume to expose the remaining volume as a separate volume. You can then create a new mirrored volume from unused space on another disk. When you restart the computer, the data from the working volume is copied to the new member of the mirrored volume. If a member of a RAID-5 volume fails, the computer continues to operate with access to all data. As data is requested, the fault-tolerant driver uses the data and parity bits on the remaining members to regenerate the missing data in RAM. During this regeneration, computer performance decreases. To restore fault tolerance to your system, you should replace the failed hard disk and then repair the RAID-5 volume. The fault tolerance driver reads the parity information from the parity information stripes on the remaining members, and then re-creates the data contained on the missing member.

To answer the questions in this objective, you should know how to recover a mirrored volume and a RAID-5 volume. You must be familiar with the Disk Management snap-in and know how to use it to identify failed disks and failed redundancy and to repair a volume and reimplement fault tolerance. You should also know how to use Safe Mode to start Windows 2000, use the Recovery Console to gain access to a hard disk, and use the Emergency Repair Disk to try to repair a Windows 2000 Server installation.

Objective 5.4 Questions

70-215.05.04.001

How can you repair the RAID-5 volume? (Choose all that apply.)

Examine the Disk Management detail pane shown in the image below to view disk configuration information.

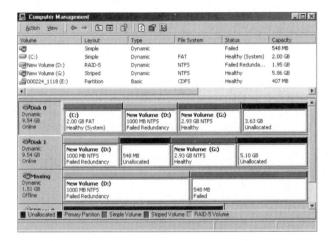

A. Replace the failed disk with a new one.

B. In the Disk Management snap-in, select the D: volume in the Missing row (in the lower window), and then select the Repair Volume command.

C. In the Disk Management snap-in, select the D: volume in the Disk 0 row (in the lower window), and then select the Repair Volume command.

D. In the Disk Management snap-in, select Disk 0 (in the lower window), and then select the Repair Volume command.

70-215.05.04.002

The master boot record and the system volume boot sector of your Windows 2000 Server computer have been damaged. You want to recover from this situation without reinstalling Windows 2000 Server. What should you do?

A. Use the Safe Mode option to start Windows 2000 Server.

B. Use the Last Known Good Configuration option to start Windows 2000 Server.

C. Use the Windows 2000 Server Setup floppy diskettes to start Setup and perform an upgrade over the existing installation.

D. Use the Windows 2000 Server Setup floppy diskettes to start Setup and launch the Recovery Console.

70-215.05.04.003

How can you recover the RAID-5 volume if Disk 0 fails? (Choose all that apply.)

Examine the Disk Management detail pane shown in the image below to view disk configuration information.

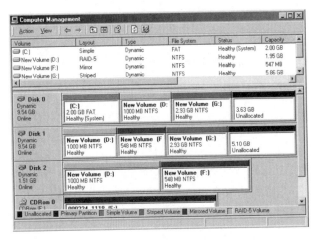

A. Replace the failed Disk 0 with a new disk.

B. Install Windows 2000 Server in a volume on Disk 0.

C. In the Disk Management snap-in, select Disk 1 (in the lower window), and then select the Repair Volume command.

D. In the Disk Management snap-in, select the D: volume in the Disk 0 row (in the lower window), and then select the Repair Volume command.

E. In the Disk Management snap-in, select the D: volume in the Disk 1 row (in the lower window), and then select the Repair Volume command.

Objective 5.4 Answers

70-215.05.04.001

▶ **Correct Answers: A and C**

A. **Correct:** When a member of a RAID-5 volume fails, it becomes an orphan. The operating system determines that it cannot be used and directs the reading and writing of all new data to the remaining members, which in this case are Disk 0 and Disk 1. Users can still access data; however, the system is no longer fault tolerant. After you replace the failed member, you can reconstruct the data for that member from the remaining members, thereby restoring fault tolerance to the system.

B. **Incorrect:** You cannot repair the volume by selecting the volume from the Missing row. You must select a volume from a disk that is online.

C. **Correct:** To replace a stripe in a RAID-5 volume, you need a dynamic disk with unallocated space that is at least as large as the stripe to repair. If you don't have a dynamic disk with enough unallocated space, the Repair Volume command is unavailable. However, once enough unallocated space is available (through the replacement of the failed disk), you can repair the volume by regenerating the data for the orphaned member from the remaining members of the RAID-5 volume. The RAID-5 volume does not display a healthy status in Disk Management until regeneration is complete.

D. **Incorrect:** You cannot repair a volume by selecting one of the disks. The only actions that you can perform by selecting a disk are those actions that affect the entire disk, such as upgrading from a basic disk to a dynamic disk.

70-215.05.04.002

▶ **Correct Answers: D**

A. **Incorrect:** Safe Mode allows you to start your system with a minimal set of device drivers and services. Safe Mode does not work in all circumstances, especially if your system files are corrupted or missing or your hard disk is damaged or has failed. Safe Mode will not work if the master boot record and the system volume boot sector have been damaged.

B. **Incorrect:** The Last Known Good Configuration option is an advanced startup option that starts Windows 2000 with the registry information that Windows saved at the last shutdown. The Last Known Good Configuration is best used in cases of an incorrect configuration. It does not solve problems caused by corrupted or missing files. The Last Known Good Configuration option will not work if the master boot record and the system volume boot sector have been damaged.

C. **Incorrect:** Although you can repair the master boot record and the system volume boot sector by performing an upgrade, this is the last resort before reinstalling the operating system. You should first try using the Recovery Console.

D. **Correct:** The Recovery Console is a text-mode command interpreter that is separate from the Windows 2000 command prompt. The Recovery Console allows you to gain access to the hard disk, regardless of the file system being used, for basic troubleshooting and system maintenance. Because starting Windows 2000 is not a prerequisite for using the Recovery Console, you can use it to access volumes without starting the graphical interface. The Recovery Console allows you to start and stop services and repair the system in a granular way. It can also be used to repair the master boot record and the boot sector and to format volumes. If the Recovery Console was installed on the local hard disk, it can be accessed from the Windows 2000 startup menu. However, if the master boot record or the system volume boot sector has been damaged, you need to start the computer by using either the Windows 2000 Setup floppy disks or the Windows 2000 installation CD-ROM to access the Recovery Console.

70-215.05.04.003

▶ **Correct Answers: A, B, and E**

A. **Correct:** When a member of a RAID-5 volume fails, it becomes an orphan. The operating system determines that it cannot be used and directs the reading and writing of all new data to the remaining members, which in this case are Disk 1 and Disk 2. Users can still access data; however, the system is no longer fault tolerant. After you replace the failed member, you can reconstruct the data for that member from the remaining members, thereby restoring fault tolerance to the system.

B. **Correct:** The C: volume is the system volume. The system volume contains the hardware-specific files needed to load Windows 2000. In addition, the C: volume is a simple volume. A simple volume contains disk space from a single disk and is not fault tolerant. If Disk 0 fails, the C: volume fails and the data in that volume is lost. As a result, Windows 2000 Server must be reinstalled.

C. **Incorrect:** You cannot repair a volume by selecting one of the disks. The only actions that you can perform by selecting a disk are those actions that affect the entire disk, such as upgrading from a basic disk to a dynamic disk.

D. **Incorrect:** You cannot repair the volume by selecting the volume from the failed disk. You must select a volume from a disk that is online.

E. **Correct:** To replace a stripe in a RAID-5 volume, you need a dynamic disk with unallocated space that is at least as large as the stripe to repair. If you don't have a dynamic disk with enough unallocated space, the Repair Volume command is unavailable. However, once enough unallocated space is available (through the replacement of the failed disk), you can repair the volume by regenerating the data for the orphaned member from the remaining members of the RAID-5 volume. The RAID-5 volume does not display a healthy status in Disk Management until regeneration is complete.

Configuring and Troubleshooting Windows 2000 Network Connections

The maintenance of network connections in a Microsoft Windows 2000 environment can include a variety of tasks that must be performed to ensure reliable, secure, and efficient network access. For example, you must be able to configure and troubleshoot shared access, which can include setting up shared folders, configuring share permissions, and troubleshooting connections to those shares if users are unable to access the necessary resources. In addition, some networks support **virtual private networks (VPNs)**, which are extensions of a private network that encompass encapsulated, encrypted, and authenticated links across shared or public internetworks. VPN connections can provide remote access and routed connections to private networks over the Internet. Maintaining network connections can also include installing, configuring, and troubleshooting network adapters and drivers. You should be able to install and uninstall network adapters; update drivers; and install, configure, and troubleshoot network protocols. Another aspect of maintaining network connections is to install and configure network services, which include the **Dynamic Host Configuration Protocol (DHCP)** service, the **Windows Internet Naming Service (WINS)**, and the **Domain Name System (DNS)**. Maintaining network connections can also include installing, configuring, monitoring, and troubleshooting Terminal Services, which allows client applications to be run on a server so that client computers can function as terminals rather than independent systems. The server provides a multisession environment and runs the Windows-based programs being used on the client. In addition, you should be able to configure, monitor, and troubleshoot remote access, which includes configuring inbound connections, creating and configuring remote access policies, and configuring remote access profiles.

Tested Skills and Suggested Practices

The skills that you need to successfully master the Configuring and Troubleshooting Windows 2000 Network Connections objective domain on the *Installing, Configuring, and Administering Microsoft Windows 2000 Server* exam include:

- **Setting up network shares on a Windows 2000 Server computer.**

    - Practice 1: On your Windows 2000 Server computer, create several shares on existing folders. Share a root directory and then share folders within that directory. If your system is configured with both NTFS and FAT volumes, configure shares on both volumes.

    - Practice 2: Configure permissions on the share you created in Practice 1. If necessary, create several user accounts to test the share access. Provide different levels of permissions for different users. For example, you might want to grant Read permission to user 1 and grant Full Control permission to user 2 to one of the shares. Once you have set the permissions on the different shares, try accessing those shares over the network from another computer. First log in as user 1 and then test your access to the various shares. Try just reading files and then try modifying files. Log in as a different user and repeat the process.

- **Configuring and monitoring remote access**

    - Practice 1: Use the Routing and Remote Access snap-in to enable Routing and Remote Access Service on your Windows 2000 Server computer. (The service is disabled by default.) Notice that, after you launch the Routing And Remote Access Setup wizard (which is used to enable and configure the Routing and Remote Access Service for a specific computer), you can select from five paths (configuration options) that you can follow in configuring the server. Choose the path that allows you to use the Routing and Remote Access snap-in to manually configure Routing and Remote Access Services. Once the service is enabled, examine the default remote access and router settings.

    - Practice 2: Use the Active Directory Users And Computers snap-in to allow and deny remote access to specific user accounts. To set the remote access options for an individual user, you must configure the remote access options in the user's properties. Allow at least one user account to have remote access, and deny at least one user account from having remote access.

- Practice 3: Enable accounting and configure logging on the remote access server. You must use the Routing and Remote Access snap-in to access the properties of the Local File object to configure account logging and to access the properties of the server object to configure event logging.

- Practice 4: Log on to a client computer as the user who has been provided remote access to the server that you configured in the previous practices. Configure the client computer as a dial-up client in order to access the remote access server. (The client computer will need to be configured with a modem.) Once the dial-up connection is configured, establish a dial-up connection to the remote server. Now log in to the computer as the user who has been denied access, and then try to establish a dial-up connection to the remote access server.

- Practice 5: After the first user in Practice 4 has established a dial-up connection, use the Routing And Remote Access snap-in (on the remote access server) to monitor that connection. Be sure to open the Status dialog box to view specific information about the connection.

- **Installing and configuring network adapters and their drivers.**

  - Practice 1: Install a network adapter on your Windows 2000 Server computer. If the only network adapter that you have is the one already installed on your computer, uninstall that adapter and reinstall it into the computer. Use Device Manager to verify that the device was properly installed in the computer. View the device's properties to review how it is configured.

  - Practice 2: Use Device Manager to open the Upgrade Device Driver wizard and update the device driver for the network adapter. You can actually start the wizard and search for a driver without having to replace the existing driver. To do this, cancel the wizard after the device is found.

  - Practice 3: Use Device Manager to launch the Hardware Troubleshooter for the network adapter. To launch the Troubleshooter, open the properties for the network adapter. Troubleshooter will walk you through steps to help you analyze problems you might be having. Try selecting different options to determine what steps you can take to address problems that you might be experiencing.

  - Practice 4: Open the properties for your local area connection for the network adapter that you installed in Practice 1, and then open the properties for TCP/IP. If your system permits, try changing the IP address, subnet mask, and default gateway. If you cannot change this information because of your system network, simply review the various options available and how they can be configured.

- **Installing and configuring network services.**

  - Practice 1: Install the DHCP service if it is not already installed on your Windows 2000 Server computer. Note that TCP/IP should be configured to use a static IP address and that you will need the physical address (the MAC address) of your computer. Once DHCP is installed, create a DHCP scope and add a reservation to the scope. If possible, test the DHCP configuration by using the client computer to automatically obtain an IP address. Verify that the client received an appropriate IP address from the scope. Then try adding a reservation for the client computer so that it always receives the same IP address.

  - Practice 2: Install WINS if it is not already installed on your Windows 2000 Server. After WINS is installed, configure the WINS settings in the DHCP snap-in to support WINS. If possible, test WINS settings on a client computer by releasing and renewing the DHCP lease, and then use the WINS snap-in on the WINS server to verify the registration of the client computer in the WINS database.

  - Practice 3: Use the DNS snap-in to delete the default lookup zone that was created when DNS was installed on your system. Create a forward lookup zone and a reverse lookup zone. Configure dynamic DNS to allow dynamic updates. Once DNS has been configured, use the DNS snap-in to confirm that the service is working properly by using the Monitoring tab in the server's Properties dialog box to test the configuration.

- **Installing and configuring Terminal Services and Terminal Services Licensing.**

  - Practice 1: Install Terminal Services to run in Remote Administration mode. You can install Terminal Services by using the Add/Remove Programs utility in Control Panel. Once Terminal Services is installed, run a remote administration session from another computer. Make certain that you are using the appropriate user name, password, and domain when logging on to the Terminal server from the remote computer.

  - Practice 2: Install Terminal Services Licensing on the terminal server to serve the license requirements of Application Server mode. You will need to use the Add/Remove Programs utility in Control Panel to install Terminal Services Licensing and to set up Terminal Services in Application Server mode.

  - Practice 3: If you have a second server networked to the Terminal server, install the Terminal Services client on the second server and then run a terminal screen from that server. From within the terminal session, run an application on the Terminal server.

Further Reading

This section lists supplemental readings by objective. Study these sources thoroughly before taking exam 70-215.

Objective 6.1

Microsoft Corporation. *Windows 2000 Server Resource Kit*. Volume: *Microsoft Windows 2000 Server Operations Guide*. Redmond, Washington: Microsoft Press, 2000. Review Chapter 3, "File Systems."

"Publishing a Shared Folder in Windows 2000 Active Directory." (This article can be downloaded for free at *http://support.microsoft.com/support/kb/articles/Q234/5/82.asp*.)

Microsoft Corporation. *MCSE Training Kit: Microsoft Windows 2000 Server*. Redmond, Washington: Microsoft Press, 2000. Review Lesson 4 in Chapter 4, "Microsoft Windows 2000 File Systems."

Objective 6.2

Microsoft Corporation. *Windows 2000 Server Resource Kit*. Volume: *Microsoft Windows 2000 Server Deployment Planning Guide*. Redmond, Washington: Microsoft Press, 2000. (This book can be downloaded for free at *http://www.microsoft.com/windows2000/library/resources/reskit/dpg/default.asp*.) Review Chapter 17, "Determining Windows 2000 Network Security Strategies." This chapter includes a discussion of VPNs.

Microsoft Corporation. *Windows 2000 Server Resource Kit*. Volume: *Microsoft Windows 2000 Server Internetworking Guide*. Redmond, Washington: Microsoft Press, 2000. Review Chapter 9, "Virtual Private Networking."

"Privacy Protected Network Access: Virtual Private Networking and Intranet Security." (This white paper can be downloaded for free at *http://www.microsoft.com/windows2000/library/howitworks/security/comsec.asp*.)

Microsoft Corporation. *MCSE Training Kit: Microsoft Windows 2000 Server*. Redmond, Washington: Microsoft Press, 2000. Review Lesson 4 in Chapter 10, "Routing and Remote Access Service."

"Windows 2000–Based Virtual Private Networking: Supporting VPN Operability." (This article can be downloaded for free at *http://www.microsoft.com/windows2000/library/howitworks/communications/remoteaccess/l2tp.asp*.)

"Virtual Private Networking: An Overview." (This article can be downloaded for free at *http://www.microsoft.com/windows2000/library/howitworks/communications/remoteaccess/vpnoverview.asp*.)

Objective 6.3

Microsoft Corporation. *Windows 2000 Server Resource Kit*. Volume: *Microsoft Windows 2000 Server Internetworking Guide*. Redmond, Washington: Microsoft Press, 2000. Review Chapter 12, "Interoperability with NetWare"; Chapter 13, "Services for Macintosh"; Chapter 14, "Asynchronous Transfer Mode"; Chapter 16, "NetBEUI"; and Chapter 17, "Data Link Control."

Microsoft Corporation. *Windows 2000 Server Resource Kit*. Volume: *Microsoft Windows 2000 Server TCP/IP Core Networking Guide*. Redmond, Washington: Microsoft Press, 2000. Review Chapter 1, "Introduction to TCP/IP"; Chapter 2, "Windows 2000 TCP/IP"; Chapter 3, "TCP/IP Troubleshooting"; and Appendix B, "Windows 2000 Network Architecture."

"Microsoft Windows 2000 TCP/IP Implementation Details." (This white paper can be downloaded for free at *http://www.microsoft.com/windows2000/library/howitworks/communications/networkbasics/tcpip_implement.asp*.)

Microsoft Corporation. *MCSE Training Kit: Microsoft Windows 2000 Server*. Redmond, Washington: Microsoft Press, 2000. Review Lessons 1 and 2 in Chapter 9, "Network Protocols and Services."

Objective 6.4

"Dynamic Host Configuration Protocol for Windows 2000 Server." (This white paper can be downloaded for free at *http://www.microsoft.com/windows2000/library/howitworks/communications/nameadrmgmt/dhcp.asp*.)

Microsoft Corporation. *Windows 2000 Server Resource Kit*. Volume: *Microsoft Windows 2000 Server TCP/IP Core Networking Guide*. Redmond, Washington: Microsoft Press, 2000. Review Chapter 4, "Dynamic Host Configuration Protocol"; Chapter 5, "Introduction to DNS"; Chapter 6, "Windows 2000 DNS"; and Chapter 7, "Windows Internet Naming Service."

Microsoft Corporation. *MCSE Training Kit: Microsoft Windows 2000 Server*. Redmond, Washington: Microsoft Press, 2000. Review Lessons 3, 4, and 5 in Chapter 9, "Network Protocols and Services."

"Windows 2000 DNS White Paper." (This article can be downloaded for free at *http://www.microsoft.com/windows2000/library/howitworks/communications/nameadrmgmt/w2kdns.asp*.)

"Windows 2000 Domain Name System Overview." (This article can be downloaded for free at *http://www.microsoft.com/windows2000/library/howitworks/communications/nameadrmgmt/dnsover.asp*.)

"Windows 2000 Server Windows Internet Naming Service (WINS) Overview." (This article can be downloaded for free at *http://www.microsoft.com/windows2000/library/ howitworks/communications/nameadrmgmt/wins.asp*.)

Objective 6.5

"Connecting Remote Users to Your Network." (This article can be downloaded for free at *http://www.microsoft.com/windows2000/library/planning/incremental/ connectremote.asp*.)

Microsoft Corporation. *Windows 2000 Server Resource Kit*. Volume: *Microsoft Windows 2000 Server Internetworking Guide*. Redmond, Washington: Microsoft Press, 2000. Review Chapter 7, "Remote Access Server"; Chapter 8, "Internet Authentication Service"; and Chapter 9, "Virtual Private Networking."

Microsoft Corporation. *MCSE Training Kit: Microsoft Windows 2000 Server*. Redmond, Washington: Microsoft Press, 2000. Review Lessons 1, 2, 3, 4, and 5 in Chapter 10, "Routing and Remote Access Service."

Objective 6.6

"Exploring Terminal Services." (This article can be downloaded for free at *http://www.microsoft.com/windows2000/guide/server/features/terminalsvcs.asp*.) This document provides links to many detailed articles about Terminal Services.

Microsoft Corporation. *Windows 2000 Server Resource Kit*. Volume: *Microsoft Windows 2000 Server Deployment Planning Guide*. Redmond, Washington: Microsoft Press, 2000. (This book can be downloaded for free at *http://www.microsoft.com/ windows2000/library/resources/reskit/dpg/default.asp*.) Review Chapter 16, "Deploying Terminal Services."

Microsoft Corporation. *MCSE Training Kit: Microsoft Windows 2000 Server*. Redmond, Washington: Microsoft Press, 2000. Review Lesson 4 in Chapter 14, "Microsoft Windows 2000 Application Servers."

Objective 6.7

Microsoft Corporation. *Windows 2000 Server Resource Kit*. Volume: *Microsoft Windows 2000 Server Operations Guide*. Redmond, Washington: Microsoft Press, 2000. Review Chapter 14, "Troubleshooting."

"Plug and Play." (This white paper can be downloaded for free at *http:// www.microsoft.com/windows2000/library/howitworks/hardware/plugnplay.asp*.)

Microsoft Corporation. *MCSE Training Kit: Microsoft Windows 2000 Server*. Redmond, Washington: Microsoft Press, 2000. Review Lesson 1 in Chapter 12, "Reliability and Availability."

"Troubleshooting Tools and Strategies." (This article can be downloaded for free at *http://www.microsoft.com/windows2000/library/resources/reskit/samplechapters/pref/ pref_tts_juhe.asp*.) Although this document is taken from the *Windows 2000 Professional Resource Kit*, it provides useful information about hardware devices, their drivers, and driver signing.

Willis, Will, David Watts, and Tillman Strahan. *Windows 2000 System Administration Handbook*. Upper Saddle River, New Jersey: Prentice-Hall Professional Technical Reference, 2000. Chapter 5, "Using the Windows Control Panel." (This document can be downloaded for free at *http://microsoft.com/technet/win2000/usingthe.asp*.) This document includes a discussion about the Add/Remove Hardware wizard and about hardware profiles.

O B J E C T I V E   6 . 1

Install, configure, and troubleshoot shared access.

To make folders and their contents available to users over a network, you must **share** the folders so that you can control access to the resources within the folders. You can share folders on a **FAT** or an **NTFS** partition. When a folder is shared, users can connect to the folder over the network and gain access to the files it contains. These files can include applications, data, or home folders. When you share a folder, you can give it a share name, provide comments to describe the folder and its contents, limit the number of users who have access to the folder, assign permissions, and share the same folder multiple times.

After you share a folder, you should specify which users have access to the shared folder. You can assign shared folder permissions to selected user accounts and groups. Unlike NTFS permissions, shared folder permissions apply only to folders, not individual files. In addition, shared folder permissions apply only to users who connect to the folder over the network. They do not restrict access to users who access the folder at the computer where it is stored. Shared folder permissions are the only way to secure network resources on a FAT volume, whereas NTFS volumes allow you to use shared folder permissions and NTFS permissions. When you share a folder, the Everyone group is granted Full Control permission to all content within the folder. You can allow or deny shared folder permissions to individual users or to user groups. However, you should deny permissions only when it is necessary to override permissions that are being allowed. Denying permissions takes precedence over the permissions that you allow.

To answer the questions in this objective, you should know how to share a folder and how to configure permissions on a shared folder to allow or deny access. You should also be familiar with how permissions are applied to a user who has been granted multiple permissions. You should also be familiar with the administrative shared folders that are created automatically in Windows 2000. In addition, you should know how to modify the properties of a shared folder after that share has been created.

Objective 6.1 Questions

70-215.06.01.001

Your Windows 2000 Server computer includes two NTFS volumes: the D: drive and the E: drive. The D:\Accounting folder is shared, and the Managers group has been granted the Full Control shared folder permission to the folder. The Managers group has also been granted the Full Control NTFS permission to the D: drive and its contents and the Read NTFS permission to the E: drive and its contents. The E: drive is not shared. You want to move the D:\Accounting folder to the E: drive. Which type of permission will network users who are members of the Managers group be granted to the E:\Accounting folder?

A. Read NTFS permission.

B. Full Control NTFS permission.

C. Full Control shared folder permission.

D. Network users who are members of the Managers group will not be able to access the folder after it is moved.

70-215.06.01.002

Your Windows 2000 Server computer includes two NTFS volumes: the D: drive and the E: drive. The D:\Accounting folder is shared, and the Managers group has been granted the Full Control shared folder permission to the folder. The Managers group has also been granted the Full Control NTFS permission to the D: drive and its contents and the Read NTFS permission to the E: drive and its contents. The E: drive is not shared. You want to copy the D:\Accounting folder to the E: drive. Which type of permission will network users who are members of the Managers group be granted to the E:\Accounting folder?

A. Read NTFS permission.

B. Full Control NTFS permission.

C. Full Control shared folder permission.

D. Network users who are members of the Managers group will not be able to access the folder after it is moved.

70-215.06.01.003

The hard disk on your Windows 2000 Server computer is configured with an NTFS volume (C:) that contains the Accounting folder. Jo Brown is the primary network user who accesses the contents in the folder. The folder is shared, and the Everyone group has been granted the Read shared folder permission to the folder, the Managers group has been granted the Change shared folder permission to the folder, and the Resource group has been granted Full Control shared folder permission to the folder. Jo is a member of the Resource group. The Everyone group has also been granted the Full Control NTFS permission on the C: drive and its contents.

Jo works on a Windows 2000 Professional client computer. The hard disk is configured with a FAT32 volume (D:) that is not shared. Jo is the only user who has local access to the computer and all its contents. You want to move the C:\Accounting folder to the D: drive on Jo's computer. Who will be able to access the Accounting folder after it is moved?

A. Jo

B. Members of the Resource group

C. Members of the Managers group

D. Members of the Everyone group

70-215.06.01.004

The hard disk on your Windows 2000 Server computer is configured with an NTFS volume (C:) that contains the Accounting folder. The folder is shared and is configured with the following shared folder permissions: The Bookkeeping group has been granted the Full Control permission, the Managers group has been granted the Change permission, the Everyone group has been granted the Read permission, and the Resource group has been denied the Full Control permission. In addition, all four groups have been granted the Full Control NTFS permission to the C: drive and its contents. Which network users can modify documents in the Accounting folder? (Choose all that apply.)

A. Members of the Bookkeeping group

B. Members of the Managers group

C. Members of the Everyone group

D. Members of the Resource group

70-215.06.01.005

The hard disk on your Windows 2000 Server computer is configured with an NTFS volume (C:) that contains the Accounting folder. The Accounting folder contains three subfolders: Managers, Accountants, and AdminAssts. The folder is shared, and the Everyone group has been granted the Read shared folder permission. In addition, the Everyone group has been granted the Full Control NTFS permission to the C: drive and its contents. What content can network users who are members of the Everyone group view?

A. All content of the Accounting folder, including the subfolder names and content

B. Content in the Accounting folder and names of the subfolders, but not content in the subfolders

C. The names of the subfolders and their content, but not content in the Accounting folder

D. The names of the subfolders, but not content in the Accounting folder or in the subfolders

Objective 6.1 Answers

70-215.06.01.001

▶ **Correct Answers: D**

A. **Incorrect:** When a folder is moved from one NTFS volume to another, the folder and its contents inherit the permissions that are set for the destination folder. In this case, the Managers group would be granted the Read NTFS permission. However, when you move a shared folder, the folder is no longer shared, and network users cannot access the folder. Sharing a folder is the only way to make that folder and its contents available over the network.

B. **Incorrect:** When a folder is moved from one NTFS volume to another, the folder and its contents inherit the permissions that are set for the destination folder. In this case, the Managers group would be granted the Read NTFS permission, not the Full Control NTFS permission. However, because the folder is no longer shared, network users cannot access the folder.

C. **Incorrect:** When you move a shared folder, the folder is no longer shared, and network users cannot access the folder.

D. **Correct:** Network users will not be able to access the folder because it is no longer shared. After you move the folder, you must create a share and set the appropriate permissions, which include the shared folder permissions and NTFS permissions. When a folder is moved from one NTFS volume to another, the folder and its contents inherit the permissions that are set for the destination folder. In this case, the Managers group would be granted the Read NTFS permission. In addition, even if you then grant the Managers group the Full Control shared folder permission to the Accounting folder, users of that group will still be limited by the Read NTFS permission that the folder inherited when it was moved. When shared folder permissions are configured for a folder and NTFS permissions are configured for folders or files within the shared folder, the most restrictive rights will become the user's effective rights to the resource. Consequently, you must modify the NTFS permission to grant the proper access to the users. In general, you should use either shared folder permissions or NTFS permissions on individual resources, but not both. NTFS permissions are preferred when applicable because permissions can be set on both files and folders within the share, and not just on the share as a whole.

70-215.06.01.002

▶ **Correct Answers: D**

A. **Incorrect:** When a folder is copied from one NTFS volume to another, the new folder and its contents inherit the permissions that are set for the destination folder. In this case, the Managers group would be granted the Read NTFS permission. However, when you copy a shared folder, the original shared folder is still shared, but the copy is not shared, and network users will not be able to access the new folder. Sharing a folder is the only way to make that folder and its contents available over the network.

B. **Incorrect:** When a folder is copied from one NTFS volume to another, the new folder and its contents inherit the permissions that are set for the destination folder. In this case, the Managers group would be granted the Read NTFS permission, not the Full Control NTFS permission. However, because the folder is not shared, network users cannot access the folder.

C. **Incorrect:** When you copy a shared folder, the new folder is no longer shared, and network users cannot access the folder.

D. **Correct:** Network users will not be able to access the folder because it is no longer shared. After you copy the folder, you must create a share and set the appropriate permissions, which include the shared folder permissions and NTFS permissions. When a folder is moved from one NTFS volume to another, the folder and its contents inherit the permissions that are set for the destination folder. In this case, the Managers group would be granted the Read NTFS permission. In addition, even if you then grant the Managers group the Full Control shared folder permission to the Accounting folder, users of that group will still be limited by the Read NTFS permission that the folder inherited when it was moved. When shared folder permissions are configured for a folder and NTFS permissions are configured for folders or files within the shared folder, the most restrictive rights will become the user's effective rights to the resource. Consequently, you must modify the NTFS permission to grant the proper access to the users. In general, you should use either shared folder permissions or NTFS permissions on individual resources, but not both. NTFS permissions are preferred when applicable because permissions can be set on both files and folders within the share, and not just on the share as a whole.

70-215.06.01.003

▶ **Correct Answers: A**

A. **Correct:** When you move a shared folder, the folder is no longer shared, and network users cannot access the folder. Sharing a folder is the only way to make that folder and its contents available over the network. After you move the folder, you must create a share and set the appropriate permissions if you want network users to be able to access the share. However, Jo can access the folder without creating a share because she is the local user on the computer and has access to the computer and its contents. In addition, NTFS permissions are not a consideration; when folders or files are moved from an NTFS volume to a FAT volume, the files and folders lose their NTFS permission because FAT volumes do not support NTFS permissions.

B. **Incorrect:** Network users will not be able to access the folder because it is no longer shared. In addition, members of the Resource group cannot access the folder locally because they have not been granted local access to the computer and its contents.

C. **Incorrect:** Network users will not be able to access the folder because it is no longer shared. In addition, members of the Managers group cannot access the folder locally because they have not been granted local access to the computer and its contents.

D. **Incorrect:** Network users will not be able to access the folder because it is no longer shared. In addition, members of the Everyone group cannot access the folder locally because they have not been granted local access to the computer and its contents.

70-215.06.01.004

▶ **Correct Answers: A and B**

A. **Correct:** The Full Control shared folder permission allows users to change file permission, take ownership of files, and perform all tasks permitted by the Change permission. The Change permission allows users to create folders, add files to folders, change data in files, append data to files, change file attributes, delete folders and files, and perform all tasks permitted by the Read permission. The Read permission allows users to display folder names, filenames, file data, and attributes; run program files; and change folders within the shared folder. When shared folder and NTFS permissions are both configured, the most restrictive permissions apply. In this case, the shared folder permission and NTFS permission are Full Control, so the users are granted Full Control access.

B. **Correct:** The Change permission allows users to create folders, add files to folders, change data in files, append data to files, change file attributes, delete folders and files, and perform all tasks permitted by the Read permission. The Read permission allows users to display folder names, filenames, file data, and attributes; run program files; and change folders within the shared folder. When shared folder and NTFS permissions are both configured, the most restrictive permissions apply. In this case, the shared folder permission is Change, and NTFS permission is Full Control, so the users are granted Change access.

C. **Incorrect:** The Read permission allows users to display folder names, filenames, file data, and attributes; run program files; and change folders within the shared folder. When shared folder and NTFS permissions are both configured, the most restrictive permissions apply. In this case, the shared folder permission is Read, and NTFS permission is Full Control, so the users are granted Read access.

D. **Incorrect:** The Resource group is denied access to the folder. When shared folder and NTFS permissions are both configured, the most restrictive permissions apply. In this case, the shared folder permission is to deny Full Control, and NTFS permission is Full Control, so the users are denied Full Control.

70-215.06.01.005

▶ **Correct Answers: A**

A. **Correct:** Members of the Everyone group can view all content in the folder, including the subfolder names and content. When a folder is shared, users can connect to the folder over the network and gain access to the files and folders that it contains. However, to gain access to the files, users must have permissions to access the shared folders. In this case, users have the Read shared folder permission. The Read permission allows users to display folder names, filenames, file data, and attributes; run program files; and change folders within the shared folder. When shared folder and NTFS permissions are both configured, the most restrictive permissions apply. Because the shared folder permission is Read and NTFS permission is Full Control, users are granted Read access to all content in the folder.

B. **Incorrect:** Members of the Everyone group can view all content in the folder, including the subfolder names and content.

C. **Incorrect:** Members of the Everyone group can view all content in the folder, including the subfolder names and content.

D. **Incorrect:** Members of the Everyone group can view all content in the folder, including the subfolder names and content.

OBJECTIVE 6.2

Install, configure, and troubleshoot a virtual private network (VPN).

A virtual private network (VPN) is a set of computers on a shared network or a public network, such as the Internet, that use encryption technology to communicate among themselves. A VPN is an extension of the private network that encompasses encapsulated, encrypted, and authenticated links across networks. The VPN mimics the properties of a dedicated private network, allowing users to connect securely to a remote server by using the routing infrastructure provided by the public internetwork. From the user's perspective, the VPN is a point-to-point connection between the user's computer and the remote server. The secure connection across the internetwork appears to the user as a virtual network interface providing private network communication. The VPN connection logically operates as a dedicated WAN link. The nature of the internetwork is not relevant because the data appears as though it is being sent over a dedicated private link.

Point-to-point connections can be simulated through the use of **tunneling**, which is a method of using an internetwork infrastructure to transfer a payload. The process of tunneling includes the encapsulation and the transmission of packets. The logical path through which the encapsulated packets travel the transit internetwork is called a **tunnel**. There are two basic types of tunnels: voluntary and compulsory. Voluntary tunnels are configured and created through a conscious action by the user at the tunnel client computer. Compulsory tunnels are configured and created automatically for users without their knowledge or intervention. Windows 2000 uses several protocols to support tunneling: **Point-to-Point Tunneling Protocol (PPTP)**, **Layer 2 Tunneling Protocol (L2TP)**, **IP Security (IPSec)**, and **IP-IP**. These protocols may work together or independently of one another.

To answer the questions in this objective, you should have a basic understanding of how VPNs and tunneling are supported in Windows 2000 Server. You should be familiar with the different types of tunnels and the primary protocols used by Windows 2000 for VPN access. In addition, you should know how to set up and manage virtual private networking and how to troubleshoot VPNs.

Objective 6.2 Questions

70-215.06.02.001

As the network administrator, you must configure the network so that 10 executives who work at home can connect to the corporate Windows 2000 network. The executives use Windows 2000 Professional desktop computers.

You must meet the following requirements:

- You must allow the executives to connect to the corporate network through the Internet.

- You must use PPP encryption.

- You must use a protocol that provides tunnel authentication.

- You must use a protocol that secures data between the endpoints of the tunnel.

You configure a virtual private network that uses PPTP.

Which requirement or requirements are met? (Choose all that apply.)

A. The executives can connect to the network through the Internet.

B. PPP encryption is used.

C. Tunnel authentication is provided.

D. Data between the endpoints of the tunnel is secured.

70-215.06.02.002

As the network administrator, you must configure the network so that 10 executives who work at home can connect to the corporate Windows 2000 network. The executives use Windows 2000 Professional desktop computers.

You must meet the following requirements:

- You must allow the executives to connect to the corporate network through the Internet.

- You must use PPP encryption.

- You must use a protocol that provides tunnel authentication.

- You must use a protocol that secures data between the endpoints of the tunnel.

You plan to configure a virtual private network that uses L2TP.

Which requirement or requirements are met? (Choose all that apply.)

A. The executives can connect to the network through the Internet.

B. PPP encryption is used.

C. Tunnel authentication is provided.

D. Data between the endpoints of the tunnel is secured.

70-215.06.02.003

As the network administrator, you must configure the network so that 10 executives who work at home can connect to the corporate Windows 2000 network. The executives use Windows 2000 Professional desktop computers.

You must meet the following requirements:

- You must allow the executives to connect to the corporate network through the Internet.

- You must use PPP encryption.

- You must use a protocol that provides tunnel authentication.

- You must use a protocol that encrypts and encapsulates entire datagram packets for secure transmissions.

You configure a virtual private network that uses L2TP and the IPSec Encapsulated Security Payload (ESP) tunnel mode.

Which requirement or requirements are met? (Choose all that apply.)

A. The executives can connect to the network through the Internet.

B. PPP encryption is used.

C. Tunnel authentication is provided.

D. The entire datagram packets are encrypted and encapsulated for secure transmissions.

Objective 6.2 Answers

70-215.06.02.001

▶ **Correct Answers: A, B, and D**

A. **Correct:** Virtual private networks allow users working at home or on the road to connect securely to a remote corporate server by using the routing infrastructure provided by a public internetwork such as the Internet. The VPN acts as an extension of the private network and enables users to send data between two computers across the internetwork in a manner that emulates the properties of a point-to-point private link. To facilitate this connection, the computers must use a protocol, such as PPTP, that supports virtual private networking in Windows 2000. PPTP encapsulates Point-to-Point Protocol (PPP) frames into IP datagrams for transmission over an IP internetwork. PPTP uses a TCP connection to create, maintain, and terminate the tunnel and uses a modified version of Generic Routing Encapsulation (GRE) to encapsulate PPP frames as tunneled data. The payloads of the encapsulated PPP frames can be encrypted or compressed or both.

B. **Correct:** PPTP uses PPP encryption to encrypt data. The PPP frame is encrypted with Microsoft Point-to-Point Encryption (MPPE) by using encryption keys generated from the Microsoft Challenge Handshake Authentication Protocol (MS-CHAP) or Extensible Authentication Protocol-Transport Level Security (EAP-TLS) authentication process. Virtual private networking clients must use either the MS-CHAP or EAP-TLS authentication protocol to encrypt PPP payloads.

C. **Incorrect:** Unlike L2TP, PPTP does not provide tunnel authentication. Tunnel authentication in L2TP provides a way to authenticate the endpoints of a tunnel during the tunnel establishment process. By default, Windows 2000 does not perform L2TP tunnel authentication.

D. **Correct:** PPTP uses PPP encryption to secure data between the endpoints of a tunnel. In Windows 2000, PPP encryption can be used only when the authentication protocol is Extensible Authentication Protocol-Transport Level Security (EAP-TLS) or Microsoft Challenge Handshake Authentication Protocol (MS-CHAP). The PPP payloads are encrypted by using Microsoft Point-to-Point Encryption (MPPE), which provides encryption between the endpoints of the tunnel. MPPE does not provide end-to-end encryption. End-to-end encryption is data encryption between the client application and the server hosting the resource or service being accessed by the client application. If end-to-end encryption is required, IPSec should be used to encrypt IP traffic after the PPTP tunnel is established.

70-215.06.02.002

▶ **Correct Answers: A and C**

A. **Correct:** Virtual private networks allow users working at home or on the road to connect securely to a remote corporate server by using the routing infrastructure provided by a public internetwork such as the Internet. The VPN acts as an extension of the private network and enables users to send data between two computers across the internetwork in a manner that emulates the properties of a point-to-point private link. To facilitate this connection, the computers must use a protocol, such as L2TP, that supports virtual private networking in Windows 2000. L2TP is a combination of PPTP and Layer 2 Forwarding (L2F) that can be used as a tunneling protocol over the Internet or in private LAN-to-LAN networking. L2TP is very similar to PPTP in function. An L2TP tunnel is created between an L2TP client and an L2TP server. However, L2TP inherits PPP compression but not encryption.

B. **Incorrect:** L2TP uses IPSec to encrypt data, not PPP. IPSec, a layer 3 protocol, is a series of standards that support the secured transfer of information across an IP internetwork. IPSec Encapsulation Security Payload (ESP) Tunnel mode supports the encapsulation and encryption of entire IP datagrams for secure transfer across a private or public IP internetwork. With IPSec ESP Tunnel mode, a complete IP datagram is encapsulated and encrypted with ESP.

C. **Correct:** Unlike PPTP, L2TP provides tunnel authentication. Tunnel authentication in L2TP provides a way to authenticate the endpoints of a tunnel during the tunnel establishment process. By default, Windows 2000 does not perform L2TP tunnel authentication.

D. **Incorrect:** L2TP, by itself, does not encrypt data. Unlike PPTP, L2TP does not inherit PPP encryption because PPP encryption does not meet the security requirements of L2TP. Data encryption is provided by using IPSec Encapsulated Security Payload (ESP) tunnel mode along with L2TP. ESP tunnel mode supports the encapsulation and encryption of entire datagrams for secure transfer across a private or public IP internetwork.

70-215.06.02.003

▶ **Correct Answers: A, C, and D**

A. **Correct:** Virtual private networks allow users working at home or on the road to connect securely to a remote corporate server by using the routing infrastructure provided by a public internetwork such as the Internet. The VPN acts as an extension of the private network and enables users to send data between two computers across the internetwork in a manner that emulates the properties of a point-to-point private link. To facilitate this connection, the computers must use a protocol, such as L2TP, that supports virtual private networking in Windows 2000. L2TP is a combination of PPTP and Layer 2 Forwarding (L2F) that can be used as a tunneling protocol over the Internet or in private LAN-to-LAN networking. L2TP is very similar to PPTP in function. An L2TP tunnel is created between an L2TP client and an L2TP server. However, L2TP inherits PPP compression but not encryption.

B. **Incorrect:** L2TP uses IPSec to encrypt data, not PPP. IPSec, a layer 3 protocol, is a series of standards that support the secured transfer of information across an IP internetwork. IPSec Encapsulation Security Payload (ESP) Tunnel mode supports the encapsulation and encryption of entire IP datagrams for secure transfer across a private or public IP internetwork. With IPSec ESP Tunnel mode, a complete IP datagram is encapsulated and encrypted with ESP.

C. **Correct:** Unlike PPTP, L2TP provides tunnel authentication. Tunnel authentication in L2TP provides a way to authenticate the endpoints of a tunnel during the tunnel establishment process. By default, Windows 2000 does not perform L2TP tunnel authentication.

D. **Correct:** L2TP, by itself, does not encrypt data. Unlike PPTP, L2TP does not inherit PPP encryption because PPP encryption does not meet the security requirements of L2TP. Data encryption is provided by using IPSec Encapsulated Security Payload (ESP) tunnel mode along with L2TP. IPSec, a layer 3 tunneling protocol, is a series of standards that support the secured transfer of information across an IP internetwork. ESP tunnel mode supports the encapsulation and encryption of entire datagrams. With IPSec ESP tunnel mode, a complete IP datagram is encapsulated and encrypted with ESP. The result is then encapsulated with a plain text IP header and sent on the transit internetwork. Upon receipt of the encrypted datagram, the tunnel server processes and discards the clear text IP header and authenticates and decrypts the ESP packet containing the IP datagram. The IP datagram is then processed normally.

O B J E C T I V E   6 . 3

Install, configure, and troubleshoot network protocols.

Windows 2000 supports a number of network **protocols** that make it possible for networks to share information. A protocol is a set of rules and conventions for sending information over the network. Protocols are specifications for standardized packets of data that are moved up and down the protocol stack and across the transmission media. They can be added or deleted as necessary and selectively bound to all network adapters in a server. Protocol binding order, which is initially determined by the order in which the protocols were installed, can be changed at any time on a per-adapter basis, allowing a greater degree of control of network traffic. In addition, network services can be selectively enabled or disabled on a per-adapter or per-protocol basis or any combination thereof. This selectivity provides administrators with fine control over networking configuration and allows them to manage security configurations with minimal difficulty.

Among the protocols supported by Windows 2000 is **Transmission Control Protocol/ Internet Protocol (TCP/IP)**, which Windows 2000 uses for logon, file and print services, replication between domain controllers, and other common functions. TCP/IP is an industry-standard suite of protocols that enables enterprise networking and connectivity on Windows 2000–based computers. TCP/IP also provides communication across networks that contain computers with various hardware architecture and operating systems. In addition to TCP/IP, Windows 2000 supports a number of other network protocols, including **Asynchronous Transfer Mode (ATM)**, **NWLink**, **NetBEUI**, **AppleTalk**, **Data Link Control (DLC)**, and **IrDA**. ATM is an advanced implementation of packet switching that is ideal for voice, video, and data communications. NWLink is Microsoft's implementation of the Novell NetWare **Internet Packet Exchange/Sequenced Packet Exchange (IPX/SPX)** protocol, which Windows 2000 most commonly uses in environments that include NetWare servers. NetBEUI was originally developed for small department LANs and provides compatibility with existing LANs that use the NetBEUI protocol. AppleTalk, a protocol suite developed by the Apple Computer Corporation, allows Windows 2000 Server computers and Macintosh clients to share files and printers. The DLC protocol was developed for IBM mainframe communications and is used by Windows 2000 to print to Hewlett-Packard printers that use the DLC protocol. IrDA is a group of short-range, high-speed, bidirectional wireless infrared protocols that allow a variety of devices to communicate with one another.

To answer the questions in this objective, you should be familiar with the primary protocols supported by Windows 2000. You should know how to add and delete protocols, change the binding order, and configure the properties for each protocol. In addition, you should be particularly attentive to TCP/IP and know how to configure TCP/IP addressing information and troubleshoot TCP/IP connectivity by using the TCP/IP utility included with Windows 2000.

Objective 6.3 Questions

70-215.06.03.001

Your company has been assigned a network ID of 132.132.0.0. Your network has five subnets. The maximum number of hosts per subnet is 8000, and the minimum number of hosts per subnet is 6500. Which subnet mask should you use for the network?

A. 255.255.192.0

B. 255.255.224.0

C. 255.255.240.0

D. 255.255.248.0

70-215.06.03.002

Your company has been assigned a network ID of 197.132.240.0. Your network has five subnets. The maximum number of hosts per subnet is 25. Which subnet mask should you use for the network?

A. 255.255.255.192

B. 255.255.255.224

C. 255.255.255.240

D. 255.255.255.248

70-215.06.03.003

Your company has been assigned a network ID of 135.132.0.0. Your network has three subnets. The first subnet has 15,000 computers, and the second subnet has 12,000 hosts. Which subnet mask should you use for the network?

A. 255.255.192.0

B. 255.255.224.0

C. 255.255.240.0

D. 255.255.248.0

70-215.06.03.004

Your company has been assigned a network ID of 121.0.0.0. Your network has 200 subnets. The maximum number of hosts per subnet is 35,000. Which subnet mask should you use for the network?

A. 255.192.0.0

B. 255.252.0.0

C. 255.254.0.0

D. 255.255.0.0

70-215.06.03.005

After configuring a Windows 2000 network with the TCP/IP protocol, you add a NetWare 3.12 server to the network. None of the Windows 2000 computers can connect to the NetWare server. How can you resolve this problem with the least administrative effort?

A. Ensure that each Windows computer is configured with the same frame type as the NetWare server.

B. Install Gateway Service for NetWare and Client Service for NetWare on the Windows computers as appropriate.

C. Remove TCP/IP from all computers, and install NWLink as the only protocol.

D. Change the frame type on the NetWare server to 802.3.

70-215.06.03.006

Your local area network consists of two Windows 2000 Server computers, five Windows 2000 Professional computers, and one NetWare 4.0 server. You must configure your network so that it uses a single protocol. In addition, each Windows 2000 Professional computer must be able to access the file, print, and directory services directly on the NetWare computer. How should you configure the computers in your network? (Choose all that apply.)

A. Configure all computers to use the TCP/IP protocol.

B. Configure all computers to use the NWLink protocol.

C. Configure the Windows 2000 Professional computers with Client Service for NetWare.

D. Configure the Windows 2000 Professional computers with Gateway Service for NetWare.

70-215.06.03.007

You are integrating 3 Windows 2000 Server computers and 100 Windows 2000 Professional computers into your NetWare 5.0 network. The network contains two NetWare servers and 200 NetWare clients.

You want to achieve the following results:

- A single protocol must be used for the entire network.

- The Windows 2000 Professional computers must be able to access files directly on the NetWare servers.

- The Windows 2000 Server computers must act as print servers for the NetWare clients.

You install the NWLink protocol on all computers.

Which result or results does your installation achieve? (Choose all that apply.)

A. A single protocol is used for the entire network.

B. The Windows 2000 Professional computers can directly access files on the NetWare servers.

C. The Windows 2000 Server computers can act as print servers for the NetWare clients.

D. The solution does not achieve any of the required results.

70-215.06.03.008

You are integrating 3 Windows 2000 Server computers and 100 Windows 2000 Professional computers into your NetWare 5.0 network. The network contains two NetWare servers and 200 NetWare clients.

You want to achieve the following results:

- A single protocol must be used for the entire network.

- The Windows 2000 Professional computers must be able to access files directly on the NetWare servers.

- The Windows 2000 Server computers must act as print servers for the NetWare clients.

You install TCP/IP on all computers and install Client Service for NetWare on the Windows 2000 Professional computers.

Which result or results does your installation achieve? (Choose all that apply.)

A. A single protocol is used for the entire network.

B. The Windows 2000 Professional computers can directly access files on the NetWare servers.

C. The Windows 2000 Server computers can act as print servers for the NetWare clients.

D. The solution does not achieve any of the required results.

70-215.06.03.009

You are integrating 3 Windows 2000 Server computers and 100 Windows 2000 Professional computers into your NetWare 5.0 network. The network contains two NetWare servers and 200 NetWare clients.

You want to achieve the following results:

- A single protocol must be used for the entire network.

- The Windows 2000 Professional computers must be able to access files directly on the NetWare servers.

- The Windows 2000 Server computers must act as print servers for the NetWare clients.

You install the NWLink protocol on all computers and install Client Service for NetWare on Windows 2000 Professional computers.

Which result or results does your installation achieve? (Choose all that apply.)

A. A single protocol is used for the entire network.

B. The Windows 2000 Professional computers can directly access files on the NetWare servers.

C. The Windows 2000 Server computers can act as print servers for the NetWare clients.

D. The solution does not achieve any of the required results.

Objective 6.3 Answers

70-215.06.03.001

▶ **Correct Answers: B**

A. **Incorrect:** The subnet mask should be 255.255.224.0, not 255.255.192.0. A subnet mask of 255.255.192.0 on a class B network (132.132.0.0) will support up to four subnets only, although each subnet will support up to 16,382 hosts.

B. **Correct:** A network ID of 132.132.0.0 is a class B network. A class B network falls in the range of 128.0.0.0 to 191.255.0.0. The 2 high-order bits of a class B network ID are always set to 1 0. The next 14 bits (completing the first two octets) identify the remaining portion of a class B network ID. In this case, the first two octets of the network ID are 132.132, which translates to a binary value of 10000100 10000100. The default subnet mask of a class B network is 255.255.0.0 (binary 11111111 11111111 00000000 00000000), indicating that the first two octets define the network ID. The remaining two octets can be used to define which bits should be used to identify the network's subnetting structure and which should be used to identify the hosts on those subnets. For a class B network, a subnet mask of 255.255.224.0 (binary 11111111 11111111 11100000 00000000) indicates that the first two octets and the first 3 bits of the third octet identify the subnetted network ID. The remaining 13 bits identify the hosts on that subnet. Because 3 bits are used to define the subnetting structure of this class B network, the network will support up to eight subnets and up to 8190 hosts per subnet.

C. **Incorrect:** The subnet mask should be 255.255.224.0, not 255.255.240.0. Although a subnet mask of 255.255.240.0 on a class B network (132.132.0.0) will support up to 16 subnets, it will support only 4094 hosts per subnet.

D. **Incorrect:** The subnet mask should be 255.255.224.0, not 255.255.248.0. Although a subnet mask of 255.255.248.0 on a class B network (132.132.0.0) will support up to 32 subnets, it will support only 2046 hosts per subnet.

70-215.06.03.002

▶ **Correct Answers: B**

A. **Incorrect:** The subnet mask should be 255.255.255.224, not 255.255.255.192. A subnet mask of 255.255.255.192 on a class C network (197.132.240.0) will support up to four subnets only, although each subnet will support up to 62 hosts.

B. **Correct:** A network ID of 197.132.240.0 is a class C network. A class C network falls in the range of 192.0.0.0 to 223.255.255.0. The 3 high-order bits of a class C network ID are always set to 1 1 0. The next 21 bits (completing the first three octets) identify the remaining portion of a class C network ID. In this case, the first three octets of the network ID are 197.132.240, which translates to a binary value of 11000101 10000100 11110000. The default subnet mask of a class C network is 255.255.255.0 (binary 11111111 11111111 11111111 00000000), indicating that the first three octets define the network ID. The remaining octet can be used to define which bits should be used to identify the network's subnetting structure and which should be used to identify the hosts on those subnets. For a class C network, a subnet mask of 255.255.255.224 (binary 11111111 11111111 11111111 11100000) indicates that the first three octets and the first 3 bits of the last octet identify the subnetted network ID. The remaining 5 bits identify the hosts on that subnet. Because 3 bits are used to define the subnetting structure of this class C network, the network will support up to eight subnets and up to 30 hosts per subnet.

C. **Incorrect:** The subnet mask should be 255.255.255.224, not 255.255.255.240. Although a subnet mask of 255.255.255.240 on a class C network (197.132.240.0) will support up to 16 subnets, it will support only 14 hosts per subnet.

D. **Incorrect:** The subnet mask should be 255.255.255.224, not 255.255.255.248. Although a subnet mask of 255.255.255.248 on a class C network (197.132.240.0) will support up to 32 subnets, it will support only six hosts per subnet.

70-215.06.03.003

▶ **Correct Answers: A**

A. **Correct:** A network ID of 135.132.0.0 is a class B network. A class B network falls in the range of 128.0.0.0 to 191.255.0.0. The 2 high-order bits of a class B network ID are always set to 1 0. The next 14 bits (completing the first two octets) identify the remaining portion of a class B network ID. In this case, the first two octets of the network ID are 135.132, which translates to a binary value of 10000111 10000100. The default subnet mask of a class B network is 255.255.0.0 (binary 11111111 11111111 00000000 00000000), indicating that the first two octets define the network ID. The remaining two octets can be used to define which bits should be used to identify the network's subnetting structure and which should be used to identify the hosts on those subnets. For a class B network, a subnet mask of 255.255.192.0 (binary 11111111 11111111 11000000 00000000) indicates that the first two octets and the first 2 bits of the third octet identify the subnetted network ID. The remaining 14 bits identify the hosts on that subnet. Because 2 bits are used to define the subnetting structure of this class B network, the network will support up to four subnets and up to 16,382 hosts per subnet.

B. **Incorrect:** The subnet mask should be 255.255.192.0, not 255.255.224.0. Although a subnet mask of 255.255.224.0 on a class B network (135.132.0.0) will support up to eight subnets, it will support only 8190 hosts per subnet.

C. **Incorrect:** The subnet mask should be 255.255.192.0, not 255.255.240.0. Although a subnet mask of 255.255.240.0 on a class B network (135.132.0.0) will support up to 16 subnets, it will support only 4094 hosts per subnet.

D. **Incorrect:** The subnet mask should be 255.255.192.0, not 255.255.248.0. Although a subnet mask of 255.255.248.0 on a class B network (135.132.0.0) will support up to 32 subnets, it will support only 2046 hosts per subnet.

70-215.06.03.004

▶ **Correct Answers: D**

A. **Incorrect:** The subnet mask should be 255.255.0.0, not 255.192.0.0. A subnet mask of 255.192.0.0 on a class A network (121.0.0.0) will support up to four subnets only, although each subnet will support up to 4,194,302 hosts.

B. **Incorrect:** The subnet mask should be 255.255.0.0, not 255.252.0.0. A subnet mask of 255.252.0.0 on a class A network (121.0.0.0) will support up to 64 subnets only, although each subnet will support up to 262,142 hosts.

C. **Incorrect:** The subnet mask should be 255.255.0.0, not 255.254.0.0. A subnet mask of 255.254.0.0 on a class A network (121.0.0.0) will support up to 128 subnets only, although each subnet will support up to 131,070 hosts.

D. **Correct:** A network ID of 121.0.0.0 is a class A network. A class A network falls in the range of 1.0.0.0 to 126.0.0.0. The high-order bit of a class A network ID is always set to 0. The next 7 bits (completing the first octet) identify the remaining portion of a class A network ID. In this case, the first octet of the network ID is 121, which translates to a binary value of 01111001. The default subnet mask of a class A network is 255.0.0.0 (binary 11111111 00000000 00000000 00000000), indicating that the first octet defines the network ID. The remaining three octets can be used to define which bits should be used to identify the network's subnetting structure and which should be used to identify the hosts on those subnets. For a class A network, a subnet mask of 255.255.0.0 (binary 11111111 11111111 00000000 00000000) indicates that the first two octets identify the subnetted network ID. The remaining 16 bits identify the hosts on that subnet. Because 8 bits are used to define the subnetting structure of this class A network, the network will support up to 256 subnets and up to 65,534 hosts per subnet.

70-215.06.03.005

▶ **Correct Answers: B**

A. **Incorrect:** The frame type defines the way in which the network adapter in a Windows 2000 computer formats data to be sent over a network. NWLink on Windows 2000 computers must be configured with the same frame type that is used by the NetWare server. However, the frame type is automatically detected when NWLink is installed. In most cases, you do not need to change the frame type. Occasionally, a misconfigured host causes an inappropriate frame type to be selected, which is usually caused by an incorrect manual setting on a computer on the network. However, frame type is not a factor in this case because NWLink has not yet been installed on these computers, and the frame type is not configured until NWLink is installed.

B. **Correct:** Client Service for NetWare and Gateway Service for NetWare work with NWLink to provide access to NetWare file, print, and directory services. NWLink is the Windows 2000 implementation of the IPX/SPX protocol, which can be used for connectivity between computers running Windows 2000 and computers running NetWare. NWLink also provides the functionality of NetBIOS and Routing Information Protocol (RIP). NWLink is included with both Windows 2000 Server and Windows 2000 Professional and is installed automatically during a Client Service for NetWare or Gateway Service for NetWare installation. Both Client Service for NetWare and Gateway Service for NetWare depend on NWLink to provide Windows 2000 computers with file, print, and directory services on a NetWare computer.

C. **Incorrect:** Although you can use NWLink as your only protocol on the network, it is not necessary and it is not the most efficient solution. The Windows 2000 computers can continue using TCP/IP—the preferred protocol—to communicate with one another and use NWLink to communicate with the NetWare server. Because NWLink is Network Driver Interface Specification (NDIS)–compliant, the Windows 2000 computers can simultaneously run other protocol stacks, such as TCP/IP. When multiple transport protocols are installed, Windows 2000 negotiates network connections in the order that the protocols are prioritized in the network services binding list. If TCP/IP is ranked at the top of the list, Windows 2000 attempts to make network connections with TCP/IP before it attempts to use other protocols. In this case, in which users make most of their network connections to servers using TCP/IP, this protocol priority would provide the best overall performance.

D. **Incorrect:** On Ethernet networks, the standard frame type for NetWare 2.2 and NetWare 3.11 is 802.3. Starting with NetWare 3.12, the default frame type was changed to 802.2. However, frame type is not a factor in this case because NWLink has not yet been installed on these computers, and the frame type is not configured until NWLink is installed.

70-215.06.03.006

▶ **Correct Answers: B and C**

A. **Incorrect:** Although TCP/IP would allow the Windows 2000 computers to communicate with one another, it will not allow them to communicate with the NetWare server. To communicate with the NetWare server, the Windows 2000 computers must be configured with NWLink. It is possible to configure the Windows 2000 computers with TCP/IP and NWLink. That way, the Windows 2000 computers can use TCP/IP—the preferred protocol—to communicate with one another and use NWLink to communicate with the NetWare server. However, because you are required to use only one protocol, you must use NWLink. Note that NetWare 5.0 actually runs on TCP/IP by default and not IPX/SPX. However, you still cannot use TCP/IP to connect Windows 2000 and NetWare networks because Gateway Service for NetWare and Client Service for NetWare work only with NWLink, not IP. So when you are integrating NetWare 5.0 with a Windows 2000 network, you have to enable IPX on the NetWare 5.0 servers.

B. **Correct:** NWLink is the Windows 2000 implementation of the IPX/SPX protocol, which can be used for connectivity between computers running Windows 2000 and computers running NetWare. NWLink also provides the functionality of NetBIOS and Routing Information Protocol (RIP). NWLink is included with both Windows 2000 Server and Windows 2000 Professional and is installed automatically during a Client Service for NetWare or Gateway Service for NetWare installation. Gateway Service for NetWare supports direct access to NetWare services from the computer running Windows 2000 Server, in the same way that Client Service for NetWare supports direct access from the client computer. Additionally, Gateway Service for NetWare supports NetWare login scripts. Both Client Service for NetWare and Gateway Service for NetWare depend on NWLink to provide Windows 2000 computers with file, print, and directory services on a NetWare computer. NWLink can be used as the only protocol on the network to allow communication among all the computers.

C. **Correct:** Client Service for NetWare works with NWLink to provide access to NetWare file, print, and directory services. Client Service for NetWare enables clients to connect directly to file and printer services on the NetWare bindery–based servers and NetWare servers running NetWare Directory Services (NDS) through IPX. Client Service for NetWare, which supports NetWare login scripts, is included with Windows 2000 Professional but not with Windows 2000 Server. (To support direct access to NetWare services from the computer running Windows 2000 Server, use Gateway Service for NetWare.) Client Service for NetWare is installed on individual Windows 2000 Professional computers and gives each client direct, high-performance access to NetWare servers.

D. **Incorrect:** Gateway Service for NetWare works with NWLink to provide access to NetWare file, print, and directory services by acting as a gateway through which multiple clients can access NetWare resources. With Gateway Service for NetWare, you can connect a computer running Windows 2000 Server to NetWare bindery–based servers and NetWare NDS servers through IPX. Multiple Windows-based clients can then use Gateway Service for NetWare as a common gateway to access NetWare services. However, clients would not be able to access the services directly, only through the Windows 2000 Server computer configured with Gateway Service for NetWare. To allow the Windows 2000 Professional computer to access the NetWare server directly, you must install Client Service for NetWare on each Windows 2000 Professional computer.

70-215.06.03.007

▶ **Correct Answers: A**

A. **Correct:** NWLink is the Windows 2000 implementation of the IPX/SPX protocol, which can be used for connectivity between computers running Windows 2000 and computers running NetWare. NWLink also provides the functionality of NetBIOS and Routing Information Protocol (RIP). NWLink is included with both Windows 2000 Server and Windows 2000 Professional and is installed automatically during a Client Service for NetWare or Gateway Service for NetWare installation. Both Client Service for NetWare and Gateway Service for NetWare depend on NWLink to provide Windows 2000 computers with file, print, and directory services on a NetWare computer. NWLink can be used as the only protocol on the network to allow communication among all the computers. Note that you must install NWLink on the NetWare computers as well as the Windows 2000 computers. Although NetWare 5.0 uses TCP/IP as its native protocol, you must use NWLink to allow communication between the Windows 2000 computers and the NetWare computers.

B. **Incorrect:** Client Service for NetWare must be installed on the Windows 2000 Professional computers to allow them to access files directly on the NetWare servers. Client Service for NetWare works with NWLink to provide access to NetWare file, print, and directory services. Client Service for NetWare enables clients to connect directly to file and printer services on the NetWare bindery–based servers and NetWare servers running NDS through IPX. Client Service for NetWare, which supports NetWare login scripts, is included with Windows 2000 Professional but not with Windows 2000 Server. (To support direct access to NetWare services from the computer running Windows 2000 Server, use Gateway Service for NetWare.) Client Service for NetWare is installed on individual Windows 2000 Professional computers and gives each client direct, high-performance access to NetWare servers.

C. **Incorrect:** File and Print Services for NetWare must be installed on the Windows 2000 Server computers to allow them to act as print servers for the NetWare clients. File and Print Services for NetWare, a separate product from Windows 2000, enables a computer running Windows 2000 Server to provide file and print services directly to NetWare client computers. No changes or additions to the NetWare client software are necessary.

D. **Incorrect:** The solution allows you to use a single protocol for the network, but it does not allow client computers to access files directly on the NetWare servers or allow the Windows 2000 Server computers to act as print servers for the NetWare clients.

70-215.06.03.008

▶ **Correct Answers: B**

A. **Incorrect:** When you install Client Service for NetWare on the computers, NWLink is automatically installed, which means that two protocols would be used on the network. If you could use only TCP/IP, the Windows 2000 computers would be able to communicate with one another and the NetWare computers would be able to communicate with one another, but the Windows 2000 computers could not communicate with the NetWare computers. For the Windows 2000 computers to be able to communicate with the NetWare computers, the Windows 2000 computers must be configured with NWLink. It is possible to configure the Windows 2000 computers with TCP/IP and NWLink. That way, the Windows 2000 computers can use TCP/IP—the preferred protocol—to communicate with one another, the NetWare computers can use TCP/IP to communicate with one another, and the Windows 2000 computers can use NWLink to communicate with the NetWare computers. However, because you are required to use only one protocol, you must use NWLink.

B. **Correct:** Client Service for NetWare must be installed on the Windows 2000 Professional computers to allow them to access files directly on the NetWare servers. Client Service for NetWare works with NWLink to provide access to NetWare file, print, and directory services. Client Service for NetWare enables clients to connect directly to file and printer services on the NetWare bindery–based servers and NetWare servers running NDS through IPX. Client Service for NetWare, which supports NetWare login scripts, is included with Windows 2000 Professional but not with Windows 2000 Server. Client Service for NetWare is installed on individual Windows 2000 Professional computers and gives each client direct, high-performance access to NetWare servers. When you install Client Service for NetWare on a Windows 2000 Professional computer, NWLink is also installed. You cannot run Client Service for NetWare without NWLink. You cannot remove NWLink from a Windows 2000 Professional computer without first removing Client Service for NetWare. As a result, installing Client Service for NetWare fulfills the requirement of directly accessing files on the NetWare server; however, it prevents TCP/IP from being the only protocol used on the network.

C. **Incorrect:** File and Print Services for NetWare must be installed on the Windows 2000 Server computers to allow them to act as print servers for the NetWare clients. File and Print Services for NetWare, a separate product from Windows 2000, enables a computer running Windows 2000 Server to provide file and print services directly to NetWare client computers. No changes or additions to the NetWare client software are necessary.

D. **Incorrect:** The solution allows the Windows 2000 Professional computers to access files directly on the NetWare server, but the solution does not allow a single protocol to be used, and it does not allow the Windows 2000 Server computers to act as print servers for the NetWare clients.

70-215.06.03.009

▶ **Correct Answers: A and B**

A. **Correct:** NWLink is the Windows 2000 implementation of the IPX/SPX protocol, which can be used for connectivity between computers running Windows 2000 and computers running NetWare. NWLink also provides the functionality of NetBIOS and Routing Information Protocol (RIP). NWLink is included with both Windows 2000 Server and Windows 2000 Professional and is installed automatically during a Client Service for NetWare or Gateway Service for NetWare installation. Both Client Service for NetWare and Gateway Service for NetWare depend on NWLink to provide Windows 2000 computers with file, print, and directory services on a NetWare computer. NWLink can be used as the only protocol on the network to allow communication among all the computers. Note that you must install NWLink on the NetWare network computers as well as the Windows 2000 computers. NetWare 5.0 uses TCP/IP as its native protocol; however, you must use NWLink to allow communication between the Windows 2000 computers and the NetWare computers.

B. **Correct:** Client Service for NetWare must be installed on the Windows 2000 Professional computers to allow them to access files directly on the NetWare servers. Client Service for NetWare works with NWLink to provide access to NetWare file, print, and directory services. Client Service for NetWare enables clients to connect directly to file and printer services on the NetWare bindery–based servers and NetWare servers running NDS through IPX. Client Service for NetWare, which supports NetWare login scripts, is included with Windows 2000 Professional but not with Windows 2000 Server. Client Service for NetWare is installed on individual Windows 2000 Professional computers and gives each client direct, high-performance access to NetWare servers. NWLink must be installed on the computer in order to use Client Service for NetWare. If NWLink is not installed, it is installed automatically when Client Service for NetWare is installed.

C. **Incorrect:** File and Print Services for NetWare must be installed on the Windows 2000 Server computers to allow them to act as print servers for the NetWare clients. File and Print Services for NetWare, a separate product from Windows 2000, enables a computer running Windows 2000 Server to provide file and print services directly to NetWare client computers. No changes or additions to the NetWare client software are necessary.

D. **Incorrect:** The solution allows you to use one protocol on your network and allows the Windows 2000 Professional computers to access files directly on the NetWare server, but the solution does not allow the Windows 2000 Server computers to act as print servers for the NetWare clients.

Install and configure network services.

Windows 2000 Server includes several network services that support the allocation of TCP/IP configuration information and the resolution of computer names to IP addresses. The Dynamic Host Configuration Protocol (DHCP) service centralizes and manages the allocation of TCP/IP configuration information by assigning IP addressing information automatically to computers that are set up as DHCP clients. Each time a DHCP client starts, it requests IP addressing information from a DHCP server. This information includes an IP address, a subnet mask, and optional values such as a default gateway address, a DNS server address, or a WINS server address. When a DHCP server receives a request from a DHCP client, the server offers IP addressing information to the client. The IP address is selected from a pool of addresses defined in the DHCP database. If the client accepts the offer, the DHCP server leases the IP address to the client for a specified period.

Windows Internet Naming Service (WINS) is an enhanced **Network Basic Input/ Output System (NetBIOS)** name server that registers NetBIOS computer names and resolves them to IP addresses. WINS maintains a dynamic database that maps computer names to IP addresses. In a mixed network environment, down-level clients, such as Windows 98 or Windows NT 4.0 computers, use NetBIOS names to communicate. As a result, a Windows 2000 network with down-level clients requires a means of resolving NetBIOS names to IP addresses. The WINS name resolution process allows each WINS client to register its name and IP address with WINS servers. WINS clients can query the WINS servers to locate and communicate with other resources on the network.

Domain Name System (DNS) is a distributed database used in TCP/IP networks to translate computer names to IP addresses. Unlike WINS, DNS resolves IP **host names** to IP addresses. Host names refer to specific computers on the Internet or a private network. DNS relies on the **domain namespace** for name-to-IP-address resolution. The domain namespace is the naming scheme that provides the hierarchical structure for the DNS database. Each node represents a partition of the DNS database. The nodes are referred to as **domains**. DNS uses **zones** to partition the domain namespace into manageable sections. A zone represents a discrete portion of the domain namespace. A DNS name server stores data for one zone or multiple zones. The DNS service in Windows 2000 includes a dynamic update capability called Dynamic DNS (DDNS). With DDNS, name servers and clients within a network automatically update the zone database files.

To answer the questions in this objective, you should know how to install, implement, configure, and troubleshoot the DHCP service, WINS, and the DNS service, and you should be familiar with how each of these services operate within the network and with the client computers. You should also know how to set up the DHCP, WINS, and DNS clients.

Objective 6.4 Questions

70-215.06.04.001

Your company recently purchased another company, and you are in charge of configuring the DNS naming scheme for the two companies. The two organizations will continue to operate independently, yet they need to communicate with each other. As a result, the naming scheme must be set up so that the DNS name of the original company remains separate from the DNS name of the new company. How should you configure the domain naming scheme?

A. As two trees

B. As a forest with two trees

C. As a tree with two zones

D. As a tree with two contiguous namespaces

70-215.06.04.002

You are setting up a TCP/IP network. The network will be configured as a Windows 2000 mixed-mode network that will contain four subnets. Each subnet will correspond to a node in the domain namespace and will include Windows 2000 Server computers, Windows 2000 Professional computers, and Windows 98 computers.

You want to achieve the following results:

- The client computers must be assigned IP addressing information automatically.

- The network must be able to automatically resolve the NetBIOS names of the Windows 98 computers to their IP addresses.

- The network must be able to automatically resolve the host names of the Windows 2000 Professional computers to their IP addresses.

You configure a DHCP server and WINS server on each subnet, and then you configure the Windows 2000 Professional and Windows 98 computers as DHCP clients and WINS clients.

Which result or results does your configuration achieve? (Choose all that apply.)

A. The client computers will be assigned IP addressing information automatically.

B. The network will be able to automatically resolve the NetBIOS names of the Windows 98 computers to their IP addresses.

C. The network will be able to automatically resolve the host names of the Windows 2000 Professional computers to their IP addresses.

D. The solution will not achieve any of the required results.

70-215.06.04.003

You are setting up a TCP/IP network. The network will be configured as a Windows 2000 mixed-mode network that will contain four subnets. Each subnet will correspond to a node in the domain namespace and will include Windows 2000 Server computers, Windows 2000 Professional computers, and Windows 98 computers.

You want to achieve the following results:

- The client computers must be assigned IP addressing information automatically.

- The network must be able to automatically resolve the NetBIOS names of the Windows 98 computers to their IP addresses.

- The network must be able to automatically resolve the host names of the Windows 2000 Professional computers to their IP addresses.

You configure a DHCP server on each subnet, and then you configure the Windows 2000 Professional and Windows 98 computers as DHCP clients.

Which result or results does your configuration achieve? (Choose all that apply.)

A. The client computers will be assigned IP addressing information automatically.

B. The network will be able to automatically resolve the NetBIOS names of the Windows 98 computers to their IP addresses.

C. The network will be able to automatically resolve the host names of the Windows 2000 Professional computers to their IP addresses.

D. The solution will not achieve any of the required results.

70-215.06.04.004

You are setting up a TCP/IP network. The network will be configured as a Windows 2000 mixed-mode network that will contain four subnets. Each subnet will correspond to a node in the domain namespace and will include Windows 2000 Server computers, Windows 2000 Professional computers, and Windows 98 computers.

You want to achieve the following results:

- The client computers must be assigned IP addressing information automatically.

- The network must be able to automatically resolve the NetBIOS names of the Windows 98 computers to their IP addresses.

- The network must be able to automatically resolve the host names of the Windows 2000 Professional computers to their IP addresses.

You configure a DHCP server on each subnet. Next you establish a DNS zone for each subnet, configure a DNS server for each zone, and then configure the DNS service in each zone to support dynamic updates. Then you configure the Windows 2000 Professional and Windows 98 computers as DHCP clients and DNS clients.

Which result or results does your configuration achieve? (Choose all that apply.)

A. The client computers will be assigned IP addressing information automatically.

B. The network will be able to automatically resolve the NetBIOS names of the Windows 98 computers to their IP addresses.

C. The network will be able to automatically resolve the host names of the Windows 2000 Professional computers to their IP addresses.

D. The solution will not achieve any of the required results.

Objective 6.4 Answers

70-215.06.04.001

▶ **Correct Answers: B**

A. **Incorrect:** A tree is a grouping or hierarchical arrangement of one or more Windows 2000 domains that allows global resource sharing. A tree can consist of a single Windows 2000 domain or can consist of a larger contiguous namespace by joining multiple domains into a hierarchical structure. All domains within a single tree share a common namespace and a hierarchical naming structure. A tree alone would not allow you to set up a naming scheme in which the DNS name of the original company remains separate from the DNS name of the new company. You must create a forest.

B. **Correct:** A forest is a grouping of one or more trees. Forests allow organizations to group two organizations that do not use the same naming scheme and operate independently yet need to communicate with the entire organization. The trees in the forest share the same schema and rules on how objects work together. All domains in a forest have the same global catalog and configuration container. The objects of the domain trees that make up a forest are available to all user objects in the forest. However, when accessing objects in the forest but in different trees, the user must know the fully qualified domain name or must at least become comfortable with viewing multiple fully qualified domain names when browsing the internal network for resources.

C. **Incorrect:** A zone represents a discrete portion of the domain namespace. Zones provide a way to divide the namespace into manageable sections. A zone must encompass a contiguous domain namespace. Although you can break a tree into two zones, a tree alone would not allow you to set up a naming scheme in which the DNS name of the original company remains separate from the DNS name of the new company. You must create a forest.

D. **Incorrect:** A tree can contain only one contiguous namespace. All domains within a single tree must share a common namespace and a hierarchical naming structure.

70-215.06.04.002

▶ **Correct Answers: A and B**

A. **Correct:** The DHCP servers will assign IP addressing information automatically to computers that are configured as DHCP clients, which in this case are the Windows 2000 Professional and Windows 98 computers. Windows 2000 Server provides the DHCP service, which enables a computer to function as a DHCP server and to configure DHCP-enabled client computers on your network. The DHCP server automatically allocates IP addresses and related TCP/IP configuration settings to the DHCP clients. Without DHCP, IP configuration must be done manually for new computers, computers moving from one subnet to another, and computers removed from the network. If you deploy DHCP in the network, this entire process is automated and centrally managed. The DHCP server maintains a pool of IP addresses and leases an address to any client that logs on to the network.

B. **Correct:** The WINS server and WINS-enabled clients will allow the network to resolve the NetBIOS names of the Windows 98 computers to their IP addresses. In a mixed-mode network, down-level clients, such as Windows NT 4.0 and Windows 98 clients, use NetBIOS names to communicate. WINS is an enhanced NetBIOS name server that registers NetBIOS computer names and resolves them to IP addresses. WINS also provides a dynamic database that maintains a mapping of computer names to IP addresses. When WINS clients log on to a network, their NetBIOS names and IP addresses are registered and added to the WINS server database, providing support for dynamic updates. The WINS server database is replicated among multiple WINS servers in a LAN or WAN. This replication prevents users from registering duplicate NetBIOS names for different computers. WINS automatically updates the WINS database when dynamic addressing through DHCP assigns new IP addresses.

C. **Incorrect:** For the network to be able to resolve the host names of the Windows 2000 Professional computers to their IP addresses, you must implement the DNS service into your network. DNS is a distributed database used in TCP/IP networks to translate host names to IP addresses. The DNS service in Windows 2000 works with the structure of the domain namespace for name resolution. Domain namespace is the naming scheme that provides the hierarchical structure for the DNS database. A DNS name server stores the database file for each zone; there must be at least one name server for a zone. The DNS service includes a dynamic update capability that allows name servers and client computers within a network to automatically update the zone database.

D. **Incorrect:** The solution allows client computers to be assigned IP addressing information and allows the network to automatically resolve the NetBIOS names of the Windows 98 computers to their IP addresses. However, the solution does not allow the network to automatically resolve the host names of the Windows 2000 Professional computers to their IP addresses.

70-215.06.04.003

▶ **Correct Answers: A**

A. **Correct:** The DHCP servers will assign IP addressing information automatically to computers that are configured as DHCP clients, which in this case are the Windows 2000 Professional and Windows 98 computers. Windows 2000 Server provides the DHCP service, which enables a computer to function as a DHCP server and to configure DHCP-enabled client computers on your network. The DHCP server automatically allocates IP addresses and related TCP/IP configuration settings to the DHCP clients. Without DHCP, IP configuration must be done manually for new computers, computers moving from one subnet to another, and computers removed from the network. If you deploy DHCP on the network, this entire process is automated and centrally managed. The DHCP server maintains a pool of IP addresses and leases an address to any client that logs on to the network.

B. **Incorrect:** For the network to be able to resolve the NetBIOS names of the Windows 98 computers to their IP addresses, you must implement WINS on your network. WINS is an enhanced NetBIOS name server that registers NetBIOS computer names and resolves them to IP addresses. WINS also provides a dynamic database that maintains a mapping of computer names to IP addresses. When WINS clients log on to a network, their NetBIOS names and IP addresses are registered and added to the WINS server database, providing support for dynamic updates. The WINS server database is replicated among multiple WINS servers in a LAN or WAN. This replication prevents users from registering duplicate NetBIOS names for different computers. WINS automatically updates the WINS database when dynamic addressing through DHCP assigns new IP addresses.

C. **Incorrect:** For the network to be able to resolve the host names of the Windows 2000 Professional computers to their IP addresses, you must implement the DNS service on your network. DNS is a distributed database used in TCP/IP networks to translate host names to IP addresses. The DNS service in Windows 2000 works with the structure of the domain namespace for name resolution. Domain namespace is the naming scheme that provides the hierarchical structure for the DNS database. A DNS name server stores the database file for each zone; there must be at least one name server for a zone. The DNS service includes a dynamic update capability that allows name servers and client computers within a network to automatically update the zone database.

D. **Incorrect:** The solution allows client computers to be assigned IP addressing information. However, the solution does not allow the network to automatically resolve the NetBIOS names of the Windows 98 computers to their IP addresses and does not allow the network to automatically resolve the host names of the Windows 2000 Professional computers to their IP addresses.

70-215.06.04.004

▶ **Correct Answers: A and C**

A. **Correct:** The DHCP servers will assign IP addressing information automatically to computers that are configured as DHCP clients, which in this case are the Windows 2000 Professional and Windows 98 computers. Windows 2000 Server provides the DHCP service, which enables a computer to function as a DHCP server and to configure DHCP-enabled client computers on your network. The DHCP server automatically allocates IP addresses and related TCP/IP configuration settings to the DHCP clients. Without DHCP, IP configuration must be done manually for new computers, computers moving from one subnet to another, and computers removed from the network. As a result of deploying DHCP on the network, this entire process is automated and centrally managed. The DHCP server maintains a pool of IP addresses and leases an address to any client that logs on to the network.

B. **Incorrect:** For the network to be able to resolve the NetBIOS names of the Windows 98 computers to their IP addresses, you must implement WINS on your network. WINS is an enhanced NetBIOS name server that registers NetBIOS computer names and resolves them to IP addresses. WINS also provides a dynamic database that maintains a mapping of computer names to IP addresses. When WINS clients log on to a network, their NetBIOS names and IP addresses are registered and added to the WINS server database, providing support for dynamic updates. The WINS server database is replicated among multiple WINS servers in a LAN or WAN. This replication prevents users from registering duplicate NetBIOS names for different computers. WINS automatically updates the WINS database when dynamic addressing through DHCP assigns new IP addresses.

C. **Correct:** The DNS service in Windows 2000 will allow the network to resolve the host names of the Windows 2000 Professional computers to their IP addresses. DNS is a distributed database used in TCP/IP networks to translate host names to IP addresses. The DNS service in Windows 2000 works with the structure of the domain namespace for name resolution. Domain namespace is the naming scheme that provides the hierarchical structure for the DNS database. A DNS name server stores the database file for each zone; there must be at least one name server for a zone. A zone represents a discrete portion of the domain namespace. Zones provide a way to divide the namespace into manageable sections. A zone must encompass a contiguous domain namespace. In this case, each subnet corresponds to a node in the domain namespace, and each node corresponds to a zone, so a DNS server is configured for each subnet, which means that a DNS database file will be maintained for each zone. The DNS service includes a dynamic update capability that allows name servers and client computers within a network to automatically update the zone database. With dynamic updates, clients can automatically send updates to the name server that is authoritative for the record that they want to change. Dynamic updates enable clients to dynamically register A and PTR resource records with a primary server. It also enables DHCP servers to register A and PTR resource records on behalf of DHCP clients.

D. **Incorrect:** The solution allows client computers to be assigned IP addressing information and allows the network to automatically resolve the host names of the Windows 2000 Professional computers to their IP addresses. However, the solution does not allow the network to automatically resolve the NetBIOS names of the Windows 98 computers to their IP addresses.

Configure, monitor, and troubleshoot remote access.

With Windows 2000 remote access, remote access clients connect to remote access servers and are transparently connected to the server or to the network to which the server is attached. This transparent connection allows remote access clients to dial in from remote locations and access resources as if they were physically attached to the network. Windows 2000 provides two types of remote access connectivity: dial-in remote access and virtual private network (VPN) remote access. A dial-up remote access connection consists of a remote access client, a remote access server, and a WAN infrastructure. The Windows 2000 remote access server accepts dial-up connections and forwards packets between remote access clients and the network. The physical or logical connection between the remote access server and the remote access client is facilitated by dial-up equipment installed at the client, server, and telecommunications infrastructure. Remote access protocols control the connection establishment and transmission of data over WAN links. The operating system and LAN protocols used on remote access clients and servers dictate which remote access protocol clients can use. Windows 2000 supports three remote access protocols: **Point-to-Point Protocol (PPP)**, **Serial Line Internet Protocol (SLIP)**, and **Microsoft RAS protocol**, which is also known as **Asynchronous NetBEUI (AsyBEUI)**.

Windows 2000 remote access connections are accepted based on the dial-in properties of a user account and the remote access policies. A remote access policy is a set of conditions and connection settings that define the characteristics of the incoming connection and set the constraints imposed on it. With remote access policies, you can grant remote access by configuring individual user accounts or by configuring specific remote access policies. Each user account contains a set of dial-in properties that are used when allowing or denying a connection attempt made by a user. You can set the remote access permission, verify caller ID, set callback options, assign a static IP address, and apply static routes. The access by policy administrative model is intended for Windows 2000 remote access servers that are either standalone servers or members of a Windows 2000 native mode domain. The remote access server can be configured to use either Windows or **Remote Authentication Dial-In User Service (RADIUS)** as an authentication provider. If Windows is used, user credentials are authenticated by using normal Windows authentication mechanisms. If RADIUS is used, user credentials are sent as a series of RADIUS request messages to a RADIUS server. The remote access server can also be configured to use either Windows or RADIUS as an accounting provider.

To answer the questions in this objective, you should have a thorough understanding of Windows 2000 remote access technology and how remote access connections are established. You should be familiar with various types of dial-up equipment and the different types of WAN infrastructures that can be used to establish a dial-up connection. You should also know how to manage remote access by configuring user accounts and remote access policies. In addition, you should understand the difference between and know how to set up Windows and RADIUS authentication and accounting.

Objective 6.5 Questions

70-215.06.05.001

You are configuring the Remote Access Service on your Windows 2000 Server computer. To make remote access more secure, you plan to configure the server so that it always calls back the remote access client at a specified location. Which type of security should you implement?

A. Callback

B. Caller ID

C. Secure user authentication

D. Mutual authentication

70-215.06.05.002

You are configuring the Remote Access Service on your Windows 2000 Server computer. To make remote access more secure, you plan to use the caller ID option so that the server verifies that a remote access client is calling from the specified number. Which device or devices must support caller ID? (Choose all that apply.)

A. Caller's telephone line

B. Server's telephone line

C. Phone system

D. Windows 2000 driver for the dial-up equipment on the server side

E. Windows 2000 driver for the dial-up equipment on the client side

70-215.06.05.003

You are configuring the Remote Access Service on your Windows 2000 Server computer. To make remote access more secure, you plan to configure the server so that it ensures that a remote access client can dial in only from a specified number. Which type of security should you implement?

A. Callback

B. Caller ID

C. Secure user authentication

D. Mutual authentication

70-215.06.05.004

You are configuring the default remote access policy on a Windows 2000 Server computer. You configure the access times so that users can dial in to the server during specified hours only. When will users be able to dial in to the remote access server?

Examine the settings shown in the image below to view the properties of the remote access profile.

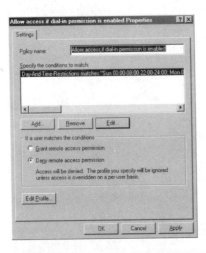

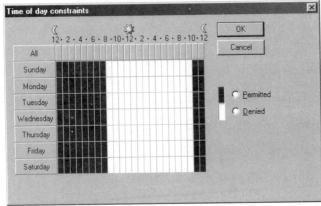

A. 9:00 A.M.

B. 11:00 P.M.

C. 9:00 P.M.

D. Never

70-215.06.05.005

You are configuring the default remote access policy on a Windows 2000 Server computer. You configure the access times so that users can dial in to the server during specified hours only. When will users be able to dial in to the remote access server?

Examine the settings shown in the image below to view the properties of the remote access profile.

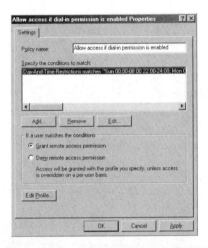

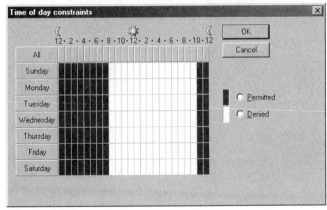

A. 9:00 A.M.

B. 11:00 P.M.

C. 9:00 P.M.

D. Never

70-215.06.05.006

You are configuring the default remote access policy on a Windows 2000 Server computer. You configure the access times so that users can dial in to the server during specified hours only. When will users be able to dial in to the remote access server?

Examine the settings shown in the image below to view the properties of the remote access profile.

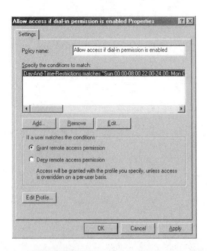

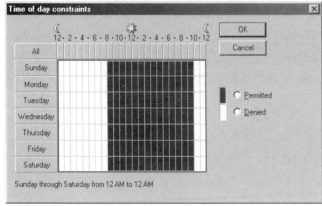

A. 9:00 A.M.

B. 11:00 P.M.

C. 9:00 P.M.

D. Never

Objective 6.5 Answers

70-215.06.05.001

▶ **Correct Answers: A**

A. **Correct:** The callback component of the Remote Access Service allows the remote access server to call the remote access client after the user credentials have been verified. Callback is configured as part of the dial-in properties of the user account. Callback can be configured on the server to call back the remote access client at a number specified by the user of the remote access client during the time of the call. This process allows a traveling user to dial in and have the remote access server call back the remote access client at the current location, saving telephone charges. Callback can also be configured to always call back the remote access client at a specific number, which is the secure form of callback.

B. **Incorrect:** The caller ID component of the Remote Access Service allows the remote access server to verify that an incoming call is coming from a specified phone number. Caller ID is configured as part of the dial-in properties of the user account. If the caller ID number of the incoming connection for that user does not match the configured caller ID, the connection is denied. Caller ID requires that the caller's telephone line, the phone system, the remote access server's telephone line, and the Windows 2000 Server driver for the dial-up equipment all support caller ID. If caller ID is configured for a user account and the caller ID is not being passed from the caller to the remote access server, the connection is denied. Although the use of the caller ID component of the Remote Access Service can make remote access more secure, caller ID cannot be used to configure the server so that it always calls back the remote access client at a specified location.

C. **Incorrect:** Secure user authentication is obtained through the encrypted exchange of user credentials. This process is possible through the use of PPP along with one of the following authentication protocols: Extensible Authentication Protocol (EAP), Microsoft Challenge Handshake Authentication Protocol (MS-CHAP), Challenge Handshake Authentication Protocol (CHAP), or Shiva Password Authentication Protocol (SPAP). The remote access server can be configured to require a secure authentication method. If the remote access client cannot perform the required secure authentication, the connection is denied. Although the use of secure user authentication can make remote access more secure, it cannot be used to configure the server so that it always calls back the remote access client at a specified location.

D. **Incorrect:** Mutual authentication is obtained by authenticating both ends of the connection through the encrypted exchange of user credentials. This process is possible through the use of PPP along with EAP-Transport Level Security (EAP-TLS) or MS-CHAP v2. During mutual authentication, the remote access client authenticates itself to the remote access server, and then the remote access server authenticates itself to the remote access client. If the remote access server does not respond to the authentication request, the connection is terminated by the client. Although the use of mutual authentication can make remote access more secure, it cannot be used to configure the server so that it always calls back the remote access client at a specified location.

70-215.06.05.002

► **Correct Answers: A, B, C, and D**

A. **Correct:** The caller ID component of the Remote Access Service allows the remote access server to verify that an incoming call is coming from a specified phone number. Caller ID is configured as part of the dial-in properties of the user account. If the caller ID number of the incoming connection for that user does not match the configured caller ID, the connection is denied. Caller ID requires that the caller's telephone line, the phone system, the remote access server's telephone line, and the Windows 2000 Server driver for the dial-up equipment all support caller ID. If caller ID is configured for a user account and the caller ID is not being passed from the caller to the remote access server, the connection is denied.

B. **Correct:** Caller ID requires that the caller's telephone line, the phone system, the remote access server's telephone line, and the Windows 2000 Server driver for the dial-up equipment all support caller ID.

C. **Correct:** Caller ID requires that the caller's telephone line, the phone system, the remote access server's telephone line, and the Windows 2000 Server driver for the dial-up equipment all support caller ID.

D. **Correct:** Caller ID requires that the caller's telephone line, the phone system, the remote access server's telephone line, and the Windows 2000 Server driver for the dial-up equipment all support caller ID.

E. **Incorrect:** The driver must exist on the server side, not the client side. The remote access server is the computer that verifies that an incoming call is from a specified phone number. The remote access client does not verify the incoming number.

70-215.06.05.003

▶ **Correct Answers: B**

A. **Incorrect:** The callback component of the Remote Access Service allows the remote access server to call the remote access client after the user credentials have been verified. Callback is configured as part of the dial-in properties of the user account. Callback can be configured on the server to call back the remote access client at a number specified by the user of the remote access client during the time of the call. This process allows a traveling user to dial in and have the remote access server call back the remote access client at the current location, saving telephone charges. Callback can also be configured to always call back the remote access client at a specific number, which is the secure form of callback. Although the use of the callback component of the Remote Access Service can make remote access more secure, callback cannot be used to configure the server so that it ensures that a remote access client can dial in only from a specified number.

B. **Correct:** The caller ID component of the Remote Access Service allows the remote access server to verify that an incoming call is coming from a specified phone number. Caller ID is configured as part of the dial-in properties of the user account. If the caller ID number of the incoming connection for that user does not match the configured caller ID, the connection is denied. Caller ID requires that the caller's telephone line, the phone system, the remote access server's telephone line, and the Windows 2000 Server driver for the dial-up equipment all support caller ID. If caller ID is configured for a user account and the caller ID is not being passed from the caller to the remote access server, the connection is denied.

C. **Incorrect:** Secure user authentication is obtained through the encrypted exchange of user credentials. This process is possible through the use of PPP along with one of the following authentication protocols: Extensible Authentication Protocol (EAP), Microsoft Challenge Handshake Authentication Protocol (MS-CHAP), Challenge Handshake Authentication Protocol (CHAP), or Shiva Password Authentication Protocol (SPAP). The remote access server can be configured to require a secure authentication method. If the remote access client cannot perform the required secure authentication, the connection is denied. Although the use of secure user authentication can make remote access more secure, it cannot be used to configure the server so that it ensures that a remote access client can dial in only from a specified number.

D. **Incorrect:** Mutual authentication is obtained by authenticating both ends of the connection through the encrypted exchange of user credentials. This process is possible through the use of PPP along with EAP-Transport Level Security (EAP-TLS) or MS-CHAP v2. During mutual authentication, the remote access client authenticates itself to the remote access server, and then the remote access server authenticates itself to the remote access client. If the remote access server does not respond to the authentication request, the connection is terminated by the client. Although the use of mutual authentication can make remote access more secure, it cannot be used to configure the server so that it ensures that a remote access client can dial in only from a specified number.

70-215.06.05.004

▶ **Correct Answers: D**

A. **Incorrect:** Users will not be granted remote access because the remote access policy is set to deny access. However, even if the policy were set to allow access, users would be denied dial-in access at 9:00 A.M. because the time-of-day constraints prevent a connection at that time. If the remote access policy were set to allow access, users would be able to connect only from 10:00 P.M. through 8:00 A.M.

B. **Incorrect:** Users will not be granted remote access because the remote access policy is set to deny access. However, if the policy were set to allow access, users would be allowed dial-in access at 11:00 P.M. because the time-of-day constraints allow users to connect to the remote access server from 10:00 P.M. through 8:00 A.M.

C. **Incorrect:** Users will not be granted remote access because the remote access policy is set to deny access. However, even if the policy were set to allow access, users would be denied dial-in access at 9:00 P.M. because the time-of-day constraints prevent a connection at that time. Users would be able to connect only from 10:00 P.M. through 8:00 A.M.

D. **Correct:** Users will not be granted remote access because the remote access policy is set to deny access. A remote access policy is a set of conditions and connection parameters that define the characteristics of the incoming connection and the set of constraints imposed on it. Remote access policies can be used to impose connection parameters, such as maximum session time, idle disconnect time, required secure authentication methods, and required encryption. With multiple remote access policies, different sets of conditions can be applied to different remote access clients, or different requirements can be applied to the same remote access client based on the parameters of the connection attempt. Windows 2000 uses remote access policies to determine whether to accept or reject connection attempts. A connection that does not match any configured remote access policy is denied, even if the remote access permission on the individual user account is set to allow access. If the policy itself is set to deny remote access, as in this case, remote access is denied to any user who tries to establish a remote access connection to the server.

70-215.06.05.005

▶ **Correct Answers: B**

A. **Incorrect:** Users would be denied access to the remote access server at 9:00 A.M. because the time-of-day constraints prevent a dial-in connection at that time. Users would be able to connect only from 10:00 P.M. through 8:00 A.M.

B. **Correct:** Users can connect to the remote access server at 11:00 P.M. because the time-of-day constraints permit a dial-up connection at that time. Users can connect to the remote access server only from 10:00 P.M. through 8:00 A.M.

C. **Incorrect:** Users would be denied access to the remote access server at 9:00 P.M. because the time-of-day constraints prevent a dial-in connection at that time. Users would be able to connect only from 10:00 P.M. through 8:00 A.M.

D. **Incorrect:** Because the remote access policy is set to allow access, users will be granted remote access as long as they try to establish a dial-in connection between 10:00 P.M. and 8:00 A.M. A remote access policy is a set of conditions and connection parameters that define the characteristics of the incoming connection and the set of constraints imposed on it. Remote access policies can be used to impose connection parameters, such as maximum session time, idle disconnect time, required secure authentication methods, and required encryption. With multiple remote access policies, different sets of conditions can be applied to different remote access clients, or different requirements can be applied to the same remote access client based on the parameters of the connection attempt. Windows 2000 uses remote access policies to determine whether to accept or reject connection attempts. A connection that does not match any configured remote access policy is denied, even if the remote access permission on the individual user account is set to allow access. If the policy itself is set to deny remote access, remote access is denied to any user who tries to establish a remote access connection to the server.

70-215.06.05.006

▶ **Correct Answers: A and C**

A. **Correct:** Users can connect to the remote access server at 9:00 A.M. because the time-of-day constraints permit a dial-up connection at that time. Users can connect to the remote access server only from 8:00 A.M. through 10:00 P.M.

B. **Incorrect:** Users would be denied access to the remote access server at 11:00 P.M. because the time-of-day constraints prevent a dial-in connection at that time. Users would be able to connect only from 8:00 A.M. through 10:00 P.M.

C. **Correct:** Users can connect to the remote access server at 9:00 P.M. because the time-of-day constraints permit a dial-up connection at that time. Users can connect to the remote access server only from 8:00 A.M. through 10:00 P.M.

D. **Incorrect:** Because the remote access policy is set to allow access, users will be granted remote access as long as they try to establish a dial-in connection between 8:00 A.M. and 10:00 P.M. A remote access policy is a set of conditions and connection parameters that define the characteristics of the incoming connection and the set of constraints imposed on it. Remote access policies can be used to impose connection parameters, such as maximum session time, idle disconnect time, required secure authentication methods, and required encryption. With multiple remote access policies, different sets of conditions can be applied to different remote access clients, or different requirements can be applied to the same remote access client based on the parameters of the connection attempt. Windows 2000 uses remote access policies to determine whether to accept or reject connection attempts. A connection that does not match any configured remote access policy is denied, even if the remote access permission on the individual user account is set to allow access. If the policy itself is set to deny remote access, remote access is denied to any user who tries to establish a remote access connection to the server.

O B J E C T I V E   6 . 6

Install, configure, monitor, and troubleshoot Terminal Services.

Terminal Services is a built-in feature of Windows 2000 Server that enables all client application execution, data processing, and data storage to occur on the server. Terminal Services provides remote access to a server desktop through terminal emulation software. The software runs on a client hardware device and sends keystrokes and mouse movements to the Terminal server, which manipulates the data locally and passes back the display. Users can access Terminal Services over any TCP/IP connection, including remote access, Ethernet, the Internet, wireless, WAN, or virtual private network (VPN). The user is limited only by the weakest link in the connection, and the security of the connection is governed by the TCP/IP deployment in the data center. Terminal Services contains its own methods for licensing clients that log on to the Terminal servers. The Terminal Services licensing method is separate from the method used for Windows 2000 Server clients. Terminal Services Licensing includes four primary components: the **Microsoft Clearinghouse**, a license server, a **Terminal server**, and client licenses.

You can enable Terminal Services in Remote Administration mode or Application Server mode. Remote Administration allows you to administer a Windows 2000 Server computer remotely over any TCP/IP connection. You can administer file and print sharing, edit the registry, or perform any task as if you were sitting at the console. Remote Administration installs only the remote access components of Terminal Services. It does not install application sharing components, which means you can use Remote Administration with little overhead. Terminal Services allows up to two concurrent Remote Administration connections. No additional licensing is required, and you do not need a license server. In Application Server mode, you can deploy and manage applications from a central location. You can install applications directly on the Terminal server, or you can use remote administration. After an application is deployed in Terminal Services, clients can connect through a remote access connection, a LAN or WAN, and from many types of clients. Client licensing is required when deploying a Terminal server as an application server. Each client computer must have the **Terminal Services Client Access License** as well as the **Windows 2000 Server Client Access License**.

To answer the questions in this objective, you should have a thorough understanding of the components of Terminal Services and Terminal Services Licensing. You should know how to set up Terminal Services in Remote Administration mode and Application Server mode, and you should be familiar with the licensing requirements for both modes. You should also know how to configure applications for use with Terminal Services.

Objective 6.6 Questions

70-215.06.06.001

You are the administrator of a Windows 2000 Server computer. You want to be able to administer the computer remotely, but you do not want to incur unnecessary overhead on the server.

You want to achieve the following results:

- You must be able to administer the Windows 2000 Server computer over a virtual private network (VPN) connection.

- You must be able to administer file and print sharing on the Windows 2000 Server computer remotely.

- You must not be required to implement a license server or connect to the Microsoft Clearinghouse.

You implement Terminal Services in Remote Administration mode on the Windows 2000 Server computer.

What result or results does this configuration achieve? (Choose all that apply.)

A. You can administer the Windows 2000 Server computer over a VPN.

B. You can administer file and print sharing on the Windows 2000 Server computer remotely.

C. You will not be required to implement a license server or connect to the Microsoft Clearinghouse.

D. The solution does not achieve any of the required results.

70-215.06.06.002

You are the administrator of a Windows 2000 Server computer. You want to be able to administer the computer remotely, but you do not want to incur unnecessary overhead on the server.

You want to achieve the following results:

- You must be able to administer the Windows 2000 Server computer over a virtual private network (VPN) connection.

- You must be able to administer file and print sharing on the Windows 2000 Server computer remotely.

- You must not be required to implement a license server or connect to the Microsoft Clearinghouse.

You implement Terminal Services in Application Server mode on the Windows 2000 Server computer.

What result or results does this configuration achieve? (Choose all that apply.)

A. You can administer the Windows 2000 Server computer over a VPN.

B. You can administer file and print sharing on the Windows 2000 Server computer remotely.

C. You will not be required to implement a license server or the Microsoft Clearinghouse.

D. The solution does not achieve any of the required results.

70-215.06.06.003

Several of your Windows 95 client computers are configured as Terminal Services clients. You want to optimize the client computers in order to improve Terminal Services performance. How can you optimize the clients? (Choose all that apply.)

A. Disable Active Desktop.

B. Use 16-bit applications when possible.

C. Configure the Terminal server to return the user's computer name and not the user's logon name.

D. Minimize the use of graphics and animation.

Objective 6.6 Answers

70-215.06.06.001

▶ **Correct Answers: A, B, and C**

A. **Correct:** Users can access Terminal Services over any TCP/IP connection, including dial-up remote access, VPN remote access, Ethernet, the Internet, wireless, or WAN. The user's experience is limited only by the characteristics of the weakest link in the connection, and the security of the link is governed by the TCP/IP deployment in the data center.

B. **Correct:** The Terminal Services Remote Administration mode allows you to remotely administer a Windows 2000 Server computer. You can administer file and print sharing, edit the registry, or perform any task as if you were sitting at the console. You can use the Remote Administration mode to manage servers not normally compatible with the Application Server mode of Terminal Services, such as servers running the Cluster service.

C. **Correct:** The Remote Administration mode installs only the remote access components of Terminal Services. It does not install application-sharing components. Terminal Services allows a maximum of two concurrent remote administration connections. No additional licensing is required for those connections, and a license server is not necessary.

D. **Incorrect:** The solution achieves all the required results.

70-215.06.06.002

▶ **Correct Answers: A and B**

A. **Correct:** Users can access Terminal Services over any TCP/IP connection, including dial-up remote access, VPN remote access, Ethernet, the Internet, wireless, or WAN. The user's experience is limited only by the characteristics of the weakest link in the connection, and the security of the link is governed by the TCP/IP deployment in the data center.

B. **Correct:** The Terminal Services Application Server mode, like the Remote Administration mode, allows you to remotely administer a Windows 2000 Server computer. You can administer file and print sharing, edit the registry, or perform any task as if you were sitting at the console. Unlike the Remote Administration mode, the Application Server mode also allows you to deploy and manage applications from a Terminal server. The server provides clients with access to Windows-based applications running entirely on the server and supports multiple client sessions.

C. **Incorrect:** Client licensing is required when deploying a Terminal server as an application server. Each client computer, regardless of the protocol used to connect to the Terminal server, must have the Terminal Services Client Access License as well as the Windows 2000 Server Client Access License. The Terminal Services Application Server mode requires a license server, a connection to the Microsoft Clearinghouse database, a Terminal server, and a client license.

D. **Incorrect:** The solution allows you to administer file and print sharing on the Windows 2000 Server computer over a VPN connection. However, the solution requires that you implement a license server and the Microsoft Clearinghouse.

70-215.06.06.003

▶ **Correct Answers: A and D**

A. **Correct:** To optimize performance on a Terminal Services client, you should disable the Active Desktop and smooth scrolling. In addition, you should enable file sharing on client computers and use easily identifiable names when you share drivers. However, you should be aware of the security implications when sharing drivers. You should also train users to use Terminal Services hot key sequences, some of which are different from those used in Windows 2000 sessions.

B. **Incorrect:** You should avoid the use of MS-DOS or Windows 16-bit applications when possible. MS-DOS applications are not recommended because they can consume all the available CPU time.

C. **Incorrect:** You should configure the Terminal server to return the user's logon name (rather than the computer name) to applications that use NetBIOS functions to call the computer name.

D. **Correct:** You should minimize the use of graphics and animation, such as screen savers, blinking cursors, Office Assistant, and cascading menus on the desktop. You should place shortcuts on the desktop and keep the Programs submenu as flat as possible. Avoid using wallpaper.

Install, configure, and troubleshoot network adapters and drivers.

Many of the tasks associated with installing, configuring, and troubleshooting network adapters and drivers are similar to the maintenance of any hardware devices on a Windows 2000 Server computer. Most network adapters are connected to expansion slots inside the computer or consist of PC cards connected to the PC card slot on a portable computer. Each network adapter connected to your computer must have its own device driver, which is a program that allows a specific device to communicate with Windows 2000 Server. Windows 2000 cannot use a device until the appropriate driver is installed and configured. If a network adapter is listed on the Hardware Compatibility List (HCL), the device driver is usually included with Windows 2000. Device drivers load automatically when a computer is started unless the device is disabled. Once the drivers are loaded, Windows 2000 configures the properties and settings for the devices. Although you can manually configure device properties and settings, you should allow Windows 2000 to do this automatically whenever possible.

In addition to the tasks associated with most hardware devices on a Windows 2000 computer, the management of network adapters can include the addition, deletion, and configuration of network protocols, which are bound to the individual adapter. As pointed out earlier in this domain (in Objective 6.3), Windows 2000 supports a number of network protocols that make it possible for networks to share information. Protocols can be added or deleted as necessary and selectively bound to all network adapters in a server. In addition, protocol binding order can be changed at any time. Among the protocols supported by Windows 2000 is **Transmission Control Protocol/Internet Protocol (TCP/IP)**, which Windows 2000 uses for logon, file and print services, replication between domain controllers, and other common functions. Windows 2000 also supports a number of other network protocols, including **Asynchronous Transfer Mode (ATM)**, NWLink, NetBEUI, AppleTalk, Data Link Control (DLC), and IrDA.

To answer the questions in this objective, you should know how to use the Device Manager snap-in and the Add/Remove Hardware wizard to install, view, remove, and troubleshoot network adapters. You should also know how to use the Device Manager snap-in to access a device's properties and update the driver for that device. In addition, you should be able to add, delete, and configure the network protocols bound to your computer's network adapters.

Objective 6.7 Questions

70-215.06.07.001

You are configuring your Windows 2000 Server computer as a multihomed computer with a 10-Mbps network adapter and a 100-Mbps network adapter. You set up the network adapters as follows:

- The 10-Mbps network adapter connects to the Internet through a cable modem. The network adapter is configured with TCP/IP, NWLink, and Client for Microsoft Network.

- The 100-Mbps network adapter connects to a TCP/IP LAN. The network adapter is configured with NWLink and Client for Microsoft Networks.

Your server can connect to the Internet, but it cannot connect to the LAN. How should you resolve the connectivity problem to the LAN? (Choose all that apply.)

A. Add the TCP/IP protocol to the 100-Mbps network adapter.

B. Add Gateway Service for NetWare to the 100-Mbps network adapter.

C. Remove the TCP/IP protocol from the 10-Mbps network adapter.

D. Add the AppleTalk protocol to the 100-Mbps network adapter.

70-215.06.07.002

You have a Pentium III 366-MHz laptop computer with a built-in network adapter on your mother-board. You want to configure the computer so that the network adapter will be unavailable when you are not connected to the network. You duplicate the only existing hardware profile, name the new version "Undocked Configuration," and configure Windows 2000 so that it will not start until you select a profile. Then you restart your computer and select the new profile. What should you do next?

A. Use Device Manager to remove the network adapter.

B. Use Device Manager to disable the network adapter.

C. Use the Add/Remove Hardware wizard to uninstall the network adapter.

D. Use the Add/Remove Hardware wizard to disable the network adapter.

70-215.06.07.003

You must update a driver for a network adapter on your Windows 2000 Server computer. How can you best update the driver?

A. Use Device Manager to disable the network adapter, and then restart your computer.

B. Use Device Manager to scan the network adapter for hardware changes.

C. Use the Add/Remove Hardware wizard in Control Panel to remove the network adapter, and then restart the computer.

D. Use Device Manager to access the network adapter's Properties dialog box to update the driver.

Objective 6.7 Answers

70-215.06.07.001

▶ **Correct Answers: A**

A. **Correct:** A network adapter must be configured with the same protocol that is used in the network the adapter is connecting to. In this case, the network adapter must be configured with TCP/IP. TCP/IP is an industry standard suite of protocols that enable enterprise networking and connectivity on Windows 2000 computers. TCP/IP provides a set of standards for how computers communicate and how networks are interconnected. TCP/IP is the primary transport protocol used for Internet communication. It was designed for large internetworks spanning WAN links. TCP/IP provides networks with a standard routable enterprise networking protocol that is the most complete and accepted protocol available.

B. **Incorrect:** Gateway Service for NetWare allows you to create a gateway through which a Windows client computer not configured with NetWare client software can access NetWare file and print resources. Gateway Service for NetWare depends on and works with NWLink to communicate with the NetWare servers. However, because you are trying to connect to a TCP/IP network, you should configure the network adapter with TCP/IP, not Gateway Service for NetWare. If your network includes NetWare servers, you might want to include Gateway Service for NetWare, but you will still need TCP/IP to communicate with other TCP/IP hosts.

C. **Incorrect:** You should not remove TCP/IP because TCP/IP is the primary transport protocol used to communicate with the Internet. Without TCP/IP, the server could not establish an Internet connection.

D. **Incorrect:** AppleTalk is a protocol suite developed by Apple Computer, Inc. It allows Windows 2000 Server computers and Macintosh clients to share files and printers. However, because you are trying to connect to a TCP/IP network, you should configure the network adapter with TCP/IP, not AppleTalk. If your network includes Macintosh computers, you might want to include AppleTalk, but you will still need TCP/IP to communicate with other TCP/IP hosts.

70-215.06.07.002

▶ **Correct Answers: B**

A. **Incorrect:** When you use Device Manager to remove the network adapter, you are uninstalling the device but not removing the device drivers from your hard disk. You should then physically remove or disconnect the device from your computer, which you cannot do with a built-in network adapter. If you do not physically remove the device, Windows 2000 will detect it the next time you start the operating system and reinstall it, and you will have to uninstall it again. It is better to disable the network adapter rather than uninstall it. That way, you can keep the device connected to the computer and simply log on with the applicable hardware profile rather than uninstall the network adapter each time you connect to the network.

B. **Correct:** Once you create a hardware profile, you can use Device Manager to disable and enable a device in a profile. When you disable a device, the device drivers for the device are not loaded when you start the computer. This is preferable to removing a device, which means that you plan to uninstall the device from your system. Device Manager is an MMC snap-in that provides you with a graphical view of the hardware that is installed on your computer. Device Manager allows you to change the way your hardware interacts with your computer's microprocessor. Any hardware configuration changes that you make are implemented in the current hardware profile.

C. **Incorrect:** When you use the Add/Remove Hardware wizard to uninstall the network adapter, you are telling Windows 2000 that the device is going to be removed from the computer. You should then physically remove or disconnect the device from your computer, which you cannot do with a built-in network adapter. If you do not physically remove the device, Windows 2000 will detect it the next time you start the operating system and reinstall it if it can locate the device drivers, or you will be prompted for the location of the device drivers. Either you will have to cancel the installation or you will have to uninstall the device again. It is better to use Device Manager to disable the network adapter rather than remove it. That way, you can keep the device connected to the computer and simply log on with the original hardware profile, and you do not have to be concerned about Windows 2000 attempting to reinstall the device.

D. **Incorrect:** You cannot use the Add/Remove Hardware wizard to disable the network adapter. You must use Device Manager.

70-215.06.07.003

▶ **Correct Answers: D**

A. **Incorrect:** Disabling the network adapter will not update the device driver. When you disable a device, Windows 2000 updates the registry so that the device drivers are no longer loaded when you start your computer. The device drivers are available again when you enable the device. Disabling a device is useful if you want to have more than one hardware configuration for your computer or if you have a portable computer and you use it at a docking station. You should use Device Manager to update the device driver, not disable the device.

B. **Incorrect:** Scanning the network adapter will not update the device driver. The Scan For Hardware Changes option in Device Manager is used to scan for Plug and Play–compliant hardware connected to your computer. It will not reinstall a Plug and Play device if it detects a device and its driver, and it will not update the driver. If you scan the camera, Device Manager will most likely not find any hardware changes.

C. **Incorrect:** You can use the Add/Remove Hardware wizard to update the device driver, although it is not the most efficient method. If you use the Add/Remove Hardware wizard to uninstall the network adapter and its device drivers, and you leave the network adapter connected to the computer when you restart the computer, Windows 2000 should automatically redetect the network adapter. If device drivers are found on your hard disk, which is possible even though you specified removing the device drivers, the hardware is reinstalled and the existing drivers are used. If no device drivers are found, you will be prompted for the source of the device driver. At this point, you can provide the updated driver. However, it is simpler to use Device Manager to access the device's properties and update the driver from there without having to uninstall or reinstall hardware.

D. **Correct:** Device Manager is an MMC snap-in that provides you with a graphical view of the hardware that is installed on your computer. Device Manager allows you to change the way your hardware interacts with your computer's microprocessor. You can use Device Manager to access a device's properties. From there, you can install an updated device driver. To install the updated driver, click the Update Driver button on the Drivers tab of the device's Properties dialog box. This will launch the Update Device Driver wizard, which will step you through the process of updating the driver. During this process, you will be prompted for the source of the new driver. Be certain that you have the driver ready when you launch the wizard.

Implementing, Monitoring, and Troubleshooting Security

The configuration and maintenance of security in a Microsoft Windows 2000 environment represents a significant component of network administration. An administrator must be able to coordinate many security-related functions in order to implement a distributed security policy that protects both individual computers and the network as a whole. An effective distributed security policy enables users to log on to appropriate computer systems, find the information that they need, and use that information, while protecting the data as it is transferred over internal networks, public telephone networks, or the Internet. Windows 2000 includes a variety of technologies that you can use to protect your organization's internal and external network connections. For example, you can use the security policies within a **Group Policy Object (GPO)** to allow consistent security settings to be applied and enforced on classes of computers, such as the domain controller class. You can also use the **Encrypting File System (EFS)** technology to encrypt designated files and folders on a local computer, or you can configure local accounts on that computer to restrict access and protect data. Windows 2000 also allows you to audit network activity, enabling you to monitor a wide variety of events that can be used to track the activities of an intruder. In addition, Windows 2000 provides a set of tools that can be used to configure security settings and perform periodic analysis of the system to ensure that the configuration remains intact and to make security-related changes as necessary.

Tested Skills and Suggested Practices

The skills that you need to successfully master the Implementing, Monitoring, and Troubleshooting Security domain on the *Installing, Configuring, and Administering Microsoft Windows 2000 Server* exam include:

- **Using EFS to encrypt data on a hard disk.**

  - Practice 1: Set up a test folder on your Windows 2000 Server computer that contains three subfolders. The parent folder and its three subfolders should each contain a test document. (Be sure to use a folder and files that contain noncritical data.) Configure the folder and all its content with data encryption. If you have Windows Explorer set up to display file and folder attributes, you should see that an E has been added to the Attributes column. Verify that all subfolders and files within the parent folder are now encrypted.

  - Practice 2: Open a file in the test folder, and view its contents. Log off the computer, and log back on as a different user. Try opening one of the encrypted files to view it. You should receive a message saying that you have been denied access to that file. Now try changing the attribute of the file. Again, you should be denied access. Log off the computer, and log back on as the original user. Remove data encryption from the test folder and its content.

  - Practice 3: Configure one of the subfolders and its content with data compression. Configure another subfolder and its content with data encryption. Now configure the parent folder and its content with data encryption. Verify whether all the content in the test folder is now encrypted.

- **Creating a Group Policy object and modifying security settings within that object.**

  - Practice 1: Perform these practices on a Windows 2000 Server computer that is configured as a domain controller. Be sure to use a server that is set up in a test environment and is not part of a production network environment. Use the Active Directory Users And Computers snap-in to access the properties for the domain and create a new Group Policy Object (GPO). Open the properties for the GPO, and view—but do not change—the default settings.

  - Practice 2: Open the Group Policy snap-in that is associated with the GPO that you created in Practice 1. Access the Security Settings node under Computer Configuration. Thoroughly review the default security settings. Notice that most individual policies are, by default, not defined.

  - Practice 3: Configure several individual policies. You will be deleting the GPO as soon as you complete this practice, so configure whichever policies you like. Be certain to select a variety of types of policies from the various security nodes. Notice that some policies rely on other policies having to be configured. After you have completed configuring individual policies, close the Group Policy snap-in, and then delete the GPO that you created from the domain's properties. The domain's Properties dialog box should still be open from when you created the GPO. Be certain to delete the GPO permanently.

- **Setting up auditing and viewing the Security log in the Event Viewer snap-in.**

  - Practice 1: On a standalone Windows 2000 Server computer, open the Group Policy snap-in associated with the Local Computer Policy GPO, and access the Audit Policy node under Windows Settings. In the detail pane, double-click the Audit Object Access policy, and define the policy settings for successful attempts and failed attempts. Close the Group Policy snap-in, and use the proper SECEDIT command to update group policies.

  - Practice 2: In Windows Explorer, select a folder and set up auditing on that specific folder and its contents. Auditing is set up on a per-user basis, so configure auditing for the user who will log in to the network and access the folder that you just configured.

  - Practice 3: Log in to the computer as the user who is being audited, and attempt to access resources on the audited folder. Try connecting to the folder, viewing its contents, and then modifying one of the files. After you have finished accessing the folder, view the Security log in the Event Viewer snap-in to view audited events. Notice the different types of events that have been logged.

- **Configuring local accounts on a standalone Windows 2000 Server computer.**

  - Practice 1: Use the Computer Management console to create several test user accounts. Configure the properties for each account differently. Set one account so that the user must change the password the first time he or she logs on to the computer. Try logging on as that user.

  - Practice 2: Use the Computer Management console to create test user groups. Add some of the test user accounts to the groups. Grant different NTFS permissions on different folders to the users and groups. Vary which types of permissions you grant the users. Try logging on as one of the test users and then access the folders that you configured. Now log on as a different user.

- **Creating and using a security-related MMC console.**

  - Practice 1: Open the Microsoft Management Console (MMC) interface and add the Security Configuration And Analysis snap-in and the Security Templates snap-in. Configure the console in User mode with limited access and a single window. Save the MMC console as Security, and then close the console. From the Administrative Tools group, open the Security console that you just created.

  - Practice 2: Use the Security Configuration And Analysis snap-in to create a database. Base the new database on the BASICSV.INF template. Run a system analysis of your computer's security settings. After the analysis is complete, review the results by expanding the Security Configuration And Analysis snap-in.

■ Practice 3: Expand the Security Templates snap-in to view the various templates available when configuring and analyzing security. Compare the results of your analysis in the Security Configuration And Analysis snap-in to the settings in the Basicsv template.

Further Reading

This section lists supplemental readings by objective. Study these sources thoroughly before taking exam 70-215.

Objective 7.1

"Best Practice for Encrypting File System." (This article can be downloaded for free at *http://support.microsoft.com/support/kb/articles/Q223/3/16.asp.*)

"Encrypting File System for Windows 2000." (This document can be downloaded for free at *http://www.microsoft.com/windows2000/library/howitworks/security/encrypt.asp.*)

Microsoft Corporation. *Windows 2000 Server Resource Kit*. Volume: *Microsoft Windows 2000 Server Deployment Planning Guide*. Redmond, Washington: Microsoft Press, 2000. (This book can be downloaded for free at *http://www.microsoft.com/windows2000/library/resources/reskit/dpg/default.asp.*) Review Chapter 11, "Planning Distributed Security." This chapter includes a short discussion on EFS.

Microsoft Corporation. *Windows 2000 Server Resource Kit*. Volume: *Microsoft Windows 2000 Server Distributed Systems Guide*. Redmond, Washington: Microsoft Press, 2000. Review Chapter 15, "Encrypting File System."

Microsoft Corporation. *MCSE Training Kit: Microsoft Windows 2000 Server*. Redmond, Washington: Microsoft Press, 2000. Review Lesson 2 in Chapter 11, "Microsoft Windows 2000 Security."

"Step-by-Step Guide to Encrypting File System (EFS)." (This document can be downloaded for free at *http://www.microsoft.com/windows2000/library/planning/security/efssteps.asp.*)

"The Encrypted Data Recovery Policy for Encrypting File System." (This article can be downloaded for free at *http://support.microsoft.com/support/kb/articles/Q230/4/90.asp.*)

Objective 7.2

"Introduction to Windows 2000 Group Policy." (This paper can be downloaded for free at *http://www.microsoft.com/windows2000/library/howitworks/management/grouppolicyintro.asp.*)

Microsoft Corporation. *Windows 2000 Server Resource Kit*. Volume: *Microsoft Windows 2000 Server Deployment Planning Guide*. Redmond, Washington: Microsoft Press, 2000. (This book can be downloaded for free at *http://www.microsoft.com/windows2000/library/resources/reskit/dpg/default.asp.*) Review Chapter 11, "Planning Distributed Security." This chapter includes a discussion about setting security policies.

Microsoft Corporation. *Windows 2000 Server Resource Kit.* Volume: *Microsoft Windows 2000 Server Distributed Systems Guide.* Redmond, Washington: Microsoft Press, 2000. Review Chapter 22, "Group Policy."

Microsoft Corporation. *MCSE Training Kit: Microsoft Windows 2000 Server.* Redmond, Washington: Microsoft Press, 2000. Review Lesson 4 in Chapter 7, "Administering Microsoft Windows 2000 Server."

"Step-by-Step Guide to Configuring Enterprise Security Policies." (This article can be downloaded for free at *http://www.microsoft.com/windows2000/library/planning/security/entsecsteps.asp.*)

"Windows 2000 Group Policy White Paper." (This paper can be downloaded for free at *http://www.microsoft.com/TechNet/win2000/win2ksrv/technote/nt5polcy.asp.*)

Objective 7.3

Microsoft Corporation. *Windows 2000 Server Resource Kit.* Volume: *Microsoft Windows 2000 Server Deployment Planning Guide.* Redmond, Washington: Microsoft Press, 2000. (This book can be downloaded for free at *http://www.microsoft.com/windows2000/library/resources/reskit/dpg/default.asp.*) Review Chapter 11, "Planning Distributed Security." This chapter includes a discussion about auditing.

Microsoft Corporation. *Windows 2000 Server Resource Kit.* Volume: *Microsoft Windows 2000 Server Distributed Systems Guide.* Redmond, Washington: Microsoft Press, 2000. Review Chapter 12, "Access Control." This chapter includes a discussion on auditing.

Microsoft Corporation. *MCSE Training Kit: Microsoft Windows 2000 Server.* Redmond, Washington: Microsoft Press, 2000. Review Lesson 5 in Chapter 11, "Microsoft Windows 2000 Security."

Objective 7.4

Microsoft Corporation. *Windows 2000 Server Resource Kit.* Volume: *Microsoft Windows 2000 Server Deployment Planning Guide.* Redmond, Washington: Microsoft Press, 2000. (This book can be downloaded for free at *http://www.microsoft.com/windows2000/library/resources/reskit/dpg/default.asp.*) Review Chapter 11, "Planning Distributed Security." This chapter includes a discussion about security groups.

Microsoft Corporation. *MCSE Training Kit: Microsoft Windows 2000 Server.* Redmond, Washington: Microsoft Press, 2000. Review Lessons 2 and 3 in Chapter 7, "Administering Microsoft Windows 2000 Server."

Objective 7.5

"Introduction to Windows 2000 Group Policy." (This paper can be downloaded for free at *http://www.microsoft.com/windows2000/library/howitworks/management/grouppolicyintro.asp.*)

Microsoft Corporation. *Windows 2000 Server Resource Kit*. Volume: *Microsoft Windows 2000 Server Deployment Planning Guide*. Redmond, Washington: Microsoft Press, 2000. (This book can be downloaded for free at *http://www.microsoft.com/windows2000/library/resources/reskit/dpg/default.asp*.) Review Chapter 11, "Planning Distributed Security." This chapter includes a discussion about setting security policies.

Microsoft Corporation. *Windows 2000 Server Resource Kit*. Volume: *Microsoft Windows 2000 Server Distributed Systems Guide*. Redmond, Washington: Microsoft Press, 2000. Review Chapter 22, "Group Policy."

Microsoft Corporation. *MCSE Training Kit: Microsoft Windows 2000 Server*. Redmond, Washington: Microsoft Press, 2000. Review Lesson 4 in Chapter 7, "Administering Microsoft Windows 2000 Server."

"Step-by-Step Guide to Configuring Enterprise Security Policies." (This article can be downloaded for free at *http://www.microsoft.com/windows2000/library/planning/security/entsecsteps.asp*.)

"Windows 2000 Group Policy White Paper." (This paper can be downloaded for free at *http://www.microsoft.com/TechNet/win2000/win2ksrv/technote/nt5polcy.asp*.)

Objective 7.6

"Introduction to Windows 2000 Group Policy." (This paper can be downloaded for free at *http://www.microsoft.com/windows2000/library/howitworks/management/grouppolicyintro.asp*.)

Microsoft Corporation. *Windows 2000 Server Resource Kit*. Volume: *Microsoft Windows 2000 Server Deployment Planning Guide*. Redmond, Washington: Microsoft Press, 2000. (This book can be downloaded for free at *http://www.microsoft.com/windows2000/library/resources/reskit/dpg/default.asp*.) Review Chapter 11, "Planning Distributed Security."

Microsoft Corporation. *Windows 2000 Server Resource Kit*. Volume: *Microsoft Windows 2000 Server Distributed Systems Guide*. Redmond, Washington: Microsoft Press, 2000. Review Chapter 22, "Group Policy."

Microsoft Corporation. *MCSE Training Kit: Microsoft Windows 2000 Server*. Redmond, Washington: Microsoft Press, 2000. Review Lesson 4 in Chapter 11, "Microsoft Windows 2000 Security."

"Step-by-Step Guide to Configuring Enterprise Security Policies." (This article can be downloaded for free at *http://www.microsoft.com/windows2000/library/planning/security/entsecsteps.asp*.)

"Step-by-Step Guide to Using the Security Configuration Tool Set." (This article can be downloaded for free at *http://www.microsoft.com/windows2000/library/planning/security/secconfsteps.asp*.)

OBJECTIVE 7.1

Encrypt data on a hard disk by using Encrypting File System (EFS).

The Encrypting File System (EFS) feature in Windows 2000 protects sensitive data in files that are stored on NTFS volumes. EFS uses **symmetric key encryption** in conjunction with **public key** technology to protect a file. It runs as an integrated system service, making it easy to manage and difficult to attack. EFS provides its users with privacy, transparent operation, and a means of data recovery. Only the owner of the file and designated user accounts can decrypt the file. Other users are denied access. Users who have permissions for that file—even the Take Ownership permission—cannot open the file without the encryptor's public key. An owner of an encrypted file is issued a digital certificate with a public key and **private key** pair that is used for EFS operations. EFS uses the key set for the user who is logged on to the local computer on which the private key is stored. It also ensures that encryption is not inadvertently defeated by copying or moving files. File encryption does not require the file owner to decrypt or re-encrypt the file on each use. EFS operations are transparent to the file owner and to applications. Decryption and encryption take place transparently as the file is read from and written to the disk. EFS is tightly integrated with NTFS. You can set the encryption attribute for folders and files as you set other attributes. However, you cannot compress and encrypt files or folders at the same time. You can use EFS for file systems on remote computers, but only if the remote computers are trusted for delegation.

Besides the user who encrypts a file, only designated recovery agents can decrypt it. EFS can be used only if at least one user account has been designated as a recovery agent. Recovery agent accounts are issued recovery agent certificates with public keys and private keys that are used for EFS data recovery operations. Recovery agent accounts are designated by EFS recovery policy. By default, the recovery agent account is the highest-level administrator account. On a standalone computer, this is the local administrator. In a domain, the domain administrator for the first domain controller installed in the domain is the default recovery agent account for all computers in the domain. Different recovery agent accounts can be assigned by changing EFS recovery policy, and different recovery policies can be configured for different parts of the organization. There can be more than one recovery agent account for an EFS file, each with a different private key. However, EFS is disabled if you configure an EFS recovery policy with no recovery agent.

To answer the questions in this objective, you should have a basic understanding of how EFS works and how it uses public key technology to protect data. You should know how to configure EFS recovery policy to designate specific users as recovery agent accounts. You should also know how to use Windows Explorer and the CIPHER command-line utility to encrypt files and folders and know how encryption is affected if files are copied or moved.

Objective 7.1 Questions

70-215.07.01.001

You are the administrator of the Windows 2000 Server computer, and you want to enable encryption on one of its folders and the folder's contents. However, the folder and its contents are already compressed because there is limited space on the hard disk. How can you set up encryption on the folder and its contents while maintaining compression?

A. Use the Active Directory Users And Computers snap-in to configure encryption.

B. Open the folder's properties and enable encryption on the folder and its contents.

C. Decompress the folder only and enable encryption on the folder and its contents.

D. You cannot enable encryption and compression on folders or files at the same time.

70-215.07.01.002

You are the administrator of a Windows 2000 Server computer, and you want to encrypt one of the folders and its contents. You back up the computer's hard disk, and then you begin to encrypt the data. During the encryption process, the computer loses power. Once power is restored, you reboot the computer. You now want to ensure that any content that was not successfully encrypted is restored to its original state before you try to encrypt it once more. What should you do?

A. Use the CIPHER command-line utility to create a new file encryption certificate on the computer.

B. Restore the most recent backup of the hard disk.

C. Use the CIPHER command-line utility to decrypt the folder and its contents.

D. Do nothing. EFS undoes the encryption operation on startup.

70-215.07.01.003

You create the Accounting folder on the C: drive of a Windows 2000 Server computer. You want any files added to the folder to be encrypted. You open a command window and go to the C: prompt. Which command should you use to configure encryption on the folder?

A. **cipher /e accounting**

B. **cipher /e /a accounting***

C. **cipher /d accounting**

D. **cipher /d /a accounting***

70-215.07.01.004

In the past, the C:\Accounting folder of a Windows 2000 Server computer had been used to store encrypted data. Currently, the folder contains no subfolders or files, and you now want to ensure that no unencrypted files that are added to the folder are encrypted. You open a command window and go to the C: prompt. Which command should you use to ensure that files added to the folder are not encrypted?

A. **cipher /e accounting**

B. **cipher /e /a accounting***

C. **cipher /d accounting**

D. **cipher /d /a accounting***

Objective 7.1 Answers

70-215.07.01.001

▶ **Correct Answers: D**

A. **Incorrect:** The Active Directory Users And Computers snap-in is a directory administration tool that allows you to add, modify, delete, and organize the Windows 2000 user accounts, computer accounts, security and distribution groups, and published resources in your organization's directory. The Active Directory Users And Computers snap-in cannot be used to enable encryption on files and folders.

B. **Incorrect:** You can enable encryption on a folder and its contents by accessing the folder's properties or by using the CIPHER command-line utility. When a file is encrypted, only the user who encrypted the file or the designated recovery agent can decrypt that file. All other users are denied access to the file. However, you cannot enable encryption and compression at the same time. The two are mutually exclusive. If you enable encryption on the folder and its contents, they are first decompressed, and then they are encrypted.

C. **Incorrect:** Although you can decompress only the folder, this will not prevent the folder's contents from being decompressed when you enable encryption. If you enable encryption on the folder and its contents, any object that is compressed will first be decompressed, and the folder and its contents will be encrypted.

D. **Correct:** Encryption and compression are mutually exclusive. If you enable encryption on the folder and its contents, they are first decompressed, and then they are encrypted.

70-215.07.01.002

▶ **Correct Answers: D**

A. **Incorrect:** The CIPHER command-line utility allows you to encrypt and decrypt files from a command prompt. You can also use the CIPHER command to display the encryption status of the current folder and any files that it contains. In addition, you can use the CIPHER command to create a new file encryption certificate on the computer on which you run the command. However, you do not need to create a new certificate if the encryption process is disrupted. If an encryption operation cannot be completed, it is completely undone, and the files are returned to their original encrypted state. The original certificate is unaffected.

B. **Incorrect:** It is not necessary to restore the most recent backup of the hard disk. If an encryption operation cannot be completed, it is completely undone, and the files are returned to their original encrypted state.

C. **Incorrect:** You do not have to use the CIPHER command to decrypt the folder and its contents. If the encryption process is disrupted, the process cannot be completed, and the files are returned to their original encrypted state. Consequently, those files for which encryption was not completed will not need to be decrypted.

D. **Correct:** Encryption and decryption are sensitive operations, and failure can result in data loss. Therefore, EFS makes all operations automatic. If an encryption operation cannot be completed, it is completely undone. As a result, if a computer loses power during an encryption operation, EFS undoes the operation on restart so that the file is in a consistent state.

70-215.07.01.003

▶ **Correct Answers: A**

A. **Correct:** The CIPHER command-line utility allows you to encrypt and decrypt files from a command prompt. You can also use the CIPHER command to display the encryption status of the current folder and any files that it contains. In addition, you can use the CIPHER command to create a new file encryption certificate on the computer on which you run the command. The CIPHER command must be used with specific parameters to encrypt and decrypt files. The /e switch is used to encrypt a specified folder, which in this case is the Accounting folder. Any files that are then added to the folder will be encrypted.

B. **Incorrect:** The /a switch, when used with the /e switch, is used to encrypt any specified files. In this case, a wild card (*) is used to specify that all files in the Accounting folder should be encrypted. However, the Accounting folder is a new folder and does not contain any files. In addition, the cipher /e /a accounting* command does not encrypt the folder itself. If the folder did contain content—and you wanted to encrypt the folder, its files, and its subfolders—you would use the cipher /e /s:accounting /a command.

C. **Incorrect:** The /d switch of the CIPHER command is used to decrypt a specified folder, which in this case is the Accounting folder. Because you want files to be encrypted, you should use the /e switch, not the /d switch.

D. **Incorrect:** The /a switch, when used with the /d switch, is used to decrypt any specified files. In this case, a wild card (*) is used to specify that all files in the Accounting folder should be decrypted. Because you want files to be encrypted, you should use the /e switch, not the /d switch. In addition, the Accounting folder is a new folder and does not contain any content, and the cipher /d /a accounting* command does not affect the actual folder, only files within the folder.

70-215.07.01.004

▶ **Correct Answers: C**

A. **Incorrect:** The /e switch is used to encrypt a specified folder, which in this case is the Accounting folder. Any files that are then added to the folder will be encrypted. Because you do not want files to be encrypted, you should use the /d switch, not the /e switch.

B. **Incorrect:** The /a switch, when used with the /e switch, is used to encrypt any specified files. In this case, a wild card (*) is used to specify that all files in the Accounting folder should be encrypted. However, the Accounting folder does not contain any files. In addition, the cipher /e /a accounting* command does not prevent files that are added to the folder from being encrypted. If the folder did contain content—and you wanted to decrypt the folder and its content—you would use the cipher /d /s:accounting /a command.

C. **Correct:** The CIPHER command-line utility allows you to encrypt and decrypt files from a command prompt. You can also use the CIPHER command to display the encryption status of the current folder and any files that it contains. In addition, you can use the CIPHER command to create a new file encryption certificate on the computer on which you run the command. The CIPHER command must be used with specific parameters to encrypt and decrypt files. The /d switch is used to decrypt a specified folder, which in this case is the Accounting folder. No unencrypted files that are then added to the folder will be encrypted.

D. **Incorrect:** The /a switch, when used with the /d switch, is used to decrypt any specified files. In this case, a wild card (*) is used to specify that all files in the Accounting folder should be decrypted. However, the Accounting folder does not contain any content, and the cipher /d /a accounting* command does not affect the actual folder, only files within the folder. So this command will not prevent files from being encrypted when they are added to the folder.

OBJECTIVE 7.2

Implement, configure, manage, and troubleshoot policies in a Windows 2000 environment.

Windows 2000 **group policies** are a set of configuration settings that can be applied to one or more objects in the Active Directory store or applied locally to individual Windows 2000 computers. Group policies can be used to control the work environment of users in a domain, or users with accounts located in a specific **organizational unit (OU)**. Group policies can also be set at the site level. With group policies, you can configure how an object and its child objects should behave. You can provide users with a fully populated desktop environment that can include a customized Start menu or with applications that are automatically set up. You can also restrict user access to files, folders, and Windows 2000 system settings. In addition, group policies can affect rights that are granted to user accounts and groups. By implementing appropriate group policy settings for specific users, combined with NTFS permissions, mandatory profiles, and other Windows 2000 security features, you can prevent users from installing software and accessing unauthorized programs or data. You can also prevent users from deleting files that are important to the proper functioning of their applications and operating system. Group policies influence a variety of network components and Active Directory objects, including software settings, script execution, security settings, administrative templates, **Remote Installation Services (RIS)** options, and folder redirection.

Group policies are contained within a **Group Policy Object (GPO)**. One or more GPOs can be applied to a site, domain, or OU. Multiple containers in the Active Directory store can be associated with the same GPO, and a single container can have more than one GPO associated with it. In addition, a local GPO exists on every Windows 2000 computer, and, by default, only the security settings are configured. A GPO stores group policy information in **Group Policy Containers (GPCs)** and **Group Policy Templates (GPTs)**. The GPC is an Active Directory object that stores GPO properties and includes subcontainers for computer and user group policy information. The GPC also includes version information to ensure that the GPC is synchronized with the GPT and includes status information that indicates whether the GPO is enabled or disabled. The GPTs make up a folder structure that stores the policy settings for administrative templates, security settings, script files, and software settings. When a GPO is created, the corresponding GPT folder structure is created. In general, group policy data that is small in size and changes infrequently is stored in the GPCs. Group policy data that is large and can change frequently is stored in the GPT.

To answer the questions in this objective, you should have a thorough understanding of how group policies work and how they can be used to administer a Windows 2000 environment. You should also have an understanding of how GPOs store group policy information. In addition, you should know how to create a GPO, configure GPO permissions, and administer the various types of group policies.

Objective 7.2 Questions

70-215.07.02.001

You are the administrator of a Windows 2000 network that includes three member servers that are used by the Accounting department. The member servers are contained within the AccountServers organizational unit (OU) within the Active Directory directory service. The OU contains no other computer objects. The Accounting department recently hired 15 temporary employees. User accounts were created for each of these employees, and the accounts were added to the AccountTemp group. The users each work on a Windows 2000 Professional computer that is a client computer in the domain. You want to prevent members of the AccountTemp group from being able to log on locally to the three member servers used by the Accounting department. What should you do?

A. In the Group Policy Object (GPO) linked to the AccountServers OU, define the Deny Access To This Computer From The Network policy, and add the AccountTemp group to the policy.

B. In the GPO linked to the AccountServers OU, define the Deny Logon Locally policy, and add the AccountTemp group to the policy.

C. In the GPO linked to the domain, define the Deny Logon Locally policy, and add the AccountDept OU and the AccountTemp group to the policy.

D. In the GPO linked to the Computers container, define the Deny Access To This Computer From The Network policy, and add the three Accounting department computers and the AccountTemp group to the policy.

Objective 7.2 Answers

70-215.07.02.001

▶ **Correct Answers: B**

A. **Incorrect:** When you have an OU that contains specific computers, you can set policies for those computers by modifying the GPO associated with that OU. In this case, you can modify the GPO linked to the AccountServers OU. However, to prevent the AccountTemp group from being able to log on locally to these servers, you should configure the Deny Logon Locally policy, not the Deny Access To This Computer From The Network policy. The latter policy prevents network access, not local logon.

B. **Correct:** A GPO can contain group policy settings for local computers, sites, domains, or OUs. A GPO associated with an OU contains group policies that affect only the objects contained within that OU. If you modify the GPO linked to the AccountServers OU, the policies are applied to the three member servers that are contained within that OU. In this case, the Deny Logon Locally policy will be applied to the member servers, and members of the AccountTemp group will be unable to log on locally to the servers. Group policy settings are processed in a specific order: local computer, site, domain, and organizational unit or units. This order means that the local computer's group policy object is processed first, and group policy objects linked to the organizational unit of which the computer or user is a direct member are processed last, overriding the earlier group policy objects. Policy settings are inherited unless they are overridden by incompatible settings in another policy.

C. **Incorrect:** Although you should configure the Deny Logon Locally policy, you should set the policy in the GPO linked to the AccountServers OU, not the GPO linked to the domain. The domain GPO applies to all containers beneath the domain, including user and computer objects in each container. Consequently, the members of the AccountTemp group will not be able to log on to any computers, including their own Windows 2000 Professional computers.

D. **Incorrect:** You should configure the GPO associated with the AccountServers OU. There is no GPO associated with the Computers container. In addition, you should configure the Deny Logon Locally policy, not the Deny Access To This Computer From The Network policy.

Implement, configure, manage, and troubleshoot auditing.

Windows 2000 **auditing** allows you to track both user activities and Windows 2000 activities on a computer. The types of activities that you can audit are predefined **events**. Through auditing, you can specify that Windows 2000 writes a record of an event to a log that can be viewed by using the Event Viewer snap-in. Security-related events in Windows 2000 are written to the Security log. The Security log can maintain a record of valid and invalid logon attempts and events related to creating, opening, or deleting files or other objects. An audit entry in the Security log includes information about the event that was performed, the user who performed the event, and the success or failure of the event. When you first start Event Viewer, it displays all events that are recorded to the selected log. You can filter the log to display specific events, or you can search the log to find a specific event. You can also archive event logs so that you can track trends by comparing logs from different periods.

To implement auditing on your Windows 2000 computer, you must configure the appropriate Audit Policy. The Audit Policy defines the types of security events that Windows 2000 records in the Security log on the computer on which the events occur. You can audit access to files and folders, users logging on and off, users shutting down and restarting the computer, changes to user accounts and groups, and attempts to change Active Directory objects. When you set up auditing for specialized resources, such as files, folders, printers, or Active Directory objects, you must first configure the appropriate audit policy, and then you must enable auditing for that resource.

To answer the questions in this objective, you should know how to configure Audit Policy on a Windows 2000 domain controller as well as on a member or standalone server. You should also know how to enable auditing on specific resources, such as files and folders. After you have set up auditing, you should be able to use Event Viewer to view the Security log for the specific computer.

Objective 7.3 Questions

70-215.07.03.001

You are creating a Group Policy Object (GPO) for your Windows 2000 network.

You want to achieve the following results:

- You must audit the success and failure of account logon events.

- You must audit the success of changes to user accounts.

- You must audit the success and failure of directory service access.

- You must audit all successful changes to policies.

You configure a new GPO for the domain.

Which result or results do you achieve? (Choose all that apply.)

Examine the Group Policy snap-in shown in the image below to view the security settings of the Group Policy Object.

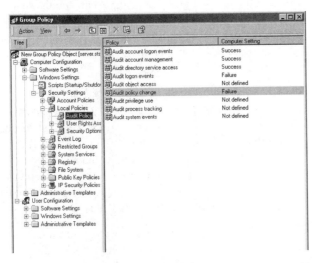

A. The success and failure of account logon events will be audited.

B. The success of changes to user accounts will be audited.

C. The success and failure of directory service access will be audited.

D. All successful changes to policies will be audited.

70-215.07.03.002

You are creating a Group Policy Object (GPO) for your Windows 2000 network.

You want to achieve the following results:

■ You must audit the success and failure of account logon events.

■ You must audit the success of changes to user accounts.

■ You must audit the success and failure of directory service access.

■ You must audit all successful changes to policies.

You configure a new GPO for the domain.

Which result or results do you achieve? (Choose all that apply.)

Examine the Group Policy snap-in shown in the image below to view the security settings of the Group Policy Object.

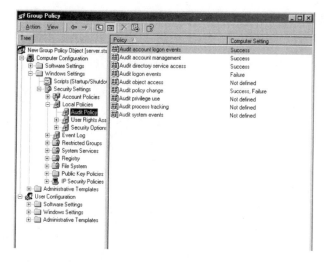

A. The success and failure of account logon events will be audited.

B. The success of changes to user accounts will be audited.

C. The success and failure of directory service access will be audited.

D. All successful changes to policies will be audited.

70-215.07.03.003

You are creating a Group Policy Object (GPO) for your Windows 2000 network.

You want to achieve the following results:

- You must audit the success and failure of account logon events.

- You must audit the success of changes to user accounts.

- You must audit the success and failure of directory service access.

- You must audit all successful changes to policies.

You configure a new GPO for the domain.

Which result or results do you achieve? (Choose all that apply.)

Examine the Group Policy snap-in shown in the image below to view the security settings of the Group Policy Object.

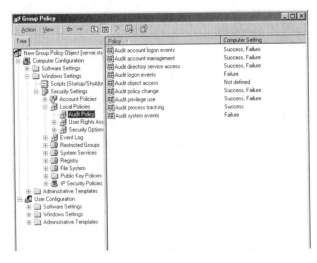

A. The success and failure of account logon events will be audited.

B. The success of changes to user accounts will be audited.

C. The success and failure of directory service access will be audited.

D. All successful changes to policies will be audited.

70-215.07.03.004

You want to set up auditing on a Hewlett-Packard LaserJet 5P printer. You want to log an event whenever a member of the Administrators groups successfully prints a document to this printer. Which permission or permissions (for successful events) should be selected? (Choose all that apply.)

Examine the dialog box shown in the image below to view the auditing options for the HP LaserJet 5P printer.

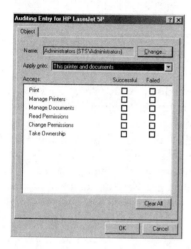

A. Print

B. Manage Printers

C. Manage Documents

D. Read Permissions

E. Change Permissions

F. Take Ownership

Objective 7.3 Answers

70-215.07.03.001

▶ **Correct Answers: B**

A. **Incorrect:** To audit the success and failure of account logon events, you must configure the Audit Account Logon Events policy to write an audit entry to the Security log whenever there is a successful or failed account logon attempt. Although the policy is currently configured to log successful events, it is not configured to log failed events. You must configure the policy to log both kinds of events to meet this requirement.

B. **Correct:** By using the Group Policy snap-in, you can configure auditing-related group policies that are contained in a GPO. A GPO contains nine types of security policies. One of these types is Local Policies. Local Policies includes Audit Policy. Audit Policy allows you to audit account logon, account management, directory service access, logon events, object access, policy change, privilege use, process tracking, and system events. You can audit both successful and failed events, which are written to the Security log whenever the event occurs. To audit the success of changes to user accounts, you must configure the Audit Account Management policy to write an audit entry to the Security log whenever there is a successful attempt to modify a user account. You can also configure the policy to log failed attempts at modifying user accounts.

C. **Incorrect:** To audit the success and failure of directory service access, you must configure the Audit Directory Service Access policy to write an audit entry to the Security log whenever there is a successful or failed attempt to access directory services. Although the policy is currently configured to log successful events, it is not configured to log failed events. You must configure the policy to log both types of events to meet this requirement.

D. **Incorrect:** To audit successful changes to policies, you must configure the Audit Policy Change policy to write an audit entry to the Security log whenever there is a successful change to a policy. Currently, the policy is configured to log only failed attempts to change policies, not successful attempts.

70-215.07.03.002

▶ **Correct Answers: B and D**

A. **Incorrect:** To audit the success and failure of account logon events, you must configure the Audit Account Logon Events policy to write an audit entry to the Security log whenever there is a successful or failed account logon attempt. Although the policy is currently configured to log successful events, it is not configured to log failed events. You must configure the policy to log both kinds of events to meet this requirement.

B. **Correct:** By using the Group Policy snap-in, you can configure auditing-related group policies that are contained in a GPO. A GPO contains nine types of security policies. One of these types is Local Policies. Local Policies includes Audit Policy. Audit Policy allows you to audit account logon, account management, directory service access, logon events, object access, policy change, privilege use, process tracking, and system events. You can audit both successful and failed events, which are written to the Security log whenever the event occurs. To audit the success of changes to user accounts, you must configure the Audit Account Management policy to write an audit entry to the Security log whenever there is a successful attempt to modify a user account. You can also configure the policy to log failed attempts at modifying user accounts.

C. **Incorrect:** To audit the success and failure of directory service access, you must configure the Audit Directory Service Access policy to write an audit entry to the Security log whenever there is a successful or failed attempt to access directory services. Although the policy is currently configured to log successful events, it is not configured to log failed events. You must configure the policy to log both types of events to meet this requirement.

D. **Correct:** To audit successful changes to policies, you must configure the Audit Policy Change policy to write an audit entry to the Security log whenever there is a successful change to a policy. Currently, the policy is configured to log successful and failed attempts to change policies. Logging failed events does not affect whether successful events are logged. You can log only successful events, log only failed events, or log both types of events.

70-215.07.03.003

▶ **Correct Answers: A, B, C, and D**

A. **Correct:** By using the Group Policy snap-in, you can configure auditing-related group policies that are contained in a GPO. A GPO contains nine types of security policies. One of these types is Local Policies. Local Policies includes Audit Policy. Audit Policy allows you to audit account logon, account management, directory service access, logon events, object access, policy change, privilege use, process tracking, and system events. You can audit both successful and failed events, which are written to the Security log whenever the event occurs. To audit the success and failure of account logon events, you must configure the Audit Account Logon Events policy to write an audit entry to the Security log whenever there is a successful or failed account logon attempt. Currently, the policy is configured to log successful and failed attempts to log on.

B. **Correct:** To audit the success of changes to user accounts, you must configure the Audit Account Management policy to write an audit entry to the Security log whenever there is a successful attempt to modify a user account. Currently, the policy is configured to log successful and failed attempts to change user accounts. Logging failed events does not affect whether successful events are logged. You can log only successful events, log only failed events, or log both types of events.

C. **Correct:** To audit the success and failure of directory service access, you must configure the Audit Directory Service Access policy to write an audit entry to the Security log whenever there is a successful or failed attempt to access directory services. Currently, the policy is configured to log successful and failed attempts to access directory services.

D. **Correct:** To audit successful changes to policies, you must configure the Audit Policy Change policy to write an audit entry to the Security log whenever there is a successful change to a policy. Currently, the policy is configured to log successful and failed attempts to change policies.

70-215.07.03.004

► **Correct Answers: A and D**

A. **Correct:** Auditing a printer allows you to track that printer's usage. You can specify which groups or users to audit and which actions to audit. For each event that can be audited, you can log both successful and failed attempts to perform that action. Auditing is configured on a printer by selecting the appropriate permissions. Specific events are associated with each permission. If the Print permission is selected, an event is added to the Security log whenever the specified users or groups attempt to print a document to the printer. An event is also logged when those users change document printing preferences on the printer. In the case of the Administrators, you need to log only successful events to meet the requirements; however, you can log failed events as well.

B. **Incorrect:** If the Manage Printers permission is selected, an event is added to the Security log whenever the specified users or groups attempt to change a document's printing defaults, create a printer share, change printer properties, or delete a printer. However, an event is not logged if the users attempt to print a document to the printer unless the Print permission is selected.

C. **Incorrect:** If the Manage Documents permission is selected, an event is added to the Security log whenever the specified users or groups attempt to change a document's job properties; pause, restart, move, or delete a document; or change document printing defaults. However, an event is not logged if the users attempt to print a document to the printer unless the Print permission is selected.

D. **Correct:** By default, the Read Permissions permission is automatically selected when you select the Print permission. When Read Permissions is selected, an event is added to the Security log whenever the specified users or groups attempt to read printer permissions.

E. **Incorrect:** If the Change Permissions permission is selected, an event is added to the Security log whenever the specified users or groups attempt to change printer permissions. However, an event is not logged if the users attempt to print a document to the printer unless the Print permission is selected.

F. **Incorrect:** If the Take Ownership permission is selected, an event is added to the Security log whenever the specified users or groups attempt to take ownership of a document or printer. However, an event is not logged if the users attempt to print a document to the printer unless the Print permission is selected.

Implement, configure, manage, and troubleshoot local accounts.

Windows 2000 allows you to create and manage local **user accounts** on standalone and member servers. A user account is a user's unique credentials that define the user to Windows 2000. A local user account allows a user to log on to and gain resources on the computer where the account is created. The account applies only to that computer and no other computers in the domain. When you create a local user account on a standalone or member server, Windows 2000 Server creates the account in that computer's security database. Windows 2000 does not replicate the account information to domain controllers. After the user account is created, the computer uses its local security database to authenticate the local user account, which allows the user to log on to that computer. You can create a user account and modify its properties by using the Local Users And Groups snap-in, which is included in the Computer Management console on a standalone or member server. The Local Users And Groups snap-in is disabled on a domain controller. As with domain user accounts, a set of default properties is associated with each local user account that is created. However, local user account properties represent only a subset of domain user account properties.

In addition to user accounts, you can create local **group accounts** on Windows 2000 Server computers. A group is a collection of user accounts. Groups simplify administration by allowing you to assign permissions to groups of users rather than having to assign permissions to individual user accounts. Windows 2000 supports two types of local groups: domain local groups and computer local groups. A domain local group can contain members from anywhere in the forest, in trusted forests, or in a trusted pre–Windows 2000 domain. However, this objective is concerned with computer local groups. Unlike domain local groups, computer local groups are created on standalone servers and member servers and can be used only on the computer on which the group is created. Therefore, you should not use computer local groups on computers that are part of a domain because it prevents you from centralizing group administration. Computer local groups do not appear in the Active Directory store. They must be maintained separately for each computer. You can use the Local Users And Groups snap-in to create computer local groups. You can assign permissions to computer local groups for access only to resources on the computer on which you create the group. Computer local groups can contain local user accounts only from the computer on which you create the local groups.

To answer the questions in this objective, you should know how to implement local user accounts and group accounts on standalone and member servers. You should be able to create the accounts and modify their properties. You should also be able to set user account passwords, unlock those accounts, and disable, enable, rename, or delete the accounts. In addition, you should be able to add and delete user accounts from local groups.

Objective 7.4 Questions

70-215.07.04.001

You are the domain administrator of a Windows 2000 network that includes 10 Windows 2000 Server computers and 100 Windows 2000 Professional computers. The network contains only one site. Linda, a new user in your organization, must be able to log on locally to a Windows 2000 Server computer that is a member server in the domain. Linda must also be able to log on to the domain through her Windows 2000 Professional computer. You create a local user account on the Windows 2000 Server computer. Linda can log on locally to the server, but she cannot log on to the domain through her workstation. What should you do?

A. Create a domain user account for Linda.

B. Configure the local user account to permit domain logon.

C. Force the replication of the Active Directory store.

D. Tell Linda to wait at least five minutes and then try again to log on to the domain.

70-215.07.04.002

You are the domain administrator of a Windows 2000 network that includes 10 Windows 2000 Server computers and 100 Windows 2000 Professional computers. The network contains only one site. Linda, a new user in your organization, must be able to log on locally to a Windows 2000 Server computer that is a member server in the domain. Linda should not be able to log on to the domain. You create a domain user account, but this allows Linda to log on to the domain. What should you do?

A. Delete the domain user account, and create a local user account on the server.

B. Configure the domain user account to allow local logon only to the server.

C. Delete the domain user account, disable Active Directory on the member server, and create a domain user account on the server.

D. Disable directory replication on the member server, and configure the domain user account to allow local logon to the server.

70-215.07.04.003

You are creating a local user account for an employee named Jennifer. You plan to assign to her account the initial password of "temporary." You want her to create her own password when she first logs on to the computer. Which option or options in the New User dialog box should you select? (Choose all that apply.)

Examine the dialog box shown in the image below to view the user's password configuration options.

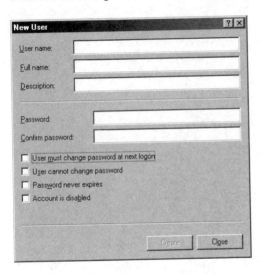

A. User Must Change Password At Next Logon

B. User Cannot Change Password

C. Password Never Expires

D. Account Is Disabled

Objective 7.4 Answers

70-215.07.04.001

▶ **Correct Answers: A**

A. **Correct:** A domain user account allows users to log on to the domain and gain access to resources anywhere on the network. In this case, Linda would provide her user name and password during the logon process. Windows 2000 uses this information to authenticate Linda and build an access token that contains information about Linda and about security settings. The access token identifies Linda to Windows 2000 computers (in the domain) on which Linda tries to access resources. Windows 2000 provides the access token for the duration of the logon session. You can create a user account in an Active Directory organizational unit (OU) on a domain controller. The domain controller replicates the new user account information to all domain controllers in the domain. After Windows 2000 replicates the account, all domain controllers in the domain tree can authenticate Linda during the logon process.

B. **Incorrect:** A local user account cannot be configured to permit domain logon. A local user account allows users to log on to and access resources only on the computer on which you create the local user account. When you create a local user account, Windows 2000 creates the account in that computer's security database. Windows 2000 does not replicate the local user account information to domain controllers. After the account is created, the computer uses its local security database to authenticate the local user account, which allows the user to log on to that computer. Because you created only a local user account on the member server, that server is the only computer that Linda can access. If you had created a domain user account, you would not have needed to create a local user account. The domain user account would have allowed Linda to access resources anywhere on the network.

C. **Incorrect:** Active Directory replication within a site is triggered by a change notification mechanism when an update occurs, moderated by a short, configurable delay (because groups of updates frequently occur together). You do not have to force a replication. However, Windows 2000 does not replicate local user account information to domain controllers, so Active Directory cannot allow Linda to access network resources. For Linda to be able to log on to the domain, a domain user account must be created. Once that account is created, it will be automatically replicated to other domain controllers.

D. **Incorrect:** The reason you might suggest that Linda try again in five minutes would be if you were waiting for Active Directory replication to occur. If, for example, you created a domain user account for Linda—which would allow her to access network resources—Linda might have to wait until the Active Directory store has been replicated to other domain controllers before she could access all network resources. However, because you created only a local user account, waiting will not help because local user accounts are not replicated.

70-215.07.04.002

▶ **Correct Answers: A**

A. **Correct:** A domain user account allows users to log on to the domain and gain access to resources anywhere on the network. However, a local user account allows users to log on to and access resources on only the computer where you create the local user account. When you create a local user account, Windows 2000 creates the account in that computer's security database. Windows 2000 does not replicate the local user account information to domain controllers. After the account is created, the computer uses its local security database to authenticate the local user account, which allows the user to log on to that computer. Because you want to prevent Linda from accessing the domain, you must delete the domain user account and then create a local user account to allow her to access the member server.

B. **Incorrect:** You cannot configure a domain user account to allow local logon only. A domain user account applies to an entire domain, allowing a user to log on to the domain and gain access to resources anywhere on the network. You can, however, use other methods of security to prevent Linda from accessing resources, such as NTFS permissions or specific object permissions. However, to prevent Linda from being able to log on to the domain, you must delete her domain user account and create a local user account on the member server to allow her access to that server only.

C. **Incorrect:** Although you should delete the domain user account, you cannot disable Active Directory on a member server because the service does not run on a member server. Active Directory runs only on domain controllers. In addition, you can create domain user accounts only on domain controllers. The only type of user account that you can create on a member server is a local user account.

D. **Incorrect:** Directory replication does not occur on the member server. Directory replication occurs only on domain controllers, which are configured with Active Directory. Active Directory does not run on a member server. In addition, you cannot configure a domain user account to allow local logon only.

70-215.07.04.003

▶ **Correct Answers: A**

A. **Correct:** You should select the User Must Change Password At Next Logon check box if you want Jennifer to change her password the first time she logs on. This ensures that she is the only person who knows her password. It is a good practice to always require new users to change their passwords the first time that they log on. This will force users to use passwords that only they know. For added security on networks, you can create random initial passwords for all new user accounts by combining letters and numbers. Creating a random initial password will help keep the user account more secure.

B. **Incorrect:** You should not select the User Cannot Change Password check box. You should select this option only if you have more than one person using the same domain user account (such as Guest) or to maintain control over user account passwords. This feature is commonly used for background service account password control.

C. **Incorrect:** You should not select the Password Never Expires check box. You should select this option only if the password should never change (for example, for a domain user account that will be used by a program or a Windows 2000 service). The Password Never Expires setting overrides the User Must Change Password At Next Logon setting. If both check boxes are selected, Windows 2000 will automatically clear the User Must Change Password At Next Logon check box.

D. **Incorrect:** You should not select the Account Is Disabled check box. You should select this option only if you want to prevent the use of this user account (for example, for a new employee who has not yet started working).

OBJECTIVE 7.5

Implement, configure, manage, and troubleshoot Account Policy.

Group policies include several types of security settings that allow you to perform such administrative tasks as restricting access to files and folders, restricting registry access, setting public key access, and configuring IP Security (IPSec) policy. Each type of security setting is a subcategory, or node, under the Security Settings node of the Group Policy Object (GPO). One of these nodes is Account Policies. The Account Policies node includes three categories of account policies: Password Policy, Account Lockout Policy, and Kerberos Policy. Password Policy allows you to modify password settings to meet your organization's security needs. For example, you can specify minimum password length and maximum password age. You can also require complex passwords or simple variations of passwords. Account Lockout Policy allows you to automatically lock out users after a specified number of failed logon attempts. You can also specify how long the accounts are frozen. Kerberos Policy allows you to modify the default Kerberos authentication settings for each domain. For example, you can set the maximum lifetime of a user ticket.

The policies that you configure affect the level of help desk support for users as well as the vulnerability of your network to security breaches and attacks. For example, specifying restrictive password policies might increase your network's security, but it can result in increased help desk calls from users who cannot log on to the network. In addition, specifying restrictive password policies can actually reduce security. If you require passwords that are too long, many users might not be able to remember them and, as a result, will write them down where an intruder can easily find them.

To answer the questions in this objective, you should know how group policies work and know how to configure policies within a GPO. Specifically, you should know how to configure the policies under the Account Policies node of a GPO and know how each of these policies affects your network's security.

Objective 7.5 Questions

70-215.07.05.001

You are creating a domainwide Group Policy Object (GPO) for your Windows 2000 network.

You want to achieve the following results:

- Passwords must be the longest minimum length that Windows 2000 allows.

- Passwords must not be changed before they are 30 days old.

- Passwords must meet complexity requirements.

- Passwords must be stored by using reversible encryption.

You configure a new GPO for the domain.

Which result or results do you achieve? (Choose all that apply.)

Examine the Group Policy snap-in shown in the image below to view the security settings of the Group Policy Object.

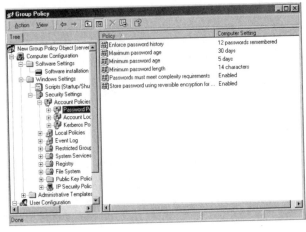

A. Passwords must be the longest minimum length that Windows 2000 allows.

B. Passwords cannot be changed before they are 30 days old.

C. Passwords meet complexity requirements.

D. Passwords are stored by using reversible encryption.

70-215.07.05.002

You are creating a domain-wide Group Policy Object (GPO) for your Windows 2000 network.

You want to achieve the following results:

- Passwords must be the longest minimum length that Windows 2000 allows.

- Passwords must not be changed before they are 30 days old.

- Passwords must meet complexity requirements.

- Passwords must be stored by using reversible encryption.

You configure a new GPO for the domain.

Which result or results do you achieve? (Choose all that apply.)

Examine the Group Policy snap-in shown in the image below to view the security settings of the Group Policy Object.

A. Passwords must be the longest minimum length that Windows 2000 allows.

B. Passwords cannot be changed before they are 30 days old.

C. Passwords meet complexity requirements.

D. Passwords are stored by using reversible encryption.

70-215.07.05.003

You are creating a domainwide Group Policy Object (GPO) for your Windows 2000 network.

You want to achieve the following results:

- Passwords must be the longest minimum length that Windows 2000 allows.

- Passwords must not be changed before they are 30 days old.

- Passwords must meet complexity requirements.

- Passwords must be stored by using reversible encryption.

You configure a new GPO for the domain.

Which result or results do you achieve? (Choose all that apply.)

Examine the Group Policy snap-in shown in the image below to view the security settings of the Group Policy Object.

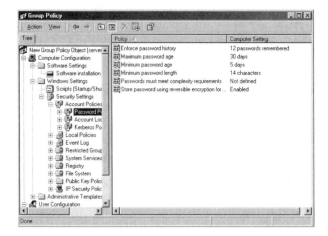

A. Passwords must be the longest minimum length that Windows 2000 allows.

B. Passwords cannot be changed before they are 30 days old.

C. Passwords meet complexity requirements.

D. Passwords are stored by using reversible encryption.

Objective 7.5 Answers

70-215.07.05.001

▶ **Correct Answers: A, C, and D**

A. **Correct:** By using the Group Policy snap-in, you can view and configure security-related group policies that are contained in a GPO. A GPO contains nine types of security policies. One of these types is Account Policies. Account Policies includes Password Policy. Password Policy allows you to enforce password history, set a maximum and minimum password age, set a minimum password length, make passwords meet complexity requirements, and store passwords by using reversible encryption. To set a minimum number of characters that a password is required to have, you must configure the Minimum Password Length policy, which allows you to set the length from 0 to 14 characters. If the number of characters is set to 0, no password is required. If the number of characters is set to greater than 0 (but not more than 14), the password must contain at least the number of characters specified in the policy. Because the number in this policy is set to 14, the largest number that can be configured in this policy, passwords will be the longest minimum length that Windows 2000 allows.

B. **Incorrect:** To prevent passwords from being changed before they are 30 days old, you must configure the Minimum Password Age policy. When this policy is configured, user accounts must retain their passwords until after the specified number of days has passed. If the number of days is set to 0, passwords can be changed immediately. If the number of days is set to greater than 0, users can change their passwords after that number has passed. In this case, the number of days is set to 5, so users can change their passwords on day 6. The number of days can be set up to 998 days, but the number must be less than the maximum password age. In addition, the maximum and minimum password ages should take into consideration when users are scheduled to receive password expiration notifications. By default, users are sent password expiration notices 14 days prior to the day that their passwords must be changed, so the maximum password age should be at least 14 days greater than the minimum password age.

C. **Correct:** To require that passwords meet complexity requirements, you must configure the Passwords Must Meet Complexity Requirements policy. For a password to meet the complexity requirements, it must be at least six characters long, and it cannot contain the user name or part of the user's full name. In addition, the password must contain characters from at least three of the following four classes: (1) English uppercase letters, (2) English lowercase letters, (3) westernized Arabic numerals, and (4) special characters, such as punctuation symbols. When you define this policy, you can configure it as enabled or disabled. When this policy is enabled, user passwords must meet the complexity requirements.

D. **Correct:** To ensure that passwords are being stored by using reversible encryption, you must configure the Store Password Using Reversible Encryption For All Users In The Domain policy. By default, passwords in the password database are encrypted. This encryption cannot normally be reversed. If you enable this policy, passwords are then stored with reversible encryption and can be recovered in case of emergency. When you define this policy, you can configure it as enabled or disabled. When this policy is enabled, user passwords are stored by using reversible encryption.

70-215.07.05.002

▶ **Correct Answers: A, B, C, and D**

A. **Correct:** By using the Group Policy snap-in, you can view and configure security-related group policies that are contained in a GPO. A GPO contains nine types of security policies. One of these types is Account Policies. Account Policies includes Password Policy. Password Policy allows you to enforce password history, set a maximum and minimum password age, set a minimum password length, make passwords meet complexity requirements, and store passwords by using reversible encryption. To set a minimum number of characters that a password is required to have, you must configure the Minimum Password Length policy, which allows you to set the length from 0 to 14 characters. If the number of characters is set to 0, no password is required. If the number of characters is set to greater than 0 (but not more than 14), the password must contain at least the number of characters specified in the policy. Because the number in this policy is set to 14, the largest number that can be configured in this policy, passwords will be the longest minimum length that Windows 2000 allows.

B. **Correct:** To prevent passwords from being changed before they are 30 days old, you must configure the Minimum Password Age policy. When this policy is configured, user accounts must retain their passwords until after the specified number of days has passed. If the number of days is set to 0, passwords can be changed immediately. If the number of days is set to greater than 0, users can change their passwords after that number has passed. In this case, the number of days is set to 29, so users can change their passwords on day 30. The number of days can be set up to 998 days, but the number must be less than the maximum password age.

One of the problems with the current configuration is that the maximum password age is 30 days, but the minimum password age is 29 days. By default, users are sent password expiration notices 14 days prior to the day that their passwords must be changed. If the maximum password age is 30 days, the password expiration notification begins on day 16. However, the Minimum Password Age policy prevents users from changing their passwords prior to day 30. If users attempt to change passwords before that day, they will not be able to make this change. To prevent this type of situation, the maximum and minimum password ages should take into consideration when users are scheduled to receive password expiration notifications.

C. **Correct:** To require that passwords meet complexity requirements, you must configure the Passwords Must Meet Complexity Requirements policy. For a password to meet the complexity requirements, it must be at least six characters long, and it cannot contain the user name or part of the user's full name. In addition, the password must contain characters from at least three of the following four classes: (1) English uppercase letters, (2) English lowercase letters, (3) westernized Arabic numerals, and (4) special characters, such as punctuation symbols. When you define this policy, you can configure it as enabled or disabled. When this policy is enabled, user passwords must meet the complexity requirements.

D. **Correct:** To ensure that passwords are being stored by using reversible encryption, you must configure the Store Password Using Reversible Encryption For All Users In The Domain policy. By default, passwords in the password database are encrypted. This encryption cannot normally be reversed. If you enable this policy, passwords are then stored with reversible encryption and can be recovered in case of emergency. When you define this policy, you can configure it as enabled or disabled. When this policy is enabled, user passwords are stored by using reversible encryption.

70-215.07.05.003

▶ **Correct Answers: A and D**

A. **Correct:** By using the Group Policy snap-in, you can view and configure security-related group policies that are contained in a GPO. A GPO contains nine types of security policies. One of these types is Account Policies. Account Policies includes Password Policy. Password Policy allows you to enforce password history, set a maximum and minimum password age, set a minimum password length, make passwords meet complexity requirements, and store passwords by using reversible encryption. To set a minimum number of characters that a password is required to have, you must configure the Minimum Password Length policy, which allows you to set the length from 0 to 14 characters. If the number of characters is set to 0, no password is required. If the number of characters is set to greater than 0 (but not more than 14), the password must contain at least the number of characters specified in the policy. Because the number in this policy is set to 14, the largest number that can be configured in this policy, passwords will be the longest minimum length that Windows 2000 allows.

B. **Incorrect:** To prevent passwords from being changed before they are 30 days old, you must configure the Minimum Password Age policy. When this policy is configured, user accounts must retain their passwords until after the specified number of days has passed. If the number of days is set to 0, passwords can be changed immediately. If the number of days is set to greater than 0, users can change their passwords after that number has passed. In this case, the number of days is set to 5, so users can change their passwords on day 6. The number of days can be set up to 998 days, but the number must be less than the maximum password age. In addition, the maximum and minimum password ages should take into consideration when users are scheduled to receive password expiration notifications. By default, users are sent password expiration notices 14 days prior to the day that their passwords must be changed, so the maximum password age should be at least 14 days greater than the minimum password age.

C. **Incorrect:** To require that passwords meet complexity requirements, you must configure the Passwords Must Meet Complexity Requirements policy. For a password to meet the complexity requirements, it must be at least six characters long, and it cannot contain the user name or part of the user's full name. In addition, the password must contain characters from at least three of the following four classes: (1) English uppercase letters, (2) English lowercase letters, (3) westernized Arabic numerals, and (4) special characters, such as punctuation symbols. When you define this policy, you can configure it as enabled or disabled. When this policy is enabled, user passwords must meet the complexity requirements. In this case, the policy is not defined, so passwords will not be required to meet the complexity requirements.

D. **Correct:** To ensure that passwords are being stored by using reversible encryption, you must configure the Store Password Using Reversible Encryption For All Users In The Domain policy. By default, passwords in the password database are encrypted. This encryption cannot normally be reversed. If you enable this policy, passwords are then stored with reversible encryption and can be recovered in case of emergency. When you define this policy, you can configure it as enabled or disabled. When this policy is enabled, user passwords are stored by using reversible encryption.

O B J E C T I V E   7 . 6

Implement, configure, manage, and troubleshoot security by using the Security Configuration Tool Set.

Windows 2000 Server includes a set of Microsoft Management Console (MMC) snap-ins that allow you to configure security settings and perform periodic analysis of the system to ensure that the configuration remains intact or to make changes to that configuration. The security-related configuration tools include three snap-ins: the Security Configuration And Analysis snap-in, the Security Templates snap-in, and the Group Policy snap-in. The Security Configuration And Analysis snap-in allows you to analyze local system security. You can import templates created with the Security Templates snap-in, and apply those templates to the Group Policy Object (GPO) for the local computer. You can also perform regular analysis that allows you to track and ensure an adequate level of security on each computer as part of a risk management program. With the Security Configuration And Analysis snap-in, you can perform quick reviews of security analysis results. Recommendations are presented along with concurrent system settings, and you can use the snap-in to resolve any discrepancies revealed by the analysis. If frequent analysis of a large number of computers is required, the SECEDIT command-line utility can be used as a method of batch analysis. The SECEDIT utility, when called from a batch file or automatic task scheduler, can be used to automatically create and apply templates and analyze system security. However, analysis results must be viewed by using the Security Configuration And Analysis snap-in.

The Security Template snap-in allows you to create and assign security templates for one or more computers. A security template is a physical representation of a security configuration. Windows 2000 includes a set of security templates. Each one is based on the role of a computer. The templates range from security settings for low-security domain clients to highly secure domain controllers. The templates can be used as provided, modified, or used as a basis for creating custom templates. A template can be applied to a local computer GPO or imported to a GPO in Active Directory. To view the contents of a GPO, you can use the Group Policy snap-in, which allows you to configure security centrally for a local computer or in Active Directory. The Group Policy snap-in includes a Security Settings node beneath the Computer Configuration node and the User Configuration node. The security settings can be used to define the security-relevant behavior of the system. Through the use of GPOs, you can centrally apply the security levels required to protect your organization's systems.

To answer the questions in this objective, you should understand the purpose of each security configuration tool and know how to use those tools to analyze and configure your system's security. You should also have an understanding of how security templates and GPOs can be used to centrally manage security in your organization.

Objective 7.6 Questions

70-215.07.06.001

You plan to use a security template to implement a security structure into your Windows 2000 network. You want to modify one of the default security templates provided with Windows 2000. Which tool should you use to modify the template?

A. Security Templates snap-in

B. Security Configuration And Analysis snap-in

C. Group Policy snap-in

D. Active Directory Users And Computers snap-in

70-215.07.06.002

You are setting up security for your Windows 2000 network, and you want to configure security centrally in the Active Directory store. Which tool should you use?

A. Security Templates snap-in

B. Security Configuration And Analysis snap-in

C. Group Policy snap-in

D. Active Directory Users And Computers snap-in

Objective 7.6 Answers

70-215.07.06.001

▶ **Correct Answers: A**

A. **Correct:** The Security Templates snap-in allows you to create and assign security templates for one or more computers. You can use the snap-in to customize a predefined security template, define a security template, refresh the security template list, and set a description for a security template. A security template is a physical file representation of a security configuration, and can be applied to a local computer or imported to a Group Policy Object (GPO) in Active Directory. When you import a security template to a GPO, Group Policy processes the template and makes the corresponding changes to the members of that GPO, which may be users or computers. Windows 2000 includes a set of security templates, each based on the role of a computer. The templates range from security settings for low-security domain clients to highly secure domain controllers. They can be used as provided, modified, or serve as a basis for creating custom templates.

B. **Incorrect:** The Security Configuration And Analysis snap-in allows you to review and analyze your system security settings and recommends modifications to the current system settings. You can also use the snap-in to directly configure local system security. In addition, you can import security templates created with the Security Templates snap-in, and apply these templates to the Group Policy Object (GPO) for the local computer. This process immediately configures the system security with the levels specified in the template. However, you cannot use the Security Configuration And Analysis snap-in to modify one of the default security templates.

C. **Incorrect:** The Group Policy snap-in allows you to configure security centrally in the Active Directory store. A Security Settings folder is located on the Computer Configuration node and the User Configuration node in the GPO. The security settings allow administrators to set policies that can restrict user access to network resources. However, you cannot use the Group Policy snap-in to modify a security template.

D. **Incorrect:** The Active Directory Users And Computers snap-in is a directory administration tool that allows you to add, modify, delete, and organize the Windows 2000 user accounts, computer accounts, security and distribution groups, and published resources in your organization's directory. The Active Directory Users And Computers snap-in cannot be used to modify a security template.

70-215.07.06.002

▶ **Correct Answers: C**

A. **Incorrect:** The Security Templates snap-in allows you to create and assign security templates for one or more computers. You can use the snap-in to customize a predefined security template, define a security template, refresh the security template list, and set a description for a security template. The Security Templates snap-in is used only indirectly to configure security centrally because a template created or modified with the snap-in can be imported to a GPO. However, to actually configure the security, you need to use the Group Policy snap-in.

B. **Incorrect:** The Security Configuration And Analysis snap-in allows you to review and analyze your system security settings and recommends modifications to the current system settings. You can also use the snap-in to directly configure local system security. In addition, you can import security templates created with the Security Templates snap-in, and apply these templates to the Group Policy Object (GPO) for the local computer. This process immediately configures the system security with the levels specified in the template. However, you cannot use the Security Configuration And Analysis snap-in to configure security centrally in the Active Directory store.

C. **Correct:** The Group Policy snap-in allows you to configure security centrally in the Active Directory store. A Security Settings folder is located on the Computer Configuration node and the User Configuration node in the GPO. The security settings allow administrators to set policies that can restrict user access to network resources. Security settings define the security-relevant behavior of the system. Through the use of GPOs in Active Directory, administrators can centrally apply the security levels required to protect the enterprise systems.

D. **Incorrect:** The Active Directory Users And Computers snap-in is a directory administration tool that allows you to add, modify, delete, and organize the Windows 2000 user accounts, computer accounts, security and distribution groups, and published resources in your organization's directory. The Active Directory Users And Computers snap-in is not used to directly configure security centrally. However, the snap-in can facilitate the administration of security. For example, you can create an organization unit (OU) that allows you to group similar resources into one location. You can then edit the GPO associated with that OU by using the Group Policy snap-in, which allows you to configure security centrally for the objects in the OU.

APPENDIX A

Questions and Answers

The following questions and answers are for Part 1 of this book.

Chapter 1

Review

1. A client has asked you to recommend the appropriate server edition(s) of Windows 2000 for his environment. Your recommendation is based on the following characteristics:

   - All remote offices are connected to the corporate headquarters and data center by high-speed (greater than 10 Mbps) connections.

   - All 10,000 users run Windows 2000 Professional or Windows 98.

   And the following functional requirements:

   - All sites will access a high-availability server cluster running a Microsoft SQL Server 7.0 database. A two-server cluster with six processors per computer is adequate, and there are no plans to upgrade the cluster.

   - All other servers will run an edition of Windows 2000 to provide Active Directory services, basic file and print services, and dial-in access to the network.

   - These servers will run anywhere between one to four processors. Processor sizing will be based on the number of users supported at each site. For example, a small remote site will contain a single processor server while all servers in the corporate site will contain four processors. For simplicity, one server edition of Windows 2000 will be selected for all computers serving this role.

   - Each domain in Active Directory services will support 2,500 users.

Windows 2000 Advanced Server is recommended for the SQL Server two-node cluster. Windows 2000 Advanced Server supports two-node clustering, eight-way SMP, and high availability. Windows 2000 Datacenter is also an option; however, this edition of the operating system exceeds the customer's requirements for clustering and SMP. Windows 2000 Server will not meet the customer's requirements for the SQL Server application because it does not support clustering or six-way SMP.

All other servers should run Windows 2000 Server because it meets the customer's requirements for a maximum of 4-way SMP, Active Directory services, dial-in via RAS, and file and print services. It easily scales to support 2,500 users/domain and over 10,000 users in the network.

2. Why is a WDM driver preferred over legacy Windows NT drivers?

WDM device drivers benefit from a common set of WDM I/O services. Therefore, a driver developed using the WDM driver development model should be binary-compatible with Windows 2000 and Windows 98.

The WDM driver model is based on a class/miniport structure that provides modular, extensible architectures for device support. This model allows each WDM class to abstract many of the common details involved in controlling similar devices.

3. How does Windows 2000 protect Executive services from user mode applications?

User mode applications request system services through the appropriate subsystem. The subsystem then makes a request on behalf of the application to the Windows 2000 Executive running in Kernel mode. While system services are available to both user mode subsystems and other components of the Windows 2000 Executive, the subsystem or component must call the exported support routine to make a request for Executive service.

4. What component of the Executive makes Windows 2000 preemptible?

The Process Manager suspends and resumes threads of running processes. This is an important feature of any multitasking operating system because the Process Manager will not allow a properly functioning process to monopolize the operating system and therefore stop all other processes from running.

5. What is the primary difference between a workgroup and a domain?

A workgroup is a distributed directory maintained on each computer within the workgroup. A domain is a centralized directory of resources maintained on domain controllers and presented to the user through Active Directory services.

6. What is the structure and purpose of a directory service?

A directory service consists of a database that stores information about network resources, such as computer and printers, and the services that make this information available to users and applications.

Chapter 2

Review

1. If you are installing Microsoft Windows NT in a dual-boot configuration on the same computer, which file system should you choose? Why?

The best choice is FAT. Although both Windows 2000 and Windows NT support NTFS, Windows 2000 supports advanced features provided by NTFS 5.0. For example, file encryption is supported in NTFS 5.0, but previous versions of NTFS did not support file encryption. Therefore, when Windows NT is running on a dual-boot computer, it will not be able to read encrypted files created in Windows 2000.

2. Which licensing mode should you select if users in your organization require frequent access to multiple servers? Why?

Per Seat licensing is the best choice for this environment. A Per-Seat license is more expensive per client computer than Per-Server licensing but becomes much less expensive when many client computers access several servers. If Per-Server licensing is used in this environment, each server must be individually licensed for client computer access.

3. You are installing Windows 2000 Server on a computer that will be a member server in an existing Windows 2000 domain. You want to add the computer to the domain during installation. What information do you need, and what computers must be available on the network, before you run the Setup program?

You need the DNS domain name of the domain that you are joining. You must also make sure that a computer account for the member server exists in the domain or you must have the user name and password of a user account in the domain with the authority to create computer accounts in the domain. A server running the DNS

service and a domain controller in the domain you are joining must be available on the network. If dynamic IP addressing is configured during setup, a server supporting DHCP must be available to assign an address to the computer.

4. You are using a CD-ROM to install Windows 2000 Server on a computer that was previously running another operating system. There is not enough space on the hard disk to run both operating systems, so you have decided to repartition the hard disk and install a clean copy of Windows 2000 Server. Name two methods for repartitioning the hard disk.

   Answer 1: Use a disk partitioning tool like MS-DOS fdisk to remove any existing partitions, and then create and format a new partition for the Windows 2000 installation.

   Answer 2: Start the computer by booting from the Windows 2000 Server Setup disk. During the text-mode portion of installation, you can delete the partition and then create and format a new one. Continue the installation of Windows 2000 Server to the new partition.

5. You are installing Windows 2000 over the network. Before you install to a client computer, what must you do?

   Locate the path to the shared installation files on the distribution server. Create a 1 GB FAT partition on the target computer (2 GB recommended). Create a client disk with a network client so that you can connect from the computer, without an operating system, to the distribution server.

6. A client is running Windows NT 3.5 Server and is interested in upgrading to Windows 2000. From the list of choices, choose all possible upgrade paths:

   a. Upgrade to Windows NT 3.51 Workstation and then to Windows 2000 Server.

   b. Upgrade to Windows NT 4.0 Server and then to Windows 2000 Server.

   c. Upgrade directly to Windows 2000 Server.

   d. Run Convert.exe to modify any NTFS partitions for file system compatibility with Windows 2000, and then upgrade to Windows 2000 Server.

   e. Upgrade to Windows NT 3.51 Server and then to Windows 2000 Server.

Answer: b and e

Answer a is wrong because Windows NT Workstation (3.5*x* or 4.0) cannot be upgraded to Windows 2000 Server.

Answer c is wrong because Windows NT 3.5 cannot be directly upgraded to Windows 2000 Server.

Answer d is wrong because the Windows 2000 Setup process automatically upgrades NTFS to NTFS version 5.0.

7. In your current network environment, user disk space utilization has been a major issue. Describe three services in Windows 2000 Server to help you manage this issue.

Answer 1: Disk quotas in NTFS version 5.0 allow you to control per-user disk space usage by disk.

Answer 2: Disk compression allows you to compress data at the disk, directory, or file level. Disk compression does not affect a user's allocated quota. Quotas are calculated based on the uncompressed file size.

Answer 3: Remote Storage Services provides an extension to disk space by making removable media accessible for file storage. Infrequently used data is automatically archived to removable media. Archived data is still easily accessible to the user; however, data retrieval is slower than with unarchived data.

Chapter 3

Page 115

5. What folder appears directly under the win2000dist folder that does not appear in the i386 folder?

oem

Page 116

18. What is the purpose of the UDF file?

The UDF file allows each automated setup to be customized with the unique settings contained in the file. To start an unattended setup, the UniqueID contained in the UDF file is specified on the command line. During setup the unique data in the UDF file is merged into the answer file.

Review

1. What is the purpose of using the /tempdrive: or /t: installation switches with Winnt32.exe or Winnt.exe, respectively?

   The Winnt32.exe /tempdrive: switch and the Winnt.exe /t: switch copy the Windows 2000 Server installation files to the drive specified with the switch. For example, Winn32.exe /tempdrive:d copies all Windows 2000 installation files to the D: partition. Using this switch also tells Setup which partition should be the boot partition for the installation of Windows 2000 Server.

2. You are asked to develop a strategy for rapidly installing Windows 2000 Server for one of your clients. You have assessed their environment and have determined that the following three categories of computers require Windows 2000 Server:

   - There are 30 unidentical computer configurations currently running Windows NT Server 4.0 that need to be upgraded to Windows 2000 Server.

   - There are 20 identical computers that need a new installation of Windows 2000 Server.

   - Remote sites will run a clean installation of Windows 2000 Server. You want to make sure that they install a standard image of Windows 2000 Server that is consistent with your local configuration of the operating system. You will provide them with hard disks that they will install in their servers.

   What are the steps for your installation strategy?

   For the 30 computers that need to be upgraded, build an answer file and a distribution share using Setup Manager. Further customize the answer file with a text editor. Use a product such as SMS to automate the distribution of operating system upgrades. If SMS is not available, run winnt32 with the /unattend switch and the other switches described in Lesson 1 that are designed to automate the installation process.

   For the 20 identical computers, set up one computer with the operating system and all applications that you need to replicate on all other computers. Copy sysprep.exe, sysprepcl.exe, and sysprep.inf (answer file format) into the OEM\\$1\\Sysprep folder. Make sure the [GuiRunOnce] section of the answer file calls sysprep.exe with the -quiet switch to continue the setup without any user interaction. Create an image with a third-party image utility, and copy this image to each of the 20 identical computers. Upon reboot, Mini-Setup will run using information in sysprep.inf to complete the setup.

For the remote sites, use /Syspart to prepare the disks for the second half of the installation. Ship the disks to the remote sites and instruct the local administrators to install them in their servers as the bootable drive, usually by setting the SCSI ID to 0 or 7, depending on the SCSI hardware.

You can also use the bootable CD-ROM method. If you use this method, include a floppy disk containing the winnt.sif file to automate Setup.

3. What is the purpose of the OEM folder and the subfolders created beneath it by Setup Manager?

The oem folder contains the optional cmdlines.txt file and subfolders for original equipment manufacturer (OEM) files and other files needed to complete or customize automated installation. Folders below oem hold all files that are not part of a standard installation of Windows 2000 Server. These folders map to specific partitions and directories on the computer running an unattended installation. The following list describes the purpose of each folder below oem:

$$ – copies files from this distribution folder location to $windir$ or $systemroot$. For a standard installation of Windows 2000 Server, these variables map to C:\Winnt. There are other folders below this one too, such as Help for OEM help files and System32 for files that must be copied to the System32 directory.

$1 – copies files from this distribution folder location to the root of the system drive. This location is equivalent to the %systemdrive% variable. In a typical installation of Windows 2000 Server, this variable maps to the C:\ root. The $1 folder contains a drivers folder for third-party driver installation.

Drive letter – folders named after a specific drive letter map to the drive letter on the local computer. For example, if you need to copy files to the E: drive during setup, create an E folder and place files or folders in this folder.

Textmode – contains any special HALs or mass storage device drivers required for installing and running Windows 2000 Server.

4. How does Cmdlines.txt differ from [GuiRunOnce]?

Cmdlines.txt runs commands before a user is logged on and in the context of the system account. Any command line or installation that can occur without a user logon can complete using Cmdlines.txt. [GuiRunOnce], a section in the answer file, runs in the context of a user account and after the user logs on for the first time. This is an ideal place to run user specific scripts, such as scripts that add printers or scripts that automatically configure a user's e-mail configuration.

5. How does Syspart differ from Sysprep?

Syspart is a switch of Winnt32.exe. This switch completes the Pre-Copy phase of Windows 2000 Server Setup. After it is complete, the disk used for the Pre-Copy phase can be installed in another computer. Upon booting from this disk, the text mode phase of setup continues. Syspart is ideal for dissimilar systems that require a faster setup procedure than is provided by running Windows 2000 Setup manually. Syspart can be further automated by calling an answer file as well as Syspart from the Winnt32 command line.

Sysprep prepares a computer for imaging. After the operating system and applications are installed on a computer, Sysprep is run to prepare it for imaging. Next, an imaging utility is used to create an image of the prepared disk. The image is downloaded to identical or nearly identical computers, and Sysprep Mini-Setup continues to complete the installation. The Mini-Setup process can be further automated with a Sysprep.inf file.

Chapter 4

Review

1. You install a new 10-GB disk drive that you want to divide into five equal 2-GB sections. What are your options?

You can leave the disk as a basic disk and then create a combination of primary partitions (up to three) and logical drives in an extended partition; or you can upgrade the disk to a dynamic disk and create five 2-GB simple volumes.

2. You are trying to create a striped volume on your Windows 2000 Server to improve performance. You confirm that you have enough unallocated disk space on two disks in your computer, but when you right-click an area of unallocated space on a disk, your only option is to create a partition. What is the problem, and how would you resolve it?

You can create striped volumes on dynamic disks only. The option to create a partition rather than a volume indicates that the disk you are trying to use is a basic disk. You will need to upgrade all the disks that you want to use in your striped volume to dynamic disks before you stripe them.

3. You dual boot your computer with Windows 98 and Windows 2000. You upgrade Disk 1, which you are using to archive files, from basic storage to dynamic storage. The next time you try to access your files on Disk 1 from Windows 98, you are unable to read the files. Why?

Only Windows 2000 is able to read dynamic storage.

4. What is the default permission when a partition is formatted with NTFS? Who has access to the volume?

The Everyone group is granted Full Control permission. All users are members of the Everyone group, so they all have access.

The default permission is Full Control. The Everyone group has access to the volume.

5. If a user has Write permission for a folder and is also a member of a group with Read permission for the folder, what are the user's effective permissions for the folder?

The user has both Read permission and Write permission for the folder because NTFS permissions are cumulative.

6. What happens to permissions that are assigned to a file when the file is moved from one folder to another folder on the same NTFS partition? What happens when the file is moved to a folder on another NTFS partition?

When the file is moved from one folder to another folder on the same NTFS partition, the file retains its permissions. When the file is moved to a folder on a different NTFS partition, the file inherits the permissions of the destination folder.

7. If an employee leaves the company, what must you do to transfer ownership of his or her files and folders to another employee?

You must be logged on as Administrator to take ownership of the employee's folders and files. Assign the Take Ownership special access permission to another employee to allow that employee to take ownership of the folders and files. Notify the employee to whom you assigned Take Ownership to take ownership of the folders and files.

8. What is the best way to secure files and folders that you share on NTFS partitions?

Put the files that you want to share in a shared folder, and keep the default shared folder permission (the Everyone group with the Full Control permission for the shared folder). Assign NTFS permissions to users and groups to control access to all contents in the shared folder or to individual files.

Chapter 5

Page 227

9. Which folder represents a location on a server other than Server01?

The intranet folder's physical path on Server02 is C:\inetput\wwwroot.

10. Which folder represents a mounted drive to a previously empty folder?

The ftp folder was a previously empty folder on Server01. The empty folder path is C:\inetput\ftproot. This directory points to an extended partition on Disk0.

Page 228

11. Earlier in this exercise, you created a replica of the Press Dfs link. The name of that replica is \\SERVER01\PressRepl. This Dfs link is a shared folder by the name of PressRepl and is located in C:\Public\Press. If you examine the contents of this directory, you will notice that it is empty. However, when you view the News Dfs link, you will notice that there is a file named Press.wri. Why is the PressRepl Dfs replica empty?

Because replication and synchronization are not supported in a stand-alone Dfs. Therefore, you must manually copy any files appearing in H:\Press (the \\Server01\Press share) to the directory C:\Public\Press (the \\Server01\PressRepl share) so that \\Server01\PressRepl can serve as a replica of \\Server01\Press. Once the files are copied over, the \\Server01\Public\News Dfs link will be fault tolerant because \\Server01\PressRepl will take over if \\Server01\Press becomes unavailable.

Review

1. How does a mounted drive to an empty folder differ from a Dfs root?

   A mounted drive to an empty folder allows for folder redirection. When you store files in a folder that points to a mounted partition, the files are redirected to the partition. This feature provides limited resource consolidation. A Dfs root provides a central point where disparate resources are consolidated through Dfs links. These links are then presented to the users as a single share containing folders. This feature provides robust resource consolidation.

2. In Exercise 1, you were asked to notice that New Root Replica and Replication Policy were not available options in the Distributed File System snap-in. Explain why these options are not available.

   New Root Replica and Replication Policy are available only for domain Dfs roots. In Exercise 1 you configured a stand-alone Dfs root. A new root replica allows you to replicate the Dfs root to other servers on the network. This feature provides fault tolerance and load balancing. If a server hosting the Dfs root fails, users access the Dfs root from the other replicas. If all servers replicating the Dfs root are available, they will load balance user requests. Replication policy allows you to configure the settings for replicating the Dfs root and Dfs shares below it.

3. Why doesn't Dfs directly provide a security infrastructure?

   Security is provided by the underlying file system. A Dfs link that points to an NTFS partition is secured using NTFS permissions or share rights; a FAT partition is secured with share rights. A Dfs link to another network operating system (NOS) is secured with native security provided by the operating system. For example, NetWare provides trustee directory and file assignments for security. A NetWare resource can be made available to Dfs through Gateway Services for NetWare.

4. How is the KCC involved in maintaining Active Directory store synchronization between domain controllers?

   KCC creates a ring topology for intra-domain replication. This topology provides a path for Active Directory store updates to flow from one domain controller to the next. It also provides two replication paths, a path on either side of the ring to continue replication even if the ring structure is temporarily broken.

5. What data does the FRS replicate?

   System Volume data and domain Dfs roots and Dfs links configured for replication.

Chapter 6

Page 276

3. Examine each of the nodes below microsoft.com. Do not modify any information that you see in these nodes.

What selections are listed under microsoft.com and what is their purpose? Hint, choose the properties of each node in the console tree to view their purpose.

Built-in – contains local groups created during installation of the domain controller.

Computers – this is the default container for upgraded computer accounts. You can move these computers to other containers if your design requires it.

Domain Controllers – this is the default container for new Windows 2000 domain controllers. You will see Server01 in this container.

ForeignSecurityPrincipals – this is the default container for object SIDs from external, trusted domains.

Users – this is the default container for upgraded and built-in user accounts.

Page 279

4. Click the Start button, point to Programs, and then point to Administrative Tools.

Notice that all installed Administrative Tools applications appear under Administrative Tools rather than just the most recently used applications.

When Server01 was a stand-alone server, all the applications appeared under Administrative Tools except those specific to Active Directory, domain, and DNS maintenance. Using your mouse, point to each of the applications listed below to see the screen hint, and then write a description in the space provided.

Active Directory Domains and Trusts

Active Directory Sites and Services

Active Directory Users and Computers

DNS

Active Directory Domains and Trusts – manages the trust relationships between domains.

Active Directory Sites and Services – creates sites to manage the replication of Active Directory data information.

Active Directory Users and Computers – manages users, computers, security groups, and other objects in the Active Directory store.

DNS – manages the DNS Domain Naming System (DNS) service for IP host name resolution.

Review

1. What is Ntds.dit, and what is its purpose?

   NTDS.DIT is the file that contains the Active Directory store.

2. What is the one SYSVOL location requirement?

   SYSVOL must be located on an NTFS 5.0 partition.

3. What is the function of SYSVOL, and what is the one disk requirement for SYSVOL?

   SYSVOL stores the domain controllers copy of the domain's public files. The contents of this directory are replicated to all domain controllers in the domain.

4. What is the difference between an attribute and an attribute value? Give examples.

   Attributes (also referred to as properties) are categories of information and define the characteristics for all objects of a defined object type. All objects of the same type have the same attributes. Values of the attributes make the objects unique. For example, all user account objects have a First Name attribute; however, the value for the First Name attribute can be any name, such as John or Jane.

5. What is the difference between modifying an object and modifying the attribute values of an object instance?

   Modifying an object is an advanced procedure completed in tools such as the Schema Manager snap-in (Schmmgmt.msc). Modifying the attribute values of an object instance involves changing data stored with an instance of an object, for example, changing the primary phone number data for a user object named John Smith.

6. You want to allow the manager of the sales department to create, modify, and delete only user accounts for sales personnel. How can you accomplish this?

   Place all the sales personnel user accounts in an OU, and then delegate control of the OU to the manager of the sales department.

7. What is the global catalog, and what is its purpose?

The global catalog stores key information about every object in a domain tree or forest. It contains a partial replica of the Entire Directory. Only the most important data about objects are stored in the global catalog, so replicating the global catalog is more efficient than replicating the entire Active Directory store. The global catalog enables a user to find information regardless of which domain in the tree or forest contains the data.

Chapter 7

Page 315

6. In what mode is the console running?

The console is running in author mode as shown in the Console Mode drop-down list box.

Page 329

13. When will the account expire?

According to the current settings, the account will never expire. The Account Expires section at the bottom of the Account page shows that the expiration is set to Never.

Page 330

5. Click OK to close the Change Password message box.

Were you able to log on successfully? Why or why not?

You were not allowed to log on locally since this right is not granted to regular user accounts. By default administrators have the right to log on locally to a domain controller, but regular users, like Jane Doe, do not.

Review

1. When you use the Administrative Tools program group to open an MMC console provided with Windows 2000 Server, can you add snap-ins to it? Why or why not?

No, snap-ins cannot be added to the MMC consoles provided with the product when the consoles are opened from the Administrative Tools program group. These consoles are configured for User Mode operation. You can open these consoles in author mode by appending the name of the path and the name of the .msc file with MMC /a. For example:

mmc /a %SystemRoot%\system32\compmgmt.msc /s

opens the Computer Management console in author mode.

2. You receive a call from a member of the Help Desk support team. She tells you that a number of users are complaining of a window that appears every time they log on. The support person tells you there is nothing in the Startup menu. Additionally, she has closed the window and shut down and restarted the computer, but the window still appears at logon. What is the most likely cause of this issue, and how can you resolve it?

   All the users complaining of this problem are using a mandatory shared profile. When the profile template was built, a window was left open on the desktop. To resolve this problem, make sure no users are accessing the profile, rename Ntuser.man to Ntuser.dat so that it is no longer mandatory. Log on with a user account that points to this profile, close the window that appears, and then log off. Upon logoff, the profile change will be saved to the network shared profile location. Next, rename Ntuser.dat back to Ntuser.man and instruct the users to log on again.

3. When should you use security groups instead of distribution groups?

   Use security groups to assign permissions. Use distribution groups when the only function of the group is not security related, such as an e-mail distribution list. You cannot use distribution groups to assign permissions.

4. What are the implications of changing the domain mode from Mixed mode to Native mode?

   Pre–Windows 2000 domain controllers cannot participate in a Native-mode domain.

   Pre–Windows 2000 stand-alone servers and computers running Windows NT Workstation can still participate in the domain.

   After you change to Native mode, you cannot change back to Mixed mode.

5. By default, in what order is group policy implemented through the Active Directory store hierarchy? How can you control this behavior?

   Group policy is implemented in the following order: site, domain, and then organizational unit (OU).

   You can control group policy inheritance through the Block Policy Inheritance check box. However, the No Override Link option set in higher levels of the hierarchy supersedes this option. Additionally, you can restrict who group policies are applied to by modifying the security settings for the group policy.

6. What is a GPO, GPC, and GPT?

A GPO is a group policy object. Group Policy configuration settings are contained within a GPO. You establish group policy settings in a GPO that you apply to a site, domain, or OU. GPOs store group policy information in two locations: a GPC and a GPT.

A GPC, or group policy container, is an Active Directory object that contains GPO properties and includes subcontainers for computer and user group policy information. The GPC contains the class store information for application deployment. The Windows 2000 class store is a server-based repository for all applications, interfaces, and application programming interfaces (APIs) that provide application publishing and assigning functions.

A GPT, or group policy template, is a folder structure in the system volume folder (Sysvol) of domain controllers. The GPT is the container for all software policy, script, file and application deployment, and security settings information. The folder name of the GPT is the globally unique identifier (GUID) of the GPO you created.

Chapter 8

Review

1. Explain the difference between a print device and a printer.

A print device is the hardware that creates printable pages or a file on a disk (print to file) that has been processed through a printer. A printer is the software interface to one or more print devices.

2. You are told by a colleague never to remove the Everyone system group from the permissions of a printer or no one will be able to manage the printer or its documents. Why is this statement incorrect? How could you configure this undesirable behavior?

Removing the Everyone system group from a printer's permissions still leaves a number of groups (Administrators, CREATOR OWNER, Printer Operators, and Server Operators) that have access to the printers by default. Removing the Everyone system group is not the same as specifically denying the Everyone system group with access to the printer. This configuration would result in the inability to manage the printer until the deny permission is removed by the CREATOR OWNER system account.

3. You have configured two Windows 2000 print servers on your network. When a user connects to one from Windows 95, printing is automatic. When the same user connects to the same print server for a different printer, she gets prompted to install a driver. Why is this happening?

One printer installed on the print server has been configured with additional drivers, specifically the Windows 95 or 98 printer driver. The other printer has not been configured with additional drivers.

4. In an environment where many users print to the same print device, how can you help reduce the likelihood of users picking up the wrong documents?

Create a separator page that identifies and separates printed documents.

5. Can you redirect a single document?

No. You can change only the configuration of the print server to send documents to another printer or print device; this change redirects all documents on that printer. The currently spooled or active document cannot be redirected.

6. A user needs to print a very large document. How can the user print the job after hours without being present while the document prints?

You can control print jobs by setting the printing time. You set the printing time for a document on the General tab of the Properties dialog box for the document. To open the Properties dialog box for a document, select the document in the Printers window, click Document on the Printers window menu bar, and then click Properties. Click Only From in the Schedule section of the Properties dialog box, and then set the Only From hour to the earliest time you want the document to begin printing after regular business hours. Set the To time to a couple of hours before normal business hours start. To set the printing time for a document, you must be the owner of the document or have the Manage Documents permission for the appropriate printer.

Chapter 9

Review

1. Your computer receives its TCP/IP configuration information from a DHCP server in the network. After DHCP information is received, you can connect to any host on your own subnet, but you cannot connect to or successfully ping any host on a remote subnet. You checked the DHCP Service to ensure that the router information specified for your address scope is correct. What is the likely cause of the problem and how would you fix it?

   The default gateway is incorrectly specified on your computer. If default gateway information is specified on a client computer, these settings take precedence over settings downloaded from a DHCP server. To solve this configuration problem, simply remove the default gateway information from the client computer and then run IPCONFIG /renew from the command line. Other possibilities are that the default gateway is offline or that the subnet mask is incorrect.

2. You installed NWLink IPX/SPX and GSNW. After installing these components, you cannot communicate with one of the NetWare servers on your network. You have no trouble accessing this NetWare server from your client computer running Windows 2000 Professional, NWLink IPX/SPX, and CSNW. You must communicate with this NetWare server from your Windows 2000 Server because the NetWare server contains resources you must make available to users running the Microsoft Network Client. What is the likely cause of the problem?

   Although the NWLink implementation in Windows 2000 can automatically detect a frame type for IPX/SPX-compatible protocols, it can only automatically detect one frame type. It's possible that the Windows 2000 Server detected the wrong frame type. If the network is configured for multiple frame types, you must manually configure the frame type that matches the frame type of the NetWare server you are attempting to access.

3. You notice that access to network resources seems slower on your computer running Windows 2000 Server than from another identical computer running Windows 2000 Server on the same network. The only difference you can determine is that the slower Windows 2000 Server computer is running multiple protocols. How could network protocol binding order potentially resolve this problem?

You specify the binding order to optimize network performance. For example, a computer running Windows 2000 Server has NetBEUI, NWLink IPX/SPX, and TCP/IP installed. However, most of the servers to which this computer connects are running only TCP/IP. You would adjust the binding order so that the Workstation service binding to TCP/IP is listed before the other Workstation service bindings for the other protocols. In this way, when you attempt to connect to another computer, the Workstation service first attempts to use TCP/IP to establish the connection.

4. When do DHCP clients attempt to renew their leases?

When 50 percent of the lease life has expired, the DHCP client attempts to renew its lease with the DHCP server that leased the address originally. If the lease isn't renewed, the DHCP client will renew its lease with any DHCP server after 87.5 percent of its current lease life has expired.

5. Why might you create multiple scopes on a DHCP server?

You might create multiple scopes on a DHCP server to centralize administration and to assign IP addresses specific to a subnet (for example, a default gateway). You can assign only one scope to a specific subnet.

6. How can you manually restore the DHCP database?

You can change the RestoreFlag key HKEY_LOCAL_MACHINE\SYSTEM\CurrentControlSet\Services\DHCPServer\Parameters to 1 in the registry and then restart the DHCP Service, or you can manually copy the files in the DHCP backup folder to the DHCP directory and then restart the service.

7. What are the configuration requirements for a WINS server?

The requirements are a computer running Windows 2000 Server configured with WINS, and a static IP address, subnet mask, and default gateway.

You can also configure a static mapping for all non-WINS clients on the WINS server, WINS support on a DHCP server, and a WINS proxy agent on WINS-enabled clients.

8. Why would you want to have multiple name servers?

Installing multiple name servers provides redundancy, reduces the load on the server that stores the primary zone database file, and allows for faster access speed for remote locations.

9. Why do you create forward and reverse lookup zones?

A name server must have at least one forward lookup zone. A forward lookup zone enables name resolution.

A reverse lookup zone is needed for troubleshooting utilities, such as nslookup, and to record names instead of IP addresses in IIS logs.

10. What is the difference between dynamic DNS and DNS?

Dynamic DNS allows automatic updates to the primary server's zone file. In DNS, you must manually update the file when new hosts or domains are added.

Dynamic DNS also allows a list of authorized servers to initiate updates. This list can include secondary name servers, domain controllers, and other servers that perform network registration for clients, such as servers running WINS and the DHCP Service.

Chapter 10

Review

1. What is the purpose of demand-dial routing?

Demand-dial routing provides a facility for connecting one dial-up router to another dial-up router. This allows two routers on separate networks to use a dial-up infrastructure such as the public switched telephone network or the Internet to connect to each other and transfer information. A two-way initiated connection allows each router to accept inbound data from an opposing router and initiate outbound data to the opposing router.

2. What authentication providers are available in RRAS and how are they different from authentication methods?

There are two authentication providers: Windows authentication and RADIUS authentication. Windows authentication uses the Windows 2000 directory for authenticating user accounts. RADIUS authentication uses either the Microsoft IAS RADIUS server or a third-party RADIUS server to authenticate user accounts. Authentication methods are a security process where by the client and the server agree on a procedure for authenticated account information. RRAS supports EAP, MS-CHAP v2, MS-CHAP, CHAP, SPAP, PAP, and clear text authentication.

3. What is the purpose of VPN and what two VPN technologies are supported in Windows 2000 RRAS?

VPN or virtual private networking provides a facility to securely transfer data over a public network. The two VPN technologies supported in Windows 2000 RRAS are PPTP and L2TP.

4. If a remote access client begins to connect to the RAS server but the connection is dropped, what troubleshooting steps will help you to solve this error?

1. **Verify that Event Logging is enabled and view the System Event log on the computer running RRAS.**

2. **On the remote access client, access the properties of the dial-up device, such as a modem, click the Diagnostics tab, and check the Record a Log check box. After attempting a connection, review the log file.**

3. **On the server, open the Authentication Methods dialog box and check the Allow remote systems to connect without authentication check box. After selecting this check box, attempt to reconnect from the client computer.**

5. How is the remote access permission of Deny Access (in Mixed mode or Native mode), similar in function to the Native-mode domain default remote access policy?

The Deny Access remote access permission does not allow a user with this setting to use remote access to connect to the server. The native-mode domain remote access policy is Allow Access If Dial-In Permission Is Enabled. The default policy's properties, however, are Deny Remote Access Permission At All Times.

6. You need to configure 10 RRAS servers for a client. All 10 servers will have identical RRAS configurations. What is the most efficient way to complete this configuration?

Configure one RRAS server to act as the master configuration for all other RRAS servers. Then, use netsh to dump the configuration and then use the –f or exec command to run the script. For example, to dump the RAS configuration from a server named RRAS1 to a script file named Ras.scr, from RRAS1 type:

```
netsh -c RAS dump > ras.scr
```

Next, to apply this policy to a RRAS server named RRAS2 from RRAS1, type:

```
netsh -r RRAS2 -f ras.scr
```

Chapter 11

Review

1. Which key is associated with the creation of digital signatures, the public key or the private key? Explain your answer.

   Private keys are associated with the creation of digital signatures. You use a private key to transform data in such a way that users are able to verify that only you could have created the encrypted data. Decrypting the data is achieved through the application of the public key. However, only the private key is used to create the digital signature.

2. What security credential(s) will be in use if you are supporting client computers running Windows 2000 and Windows NT that authenticate to servers running Windows 2000 Server, and Windows NT Server?

   Windows NT client computers will authenticate to both Windows 2000 and Windows NT Servers using NTLM credentials (Windows NT domain name, username, and encrypted password). Windows 2000 client computers will authenticate to the computers running Windows 2000 Server using Kerberos authentication (domain name, username, Kerberos encrypted password), and they will authenticate to the computers running Windows NT Server using NTLM authentication.

3. How can a security template be used to facilitate configuration and analysis of security settings?

   A template can be applied to a security configuration database created by the Security Analysis and Configuration snap-in. After the database is created, the current settings of the computer can be compared to the settings dictated by the policy. After reviewing discrepancies between policy and computer security settings, the same snap-in can be used to configure the computer's security settings to the template's settings.

4. Where is the Certificate Services Enrollment page and what is its purpose?

   The Certificate Services Enrollment page is a Web page that allows for the easy creation and monitoring of certificate requests, and for the retrieval of CRLs and certificates.

5. What steps must you follow to enable auditing of specific file objects on domain controllers in a domain where Group Policy is enabled?

Use Active Directory Users And Computers to open a group policy (typically the Default Domain GPO or the Default Domain controller Policy GPO). Navigate to the Audit Policy node below the Windows Settings - Security Settings – Local Policies node. In the details pane, double-click Audit Object Access and enable success or failure attempts as appropriate. Using Windows Explorer, navigate to the specific file or folder that you need to access. Access the properties of the file or folder object, click the Security tab, then click the Advanced button. From the Access Control Settings dialog box, select View/Edit to modify the audit policy of a selected user or group or add a new user or group to audit. Be cautious about how much file object auditing you configure. This feature can be processor intensive if it is configured improperly.

Chapter 12

Review

1. You have configured a computer to boot Windows 2000 Server as the default operating system, and Windows NT 4.0 Server as the optional operating system. After modifying the attributes of files on %systemdrive% and deleting some of the files, the computer does not display Windows NT 4.0 Server as an operating system to start. Windows 2000 Server starts up properly. The problem is caused because you deleted a file. What is the name of the file, and what can you do to recover from this error?

You deleted the Boot.ini file. Boot.ini allows for multiboot. If this file is missing, the default operating system starts. To recover this file, run the ERD, choose Manual Repair, and then choose Inspect Startup Environment.

2. You have created three hardware profiles for your mobile computer: Docked, Undocked On The Network, and Undocked At Home. When you reboot the computer, the first two hardware profiles appear, but the third one does not. What is the most likely reason that the Undocked At Home profile does not appear?

In the properties of the Undocked At Home profile, the Always Include This Profile As An Option When Windows Starts check box is not selected.

3. Why would the Use Hardware Compression, If Available check box be unavailable in the Backup wizard?

This option is available only if an installed tape device and its driver supports hardware compression.

4. You performed a normal backup on Monday. For the remaining days of the week, you only want to back up files and folders that have changed since the previous day. What backup type do you select?

Incremental. The incremental backup type backs up changes since the last markers were set and then clears the markers. Thus, for Tuesday through Friday, you only back up changes made since the previous day.

5. How can you test the configuration of the UPS service on a computer?

You can simulate a power failure by disconnecting the main power supply to the UPS device. During the test, the computer and peripherals connected to the UPS device should remain operational, messages should display, and events should continue to be logged.

In addition, you should wait until the UPS battery reaches a low level to verify that a graceful shutdown occurs. Then restore the main power to the UPS device and check the event log to ensure that all actions were logged and there were no errors.

Note that this procedure requires a UPS that communicates with the computer through a COM port or a proprietary interface provided with the UPS.

Chapter 13

Review

1. You have used the Compact utility to compress the files contained in the Users subfolders on an NTFS partition. You have enabled the Folder Option, Display Compressed Files And Folders With Alternate Color. A week later you use Windows Explorer to see if files are being compressed. To your surprise, user account subfolders, located directly under the Users folder created after you ran the compress utility, are not compressed. Why did this happen and how can you fix it?

You ran the Compact utility and compressed each of the subfolders under the Users subfolder. As a result, all subfolders were marked for compression but the Users parent folder was not marked for compression. Therefore, new folders created directly below the

Users folder are not compressed. There are a number of ways to fix this. You can use the Compact utility to mark the Users folder for compression and all subfolders below users. Open a command prompt, go to the driver containing the Users parent folder, and type compact /s:Users /c. Or you can use the Windows Explorer to compress the Users subfolder and then choose the Apply changes to this folder, subfolders and files radio button.

2. Your department has recently archived several GB of data from a computer running Windows 2000 Server to CD-ROMs. As users have added files to the server, you have noticed that the server has been taking longer than usual to gain access to the hard disk. How can you increase disk access time for the server?

Use Disk Defragmenter to defragment files on the server's hard disk.

3. You are the administrator for a computer running Windows 2000 Server that is used to store user's home folders and roaming user profiles. You want to restrict users to 25 MB of available storage for their home folder while monitoring, but not limiting, the disk space used for the roaming user profiles. How should you configure the volumes on the server?

Create two volumes: one to store home folders and another to store roaming user profiles. Format both volumes with NTFS, and enable disk quotas for both volumes. For the home folder volume, specify a limit of 25 MB and select the Deny Disk Space To Users Exceeding Quota Limit check box. For the roaming user profile volume, do not specify a limit and clear the Deny Disk Space To Users Exceeding Quota Limit check box.

4. You notice that a new server is not performing as well as you expected. You need to obtain summary information on a server's performance, and then you want to use a utility to obtain detailed reports of performance bottlenecks. After you have resolved the performance problem, what should you do to track the performance of the server as more users begin to access the server?

To obtain summary information on a server's performance, run Task Manager to observe common data points contained under the Performance tab. This can give you an idea of where your performance bottleneck is. Next, run the System Monitor snap-in and observe detailed performance metrics. Add resources as necessary or remove applications that are creating the bottleneck. After you have resolved the performance issue, use the Performance Logs And Alerts to log performance activity. These logs serve as your baseline for future performance monitoring. So that you are not caught off-guard by poor performance or a potential hardware failure, create

alerts to track the activity of the server. If you think poor performance might be related to network activity, run the Network Monitor to analyze network activity.

5. You want to filter out all network traffic except for traffic between two computers, and you also want to locate specific data within the packets. Which Network Monitor filter features should you specify?

   Filter for Address Pairs where you specify the media access control address of each computer, and then specify Pattern Matches where you filter for specific patterns in Hex or ASCII contained in the frames.

6. You goal is to make sure that only two network management stations in your organization are able to communicate with the SNMP agents. What measures can you take when configuring the SNMP service to enhance security?

   Using the Security tab of the SNMP Service Properties dialog box, make the following configuration changes:

   - **Specify a unique community name and remove the public community name.**

   - **Adjust the community rights settings so that the NMS can complete the functions you want to enable. If you aren't sure of the community rights you need, configure this for READ ONLY and adjust it by NMS to SNMP service testing.**

   - **Select the Accept SNMP packets from these hosts radio button, and then specify the host name, IP, or IPX address of the two network management stations.**

   - **If you will be sending Traps to an NMS, make sure to specify the Trap destination(s) under the Traps tab.**

Chapter 14

Page 852

7. With the Web Site tab active, record the TCP Port value appearing in the TCP Port text box.

   Port value will vary but should be between 2000-9999.

Review

1. Compare a virtual directory to a Dfs root.

   A virtual directory is a term used to describe Web server directories that appear to be located below a Web server's home directory but could be located in any location accessible to the Web server. An alias is used to describe the virtual directory so that Web browser users are unaware of the virtual directories' physical location or path.

   A Dfs root is also a symbolic share that provides centralized access to shares located throughout the network. The user is unaware of the physical location of the shares but is able to reach them by starting from the Dfs root. The Dfs root is similar to an Internet Information Services (IIS) home directory and the shares below the Dfs root are similar to virtual directories in IIS.

2. You are accessing the IIS 5.0 documentation from Internet Services Manager (HTML). All of the documentation appears and you are able to access information via the Index tab. Under the Index tab, you find the phrase Process Accounting. However, when you perform a search on this phrase, the Web browser reports that your search phrase cannot be found. What is the most likely reason that this is happening?

   The indexing service has been started since the Web browser did not report the inability to perform a search. Because the phrase was not found it could be that you have not configured the Indexing Service to catalog the iisHelp folder or the Indexing Service has not completed the task of indexing this folder's contents.

3. You have created a virtual directory for the purpose of WebDAV publishing. The home directory of the Web site is accessible from Internet Explorer 5, but when you attempt to access the virtual directory for WebDAV publishing, access is denied. Name two reasons why this may happen and how you can solve this access problem.

   WebDAV security is managed by the file system and Internet Services. Therefore, access could be denied because the physical directory for WebDAV has an ACL that does not allow the browser client to access the folder. If access is allowed at the file system level, verify that Read, Write, and Directory Browsing on the WebDAV virtual directory is enabled. For ASP support also make sure to enable Script source access.

4. Why is it important that the Microsoft Telnet Client and the Microsoft Telnet service support NTLM authentication?

   NTLM authentication protects authentication information from being transmitted across a network from the Telnet client to the Telnet server. A user is authenticated in the context of the current logon. If authentication is necessary, NTLM challenge/response authentication protects logon information. This is an important security feature of Windows 2000 Telnet.

5. If Terminal Services is not licensed, what features of Terminal Services will work and for how long?

   Remote Administration mode allows for two remote control sessions with the computer running Terminal Services. No Terminal Service client license is necessary for this function. In Application Server mode, a Terminal Service client license is required for each session. The Terminal Service will continue to function for 90 days without Terminal Service client licenses installed on the Terminal Services License server.

A P P E N D I X   B

Sample Answer Files for Unattended Setup

Unattended Setup in Microsoft Windows 2000 uses an ASCII text file that is called an answer file to supply data that would otherwise be entered interactively when you run the Setup wizard. The answer file is specified on either a Winnt.exe or Winnt32.exe command line when the Unattended Setup option is used.

This appendix includes sample answer files that are appropriate for common installation configurations. You can customize the default answer file (Unattend.txt) that comes with Windows 2000 or write a new one based on the samples that are provided in this appendix.

In This Appendix

- Answer file format
- Sample answer files

Answer File Format

An answer file consists of section headers, keys, and the values for each key. Most of the section headers are predefined, but some can be user defined. You do not need to specify all the possible keys in an answer file if the installation does not require them. Invalid key values generate errors or can cause incorrect behavior after setup. The file format is as follows:

```
[section_name]
```

Sections contain keys and the corresponding values for those keys. Each key and value are separated by a space, an equal sign, and a space. The following is an example:

```
key = value
```

Values that have spaces in them require double quotes around them. The following is an example:

```
key = "value with spaces"
```

Some sections have no keys and merely contain a list of values. The following is an example:

```
[OEMBootFiles]
Txtsetup.oem
```

Comment lines start with a semicolon.

```
; This is an example of a comment line.
```

Answer File Keys and Values

Every key in an answer file must have a value assigned to it; however, some keys are optional, and some keys have default values that are used if the key is omitted.

Key values are strings of text unless numeric is specified. If numeric is specified, the value is decimal unless otherwise noted.

Note Keys are not case sensitive; they can be uppercase or lowercase.

The Unattend.doc file has detailed information about the answer file keys and values. To find this file, look on the Windows 2000 installation CD-ROM in the \Support\Tools folder for Deploy.cab. To extract or view the contents of the Deploy.cab file, use Windows Explorer.

Sample Answer Files

The sample answer files that are provided in this section are examples of the more common installation configurations of the keys commonly used in those configurations. Consider these files as examples only, and modify them as appropriate for your organization.

Note In the answer files that follow, the use of italic font style indicates that the user must supply the required information.

Sample 1 – Default Unattend.txt.

The following answer file is the default Unattend.txt file provided on the Windows 2000 CD.

```
; Microsoft Windows 2000 Professional, Server, Advanced
Server and Datacenter
; (c) 1994 - 1999 Microsoft Corporation. All rights re-
served.
;
; Sample Unattended Setup Answer File
;
; This file contains information about how to automate the
installation
; or upgrade of Windows 2000 Professional and Windows 2000
Server so the
; Setup program runs without requiring user input.
;


[Unattended]
Unattendmode = FullUnattended
OemPreinstall = NO
TargetPath = WINNT
Filesystem = LeaveAlone

[UserData]
FullName = "Your User Name"
OrgName = "Your Organization Name"
ComputerName = "COMPUTER_NAME"

[GuiUnattended]
; Sets the Timezone to the Pacific Northwest
; Sets the Admin Password to NULL
; Turn AutoLogon ON and login once
TimeZone = "004"
AdminPassword = *
AutoLogon = Yes
AutoLogonCount = 1
```

```
;For Server installs
[LicenseFilePrintData]
AutoMode = "PerServer"
AutoUsers = "5"

[GuiRunOnce]
; List the programs that you want to lauch when the machine
is logged into for the first time

[Display]
BitsPerPel = 8
XResolution = 800
YResolution = 600
VRefresh = 70

[Networking]
; When set to YES, setup will install default networking
components. The components to be set are
; TCP/IP, File and Print Sharing, and the Client for
Microsoft Networks.
InstallDefaultComponents = YES

[Identification]
JoinWorkgroup = Workgroup
```

Sample 2 – Unattended Installation of Windows 2000 Professional from CD-ROM

The following answer file installs Microsoft Windows 2000 Professional from CD-ROM. For this answer file to function properly, you must name it Winnt.sif and place it on a floppy disk.

```
; Microsoft Windows 2000 Professional
; © 1994-1999 Microsoft Corporation. All rights reserved.
;
; Sample Answer File for Unattended Setup
;
; This file contains information about how to automate the
installation
; or upgrade of Windows 2000 Professional so that the Setup
program runs
; without requiring user input.
;

[Data]
; This section is required when you perform an unattended
installation
; by starting Setup directly from the Windows 2000 installa-
tion CD-ROM.
Unattendedinstall = Yes
; If you are running Unattended Setup from the CD-ROM, you
```

```
must set the
; Msdosinitiated key to 0.
Msdosinitiated = "0"
; AutoPartition allows Windows 2000 Unattended Setup to
choose a
; partition to install to.
AutoPartition = 1

[Unattended]
UnattendMode = FullUnattended
; The OemPreinstall key tells Unattended Setup that the
installation is
; being performed from distribution shares if the value is
set to Yes.
OemPreinstall = Yes
TargetPath = Winpro
FileSystem = LeaveAlone
; If the OemSkipEula key is set to Yes, it informs Unat-
tended Setup that
; the user should not be prompted to accept the End User
License
; Agreement (EULA). A value of Yes signifies agreement to
the EULA and
; should be used in conjunction with the terms of your
license
; agreement.
OemSkipEula = Yes

[GuiUnattended]
; Sets the TimeZone. For example, to set the TimeZone for
the Pacific Northwest, use a
; value of "004." Be sure to use the numeric value that
represents your own time zone. To look up
; a numeric value, see the Unattend.doc file on the Win-
dows 2000 CD.
TimeZone = "YourTimeZone"
; It is recommended that you change the administrator pass-
word before the computer
; is placed at it's final destination.
AdminPassword = adminpassword
; Tells Unattended Setup to turn AutoLogon ON and log on
once.
AutoLogon = Yes
AutoLogonCount = 1
; The OemSkipWelcome key specifies whether the welcome page
in the
; wizard phase of Setup should be skipped. A value of 1
causes the page
; to be skipped.
OemSkipWelcome = 1
; The OemSkipRegional key allows Unattended Setup to skip
RegionalSettings
```

```
; when the final location of the computer is unknown.
OemSkipRegional = 1

[UserData]
FullName = "Your user name"
OrgName = "Your organization name"
;It is recommended that you avoid using spaces in the
ComputerName value.
ComputerName = "YourComputer_name"
; To ensure a fully unattended installation, you must pro-
vide a value
; for the ProductId key.
ProductId = "Your product ID"

[Display]
BitsPerPel = 8
XResolution = 800
YResolution = 600
VRefresh = 60

[Networking]
; When you set the value of the InstallDefaultComponents key
to Yes, Setup will install
;default networking components. The components to be set are
TCP/IP, File and Print Sharing,
; and the Client for Microsoft Networks.
InstallDefaultComponents = Yes
```

Sample 3 – Install and Configure Windows 2000 and Configure Microsoft Internet Explorer with Proxy Settings

The following answer file installs and configures Microsoft Internet Explorer and configures proxy settings.

```
; Microsoft Windows 2000 Professional, Server, Advanced
Server
; © 1994-1999 Microsoft Corporation. All rights reserved.
;
; Sample Answer File for Unattended Setup
;
; This file contains information about how to automate the
installation
; or upgrade of Windows 2000 Professional and Windows 2000
Server so
; that the Setup program runs without requiring user input.
;

[Unattended]
UnattendMode = FullUnattended
TargetPath = Windows
FileSystem = LeaveAlone
```

```
OemPreinstall = Yes
OemSkipEula = Yes

[GuiUnattended]
; Sets the TimeZone. For example, to set the TimeZone for
the Pacific Northwest, use a
; value of "004." Be sure to use the numeric value that
represents your own time zone. To look up
; a numeric value, see the Unattend.doc file on the Win-
dows 2000 CD.
TimeZone = "YourTimeZone"
; It is recommended that you change the administrator pass-
word before the computer
; is placed at it's final destination.
AdminPassword = adminpassword
; Tells Unattended Setup to turn AutoLogon ON and log on
once.
AutoLogon = Yes
AutoLogonCount = 1
OemSkipWelcome = 1
; The OemSkipRegional key allows Unattended Setup to skip
RegionalSettings
; when the final location of the computer is unknown.
OemSkipRegional = 1

[UserData]
FullName = "Your user name"
OrgName = "Your organization name"
;It is recommended that the use of spaces be avoided in the
ComputerName value.
ComputerName = "YourComputername"
; To ensure a fully unattended installation, you must pro-
vide a value
; for the ProductId key.
ProductId = "Your product ID"

[LicenseFilePrintData]
; This section is used for server installs.
AutoMode = "PerServer"
AutoUsers = "50"

[Display]
BitsPerPel = 8
XResolution = 800
YResolution = 600
VRefresh = 60

[Components]
; This section contains keys for installing the components
of Windows 2000.
; A value of On installs the components, and a value of Off
prevents the
```

```
; component from being installed.
iis_common = On
iis_inetmgr = Off
iis_www = Off
iis_ftp = Off
iis_htmla = Off
iis_doc = Off
iis_pwmgr = Off
iis_smtp = On
iis_smtp_docs = Off
Mts_core = On
; The Fp key installs Front Page Server Extensions.
Fp = On
Msmq = Off
; If you set the TSEnable key to On, Terminal Services is
installed on
; Windows 2000 Server.
TSEnable = On
; If you set the TSClients key to On, the files required to
create
; Terminal Services client disks are installed. If you set
this key to On, you must also set the
; TSEnable key to On.
TSClients = On
; TSPrinterDrivers and TSKeyboardDrivers are optional keys.
If enabled,
; they require additional disk space.
TSPrinterDrivers = Off
TSKeyboardDrivers = Off
Netoc = On
Reminst = On
Certsrv = Off
Rstorage = Off
Indexsrv_system = On
Certsrv_client = Off
Certsrv_server = Off
Certsrv_doc = Off
Accessopt = On
Calc = On
Cdplayer = On
Charmap = On
Chat = Off
Clipbook = On
Deskpaper = On
Dialer = On
Freecell = Off
Hypertrm = On
Media_blindnoisy = On
Media_blindquiet = On
Media_clips = On
Media_jungle = On
Media_musica = On
```

```
Media_robotz = On
Media_utopia = On
Minesweeper = Off
Mousepoint = Off
Mplay = On
Mswordpad = On
Objectpkg = On
Paint = On
Pinball = Off
Rec = On
Solitaire = Off
Templates = On
Vol = On

[TapiLocation]
CountryCode = "1"
Dialing = Pulse
; Indicates the area code for your telephone. This value
should be a 3-digit number.
AreaCode = "Your telephone area code"
LongDistanceAccess = 9

[Networking]
; When you set the value of the InstallDefaultComponents key
to Yes, Setup will install
;default networking components. The components to be set are
TCP/IP, File and Print Sharing,
; and the Client for Microsoft Networks.
InstallDefaultComponents = Yes

[Identification]
JoinDomain = YourCorpNet
DomainAdmin = YourCorpAdmin
DomainAdminPassword = YourAdminPassword

[NetOptionalComponents]
; This section contains a list of the optional network
components to install.
Wins = Off
Dns = Off
Dhcpserver = Off
ils = Off
Snmp = Off
Lpdsvc = Off
Simptcp = Off
Netmontools = On
Dsmigrat = Off

[Branding]
; This section brands Microsoft Internet Explorer with
custom
; properties from the Unattended answer file.
BrandIEUsingUnattended = Yes
```

```
[URL]
; This section contains custom URL settings for Microsoft
Internet Explorer. If these settings
; are not present, the default settings are used.
; Specifies the URL for the browser's default home page. For
example,
; you might use: Home_Page = www.microsoft.com.
Home_Page = YourHomePageURL
; Specifies the URL for the default search page. For ex-
ample, you might
; use: Search Page = www.msn.com
Search_Page = YourSearchPageURL
; Specifies a shortcut name in the link folder of Favorites.
For example,
; you might use: Quick_Link_1_Name = "Microsoft Product
Support Services"
Quick_Link_1_Name = "Your Quick Link Name"
; Specifies a shortcut URL in the link folder of Favorites.
For example,
; you might use: Quick_Link_1 = http://
support.microsoft.com/.
Quick_Link_1 = YourQuickLinkURL

[Proxy]
; This section contains custom proxy settings for Microsoft
Internet Explorer. If these settings are
; not present, the default settings are used. If proxysrv:80
is not accurate for yourconfiguration,
; be sure to replace the proxy server and port number with
your own parameters.
HTTP_Proxy_Server = proxysrv:80
Use_Same_Proxy = 1
Proxy_Enable = 1
Proxy_Override = <local>
```

Sample 4 – Install and Configure Windows 2000 Server with Two Network Adapters

The following answer file installs Microsoft Windows 2000 Server with two network adapters; one adapter uses Dynamic Host Configuration Protocol (DHCP), and the other uses static information.

```
; Microsoft Windows 2000 Server, Advanced Server
; © 1994-1999 Microsoft Corporation. All rights reserved.
;
; Sample Answer File for Unattended Setup
;
; This file contains information about how to automate the
installation
; or upgrade of Windows 2000 Server or Windows 2000 Advanced
```

```
Server so that
; that the Setup program runs without requiring user input.
;

[Unattended]
UnattendMode = FullUnattended
TargetPath = Winnt
Filesystem = ConvertNTFS

[GuiUnattended]
; Sets the TimeZone. For example, to set the TimeZone for
the Pacific Northwest, use a
; value of "004." Be sure to use the numeric value that
represents your own time zone. To look up
; a numeric value, see the Unattend.doc file on the Win-
dows 2000 CD.
TimeZone = "YourTimeZone"
; It is recommended that you change the administrator pass-
word before the computer
; is placed at it's final destination.
AdminPassword = adminpassword
; Tells Unattended Setup to turn AutoLogon ON and log on
once.
AutoLogon = Yes
AutoLogonCount = 1

[LicenseFilePrintData]
; This section is used for server installs.
AutoMode = "PerServer"
AutoUsers = "50"

[UserData]
FullName = "Your user name"
OrgName = "Your organization name"
;It is recommended that you avoid the use of spaces in the
ComputerName value.
ComputerName = "YourComputer_name"
; To ensure a fully unattended installation, you must pro-
vide a value
; for the ProductId key.
ProductId = "Your product ID"

[Display]
BitsPerPel = 8
XResolution = 800
YResolution = 600
VRefresh = 70

[Networking]
; When you set the value of the InstallDefaultComponents key
to Yes, Setup will install
;default networking components. The components to be set are
```

```
TCP/IP, File and Print Sharing,
; and the Client for Microsoft Networks.
InstallDefaultComponents = Yes

[Identification]
JoinDomain = YourCorpNet
DomainAdmin = YourCorpAdmin
DomainAdminPassword = YourAdminPassword

[NetAdapters]
; In this example, there are two network adapters, Adapter01
and Adapter02.
; Note that the adapter specified here as 01 is not always
local area network (LAN)
; connection 1 in the user interface.
Adapter01 = Params.Adapter01
Adapter02 = Params.Adapter02

[Params.Adapter01]
; Specifies which adapter is number one.
; Note that the InfID key must match a valid PNP ID in the
system. For example, a valid PNP ID
; might look as follows: InfID = "pci\ven_0e11&dev_ae32"
InfID = "Your_PNP_ID_for_Adapter01"

[Params.Adapter02]
; Specifies which adapter is number two.
; Note that the InfID key must match a valid PNP ID in the
system. For example, a valid PNP ID
; might look as follows: InfID =
"pci\ven_8086&dev_1229&subsys_00018086"
InfID = "Your_PNP_ID_for_Adapter02"

[NetClients]
; Installs the Client for Microsoft Networks.
MS_MSClient· = params.MS_MSClient

[Params.MS_MSClient]

[NetProtocols]
; Installs only the TCP/IP protocol.
MS_TCPIP = params.MS_TCPIP

[params.MS_TCPIP]
; This section configures the TCP/IP properties.
AdapterSections =
Params.MS_TCPIP.Adapter01,params.MS_TCPIP.Adapter02

[Params.MS_TCPIP.Adapter01]
; Adapter01 uses DHCP server information.
SpecificTo = Adapter01
```

```
        DHCP = Yes
        Wins = Yes

        [Params.MS_TCPIP.Adapter02]
        ; Adapter02 uses static TCP/IP configuration.
        SpecificTo = Adapter02
        IPAddress = 1.1.1.1
        SubnetMask = 255.255.248.0
        DefaultGateway = 2.2.2.2
        DHCP = No
        Wins = No

        [NetServices]
        ; Install File and Print services.
        MS_Server = Params.MS_Server

        [Params.MS_Server]
```

Sample 5 – Install Windows 2000 Advanced Server with Network Load Balancing

The following answer file installs Microsoft Windows 2000 Advanced Server with Network Load Balancing.

```
        ; Microsoft Windows 2000 Advanced Server
        ; © 1994-1999 Microsoft Corporation. All rights reserved.
        ;
        ; Sample Answer File for Unattended Setup
        ;
        ; This file contains information about how to automate the
        installation
        ; or upgrade of Windows 2000 Advanced Server so that the
        ; Setup program runs without requiring user input.
        ;

        [Unattended]
        UnattendMode = FullUnattended
        TargetPath = Windows
        FileSystem = ConvertNTFS

        [GuiUnattended]
        ; Sets the TimeZone. For example, to set the TimeZone for
        the Pacific Northwest, use a
        ; value of "004." Be sure to use the numeric value that
        represents your own time zone. To look up
        ; a numeric value, see the Unattend.doc file on the Win-
        dows 2000 CD.
        TimeZone = "YourTimeZone"
        ; It is recommended that you change the administrator pass-
        word before the computer
        ; is placed at it's final destination.
```

```
AdminPassword = adminpassword
; Tells Unattended Setup to turn AutoLogon ON and log on
once.
AutoLogon = Yes
AutoLogonCount = 1
AdvServerType = Servernt

[LicenseFilePrintData]
; This section is used for server installs.
AutoMode = "PerServer"
AutoUsers = "50"

[UserData]
FullName = "Your user name"
OrgName = "Your organization name"
;It is recommended that you avoid the use of spaces in the
ComputerName value.
ComputerName = "YourComputer_name"
; To ensure a fully unattended installation; you must pro-
vide a value
; for the ProductId key.
ProductId = "Your product ID"

[Display]
BitsPerPel = 8
XResolution = 800
YResolution = 600
VRefresh = 70

[Networking]
; When you set the value of the InstallDefaultComponents key
to Yes, Setup will install
;default networking components. The components to be set are
TCP/IP, File and Print Sharing,
; and the Client for Microsoft Networks.
InstallDefaultComponents=Yes

[Identification]
JoinDomain = YourCorpNet
DomainAdmin = YourCorpAdmin
DomainAdminPassword = Your AdminPassword

[NetAdapters]
 ; In this example, there are two network adapters,
Adapter01 and Adapter02.
; Note that the adapter specified here as 01 is not always
local area network (LAN)
; connection 1 in the user interface. The network adapters
in this example are
; not identical.
Adapter01 = Params.Adapter01
Adapter02 = Params.Adapter02
```

```
[NetBindings]
Enable = MS_WLBS, Adapter01
Enable = MS_TCPIP, Adapter02

[Params.Adapter01]
; Specifies which adapter is number one.
PseudoAdapter = No
PreUpgradeInstance = E100B1
; Note that the InfID key must match a valid PNP ID in the
system. For example, a valid PNP ID
; might look as follows: InfID = PCI\VEN_8086&DEV_1229.
InfID = Your_PNP_ID_for_Adapter01
BusType = PCI
; The ConnectionName key specifies the name for the network
connection
; associated with the network adapter that you are install-
ing.
ConnectionName = "Connection1"

[Params.Adapter02]
; Specifies which adapter is number two.
PseudoAdapter = No
PreUpgradeInstance = E190x2
; Note that the InfID key must match a valid PNP ID in the
system. For example, a valid PNP ID
; might look as follows: InfID = PCI\VEN_10b7&DEV_9050
InfID = Your_PNP_ID_for_Adapter02
BusType = PCI
; The ConnectionName key specifies the name for the network
connection associated with the
; network adapter that you are installing.
ConnectionName = "Connection2"

[NetProtocols]
MS_TCPIP = Params.MS_TCPIP
MS_NetMon = Params.MS_NetMon

[Params.MS_TCPIP]
AdapterSections =
params.MS_TCPIP.Adapter01,params.MS_TCPIP.Adapter02

[Params.MS_TCPIP.Adapter01]
SpecificTo = Adapter01
DNSServerSearchOrder = 192.31.56.150
Wins = Yes
WinsServerList = 192.31.56.150
NetBIOSOptions = 0
DHCP = No
IPAddress = 192.31.56.90,192.31.56.91
SubnetMask = 255.255.255.0,255.255.255.0
DefaultGateway = 192.31.56.150
```

```
[Params.MS_TCPIP.Adapter02]
SpecificTo = Adapter02
DNSServerSearchOrder = 192.31.56.150
Wins = Yes
WinsServerList = 192.31.56.150
NetBIOSOptions = 0
DHCP = No
IPAddress = 192.31.56.92
SubnetMask = 255.255.255.0
DefaultGateway = 192.31.56.150

[Params.MS_NetMon]

[Params.MS_WLBS]
; This section contains keys specific to setting the proper-
ties of Network Load Balancing.
HostPriority = 1
ClusterModeOnStart = 0
ClusterIPAddress = 192.31.56.91
ClusterNetworkMask = 255.255.255.0
DedicatedIPAddress = 192.31.56.90
DedicatedNetworkMask = 255.255.255.0
ClusterName = cluster.yourcompany.com
MulticastSupportEnable = 0
MaskSourceMAC = 1
RemoteControlCode = 0x00000000
RemoteControlUDPPort = 2504
RemoteControlEnabled = 1
Ports =
80,80,Both,Multiple,None,Equal,443,443,Both,Multiple,Single,Equal
AliveMsgPeriod = 2000
AliveMsgTolerance = 10
NumActions = 50
NumPackets = 100
NumAliveMsgs = 10
DescriptorsPerAlloc = 512
MaxDescriptorAllocs = 512
ConnectionCleanupDelay = 300000
NBTSupportEnable = 1

[NetClients]
MS_MSClient = Params.MS_Client

[Params.MS_Client]

[NetServices]
MS_Server = Params.MS_Server
MS_WLBS = Params.MS_WLBS

[Params.MS_Server]
Optimizations = Balance

[NetOptionalComponents]
Netmontools = 1
```

Sample 6 – Install Windows 2000 Advanced Server with Windows Clustering

The following answer file installs Windows 2000 Advanced Server with Windows Clustering.

```
; Microsoft Windows 2000 Advanced Server.
; © 1994-1999 Microsoft Corporation. All rights reserved.
;
; Sample Answer File for Unattended Setup
;
; This file contains information about how to automate the
installation
; or upgrade of Windows 2000 Advanced Server so that the
Setup program
; runs without requiring user input.
;

[Unattended]
UnattendMode = FullUnattended
TargetPath = Advsrv
FileSystem = ConvertNTFS
OemPreinstall = Yes
OemSkipEula = Yes

[GuiUnattended]
; Sets the TimeZone. For example, to set the TimeZone for
the Pacific Northwest, use a
; value of "004." Be sure to use the numeric value that
represents your own time zone. To look up
; a numeric value, see the Unattend.doc file on the Win-
dows 2000 CD.
TimeZone = "YourTimeZone"
; It is recommended that you change the administrator pass-
word before the computer
; is placed at it's final destination.
AdminPassword = adminpassword
; Tells Unattended Setup to turn AutoLogon ON and log on
once.
AutoLogon = Yes
AutoLogonCount = 1
AdvServerType = Servernt
OemSkipWelcome = 1
; The OemSkipRegional key allows Unattended Setup to skip
RegionalSettings
; when the final location of the computer is unknown.
OemSkipRegional = 1

[LicenseFilePrintData]
; This section is used for server installs.
AutoMode = "PerServer"
AutoUsers = "50"
```

```
[UserData]
FullName = "Your user name"
OrgName = "Your organization name"
;It is recommended that you avoid the use of spaces in the
ComputerName value.
ComputerName = "YourComputer_name"
; To ensure a fully unattended installation, you must pro-
vide a value for the ProductId key.
ProductId = "Your product ID"

[Display]
BitsPerPel = 8
XResolution = 800
YResolution = 600
VRefresh = 70

[Networking]
; When you set the value of the InstallDefaultComponents key
to Yes, Setup will install
;default networking components. The components to be set are
TCP/IP, File and Print Sharing,
; and the Client for Microsoft Networks.
InstallDefaultComponents = Yes

[Identification]
JoinDomain = YourCorpNet
DomainAdmin = YourCorpAdmin
DomainAdminPassword = YourAdminPassword

[NetAdapters]
; In this example there are three network adapters,
Adapter 01, Adapter 02,
; and Adapter 03. The adapter specified here as 01 is not
always
; LAN connection 1 in the user interface. The network adapt-
ers in this example are
; not identical.

Adapter01 = Params.Adapter01
Adapter02 = Params.Adapter02
Adapter03 = Params.Adapter03

[Params.Adapter01]
; Specifies which adapter is number one.
; Note that the NetCardAddress key must match a valid ad-
dress of the adapter in the system. For
; example, a valid address might look like the following:
NetCardAddress = 0x00C04F778A5A
NetCardAddress = YourNetCardAddress
; The ConnectionName key specifies the name for the network
connection associated with
; the network adapter that you are installing.
ConnectionName = CorpNet
```

```
[Params.Adapter02]
; Specifies which adapter is number two.
; Note that the NetCardAddress key must match a valid ad-
dress of the adapter in the system. For
; example, a valid address might look like the following:
NetCardAddress = 0x00C04F778A5A
NetCardAddress = YourNetCardAddress
; The ConnectionName key specifies the name for the network
connection associated with
; the network adapter that you are installing.
ConnectionName = VendorNet

[Params.Adapter03]
; Specifies which adapter is number three.
; Note that the NetCardAddress key must match a valid ad-
dress of the adapter in the system. For
; example, a valid address might look like the following:
NetCardAddress = 0x00C04F778A5A
NetCardAddress = YourNetCardAddress
;The ConnectionName key specifies the name for the network
connection
; associated with the network adapter that you are install-
ing.
ConnectionName = PrivateNet

[NetClients]
; Installs the Client for Microsoft Networks.
MS_MSClient = Params.MS_MSClient

[Params.MS_MSClient]

[NetProtocols]
; Installs only the TCP/IP protocol.
MS_TCPIP = Params.MS_TCPIP

[Params.MS_TCPIP]
; This section configures TCP/IP properties.
AdapterSections =
Params.MS_TCPIP.Adapter01,params.MS_TCPIP.Adapter02,params.MS_TCPIP.Adapter03

[Params.MS_TCPIP.Adapter01]
; CorpNet on Adapter01 uses DHCP server information.
SpecificTo = Adapter01
DHCP = Yes
DNSServerSearchOrder = 172.31.240.226, 172.31.240.225
DNSSuffixSearchOrder = CorpNet, dns.yourcompany.com
DNSDomain = CorpNet

[Params.MS_TCPIP.Adapter02]
; VendorNet on Adapter02 uses local DHCP information.
SpecificTo = Adapter02
DHCP = Yes
```

```
[Params.MS_TCPIP.Adapter03]
; PrivateNet on Adapter03 uses static information.
SpecificTo = Adapter03
DHCP = No
WINS = No
IPAddress = 10.2.0.41
SubnetMask = 255.255.0.0
DefaultGateway = 2.2.2.2
DNSServerSearchOrder = 10.2.0.253, 10.2.0.254

[NetServices]
; Installs File and Print services.
MS_Server = Params.MS_Server

[Params.MS_Server]

[Components]
; Installs Windows Clustering and Administration components
on
; Advanced Server when you set the value to On.
Cluster = On

[Cluster]
Name = CorpCluster
Action = Form
Account = CorpAdmin
Domain = CorpNet
IPAddr = 172.31.240.227
Subnet = 255.255.248.0
Network = CorpNet,ALL
Network = VendorNet,ALL

[GuiRunOnce]
; You can automate the running of Cluscfg.exe by placing
Cluscfg.exe in the [GuiRunOnce]
; section of the Unattended answer file. This executes
Cluscfg.exe and configures
; clustering on the first startup after GUI mode Setup has
completed.
; You must include the full path to the program between the
quotes.
"%Windir%\Cluster\Cluscfg.exe -unattend"

[NetOptionalComponents]
NETMONTOOLS = 1
```

APPENDIX   C

Installing Service Packs

Windows 2000 makes it easier for administrators to add service packs. With older operating systems service packs had to be installed separately, after the operating system had been installed. Windows 2000 supports service pack slipstreaming, which means that the service pack is added directly to the operating system's distribution share during installation.

Windows 2000 also eliminates the need to reinstall components that were applied before a service pack was installed. This makes it much easier to install service packs on existing systems. In the past, when service packs were applied, many previously installed components had to be reinstalled. For example, when a service pack is applied to Windows NT 4.0, services such as IPX or RAS (that had been installed previously) have to be reinstalled. To address the problems that existed with Windows NT 4.0 service packs, Windows 2000 provides service pack slipstreaming and post-setup installation of service packs.

Service Pack Slipstreaming

Service pack slipstreaming refers to a service pack being integrated with an updated version of Windows 2000 on a CD-ROM or on a network share. When Windows 2000 is installed from either source, the appropriate files from the service pack are installed without having to manually apply the service pack after the installation.

To apply a new service pack, you will have to use update.exe with the -s:*distribution_folder* switch, where *distribution_folder* is the name of the folder that contains the Windows 2000 installation files. This will copy the updated service pack files over the existing Windows 2000 files. Some of the key files that will be replaced include the following:

- New layout.inf, dosnet.inf, and txtsetup.sif with updated checksums for all the service pack files. These files will need additional entries if any additional files have been added.

- A new driver.cab if the drivers in the cabinet file have been changed.

Post-Setup Installation of a Service Pack

A service pack is applied on an existing Windows 2000 system by running update.exe and updating the system to Windows 2000 plus the service pack. When the system state changes (adding or removing services), this tells the base system that a service pack was installed, what files were replaced or updated by the service pack, and where to install the service pack from. This means that the right files are copied from the service pack install location (network share, CD-ROM, Web site) and the right files are copied from the Windows 2000 installation source (network share or CD-ROM). This eliminates the need to reapply a service pack once the system state has changed.

Once the service pack has been applied, if the system state changes (for example, adding RAS after the service pack is applied), Windows 2000 installs the correct files, whether those files originate from the Windows 2000 CD-ROM or from the service pack. The eliminates the need to re-apply the service pack whenever the system state changes.

Glossary

5-4-3 rule A rule that states that a thinnet network can combine as many as five cable segments connected by four repeaters. However, only three segments can have stations attached, which leaves two segments untapped.

10Base2 Ethernet topology that transmits at 10 Mbps over a baseband wire, and can carry a signal 185 meters. *See also* thinnet.

10Base5 *See* standard Ethernet.

10BaseFL An Ethernet network that typically uses fiber-optic cable to connect computers and repeaters.

10BaseT A 10 Mbps Ethernet network topology that typically uses unshielded twisted-pair (UTP) cable to connect computers. The maximum length of a 10BaseT segment is 100 meters (328 feet).

100BaseX Ethernet *See* Fast Ethernet.

100VG (Voice Grade) AnyLAN (100VGAnyLAN) An emerging networking technology that combines elements of both Ethernet and Token Ring.

A

access method The set of rules that defines how a computer puts data onto the network cable and takes data from the cable. When data is moving on the network, access methods help to regulate the flow of network traffic.

access permissions Features that control access to sharing in Windows NT Server. Permissions can be set for the following access levels: No Access—Prevents access to the shared directory, its subdirectories, and its files. Read—Allows viewing of file and subdirectory names, changing to a shared directory's subdirectory, viewing data in files, and running applications. Change—Allows viewing of file and subdirectory names, changing to a shared directory's subdirectories, viewing data in files and running application files, adding files and subdirectories to a shared directory, changing data in files, and deleting subdirectories and files. Full Control—Includes the same permissions as Change, plus changing permissions (taking ownership of the Windows NT file system [NTFS] files and directories only).

account *See* user account.

account lockout A Windows 2000 security feature that locks a user account if a number of failed logon attempts occur within a specified amount of time, based on security policy lockout settings. Locked accounts cannot log on.

account policy Controls how passwords must be used by all user accounts in a domain or in an individual computer.

Active Directory services The directory service included with Windows 2000 Server. It stores information about objects on a network and makes this information available to users and network administrators. Active Directory services allows users to use a single logon process to access permitted resources anywhere on the network. Active Directory services provides network administrators with an intuitive hierarchical view of the network and a single point of administration for all network objects.

Address Resolution Protocol (ARP) Determines hardware addresses (MAC addresses) that correspond to an IP address.

ADSL *See* Asymmetric Digital Subscriber Line (ADSL).

advanced cable testers Cable testers that work beyond the physical layer of the OSI reference model up into layers 2, 3, and even 4. They can display information about the condition of the physical cable as well as message-frame counts, excess collisions, late collisions, error-frame counts, congestion errors, and beaconing. These testers can monitor overall network traffic, certain kinds of error situations, and traffic to and from a particular computer. They indicate if a particular cable or network interface card (NIC) is causing problems.

advanced program-to-program communication (APPC) A specification developed as part of IBM's SNA (Systems Network Architecture) model and designed to enable application programs running on different computers to communicate and exchange data directly. *See also* Systems Network Architecture.

AFP *See* AppleTalk filing protocol (AFP).

agent A program that performs a background task for a user and reports to the user when the task is done or when some expected event has taken place.

American National Standards Institute (ANSI) An organization of American industry and business groups dedicated to the development of trade and communications standards. ANSI is the American representative to the International Organization for Standardization (ISO). *See also* International Organization for Standardization (ISO).

amplifier A device, such as a repeater or bridge, that amplifies or increases the power of electrical signals, allowing them to travel on additional cable segments at their original strength. Amplifiers strengthen signals that have been weakened by attenuation.

analog Related to a continuously variable physical property, such as voltage, pressure, or rotation. An analog device can represent an infinite number of values within the range the device can handle. *See also* analog line, digital.

analog line A communications line, such as a telephone line, that carries information in analog (continuously variable) form. To minimize distortion and noise interference, an analog line uses amplifiers to strengthen the signal periodically during transmission.

ANSI *See* American National Standards Institute (ANSI).

APPC *See* advanced program-to-program communication (APPC).

AppleShare AppleShare is the Apple network operating system. Features include file sharing, client software that is included with every copy of the Apple operating system, and the AppleShare print server, a server-based print spooler.

AppleTalk The Apple network architecture that is included in the Macintosh operating system software. It is a collection of protocols that correspond to the OSI model. Thus network capabilities are built into every Macintosh. AppleTalk protocols support LocalTalk, Ethernet (EtherTalk), and Token Ring (TokenTalk).

AppleTalk filing protocol (AFP) Describes how files are stored and accessed on the network. AFP is responsible for the Apple hierarchical filing structure of volumes, folders, and files and provides for file sharing between Macintoshes and MS-DOS–based computers. It provides an interface for communication between AppleTalk and other network operating systems, allowing Macintoshes to be integrated into any network that uses an operating system that recognizes AFP.

application layer The top (seventh) layer of the OSI reference model. This layer serves as the window that application processes use to access network services. It represents the services that directly support user applications, such as software for file transfers, database access, and e-mail.

application programming interface (API) A set of routines that an application program uses to request and carry out lower-level services performed by the operating system.

application protocols Protocols that work at the higher end of the OSI reference model, providing application-to-application interaction and data exchange. Popular application protocols include: FTAM (file transfer access

and management)—A file access protocol. SMTP (simple mail transfer protocol)—A TCP/IP protocol for transferring e-mail. Telnet—A TCP/IP protocol for logging on to remote hosts and processing data locally. NCP (NetWare core protocol)—The primary protocol used to transmit information between a NetWare server and its clients.

ArcNet (Attached Resource Computer Network) Developed by Datapoint Corporation in 1977, designed as a baseband, token-passing, bus architecture, transmitting at 2.5 Mbps. A successor to the original ArcNet, *ArcNetplus* supports data transmission rates of 20 Mbps. A simple, inexpensive, flexible network architecture designed for workgroup-sized LANs, ArcNet runs on coaxial, twisted-pair, and fiber-optic cable and supports up to 255 nodes. ArcNet technology predates IEEE Project 802 standards but loosely maps to the 802.4 document. *See also* Project 802.

ARP *See* Address Resolution Protocol (ARP).

ARPANET (Advanced Research Projects Agency Network) Acronym for the Department of Defense Advanced Research Projects Agency. A pioneering wide area network (WAN), ARPANET was designed to facilitate the exchange of information between universities and other research organizations. ARPANET, which became operational in the 1960s, is the network from which the Internet evolved.

ASCII (American Standard Code for Information Interchange) A coding scheme that assigns numeric values to letters, numbers, punctuation marks, and certain other characters. By standardizing the values used for these characters, ASCII enables computers and computer programs to exchange information.

Asymmetric Digital Subscriber Line (ADSL)
A recent modem technology that converts existing twisted-pair telephone lines into access paths for multimedia and high-speed data communications. These new connections can transmit more than 8 Mbps to the subscriber and up to 1 Mbps from the subscriber. ADSL is recognized as a physical layer transmission protocol for unshielded twisted-pair media.

asynchronous transfer mode (ATM) An advanced implementation of packet switching that provides high-speed data transmission rates to send fixed-size cells over broadband LANs or WANs. Cells are 53 bytes—48 bytes of data with five additional bytes of address. ATM accommodates voice, data, fax, real-time video, CD-quality audio, imaging, and multimegabit data transmission. ATM uses switches as multiplexers to permit several computers to put data on a network simultaneously. Most commercial ATM boards transmit data at about 155 Mbps, but theoretically a rate of 1.2 gigabits per second is possible.

asynchronous transmission A form of data transmission in which information is sent one character at a time, with variable time intervals between characters. Asynchronous transmission does not rely on a shared timer that allows the sending and receiving units to separate characters by specific time periods. Therefore, each transmitted character consists of a number of data bits (that compose the character itself), preceded by a start bit and ending in an optional parity bit followed by a 1-, 1.5-, or 2-stop bit.

ATM *See* asynchronous transfer mode (ATM).

attachment unit interface (AUI) The connector used with standard Ethernet that often includes a cable running off the main, or backbone, coaxial cable. Also known as a DIX connector.

attenuation The weakening or degrading (distorting) of a transmitted signal as it travels farther from its point of origin. This could be a digital signal on a cable or the reduction in amplitude of an electrical signal, without the appreciable modification of the waveform. Attenuation is usually measured in decibels. Attenuation of a signal transmitted over a long cable is corrected by a repeater, which amplifies and cleans up an incoming signal before sending it farther along the cable.

auditing A process that tracks network activities by user accounts and a routine element of network security. Auditing can produce records of list users who have accessed—or attempted to access— specific resources; help administrators identify unauthorized activity; and track activities such as logon attempts, connection and disconnection from designated resources, changes made to files and directories, server events and modifications, password changes, and logon parameter changes.

AUI *See* attachment unit interface (AUI).

authentication Verification based on user name, passwords, and time and account restrictions.

AWG (American Wire Gauge) A standard that determines wire diameter. The diameter varies inversely to the gauge number.

B

backbone The main cable, also known as the trunk segment, from which transceiver cables connect to computers, repeaters, and bridges.

back end In a client/server application, the part of the program that runs on the server.

backup A duplicate copy of a program, a disk, or data, made to secure valuable files from loss.

backup domain controller (BDC) In a Windows NT Server domain, a computer that receives a copy of the domain's security policy and domain database and authenticates network logons. It provides a backup if the primary domain controller (PDC) becomes unavailable. A domain is not required to have a BDC, but it is recommended to have a BDC to back up the PDC. *See also* domain, domain controller, primary domain controller.

bandwidth In communications, the difference between the highest and lowest frequencies in a given range. For example, a telephone accommodates a bandwidth of 3000 Hz, or the difference between the lowest (300 Hz) and highest (3300 Hz) frequencies it can carry. In computer networks, greater bandwidth indicates faster or greater data-transfer capability.

barrel connector A component that can connect two pieces of cable to make a longer piece of cable.

baseband A system used to transmit the encoded signals over cable. Baseband uses digital signaling over a single frequency. Signals flow in the form of discrete pulses of electricity or light. With baseband transmission, the entire communication-channel capacity is used to transmit a single data signal.

base I/O port Specifies a channel through which information is transferred between a computer's hardware, such as the network interface card (NIC), and its CPU.

base memory address Defines the address of the location in a computer's memory (RAM) that is used by the NIC. This setting is sometimes called the RAM start address.

basic input/output system (BIOS) On PC-compatible computers, the set of essential software routines that test hardware at startup, start the operating system, and support the transfer of data among hardware devices. The BIOS is stored in read-only memory (ROM) so that it can be executed when the computer is turned on. Although critical to performance, the BIOS is usually invisible to computer users.

baud A measure of data-transmission speed named after the French engineer and telegrapher Jean-Maurice-Emile Baudot. It is a measure of the speed of oscillation of the sound wave on which a bit of data is carried over telephone lines. Because baud was originally used to measure the transmission speed of telegraph equipment, the term sometimes refers to the data-transmission speed of a modem. However, current modems can send at a speed higher than one bit per oscillation, so baud is being replaced by the more accurate bps (bits per second) as a measure of modem speed.

baud rate Refers to the speed at which a modem can transmit data. Often confused with bps (the number of bits per second transmitted), baud rate actually measures the number of events, or signal changes, that occur in one second. Because one event can actually encode more than one bit in high-speed digital communication, baud rate and bps are not always synonymous, and the latter is the more accurate term to apply to modems. For example, the 9600-baud modem that encodes four-bits per event actually operates at 2400 baud, but transmits at 9600 bps (2400 events times 4 bits per event), and thus should be called a 9600-bps modem.

BBS *See* bulletin board system (BBS).

BDC *See* backup domain controller (BDC).

beaconing The process of signaling computers on a ring system that token passing has been interrupted by a serious error. All computers in an FDDI or Token Ring network are responsible for monitoring the token-passing process. To isolate serious failures in the ring, FDDI and Token Ring use beaconing in which a computer that detects a fault sends a signal, called a beacon, onto the network. The computer continues to send the beacon until it notices a beacon from its upstream neighbor. This process continues until the only computer sending a beacon is the one directly downstream of the failure. When the beaconing computer finally receives its own beacon, it assumes the problem has been fixed and regenerates a token.

bind To associate two pieces of information with one another.

binding A process that establishes the communication channel between a protocol driver and a NIC driver.

BIOS (basic input/output system) *See* basic input/output system (BIOS).

BISDN *See* broadband Integrated Services Digital Network (BISDN).

bisync (binary synchronous communications protocol) A communications protocol developed by IBM. Bisync transmissions are encoded in either ASCII or EBCDIC. Messages can be of any length and are sent in units called frames, optionally preceded by a message header. Because bisync uses

synchronous transmission, in which message elements are separated by a specific time interval, each frame is preceded and followed by special characters that enable the sending and receiving machines to synchronize their clocks.

bit Short for binary digit: either 1 or 0 in the binary number system. In processing and storage, a bit is the smallest unit of information handled by a computer. It is represented physically by an element such as a single pulse sent through a circuit or small spot on a magnetic disk capable of storing either a 1 or 0. Eight bits make a byte.

bits per second (bps) A measure of the speed at which a device can transfer data. *See also* baud rate.

bit time The time it takes for each station to receive and store a bit.

BNC cable connector A connector for coaxial cable that locks when one connector is inserted into another and is rotated 90 degrees.

BNC components A family of components that include the BNC cable connector, BNC T connector, BNC barrel connector, and the BNC terminator. The origin of the acronym "BNC" is unclear; names ascribed to these letters range from "British Naval Connector" to "Bayonet Neill-Councelman."

boot-sector virus A type of virus that resides in the first sector of a floppy disk or hard drive. When the computer is booted, the virus executes. In this common method of transmitting viruses from one floppy disk to another, the virus replicates itself onto the new drive each time a new disk is inserted and accessed.

bottleneck A device or program that significantly degrades network performance. Poor network performance results when a device uses noticeably more CPU time than it should, consumes too much of a resource, or lacks the capacity to handle the load. Potential bottlenecks can be found in the CPU, memory, NIC, and other components.

bounce *See* signal bounce.

bps *See* bits per second (bps).

bridge A device used to join two LANs. It allows stations on either network to access resources on the other. Bridges can be used to increase the length or number of nodes for a network. The bridge makes connections at the data-link layer of the OSI reference model.

bridged network A network that is connected by bridges.

Broadband Integrated Services Digital Network (BISDN) A consultative committee for the CCITT that recommends definitions for voice, data, and video in the megabit/gigabit range. BISDN is also a single ISDN network that can handle voice, data, and video services. BISDN works with an optical cable transport network called Synchronous Optical Network (SONET) and an asynchronous transfer mode (ATM) switching service. SMDS (Switched Multimegabit Data Services) is a BISDN service that offers high bandwidth to WANs. *See also* Synchronous Optical Network (SONET), asynchronous transfer mode (ATM), Switched Multimegabit Data Services (SMDS).

broadband network A type of LAN on which transmissions travel as analog (radio-frequency) signals over separate inbound and outbound channels. Devices on a broadband network are connected by coaxial or fiber-optic cable, and signals flow across the physical medium in the form of electromagnetic or optical waves. A broadband system

uses a large portion of the electromagnetic spectrum with a range of frequencies from 50 Mbps to 600 Mbps. These networks can simultaneously accommodate television, voice, data, and other services over multiple transmission channels.

broadcast A transmission sent simultaneously to more than one recipient. In communication and on networks, a broadcast message is one distributed to all stations or computers on the network.

broadcast storm An event that occurs when there are so many broadcast messages on the network that they approach or surpass the capacity of the network bandwidth. This can happen when one computer on the network transmits a flood of frames saturating the network with traffic so it can no longer carry messages from any other computer. Such a broadcast storm can shut down a network.

brouter A network component that combines the best qualities of a bridge and a router. A brouter can act as a router for one protocol and as a bridge for all the others. Brouters can route selected routable protocols, bridge nonroutable protocols, and deliver more cost-effective and manageable internetworking than separate bridges and routers. A brouter is a good choice in an environment that mixes several homogeneous LAN segments with two different segments.

buffer A reserved portion of RAM in which data is held temporarily, pending an opportunity to complete its transfer to or from a storage device or another location in memory.

built-in groups One of four kinds of group accounts used by Microsoft Windows NT and Windows NT Server. Built-in groups, as the name implies, are included with the network operating system. Built-in groups have been granted useful collections of rights and built-in abilities. In most cases, a built-in group provides all the capabilities needed by a particular user. For example, if a domain user account belongs to the built-in Administrators group, logging on with that account gives a user administrative capabilities over the domain and the servers in the domain. *See also* user account.

bulletin board system (BBS) A computer system equipped with one or more modems or other means of network access that serves as an information and message-passing center for remote users. Many software and hardware companies run proprietary BBSs for customers that include sales information, technical support, and software upgrades and patches.

bus Parallel wires or cabling that connect components in a computer.

bus topology A topology that connects each computer, or station, to a single cable. At each end of the cable is a terminating resistor, or terminator. A transmission is passed back and forth along the cable, past the stations and between the two terminators, carrying a message from one end of the network to the other. As the message passes each station, the station checks the message's destination address. If the address in the message matches the station's address, the station receives the message. If the addresses do not match, the bus carries the message to the next station, and so on.

byte A unit of information consisting of 8 bits. In computer processing or storage, a byte is equivalent to a single character, such as a letter, numeral, or punctuation mark. Because a byte represents only a small amount of information, amounts of computer memory are usually given in kilobytes (1024

bytes or 2 raised to the 10th power), megabytes (1,048,576 bytes or 2 raised to the 20th power), gigabytes (1024 megabytes), terabytes (1024 gigabytes), petabytes (1024 terabytes), or exabytes (1024 petabytes).

C

CA (certificate authority) *See* certificate authority (CA).

cable categories The three major groups of cabling that connect the majority of networks: coaxial, twisted-pair (unshielded twisted-pair and shielded twisted-pair), and fiber-optic cabling.

cable testers *See* advanced cable testers.

cache A special memory subsystem or part of RAM in which frequently used data values are duplicated for quick access. A memory cache stores the contents of frequently accessed RAM locations and the addresses where these data items are stored. When the processor references an address in memory, the cache checks to see whether it holds that address. If it does hold the address, the data is returned to the processor; if it does not, regular memory access occurs. A cache is useful when RAM accesses are slow as compared to the microprocessor speed.

carrier-sense multiple access with collision avoidance (CSMA/CA) access method An access method by which each computer signals its intent to transmit before it actually transmits data, thus avoiding possible transmission collisions. *See also* access method.

carrier-sense multiple access with collision detection (CSMA/CD) access method An access method generally used with bus topologies. Using CSMA/CD, a station "listens" to the physical medium to determine whether another station is currently transmitting a data frame. If no other station is transmitting, the station sends its data. A station "listens" to the medium by testing the medium for the presence of a carrier, a specific level of voltage or light—thus the term carrier-sense. The multiple access indicates that there are multiple stations attempting to access or put data on the cable at the same time. The collision detection indicates that the stations are also listening for collisions. If two stations attempt to transmit at the same time and a collision occurs, the stations must wait a random period of time before attempting to transmit. *See also* access method.

CCEP *See* Commercial COMSEC Endorsement Program (CCEP).

CCITT (Comité Consultatif Internationale de Télégraphie et Téléphonie) An organization based in Geneva, Switzerland, and established as part of the United Nations International Telecommunications Union (ITU). The CCITT recommends use of communication standards that are recognized throughout the world. Protocols established by the CCITT are applied to modems, networks, and facsimile transmission.

Cellular Digital Packet Data (CDPD) A communication standard that uses very fast technology, similar to that of cellular telephones, to offer computer data transmissions over existing analog voice networks between voice calls, when the system is not occupied with voice communication.

central file server A network in which specific computers take on the role of server with other computers on the network sharing the resources. *See also* client/server.

certificate A collection of data used for authentication and secure exchange of information on nonsecured networks, such as the Internet. A certificate securely binds a public key to the entity that holds the corresponding private key. Certificates are digitally signed by the issuing CA and can be managed for a user, computer, or service. The most widely accepted format for certificates is defined by ITU-T X.509 international standards.

certificate authority (CA) An entity responsible for establishing the couching for the authenticity of public keys belonging to users or other CAs. Activities of a CA may include binding public keys to distinguished names through signed certificates, managing certificate serial numbers, and revoking certificates.

central processing unit (CPU) The computational and control unit of a computer, the device that interprets and carries out instructions. Single-chip CPUs, called microprocessors, made personal computers possible. Examples include the 80286, 80386, 80486, and Pentium processors.

cladding The concentric layer of glass that surrounds the extremely thin, cylindrical glass core in fiber-optic cable.

client A computer that accesses shared network resources provided by another computer, called a server.

client/server A network architecture designed around the concept of distributed processing in which a task is divided between a back end (server), that stores and distributes data, and a front end (client) that requests specific data from the server. *See also* central file server.

coaxial cable (coax) A conductive center wire surrounded by an insulating layer, a layer of wire mesh (shielding), and a non-conductive outer layer. Coaxial cable is resistant to interference and signal weakening that other cabling, such as unshielded twisted-pair cable, can experience.

codec (compression/decompression) Compression/decompression technology for digital video and stereo audio.

Commercial COMSEC Endorsement Program (CCEP) A data-encryption standard introduced by the National Security Agency. Vendors who have the proper security clearance can join CCEP and be authorized to incorporate classified algorithms into communications systems. *See also* encryption.

companion virus A virus that uses the name of a real program, but has a different file extension from that of the program itself. The virus is activated when its companion program is opened. The companion virus uses a .COM file extension, which overrides the .EXE file extension and activates the virus.

concentrator A network physical-layer device that serves as a central connection for other network devices. *See also* hub.

contention Competition among stations on a network for the opportunity to use a communication line or network resource. Two or more computers attempt to transmit over the same cable at the same time, thus causing a collision on the cable. Such a system needs regulation to eliminate data collisions on the cable which can destroy data and bring network traffic to a halt. *See also* carrier-sense multiple access with collision detection (CSMA/CD) access method.

core In coaxial cable, the innermost part of the cable that carries the electronic signals

which make up the data. It can be solid (usually copper) or stranded. In fiber-optic cable, digital data signals travel through an extremely thin cylindrical glass core surrounded by cladding.

CPU *See* central processing unit (CPU).

CRC *See* cyclical redundancy check (CRC).

crossover cable Used to connect two computers directly with a single patch cable, so that the send wire from one computer is connected to the receive port on the other computer. Crossover cables are useful in troubleshooting network connection problems.

crosstalk Signal overflow from an adjacent wire. When a second faint telephone conversation is heard in the background while one is making a phone call, crosstalk is occurring.

cryptography The processes, art, and science of keeping messages and data secure. Cryptography is used to enable and ensure confidentiality, data integrity, authentication (entity and data origin), and nonrepudiation.

CSMA/CD *See* carrier-sense multiple access with collision detection (CSMA/CD) access method.

cyclical redundancy check (CRC) A form of error checking in transmitting data. The sending packet includes a number produced by a mathematical calculation made at the transmission source. When the packet arrives at its destination, the calculation is redone. If the two figures are the same, this indicates that the data in the packet has remained stable. If the calculation at the destination differs from the calculation at the source, this indicates that the data has changed during the transmission. In that case, the CRC routine signals the source computer to retransmit the data.

D

daisy chain A set of devices, such as Small Computer System Interfaces (SCSIs) and Universal Serial Buses (USBs), that are connected in a series. When devices are daisy-chained to a microcomputer, the first device is connected to the computer, the second device is connected to the first, and so on down the line. Signals are passed through the chain from one device to the next. *See also* Small Computer System Interface (SCSI) and Universal Serial Bus (USB).

database management system (DBMS) A layer of software between the physical database and the user. The DBMS manages all requests for database action from the user, including keeping track of the physical details of file locations and formats, indexing schemes, and so on. In addition, a DBMS permits centralized control of security and data integrity requirements.

Data Communications Equipment (DCE) One of two types of hardware connected by an RS-232 serial connection, the other being a DTE (data terminal equipment) device. A DCE device takes input from a DTE device and often acts as an intermediary device, transforming the input signal in some way before sending it to the actual recipient. For example, an external modem is a DCE device that accepts data from a microcomputer (DTE), modulates it, then sends the data along a telephone connection. In communication, an RS-232 DCE device receives data over line 2 and transmits over line 3. In contrast, a DTE device receives over line 3 and transmits over line 2. *See also* Data Terminal Equipment (DTE).

data encryption *See* encryption.

data encryption standard (DES) A commonly used, highly sophisticated algorithm devel-

oped by the U.S. National Bureau of Standards for encrypting and decoding data. *See also* encryption.

data frames Logical, structured packages in which data can be placed. Data being transmitted is segmented into small units and combined with control information such as message start and message end indicators. Each package of information is transmitted as a single unit, called a frame. The data-link layer packages raw bits from the physical layer into data frames. The exact format of the frame used by the network depends on the topology. *See also* frame.

data-link layer The second layer in the OSI reference model. This layer packages raw bits from the physical layer into data frames. *See also* Open Systems Interconnection (OSI) reference model.

data stream An undifferentiated, byte-by-byte flow of data.

Data Terminal Equipment (DTE) According to the RS-232 hardware standard, a device, such as a microcomputer or a terminal, that has the ability to transmit information in digital form over a cable or a communication line. A DTE is one of two types of hardware connected by an RS-232 serial connection, the other being a DCE (Data Communications Equipment) device, such as a modem, that normally connects the DTE to the communication line itself. In communication, an RS-232 DTE device transmits data over line 2 and receives it over line 3. A DCE receives over line 2 and transmits over line 3. *See also* Data Communications Equipment (DCE).

DB connector A connector that facilitates parallel input and output. The initials DB stand for *data bus*. The numbers which follow DB indicate the number of wires within the connector. For example, a DB-15 connector has 15 pins and supports up to 15 lines, each of which can connect to a pin on the connector; a DB-25 connector has 25 of each.

DBMS *See* database management system (DBMS).

DCE *See* Data Communications Equipment (DCE).

DECnet Digital Equipment Corporation hardware and software products that implement the Digital Network Architecture (DNA). DECnet defines communication networks over Ethernet LANs, Fiber Distributed Data Interface metropolitan area networks (FDDI MANs), and WANs that use private or public data transmission facilities. It can use TCP/IP and OSI protocols as well as Digital's DECnet protocols. *See also* Fiber Distributed Data Interface, metropolitan area network (MAN).

dedicated server A computer on a network that functions only as a server and is not also used as a client. *See also* server, server-based network.

DES *See* data encryption standard (DES).

device A generic term for a computer subsystem. Printers, serial ports, and disk drives are referred to as devices.

Dfs (distributed file system) *See* distributed file system (Dfs).

DHCP *See* Dynamic Host Configuration Protocol (DHCP).

dial-up connection The connection to your network if you are using a device that uses the telephone network. This includes modems with a standard phone line, ISDN cards with high speed ISDN lines, or X.25 net-

works. If you are a typical user, you may have one or two dial-up connections, perhaps to the Internet and to your corporate network. In a more complex server situation, multiple network modem connections might be used to implement advanced routing.

digital A system that encodes information numerically, such as 0 and 1, in a binary context. Computers use digital encoding to process data. A digital signal is a discrete binary state, either on or off. *See also* analog.

digital line A communication line that carries information only in binary-encoded (digital) form. To minimize distortion and noise interference, a digital line uses repeaters to regenerate the signal periodically during transmission. *See also* analog line.

digital signature A means for originators of a message, file, or other digitally encoded information to bind their identity to the information. The process of signing information entails transforming the information, as well as some secret information held by the sender, into a tag called a signature. Digital signatures are used in public key environments. and they provide nonrepudiation and integrity services.

digital video disc (DVD) An optical storage medium with higher capacity and bandwidth than a compact disc. A DVD can hold a full-length film with up to 133 minutes of high-quality video, in MPEG-2 format, and audio. Also known as digital versatile disc.

digital voltmeter (DVM) A basic, all-purpose electronic measuring tool. In addition to indicating the amount of voltage passing through resistance, in network cable testing, voltmeters measure continuity to determine if a cable is able to carry current.

DIP (dual inline package) switch One or more small rocker or sliding switches that can be set to one of two states—closed or open—to control options on a circuit board.

direct memory access (DMA) Memory access that does not involve the microprocessor, frequently employed for data transfer directly between memory and an "intelligent" peripheral device such as a disk drive.

direct memory access (DMA) channel A channel for direct memory access that does not involve the microprocessor, providing data transfer directly between memory and a disk drive.

disk duplexing *See* disk mirroring, fault tolerance.

disk duplicating *See* disk mirroring.

diskless computers Computers that have neither a floppy disk nor a hard disk. Diskless computers depend on special ROM in order to provide users with an interface through which they can log on to the network.

disk mirroring A technique, also known as disk duplicating, in which all or part of a hard disk is duplicated onto one or more hard disks, each of which ideally is attached to its own controller. With disk mirroring, any change made to the original disk is simultaneously made to the other disk(s). Disk mirroring is used in situations in which a backup copy of current data must be maintained at all times. *See also* disk striping, fault tolerance.

disk striping Divides data into 64 K blocks and spreads it equally in a fixed rate and order among all disks in an array. However, disk striping does not provide any fault tolerance because there is no data redundancy. If any

partition in the set fails, all data is lost. *See also* disk mirroring, fault tolerance.

distributed file system (Dfs) A single, logical, hierarchical file system. Dfs organizes shared folders on different computers in a network to provide a logical tree structure for file system resources.

DIX (Digital, Intel, Xerox) connector The connector used with standard Ethernet that often includes a cable running off the main, or backbone, coaxial cable. This is also known as an AUI connector. *See also* attachment unit interface (AUI).

DMA *See* direct memory access (DMA).

DMA channel *See* direct memory access (DMA) channel.

DNS *See* Domain Name System (DNS).

domain For Microsoft networking, a collection of computers and users that share a common database and security policy that are stored on a Windows NT Server domain controller. Each domain has a unique name. *See also* workgroup.

domain controller For Microsoft networking, the Windows NT Server–based computer that authenticates domain logons and maintains the security policy and master database for a domain. *See also* backup domain controller (BDC), primary domain controller (PDC).

Domain Name System (DNS) A general-purpose distributed, replicated, data-query service used primarily on the Internet for translating host names into Internet addresses.

downtime The amount of time a computer system or associated hardware remains nonfunctioning. Although downtime can occur because hardware fails unexpectedly, it can also be a scheduled event, such as when a network is shut down to allow time for maintaining the system, changing hardware, or archiving files.

driver A software component that permits a computer system to communicate with a device. For example, a printer driver is a device driver that translates computer data into a form understood by the target printer. In most cases, the driver also manipulates the hardware in order to transmit the data to the device.

DTE *See* Data Terminal Equipment (DTE).

dual boot A computer configuration that can start two different operating systems.

dual shielded cable Cable that contains one layer of foil and insulation and one layer of braided metal shielding.

dumb terminal A device used for obtaining or entering data on a network that does not contain any "intelligence" or processing power provided by a CPU.

duplex transmission Also called full-duplex transmission. Communication that takes place simultaneously, in both directions, between the sender and the receiver. Alternative methods of transmission are simplex, which is one-way only, and half-duplex, which is two-way communication that occurs in only one direction at a time.

DVD (digital video disc, also known as digital versatile disc) *See* digital video disc (DVD).

Dynamic Host Configuration Protocol (DHCP) A protocol for automatic TCP/IP configuration that provides static and dynamic address allocation and management. *See also* Transport Control Protocol/Internet Protocol (TCP/IP).

E

EBCDIC *See* Extended Binary Coded Decimal Interchange Code (EBCDIC).

EFS (encrypting file system) *See* encrypting file system (EFS)

EISA *See* Extended Industry Standard Architecture (EISA).

encrypting file system (EFS) Windows 2000 file system that enables users to encrypt files and folders on an NTFS volume disk to keep them safe from access by intruders.

encryption The process of making information indecipherable to protect it from unauthorized viewing or use, especially during transmission or when the data is stored on a transportable magnetic medium. A key is required to decode the information. *See also* CCEP, data encryption standard (DES).

Enhanced Small Device Interface (ESDI) A standard that can be used with high-capacity hard disks and tape drives to enable high-speed communication with a computer. ESDI drivers typically transfer data at about 10 Mbps.

ESDI *See* Enhanced Small Device Interface (ESDI).

Ethernet A LAN developed by Xerox in 1976. Ethernet became a widely implemented network from which the IEEE 802.3 standard for contention networks was developed. It uses a bus topology and the original Ethernet relies on CSMA/CD to regulate traffic on the main communication line.

EtherTalk Allows the AppleTalk network protocols to run on Ethernet coaxial cable. The EtherTalk card allows a Macintosh computer to connect to an 802.3 Ethernet network. *See also* AppleTalk.

event An action or occurrence to which a program might respond. Examples of events are mouse clicks, key presses, and mouse movements. Also, any significant occurrence in the system or in a program that requires users to be notified or an entry to be added to a log.

exabyte *See* byte.

Extended Binary Coded Decimal Interchange Code (EBCDIC) A coding scheme developed by IBM for use with IBM mainframe and Personal Computers as a standard method of assigning binary (numeric) values to alphabetic, numeric, punctuation, and transmission-control characters.

Extended Industry Standard Architecture (EISA) A 32-bit bus design for x86-based computers introduced in 1988. EISA was specified by an industry consortium of nine computer-industry companies (AST Research, Compaq, Epson, Hewlett-Packard, NEC, Olivetti, Tandy, Wyse, and Zenith). An EISA device uses cards that are upwardly compatible from ISA. *See also* Industry Standard Architecture (ISA).

extended partition A portion of a basic disk that can contain logical drives. Use an extended partition if you want to have more than four volumes on your basic disk. Only one of the four partitions allowed per physical disk can be an extended partition, and no primary partition needs to be present to create an extended partition. Extended partitions can be created only on basic disks.

F

fast Ethernet Also called 100BaseX Ethernet. An extension to the existing Ethernet standard, it runs on UTP Category 5 data-grade cable and uses CSMA/CD in a star-wired bus topology, similar to 10BaseT in which all cables are attached to a hub.

FAT (file allocation table) *See* file allocation table (FAT).

fault tolerance The ability of a computer or an operating system to respond to an event such as a power outage or a hardware failure in such a way that no data is lost and any work in progress is not corrupted.

Fiber Distributed Data Interface (FDDI) A standard developed by the ANSI for high-speed, fiber-optic local area networks. FDDI provides specifications for transmission rates of 100 Mbps on networks based on the Token Ring standard.

fiber-optic cable Cable that uses optical fibers to carry digital data signals in the form of modulated pulses of light.

file allocation table (FAT) A table or list maintained by some operating systems to keep track of the status of various segments of disk space used for file storage.

file infector A type of virus that attaches itself to a file or program and activates any time the file is used. Many subcategories of file infectors exist. *See also* companion virus, macro virus, polymorphic virus, stealth virus.

file replication service (FRS) Provides multi-master file replication for designated directory trees between designated Windows 2000 servers. The designated directory trees must be on disk partitions formatted with the version of NTFS used with Windows 2000. FRS is used by the Microsoft distributed file system (Dfs) to automatically synchronize content between assigned replicas, and by Active Directory services to automatically synchronize content of the system volume information across domain controllers.

File Transfer Protocol (FTP) A process that provides file transfers between 'local and remote computers. FTP supports several commands that allow bidirectional transfer of binary and ASCII files between computers. The FTP client is installed with the TCP/IP connectivity utilities. *See also* ASCII (American Standard Code for Information Interchange), Transport Control Protocol/Internet Protocol (TCP/IP).

firewall A security system, usually a combination of hardware and software, intended to protect a network against external threats coming from another network, including the Internet. Firewalls prevent an organization's networked computers from communicating directly with computers that are external to the network, and vice versa. Instead, all incoming and outgoing communication is routed through a proxy server outside the organization's network. Firewalls also audit network activity, recording the volume of traffic and information about unauthorized attempts to gain access. *See also* proxy server.

firmware Software routines stored in ROM. Unlike RAM, ROM stays intact even in the absence of electrical power. Startup routines and low-level I/O instructions are stored in firmware.

flow control Regulating the flow of data through routers to ensure that no segment becomes overloaded with transmissions.

FQDN (fully qualified domain name) *See* fully qualified domain name (FQDN).

frame A package of information transmitted on a network as a single unit. Frame is a term most often used with Ethernet networks. A frame is similar to the packet used in other networks. *See also* data frame, packet.

frame preamble Header information, added to the beginning of a data frame in the physical layer of the OSI reference model.

frame relay An advanced, fast-packet, variable-length, digital, packet-switching technology. It is a point-to-point system that uses a private virtual circuit (PVC) to transmit variable-length frames at the data-link layer of the OSI reference model. Frame relay networks can also provide subscribers with bandwidth, as needed, that allows users to make nearly any type of transmission.

front end In a client/server application, front end refers to the part of the program carried out on the client computer.

FRS (file replication service) *See* file replication service (FRS).

FTP *See* File Transfer Protocol (FTP).

full-duplex transmission Also called duplex transmission. Communication that takes place simultaneously, in both directions. *See also* duplex transmission.

fully qualified domain name (FQDN) A DNS domain name that has been stated unambiguously so as to indicate with absolute certainty its location in the domain namespace tree. Fully qualified domain names differ from relative names in that they are typically stated with a trailing period (.), for example, host.example.microsoft.com, to qualify their position to the root of the namespace.

G

gateway A device used to connect networks using different protocols so that information can be passed from one system to the other. Gateways functions at the network layer of the OSI reference model.

Gb *See* gigabit.

GB *See* gigabyte.

gigabit 1,073,741,824 bits. Also referred to as 1 billion bits.

gigabyte Commonly, a thousand megabytes. However, the precise meaning often varies with the context. A gigabyte is 1 billion bytes. In the context of computing, bytes are often expressed in multiples of powers of two. Therefore, a gigabyte can also be either 1000 megabytes or 1024 megabytes, where a megabyte is considered to be 1,048,576 bytes (2 raised to the 20th power).

global group One of four kinds of group accounts used by Microsoft Windows NT and Windows NT Server. Used across an entire domain, global groups are created on a Primary Domain Controller (PDC) in the domain in which the user accounts reside. Global groups can contain only user accounts from the domain in which the global group is created. Members of global groups obtain resource permissions when the global group is added to a local group. *See also* group, primary domain controller (PDC).

group In networking, an account containing other accounts that are called members. The permissions and rights granted to a group are also provided to its members; thus, groups offer a convenient way to grant common capabilities to collections of user accounts. For Windows NT, groups are managed with User Manager. For Windows NT Server, groups are managed with User Manager for Domains.

H

half-duplex transmission Two-way communication occurring in only one direction at a time.

handshaking A term applied to modem-to-modem communication. Refers to the process by which information is transmitted between the sending and receiving devices to maintain and coordinate data flow between them. Proper handshaking ensures that the receiving device will be ready to accept data before the sending device transmits.

hard disk One or more inflexible platters coated with material that allows the magnetic recording of computer data. A typical hard disk rotates at up to 7200 revolutions per minute (RPM), and the read/write heads ride over the surface of the disk on a cushion of air 10 to 25 millionths of an inch deep. A hard disk is sealed to prevent contaminants from interfering with the close head-to-disk tolerances. Hard disks provide faster access to data than floppy disks and are capable of storing much more information. Because platters are rigid, they can be stacked so that one hard-disk drive can access more than one platter. Most hard disks have between two and eight platters.

hardware The physical components of a computer system, including any peripheral equipment such as printers, modems, and mouse devices.

hardware compatibility list (HCL) A list of computers and peripherals that have been tested and have passed compatibility testing with the product for which the HCL is being developed. For example, the Windows NT 3.51 HCL lists the products which have been tested and found to be compatible with Window NT 3.51.

hardware loopback A connector on a computer that is useful for troubleshooting hardware problems, allowing data to be transmitted to a line, then returned as received data. If the transmitted data does not return, the hardware loopback detects a hardware malfunction.

HCL *See* hardware compatibility list (HCL).

HDLC *See* High-Level Data Link Control (HDLC).

header In network data transmission, one of the three sections of a packet component. It includes an alert signal to indicate that the packet is being transmitted, the source address, the destination address, and clock information to synchronize transmission.

hermaphroditic connector A connector that is neither male nor female, such as IBM cable connectors in which any two can be connected together, as opposed to BNC connectors that require both a male part and female part before a connection can be made.

hertz (Hz) The unit of frequency measurement. Frequency measures how often a periodic event occurs, such as the manner in which a wave's amplitude changes with time. One hertz equals one cycle per second. Frequency is often measured in kilohertz (KHz, 1000 Hz), megahertz (MHz), gigahertz (GHz, 1000 MHz), or terahertz (THz, 10,000 GHz).

High-Level Data Link Control (HDLC) HDLC is a widely accepted international protocol, developed by the International Organization for Standardization (ISO), that governs information transfer. HDLC is a bit-oriented, synchronous protocol that applies to the data-link (message packaging) layer of the OSI reference model. Under the HDLC protocol, data is transmitted in frames, each of which can contain a variable amount of data, but which must be organized in a particular way. *See also* data frames, frame.

hop In routing through a mesh environment, the transmission of a data packet through a router.

host *See* server.

hot fixing *See* sector sparing.

HTML *See* Hypertext Markup Language (HTML).

hub A connectivity component that provides a common connection among computers in a star-configured network. Active hubs require electrical power but are able to regenerate and retransmit network data. Passive hubs simply organize the wiring. *See also* Multistation Access Unit (MAU).

hybrid hub An advanced hub that can accommodate several different types of cables.

hybrid network A network made up of mixed components.

Hypertext Markup Language (HTML) A language developed for writing pages for the World Wide Web. HTML allows text to include codes that define fonts, layout, embedded graphics, and hypertext links. Hypertext provides a method for presenting text, images, sound, and videos that are linked together in a nonsequential web of associations.

Hypertext Transport Protocol (HTTP) The method by which World Wide Web pages are transferred over the network.

I

IAB *See* Internet Architecture Board (IAB).

IBM cabling system Used in a Token Ring environment. Introduced by IBM in 1984 to define cable connectors, face plates, distribution panels, and cable types. Many parameters are similar to non-IBM specifications. Uniquely shaped, the IBM connector is hermaphroditic. *See also* hermaphroditic connector.

ICMP *See* Internet Control Message Protocol (ICMP).

IDE *See* Integrated Device Electronics (IDE).

IEEE *See* Institute of Electrical and Electronics Engineers (IEEE).

IEEE Project 802 A networking model developed by the IEEE. Named for the year and month it began (February 1980), Project 802 defines LAN standards for the physical and data-link layers of the OSI reference model. Project 802 divides the data-link layer into two sublayers: Media Access Control (MAC) and Logical Link Control (LLC).

impedance Impedance has two aspects: the first is resistance, which impedes direct and alternating current. Resistance is always greater than zero. The second is reactance, which impedes alternating current only. Reactance varies with frequency and can be positive or negative.

Industry Standard Architecture (ISA) An unofficial designation for the bus design of the IBM Personal Computer (PC) PC/XT. It allows various adapters to be added to the system by inserting plug-in cards into expansion slots. Commonly, ISA refers to the expansion slots themselves; such slots are called 8-bit slots or 16-bit slots. *See also* Extended Industry Standard Architecture (EISA), Micro Channel Architecture.

infrared transmission Electromagnetic radiation with frequencies in the electromagnetic spectrum in the range just below that of visible red light. In network communications, infrared technology offers extremely high transmission rates and wide bandwidth in line-of-sight communications.

Institute of Electrical and Electronics Engineers (IEEE) An organization of engineering and electronics professionals; noted in networking for developing the IEEE 802.x standards for the physical and data-link layers of the OSI reference model, applied in a variety of network configurations.

Integrated Device Electronics (IDE) A type of disk-drive interface in which the controller electronics reside on the drive itself, eliminating the need for a separate network interface card. The IDE interface is compatible with the Western Digital ST-506 controller.

Integrated Services Digital Network (ISDN) A worldwide digital communication network that evolved from existing telephone services. The goal of the ISDN is to replace current telephone lines, which require digital-to-analog conversions, with completely digital switching and transmission facilities capable of carrying data ranging from voice to computer transmissions, music, and video. The ISDN is built on two main types of communications channels: B channels, that carry voice, data, or images at a rate of 64 Kbps (kilobits per second), and a D channel, that carries control information, signaling, and link-management data at 16 Kbps. Standard ISDN Basic Rate desktop service is called 2B+D. Computers and other devices connect to ISDN lines through simple, standardized interfaces.

interfaces Boundaries that separate the layers from each other. For example, in the OSI reference model, each layer provides some service or action that prepares the data for delivery over the network to another computer.

intermediate systems Equipment that provides a network communication link, such as bridges, routers, and gateways.

International Organization for Standardization (ISO) An organization made up of standards-setting groups from various countries. For example, the United States member is the American National Standards Institute (ANSI). The ISO works to establish global standards for communications and information exchange. Primary among its accomplishments is development of the widely accepted OSI reference model. Note that the ISO is often wrongly identified as the International Standards Organization, probably because of the abbreviation "ISO"; however, ISO is derived from "isos," which means "equal" in Greek, rather than an acronym.

International Telecommunications Union (ITU) The organization responsible for setting the standards for international telecommunications.

International Telecommunications Union-Telecommunication (ITU-T) The sector of the ITU responsible for telecommunication standards. ITU-T replaces the Comité Consultatif Internationale de Télégraphie et Téléphonie (CCITT). Its responsibilities include standardizing modem design and operations, and standardizing protocols for networks and facsimile transmission. ITU is an international organization within which governments and the private sector coordinate global telecom networks and services.

Internet Architecture Board (IAB) A body that develops and maintains Internet architectural standards as part of the Internet Society (ISOC). It also adjudicates disputes in the standards process.

Internet Control Message Protocol (ICMP) Used by IP and higher-level protocols to send and receive status reports about information being transmitted.

Internet Protocol (IP) The TCP/IP protocol for packet forwarding. *See also* Transport Control Protocol/Internet Protocol (TCP/IP).

Internetworking The intercommunication in a network that is made up of smaller networks.

Internetwork Packet Exchange/Sequenced Packet Exchange (IPX/SPX) A protocol stack that is used in Novell networks. IPX is the NetWare protocol for packet forwarding and routing. It is a relatively small and fast protocol on a LAN, is a derivative of Xerox Network System (XNS), and supports routing. SPX is a connection-oriented protocol used to guarantee the delivery of the data being sent. NWLink is the Microsoft implementation of the IPX/SPX protocol.

interoperability The ability of components in one system to work with components in other systems.

interrupt request (IRQ) An electronic signal sent to a computer's CPU to indicate that an event has taken place that requires the processor's attention.

IP *See* Internet Protocol (IP). *See also* Transport Control Protocol/Internet Protocol (TCP/IP).

ipconfig A diagnostic command that displays all current TCP/IP network configuration values. It is of particular use on systems running DHCP because it allows users to determine which TCP/IP configuration values have been configured by the DHCP server. *See also* winipcfg.

IPX/SPX *See* Internetwork Packet Exchange/Sequenced Packet Exchange (IPX/SPX).

IRQ *See* interrupt request (IRQ).

ISA *See* Industry Standard Architecture (ISA).

ISDN *See* Integrated Services Digital Network (ISDN).

ISO *See* International Organization for Standardization (ISO).

ITU *See* International Telecommunications Union (ITU).

(ITU-T) International Telecommunications Union-Telecommunication *See* International Telecommunications Union-Telecommunication (ITU-T).

J

jitter Instability in a signal wave form over time that can be caused by signal interference or an unbalanced ring in FDDI or Token Ring environments.

jumper A small plastic-and-metal plug or wire for connecting different points in an electronic circuit. Jumpers are used to select a particular circuit or option from several possible configurations. Jumpers can be used on network interface cards to select the type of connection through which the card will transmit, either DIX or BNC.

K

Kevlar A brand name of the DuPont Corporation for the fibers in the reinforcing layer of plastic that surrounds each glass strand of a fiber-optic connector. The name is sometimes used generically.

key In database management, an identifier for a record or group of records in a data file. Most often, the key is defined as the contents of a single field, called the key field in some database management programs and the index field in others. Keys are maintained in tables and are indexed to speed record retrieval. Keys also refer to code that deciphers encrypted data.

kilo (K) Refers to 1000 in the metric system. In computing terminology, because computing is based on powers of 2, kilo is most often used to mean 1024 (2 raised to the 10th power). To distinguish between the two contexts, a lowercase k is often used to indicate 1000, an uppercase K for 1024. A kilobyte is 1024 bytes.

kilobit (Kbit) One thousand twenty-four bits. *See also* bit, kilo.

kilobyte (KB) Refers to 1024 bytes. *See also* byte, kilo.

L

LAN *See* local area network (LAN).

LAN requester *See* requester (LAN requester).

laser transmission Wireless network that uses a laser beam to carry data between devices.

LAT *See* local area transport (LAT).

layering The coordination of various protocols in a specific architecture that allows the protocols to work together to ensure that the data is prepared, transferred, received, and acted upon as intended.

link The communication system that connects two LANs. Equipment that provides the link, including bridges, routers, and gateways.

local area network (LAN) Computers connected in a geographically confined network, such as in the same building, campus, or office park.

local area transport (LAT) A nonroutable protocol from Digital Equipment Corporation.

local group One of four kinds of group accounts used by Microsoft Windows NT and Windows NT Server. Implemented in each local computer's account database, local groups contain user accounts and other global groups that need to have access, rights, and permissions assigned to a re-source on a local computer. Local groups cannot contain other local groups.

LocalTalk Cabling components used in an AppleTalk network, including cables, connector modules, and cable extenders. These components are normally used in a bus or tree topology. A LocalTalk segment supports a maximum of 32 devices. Because of LocalTalk's limitations, clients often turn to vendors other than Apple for AppleTalk cabling. Farallon PhoneNet, for example, can accommodate 254 devices.

local user The user at the computer.

Logical Link Control (LLC) sublayer One of two sublayers created by the IEEE 802 project out of the data-link layer of the OSI reference model. The Logical Link Control (LLC) is the upper sublayer that manages data-link communication and defines the use of logical interface points, called service access points (SAPs), used by computers to transfer information from the LLC sublayer to the upper OSI layers. *See also* Media Access Control (MAC) sublayer, service access point (SAP).

lost token Refers to an error on a Token Ring network that causes an errant station to halt the token, leaving the ring without a token.

M

MAC (Message Authentication Code) *See* Message Authentication Code (MAC).

macro virus A file-infector virus named because it is written as a macro for a specific application. Macro viruses are difficult to detect and becoming more common, often infecting widely used applications, such as word-processing programs. When an infected file is opened, the virus attaches itself to the application, then infects any files accessed by that application. *See also* file infector.

magneto-optical (MO) disc A plastic or glass disc, coated with a compound containing special properties, that is read by bouncing a low-intensity laser beam off the disc.

MAN (metropolitan area network) *See* metropolitan area network (MAN).

MAU *See* Multistation Access Unit (MSAU or MAU).

Mb *See* megabit (Mb).

MB *See* megabyte (MB).

Mbps *See* millions of bits per second (Mbps).

media The vast majority of LANs today are connected by some sort of wire or cabling that acts as the LAN transmission medium, carrying data between computers. The cabling is often referred to as the media.

Media Access Control (MAC) driver The device driver located at the Media Access Control sublayer of the OSI reference model.

This driver is also known as the NIC driver. It provides low-level access to NICs by providing data-transmission support and some basic NIC management functions. These drivers also pass data from the physical layer to transport protocols at the network and transport layers.

Media Access Control (MAC) sublayer One of two sublayers created by the IEEE 802 project out of the data-link layer of the OSI reference model. The Media Access Control (MAC) sublayer communicates directly with the network interface card and is responsible for delivering error-free data between two computers on the network. *See also* Logical Link Control (LLC) sublayer.

megabit (Mb) Usually, 1,048,576 bits; sometimes interpreted as 1 million bits. *See also* bit.

megabyte (MB) 1,048,576 bytes (2 raised to the 20th power); sometimes interpreted as 1 million bytes. *See also* byte.

mesh network topology Connects remote sites over telecommunication links. Common in wide area networks (WANs), meshes use routers to search among multiple active paths (the mesh) and determine the best path at that particular moment.

Message Authentication Code (MAC) An algorithm that insures the quality of a block of data.

metropolitan area network (MAN) A data network designed for a town or city. In geographic breadth, MANs are larger than local area networks but smaller than wide area networks. MANs are usually characterized by very-high-speed connections using fiber-optic cable or other digital media.

Micro Channel Architecture The design of the bus in IBM PS/2 computers (except Models 25 and 30). The Micro Channel is electrically and physically incompatible with the IBM PC/AT bus. Unlike the PC/AT bus, the Micro Channel functions as either a 16-bit or 32-bit bus. The Micro Channel also can be driven independently by multiple bus master processors. *See also* Extended Industry Standard Architecture (EISA), Industry Standard Architecture (ISA).

Microcom Network Protocol (MNP) The standard for asynchronous data-error control developed by Microcom Systems. The method works so well that other companies have adopted not only the initial version of the protocol, but later versions as well. Currently, several modem vendors incorporate MNP Classes 2, 3, 4, and 5.

Microsoft Management Console (MMC) A framework for hosting administrative tools, called consoles. A console may contain tools, folders or other containers, World Wide Web pages, and other administrative items. These items are displayed in the left pane of the console, called a console tree. A console has one or more windows that can provide views of the console tree. The main MMC window provides commands and tools for authoring consoles. The authoring features of MMC and the console tree itself may be hidden when a console is in User mode.

Microsoft Technical Information Network (TechNet) Provides informational support for all aspects of networking, with an emphasis on Microsoft products.

millions of bits per second (Mbps) The unit of measure of supported transmission rates on the following physical media: coaxial cable, twisted-pair cable, and fiber-optic cable. *See also* bit.

MMC (Microsoft Management Console) *See* Microsoft Management Console (MMC).

MNP *See* Microcom Network Protocol (MNP).

MO (magneto-optical) disc *See* magneto-optical (MO) disc.

mobile computing Incorporates wireless adapters using cellular telephone technology to connect portable computers with the cabled network.

modem A communication device that enables a computer to transmit information over a standard telephone line. Because a computer is digital, it works with discrete electrical signals representing binary 1 and binary 0. A telephone is analog and carries a signal that can have many variations. Modems are needed to convert digital signals to analog and back. When transmitting, modems impose (modulate) a computer's digital signals onto a continuous carrier frequency on the telephone line. When receiving, modems sift out (demodulate) the information from the carrier and transfer it in digital form to the computer.

mounted drive A drive attached to an empty folder on an NTFS volume. Mounted drives function the same as any other drive, but are assigned a label or name instead of a drive letter. The mounted drive's name is resolved to a full file system path instead of just a drive letter. Members of the Administrators group can use Disk Management to create mounted drives or reassign drive letters.

MSAU *See* Multistation Access Unit (MAU).

multiplexer (mux) A device used to divide a transmission facility into two or more chan-

nels. It can be a program stored in a computer. Also, a device for connecting a number of communication lines to a computer.

Multistation Access Unit (MAU) The name for a Token Ring wiring concentrator. Also referred to as a hub. MAUs are sometimes referred to as MSAUs.

multitasking A mode of operation offered by an operating system in which a computer works on more than one task at a time. There are two primary types of multitasking: preemptive and nonpreemptive. In preemptive multitasking, the operating system can take control of the processor without the task's cooperation. In nonpreemptive multitasking, the processor is never taken from a task. The task itself decides when to give up the processor. A true multitasking operating system can run as many tasks as it has processors. When there are more tasks than processors, the computer must "time slice" so that the available processors devote a certain amount of time to one task and then move on to the next task, alternating between tasks until all the tasks are completed.

mux *See* multiplexer (mux).

N

Name Binding Protocol (NBP) An Apple protocol responsible for keeping track of entities on the network and matching names with Internet addresses. It works at the transport layer of the OSI reference model.

namespace A set of unique names for resources or items used in a shared computing environment. For MMC, the namespace is represented by the console tree, which displays all of the snap-ins and resources that are accessible to a console. *See also* console tree;

MMC; resource; snap-in. For DNS, namespace is the vertical or hierarchical structure of the domain name tree. For example, each domain label, such as host1 or example, used in a fully qualified domain name, such as host1.example.microsoft.com, indicates a branch in the domain namespace tree.

narrowband (single-frequency) transmission
High-frequency radio transmission similar to broadcasting. The user tunes both the transmitter and the receiver to a certain frequency to send and receive data.

NAS (network access server) *See* network access server (NAS).

NBP *See* Name Binding Protocol (NBP).

nbtstat A diagnostic command that displays protocol statistics and current TCP/IP connections using NBT (NetBIOS over TCP/IP). This command is available only if the TCP/IP protocol has been installed. *See also* netstat.

NDIS *See* Network Device Interface Specification (NDIS).

NetBEUI (NetBIOS extended user interface) A protocol supplied with all Microsoft network products. NetBEUI advantages include small stack size (important for MS-DOS–based computers), speed of data transfer on the network medium, and compatibility with all Microsoft-based net-works. The major drawback of NetBEUI is that it is a LAN transport protocol and therefore does not support routing. It is also limited to Microsoft-based networks.

NetBIOS (network basic input/output system)
An application programming interface (API) that can be used by application programs on a LAN consisting of IBM-compatible micro-computers running MS-DOS, OS/2, or some version of UNIX. Primarily of interest to programmers, NetBIOS provides application programs with a uniform set of commands for requesting the lower-level network services required to conduct sessions between nodes on a network and transmit information between them.

netstat A diagnostic command that displays protocol statistics and current TCP/IP network connections. This command is available only if the TCP/IP protocol has been installed. *See also* nbtstat.

NetWare Core Protocol (NCP) Defines the connection control and service-request encoding that make it possible for clients and servers to interact. This is the protocol that provides transport and session services. NetWare security is also provided within this protocol.

network In the context of computers, a system in which a number of independent computers are linked together to share data and peripherals, such as hard disks and printers.

network access server (NAS) The device that accepts PPP connections and places clients on the network that the NAS serves.

network adapter card *See* network interface card (NIC).

network analyzers Network troubleshooting tools, sometimes called protocol analyzers. They perform a number of functions in real-time network traffic analysis and carry out packet capture, decoding, and transmission. They can also generate statistics based on the network traffic to help create a picture of the network's cabling, software, file server, clients, and NICs. Most analyzers have a built-in TDR. *See also* time-domain reflecto-meter (TDR).

Network Device Interface Specification (NDIS)
A standard that defines an interface for communication between the Media Access Control (MAC) sublayer and protocol drivers. NDIS allows for a flexible environment of data exchange. It defines the software interface, called the NDIS interface, which is used by protocol drivers to communicate with the network interface card. The advantage of NDIS is that it offers protocol multiplexing so that multiple protocol stacks can be used at the same time. *See also* Open Data-Link Interface (ODI).

network interface card (NIC) An expansion card installed in each computer and server on the network. The NIC acts as the physical interface or connection between the computer and the network cable.

network layer The third layer in the OSI reference model. This layer is responsible for addressing messages and translating logical addresses and names into physical addresses. This layer also determines the route from the source to the destination computer. It determines which path the data should take based on network conditions, priority of service, and other factors. It also manages traffic problems such as switching, routing, and controlling the congestion of data packets on the network. *See also* Open Systems Interconnection (OSI) reference model.

network monitors Monitors that track all or a selected part of network traffic. They examine frame-level packets and gather information about packet types, errors, and packet traffic to and from each computer.

Network News Transfer Protocol (NNTP) A protocol defined in RFC 977. It is a de facto protocol standard on the Internet used for the distribution, inquiry, retrieval, and posting of Usenet news articles over the Internet.

NIC *See* network interface card (NIC).

NNTP *See* Network News Transfer Protocol (NNTP).

node On a LAN, a device that is connected to the network and is capable of communicating with other network devices. For example, clients, servers, and repeaters are called nodes.

noise Random electrical signals that can get onto the cable and degrade or distort the data. Noise is generated by power lines, elevators, air conditioners, or any device with an electric motor, relays, and radio transmitters. *See also* shielding.

nonpreemptive multitasking A form of multitasking in which the processor is never taken from a task. The task itself decides when to give up the processor. Programs written for nonpreemptive multitasking systems must include provisions for yielding control of the processor. No other program can run until the non-preemptive program gives up control of the processor. *See also* multitasking, preemptive multitasking.

Novell NetWare One of the leading network architectures.

O

ODI *See* Open Data-Link Interface (ODI).

ohm The unit of measure for electrical resistance. A resistance of 1 ohm will pass 1 ampere of current when a voltage of 1 volt is applied. A 100-watt incandescent bulb has a resistance of approximately 130 ohms.

Open Data-Link Interface (ODI) A specification defined by Novell and Apple to simplify driver development and to provide support for multiple protocols on a single network interface card. Similar to NDIS in many respects, ODI allows Novell NetWare drivers to be written without concern for the protocol that will be used on top of them.

Open Shortest Path First (OSPF) A routing protocol for IP networks, such as the Internet, that allows a router to calculate the shortest path to each node for sending messages.

Open Systems Interconnection (OSI) reference model A seven-layer architecture that standardizes levels of service and types of interaction for computers exchanging information through a network. It is used to describe the flow of data between the physical connection to the network and the end-user application. This model is the best known and most widely used model for describing networking environments.

OSI layer Focus 7. application layer Program-to-program transfer of information 6. presentation layer Text formatting and display code conversion 5. session layer Establishing, maintaining, and coordinating communication 4. transport layer Accurate delivery, service quality 3. network layer Transport routes, message handling, and transfer 2. data-link layer Coding, addressing, and transmitting information 1. physical layer Hardware connections.

optical drive A drive that accommodates optical discs.

optical fiber Medium that carries digital data signals in the form of modulated pulses of light. An optical fiber consists of an extremely thin cylinder of glass, called the core, surrounded by a concentric layer of glass, known as the cladding.

oscilloscope An electronic instrument that measures the amount of signal voltage per unit of time and displays the results on a monitor.

OSI *See* Open Systems Interconnection (OSI) reference model.

OSPF *See* Open Shortest Path First (OSPF).

P

packet A unit of information transmitted as a whole from one device to another on a network. In packet-switching networks, a packet is defined more specifically as a transmission unit of fixed maximum size that consists of binary digits representing data; a header containing an identification number, source, and destination addresses; and sometimes error-control data. *See also* frame.

packet assembler/disassembler (PAD) A device that breaks large chunks of data into packets, usually for transmission over an X.25 network, and reassembles them at the other end. *See also* packet switching.

Packet Internet Groper (ping) A simple utility that tests if a network connection is complete, from the server to the workstation, by sending a message to the remote computer. If the remote computer receives the message, it responds with a reply message. The reply consists of the remote workstation's IP address, the number of bytes in the message, how long it took to reply—given in milliseconds (ms)—and the length of time-to-live (TTL) in seconds. Ping works at the IP level and will often respond even when higher level TCP-based services cannot.

packet switching A message delivery technique in which small units of information (packets) are relayed through stations in a computer network along the best route available between the source and the destination. Data is broken into smaller units and then repacked in a process called packet assembly and disassembly (PAD). Although each packet can travel along a different path, and the packets composing a message can arrive at different times or out of sequence, the receiving computer reassembles the original message. Packet-switching networks are considered fast and efficient. Standards for packet switching on networks are documented in the CCITT recommendation X.25.

PAD *See* packet assembler/disassembler (PAD).

page-description language (PDL) A language that communicates to a printer how printed output should appear. The printer uses the PDL to construct text and graphics to create the page image. PDLs are like blueprints in that they set parameters and features such as type sizes and fonts, but leave the drawing to the printer.

parity An error-checking procedure in which the number of 1s must always be the same— either odd or even—for each group of bits transmitted without error. Parity is used for checking data transferred within a computer or between computers.

partition A portion of a physical disk that functions as if it were a physically separate unit.

partition boot sector A portion of a hard disk partition that contains information about the disk's file system and a short machine language program that loads the Windows operating system.

password-protected share Access to a shared resource that is granted when a user enters the appropriate password.

PBX Private Branch Exchange (PABX Private Automated Branch Exchange) A switching telephone network that allows callers within an organization to place intraorganizational calls without going through the public telephone system.

PDA *See* Personal Digital Assistant (PDA).

PDC *See* Primary Domain Controller (PDC).

PDL *See* page-description language (PDL).

PDN *See* public data network (PDN).

peer-to-peer network A network in which there are no dedicated servers or hierarchy among the computers. All computers are equal and, therefore, known as peers. Generally, each computer functions as both client and server.

Per-Seat Licensing A licensing mode that requires a separate Client Access License for each client computer that accesses Windows 2000 Server, regardless of whether all the clients access the server at the same time.

Per-Server Licensing A licensing mode that requires a separate Client Access License for each concurrent connection to the server, regardless of whether there are other client computers on the network that do not happen to connect concurrently.

performance monitor A tool for monitoring network performance that can display statistics, such as the number of packets sent and received, server-processor utilization, and the amount of data going into and out of the server.

peripheral A term used for devices such as disk drives, printers, modems, mouse devices, and joysticks that are connected to a computer and controlled by its microprocessor.

Peripheral Component Interconnect (PCI)
32-bit local bus used in most Pentium computers and in the Apple Power Macintosh. Meets most of the requirements for providing Plug and Play functionality.

permanent virtual circuit (PVC) A permanent logical connection between two nodes on a packet-switching network; similar to leased lines that are permanent and virtual, except that with PVC the customer pays only for the time the line is used. This type of connection service is gaining importance because both frame relay and ATM use it. *See also* packet switching, virtual circuit.

permissions *See* access permissions.

Personal Digital Assistant (PDA) A type of hand-held computer that provides functions including personal organization features—like a calendar, note taking, database manipulation, calculator, and communications. For communication, a PDA uses cellular or wireless technology that is often built into the system, but that can be supplemented or enhanced by means of a PC Card.

petabyte *See* byte.

phase change rewritable (PCR) A type of rewritable optical technology in which the optical devices come from one manufacturer (Matsushita/Panasonic) and the media comes from two (Panasonic and Plasmon).

physical layer The first (bottommost) layer of the OSI reference model. This layer addresses the transmission of the unstructured raw bit stream over a physical medium (the networking cable). The physical layer relates the electrical/optical, mechanical, and functional interfaces to the cable and also carries the signals that transmit data generated by all of the higher OSI layers. *See also* Open Systems Interconnection (OSI) reference model.

piercing tap A connector for coaxial cable that pierces through the insulating layer and makes direct contact with the conducting core.

ping *See* Packet Internet Groper (ping).

PKI (public key infrastructure) *See* public key infrastructure (PKI).

plenum The space in many buildings between the false ceiling and the floor above, used to circulate warm and cold air throughout the building. The space is often used for cable runs. Local fire codes specify the types of wiring that can be routed through this area.

Plug and Play (PnP) Refers to the ability of a computer system to automatically configure a device added to it. Plug and Play capability exists in Macintoshes based on the NuBus and, since Windows 95, on PC-compatible computers. Also, refers to specifications developed by Intel and Microsoft that allow a PC to configure itself automatically to work with peripherals such as monitors, modems, and printers.

point-to-point configuration Dedicated circuits that are also known as private, or leased, lines. They are the most popular WAN communication circuits in use today. The carrier guarantees full-duplex bandwidth by setting up a permanent link from each end point, using bridges and routers to connect LANs through the circuits. *See also* Point-to-Point Protocol (PPP), Point-to-Point Tunneling Protocol (PPTP), and duplex transmission.

Point-to-Point Protocol (PPP) A data-link protocol for transmitting TCP/IP packets over dial-up telephone connections, such as between a computer and the Internet. PPP was developed by the Internet Engineering Task Force in 1991.

Point-to-Point Tunneling Protocol (PPTP)
PPTP is an extension of the Point-to-Point
Protocol that is used for communications on
the Internet. It was developed by Microsoft
to support virtual private networks (VPNs),
which allow individuals and organizations to
use the Internet as a secure means of communication. PPTP supports encapsulation of
encrypted packets in secure wrappers that
can be transmitted over a TCP/IP connection. *See also* Virtual Private Networks
(VPN).

polymorphic virus A variant of file-infector
virus that is named for the fact that it
changes its appearance each time it is
replicated. This makes it difficult to detect,
because no two versions of the virus are
exactly the same. *See also* file infector.

preemptive multitasking A form of multitasking (the ability of a computer's operating
system to work on more than one task at a
time). With preemptive multitasking—as
opposed to nonpreemptive multitasking—the
operating system can take control of the
processor without the task's cooperation. *See
also* nonpreemptive multitasking.

presentation layer The sixth layer of the OSI
reference model. This layer determines the
form used to exchange data between networked computers. At the sending computer,
this layer translates data from a format sent
down from the application layer into a
commonly recognized, intermediary format.
At the receiving end, this layer translates the
intermediary format into a format useful to
that computer's application layer. The
presentation layer manages network security
issues by providing services such as data
encryption, provides rules for data transfer,
and performs data compression to reduce the
number of bits that need to be transmitted.

See also Open Systems Interconnection
(OSI) reference model.

primary domain controller (PDC) The server
that maintains the master copy of the
domain's user-accounts database and that
validates logon requests. Every network
domain is required to have one, and only one,
PDC. *See also* domain, domain controller.

primary partition A volume you create using
unallocated space on a basic disk. Windows
2000 and other operating systems can start
from a primary partition. You can create up
to four primary partitions on a basic disk, or
three primary partitions and an extended
partition. Primary partitions can be created
only on basic disks and cannot be
subpartitioned.

print queue A buffer in which a print job is
held until the printer is ready to print it.

private key The secret half of a cryptographic key pair that is used with a public
key algorithm. Private keys are typically
used to decrypt a symmetric session key,
digitally sign data, or decrypt data that has
been encrypted with the corresponding
public key.

Project 802 A subgroup of the IEEE, originally formed in 1980, that defined network
standards for the physical components of a
network, the network interface card, and the
cabling, which are accounted for in the
physical and data-link layers of the OSI
reference model.

protocol The system of rules and procedures
that govern communication between two or
more devices. Many varieties of protocols
exist, and not all are compatible, but as long
as two devices are using the same protocol,
they can exchange data. Protocols exist

within protocols as well, governing different aspects of communication. Some protocols, such as the RS-232 standard, affect hardware connections. Other standards govern data transmission, including the parameters and handshaking signals such as XON/OFF used in asynchronous (typically, modem) communications, as well as such data-coding methods as bit- and byte-oriented protocols. Still other protocols, such as the widely used XMODEM, govern file transfer, and others, such as CSMA/CD, define the methods by which messages are passed around the stations on a LAN. Protocols represent attempts to ease the complex process of enabling computers of different makes and models to communicate. Additional examples of protocols include the OSI model, IBM's SNA, and the Internet suite, including TCP/IP. *See also* Systems Network Architecture (SNA), Transport Control Protocol/Internet Protocol (TCP/IP).

protocol analyzers *See* network analyzers.

protocol driver The driver responsible for offering four or five basic services to other layers in the network, while "hiding" the details of how the services are actually implemented. Services performed include session management, datagram service, data segmentation and sequencing, acknowledgment, and possibly routing across a WAN.

protocol stack A layered set of protocols that work together to provide a set of network functions.

proxy server A firewall component that manages Internet traffic to and from a local area network (LAN). The proxy server decides whether it is safe to let a particular message or file pass through to the organization's network, providing access control to the network, and filters and discards requests as specified by the owner, including requests for unauthorized access to proprietary data. *See also* firewall.

public data network (PDN) A commercial packet-switching or circuit-switching WAN service provided by local and long-distance telephone carriers.

public key The nonsecret half of a cryptographic key pair that is used with a public key algorithm. Public keys are typically used when encrypting a session key, verifying a digital signature, or encrypting data that can be decrypted with the corresponding private key.

public key cryptography A method of cryptography in which two different keys are used: a public key for encrypting data and a private key for decrypting data.

public key infrastructure (PKI) The term generally used to describe the laws, policies, standards, and software that regulate or manipulate certificates and public and private keys. In practice, it is a system of digital certificates, certification authorities, and other registration authorities that verify and authenticate the validity of each party involved in an electronic transaction. Standards for PKI are still evolving, even though they are being widely implemented as a necessary element of electronic commerce. Public key infrastructure is also called PKI.

punchdown block A wiring terminal, or series of terminals, into which cable can be plugged or "punched down." It is designed for environments that require a centralized location for all cabling to facilitate making changes; wiring running to the jacks can be more easily organized and maintained.

punchdown tool A specialized tool used to "punch down" cable wires into a wiring terminal. Using this tool ensures a solid connection.

PVC (permanent virtual circuit) *See* permanent virtual circuit (PVC).

PVC (polyvinyl chloride) The material most commonly used for insulating and jacketing cable.

Q

QoS (Quality of Service) *See* Quality of Service (QoS).

quad shielding Cable that contains two layers of foil insulation and two layers of braided metal shielding.

Quality of Service (QoS) A set of quality-assurance standards and mechanisms for data transmission, implemented in Windows 2000.

R

RADIUS (Remote Authentication Dial-In User Service) *See* Remote Authentication Dial-In User Service (RADIUS).

RAID *See* redundant array of independent disks (RAID).

random access memory (RAM) Semiconductor-based memory that can be read and written to by the microprocessor or other hardware devices. The storage locations can be accessed in any order. Note that the various types of ROM memory are also capable of random access. However, the term RAM is generally understood to refer to volatile memory, which can be written as well as read. *See also* read-only memory (ROM).

read-only memory (ROM) Semiconductor-based memory that contains instructions or

data which can be read but not modified. *See also* random access memory (RAM).

redirector Networking software that accepts I/O requests for remote files, named pipes, or mail slots and sends (redirects) the requests to a network service on another computer.

Reduced Instruction Set Computing (RISC) A type of microprocessor design that focuses on rapid and efficient processing of a relatively small set of instructions. RISC design is based on the premise that most of the instructions that a computer decodes and executes are simple. As a result, RISC architecture limits the number of instructions that are built into the microprocessor, but optimizes each so it can be carried out very rapidly, usually within a single clock cycle. RISC chips execute simple instructions faster than microprocessors designed to handle a much wider array of instructions. They are, however, slower than general-purpose CISC (complex instruction set computing) chips when executing complex instructions, which must be broken down into many machine instructions before they can be carried out by RISC microprocessors.

redundancy system A fault-tolerant system that protects data by duplicating it in different physical sources. Data redundancy allows access to data even if part of the data system fails. *See also* fault tolerance.

redundant array of independent disks (RAID) A standardization of fault-tolerant options in five levels. The levels offer various combinations of performance, reliability, and cost. Formerly known as redundant array of inexpensive disks (RAID).

redundant array of inexpensive disks (RAID) *See* redundant array of independent disks (RAID).

Remote Authentication Dial-In User Service (RADIUS) A security authentication protocol based on clients and servers and widely used by Internet service providers (ISPs) on non-Microsoft remote servers. RADIUS is the most popular means of authenticating and authorizing dial-up and tunneled network users today.

remote-boot PROM (programmable read-only memory) A special chip in the network interface card that contains the hardwired code that starts the computer and connects the user to the network, used in computers for which there are no hard-disk or floppy drives. *See also* diskless computers.

remote user A user who dials in to the server over modems and telephone lines from a remote location.

repeater A device that regenerates signals so that they can be transmitted on additional cable segments to extend the cable length or to accommodate additional computers on the segment. Repeaters operate at the physical layer of the OSI reference model and connect like networks, such as an Ethernet LAN to an Ethernet LAN. Repeaters do not translate or filter data. For a repeater to work, both segments that the repeater joins must have the same media-access scheme, protocol, and transmission technique.

requester (LAN requester) Software that resides in a computer and forwards requests for network services from the computer's application programs to the appropriate server. *See also* redirector.

resources Any part of a computer system. Users on a network can share computer resources, such as hard disks, printers, modems, CD-ROM drives, and even the processor.

rewritable optical disc An optical disc that can be written to more than once.

RG-58 A/U Stranded-core coaxial cable. The version of this cable used by the United States military is known as RG-58 C/U.

RG-58 /U Solid-core coaxial cable.

rights Authorization with which a user is entitled to perform certain actions on a computer network. Rights apply to the system as a whole, whereas permissions apply to specific objects. For example, a user might have the right to back up an entire computer system, including the files that the user does not have permission to access. *See also* access permissions.

ring topology A topology in which computers are placed on a circle of cable. There are no terminated ends. The data travels around the loop in one direction and passes through each computer. Each computer acts as a repeater to boost the signal and send it on. Because the signal passes through each computer, the failure of one computer can bring the entire network down. The ring can incorporate features that disconnect failed computers so that the network can continue to function despite the failure. *See also* token passing, Token Ring network.

RIP *See* Routing Information Protocol (RIP).

RISC *See* Reduced Instruction Set Computing (RISC).

RJ-11 A four-wire modular connector used to join a telephone line to a wall plate or a communications peripheral such as a modem.

RJ-45 An eight-wire modular connector used to join a telephone line to a wall plate or some other device. It is similar to an RJ-11 telephone connector but has twice the number of conductors.

ROM *See* read-only memory (ROM).

routable protocols The protocols that support multipath LAN-to-LAN communications. *See also* protocol.

router A device used to connect networks of different types, such as those using different architectures and protocols. Routers work at the network layer of the OSI reference model. This means they can switch and route packets across multiple networks, which they do by exchanging protocol-specific information between separate networks. Routers determine the best path for sending data and filter broadcast traffic to the local segment.

Routing Information Protocol (RIP) A protocol that uses distance-vector algorithms to determine routes. With RIP, routers transfer information among other routers to update their internal routing tables and use that information to determine the best routes based on hop counts between routers. TCP/IP and IPX support RIP.

RS-232 standard An industry standard for serial communication connections. Adopted by the Electrical Industries Association (EIA), this recommended standard defines the specific lines and signal characteristics used by serial communications controllers to standardize the transmission of serial data between devices.

S

safe mode A method of starting Windows 2000 using basic files and drivers only, without networking. Safe mode is available by pressing the F8 key when prompted during startup. This allows you to start your computer when a problem prevents it from starting normally.

SAP (service access point) *See* service access point (SAP).

SAP (Service Advertising Protocol) *See* Service Advertising Protocol (SAP).

SCSI *See* Small Computer System Interface (SCSI).

SDLC *See* Synchronous Data Link Control (SDLC).

sector A portion of the data-storage area on a disk. A disk is divided into sides (top and bottom), tracks (rings on each surface), and sectors (sections of each ring). Sectors are the smallest physical storage units on a disk and are of fixed size—typically capable of holding 512 bytes of information apiece.

sector sparing A fault-tolerant system also called hot fixing. It automatically adds sector-recovery capabilities to the file system during operation. If bad sectors are found during disk I/O, the fault-tolerant driver will attempt to move the data to a good sector and map out the bad sector. If the mapping is successful, the file system is not alerted. It is possible for SCSI devices to perform sector sparing, but AT devices (ESDI and IDE) cannot.

security Making computers and data stored on them safe from harm or unauthorized access.

security identifier *or* **security ID (SID)** A unique number that identifies user, group, and computer accounts. Every account on your network is issued a unique SID when the account is first created. Internal processes in Windows 2000 refer to an account's SID rather than the account's user or group name. If you create an account, delete it, and then create an account with the same user name, the new account will not have the rights or permissions previously granted to the old account because the accounts have different SID numbers.

segment The length of cable on a network between two terminators. A segment can also refer to messages that have been broken up into smaller units by the protocol driver.

Sequenced Packet Exchange (SPX) Part of Novell's IPX/SPX protocol suite for sequenced data. *See also* Internetwork Packet Exchange/Sequenced Packet Exchange (IPX/SPX).

Serial Line Internet Protocol (SLIP) Defined in RFC 1055. SLIP is normally used on Ethernet, over a serial line; for example, an RS-232 serial port connected to a modem.

serial transmission One-way data transfer. The data travels on a network cable with one bit following another.

server A computer that provides shared resources to network users. *See also* client.

server-based network A network in which resource security and most other network functions are provided by dedicated servers. Server-based networks have become the standard model for networks serving more than 10 users. *See also* peer-to-peer network.

server message block (SMB) The protocol developed by Microsoft, Intel, and IBM that defines a series of commands used to pass information between network computers. The redirector packages SMB requests into a network control block (NCB) structure that can be sent over the network to a remote device. The network provider listens for SMB messages destined for it and removes the data portion of the SMB request so that it can be processed by a local device.

service access point (SAP) The interface between each of the seven layers in the OSI protocol stack that has connection points, similar to addresses, used for communication between layers. Any protocol layer can have multiple SAPs active at one time.

Service Advertising Protocol (SAP) Allows service-providing nodes (including file, printer, gateway, and application servers) to advertise their services and addresses.

session A connection or link between stations on the network.

session layer The fifth layer of the OSI reference model. This layer allows two applications on different computers to establish, use, and end a connection called a session. This layer performs name recognition and functions, such as security, needed to allow two applications to communicate over the network. The session layer provides synchronization between user tasks. This layer also implements dialog control between communicating processes, regulating which side transmits, when, for how long, and so on. *See also* Open Systems Interconnection (OSI) reference model.

session management Establishing, maintaining, and terminating connections between stations on the network.

share To make resources, such as folders and printers, available to others.

sharing Means by which files are publicly posted on a network for access by anyone on the network.

shell A piece of software, usually a separate program, that provides direct communication between the user and the operating system. This usually, but not always, takes the form of a command-line interface. Examples of shells are Macintosh Finder and the MS-DOS command interface program COMMAND.COM.

shielded twisted-pair (STP) cable An insulated cable with wires that are twisted around each other with a minimum number of twists per foot. The twists reduce signal interference between the wires, and the more twists per foot, the greater the reduction in interference (crosstalk).

shielding The woven or stranded metal mesh that surrounds some types of cabling. Shielding protects transmitted data by absorbing stray electronic signals, sometimes called noise (random electrical signals that can degrade or distort communications), so that they do not get onto the cable and distort the data.

short A disruption in an electrical circuit that occurs when any two conducting wires or a conducting wire and ground come in contact with each other.

SID (security identifier *or* **security ID)** *See* security identifier *or* security ID (SID).

signal bounce The process by which, on a bus network, the signal is broadcast to the entire network. The signal travels from one end of the cable to the other. If the signal were allowed to continue uninterrupted, it would keep bouncing back and forth along the cable and prevent other computers from sending signals. To stop the signal from bouncing, a component called a terminator is placed at each end of the cable to absorb free signals. Absorbing the signal clears the cable so that other computers can send data. *See also* terminator.

Simple Mail Transfer Protocol (SMTP) A TCP/IP protocol for transferring e-mail. *See also* application protocols, Transport Control Protocol/Internet Protocol (TCP/IP).

Simple Network Management Protocol (SNMP) A TCP/IP protocol for monitoring networks.

SNMP uses a request and response process. In SNMP, short utility programs, called agents, monitor the network traffic and behavior in key network components in order to gather statistical data which they put into a management information base (MIB). To collect the information into a usable form, a special management console program regularly polls the agents and downloads the information in their MIBs. If any of the data falls either above or below parameters set by the manager, the management console program can present signals on the monitor locating the trouble and notify designated support staff by automatically dialing a pager number.

simplex transmission One-way transmission of data.

simultaneous peripheral operation on line (spool) Facilitates the process of moving a print job from the network into a printer.

SLIP *See* Serial Line Internet Protocol (SLIP).

Small Computer System Interface (SCSI) A standard, high-speed parallel interface defined by the ANSI. A SCSI interface is used for connecting microcomputers to peripheral devices, such as hard disks and printers, and to other computers and LANs. SCSI is pronounced "scuzzy."

smart card A credit card-sized device used to securely store public and private keys, passwords, and other types of personal information. To use a smart card, you need a smart card reader attached to the computer and a personal PIN number for the smart card. In Windows 2000, smart cards can be used to enable certificate-based authentication and single sign-on to the enterprise.

smart card reader A standard device within the smart card subsystem. A smart card reader is an interface device (IFD) that supports bidirectional input/output to a smart card.

SMB *See* server message block (SMB).

SMDS *See* Switched Multimegabit Data Services (SMDS).

SMP *See* symmetric multiprocessing (SMP).

SMTP *See* Simple Mail Transfer Protocol (SMTP).

SNA *See* Systems Network Architecture (SNA).

SNMP *See* Simple Network Management Protocol (SNMP).

software Computer programs or sets of instructions that allow the hardware to work. Software can be grouped into four categories: system software, such as operating systems, that control the workings of the computer; application software, such as word-processing programs, spreadsheets, and databases, which perform the tasks for which people use computers; network software, which enables groups of computers to communicate; and language software, which provides programmers with the tools they need to write programs.

SONET *See* Synchronous Optical Network (SONET).

spanning tree algorithm (STA) An algorithm (mathematical procedure) implemented to eliminate redundant routes and avoid situations in which multiple LANs are joined by more than one path by the IEEE 802.1 Network Management Committee. Under STA, bridges exchange certain control information in an attempt to find redundant routes. The bridges determine which would be the most efficient route, then use that one and disable the others. Any of the disabled routes can be reactivated if the primary route becomes unavailable.

spread-spectrum radio technology A technology that provides for a truly wireless network. Spread-spectrum radio broadcasts signals over a range of frequencies, avoiding the communication problems of narrowband radio transmission.

SPX *See* Sequenced Packet Exchange (SPX).

SQL *See* structured query language (SQL).

STA *See* spanning tree algorithm (STA).

stand-alone computer A computer that is not connected to any other computers and is not part of a network.

stand-alone environment A work environment in which each user has a personal computer but works independently, unable to share files and other important information that would be readily available through server access in a networking environment.

standard Ethernet A network topology that transmits at 10 Mbps over a baseband wire and can carry a signal 500 meters (five 100-meter segments). *See also* thicknet.

star topology A topology in which each computer is connected by cable segments to a centralized component called a hub. Signals transmitted by a computer on the star pass through the hub to all computers on the network. This topology originated in the early days of computing with terminals connected to a centralized mainframe. The star topology offers centralized resources and management. However, because each computer is connected to a central point, much cable is required in a large installation, and if the central point fails, the entire network goes down. *See also* hub.

stealth virus A variant of file-infector virus. This virus is so named because it attempts to hide from detection. When an antivirus program attempts to find it, the stealth virus tries to intercept the probe and return false information indicating that it does not exist.

STP *See* shielded twisted-pair (STP).

stripe set A form of fault tolerance that combines multiple areas of unformatted free space into one large logical drive, distributing data storage across all drives simultaneously. In Windows NT, a stripe set requires at least two physical drives and can use up to 32 physical drives. Stripe sets can combine areas on different types of drives, such as Small Computer System Interface (SCSI), Enhanced Small Device Interface (ESDI), and Integrated Device Electronics (IDE) drives.

structured query language (SQL) A database sublanguage used to query, update, and manage relational databases. Although not a programming language in the same sense as C or Pascal, SQL can be used either in formulating interactive queries or embedded in an application as instructions for handling data. The SQL standard also contains components for defining, altering, controlling, and securing data.

SVC *See* switched virtual circuit (SVC).

Switched Multimegabit Data Services (SMDS) A high-speed, switched-packet service that can provide speeds of up to 34 Mbps.

switched virtual circuit (SVC) A logical connection between end computers that uses a specific route across the network. Network resources are dedicated to the circuit, and the route is maintained until the connection is terminated. These are also known as point-to-multipoint connections. *See also* virtual circuit.

switching *See* packet switching.

symmetric multiprocessing (SMP) SMP systems, such as Windows NT Server, use any available processor on an as-needed basis. With this approach, the system load and application needs can be distributed evenly across all available processors.

synchronous A form of communication that relies on a timing scheme coordinated between two devices to separate groups of bits and transmit them in blocks called frames. Special characters are used to begin the synchronization and check its accuracy periodically. Because the bits are sent and received in a timed, controlled (synchronized) fashion, start and stop bits are not required. Transmission stops at the end of one transmission and starts again with a new one. It is a start/stop approach, and more efficient than asynchronous transmission. If an error occurs, the synchronous error detection and correction scheme implements a retransmission. However, because more sophisticated technology and equipment is required to transmit synchronously, it is more expensive than asynchronous transmission.

Synchronous Data Link Control (SDLC) The data link (data transmission) protocol most widely used in networks conforming to IBM's SNA. SDLC is a communications guideline that defines the format in which information is transmitted. As its name implies, SDLC applies to synchronous transmissions. SDLC is also a bit-oriented protocol and organizes information in structured units called frames.

Synchronous Optical Network (SONET) A fiber-optic technology that can transmit data at more than one gigabit per second. Networks based on this technology are capable of delivering voice, data, and video. SONET is a standard for optical transport formulated by the Exchange Carriers Standards Association (ECSA) for the ANSI.

Systems Network Architecture (SNA) A widely used communication framework developed by IBM to define network functions and establish standards for enabling its different models of computers to exchange and process data. SNA is a design philosophy that separates network communication into five layers. Each layer, like those in the similar ISO/OSI model, represents a graduated level of function moving upward from physical connections to applications software.

SYSVOL A shared directory that stores the server copy of the domain's public files, which are replicated among all domain controllers in the domain.

T

T1 line A high-speed communications line that can handle digital communication and Internet access at a rate of 1.544 Mbps (megabits per second).

T1 service The standard digital line service. It provides transmission rates of 1.544 Mbps and can carry both voice and data.

tap A connection to a network. This usually refers specifically to a connection to a cable.

T connector A T-shaped coaxial connector that connects two thinnet Ethernet cables while supplying an additional connector for a network interface card.

TCP *See* Transmission Control Protocol (TCP).

TCP/IP *See* Transport Control Protocol/Internet Protocol (TCP/IP).

TDI *See* transport driver interface (TDI).

TDR *See* time-domain reflectometer (TDR).

Technet *See* Microsoft Technical Information Network (TechNet).

Telnet The command and program used to log in from one Internet site to another. The Telnet command and program brings the user to the login prompt of another host.

terabyte *See* byte.

terminator A resistor used at each end of an Ethernet cable to ensure that signals do not reflect back and cause errors. It is usually attached to an electrical ground at one end. *See also* signal bounce.

terminator resistance The level of resistance in a terminator, measured in ohms. It must match the network architecture specification. For example, Ethernet using RG-58 A/U thinnet cable requires a 50-ohm resistor in the terminator. Terminating resistance that does not match the specifications can cause the network to fail. *See also* ohm.

thicknet (standard Ethernet) A relatively rigid coaxial cable about 0.5-inch in diameter. Typically, thicknet is used as a backbone to connect several smaller thinnet-based networks because of its ability to support data transfer over longer distances. Thicknet can carry a signal for 500 meters (about 1640 feet) before needing a repeater.

thinnet (ThinWire Ethernet) A flexible coaxial cable about 0.25-inch thick. It is used for relatively short-distance communication and is fairly flexible to facilitate routing between computers. Thinnet coaxial cable can carry a signal up to approximately 185 meters (about 607 feet) before needing a repeater.

throughput A measure of the data transfer rate through a component, connection, or system. In networking, throughput is a good indicator of the system's total performance because it defines how well the components work together to transfer data from one computer to another. In this case, the throughput would indicate how many bytes or packets the network could process per second.

ticket A set of identification data for a security principle, issued by a domain controller for purposes of user authentication. Two forms of tickets in Windows 2000 are ticket-granting tickets (TGTs) and service tickets.

time-domain reflectometer (TDR) A troubleshooting tool that sends sonar-like pulses along a cable looking for any kind of a break, short, or imperfection that might affect performance. If the pulse finds a problem, the TDR analyzes it and displays the result. A good TDR can locate a break to within a few feet of the actual separation in the cable.

Time-to-Live (TTL) A timer value included in packets sent over TCP/IP-based networks that tells the recipients how long to hold or use the packet or any of its included data before expiring and discarding the packet or data. For DNS, TTL values are used in resource records within a zone to determine how long requesting clients should cache and use this information when it appears in a query response answered by a DNS server for the zone.

token A predetermined formation of bits that permits a network device to communicate with the cable. A computer cannot transmit unless it has possession of the token. Only one token at a time can be active on the network, and the token can travel in only one direction around the ring. *See also* token passing, Token Ring network.

token passing A media access control method in a Token Ring network in which a data frame, called a token, is passed from one station to the next around the ring. *See also* token, Token Ring network.

Token Ring network A network in which computers are situated on a continuous network loop through which a token is passed from one computer to the next. Computers are centrally connected to a hub called a Multistation Access Unit (MAU) and are wired in a star configuration. Computers use a token to transmit data and must wait for a free token in order to transfer data. *See also* token, token passing.

TokenTalk An expansion card that allows a Macintosh II to connect to an 802.5 Token Ring network.

tone generator and tone locator Standard wiring tools used for troubleshooting. The tone generator is used to apply an alternating or continuous tone signal to a cable or conductor and is attached to one end of the cable. A matching tone locator is used to detect the correct cable at the other end of the run. These tools are also referred to as a "fox and hound."

tone locator *See* tone generator and tone locator.

topology The arrangement or layout of computers, cables, and other components on a network. Topology is the standard term that most network professionals use when referring to the network's basic design.

tracert A Trace Route command-line utility that shows every router interface through which a TCP/IP packet passes on its way to a destination.

trailer One of the three sections of a packet component. The exact content of the trailer varies depending on the protocol, but it usually includes an error-checking component (CRC).

transceiver A device that connects a computer to the network. The term is derived from transmitter/receiver; thus, a transceiver is a device that receives and transmits signals. It switches the parallel data stream used on the computer's bus into a serial data stream used in the cables connecting the computers.

Transmission Control Protocol (TCP) The TCP/IP protocol for sequenced data. *See also* Transport Control Protocol/Internet Protocol (TCP/IP).

Transport Control Protocol/Internet Protocol (TCP/IP) An industry standard suite of protocols providing communications in a heterogeneous environment. In addition, TCP/IP provides a routable, enterprise networking protocol and access to the Internet and its resources. It is a transport layer protocol that actually consists of several other protocols in a stack that operates at the session layer. Most networks support TCP/IP as a protocol.

transport driver interface (TDI) An interface that works between the file-system driver and the transport protocols, allowing any protocol written to TDI to communicate with the file-system drivers.

transport layer The fourth layer of the OSI reference model. It ensures that messages are delivered error free, in sequence, and without losses or duplications. This layer repackages messages for efficient transmission over the network. At the receiving end, the transport layer unpacks the messages, reassembles the original messages, and sends an acknowledgment of receipt. *See also* Open Systems Interconnection (OSI) reference model.

transport protocols Protocols that provide for communication sessions between computers and ensure that data is able to move reliably between computers.

"Trojan horse" virus A type of virus that appears to be a legitimate program that might be found on any system. The Trojan horse virus can destroy files and cause physical damage to disks.

trunk A single cable, also called a backbone, or segment.

trust relationship Trust relationships are links between domains that enable pass-through authentication, in which a user has only one user account in one domain, yet can access the entire network. User accounts and global groups defined in a trusted domain can be given rights and resource permissions in a trusting domain even though those accounts do not exist in the trusting domain's database. A trusting domain honors the logon authentication of a trusted domain.

TTL (Time-to-Live) *See* Time-to-Live (TTL).

twisted-pair cable A cable that consists of two insulated strands of copper wire twisted together. A number of twisted-wire pairs are often grouped together and enclosed in a protective sheath to form a cable. Twisted-pair cable can be shielded or unshielded. Unshielded twisted-pair cable is commonly used for telephone systems. *See also* shielded twisted-pair (STP) cable, unshielded twisted-pair (UTP) cable.

U

UART *See* universal asynchronous receiver transmitter (UART).

UDP *See* User Datagram Protocol (UDP).

Uniform Resource Locator (URL) Provides the hypertext links between documents on the World Wide Web (WWW). Every resource on the Internet has its own location identifier, or URL, that specifies the server to access as well as the access method and the location. URLs can use various protocols including FTP and HTTP.

UNC (Universal Naming Convention) *See* Universal Naming Convention (UNC).

uninterruptible power supply (UPS) A device connected between a computer or another piece of electronic equipment and a power source, such as an electrical outlet. The UPS ensures that the electrical flow to the computer is not interrupted because of a blackout and, in most cases, protects the computer against potentially damaging events such as power surges and brownouts. Different UPS models offer different levels of protection. All UPS units are equipped with a battery and loss-of-power sensor. If the sensor detects a loss of power, it immediately switches over to the battery so that users have time to save their work and shut off the computer. Most higher-end models have features such as power filtering, sophisticated surge protection, and a serial port so that an operating system capable of communicating with a UPS (such as Windows NT) can work with the UPS to facilitate automatic system shutdown.

universal asynchronous receiver transmitter (UART) A module, usually composed of a single integrated circuit, that contains both the receiving and transmitting circuits required for asynchronous serial communication. Two computers, each equipped with a UART, can communicate over a simple wire connection. The operation of the sending and receiving units are not synchronized by a common clock signal, so the data stream itself must contain information about when packets of information (usually bytes) begin and end. This information about the beginning and ending of a packet is provided by the start and stop bits in the data stream. A UART is the most common type of circuit used in personal-computer modems.

Universal Naming Convention (UNC) The standard used for a full Windows 2000 name of a resource on a network. It conforms to the *server**share* syntax, where servername is the name of the server and sharename is the name of the shared resource. UNC names of directories or files can also include the directory path under the share name, with the following syntax:*server**share**directory**filename*.

Universal Serial Bus (USB) A serial bus with a data transfer rate of 12 megabits per second (Mbps) for connecting peripherals to a microcomputer. USB can connect up to 127 peripheral devices to the system through a single, general-purpose port. This is accomplished by daisy chaining peripherals together. USB is designed to support the ability to automatically add and configure new devices and the ability to add such devices without having to shut down and restart the system.

unshielded twisted-pair (UTP) cable A cable with wires that are twisted around each other with a minimum number of twists per foot. The twists reduce signal interference between the wires. The more twists per foot, the greater the reduction in interference (crosstalk). This cable is similar to shielded twisted-pair (STP) cable, but lacks the insulation or shielding found in STP cable.

UPS *See* uninterruptible power supply (UPS).

URL *See* Uniform Resource Locator (URL).

USB *See* Universal Serial Bus (USB).

user account Consists of all of the information that defines a user on a network. This includes the user name and password required for the user to log on, the groups in which the user account has membership, and the rights and permissions the user has for using the system and accessing its resources.

User Datagram Protocol (UDP) A connectionless protocol, responsible for end-to-end data transmission.

user groups Groups of users who meet online or in person to discuss installation, administration, and other network challenges for the purpose of sharing and drawing on each other's expertise in developing ideas and solutions.

UTP *See* unshielded twisted-pair (UTP) cable.

V

vampire tap (piercing tap transceiver) An Ethernet transceiver housed in a clamp-like device with sharp metal prongs that "bite" through thicknet cable insulation and make contact with the copper core. The transceiver's DIX (DB15) connector provides an attachment for an AUI cable that runs from the transceiver to either the computer or a hub or repeater. Along thick coaxial cable that includes bands spaced 2.5 meters (8 feet) apart, a vampire tap is inserted into each band; an AUI, DIX, or

DB15 connector then attaches a cable from the tap to the computer or other device to be added to the Ethernet network.

virtual circuit A series of logical connections between a sending computer and receiving computer. The connection is made after both computers exchange information and agree on communication parameters that establish and maintain the connection, including maximum message size and path. Virtual circuits incorporate communication parameters such as acknowledgments, flow control, and error control to ensure reliability. They can be either temporary, lasting only as long as the conversation, or permanent, lasting as long as the users keep the communication channel open.

Virtual Private Network (VPN) A set of computers on a public network such as the Internet that communicate among themselves using encryption technology. In this way their messages are safe from being intercepted and understood by unauthorized users. VPNs operate as if the computers were connected by private lines.

virus Computer programming, or code, that hides in computer programs or on the boot sector of storage devices such as hard-disk drives and floppy-disk drives. The primary purpose of a virus is to reproduce itself as often as possible; a secondary purpose is to disrupt the operation of the computer or the program.

voltmeter *See* digital voltmeter (DVM).

volume set A collection of hard-disk partitions that are treated as a single partition, thus increasing the disk space available in a single drive letter. Volume sets are created by combining between 2 and 32 areas of unformatted free space on one or more physical drives. These spaces form one large logical volume set which is treated like a single partition.

W

wide area network (WAN) A computer network that uses long-range telecommunication links to connect networked computers across long distances.

winipcfg A diagnostic command specific to Microsoft Windows 95 and 98. Although this graphical user interface (GUI) utility duplicates the functionality of ipconfig, its GUI makes it easier to use. *See also* ipconfig.

wireless bridge A component that offers an easy way to link buildings without using cable.

wireless concentrator A component that acts as a transceiver to send and receive signals while communicating with network interface cards.

wireless network An emerging networking option consisting of wireless components that communicate with a network that uses cables in a mixed-component network called a hybrid.

workgroup A collection of computers grouped for sharing resources such as data and peripherals over a LAN. Each workgroup is identified by a unique name. *See also* domain, peer-to-peer network.

World Wide Web (the Web, or WWW) The Internet multimedia service that contains a vast store-house of hypertext documents written in HTML. *See also* Hypertext Markup Language (HTML).

WORM *See* Write-Once Read-Many (WORM).

Write-Once Read-Many (WORM) Any type of storage medium to which data can be written only once, but can be read any number of

times. Typically, this is an optical disc whose surface is permanently etched using a laser, in order to record information.

X

X.25 A recommendation published by the CCITT that defines the connection between a terminal and a packet-switching network. A packet-switching network routes packets whose contents and format are controlled standards such as those defined in the X.25 recommendation. X.25 incorporates three definitions: the electrical connection between the terminal and the network, the transmission or link-access protocol, and the implementation of virtual circuits between network users. Taken together, these definitions specify a synchronous, full-duplex, terminal-to-network connection. Packets transmitted in such a network can contain either data or control commands. Packet format, error control, and other features are equivalent to portions of the HDLC protocol defined by the ISO. X.25 standards are related to the lowest three levels of the OSI reference model.

X.400 A CCITT protocol for international e-mail transmissions.

X.500 A CCITT protocol for file and directory maintenance across several systems.

XNS (Xerox Network System) Protocol developed by Xerox for its Ethernet LANs.

Z

Zones Logical groupings of users and resources in an AppleTalk network.

Index

Pipe and Tube Cutter

Many simple plumbing jobs require cutting pipes. The tools you need for working with pipe depend on whether the pipe is galvanized steel, copper, or plastic. You can cut pipe with a hacksaw, but **pipe and tube cutters** work faster and make it easier to get a square cut. Most pipe and tube cutters have two rollers and one cutting wheel, but some allow you to exchange the rollers so you have three cutting wheels. The pipe fits between these three points. Turn the handle until the pipe fits snugly between them, then tighten the handle slightly until the wheels begin to bite. Next, revolve the cutter around the pipe, gradually tightening the wheels as it cuts through the pipe. In short order, you will cut all the way through the pipe. You have to avoid the temptation to cut too fast, which can raise a lip on the outside of the pipe that you'll have to file off. You might also have to smooth any burrs off the pipe when you're done cutting.*

At Microsoft Press, we use tools to illustrate our books for software developers and IT professionals. Tools very simply and powerfully symbolize human inventiveness. They're a metaphor for people extending their capabilities, precision, and reach. From simple calipers and pliers to digital micrometers and lasers, these stylized illustrations give each book a visual identity, and a personality to the series. With tools and knowledge, there's no limit to creativity and innovation. Our tagline says it all: *the tools you need to put technology to work.*

*From THE GREAT TOOL EMPORIUM by David X. Manners (published by E.P. Dutton/Times Mirror Magazines, Inc., 1979)

MICROSOFT LICENSE AGREEMENT

Book Companion CD

IMPORTANT—READ CAREFULLY: This Microsoft End-User License Agreement ("EULA") is a legal agreement between you (either an individual or an entity) and Microsoft Corporation for the Microsoft product identified above, which includes computer software and may include associated media, printed materials, and "online" or electronic documentation ("SOFTWARE PRODUCT"). Any component included within the SOFTWARE PRODUCT that is accompanied by a separate End-User License Agreement shall be governed by such agreement and not the terms set forth below. By installing, copying, or otherwise using the SOFTWARE PRODUCT, you agree to be bound by the terms of this EULA. If you do not agree to the terms of this EULA, you are not authorized to install, copy, or otherwise use the SOFTWARE PRODUCT; you may, however, return the SOFTWARE PRODUCT, along with all printed materials and other items that form a part of the Microsoft product that includes the SOFTWARE PRODUCT, to the place you obtained them for a full refund.

SOFTWARE PRODUCT LICENSE

The SOFTWARE PRODUCT is protected by United States copyright laws and international copyright treaties, as well as other intellectual property laws and treaties. The SOFTWARE PRODUCT is licensed, not sold.

1. **GRANT OF LICENSE.** This EULA grants you the following rights:

   a. **Software Product.** You may install and use one copy of the SOFTWARE PRODUCT on a single computer. The primary user of the computer on which the SOFTWARE PRODUCT is installed may make a second copy for his or her exclusive use on a portable computer.

   b. **Storage/Network Use.** You may also store or install a copy of the SOFTWARE PRODUCT on a storage device, such as a network server, used only to install or run the SOFTWARE PRODUCT on your other computers over an internal network; however, you must acquire and dedicate a license for each separate computer on which the SOFTWARE PRODUCT is installed or run from the storage device. A license for the SOFTWARE PRODUCT may not be shared or used concurrently on different computers.

   c. **License Pak.** If you have acquired this EULA in a Microsoft License Pak, you may make the number of additional copies of the computer software portion of the SOFTWARE PRODUCT authorized on the printed copy of this EULA, and you may use each copy in the manner specified above. You are also entitled to make a corresponding number of secondary copies for portable computer use as specified above.

   d. **Sample Code.** Solely with respect to portions, if any, of the SOFTWARE PRODUCT that are identified within the SOFTWARE PRODUCT as sample code (the "SAMPLE CODE"):

      i. **Use and Modification.** Microsoft grants you the right to use and modify the source code version of the SAMPLE CODE, *provided* you comply with subsection (d)(iii) below. You may not distribute the SAMPLE CODE, or any modified version of the SAMPLE CODE, in source code form.

      ii. **Redistributable Files.** Provided you comply with subsection (d)(iii) below, Microsoft grants you a nonexclusive, royalty-free right to reproduce and distribute the object code version of the SAMPLE CODE and of any modified SAMPLE CODE, other than SAMPLE CODE, or any modified version thereof, designated as not redistributable in the Readme file that forms a part of the SOFTWARE PRODUCT (the "Non-Redistributable Sample Code"). All SAMPLE CODE other than the Non-Redistributable Sample Code is collectively referred to as the "REDISTRIBUTABLES."

      iii. **Redistribution Requirements.** If you redistribute the REDISTRIBUTABLES, you agree to: (i) distribute the REDISTRIBUTABLES in object code form only in conjunction with and as a part of your software application product; (ii) not use Microsoft's name, logo, or trademarks to market your software application product; (iii) include a valid copyright notice on your software application product; (iv) indemnify, hold harmless, and defend Microsoft from and against any claims or lawsuits, including attorney's fees, that arise or result from the use or distribution of your software application product; and (v) not permit further distribution of the REDISTRIBUTABLES by your end user. Contact Microsoft for the applicable royalties due and other licensing terms for all other uses and/or distribution of the REDISTRIBUTABLES.

2. **DESCRIPTION OF OTHER RIGHTS AND LIMITATIONS.**

   - **Limitations on Reverse Engineering, Decompilation, and Disassembly.** You may not reverse engineer, decompile, or disassemble the SOFTWARE PRODUCT, except and only to the extent that such activity is expressly permitted by applicable law notwithstanding this limitation.

   - **Separation of Components.** The SOFTWARE PRODUCT is licensed as a single product. Its component parts may not be separated for use on more than one computer.

   - **Rental.** You may not rent, lease, or lend the SOFTWARE PRODUCT.

- **Support Services.** Microsoft may, but is not obligated to, provide you with support services related to the SOFTWARE PRODUCT ("Support Services"). Use of Support Services is governed by the Microsoft policies and programs described in the user manual, in "online" documentation, and/or in other Microsoft-provided materials. Any supplemental software code provided to you as part of the Support Services shall be considered part of the SOFTWARE PRODUCT and subject to the terms and conditions of this EULA. With respect to technical information you provide to Microsoft as part of the Support Services, Microsoft may use such information for its business purposes, including for product support and development. Microsoft will not utilize such technical information in a form that personally identifies you.

- **Software Transfer.** You may permanently transfer all of your rights under this EULA, provided you retain no copies, you transfer all of the SOFTWARE PRODUCT (including all component parts, the media and printed materials, any upgrades, this EULA, and, if applicable, the Certificate of Authenticity), and the recipient agrees to the terms of this EULA.

- **Termination.** Without prejudice to any other rights, Microsoft may terminate this EULA if you fail to comply with the terms and conditions of this EULA. In such event, you must destroy all copies of the SOFTWARE PRODUCT and all of its component parts.

3. **COPYRIGHT.** All title and copyrights in and to the SOFTWARE PRODUCT (including but not limited to any images, photographs, animations, video, audio, music, text, SAMPLE CODE, REDISTRIBUTABLES, and "applets" incorporated into the SOFTWARE PRODUCT) and any copies of the SOFTWARE PRODUCT are owned by Microsoft or its suppliers. The SOFT-WARE PRODUCT is protected by copyright laws and international treaty provisions. Therefore, you must treat the SOFTWARE PRODUCT like any other copyrighted material **except** that you may install the SOFTWARE PRODUCT on a single computer provided you keep the original solely for backup or archival purposes. You may not copy the printed materials accompanying the SOFTWARE PRODUCT.

4. **U.S. GOVERNMENT RESTRICTED RIGHTS.** The SOFTWARE PRODUCT and documentation are provided with RESTRICTED RIGHTS. Use, duplication, or disclosure by the Government is subject to restrictions as set forth in subparagraph (c)(1)(ii) of the Rights in Technical Data and Computer Software clause at DFARS 252.227-7013 or subparagraphs (c)(1) and (2) of the Commercial Computer Software—Restricted Rights at 48 CFR 52.227-19, as applicable. Manufacturer is Microsoft Corporation/One Microsoft Way/Redmond, WA 98052-6399.

5. **EXPORT RESTRICTIONS.** You agree that you will not export or re-export the SOFTWARE PRODUCT, any part thereof, or any process or service that is the direct product of the SOFTWARE PRODUCT (the foregoing collectively referred to as the "Restricted Components"), to any country, person, entity, or end user subject to U.S. export restrictions. You specifically agree not to export or re-export any of the Restricted Components (i) to any country to which the U.S. has embargoed or restricted the export of goods or services, which currently include, but are not necessarily limited to, Cuba, Iran, Iraq, Libya, North Korea, Sudan, and Syria, or to any national of any such country, wherever located, who intends to transmit or transport the Restricted Components back to such country; (ii) to any end user who you know or have reason to know will utilize the Restricted Components in the design, development, or production of nuclear, chemical, or biological weapons; or (iii) to any end user who has been prohibited from participating in U.S. export transactions by any federal agency of the U.S. government. You warrant and represent that neither the BXA nor any other U.S. federal agency has suspended, revoked, or denied your export privileges.

DISCLAIMER OF WARRANTY

NO WARRANTIES OR CONDITIONS. MICROSOFT EXPRESSLY DISCLAIMS ANY WARRANTY OR CONDITION FOR THE SOFTWARE PRODUCT. THE SOFTWARE PRODUCT AND ANY RELATED DOCUMENTATION ARE PROVIDED "AS IS" WITHOUT WARRANTY OR CONDITION OF ANY KIND, EITHER EXPRESS OR IMPLIED, INCLUDING, WITHOUT LIMITA-TION, THE IMPLIED WARRANTIES OF MERCHANTABILITY, FITNESS FOR A PARTICULAR PURPOSE, OR NONINFRINGEMENT. THE ENTIRE RISK ARISING OUT OF USE OR PERFORMANCE OF THE SOFTWARE PRODUCT REMAINS WITH YOU.

LIMITATION OF LIABILITY. TO THE MAXIMUM EXTENT PERMITTED BY APPLICABLE LAW, IN NO EVENT SHALL MICROSOFT OR ITS SUPPLIERS BE LIABLE FOR ANY SPECIAL, INCIDENTAL, INDIRECT, OR CONSEQUENTIAL DAM-AGES WHATSOEVER (INCLUDING, WITHOUT LIMITATION, DAMAGES FOR LOSS OF BUSINESS PROFITS, BUSINESS INTERRUPTION, LOSS OF BUSINESS INFORMATION, OR ANY OTHER PECUNIARY LOSS) ARISING OUT OF THE USE OF OR INABILITY TO USE THE SOFTWARE PRODUCT OR THE PROVISION OF OR FAILURE TO PROVIDE SUPPORT SERVICES, EVEN IF MICROSOFT HAS BEEN ADVISED OF THE POSSIBILITY OF SUCH DAMAGES. IN ANY CASE, MICROSOFT'S ENTIRE LIABILITY UNDER ANY PROVISION OF THIS EULA SHALL BE LIMITED TO THE GREATER OF THE AMOUNT ACTUALLY PAID BY YOU FOR THE SOFTWARE PRODUCT OR US$5.00; PROVIDED, HOWEVER, IF YOU HAVE ENTERED INTO A MICROSOFT SUPPORT SERVICES AGREEMENT, MICROSOFT'S ENTIRE LIABILITY REGARDING SUPPORT SERVICES SHALL BE GOVERNED BY THE TERMS OF THAT AGREEMENT. BECAUSE SOME STATES AND JURISDICTIONS DO NOT ALLOW THE EXCLUSION OR LIMITATION OF LIABILITY, THE ABOVE LIMITATION MAY NOT APPLY TO YOU.

MISCELLANEOUS

This EULA is governed by the laws of the State of Washington USA, except and only to the extent that applicable law mandates governing law of a different jurisdiction.

Should you have any questions concerning this EULA, or if you desire to contact Microsoft for any reason, please contact the Microsoft subsidiary serving your country, or write: Microsoft Sales Information Center/One Microsoft Way/Redmond, WA 98052-6399.

PN 097-0002296

Get a *Free*
e-mail newsletter, updates, special offers, links to related books, and more when you
register on line!

Register your Microsoft Press® title on our Web site and you'll get a FREE subscription to our e-mail newsletter, *Microsoft Press Book Connections.* You'll find out about newly released and upcoming books and learning tools, online events, software downloads, special offers and coupons for Microsoft Press customers, and information about major Microsoft® product releases. You can also read useful additional information about all the titles we publish, such as detailed book descriptions, tables of contents and indexes, sample chapters, links to related books and book series, author biographies, and reviews by other customers.

Registration is easy. Just visit this Web page and fill in your information:

http://www.microsoft.com/mspress/register

Microsoft®

System Requirements

To complete the exercises in Part 1 and to use the book's Supplemental Course Materials CD-ROM, you need two computers each equipped with the following minimum configuration:

- 133 MHz or higher Pentium-compatible CPU
- Microsoft Windows 95, Windows 98, or Windows NT 4.0 or later
- 128 MB of RAM
- 2 GB hard disk with a minimum of 500 MB free space
- 12X CD-ROM drive
- Microsoft Mouse or compatible pointing device (recommended)
- A modem

To use the online version of this book from the Supplemental Course Materials CD-ROM, you need a computer additionally equipped with the following:

- Internet Explorer 5.01 or later

To use the electronic assessment program on the Supplemental Course Materials CD-ROM, you need a computer equipped with the following minimum configuration:

- Microsoft Windows 95 or Windows NT 4 with Service Pack 3 or later, or Microsoft Windows 98 or Microsoft Windows 2000 Professional
- Microsoft Internet Explorer 5.01 or later
- Multimedia PC with a 75-MHz Pentium or higher processor
- 16 MB RAM for Windows 95 or Windows 98 (minimum)
- 32 MB RAM for Windows NT (minimum)
- 64 MB RAM for Windows 2000 (minimum)
- 17 MB available hard disk space for installation
- A double-speed CD-ROM drive or better
- Super VGA display with at least 256 colors
- Microsoft Mouse or compatible pointing device

For the location of a VUE testing center near you, visit www.vue.com/mspress. There are more than 3000 quality VUE testing centers in over 130 countries to choose from.

To learn about other special offers and promotions, go to www.vue.com/resources. While you're there, be sure to sign up for VUE News! We'll send you infrequent emails about special IT promotions and offers.

Register online only at
www.vue.com/mspress

X08-98810   0-7356-1767-8